Rick Steves'
BEST OF
EUROPE
2001

Europe

500 KM
300 MI

AVALON
TRAVEL
publishing

Other ATP travel guidebooks by Rick Steves
Rick Steves' Europe Through the Back Door
Rick Steves' Europe 101: History and Art for the Traveler
  (with Gene Openshaw)
Rick Steves' Mona Winks: Self-Guided Tours of Europe's Top Museums
  (with Gene Openshaw)
Rick Steves' Postcards from Europe
Rick Steves' France, Belgium & the Netherlands (with Steve Smith)
Rick Steves' Germany, Austria & Switzerland
Rick Steves' Great Britain & Ireland
Rick Steves' Italy
Rick Steves' Scandinavia
Rick Steves' Spain & Portugal
Rick Steves' London (with Gene Openshaw)
Rick Steves' Paris (with Steve Smith and Gene Openshaw)
Rick Steves' Rome (with Gene Openshaw)
Rick Steves' Phrase Books: German, French, Italian,
  Spanish/Portuguese, and French/Italian/German

Avalon Travel Publishing, 5855 Beaudry Street, Emeryville, CA 94608

Printed in the United States of America
Second printing March 2001

For the latest on Rick Steves' lectures, guidebooks, tours, and public television series, contact Europe Through the Back Door, Box 2009, Edmonds, WA 98020, tel. 425/771-8303, fax 425/771-0833, www.ricksteves.com, or e-mail: rick@ricksteves.com.

ISBN: 1-56691-239-3
ISSN: 1096-7702

Europe Through the Back Door Editors Risa Laib, Jacquie Maupin
Avalon Travel Publishing Editor Kate Willis
Research Assistance Risa Laib, Brent A. Hurd, and Steve Smith
Production & Typesetting Kathleen Sparkes, White Hart Design
Design Linda Braun
Cover Design Janine Lehmann
Maps David C. Hoerlein
Printer Publishers Press
Cover Photo Il Duomo (cathedral and temple), Siena, Italy;
  Leo de Wys Inc./Jacobs

Distributed to the book trade
by Publishers Group West, Berkeley, California

CONTENTS

Europe's Best Destinations

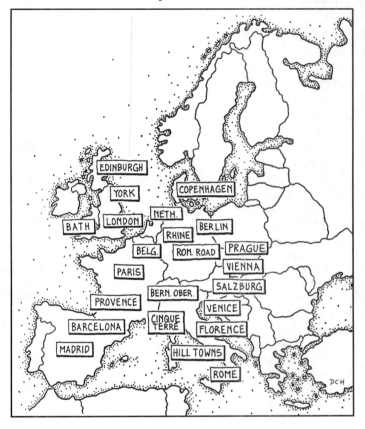

INTRODUCTION

This book breaks Europe into its top big-city, small-town, and rural destinations. It then gives you all the information and opinions necessary to wring the maximum value out of your limited time and money in each of them. If you plan to stay for two months or less in Europe, this lean and mean book is all you need.

Experiencing Europe's culture, people, and natural wonders economically and hassle-free has been my goal for more than 25 years of traveling, tour guiding, and travel writing. With this book, I pass on to you the lessons I've learned, updated for 2001.

Rick Steves' Best of Europe is the crème de la crème of places featured in my Country Guides. This book is balanced to include a comfortable mix of exciting big cities and cozy small towns: from Paris, London, and Rome to traffic-free Riviera ports, avalanche-zone Alpine villages, and mom-and-pop châteaus. It covers the predictable biggies and mixes in a healthy dose of Back Door intimacy. Along with Leonardo in the Louvre, you'll enjoy Caterina in her Cantina. I've been selective. For example, rather than listing countless castles and hill towns, I recommend the best three or four of each.

The best is, of course, only my opinion. But after more than two decades of travel research, I've developed a sixth sense for what tickles the traveler's fancy.

This Information Is Accurate and Up-to-Date

This book is updated every year. Most publishers of guidebooks that cover Europe from top to bottom can afford an update only every two or three years (and even then, it's often by letter). Since this book covers only my favorite places, I am able to update it personally each year. Even with an annual update, things change. But if you're traveling with the current edition of this book, I guarantee you're using the most up-to-date information available (for the latest, visit www.ricksteves.com/update). If you're packing an old book, you'll learn the seriousness of your mistake...in Europe. Your trip costs at least $10 per waking hour. Your time is valuable. This guidebook saves lots of time.

Planning Your Trip

This book is organized by destinations. Each destination is covered as a mini-vacation on its own, filled with exciting sights and homey, affordable places to stay. In each chapter, you'll find the following:

Planning Your Time contains a suggested schedule, with thoughts on how to best use your limited time.

Orientation includes tourist information, city transportation, and an easy-to-read map designed to make the text clear and your arrival smooth.

Exchange Rates

I've priced things in local currencies throughout this book.

Country	$1 equals roughly . . .
Austria	15 Austrian schillings (AS)
Belgium	45 Belgian francs (BF)
Czech Republic	38 koruna (kč)
Denmark	8 kroner (kr)
France	6.50 francs (F)
Germany	2 Deutsche marks (DM)
Great Britain	.65 pound (£)
Italy	2,000 lire (L)
Netherlands	2.50 guilders (f)
Spain	180 pesetas (ptas)
Switzerland	1.70 Swiss francs (SF)

Euro: The euro was adopted as a standard currency by 11 of the countries belonging to the European Union. However, euros won't concern you until 2002 when they materialize into actual bills and coins. For a preview, the countries switching to the euro are Austria, Belgium, France, Germany, Italy, the

Sights are rated: ▲▲▲—Don't miss; ▲▲—Try hard to see; ▲—Worthwhile if you can make it; No rating—Worth knowing about.

Sleeping and Eating includes addresses and phone numbers of my favorite budget hotels and restaurants.

Transportation Connections covers how to reach nearby destinations by train, bus, or car.

The **appendix** is a traveler's tool kit, with telephone tips, a climate chart, and a list of national tourist offices.

Browse through this book, choose your favorite destinations, and link them up. Then have a great trip! You'll travel like a temporary local, getting the most out of every mile, minute, and dollar.

To roughly convert prices into dollars . . .

Drop the last zero off Austrian prices and subtract one-third (e.g., 300 AS = about $20, actually $21).

Knock off the last digit from Belgian prices and divide by two (235BF = about $12).

Drop the last zero off Czech prices and divide by three (2,000-kč = about $67).

Divide Danish prices by eight (90 kr = about $11).

Divide French prices by six (160F = about $27).

Divide German prices in half (e.g., 37 DM = about $18).

Add 50 percent to British prices: £6 is about $9 (actually $9.60), £3 is about $4.50, and 80p is about $1.20.

Ignore the last three digits of Italian prices and cut what's left by half (e.g., a L27,000 dinner costs about $13.50).

Divide Dutch prices by two, then subtract 10 percent (f98 = about $40).

Drop the last two digits of Spanish pesetas and cut in half (3,200 ptas = about $16, actually $18)

Divide prices in Swiss francs by half (e.g., 60 SF = about $30, actually $36) or, more precisely, multiply by 6 and drop the last digit (e.g., 60 SF: 60 x 6 = 360, or $36)

Netherlands, and Spain (plus Finland, Ireland, Luxembourg, and Portugal—not covered in this book). Holdouts include Britain and Denmark. The Czech Republic and Switzerland, which don't belong to the European Union, will keep their currencies. Regardless, for travelers in 2001, euros are not an issue.

You won't waste time on mediocre sights because this guidebook, unlike others, covers only the best. Since your major financial pitfalls are lousy, expensive hotels, I've worked hard to assemble the best accommodations values for each stop. And as you travel the route I know and love, I'm happy you'll be meeting some of my favorite Europeans.

Trip Costs

Five components make up your trip cost: airfare, surface transportation, room and board, sightseeing/entertainment, and shopping/miscellany.

Airfare: Don't try to sort through the mess yourself.

Get and use a good travel agent. A basic round-trip U.S.A.-to-Europe flight should cost $600 to $1,000, depending on where you fly from and when. Always consider saving time and money in Europe by flying "open-jaw" (flying into one city and out of another, such as flying into London and out of Rome).

Surface Transportation: Your best mode depends upon the time you have and the scope of your trip. For many it's a Eurailpass (3 weeks-$718; 1 month-$890; 2 months-$1,260; 15 days in 2 months-$862). Train passes are normally available only outside of Europe. You may save money by simply buying tickets as you go (see "Transportation," below).

Drivers can figure $200 per person per week (based on 2 people splitting the cost of the car, tolls, gas, and insurance). Car rental is cheapest to arrange from the U.S.A. Leasing, for trips over three weeks, is even cheaper.

Room and Board: You can thrive in Europe in 2001 on an overall average of $70 a day per person for room and board (less for the smaller cities). A $70 a day budget allows $10 for lunch, $15 for dinner, and $45 for lodging (based on 2 people splitting the cost of a $90 double room that includes breakfast). That's doable. Students and tightwads will do it on $35 or $40 ($15–20 per bed, $20 for meals and snacks). But budget sleeping and eating require the skills and information covered below (or much more extensively in *Rick Steves' Europe Through the Back Door*).

Sightseeing and Entertainment: In big cities, figure $5 to $10 per major sight, $2 for minor ones, and $25 for splurge experiences (e.g., tours, concerts, gelato binges). An overall average of $15 a day works for most. Don't skimp here. After all, this category directly powers most of the experiences all the other expenses are designed to make possible.

Shopping and Miscellany: Figure $1 per postcard and $2 per coffee, beer, and ice-cream cone. Shopping can vary in cost from nearly nothing to a small fortune. Good budget travelers find that this category has little to do with assembling a trip full of lifelong and wonderful memories.

Prices, Times, and Discounts

The prices in this book, as well as the hours and telephone numbers, are accurate as of late 2000. But Europe is always changing. I know you'll understand that this, like any other guidebook, starts to yellow even before it's printed.

In Europe—and in this book—you'll be using the 24-hour clock. After 12:00 noon, keep going—13:00, 14:00, and so on. For anything over 12, subtract 12 and add p.m. (14:00 is 2 p.m.).

While discounts for sights and transportation are not listed in this book, seniors (60 and over), students (with International Student Identity Cards), and youths (under 18) may snare

Europe's Best 70 Days

discounts—but only by asking. Some discounts (particularly for sights) are granted only to European residents.

When to Go

May, June, September, and October are the best travel months. Peak season (July and August) offers the sunniest weather and the most exciting slate of activities—but the worst crowds. During this busy time, it's best to reserve rooms well in advance, particularly for the big cities (see "Making Reservations," below).

Off-season, October through April, expect generally shorter hours at attractions, more lunchtime breaks, fewer activities, and fewer guided tours in English. If you're traveling off-season, be careful to confirm opening times.

As a general rule of thumb any time of year, the climate north of the Alps is mild (like Seattle), and south of the Alps it's like southern California. For specifics, check the Climate Chart in the appendix. If you wilt in the heat, avoid the Mediterranean in summer. If you want blue skies in the Alps, Britain, and Scandinavia, travel in the height of summer. Plan your itinerary to beat the heat (for a spring trip, start in the south and work north) but also to moderate culture shock (start in mild Britain and work

The Best of Europe in Three Weeks

Day 1   Arrive in Amsterdam, stay in Haarlem
Day 2   Amsterdam
Day 3   To Rhine, Bacharach
Day 4   Cruise Rhine, tour Rheinfels Castle
Day 5   Rothenburg
Day 6   Munich
Day 7   Castle Day in Bavaria and Tirol, Reutte
Day 8   To Venice
Day 9   Venice
Day 10   Florence
Day 11   Siena, Florence
Day 12   Rome
Day 13   Rome
Day 14   Civita di Bagnoregio
Day 15   Italian Riviera, Cinque Terre, Vernazza
Day 16   Beach time or hiking Riviera trails
Day 17   To the Alps, Gimmelwald
Day 18   Alps Appreciation Day
Day 19   To Beaune in Burgundy
Day 20   Versailles, drop car
Day 21   Paris
Day 22   Paris

While this itinerary is designed to be done by car, with a few small modifications, it works great by train. Stay in Füssen in Bavaria rather than Reutte in Triol. The hill town of Orvieto is easier to reach than Civita. Consider skipping Beaune if you'd perfer to take an overnight train from Switzerland to Paris. Do Versailles as an easy day trip from Paris.

south and east) and minimize crowds. Touristy places in the core of Europe (Germany, the Alps, France, Italy, and Greece) suffer most from crowds.

Sightseeing Priorities

Depending on the length of your trip, here are my recommended priorities. Assuming you're traveling by train, I've taken geographical proximity into account.

5 days:	London, Paris
7 days, add:	Amsterdam, Haarlem
10 days, add:	Rhine, Rothenburg
14 days, add:	Salzburg, Swiss Alps
17 days, add:	Venice, Florence
21 days, add:	Rome, Cinque Terre

Europe's Best Three Weeks

24 days, add:	Siena, Bavarian sights
30 days, add:	Arles (Provence), Barcelona, Madrid
36 days, add:	Vienna, Prague, Berlin
40 days, add:	Copenhagen, Bath
70 days:	See Europe's Best 70 Days map on page 5.

Red Tape, News, and Banking

Red Tape: You currently need a passport but no visa and no shots to travel in Europe. Crossing borders is easy. Sometimes you won't even realize it's happened. When you do change countries, however, you change money, postage stamps, phone cards, gas prices, ways to flush a toilet, words for "hello," figurehead monarchs, and breakfast breads. Plan ahead for these changes. Coins and stamps are worthless outside their home countries. Just before crossing a border, I use up my coins on gas, candy, souvenirs, or a telephone call home.

News: Americans keep in touch with the *International Herald Tribune* (published almost daily via satellite throughout Europe).

Every Tuesday, the European editions of *Time* and *Newsweek* hit the stands with articles of particular interest to European travelers. Sports addicts can get their fix from *USA Today*. News in English will only be sold where there's enough demand: in big cities and tourist centers. If you're concerned about how some event might affect your safety as an American traveling abroad, call the U.S. consulate or embassy in the nearest big city for advice.

Banking: Bring plastic (ATM, credit, or debit cards) along with some traveler's checks in dollars as a backup.

To get a cash advance from a bank machine, you'll need a four-digit PIN (numbers only, no letters) with your bank card. Before you go, verify with your bank that your card will work, then use it whenever possible (bring 2 cards in case one gets demagnetized or eaten by a machine). If you are planning on getting cash advances from your regular credit card, make sure to ask the card company about fees before you leave.

Visa and MasterCard are more commonly accepted than American Express. Just like at home, credit or debit cards work easily at larger hotels, restaurants, and shops, but smaller businesses prefer payment in local currency.

Regular banks have the best rates for cashing traveler's checks. For a large exchange, it pays to compare rates and fees. Post offices and train stations usually change money if you can't get to a bank.

You should use a money belt. Thieves target tourists. A money belt (call 425/771-8303 for our free newsletter/catalog) provides peace of mind. You can carry lots of cash safely in a money belt.

Don't be petty about changing money. You don't need to waste time every few days returning to a bank or tracking down a cash machine. Change a week's worth of money, get big bills, stuff it in your money belt, and travel!

Travel Smart

Upon arrival in a new town, lay the groundwork for a smooth departure. Reread this book as you travel and visit local tourist information offices. Buy a phone card and use it for reservations, reconfirmations, and double-checking hours. Enjoy the friendliness of the local people. Ask questions. Most locals are eager to point you in their idea of the right direction. Wear your money belt, learn the local currency, and develop a simple formula to estimate rough prices in dollars quickly. Keep a notepad in your pocket for organizing your thoughts. Those who expect to travel smart, do.

As you read this book, note the days of markets and festivals and when sights are closed. Anticipate problem days: Mondays are bad in Florence, Tuesdays are bad in Paris. Museums and sights, especially large ones, usually stop admitting people 30 to 60 minutes before closing time.

Sundays have the same pros and cons as they do for travelers in the United States. Sightseeing attractions are generally open, shops and banks are closed, and city traffic is light. Rowdy evenings are rare on Sundays. Saturdays in Europe are virtually weekdays with earlier closing hours. Hotels in tourist areas are most crowded on Fridays and Saturdays.

Plan ahead for banking, laundry, post office chores, and picnics. Mix intense and relaxed periods. Every trip (and every traveler) needs at least a few slack days. Pace yourself. Assume you will return.

Tourist Information

The tourist information office is your best first stop in any new city. Try to arrive, or at least telephone, before it closes. In this book, I'll refer to a tourist information office as a TI. Throughout Europe, you'll find TIs are usually well organized and English speaking.

As national budgets tighten, many TIs have been privatized. This means they become sales agents for big tours and hotels, and their "information" becomes unavoidably colored. While the TI has listings of all the rooms and is eager to book you one, use their room-finding service only as a last resort. Across Europe, room-finding services are charging commissions from hotels, taking fees from travelers, blacklisting establishments that buck their material-istic rules, and are unable to give hard opinions on the relative value of one place over another. The accommodations stakes are too high to go potluck through the TI. By using the listings in this book, you can avoid that kind of "help."

Tourist Offices, U.S.A. Addresses: Each country has a national tourist office in the U.S.A. (see the appendix for addresses). Before your trip, you can ask for the free general information packet and any specific information you may want (such as city maps and schedules of upcoming festivals).

Recommended Guidebooks

You may want some supplemental information, especially if you'll be traveling beyond my recommended destinations. When you consider the improvements they'll make in your $3,000 vacation, $25 or $35 for extra maps and books is money well spent. Especially for several people traveling by car, the weight and expense are negligible.

The Lonely Planet guides to various European countries are thorough, well researched (though not updated annually), and packed with good maps and hotel recommendations for low-to moderate-budget travelers. The hip, insightful Rough Guide series (by British researchers, not updated annually) and the highly opinionated Let's Go series (annually updated by Harvard students) are great for students and vagabonds. If you're a backpacker with a train pass and interested in the youth and night scene, get Let's Go. The popular, skinny green Michelin guides to most southern countries and French regions are excellent, especially if you're driving. They're known for their city and sightseeing maps, dry but concise and helpful information on all major sights, and good cultural and historical background. English editions are sold locally at tourist shops and gas stations.

Rick Steves' Books and Videos

Rick Steves' Europe Through the Back Door 2001 gives you budget travel tips on minimizing jet lag, packing light, planning your itinerary, traveling by car or train, finding budget beds without reservations, changing money, avoiding rip-offs, outsmarting thieves, hurdling the language barrier, staying healthy, taking great photographs, using your bidet, and much more. The book also includes chapters on my 35 favorite "Back Doors."

Rick Steves Country Guides are a series of seven guide-books—including this one—covering Britain/Ireland; France/Belgium/the Netherlands; Italy; Spain/Portugal; Germany/Austria/Switzerland; and Scandinavia. These are updated annually and come out each December. If you wish this book covered more of any particular country, my Country Guides are for you.

My **City Guides** cover Paris, London, and Rome. For more thorough coverage of Europe's three greatest cities, complete with self-guided, illustrated tours through the grandest museums, consider these handy, easy-to-pack guidebooks (updated annually and available in January).

Rick Steves' Europe 101: History and Art for the Traveler (with Gene Openshaw, 2000) gives you the story of Europe's people, history, and art. Written for smart people who were sleeping in their history and art classes before they knew they were going to Europe, *101* helps Europe's sights come alive.

Rick Steves' Mona Winks (with Gene Openshaw, 1998) gives you fun, easy-to-follow self-guided tours of the major museums and historic highlights in cities covered in this book, including Amsterdam (Rijksmuseum and Van Gogh Museum), London (British Museum, British Library, National Gallery, Tate Britain, Westminster Abbey, and a Westminster Walk), Venice (St. Mark's, Doge's Palace, and Accademia Gallery), Florence (Uffizi Gallery, Bargello, Michelangelo's *David*, and a Renaissance Walk), Rome (Colosseum, Forum, Pantheon, Vatican Museum, and St. Peter's Basilica), Madrid (Prado), and Paris (Louvre, Orsay Museum, and a tour of Europe's greatest palace, Versailles). If you're planning on touring these sights, *Mona* will be a valued friend.

Rick Steves' Phrase Books: After more than 25 years as an English-only traveler struggling with other phrase books, I've designed a series of practical, fun, and budget-oriented phrase books to help you ask the *gelato* man for a free little taste and the hotel receptionist for a room with no street noise. If you want to chat with your cabbie and make hotel reservations over the phone, my pocket-sized Rick Steves' Phrase Books (for French; German; Italian; combined French/Italian/German; and Spanish/Portuguese, 1999) will come in handy.

My brand-new public television series, *Rick Steves' Europe*, airs in 2001 with 16 new shows on Europe. My first series, *Travels in Europe with Rick Steves*, features 52 half-hour shows on Europe. The shows run throughout the United States on public television and the Travel Channel. They're also available as information-packed videotapes, along with my two-hour slideshow lectures (call 425/771-8303 for free newsletter/catalog).

Rick Steves' Postcards from Europe (1999), my autobiographical book, packs 25 years of travel anecdotes and insights into the ultimate 3,000-mile European adventure. Through my guidebooks, I share my favorite European discoveries with you. *Postcards* introduces you to my favorite European friends.

All of my books are published by Avalon Travel Publishing (www.travelmatters.com).

Maps

The maps in this book, drawn by Dave Hoerlein, are concise and simple. Dave, who is well-traveled in Europe, has designed the maps to help you locate recommended places and get to the tourist offices, where you can pick up a more in-depth map (usually free) of the city or region.

For an overall map of Europe, consider my new Rick Steves' Europe Planning Map—geared to travelers' needs—with sight-seeing destinations listed prominently (for our free newsletter/catalog, contact us at 425/771-8303 or www.ricksteves.com).

European bookstores, especially in tourist areas, have good selections of maps. For drivers, I'd recommend a 1:200,000 or 1:300,000 scale map for each country. Train travelers can usually manage fine with the freebies they get with their train pass and at the local tourist offices.

Tours of Europe

Travel agents will tell you about typical tours of Europe, but they won't tell you about ours. At Europe Through the Back Door, we run 21-day tours of Europe featuring most of the highlights in this book (departures April–October, 26 people on a big roomy bus with 2 great guides). We also offer regional tours of Britain, Ireland, France, Spain/Portugal, Italy, Germany/Austria/Switzerland, Scandinavia, Turkey, and new in 2001, Eastern Europe. And we lead week-long getaways in winter and spring to London, Paris, and Rome. For details, call us at 425/771-8303 or visit www.ricksteves.com.

Transportation in Europe

By Car or Train?

Each has pros and cons. Cars are an expensive headache in big cities but give you more control for delving deep into the countryside. Groups of three or more go cheaper by car. If you're packing heavy (with kids), go by car. Trains are best for city-to-city travel and give you the convenience of doing long stretches overnight. By train, I arrive relaxed and well rested—not so by car. A rail 'n' drive pass allows you to mix train and car travel. When thoughtfully used, this pass economically gives you the best of both transportation worlds.

Traveling by Train

A major mistake Americans make is relating public transportation in Europe to the pathetic public transportation they're used to at home. By rail you'll have the Continent by the tail. While many simply buy tickets as they go ("point to point"), the various train passes give you the simplicity of ticket-free, unlimited travel and, depending on how much traveling you do, often offer a tremendous savings over regular point-to-point tickets. The Eurailpass gives you several options (explained in the box on page 13).

For a free 40-page Railpass Guide analyzing the railpass and point-to-point ticket deals available in both the U.S.A. and in Europe, call my office at 425/771-8303 (or find it at www.ricksteves .com). This booklet is updated each January. Regardless of where you get your train pass, this information will help you know you're getting the right one for your trip. To study train schedules in advance on the Web, check http://bahn.hafas.de/english.html.

Eurailpass, Europass, and Eurail Selectpass

The granddaddy of European railpasses, Eurail, gives you unlimited rail travel on the national trains of 17 European countries. That's 100,000 miles of track through all of western Europe, including Ireland, Greece, and Hungary (but excluding Great Britain and most of eastern Europe). The pass includes many bonuses, such as free boat rides on the Rhine, Mosel, Danube, and lakes of Switzerland; several international ferries (Sweden–Finland and Italy–Greece, plus a 50 percent discount on the Ireland–France route); and a 75 percent discount on the Romantic Road bus tour through Germany. The Europass is more focused (and cheaper) than the Eurailpass, covering five countries (France, Germany, Switzerland, Italy, and Spain), with an extra-cost option to add adjacent countries.

The new Eurail Selectpass, which covers any three Eurail countries connected by rail or ferry (such as Austria, Italy, and Greece) is fine for a focused trip, but to see the Best of Europe, you'd do best with a Eurailpass. All of these passes give a 15 percent Saverpass discount to two or more companions traveling together.

Railpasses

My free *Rick Steves' Guide to European Railpasses* has our latest information. To get the railpass guide, call us at 425/771-8303 or visit www.ricksteves.com/rail (you can order most passes online).

2001 EURAILPASSES

These passes cover all 17 Eurail countries: Austria, Belgium, Denmark, Finland, France, Germany, Greece, Hungary, Ireland, Italy, Luxembourg, Netherlands, Norway, Portugal, Spain, Sweden, and Switzerland.

	1st class	1st class Saver*	2nd class Youth**
10 days in 2 months flexi	$654	$556	$458
15 days in 2 months flexi	862	732	599
15 consecutive days	554	470	388
21 consecutive days	718	610	499
1 month consec. days	890	756	623
2 months consec. days	1260	1072	882
3 months consec. days	1558	1324	1089

2001 EUROPASSES

All Europasses include France, Germany, Italy, Spain and Switzerland. Up to two of the following extra-cost "zones" may be added: Austria/Hungary; Belgium/Netherlands/Luxembourg; Portugal; Greece (includes the Brindisi, Italy to Patras, Greece boat).

	1st class	1st class Saver*	2nd class Youth**
5 days in 2 months	$323	$280	$230
6 days in 2 months	360	306	252
8 days in 2 months	420	358	294
10 days in 2 months	476	406	334
15 days in 2 months	688	586	482
With one add-on zone	+60	+52	+42
With two add-on zones	+100	+86	+70

* Saverpass: when 2 or more adults travel together at all times, they each save 15% by sharing a Saverpass, compared to buying individual Eurail or Europasses

** Youthpasses: Under age 26 only. Kids 4-11 pay half adult fare; under 4: free.

2001 EURAIL SELECTPASSES

This pass covers travel in three adjacent countries. For details, visit www.ricksteves.com/rail or see *Rick Steves' Guide to European Railpasses.*

	1st class Selectpass	1st class Saverpass	2nd class Youthpass
5 days in 2 months	$328	$280	$230
6 days in 2 months	360	306	252
8 days in 2 months	420	358	294
10 days in 2 months	476	406	334

Saverpass prices are per person for two or more people traveling together. Prices subject to change.

Europe by Rail: Time and Cost

This map can help you determine if a railpass is right for you. Add up the ticket prices for your route. If your total is about the same or more than the cost of a pass, buy the pass (unless you like waiting in lines at train stations).

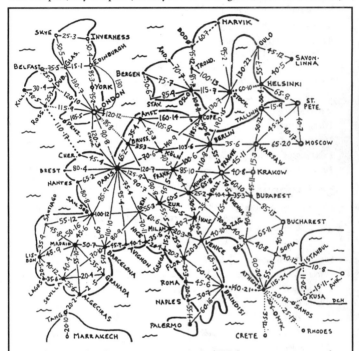

The **first number** between cities = **cost** in $US for a one-way, second-class ticket. The **second number** = number of **hours** the trip takes.
- ● = Cities served by Eurailpass
- ○ = Cities not served by Eurailpass (for example, if you want to go from Berlin to Prague, you'll need to pay extra for the portion through the Czech Republic)
- ••• = Boat Crossings

Important: These fares and times are based on the Eurail Tariff Guide. Actual prices may vary due to currency fluctuations and local promotions. Local competition can cut the actual price of some boat crossings (from Italy to Greece, for example) by 50% or more. For approximate first-class rail prices, multiply the prices shown by 1.5. In some cases, faster trains (like the TGV in France) are available, cutting the hours indicated on the map. Travelers under age 26 can receive up to 1/3 off the second-class fares shown. Eurailpasses are not honored in the United Kingdom, Turkey, or Eastern Europe (except for Hungary).

Rail 'n' Drive Passes

2000 FIRST CLASS EURAILDRIVE PASSES

4 first class rail days and 2 car days in a 2 month period.

Car categories	2 adults	1 adult	Extra car day	Extra rail day
Economy	$339	$399	$61	$59
Compact	359	439	80	59
Intermediate	369	459	90	59

Prices are per person. Third and fourth persons sharing car get a 4-day out of 2-month railpass for approx. $280 (kids 4-11: $140). You can add rail days (max. 5) and car days (no limit).

2000 FIRST CLASS EUROPASS DRIVE

3 first class rail days and 2 car days in a 2 month period.

Car categories	2 adults	1 adult	Extra car day	Extra rail day
Economy	$284	$345	$59	$45
Compact	304	379	79	45
Intermediate	314	399	89	45
Small Automatic	334	445	109	45

Prices are per person. You can add rail days (max. 7) and car days (no limit). ***Prices may vary in 2000. To order Rail 'n Drive passes, call Rail Europe at 800/438-7245 or DER at 800/549-3737.***

Eurail Analysis

Break-even point? For an at-a-glance break-even point, remember that a one-month Eurailpass pays for itself if your route is Amsterdam–Rome–Madrid–Paris on first class or Copenhagen–Rome–Madrid–Copenhagen on second class. A one-month Eurail Youthpass saves you money if you're traveling from Amsterdam to Rome to Madrid and back to Amsterdam. Passes pay for themselves quicker in the north, where the cost per kilometer is higher. Check the "Europe by Rail: Time and Cost" map, on page 14 to see if your planned travels merit the purchase of a train pass. If it's about even, go with the pass for the convenience of not having to wait in line to buy tickets and for the fun and freedom to travel "free."

Using one Eurailpass versus a series of country passes: While nearly every country has its own mini-version of the Eurailpass, trips covering several countries are usually cheapest with the budget whirlwind traveler's old standby, the Eurailpass, or its budget cousins, the Europass and Eurail Selectpass. This is because the more rail days included in a pass, the cheaper your per-day cost is. A group of country passes with a few rail days apiece will have a high per-day cost, while a Eurailpass with a longer life span offers a better deal overall. However, if you're traveling in a single country, an individual country railpass (such as Francerail or Germanrail) is often a better value than any of the Eurail passes.

EurailDrive Pass: The EurailDrive Pass is for those who want to combine train travel with the freedom of having a car a day here and a day there. Great areas for a day of joyriding include the

Dutch countryside; Germany's Rhine, Mosel, or Bavaria; France's
Provence; Italy's Tuscany and Umbria; or "car hiking" in the Alps.
When comparing prices, remember that each day of car rental
comes with about $30 of extra expenses (CDW insurance, gas,
parking), which you'll divide among the people in your party.

Car Rental

It's cheaper to arrange European car rentals in the United States, so
check rates with your travel agent or directly with the companies.
Rent by the week with unlimited mileage. If you'll be renting for
three weeks or more, ask your agent about leasing, which is a
scheme to save on insurance and taxes. I normally rent the smallest,
least expensive model. Explore your drop-off options (and costs).

For peace of mind, I spring for the Collision Damage Waiver
insurance (CDW, about $10–15 per day), which has a zero-
deductible rather than the standard value-of-the-car "deductible."
Ask your travel agent about money-saving alternatives to CDW.
A few gold credit cards cover CDW insurance; quiz your credit
card company on the worst-case scenario. Or consider Travel
Guard, which offers CDW insurance for $6 a day (U.S. tel. 800/
826-1300, www.travelguard.com); it'll cover you throughout
Europe but not in Scotland, Ireland, and Italy.

Note that if you'll be driving in Italy, theft insurance (separate from CDW insurance) is mandatory. The insurance usually
costs about $10 to $15 a day, payable when you pick up the car.

If you plan to drive your rental car into the Czech Republic,
keep these tips in mind: State your travel plans up front to the
rental company. Some won't allow any of their rental cars to enter
eastern European countries due to the high theft rate. Some won't
allow certain types of cars: BMWs, Mercedes, and convertibles.
Ask about extra fees—some companies automatically tack on theft
and collision coverage for a Czech excursion. To avoid hassles at
the Czech border, ask the rental agent to mark your contract with
the company's permission to cross.

Driving

For much of Europe, all you need is your valid U.S. driver's
license and a car. Confirm with your rental company if an international license is required in the countries you plan to visit. Those
traveling in Austria, Germany, Greece, Italy, Portugal, Spain, and
eastern Europe should probably get an international driver's
license (at your local AAA office—$10 plus the cost of two pass-
port-type photos).

While gas is expensive, if you keep an eye on the big picture,
paying $4 per gallon is more a psychological trauma than a finan-
cial one. I use the freeways whenever possible. They are free in
the Netherlands and Germany. You'll pay a one-time road fee of

Standard European Road Signs

| STOP | No Entry For Cars | All Vehicles Prohibited | No Entry | Speed Limit (in km) | Yield | No Passing | Danger | Parking |

red

Duh

about $25 as you enter Switzerland and about $7 for Austria. The Italian autostradas and French autoroutes are punctuated by toll booths (charging about $1 for every 10 minutes). The alternative to these superfreeways often is being marooned in rural traffic. The autostrada/autoroute usually saves enough time, gas, and nausea to justify its expense. Mix scenic country-road rambling with high-speed autobahning, but don't forget that in Europe, the shortest distance between two points is the autobahn.

Metric: Outside of Britain, get used to metric. A liter is about a quart, four to a gallon. A kilometer is six-tenths of a mile. I figure kilometers to miles by cutting them in half and adding back 10 percent of the original (120 km: 60 + 12 = 72 miles, 300 km: 150 + 30 = 180 miles).

Parking: Parking is a costly headache in big cities. You'll pay about $20 a day to park safely. Ask at your hotel for advice. I keep a pile of coins in my ashtray for parking meters, public phones, Laundromats, and wishing wells.

Telephones, Mail, and E-mail

Smart travelers learn the phone system and use it daily to reserve or reconfirm rooms, find out tourist information, or phone home. Many European phone booths take phone cards rather than coins. Each country sells phone cards good for use in that country's phones. (For example, you can use a Swiss phone card to make local and international calls from Switzerland, but it won't do a thing for you in France.) Buy a phone card from post offices, newsstands, or tobacco shops. Insert the card into the phone and make your call, and the value is automatically deducted from your card. If you use coins instead, have a bunch handy. The new PIN cards allow you to dial from any phone, even your hotel room; after you buy the card (at exchange bureaus, newsstands, or mini-marts), just follow the instructions. You'll end up dialing lots more numbers (whether it's a local or international call), but you'll save money per minute, especially on overseas calls. There's no one brand name; just ask for an international calling card. Available in Britain, Ireland, France, and Italy, these will likely catch on soon throughout Europe.

Dialing Direct: You'll usually save money by dialing direct. You just need to learn to break the codes.

Here are the general guidelines: When calling long-distance within a country, first dial the area code (which starts with zero), then dial the local number. For example, Berlin's area code is 030, and the number of one of my recommended Berlin hotels is 3150-3944. To call it from Frankfurt, dial 030/3150-3944. When dialing internationally, dial the international access code (of the country you're calling from), the country code (of the country you're calling to), the area code (without the initial zero), and the local number. To call the Berlin hotel from the U.S.A., dial 011 (U.S.A.'s international access code), 49 (Germany's country code), 30 (Berlin's area code without the initial zero), then 3150-3944. To call my office from Berlin, I dial 00 (Europe's international access code), 1 (U.S.A.'s country code), 425 (Edmonds' area code), and 771-8303.

There are always exceptions. Some countries don't use area codes at all, such as Denmark, France, Italy, Norway, Portugal, and Spain. To make an international call to these countries, dial the international access code of the country you're calling from, the country code of the country you're calling, and the local number in its entirety. (Okay, so there's one exception to the exception; for France, you drop the initial zero of the local number.) To make long-distance calls within any of these countries, simply dial the local number in its entirety (whether you're calling across the street or across the country).

European time is six/nine hours ahead of the east/west coast of the U.S.A. For a listing of international access codes and country codes, see the appendix.

USA Direct Services: Calling home from Europe is easy with AT&T, MCI, or Sprint calling cards, but since direct-dial rates have dropped, calling cards aren't as good a deal as they were a few years ago. It's cheaper to call direct. But if you prefer to use a calling card, here's the scoop: Each card company has a toll-free number in each European country that puts you in touch with an English-speaking operator who takes your card number and the number you want to call, puts you through, and bills your home phone number for the call (about $2 per minute plus a $4 service charge). Calling an answering machine is a $6 mistake. Avoid this by making a five-second call using a small-value coin or a phone card. For about 25 cents you can get through long enough to make sure an answering machine is off so you can call back using your USA Direct number. For a list of AT&T, MCI, and Sprint calling-card operators, see the appendix. It's a rip-off to use your calling card to make calls between European countries; it's much cheaper to call direct using a phone card or coins.

Mail: To arrange for mail delivery, reserve a few hotels along your route in advance and give their addresses to friends or use American Express Company's mail services (available to anyone who has at least one Amex traveler's check). Allow 10 days for a letter to arrive. Federal Express makes two-day deliveries—for a price. Phoning is so easy that I've dispensed with mail stops all together.

E-mail: More and more hoteliers have e-mail addresses and Web sites (listed in this book). And cybercafés are available in most cities, giving you reasonably inexpensive and easy Internet access.

Sleeping

In the interest of smart use of your time, I favor hotels and restaurants handy to your sightseeing activities. Rather than list hotels scattered throughout a city, I describe my favorite two or three neighborhoods and recommend the best accommodations values in each, from $10 bunks to $150 doubles.

Now that hotels are so expensive and tourist information offices' room-finding services are so greedy, it's more important than ever for budget travelers to have a good listing of rooms and call directly to make reservations. This book gives you a wide range of budget accommodations to choose from: hostels, bed-and-breakfasts, guest houses, pensions, small hotels, and splurges. I like places that are quiet, clean, small, central, traditional, friendly, and not listed in other guidebooks. Most places I list are a good value, having at least five of these seven virtues.

Rooms with private bathrooms are often bigger and renovated, while the cheaper rooms without bathrooms often will be on the top floor or not yet refurbished. Any room without a bathroom has access to a bathroom in the corridor (free unless otherwise noted). Rooms with tubs often cost more than rooms with showers. All rooms have a sink. Unless I note a difference, the cost of a room includes a continental breakfast. When breakfast is not included, the price is usually posted in your hotel room.

Before accepting a room, confirm your understanding of the complete price. The only tip my recommended hotels would like is a friendly, easygoing guest. I appreciate feedback on your hotel experiences.

Hotels

While most hotels listed in this book cluster around $60 to $80 per double, they range from $25 (very simple, toilet and shower down the hall) to $150 (maximum plumbing and more) per double. The cost is higher in big cities and heavily touristed cities and lower off the beaten track. Three or four people can save money by requesting one big room. Traveling alone can get expensive: A single room is

Sleep Code

To give maximum information in a minimum of space, I use this code to describe accommodations listed in this book. Prices listed are per room, not per person. When there is a range of prices in one category, the price will fluctuate with the season, size of room, or length of stay.

S = Single room (or price for one person in a double).

D = Double or Twin. Double beds are usually big enough for non-romantic couples.

T = Triple (often a double bed with a single bed moved in).

Q = Quad (an extra child's bed is usually less).

b = Private bathroom with toilet and shower or tub.

t = Private toilet only (the shower is down the hall).

s = Private shower or tub only (the toilet is down the hall).

CC = Accepts credit cards (**V**isa, **M**asterCard, **A**merican Express). If CC isn't mentioned, assume you'll need to pay cash.

SE = Speaks English. This code is used only when it seems predictable that you'll encounter English-speaking staff.

NSE = Does not speak English. Used only when it's unlikely you'll encounter English-speaking staff.

According to this code, a couple staying at a "Db-6,000 ptas, CC:V, SE" hotel in Spain would pay a total of 6,000 pesetas (about $27) for a double room with a private bathroom. The hotel will accept Visa or Spanish cash in payment, and the staff speaks English.

often only 20 percent cheaper than a double. If you'll accept a room with twin beds and you ask for a double, you may be turned away. Ask for "a room for two people" if you'll take a twin or a double.

Rooms are generally safe, but don't leave valuables lying around. More (or different) pillows and blankets are usually in the closet or available on request. Remember, in Europe towels and linen aren't always replaced every day. Drip-dry and conserve.

A very simple continental breakfast is almost always included. (Breakfasts in Europe, like towels and people, get smaller as you go south.) If you like juice and protein for breakfast, supply it yourself. I enjoy a box of juice in my hotel room and often supplement the skimpy breakfast with a piece of fruit and cheese.

Pay your bill the evening before you leave to avoid the time-wasting crowd at the reception desk in the morning.

Making Reservations

It's possible to travel at any time of year without reservations
(especially if you arrive early in the day), but given the high stakes,
erratic accommodations values, and the quality of the gems I've
found for this book, I'd highly recommend calling for rooms at
least a day or two in advance as you travel (your fluent receptionist
will likely help you call your next hotel if you pay for the call).
Even if a hotel clerk says the hotel is fully booked, you can try
calling between 9:00 and 10:00 on the day you plan to arrive.
That's when the hotel clerk knows who'll be checking out and
just which rooms will be available. I've taken great pains to list
telephone numbers with long distance instructions (see "Telephones," above and the appendix). Use the telephone and the
convenient phone cards. Most hotels listed are accustomed to
English-only speakers. A hotel receptionist will trust you and hold
a room until 16:00 (4:00 p.m.) without a deposit, though some
will ask for a credit card number. Honor (or cancel by phone)
your reservations. Long distance is cheap and easy from public
phone booths. Don't let these people down—I promised you'd
call and cancel if for some reason you won't show up. Don't
needlessly confirm rooms through the tourist office; they'll take
a commission.

If you know exactly which dates you need and really want a
particular place, reserve a room well in advance before you leave
home. To reserve from home, call, fax, e-mail, or write the hotel.
Phone and fax costs are reasonable, e-mail is a steal, and simple
English is usually fine. To fax, use the form in the appendix
(or find it online at www.ricksteves.com/reservation). If you're
writing, add the zip code and confirm the need and method for a
deposit. A two-night stay in August would be "two nights, 16/8/01
to 18/8/01" (Europeans write the date in this order—day/month/
year—and hotel jargon counts your stay from your day of arrival
through your day of departure). You'll often receive a response
requesting one night's deposit. A credit card number and expiration date will usually work. If you use your credit card for the
deposit, you can pay with your card or cash when you arrive; if
you don't show up, you'll be billed for one night. Reconfirm
your reservations a day in advance for safety.

Bed-and-Breakfasts

You can stay in private homes throughout Europe and enjoy
double the cultural intimacy for about half the cost of hotels.
You'll find them mainly in smaller towns and in the countryside
(so they are most handy for those with a car). In Germany, look
for *Zimmer* signs. For Italian *affitta camere* and French *chambre
d'hôte* (CH), ask at local tourist offices. Doubles cost about $50,
and you'll often share a bathroom with the family. While your

European hosts will rarely speak English (except in Switzerland, the Netherlands, Belgium, and Scandinavia), they will almost always be enthusiastic, delightful hosts.

Hostels
For $10 to $20 a night, you can stay at one of Europe's 2,000 youth hostels. While most hostels admit nonmembers for an extra fee, it's best to join the club and buy a youth hostel card before you go (call Hostelling International at 202/783-6161 or order online at www.hiayh.org). Except in Bavaria (where you must be under 27 to stay in a hostel), travelers of any age are welcome as long as they don't mind dorm-style accommodations and making lots of traveling friends. Cheap meals are sometimes available, and kitchen facilities are usually provided for do-it-yourselfers. Expect crowds in the summer, snoring, and lots of youth groups giggling and making rude noises while you try to sleep. Family rooms and doubles are often available on request, but it's basically boys' dorms and girls' dorms. Many hostels are locked up from about 10:00 until 17:00, and a 23:00 curfew is often enforced. Hosteling is ideal for those traveling single: prices are per bed, not per room, and you'll have an instant circle of friends. More and more hostels are getting their business acts together, taking credit card reservations over the phone and leaving sign-in forms on the door for each available room. If you're serious about traveling cheaply, get a card, carry your own sheets, and cook in the members' kitchens.

Camping
For $4 to $10 per person per night, you can camp your way through Europe. "Camping" is an international word, and you'll see signs everywhere. All you need is a tent and a sleeping bag. Good campground guides are published, and camping information is also readily available at local tourist information offices. Europeans love to holiday camp. It's a social rather than a nature experience and a great way for traveling Americans to make local friends. Camping is ideal for families traveling by car on a tight budget.

Eating European
Europeans are masters at the art of fine living. That means eating long and eating well. Two-hour lunches, three-hour dinners, and endless hours sitting in outdoor cafés are the norm. Americans eat on their way to an evening event and complain if the check is slow in coming. For Europeans, the meal is an end in itself, and only rude waiters rush you.

Even those of us who liked dorm food will find that the local cafés, cuisine, and wines become a highlight of our European adventure. This is sightseeing for your palate, and even if the rest of you is sleeping in cheap hotels, your taste buds will want an occasional first-class splurge. You can eat well without going broke. But be careful: You're just as likely to blow a small fortune on a mediocre meal as you are to dine wonderfully for $15.

Restaurants

When restaurant hunting, choose a place filled with locals, not the place with the big neon signs boasting "We Speak English and Accept Credit Cards." Look for menus posted outside; if you don't see one, move along. Especially in France and Italy, look for set-price menus (called the tourist menu, *menu del giorno*, *prix-fixe*, or simply *le menu*) that give you several choices of courses.

At some restaurants, the *menu* is cheaper at lunch than dinner. Combination plates (*le plat* in France, *plato combinado* in Spain) provide house specialties at reasonable prices. Galloping gourmets bring a menu translator. (The *Marling Menu Master*, available in French, Italian, and German editions, is excellent.)

These days, tipping is included in the bill in most cafés and restaurants. If it's not, the menu will tell you. Still, it's polite to leave the change (up to 5 percent) if the service was good.

When you're in the mood for something halfway between a restaurant and a picnic meal, look for take-out food stands, delis with stools or a table, a department store cafeteria, or simple little eateries for fast and easy sit-down restaurant food.

Picnics

So that I can afford the occasional splurge in a nice restaurant, I like to picnic. In addition to the savings, picnicking is a great way to sample local specialties. And, in the process of assembling your meal, you get to plunge into local markets like a European.

Gather supplies early. Many shops close for a lunch break. While it's fun to visit the small specialty shops, a *supermarché* gives you more efficiency with less color for less cost.

When driving, I organize a backseat pantry in a cardboard box: plastic cups, paper towels, a water bottle (the standard disposable European half liter plastic mineral water bottle works fine), a damp cloth in a Zip-loc baggie, a Swiss army knife, and a petite tablecloth. To take care of juice once and for all, stow a rack of liter boxes of orange juice in the trunk. (Look for "100%" on the label or you'll get a sickly sweet orange drink.)

Picnics (especially French ones) can be an adventure in high cuisine. Be daring: Try the smelly cheeses, midget pickles, ugly pâtés, and minuscule yogurts. Local shopkeepers sell small quantities of produce and even slice and stuff a sandwich for you.

A typical picnic for two might be fresh bread (half loaves on request), two tomatoes, three carrots, 100 grams of cheese (about a quarter-pound, called an *etto* in Italy), 100 grams of meat, two apples, a liter box of orange juice, and yogurt. Total cost for two: about $8.

Stranger in a Strange Land

We travel all the way to Europe to enjoy differences—to become temporary locals. You'll experience frustrations. Certain truths that we find "God-given" or "self-evident," like cold beer, ice in drinks, bottomless cups of coffee, hot showers, body odor smelling bad, and bigger being better, are suddenly not so true. One of the benefits of travel is the eye-opening realization that there are logical, civil, and even better alternatives. A willingness to go local ensures that you'll enjoy a full dose of local hospitality.

If there is a negative aspect to the European image of Americans, we can appear loud, aggressive, impolite, rich, and a bit naive. While Europeans look bemusedly at some of our Yankee excesses—and worriedly at others—they nearly always afford us individual travelers all the warmth we deserve.

Back Door Manners

While updating this book, I heard over and over again that my readers are considerate and fun to have as guests. Thank you for traveling as temporary locals who are sensitive to the culture. It's fun to follow you in my travels.

Send Me a Postcard, Drop Me a Line

If you enjoy a successful trip with the help of this book and would like to share your discoveries, please fill out the survey at the end of this book and send it to me at Europe Through the Back Door, Box 2009, Edmonds, WA 98020. I personally read and value all feedback.

For our latest travel information, tap into our Web site: www.ricksteves.com. To check on updates for this book, visit www.ricksteves.com/update. My e-mail address is rick @ricksteves.com. Anyone is welcome to request a free issue of our *Back Door* quarterly newsletter.

Judging from all the positive feedback I receive from travelers who have used this book, it's safe to assume you'll enjoy a great, affordable vacation—with the finesse of an experienced, independent traveler. Thanks, and happy travels!

BACK DOOR TRAVEL PHILOSOPHY
As Taught in Rick Steves' Europe Through the Back Door

Travel is intensified living—maximum thrills per minute and one of the last great sources of legal adventure. Travel is freedom. It's recess, and we need it.

Experiencing the real Europe requires catching it by surprise, going casual... "Through the Back Door."

Affording travel is a matter of priorities. (Make do with the old car.) You can travel—simply, safely, and comfortably—anywhere in Europe for $70 a day plus transportation costs. In many ways, spending more money only builds a thicker wall between you and what you came to see. Europe is a cultural carnival and, time after time, you'll find that its best acts are free and the best seats are the cheap ones.

A tight budget forces you to travel close to the ground, meeting and communicating with the people, not relying on service with a purchased smile. Never sacrifice sleep, nutrition, safety, or cleanliness in the name of budget. Simply enjoy the local-style alternatives to expensive hotels and restaurants.

Extroverts have more fun. If your trip is low on magic moments, kick yourself and make things happen. If you don't enjoy a place, maybe you don't know enough about it. Seek the truth. Recognize tourist traps. Give a culture the benefit of your open mind. See things as different but not better or worse. Any culture has much to share.

Of course, travel, like the world, is a series of hills and valleys. Be fanatically positive and militantly optimistic. If something's not to your liking, change your liking. Travel is addicting. It can make you a happier American as well as a citizen of the world. Our Earth is home to 6 billion equally important people. It's humbling to travel and find that people don't envy Americans. They like us, but with all due respect, they wouldn't trade passports.

Globetrotting destroys ethnocentricity. It helps you understand and appreciate different cultures. Travel changes people. It broadens perspectives and teaches new ways to measure quality of life. Many travelers toss aside their hometown blinders. Their prized souvenirs are the strands of different cultures they decide to knit into their own character. The world is a cultural yarn shop. And Back Door Travelers are weaving the ultimate tapestry. Come on, join in!

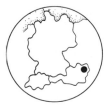

VIENNA
(WIEN)

Vienna is a head without a body. For 640 years the capital of the once-grand Hapsburg Empire, she started and lost World War I and, with it, her far-flung holdings. Today you'll find an elegant capital of 1.6 million people (20 percent of Austria's population) ruling a small, relatively insignificant country. Culturally, historically, and from a sightseeing point of view, this city is the sum of its illustrious past. The city of Freud, Brahms, a gaggle of Strausses, Maria Theresa's many children, and a dynasty of Holy Roman Emperors is right up there with Paris, London, and Rome.

Vienna has always been the easternmost city of the West. In Roman times it was Vindobona, on the Danube facing the Germanic barbarians. In medieval times Vienna was Europe's bastion against the Ottoman Turks (a "horde" of 300,000 was repelled in 1683). While the ancient walls held out the Turks, World War II bombs destroyed nearly a quarter of the city's buildings. In modern times Vienna took a big bite out of the USSR's Warsaw Pact buffer zone.

The truly Viennese person is not Austrian but a second-generation Hapsburg cocktail, with grandparents from the distant corners of the old empire—Polish, Serbian, Hungarian, Romanian, Czech, or Italian. Vienna is the melting-pot capital of an empire of 60 million—of which only 8 million were Austrian.

In 1900, Vienna's 2.2 million inhabitants made it the world's fifth-largest city (after New York, London, Paris, and Berlin). But the average Viennese mother has 1.3 children, and the population is down to 1.6 million. (Dogs are the preferred "child.")

Some ad agency has convinced Vienna to make Elisabeth, wife of Emperor Franz Josef, with her narcissism and difficulties with

Vienna Overview

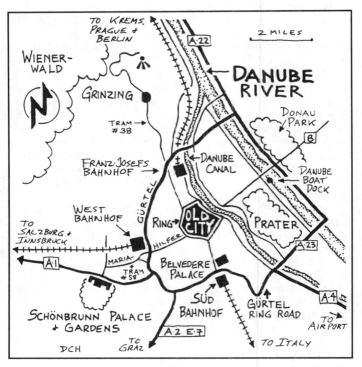

royal life, the darling of the local tourist scene. You'll see "Sissy" all over town. But stay focused on the Hapsburgs who mattered.

Of the Hapsburgs who ruled Austria from 1273 to 1918, Maria Theresa (ruled 1740–1765) and Franz Josef (ruled 1848–1916) are the most famous. People are quick to remember Maria Theresa as the mother of 16 children (12 survived). This was actually no big deal back then (one of her daughters had 18 kids, and a son fathered 16). Maria Theresa's reign followed the Austrian defeat of the Turks, when Europe recognized Austria as a great power. She was a strong and effective queen. (Her rival, the Prussian emperor, said, "When at last the Hapsburgs get a great man, it's a woman.")

Maria Theresa was a great social reformer. During her reign she avoided wars and expanded her empire by skillfully marrying her children into the right families. With daughter Marie Antoinette's marriage into the French Bourbon family (to Louis XVI), for instance, a country that had been an enemy became an ally. (Unfortunately for Marie, she arrived in time for the Revolution, and she lost her head.)

In tune with her age and as a great reformer, Maria Theresa's "Robin Hood" policies helped Austria glide through the "age of revolution" without turmoil. She taxed the church and the nobility and provided six years of obligatory education to all children and free health care to all in her realm. And she welcomed the boy genius Mozart into her court.

As far back as the 12th century, Vienna was a mecca for musicians—both sacred and secular (troubadours). The Hapsburg emperors of the 17th and 18th centuries were not only generous supporters of music but fine musicians and composers themselves. (Maria Theresa played a mean double bass.) Composers such as Haydn, Mozart, Beethoven, Schubert, Brahms, and Mahler gravitated to this music-friendly environment. They taught each other, jammed together, and spent a lot of time in Hapsburg palaces. Beethoven was a famous figure, walking—lost in musical thought—through Vienna's woods.

After the defeat of Napoleon and the Congress of Vienna in 1815 (which redrew the map of 19th-century Europe), Vienna enjoyed its violin-filled belle époque, which shaped our romantic image of the city—fine wine, chocolates, cafés, and waltzes. "Waltz King" Johann Strauss and his brothers kept Vienna's 300 ballrooms spinning.

This musical tradition continues in our century leaving some prestigious Viennese institutions for today's tourists to enjoy: the Opera, the Boys' Choir, and the great Baroque halls and churches, all busy with classical and waltz concerts.

Planning Your Time

For a big city, Vienna is pleasant and laid-back. Vienna is worth two days and two nights on the speediest trip. Not only is it packed with great sights, but it's also a joy to simply spend time in. It seems like Vienna was designed to help people just meander through a day. To be grand-tour efficient, you could sleep in and sleep out on the train (Berlin, Venice, Rome, the Swiss Alps, Paris, and the Rhine are each handy night trains away). I'd come in from Salzburg via Hallstatt and spend two days this way:

Day 1: 9:00–Circle the "Ring" by tram, following the self-guided tour (see "Do-It-Yourself Bus Orientation Tour," below), 10:00–Tour Opera (take care of any TI and ticket needs), 11:00–Horse lovers tour the Lipizzaner Museum and see the horses practicing; art fans can visit the Academy of Fine Arts; people watchers and picnic gatherers wander Naschmarkt, 12:00–Lunch at Buffet Trzesniewski or Rosenberger Markt Restaurant, 13:00–Tour Hofburg, visiting royal apartments, treasury, and Kaisergruft, 16:30–Stroll Kärntner Strasse, tour St. Stephan's cathedral, and stroll Graben and Kohlmarkt, 19:00–Choose classical music (concert or opera), House of Music museum, or Heurige wine garden.

Day 2: 9:00–Schönbrunn Palace (drivers: this is conveniently on the way out of town toward Salzburg), 13:00–Kunsthistorisches Museum after lunch, 15:00–Your choice of the many sights left to see in Vienna, Evening–See Day 1 evening options.

Orientation (area code: 01)

Vienna, or Wien (veen) in German, is bordered on three sides by the Vienna Woods (Wienerwald) and on one side by the Danube (Donau). To the southeast is industrial sprawl. The Alps, which arc across Europe from Marseilles, end at Vienna's wooded hills. These provide a popular playground for walking and new-wine drinking. This greenery's momentum carries on into the city. You'll notice more than half of Vienna is parkland, filled with ponds, gardens, trees, and statue memories of Austria's glory days.

Think of the city map as a target. The bull's-eye is the cathedral, the first circle is the Ring, and the second is the Gürtel. The old town snuggles around towering St. Stephan's Cathedral south of the Donau, and is bound tightly by the Ringstrasse. The Ring, marking what was the city wall, circles the first district (or *Bezirk*). The Gürtel, a broader ring road, contains the rest of downtown (*Bezirkes* 2–9).

Addresses start with the *Bezirk*, followed by street and building number. Any address higher than the ninth *Bezirk* is beyond the Gürtel, far from the center. The middle two digits of Vienna's postal codes show the district, or *Bezirk*. The address "7, Lindengasse 4" is in the seventh district, #4 on Linden Street. Its postal code would be 1070. Nearly all your sightseeing will be done in the core first district or along the Ringstrasse. As a tourist, concern yourself only with this compact old center. When you do, sprawling Vienna suddenly becomes manageable.

Tourist Information

Vienna has one real tourist office (near the Opera in the old center). Hotel and ticket booking agencies answer questions and give out maps and brochures at the train stations and airport.

The main Vienna tourist office is at a slick and spacious location a block behind the Opera House at Albertinaplatz (daily 9:00–19:00, tel. 01/211-140, www.info.wien.at). Confirm your sightseeing plans and pick up the free and essential city map (also available at most hotels), the museum brochure (listing hours), the monthly program of concerts (called "Programm"), the fact-filled *Vienna Scene* magazine, and the youth guide ("Ten Good Reasons For Vienna").

Consider the TI's handy 50-AS *Vienna from A to Z* booklet. Every important building sports a numbered flag banner that keys into this guidebook. A to Z numbers are keyed into the TI's city map. When lost, find one of the "famous-building flags" and match its number to your map. If you're at a "famous building," check the map to see what other key numbers are nearby, then check the A to Z book description to see if you want to go in. This system is especially helpful for those just wandering aimlessly among Vienna's historic charms.

Skip the much promoted 210-AS "Vienna Card." It gives you a 72-hour transit pass (worth 150 AS) and insignificant discounts at museums on the push list.

Arrival in Vienna

By Train at the West Station (Westbahnhof): Train travelers arriving from Munich, Salzburg, and Melk land at the Westbahnhof. The Reisebüro am Bahnhof books hotels (for a fee), has free maps, and answers questions (daily 7:00–22:00). To get to the city center (and most likely, your hotel), catch the U-3 metro (buy the 60-AS 24-hr pass from a *Tabak* shop in the station or from a machine—good on all city transit). U-3 signs lead down to the metro tracks. Catch a train in the direction of U-3 Erdberg. If your hotel is along Mariahilfer Strasse, your stop is on this line (see "Sleeping," below). If you're sleeping in the center or just sightseeing, ride five stops to Stephansplatz, escalate in the exit direction "Stephansplatz," and you'll hit the cathedral. The TI is a five-minute stroll down the busy Kärntner Strasse pedestrian street.

The Westbahnhof has a grocery store (daily 5:30–23:00), change offices (station ticket windows offer better rates and shorter lines than change offices), storage facilities, and rental bikes (see "Getting around Vienna," below). Airport buses and taxis await in front of the station.

By Train at the South Station (Südbahnhof): Those arriving from Italy and Prague land here. The Sudbahnhof has all the services, including bike rental, left luggage, and a TI (9:00–19:00). To reach Vienna's center, follow the "S" (Schnellbahn) signs to the right and down the stairs, and take any train in the direction "Floridsdorf"; transfer in two stops (at Landsstrasse/Wien Mitte) to the U3 (yellow) line, direction "Ottakring" which goes directly to Stephansplatz and Mariahilfer Strasse hotels. Also, tram D goes to the Ring and bus #13A goes to Mariahilfer Strasse.

By Plane: The airport (10 miles from town, tel. 01/7007-22233) is connected by 70 AS shuttle buses (2/hrly) to either the Westbahnhof (35 min) or the City Air Terminal (20 min) near the river in the old center. Taxis into town cost about 400 AS. Hotels arrange for fixed-rate car service to the airport (30-minute ride, 400 AS).

Getting around Vienna

By Bus, Tram, and Metro: Take full advantage of Vienna's simple, cheap, and super-efficient transit system. Buses, trams, and the metro all use the same tickets. Buy your tickets from *Tabak*

shops, station machines, or Vorverkauf offices in the station.
You have lots of choices:

- single tickets (19 AS, 22 AS if bought on tram—exact change only, good for 1 journey with necessary transfers)
- 24-hour pass (60 AS)
- 72-hour pass (150 AS)
- 7-day pass (155 AS, Mon–Sun)
- 8 Tage Umwelt Streifennetzkarte: eight all-day strips for 300 AS (can be shared, e.g., 4 people for 2 days each). Per person cost: 38 AS/day (compared to 60 AS/day for a 24-hour pass—a big savings for groups).

Take a moment to study the eye-friendly city center map on metro station walls to internalize how the metro and tram system can help you (metro routes are signed by the end-of-the-line stop). I use it mostly to zip along the Ring (tram #1 or #2), and take the metro to more outlying sights or hotels. The 30-AS transit map is overkill. All necessary routes are listed on the free tourist city map. Numbered lines (e.g., #38) are trams, numbers followed by an "A" (e.g., #38A) are buses.

Stamp a time on your ticket or transit pass as you enter the system or tram (stiff 600-AS fine if caught without a validated ticket—then they make you buy a ticket). Rookies miss stops because they fail to open the door. Push buttons, pull latches—do whatever it takes. Study your street map before you exit the metro. Choosing the right exit—signposted from the moment you step off the train—saves lots of walking (for information call 01/790-9105).

By Taxi: Vienna's comfortable, civilized, and easy-to-flag-down taxis start at 27 AS. You'll pay 90 AS to go from the Opera to the South or West Train Station.

By Bike: Good as the city's transit system is, you may want to rent a bike and follow one of the routes recommended in the TI's biking brochure. Bikes are available at any train station (daily 04:00–24:00, 100 AS/day with railpass or train ticket, 150 AS without; rent early in morning before supply runs out, tel. 01/5800-32985). Pedal Power offers rental bikes (300 AS/half day, 395 AS/24 hrs, includes delivery and pick up from your hotel) and 3.5-hour, two-language city tours (daily at 10:00, 280 AS includes bike, Austellungsstrasse 3, U-1 to Praterstern and 5-minute walk, tel. 01/729-7234, www.pedalpower.co.at).

By Buggy: Rich romantics get around by traditional horse and buggy. You'll see the horse buggies, called Fiakers, clip-clopping tourists on tours lasting 20 minutes (500 AS), 40 minutes (800 AS), or one hour (1,300 AS).

Helpful Hints

Bank Alert: Abundant ATMs are the smart way to change money. Banking is expensive in Vienna. Save three percent by comparing rates. (Warning: "Rieger Bank" is an expensive exchange bureau in disguise.) Banks are open weekdays roughly from 8:00 to 15:00 and until 17:30 on Tuesday and Thursday. After hours you can change money at train stations, the airport, or post offices. Commissions of 100 AS are sadly normal (American Express charges no commissions on its checks, Mon–Fri 9:00–17:30, Sat 9:00–12:00, Kärntner Strasse 21–23, tel. 01/5154-0456).

Post Offices: Choose from the main post office (Postgasse in center, open 24 hrs daily, handy metered phones), West and South Train Stations (open 04:00–24:00), and one near the Opera (Mon–Fri 7:00–19:00, Krugerstrasse 13).

English Bookstores: Consider the British Bookshop (at the corner of Weihburggasse and Seilerstätte) or Shakespeare & Co. (Sterngasse 2, north of Höher Markt square, tel. 01/535-5053).

Internet Access: The TI has an updated list. Amadeus in Steffl is central (Mon–Fri 9:30–19:00, Sat–Sun 9:30–17:00, Kärntner Strasse 19, tel. 01/513-1450) and Internet Aktiv is near the Mariahilfer Strasse hotels (Zieglergasse 29, tel. 01/526-7389). Coffeeshop Company (a Starbucks-like place just off Kärntner Strasse at Krugerstrasse 6) gives free Internet access to customers.

Laundry: These are few and far between; ask at your hotel. Gottshalks will do your laundry in a day (50 AS/1 kilo, Mon–Fri 8:00–18:00, Sat 9:00–12:00, near St. Stephan's at Singerstrasse 22). Launderette, near Mariahilfer Strasse, is handy (Mon–Fri 8:00–18:00, closed Sat–Sun, Siebensternstrasse 52, walk 4 blocks up Zollergasse from Mariahilfer Strasse).

City Tours

Walks: The *Walks in Vienna* brochure at the TI describes Vienna's guided walks in English (basic 90-minute intro, 140 AS, daily at 14:00 from TI and other locations, tel. 01/876-7111, www .wienguide.at). Monika Tentschert, a local teacher and private guide who knows her stuff, charges 1,500 AS for a half-day tour (tel. 01/212-0640).

Bus Tours: Vienna Line offers hop-on hop-off tours covering the 14 predictable sightseeing stops. Given Vienna's excellent public transportation and this outfit's meager one-bus-per-hour frequency, I'd take this not to hop on and off, but only to get the narrated orientation drive through town (in German and English, 250 AS, good for 2 days, or 140 AS if you stay on for 1 ride). The basic Vienna city sights tour includes a visit to the Schönnbrun Palace and a bus tour around town (3.5 hrs, 400 AS, 3/day from Opera, to book this or get info on other tours, call 01/712-46830).

Do-It-Yourself Bus Orientation Tour

▲▲**Ringstrasse Tram #2 Tour**—In the 1860s Emperor Franz Josef had the city's ingrown medieval wall torn down and replaced

Vienna

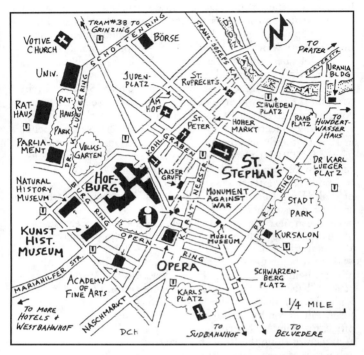

with a grand boulevard 190 feet wide. The road, arcing nearly three miles around the city's core, predates all the buildings that line it. So what you'll see is neo-Gothic, neoclassical, and neo-Renaissance. One of Europe's great streets, it's lined with many of the city's top sights. Trams #1 and #2 and a great bike path circle the whole route and so should you.

This self-service tram tour gives you a fun orientation and a ridiculously quick glimpse of the major sights as you glide by (19 AS, 30-minute circular tour). For an actual look at these sights, consider biking or hiking most of the route. Tram #1 goes clockwise; tram #2, counterclockwise. Most sights are on the outside, so tram #2 is best (sit on right—ideally in the front of the front car). Start at the Opera House. You can jump on and off as you go—trams come every five minutes. Read ahead and pay attention, these sights can fly by. Let's go:

☛ Immediately on the left: The city's main pedestrian drag, Kärntner Strasse, leads to the zigzag roof of **St. Stephan's Cathedral**. This tram tour makes a 360-degree circle around the cathedral, staying about this same distance from it.

☛ At first bend (before first stop): Look right toward the tall fountain and the guy on a horse. Schwartzenberg Platz shows off its **equestrian statue** of Prince Charles Schwartzenberg, who fought Napoleon. Behind that is the Russian monument (behind the fountain), which was built in 1945 as a forced thanks to the Soviets for liberating Austria from the Nazis. Formerly a sore point, now it's just ignored.

☛ Going down Schubertring, you reach the huge *Stadtpark* (city park) on the right, which honors 20 great Viennese musicians and composers with statues. At the beginning of the park, the white-and-yellow concert hall behind the trees is the **Kursalon**, opened in 1867 by the Strauss brothers, who directed many waltzes here (closed in 2001 for restoration, normally site of great waltz concerts, may reopen late in 2001, more likely in 2002).

☛ Immediately after next stop: In the same park, the gilded statue of Waltz King **Johann Strauss** holds his violin as he did when he conducted his orchestra.

☛ While at next stop at end of park: On the left, a green statue of Dr. Karl Lueger honors the popular man who was mayor of Vienna until 1910.

☛ At next bend: On the right, the quaint white building with military helmets decorating the windows was the Austrian ministry of war—back when that was a serious operation. Field Marshal Radetzky, a military big shot in the 19th century under Franz Josef, still sits on his high horse. He's pointing towards the post office, the only Art Nouveau building on the Ring. Locals call the architecture along the Ring "**historicism**" because it's all neo-this and neo-that—generally fitting the purpose of the building (farther along the Ring, we'll see: a neo-Gothic city hall—recalling when medieval burgers ran the city government in Gothic days; a neoclassical parliament building—celebrating ancient Greek notions of democracy; and a neo-Renaissance opera house—venerating the high culture filling it).

☛ At next corner: The white-domed building over your right shoulder as you turn is the Urania, Franz Josef's 1910 **observatory**. Lean forward and look behind it for a peek at the huge red cars of the giant 100-year-old Ferris wheel in Vienna's Prater Park (fun for families, described in "Top People-Watching and Strolling Sights," below).

☛ Now you're rolling along the **Danube Canal**. This "Baby Danube" is one of the many small arms of the river that once made up the Danube at this location. The rest have been gathered together in a mightier modern-day Danube, farther away. This was the site of the original Roman town, Vindobona. In three long blocks, on the left (opposite BP station, be ready—it passes fast), you'll see the ivy-covered walls and round Romanesque arches of St. Ruprechts, the oldest church in Vienna (built in the

11th century on a bit of Roman ruins). By about 1200, Vienna had grown to fill the area within this ring road.

☞ Leaving the canal, turning up Schottenring, at first stop: On the left, the orange-and-white, neo-Renaissance temple of money, the **Börse**, is Vienna's stock exchange.

☞ Next stop, at corner: The huge, frilly, neo-Gothic church on the right is a "votive church," built as a thanks to God when an 1853 assassination attempt on Emperor Franz Josef failed. Ahead on the right (in front of tram stop) is the Vienna University building (established in 1365, it has no real campus as the buildings are scattered around town). It faces (on the left, behind gilded angel) a chunk of the old city wall.

☞ At next stop on right: The neo-Gothic city hall, flying the flag of Europe, towers over **Rathaus Platz**, a festive site in summer with a huge screen showing outdoor movies, opera, and concerts. Immediately across the street (on left) is the **Hofburg Theater**, Austria's national theater.

☞ At next stop on right: The neo-Greek temple of democracy houses the **Austrian Parliament**. The lady with the golden helmet is Athena, goddess of wisdom. Across the street (on left) is the royal park called the "Volksgarten."

☞ After next stop on the right is the **Natural History Museum**, the first of Vienna's huge twin museums. It faces the **Kunsthistorisches Museum**, containing the city's greatest collection of paintings. A hefty statue of Empress Maria Theresa sits between the museums, facing the grand gate to the **Hofburg**, the emperor's palace (on left). Of the five arches, only the center one was used by the emperor.

☞ Fifty meters after the next stop, on the left through a gate in the black iron fence is the statue of Mozart. It's one of many charms in the **Burggarten**, which until 1880 was the private garden of the emperor. Vienna had more than its share of intellectual and creative geniuses. A hundred meters farther (on left, just out of the park), Goethe sits in a big, thought-provoking chair playing trivia with Schiller (across the street on your right). Behind the statue of Schiller is the Academy of Fine Arts.

☞ Hey, there's the **Opera** again. Jump off the bus and see the rest of the city.

Sights—Vienna's Old Center
Sights are listed in a logical walking order.

▲▲▲**Opera (Staatsoper)**—The Opera, facing the Ring and near the TI, is a central point for any visitor. While the critical reception of the building 130 years ago led the architect to commit suicide, and though it's been rebuilt since the WWII bombings, it's still a dazzling place (65 AS, by guided 35-minute tour only, daily in English, July–Aug at 11:00, 13:00, 14:00, 15:00, and often at 10:00 and 16:00; Sept–June afternoons only). Tours are often canceled for rehearsals and shows, so check the posted schedule or call 01/514-442-959.

The Vienna State Opera is one of the world's top opera houses, even though the Vienna Philharmonic Orchestra doesn't perform here. Instead its farm team plays in the pit (you can't get into the best orchestra in town without doing time here first). There are 300 performances a year—nearly nightly, except in July and August when the singers rest their voices. Expensive seats are normally sold out.

Tickets for seats: For ticket information call 01/513-1513 (phone answered daily 10:00–21:00, www.culturall.com, e-mail: tickets@volksoper.at). Last-minute tickets are sold for 400 AS from 9:00 to 12:00 the day before.

Standing room: Unless Pavarotti is in town, it's easy to get one of 567 *Stehplatz* (standing-room spots, 30–50 AS at the very top or—better—downstairs). The *Stehplatz* ticket window in the front lobby opens 80 minutes before each performance (tel. 01/5144-42419). If fewer than 567 people are in line, there's no need to line up early. Dress is casual (but do your best) at the standing-room bar.

Rick's crude tip: For me, three hours is a lot of opera. But just to see and hear the Opera House in action for half an hour is a treat. You can buy a standing room spot intending to just drop in for part of the show. Ushers don't mind letting tourists with standing-room tickets in for a short look. Ending time is posted in the lobby—you could drop in for just the finale. If you go for the start or finish you'll see Vienna dressed up. With all the time you save, consider stopping by...

Sacher Café, home of every chocoholic's fantasy, the *Sachertorte*, faces the rear of the Opera (on Philharmoniker Strasse). While locals complain that the cakes have gone down-hill, a coffee and slice of cake here is 100 AS well invested.

▲**Monument against War and Fascism**—A powerful four-part statue stands behind the Opera House, on Albertinaplatz. The split white statue, "The Gates of Violence," remembers the victims of the 1938 to 1945 Nazi rule of Austria. A montage of wartime images—clubs and gas masks, a dying woman birthing a future soldier, slave laborers—sits on a pedestal of granite cut from the infamous quarry at Mathausen, a nearby concentration camp. The hunched-over figure on the ground behind is a Jew forced to wash anti-Nazi graffiti off a street with a toothbrush. The statue with its head buried in the stone reminds Austrians of the consequences of not keeping their government on track. The 1945 declaration of Austria's second republic is cut into the stone behind that. The monument stands over the spot where a hundred people were buried alive while hiding in the cellar of a fancy building, demolished in a WWII bombing attack.

Austria was pulled into World War II by Germany, who annexed the country in 1938, saying Austrians were wannabe Germans anyway. But Austrians are not Germans—never were, never will be. They're quick to tell you that, while Austria was founded in 976, Germany wasn't born until 1870. For seven years during World War II (1938–1945), there was no Austria. In 1955, after 10 years of joint occupation by the victorious Allies, Austria regained her independence.

▲**Kärntner Strasse**—This grand mall (traffic free since 1974) is the people-watching delight of this in-love-with-life city. It points south in the direction of the southern Austrian state of Kärnten (for which it's named). Starting from the Opera, you'll find lots of action—shops, street music, the city casino (at #41), American Express (#21–23), and then, finally, the cathedral.

▲▲**Haus der Musik**—Vienna's newest museum is long overdue— the House of Music. While it has a floor devoted to the Vienna Philharmonic and fine audio-visual exhibits on each of the famous hometown boys (Haydn, Mozart, Beethoven, Strauss, and Mahler), this museum is unique for its effective use of interactive touch-screen computers and headphones to literally put you in the musical driving seat. You can twist, dissect, and bend sounds to make your own musical language, merge your voice with a duck's quack or a city's traffic roar. Wander through the "sonosphere" and marvel at the amazing acoustics—I could actually hear what I thought only a piano tuner can hear. Pick up a virtual baton to conduct the Vienna Philharmonic Orchestra (each time you screw up, the orchestra stops and ridicules you). Really seeing the place takes time. It's open late and makes a good evening activity (110 AS, daily 10:00– 22:00, 2 blocks from Opera at Seilerstatte 30, tel. 01/51648).

▲▲**St. Stephan's Cathedral**—Stephansdom is the Gothic needle around which Vienna spins. It's survived Vienna's many wars and symbolizes the city's freedom (daily 6:00–22:00, entertaining English tours daily April–Oct at 15:45, information board inside entry has tour schedules and time of impressive 50-minute daily mass).

This is the third church to stand on this spot. (In fact, an older Romanesque chapel—the Virgilkapelle—is on display in the adjacent metro station.) The last bit of the 11th-century Roman-esque church can be seen on the west end (above the entry): the portal and the round windows of the towers. The church survived the bombs of World War II, but, in the last days of the war, fires from the street fighting between Russian and Nazi troops leapt to the rooftop; the original timbered Gothic rooftop burned, and the cathedral's huge bell crashed to the ground. With a financial out-pouring of civic pride, the roof of this symbol of Austria was rebuilt in its original splendor by 1952. The ceramic tiles are purely deco-rative (locals each "own" one for the many small post-war donations made to finance the rebuilding).

Inside, find the Gothic sandstone **pulpit** in the middle of the nave (on left). A spiral stairway winds up to the lectern, surrounded and supported by the four Latin Church fathers: Saints Ambrose, Jerome, Gregory, and Augustine. The railing leading up swarms with symbolism: lizards (animals of light), battle toads (animals of darkness), and the "Dog of the Lord" standing at the top to be sure none of those toads pollute the sermon. Below the toads, wheels with three parts (the Trinity) roll up while wheels with four parts (standing for the four seasons, symbolizing mortal life) roll down. This work, by Anton Pilgram, has all the elements of flamboyant Gothic in miniature. But this was around 1500, and the Italian Renaissance was going strong in Italy. While Gothic persisted in the north, the Renaissance spirit had already arrived. Pilgram included a rare self-portrait bust in his work (the guy with sculptor's tools, looking out a window under the stairs). Gothic art was to the glory of God. Artists were anonymous. In the more humanist Renaissance, man was allowed to shine—and artists became famous.

St. Stephan's is draped in history—carved in its walls and buried in its **crypt** (left transept, 40 AS, open at odd times, tel. 01/5155-23526). You can ascend both towers, the north (via crowded elevator inside on the left) and the south (outside right transept, by spiral staircase). The north shows you a big bell (the 21-ton Pummerin, cast from the cannon captured from the Turks in 1683, supposedly the second biggest bell in the world that rings by swinging) but a mediocre view (50 AS, Mon–Sat 9:00–18:00, Sun 13:00–17:00). The 450-foot-high **south tower**, called St. Stephan's Tower, offers a great view—343 tightly wound steps up the spiral staircase (30 AS, daily 9:00–17:30, this hike burns about one *Sachertorte* of calories). From the top, use your *Vienna from A to Z* to locate the famous sights.

The peaceful Cathedral Museum (Dom Museum, outside left transept past horses) gives a close-up look at piles of religious paintings, statues, and a treasury (50 AS, Tue–Sat 10:00–17:00, closed Mon, behind church and past buggy stand, Stephansplatz 6).

▲▲**Stephansplatz, Graben, and Kohlmarkt**—The atmosphere of the church square, Stephansplatz, is colorful and lively. At nearby Graben Street (which was once a *Graben* or "ditch"), top-notch street entertainment dances around an exotic plague monument (at Brauner Strass). In medieval times people did not understand the causes of plagues and figured they were a punishment from God. It was common for survivors to thank God with a monument like this one from the 1600s. Find Emperor Leopold, who ruled during the plague and made this statue in gratitude. (Hint: The typical inbreeding of royal families left him with a gaping underbite.) Below Leopold, "Faith" (with the help of a disgusting little cupid) tosses old naked women—symbolizing the plague—into the abyss.

Just beyond the monument is a fine set of Jugendstil public toilets (5.50 AS). St. Peter's Church faces the toilets. Step into this festival of Baroque (from 1708) and check out the jeweled skeletons (flanking the altar—anonymous martyrs donated by the pope.

At the end of Graben, turn left on **Kohlmarkt**, Vienna's most elegant shopping street (except for "American Catalog Shopping," at #5, second floor). Kohlmarkt leads to the palace. En route, check out the edible window displays at Demel (Kohlmarkt 14). Then drool through the interior (coffee and cake for 100 AS). Shops like this boast "K. u. K." This means a shop considered good enough for the *König und Kaiser* (king and emperor—same guy).

Kohlmarkt ends at Michaelerplatz. The stables of the Spanish Riding School face this square a block to the left. Notice the Roman excavation in the center. Enter the Hofburg Palace by walking through the gate, under the dome, and into the first square (In der Burg).

Sights—Vienna's Hofburg Palace

▲▲**Hofburg**—The complex, confusing, and imposing Imperial Palace, with 640 years of architecture, demands your attention. This first Hapsburg residence grew with the family empire from the 13th century until 1913, when the new wing was opened. The winter residence of the Hapsburg rulers until 1918, it's still the home of the Spanish Riding School, the Vienna Boys' Choir, the Austrian president's office, 5,000 government workers, and several important museums.

Rather than lose yourself in its myriad halls and courtyards, focus on three things: the Imperial Apartments, Treasury, and Neue Burg (New Palace).

Orient from **In der Burg Square**. The statue is of Emperor Franz II, grandson of Maria Theresa, grandfather of Franz Josef, and father-in-law of Napoleon. Behind him is a tower with three kinds of clocks (the yellow disc shows the stage of the moon tonight). On the right, a door leads to the Imperial Apartments and Hofburg model. Franz II faces the oldest part of the palace. The colorful gate, which used to have a drawbridge, leads to the 13th-century Swiss Court (named for the Swiss mercenary guards once stationed here), the Schatzkammer (treasury), and the Hof-burgkappelle (palace chapel, where the Boys' Choir sings the mass). For the Hero's Square and the New Palace, continue opposite the way you entered In der Burg, passing through the left-most tunnel (with a tiny but handy sandwich bar—Hofburg Stüberl).

Tour the Imperial Apartments first.

▲▲**Imperial Apartments (Kaiserappartements)**—These lavish, Versailles-type "wish-I-were-God" royal rooms are a small, downtown version of the grander Schönbrunn Palace. If rushed

Vienna's Hofburg Palace

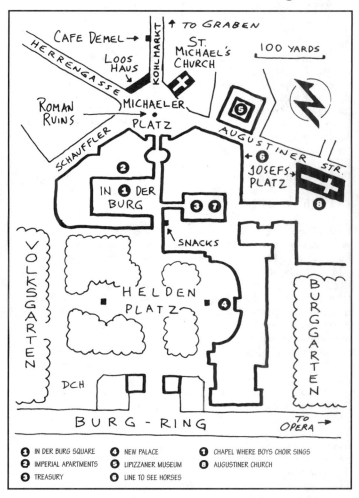

1 IN DER BURG SQUARE   **4** NEW PALACE   **7** CHAPEL WHERE BOYS CHOIR SINGS

2 IMPERIAL APARTMENTS   **5** LIPIZZANER MUSEUM   **8** AUGUSTINER CHURCH

3 TREASURY   **6** LINE TO SEE HORSES

and you have time for only one, these suffice (95 AS, daily 9:00–
17:00, from courtyard through St. Michael's Gate, just off
Michaelerplatz, tel. 01/533-7570). Study the great Hofburg
model outside near the ticket line. Palace visits are a one-way
romp through 20 rooms. You'll find some helpful English information within, and, together with the following description, you
won't need the 95-AS Hofburg guidebook. Tickets include the
royal silver and porcelain collection near the turnstile.

Get your ticket and climb two flights. The first two rooms give an overview (in English) of Empress Elisabeth's assortment of luxury homes, including the Hofburg.

Amble through the first several furnished rooms to the ...

Audience chamber: Every citizen had the right to meet privately with the emperor. Three huge paintings would entertain guests while they waited. They were propaganda, showing crowds of commoners enthusiastic about their Hapsburg royalty. On the right: The emperor returning to Vienna celebrating news that Napoleon had begun his retreat in 1809. Left: The return of the emperor from the 1814 Peace of Paris, the treaty that ended the Napoleonic wars. (The 1815 Congress of Vienna that followed was the greatest assembly of diplomats in European history. Its goal: to establish peace through a "balance of power" among nations. While rulers ignored nationalism in favor of continued dynastic rule, this worked for about 100 years, when a colossal war—World War I—wiped out Europe's royal families.) Center: Less important, the emperor makes his first public appearance to adoring crowds after recovering from a life-threatening illness (1826). The chandelier—considered the best in the palace—is Baroque of Bohemian crystal.

Audience room: Suddenly you were face-to-face with the emp. The portrait on the easel shows Franz Josef (who gets my vote for the greatest Hapsburg emperor) in 1915 when he was over 80 years old. Famously energetic, he lived a spartan life dedicated to duty. He'd stand at the high table here to meet with commoners who came to show gratitude or make a request. (Standing kept things moving.) On the table you see a partial list of 56 appointments he had on January 3, 1910.

Conference room: The emperor presided here over the equivalent of cabinet meetings. Remember, after 1867, he ruled the Austro-Hungarian Empire and Hungarians sat at these meetings. The paintings on the wall show the military defeat of a popular Hungarian uprising ... subtle.

Emperor Franz Josef's study: The desk was originally between the windows. Franz Josef could look up from his work and see his lovely empress Elisabeth's reflection in the mirror. Notice the trompe l'oeil paintings above each door giving the believable illusion of marble relief.

The walls between the rooms are wide enough to hide servants' corridors (the door to his valet's room is open). The emperor lived with a personal staff of 14: "3 valets, 4 lackeys, 2 doormen, 2 manservants, and 3 chambermaids."

Emperor's bedroom: This features his famous spartan iron bed and portable washstand (necessary until 1880 when the palace got running water). A small painted porcelain portrait of the newlywed royal couple sits on the dresser. Franz Josef lived

Sissy

Empress Elisabeth, Emperor Franz Joseph's mysterious, nar-
cissistic, and beautiful wife, is in vogue. She was mostly
silent, worked out frantically to maintain her Barbie Doll figure, and spent hours each day tending to her ankle-length
hair. Sissy's main purpose in life seemed to be to preserve
her reputation as a beautiful empress and maintain her fairy-
tale hair. In spite of severe dieting and fanatic exercise, age
took its toll. After turning 30, she allowed no more portraits
painted and was seen in public generally with a delicate fan
covering her face. Complex and influential, she was adored
by Franz Joseph whom she respected. Her political cause was
promoting Hungary's bid for nationalism, her tragedy was
the death of her son Rudolf, the crown prince, by suicide.
Hating Vienna and the confines of the court, she traveled
more and more frequently. Over the years, the restless Sissy
and her hardworking husband became estranged. In 1898,
while visiting Geneva, Switzerland, she was murdered by an
Italian anarchist. Sissy has been compared to Princess Diana
because of her beauty, bittersweet life, and tragic death.

here after his estrangement from Sissy. An etching shows the
empress—an avid hunter—riding sidesaddle while jumping a
hedge. The big ornate stove in the corner was fed from behind.
Through the 19th century, this was a standard form of heating.

Great salon: See the paintings of the emperor and empress in
grand gala ballroom outfits from 1865. Look for window shades
with English descriptions of royal life in the next several rooms.

Emperor's smoking room: This is dedicated to the memory
of the assassinated Emperor Maximillian of Mexico (bearded
portrait, killed in 1867). A smoking room was necessary in the
early 19th century, when smoking was newly fashionable but only
for men and then not in the presence of women.

Empress' bedroom and drawing room: This was Sissy's,
refurbished neo-rococo in 1854. She lived here—the bed was
rolled in and out daily—until her death in 1898.

Sissy's dressing/gymnastic room: This was the marital
bedroom of the newlywed couple. The open bathroom door shows
her huge copper tub. Servants worked two hours a day on Sissy's
famous hair here. She'd exercise on the wooden structure. While
she had a tough time with people, she did fine with animals. Her
favorite circus horses, Flick and Flock, prance on the wall.

Empress' great salon: The royal room is painted with

Mediterranean escapes, the 19th-century equivalent of travel posters. The statue is of Elisa, Napoleon's oldest sister (by the neoclassical master Canova). At the end of the hall admire the Empress' hard-earned thin waist. Turn the corner and pass through the anterooms of Alexander's apartments.

Reception room: The Gobelin wall hangings were a 1776 gift from Marie Antoinette and Louis XVI in Paris to their Viennese counterparts.

Dining room: It's dinner time, and Franz Josef has called his large family together. The settings are modest...just silver. Gold was saved for formal state dinners. Next to each name card was a menu with the chef responsible for each dish. (Talk about pressure.) While the Hofburg had tableware for 4,000, feeding 3,000 was a typical day. The cellar was stocked with 60,000 bottles of wine. The kitchen was huge—50 birds could be roasted on the hand-driven spits at once.

Small salon: The last room is dedicated to Franz Josef's first two heirs: Rudolf (his troubled son, who committed suicide in 1889) and Franz Ferdinand (his liberal nephew, assassinated in Sarajevo in 1914). Back on the street, two quick lefts take you back to the palace square (In der Burg) and the treasury.

▲▲▲Treasury (Weltliche und Geistliche Schatzkammer)— This Secular and Religious Treasure Room contains the best jewels on the Continent. Slip through the vault doors and reflect on the glitter of 21 rooms filled with scepters, swords, crowns, orbs, weighty robes, double-headed eagles, gowns, gem-studded bangles, and a 2.5-meter-tall, 500-year-old unicorn horn (or maybe the tusk of a narwhal)—which was incredibly powerful in the old days, giving its owner the grace of God. Remember that these were owned by the Holy Roman Emperor—a divine monarch (100 AS, Wed–Mon 10:00–18:00, closed Tue, follow "Schatzkammer" signs through the black, red, and gold arch leading from the main courtyard into Schweizerhof, tel. 01/533-7931). Take advantage of the ingenious and extremely helpful Art-Guide mini-video (free, deposit: passport or 100 AS). Point this infrared computer at display cases to get information.

Room 2: The personal crown of Rudolf II survived since 1602 because it was considered too well crafted to cannibalize for other crowns. This crown is a big deal because it's the adopted crown of the Austrian Empire, established in 1806 after Napoleon dissolved the Holy Roman Empire (so named because it had tried to be the grand continuation of the Roman Empire). Pressured by Napoleon, the Austrian Francis II—who'd been Holy Roman Emperor—became Francis I, Emperor of Austria. Francis I/II (the stern guy on the wall) ruled from 1792 to 1835. Look at the crown. Its design merges the typical medieval king's crown and a bishop's miter.

Rooms 3 and 4: These contain some of the coronation vestments and regalia needed for the new Austrian emperor.

Room 5: Ponder the Throne Cradle. Napoleon's son was born in 1811 and made king of Rome. The little eagle at the foot is symbolically not yet able to fly but glory bound. Glory is symbolized by the star with dad's big "N" raised high.

Room 11: The collection's highlight is the 10th-century crown of the Holy Roman Emperor. The imperial crown swirls with symbolism "proving" that the emperor is both holy and Roman. The jeweled arch over the top is reminiscent of the parade helmet of ancient Roman emperors whose successors the HRE claimed to be. The cross on top says that the HRE rules as Christ's representative on earth. King Solomon's portrait (right of cross) is Old Testament proof that kings can be wise and good. King David (next panel) is similar proof that they can be just. The crown's eight sides represent the celestial city of Jerusalem's eight gates. The jewels on the front panel symbolize the Twelve Apostles. The nearby 11th-century Imperial Cross preceded the emperor in ceremonies. Crusted with jewels, it carried a substantial chunk of *the* cross (see it below).

Two cases in this room have jewels from the reign of Karl der Grosse (Charlemagne), the greatest ruler of medieval Europe. Notice Charlemagne modeling the crown in the tall painting adjacent.

Room 12: This features a painting of the coronation of Josef II in 1764, wearing the crown and royal garb you've just seen.

Room 16: Most tourists walk right by perhaps the most exquisite workmanship in the entire treasury, the royal vestments (15th century). Look closely—they are painted with gold and silver threads.

▲**Hero's Square and the New Palace (Heldenplatz and the Neue Burg)**—This last grand addition to the palace, from just before World War I, was built for Franz Ferdinand but never used. (It was tradition for rulers not to move into their predecessor's quarters.) Its grand facade arches around Heldenplatz, or Hero's Square. Notice statues of the two great Austrian heroes on horseback: Prince Eugene of Savoy (who saved the city from the Turks) and Archduke Charles (first to beat Napoleon in a battle, breaking Nappy's image of invincibility and heralding the end of the Napoleonic age). The frilly spires of Vienna's neo-Gothic city hall break the horizon and a line of horse-drawn carriages await their customers.

▲**New Palace Museums: Armor, Music, and Ancient Greek Statues**—The Neue Burg—labeled "Kunsthistorisches Museum" because it contains one wing from the main museum across the way—houses three small but fine museums (same ticket): an armory, historical musical instruments, and classical statuary from ancient

Ephesus. The musical instruments are particularly entertaining.
Free radio headsets—when they work—play appropriate music
in each room. Wait for the brief German description to finish, and
you might hear the instruments you're seeing. Stay tuned in, as
graceful period music accompanies your wander through the neighboring halls of medieval weaponry—a killer collection of crossbows,
swords, and armor. An added bonus is the chance to wander all
alone among those royal Hapsburg halls, stairways, and painted
ceilings (60 AS, Wed–Mon 10:00–18:00, closed Tue, almost no
tourists, not a word of English—and proud of it).

More Hofburg Sights

These sights are near—and associated with—the palace.
▲**Lipizzaner Museum**—A must for horse lovers, this tidy
museum in the Renaissance Stallburg Palace shows (and tells
in English) the 400-year history of the famous riding school.
Videos show the horses in action (on TVs throughout and in
the basement theater—45-minute movie in German, but great
horse footage). A highlight for many is the opportunity to view
the stable from a museum window and actually see the famous
white horses just sitting there looking common (70 AS, daily
9:00–18:00, Reitschulgasse 2 between Josefsplatz and Michaelerplatz, tel. 01/533-7811). Part of the exhibit explains how, at the
end of World War II, U.S. General Patton—knowing that the
Soviets were about to take control of Vienna—ordered a raid
on the stable to save the horses and insure the survival of their
fine old bloodlines.
   Seeing the Lipizzaner Stallions: Seats for performances
by Vienna's prestigious Spanish Riding School book up long in
advance, but standing room is usually available the same day
(tickets-250–900 AS, standing room-200 AS, 1 or 2 shows/week
May–June and Sept–Dec). Lucky for the masses, training sessions
in a chandeliered Baroque hall are open to the public (100 AS at
the door, Tue–Fri 10:00–12:00 roughly Feb–June and Sept–Dec;
occasional rehearsals with music on Sat are more entertaining than
the generally low-energy training sessions). The gang lines up
early at Josefsplatz, gate 2. Save money and avoid the wait by
buying the 140-AS combo ticket covering both the museum and
the training session. Or, better yet, simply show up late. Tourists
line up for hours to get in at 10:00. Since almost no one stays for
the full two hours—except for the horses—you can just waltz in
with no wait at all after 11:00.
▲**Augustinian Church**—Step into the nearby Augustinerkirche
(on Josefsplatz), the Gothic and neo-Gothic church where the
Hapsburgs latched, then buried, their hearts (weddings took place
here and the royal hearts are in the vault). Don't miss the exquisite
Canova tomb (neoclassical, 1805) of Maria Theresa's favorite

daughter, Maria Christina, with its incredibly sad white-marble procession. The church's 11:00 Sunday mass is a hit with music lovers (pipe organ and choral, especially outside of summer).

▲▲**Kaisergruft, the Remains of the Hapsburgs**—Visiting the imperial remains is not as easy as you might imagine. These original organ donors left their bodies—147 in all—in the Kaisergruft (Capuchin Crypt), their hearts in the Augustinian Church (church open daily, but to see the goods you'll have to talk to a priest; Augustinerstrasse 3), and their entrails in the crypt below St. Stephan's Cathedral. Don't tripe.

Upon entering the Kaisergruft (40 AS, daily 9:30–16:00, behind Opera on Neuer Markt), see the Capuchin brother at the door and buy the 5-AS map with a Hapsburg family tree and a chart locating each coffin. The double coffin of Maria Theresa and her husband is worth a close look for its artwork. Don't miss the tombs of Franz Josef, Sissy (always with fresh flowers), and—the latest addition—Empress Zita, buried in 1989. Her burial procession was probably the last such Old Regime event in European history. The monarchy died hard in Austria. Take a whiff. The crypt is smelling funny and will probably be closed sometime in the near future for restoration and freshening up.

Rather than chasing down all these body parts, remember that the magnificence of this city is the real remains of the Hapsburgs. Pan up. Watch the clouds glide by the ornate gables of Vienna.

Sights—Schönbrunn Palace

▲▲▲**Schönbrunn Palace**—Among Europe's palaces, only Schloss Schönbrunn rivals Versailles. Located four miles from the center, it was the Hapsburgs' summer residence. It's big—1,441 rooms—but don't worry, only 40 rooms are shown to the public. (The families of 260 civil servants actually rent simple apartments in the rest of the palace.)

While the exterior is Baroque, the interior was finished under Maria Theresa in let-them-eat-cake rococo. The chandeliers are either of hand-carved wood with gold-leaf gilding or of Bohemian crystal. Thick walls hid the servants as they ran around stoking the ceramic stoves from the back, and so on. Most of the public rooms are decorated in neo-Baroque as they were under Franz Josef (ruled 1848–1916). When World War II bombs rained on the city and the palace grounds, the palace itself took only one direct hit. Thankfully, that bomb, which crashed through three floors, including the sumptuous central ballroom, was a dud.

Reservations, Hours: Schönbrunn suffers from crowds. To avoid the long delays, make a reservation by telephone (01/8111-3239, they answer daily 8:00–17:00). You'll get an appointment time and ticket number. Check in at least 30 minutes early. Upon arrival, go to the first desk for group leaders, give your number, pick up your ticket, and jump in ahead of the masses. If you show up without calling first, you deserve the frustration. Wait in line, buy your ticket, and wait until the listed time to enter (which could be tomorrow). Kill time in the gardens or coach museum (palace open daily 8:30–17:45, last entry 17:00, off-season until 17:15, last entry 16:30). Crowds are worst from 9:30 to 11:30 and on weekends; it's least crowded from 12:00 to 14:00 and after 16:00.

Cost, Tours: The admission price is the price of the tour you select. Choose among two recorded audioguide tours (Imperial Tour or the bigger Grand Tour) or a live tour. The Imperial Tour covers 22 rooms (95 AS, 35 min, Grand Palace rooms plus apartments of Franz Josef and Elisabeth). I'd recommend the Grand Tour, which covers those 22 rooms plus 18 more (125 AS, 75 min, adds apartments of Maria Theresa). While there are occasional live guided tours doing all 40 rooms (150 AS, call day before your visit to ask if English tour is scheduled), I prefer the headphones.

Getting to Palace: Take tram #58 from Westbahnhof directly to the palace or ride U-4 to Schönbrunn and walk 300 meters. The main entrance is in the left side of the palace (as you face it).

Coach Museum Wagenburg—The Schönbrunn coach museum is a 19th-century traffic jam of 50 impressive royal carriages and sleighs. Highlights include silly sedan chairs, the death-black hearse carriage (used for Franz Josef in 1916 and most recently for Empress Zita in 1989), and an extravagantly gilded imperial carriage pulled by eight Cinderella horses (60 AS, daily 9:00–18:00, off-season 10:00–16:00 and closed on winter Mon, 200 meters from palace, walk through right arch as you face palace).

Palace Gardens—After strolling through all the Hapsburgs tucked neatly into their crypts, a stroll through the emperor's garden with countless commoners is a celebration of the natural (and necessary) evolution of civilization from autocracy into real democracy. As a civilization, we're doing well. The sculpted gardens (with a palm house, 60 AS, 9:30–18:00) lead past Europe's oldest zoo (Tiergarten, 120 AS, built by Maria Theresa's husband for the entertainment and education of the court in 1752) up to the Gloriette, a purely decorative monument celebrating an obscure Austrian military victory and offering a fine city view (and an expensive cup of coffee). The park is free (daily 6:00–20:30, entrance on either side of the palace).

Vienna's Other Top Sights
▲▲▲**Kunsthistorisches Museum**—This exciting museum across the Ring from the Hofburg Palace showcases the great Hapsburg art collection—masterpieces by Dürer, Rubens, Titian, Raphael, and especially Brueghel. There's also a fine display of Egyptian, classical, and applied arts, including a divine golden salt bowl by

Cellini. The paintings are hung on one glorious floor (100 AS, higher depending on special exhibitions, Tue–Sun 10:00–18:00, Thu until 21:00, closed Mon, sporadic 90-minute English tours April–Oct Tue–Sun, could be at 11:00 and 15:00, tel. 01/525-240).

▲**Natural History Museum**—In the twin building facing the art museum, you'll find moon rocks, dinosaur stuff, and the fist-sized *Venus of Willendorf*—at 30,000 years old, the world's oldest sex symbol, found in the Danube Valley (30 AS, Wed–Mon 9:00–18:30, Wed until 21:00, closed Tue, off-season 9:00–15:00, tel. 01/521-770).

▲**Academy of Fine Arts**—This small but exciting collection includes works by Bosch, Botticelli, and Rubens; a Venice series by Guardi; and a self-portrait by 15-year-old Van Dyck (50 AS, Tue–Sun 10:00–16:00, closed Mon, 3 blocks from Opera at Schillerplatz 3, tel. 01/5881-6225). As you wander the halls of this academy, ponder how history might have been different if Hitler—who applied to study architecture here but was rejected—would have been accepted.

KunstHausWien—This "make yourself at home" modern-art museum is a hit with lovers of modern art. It features the work of local painter/environmentalist Hundertwasser (95 AS, 48 AS on Mon, daily 10:00–19:00; Weissgerberstrasse 13, metro: U-3 Landstrasse, tel. 01/712-0491).

Nearby, the one-with-nature **Hundertwasserhaus** (at Löwengasse and Kegelgasse) is a complex of 50 lived-in apartments. This was built in the 1980s as a breath of architectural fresh air in a city of boring blocky apartment complexes. It's not open to visitors but is worth visiting for its fun-loving and colorful patchwork exterior, the Hundertwasser festival of shops across the street, and for the pleasure of annoying its neighbors. People wait for years to get an apartment here.

▲**Belvedere Palace**—The elegant palace of Prince Eugene of Savoy (the still-much-appreciated conqueror of the Turks), and later home of Franz Ferdinand, houses the Austrian Gallery of 19th- and 20th-century art. Skip the lower palace and focus on the garden and the top floor of the upper palace (Oberes Belvedere) for a winning view of the city and a fine collection of Jugendstil art, Klimt, and Kokoschka (80 AS, Tue–Sun 10:00–17:00, closed Mon, entrance at Prinz Eugen Strasse 27, tel. 01/7955-7134). Your ticket includes the Austrian Baroque and Gothic art in the Lower Palace.

Honorable Mention—There's much, much more. The city museum brochure lists everything. If you're into butterflies, Esperanto, undertakers, tobacco, clowns, fire fighting, Freud, or the homes of dead composers, you'll find them all in Vienna. Several good museums that try very hard but are submerged in the greatness of Vienna include: **Historical Museum of the**

Jugendstil

Vienna gave birth to its own curvaceous brand of Art Nouveau around the early 1900s: Jugendstil. The TI has a brochure laying out Vienna's 20th-century architecture. The best of Vienna's scattered Jugendstil sights: the Belvedere Palace collection, the clock on Höher Markt (which does a musical act at noon), and the Karlsplatz metro stop, where you'll find the gilded-cabbage-domed gallery with the movement's slogan: "To each century its art and to art its liberty." Klimt, Wagner, and friends (who called themselves the Vienna Succession) first exhibited their "liberty style" art here in 1897.

City of Vienna (Tue–Sun 9:00–16:30, Karlsplatz), **Folkloric Museum of Austria** (Laudongasse 15, tel. 01/406-8905), and **Museum of Military History**, one of Europe's best if you like swords and shields (Heeresgeschichtliches Museum, Sat–Thu 9:00–17:00, closed Fri, Arsenal district, Objekt 18, tel. 01/795-610). The **Albertina Museum**, with its superb collection of sketches and graphic art, is closed until 2002.

For a walk in the **Vienna Woods**, catch the U-4 metro to Heiligenstadt, then bus #38A to Kahlenberg, for great views and a café overlooking the city. From there it's a peaceful 45-minute downhill hike to the *Heurigen* of Nussdorf or Grinzing to enjoy some wine (see "Vienna's Wine Gardens," below).

Top People-Watching and Strolling Sights

▲**City Park**—Vienna's Stadtpark is a waltzing world of gardens, memorials to local musicians, ponds, peacocks, music in bandstands, and locals escaping the city. Notice the Jugendstil entry at the Stadtpark metro station. The Kursalon is where Strauss was the violin-toting master of waltzing ceremonies.

▲**Prater**—Vienna's sprawling amusement park tempts many visitors with its huge 220-foot-high, famous, and lazy Ferris wheel (*Riesenrad*), roller coaster, bumper cars, Lilliputian railroad, and endless eateries. Especially if you're traveling with kids, this is a fun, goofy place to share the evening with thousands of Viennese (daily 9:00–24:00 in summer, metro: Praterstern). For a local-style family dinner, eat at Schweizerhaus (good food, great beer) or Wieselburger Bierinsel.

Sunbathing—Like most Europeans, the Austrians worship the sun. Their lavish swimming centers are as much for tanning as for swimming. For the best man-made island beach, head for the "Danube Sea," Vienna's 30-kilometer beach along Danube Island (metro: Donauinsel).

▲**Naschmarkt**—Vienna's ye olde produce market bustles daily, near the Opera along Wienzeile Street. It's likably seedy and surrounded by sausage stands, Turkish *döner kebab* stalls, cafés, and theaters. Each Saturday it's infested by a huge flea market where, in olden days, locals would come to hire a monkey to pick little critters out of their hair (Mon–Fri 7:00–18:00, Sat 6:00–13:00, metro: Kettenbruckengasse). For a picnic park, walk a block down Schleifmuhlgasse.

Summer Music Scene

Vienna is Europe's music capital. It's music *con brio* from October through June, reaching a symphonic climax during the Vienna Festival each May and June. Sadly, in July and August, the Boys' Choir, the Opera, and many more music companies are—like you—on vacation. But Vienna hums year-round with live classical music. In the summer, you have these basic choices:

Touristy Mozart and Strauss Concerts—If the music comes to you, it's touristy—designed for flash-in-the-pan Mozart fans. Powdered-wig orchestra performances are given almost nightly in grand traditional settings (400–700 AS). Pesky wigged and powdered Mozarts peddle tickets in the streets with slick sales pitches about the magic of the venue and the quality of the musicians. Second-rate orchestras, clad in historic costumes, perform the greatest hits of Mozart and Strauss. While there's not a local person in the audience, the tourists generally enjoy the evening. To sort through all your options, check with the ticket office in the TI (same price as on the street but with all venues to choose from).

Strauss in the Palais Borse—For years Strauss concerts have been held in the Kursalon, where the Waltz King himself directed wildly popular concerts 100 years ago. Until 2002, while the Kursalon is renovated, concerts are in the less exciting but still classy Palais Borse (north end of the Ring, daily July–Sept at 20:00, 390–590 AS, tel. 01/718-9666). Shows are a touristy mix of ballet, waltzes, 15-piece orchestra in wigs and old outfits, and a chance for anyone in the audience to get on the floor and waltz.

Serious Concerts—These events, including the Opera, are listed in the monthly *Programm* (available at the TI). Tickets run from 300 to 1000 AS (plus a stiff 22 percent booking fee when booked in advance or through a box office like the one at the TI). If you call a concert hall directly, they can advise you on the availability of (cheaper) tickets at the door. Vienna takes care of its starving artists (and tourists) by offering cheap standing-room tickets to top-notch music and opera (1 hr before show time).

Vienna's **Summer of Music Festival** assures that even from June through September you'll find lots of great concerts, choirs, and symphonies (special *Klang Bogen* brochure at TI; get tickets at

Wien Ticket pavilion off Kärntner Strasse next to Opera House,
or go directly to location of particular event, tel. 01/4000-8410
for information).

▲▲**Vienna Boys' Choir**—The boys sing (heard but not seen,
from a high balcony) at mass in the Imperial Chapel (Hofburg-
kapelle) of the Hofburg (entrance at Schweizerhof) at 9:15 on
Sundays, except in July and August. While seats must be reserved
two months in advance (70–380 AS), standing room inside is free
and open to the first 60 who line up. Rather than line up early,
you can simply swing by and stand in the narthex just outside,
from where you can hear the boys and see the mass on a TV
monitor. Boys' Choir concerts (on stage in the Konzerthaus) are
also given Fridays at 15:30 in May, June, September, and October
(390–430 AS, tel. 01/5880-4141 or 01/533-9927, fax 011-431-
533-992-775 from the U.S., or write Hofmusikkapelle, Hofburg,
A-1010 Wien). They're nice kids, but, for my taste, not worth all
the commotion.

Vienna's Cafés and Wine Gardens

▲**Viennese Coffeehouses**—In Vienna the living room is down
the street at the neighborhood coffeehouse. This tradition is just
another example of the Viennese expertise in good living. Each of
Vienna's many long-established (and sometimes even legendary)
coffeehouses has its individual character (and characters). They
offer newspapers, pastries, sofas, elegance, a smoky ambience,
and a "take all the time you want" charm for the price of a cup
of coffee. Order it *malange* (with a little milk) or *schwarzer* (black).
Rather than buy the *Herald Tribune* ahead of time, buy a cup of
coffee and read it for free Vienna-style.

My favorites are: **Café Hawelka**, with a dark, "brooding
Trotsky" atmosphere, paintings on the walls by struggling artists
who couldn't pay, a saloon-wood flavor, chalkboard menu, smoked
velvet couches, an international selection of newspapers, and a
phone that rings for regulars (8:00–02:00, Sun from 16:00, closed
Tue, Dorotheergasse 6, just off Graben); **Café Central**, with
Jugendstil decor and great *Apfelstrudel* (high prices and rude staff,
Mon–Sat 8:00–20:00, closed Sun, Herrengasse 14); the **Jugendstil
Café Sperl**, dating from 1880 (Mon–Sat 7:00–23:00, closed Sun in
summer, Gumpendorfer 11, just off Naschmarkt near Mariahilfer
Strasse); and the basic, untouristy **Café Ritter** (daily 8:00–20:00,
Mariahilfer Strasse 73, at Neubaugasse metro stop near several
recommended hotels).

▲**Wine Gardens**—The *Heurige* is a uniquely Viennese institution
celebrating the *Heurige*, or new wine. When the Hapsburgs let
Vienna's vintners sell their own wine tax free for 300 days a year,
several hundred families opened *Heurigen* (wine-garden restaurants
clustered around the edge of Vienna), and a tradition was born.

Today they do their best to maintain their old-village atmosphere, serving the homemade new wine (the last vintage, until November 11) with light meals and strolling musicians. For a *Heurige* evening, rather than go to a particular place, tram to the wine-garden district of your choice and wander around, choosing the place with the best ambience. Here are some options:

Grinzing: Of the many *Heurige* suburbs, Grinzing (tram #38 or bus #38A) is the most famous, lively...and touristy—with lots of tour buses. Many people precede their Grinzing meal and drinking by riding bus #38A to its end, high up at Kahlenberg for a grand Vienna view and then ride 20 minutes back into the *Heurige* action. Away from the commotion, consider **Heuriger am Oberen** at Reisenbergweg 15 (tram #38 to end, hike 200 meters uphill, through gate, 400 meters through vineyard to restaurant).

Nussdorf: Less touristy but still characteristic and popular with locals, Nussdorf has plenty of *Heurige* ambience. Two fine places are right at the end of tram D.

Bus #38A connects Grinzing and Nussdorf. Midway, Pfarr-platz has many decent spots including the famous and touristy **Beethoven's home** (Heiligenstadt, with live music, 10-minute walk from bus stop, tel. 01/370-3361). Beethoven lived—and composed his Sixth Symphony—here in 1817. (He hoped the local spa would cure his worsening deafness.)

Neustift am Walde: This neighborhood has lots of *Heuri-gen*, plenty of charm, and the fewest tourists of all (metro: U-6 Nussdorferstrasse, then bus #35A).

Gumpoldskirchen: This small medieval village farther out-side of Vienna has more *Heurige* ambience than tourists. Ride the commuter train from the Opera to Gumpoldskirchen, and you'll find plenty of places to choose from.

At any *Heurige*, fill your plate at a self-serve cold-cut buffet (75–125 AS for dinner). Dishes to look out for: *Stelze* (grilled knuckle of pork), *Fleischlaberln* (fried ground meat patties), *Schinkenfleckerln* (pasta with cheese and ham), *Blunzen* (black pudding...sausage made from blood), *Presskopf* (jellied brains and innards), *Liptauer* (spicy cheese spread), *Kornspitz* (wholemeal bread roll), and *Kummelbraten* (crispy roast pork with caraway). Waitresses will then take your wine order (30 AS per quarter liter). Many locals claim it takes several years of practice to distinguish between *Heurige* and vinegar. For a near-*Heurige* experience right downtown, drop by Gigerl Stadtheuriger (see "Eating," below).

Shopping

The best-value shopping street, with more than 2,000 shops, is Mariahilfer Strasse. For an aristocrat's flea market, drop by Austria's answer to Sotheby's, the **Dorotheum**—five floors of antique furniture and fancy knickknacks put up either for immediate sale or auction (often by people who inherited old things they don't have room for, Mon–Fri 10:00–18:00, Sat 9:00–17:00, closed Sun, between Graben and the Hofburg at Dorotheergasse 17).

Nightlife

If old music or new wine isn't your thing, Vienna has plenty of alternatives. For an up-to-date rundown on fun after dark, get the TI's free *Ten Reasons for Vienna* booklet. An area known as the "Bermuda Dreieck" (Triangle), north of the cathedral between Rotenturmstrasse and Judengasse, is the hot local nightspot, with lots of classy pubs, or *Beisl* (such as Krah Krah, Salzamt, Slammer, and Bermuda Brau), and music spots. On balmy summer evenings the liveliest scene is at Danube Island. If you're just want a good movie, the English Cinema Haydn plays English movies nightly (Mariahilfer Strasse 57, tel. 01/587-2262).

Sleeping in Vienna
(15 AS = about $1, country code: 43, area code: 01)
Sleep Code: **S** = Single, **D** = Double/Twin, **T** = Triple, **Q** = Quad, **b** = bathroom, **t** = toilet only, **s** = shower only, **CC** = Credit Card (Visa, MasterCard, Amex). English is spoken at each place.

Book accommodations by phone a few days in advance. Most places will hold a room without a deposit if you promise to arrive before 17:00. My recommendations stretch mainly along the likeable Mariahilfer Strasse from the Westbahnhof (West Station) to the town center. These hotels are listed starting from the not-so-appealing Westbahnof and working toward the city center. Unless otherwise noted, prices include a continental breakfast. Postal code is 1XX0, with XX being the district.

Sleeping near the Westbahnhof Train Station
Pension Funfhaus is big, clean, stark, and quiet. Although the neighborhood is run-down, this place is a good value (S-395 AS, Sb-480 AS, D-570 AS, Db-650 AS, T-850 AS, Tb-930 AS, 2-bedroom apartments for 4 people-1,140 AS, closed mid-Nov–Feb, Sperrgasse 12, 1150 Wien, tel. 01/892-3545 or 01/892-0286, fax 01/892-0460, Frau Susi Tersch). Half the rooms are in the fine main building and half are in the annex, which has good rooms but is near the train tracks and a bit scary on the street at night. From the station, ride tram #52 or #58 two stops down Mariahilfer Strasse to Sperrgasse.

Hotel Ibis Wien, a modern high-rise hotel with American charm, is ideal for anyone tired of quaint old Europe. Its 340 cookie-cutter rooms are bright, comfortable, modern, and have all the conveniences (Sb-890 AS, Db-1,090 AS, Tb-1,290 AS, breakfast-125 AS, CC:VMA, elevator, smoke-free rooms,

air-con, 400 meters to the right leaving Westbahnhof, Mariahilfer
Gürtel 22–24, A-1060 Wien, tel. 01/59998, fax 01/597-9090,
e-mail: resamariahilf@hotel-ibis.co.at).

Hotel Furstenhof, right across from the station, charges
top schilling for its Old World, red-floral, spacious rooms and
Internet access (S-560 AS, Sb-880–1,220 AS, D-890 AS, Db-1,390
AS, Tb-1,440 AS, Qb-1,480 AS, CC:VMA, Europlatz 4, tel.
01/523-3267, fax 01/523-326-726, www.hotelfuerstenhof.com).

Hotels along Mariahilfer Strasse

Lively Mariahilfer Strasse connects the West Station with the
center. The U-3 metro line, starting at the Westbahnhof, goes
down Mariahilfer Strasse to the cathedral. This very Viennese
street is a comfortable and vibrant area filled with local shops and
cafés. Most hotels are within a few steps of a metro stop, just one
or two stops from the West Train Station.

Pension Hargita, with 19 generally small, bright, and
tidy rooms (mostly twins), is right at the U-3 Zieglergasse stop
(S-400 AS, Ss-450 AS, D-600 AS, Ds-700 AS, Db-800–900 AS,
Ts-850 AS, Tb-1,050 AS, Qb-1,100 AS, CC:VM, breakfast-40 AS,
cheaper off-season, corner of Mariahilfer Strasse and Andreasgasse, Andreasgasse 1, 1070 Wien, tel. 01/526-1928, fax 01/
526-0492, www.hargita.at, e-mail: pension@hargita.at).

Astron Suite Hotel Wien is two stern, business hotels a few
blocks apart on Mariahilfer Strasse. Both rent ideal-for-families
suites, each with a living room, two TVs, bathroom, desk, and
kitchenette (Db suite-1,980 AS, apartment for 2–3 adults-2,880 AS,
kids under 12 free, kids over 12-490 AS each, CC:VMA, nonsmoking rooms, elevator, www.astron-hotels.de). One is at
Mariahilfer Strasse 78 (at U-3 Zieglergasse metro stop, tel. 01/
5245-6000, fax 01/524-560-015), the other is at Mariahilfer Strasse
32 (metro: U-3 Neubaugasse, tel. 01/521-720, fax 01/521-7215).

Pension Corvinus is small, bright, modern, and warmly
run. Its comfortable rooms have small bathrooms (Sb-750 AS,
Db-1,150 AS, Tb-1,350 AS, prices promised through 2001 with
this book, extra bed-350 AS, CC:VM, elevator, air-con available,
garage-150 AS, Mariahilfer Strasse 57, tel. 01/587-7239, fax
01/587-723-920, e-mail: hotel@corvinus.at). In the same building,
Haydn Hotel is a big, hotelesque place with spacious rooms (Sb-
890 AS, Db-1,290 AS, extra bed-400 AS, garage-150 AS, CC:VM,
Mariahilfer Strasse 57, tel. 01/587-4414, fax 01/586-1950, e-mail:
info@haydn-hotel.at).

Pension Mariahilf is a four-star place offering a clean aristocratic air in an affordable and cozy pension package. Its 12 rooms
are spacious and feel new, but with an art deco flair. With four
stars, everything's done right. You'll find the latest American
magazines and even free Mozart balls at the reception desk

Vienna: Hotels Outside the Ring

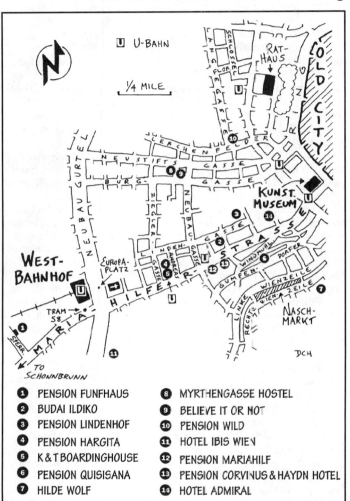

❶ PENSION FUNFHAUS	❽ MYRTHENGASSE HOSTEL
❷ BUDAI ILDIKO	❾ BELIEVE IT OR NOT
❸ PENSION LINDENHOF	❿ PENSION WILD
❹ PENSION HARGITA	⓫ HOTEL IBIS WIEN
❺ K & T BOARDINGHOUSE	⓬ PENSION MARIAHILF
❻ PENSION QUISISANA	⓭ PENSION CORVINUS & HAYDN HOTEL
❼ HILDE WOLF	⓮ HOTEL ADMIRAL

(Sb-800 AS, Db-1,300 AS, Tb-1,700 AS, at U-3 Neubaugasse metro stop, Mariahilfer Strasse 49, tel. 01/586-1781, fax 01/586-178-122, e-mail: penma@atnet.at, warmly run by Frau and Herr Ender).

Beyond its plain lobby, **Hotel Admiral** is a huge, quiet, family-run hotel that has large, comfortable rooms. Alexandra works hard to keep her guests happy (Sb-750–860 AS, Db-1,000

AS, special price with this book through 2001, extra bed-310 AS, free parking, metro: U-2 or U-3 Volkstheater, a block off Mariahilfer Strasse at Karl Schweighofer Gasse 7, tel. 01/521-410, fax 01/521-4116, e-mail: hoteladmiralwien@aon.at).

At **K&T Boardinghouse**, Tina and Fred Kaled rent four big, comfortable rooms (3 with full bathrooms) with the comforts you'd pay lots for in a hotel. This place—with the best cheap doubles in town—is homey with accommodating hosts (D-600 AS, Db-700 AS, Tb-950 AS, Qb-1,200 AS, no breakfast, Internet access, laundry, nonsmoking, 3 flights up, no elevator, Mariahilfer Strasse #72, tel. 01/523-2989, fax 01/522-0345, http://members .chello.at/timea.fetoui/, e-mail: kaled@chello.at).

Two women rent rooms out of their dark and homey apartments in the same building at Lindengasse 39 (1070 Wien). Each have high ceilings and Old World furnishings with two cavernous rooms sleeping two to four and a skinny twin room, all sharing one bathroom. These places are great if you're on a tight budget and wish you had a grandmother to visit in Vienna: **Maria Pribojszki** (S-400 AS, D-550 AS, T-800 AS, Q-1,000 AS, breakfast-50 AS, free laundry service for 4-night stays, tel. 01/523-9006, e-mail: e.boehm@xpoint.at) or **Budai Ildiko** (S-390 AS, D-600 AS, T-870 AS, Q-1,120 AS, no breakfast but free coffee, laundry-40 AS, tel. 01/523-1058, tel. & fax 01/526-2595, e-mail: budai@hotmail.com).

Pension Lindenhof is worn but clean, filled with plants, and run with Bulgarian and Armenian warmth (S-380 AS, Sb-480 AS, D-640 AS, Db-860 AS, cheaper in winter, hall showers-20 AS, metro: U-3 Neubaugasse, Lindengasse 4, 1070 Wien, tel. 01/523-0498, fax 01/523-7362).

Pension Quisisana—a tired and ramshackle time warp—is cheap and sleep-worthy for vagabonds (S-340 AS, Ss-390 AS, D-540 AS, Ds-610–650 AS, Db-710–750 AS, third person-260 AS, Windmuhlgasse 6, 1060 Wien, tel. 01/587-7155, fax 01/587-715-633).

Hilde Wolf shares her homey apartment with travelers (7 blocks off Mariahilfer Strasse and 3 blocks below Naschmarkt). Her four huge but stuffy rooms are like old libraries. Hilde won't overwhelm you with friendliness but she may do your laundry if you stay two nights (S-450 AS, D-650 AS, T-955 AS, Q-1,225 AS, prices good through 2001, reserve with CC but pay in cash, small breakfast, elevator, metro: U-2 Karlsplatz, Schleifmühlgasse 7, 1040 Vienna, tel. 01/586-5103).

Dorms and Hostels near Mariahilfer Strasse

Jugendherbergen Myrthengasse is a well-run youth hostel (185–215-AS beds, nonmembers-40 AS extra, includes sheets and breakfast, 3- to 6-bed rooms, some private rooms for couples and families, Myrthengasse 7, 1070 Wien, tel. 01/523-6316, fax 01/523-5849, e-mail: hostel@chello.at). Other hostels near

Mariahilfer Strasse are **Wombats City Hostel** (Grangasse 6,
tel. 01/897-2336, e-mail: wombats@chello.at) and **Hostel
Ruthensteiner** (Robert-Hamerling-Gasse 24, tel. 01/893-4202,
e-mail: hostel.ruthensteiner@telecom.at).

Believe It or Not is a friendly and basic place with two
coed rooms for up to 10 travelers under age 30. It's locked up
from 10:30 to 12:30, has kitchen facilities, and no curfew
(160 AS per bed, 110 AS Nov–Easter, Myrthengasse 10, ring
Apt. #14, tel. 01/526-4658, run by Gosha).

Sleeping within the Ring, in the Old City Center

You'll pay extra to sleep in the old center. The first two are in
the shadow of St. Stephan's Cathedral, on or near the Graben,
where the elegance of Old Vienna strums happily over the cobbles. The next two are near the Opera and TI, five minutes from
the cathedral. If you can afford it, staying here gives you the best
classy Vienna experience.

At **Pension Nossek**, an elevator takes you above any street
noise into Frau Bernad's and Frau Gundolf's world, where the
children seem to be placed among the lace and flowers by an interior designer. Right on the wonderful Graben, this is particularly
good value (Ss-700 AS, Sb-800–1,100 AS, Db-1,300 AS, Tb-1,700
AS, 300 AS extra for sprawling suites, Graben 17, tel. 01/5337-
0410, fax 01/535-3646, e-mail: pension.nossek@faxvia.net).

Pension Pertschy circles an old courtyard and is bigger and
more hotelesque than the others. The rooms are huge but musty.
Those on the courtyard are quietest (Sb-940 AS, Db-1,460–1,660
AS depending on size, cheaper off-season, extra person-380 AS,
CC:VM, Hapsburgergasse 5, tel. 01/534-490, fax 01/534-4949,
www.pertschy.com, e-mail: pertschy@pertschy.com).

Baroque and doily as you'll find in this price range, **Pension
Suzanne** is wonderfully located a few meters from the Opera. It's
quiet and simple but run with the class of a bigger hotel (Sb-950 AS,
Db-1,150–1,450 AS depending on size, third person-500 AS, huge
discounts in winter, reserve with CC but pay cash, a block from
Opera, at metro: Karlsplatz take Opera exit, Walfischgasse 4, 1010
Wien, tel. 01/513-2507, fax 01/513-2500, www.pension-suzanne.at,
e-mail: info@pension-suzanne.at).

Hotel zur Wiener Staatsoper is quiet, rich, and hotelesque.
Its rooms come with high ceilings, chandeliers, and fancy carpets
on parquet floors—a good value for this locale and ideal for
people whose hotel tastes are a cut above mine (Sb-1,200 AS,
Db-1,500–1,750 AS, depending on season, summer is cheaper,
extra bed-300 AS, family deals, CC:VMA, a block from Opera
at Krugerstrasse 11, 1010 Wien, tel. 01/513-1274, fax 01/5131-
27415, e-mail: office@zurwienerstaatsoper.at).

Schweizer Pension Solderer, family owned for three

Hotels in Central Vienna

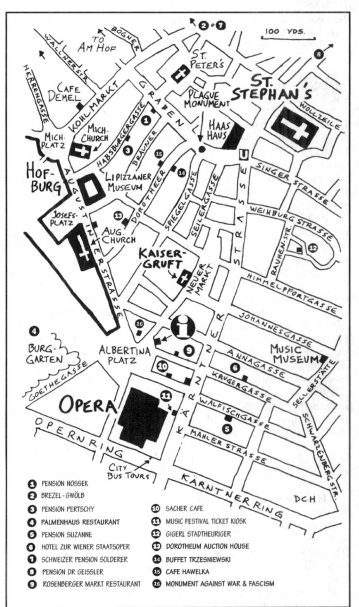

100 YDS.

1. PENSION NOSSEK
2. BREZEL - GWÖLB
3. PENSION PERTSCHY
4. PALMENHAUS RESTAURANT
5. PENSION SUZANNE
6. HOTEL ZUR WIENER STAATSOPER
7. SCHWEIZER PENSION SOLDERER
8. PENSION DR GEISSLER
9. ROSENBERGER MARKT RESTAURANT
10. SACHER CAFE
11. MUSIC FESTIVAL TICKET KIOSK
12. GIGERL STADTHEURIGER
13. DOROTHEUM AUCTION HOUSE
14. BUFFET TRZESNIEWSKI
15. CAFE HAWELKA
16. MONUMENT AGAINST WAR & FASCISM

generations, is warmly run by two friendly sisters, Monica and
Anita. Enjoy the homey feel, 11 big, comfortable rooms, parquet
floors, and lots of tourist info (S-490 AS, Ss-700–800 AS, D-780
AS, Ds-980 AS, Db-1,050–1,100 AS, elevator, laundry-150 AS,
nonsmoking, metro: U-2 Schottenring, Heinrichsgasse 2, 1010
Wien, tel. 01/533-8156, fax 01/535-6469, e-mail: schweizer
.pension@chello.at).

Pension Dr. Geissler has comfortable rooms on the eighth
floor of a modern building about 10 blocks northeast of St.
Stephan's, just below the canal (S-580 AS, Sb-800–900 AS,
D-800 AS, Ds-980 AS, Db-1000–1,200 AS, prices vary with
season, CC:VMA, metro: Schwedenplatz, Postgasse 14, 1010
Wien, tel. 01/533-2803, fax 01/533-2635).

Pension Wild is outside of the old center, behind the City
Hall. But with 20 delightful, just-renovated rooms, two family
apartments, and a good, keep-it-simple-and-affordable attitude,
it's one of Vienna's top values (S-490 AS, Sb-690 AS, D-590 AS,
Db-990 AS, reserve with CC but pay cash, elevator, metro: U-2
Rathaus, Langegasse 10, 1080 Vienna, tel. 01/406-5174, fax 01/
402-2168, www.pension-wild.com).

Eating in Vienna

The Viennese appreciate the fine points of life, and right up there
with waltzing is eating. The city has many atmospheric restaurants.
As you ponder the Slavic and eastern European specialties on menus,
remember that Vienna's diverse empire may be gone, but its flavor
lingers.

While cuisines are routinely named for countries, Vienna
claims to be the only city with a cuisine of its own: Vienna soups
come with fillings (semolina dumpling, liver dumpling, or pancake
slices). *Gulasch* is a beef ragout of Hungarian origin (spiced with
onion and paprika). Of course, Vienna Schnitzel (*Wiener Schnitzel*)
is a breaded and fried veal cutlet. Another meat specialty is boiled
beef (*Tafelspitz*). While you're sure to have *Apfelstrudel*, try the
sweet cheese strudel, too (*Topfenstrudel*, wafer-thin strudel pastry
filled with sweet cheese and raisins).

On nearly every corner you can find a colorful *Beisl* (Viennese
tavern) filled with poetry teachers and their students, couples
loving without touching, housewives on their way home from cello
lessons, and waiters who enjoy serving hearty food and good drink
at an affordable price. Ask at your hotel for a good *Beisl*.

Wherever you're eating, some vocabulary will help. Try the
grüner Veltliner (dry white wine, any time), *Traubermost* (a heavenly
grape juice on the verge of wine, autumn only, sometimes just called
Most), and *Sturm* (barely fermented *Most*, autumn only). The local
red wine (called *Portuguese*) is pretty good. Since the Austrian wine is
often very sweet, remember the word *Trocken* (dry). You can order

your wine by the *Viertel* (quarter liter) or *Achtel* (eighth liter). Beer comes in a *Krugel* (half liter) or *Seidel* (.3 liter).

Eating in the City Center

These eateries are within a five-minute walk of the cathedral.

Gigerl Stadtheuriger offers a near-*Heurige* experience (à la Grinzing, see "Vienna's Cafes and Wine Gardens," above) without leaving the center. Just point to what looks good. Food is sold by the weight (cheese and cold meats cost about 35 AS/100 grams, salads are about 15 AS/100 grams; price sheet is posted, 10 dag equals 100 grams). They also have menu entrées, along with spinach strudel, quiche, *Apfelstrudel*, and, of course, casks of new and local wines. Meals run from 100 AS to 150 AS (daily 11:00–24:00, indoor/outdoor seating, behind cathedral, a block off Kärntner Strasse, a few cobbles off Rauhensteingasse on Blumenstock, tel. 01/513-4431).

The next five places are within a block of Am Hof square (metro: U-3 Herrengasse). **Restaurant Ofenloch** serves good old-fashioned Viennese cuisine with friendly service both indoors and out. This 300-year-old eatery, with great traditional ambience, is very central but not overrun with tourists (150–200 AS meals, daily 10:00–24:00, Kurrentgasse 8, tel. 01/533-8844). **Brezel-Gwölb**, a wonderfully atmospheric wine cellar with outdoor dining on a quiet square, serves delicious light meals, fine *Krautsuppe*, and old-fashioned local dishes. It's ideal for a romantic late-night glass of wine (daily 11:30–01:00, take Drahtgasse 20 meters off Am Hof, Ledererhof 9, tel. 01/533-8811). Around the corner, **Zum Scherer Sitz u. Stehbeisl** is just as untouristy, with indoor or outdoor seating, a soothing woody atmosphere, intriguing decor, and local specialties (Mon–Sat 11:00–01:00, Sun 17:00–24:00, Judenplatz 7, near Am Hof). Just below Am Hof, **Stadtbeisl** offers a good mix of value, local cuisine, and atmosphere (nightly, Naglergasse 21, tel. 01/533-3507). Around the corner, the ancient and popular **Esterhazykeller** has traditional fare deep underground or outside on a delightful square (daily, self-service buffet in lowest cellar or from menu, Haarhof 1, tel. 01/533-9340).

These wine cellars are fun and touristic but typical, in the old center of town, with reasonable prices and plenty of smoke: **Melker Stiftskeller**, less touristy, is a *Stadtheurige* in a deep and rustic cellar with hearty, inexpensive meals and new wine (Tue–Sat 17:00–24:00, closed Sun–Mon, between Am Hof and the Schottentor metro stop at Schottengasse 3, tel. 01/533-5530). **Zu den Drei Hacken** is famous for its local specialties (Mon–Fri 9:00–24:00, Sat 10:00–24:00, closed Sun, indoor/outdoor seating, CC:VA, Singerstrasse 28).

Cafe Restaurant Palmenhaus, overlooking the palace garden (*Burggarten*), tucked away in a green and peaceful corner two blocks behind the Opera in the Hofburg's backyard, is a world apart. If you want to eat modern Austrian cuisine with palm trees rather than tourists, this is it. And at the edge of a huge park, it's great for families (150-AS lunches, 200-AS dinners, serious vegetarian dishes and good wine, daily 10:00–24:00, indoors in greenhouse or outdoors, cool parkside outdoor pub just below, at Burggarten, tel. 01/533-1033).

Rosenberger Markt Restaurant is my favorite for a fast, light, and central lunch. Just a block toward the cathedral from the Opera, this place—while not cheap—is brilliant. Friendly and efficient, with special theme rooms for dining, it offers a fresh, smoke-free, and healthy cornucopia of food and drink (daily 10:30–23:00, lots of fruits, veggies, fresh-squeezed juices, addictive banana milk, ride the glass elevator downstairs, Mayseder-gasse 2). You can stack a small salad or veggie plate into a tower of gobble for 35 AS.

Buffet Trzesniewski is an institution—justly famous for its elegant and cheap finger sandwiches and small beers (10 AS each). Three different sandwiches and a *kleines Bier* (*Pfiff*) make a fun, light lunch. Point to whichever delights look tasty and pay for them and a drink. Take your drink tokens to the lady on the right. Sit on the bench and scoot over to a tiny table when a spot opens up (Mon–Fri 8:30–19:30, Sat 9:00–17:00, closed Sun, 50 meters off Graben, nearly across from brooding Café Hawelka, on Dorotheergasse 2).

Akakiko Sushi: If you're just schnitzeled out, a small chain of Japanese restaurants with an easy sushi menu may suit you (next to downtown recommended eateries in the heart of old center at Heidenschuss 3 or at Mariahilfer Strasse 40, tel. 01/533-8514).

Eating near Mariahilfer Strasse

Mariahilfer Strasse is filled with reasonable cafés serving all types of cuisine. A few blocks away, on the romantic streets just north of Siebensterngasse (take Stiftgasse from Mariahilfer Strasse), several cobbled alleys open their sidewalks and courtyards to appreciative locals (ideal for dinner or a relaxing drink). Stroll Spitellberggasse, Schrankgasse, and Gutenberggassse and pick your favorite place. Check out the courtyard inside Spittelberggasse 3, and don't miss the vine-strewn wine garden inside Schrankgasse 1. For traditional Viennese cuisine, consider **Witwe Bolte** (Gutenberggasse 13, daily 11:30–24:00, tel. 01/523-1450).

Restaurant Beim Novak serves good local cuisine away from the modern rush (Mon–Sat 18:00–24:00, closed Sun, a block down Andreasgasse from Mariahilfer Strasse at Richtergasse 12, tel. 01/ 523-3244).

Naschmarkt is Vienna's best Old World market, with plenty of fresh produce, cheap local-style eateries, cafés, and *döner kebab* and sausage stands (Mon–Fri 7:00–18:00, Sat until 12:00, closed Sun).

Transportation Connections—Vienna

Vienna has two main train stations: the Westbahnhof (West Train Station), serving Munich, Salzburg, Melk, and Budapest; and the Südbahnhof (South Train Station), serving Italy, Budapest, and Prague. A third station, Franz Josefs, serves Krems and the Danube Valley (but Melk is served by the Westbahnhof). Metro line U-3 connects the Westbahnhof with the center, tram D takes you from the Südbahnhof and the Franz Josefs to downtown, and tram #18 connects West and South Stations. Train info: tel. 051717 (wait through long German recording for operator).

By train to: Melk (hrly, 75 min), **Krems** (hrly, 1 hr), **Salzburg** (hrly, 3 hrs), **Innsbruck** (3/day, 5.5 hrs), **Budapest** (3/day, 3 hrs), **Prague** (4/day, 5.5 hrs), **Munich** (10/day, 4.5 hrs), **Berlin** (2/day 14 hrs), **Zurich** (4/day, 9 hrs), **Rome** (3/day, 14 hrs), **Venice** (6/day, 9 hrs), **Frankfurt** (7/day, 7.5 hrs), **Amsterdam** (2/day, 14 hrs).

To Eastern Europe: Vienna is the springboard for a quick trip to Prague and Budapest—three hours by train from Budapest (370 AS, 740 AS round-trip, free with Eurail) and 5.5 hours from Prague (486 AS one-way, 1,030 AS round-trip, 710 AS round-trip with Eurail). Visas are not required. Purchase tickets at most travel agencies. Eurail passholders bound for Prague must pay to ride the rails in the Czech Republic; for details, see "Transportation Connections" in the Berlin chapter.

SALZBURG, SALZKAMMERGUT, AND WEST AUSTRIA

Enjoy the sights, sounds, and splendor of Mozart's hometown, Salzburg, then commune with nature in the Salzkammergut, Austria's *Sound of Music* country. Amid hills alive with the S.O.M., you'll find the tiny town of Hallstatt, as pretty as a postcard (and not much bigger).

SALZBURG

Salzburg is forever smiling to the tunes of Mozart and *The Sound of Music*. Thanks to its charmingly preserved old town, splendid gardens, Baroque churches, and Europe's largest intact medieval castle, Salzburg feels made for tourism.

But even without Mozart and the von Trapp family, Salzburg is steeped in history. In about A.D. 700, Bavaria gave Salzburg to Bishop Rupert for his promise to Christianize the area. Salzburg remained an independent state until Napoleon stormed in (around 1800). Salzburg managed to avoid the ravages of war for 1,200 years...until World War II. Half of the town was destroyed by WWII bombs, but the historic old town survived.

Eight million tourists crawl its cobbles each year. That's a lot of Mozart balls—and all that popularity has led to a glut of businesses hoping to catch the tourist dollar. Still, Salzburg makes for a pleasant visit.

Planning Your Time

While Vienna measures much higher on the Richter scale of sight-seeing thrills, Salzburg is simply a stroller's delight—a touristy delight. If you're going into the nearby Salzkammergut lake country, skip the *Sound of Music* tour—if not, allow half a day for it. The S.O.M. tour kills a nest of sightseeing birds with one ticket (city

Salzburg

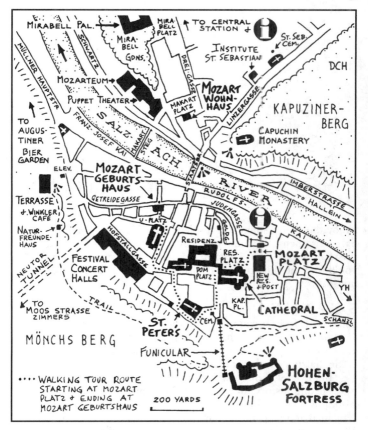

overview, S.O.M. sights, a fun luge ride, and a fine drive through the lakes).

You'll probably need two nights for Salzburg; nights are important for swilling beer in atmospheric local gardens and attending concerts in Baroque halls and chapels. Seriously consider one of Salzburg's many evening musical events (about 350–400 AS). While the sights are mediocre, the town is an enjoyable Baroque museum of cobbled streets and elegant buildings. And to get away from it all, bike down the river or hike across the Mönchsberg.

Orientation (area code: 0662)

Salzburg, a city of 150,000 (Austria's fourth largest), is divided into old and new. The old town, sitting between the Salzach River and the 1,600-foot-high hill called Mönchsberg, holds nearly all the charm and most of the tourists.

Tourist Information: Salzburg's many TIs are helpful (at the train station—daily 8:15–21:00; on Mozartplatz in the old center—daily 9:00–20:00 in summer, closes at 19:00 off-season; on freeway exits; and at the airport, tel. 0662/8898-7330, www.salzburginfo .or.at). You can pick up a city map (10 AS, free at most hotels), a list of sights with current hours, and a schedule of events. The TI sells a "Salzburg Card" which covers all your bus transportation and admission to all the city sights (225 AS/24 hrs, 320 AS/48 hrs); it pays for itself after two admissions and one bus ride. The new "Salzburg Plus Light" adds 150 AS to the Salzburg Card for a dinner and two drinks at your choice of the city's big hotels. Book a concert upon arrival. The TIs also book rooms (30-AS fee, or 60 AS for 3 people or more).

Arrival in Salzburg

By Train: The little Salzburg station makes it easy. The TI is at track 2A. Downstairs, at street level, you'll find a place to store your luggage, rent bikes, buy tickets, and get train information. The bus station is across the street (where buses #1, #5, #6, #51, and #55 go to the old center; get off at the first stop after you cross the river for most sights and city center hotels, or just before the bridge for Linzergasse hotels). Figure 90 AS for a taxi to the center. To walk downtown (15 min), leave the station ticket hall to the left near the Bankomat and walk straight down Rainer-strasse, which leads under the tracks past Mirabelplatz, turning into Dreitaltigkeitsgasse. From here you can turn left onto Paris-Lodron Strasse or Linzergasse for many hotels listed in this book or cross the *Staatsbrücke* (bridge) for the old town (and more hotels). For a more dramatic approach, leave the station the same way but follow the tracks to the river, turn left, and walk the riverside path toward the castle.

By Car: Follow Zentrum signs to the center and park short-term on the street or longer under Mirabellplatz. Ask at your hotel for suggestions.

Getting around Salzburg

By Bus: Single-ride tickets are sold on the bus for 20 AS. Daily passes called *Tageskarte* cost 40 AS (good for 1 calendar day only). Bus info: tel. 0662/4480-6262.

By Bike: Salzburg is bike friendly. From 7:00 until midnight, the train station rents good road bikes for 100 AS and mountain bikes for 175 AS; if you don't have a railpass or train ticket, you'll pay 25 to 50 AS more (no deposit required, pay at counter #3, pick bike up at "left luggage"). Velo-Active rents bikes on Resi-denzplatz under the Glockenspiel in the old town (60 AS/hr,

190 AS/24 hrs, 150 AS/24 hrs with this book, daily 9:00–19:00 but hours unreliable, less off-season and in bad weather, passport number for security, extra charge for mountain bikes, tel. 0662/435-5950).

By Funicular and Elevator: The old town is connected to Mönchsberg (and great views) via funicular and elevator. The funicular whisks you up to the imposing Hohensalzburg fortress (76-AS round-trip includes fortress admission; 34 AS for ride and grounds only; last ride up at 21:30, last down at 22:00). The elevator on the east side of the old town propels you to Café Winkler, the recommended Naturfreundehaus (see "Sleeping in the Old Town," below), and lots of wooded paths (16 AS one-way, 27 AS round-trip).

By Taxi: Salzburg is a fine taxi town. Meters start at 33 AS. A ride from the station to the old town runs about 90 AS.

Helpful Hints

Guide Association: Salzburg's many guides can give you a good three-hour walk through town for 1,600 AS (tel. 0662/840-406). Barbel Boxrainer packs in the information and enjoys leaving the touristy places (tel. 0662/632-225).

Laundromat: You'll find it near recommended Linzergasse hotels at the corner of Paris-Lodron Strasse and Wolf-Dietrich Strasse (Mon–Fri 7:30–18:00, Sat 8:00–12:00, self-serve or drop-off service, tel. 0662/876-381).

Internet Access: The Internet Café on Mozartplatz is fast and handy, right next to the TI (20 AS/10 min, 120 AS/hr, daily 10:00–24:00, 12 stations, Mozartplatz 5, tel. 0662/844-822). Another cybercafé is at Gstattengasse 27; turn right where Griesgasse meets the hill (80 AS/hr, daily 14:00–20:00, tel. 0662/8426-1622).

American Express: Amex charges no commission to cash Amex checks (Mon–Fri 9:00–17:30, Sat 9:00–12:00, Mozartplatz 5, A-5010 Salzburg, tel. 0662/8080).

City View: For a painless, grand view, ride Hotel Stein's elevator to the seventh floor (near where Linzergasse meets the main bridge).

Old Town Walking Tour

The two-language, one-hour guided walks of the old town are informative and worthwhile if you don't mind listening to a half hour of German (100 AS, daily at 12:15, not on winter Sun, start at TI on Mozartplatz, tel. 0662/88987), but you can easily do it on your own.

Here's a basic old-town orientation walk (start on Mozartplatz in the old town):

Mozartplatz: This square features a statue of Mozart erected in 1842. Mozart spent most of his first 20 years (1756–1777) in

Salzburg, the greatest Baroque city north of the Alps. But the
city's much older. The Mozart statue actually sits on bits of
Roman Salzburg. And the pink church of St. Michael overlooking
the square is from A.D. 800. Surrounding you are Café Glockenspiel, an Internet café, the American Express office, and the tourist
information office with a concert box office. Just around the
corner is a pedestrian bridge leading over the Salzach River to
the quiet, most medieval street in town, Steingasse (see "Sights—
Across the River," below). Walk toward the cathedral into the
big square with the huge fountain.

Residenz Platz: Salzburg's energetic Prince-Archbishop
Wolf Dietrich (who ruled from 1587–1612) was raised in Rome,
counted the Medicis as his buddies, and had grand Renaissance
ambitions for Salzburg. After a convenient fire destroyed much
of the old town, he set about building "the Rome of the North."
This square, with his new cathedral and palace, was the centerpiece of his Baroque dream city. A series of interconnecting
squares lead from here through the old town.

For centuries, Salzburg's leaders were both important church
officials and princes of the Holy Roman Empire, hence their title—
mixing sacred and secular authority. Wolf Dietrich abused his power
and spent his last five years imprisoned in the Salzburg castle.

The fountain is as Italian as can be, with a Triton matching
Bernini's *Triton Fountain* in Rome. As the north became aware of
the exciting things going on in Italy, things Italian were respected.
(You know, when a bumpkin in a faraway land "stuck a feather in
his cap and called it macaroni.") Local architects even Italianized
their names in order to raise their rates.

Near the fountain is a picnic-friendly grocery with an orange
awning (Mon–Fri 8:30–18:00, Sat 8:00–17:00).

Residenz: Dietrich's palace is connected to the cathedral by a
skyway. A series of ornately decorated rooms and an art gallery are
open to visitors with time to kill (90 AS includes audioguide, daily
10:00–17:00, tel. 0662/8042-2690).

Opposite the old Residenz is the new Residenz, which has
long been a government administration building with the central
post office and the Hiematwerk, a shop showing off all the best
local handicrafts (Mon–Fri 9:00–18:00, Sat 9:00–13:00). Atop the
new Residenz is the famous...

Glockenspiel: This bell tower has a carillon of 35 17th-
century bells (cast in Antwerp) that chimes throughout the day
and plays tunes (appropriate to the month) at 7:00, 11:00, and 18:00.
There was a time when Salzburg could afford to take tourists
to the top of the tower to actually see the big adjustable barrel
turn...pulling the right bells in the right rhythm—a fascinating
show. Notice the ornamental top: an upside-down heart in flames
surrounding the solar system (symbolizing that God loves all).

Look back past Mozart's statue to the 4,220-foot-tall Gais-
berg (the forested hill with the television tower). A road leads
to the top for a commanding view. It's a favorite destination for
local bikers. Walking under the Prince-Archbishop's skyway, step
into Domplatz, the cathedral square.

Salzburg Cathedral: Built in the 17th century, this was
one of the first Baroque buildings north of the Alps (free, daily
10:00–18:30). The dates on the iron gates refer to milestones in
the church's history: In 774 the previous church (long since
destroyed) was founded by St. Virgil, to be replaced in 1628 by
the church you see today. In 1959 the reconstruction was completed after a WWII bomb blew through the dome.

Wander inside. Built in just 14 years (1614–1628), the architecture is harmonious. When the pope visited in 1998, 5,000 people
filled the cathedral (dimensions: 110 meters long, 70 meters tall).
The baptismal font, left of the entry, is from the previous cathedral.
Mozart was baptized here (Amadeus means "beloved by God").
Gape up. The interior is marvelous. Concert and mass schedules
are posted at the entrance; the Sunday mass at 10:00 is famous for
its music. (The 11:30 mass also has music. Acoustics are best in pews
immediately under the dome.)

Under the skyway, a stairway leads down to the excavation
site under the church with a few second-century Christian Roman
mosaics and the foundation stones of the previous Romanesque and
Gothic churches (20 AS, Wed–Sun 9:00–17:00). The Cathedral (or
Dom) Museum has a rich collection of church art (entry at portico).

From Cathedral Square to St. Peter's: The cathedral square
is surrounded by "ecclesiastical palaces." The statue of Mary (1771)
is looking away from the church, but if you stand in the rear of the
square immediately under the middle arch, you'll see how she's
positioned to be crowned by the two angels on the church facade.

From the arch, walk back across the square to the front
of the cathedral and turn right (going past the underground public toilets) into the next square. Walk past the giant chessboard
to the pond. This was a horse bath, the 18th-century equivalent
of a car wash. Notice the puzzle above it—the artist wove the
date of the structure into a phrase. It says, "Leopold the Ruler
Built Me," using the letters LLDVICMXVXI, which totals
1732—the year it was built. A small road leads up to the castle
(and castle lift). Leave the square through a gate on the right
(past the souvenir stalls) which reads "St. Peter." It leads to a
waterfall and St. Peter's Cemetery.

The waterfall is part of a canal system that has brought water
into Salzburg from Berchtesgaden, 25 kilometers away, since 1150.
The busy water used to flush out the streets (Saturday morning was
flood-the-streets day) and power factories (over 100 firms as late as
the 19th century). Drop into the traditional bakery at the waterfall

(hard to beat their rocklike *Roggenbrot*, sold 7:00–17:30) and then step into the cemetery.

St. Peter's Cemetery: This collection of lovingly tended mini-gardens is butted up against the Mönchberg's rock wall. The graves are cared for by relatives. (In Austria, grave sites are rented not owned. Rent bills are sent out every 10 years. If no one cares enough to make the payment, you're gone.) Look up the cliff. Medieval hermit monks lived in the hillside. You can climb up to see their chapel (12 AS, Tue–Sun 10:30–17:00, closed Mon). While the cemetery the von Trapp family hid out in was actually in Hollywood, it was inspired by this one. Walk through the cemetery (silence is requested) and out the opposite end. Drop into St. Peter's Church, a Romanesque basilica done up beautifully Baroque. Continue (through arch opposite hillside, left at church, take the second right, pass the public WC, another square, and church) to . . .

Universitätsplatz: This square comes with a busy open-air produce market—Salzburg's liveliest (mornings Mon–Sat, best on Sat when the farmers are in town—60 percent of Austria's produce is now grown organically). You can see the market stall numbers in the pavement. Exit through the covered arcade at #10 to Getreidegasse. Several of these characteristic and nicely arcaded medieval tunnel passages connect Salzburg's streets.

Getreidegasse: This street was old Salzburg's busy, colorful main drag. Famous for its old wrought-iron signs, it still looks much as it did in Mozart's day. (The Nordsee Restaurant was even more of a scandal than the coming of McDonald's—notice the medieval golden arches street sign.) *Schmuck* means jewelry. Wolfgang was born on this street. Find his very gold house.

Mozart's Birthplace (Geburtshaus): Mozart was born here in 1756. It was in this building that he composed most of his boy-genius works. This is the most popular Mozart sight in town. Filled with scores of scores, portraits, old keyboard instruments and violins, and a furnished middle class apartment from Mozart's time (all well-described in English), it's almost a pilgrimage. If you're a fan, you'll have to check it out (70 AS, or 110 AS for combined ticket to Mozart's *Wohnhaus*—see "Sights—Across the River," below, daily 9:00–18:00, shorter hours off-season, Getreidegasse 9). Note that Mozart's *Wohnhaus* provides a more informative visit than this more visited site.

Sights—Above the Old Town
▲**Hohensalzburg Fortress**—Built on a rock 400 feet above the Salzach River, this castle is a testament to the importance of the salt trade. One of Europe's mightiest, it dominates Salzburg's skyline and offers incredible views. You can hike up or ride the *Festungsbahn* (funicular, 76-AS round-trip includes fortress

courtyard, 66 AS one-way, pleasant to walk down). The castle visit has two parts—a relatively dull courtyard with some fine views (42 AS or included in 76-AS funicular fare) and the palatial interior (worth the 42-AS extra admission). The included audio-guide gives a 40-minute room-by-room narration—good information but makes a short story long (feel free to skip rooms). The highlight is the commanding city view from the top of a tower. It ends at the museum showing the fortress through its battle-torn years including World War II (fortress open daily 8:00–19:00, off-season 9:00–17:00, tel. 0662/842-430). Kids may enjoy the marionette exhibit in the fortress courtyard (adults-35 AS, kids-20 AS, daily 10:00–17:00).

▲**The Hills Are Alive Walk**—For a most enjoyable approach to the castle, consider riding the elevator to Café Winkler and walking 20 minutes across Salzburg's little mountain, Mönchsberg. A trail goes through the woods high above the city to Festung Hohensalzburg (stay on the high paved paths, or you'll have a needless climb back up to the castle).

In 1669, a huge Mönchsberg landslide killed over 200 towns-people. Since then the cliffs have been carefully checked each spring and fall. Even today, you'll see crews of three on the cliff monitoring its stability.

Sights—Across the River

Salzach River—Cross the river (ideally on a pedestrian bridge—the one farthest upstream, built in 1903, is just a block off Mozartplatz). It's called "salt river" not because it's salty but because the important salt mines of Hallein are just 15 kilometers upstream. Salt could be transported from here all the way to the Danube and on to Russia. The riverbanks and roads were built in 1860. Before that, the Salzach was much wider and slower moving. Houses opposite the old town fronted the river with docks and garages for boats.

▲**Steingasse**—This street, a block in from the river, was the only street in the Middle Ages going south to Hallein. Today it's won-derfully peaceful and free of Salzburg's touristy crush. Wander down Steingasse (from Mozartplatz, cross the pedestrian bridge, go a block inland, and turn left).

There's a great castle viewpoint midway up Steingasse. Notice the oldest nunnery in the German-speaking world (estab-lished in 712) under the castle and to the left. Maria from *The Sound of Music* taught in this nunnery's school. In 1927, she and Herr von Trapp were married in the church you see here (not the church filmed in the movie). He was 47. She was 22. Hmmmm.

At #19 find the carvings on the old door. Look for the notices from beggars to the begging community (more numerous after the economic dislocation caused by the wars over religion following the Reformation) indicating whether the residents would give or not. The four ringers indicate four families lived at this address.

Across the street, the wall is gouged out. This was left even after the building was restored so locals could remember the American GI who tried to get a tank down this road during a visit to the Steingasse brothel.

At #9 a plaque shows where Joseph Mohr, who wrote the words to *Silent Night*, was born, poor and illegitimate, in 1792.

▲**St. Sebastian Cemetery**—Wander through this peaceful place—so Baroque and so Italian (daily 9:00–19:00, Linzergasse 43). Mozart's father and most of his family are buried here (near entry on left). When Prince-Archbishop Wolf Dietrich had the cemetery moved from around the cathedral and put here, across the river, people didn't like it. To help popularize it, he had his mausoleum built as its centerpiece. Step into his dome, read the legalistic epitaph (posted in English), and look at the tomb through the grate in the floor. To get to the cemetery (Friedhof St. Sebastian), take Linzergasse, the best shopping street in Salzburg.

▲▲**Mozart's Wohnhaus**—This reconstruction of Mozart's second home (his family moved here when he was 17) is the most informative Mozart sight in town. The English-language audio-guides (free with admission, keep it carefully pointed at the trans-mitters and don't move while listening) provide a fascinating insight into Mozart's life and music. Along with the usual scores and old pianos, the highlight is an intriguing film (30 min, runs continu-ously, in English) that leaves you wanting to know more about Mozart and his remarkable family (65 AS, or 110 AS for combined ticket to birthplace, guidebook-59 AS, daily 9:00–18:00, until 19:00 July–Aug, allow 1 hr for visit, just over the river at Marktplatz 8, tel. 0662/8742-2740). The gift shop here sells unique CDs featuring Mozart's music performed on Mozart's piano.

▲**Mirabell Gardens and Palace (Schloss)**—The bubbly gardens, laid out in 1730, are always open and free. You may recognize the statues and the arbor featured in *The S.O.M.* A brass band plays free park concerts twice weekly (Sun 10:30, Wed 20:30). To properly enjoy the lavish Mirabell Palace—once Wolf Dietrich's summer palace and now the seat of the mayor—get a ticket to a *Schlosskonzert* (my favorite venue for a classical concert). Baroque music flying around a Baroque hall is a happy bird in the right cage. Tickets are around 400 AS (student-250 AS) and are rarely sold out (tel. 0662/848-586). The Café Bazar, nearby and overlooking the river, is a great place for a classy drink with an old town and castle view.

More Sights—Salzburg

▲▲**Riverside Bike Ride**—The Salzach River has smooth, flat, and scenic bike paths along each side. On a sunny day I can think of no more shout-worthy escape from the city. Hallein is a

Sound of Music **Debunked**

Rather than visit the real-life sights from the life of Maria von Trapp and family, most tourists want to see the places Hollywood chose to film this fanciful story. Local guides are happy not to burst any *S.O.M* pilgrim's bubble, but keep these points in mind:

- "Edelweiss" is not a cherished Austrian folk tune or national anthem. It was composed by Rodgers and Hammerstein for the movie.
- Maria was never a nun. She taught at the nunnery school.
- The colonel didn't run a tight domestic ship. In fact, his seven children were as unruly as most. He did use a whistle to call them. Each kid was trained to respond to a certain pitch.
- The family never escaped to Switzerland (which is a five-hour drive away). Rather, they went, legally, on a singing tour of the USA. The scene showing them climbing into Switzerland is actually near Berchtesgaden...home to Hitler's Eagle's Nest, and certainly not a smart place to flee.
- The actual von Trapp family house exists...but it's not the one you see in the film. In fact, the mansion in the movie is actually two different buildings (one used for the exterior and the other for the interior).
- Maria was given the choice: royalties or $8,000 for her story. She didn't think her story would sell so she traded all the rights for $8,000.

pleasant destination (with a salt mine tour, 9:00–17:00, 15 kilometers away, the north or "new town" side of river is most scenic). Even a quickie ride from one end of town to the other is a great Salzburg experience. In the evening, the riverbanks are a hand-in-hand, floodlit-spires world.

▲▲*Sound of Music* **Tour**—I took this tour skeptically (as part of my research chores) and liked it. It includes a quick but good general city tour, stops for a luge ride (45 AS extra, in season, fair weather), hits some *S.O.M.* spots (including the stately home, gazebo, and wedding church), and shows you a lovely stretch of the Salzkammergut. The Salzburg Panorama Tours Company charges 400 AS for the four-hour, English-only tour (from Mirabellplatz daily at 9:30 and 14:00, ask for a reservation and a free hotel pickup; travelers with this book who buy their tickets with cash at the Mirabellplatz ticket booth get a 10 percent discount on this and any other tour they do; tel. 0662/874-029,

Greater Salzburg

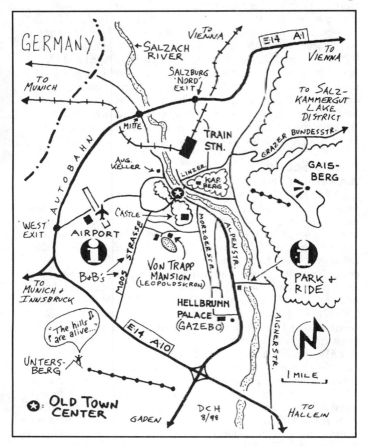

www.panoramatours.at). This is worthwhile for *S.O.M.* fans and those who won't otherwise be going into the Salzkammergut. Warning: Many think rolling through the Austrian countryside with 30 Americans singing "Doe, a deer" is pretty schmaltzy. Local Austrians don't understand all the commotion.

   Several similar and very competitive tour companies offer every conceivable tour of and from Salzburg (Mozart sights, Berchtesgaden, salt mines, Salzkammergut lakes and mountains). Some hotels have their brochures and get a healthy commission. Bob's Special Tours uses a minibus (several different tours, Kaigasse 10, tel. 0662/849-511, www.austria.at/bob/, e-mail: bobs-special-tours@net4you.co.at).

▲**Hellbrunn Castle**—The attractions here are a garden full of clever trick fountains and the sadistic joy the tour guide gets from soaking tourists. The Baroque garden, one of the oldest in Europe, is pretty enough and now features the "I am 16, going on 17" gazebo (80 AS for 35-minute tour and admission, daily 9:00–17:30, until 22:00 July–Aug, until 16:30 in April and Oct, closed Nov–March, tel. 0662/820-372). The archbishop's mediocre 17th-century palace, in the courtyard, is open by tour only (40 AS, 2/hrly, 20 min). Hellbrunn is three miles south of Salzburg (bus #55 from station or downtown, 2/hrly, 20 min). It's most fun on a sunny day or with kids, but, for many, it's a lot of trouble for a few water tricks.

Music Scene

▲▲**Salzburg Festival**—Each summer, from late July to the end of August, Salzburg hosts its famous Salzburger Festspiele, founded in 1920 partly to employ Vienna's musicians in the summer. This fun and festive time is crowded, but there are plenty of beds (except for a few August weekends). Tickets are normally available the day of the concert unless it's a really big show (the ticket office on Mozartplatz, in the TI, prints a daily list of concerts). You can contact the Austrian National Tourist Office in the United States for specifics on this year's festival schedule and tickets (Box 1142, New York, NY 10108-1142, tel. 212/944-6880, fax 212/730-4568, www.experienceaustria.com, e-mail: info@oewnyc.com), but I've never planned in advance and have enjoyed great concerts with every visit.

▲▲**Musical Events outside of Festival Time**—Salzburg is busy throughout the year with 2,000 classical performances in its palaces and churches annually. Pick up the events calendar at the TI (free, comes out monthly). Whenever you visit, you'll have a number of concerts to choose from. There are nearly nightly concerts at the Mirabell Palace and up in the fortress (both with open seating and 400-AS tickets, concerts at 19:30 or 20:30, doors open 30 min early). The *Schlosskonzerte* at the Mirabell Palace offer a fine Baroque setting for your Mozart (tel. 0662/848-586). The fortress concerts, called *Festungskonzerte*, are held in the "prince's chamber" (usually chamber music—a string quartet, tel. 0662/825-858 to reserve, you can pick up tickets at the door). This medieval-feeling room atop the castle has windows overlooking the city and the concert gives you a chance to enjoy a stroll through the castle courtyard and the grand city view (76-AS funicular, round-trip; only 34 AS if you have a concert ticket).

The almost daily "5:00 Concert" next to St. Peter's is cheaper, since it features young artists (120 AS, daily except Wed, 45 min, tel. 0662/8445-7619). While the series is named after the brother of Joseph Haydn, it features music from various masters.

Salzburg's impressive Marionette Theater performs operas with remarkable marionettes and recorded music (350–480 AS, nearly nightly May–Sept, tel. 0662/872-406, www.marionetten.at).

For those who'd like some classical music but would rather not sit through a concert, Stiftskeller St. Peter offers a **Mozart Dinner Concert** with a traditional candlelit three-course meal mixed with Mozart performed in historic costumes in an elegant Baroque setting (560 AS, nightly at 20:00, see "Eating," below, call to reserve at 0662/828-6950).

The *S.O.M.* musical at the Sternbrau restaurant (see "Eating," below) gets good reviews from couples and families.

Sights—Near Salzburg

▲**Bad Dürnberg Salzbergwerke**—Like its salty neighbors, this salt mine tour and cable-car ride above the town of Hallein (15 kilometers from Salzburg) is a fun experience while wearing white overalls, sliding down the sleek wooden chutes, and crossing underground from Austria into Germany (200 AS, daily 9:00– 17:00, English-speaking guides and information sheets, easy bus and train connections from Salzburg, tel. 06245/852-8515). A convenient "Salt Ticket" from Salzburg's train station covers admission, train, and cable-car fees for 289 AS.

Sleeping in Salzburg
(15 AS = about $1, country code: 43, area code: 0662, zip code: 5020)
Sleep Code: **S** = Single, **D** = Double/Twin, **T** = Triple, **Q** = Quad, **b** = bathroom, **t** = toilet only, **s** = shower only, **CC** = Credit Card (Visa, MasterCard, Amex), **SE** = Speaks English, **NSE** = No English.

Finding a room in Salzburg, even during the music festival, is usually easy. Unless otherwise noted, all my listings come with breakfast and at least some English is spoken. Rates rise significantly during the music festival (late July and Aug).

Sleeping in (or above) the Old Town
Gasthaus zur Goldenen Ente, run by the family Steinwender, is a good splurge if you'd like to sleep in a 600-year-old building above a fine restaurant as central as you can be on a pedestrian street in old Salzburg. Somehow the 15 modern and comfortable doubles fit into this building's medieval-style stone arches and narrow stairs (Sb-720–820 AS, Db-1,080–1,280 AS with this book, extra person-400 AS, the higher prices occur July–Aug, CC:VMA, elevator, parking-80 AS/day, Goldgasse 10, tel. 0662/845-622, fax 0662/845-6229, www.ente.at, e-mail: ente@eunet.at). The breakfast is buffet-big and their restaurant is a treat (see "Eating," below).

Hotel Restaurant Weisses Kreuz is a classy, comfy, family-run place on a cobbled back street under the castle away from the crowds with a fine restaurant (Sb-800 AS, Db-1,200 AS, Tb-1,600 AS, CC:VMA, peaceful roof garden, garage, Bierjodlgasse 6, tel. 0662/845-641, fax 0662/845-6419, e-mail: weisseskreuz@eunet.at).

Gasthof Hinterbrühl is a smoky, ramshackle old place with a handy location, minimal plumbing, and not a tourist in sight (S-450 AS, D-570 AS, T-600 AS, optional breakfast-60 AS, above a bar that can be noisy, workable parking, on a villagelike square under the castle's river end at Schanzlgasse 12, tel. 0662/846-798, fax 0662/841-859, e-mail: hinterbruhl@kronline.at).

Naturfreundehaus, also called "Gasthaus Bürgerwehr," is a local version of a mountaineer's hut. It's a great budget alternative in a forest guarded by singing birds and snuggled in the remains of a 15th-century castle wall overlooking Salzburg, with magnificent town and mountain views (D-280 AS, 120 AS/person in 4- to 6-bed dorms, breakfast-30 AS, dinner-63–108 AS, 01:00 curfew, open May–Sept, 2 min from the top of the 27-AS roundtrip Mönchsberg elevator, Mönchsberg 19, tel. 0662/841-729). High above the old town, it's the stone house to the left of the glass Café Winkler.

Sleeping on Linzergasse and Rupertgasse

These listings are between the train station and the old city in a pleasant neighborhood (with easy parking), a 15-minute walk from the train station (for directions, see "Arrival In Salzburg/By Train," above) and 10 to 15 minutes to the old city. If you're coming from the old city, simply cross the main bridge (Staatsbrücke) to nearly traffic-free Linzergasse. The first listings are on or very near Linzergasse, across the bridge from Mozartville. The last ones are farther out with easier parking.

Hotel Trumer Stube, a comfy little hotel-pension a few blocks from the river just off Linzergasse, has clean new rooms and a friendly can-do owner (Sb-780 AS, Db-1,320 AS, Tb-1,490 AS, Qb-1,826 AS, higher in Aug, lower in winter, CC to reserve but pay cash, elevator, parking-100 AS, Bergstrasse 6, tel. 0662/874-776, fax 0662/874-326, www.members.eunet.at/hotel.trumer-stube.sbg, e-mail: hotel.trumer-stube.sbg@eunet.at, Sylvia SE).

Hotel Goldene Krone, about five blocks from the river, is big, quiet, and creaky-traditional but modern, with comforts rare in this price range (Sb-500–570 AS, D-750–800 AS, Db-850–970 AS, Tb-1,000–1,300 AS, elevator, Linzergasse 48, tel. 0662/872-300, fax 0662/8723-0066).

Institute St. Sebastian—a somewhat sterile but very clean, historic building—has spacious public areas, a roof garden, and rents some of the best rooms and dorm beds in town for the money. The doubles come with modern baths and head-to-toe twin beds (Sb-400 AS, Db-700 AS, Tb-900 AS, elevator, reception closes at 21:00, Linzergasse 41, enter through arch at #37, tel. 0662/871-386,

Salzburg Hotels

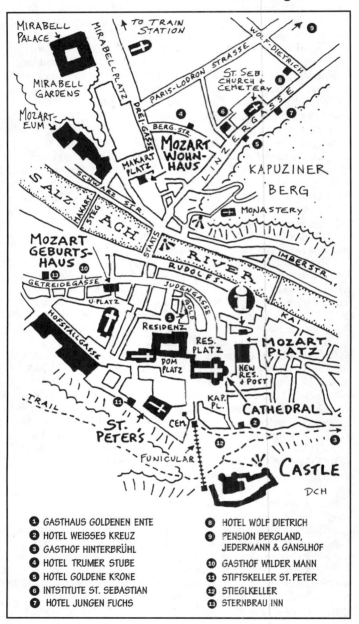

1. GASTHAUS GOLDENEN ENTE
2. HOTEL WEISSES KREUZ
3. GASTHOF HINTERBRÜHL
4. HOTEL TRUMER STUBE
5. HOTEL GOLDENE KRONE
6. INTSTITUTE ST. SEBASTIAN
7. HOTEL JUNGEN FUCHS
8. HOTEL WOLF DIETRICH
9. PENSION BERGLAND, JEDERMANN & GANSLHOF
10. GASTHOF WILDER MANN
11. STIFTSKELLER ST. PETER
12. STIEGLKELLER
13. STERNBRAU INN

fax 0662/8713-8685). Students like the 210-AS bunks in 10-bed
dorms (30 AS less if you have sheets, no lockout time, lockers, free
showers). Self-service kitchens on each floor (fridge space is free;
just request a key). Ask about their washer and dryer.

Hotel zum Jungen Fuchs turns on troglodytes. It's plain
but clean and wonderfully located in a funky, dumpy old building
(S-300 AS, D-400 AS, T-500 AS, no breakfast, just up from Hotel
Krone at Linzergasse 54, tel. 0662/875-496).

Rudolf Schneider Zimmer—a basic, no breakfast, no-
speak-English place perfectly located on Linzergasse—rents
six fine rooms at a great price (Sb-350 AS, Db-600–700 AS,
Linzergasse 70, tel. & fax 0662/876-327).

Altstadthotel Wolf Dietrich, one block above Hotel zum
Jungen Fuchs, around the corner on Wolf-Dietrich Strasse, is
well located and a reasonable option if you want a formal hotel
(Sb-1,000 AS, Db-1,460–1,860 AS, prices go up 500 AS in Aug,
CC:VMA, Wolf-Dietrich Strasse 7, tel. 0662/871-275, fax 0662/
882-320, e-mail: office@salzburg-hotel.at).

These three hotels are about five blocks farther from the river
up Paris-Lodron Strasse to Rupertgasse, a breeze for drivers.

Pension Bergland is a charming, classy oasis of calm with
rustic rooms and musical evenings (Sb-590 AS, Db-970 AS, Tb-
1,100 AS, music room open 17:00–21:30, Internet access, bike
rental, English library, Rupertgasse 15, tel. 0662/872-318, fax
0662/872-3188, www.sol.at/bergland, e-mail: pkuhn@sol.at).

The similar boutiquelike **Hotel Jedermann**, a few doors
down, is tastefully done and comfortable with friendly owners, a
cheery breakfast room, and a bird-chirping backyard garden (Sb-
690–790 AS, Db-920–1,250 AS, Qb-1,700–1,840 AS, CC:VMA,
cable TV, Internet access, Rupertgasse 25, tel. 0662/873-241, fax
0662/873-2419, e-mail: jedermann@salzburginfo.at, Walter SE).

Gasthaus Ganslhof, around the corner to the right, facing a
hill of trees, is decent and clean with Motel 6 ambience, a parking
lot, and 25 surprisingly comfortable rooms (Db-850–1,100 AS,
CC:VMA, elevator, TV, phone, Vogelweiderstrasse 6, tel. 0662/
873-853, fax 0662/8738-5323, e-mail: office.ganslhof@aon.at).

Zimmer

These are generally roomy and comfortable and come with a
good breakfast, easy parking, and tourist information. Off-season,
competition softens prices. They are a bus ride from town, but, with
a day pass and the frequent service, this shouldn't keep you away.
Unsavory *Zimmer* skimmers lurk at the station. Ignore them.

Brigitte Lenglachner fills her big, traditional home with a
warm welcome (S-290 AS, D-480 AS, bunk bed D-390 AS, Db-550
AS, T-690 AS, Tb-830 AS, Qb-1,100 AS, fifth person-280 AS,
apartment with kitchen available: Sb-500, Db-800, Scheibenweg 8,

tel. & fax 0662/438-044). It's a 10-minute walk northeast of the
station (cross pedestrian Pioneer bridge, turn right, walk along
the river 300 meters, cross canal, left on linke Glanzeile for 3 min,
right onto Wachtelgasse).

Trude Poppenberger's three pleasant rooms offer a moun-
tain-view balcony (S-280 AS, D-480 AS, T-720 AS; stay 2 nights
and she'll do your laundry for 100 AS; Wachtelgasse 9, tel. & fax
0662/430-094, e-mail: trudeshome@yline.com). She offers free
pick up at the station. Or it's a 30-minute walk northwest of the
station (cross pedestrian Pioneer bridge, turn right, walk along
river 300 meters, cross canal, left on Linke Glanzeile for 3 min,
right onto Wachtelgasse).

Zimmers **on Moosstrasse:** The street called Moosstrasse,
southwest of Mönchsberg, is lined with *Zimmer*. Those farther out
are farmhouses. From the station, catch bus #1 and change to bus
#60 immediately after crossing the river. From the old town, ride
bus #60. If you're driving from the center, go through the tunnel,
straight on Neutorstrasse, and take the fourth left onto Moosstrasse.

Maria Gassner rents 10 sparkling clean, comfortable rooms
in her modern house (St-300 AS, Sb-400 AS, D-450 AS, Db-500
AS, big Db-600 AS, 10 percent more for 1-night stays, family
deals, CC:VM, 60-AS coin-op laundry, Moosstrasse 126-B, tel.
0662/824-990, fax 0662/822-075).

Frau Ballwein offers cozy, charming rooms in an old farmhouse (S-220 AS, Ss-260 AS, D-420 AS, Db-500 AS, farm-fresh
breakfasts, Moosstrasse 69A, tel. & fax 0662/824-029).

Haus Reichl also has good rooms (Db-600 AS, Tb-850 AS,
Qb-1,000 AS, family deals, Q rooms have balcony and view,
between Ballwein and Bankhammer B&Bs at Reiterweg 52, tel.
& fax 0662/826-248, www.privatzimmer.at, e-mail:
haus.reichl@telering.at).

Helga Bankhammer rents recently renovated, pleasant
rooms in a farmhouse with farm animals nearby (D-450 AS,
Db-520 AS, Moosstrasse 77, tel. & fax 0662/830-067, e-mail:
helga.bankhammer@telering.at).

Gästehaus Blobergerhof is rural and comfortable (Sb-350–
400 AS, Db-550–650 AS, 10 percent more for 1-night stays,
CC:VM; breakfast buffet, free bike usage, laundry service, will
pick up at station, Hammerauerstrasse 4, Querstrasse zur Moosstrasse, tel. 0662/830-227, fax 0662/827-061, www.privatzimmer
.at, e-mail: keuschnigg@eunet.at).

Sleeping near the Train Station
Pension Adlerhof, a plain and decent old place, is two blocks in
front of the train station (left off Kaiserschutzenstrasse), but a 15-
minute walk from the sightseeing action. It has a quirky staff and
well-maintained rooms (S-420–440 AS, Sb-650 AS, D-670 AS,

Db-850 AS, Elisabethstrasse 25, tel. 0662/875-236, fax 0662/873-6636, e-mail: adlerhof@pension-adlerhof.at).

Gottfried's International Youth Hotel, a.k.a. the "Yo-Ho," is the most fun, handy, and American of Salzburg's many hostels (150 AS in 6- to 8-bed dorms, D-200 AS/person, T or Q-170 AS/person, sheets-20 AS, 6 blocks from station toward Linzergasse and 6 blocks from river at Paracelsusstrasse 9, tel. 0662/879-649, www.yoho.at). This easygoing place speaks English first; has cheap meals, 400 beds, lockers, a laundry, tour discounts, and a soft 01:00 curfew; plays *The Sound of Music* free daily about noon; runs a lively bar; and welcomes anyone of any age. The fun, noisy atmosphere can make it hard to sleep.

Eating in Salzburg

Salzburg boasts many inexpensive, fun, and atmospheric places to eat. I'm a sucker for big cellars with their smoky, Old World atmosphere, heavy medieval arches, time-darkened paintings, antlers, hearty meals, and plump patrons. These places are famous with visitors but are also enjoyed by the locals. All but the last two places are central in the old city.

Gasthaus zum Wilder Mann is the place if the weather's bad and you're in the mood for Hofbräu atmosphere and a hearty, cheap meal at a shared table in one small, well-antlered room (Mon–Sat 11:00–21:00, closed Sun, smoky, 2 min from Mozart's birthplace, enter from Getreidegasse 20 or Griesgasse 17, tel. 0662/841-787). For a quick lunch, get the *Bauernschmaus*, a mountain of dumplings, kraut, and peasant's meats.

Stiftskeller St. Peter has been in business for more than 1,000 years—it was mentioned in the biography of Charlemagne. It's classy (with strolling musicians), more central, and a good splurge for traditional Austrian cuisine in medieval sauce (meals 100–200 AS, daily 11:00–24:00, indoor/outdoor seating, hosts Mozart Dinner Concert mentioned in "Music Scene," above: 560 AS, nightly at 20:00, call to reserve, CC:VMA, next to St. Peter's church at foot of Mönchsberg, tel. 0662/841-268).

Gasthaus zur Goldenen Ente (see "Sleeping," above) serves great food in a classy, subdued hotel dining room. The chef, Robert, specializes in roast duck (*Ente*) and seafood, along with "Salzburger *Nockerl*," the mountainous sweet soufflé served all over town. It's big enough for four (Mon–Fri 11:00–21:00, closed Sat–Sun, Goldgasse 10, tel. 0662/845-622).

Stieglkeller is a huge, atmospheric institution that has several rustic rooms and outdoor garden seating with a great rooftop view of the old town (daily 10:00–23:00, 50 meters uphill from the lift to the castle, Festungsgasse 10, tel. 0662/842-681).

Sternbrau Inn is a sprawling complex of popular eateries (traditional and vegetarian). One elegant room hosts the *Sound of*

Music dinner show. A piano player and a hard-working quartet of singers perform an entertaining mix of *Sound of Music* hits and traditional folk songs (570 AS includes a schnitzel and crisp apple strudel dinner at 19:30, 370 AS for 20:30 show only, ideal for families, daily May–Sept, Griesgasse 23, tel. 0662/826-617).

Resch & Lieblich Bierhaus, wedged between the cliff side and the back of the big concert hall, is a rough and characteristic place popular with locals for salads, goulash, and light meals (indoor/outdoor seating: in rustic little cellar or under umbrellas on square, Toscaninihof, tel. 0662/843-675).

Café Glockenspiel, on Mozartplatz 2, is the place to see and be seen (daily 9:00–24:00).

Nestled behind the cathedral and under the castle, **Restaurant Weisses Kreuz** serves fine Balkan cuisine in a pleasant dining room (nightly, Bierjodlgasse 6, tel. 0662/845-641).

Picnickers will appreciate the bustling morning produce market (daily except Sun) on Universitätsplatz, just behind Mozart's house. **Restaurant Zipfer Bierhaus**, facing Universitätsplatz, serves good salads and traditional meals at a decent price (closed Sun).

Sausage stands serve the local fast food. The best places (such as the one on the side of the Collegiate Church just off Universitätsplatz) use the same boiling water all day, which fills the wienies with more flavor. Key wienie words: *bratwurst:* boiled white sausage, *bosna:* with onions and curry, *kas krainer:* with melted cheese inside, and *senf:* mustard (ask for sweet: *süss* or sharp: *scharf*). Only a tourist puts the sausage in a bun like a hot dog. Munch alternately between the meat and the bread (that's why you have two hands), and you'll look like a local.

The next two places are on the old-town side of the river, about a 10-minute walk along the river (river on your right) from the Staatsbrücke bridge.

Krimplestätter employs 450 years of experience serving authentic old-Salzburger food in its authentic old-Austrian interior or its cheery garden (Tue–Sun 10:00–24:00, closed Mon all year and Sun in winter, Müllner Hauptstrasse 31). For fine food with a wild finale, eat here and drink at the nearby Augustiner Bräustübl.

Augustiner Bräustübl, a monk-run brewery, is rustic and crude. On busy nights it's like a Munich beer hall with no music but the volume turned up. When it's cool you'll enjoy a historic setting with beer-sloshed and smoke-stained halls. On balmy evenings it's a Monet painting with beer breath under chestnut trees in the garden. Local students mix with tourists eating hearty slabs of schnitzel with their fingers or cold meals from the self-serve picnic counter while children frolic on the playground kegs. Waiters only bring drinks. For food, go up the stairs, survey the hallway of deli counters, and assemble your meal (or, as long as you buy a drink, you can bring in your picnic, open daily 15:00–23:00, Augustinergasse 4, head

up Müllner Hauptstrasse northwest along the river, and ask for
"Müllnerbräu," its local nickname). Don't be fooled by second-rate
gardens serving the same beer nearby. Augustiner Bräustübl is a
huge, 1,000-seat place within the Augustiner brewery. For your
beer: Pick up a half-liter or full-liter mug ("*shank*" means self-serve
price, "*bedienung*" is the price with waiter service), pay the lady,
wash your mug, and give Mr. Keg your receipt and empty mug
to be filled. For dessert—after a visit to the strudel kiosk—enjoy
the incomparable floodlit view of old Salzburg from the nearby
pedestrian bridge and a riverside stroll home.

Eating on or near Linzergasse

These cheaper places are near the recommended hotels on
Linzergasse. **Frauenberger** is friendly, picnic-ready, and inexpensive, with indoor or outdoor seating (Mon–Fri 8:00–14:00, across
from Linzergasse 16). **Spicy Spices** is a vegetarian-Indian lunch
take-out restaurant (with a few tables) serving tasty curry and rice
boxes, *samosas*, organic salads, and fresh juices (Mon–Sat 10:00–
22:00, closed Sun, Wolf-Dietrich Strasse 1, tel. 0662/870-712).
Nearby, **Restaurant Ahrlich** offers a delicious variety of organic
meals (Mon–Sat 18:00–22:00, also 12:00–14:00 July–Aug, closed
Sun, Wolf-Dietrich Strasse 7, tel. 0662/8712-7539). **Mensa
Aicherpassage** serves some of Salzburg's cheapest meals in the
basement (Mon–Fri 11:30–14:30, near Mirabellplatz, walk into
Aicherpassage, go under arch, enter metal door to "Mozarteum,"
and go down 1 floor). Closer to the hotels on Rupertgasse and
away from the tourists is the very local **Biergarten Weisse** (daily
11:00–24:00, on Rupertgasse east of Bayerhamerstrasse).

Transportation Connections—Salzburg

By train to: Innsbruck (every 2 hrs, 2 hrs), **Vienna** (2/hrly, 3.5
hrs), **Hallstatt** (hrly, 50 min to Attnang Puchheim, 20-minute
wait, 90 min to Hallstatt), **Reutte** (every 2 hrs, 4 hrs, transfer to a
bus in Innsbruck), **Munich** (hrly, 90 min). Train info: tel. 051717
(wait through long German recording for operator).

By car: To leave town driving west, go under the Mönchsberg tunnel and follow blue A1 signs to Munich. It's 90 minutes
from Salzburg to Innsbruck.

SALZKAMMERGUT LAKE DISTRICT AND HALLSTATT

Commune with nature in Austria's Lake District. "The hills are
alive," and you're surrounded by the loveliness that has turned on
everyone from Emperor Franz Josef to Julie Andrews. This is *The
Sound of Music* country. Idyllic and majestic, but not rugged, it's a
gentle land of lakes, forested mountains, and storybook villages,

Hallstatt

NOT TO SCALE—
BUS STOP TO MARKTPLATZ
IS A 10 MINUTE WALK

SALT MINE

CATHOLIC CHURCH

TO ECHERNTAL VALLEY

FUNICULAR

SMALL UPPER PARKING LOT #1 IN TUNNEL

TUNNEL

TO BAD ISCHL + SALZBURG

MAIN ROAD

DR. MORTON WEG

GROC ROAD

MUSEUM

MARKT PLATZ

GOSAUMÜHL

MAIN

BUS STOP W.C. + PARKING LOT #2

BOAT RENTAL

PROT. CHURCH

MARKT DOCK

BOAT RENTAL

TO OBERTRAUN

LAHN DOCK

Post

HALLSTATTERSEE

TO HALLSTATT TRAIN STATION

1 GASTHOF SIMONY   4 PENSION SEETHALER   7 PENSION SARSTEIN
2 GASTHOF ZAUNER   5 HELGA LENZ ZIMMER
3 GASTHAUS ZUR MÜHLE   6 FRAU ZIMMERMAN ZIMMER

rich in hiking opportunities and inexpensive lodging. Settle down in the postcard-pretty, fjord-cuddling town of Hallstatt.

Planning Your Time

While there are plenty of lakes and charming villages, Hallstatt is really the only one that matters. One night and a few hours to browse are all you'll need to fall in love. To relax or take a hike in the surroundings, give it two nights and a day. It's a relaxing break between Salzburg and Vienna. My best Austrian week: the two big cities—Salzburg and Vienna, a bike ride along the Danube, and a stay in Hallstatt.

Orientation (area code: 06134)

Lovable Hallstatt is a tiny town bullied onto a ledge between a selfish mountain and a swan-ruled lake, with a waterfall ripping furiously through its middle. It can be toured on foot in about 15 minutes. The town is one of Europe's oldest, going back centuries before Christ. The charm of Hallstatt is the village and its lakeside setting. Go there to relax, nibble, wander, and paddle. While tourist crowds can trample much of Hallstatt's charm in August, the place is almost dead in the off-season. The lake is famous for its good fishing and pure water.

Tourist Information: The TI, on the main drag, can explain hikes and excursions, arrange private tours of Hallstatt (600 AS), and find you a room (Mon–Fri 9:00–17:00, Sat–Sun 10:00–14:00, less off-season, a block from Marktplatz toward the lakefront parking, above post office, Seestrasse 169, tel. 06134/8208, www.tiscover.com/hallstatt, e-mail: hallstatt-info@eunet.at). Hallstatt gives anyone spending the night a "guest card" allowing free parking and discounts to local attractions (free, from your hotel, ask for it).

Arrival in Hallstatt

By Train: Hallstatt's train station is a wide spot on the tracks across the lake. *Stefanie* (a boat) meets you at the station and glides scenically across the lake into town (25 AS, meets each train until 18:40—don't arrive after that). Last departing boat-train connection leaves Hallstatt at 18:15. Walk left from the boat dock for the TI and most hotels. Since there's no train station in town, the TI provides schedule information (10 AS).

By Car: The main road skirts Hallstatt via a long tunnel above the town. Parking is tight mid-June through mid-October. Hallstatt has several numbered parking areas outside the town center. Parking lot #1 is in the tunnel above the town (swing through to check for a spot, free with guest card). Otherwise several numbered lots are just after the tunnel. If you have a hotel reservation, the guard will let you drive into town to drop your bags (ask if your hotel has any in-town parking). It's a lovely 10- to 20-minute lakeside walk to the center of town from the lots. Without a guest card, you'll pay 50 AS per day for parking. Off-season parking in town is easy and free.

Helpful Hints

Laundromat: A small full-service Laundromat is at the campground near the island of Bade-Insel (100 AS per load, based on weight). In the center, Hotel Gruner Baum also does laundry for nonguests (more expensive) and rents bikes (80 AS/half day, 120 AS/day, facing market square).

Parks and Swimming: Green and peaceful lakeside parks line the south end of Lake Hallstatt. If you walk 10 minutes south of town to Hallstatt-Lahn, you'll find a grassy public park, playground, and swimming area with a fun man-made play island (Badestrand and Bade-Insel).

Views: For a great view over Hallstatt, hike above Helga Lenz's *Zimmer* as far as you like (see "Sleeping," below), or climb any path leading up the hill. The 40-minute steep hike down from the salt mine tour gives the best views (see "Sights," below).

Hallstatt Historic Town Walk

This short walk starts at the dock.

Boat Landing: There was a Hallstatt before there was a Rome. In fact, because of the importance of salt mining here, an entire epoch—the Hallstatt era from 800 to 400 B.C.—is named for this important spot. Through the centuries salt was traded and people came and went by boat. You'll still see the traditional "Fuhr" boats, designed to carry heavy loads in shallow water.

Towering above the town is the Catholic church. Its faded St. Christopher—patron saint of travelers with his cane and baby Jesus on his shoulder—watched over those sailing in and out. Until 1875, the only way into town was by boat. Then came the train and the road. The good ship *Stefanie* shuttles travelers back and forth from here to the Hallstatt train station immediately across the lake. The *Bootverleih* sign advertises boat rentals (see "Lake Trip," below).

Notice the one-lane road out of town (with the waiting time, width, and height posted). Until 1966, when a bigger tunnel was built above Hallstatt, all the traffic crept single file right through the town.

Look down the shore at the huge homes. Housing several families back when Hallstatt's population was about double its present 1,000, many of these rent rooms to visitors today.

Parking is tight here in the tourist season. Locals and hotels have cards getting them into the prime town center lot. From October through May, the barricade is lifted and anyone can park here. Hallstatt is snowbound for about three months each winter. But the lake hasn't frozen over since 1981.

See any swans? They've patrolled the lake like they own it since the 1860s when Emperor Franz Josef and Empress Sissy—the Lady Diana of her day—made this region their annual holiday retreat. Sissy loved swans, so locals made sure she'd see them here. During this period, the Romantics discovered Hallstatt, many top painters worked here, and the town got its first hotel.

Tiny Hallstatt has two big churches—Protestant (step into its cemetery, which is actually a grassy lakeside playground) and Catholic up above (described below with its fascinating bone chapel). After the Reformation, most of Hallstatt was Protestant. Then, under Hapsburg rule, it was mostly Catholic. Today, 60 percent of the town is Catholic. Walk over the town's stream, past the Protestant church one block to...

Market Square: In 1750, a fire leveled this part of town. The buildings you see now are all late 18th century and built of stone rather than burnable wood. Take a close look at the two-dimensional, up-against-the-wall pear tree (it likes the sun-warmed wall). The statue features the Holy Trinity. At #58 study the painting of Hallstatt in 1750. Continue a block past Hotel Simony to the pair of phone booths and step into the...

City Museum Square: Because 20th-century Hallstatt was of no industrial importance, it was untouched by World War II. But once upon a time its salt was worth defending. High above, peeking out of the trees, is Rudolf's Tower (*Rudolfsturm*). Originally a 13th-century watchtower protecting the salt mines and later the mansion of a salt mine boss, today it's a restaurant with a great view. A zigzag trail connects the town with *Rudolfsturm* and the salt mines just beyond. The big white houses by the waterfall were water-powered mills that once ground Hallstatt's grain. If you hike up a few blocks, you'll see the river raging through town. Around you are the town's TI, post office, two museums, city hall, and the Janu Sport shop (with its prehistoric basement—described below). The statue on the square is of the mine manager who excavated prehistoric graves around 1850. Much of the *Schmuck* (jewelry) sold locally is inspired by the jewelry found in the area's Bronze Age tombs.

For thousands of years people have been leaching salt out of this mountain. A brine spring sprung here, attracting Bronze Age people around 1500 B.C. Later, they dug tunnels to mine the rock, which was 70 percent salt, dissolved it into a brine, and distilled out salt—precious for preserving meat (and making French fries so tasty). For a look at early salt mining implements, visit the museum.

Sights—Hallstatt

Prehistory Museum—The humble Prehistory Museum adjacent to the TI is interesting because little Hallstatt was the important salt-mining hub of a culture that spread from France to the Balkans during the "Hallstatt Period" (800–400 B.C.). Back then, Celtic tribes dug for precious salt, and Hallstatt was, as its name means, the "place of salt." Your 50-AS Prehistory Museum ticket also gets you into the cute Heimatmuseum of folk culture (both open daily 10:00–18:00 in summer, tel. 06134/8398). Historians like the English booklet that covers both museums (25 AS). The Janu Sport shop across from the TI dug into a prehistoric site, and now its basement is another small museum (free).

▲▲**Hallstatt's Catholic Church and Bone Chapel**—The Catholic church overlooks the town from above. From near the boat dock, hike up the covered wooden stairway to the church. The lovely church has 500-year-old altars and frescoes dedicated to St. Barbara (patron of miners) and St. Catherine (patron of foresters—lots of wood was needed to fortify the miles of tunnels and boil the brine to distill out the salt).

Behind the church, in the well-tended graveyard, is the 12th-century Chapel of St. Michael (even older than the church). Its bone chapel—or charnel house—contains over 600 painted skulls. Each skull has been lovingly named, dated, and decorated (skulls with dark, thick garlands are oldest—18th century, flowers

Salzkammergut Lakes

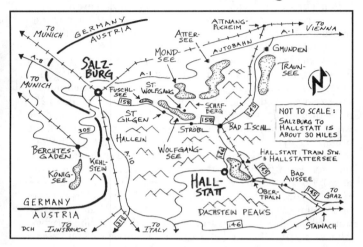

indicate more recent—19th century). Space was so limited in this cemetery that bones had only 12 peaceful, buried years here before making way for the freshly dead. Many of the dug-up bones and skulls ended up in this chapel. They stopped this practice in the 1960s, about the same time the Catholic Church began permitting cremation (Beinhaus, 10 AS, daily 10:00–18:00).

▲**Lake Trip**—While there are full lake tours, you can ride *Stefanie* across the lake and back for 50 AS. It stops at the tiny Hallstatt train station for 30 minutes giving you time to walk to a hanging bridge and enjoy the peaceful, deep part of the lake. Those into relaxation can rent a sleepy electric motorboat to enjoy town views from the water (75 AS/30 min, 120 AS/60 min, until 19:00; boats have 2 speeds: slow and stop; spend 20 AS more for faster 500-watt boats, rental place next to ferry dock).

▲▲**Salt Mine Tour**—If you have yet to do a salt mine, Hallstatt's—which claims to be the oldest in the world—is a good one. You'll ride a steep funicular high above the town (105 AS round-trip, 65 AS one-way, May–Sept 9:00–18:00, until 16:30 in Oct, tel. 06134/8400), take a 10-minute hike, check your bag and put on old miners' clothes, hike 200 meters higher in your funny outfit to meet your guide, load onto the train, and ride into the mountain through a tunnel actually made by prehistoric miners. Inside, you'll listen to a great video (English headsets), slide down two banisters, and follow your guide. While the tour is mostly in German, the guide is required to speak English if you ask—so ask (140 AS, May–Oct daily 9:30–16:30, the 16:00 funicular departure catches the last tour at 16:30, no children under age 4, rarely a long wait but arrive

after 15:00 and you'll find no lines and a smaller group, tel. 06134/
8400). The well-publicized ancient Celtic graveyard excavation
sites nearby are really dead (precious little to see). If you skip the
funicular, the scenic 40-minute hike back into town is (with strong
knees) a joy.

At the base of the funicular, notice train tracks leading to the
Erbstollen tunnel entrance. This lowest of the salt tunnels goes
miles into the mountain where a shaft connects it to the tunnels you
just explored. Today the salty brine from these tunnels flows 25
miles through the world's oldest pipeline to the huge modern salt
works (next to the highway) at Ebensee. You'll pass a stack of the
original 120-year-old wooden pipes between the lift and the mine.

▲**Local Hikes**—Mountain lovers, hikers, and spelunkers keep
busy for days using Hallstatt as their home base (ask the TI for
ideas). Local hikes are well described in the TI's *Dachstein Hiking
Guide* (80 AS, English). A good, short, and easy walk is the two-
hour round-trip up the Echerntal Valley to the Waldbachstrub
waterfall and back. With a car, consider hiking around nearby
Altaussee (flat, 3-hour hike) or along Grundlsee to Tolpitzsee.
Regular buses connect Hallstatt with Gosausee for a pleasant
hour-long walk around that lake. The TI can recommend a great
two-day hike with an overnight in a nearby mountain hut.

Sights—Near Hallstatt

▲▲**Dachstein Mountain Cable Car and Caves**—For a refreshing activity, ride a scenic cable car up a mountain to visit huge,
chilly caves.

Dachstein Cable Car: From Obertraun, five kilometers
beyond Hallstatt, a mighty gondola goes in three stages high up
the Dachstein Plateau—crowned by Dachstein, the highest mountain in the Salzkammergut (over 9,000 feet). The first segment
stops at Schonbergalm (4,500 feet) with a mountain restaurant
and two huge caves (described below). The second segment goes
to Krippenstein, a 6,600-foot summit with a classy hotel/restau-
rant and a rustic chalet restaurant. The third segment descends
a bit to Gjaidalm (5,800 feet) from which several hikes begin.
For a quick high-country experience, Krippenstein is better than
Gjaidalm. From Krippenstein you'll survey a scrubby limestone
"karst" landscape (which absorbs rainfall through its many cracks
and ultimately carves all those caves) with 360-degree views of
the surrounding mountains (cable car ride to the caves-170 AS,
to Krippenstein-260 AS, tel. 06131/273).

Giant Ice Caves (Riesen-Eishohle, 4,500 feet): These were
discovered in 1910. Today, guides lead tours in German and
English on an hour-long, one-kilometer hike through an eerie, icy,
subterranean world, passing limestone canyons the size of subway
stations. The limestone caverns, carved by rushing water, are

named for scenes from Wagner operas—the favorite of the mountaineers who first came here. If you're nervous, note that the iron oxide covering the ceiling takes 5,000 years to form. Things are very stable.

At the lift station, report to the ticket window to get your cave appointment. While the temperature is just above freezing and the 600 steps help keep you warm, bring a sweater. Allow 90 minutes, including the 10-minute hike from the station (90 AS, or 150-AS combo ticket with Mammoth Caves, open mid-May– mid-Oct, hour-long tours from 9:00–16:00, stay in front and assert yourself for English information, tel. 06134/8400).

Drop by the little free museum near the lift station—in a local-style wood cabin designed to support 200 tons of snow— to see the huge cave system model, exhibits about its exploration, and life in the caves.

Mammoth Caves: While huge and well promoted, these are much less interesting than the Ice Caves and—for most—not worth the time. Of the 50-kilometer limestone labyrinth excavated so far, you'll walk a kilometer with a German-speaking guide (90 AS, or 150-AS combo ticket with Ice Caves, hour-long tours 10:00–15:00, entrance a 10-minute hike from lift station).

Luge Rides on the Hallstatt–Salzburg Road—If you're driving between Salzburg and Hallstatt, you'll pass two luge rides. Each is a ski lift which drags you backwards up the hill as you sit on your go-cart. At the top you ride the cart down the winding metal course. Operating the sled is simple. Push to go, pull to stop, take your hands off your stick and you get hurt.

Each course is just off the road with easy parking. The ride up and down takes about 15 minutes. Look for *Riesen-Rutschbahn* or *Sommerrodelbahn* signs. The one near Fuschlsee (closest to Salzburg) is half as long and half the price (45 AS/ride, 320 AS/10 rides, 600 meters). The one near Walfgangsee is a double course, more fun and scenic with grand lake views (70 AS/ride, 480 AS/10 rides, 1,300 meters, each track is the same speed). Courses are open April through October from 10:00 to 18:00 (July–Aug 9:30–19:00, tel. 06235/7297). While these are fun, the concrete courses near Reutte are better.

Sleeping in Hallstatt
(15 AS = about $1, country code: 43, area code: 06134, zip code: 4830)
Sleep Code: **S** = Single, **D** = Double/Twin, **T** = Triple, **Q** = Quad, **b** = bathroom, **t** = toilet only, **s** = shower only, **CC** = Credit Card (Visa, MasterCard, Amex), **SE** = Speaks English, **NSE** = No English.

Hallstatt's TI can almost always find you a room (either in town or at B&Bs and small hotels outside of town—which are more likely to have rooms available and come with easy parking).

Mid-July and August can be tight. Early August is worst. A bed in a private home costs about 200 AS with breakfast. It's hard to get a one-night advance reservation. But if you drop in and they have a spot, one-nighters are welcome. Prices include breakfast, lots of stairs, and a silent night. "*Zimmer mit Aussicht?*" means "Room with view?"—worth asking for. Only two of my listings accept plastic, which goes for most businesses here.

Gasthof Simony is my stocking-feet-tidy, 500-year-old favorite. It's right on the square with a lake view, balconies, creaky wood floors, slippery rag rugs, antique furniture, a lakefront garden, and a huge breakfast. Reserve in advance. For safety, reconfirm a day or two before you arrive and call again if arriving late (S-380 AS, Sb-650 AS, D-550 AS, Db-900–950 AS, third person-350–450 AS, Markt 105, tel. & fax 06134/8231, Susan Scheutz SE). Downstairs and in the lakefront garden, Frau Zopf runs a traditional Austrian restaurant—try her delicious homemade desserts. Grab a lakeside table.

Braugasthof Hallstatt is another creaky old place—a former brewery—with eight mostly lake-view rooms near the town center (Db-920 AS, less off-season, CC:VM, Seestrasse 120, tel. 06134/8221, fax 06134/82214, Lobisser family).

Gasthof Zauner, at the opposite end of the square from the Simony, is my second listing that accepts credit cards. It's a business machine offering modern pine-flavored rooms with all the comforts on the main square, and a restaurant specializing in grilled meat and fish (12 rooms, Db-1,230 AS, CC:VM, Marktplatz 51, tel. 06134/8246, fax 06134/82468, e-mail: zauner@hallstatt.at).

Gasthaus zur Mühle Jugendherberge, below the waterfall with the best cheap beds in town, is popular for its great pizzas and cheap grub (bed in 3- to 20-bed coed dorms-120 AS, D-270 AS, sheets-40 AS extra, family quads, breakfast-40 AS, big lockers, closed Nov, below tunnel car park, Kirchenweg 36, tel. & fax 06134/8318, e-mail: toeroe.f@magnet.at, run by Ferdinand Törö).

Pension Seethaler is a homey old lodge with 45 beds and a breakfast room mossy with antlers, perched above the lake. The place is very simple with coin-op showers downstairs (215 AS/person in S, D, T, or Q, 280 AS/person in rooms with private bath, multinight stays-20 AS less; from the Boote paddleboats between the lake parking lot and Marktplatz, find and climb the steps then turn right, Dr. Morton Weg 22, tel. 06134/8421, fax 06134/84214, Frau Seethaler).

Helga Lenz is a five-minute climb above the Seethaler (look for the green *Zimmer* sign). This big, sprawling, woodsy house has a nifty garden perch, wins the best-view award, and is ideal for those who sleep well in tree houses (D-400 AS, T-570 AS, 1-night stays-20 AS extra, family room, Hallberg 17, tel. 06134/8508, e-mail: haus-lenz@aon.at).

These two listings are 200 meters to the right of the ferry boat dock, with your back to the lake: **Frau Zimmermann** runs a three-room *Zimmer* (as her name implies) in a 500-year-old ramshackle house with low beams, time-polished wood, and fine lake views (S-210 AS, D-420 AS, can be musty, Gosaumühlstrasse 69, tel. 06134/86853). She speaks little English, but you'll find yourself caught up in her charm and laughing together like old friends. A block away, **Pension Sarstein** has 25 beds in basic, dusty rooms with flower-bedecked, lake-view balconies, in a charming building run by friendly Frau Fisher. You can swim from her lakeside garden (D-440 AS, Ds-640 AS with this book, 1-night stays-20 AS per person extra, Gosaumühlstrasse 83, tel. 06134/8217).

Gasthof Pension Gruner Anger is a practical and modern place away from the medieval town center. It's big, quiet, with a normal parking lot, well situated a block from the base of the salt mine lift, and a 10-minute walk from the town center (12 rooms, Sb-450 AS, Db-740 AS, 780 AS in July–Aug, 1-night stays-820 AS, third person-200 AS, CC:VM, Lahn 10, tel. 06134/8397, fax 06134/83974, e-mail: anger@aon.at, Sulzbacher family).

Eating in Hallstatt

You can enjoy good food inexpensively with delightful lakeside settings. While everyone cooks the typical Austrian fare, your best bet here is trout. Reinanke trout is from Lake Hallstatt. Grab a front table at **Gasthof Simony's** garden restaurant (see "Sleeping," above). **Hotel Gruner Baum's** romantic restaurant is fancier and also good. Or feed the swans while your trout cooks at **Restaurant Braugasthof** (they have a fun menu, tel. 06134/20012). While it lacks a lakeside setting, **Gasthof Zauner's** restaurant is well respected for its grilled meat and fish (see "Sleeping," above). For the best pizza in town with a fun-loving local crowd, chow down cheap and hearty at **Gasthaus zur Mühle** (see "Sleeping," above). And every local's favorite place for a good dinner is a 10-minute lakeside hike away near the town beach at the **Strand Café** (great garden setting on the lake, Seelande 102, tel. 06134/8234). For your late-night drink, savor the Market Square from the trendy little pub called the **Ruth Zimmermann**.

Transportation Connections—Hallstatt

By train to: Salzburg (hrly, 90 min to Attnang Puchheim, short wait, 50 min to Salzburg), **Vienna** (hrly, 90 min to Attnang Puchheim, short wait, 2.5 hrs to Vienna). Day-trippers to Hallstatt can check bags at the Attnang Puchheim station. (Note: Connections there and back can be very fast—about 5 minutes. Have three 10-AS coins ready for the lockers.)

BRUGES
(BRUGGE)

With Renoir canals, pointy gilded architecture, time-tunnel art, and stay-awhile cafés, Bruges is a heavyweight sightseeing destination as well as a joy. Where else can you ride a bike along a canal, munch mussels, wash them down with the world's best beer, savor heavenly chocolate, and see Flemish Primitives and a Michelangelo, all within 300 meters of a bell tower that rings out "Don't worry, be happy" jingles every 15 minutes? And there's no language barrier.

The town is Brugge (broo-gha) in Flemish, Bruges (broozh) in French and English. Before it was Flemish or French, the name was a Viking word for "wharf" or "embarkment." Right from the start, Bruges was a trading center. In the 11th century the city grew wealthy on the cloth trade. By the 14th century Bruges' population was 40,000, in a league with London and one of the largest cities in the world. At the time, Bruges was the most important cloth market in northern Europe. In the 15th century Bruges was the favored residence of the powerful Dukes of Burgundy. Commerce and the arts boomed. The artists Jan van Eyck and Hans Memling had studios here. But by the 16th century the harbor had silted up, and the economy collapsed. The Burgundian court left, Spain conquered Belgium in 1548, and Bruges' golden age abruptly ended. For generations Bruges was known as a mysterious and dead city. In the 19th century a new port, Zeebrugge, brought renewed vitality to the area. And 20th-century tourists discovered the town. Today, Bruges prospers because of tourism: It's a uniquely well-preserved Gothic city and a handy gateway to Europe. It's no secret, but even with the crowds Bruges is the kind of city where you don't mind being a tourist.

Planning Your Time

Bruges needs at least two nights and a full, well-organized day.
Even nonshoppers enjoy browsing here, and the Belgian love of
life makes a hectic itinerary seem a little senseless. With one day,
the speedy visitor could do this: 9:30–Climb the belfry, 10:00–
Tour the Burg sights (visit the TI if necessary), 11:30–Take a
boat tour, 12:15–Walk to the brewery, have lunch, and catch the
13:00 tour, 14:30–Walk through the Begijnhof, 15:00–Tour the
Memling Museum (6 paintings), 15:45–See the Michelangelo in
the church, 16:00–Tour the Groeninge Museum (closes at 17:00).
Rent a bike for an evening ride through the quiet backstreets (or
take a 1,000BF half-hour horse-and-buggy tour). Lose the tourists
and find a dinner. (If this schedule seems insane, skip the belfry
and the brewery—or stay another day.)

Orientation (area code: 050)

The tourists' Bruges (you'll be sharing it) is contained within a
one-kilometer-square canal, or moat. Nearly everything of interest
and importance is within a cobbled and convenient swath between
the train station and Market Square (a 15-min walk).

Tourist Information: The main office is on Burg Square
(Mon–Fri 9:30–18:30, Sat–Sun 10:00–12:00, 14:00–18:30, off-
season closes at 17:00, lockers and money-exchange desk, tel.
050/448-686, public WC in courtyard). The other TI is at the
train station (Mon–Sat 10:30–13:15, 14:00–18:30, closed Sun and
off-season at 17:30, www.brugge.be). Both TIs sell a great 25BF
all-inclusive Bruges visitors guide with a map and listings of all of
the sights and services. The free *Exit* includes a monthly calendar
of the many events the town puts on to keep its hordes of tourists
entertained. It's in Dutch but almost readable (i.e., van Gershwin
tot Clapton). Skip the TI's "combo" museum ticket. They also
have train-schedule information and specifics on the various
kinds of tours available. Bikers will want the *5X on the Bike around
Bruges* map/guide, which sells for 50BF and shows five routes
through the countryside.

Internet Access: The relaxing Coffee Link, with mellow
music and pleasant art, is located between the train station and
the center of town (60BF/15 min, Mon–Sat 10:00–21:30, Sun
13:30–18:30, across from Church of Our Lady at Mariastraat 38).

Arrival in Bruges

By Train: From the train (and from the TI near the station), you'll
see the square belfry tower marking the main square. Upon arrival,
stop by the station TI (has lockers) to pick up the Bruges visitors
guide (map in centerfold). There are no ATMs at the station, but
you can change money at ticket windows. Buses marked "CEN-
TRUM" speed to the Market Square (40BF ticket, buy from driver,

good for 1 hr). Buses #4 and #8 go farther, near the recommended Carmerstraat-area hotels. The taxi fare to most hotels is 250BF. It's a 15-minute walk from the station to the center: Cross the busy street and canal in front of the station, head up Oostmeers, and turn right on Steenstraat to reach Market Square. You could rent a bike at the station for the duration of your stay (350BF/day with a 500BF deposit, tel. 050/302-328), but other bike-rental shops are closer to the center (see "Bruges Experiences," below).

By Car: Park at the train station for just 100BF per day; show your parking receipt on the bus to get a free ride into town. The pricier underground parking garage at t'Zand costs 350BF per day.

Helpful Hints

The information number for all **museums** is 050/448-711. Off-season is October through March (when some museums close on Tuesday).

You can change traveler's checks at **Best Change** (daily 9:00–21:00, until 19:00 in winter, just off Market Square on Steenstraat). The **post office** is on Market Square near the belfry (Mon–Fri 9:00–19:30, Sat 9:30–12:30, tel. 050/331-411).

Shops are open from 9:00 to 18:00, a little later on Friday. Grocery stores are usually closed on Sunday. **Market day** is Wednesday morning (Market Square) and Saturday morning (t'Zand). On Saturday and Sunday afternoons, there's a flea market along Dijver in front of the Groeninge Museum.

Sights—Bruges

Bruges' sights are listed here in walking order, from Market Square to the Burg to the cluster of museums around the Church of Our Lady to the Begijnhof (10-min walk from beginning to end). Like Venice, the ultimate sight is the town itself, and the best way to enjoy that is to get lost on the backstreets away from the lace shops and ice-cream stands.

Market Square (Markt)—Ringed by banks, the post office, lots of restaurant terraces, great old gabled buildings, and the belfry, this is the modern heart of the city. Most city buses go from here to the station. Under the belfry are two great Belgian French fry stands, a quadrilingual Braille description, and a metal model of the tower. In its day, a canal went right up to the central square of this formerly great trading center. **Geldmuntstraat**, just off the square, is a delightful street with many fun and practical shops and eateries.

▲▲**Belfry (Belfort)**—Most of this bell tower has stood over Market Square since 1300. In 1486 the octagonal lantern was added, making it 88 meters high—that's 366 steps (daily 9:30–17:00, Oct–March closed 12:30–13:30, ticket window closes 45 min early, WC in courtyard). The view is worth the climb and

Bruges

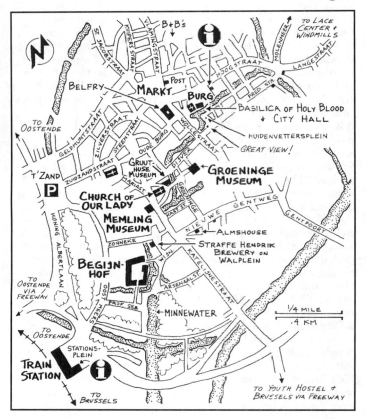

the 100BF. Survey the town. On the horizon you can see the towns along the coast. Just before you reach the top, peek into the carillon room. The 47 bells can be played mechanically with the giant barrel and movable tabs (as they do on each quarter hour), or with a manual keyboard (as it does for regular concerts) with fists and feet rather than fingers. Be there on the quarter hour, when things ring. It's *bellissimo* at the top of the hour. Carillon concert times are listed at the base of the belfry (usually Mon, Wed, and Sat at 21:00 and Sun at 14:15). Back on the square, with your back to the belfry, turn right onto pedestrian-only Breidelstraat and thread yourself through the lace and *wafels* to Burg Square.

▲▲**Burg Square**—The opulent square called Burg is Bruges' civic center, historically the birthplace of Bruges and the site of the ninth-century castle of the first Count of Flanders. Today it's

the scene of outdoor concerts and home of the TI (with a 10BF
WC). It's surrounded by six centuries of architecture. Sweeping
counterclockwise 360 degrees, you'll go from Romanesque (the
round arches and thick walls of the brick basilica in the corner,
best seen inside the lower chapel) to the pointed Gothic arches of
the City Hall (with its "Gothic Room") to the well-proportioned
Renaissance windows of the Old Recorder's House (next door,
under the gilded statues) and past the TI and the park to the
elaborate 17th-century Baroque of the Provost's House. Complete
your spin and walk to that corner.

▲**Basilica of the Holy Blood**—Originally the Chapel of Saint
Basil, it is famous for its relic of the blood of Christ, which,
according to tradition, was brought to Bruges in 1150 after the
Second Crusade (and is displayed only during Friday worship
services). The lower chapel (through the door labeled "Basiliek")
is dark and solid—a fine example of Romanesque style (with some
beautiful statues). The upper chapel (separate entrance, climb the
stairs) is decorated Gothic and usually accompanied by appropri-
ately contemplative music. A 10BF English flier tells about the
relic, art, and history. The small but sumptuous Basilica Museum
(well described in English) contains the gem-studded hexagonal
reliquary (c. 1600) that carries the relic on its yearly Ascension
Day trip through the streets of Bruges (museum is next to upper
chapel, 40BF, daily 9:30–12:00, 14:00–18:00; shorter hours and
closed Wed afternoon off-season).

▲**City Hall's Gothic Room**—Your ticket gives you a room full
of old town maps and paintings and a grand, beautifully restored
"Gothic Hall" from 1400. Its painted and carved wooden ceiling
features hanging arches (explained by an English flier). Notice the
New Testament themes carved into the circular "vault keys." The
wall murals are late-19th-century Romantic paintings of episodes
from the city's history (described in the flier). The free ground-
level lobby (closed on weekends) is a picture gallery of Belgium's
colonial history, from the Spanish Bourbon king to Napoleon
(150BF, includes audioguide and admission to Renaissance Hall,
daily 9:30–17:00, Burg 12).

Renaissance Hall (Brugse Vrije)—This is just one ornate room
with an impressive Renaissance chimney. If you're into heraldry,
the symbolism, explained in the free English flier, makes this
worth a five-minute stop. If you're not, you'll wonder where the
rest of the museum is (150BF, includes admission to City Hall,
daily 9:30–17:00, entry in the corner of the square).

From Burg to Fish Market to View—From Burg, walk under
the Goldfinger family down Blinde Ezelstraat. Just after you
cross the bridge, the persistent little fish market (*Vismarkt*, fresh
North Sea catch sold Tue–Fri 6:00–13:00) is on your left. Take
an immediate right to Huidevettersplein, a tiny, picturesque,

restaurant-filled square. Continue a few steps to Rozenhoedkaai Street, where you can get a great photo of the belfry reflected in the canal. Can you see its tilt? It leans about four feet. Down the canal (past a flea market on weekends) looms the huge spire of the Church of Our Lady (tallest brick spire in the Low Countries). Between you and the church are the next three museums.

▲▲▲**Groeninge Museum**—This diverse and classy collection shows off mostly Flemish art from Memling to Magritte. Rooms 1 through 18 take you from 1400 to 1945. While it has plenty of worthwhile modern art, the highlights are its vivid and pristine Flemish Primitives. (*Primitive* here means before the Renaissance.) Flemish art is shaped by its love of detail, its merchant patrons' egos, and the power of the Church. Lose yourself in the halls of Groeninge: Gaze across 15th-century canals, into the eyes of reassuring Marys, and through town squares littered with leotards, lace, and lopped-off heads (250BF, daily 9:30–17:00, Oct–March closed Tue, Dijver 12). The **Brangwyn Museum** (Arentshuis), next door, is only interesting if you are into lace or the early-20th-century art of Brangwyn (80BF, daily 9:30–17:00, off-season closed Tue, Dijver 16).

▲**Gruuthuse Museum**—A wealthy brewer's home, this is a sprawling smattering of everything from medieval bedpans to a guillotine. There's no information inside, so to understand the crossbows, dark old paintings, and what a beer merchant's doing with box seats peeking down on the altar of the Church of Our Lady next door, you'll have to buy or browse through the 600BF guidebook (130BF, daily 9:30–17:00, Dijver 17). Leaving the museum, contemplate the mountain of bricks towering 120 meters above as they have for 600 years.

▲▲**Church of Our Lady**—The church stands as a memorial to the power and wealth of Bruges in its heyday. A delicate *Madonna and Child*, by Michelangelo, is near the apse (to the right if you're facing the altar). It's said to be the only Michelangelo statue to leave Italy in his lifetime (thanks to the wealth generated by Bruges' cloth trade). If you like tombs and church art, pay to wander through the apse (70BF, Michelangelo free, art-filled apse Mon–Fri 10:00–12:00, 14:00–17:00, closes at 16:00 on Sat, Sun 14:00–16:00, closes off-season at 16:30, on Mariastraat).

▲▲**St. Jans Hospital/Memling Museum**—Across the street from the Church of Our Lady is a medieval hospital with six much-loved paintings by the greatest of the Flemish Primitives, Hans Memling. His *Mystical Wedding of St. Catherine* triptych deserves a close look. Catherine and her "mystical groom," the baby Jesus, are flanked by a headless John the Baptist and a pensive John the Evangelist. The chairs are there so you can study it. If you understand the Book of Revelations, you'll understand St. John's wild and intricate vision. The Reliquary of St. Ursula, an ornate little mini-church in the same room, is filled with

impressive detail (100BF, daily 9:30–17:00, off-season closed
Wed, Mariastraat 38).

▲▲**Straffe Hendrik Brewery Tour**—Belgians are Europe's beer
connoisseurs. This fun and handy tour is a great way to pay your
respects. The happy gang at this working family brewery gives
entertaining and informative 45-minute, four-language tours (usually
by friendly Inge, 150BF including a beer, piles of very steep steps, a
great rooftop panorama, daily on the hour 11:00–16:00, 11:00 and
15:00 are your best times to avoid groups, Oct–March 11:00 and
15:00 only, 1 block past church and canal, take a right down skinny
Stoofstraat to #26 on Walplein square, tel. 050/332-697). At Straffe
Hendrik ("Strong Henry") they remind their drinkers: "The components of the beer are vitally necessary and contribute to a well-bal-
anced life-pattern. Nerves, muscles, visual sentience, and a healthy
skin are stimulated by these in a positive manner. For longevity and
lifelong equilibrium, drink Straffe Hendrik in moderation!"

Their bistro, where you'll be given your included-with-the-
tour beer, serves a quick and hearty lunch plate (the 170BF "bread
with pâté and vegetables" is the best value, although the 250BF
"meat selection and vegetables" is a beer-drinker's picnic for 2).
On sunny summer days they offer a barbecue and salad bar for
350BF. You can eat indoors with the smell of hops or outdoors
with the smell of hops. This is a great place to wait for your tour
or to linger afterward. From here the lacy cuteness of Bruges
crescendos as you approach the Begijnhof.

▲▲**Begijnhof**—For military (and various other) reasons, there
were more women than men in the medieval Low Countries.
Towns provided Begijnhofs (buh-HINE-hofs), dignified places
in which these "Begijns" could live a life of piety and service
(without having to take the same vows a nun would). You'll find
Begijnhofs all over Belgium and Holland. Bruges' Begijnhof—
now inhabited not by Begijns but by Benedictine nuns—almost
makes you want to don a habit and fold your hands as you walk
under its wispy trees and whisper past its frugal little homes.
For a good slice of Begijnhof life, walk through the simple
museum (Begijn's House, left of entry gate, 60BF with English
flier, daily 10:00–12:00, 13:45–17:00, shorter hours off-season).

Minnewater—Just south of the Begijnhof is Minnewater, an
idyllic, clip-clop world of flower boxes, canals, swans, and tour
boats packed like happy egg cartons.

Almshouses—Walking from the Begijnhof back to the center,
you might detour along Nieuwe Gentweg to visit one of about
20 almshouses in the city. At #8, go through the door dated 1613
(free) into the peaceful courtyard. This was a medieval form of housing for the poor. The rich would pay for someone's tiny room here
in return for lots of prayers. The Diamond Museum (at the start of
Nieuwe Gentweg) is less interesting than an encyclopedia (200BF).

Bruges Experiences

Chocolate—Bruggians are connoisseurs of fine chocolate. You'll be tempted by chocolate-filled display windows all over town. Godiva is the best big-factory/high-price/high-quality local brand, but for the finest small-family operation, drop by **Maitre Chocolatier Verbeke**. While Mr. Verbeke is busy downstairs making chocolates, Mrs. Verbeke makes sure customers in the shop get the chocolate of their dreams. Ask her to assemble a bag of your favorites (the smallest amount sold is 100 grams—about seven pieces—for 90BF). Most are pralines, which means they're filled. While the "hedgehogs" are popular, be sure to get a "pharaoh's head." Pray for cool weather, since it's closed when it's very hot. (Open at least in the mornings on Tue, Wed, Fri, and Sat; open cooler afternoons as well, a block off Market Square at Geldmuntstraat 25, can ship overseas except during hot summer months, tel. 050/334-198.)

Lace and Windmills by the Moat—A 10-minute walk from the center to the northeast end of town brings you to four windmills strung out along a pleasant grassy setting on the "big moat" canal (between Kruispoort and Dampoort, on Bruges side of the moat). One of the windmills (St. Janshuismolen) is open to visitors (40BF, daily 9:30–12:30, 13:30–17:00, closed Oct–April, at the end of Carmersstraat).

To actually see lace being made, drop by the nearby Lace Centre, where ladies toss bobbins madly while their eyes go bad (60BF includes afternoon demonstrations and a small lace museum called Kantcentrum, as well as the adjacent Jerusalem church; Mon–Fri 10:00–12:00, 14:00–18:00, until 17:00 on Sat, closed Sun, Peperstraat 3). The Folklore Museum, in the same neighborhood, is cute but forgettable (80BF, daily 9:30–17:00, Oct–March closed Tue, Rolweg 40). To find either place, ask for the Jerusalem church.

▲▲**Biking**—While the sights are close enough for easy walking, the town is a treat to bike through, and you can to get away from the tourist center. Consider a peaceful evening ride through the backstreets and around the outer canal. Rental shops have maps and ideas. The TI sells a handy *5X on the Bike around Bruges* map/guide for 50BF; it narrates five different bike routes (18–30 kilometers) through the idyllic countryside nearby. The best trip is 30 minutes along the canal out to Damme and back. The Netherlands/Belgium border is a 40-minute pedal beyond Damme. Two shops rent bikes in the center of town (100–110BF for 1 hr, 200–225BF for 4 hrs, or 325BF/day). Both offer free city maps and child seats. **Popelier Eric's** doesn't require a deposit and sells a good map of the country-side for 75BF (daily 9:00–21:00 in summer, 10:00–19:00 in winter, 50 meters from Church of Our Lady at Mariastraat 26, tel. 050/343-262). **'T Koffieboontje** asks for a 1,000BF deposit, your passport, or a credit-card imprint (also rents mountain and tandem bikes, Hallestraat 4, closer to belfry, tel. 050/338-027). The less central **De Ketting** rents bikes for less (150BF/day, daily 9:00–19:00, Gentpoortstraat 23, tel. 050/344-196).

Tours of Bruges

Bruges by Boat—The most relaxing and scenic (if not informative) way to see this city of canals is by boat, with the captain narrating. Boats leave from all over town (190BF, 4/hrly, 10:00–18:00, copycat 30-min rides). Boten Stael (just over the canal from the Memling Museum) offers a 30BF discount with this book.

City Minibus Tours—"City Tour Bruges" gives 50-minute/380BF rolling overviews of the town in an 18-seat, two-skylight minibus with dial-a-language headsets and video support. The tour leaves hourly (on the hr, 10:00–19:00 in summer, until 18:00 in spring and fall, less in winter) from Market Square. The narration, while clean, is slow-moving and boring. But the tour is a lazy way to cruise by virtually every sight in Bruges.

Walking Tours—Local guides walk small groups through the core of town daily in July and August (150BF, depart from TI at 15:00). The tours, while earnest, are heavy on history and in two languages, so they may be less than peppy. Still, to propel you beyond the pretty gables and canal swans of Bruges, they are good medicine. A private guided tour costs 1,500BF (reserve at least 3 days in advance through the TI).

Bus Tours of Countryside—Quasimodo Tours offers those with extra time two excellent all-day tours through the rarely visited Flemish countryside. The "Flanders Fields" tour concentrates on WWI battlefields, trenches, memorials, and poppy-splattered fields (Sun, Tue, and Thu 9:00–16:30). The other is "Triple Treat": the port of Damme, a castle, a monastery, a brewery, and a chocolate factory as well as a sampling of the treats—a waffle, chocolate, and beer (Mon, Wed, and Fri 9:00–16:00). Hardworking Lote leads all the tours himself, in English only (1,500BF, 1,200BF if under 26, CC:VM, 29-seat nonsmoking bus, includes lunch, lots of walking, pickup at your hotel or the train station, tel. 050/370-470 to book, fax 050/374-960, www.quasimodo.be).

Bruges by Bike—The Backroad Bike Company leads daily bike tours through the nearby countryside at 10:00, 13:00, and 19:00 (550–650BF, 30 km, 3 hrs, tel. 050/370-470). Shorter, longer, and evening tours are available.

Bus and Boat Tour—The Sightseeing Line offers a bus trip to Damme and a boat ride back (660BF, April–Sept daily at 14:00 and 16:00, 2 hrs, leaves from Market Square).

Sights—Near Bruges

Dolfinarium—At Boudewijnpark, just outside of town, dolphins make a splash several times a day (call for show times—tel. 050/383-838, 280BF for 40-min show, Debaeckestraat 12, www.boudewijnpark.be). The theme park's roller-skating rink is open in the afternoon (and turns into an ice-skating rink off-season). From Bruges, catch the "Sint Michiels" bus #7 or #17 from Kuipersstraat.

Flanders Fields—This WWI museum, 60 kilometers southwest of Bruges, provides a moving look at the battles fought near Ieper (Ypres in French). Use interactive computers to trace the wartime lives of individual soldiers and citizens. Powerful videos and ear-shattering audio complete the story (250 BF, April–Sept daily 10:00–18:00, Oct–March Tue–Sun 10:00–17:00, Grote Markt 34, Ieper, tel. 057/228-584, fax 057/218-589, www.inflandersfields.be). From Bruges, catch a train to Ieper via Kortrijk (2 hrs). Drivers follow A17 to Kortrijk, then take A19 to Ieper.

Sleeping in Bruges
(45BF = about $1, country code: 32, area code: 050, zip code: 8000)

Sleep Code: **S** = Single, **D** = Double/Twin, **T** = Triple, **Q** = Quad, **b** = bathroom, **t** = toilet only, **s** = shower only, **CC** = Credit Card (**V**isa, **M**asterCard, **A**mex). Everyone speaks English.

Most places are located between the train station and the old center, with the most distant (and best) being a few blocks beyond Market Square to the north and east. B&Bs offer the best value. All include breakfast, are on quiet streets, and (with a few exceptions) keep the same prices throughout the year. Bruges is most crowded Friday and Saturday evenings Easter through October—with July and August weekends being worst. Otherwise, finding a room is easy.

You'll find a **Laundromat** at Gentportstraat 28 (daily 7:00–22:00, English instructions, machines use 20BF coins; you'll need about 14 total) or at Mr. Wash (near Hotel Hansa on St. Jakobsstraat).

Hotels

Hansa Hotel offers 24 rooms in a completely modernized old building. It's tastefully decorated in elegant pastels and has all the amenities. It's a great splurge (Db-4,520–5,970BF depending on room size, extra bed-1,250BF, suites available, CC:VMA, air-con, nonsmoking, elevator, Niklaas Desparsstraat 11, a block north of Market Square, tel. 050/338-444, fax 050/334-205, www.hansa.be, e-mail: information@hansa.be, cheery and hard-working Johan and Isabelle).

Hotel Aarendshuis, an old merchant's mansion, is well worn but comfortable. It's family run and has 25 spacious rooms, dingy carpets, chandeliered public places, and a small garden (prices vary with size and luxury: Sb-2,700BF, Db-3,000–4,000BF, Tb-4,000BF, Qb-4,500BF, kids under 10 free, car park-400BF, CC:VMA, elevator, 2 blocks off Burg Square at Hoogstraat 18, tel. 050/337-889, fax 050/330-816, e-mail: hotelaarendshuis @village.uunet.be).

Hotel Cordoeanier, another family-run place, rents 22 bright, simple, modern rooms on a quiet street two blocks off Market Square (Sb-1,950BF, Db-2,300BF, Tb-2,900–3,200BF, Qb-3,400BF, 5b-3,900BF, CC:VM, nearly free Internet access, Cordoeanierstraat 16, tel. 050/339-051, fax 050/346-111, www .cordoeanier.be, Kris and Veerie). **Hotel Nicolas** is equally central and even cheaper but smoky and not the same value (Sb-1,800BF, Db-2,100BF, CC:VMA, elevator, next to Hotel Hansa at N. Desparsstraat 9, tel. 050/335-502, fax 050/343-544).

Hotel Cavalier, which has more stairs than character, serves a hearty buffet breakfast in a royal setting (Sb-2,900BF, Db-2,400BF, Tb-3,000BF, Qb-3,300BF, 2 lofty "backpackers' doubles" on the 4th floor-1,600BF or 1,800BF with WC, CC:VMA, Kuipersstraat 25, tel. 050/330-207, fax 050/347-199, e-mail: hotel.cavalier@skynet.be, run by friendly Viviane De Clerck).

Hotel Botaniek has three stars, nine small rooms, and a quiet location a block from Astrid Park. This friendly hotel is basic, small, and comfy (Sb-2,600BF, Db-3,000BF, Tb-3,600BF, Qb-4,000BF, CC:VMA, Waalsestraat 23, tel. 050/341-424, fax 050/345-939, e-mail: hotel.botaniek@ping.be).

Hotel Rembrandt-Rubens has 15 rooms in a creaky 500-year-old building with tipsy floors, a mysterious floor plan, tacky rooms, ancient dippy beds, elephant tusks, a gallery of creepy old paintings, and probably the Holy Grail in a drawer somewhere (S-1,100BF, Ss-1,500BF, one D-1,600BF, Ds-2,100BF, Db-2,400BF, Tb-3,000BF, Qb-3,900BF, locked up at 24:00, on a quiet square between the Memlings and the brewery at Walplein 38, tel. 050/ 336-439, fax 050/677-780). The breakfast room (which must have been the knights' hall) overlooks a canal (while Rembrandt and Rubens overlook you from an ornately carved and tiled 1648 chimney). There's a little warmth behind Mrs. De Buyser's crankiness. The hotel has been in her family for 50 years.

Hotel Adornes, a great value, has 20 comfy new rooms with full, modern bathrooms in a 17th-century canalside house. They offer free parking, free loaner bikes, and a cellar game and video lounge (Db-3,000–3,800BF depending upon size, CC:VMA, elevator, near Van Nevel B&B, below, and Carmersstraat at St. Annarei 26, tel. 050/341-336, fax 050/342-085, e-mail: hotel .adornes@proximedia.be, Nathalie runs the family business).

Hotel De Pauw is tall, skinny, and family run, with straight-forward rooms on a quiet street across from a church (2 top-floor

Hotels in Bruges

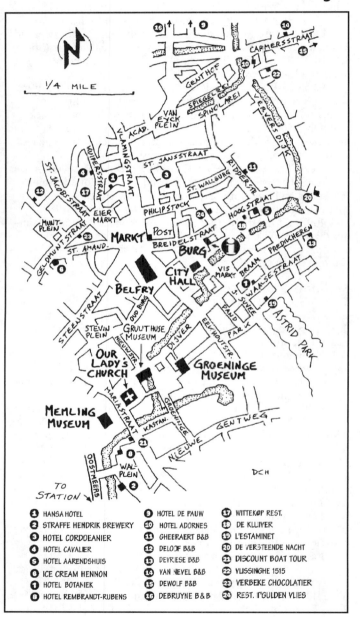

① HANSA HOTEL	⑨ HOTEL DE PAUW	⑰ WITTEKOP REST.
② STRAFFE HENDRIK BREWERY	⑩ HOTEL ADORNES	⑱ DE KLUIVER
③ HOTEL CORDOEANIER	⑪ GHEERAERT B&B	⑲ L'ESTAMINET
④ HOTEL CAVALIER	⑫ DELOOF B&B	⑳ DE VERSTEENDE NACHT
⑤ HOTEL AARENDSHUIS	⑬ DEVRESE B&B	㉑ DISCOUNT BOAT TOUR
⑥ ICE CREAM HENNON	⑭ VAN NEVEL B&B	㉒ VLISSINGHE 1515
⑦ HOTEL BOTANIEK	⑮ DEWOLF B&B	㉓ VERBEKE CHOCOLATIER
⑧ HOTEL REMBRANDT-RUBENS	⑯ DEBRUYNE B&B	㉔ REST. I'GULDEN VLIES

D-1,950BF, Db-2,200–2,550BF, CC:VM, free and easy parking, cable TV and phones, Sint Gilliskerkhof 8, tel. 050/337-118, fax 050/345-140, www.hoteldepauw.be, Philippe and Hilde).

Hotel Egmond is quietly located in the middle of the placid Minnewater. Its 18th-century rooms have all the comforts (Sb-3,600BF, Db-4,200BF, Tb-5,200BF, CC:VM, Minnewater 15, tel. 050/341-445, fax 050/342-940, www.egmond.be).

Crowne Plaza Hotel Brugge is the most modern, comfortable, and central hotel option. Each of its 96 air-conditioned rooms comes with a magnifying mirror and trouser press (rack rate: Db-8,300BF, prices drop as low as 5,500BF on weekdays and off-season, CC:VMA, elevator, pool, Burg 10, tel. 050/446-844, fax 050/446-868, www.crowneplaza.com).

Near Train Station: The **Hotel t'Keizershof** is a dollhouse of a hotel that lives by its motto, "Spend a night, not a fortune." It's simple and tidy, with seven small, cheery, old-time rooms split between two floors, a shower and toilet on each (S-950BF, D-1,400BF, T-2,100BF, Q-2,500BF, free and easy parking, laundry service-300BF, Oostmeers 126, a block in front of train station, tel. 050/338-728, e-mail: hotel.keizershof@12move.be, run by Stefaan and Hilde).

Bed-and-Breakfasts

These places, run by people who enjoy their work, offer the best value. Each is central and offers lots of stairs and three or four doubles you'd pay 4,000BF for in a hotel. Parking is generally easy on the street.

Koen and Annemie Dieltiens are a friendly couple who enjoy getting to know their guests and sharing a wealth of information on Bruges. You'll eat a hearty breakfast around a big table in their bright, homey, comfortable house. In April they'll move several blocks away, but will keep the same contact information (S-1,300BF, Sb-1,700BF, D-1,600BF, Db-1,900BF, T-2,100BF, Tb-2,400BF, Qb-2,900BF, 1-night stays pay 200BF extra per room, nonsmoking, Sint-Walburgastraat 14, 3 blocks east of Market Square, moving on April 2 to Waalse Straat 40, 3 blocks southeast of Burg Square, tel. 050/334-294, fax 050/335-230, http://users.skynet.be/dieltiens, e-mail: koen.dieltiens@skynet.be). The Dieltiens also rent a cozy studio and apartment for two to six people in a nearby 17th-century house (2 pay 13,300BF per week for studio, 14,700BF for apartment, prices higher for shorter stays and more people, cheaper off-season).

Paul and Roos Gheeraert live on the first floor while their guests take the second. This neoclassical mansion with big, bright, comfy rooms is another fine value (Sb-1,700BF, Db-1,900BF, Tb-2,400BF; rooms have coffeemakers and fridges; Ridderstraat 9, 4 blocks east of Market, tel. 050/335-627, fax 050/345-201, e-mail: paul.gheeraert@skynet.be). They also rent three modern, fully-equipped apartments and a large loft nearby (minimum 3 nights, view at http://users.skynet.be/brugge-gheeraert).

Chris Deloof's big, homey rooms are a good bet in the old center. Check out the fun, lofty A-frame room upstairs (Sb-1,800BF, Db-1,900–2,100BF, pleasant breakfast room, nonsmoking, Geerwiynstraat 14, tel. & fax 050/340-544, www.sin.be/chrisdeloof, e-mail: chris.deloof@ping.be). Chris also rents a nearby apartment, great for a family or group (Qb-3,500BF).

The **Van Nevel family** rents two attractive top-floor rooms with built-in beds in a 16th-century house (S-1,300–1,600BF, D-1,600–1,900BF, T-2,500BF, includes breakfast, CC:VM but cash preferred, nonsmoking, Carmersstraat 13, 10-min walk from Market Square, tel. 050/346-860, fax 050/347-616, http://home .worldonline.be/~rvanneve, e-mail: Robert.VanNevel@advalvas .be). Robert enthusiastically shares the culture and history of Bruges with his guests.

Yvonne De Vriese rents three tidy B&B rooms on a corner overlooking two canals (1 S-1,000BF, D-1,500BF, Db-1,800BF, third or fourth person-500BF extra, breakfast served in your room, CC:VMA, Predikherenstraat 40, 4 blocks east of Burg Square, take bus #6 or #16 from station and get off at the first stop on Predikheren Rei, tel. 050/334-224, fax 050/336-491).

Arnold Dewolf's B&B is in a stately, quiet neighborhood (D-1,400BF, T-1,800BF, Q-2,200BF, family-friendly, near windmills, Oostproosse 9, tel. 050/338-366). From the train station, take bus #4 to Sasplein. Walk to the path behind the first windmill and turn left on Oostproosse.

Debruyne B&B, run by Marie-Rose and architect Ronny Debruyne, offers artsy, original decor and genuine friendliness (Db-1,900BF, Tb-2,400BF, Qb-2,900BF, 1-night stay-200BF extra per room, 5-min walk north of Market Square, Lange Raamstraat 18, tel. 050/347-606, fax 050/340-285, www .bedandbreakfastbruges.com).

Hostels

Bruges has several good hostels offering beds for around 400 to 450BF in two- to eight-bed rooms (singles go for around 600BF). Pick up the hostel info sheet at the station TI. The new American-style **Charlie Rockets** bar and hostel is the liveliest and most central (56 beds, 500BF per bed, 2–6 per room, Hoogstraat 19, tel. 050/330-660). These hostels are small, loose, and central: the dull **Snuffel Travelers Inn** (Ezelstraat 47, tel. 050/333-133), **Bauhaus International Party Hotel** (Langestraat 135, tel. 050/ 341-093), and the funky **Passage** (Dweerstraat 26, tel. 050/340-232; its hotel next door rents 1,400BF doubles).

Eating in Bruges

Specialties include mussels cooked a variety of ways (one order can feed 2 people), fish dishes, grilled meats, and French fries. Touristy places on the square come with great views and are affordable; candle-cool bistros flicker on backstreets. Don't eat before 19:30 unless you like eating alone. Tax and service are always included.

Wittekop is very Flemish—a cluttered, laid-back, old-time place specializing in the beer-soaked equivalent of beef bourguig-nonne (395–675BF main courses, Tue–Sat 18:00–24:00, closed Sun-Mon, terrace in the back, Sint Jakobsstraat 14, tel. 050/332-059).

De Kluiver is a pub serving hot snacks, light 400BF meals, and great "seasnails in spiced bouillon" simmered in a whispering jazz ambience (Wed–Mon 18:00–01:00, closed Tue, Hoogstraat 12, tel. 050/338-927).

Pannekoekenhuisje, the little pancake house, is a cute restau-rant serving delicious, inexpensive pancake meals (daily 12:00–21:00, just off Geldmuntstraat at Helmstraat 3, tel. 050/340-086). In 2001, enthusiastic chefs Mario and Rik open **The Flemish Pot** next door, offering vintage Flemish cuisine and homemade *wafels*.

Lotus Vegetarisch Restaurant serves good veggie lunches only (300BF plates, Mon–Sat 11:45–13:45, closed Sun, just off Burg at Wapenmakersstraat 5, tel. 050/331-078).

Two youthful, trendy, jazz-filled eateries: For hearty budget spaghetti (230BF), head for **L'Estaminet**, on the northern border of peaceful Astrid Park (11:30–3:00, closed Mon afternoon and all day Thu, Park 5). Or try **De Versteende Nacht Jazzcafe** on Lange-straat 11 (500BF meals, Tue–Sat 19:00–02:00, closed Sun–Mon).

Vlissinghe 1515, the oldest pub in town, serves hot snacks in a great atmosphere (open from 11:30 on, closed Tue, Blekers-straat 2). **Restaurant 't Gulden Vlies**, just off Burg, is good for a late dinner (650BF plates, closed Mon–Tue, Mallebergplaats 17, tel. 050/334-709).

Restaurant de Eetkamer (the living room) offers stay-a-while elegance, fine service, and fine food (daily 12:00–14:30, 18:30–23:00, just south of Markt, Eeekhout 6, tel. 050/337-886). Drop by **Bistro De Schaar** for good food and fun atmosphere (Fri–Wed 12:00–14:30, 18:00–23:00, Hooistraat 2, tel. 050/335-979).

Picnics: Geldmuntstraat is a handy street when you're hungry. A block off Market Square, **Pickles Frituur** serves the best sit-down fries in town (Mon–Sat 11:00–24:00, closed Sun). A block farther, past the Verbeke chocolate shop, **Nopri Supermarket** is great for picnics (push-button produce pricer lets you buy as little as one mushroom, Mon–Sat 9:00–18:30, closed Sun). The small **Delhaize grocery** is on Market Square opposite the belfry (Mon–Sat 8:00–12:00, 13:30–18:00, closed Sun). **Selfi** has cheap sandwiches to go (Breidelstraat 16, between Burg and Market Square). For midnight munchies, you'll find Indian-run corner grocery stores.

Frietjes: These local French fries are a treat. Proud and traditional *frituurs* serve tubs of fries and various local-style shish kebabs. Belgians dip their *frietjes* in mayonnaise, but ketchup is there for the Yankees (along with spicier sauces). For a quick, cheap, and scenic meal, hit a *frituur* and sit on the steps or benches overlooking Market Square, about 50 meters past the post office.

Beer: Belgium boasts more than 350 types of beer. Straffe Hendrik ("Strong Henry"), a potent and refreshing local brew, is, even to a Bud Lite kind of guy, obviously great beer. Among the more unusual of the others to try: Dentergems (with coriander and orange peel) and Trappist (a dark, malty, monk-made beer). Non–beer drinkers enjoy Kriek (a cherry-flavored beer) and Frambozen Bier (raspberry-flavored beer). Each beer is served in its own unique glass. Any pub carries the basic beers, but for a selection of more than 300 types, drink at t'**Brugs Beertje** (16:00–01:00, closed Wed, Kemelstraat 5). When you've finished those, step next door, where **Dreupel Huisje "1919"** serves more than 100 Belgian gins and liqueurs (closed Tue). Another good place is **de Garre**. Rather than a noisy pub scene, it has a sit-down-and-focus-on-your-friend-and-the-fine-beer ambience (huge selection, off Breidelstraat, between Burg and Markt, on the tiny Garre alley, daily 12:00–24:00, tel. 050/341-029).

Belgian Waffles: While Americans think of "Belgian" waffles for breakfast, the Belgians (who don't eat waffles or pancakes for breakfast) think of *wafels* as Liege-style (dense, sweet, eaten plain and heated up, served take-away) and Brussels-style (lighter, often with powdered sugar or whipped cream and fruit, served in teahouses). For the best Liege-style *wafels* in town, drop by **Ice Cream Hennon** for a Luikse Wafel (50BF, daily 10:00–24:00, across from Nopri Supermarket, corner of Guldmuntstraat and Sind Amandstraat). Hennon's *wafels* and ice cream (18 flavors) are fresh and tasty.

Transportation Connections—Bruges

From nearby Brussels, all of Europe is at your fingertips. Train info: tel. 050/382-382.

By train to: Brussels (2/hrly, at :33 and :59, 1 hr), **Ghent** (4/hrly, 40 min), **Ostende** (3/hrly, 15 min), **Köln** (6/day, 4 hrs), **Paris** (hrly via Brussels, 2.5 hrs, 420BF supplement for Eurail), **Amsterdam** (hrly, 3.5 hrs).

Trains from England: Bruges is an ideal "welcome to Europe" stop after London. Take the Eurostar train from London to Brussels under the English Channel (10/day, 3 hrs), then transfer to Bruges (hrly, 1 hour). Or, to cross the Channel by boat, catch the London-to-Dover train (2 hrs, from London's Victoria station), then the catamaran to Ostende (2 hrs; train station at Ostende catamaran terminal), then the train to Bruges (15 min). Five boats run daily (1,650BF one-way, same price for 5-day return ticket, call to reserve a seat and pay at the dock, CC:VMA, tel. 059/559-955).

PRAGUE

It's amazing what 10 years of freedom can do. Prague has always been historic. Now it's fun, too. No place in Europe has become so popular so quickly. And for good reason: The capital of the Czech Republic—the only major city of central Europe to escape the bombs of the last century's wars—is Europe's best-preserved Baroque city. It's slinky with sumptuous Art Nouveau facades, it offers tons of cheap Mozart and Vivaldi, and it brews the best beer in Europe. But more than the architecture and traditional culture, it's an explosion of pent-up entrepreneurial energy jumping for joy after 50 years of Communist rule. And its low prices will make your visit enjoyable and nearly stressless.

Planning Your Time

Two days (with 3 nights, or 2 nights and a night train) makes the long train ride in and out worthwhile and gives you time to get beyond the sightseeing and enjoy Prague's ambience. You'll wish you had more time. From Munich, Berlin, and Vienna, it's a six-hour train ride (during the day) or an overnight ride.

With two days in Prague, I'd spend a morning seeing the castle and a morning in the Jewish Quarter—the only two chunks of sightseeing that demand any brainpower. Spend your afternoons loitering around the Old Town, Charles Bridge, and the Little Quarter and your nights split between beer halls and live music. Keep in mind that state museums close on Monday, and Jewish sites close on Saturday.

History

Medieval Prague: Prague's castle put it on the map in the ninth century. In the 10th century the region was incorporated into the

Prague

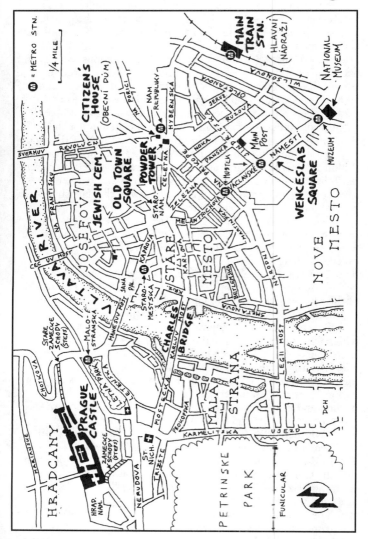

German "Holy Roman" Empire. The 14th century was Prague's Golden Age, when Holy Roman Emperor Charles IV ruled from here, and Prague was one of Europe's largest and most highly cultured cities. During this period Prague built St. Vitus Cathedral and Charles Bridge and established the first university in central Europe.

Bucking the Pope and Germany: Jan Hus was a local preacher who got in trouble with the Vatican a hundred years before Martin Luther. Like Luther, he preached in the people's language rather than Latin. To add insult to injury, he complained about church corruption. Tried for heresy and burned in 1415, Hus roused nationalist (Bohemian) as well as religious feelings and became a symbol of Czech martyrdom. His followers are Hussites.

Religious Wars: The reformist times of Jan Hus (around 1400, when Czechs rebelled against both German and Roman Catholic control) led to a period of religious wars and ultimately subjugation under Austrian rule. Prague stagnated under the Hapsburgs of Austria with the brief exception of Rudolf II's reign.

Under the late 16th-century rule of the Hapsburg King Rudolf II, Prague emerged again as a cultural and intellectual center. Johannes Kepler, Tycho Brahe, and others worked here. Much of Prague's great art can be attributed to this Hapsburg king who lived not in Vienna but in Prague.

The Thirty Years' War (1618–1648) began in Prague when locals tossed two Catholic/Hapsburg officials (Czechs sympathetic to the Germans) out the window of the Prague Castle. Often called "the first world war" because it engulfed so many nations, these 30 years were particularly tough on Prague. During this period its population dropped from 60,000 to 25,000. The result of this war was 300 years of Hapsburg rule: German and Catholic culture, not Czech. Prague became a backwater of Vienna.

Czech Nationalist Revival: The 19th century was a time of nationalism for people throughout Europe, including the Czechs, as the age of divine kings and ruling families was coming to a fitful end. The arts (such as the paintings by Mucha and the building of the massive National Museum atop Wenceslas Square) stirred the national spirit. With the end of World War I, the Hapsburgs were history, and in 1918 the independent country of Czechoslovakia was proclaimed with Prague as its capital.

Troubled 20th Century: Independence lasted only until 1939 when the Nazis swept in. Prague escaped the bombs of World War II but went almost directly from the Nazi frying pan into the Communist fire. Almost. A local uprising freed the city from the Nazis on May 8, 1945. The Russians "liberated" them again on May 9.

The Communist chapter of Czech subjugation (1948–1989) was grim. The student- and artist-led "Prague Spring" revolt in 1968 was crushed. The charismatic leader Alexander Dubcek was exiled into a job in the backwoods, and the years after 1968 were particularly tough. But eventually the Soviet empire crumbled. Czechoslovakia regained its freedom in the 1989 "Velvet Revolution" (so called because there were no casualties). Until 1989, May 9 was the Czech day of liberation. Now Czechs celebrate their liberation on May 8. In 1993, the Czech and Slovak Republics agreed on the "Velvet Divorce" and became two separate countries.

Today, while not without its problems, the Czech Republic is enjoying a growing economy and a strong democracy. Prague has emerged as one of the most popular tourist destinations in Europe. It's a huge entrepreneurial spanking machine... and it's your turn.

Orientation (area code: 02)

Locals call their town "Praha." It's big, with 1.2 million people, but for a quick visit, focus on its small old-town core. I will refer to the tourist landmarks in English (with the Czech name in parentheses). Study the map and learn these key places:

Main Train Station:	*Hlavní Nádraží* (hlav-nee nah-dra-shzee)
Old Town:	*Staré Město* (sta-rey mnyess-toh)
Old Town Square:	*Staroměstské Náměstí* (starro-min-yes-ststi-keh nah-mnyess-tee)
New Town:	*Nové Město* (no-vay mnyess-toh)
Little Quarter:	*Malá Strana* (mah-lah strah-nah)
Jewish Quarter:	*Josefov* (yoo-zef-fohf)
Castle Area:	*Hradčany* (hrad-chah-nee)
Charles Bridge:	*Karluv Most* (kar-loov most)
Wenceslas Square:	*Václavske Náměstí* (vah-slawf-skeh nah-mnyess-tee)
The River:	*Vltava* (vul-tah-vah)

The Vltava River divides the west side (castle and Little Quarter) from the east side (train station, Old Town, New Town, and nearly all of the recommended hotels). Prague addresses come with a general zone. Praha 1 is in the old center on either side of the river. Praha 2 is in the new city south of Wenceslas Square. Praha 3 and higher indicates a location farther from the center.

Tourist Information

TIs are at four key locations: main train station, Old Town Square, below Wenceslas Square at Na Příkope 20, and the castle side of Charles Bridge (generally 9:00–18:00 or 19:00, tel. 02/2448-2202). They offer maps, information on guided walks and bus tours, and bookings for concerts, hotel rooms, and rooms in private homes. Get the brochure listing all of Prague's museums and hours.

Helpful Hints

Formalities: Travel in Prague is like travel in Western Europe— 15 years ago and for half the price. Americans and Canadians need no visa. Just flash your passport at the border. The U.S. embassy in Prague is near the Little Quarter Square, or Malostranske Náměstí (Trziste 15, tel. 02/5753-0663). Since Eurailpasses don't cover the Czech Republic, you'll need to buy train tickets or a Prague Excursion pass for your travels to and from Prague (see "Transportation Connections," below).

Rip-offs: Prague's new freedom comes with new scams. There's no particular risk of violent crime, just green, rich tourists getting taken by con artists. Simply be on guard: on trains (thieves on overnight trains and corrupt conductors intimidating Western tourists for a bribe); changing money (tellers anywhere with bad arithmetic and inexplicable pauses while counting back your change); and dealing with taxis (see "Getting around Prague," below). In restaurants, understand the price clearly before ordering. Plainclothes policemen "looking for counterfeit money" are con artists. Don't show them your cash.

Telephoning: Czech phones work like any in Europe. For international calls, buy a phone card at a kiosk or your hotel (180 kč). It costs about $1 a minute to call the United States directly (dial 001, the area code, and the number) from a public phone booth that accepts the local phone card. To call Prague from abroad, dial the international code (00 in Europe or 011 in the U.S.), the Czech Republic code (420), then Prague's area code (2), followed by the local number. Hotels often list phone numbers with the country code (420), a number you don't need to dial when inside the Czech Republic.

Money: 38 koruna (kč) = about U.S. $1. There is no black market. Assume anyone trying to sell money on the streets is peddling obsolete currency. Buy and sell easily at the station (5 percent fees), banks, or hotels. ATMs are everywhere. Czech money is tough to change in the West. Before leaving the Czech Republic, change your remaining koruna into your next country's currency (at Prague's train station change bureaus).

American Express: Václavske Náměstí 56, Praha 1 (9:00–19:00, closed Sun) or Mosteka 12, Praha 1 (open 9:30–19:30, tel. 02/5731-3636).

Internet Access: Internet cafés beg for business all along Karlova street on the city side of the bridge.

Local Help: Magic Praha is a tiny travel service run by hardworking, English-speaking Lida Steflova. A charming jack-of-all-trades who takes her clients' needs seriously, she's particularly helpful with accommodations, private tours, and airport or train station transfers anywhere in the Czech Republic (tel. 02/302-5170, cellular 060-420-7225, e-mail: mp.ludmila@post.cz).

Best Views: Enjoy "the golden city of a hundred spires" during the early evening when the light is warm and the colors are rich. Good viewpoints include the castle square, the top of the east tower of Charles Bridge, the Old Town Square clock tower, and the steps of the National Museum overlooking Wenceslas Square.

Language: Czech, a Slavic language, has little resemblance to

Western European languages. These days, English is "modern" and you'll find the language barrier minimal. If you speak German, it's helpful. An acute accent means you linger on that vowel. The little smile above the c, s, or z makes it ch, sh, or zh.

Learn these key Czech words:

Hello/Goodbye (familiar)	*Ahoj* (ah-hoi)
Good day, Hello (formal)	*Dobrý den* (DOH-bree den)
Yes/No	*Ano* (AH-no)/*Ne* (neh)
Please	*Prosím* (proh-zeem)
Thank you	*Děkuji* (dyack-quee)
You're welcome	*Prosím* (proh-zeem)
Where is...?	*Kde je...?* (gday yeh)
Do you speak English?	*Mluvíte anglicky?*
	(MLOO-vit-eh ANG-litz-key)
krown (the money)	*koruna* (koh-roo-nah)

Arrival in Prague

Prague unnerves many travelers—it's relatively run-down, it's behind the former Iron Curtain, and you've heard stories of rip-offs and sky-high hotel prices. But, in reality, Prague is charming, safe, and welcomes you with open cash registers and smiles.

By Train: Most travelers coming from and going to the West use the main station (Hlavní Nádraží) or the secondary station (Holešovice Nádraží). Trains to other points within the country use Masarykovo or Smíchov stations.

Upon arrival, change money. Rates vary—compare by asking at two exchange windows what you'll get for $100. Count carefully. At the same window, buy a city map (50 kč, with trams and metro lines marked and tiny sketches of the sights for ease in navigating). You'll be constantly referring to this map. Confirm your departure plans at the train information window. Consider arranging a room or tour at the TI or AVE travel agency. The left-luggage counter is reportedly safer than the lockers.

At Prague's main train stations, anyone arriving on an international train will be met at the tracks by room hustlers (snaring tourists for cheap rooms). The orange low-ceilinged main hall is a fascinating mix of travelers, kiosks, loitering teenagers, and older riffraff.

From the main station, it's a 10-minute walk to Wenceslas Square (turn left out of the station and follow Washingtonova to the huge Narodini Museum and you're there). You can also catch trams #5, #9, or #26 (to find the stop, walk into park, head 2 minutes to right), or take the metro (inside station, look for the red "M" with 2 directions: Muzeum or Florenc; take Muzeum, then transfer to the green line—direction Dejvicka—and get off at either Můstek or Staroměstske; these stops straddle the Old Town). The courageous and savvy get a cabby to treat them fairly and get to their hotel fast and sweat-free for no more than 130 kč (see "Getting around Prague," below; to avoid the train station taxi stand, go out the front door and downhill through the park to the first street for a rank of less criminal cabbies or ride the metro a stop and catch one on the street).

Holešovice Nádraží station is suburban mellow. The main hall has all the services of the main station in a compact area. Outside the first glass doors, the ATM is on the left, the metro is straight ahead (follow "Vstup" which means "entrance," take it 3 stops to the main station, 4 stops to the city center Muzeum stop), and taxis and trams are outside to the right (allow 150 kč for a cab to the center).

By Plane: Your hotel can arrange for a shuttle minibus to take you economically to the airport. Airport info tel. 02/367-814.

Getting around Prague

You can walk nearly everywhere. But the metro is slick, the trams fun, and the taxis quick and easy once you're initiated.

Public Transport: The trams and metro work on the same cheap tickets. Buy from machines (press enter after the ticket type before inserting coins) at kiosks or purchase at hotels. For convenience, buy all the tickets you think you'll need: 15-minute ticket— 8 kč, 60-minute ticket—12 kč, 24-hour ticket—70 kč, three-day pass—180 kč. Cheaters, when caught, are fined 800 kč. The metro closes at midnight, but some trams keep running all night (identified with white numbers on blue backgrounds at tram stops).

City maps show the tram/bus/metro lines. The metro system is handy and simple (just 3 lines) but doesn't get to many hotels and sights. Trams are also easy to use; track your route with your city map. They run every 5 to 10 minutes, less on weekends. Get used to hopping on and off. Validate your ticket on the bus by sticking it in the machine (which stamps a time on it).

Taxis: Prague's taxis—notorious for meters that spin for tourists like pinwheels—are being tamed. Still, many cabbies consider one sucker a good day's work. While most hotel receptionists and guidebooks advise avoiding taxis, this is defeatist. I find Prague is a great taxi town and use them routinely. Get the local rate, and they're cheap. Use only registered taxis: These are marked by a fixed (not magnetic) roof lamp with the word "TAXI" in black on both sides, and the front doors sport a company name, license number, and rates (3 rows: drop charge—25 kč, per-kilometer charge—17 kč, and wait time per minute—4 kč). The key is the tiny "*sazba*" box on the magic meter showing the rate. This should read "1," unless you called for a pickup (which adds 30 to 50 kč). If a cabby tries to rip you off, simply pay 100 kč or 150 kč for a long ride. Let him follow you into the hotel if he insists you owe him more. (He won't.) The receptionist will

Prague Metro

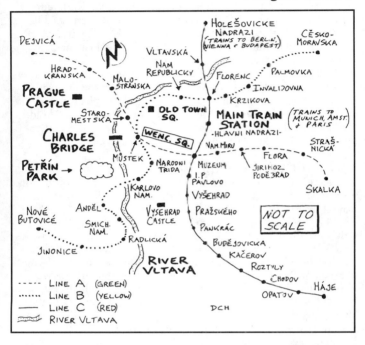

defend you. Don't bother with any taxi parked in a touristed zone. To remind him to turn on the meter, say *"Zapnete taximetr"* (zapp-nyet-ay tax-ah-met-er). The AAA and ProfiTaxi companies are considered honest. Any taxi with an excuse not to use the meter ("personal transport") is ripping you off. In 2001, 150 kč is the most any Old Town ride should cost.

Tours of Prague

Walking Tours—Prague Walks offers walking tours of the Old Town, the castle, and Jewish Quarter (mostly 2 hrs, 250 kč, tel. 02/627-0981, e-mail: pwalks@comp.cz). Consider their clever Good Morning Walk (7:00, before the crowds hit). Several decent companies give guided walks. For the latest, pick up the walking tour fliers at the TI. The TI has plenty of private guides available for hire on very short notice (3 hrs for 1,000 kč, desk at Old Town Square TI, tel. 02/2448-2562).

Bus Tours—Cheap big-bus orientation tours provide an efficient once-over-lightly look at Prague and a convenient way to see the castle. Premiant City Tours offers 15 different tours including: quick city (350 kč, 2 hrs, 5/day), grand city (590 kč, 3.5 hrs,

2/day), Jewish Quarter (620 kč, 2 hrs), Prague by night, Bohemian glass, Terezin Concentration Camp memorial, Karlštejn Castle, Český Krumlov (1,600 kč, 8 hrs), and a river cruise. The tours feature live guides (in German and English) and depart from near the bottom of Wenceslas Square at Na Príkope 23. Get tickets at an AVE travel agency, hotel, on the bus, or at Na Príkope 20 (tel. 02/2494-6922, www.premiant.cz).

Tram Joyride—Tram #22 makes a fine joyride through town. Consider this as a scenic lead-up to touring the castle. Catch it at metro: Náměstí Míru, roll through a bit of new town, the old town, across the river, and hop out just above the castle (at Pyramid Hotel and hike down the hill into castle area).

Self-Guided Walking Tour

The King's Walk (Královská cesta), the ancient way of coronation processions, is touristy but great. Pedestrian friendly and full of playful diversions, it connects the essential Prague sites. The king would be crowned in St. Vitus Cathedral in the Prague Castle, walk through the Little Quarter to the Church of St. Nicholas, cross Charles Bridge, and finish at the Old Town Square. If he hurried, he'd be done in 20 minutes. Like the main drag in Venice between St. Mark's and the Rialto bridge, this walk mesmerizes tourists. Use it as a spine, but venture off it—especially to eat.

While you could cover this route in the same direction, the king's long gone and it's a new morning in Prague, so I'll lay out Prague's essential sights in walking order, starting where modern independence was proclaimed, on Wenceslas Square, proceeding through the Old Town, across the bridge, and finishing at the castle. This walk laces together all the following recommended sights except the Jewish Quarter.

▲▲**Wenceslas Square (Václavske Náměstí)**—More a broad boulevard than a square (until recently trams rattled up and down its parklike median strip), it's named for the equestrian statue of King Wenceslas that stands at the top of the boulevard.

The square is a stage for modern Czech history: The Czechoslovak state was proclaimed here in 1918. In 1968 the Soviets put down huge popular demonstrations here. Starting at the top (metro: Muzeum), stroll down the square:

The **National Museum** stands grandly at the top. The only thing exciting about it is the view (80 kč, daily 10:00–18:00, halls of Czech fossils and animals).

The metro stop (Muzeum) is the cross point of two metro lines. From here you could roll a ball straight down the boulevard and through the heart of Prague to Charles Bridge.

St. Wenceslas (Václave), commemorated by the statue, is the "good king" of Christmas carol fame. He was never really a king but the wise and benevolent 10th-century Prince of Bohemia.

After being assassinated in 929, he became a symbol of Czech nationalism. Now his equestrian statue is a popular meeting point. Locals say, "I'll see you under the horse's ass."

Thirty meters below the big horse is a small round garden with a low-key **memorial** "to the victims of Communism." Pictured here is Jan Palach. In 1969, a group of patriots decided a self-immolation would stoke the fires of independence. They drew straws and Jan Palach got the short one. He set himself on fire for the cause of Czech independence. Twenty years later massive demonstrations here led to the overthrow of the Czech Communist government. From the balcony of Melantrich (opposite the Grand Hotel Europa—farther down), Vaclav Havel stood with Alexander Dubcek, hero of the 1968 revolt, and declared the free Republic of Czechoslovakia in December 1989.

Havel is still president and popular, although his popularity took a hit when he married for the second time to an actress 17 years his junior (some say his brain dropped about one meter). His second (and last) five-year term ends in 2003.

As you wander, notice the fun mix of **architectural styles**, all post-1850: Romantic neo-Gothic, neo-Renaissance, neo-Baroque from the 19th century, Art Nouveau from 1900, ugly functionalism from the mid-20th century, and Stalin Gothic from the "Communist epoch." The Grand Hotel Europa (halfway down Wenceslas Square) is hard to miss with its dazzling Art Nouveau exterior.

▲**Na Príkope (the Moat)**—The bottom of Wenceslas Square meets another spacious pedestrian mall. Na Príkope (meaning "the moat") leads from Wenceslas Square right to the Powder Tower (the Powder Tower sounds interesting but is a dud). While probably not worth the detour on this walk, consider these reasons to explore the Tower area later: City tour buses leave from along this street. A fancy Bohemian crystal shop, Moser's (described below in "Shopping"), is at #12. Next to the Powder Tower is the dazzling **Municipal House**, with a great Art Nouveau facade and three recommended restaurants.

▲**Havelská Market**—Central Prague's best open-air flower and produce market scene is a block toward the Old Town Square from the bottom of Wenceslas Square. Laid out in the 13th century by King Wenceslas for the German trading community, it keeps hungry locals and vagabonds fed cheaply today.

▲▲▲**Old Town Square (Staroměstske Náměstí)**—The focal point for most visits, this has been a market square since the 11th century. It became the nucleus of a town (Staré Město) in the 13th century when its city hall was built. Today the old-time market stalls have been replaced by cafés, touristic horse buggies, and souvenir hawkers.

The **Hus Memorial**—erected in 1915, 500 years after his

Prague

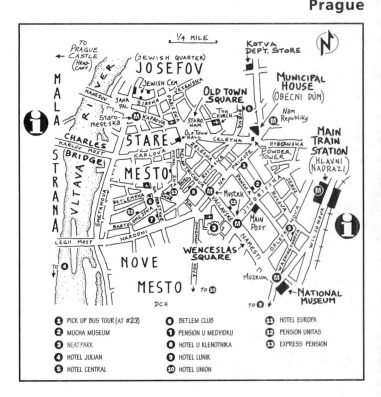

TO PRAGUE CASTLE (HRAD ČANY)

KOTVA DEPT. STORE

¼ MILE

(JEWISH QUARTER)
JOSEFOV

Jewish Cem.

MUNICIPAL HOUSE (OBECNÍ DŮM)

MALA STRANA

MANESUV

JANA PAL

SIROKA

VEZENSKA

OLD TOWN SQUARE

Nam Republiky

Staro mestska

KAPROVA

STARO NAM.

TYN CHURCH

MAIN TRAIN STATION (HLAVNI NADRAZI)

CHARLES BRIDGE

KARLUV MOST

STARE

Old Town Hall

CELETNA

HYBERNSKA

POWDER TOWER

KARLOVA

ZELEZNA

MESTO

RYTIRSKA

NA PRIKOPE

PANSKA

Mustek

JINDRISSKA

VLTAVA

SMETANOVA

BETLEMSKA

BARTOLOMEJSKA

NARODNI

VODICKOVA

VACLAVSKE

JUNGMANNOVA

Main Post

WASHINGTONOVA

WILSONOVA

LEGII MOST

NOVE MESTO

WENCESLAS SQUARE

NAMESTI

OPLETALOVA

Muzeum

NATIONAL MUSEUM

TO ④

TO ⑩

TO ⑬

DCH

① PICK UP BUS TOUR (AT #23)	⑥ BETLEM CLUB	⑪ HOTEL EUROPA
② MUCHA MUSEUM	⑦ PENSION U MEDVIDKU	⑫ PENSION UNITAS
③ NEAT PARK	⑧ HOTEL U KLENOTNIKA	⑬ EXPRESS PENSION
④ HOTEL JULIAN	⑨ HOTEL LUNIK	
⑤ HOTEL CENTRAL	⑩ HOTEL UNION	

burning—marks the center of the square and symbolizes the long struggle for Czech freedom. Walk around the memorial. The Czech reformer Jan Hus stands tall between two groups of people: victorious Hussite patriots and Protestants defeated by the Hapsburgs. One of the patriots holds a cup—in the medieval Church, only priests could drink the wine at communion. Hussites fought for the right to take both the wine and the bread. A mother with her children behind Hus represents the ultimate rebirth of the Czech nation. Hus was excommunicated and burned in Germany a century before the age of Martin Luther.

Do a spin tour in the center of the square to get a look at architectural styles: Romanesque, Gothic, Renaissance, Baroque, and Art Nouveau.

Spin clockwise, from the green domes of the Baroque Church of St. Nicholas. There has been a church on this site since the 12th century. This one, dating from the early 18th century, is now a Hussite church (evening concerts). The Jewish Quarter (Josefov) is a few blocks behind it down the uniquely tree-lined Paris Street (Parizska), a festival of mostly Art Nouveau facades. Spin to the right past the Hus Memorial and the fine golden and mosaic Art Nouveau facade of the Ministry of the Economy. Notice the Gothic Tyn Church (described below) with its Disneyesque spires flanking a solid gold effigy of the Virgin Mary. Lining the uphill side of the square is an interesting row of pastel houses with Gothic, Renaissance, and Baroque facades. The pointed 75-meter-tall spire marks the 14th-century Old Town Hall, famous for its astronomical clock (described below). In front of the city hall, 27 white inlaid crosses mark the spot where 27 Protestant nobles and intellectuals were beheaded in 1621 after rebelling against the Catholic Hapsburgs.

Tyn Church—The fanciful church (pronounced "teen") facing the Old Town Square was rebuilt fancier than the original—but enjoy it. For 200 years after Hus's death, this was Prague's leading Hussite church. Enter through the Gothic arcade facing the square (a diagram at the door locates spots of interest, such as the tomb of astronomer Tycho Brahe).

The lane leading to the church from the Old Town Square has a public WC and the most central box office in town (see "Entertainment," below).

▲Old Town Hall Astronomical Clock—Join the gang—ignoring the ridiculous human sales racks—for the striking of the hour (daily 8:00–20:00) on the 15th-century town hall clock. As you wait, see if you can figure out how the clock works.

With revolving disks, celestial symbols, and sweeping hands, this clock keeps several versions of time. Two outer rings show the hour: Bohemian time (Gothic numbers, counts from sunset—find the zero, next to 23 ... supposedly the time of tonight's sunset) and modern time (24 Roman numerals, XII at the top being noon, XII at the bottom being midnight). Five hundred years ago, everything revolved around the earth (the fixed middle background).

To indicate the times of sunrise and sunset, arcing lines and moving spheres combine with the big hand (a sweeping golden sun) and the little hand (the moon showing various stages). Look for the orbits of the sun and moon as they rise through day (the blue zone) and night (the black zone).

If this seems complex today, it must have been a marvel 500 years ago. The circle below (added in the 19th century) shows the zodiac, scenes from the seasons of a rural peasant's life, and a ring of saints' names—one for each day of the year with a marker showing today's special saint (out of order).

Four statues flanking the clock represent 15th-century Prague's four biggest worries: invasion (a Turkish conqueror ... his hedonism symbolized by a mandolin), death (a skeleton), greed (a miserly moneylender, which used to have "Jewish" features until after World War II, when anti-Semitism became politically incorrect), and vanity (enjoying the mirror).

At the top of the hour (don't blink—the show lasts 20 seconds): (1) Death tips his hourglass and pulls the cord ringing the bell; (2) the windows open and the Twelve Apostles parade by acknowledging the gang of onlookers; (3) the rooster crows; and (4) the hour is rung. The hour is often off because of daylight saving time (completely senseless to 15th-century clockmakers). At the top of the next hour, stand under the tower—protected by a line of banner-wielding, powdered-wigged concert salespeople—and watch the tourists.

Left of the clock is the main TI, a local guides' desk, and an opportunity to pay three admissions: for the city hall (by tour only), a Gothic chapel (only interesting for a close-up of the Twelve Apostles, and the clock mechanism well described in English), and the tower (long climb, fine view).

To reach the bridge, turn your back to the fancy Tyn Church and march with the crowds.

Karlova Street—This street winds through medieval old Prague from the City Hall Square to the Charles Bridge. This is a commercial gauntlet, and it's here that the touristic feeding frenzy of Prague is most ugly. Street signs keep you on track and "Karluv Most" signs point to the bridge. Obviously, you'll find great people watching but no good values on this drag.

Torture Museum—This gimmicky moneymaker is no different from any other European torture museum—but nevertheless interesting, showing 60 models of gruesome medieval tortures with well-written English descriptions (100 kč, daily 10:00–22:00, just before the bridge at Karlova 2).

▲▲▲**Charles Bridge (Karluv Most)**—This much-loved bridge, commissioned by the Holy Roman Emperor Charles IV in 1357, offers one of the most pleasant 500-meter strolls in Europe. Until 1850 it was the only bridge crossing the river here. Be on the bridge when the sun is low for the warmest people watching and best photo opportunities.

Before crossing the bridge, step into the little square on the right with the statue of the Holy Roman Emperor Charles IV (Karlo Quatro). Charles ruled his vast empire from Prague in the 14th century. He's holding a contract establishing Prague university—the first in central Europe. The women around his pedestal symbolize the university's four faculties: medicine, law, theology, and the arts. The statue was erected in 1848 to celebrate the university's 500th birthday. Enjoy the view across the river. The bridge tower above you—once a toll booth—is considered one of the finest Gothic gates anywhere. Climb it for a fine view but nothing else (30 kč, daily 10:00–22:00).

Charles Bridge is famous for its statues. But those you see

today are replicas—the originals are in city museums and out of the pollution.

Two statues on the bridge are worth a comment: the crucifix (facing the castle, near the start on the right) is the spot where convicts would pause to pray on their way to execution on the Old Town Square. Further on (midstream, on right) the statue of John Nepomuk—patron saint of the Czech people—draws a crowd (look for the guy with the five golden stars and the shiny dog). Back in the 14th century, he was the priest to whom the queen confessed all her sins. The king wanted to know her secrets but John dutifully refused to tell. He was tortured, eventually killed, and tossed off the bridge. When he hit the water five stars appeared. The shiny spot on the base of the statue shows the heave-ho. Locals touch it to help wishes come true. The shiny dog killed the queen...but that's another story. From the end of the bridge (TI in tower on castle side), the street leads two blocks to the Little Quarter Square at the base of the huge St. Nicholas church.

▲▲**Little Quarter (Malá Strana)**—This is the most characteristic, fun-to-wander old section of town. It's one of four medieval towns (along with Hradčany, Staré Město, and Nové Město) that united in the 1700s to make modern Prague. It centers on the Little Quarter Square (Malostranské Náměstí, on downhill side of huge St. Nicholas church) with its plague monument facing the entry to the commanding church, at the upper end of the square. **Church of St. Nicholas**—Dominating the Little Quarter, this is the best example of High Baroque in town. It's a Jesuit church, giddy with curves and illusions. The altar features a lavish gold-plated Nicholas flanked by the two top Jesuits: St. Ignatius Loyola and St. Francis Xavier (45 kč, daily 9:00–16:00, built 1703–1760, 75-meter-high dome, tower climbable from outside right transept). From here, hike 10 minutes uphill to the castle.

Sights—Prague's Castle Area

▲▲**Prague Castle**—For a thousand years, Czech rulers have ruled from the Prague Castle. It's huge (by some measures, the biggest castle on earth) and confusing—with plenty of sights not worth seeing. Rather than worry about rumors that you should spend all day here with long lists of museums to see, keep things simple. Five stops matter and are explained here: Castle Square, St. Vitus Cathedral, the old Royal Palace, Basilica of St. George, and the Golden Lane. One 120-kč ticket gets you into all these sights (Tue–Sun 9:00–17:00, last entry at 16:00, closed Mon; the 145 kč audioguide is good but requires 2 hrs and, since you need to return it where you got it, makes it impossible to exit the castle area from the bottom).

To reach the castle, choose one of four ways: metro to Malostranská (and climb up); tram #22 or #23 (which stop above

the castle, and hike down); take a cab directly to Castle Square; or—the best—walk through the Little Quarter from the bridge.
Castle Square (Hradčanske Náměstí)—The big square facing the castle feels like the castle's entry, but it's actually the central square of a fortified town called Prague Castle, which until the 1700s was independent. Enjoy the awesome city view and the Prague Fun Fair Orchestra—a string quartet which plays regularly at the gate (their CD is terrific, say hello to friendly, mustachioed Josef). A tranquil café hides a few steps down immediately to the right as you face the castle. From here stairs lead into the Lesser Town. Uphill from the gate is a plague monument in the center, the Renaissance Schwarzenberg Palace (on the left, now an armory museum), a lane on the right leading to the Sternberg Palace (filled with the National Gallery's skippable collection of European paintings—mostly minor works by Dürer, Rubens, Rembrandt, El Greco, 90 kč, Tue–Sun 10:00–18:00, closed Mon).

Survey the castle from this square—the tip of a 500-meter-long series of courtyards, churches, and palaces. The offices facing this first courtyard belong to the Czech president, Vaclav Havel (left side). The guard changes on the hour (with the most ceremony at noon). Walk under the fighting giants, under an arch, to the ticket booth. You can walk through the castle and enter the cathedral without a ticket, but you'll need a ticket to see the castle properly (120-kč ticket covers cathedral apse and spire, Old Royal Palace, Basilica of St. George, and Powder Tower; hour-long, 60-kč English tours depart from ticket office regularly but cover Cathedral and Old Palace only; private guides-500 kč, tel. 02/2437-3368).
▲St. Vitus Cathedral—This Roman Catholic cathedral symbolizes the Czech spirit. Started in 1344, Prague's top church wasn't finished until 1929 in time for the 1,000th anniversary of the assassination of St. Wenceslas, patron saint of the Czechs. It looks all Gothic, but it's two distinct halves: modern neo-Gothic first and the original 14th-century Gothic from the high altar to the far end. Wars and plagues stalled the building, and for 400 years a temporary wall sealed off the unfinished cathedral. With the 19th-century rise of Czech nationalism, it was finally finished in the last century.

In the neo-Gothic section, the stained glass is all 20th century. The masterful Art Nouveau window on the left is from 1931 by Czech artist Alfons Mucha (if you like this, you'll love the Mucha museum downtown—described below in "Art Nouveau").

Show your ticket and circulate around the apse past a carved wood relief of Prague in 1630, lots of faded Gothic paintings, and tombs of local saints. A fancy roped-off chapel (right transept) houses the tomb of Prince Wenceslas surrounded by murals showing scenes of his life, and a locked door leading to the crown jewels. More kings are buried in the royal mausoleum in front of the high altar and in the crypt underneath. You can climb

Prague's Castle Area

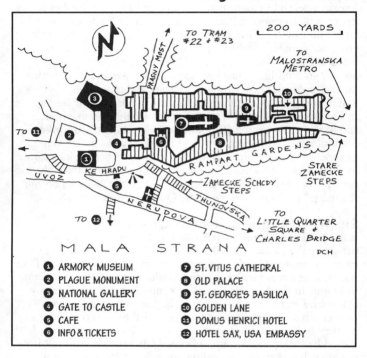

TO TRAM #22 & #23

200 YARDS

TO MALOSTRANSKA METRO

PRASNY MOST

TO

UVOZ

KE HRADU

RAMPART GARDENS

STARE ZAMECKE STEPS

ZAMECKE SCHODY STEPS

NERUDOVA

THUNOVSKA

TO

LITTLE QUARTER SQUARE & CHARLES BRIDGE

DCH

M A L A   S T R A N A

❶ ARMORY MUSEUM
❷ PLAGUE MONUMENT
❸ NATIONAL GALLERY
❹ GATE TO CASTLE
❺ CAFE
❻ INFO & TICKETS

❼ ST. VITUS CATHEDRAL
❽ OLD PALACE
❾ ST. GEORGE'S BASILICA
❿ GOLDEN LANE
⓫ DOMUS HENRICI HOTEL
⓬ HOTEL SAX, USA EMBASSY

the spire for a fine view (daily except Sunday morning, 9:00–17:00, 287 steps).

Leaving the cathedral, turn left. Find the 14th-century mosaic of the Last Judgment outside on the right transept. Across from that is the . . .

Old Royal Palace—This was the seat of the Bohemian princes in the 12th century. While extensively rebuilt, the large hall is late Gothic. It's big enough for jousts—even the staircase was designed to let a mounted soldier gallop in. Look up at the impressive vaulted ceiling, look down on the chapel from the end, and go out on the balcony for a fine Prague view. Is that Paris in the distance? No, it's an observation tower built for an exhibition in 1891 (60 meters tall; a quarter of the height of its Parisian big brother that was built in 1889). The spiral stairs on the left lead up to several rooms with painted coats of arms and no English explanations. There's nothing to see downstairs in the palace. Across from the palace exit is the basilica.

Basilica of St. George and Convent—The first Bohemian convent was established here near the palace in 973. Today the convent houses the Czech Gallery (best Czech paintings from Gothic, Renaissance, and Baroque periods). The beautifully lit basilica is Prague's best-preserved Romanesque church. St. Ludmila was buried here in 973. Continue walking downhill through the castle grounds. Turn left on the first street, which leads into a cute lane. **Golden Lane**—This street of old buildings, which originally housed goldsmiths, is now jammed with tourists and lined with expensive gift shops, boutiques, galleries, and cafés. The Czech writer Franz Kafka lived at #22. There's a deli/bistro at the top and a convenient public WC at the bottom. Beyond that, at the end of the castle, are fortifications beefed up in anticipation of the Turkish attack—the cause for most medieval arms buildups in Europe—and steps funneling the mobs of tourists back into town. At the bottom of the castle, follow its walls around to the right and pay (40 kč, 10:00–18:00) to shortcut through the "Garden on the Ramparts" back down to the Little Quarter (Malá Strana).

Sights—Prague's Jewish Quarter

▲▲▲**Jewish Quarter (Josefov)**—The Jewish people were dispersed by the Romans 2,000 years ago. Over the centuries, their culture survived in enclaves throughout the Western world: "Time was their sanctuary which no army could destroy." Jews first came to Prague in the 10th century. The main intersection of Josefov (Maiselova and Siroka Streets) was the meeting point of two medieval trade routes. Jewish traders settled here in the 13th century and built a synagogue.

When the pope declared Jews and Christians should not live together, Jews had to wear yellow badges, and their quarter was walled in so that it became a ghetto. In the 16th and 17th centuries Prague had the biggest ghetto in Europe with 11,000 inhabitants—nearly half the population of Prague. Within its six gates, Prague's Jewish Quarter was a gaggle of two hundred wooden buildings. Someone wrote: "Jews nested rather than dwelled."

The "outcasts" of Christianity relied on profits from money lending (forbidden to Christians) and community solidarity to survive. While their money protected them, it was also a curse. Throughout Europe, when times got tough and Christian debts to the Jewish community mounted, entire Jewish communities were evicted or killed.

In the 1780s Emperor Joseph II eased much of the discrimination against Jews. In 1848 the walls were torn down and the neighborhood, named Josefov in honor of the emperor who was less anti-Semitic than the norm, was incorporated as a district of Prague.

In 1897, ramshackle Josefov was razed and replaced with a new modern town—the original 31 streets and 220 buildings became 10 streets and 83 buildings. This is what you'll see today: an attractive neighborhood of fine, mostly Art Nouveau buildings, with a few

Prague's Jewish Quarter

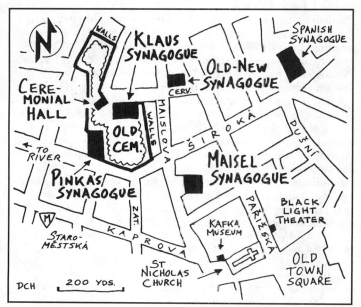

surviving historic Jewish buildings. In the 1930s some 50,000 Jews lived in Josefov. Today only a couple of thousand remain.

Strangely, the museums of the Jewish Quarter are, in part, the work of Hitler. He preserved Josefov to be his museum of the "exterminated race." Seven sites scattered over a three-block area make the tourists' Jewish Quarter. Six, called "the Museum," are treated as one admission. Your ticket comes with a map locating the sights and admission appointments: times you'll be let in if it's very crowded. (Without crowds, ignore the times.)

For all seven sights you'll pay 480 kč (280 kč for the "Museum" and 200 kč for the Old-New Synagogue). The sites are open from Sunday to Friday 9:00 to 17:30, and closed on Saturday (the Jewish Sabbath). There are occasional guided walks in English (often at 14:00, 40 kč, 2.5 hrs, starts at Maisel Synagogue, tel. 02/231-7191). Most stops are well described in English. These museums are well presented and profoundly moving: For me, this is the most interesting Jewish site in Europe.

Maisel Synagogue—This shows a thousand years of Jewish history in Bohemia and Moravia. Ironically, the collection was assembled from synagogues throughout the region by Nazis planning to archive the "extinct Jewish culture" here in Josefov with a huge museum. Exhibits include topics such as the origin of the Star of

David, Jewish mysticism, discrimination, and the creation of the
Prague Ghetto.

Spanish Synagogue—This 19th-century, ornate, Moorish-style
synagogue continues the history the Maisel Synagogue started,
covering the 18th, 19th, and tumultuous 20th centuries. The
upstairs is particularly interesting (with c. 1900 photos of Josefov).

Pinkas Synagogue—A site of Jewish worship for 400 years, today
this is a poignant memorial to the victims of the Nazis. Of the
120,000 Jews living around here in 1939, only 15,000 lived to see
liberation in 1945. The walls are covered with the handwritten
names of 77,297 local Jews who were sent from here to the gas
chambers of Auschwitz. Family names are in gold, followed by the
individuals' first names in black, with birthdays and the last date
known to be alive (usually the date of transport—to one of the
camps listed by the altar). Notice that families generally perished
together. Climb six steps into the women's gallery. The names
near the ceiling in poor condition are from 1953. When the
Communists moved in, they closed the synagogue and erased
everything. With freedom, in 1989, the Pinkas Synagogue was
reopened and all the names rewritten.

Upstairs is the Terezin Children's Art Exhibit. Terezin, near
Prague, was a fortified town of 7,000 Czechs. The Nazis moved
these people out and moved in 60,000 Jews, creating their model
"Jewish town," a concentration camp dolled up for propaganda
purposes. The town's medieval walls, originally to keep people
from getting in, were used by Nazis to prevent people from getting out. Jewish culture seemed to thrive in Terezin as "citizens"
put on plays and concerts, published a magazine, and raised their
families in ways impressive to Red Cross inspectors. But virtually
all of the Jews ended up dying at concentration camps in the East
such as Auschwitz. The art of the children of Terezin survives as a
striking testimony to the horror of the Holocaust. While the
Communists kept the art away from the public, today it's well
displayed and described in English.

Terezin is a powerful day trip from Prague for those interested in touring the concentration camp memorial/museum; you
can either take a public bus (6/day, 60 min, leaves from Prague's
Florenc bus station) or a tour bus (see "Tours of Prague," above).

Old Jewish Cemetery—As you wander among 12,000 evocative
tombstones, remember that from 1439 until 1787 this was the only
burial ground allowed for the Jews of Prague. With limited space
and over 100,000 graves, tombs were piled atop each other. With
as many as 12 layers, the cemetery became a small plateau. The
Jewish word for cemetery means "House of Life"; like Christians,
Jews believe that death is the gateway into the next world. Pebbles
on the tombstones are "flowers of the desert," reminiscent of the
old days when a rock was placed upon the sand gravesite to keep

the body covered. Often a scrap of paper with a prayer on it is under a pebble.

Ceremonial Hall—Leaving the cemetery you'll find a neo-Romanesque mortuary house built in 1911 for the purification of the dead (on left). It's filled with an interesting and well-described exhibition on Jewish burial traditions with historic paintings of the cemetery.

Klaus Synagogue—This 17th-century synagogue (also at the exit of the cemetery) is the final wing of this museum, devoted to Jewish religious practices. On the ground floor, exhibits explain the festive Jewish calendar. Upstairs features the ritual stages of Jewish life.

Old-New Synagogue—For over 700 years this has been the most important synagogue and central building in Josefov. Standing like a bomb-hardened bunker, it feels like it's survived plenty of hard times. Stairs take you down to the street level of the 13th century and into the Gothic interior. Built in 1270, it's the oldest synagogue in Europe. Originally called the "New Synagogue," it was renamed "Old-New" as other synagogues were built. The Shrine of the Arc in front is the focus of worship. It holds the sacred scrolls of the Torah, the holiest place in the synagogue. The old rabbi's chair to the right remains empty out of respect. Twelve is a popular number (e.g., windows) because it symbolizes the 12 tribes of Israel. The slitlike windows on the left are an 18th-century addition allowing women to view the men-only services (separate 200 kč admission, open 9:30–18:00).

Art Nouveau

Prague is the best Art Nouveau town in Europe with fun-loving facades gracing streets all over town. The streets of Josefov, the Mucha window in the St. Vitus Cathedral, and Hotel Europa and its sisters on Wenceslas Square are just a few highlights. The top two places for Art Nouveau fans are the Mucha Museum and the Municipal House.

▲▲**Mucha Museum**—This is one of Europe's most enjoyable little museums. I find the art of Alfons Mucha (moo-kah, 1860–1939) insistently likeable. Read how this popular Czech artist's posters were patriotic banners in disguise, see the crucifixion scene he painted as an eight-year-old, and check out the photographs of his models. Prague isn't much on museums, but if you're into Art Nouveau, this one is great. Run by Mucha's grandson, it's two blocks off Wenceslas Square and wonderfully described and displayed on one comfortable floor (120 kč, daily 10:00–18:00, Panska 7, tel. 02/628-4162, www.mucha.cz). While the exhibit is well described in English, the 30-kč English brochure on the art is a good supplement. The video is also worthwhile (30 min, hrly in English, ask upon entry).

Municipal House—The Municipal House (Obecní Dum, built 1905–1911, near Powder Tower) features Prague's largest concert hall, a great Art Nouveau café with handy cyber access, and two other restaurants. Look for the *Homage to Prague* mosaic—with a goddesslike Praha presiding over a land of peace and high culture—on the building's striking facade; it stoked cultural pride and nationalist sentiment. Then choose your place for a meal or drink (described below in "Eating").

Entertainment

Prague booms with live (and inexpensive) theater, opera, classical, jazz, and pop entertainment. Everything's listed in Prague's monthly cultural events program (free at TI).

Black Light Theater, a kind of mime/modern dance variety show, has no language barrier and is, for many, more entertaining than a classical concert.

Six or eight classical "tourist" concerts a day resound throughout the famous Old Town halls and churches generally within a three-minute walk of the Old Town Square or bridge. The music is of the crowd-pleasing sort: Vivaldi, Best of Mozart, Most Famous Arias, and works by local boy Anton Dvořák. Leafleteers are everywhere announcing the evening's events. Concerts typically cost 400 to 1000 kč, start anywhere from 17:00 to 20:00, last one hour, and are usually quartets (e.g., flute, French horn, cello violin).

Common venues are in the Little Quarter Square—Malostranské Náměstí (at the Church of St. Nicholas and the Prague Academy of Music in Lichtenstein Palace), at the city end of Charles Bridge (St. Francis Church), and on the Old Town Square (another St. Nicholas Church).

To really understand all your options (the street Mozarts are pushing only their concert), drop by the box office at the Tyn Church. The wall display clearly shows what's playing today and tomorrow (concerts, Black Light Theater, marionette shows, photos of each venue, and a map locating everything, daily 10:00–18:00, tel. 02/231-4936).

Shopping

Moser's Bohemian Crystal shop offers a top-end look at this local specialty. Climb the stairs into the elegant showrooms, housed in the 19th-century mansion of a local Jewish family that's sold crystal since 1925. It's like a museum (Mon–Fri 9:00–20:00, Sat–Sun 10:00–18:00, midway between bottom of Wenceslas Square and Powder Tower at Na Príkope 12, tel. 02/2421-1293).

The huge Kotva department store (the name means "anchor") on the edge of the Old Town is a fun opportunity to see work-a-day Czech consumerism. Since cosmetics were scarce in the Communist days, that's the big draw even today; cosmetics and perfume routinely are placed by the front door of department stores (latest Czech fashions, cheap manicures, sprawling grocery store in basement, Mon–Fri 9:00–20:00, Sat–Sun 10:00–18:00, few minutes' walk from Old Town Square on Kraládvorská).

Sleeping in Prague
(38 kč = about $1, country code: 420, area code: 02)
Sleep Code: **S** = Single, **D** = Double/Twin, **T** = Triple, **Q** = Quad, **b** = bathroom, t = toilet only, s = shower only, **CC** = Credit Card (Visa, MasterCard, Amex).

Finding a bed in Prague worries Western tourists. It shouldn't. You have several options. Capitalism is working as Adam Smith promised: With a huge demand, the supply is increasing and the price is going up. Peak time is May, June, September, October, Christmas, and Easter. July and August are not too bad. Expect crowds on weekends. I've listed peak time prices. If you're traveling in July or August, you'll save about 20 percent. English is generally spoken. Reserve by phone or e-mail. Generally you simply promise to come and need no deposit.

Room-Booking Services
The city is awash with fancy rooms on the push list, private, small-time operators with rooms to rent in their apartments, and roving agents eager to book you a bed and win a commission. You can save about 30 percent by showing up in Prague without a reservation and finding accommodations upon arrival.

AVE, at the main train station (Hlavní Nádraží), is a helpful and well-organized booking service (daily 6:00–23:00, tel. 02/2422-3226, fax 02/2423-0783, e-mail: ave@avetravel.cz). With the tracks at your back, walk down to the orange ceiling—their office is in the left corner by the exit to the rip-off taxis. Another AVE office is at Holešovice station. Their display board shows discounted hotels. They have a slew of private rooms and small pensions available ($50 pension doubles in the old center, $35 doubles a metro ride away). You can reserve by e-mail (using your credit card as a deposit) or just show up at the office and request a room.

Athos Travel, run by Filip Antos, is basically a Web site designed to set you up with budget beds in Prague. It's a work in progress, but log onto www.athos.cz and see what happens (e-mail: filip@antos.cz).

For a more personal touch, contact Lida at **Magic Praha** for help with accommodations (tel. 02/302-5170, e-mail: mp .ludmila@post.cz, see "Helpful Hints," above).

Three-Star Hotels
Prague's three-star hotels—each plenty professional and comfortable—are often beholden to agencies that have a lock on rooms

(generally until 6 weeks in advance). Agencies get a 30 percent discount and can sell the rooms at whatever price they like between that and the "rack rate." Consequently, Prague has a reputation of being perpetually booked up. But as the agencies rarely use up their allotment, the "crowds" are only an illusion. You need to make reservations either long in advance, when the few rooms not reserved for agencies are still available, or a few weeks in advance, after the agencies have released their rooms.

Hotel Julian—an oasis of professional, predictable decency in a quiet, untouristy neighborhood—is a five-minute taxi or tram ride from the action on the castle side of the river. Its 29 spacious, fresh, well-furnished rooms and big, homey public spaces hide behind a noble neoclassical facade. The staff is friendly and helpful (Sb-3,080 kč, Db-3,380 kč, suite Db-4,180 kč, extra bed-900 kč, family room, CC:VMA, 5 percent discount off best quoted rate with this book, parking lot, elevator, Internet services, Elisky Peskove 11, Prague 5, tel. 02/5731-1150, reception tel. 02/5731-1144, fax 02/5731-1149, www.julian.cz, e-mail: casjul@vol.cz,). Free lockers and a shower are available for those needing to check out early but stay until late (e.g., for an overnight train). Mike's Chauffeur Service based here is reliable and affordable (see "Transportation Connections," below).

Hotel Central is as likeable as an old horse I stayed there in the Communist days, and—while the rooms are modestly renovated—it hasn't changed a lot since. Even Charlie is still at the reception desk. The 68 rooms are proletarian plain, but the place is well run and the location, three blocks east of the old square, is excellent (Sb-3,000 kč, Db-3,500 kč, Tb-4,000 kč, CC:VMA, elevator, Rybna 8, Praha 1, metro: Náměstí Republiky, tel. 02/2481-2041, fax 02/232-8404, e-mail: what's that?).

Betlem Club is a shiny jewel of comfort on a pleasant medieval square in the heart of the Old Town across from the Betlem Chapel where Jan Hus preached his trouble-making sermons. Its 22 modern and comfy rooms face a quiet inner courtyard, and breakfast is served in a Gothic cellar (Sb-2,500 kč, Db-3,600 kč, extra bed-900 kč, elevator, Betlémské Náměstí 9, Praha 1, tel. 02/2222-1575, fax 02/2222-0580, e-mail: betlem.club@login.cz).

Hotel U Klenotnika, with 10 modern and comfortable rooms in a plain building, is three blocks off the old square (Sb-2,500 kč, Db-3,800 kč, Tb-4,500 kč, 10 percent off when booking direct with this book, CC:VMA, no elevator, Rytirska 3, Praha 1, tel. 02/2421-1699, fax 02/2422-1025).

Hotel Lunik is a stately no-nonsense place out of the medieval faux-rustic world and in a normal, pleasant business district two metro stops from the main station (metro: Pavlova) or a 10-minute walk from Wenceslas Square. It's friendly, spacious, and rents 35 pleasant rooms (Db-2,500 kč, Tb-2,900 kč, CC:VMA, elevator, no reservations more than 6 weeks in advance, Londynska 50, Praha 2, tel. 02/2425-3974, fax 02/2425-3986, e-mail: hotel.lunik@email.cz).

Hotel Union is a grand 1906 Art Nouveau building filling its street corner. Like Hotel Lunik, it's away from the touristic center in a more laid-back neighborhood a direct 10-minute ride to the station on tram #24 or to Charles Bridge on tram #18 (57 rooms, Sb-2,815 kč, Db-3,380 kč, Db deluxe-3,580 kč, extra bed-865 kč, CC:VMA, elevator, Nusle Ostrcilovo Náměstí 1, Praha 2, tel. 02/6121-4812, fax 02/6121-4820, e-mail: hotel.union@telecom.cz).

Hotel 16, a stately little place with an intriguing Art Nouveau facade, a garden, high ceilings, and a clean, sleek interior, rents 13 fine rooms (Sb-2,300 kč, Db-3,100 kč, Tb-3,500 kč, CC:VM, elevator, a 10-minute walk south of Wenceslas Square, metro: Pavlova, Katerinska 16, 12800 Praha 2, tel. 02/2492-0636, fax 02/2492-0626, www.hotel16.cz).

Hotel Adria, with a prime Wenceslas Square location, cool Art Nouveau facade, and completely modern and business-class interior, is your big-time central splurge (88 air-con rooms, Db-$185, CC:VMA, elevator, minibars ... the works, Václavske Náměstí 26, tel. 02/2108-1111, fax 02/2108-1300, www.hoteladria.cz, e-mail: mailbox@hoteladria.cz).

Cloister Inn is a modern, three-star place with 70 rooms and more concrete than charm but plenty comfortable and well located (Db-3,800 kč, Konviktska 14, 11000 Praha 1, tel. 02/2421-1020, fax 02/2421-0800, www.cloister-inn.cz).

Three-Star Hotels near the Castle in the Little Quarter (Malá Strana)

Hotel Sax, on a quiet corner a block below the action, will delight the artsy yuppie with its airy atrium and modern, stylish decor (22 rooms, Sb-3,700 kč, Db-4,400 kč, Db suite-5,100 kč, CC:VMA, elevator, near St. Nicholas church, 1 block below Nerudova at Jansky Vrsek 3, tel. 02/5753-1268, fax 02/5753-4101, e-mail: hotelsax@bon.cz).

Domus Henrici, just above the castle square, is a quiet retreat that charges—and gets—top koruna for its smartly appointed rooms, some of which include good views (Db-$150/$170/$180 depending on size, extra bed-$40, pleasant breakfast terrace, Loretanska 11, tel. 02/2051-1369, fax 02/2051-1502, www.domus-henrici.cz). This is a five-minute walk above the castle gate in a stately and quiet area.

Pensions

With the rush of tourists into Prague, small 6- to 15-room pensions are popping up everywhere. Most have small, spartan rooms—often with no plumbing at all; sinks, showers, and toilets are down the hall. Breakfast is included in the price. Some of these places take bookings no more than a month in advance. All are in the Old Town, close to the Můstek metro station.

The **Laundromat** nearest most recommended hotels is at Karoliny Svetle 10, Praha 1 (200 kč/load, 200 meters from the bridge, Mon–Sat 7:30–19:00, closed Sun).

Pension Unitas rents 34 small and tidy youth hostel–type rooms with plain, minimalist furnishings and no sinks (S-1,020 kč, D-1,200 kč, T-1,650 kč, Q-2,000 kč, T and Q are cramped with bunks in D-sized rooms, Bartolomejska 9, 11000 Praha 1, tel. 02/2421-1020, fax 02/2421-0800, www .cloister-inn.cz/unitas).

Hotel Europa is in a class by itself. This landmark place, famous for its wonderful 1903 Art Nouveau facade, is the center-piece of Wenceslas Square. But someone pulled the plug on the hotel about 50 years ago, and it's a mess. It offers haunting beauty in all the public spaces with 90 dreary, ramshackle rooms and a weary staff (S-1,300 kč, Sb-2,700 kč, D-2,600 kč, Db-4,000 kč, T-3,100 kč, Tb-5,000 kč, CC:VMA, elevator, Václavské Náměstí 25, Praha 1, tel. 02/2422-8117, fax 02/2422-4544).

Express Pension rents 24 simple rooms and serves a lousy continental breakfast (Sb-2,400 kč, D-1,800 kč, Db-2,600 kč, Tb-3,000 kč, no elevator and lots of stairs, Skorepka 5, Praha 1, tel. 02/2421-1801, fax 02/2422-3309, e-mail: express@zero.cz).

Pension U Medvidku has 22 comfortably renovated rooms in a big, rustic, medieval shell (Sb-2,265 kč, Db-3,000 kč, Tb-4,000 kč, CC:VMA, Na Perstyne 7, Praha 1, tel. 02/2421-1916, fax 02/2422-0930, www.umedvidu.cz). The pension runs a popular restaurant that has live music nightly until 23:00.

Guest House Lida, with homey and spacious rooms, fills a big house in a quiet residential area that's a 10-minute walk or five-minute tram ride from the center. Jan and Jiri Prouza, who run the place, are a wealth of information and know how to make people feel at home (Db-$55, 10 percent off Nov–March, family rooms, metro: Prazskeho Povstani, Lopatecka 26, 14700 Praha 4, tel. & fax 02/6121-4766, e-mail: lida@login.cz).

Eating in Prague

The beauty of Prague is wandering aimlessly through the winding old quarters marveling at the architecture, people watching, and sniffing out restaurants. You can eat well and for very little money. What you'd pay for a basic meal in Vienna or Munich will get you an elegant meal in Prague. Choose between traditional, dark Czech beer hall–type ambience, elegant Jugendstil turn-of-the-century atmosphere, or a hip, modern place. For traditional cuisine, wander the Old Town (Staré Město).

Traditional Czech Beer Halls near Old Town Square

Plzenska Restaurace U Dvou Kocek is a typical Czech pub with cheap, local, no-nonsense, hearty Czech food, great beer, and a local crowd (150 kč for 3 courses and beer, serving original Pilsner Urquell with accordion music nightly until 23:00, under an arcade, facing the tiny square between Perlova and Skorepka Streets, tel. 02/267-729).

U Vejvodu is a rollicking place with great Czech beer, raditional grub, and lots of brass and wood. The deeper you go, the more smoky and atmospheric it gets (150 kč dinners, 2 blocks off the Old Town Square at Jilska 4).

Restaurace U Rotta is a new pub, bright and classy but low-key traditional with good beer on tap and music nightly at 20:00 under medieval arches (daily 11:00–24:00, a block toward the bridge from Old Town Square at Male Náměstí 3, tel. 02/269-537).

Art Nouveau Restaurants

The sumptuous Art Nouveau concert hall—**Municipal House**—has three special restaurants: a café, a French restaurant, and a beer cellar (Náměstí Republiky 5). The dressy cafe, **Kavarna Obecní Dům**, is drenched in chandeliered Art Nouveau elegance (light meals, 1 hot meal special daily—200 kč, live piano 16:30–20:30; cybercafé: 40 kč/10 min). **Krancouzska Restaurant**, the fine French restaurant, is in the next wing (500-kč meals). **Plzenska Restaurant**, downstairs, brags it's the most beautiful Art Nouveau pub in Europe (cheap meals, great atmosphere, 12:00–23:00 daily).

Restaurant Mucha is touristy with decent Czech food in a formal Art Nouveau dining room (300-kč meals, daily until 24:00, Melantrichova 5, tel. 02/263-586).

Uniquely Czech Places near Old Town Square

Prices go way down when you get away from the tourist areas. At least once, eat in a restaurant with no English menu.

Restaurant U Plebana is a quiet little place with good service, Czech cuisine, and a modern yet elegant setting (daily until 24:00, Betlémské Náměstí 10, tel. 02/2222-1568).

Country Life Vegetarian Restaurant is a bright and easy cafeteria that has a well-displayed buffet of salads and veggie hot dishes in a smoke-free restaurant midway between the Old Town Square and the bottom of Wenceslas Square. They are serious about their vegetarianism, serving only plant-based, unprocessed, and unrefined food (Sun–Thu 11:00–20:30, Fri 11:00–18:00, closed Sat, through courtyard at Melantrichova 15/Michalska 18, tel. 02/2421-3366).

Czech Kitchen (Ceska Kuchyne) is a new blue-collar cafeteria serving steamy old Czech cuisine to a local clientele market. There's no English. Just pick up your tally sheet at the

door, grab a tray, and point liberally to whatever you'd like. It's
extremely cheap (daily 9:30–17:00, across from Havelská market
at Havelská 23).

37 Patro Fast Food is another super-cheap cafeteria catering
to locals. This one's actually in the Můstek metro station (downstairs under Jungmannovo Náměstí).

Czech Beer

For many, *pivo* (beer) is the top Czech tourist attraction. After
all, the Czechs invented lager in nearby Pilsen. This is the famous
Pilsner Urquell, a great lager on tap everywhere. Budvar is the local
Budweiser, but it's not related to the American brew. Czechs are
among the world's biggest beer drinkers—adults drink about 80 gallons a year. The big degree symbol on bottles and menus marks the
beer's heaviness, not its alcohol content (12 degrees is darker, 10
degrees lighter). The smaller figure shows alcohol content. Order
beer from the tap (*sudove pivo*) in either small (.3 liter, *male pivo*) or
large (.5 liter, *pivo*). In many restaurants a beer hits your table like a
glass of water in the United States. *Pivo* for lunch has me sightseeing
for the rest of the day on Czech knees. Be sure to venture beyond
the Pilsner Urquell. There are plenty of other good Czech beers.

Transportation Connections—Prague

Getting to Prague: Those with railpasses need to purchase
tickets to cover the portion of their journey from the border of
the Czech Republic to Prague (buy at station before you board
train for Prague). Or supplement your pass with a "Prague Excursion" pass, giving you passage from any Czech border station into
Prague and back to any border station within seven days. Ask about
this pass (and get reservations) at the EurAide offices in Munich or
Berlin (90 DM first class, 60 DM second class, 45 DM for youths
under 26, tel. 089/593-889). EurAide's U.S. office sells these passes
for a bit less (U.S. tel. 941/480-1555, fax 941/480-1522). Direct
trains leave Munich for Prague daily around 7:00, 14:00, and 23:00,
(5–6 hr trip). Tickets cost about 100 DM from Munich or, if you
have a railpass covering Germany, 30 DM from the border.

By train to: Berlin (5/day, 5 hrs), **Munich** (3/day, 5 hrs),
Frankfurt (3/day, 6 hrs), **Vienna** (3/day, 5 hrs), **Budapest** (6/day,
9 hrs). Train info: tel. 02/2422-4200. Czech Rail Agency: tel.
02/800-805.

By car with a driver: Mike's Chauffeur Service is a reliable
little company with fair and fixed rates around town and beyond
(round-trip fares with waiting time included: Český Krumlov-
3,500 kč, Terezin-1,700 kč, Karlštejn-1,500 kč; up to 4 people,
tel. 02/5156-5161, e-mail: mike.chauffeur@cmail.cz). On the
way to Český, Mike will stop at no extra charge at Hluboka
Castle or České Budějovice, where the original Bud beer is made.

PARIS

Paris offers sweeping boulevards, sleepy parks, world-class art galleries, chatty crepe stands, Napoleon's body, sleek shopping malls, the Eiffel Tower, and people watching from outdoor cafés. Climb the Notre-Dame and the Eiffel Tower, cruise the Seine and the Champs-Élysées, and master the Louvre and Orsay Museums. Save some after-dark energy for one of the world's most romantic cities. Many people fall in love with Paris. Some see the essentials and flee, overwhelmed by the huge city. With the proper approach and a good orientation, you'll fall head over heels for Europe's capital city.

Planning Your Time
Paris in One, Two, or Three Days

Day 1
Morning: Follow "Historic Core of Paris Walk" (see "Sights," below) featuring Île de la Cité, Notre-Dame, Latin Quarter, and Sainte-Chapelle.
Afternoon: Tour Louvre Museum.
Evening: Cruise Seine River or take illuminated Paris by Night bus tour.

Day 2
Morning: Métro to l'Arc de Triomphe and saunter down the Champs-Élysées.
Midday: Tour Orsay Museum.
Afternoon: Catch RER from Orsay to Versailles. To avoid crowds, see the park first and the palace late.
Evening: Enjoy Trocadero scene and ride up Eiffel Tower.

Daily Reminder

Monday: These museums are closed today—Orsay, Rodin, Marmottan, Montmartre, Carnavalet, and Versailles. The Louvre is especially crowded today, but the Richelieu wing stays open until 21:45. Many small stores don't open until 14:00. Some restaurants are closed today. It's discount night at most cinemas.

Tuesday: Many museums are closed today, including the Louvre, Picasso, Cluny, and Pompidou Center. The Eiffel Tower, Versailles, and the Orsay are particularly busy today.

Wednesday: All museums are open, the Louvre until 21:45. The weekly *Pariscope* magazine comes out today.

Thursday: All museums are open (the Orsay until 21:45). The Sewer Tour is closed. Department stores are open late.

Friday: All sights are open (except the Sewer Tour). Afternoon trains and roads leaving Paris are crowded; TGV reservation fees are much higher.

Saturday: All sights are open (except the Jewish Art and History Museum), and the fountains run at Versailles (July–Sept). Paris department stores are busy.

Sunday: Some museums are two-thirds price all day (Louvre, Orsay, Cluny, and Picasso). The fountains run at Versailles (early April–early Oct). Most stores are closed today, but shoppers will find relief in the lively Marais neighborhood—the Jewish Quarter—where many stores are open. Look for organ concerts at St. Sulpice and possibly other churches. The American Church usually offers a free evening concert at 18:00.

Day 3
Morning: Tour the Pompidou Center and the Jewish Art and History Museum in the Marais neighborhood.
Afternoon: Visit the Rodin Museum and nearby Napoleon's Tomb and Military Museum.
Evening: Explore Montmartre and Sacre Coeur. Or consider a romantic dinner on the Île St. Louis, near the floodlit Notre-Dame.

Orientation

Paris is split in half by the Seine River, divided into 20 *arrondissements* (proud and independent governmental jurisdictions), and circled by a ring-road freeway (the *périphérique*). You'll find Paris easier to negotiate if you know which side of the river you're on, which arrondissement you're in, and which subway (Métro) stop you're closest to. If you're north of the river (above on any city

Paris Overview

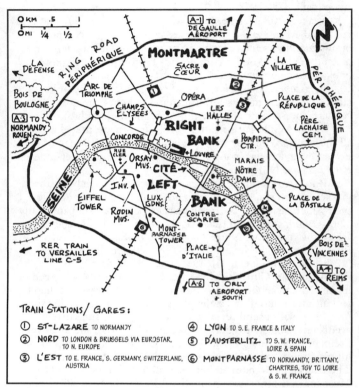

OKM .5 1
OMI ¼ ½

LA DÉFENSE

RING ROAD PÉRIPHÉRIQUE

MONTMARTRE

SACRÉ CŒUR

LA VILLETTE

A-1 TO DE GAULLE AÉROPORT

BOIS DE BOULOGNE

ARC DE TRIOMPHE

CHAMPS ELYSÉES

OPÉRA

LES HALLES

PLACE DE LA RÉPUBLIQUE

PÈRE LACHAISE CEM.

PÉRIPHÉRIQUE

A-3 TO NORMANDY ROUEN

①

②

③

CONCORDE

RIGHT BANK

RUE CLER

ORSAY MUS.

CITÉ

LEFT

INV.

SEINE

EIFFEL TOWER

RODIN MUS.

LUX. GDNS.

POMPIDOU CTR.

♦LOUVRE

MARAIS

NÔTRE DAME

BANK

CONTRE-SCARPE

PLACE DE LA BASTILLE

RER TRAIN TO VERSAILLES LINE C-5

⑥

MONT-PARNASSE TOWER

PLACE→ D'ITALIE

⑤

BOIS DE VINCENNES

A-4 TO REIMS

A-6 TO ORLY AÉROPORT + SOUTH

TRAIN STATIONS/ GARES:

① ST-LAZARE TO NORMANDY

② NORD TO LONDON & BRUSSELS VIA EUROSTAR, TO N. EUROPE

③ L'EST TO E. FRANCE, S. GERMANY, SWITZERLAND, AUSTRIA

④ LYON TO S.E. FRANCE & ITALY

⑤ D'AUSTERLITZ TO S.W. FRANCE, LOIRE & SPAIN

⑥ MONTPARNASSE TO NORMANDY, BRITTANY, CHARTRES, TGV TO LOIRE & S.W. FRANCE

map), you're on the Right Bank (*rive droite*). If you're south of it, you're on the Left Bank (*rive gauche*).

Arrondissements are numbered, starting at Notre-Dame (ground zero) and moving in a clockwise spiral out to the ring road. The last two digits in a Parisian zip code are the arrondissement number, and the notation for the Métro stop is "Mo." In Parisian jargon, Napoleon's tomb is on *la rive gauche* (the Left Bank) in the *7ème* (seventh arrondissement), zip code 75007, Mo: Invalides. Paris Métro stops are used as a standard aid in giving directions, even for those not using the Métro.

Tourist Information

Avoid the Paris tourist offices—long lines, short information, and a 5F charge for maps. This book, the *Pariscope* magazine (described below), and one of the freebie maps available at any hotel are all you need. The main TI is at 127 avenue des Champs-Élysées (daily 9:00–20:00, tel. 08 36 68 31 12), but the TIs at the Gare de Lyon (daily 8:00–20:00, tel. 01 43 43 33 24, answered by live English-speaker), Eiffel Tower (daily May–Sept 11:00–18:00), and Louvre (Wed–Mon 10:00–19:00) are less crowded. For a complete list of museum hours and scheduled English-language museum tours, pick up the free "Musées, Monuments Historiques, et Expositions" booklet from any museum.

Pariscope: The *Pariscope* weekly magazine (or one of its clones, 3F at any newsstand) lists museum hours, art exhibits, concerts, music festivals, plays, movies, and nightclubs.

Maps: While Paris is littered with free maps, they don't show all the streets. You may want the huge Michelin #10 map of Paris. For an extended stay, consider the pocket-size and street-indexed *Paris Pratique* (40F).

Bookstores: There are many English-language bookstores in Paris where you can pick up guidebooks (for nearly double their American price). A few are: Shakespeare & Company (daily 12:00–24:00, some used travel books, 37 rue de la Boucherie, across the river from Notre-Dame), W. H. Smith (248 rue de Rivoli, Mo: Concorde, tel. 01 44 77 88 99), and Brentanos (37 avenue de L'Opéra, Mo: Opéra, tel. 01 42 61 52 50).

American Church: The American Church is a nerve center for the American émigré community. It distributes a free, handy, and insightful monthly English-language newspaper, called the *Free Voice*, with useful reviews of concerts, plays, and current events (available at around 200 locations in Paris), and an advertisement paper called *France—U.S.A. Contacts*, full of helpful information for those looking for work or long-term housing. The church faces the river between the Eiffel Tower and Orsay Museum (reception open Mon–Sat 9:30–22:30, Sun 9:00–19:30, 65 quai d'Orsay, Mo: Invalides, tel. 01 40 62 05 00).

Arrival in Paris
By Train: Paris has six train stations, all connected by Métro, bus, and taxi. All have ATMs, banks or change offices, information desks, telephones, cafés, lockers (*consigne automatique*), newsstands, and clever pickpockets. Hop the Métro to your hotel (see "Getting around Paris," below).

By Plane: For detailed information on getting from Paris' airports to downtown Paris (and vice versa), see "Transportation Connections" at the end of this chapter.

Helpful Hints
Theft Alert: Use your money belt and never carry a wallet in your back pocket or a purse over your shoulder. Thieves thrive in tourist areas and the Métro (at stations and in subway cars).

Museums: Most museums offer reduced prices and shorter

hours on Sunday. Many begin closing rooms 45 minutes before
the actual closing time. For the fewest crowds, visit very early, at
lunch, or very late. The best Impressionist art museums are the
Orsay and Marmottan (another, L'Orangerie, is closed for renovation). Most museums have slightly shorter hours October
through March. French holidays can really mess up your sightseeing plans (Jan 1, May 1, May 8, July 14, Nov 1, Nov 11, and
Dec 25). See "Daily Reminder," above, for other "closed" days.

Paris Museum Pass: In Paris there are two classes of sightseers: those with a museum pass and those without. Serious sightseers save time and money by getting this pass. Sold at museums,
main Métro stations, and TIs, it pays for itself in two admissions
and gets you into sights with no lining up (1 day-80F, 3 consecutive days-160F, 5 consecutive days-240F; no discounts for kids).
Included sights (and admission prices without the pass) you're
likely to visit: Louvre (45F), Orsay (40F), Sainte-Chapelle (35F),
l'Arc de Triomphe (40F), Napoleon's Tomb (38F), Carnavalet
Museum (35F), Conciergerie (35F), Sewer Tour (25F), Cluny
Museum (38F), Pompidou Center (50F), Notre-Dame towers
(35F) and crypt (35F), Picasso Museum (30F), Rodin Museum
(28F), and the elevator to the top of the Grand Arche de la
Defense (46F). Outside Paris, the pass covers the Palace of Versailles (46F), its Grand Trianon (25F), and Château Chantilly
(43F). Notable sights not covered: Marmottan Museum, Jewish
Art and History Museum, Eiffel Tower, Montparnasse Tower,
the ladies of Pigalle, and Disneyland Paris. Tally it up—but
remember, an advantage of the pass is that you skip to the front
of the line, saving hours of waiting in the summer (though everyone must pass through the slow-moving metal-detector lines at a
few sights). With the pass, you'll pop painlessly into sights (even
for a few minutes) that you're walking by that might otherwise
not be worth the expense (e.g., Notre-Dame crypt, Cluny Museum, Conciergerie, Victor Hugo's House). The free directory that
comes with your pass lists the latest hours, phone numbers, and
prices for kids (the cutoff age for free entry varies from 5 to 18).
Most major art museums let in young people up to age 18 for free.
If you're buying a pass at a museum with a long line, skip to the
front and find the sales window.

Telephone Cards: Pick up the essential France *télécarte*
or a KOSMOS card at any *tabac* (tobacco shop), post office, or
tourist office (*une petite télécarte* is 49F; *une grande* is 98F). Smart
travelers check things by telephone. Most public phones use
télécartes (KOSMOS cards work at any phone).

Useful Telephone Numbers: American Hospital—01 46
41 25 25, American pharmacy—01 47 42 49 40 (Mo: Opéra),
Police—17, U.S. Embassy—01 43 12 22 22, Paris and France
directory assistance—12, AT&T operator—0800 99 00 11,

MCI—0800 99 00 19, Sprint—0800 99 00 87. (See appendix for additional numbers.)

Toilets: Carry small change for pay toilets, or walk into any outdoor café like you own the place and find the toilet in the back. Remember, the toilets in museums are free and generally the best you'll find. Modern super-sanitary street-booth toilets provide both relief and a memory (2F coin required, don't leave small children inside unattended).

Getting around Paris

By Métro: Europe's best subway is divided into two systems— the Métro (for puddle-jumping everywhere in Paris) and the RER (which connects suburban destinations with a few stops within central Paris). You'll be using the Métro for almost all your trips. Occasionally you'll find the RER more convenient as it makes fewer stops (like an express bus).

In Paris you're never more than a 10-minute walk from a Métro station. One ticket takes you anywhere in the system with unlimited transfers. Save 40 percent by buying a *carnet* (car-nay) of 10 tickets for 58F at any Métro station (a single ticket is 8F). Métro tickets work on city buses, though one ticket cannot be used as a transfer between subway and bus.

The *Mobilis* ticket (moh-bee-lee) allows unlimited travel for a single day on all bus and Métro lines (30F). If you're staying longer, the *Carte Orange* (pron: kart oh-rahnzh) pass gives you free run of the bus and Métro system for one week (80F, ask for the *Carte Orange Coupon Vert*, supply a photo) or a month (280F, ask for the *Carte Orange Coupon Orange*, supply a photo). These pass prices cover only central Paris; you can pay more for passes covering regional destinations (e.g., Versailles).

The weekly pass begins Monday and ends Sunday, and the monthly pass begins the first day of the month and ends the last day of that month, so midweek or midmonth purchases are generally not worthwhile. The passes are officially only for Parisian residents. While the purchase of these passes by tourists is rarely an issue, be aware that a ticket seller might refuse to sell you this pass. In this case you have three options: (1) Tell them you are living in Paris for a temporary period; (2) Go to another station to buy your pass; (3) Use carnets of 10 tickets instead. All passes can be purchased at any Métro station (most have photo booths).

To get to your destination, determine which "Mo" stop is closest to it and which line or lines will get you there. The lines have numbers, but they're best known by their direction or end-of-the-line stop. (For example, the La Défense/Château de Vincennes line runs between La Défense in the west and Vincennes in the east.)

Once in the Métro station, you'll see blue-and-white signs directing you to the train going in your direction

Paris

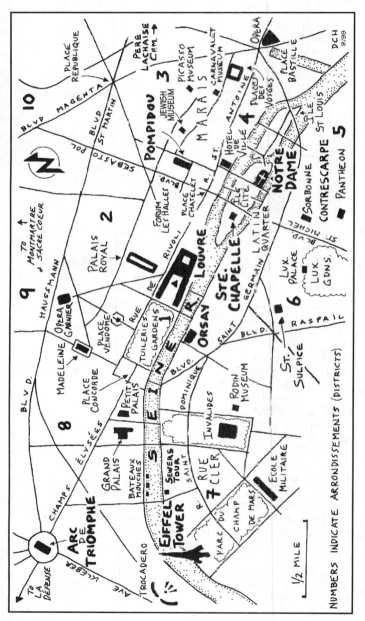

NUMBERS INDICATE ARRONDISSEMENTS (DISTRICTS)

1/2 MILE

Key Words for the Métro and RER

- *direction* (dee-rek-see-ohn): direction
- *ligne* (lean-yuh): line
- *correspondance* (kor-res-pohn-dahns): transfer
- *sortie* (sor-tee): exit
- *carnet* (kar-nay): cheap set of 10 tickets
- *Pardon, madame/monsieur* (par-dohn, mah-dahm/mes-yur): Excuse me, lady/bud.
- *Je descend* (juh day-sahn): I'm getting off.
- *Donnez-moi mon porte-monnaie!*: Give me back my wallet!

Etiquette

- When waiting at the platform, get out of the way of those exiting their train. Board only once everyone is off.
- Avoid using the hinged seats when the car is jammed; they take up valuable standing space.
- When in a crowded train, try not to block the exit. If you're blocking the door when the train stops, step out of the car and to the side, let others off, then get back on.
- Talk softly in the cars. Listen to how quietly Parisians can communicate and follow their lead.
- On escalators, stand on the right, pass on the left.

(e.g., "direction: La Défense"). Insert your ticket in the automatic turnstile, pass through, and reclaim and keep your ticket until you exit the system. Fare inspectors regularly check for cheaters and accept absolutely no excuses from anyone. I repeat, keep that ticket until you leave the Métro system.

Transfers are free and can be made wherever lines cross. When you transfer, look for the orange *correspondance* (connections) signs when you exit your first train, then follow the proper direction sign.

Before you *sortie* (exit), check the helpful *plan du quartier* (map of the neighborhood) to get your bearings, locate your destination, and decide which *sortie* you want. At stops with several *sorties*, you can save lots of walking by choosing the best exit.

Thieves spend their days in the Métro. Be on guard. For example, a pocket picked as you pass through a turnstile leaves you on the wrong side and the thief strolling away. Any jostle or commotion (especially when boarding or leaving trains) is likely the sign of a thief or team of thieves in action.

Paris has a huge homeless population and over 11 percent unemployment; expect a warm Métro welcome by panhandlers, musicians, and those selling magazines produced by the homeless community.

By RER: The RER (Réseau Express Régionale, air-ay-air) is the suburban train system, indicated by thick lines on your subway map and identified by letters A, B, C, and so on. The RER works like the Métro but can be speedier (if it serves your destination directly) because it makes only a few stops within the city. One Métro ticket is all you need for RER rides within central Paris. You can transfer between the Métro and RER systems with the same ticket. Unlike the Métro, you need to insert your ticket in a turnstile to exit the RER system. To travel outside the city (to Versailles or the airport, for example), you'll need to buy a separate, more expensive ticket at the station window before boarding. Make sure your stop is served by checking the signs over the train platform (not all trains serve all stops).

By City Bus: The trickier bus system is worth figuring out. Métro tickets are good on both bus and Métro, though you can't use the same ticket to transfer between the two systems. One ticket gets you anywhere in central Paris, but if you leave the city center (shown as section 1 on the diagram onboard the bus), you must validate a second ticket. While the Métro shuts down about 00:30, some buses continue much later. Schedules are posted at bus stops. Handy bus-system maps (*plan des autobus*) are available in any Métro station and are provided in your *Paris Pratique* map book if you invest (40F).

Big system maps, posted at each bus and Métro stop, display the routes. Individual route diagrams show the exact routes of the lines serving that stop. Major stops are painted on the side of each bus. Enter through the front doors. Punch your Métro ticket in the machine behind the driver, or pay the higher cash fare. Get off the bus using the rear door. Even if you're not certain you've figured it out, do some joyriding (outside of rush hour). Lines #24, #63, and #69 are Paris' most scenic routes and make a great introduction to the city. Bus #69 is particularly handy, running between the Eiffel Tower, rue Cler (recommended hotels), Orsay, Louvre, Marais (recommended hotels), and Père Lachaise Cemetery. The most handy bus routes are listed for each hotel area recommended (see "Sleeping," near end of chapter).

By Taxi: Parisian taxis are almost reasonable. A 10-minute ride costs about 50F (versus 5.50F to get anywhere in town on the Métro). You can try waving one down (a glowing white light on the roof means it's free, an orange light means occupied), but it's easier to ask for the nearest taxi stand (*Où est une station de taxi?*; oo ay oon stah-see-ohn duh taxi) or ask your hotel to call for you. Higher rates are charged at night from 19:00 to 7:00, all day Sunday, and to either airport. There's a 6F charge for each piece of baggage. A 3- to 5F-tip is generally plenty. If you call from your hotel, the meter starts as soon as the call is received. Taxis are tough to find on Friday and Saturday night, especially after the

Métro closes (around 00:30). If you need a taxi for a morning trip to the airport or train station, consider booking the night before.

By Foot: Be careful! Parisian drivers are notorious for ignoring pedestrians. Never assume you have the right of way, even in a crosswalk. When crossing a street, keep your pace constant and don't stop suddenly. Drivers carefully calculate your speed and will miss you, providing you don't alter your route or pace.

Organized Tours of Paris

Bus Tours: Paris Vision offers handy bus tours of Paris, day and night (advertised in hotel lobbies); their "Illuminated Paris" tour is far more interesting (see "Nightlife in Paris," below). A better daytime bus tour is the hop-on hop-off double-decker bus service called **Open Deck Tours**, offering three different routes covering most of the important sights in Paris (the Paris Grand Tour is the best to start with). Use these buses to connect the major sights (with a running commentary) and get a good city-orientation tour at the same time. Expect to wait 15 to 20 minutes for a bus at each stop. Buy your tickets from the driver (135F/one day, 150F/two days, 2 buses/hrly about 10:00–18:00, you can hop off at various sights then catch a later bus). You'll see these bright yellow topless double-decker buses all over town—pick one up at the first important sight you visit, or start your tour at the Eiffel Tower stop (the first street on the non-river side of the tower).

Boat Tours: Several companies offer one-hour boat cruises on the Seine (by far best at night; see "Nightlife in Paris," below). The huge, mass-production **Bâteaux-Mouches** boats depart every 30 minutes from Pont de l'Alma's right bank and are convenient to rue Cler hotels (40F, 20F under 14, daily 10:00–23:00, useless taped explanations in 6 languages and tour groups by the dozens, tel. 01 42 25 96 10). The much smaller and more intimate **Vedettes de Pont Neuf** boats depart only once an hour from the center of the Pont Neuf but come with a live guide giving explanations in French and English only and are convenient to Marais and Contrescarpe hotels (50F, 25F under age 14, tel. 01 46 33 98 38). From April to October, **Bâteau-Bus** operates boats on the Seine, connecting six key stops about every 25 minutes: Eiffel Tower, Orsay/place de la Concorde, Louvre, Notre-Dame, Hôtel de Ville, and St. Germain-des-Près. Pick up their schedule at any stop (or TI) and use them as a scenic alternative to the Métro. Tickets are available for single trips (20F), one day (60F), and two days (90F). Boats run from 10:00 to 19:00, until 22:00 in summer. **Paris Canal** boats depart twice daily for three-hour cruises between the Orsay and the Parc de la Vilette. You'll cruise up the Seine then along a quiet canal through untouristed Paris, accompanied by English explanations (100F-adults, 75F-ages 12–25, 55F-ages 4–11, one-way departures from the Orsay at 9:30 and from Parc de la Vilette at 14:30, tel. 01 42 40 96 97).

Walking Tours: Paris Walking Tours offers a variety of excellent two-hour walks nearly daily for 60F (tel. 01 48 09 21 40, fax 01 42 43 75 51, www.pariswalkingtours.com). They focus on the Marais, Luxembourg Gardens, Opéra Garnier, Montmartre, and Hemingway's Paris. Call a day or two ahead to learn their schedule and starting point. No reservations are required. These are thoughtfully prepared, humorous, and relaxing walking tours led by British or American guides. Don't hesitate to stand close to the guide to hear. For Lost Generation fans, **Paris Literary Promenades** takes you through areas once popular with literary giants from Joyce to Beckett to Hemingway (60F, 2 hrs, late May–mid-Oct, tours depart from place de l'Odeon daily except Wed at 14:30 and 19:00, tel. 01 48 07 80 72 or cellular 06 03 27 73 52). You can also hire a Parisian as your personal guide. Arnaud Servignat (tel. 01 42 57 03 35, fax 01 42 62 68 62, e-mail: arnotour@noos.fr) and Marianne Siegler (tel. 01 42 52 32 51) are licensed local guides who freelance for individuals and families ($150/4 hrs, $250/day).

Bike Tours: Bullfrog Bike Tours will show you Paris on two wheels at a relaxed pace (120F, 3–4-hr tours in English May–mid-Sept 11:00 and 15:30, no bikes or reservations needed, meet at fountain on avenue Joseph, 100 meters from Eiffel Tower in Champ de Mars park, ask about new evening tours, cellular 06 09 98 08 60, http://BullfrogBikes.com).

Sights—The "Historic Core of Paris" Walk

(This information is distilled from the Historic Paris Walk chapter in *Rick Steves' Mona Winks*, by Gene Openshaw and Rick Steves.)

Allow four hours for this self-guided tour, including sight-seeing. Start where the city did—on the Île de la Cité. Face Notre-Dame and follow the dotted line on the "Core of Paris" map (within this chapter). To get to Notre-Dame, ride the Métro to Cité, Hôtel de Ville, or St. Michel and walk to the big square facing the...

▲▲**Notre-Dame Cathedral**—This 700-year-old cathedral is packed with history and tourists. Study its sculpture and windows, take in a Mass, eavesdrop on guides, and walk all around the outside (free, daily 8:00–18:45, 15F for treasury open daily 9:30–17:30, free English tours normally Wed and Thu at 12:00 and Sat at 14:30, Sun masses at 8:00, 8:45, 10:00, 11:30, 12:30, and 18:30). Climb to the top for a great view of the city; you get 400 steps for only 35F (entrance outside, north tower open 9:30–17:30, closed at lunch and earlier off-season). There are clean 2.70F toilets in front of the church near Charlemagne's statue.

The **cathedral facade** is worth a close look. The church is dedicated to "Our Lady" (Notre-Dame). Mary is center stage,

Core of Paris

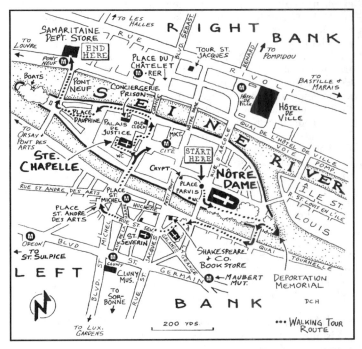

cradling Jesus, surrounded by the halo of the rose window. Adam is on the left and Eve is on the right.

Below Mary and above the arches is a row of 28 statues known as the Kings of Judah. During the French Revolution, these Biblical kings were mistaken for the hated French kings. The citizens stormed the church, crying, "Off with their heads!" All were decapitated but have since been recapitated.

Speaking of decapitation, look at the carving above the doorway on the left. The man with his head in his hands is St. Denis. Back when there was a Roman temple on this spot, Christianity began making converts. The fourth-century bishop of Roman Paris, Denis, was beheaded. But these early Christians were hard to keep down. The man who would become St. Denis got up, tucked his head under his arm, and headed north until he found just the right place to meet his maker: Montmartre, which means "mountain of the martyr." The Parisians were convinced of this miracle, Christianity gained ground, and a church soon replaced the pagan temple.

Medieval art was OK if it embellished the house of God and told Bible stories. For a fine example, move to the base of the central column (at the foot of Mary, about where the head of St. Denis could spit if he was real good). Working around from the left, find God telling a barely created Eve, "Have fun but no apples." Next, the sexiest serpent I've ever seen makes apples à la mode. Finally, Adam and Eve, now ashamed of their nakedness, are expelled by an angel. This is a tiny example in a church covered with meaning.

Now move to the right and study the carving above the **central portal**. It's the end of the world, and Christ sits on the throne of Judgment (just under the arches, holding his hands up). Below him an angel and a demon weigh souls in the balance. The "good" stand to the left, looking up to heaven. The "bad" ones to the right are chained up and led off to ... Versailles on a Tuesday. The "ugly" ones must be the crazy sculpted demons to the right, at the base of the arch.

Wander through the interior. You'll be routed around the ambulatory, much as medieval pilgrims would have been. Don't miss the rose windows filling each of the transepts. Back outside, walk around the church through the park on the riverside for a close look at the flying buttresses.

The neo-Gothic 90-meter **spire** is a product of the 1860 reconstruction. Around its base are apostles and evangelists (the green men) as well as Viollet-le-Duc, the architect in charge of the work. Notice how the apostles look outward, blessing the city, while the architect (at top, seen from behind the church) looks up, admiring his spire.

The archaeological **crypt** is a worthwhile 15-minute stop with your museum pass (35F, 50F with Notre-Dame's tower, daily 10:00–18:00, closes at 17:00 Oct–April, enter 100 meters in front of church). You'll see Roman ruins, trace the street plan of the medieval village, and see diagrams of how the earliest Paris grew and grew, all thoughtfully explained in English.

If you're hungry near Notre-Dame, the nearby Île St. Louis has inexpensive *crêperies* and grocery stores open daily on its main drag. Plan a picnic for the quiet bench-filled park immediately behind the church (public WC).

Behind Notre-Dame, squeeze through the tourist buses, cross the street, and enter the iron gate into the park at the tip of the island. Look for the stairs and head down.

▲▲**Deportation Memorial (Mémorial de la Déportation)**— This memorial to the 200,000 French victims of the Nazi concentration camps draws you into their experience. As you descend the steps, the city around you disappears. Surrounded by walls, you have become a prisoner. Your only freedom is your view of the sky and the tantalizing glimpse of the river below.

Enter the single-file chamber ahead. Inside, the circular plaque in the floor reads, "They descended into the mouth of the earth and they did not return." A hallway stretches in front of you, lined with 200,000 lighted crystals, one for each French citizen that died. Flickering at the far end is the eternal flame of hope. The tomb of the unknown deportee lies at your feet. Above, the inscription reads, "Dedicated to the living memory of the 200,000 French deportees sleeping in the night and the fog, exterminated in the Nazi concentration camps."

Above the exit as you leave is the message you'll find at all Nazi sights: "Forgive but never forget." (Free, Mon–Fri 8:30–21:45, Sat–Sun and holidays from 9:00, sometimes closes 12:00–14:00, shorter hours off-season, east tip of the island near Île St. Louis, behind Notre-Dame, Mo: Cité.)

Île St. Louis—Look across the river to the Île St. Louis. If the Île de la Cité is a tug laden with the history of Paris, it's towing this classy little residential dinghy laden only with boutiques, famous sorbet shops, and restaurants (see "Eating in Paris," below). This island wasn't developed until much later (18th century). What was a swampy mess is now harmonious Parisian architecture. The pedestrian bridge, Pont Saint Louis, connects the two islands, leading right to rue Saint Louis en l'Île. This spine of the island is lined with interesting shops. A short stroll takes you to the famous Bertillon ice-cream parlour (#31). Loop back to the pedestrian bridge along the parklike quays (walk north to the river and turn left). This walk is about as peaceful and romantic as Paris gets.

Before walking to the opposite end of the Île de la Cité, loop through the Latin Quarter (as indicated on the map). From the Deportation Memorial cross the bridge onto the Left Bank and enjoy the riverside view of the Notre-Dame and window shop among the green book stalls, browsing through used books, vintage posters, and souvenirs. At the little park and church (over the bridge from the front of Notre-Dame), venture inland a few blocks, basically arcing through the Latin Quarter and returning to the island two bridges down at place St. Michel.

▲**Latin Quarter**—This area, which gets its name from the language used here when it was an exclusive medieval university district, lies between the Luxembourg Gardens and the Seine, centering around the Sorbonne University and boulevards St. Germain and St. Michel. This is the core of the Left Bank—it's crowded with international eateries, far-out bookshops, street singers, and jazz clubs. For colorful wandering and café sitting, afternoons and evenings are best (Mo: St. Michel).

Along rue Saint-Severin you can still see the shadow of the medieval sewer system (the street slopes into a central channel of bricks). In the days before plumbing and toilets, when people still went to the river or neighborhood wells for their water, "flushing" meant throwing it out the window. Certain times of day were flushing times. Maids on the fourth floor would holler "*Garde de l'eau!*" ("Look out for the water!") and heave it into the streets, where it would eventually be washed down into the Seine.

Consider a visit to the Cluny Museum for its medieval art and unicorn tapestries (listed under "Sights—Southeast Paris," below).

Place St. Michel (facing the St. Michel bridge) is the traditional core of the Left Bank's artsy, liberal, hippie, Bohemian district of poets, philosophers, winos, and tourists. In less-commercial times, place St. Michel was a gathering point for the city's malcontents and misfits. Here, in 1871, the citizens took the streets from the government troops, set up barricades *Les Mis*–style, and established the Paris Commune. In World War II the locals rose up against their Nazi oppressors (read the plaques by the St. Michel fountain). And in the spring of 1968, a time of social upheaval all over the world, young students—battling riot batons and tear gas—took over the square and demanded change.

From place St. Michel, look across the river and find the spire of Sainte-Chapelle church and its weathervane angel (below). Cross the river on the Pont St. Michel and continue along boulevard du Palais. On your left you'll see the high-security doorway to Sainte-Chapelle. But first, carry on another 30 meters and turn right at a wide pedestrian street, the rue de Lutece.

Cité "Métropolitain" Stop—Of the 141 original turn-of-the-19th-century subway entrances, this is one of 17 survivors now preserved as a national art treasure. The curvy, plantlike iron work is a textbook example of Art Nouveau, the style that rebelled against the erector-set squareness of the Industrial Age (e.g., Mr. Eiffel's tower).

The flower market right here on place Louis Lepine is a pleasant detour. On Sundays this square chirps with a busy bird market. And across the way is the Prefecture de Police, where Inspector Clouseau of *Pink Panther* fame used to work and where the local resistance fighters took the first building from the Nazis in August 1944, leading to the Allied liberation of Paris a week later.

Pause here to admire the view. Sainte-Chapelle is a pearl in an ugly architectural oyster, part of a complex of buildings that includes the Palace of Justice (to the right of Sainte-Chapelle, behind the fancy gates). Return to the entrance of Sainte-Chapelle. You'll need to pass through a metal detector to get in. Free toilets are ahead on the left. The line into the church may be long. (Museum-card holders can go directly in; pick up the excellent English info sheet.) Enter the humble ground floor of . . .

▲▲▲Sainte-Chapelle—The triumph of Gothic church architecture is a cathedral of glass like no other. It was speedily built from 1242 to 1248 for St. Louis IX (France's only canonized king) to house the supposed Crown of Thorns. Its architectural harmony is due to the fact that it was completed under the direction of one architect in only six years—unheard of in Gothic times. (Notre-Dame took more than 200 years to build.)

The design clearly shows an Old Regime approach to worship. The basement was for staff and other common folk. Royal Christians worshiped upstairs. The ground-floor paint job, a 19th-century restoration, is a reasonably accurate copy of the original.

Climb the spiral staircase to the **Chapelle Haute**. Fill the place with choral music, crank up the sunshine, face the top of the altar, and really believe that the Crown of Thorns was there, and this becomes one awesome space.

"Let there be light." In the Bible, it's clear: Light is divine. Light shining through stained glass was a symbol of God's grace shining down to earth. Gothic architects used their new technology to turn dark stone buildings into lanterns of light. The glory of Gothic shines brighter here than in any other church.

There are 15 separate panels of stained glass (6,500 square feet—two-thirds of it 13th-century original), with more than 1,100 different scenes, mostly from the Bible. In medieval times, scenes like these helped teach Bible stories to the illiterate.

The altar was raised up high to better display the relic—the Crown of Thorns—around which this chapel was built. The supposed crown cost King Louis three times as much as this church. Today it is kept in the Notre-Dame Treasury and shown only on Good Friday.

Louis' little private viewing window is in the wall to the right of the altar. Louis, both saintly and shy, liked to go to church without dealing with the rigors of public royal life. Here he could worship still dressed in his jammies.

Lay your camera on the ground and shoot the ceiling. Those ribs growing out of the slender columns are the essence of Gothic.

Books in the gift shop explain the stained glass in English. There are concerts (120F) almost every summer evening (35F, daily 9:30–18:00, off-season 10:00–16:30, call 01 48 01 91 35 for concert information, Mo: Cité).

Palais du Justice—Back outside, as you walk around the church exterior, look down and notice how much Paris has risen in the 800 years since Sainte-Chapelle was built. You're in a huge complex of buildings that has housed the local government since ancient Roman times. It was the site of the original Gothic palace of the early kings of France. The only surviving medieval parts are the Sainte-Chapelle church and the Conciergerie prison.

Most of the site is now covered by the giant Palais de Justice, home of France's supreme court (built in 1776). "Liberté, Egalité, Fraternité" over the doors is a reminder that this was also the headquarters of the revolutionary government.

Now pass through the big iron gate to the noisy boulevard du Palais and turn left (toward the Right Bank). On the corner is the site of the oldest public clock (built in 1334) in the city. While the present clock is said to be Baroque, it somehow still manages to keep accurate time.

Turn left onto quai de l'Horologe and walk along the river. The round medieval tower just ahead marks the entrance to the Conciergerie. Pop in to visit the courtyard and lobby (free). Step past the serious-looking guard into the courtyard.

Conciergerie—The Conciergerie, a former prison, is a gloomy place. Kings used it to torture and execute failed assassins. The leaders of the Revolution put it to similar good use. The tower next to the entrance, called "the babbler," was named for the painful sounds that leaked from it.

Look at the stark lettering above the doorways. This was a no-nonsense revolutionary time. Everything, even lettering, was subjected to the test of reason. No frills or we chop 'em off.

Step inside; the lobby, with an English-language history display, is free. Marie Antoinette was imprisoned here. During a busy eight-month period in the Revolution, she was one of 2,600 prisoners kept here on the way to the guillotine. The interior, with its huge vaulted and pillared rooms, echoes with history but is pretty barren (35F, daily 9:30–18:30, 10:00–17:00 in winter, good English descriptions). You can see Marie Antoinette's cell, housing a collection of her mementos. In another room, a list of those made "a foot shorter at the top" by the "national razor" includes ex-King Louis XVI, Charlotte Corday (who murdered Marat in his bathtub), and the chief revolutionary who got a taste of his own medicine, Maximilien Robespierre.

Back outside, wink at the flak-proof vested guard, fake right, and turn left. Listen for babbles and continue your walk along the river. Across the river you can see the rooftop observatory—flags flapping—of the Samaritaine department store, where this walk will end. At the first corner, veer left past France's supreme-court building and into a sleepy triangular square called place Dauphine. Marvel at how such quaintness could be lodged in the midst of such greatness as you walk through the park to the end of the island. At the equestrian statue of Henry IV, turn right onto the bridge and take refuge in one of the nooks on the Eiffel Tower side.

Pont Neuf—This "new bridge" is now Paris' oldest. Built during Henry IV's reign (around 1600), its 12 arches span the widest part of the river. The fine view includes the park on the tip of the island (note Seine tour boats), the Orsay Museum, and the Louvre. These turrets were originally for vendors and street entertainers. In the days of Henry IV, who originated the promise of "a chicken in every pot," this would have been a lively scene.

Directly over the river, the first building you'll hit on the Right Bank is the venerable old department store, Samaritaine.

▲**Samaritaine Department Store Viewpoint**—Enter the store

and go to the rooftop. Ride the glass elevator from near the Pont Neuf entrance to the ninth floor (you'll be greeted by a WC—check out the sink). Pass the 10th-floor *terrasse* for the 11th-floor panorama (tight spiral staircase; watch your head). Quiz yourself. Working counterclockwise, find the Eiffel Tower, Invalides/ Napoleon's Tomb, Montparnasse Tower, Henry IV statue on the tip of the island, Sorbonne University, the dome of the Panthéon, Sainte-Chapelle, Notre-Dame, Hôtel de Ville (city hall), Pompidou Center, Sacré-Coeur, Opéra, and Louvre. The Champs-Élysées leads to the Arc de Triomphe. Shadowing that—even bigger, while two times as distant—is the Grand Arche de la Défense. You'll find light, reasonably priced, and incredibly scenic meals on the breezy terrace and a supermarket in the basement. (Rooftop view is free, daily 9:30–19:00, Mo: Pont Neuf, tel. 01 40 41 20 20.)

Sights—Paris' Museums near the Tuileries Gardens

The newly renovated Tuileries Gardens was once private property of kings and queens. Paris' grandest public park links these museums.

▲▲▲**Louvre**—This is Europe's oldest, biggest, greatest, and maybe most-crowded museum. There is no grander entry than through the pyramid, but metal detectors create a long line at times. To avoid the line, you have two choices. Museum-pass holders can use the group entrance in the pedestrian passageway between the pyramid and rue de Rivoli (facing the pyramid with your back to the Tuileries Gardens, go to your left, which is north; under the arches you'll find the entrance and escalator down). Or anyone can get into the Louvre from the slick under-ground shopping mall that connects with the museum; enter the mall either at 99 rue de Rivoli at the door with the red awning or get off the Métro at the "Palais Royal Musée du Louvre" stop and follow signs to "Musée du Louvre" (don't get off at the "Louvre Rivoli" Métro stop, which is farther away).

Pick up the free "Louvre Handbook" in English at the infor-mation desk under the pyramid as you enter. Don't try to cover the entire museum. The 90-minute English-language tours, which leave six times daily except Sunday, boil this overwhelming museum down to size (35F, tour tel. 01 40 20 52 09). Clever 30F digital audioguides (after ticket booths, at top of stairs) give you a receiver and a directory of about 130 masterpieces, allowing you to dial a (rather dull) commentary on included works as you stumble upon them. Rick Steves' and Gene Openshaw's museum guidebook, *Rick Steves' Mona Winks* (buy in United States), includes a self-guided tour of the Louvre.

If you can't get a guide, start in the Denon wing and visit these **highlights**, in this order: Michelangelo's *Slaves*, Ancient

Paris Museums near Tuileries Gardens

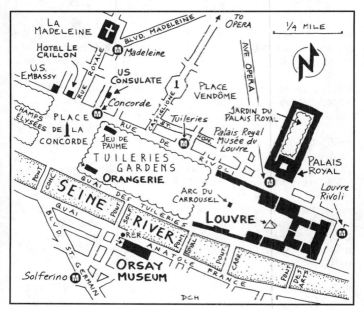

Greek and Roman works (Parthenon frieze, *Venus de Milo*,
Pompeii mosaics, Etruscan sarcophagi, Roman portrait busts,
Nike of Samothrace); Apollo Gallery (jewels); French and Italian
paintings in the Grande Galerie (a quarter-mile long and worth
the hike); the *Mona Lisa* and her Italian Renaissance roommates;
the nearby neoclassical collection (*Coronation of Napoleon*); and
the Romantic collection, with works by Delacroix (*Liberty at the
Barricades*) and Géricault (*Raft of the Medusa*).

Cost: 45F, 26F after 15:00 and on Sunday, those under 18
enter free; free on first Sunday of the month. Tickets good all
day. Reentry allowed.

Hours: Wednesday through Monday 9:00 to 18:00, closed
Tuesday, all wings open Wednesday until 21:45, Richelieu Wing
open until 21:45 on Monday. Galleries start closing 30 minutes
early. Closed January 1, Easter, May 1, November 1, and Christmas
Day. Crowds are worst on Sunday, Monday, Wednesday, and mornings. Save money by visiting after 15:00. (You can enter the pyramid
for free until 21:30. Go in at night and see it glow.) Tel. 01 40 20 51
51 or 01 40 20 53 17 for recorded information (www.louvre.fr).

The newly renovated Richelieu wing and the underground
shopping-mall extension add the finishing touches to Le Grand
Louvre Project (which started in 1989 with the pyramid entrance).

To explore this most recent extension of the Louvre, enter through the pyramid, walk toward the inverted pyramid, and uncover a post office, a handy TI and SNCF office, glittering boutiques and a dizzying assortment of good-value eateries (up the escalator), and the Palais-Royal Métro entrance. Stairs at the far end take you right into the Tuileries Gardens, a perfect antidote to the stuffy, crowded rooms of the Louvre.

Jeu de Paume—This one-time home to the Impressionist art collection (now located in the Musée d'Orsay) hosts rotating exhibits of top contemporary artists (38F, not covered by museum pass, Tue 12:00–21:30, Wed–Fri 12:00–19:00, Sat–Sun 10:00–19:00, closed Mon, on place de la Concorde, just inside Tuileries Gardens on the rue de Rivoli side, Mo: Concorde).

L'Orangerie—Closed for renovation until 2002.

▲▲▲**Orsay Museum**—Paris' 19th-century art museum (actually, art from 1848–1914) includes Europe's greatest collection of Impressionist works. The museum is housed in a former train station (Gare d'Orsay) across the river and 10 minutes downstream from the Louvre. (The RER-C train line zips you right to "Musée d'Orsay;" the Métro stop Solferino is three blocks south of the Orsay.)

Start on the ground floor. The "pretty" conservative-establishment art is on the right. Then cross left into the brutally truthful and, at that time, very shocking art of the realist rebels and Manet. Then ride the escalators at the far end (detouring at the top for a grand museum view) to the series of Impressionist rooms (Monet, Renoir, Dégas, et al). Don't miss the Grand Ballroom (room 52, Arts et Decors de la IIIème République) and Art Nouveau on the mezzanine level.

Cost: 40F, 30F on Sun and for people ages 18 to 25 or over 60, free for those under 18 and for anyone first Sun of month; tickets good all day. The booth near the entrance gives free floor plans in English. English-language tours usually run daily except Sunday at 11:30, cost 36F, take 90 minutes, and are also available on audio-guide (30F). Paris museum passes are sold in the basement; if there's a long line you can skip it by buying one there, but you can't skip the metal-detector line into the museum. Tel. 01 40 49 48 48.

Hours: Tuesday through Saturday 10:00 to 18:00, Thursday until 21:45, Sunday 9:00 to 18:00, closed Monday. The museum opens at 9:00 June 20 through September 20. Last entrance is 45 minutes before closing. Galleries start closing 30 minutes early. The Orsay is very crowded on Tuesday, when the Louvre is closed.

Sights—Southwest Paris: The Eiffel Tower Neighborhood

▲▲▲**Eiffel Tower**—It's crowded and expensive but worth the trouble. Go early (arrive by 9:15) or late in the day (after 18:00)

The Eiffel Tower Neighborhood

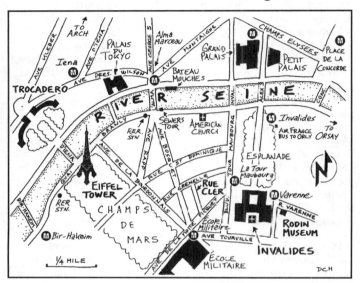

to avoid most crowds. Weekends are worst. Pilier Nord (the north pillar) has the biggest elevator and, therefore, the fastest-moving line. The stairs (yes, you can walk up) are next to the Jules Verne restaurant entry.

It's 1,000 feet tall (6 inches taller in hot weather), covers two and one-half acres, and requires 50 tons of paint. The tower's 7,000 tons of metal are spread out so well at the base that it's no heavier per square inch than a linebacker on tiptoes. Visitors to Paris may find *Mona Lisa* to be less than expected, but the Eiffel Tower rarely disappoints, even in an era of skyscrapers.

Built a hundred years after the French Revolution (and in the midst of an industrial one), the tower served no function but to impress. Gustave Eiffel won an architectural contest at the 1889 centennial world's fair by beating out such rival proposals as a giant guillotine. To a generation hooked on technology, the tower was the marvel of the age, a symbol of progress and of man's ingenuity. To others it was a cloned-sheep monstrosity. The writer de Maupassant routinely ate lunch in the tower just so he wouldn't have to look at it.

Delicate and graceful when seen from afar, it's massive—even a bit scary—from close up. You don't appreciate the size until you walk toward it—like a mountain, it seems so close but takes forever to reach. There are three observation platforms, at 200, 400, and 900 feet. The higher you go the more you pay. Each requires a

separate elevator (and a line), so plan on at least 90 minutes
if you want to go to the top and back. The view from the 400-
foot-high second level is plenty. Begin at the first floor, read the
informative signs (in English) describing the major monuments,
see the entertaining free movie on the history of the tower, and
consider a drink overlooking all of Paris at the café or at Paris'
best view/bar restaurant, Altitude 95 (260F meals, seatings at 19:00 and
21:00, reserve well ahead for a view table, tel. 01 45 55 20 04).
Take the elevator to the second floor for even greater views. As you
ascend through the metal beams, imagine being a worker, perched
high above nothing, riveting this giant erector set together.

On top you can see all of Paris, aided by a panorama guide.
On a good day you can see 40 miles. It costs 22F to go to the first
level, 44F to the second, and 62F to go all the way for the 1,000-
foot view (not included with museum pass). On a budget? You can
climb the stairs to the second level for only 18F (summers daily
9:00–24:00, off-season 9:30–23:00, tel. 01 44 11 23 23, Mo:
Trocadero, RER: Champs de Mars, tel. 01 44 11 23 23).

For a great view, especially at night, enjoy the tower—and the
wild in-line-skating scene on Trocadero square—by approaching via
the Trocadero Métro stop (from here the tower is a 10-min walk
north, across the river). Another super view is from the long, grassy
fields of the Champs du Mars (to the south). After about 21:00 the
gendarmes look the other way as Parisians stretch out or picnic on
the grass. However impressive it may be by day, it's an awesome
thing to see at twilight, when the tower becomes engorged with
light and virile Paris lies back and lets night be on top.

▲**Paris Sewer Tour (Égouts)**—This quick and easy visit takes
you along a few hundred meters of underground water tunnel lined
with interesting displays, well described in English, explaining the
evolution of the world's longest sewer system. (If you lined up Paris'
sewers they would reach beyond Istanbul.) Don't miss the slideshow,
the fine WCs just beyond the gift shop, and the occasional tours in
English (25F, Sat–Wed 11:00–17:00, closed Thu–Fri, where the
Pont de l'Alma hits the Left Bank, tel. 01 47 05 10 29).

▲▲**Napoleon's Tomb and Army Museum (Les Invalides)**—
The emperor lies majestically dead inside several coffins under a
grand dome—a goose-bumping pilgrimage for historians. Napoleon
is surrounded by the tombs of other French war heroes and a fine
military museum in Hôtel des Invalides (check out the new WWII
wing). Follow signs to the "crypt" to find Roman Empire–style
reliefs listing the accomplishments of Napoleon's administration.
The restored dome glitters with 26 pounds of gold (38F, students
and kids 12–17 pay 28F, under 12-free, daily 10:00–17:45, closes
off-season at 16:45, tel. 01 44 42 37 67, Métros: La Tour Maubourg
or Varennes).

▲▲**Rodin Museum**—This user-friendly museum is filled with

passionate works by the greatest sculptor since Michelangelo. See *The Kiss*, *The Thinker*, *The Gates of Hell*, and many more. Don't miss the room full of work by Rodin's student and mistress, Camille Claudel (28F, 18F on Sun, free for those under 18 and for anyone first Sun of month; 5F for gardens only, which may be Paris' best deal, as many works are well displayed in the beautiful gardens; Tue–Sun 9:30–17:45, closed Mon and at 17:00 off-season, 77 rue de Varennes, Mo: Varennes, near Napoleon's Tomb, tel. 01 44 18 61 10). There's a good self-serve cafeteria as well as idyllic picnic spots in the family-friendly back garden.

▲▲**Marmottan**—In this private, intimate, less-visited museum you'll find more than 100 paintings by Claude Monet (thanks to his son Michel), including the *Impressions of a Sunrise* painting that gave the movement its start—and name (40F, not covered by museum pass, Tue–Sun 10:00–17:30, closed Mon, 2 rue Louis Boilly, Mo: La Muette, follow the museum signs 6 blocks through a park to the museum, tel. 01 42 24 07 02). Combine this fine museum with a stroll down one of Paris' most pleasant shopping streets, the rue de Passy (from la Muette Mo. stop).

Sights—Southeast Paris: The Latin Quarter

▲**Latin Quarter**—This Left Bank neighborhood just opposite the Notre-Dame is the Latin Quarter. (For more information and a walking tour, see "Historic Core of Paris Walk," above.) This was a center of Roman Paris. But its touristic fame relates to the Latin Quarter's intriguing artsy, bohemian character. This was perhaps Europe's leading university district in the Middle Ages—home, since the 13th century, to the prestigious Sorbonne University. Back then, Latin was the language of higher education. And, since students here came from all over Europe, Latin served as their linguistic common denominator. Locals referred to the quarter by its language: Latin. In modern times this was the center of Paris' café culture. The neighborhood's main boulevards (St. Michel and St. Germain) are lined with cafés—once the haunts of great poets and philosophers but now the hangout of tired tourists. While still youthful and artsy, the area has become a tourist ghetto filled with cheap North African eateries.

▲**Cluny Museum (Musée National du Moyen Age)**—This treasure trove of medieval art fills the old Roman baths, offering close-up looks at stained glass, Notre-Dame carvings, fine goldsmithing and jewelry, and rooms of tapestries—the best of which is the exquisite *Lady with the Unicorn*. In five panels, a delicate-as-medieval-can-be noble lady introduces a delighted unicorn to the senses of taste, hearing, sight, smell, and touch (38F, 28F on Sun, Wed–Mon 9:15–17:45, closed Tue, 6 place Paul-Painlevé, near the corner of boulevards St. Michel and St. Germain, Mo: Cluny, tel. 01 53 73 78 00).

St. Germain des Prés—A church was first built on this site in

A.D. 452. The church you see today was constructed in 1163. The area around the church hops at night with fire eaters, mimes, and scads of artists (Mo: St. Germain-des-Prés).

▲**St. Sulpice Organ Concert**—For pipe-organ enthusiasts, this is a delight. The Grand-Orgue at St. Sulpice has a rich history, with a line of 12 world-class organists (including Widor and Dupre) going back 300 years. Widor started the tradition of opening the loft to visitors after the 10:30 service on Sundays. Daniel Roth continues to welcome guests in three languages while playing five keyboards at once. The 10:30 Sunday mass is followed by a 25-minute recital at 11:40. If you're lucky, at 12:00 the small unmarked door will open (left of entry as you face the rear) and allow visitors to scamper like sixteenth notes up spiral stairs to a world of 7,000 pipes, where they can watch the master perform the next mass, friends warming his bench, and a committee scrambling to pull and push the 102 stops (Mo: St. Sulpice or Mabillon).

▲▲**Luxembourg Gardens**—Paris' most beautiful, interesting, and enjoyable garden/park/recreational area is a great place to watch Parisians at rest and play. The brilliant flower plantings are completely changed three times a year, and the boxed trees are brought out of the *orangerie* in May. Challenge the card and chess players to a game (near the tennis courts), or find a free chair near the main pond and take a breather. Notice any pigeons? A poor Ernest Hemingway used to hand-hunt (read: strangle) them here. Paris Walks offers a good tour of the park (see "Organized Tours," above). The grand neoclassical-domed Panthéon, now a mausoleum housing the tombs of several great Frenchmen, is a block away and is only worth entering if you have a museum pass. The park is open until dusk (Mo: Odéon, RER: Luxembourg). If you enjoy the Luxembourg Gardens and want to see more, visit the elegant Parc Monceau (Mo: Monceau) and the colorful Jardin des Plantes (Mo: Jussieu or Gare d'Austerlitz, RER: Luxembourg).

Montparnasse Tower—This 59-floor superscraper—it's cheaper and easier to get to the top than to that of the Eiffel Tower—offers one of Paris' best views, since the Eiffel Tower is in it and Montparnasse Tower isn't. Buy the photo guide to the city, then go to the rooftop and orient yourself (46F, daily in summer 9:30–23:00, off-season 10:00–22:00, disappointing after dark, entrance on rue l'Arrivé, Mo: Montparnasse). This is efficient when combined with a day trip to Chartres, which begins at the Montparnasse train station.

Sights—Northwest Paris

▲▲**Place de la Concorde and the Champs-Élysées**—This famous boulevard is Paris' backbone and greatest concentration of traffic. All of France seems to converge on the place de la Concorde, the city's largest square. It was here that the guillotine took the lives of thousands—including King Louis XVI and Marie Antoinette. Back then it was called the place de la Revolution.

Catherine de Médici wanted a place to drive her carriage, so she started draining the swamp that would become the Champs-Élysées. Napoleon put on the final touches, and it's been the place to be seen ever since. The Tour de France bicycle race ends here, as do all parades (French or foe) of any significance. While the boulevard has become a bit hamburgerized, a walk here is a must. Take the Métro to the Arc de Triomphe (Mo: Étoile) and saunter down the Champs-Élysées (Métro stops every few blocks: FDR, George V, and Étoile).

▲▲▲**Arc de Triomphe**—Napoleon had the magnificent Arc de Triomphe commissioned to commemorate his victory at the Battle of Austerlitz. He died prior to its completion. Today the Arc de Triomphe is dedicated to the glory of all French armies. There's no triumphal arch bigger (50 meters high, 40 meters wide). And, with 12 converging boulevards, there's no traffic circle more thrilling to experience—either behind the wheel or on foot (take the underpass). An elevator or a spiral staircase leads to a cute museum about the arch and a grand view from the top, even after dark (40F, June–Sept daily 9:30–23:00, Oct–May daily 9:30–22:00, Mo: Étoile, tel. 01 43 80 31 31).

▲**Grande Arche de La Défense**—The centerpiece of Paris' ambitious skyscraper complex (La Défense) is the Grande Arche. Built to celebrate the 200th anniversary of the 1789 French Revolution, the place is big—38 floors on more than 200 acres. It holds offices for 30,000 people. Notre-Dame Cathedral could fit under its arch. The La Défense complex is an interesting study in 1960s land-use planning. More than 100,000 workers commute here daily, directing lots of business and development away from downtown and allowing central Paris to retain its more elegant feel. This aspect makes sense to most Parisians, regardless of whatever else they feel about the controversial complex. You'll enjoy city views from the Arche elevator (46F includes a film on its construction and art exhibits, daily 10:00–19:00, Métro or RER: La Défense, follow signs to Grande Arche, tel. 01 49 07 27 57).

Sights—Northeast Paris: Marais Neighborhood and More

▲▲**Pompidou Center**—Europe's greatest collection of far-out modern art is showcased at the Musée National d'Art Moderne, located on the top floor of this newly renovated and colorful exoskeletal building. Once ahead of its time, this 20th-century art (remember that century?) has been waiting for the world to catch up with it. After so many Madonnas and Children, a piano smashed to bits and glued to the wall is refreshing (50F, audio-guide-25F, Wed–Mon 11:00–22:00, closed Tue, to ride escalator you need a museum ticket or pass, café on mezzanine level is cheaper than cafés outside, Mo: Rambuteau, tel. 01 44 78 12 33).

The Pompidou Center and its square are lively, with lots of people, street theater, and activity inside and out—a perpetual street fair. Kids of any age enjoy the fun, colorful fountain (called *Homage to Stravinsky*) on the square.

▲▲**Museum of Art and History of Judaism (Hotel d'Aignan)**—This remarkable museum, located in a beautifully restored Marais mansion, tells the story of *Judaism* throughout Europe, from the Roman destruction of Jerusalem to the theft of famous artwork during World War II. Helpful audioguides and many English explanations make this an enjoyable history lesson. Move along at your own speed. The emphasis of the museum is to illustrate the cultural unity maintained by this continually dispersed population. You'll learn about the history of Jewish traditions, from bar mitzvahs to menorahs, and see exquisite traditional costumes and objects around which daily life revolved. Don't miss the explanation of the Dreyfus affair, a major event in early-1900 French politics.You'll also see photographs of and paintings by famous Jewish artists, including Chagall, Modigliani, and Soutine. The small section devoted to the deportation of Jews from Paris is very moving (40F, not covered with museum pass, Sun 10:00–18:00, Mon–Fri 11:00–18:00, closed Sat, 71 rue du Temple, tel. 01 53 01 86 53).

▲**Picasso Museum (Hôtel Salé)**—This is the world's largest collection of Pablo Picasso's paintings, sculpture, sketches, and ceramics and includes his personal collection of Impressionist art. It's well explained in English and worth ▲▲▲ if you're a fan (30F, Wed–Mon 9:30–18:00, closed Tue, 5 rue Thorigny, Mo: St. Paul or Chemin Vert, tel. 01 42 71 25 21).

▲**Carnavalet Museum**—The tumultuous history of Paris is well displayed in this converted Marais mansion. Unfortunately, explanations are in French only, but many displays are fairly self-explanatory. You'll see paintings of Parisian scenes, French Revolution paraphernalia, old Parisian store signs, a small guillotine, a model of 16th-century Île de la Cité (notice the bridge houses), and rooms full of 15th-century Parisian furniture (35F, Tue–Sun 10:00–17:00, closed Mon, 23 rue de Sévigné, Mo: St Paul, tel. 01 42 72 21 13).

Victor Hugo's House—France's literary giant lived in this fine house on the place des Vosges from 1832 to 1848. Inside you'll find many posters advertising theater productions of his works, paintings of some of his most famous character creations, and a few furnished rooms (22F, Tue–Sun 10:00–17:40, closed Mon, 6 place des Vosges).

Promenade Plantée Park—This three-kilometer narrow garden walk, once a train track and now a joy, runs from place de la Bastille (Mo: Bastille) along avenue Daumesnil to

Saint-Mandé (Mo: Michel Bizot). Part of the park is elevated.
At times you'll walk along the street till you pick up the next
segment. From place de la Bastille, take avenue Daumesnil
(past Opéra building) to the intersection with avenue Ledru
Rollin. Walk up the stairs and through the gate (free, hours
vary with season, open roughly 8:00–20:00).

▲**Père Lachaise Cemetery**—Littered with the tombstones of
many of the city's most illustrious dead, this is your best one-stop
look at the fascinating, romantic world of permanent Parisians. The
place is confusing, but maps will direct you to the graves of Chopin,
Molière, Edith Piaf, Oscar Wilde, Gertrude Stein, Héloïse and
Abelard, and even the American rock star Jim Morrison (who died
in Paris). In section 92, a series of statues memorializing the war
makes the French war experience a bit more real (helpful 10F maps
at the flower store near the entry, across the street from Métro stop,
closes at dusk, Mo: Père Lachaise or bus #69).

Sights—North Paris: Montmartre

▲**Sacré-Coeur and Montmartre**—This Byzantine-looking
church, while only 130 years old, is impressive. It was built as a
"praise the Lord anyway" gesture after the French were humiliated
by the Germans in a brief war in 1871. The church is open daily
until 23:00. One block from the church, the place du Tertre
was the haunt of Toulouse-Lautrec and the original Bohemians.
Today it's mobbed by tourists and unoriginal bohemians but still
fun. Wander down the rue Lepic to the two remaining windmills
(once there were 30). Rue des Saules leads to Paris' only vineyard.
Métros: Anvers (an extra Métro ticket buys your way up the funicular and avoids the stairs) or the closer but less scenic Abbesses.
A taxi to the top of the hill saves time and sweat.

Pigalle—Paris' red-light district, the infamous "Pig Alley," is at
the foot of Butte Montmartre. *Ooh la la.* More shocking than dangerous. Walk from place Pigalle to place Blanche, teasing desperate barkers and fast-talking temptresses. In bars a 1,000F bottle of
cheap champagne comes with a friend. Stick to the bigger streets,
hang on to your wallet, and exercise good judgment. Cancan can
cost a fortune, as can con artists in topless bars. After dark, tour
buses line the streets. Tour guides make big bucks by bringing
their groups to touristic nightclubs like the Moulin Rouge (Mo:
Pigalle and Abbesses).

Best Shopping

Forum des Halles is a huge subterranean shopping center. It's
fun, mod, and colorful but lacks a soul (Mo: Les Halles). The
Galeries Lafayette behind the old Opéra Garnier is your best
elegant, Old World, one-stop Parisian department store/shopping
center (Mo: Opéra). Also visit the adjacent **Printemps** store and

the historic (as well as handy) **Samaritaine** department store in several buildings near Pont Neuf (Mo: Pont Neuf). Ritzy shops surround the Ritz Hotel at place Vendôme (Mo: Tuileries).

Disappointments de Paris

While Paris can drive you in-Seine with superlatives, here are a few negatives to help you manage your limited time:

La Madeleine is a big, stark, neoclassical church with a post-card facade and a postbox interior. The famous aristocratic deli behind the church, Fauchon, is elegant, but so are many others handier to your hotel.

Paris' Panthéon (nothing like Rome's) is another stark, neo-classical edifice filled with mortal remains of great Frenchmen who mean little to the average American tourist.

The Bastille is Paris' most famous nonsight. The square is there, but confused tourists look everywhere and can't find the famous prison of Revolution fame. The building's gone, and the square is good only as a jumping-off point for the Promenade Plantée Park (see "Sights—Northeast Paris," above).

The Latin Quarter is a frail shadow of its characteristic self. It's more Tunisian, Greek, and Woolworth's than old-time Paris. The café life that turned on Hemingway and endeared boul' Miche and boulevard St. Germain to so many poets is also trampled by modern commercialism.

Palace of Versailles

Every king's dream, Versailles was the residence of the French king and the cultural heartbeat of Europe for about 100 years—until the Revolution of 1789 ended the notion that God deputized some people to rule for Him on Earth. Louis XIV spent half a year's income of Europe's richest country turning his dad's hunting lodge into a palace fit for a divine monarch. Louis XV and Louis XVI spent much of the 18th century gilding Louis XIV's lily. In 1837, about 50 years after the royal family was evicted, King Louis Philippe opened the palace as a museum. Europe's next-best palaces are Versailles wanna-bes.

Information: A helpful TI is just past the Sofitel Hôtel on your way from the station to the palace (tel. 01 39 24 88 88). You'll also find information booths inside the château (at doors A, B-2, and C). The useful brochure, "Versailles Orientation Guide," explains your sightseeing options.

Ticket Options: The self-guided one-way romp through the State Apartments, including the Hall of Mirrors, costs 46F (covered by museum pass, 36F after 15:30, on Sun, or for those over 60 or ages 18–25, under 18 free). The entry fee is payable at doors A, C, or D. If you want a guided tour through the other sections, you need to pay the 46F base price, then pay extra for the tour.

Versailles

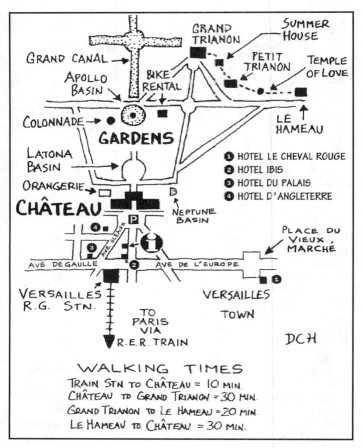

Tours: Add 25F for a 60-minute guided tour (of lesser-known nobles' apartments, like those of the well-coiffed Madame Pompadour) or 37F for a 90-minute guided tour of the King's Private Apartments (Louis XV, Louis XVI, and Marie-Antoinette), the chapel, and Opera House. Pay and get your tour appointment at entrance D. Tour times are normally all allotted for the day by 13:00. Tours leave from door F (across the courtyard from door D). Audioguides are available for 30F (choose between Louis XIV's Private Apartments at door C, or the State Apartments and Hall of Mirrors at doors A or B-2). Tours aren't covered by the museum pass. If you have extra time before your tour, wander through the state apartments or gardens.

Entrances to Versailles

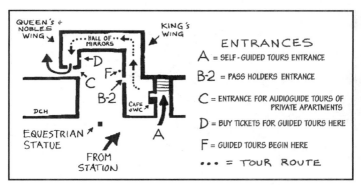

Hours: May through September Tuesday through Sunday 9:00 to 18:30, October through April Tuesday through Sunday 9:00 to 17:30, closed Monday, last entry 30 minutes before closing. Versailles is especially crowded around 10:00 and 13:00, Tuesday, and Sunday. To minimize crowds, either arrive by 9:00 or after 15:30 (admission is cheaper after 15:30, but you'll miss the last guided tours of the day, which generally depart around 15:00); tour the gardens after the palace closes. The palace is great late. On my last visit, at 18:00, I was the only tourist in the Hall of Mirrors...even on a Tuesday.

Time to Allow: Six hours round-trip from Paris (1 hour each way in transit, 2 hours for palace, 2 for gardens).

Self-Guided Tour: For the basic self-guided tour, join the line at entrance A. Those with a museum pass are allowed in through entrance B-2 without a wait. Enter the palace and take a one-way walk through the State Apartments from the "King's Wing," through the magnificent Hall of Mirrors, and out via the "Queen's Wing."

The Hall of Mirrors was the ultimate hall of the day—250 feet long, 17 arched mirrors matching 17 windows with royal garden views, 24 gilded candelabra, eight busts of Roman emperors, and eight classical-style statues (7 are ancient originals). The ceiling is decorated with stories of Louis' triumphs. Imagine this place filled with silk gowns and powdered wigs, lit by thousands of candles. The mirrors—a luxurious rarity at the time—were a reflection of a time when aristocrats felt good about their looks and their fortunes. In another age altogether, this was the room in which the Treaty of Versailles was signed, ending World War I.

Before going downstairs at the end, take a stroll clockwise around the long room filled with the great battles of France murals. If you don't have *Rick Steves' Paris* or *Rick Steves' Mona*

Winks, the guidebook called *The Châteaux, The Gardens, and Trianon* gives a room-by-room rundown.

Palace Gardens: The gardens offer a world of royal amusements. Outside the palace is L'Orangerie. Louis, the only one who could grow oranges in Paris, had an orange grove on wheels that could be wheeled in and out of his greenhouses according to the weather. A promenade leads from the palace to the Grand Canal, an artificial lake that, in Louis' day, was a mini-sea with nine ships, including a 32-cannon warship. France's royalty used to float up and down the canal in Venetian gondolas.

While Louis cleverly used palace life at Versailles to "domesticate" his nobility, turning otherwise meddlesome nobles into groveling socialites, all this pomp and ceremony hampered the royal family as well. For an escape from the public life at Versailles, they built more intimate palaces as retreats in their garden. Before the revolution there was plenty of space to retreat—the grounds were enclosed by a 25-mile-long fence.

The beautifully restored **Grand Trianon Palace** is as sumptuous as the main palace but much smaller. With its pastel-pink colonnade and more human scale, this is a place you'd like to call home. The nearby **Petit Trianon,** which has a fine neoclassical exterior with a skippable interior, was Marie Antoinette's favorite residence (25F-Grand Trianon, 15F-Petit Trianon, 30F for both, covered by museum pass, May–Sept Tue–Sun 10:00–18:00, closed Mon, Oct–April 10:00–17:00).

You can almost see princesses bobbing gaily in the branches as you walk through the enchanting forest, past the white marble temple of love (1778) to the queen's fake-peasant **Hamlet** (*Hameau;* interior not tourable). Palace life really got to Marie Antoinette. Sort of a back-to-basics queen, she retreated further and further from her blue-blooded reality. Her happiest days were at the hamlet, under a bonnet, tending her perfumed sheep and her manicured gardens in a thatch-happy wonderland.

Getting around the Gardens: It's a 30-minute hike from he palace, down the canal, past the two mini-palaces to the hamlet. You can rent bikes (30F/hr). The pokey tourist train, which costs only 10F, runs between the canal and château (30F, 5/hrly, 4 stops, you can hop on and off as you like; nearly worthless commentary).

Garden Hours: Except for fountain-filled weekends (see below), the gardens are free and open from 7:00 to sunset (as late as 21:30). There's a sandwich kiosk and a decent restaurant at the canal.

Fountain Spectacles: Classical music fills the king's backyard and the garden's fountains are in full squirt on Saturdays from July through September and on Sundays from early April through early October (schedule for both days: 11:00–12:00, 15:30–17:00, and

17:20–17:30). On these "spray days," the gardens cost 30F (not covered by museum pass). Louis had his engineers literally reroute a river to fuel these fountains. Even by today's standards they are impressive. For more information, pick up the map of the fountain show (*Les Grandes Eaux Musicales*) at any information booth.

Getting There: Take the RER-C train (29F round-trip, 30 min one-way) to Versailles R.G. or "Rive Gauche" (not Versailles C.H., which is farther from the palace). Trains, usually named "Vick," leave about five times an hour for the palace. RER-C trains leave from these RER/Métro stops: Invalides, Champ de Mars, Musée d'Orsay, St. Michel, and Gare d'Austerlitz. Get off at Versailles Rive Gauche (the end of the line), turn right out of the station, then left at the first boulevard. It's a 10-minute walk to the palace.

Your Eurailpass covers this inexpensive trip, but it uses up a valuable "flexi" day; consider seeing Versailles on your way in or out of Paris. To get free passage, show your railpass at an SCNF ticket window (for example, at the Les Invalides or Musée d'Orsay RER stops) and get a *contremarque de passage*; keep this ticket to exit the system.

When returning from Versailles, look through the windows past the turnstiles for the departure board. Any train leaving Versailles goes as far as downtown Paris (they're marked "all stations until d'Austerlitz"). If you're uncertain, confirm with a local by asking, "*À Paris?*" ("To Paris?").

Allow 225F (each way) for a taxi from Paris to Versailles. To cut your park walking by 50 percent, consider having the taxi drop you at the Hamlet (*Hameau*).

Town of Versailles (zip code: 78000): After the palace closes and the tourists go, the prosperous, wholesome town of Versailles feels a long way from Paris. The central market thrives on place du Marché on Tuesday, Friday, and Saturday until 13:00 (leaving the RER station, turn right and walk 10 min). Consider the wisdom of picking up or dropping your rental car in Versailles rather than in Paris. In Versailles, the Hertz and Avis offices are at the Gare des Chantiers (Versailles C.H., served by Paris' Montparnasse station). Versailles makes a fine home base; see Versailles accommodations under "Sleeping," below (see page 187).

More Day Trips from Paris

▲▲▲**Chartres**—In 1194 a terrible fire destroyed the church at Chartres that housed the much-venerated veil of Mary. With almost unbelievably good fortune, the monks found the veil miraculously preserved in the ashes. Money poured in for the building of a bigger and better cathedral—decorated with 2,000 carved figures and some of France's best stained glass. The cathedral feels too large for the city because it was designed to accommodate huge crowds of pilgrims. One of those pilgrims, an impressed

Chartres

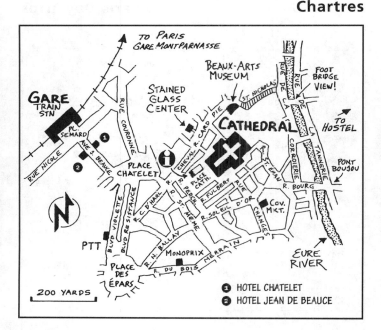

GARE · TRAIN STN

TO PARIS
GARE MONTPARNASSE

BEAUX-ARTS MUSEUM

STAINED GLASS CENTER

FOOT BRIDGE VIEW!

RUE ST. NICHOLAS

CATHEDRAL

TO HOSTEL

PL. SEMARD

RUE COURONNE

R. CARD. PIE

CHEVAL. BLANC

PONT BOUJOU

AVE J. BEAUCE

PLACE CHATELET

RUE NICOLE

R. ST. PIERRE

BLVD VIOLETTE

BLVD RESISTANCE

R.C. P. HARLI

R. MEME

R. N. RALLAY

R. PORCHE

R. FULBERT

PLACE CATH.

R. SOLEIL D'OR

R. ST. JEAN

R. BOURG

COV. MKT.

R. CORROIERIE

RUE DE LA TANNERIE

R. CHANGES

MERRAIN

EURE RIVER

PTT

MONOPRIX

R. DU BOIS

PLACE DES ÉPARS

200 YARDS

N

1 HOTEL CHATELET
2 HOTEL JEAN DE BEAUCE

Napoleon, declared after a visit in 1811: "Chartres is no place for an atheist." Rodin called it "the Acropolis of France." British Francophile Malcolm Miller or his assistant give great "Appreciation of Gothic" tours Monday through Saturday, usually at noon and 14:45 (verify times in advance, no tours off-season, call TI at 02 37 18 26 26). Each 40F tour is different; many people stay for both tours. Just show up at the church (daily 7:00–19:00).

Explore Chartres' pleasant city center and discover the picnic-friendly park behind the cathedral. The helpful TI, next to the cathedral, has a map with a self-guided tour of Chartres (daily 9:30–18:45). Chartres is a one-hour train trip from the Gare Montparnasse (about 75F one-way, 10/day). To stay overnight, try the comfy **Hôtel Chatelet***** (Db-430–510F, CC:VM, 6 avenue Jehan de Bruce, tel. 02 37 21 78 00, fax 02 37 36 23 01) or the basic **Hôtel Jehan de Beauce**** (Db-240–310F, 19 avenue Jehan de Beauce, tel. 02 37 21 01 41, fax 02 37 21 59 10).

▲**Giverny**—Monet spent 43 of his most creative years here (1883–1926). Monet's gardens and home are unfortunately split by a busy road and very popular with tourists. Buy your ticket, walk through the gardens, and take the underpass into the artist's famous lilypad land. The path leads you over the Japanese Bridge, under weeping willows, and past countless scenes that leave artists aching for an

Paris Day Trips

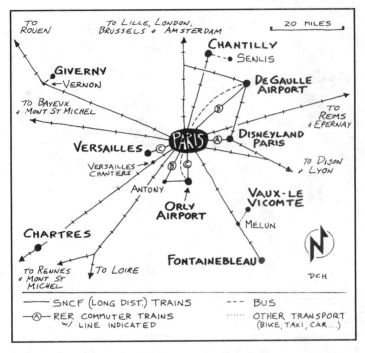

easel. Back on the other side, stroll through his more robust, struc-
tured garden and his mildly interesting home. The jammed gift shop
at the exit is Monet's actual skylit studio.

While lines may be long and tour groups may trample the
flowers, true fans still find magic in those lilypads. Minimize
crowds by arriving before 10:00 (get in line) or after 16:00 (35F,
25F for gardens only, April–Oct Tue–Sun 10:00–18:00, closed
Mon and Nov–March, tel. 02 32 51 94 65). Take the Rouen-
bound train from Paris' Gare St. Lazare station to Vernon (about
140F round-trip, long gaps in service, know the schedule before
you go). To get from the Vernon train station to Monet's garden
(4 kilometers away), take the Vernon-to-Giverny bus (5/day,
scheduled to meet most trains), hitch, taxi (60F), or rent a bike
at the station (60F, busy road). Get return bus times from the
ticket office in Giverny or ask them to call a taxi. Big tour companies do a Giverny day trip from Paris for around $60.

The new **American Impressionist Art Museum** is devoted
to American artists who followed Claude to Giverny. This bright,
modern gallery is well explained in English, has a good little Mary

Cassatt section, and gives Americans a rare chance to see French
people appreciating our artists (same price and hours as Monet's
home, pleasant café, 100 meters from Monet's place).

To sleep two blocks from Monet's home, try the adorable
Hôtel La Musardiere** (Db-400F, 132 rue Claude Monet, tel.
02 32 21 03 18, fax 02 32 21 60 00).

▲▲**Disneyland Paris**—Europe's Disneyland is basically a
modern remake of California's, with most of the same rides and
smiles. The main difference is that Mickey Mouse speaks French
(and you can buy wine with your lunch). My kids went ducky.
Locals love it. It's worth a day if Paris is handier than Florida
or California. If possible, avoid Saturday, Sunday, Wednesday,
school holidays, and July and August. The park can get very
crowded. When 60,000 have entered, they close the gates (tel.
01 64 74 30 00 for the latest). After dinner, crowds are gone,
and you'll walk right onto rides that had a 45-minute wait three
hours earlier. Food is fun but expensive. Smuggle in a picnic.

Disney brochures are in every Paris hotel. The RER (about
43F each way, direct from downtown Paris to Marne-la-Vallee in
30 minutes) drops you right into the park. The last train back to
Paris leaves shortly after midnight. (220F for adults, 170F for
kids ages 3–11, 25F less in spring and fall, daily 9:00–23:00 late
June–early Sept and Sat–Sun off-season, shoulder-season Mon–
Fri 9:00–19:00, off-season 10:00–18:00, tel. 01 50 30 60 30.)

To sleep reasonably at the huge Disney complex, try Hotel
Sante Fe (780F family rooms for 2–4 people includes breakfast,
less off-season; ask for their hotel-and-park package deal, tel.
01 60 30 60 30, fax 01 60 30 60 65). If all this ain't enough, a
new Planet Hollywood restaurant opened just outside the park.

Nightlife in Paris

Paris is brilliant after dark. Save energy from your day's sightseeing and get out at night. Whether it's a concert at Sainte-
Chapelle, an elevator up the Arc de Triomphe, or a late-night
café, experience the city of light lit. If a night bus tour or a Seine
River cruise appeals, see "Organized Tours of Paris," above.

The *Pariscope* magazine (3F at any newsstand) offers a com-
plete weekly listing of music, cinema, theater, opera, and other
special events; we decipher this useful periodical for you below.
The *Free Voice* newspaper, in English, has a monthly review of
Paris entertainment (available at any English-language bookstore,
French-American establishments, or the American Church).

A Tour of Pariscope

The weekly *Pariscope* (3F) or *L'Officiel des Spectacles* (2F) are both
cheap and essential if you want to know what's happening. For a
head start, *Pariscope* has a Web site: www.pariscope.fr.

Each begins with culture news. Skip the "Theatres" and "Dîners/Spectacles" sections and anything listed as *des environs* (outside of Paris). "Musique" or "Concerts Classiques" list each day's events (with location, time, and price). Venues with phone numbers and addresses are listed in an "Adresses des Salles de Concerts" sidebar. Touristic venues (Sainte-Chapelle, Église de la Madeleine) are often featured in display ads. "Opéras," "Musique Traditionelle," "Ballet/Danse," and "Jazz/Rock" listings follow.

Half of these magazines are devoted to **cinema**—a Paris forte. After the "Films Nouveaux" section trumpets new releases, the "Films en Exclusivite" pages list all the films playing in town. While a code marks films as "Historique," "Karate," "Erotisme," and so on, the key mark for tourists is "v.o.," which means *version original* (American films have their English soundtracks and French subtitles). Films are listed alphabetically, with theaters and their arrondissements at the end of each entry. Later films are listed by neighborhood ("Salles Paris") and by genre. First runs are shown at cinemas on the Champs-Élysées and on place de l'Odeon; art films and older films are best found in the Latin Quarter. To find a showing near your hotel, simply match the arrondissement (but don't hesitate to hop on the Métro for the film you want). "Salles Périphérie" is out in the suburbs. Film festivals are also listed.

Pariscope has a small English "Time Out" section listing the week's events. The "Musées" sections (Monuments, Jardins, Autres Curiosites, Promenades, Activites Sportives, Piscines) give hours of sights, gardens, curiosities, boat tours, sports, pools, and so on. "Clubs de Loisirs" are athletic and social clubs. "Pour les Jeunes" is for young people (kids' films, cartoons, marionettes, circuses, and amusement parks, such as Asterix and Disney). "Conferences" are mostly lectures. For cancan mischief, look under "Paris la Nuit," "Cabarets," or the busty "Spectacles Erotiques."

Finally, you'll find a **TV** listing. Paris has four country-wide stations: TF1, France 2, France 3, and the new Arte station (a German/French cultural channel). M6 is filled with American series. Canal Plus (channel 4) is a cable channel that airs an American news show at 7:00 and an American sports event on Sunday evening.

Music

Jazz Clubs

With a lively mix of American, French, and international musicians, Paris has been an internationally acclaimed jazz capital since World War II. You'll pay from 40F to 160F to enter a jazz club (a drink may be included; if not, expect to pay 30–60F per drink; beer is cheapest). See *Pariscope* under "Musique" for listings or, better, the

American Church's *Free Voice* paper for a good monthly review
(in English)—or drop by to check out their calendars posted on
the front door. Music starts after 22:00 in most clubs. Some offer
dinner concerts from about 20:30 on. Here are a few good bets:

Caveau de la Huchette, a characteristic old jazz club for visitors, fills an ancient Latin Quarter cellar with live jazz and frenzied
dancing every night (65F weekday, 80F weekend admission, 30F
drinks, 21:30–02:30 or later, closed Mon, 5 rue de la Huchette,
recorded info tel. 01 43 26 65 05).

For a hotbed of late-night activity and jazz, go to the two-
block-long rue des Lombards, at boulevard Sebastopol, midway
between the river and Pompidou Center (Mo: Chatelet). **Au Duc
des Lombards**, right at the corner, is one of the most popular and
respected jazz clubs in Paris with concerts generally at 21:30 (42
rue des Lombards, tel. 01 42 33 23 88, www.jazzvalley.com/duc).
Le Sunset is a block west and offers more traditional jazz and
fewer crowds with concerts around 21:00 (60 rue des Lombards,
Mo: Chatelet, tel. 01 40 26 46 60).

At the down-to-earth and mellow **Le Cave du Franc Pinot**,
you can enjoy a glass of chardonnay at the main-floor wine bar
then drop downstairs for a cool jazz scene (1 quai de Bourbon,
good dinner values as well, located on Île St. Louis where the
Pont Marie meets the island, Mo: Pont Marie, tel. 01 46 33 60 64).

The **American Church** regularly plays host to fine jazz
musicians for the best price in Paris (free, 65 quai d'Orsay, Mo:
Invalides, RER-C: Pont de l'Alma, tel. 01 40 62 05 00).

Classical Concerts

For classical music on any night, consult *Pariscope* magazine;
the "Musique" section under "Concerts Classique" lists concerts
(free and fee). Look for posters at churches. Churches that
regularly host concerts include St. Sulpice, St. Germain-des-Près,
Basilique de Madeleine, St. Eustache, and Sainte-Chapelle.
It's worth the 100F to 150F to hear Mozart while you're surrounded by the stained glass of the tiny Sainte-Chapelle. Even
the Galeries Lafayette department store offers concerts. Many
are free (*entrée libre*), such as the Sunday Atelier concert sponsored
by the American Church (18:00, 65 quai d'Orsay, Mo: Invalides,
RER: Pont de l'Alma, tel. 01 47 05 07 99).

Opera

Paris is home to two well-respected operas. The **Opéra Garnier**,
Paris' first opera house, hosts opera and ballet performances. Come
here for less-expensive tickets and grand belle epoque decor (Mo:
Opéra, tel. 01 44 73 13 99). The **Opéra de la Bastille** is the massive
modern opera house that dominates place de la Bastille. Come
here for state-of-the-art special effects and modern interpretations

of classic ballets and operas (Mo: Bastille, tel. 01 43 43 96 96). For tickets, either call 01 44 73 13 00, go to the opera ticket offices (open 11:00–18:00), or, best, reserve on the Web at www .ticketavenue.com (for both operas).

Seine River Cruises

The Bâteaux-Mouches offer one-hour cruises on huge glass boats with departures (every 30 min from 10:00–23:00) from the Pont de l'Alma, the centrally located Pont Neuf, and right in front of the Eiffel Tower (see "Organized Tours of Paris," above).

Bus Tours

Paris Illumination Tours, run by Paris Vision, connect all the great illuminated sights of Paris with a 100-minute bus tour in 12 languages. Double-decker buses have huge windows, but Moulin Rouge customers get the most desirable front seats. You'll stampede on with a United Nations of tourists, get a hand-held audioguide, and listen to a tape-recorded spiel (interesting but occasionally hard to hear). Uninspired as it is, this provides a fine first-night overview of the city at its floodlit scenic best. Visibility is fine in the rain. You're entirely on the bus except for one five-minute cigarette break at the Eiffel Tower viewpoint (150F-adult, 75F-ages 4–11, free-under 3, departures at 20:30 nightly all year plus 22:00 April–Oct, departs from Paris Vision office at 214 rue de Rivoli, across street from Mo: Tuileries). These trips are sold through your hotel (brochures in lobby) or direct at the address listed above. Look also for the same tour by minivan—pickup is at your hotel, the driver is a qualified guide, and there's a maximum of seven clients (295F per person, for bus and minivans tel. 01 42 60 30 01, fax 01 42 86 95 36, www.parisvision.com).

Sleeping in Paris
(6.50F = about $1, country code: 33)

Sleep Code: **S** = Single, **D** = Double/Twin, **T** = Triple, **Q** = Quad, **b** = bathroom, **t** = toilet only, **s** = shower only, **CC** = Credit Card (**V** = Visa, **M** = MasterCard, **A** = Amex), * = French hotel rating system (0–4 stars).

I've focused on three safe, handy, and colorful neighborhoods: rue Cler, Marais, and Contrescarpe. For each, I list good hotels, helpful hints, and restaurants (see "Eating," below). Before reserving, read the descriptions of the three neighborhoods closely. Each offers different pros and cons, and your neighborhood is as important as your hotel to the success of your trip.

Reserve ahead for Paris, the sooner the better. Conventions clog Paris in September (worst), October, May, and June. In August, when Paris is quiet, some hotels offer lower rates to fill their rooms (if you're planning to visit Paris in the summer, the extra expense of an air-conditioned room can be money well spent). Most hotels accept telephone reservations, require prepayment with a credit-card number, and prefer a faxed follow-up to be sure everything is in order. For more information, see "Making Reservations" in this book's introduction.

French hotels are rated by stars (indicated in this chapter by an *). One star is simple, two has most of the comforts, and three generally just adds a mini-bar and fancier lobby (though I've tried to find three-star hotels that merit the extra expense).

Old, characteristic, budget Parisian hotels have always been cramped. Retrofitted with elevators, toilets, and private showers (as most are today), they are even more cramped. Even three-star hotel rooms are small and often not worth the extra expense in Paris. Some hotels include the hotel tax (*taxe du séjour*, about 5F per person per day), though most will add this to your bill. Two- and three-star hotels are required to have an English-speaking staff. Nearly all hotels listed will have someone who speaks English.

Quad rooms usually have two double beds. Recommended hotels have an elevator unless otherwise noted. Because rooms with double beds and showers are cheaper than rooms with twin beds and baths, room prices vary within each hotel.

You can save as much as 100F by finding the increasingly rare room without a private shower, though some hotels charge for down-the-hall showers. Singles (except for the rare closet-type rooms that fit only one twin bed) are simply doubles used by one person. They rent for only a little less than a double. Continental breakfasts cost 25F to 35F, buffet breakfasts (baked goods, cereal, yogurt, and fruit) cost 50F to 60F. Café or picnic breakfasts are cheaper, but hotels usually give unlimited coffee.

Get advice from your hotel for safe parking (consider long-term parking at Orly Airport and taxi in). Meters are free in August. Garages are plentiful (90–140F/day, with special rates through some hotels). Self-serve Laundromats are common; ask your hotelier for the nearest one (*Où est un laverie automatique?*; ooh ay uh lah-vay-ree auto-mah-teek).

Rue Cler Orientation

Rue Cler, a village-like pedestrian street, is safe, tidy, and makes me feel like I must have been a poodle in a previous life. How such coziness lodged itself between the high-powered government district and the wealthy Eiffel Tower and Invalides areas, I'll never know. This is a neighborhood of wide, tree-lined boulevards, stately apartment buildings, and lots of Americans. The American Church, American Library, American University, and many of my readers call this area home.

Become a local at a rue Cler café for breakfast or join the afternoon crowd for *une bière pression* (a draft beer). On rue Cler you can eat and browse your way through a street full of tart shops, delis, cheeseries, and colorful outdoor produce stalls. For an after-dinner cruise on the Seine, it's just a short walk to the river and the Bâteaux-Mouches (see "Organized Tours of Paris," above).

Your neighborhood **TI** is at the Eiffel Tower (May–Sept daily 11:00–18:00, tel. 01 45 51 22 15). The Métro station (École Militaire) and a **post office** are at the end of rue Cler—on avenue de la Motte Piquet, and there's a handy SNCF office under the *Aérogare* at the Invalides Métro stop, where you can get information, buy tickets, and make seat reservations. The nearest Internet access is at the splashy Toyota **Cybercafé** (79 avenue Champs-Élysées, Mo: George V, tel. 01 56 89 29 79). Taxi stands are on avenue de Tourville at avenue la Motte Piquet (near Métro stop) and on avenue Bosquet at rue St. Dominique. The Banque Populaire (across from Hôtel Leveque) changes money. Rue St. Dominique is the area's boutique-browsing street. The Épicerie de la Tour **grocery** is open until midnight (197 rue de Grenelle).

The **American Church and College** is the community center for Americans living in Paris and should be one of your first stops if you're staying in Paris a while (reception open Mon–Sat 9:00–22:30, Sun 9:00–19:30, 65 quai d'Orsay, tel. 01 40 62 05 00). Pick up copies of the *Free Voice* for a monthly review of Paris entertainment, and *France-U.S.A. Contacts* for information on housing and employment through the community of 30,000 Americans living in Paris. The interdenominational service at 11:00 on Sunday, the coffee hour after church, and the free Sunday concerts (18:00, not every week) are a great way to make some friends and get a taste of émigré life in Paris.

Afternoon *boules* (lawn bowling) on the esplanade des Invalides is a relaxing spectator sport. Look for the dirt area to the upper right as you face the Invalides.

You should try at least one of these helpful **bus routes:** Line #69 runs along rue St. Dominique and serves Les Invalides, Orsay, Louvre, Marais, and Père-Lachaise cemetery. Line #92 runs along avenue Bosquet and serves the Arc de Triomphe and Champs-Elysées in one direction and Montparnasse Tower in the other. Line #87 runs on avenue de la Bourdonnais and serves St. Sulpice, Luxembourg Gardens, and the Sevres-Babylone shopping area. Line #49 runs on boulevard La Tour Maubourg and serves the St. Lazare and Gare du Nord stations.

Sleeping in the Rue Cler Neighborhood
(7th arrondissement, Mo: École Militaire, zip code: 75007)

Rue Cler is the glue that holds this pleasant neighborhood together. From here you can walk to the Eiffel Tower, Napoleon's Tomb, the Seine, and the Orsay and Rodin Museums.

Rue Cler Hotels

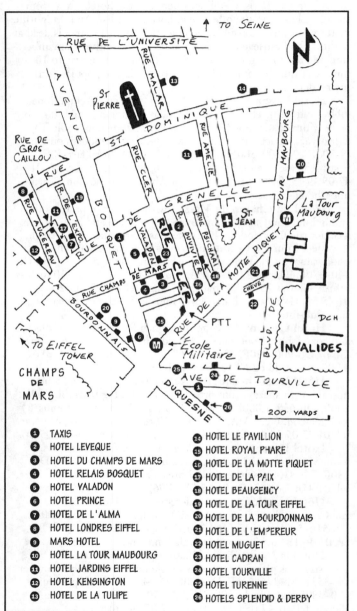

1. TAXIS
2. HOTEL LEVEQUE
3. HOTEL DU CHAMPS DE MARS
4. HOTEL RELAIS BOSQUET
5. HOTEL VALADON
6. HOTEL PRINCE
7. HOTEL DE L'ALMA
8. HOTEL LONDRES EIFFEL
9. MARS HOTEL
10. HOTEL LA TOUR MAUBOURG
11. HOTEL JARDINS EIFFEL
12. HOTEL KENSINGTON
13. HOTEL DE LA TULIPE
14. HOTEL LE PAVILLON
15. HOTEL ROYAL PHARE
16. HOTEL DE LA MOTTE PIQUET
17. HOTEL DE LA PAIX
18. HOTEL BEAUGENCY
19. HOTEL DE LA TOUR EIFFEL
20. HOTEL DE LA BOURDONNAIS
21. HOTEL DE L'EMPEREUR
22. HOTEL MUGUET
23. HOTEL CADRAN
24. HOTEL TOURVILLE
25. HOTEL TURENNE
26. HOTELS SPLENDID & DERBY

Many of my readers stay in this neighborhood. If you want to disappear in Paris, you'll do it better at the hotels away from the rue Cler, or in the other neighborhoods I list. And if nightlife matters, seriously consider sleeping elsewhere (this area is dead at night). The first seven hotels listed below are within Camembert-smelling distance of rue Cler; the others are within a 5- to 10-minute stroll. Warning: The first two hotels are popular with my readers.

Hôtel Leveque** is ideally located, with an air-conditioned lobby (and ice machine), helpful staff, and a singing maid. It's a big place with well-designed rooms that have ceiling fans, cable TV, hair dryers, direct phone lines, safes, and French modem outlets (S-300F, Db-400–500F, Tb-600F, CC:VMA, breakfast-40F, first breakfast free for readers of this book, 29 rue Cler, tel. 01 47 05 49 15, fax 01 45 50 49 36, www.hotel-leveque.com, e-mail: info@hotelleveque.com).

Hôtel du Champ de Mars**, with charming, pastel rooms and helpful English-speaking owners Françoise and Stephane, is a cozier rue Cler option. The hotel has a Provence-style, small-town feel from top to bottom. Rooms are comfortable and a very good value. Single rooms can work as tiny doubles (Sb-400F, Db-440–470F, Tb-560F, CC:VMA, cable TV, hair dryers, 30 meters off rue Cler at 7 rue de Champ de Mars, tel. 01 45 51 52 30, fax 01 45 51 64 36, www.hotel-du-champ-de-mars.com, e-mail: stg@club-internet.fr).

Hôtel Cadran*** charges too much for its fine location and cozy lobby. Rooms are tight and narrow but air-conditioned (Sb or Db-900–980F, 10 rue de Champs de Mars, tel. 01 40 62 67 00, fax 01 40 62 67 13, www.cadranhotel.com).

Hôtel Relais Bosquet*** is modern, spacious, and a bit upscale, with snazzy, comfortable rooms and big beds (Sb-600–800F, Db-650–1,000F, most at 850F, more-expensive rooms with air-con, CC:VMA, cable TV, 19 rue de Champ de Mars, tel. 01 47 05 25 45, fax 01 45 55 08 24, www.relaisbosquet.com).

Hôtel Beaugency*** has small but comfortable rooms, a lobby you can stretch out in, and a helpful staff (Sb-680F, Db-730F, Tb-830F, includes buffet breakfast, 21 rue Duvivier, tel. 01 47 05 01 63, fax 01 45 51 04 96).

Hôtel Valadon**, on a quiet street one block west of rue Cler, will be spiffed up for 2001 by new owners (Sb-400F, Db-510–560F, CC:VMA, 16 rue Valadon, tel. 01 47 53 89 85, fax 01 44 18 90 56, www.hotelvaladon.com).

Hôtel la Motte Piquet**, at the end of rue Cler on a busy street, is pleasant with reasonable rates and a helpful owner (Ss-355F, Sb-375–435F, Ds-400F, Db-420–490F, duplex suites-670–780F, extra bed-100F, CC:VM, 30 avenue de la Motte Piquet, tel. 01 47 05 09 57, fax 01 47 05 74 36).

Near rue Cler: The following listings are a 5- to 10-minute walk west of rue Cler and are listed in order of proximity.

Hôtel Prince**, just across avenue Bosquet from the École Militaire Métro stop, has fair-value rooms, many overlooking a busy street (Db-470–625F, CC:VMA, 66 avenue Bosquet, tel. 01 47 05 40 90, fax 01 47 53 06 62).

Hôtel le Tourville**** is the most classy and expensive of my Paris listings. This four-star gem is surprisingly intimate and friendly, from its welcoming lobby to its air-conditioned, pastel rooms and vaulted breakfast area (small standard Db-890F, superior Db-1,090F, Db with private terrace-1,350F, extra bed-100F, 16 avenue de Tourville, Mo: École Militaire, tel. 01 47 05 62 62, fax 01 47 05 43 90, e-mail: hotel@tourville.com).

Hôtel de Turenne**, with small air-conditioned rooms, is a good value when it's hot (Sb-370F, Db-440–510F, Tb-600F, extra bed-60F, CC:VM, cable TV, 20 avenue de Tourville, tel. 01 47 05 99 92, fax 01 45 56 06 04, e-mail: hotel.turenne.paris7 @wanadoo.fr).

Hôtel de l'Alma*** is a fair value, with 32 small but pleasant look-alike rooms, all with cable TV and minibar and a tiny lobby (Sb-450F, Db-500F, no triples but a kid's bed can be moved in for free, CC:VMA, includes breakfast, 32 rue de l'Exposition, tel. 01 47 05 45 70, fax 01 45 51 84 47, e-mail: almahotel@minitel.net).

Hôtel Londres Eiffel*** may have rooms when others don't. The helpful staff takes good care of its guests and offers small but thoughtfully appointed rooms and cozy public spaces (Sb-545F, Db-645F, Tb-825F, extra bed-70F, CC:VMA, use handy bus #69 or the RER Alma stop, 1 rue Augerau, tel. 01 45 51 63 02, fax 01 47 05 28 96, www.Londres-Eiffel.com).

Mars Hôtel** is a formal Parisian place, with spacious rooms, thin walls, reasonable rates, and a beam-me-up-Jacques, coffin-sized elevator. Front rooms are noisier but have views of the Eiffel Tower (large Sb-350F, Db-410F, Twin/b-510F, CC:VM, 117 avenue de la Bourdonnais, tel. 01 47 05 42 30, fax 01 47 05 45 91).

Hôtel de la Bourdonnais***, more famous for its highly respected restaurant, is a superb three-star hotel. This perfectly Parisian place mixes Old World elegance with top-notch service, spacious rooms, and pleasant public spaces (Sb-690F, Db-790F, Tb-850F, Qb-910F, Qb suite-1,500F, CC:VMA, cable TV, 111 aveune de la Bourdonnais, tel. 01 47 05 45 42, fax 01 45 55 75 54, e-mail: otlbourd@clubinternet.fr).

Hôtel Kensington** has warmly decorated rooms at a fair value, but a cold staff (Sb-325F, Db-410–510F, extra bed-80F, CC:VMA, 79 avenue de la Bourdonnais, tel. 01 47 05 74 00, fax 01 47 05 25 81, www.hotel-kensington.com).

Hôtel de la Tulipe** is a unique place two blocks from rue Cler toward the river, with artistically decorated rooms (each one different) surrounding a wood-beamed lounge and a peaceful, leafy courtyard (Sb-570F, Db-680F, extra bed-150F, no elevator, cable TV, 33 rue Malar, tel. 01 45 51 67 21, fax 01 47 53 96 37, www .hoteldelatulipe.com).

Near Métro stop La Tour Maubourg: The next four listings are within two blocks of the intersection of avenue de la Motte Piquet and Les Invalides.

Hôtel Les Jardins Eiffel*** merits its three stars with professional service, a spacious lobby, outdoor patio, and comfortable, air-conditioned rooms—some with private balconies. Ask for a room *avec petit balcon* (Sb-600–840F, Db-700–1,000F, extra bed-135F, CC:VMA, parking-110F/day, 8 rue Amelie, tel. 01 47 05 46 21, fax 01 45 55 28 08, e-mail: Eiffel@unimedia.fr).

Hôtel La Tour Maubourg*** feels like a slightly faded, elegant manor house with spaciously comfortable Old World rooms. It overlooks a cheery green lawn and a busy street, within sight of Napoleon's tomb (Sb-700F, Db-800–900F, suites for up to 4 people-1,100–1,800F, prices reduced mid-July–mid-Aug, CC:VM, includes breakfast with freshly squeezed juice, immediately at La Tour Maubourg Métro stop, 150 rue de Grenelle, tel. 01 47 05 16 16, fax 01 47 05 16 14, www .latour-maubourg.fr).

Hôtel de l'Empereur** is a big, modern place with all the comforts (Sb-430F, Db-470–500F, Tb-650F, Qb-750F, CC:VM, 2 rue Chevert, tel. 01 45 55 88 02, fax 01 45 51 88 54).

Hôtel Muguet** is peaceful, overlooked, and very sharp. Here, you get three-star comfort for the price of two; a pleasant owner; quiet, air-conditioned rooms; and a small garden courtyard (Sb-560F, Db-600F, Tb-780F, CC:VMA, 11 rue Chevert, tel. 01 47 05 05 93, fax 01 45 50 25 37, www.hotelmuguet.com).

Lesser values: Given this fine area, these are acceptable last choices—**Derby Eiffel Hôtel***** (Db-750F–900F, CC:VMA, air-con, 5 avenue Duquesne, tel. 01 47 05 12 05, fax 01 47 05 43 43, www.derbyeiffelhotel.com); **Hôtel Splendid***** (Db-790–930F, 29 avenue Tourville, tel. 01 45 51 24 77, fax 01 44 18 94 60, e-mail: splendid@club-internet.fr); **Hôtel de la Tour Eiffel**** (Sb-370F, Db-420F, Tb-520F, CC:VMA, 17 rue de l'Exposition, tel. 01 47 05 14 75, fax 01 47 53 99 46, Muriel SE); the quiet but tired **Hôtel le Pavillon**** (has unrealized potential and a small courtyard; Db-460F, family suites-575F, 54 rue St. Dominique, tel. 01 45 51 42 87, fax 01 45 51 32 79, e-mail: PatrickPavillon@aol.com); **Hôtel Royal Phare**** (Db-390–460F, CC:VMA, facing École Militaire Métro stop, 40 avenue de la Motte Piquet, tel. 01 47 05 57 30, fax 01 45 51 64 41); the simple, quiet **Hôtel de la Paix** (S-180F, Ds-330F, Db-350F, Tb-480F, no elevator, 19 rue du Gros-Caillou, tel. 01 45 51 86 17, fax 01 45 55 93 28); and the basic, overpriced **Hôtel la**

Serre* (Db-500F, has superb location on rue Cler but generates readers' complaints for its rude staff and bizarre hotel practices—you can't see room in advance and no refunds are given, 24 rue Cler, across from Hôtel Leveque, Mo: Ecole Militaire, tel. 01 47 05 52 33, fax 01 40 62 95 66).

Marais Orientation

Those interested in a more Soho-Greenwich Village locale should make the Marais their Parisian home. The Marais is a more happening area than rue Cler, with great access to many museums: Picasso, Carnavalet, Jewish History, and Pompidou Center. It's narrow, medieval Paris at its finest, where elegant stone mansions sit side by side with trendy bars, antique shops, and slick boutiques. Only 15 years ago it was a forgotten Parisian backwater, but now the Marais is one of Paris' most popular residential and shopping areas.

The nearest **TIs** are in the Louvre and Gare de Lyon (arrival level, daily 8:00–20:00, tel. 01 43 43 33 24). The **Banque de France** changes money, offering good rates and sometimes long lines (Mon–Fri 9:00–11:45, 13:30–15:30, at the corner where rue St. Antoine hits place de la Bastille). Most banks and other services are on the main drag, rue de Rivoli/St. Antoine. You'll find one **taxi stand** on the north side of rue St. Antoine, where it meets rue Castex, and another on the south side of St. Antoine, in front of the St. Paul church.

The new Bastille opera house, Promenade Plantée Park, place des Vosges (Paris' oldest square), and the Jewish Quarter (rue des Rosiers) are all nearby. Be sure to stroll into place des Vosges after dark. The massive budget **department store** is BHV, next to Hôtel de Ville. Marais **post offices** are on rue Castex and on the corner of rues Pavée and Francs Bourgeois. The handiest **Internet cafés** are the Café du Hamman (4 rue des Rosiers) and the Quick Cybercafé (66 rue de Rivoli, Mo. Chatelet, tel. 01 48 87 78 43).

Helpful **bus routes**: Line #69 on rue St. Antoine takes you to the Louvre, Orsay, Rodin, and Napoleon's Tomb and ends at the Eiffel Tower. Line #86 runs down boulevard Henri IV, crossing Île St. Louis and serving the Latin Quarter along boulevard St. Germain. Line #96 runs on rues Turenne and Francois Miron and serves the Louvre and boulevard St. Germain (near Luxembourg Gardens). Line #65 serves the train stations Austerlitz, Est, and Nord from place de la Bastille.

Sleeping in the Marais Neighborhood
(4th arrondissement, Mo: St. Paul or Bastille, zip code: 75004)

The Marais runs from the Pompidou Center to the Bastille (a 15-min walk), with most hotels located a few blocks north of the main east-west drag, rue de Rivoli/St. Antoine. It's about 15 minutes on foot from any hotel in this area to Notre-Dame, Île St. Louis, and the Latin Quarter. Strolling home (day or night) from Notre-Dame along the Île St. Louis is a marvelous plus of this area.

The St. Paul Métro stop puts you right in the heart of the Marais, while the Hôtel de Ville stop serves its western end and the Bastille stop serves its eastern limit.

Hôtel Castex** is a clean, well-run, and cheery place—a great value with comfortable rooms, many stairs, and a good location on a relatively quiet street. Reserve by phone and leave your credit-card number (Sb-310F, Db-360–380F, Tb-480F, CC:VM, no elevator, just off place de la Bastille and rue St. Antoine, 5 rue Castex, Mo: Bastille, tel. 01 42 72 31 52, fax 01 42 72 57 91, e-mail: info @castexhotel.com). The owners have another good-value hotel two Métro stops away in a less appealing location that often has rooms when others don't: **Hôtel de la République**** (Sb-350F, Db-400F, cable TV, 31 rue Albert Thomas, 75010 Paris, Mo: République, tel. 01 42 39 19 03, fax 01 42 39 22 66, www.republique.com).

Grand Hôtel Jeanne d'Arc**, a warm, welcoming place with thoughtfully appointed rooms and cozy public spaces, is ideally located for connoisseurs of the Marais. Rooms on the street can be noisy until the bars close. Sixth-floor rooms have a view and corner rooms are wonderfully bright in the City of Light. Reserve this place way ahead (small Db-320F, Db-435–500F, Tb-550F, family friendly Qb-620F, extra bed-75F, CC:VM, 3 rue Jarente, Mo: St. Paul, tel. 01 48 87 62 11, fax 01 48 87 37 31).

Hôtel Bastille Speria*** a short block off the Bastille, feels family-run while offering serious, business-type service. Its spacious lobby and 45 rooms are modern, cheery, and pastel. It's English-language friendly, from the *Herald Tribune*s in the lobby to the history of the Bastille posted in the elevator (Sb-540–580F, Db-600–720F, Tb-830F, extra bed-110F, CC:VMA, 1 rue de la Bastille, Mo: Bastille, tel. 01 42 72 04 01, fax 01 42 72 56 38, e-mail: speria@micronet.fr).

Hôtel Lyon-Mulhouse**, on a busy street just off place de la Bastille, is a good value, with pleasant, modern rooms and helpful owners (Sb-345–435F, Db-370–540F, Tb-545–575F, Qb-600–640F, CC:VM, 8 boulevard Beaumarchais, tel. 01 47 00 91 50, fax 01 47 00 06 31, e-mail: hotelyonmulhouse@wanadoo.fr).

Hôtel de la Place des Vosges**, quasi-classy with a linoleum/antique feel, is ideally located on a quiet street (Sb-495F, Db-660–690F, CC:VMA, elevator begins on 2nd floor, just off elegant place des Vosges and just as snooty, 12 rue de Biraque, Mo: St. Paul, tel. 01 42 72 60 46, fax 01 42 72 02 64, e-mail: hotel.place.des.vosges@gofornet.com).

Marais Hotels

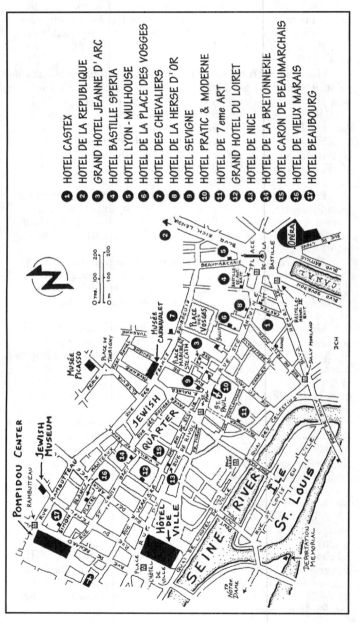

1. HOTEL CASTEX
2. HOTEL DE LA REPUBLIQUE
3. GRAND HOTEL JEANNE D' ARC
4. HOTEL BASTILLE SPERIA
5. HOTEL LYON - MULHOUSE
6. HOTEL DE LA PLACE DES VOSGES
7. HOTEL DES CHEVALIERS
8. HOTEL DE LA HERSE D'OR
9. HOTEL SEVIGNE
10. HOTEL PRATIC & MODERNE
11. HOTEL DE 7 eme ART
12. GRAND HOTEL DU LOIRET
13. HOTEL DE NICE
14. HOTEL DE LA BRETONNERIE
15. HOTEL CARON DE BEAUMARCHAIS
16. HOTEL DE VIEUX MARAIS
17. HOTEL BEAUBOURG

Hôtel des Chevaliers***, one block northwest of place des Vosges, offers small, pleasant, and comfortable rooms, with modern comforts from hair dryers to cable TV. Rooms off the street are quiet (Db-660–850F, CC:VMA, skip overpriced breakfast, 30 rue de Turenne, Mo: St. Paul, tel. 01 42 72 73 47, fax 01 42 72 54 10).

Hôtel de la Herse D'Or is industrial-strength, three-coats-of-paint simple, with a good location, tortured floor plan, and hard-to-beat prices for its relatively comfortable rooms (S-180F, D-220F, Db-310F, extra bed-50F, showers-10F, no elevator, 20 rue St. Antoine, Mo: Bastille, tel. 01 48 87 84 09, fax 01 48 87 94 01).

Hôtel Sévigné** provides two-star comfort at fair prices with the cheapest breakfast in Paris—20F (Sb-360F, Db-380–400F, Tb-512F, CC:VM, 2 rue Malher, Mo: St. Paul, tel. 01 42 72 76 17, fax 01 42 78 68 26).

Hôtel Pratic*'s greatest plus is its location on a great people-friendly square. Its pricey rooms are modern (single rooms are tiny) and stairs are many (St-250F, Dt-280F, Ds-390F, Db-460F, no elevator, 9 rue d'Ormesson, Mo: St. Paul, tel. 01 48 87 80 47, fax 01 48 87 40 04).

The bare-bones and dumpy **Hôtel Moderne**, next to Hôtel Pratic, might be better than a youth hostel if you need privacy. The only thing *moderne* about it is the name, which is illegible on the broken sign (S-170F, D-190F, Db-340F, 3 rue Caron, Mo: St. Paul, tel. 01 48 87 97 05).

Hôtel de 7ème Art**, two blocks south of rue St. Antoine, is a relaxed, Hollywood-nostalgia place, run by young, friendly, hip Marais types, with a full-service café/bar and Charlie Chaplin murals. Most rooms are average, but the few large double rooms at 690F are very nice (Sb-300F, Db-430–570F, large Db-690F, extra bed-100F, CC:VMA, 20 rue St. Paul, Mo: St. Paul, tel. 01 44 54 85 00, fax 01 42 77 69 10).

MIJE Youth Hostels: The *Maison Internationale de la Jeunesse des Étudiants* (MIJE) runs three classy old residences clustered a few blocks south of rue St. Antoine. Each offers simple, clean, single-sex, one- to four-bed rooms for families and travelers under the age of 30 (exceptions are made for families). Prices are per person; you can pay more to have your own room or be roomed with as many as three others (Sb-225F, Db-175F, Tb-155F, Qb-145F; includes breakfast but not towels—which you can get from a machine; required membership card-15F extra/person; rooms locked from 12:00–15:00 and at 01:00). **MIJE Fourcy** (cheap dinners, 6 rue de Fourcy, just south of rue Rivoli), **MIJE Fauconnier** (11 rue Fauconnier), and the best, **MIJE Maubisson** (12 rue des Barres), share the same contact information (tel. 01 42 74 23 45, fax 01 40 27 81 64, www.mije.com) and Métro stop (St. Paul). Reservations are accepted.

Near Pompidou Center: The remaining hotels are farther west, and much closer to the Pompidou than to place Bastille.

Hôtel de Nice** is a cozy "Marie Antoinette does tie-dye" place with lots of thoughtful touches on the Marais' busy main drag. Twin rooms, which cost the same as doubles, are roomier but on the street side—with effective double-paned windows (Sb-380F, Db-550F, Tb-680F, CC:VM, 42 bis rue de Rivoli, Mo: Hôtel de Ville, tel. 01 42 78 55 29, fax 01 42 78 36 07).

Hôtel de la Bretonnerie***, three blocks north and east of the Hôtel de Ville, is a fine Marais splurge. It has elegant décor; tastefully decorated and spacious rooms with an antique, open-beam coziness; and an efficient, helpful staff (standard Db-660F, Db with character-830F, the standard Db has enough character for me, family-friendly suites-1,050F, CC:VMA, between rue du Vielle du Temple and rue des Archives at 22 rue Sainte Croix de la Bretonnerie, Mo: Hôtel de Ville, tel. 01 48 87 77 63, fax 01 42 77 26 78, www.laBretonnerie.com).

Grand Hôtel du Loiret**, just north of rue de Rivoli, is a fair-enough value. It has laid-back management and is popular with American students (S-190F, Sb-270–350F, D-230F, Db-310–410F, Tb-515F, Qb-600F, CC:VMA, 8 rue des Garçons Mauvais, Mo: Hôtel de Ville, tel. 01 48 87 77 00, fax 01 48 04 96 56, e-mail: HOTELLOIRET@aol.com).

Hôtel Caron de Beaumarchais***, an 18th-century Marais manor house, has pricey, precious, comfortable rooms (Db-790–870F, CC:VMA, air-con, 12 rue Vielle du Temple, Mo: Hôtel de Ville, tel. 01 42 72 34 12, fax 01 42 72 34 63).

Hôtel de Vieux Marais**, tucked away on a quiet street two blocks east of the Pompidou Center, offers spotless and fairly spacious rooms with air-conditioning, pleasing decor, and we-try-harder owners. Make sure to greet Leeloo, the hotel hound (Sb-600–660F, Db-695–720F, extra bed-150F, CC:VM, cable TV, just off rue des Archives at 8 rue du Platre, Mo: Rambuteau/Hôtel de Ville, tel. 01 42 78 47 22, fax 01 42 78 34 32).

Hôtel Beaubourg***, is an excellent three-star value within spitting distance of the Pompidou Center on a small street. The comfortable rooms are wood-beam cozy and public spaces are warm and pleasant (Db-520–590F, Db with private terrace-690F, CC:VM, 11 rue Simon Lefranc, Mo: Rambuteau, tel. 01 42 74 34 24, fax 01 42 78 68 11, e-mail: htlbeaubourg@hotellerie.net).

Contrescarpe Orientation

This lively, colorful neighborhood is like Montmartre without all the tourists. It's just south of the Latin Quarter, encompassing the area between the Luxembourg Gardens and rue Monge.

The nearest **TI** is at the Louvre Museum. The **post office** (PTT) is between rue Mouffetard and rue Monge at 10 rue de l'Épée du Bois. Place Monge hosts a colorful **outdoor market** on Wednesday, Friday, and Sunday until 13:00. The **street market** at the bottom of rue Mouffetard bustles daily except Monday (Tue–Sat 8:00–12:00, 15:30–19:00, Sun 8:00–12:00, 5 blocks south of place Contrescarpe). The lively place Contrescarpe hops in the afternoon and evening until the wee hours. **Bus #47** runs along rue Monge north to Notre-Dame, the Pompidou Center, and Gare du Nord.

The flowery Jardin des Plantes park is just east and the sublime Luxembourg Gardens are just west. Both are ideal for afternoon walks, picnics, and naps. The doorway at 49 rue Monge leads to a hidden Roman arena (Arènes de Lutèce). Today, *boules* players occupy the stage while couples cuddle on the seats. Admire the Panthéon from the outside (it's not worth paying to go in), and go into the exquisitely beautiful St. Étienne-du-Mont church.

Sleeping in the Contrescarpe Neighborhood
(5th arrondissement, Mo: place Monge, zip code: 75005)

Hotels here are a 20-minute walk from Notre-Dame, Île de la Cité, and Île St. Louis, and a 5- to 10-minute walk from the Luxembourg Gardens and the grand boulevards St. Germain and St. Michel. Fewer tourists sleep in Contrescarpe, and I find the hotel values generally better than in most other neighborhoods. Most hotels listed are on or very near rue Mouffetard, the spine of this area, running from the perfectly Parisian place Contrescarpe south to rue Bazelles. Two thousand years ago, rue Mouffetard was the principal Roman road south to Italy. Today this small, meandering street has a split personality. The lower part thrives in the daytime as a pedestrian market street. The upper part sleeps during the day, but comes alive after dark, teeming with bars, restaurants, and nightlife. These hotels are listed in order of proximity to the Seine and Notre-Dame.

The low-energy, no-frills **Hôtel du Commerce** is run by Monsieur Mattuzzi, who must be a pirate gone good. This 300-year-old place (with vinyl that looks it) is a great rock-bottom deal and as safe as any dive next to a police station can be. In the morning, the landlady will knock and chirp, "*Restez-vous?*"—Are you staying tonight? (S-135F, D-155F, Ds-175F, Ts-225F, Qs-290F, showers-15F, no elevator, takes no reservations, call at 10:00 and monsieur will say "*oui*" or "*non*," 14 rue de La Montagne Ste. Geneviève, Mo: Maubert-Mutualité, tel. 01 43 54 89 69).

Hôtel Central* is unpretentious, with a charming location, a steep and slippery castlelike stairway, simple rooms (all with showers, though toilets are down the hall), so-so beds, and plenty of smiles. It's a fine budget value (Ss-165–213F, Ds-240–276F, no elevator, 6 rue Descartes, Mo: Cardinal Lemoine, tel. 01 46 33 57 93).

Hôtel des Grandes Écoles*** is simply idyllic. A short

Contrescarpe Hotels

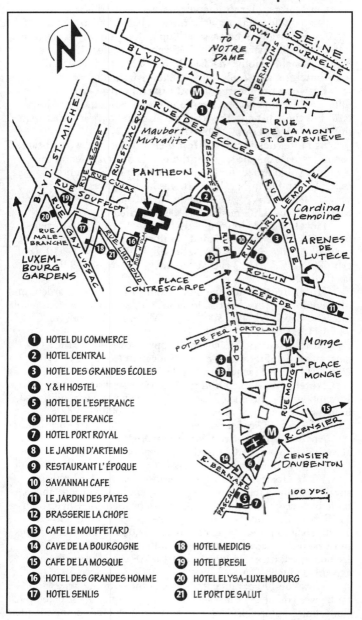

1. HOTEL DU COMMERCE
2. HOTEL CENTRAL
3. HOTEL DES GRANDES ÉCOLES
4. Y & H HOSTEL
5. HOTEL DE L'ESPERANCE
6. HOTEL DE FRANCE
7. HOTEL PORT ROYAL
8. LE JARDIN D'ARTEMIS
9. RESTAURANT L'ÉPOQUE
10. SAVANNAH CAFE
11. LE JARDIN DES PATES
12. BRASSERIE LA CHOPE
13. CAFE LE MOUFFETARD
14. CAVE DE LA BOURGOGNE
15. CAFE DE LA MOSQUE
16. HOTEL DES GRANDES HOMME
17. HOTEL SENLIS
18. HOTEL MEDICIS
19. HOTEL BRESIL
20. HOTEL ELYSA-LUXEMBOURG
21. LE PORT DE SALUT

alley leads to three buildings that protect a flowering garden courtyard, preserving a tranquility rare in a city this size. Rooms are spacious and comfortable with large beds. This romantic place is deservedly popular, so call up to four months in advance (Db-555–720F, extra bed-100F, 75 rue de Cardinal Lemoine, Mo: Cardinal Lemoine, tel. 01 43 26 79 23, fax 01 43 25 28 15, www.hotel-grandes-ecoles.com, mellow Marie SE).

Between the Panthéon and Luxembourg Gardens: The following five hotels are a five-minute walk from the rue Mouffetard. For these listings, the RER stop Luxembourg is closer than the nearest Métro stop, Maubert Mutualité.

At **Hôtel des Grandes Hommes*****, spacious, wood-beamed rooms stare across the street at the Panthéon and offer all the comforts you'd expect for the price, including air-conditioning, cable TV, and mini-bar. Some rooms have terraces (Db-850F, suite-1,100F, CC:VM, 17 place du Panthéon, tel. 01 46 34 19 60, fax 01 43 26 67 32, e-mail: henri4@hotellerie.net).

Hôtel Senlis** hides quietly two blocks from the Luxembourg Gardens with simple but comfortable rooms, all with beamed ceilings and TV (Sb-420F, Db-450–530F, Tb-530–580F, Qb-680F, CC:VMA, 7 rue Malebranche, tel. 01 43 29 93 10, fax 01 43 29 00 24).

Hôtel Brésil** lies one block from Luxembourg Gardens and offers unimaginative but comfortable, modern rooms at reasonable rates (Sb-375F, Db-400–500F, CC:VM, 10 rue le Goff, tel. 01 43 54 76 11, fax 01 46 33 45 78).

Hôtel Medicis is as cheap, stripped-down, and basic as it gets with a helpful owner and great location (S-100F, D-190–200F, 214 rue St. Jacques, tel. 01 43 54 14 66).

Hôtel Elysa-Luxembourg*** sits on a busy street at the Luxembourg Gardens and charges top franc for its air-conditioned, impressively decorated rooms (Sb-680F, Db-800F, Tb-900F, CC:VMA, 6 rue Gay Lussac, tel. 01 43 25 31 74, fax 01 46 34 56 27).

At the bottom of rue Mouffetard: Of my recommended accomodations in the Contrescarpe neighborhood, these are the farthest from the Seine. They may have rooms when others don't.

Y&H Hostel offers a great location, easygoing English-speaking management, Internet access, kitchen facilities, and basic but acceptable hostel-like conditions (beds in 4-bed rooms-117F, beds in double rooms-137F, sheets-15F, rooms closed 11:00–16:00 but reception stays open, 02:00 curfew, reservations must be paid in advance, 80 rue Mouffetard, Mo: Cardinal Lemoine, tel. 01 45 35 09 53, fax 01 47 07 22 24, e-mail: smile @youngandhappy.fr).

Hôtel de l'Esperance**, located at the bottom of rue Mouffetard, gives you nearly three stars for the price of two. It's quiet, pink, fluffy, and comfortable, with thoughtfully appointed rooms complete with canopy beds, hair dryers, cable TV, and a flamboyant owner (Sb-440F, Db-450–550F, small Tb-600F, CC:VM, 15 rue Pascal, Mo: Censier-Daubenton, tel. 01 47 07 10 99, fax 01 43 37 56 19).

Hôtel de France**, set on a busy street, has fine, modern rooms and hardworking, helpful owners (Jean and Christine). The best and quietest rooms are *sur le cour* (on the courtyard), though streetside rooms are fine (Sb-390F, Db-435–455F, CC:VM, 108 rue Monge, Mo: Censier-Daubenton, tel. 01 47 07 19 04, fax 01 43 36 62 34, e-mail: hotel.de.fce@wanadoo.fr).

Hôtel Port Royal* is well run (by the same family for 66 years), with a small, pleasant courtyard and incredibly clean, comfortable rooms at fair prices. Ask for a room off the street (S-210–260F, D-260F, Db-405F, no CC, climb stairs from rue Pascal to 8 boulevard de Port Royal, Mo: Gobelins, tel. 01 43 31 70 06, fax 01 43 31 33 67).

Sleeping near Paris, in Versailles

For a laid-back alternative to Paris within easy reach of the big city by RER train (5/hrly, 30 min), Versailles can be a good overnight stop—with easy, safe parking and reasonably priced hotels (see map on page 163).

Hôtel Le Cheval Rouge**, built in 1676 as Louis XIV's stables, now houses tourists. It's a block behind place du Marché in a quaint corner of town on a large, quiet courtyard with free, safe parking and simple but adequate rooms (Ds-300F, Db-360–410F, extra bed-90F for 1 person, 120F for 2, CC:VMA, cable TV, 18 rue Andre Chenier, tel. 01 39 50 03 03, fax 01 39 50 61 27).

Ibis Versailles**, a slick business-class place, offers all the comfort with none of the character (Db-425F, cheaper weekend rates available but can't be reserved ahead, CC:VMA, across from RER station, 4 avenue du General de Gaulle, tel. 01 39 53 03 30, fax 01 39 50 06 31, e-mail: accorhotel.com).

Hôtel du Palais, facing the RER station, has cheap and handy beds; ask for a quiet room off the street. It's a pink and funky place—dumpy enough to lack even one star but proud enough to put candy on the beds (D-180F, Ds-250F, Db-250–280F, extra person-70F, miles of stairs, 6 place Lyautey, tel. 01 39 50 39 29, fax 01 39 50 80 41).

Hôtel d'Angleterre** is a tranquil old place with comfortable and spacious rooms. Park nearby in the palace lot (Db-350–450F, extra bed-100F, CC:VMA, cable TV, mini-bar, just below palace to the right as you exit, 2 rue de Fontenay, tel. 01 39 51 43 50, fax 01 39 51 45 63).

Eating in Paris

Paris is France's wine and cuisine melting pot. While it lacks a style of its own (only French onion soup is truly Parisian), it draws from the best of France. Paris could hold a gourmet's Olympics and import nothing.

Picnic or go to bakeries for quick take-out lunches, or stop at a café for a lunch salad or *plat du jour*, but linger longer over dinner. You can eat well, restaurant style, for 100F to 150F. Your hotel can usually recommend nearby restaurants in the 80F to 100F range. Remember, cafés are happy to serve a *plat du jour* (garnished plate of the day, about 70F) or a chef-like salad (60F) day or night. Famous places are often overpriced, overcrowded, and overrated. Find a quiet neighborhood and wander, or follow a local recommendation. Restaurants open for dinner around 19:00, and small local favorites get crowded after 21:00.

To save piles of francs, review the budget eating tips in this book's introduction and consider dinner picnics (great take-out dishes available at *charcuteries*). My recommendations are centered around the same three great neighborhoods listed in "Sleeping," above; you can come home exhausted after a busy day of sight-seeing and have a good selection of restaurants right around the corner. And evening is a fine time to explore any of these delight-ful neighborhoods even if you're sleeping elsewhere.

Restaurants

The Parisian eating scene is kept at a rolling boil. Entire books (and lives) are dedicated to the subject. If you are traveling outside of Paris, save your splurges for the countryside, where you'll enjoy regional cooking for less money. I've listed places that conveniently fit a busy sightseeing schedule and places near recommended hotels. If you'd like to visit a district specifically to eat, consider the many romantic restaurants that line the cozy Ile St. Louis' main street and the colorful, touristy-but-fun string of eateries along rue Mouffetard behind the Panthéon (in the Contrescarpe neighborhood). Beware: Many restaurants close Sunday and Monday.

Cafeterias and Picnics

Many Parisian department stores have huge supermarkets hiding in the basement and top-floor cafeterias offering not really cheap but low-risk, low-stress, what-you-see-is-what-you-get meals.

For lunch and dinner picnics, you'll find hardy little groceries (*épiceries*) and delis (*charcuteries*) all over town but rarely near famous sights. Good picnic fixings include roasted chicken, drinkable yogurt, fresh bakery goods, melons, and exotic pâtés and cheeses. Great take-out deli-type foods like gourmet salads and quiches abound. *Boulangeries* make good, cheap mini-quiches and sand-wiches. While wine is taboo in public places in the United States, it's *pas de problème* in France.

Romantic Picnic Spots: My favorite dinner-picnic places are the pedestrian bridge (Pont des Arts) across from the Louvre, with unmatched views and plentiful benches; the Champ de Mars park under the Eiffel Tower; and the western tip of Île St. Louis, over-looking Île de la Cité. Bring your own dinner feast and watch the riverboats or the Eiffel Tower light up the city for you. The Palais Royal (across the street from the Louvre) is a good spot for a peaceful, royal picnic, as is the little triangular Henry IV Park on the west tip of Île de la Cité. For lunch picnics with great people watching, try the Pompidou Center (by the *Homage to Stravinsky* fountain), the elegant place des Vosges (closes at dusk), the gardens at the Rodin Museum, and Luxembourg Gardens.

Eating in the Rue Cler Neighborhood

The rue Cler neighborhood isn't famous for its restaurants. That's why I enjoy eating here. Several small family-run places serve great dinner *menus* for 100F and *plats du jour* for 60F to 80F. My first two recommendations are easygoing cafés, ideal if what you want is a light dinner (good dinner salads) or more substantial but simple meals.

Café du Marché, with the best seats, coffee, and prices on rue Cler, serves hearty salads and good 50F *plat du jour* for lunch or dinner to a trendy, mainly French crowd. Arrive before 19:30 or wait at the bar. A chalkboard listing the plates of the day—each a meal—will momentarily be hung in front of you (at the corner of rue Cler and rue Champ de Mars). You'll find the same menu and prices with better (but smoky) indoor seating at their other restaurant, **Le Comptoir du Septième**, at the École Militaire Métro stop (39 avenue de la Motte Piquet, tel. 01 45 55 90 20).

Café le Bosquet's friendly owner Jean Francois will make you feel welcome at his classic Parisian brasserie. Come here for a bowl of French onion soup, a salad, or a three-course set *menu* (98F *menu*, many choices, 46 avenue Bosquet, tel. 01 45 51 38 13).

Leo le Lion, run by Mimi for 20 years, is an easygoing place. A warm, charming souvenir of old Paris, it's popular with locals. The 115F *menu* comes with a first course that could feed two for an entire meal (but no splitting) and a fully garnished main course (closed Sun, 23 rue Duvivier, tel. 01 45 51 41 77).

Vegetarians will appreciate the Mediterranean cuisine at **7ème Sud** (closed Sun, at the corner of rue de Grenelle and rue Duvivier).

Closer to Invalides, the friendly **Le Bistrot du 7ème** opens its cozy interior onto a broad sidewalk and serves a decent 98F *menu* with many choices (open daily, 56 boulevard Latour-Maubourg, tel. 01 45 51 93 08). **La Bressanne** is a country-warm place with a good 130F *menu* (16 avenue de la Motte Piquet, tel. 01 47 05 98 37). The tiny **Au Petit Tonneau** is a totally Parisian experience, where the owner/chef prepares everything herself (open daily, 20 rue Surcouf, tel. 01 47 05 09 10)

Rue Cler Restaurants

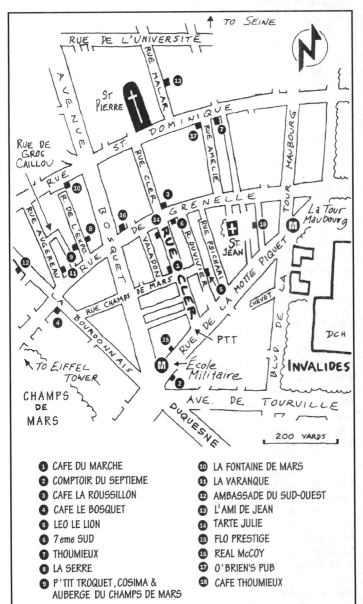

1. CAFE DU MARCHE
2. COMPTOIR DU SEPTIEME
3. CAFE LA ROUSSILLON
4. CAFE LE BOSQUET
5. LEO LE LION
6. 7eme SUD
7. THOUMIEUX
8. LA SERRE
9. P'TIT TROQUET, COSIMA & AUBERGE DU CHAMPS DE MARS
10. LA FONTAINE DE MARS
11. LA VARANQUE
12. AMBASSADE DU SUD-OUEST
13. L'AMI DE JEAN
14. TARTE JULIE
15. FLO PRESTIGE
16. REAL McCOY
17. O'BRIEN'S PUB
18. CAFE THOUMIEUX

Thoumieux, the neighborhood's classy, traditional Parisian brasserie, is deservedly popular (skippable 82F but fine 160F *menu*, complete *à la carte*, 79 rue St. Dominique, tel. 01 47 05 49 75).

For a special dinner, survey the handful of fine places that line rue de l'Exposition one block west of avenue Bosquet between rue St. Dominique and rue de Grenelle: **Restaurant La Serre**, at #29, has fun ambience, usually great food, but an unpredictable staff (*plats* 50–70F, daily from 19:00, often a wait after 21:00, good onion soup and duck specialties, tel. 01 45 55 20 96, Marie-Alice and intense Philippe speak English). **Le P'tit Troquet**, across the street at #28, is delightfully Parisian, popular with locals, and ideal for a last-night splurge—allow 160F per person for dinner (closed Sun–Mon, tel. 01 47 05 80 39). The quieter **La Maison de Cosima** at #20 offers refined, creative French cuisine and excellent 100F and 160F *menus* that include a vegetarian option (closed Sun, tel. 01 45 51 37 71, run by friendly Helene). The softly lit tables and red velvet chairs of **Auberge du Champ de Mars**, at #18, draw a romantic crowd (no inexpensive wines, closed Mon). For top *à la carte*–only cuisine, locals reserve early for the charmingly situated **La Fontaine de Mars** (allow 250F per person with wine, 129 rue St. Dominique, tel. 01 47 05 46 44). Just off rue de Grenelle, the friendly and unpretentious **La Varanque** is a good budget bet, with 60F *plats* and an 80F *menu* (27 rue Augereau, tel. 01 47 05 51 22).

Ambassade du Sud-Ouest, a wine and food boutique/restaurant, specializes in southwestern French cuisine such as *daubes de canard* (duck meatballs) and cassoulet (46 avenue de la Bourdonnais, tel. 01 45 55 59 59). **L'Ami de Jean** is a lively place to sample Basque cuisine (closed Sun, 27 rue Malar, tel. 01 47 05 86 89).

Picnicking: Rue Cler is a moveable feast that gives "fast food" a good name. The entire street is clogged with connoisseurs of good eating. Only the health-food store goes unnoticed. A festival of food, the street is lined with people whose lives seem to be devoted to their specialty: stacking polished produce, rotisserie chicken, crepes, or cheese squares.

For a magical picnic dinner at the Eiffel Tower, assemble it in no fewer than five shops on rue Cler and lounge on the best grass in Paris (the police don't mind after dusk), with the dogs, Frisbees, a floodlit tower, and a cool breeze in the Parc du Champ de Mars.

The **crepe stand** next to Café du Marché does a wonderful top-end dinner crepe for 25F. An Asian deli, **Traiteur Asie** (many in the area, one across from Hôtel Leveque), has tasty low-stress, low-price take-out treats. Its tables offer the cheapest place to sit, eat, and enjoy the rue Cler ambience. For quiche, cheese pie, or a pear/chocolate tart, try **Tarte Julie's** (takeout or stools, 28 rue Cler). The elegant **Flo Prestige** *charcuterie* (at the École Militaire Métro stop) is open until 23:00 and offers mouthwatering meals to go. **Real McCoy** is a little shop selling American food and sandwiches (194 rue de Grenelle). A good, small, late-night grocery is at 197 rue de Grenelle.

The bakery (*boulangerie*) on the corner of rue Cler and rue de Champ de Mars is the place for a fresh baguette, sandwich, tiny quiche, or *pain au chocolat*, but the almond croissants at the *boulangerie* on rue de Grenelle at rue Cler make my day. The bakery at 112 rue St. Dominique is in a league by itself and worth the detour, with classic decor and tables to enjoy your *café au lait* and croissant.

Cafés and Bars: If you want to linger over coffee or a drink at a sidewalk café, try **Café du Marché** (see above), **Petite Brasserie PTT** (local workers eat here, opposite 53 rue Cler), or **Café le Bosquet** (46 avenue Bosquet, tel. 01 45 51 38 13). **Café La Roussillon**, peopled and decorated belle epoque, also offers a quintessential café experience (at the corner of rue de Grenelle and rue Cler). **Le Sancerre** wine bar/café is wood-beam warm and ideal for a light lunch or dinner, or just a glass of wine after a long day of sightseeing. The owner's cheeks are the same color as his wine (open until 21:30, great omelets, 22 avenue Rapp, tel. 01 45 51 75 91). **Maison Altmayer** is a hole-in-the-wall place for a quiet drink (9:00–19:30, next to Hôtel Eiffel Rive Gauche, 6 rue du Gros Caillou). Cafés like this originated (and this one still functions) as a place where locals enjoyed a drink while their heating wood, coal, or gas was prepared for delivery.

Nightlife: This sleepy neighborhood is not the place for night owls, but there are four notable exceptions: **Café du Marché** and its brother, **Le Comptoir du Septième** (both listed above), hop with a Franco-American crowd until about midnight. **O'Brien's Pub** is a relaxed, Parisian rendition of an Irish pub (77 St. Dominique). **Café Thoumieux** is a sophisticated place with big-screen sports and a trendy young crowd (4 rue de la Comete, Mo: Latour Maubourg).

Eating in the Marais Neighborhood

The windows of the Marais are filled with munching sophisticates and crowd-pleasing eateries. And with Île St. Louis a short walk away (see below), those sleeping in the Marais have a great selection of good-value restaurants.

You'll find several good places at place du Marché Ste. Catherine, a tiny square just off rue St. Antoine between the St. Paul Métro stop and place des Vosges. **Le Marais Ste. Catherine** is a good value (110F *menu*, daily from 19:00, non-smoking, extra seating in candlelit cellar, 5 rue Caron, tel. 01 42 72 39 94), but if it's warm, you may prefer the outdoor tables at **Le Marché** (130F *menu*, 2 place Marché Ste. Catherine,

Marais Restaurants

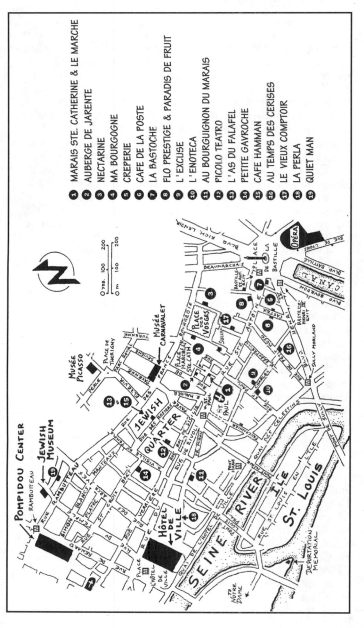

1. MARAIS STE. CATHERINE & LE MARCHE
2. AUBERGE DE JARENTE
3. NECTARINE
4. MA BOURGOGNE
5. CREPERIE
6. CAFE DE LA POSTE
7. LA BASTOCHE
8. FLO PRESTIGE & PARADIS DE FRUIT
9. L'EXCUSE
10. L'ENOTECA
11. AU BOURGUIGNON DU MARAIS
12. PICOLO TEATRO
13. L'AS DU FALAFEL
14. PETITE GAVROCHE
15. CAFE HAMMAN
16. AU TEMPS DES CERISES
17. LE VIEUX COMPTOIR
18. LA PERLA
19. QUIET MAN

tel. 01 42 77 34 88). Just off the square, **L'Auberge de Jarente** offers a well-respected cuisine with Basque specialities (120F *menu*, closed Sun–Mon, 7 rue Jarente, tel. 01 42 77 49 35).

Dinners under the candlelit arches of place des Vosges are *très* romantic. **Nectarine**, at #16, serves salads, quiches, and reasonable *plats du jour* daily and nightly (no CC), while **Ma Bourgogne** is where locals go for a splurge (open daily, reserve dinner ahead, no CC, at northwest corner, tel. 01 42 78 44 64).

For a fast, cheap change of pace, eat at (or take out from) the Chinese/Japanese **Delice House**. Two can split 200 grams of chicken curry (or whatever, 30F) and rice (20F). There's lots of seating, with pitchers of water at the ground-floor tables and a roomier upstairs (open until 21:00, 81 rue St. Antoine).

The **Crêperie** at 6 rue Castex serves a 60F all-crepe *menu* (closed Sun–Mon), and the cozy restaurant **de la Poste** (13 rue Castex) offers 60F *plats du jour* (closed Sun). **La Bastoche**'s warm ambience and reasonable 90F *menu* make it a popular place (7 rue St. Antoine, tel. 01 48 04 74 34). Across the street, **Le Paradis de Fruit** serves salads and organic foods to a young local crowd (on small square at rues Tournelle and St. Antoine). **Gaspard de le Nuit** is a cozy step up with a fine 152F *menu* (6 rue des Tournelles, tel. 01 42 77 90 53).

Near Hôtel du 7ème Art, try the romantic and traditional **L'Excuse** for a worthwhile splurge (190F *menu*, closed Sun, call ahead, 14 rue Charles V, tel. 01 42 77 98 97). Across the street, **L'Énoteca** (wine bar) has lively and reasonable Italian cuisine in a relaxed, open setting (closed Sun, 20 rue St. Paul, tel. 01 42 78 91 44).

Wine lovers shouldn't miss the superb Burgundy wines and exquisite, though limited, menu selection at **Au Bourguignon du Marais** (closed Sat–Sun, call by 19:00 to reserve, 52 rue Francois Miron, tel. 01 48 87 15 40).

Vegetarians will appreciate the excellent cuisine at the popular **Picolo Teatro** (closed Mon, 6 rue des Ecouffes, tel. 01 42 72 17 79) and **L'As du Falafel**, serving the best falafel on rue Rosier at #34.

Picnicking: Picnic at the peaceful place des Vosges (closes at dusk). Hobos stretch their francs at the supermarket in the basement of the **Monoprix** department store (close to place des Vosges on rue St. Antoine), and connoisseurs prefer the gourmet take-out places all along rue St. Antoine, such as **Flo Prestige** (open until 23:00, on the tiny square where rue Tournelle and rue St. Antoine meet). A few small grocery shops are open until 23:00 on rue St. Antoine (near intersection with rue Castex). An **open-air market**, held Sunday morning, is just off place de la Bastille on boulevard Richard Lenoir.

For a cheap breakfast, try the tiny *boulangerie/pâtisserie* where the hotels buy their croissants (coffee machine-3F, baby quiches-10F, *pain au chocolat*-5F, 1 block off place de la Bastille, corner of rue St. Antoine and rue de Lesdiguieres).

Cafés and Bars: The trendiest cafés and bars are clustered on rues Vielle du Temple, Archives, and Ste. Croix de la Bretonniere (open generally until 02:00), and are popular with gay men. The *très* local wine bar at **Au Temps des Cerises** is amiably run and a welcoming, if smoky, place (around the corner from Hôtel Castex, rue du Petit Musc and rue de Cerisaie).

Nightlife: Le Vieux Comptoir is tiny, lively, and not too hip (just off place des Vosges at 8 rue Biraque). La Perla is trendy and full of Parisian yuppies in search of the perfect margarita (26 rue Francois Miron). The Quiet Man is a traditional Irish pub with happy hour from 16:00 to 20:00 (5 rue des Haudriettes).

Eating in the Contrescarpe Neighborhood

The rue Mouffetard and rue du Pot-de-Fer are lined with inexpensive, lively, and forgettable restaurants (see map on page 185). Study the many *menus*, compare crowds, then dive in. **Le Jardin d'Artemis** is one of the better values on rue Mouffetard at #34 (89F menu). **Restaurant l'Époque**, a fine neighborhood restaurant, has excellent *menus* at 78F and 118F (a block off place Contrescarpe at 81 rue Cardinal Lemoine, tel. 01 46 34 15 84). **Savannah Café**'s creative Mediterranean cuisine attracts a loyal, artsy crowd (27 rue Descartes, tel. 01 43 29 45 77). **Le Jardin des Pates** is popular with vegetarians, serving pastas and salads at fair prices (near Jardins des Plantes, 4 rue Lacepede, tel. 01 43 31 50 71). **Le Port de Salut**, one block from the Panthéon, has ambience and inexpensive *menus* (closed Sun–Mon, 163 bis rue St. Jacques, tel. 01 46 33 63 21).

Cafés: Brasserie La Chope, a classic Parisian brasserie right on place Contrescarpe, is popular until the wee hours. Sit indoors or outdoors for good people watching. **Café Le Mouffetard** is in the thick of the street-market hustle and bustle (at the corner of rue Mouffetard and rue de l'Arbalete). The outdoor tables at **Cave de la Bourgogne** are picture-perfect (at the bottom of rue Mouffetard, on rue Bazelles). At **Café de la Mosque** you'll feel like you've been beamed to Morocco. In this purely Arab café, order a mint tea, pour in the sugar, and enjoy the authentic interior and peaceful outdoor terrace (behind mosque, 2 rue Daubenton).

Eating on Île St. Louis

Cruise the island's main street for a variety of good options, from cozy *crêperies* to romantic restaurants. Sample Paris' best sorbet and ice cream at any place advertising *les glaces Berthillon*; the original Berthillon shop is at 31 rue St. Louis en l'Île.

All listings below are on rue St. Louis en l'Île and are listed starting at the end of the island closest to the Île de la Cité. **Café Med**, at #73, serves inexpensive salads, crepes, and lighter *menus* in a cheery setting. **La Castafiore**, at #51-53, serves fine Italian dishes in a cozy atmosphere (160F *menu*). Farther down lie two fine romantic splurges: **Le Tastevin** (150F and 220F *menus*, #46, tel. 01 43 54 17 31) and, next door, **Au Gourmet de l'Isle** (150F and 185F *menus*, closed Mon–Tue).

For a crazy, touristy, cellar atmosphere and hearty, fun food, feast at **La Taverne du Sergeant Recruiter**. The "Sergeant Recruiter" used to get young Parisians drunk and stuffed here, then sign them into the army. It's all-you-can-eat, including wine and service, for 190F (daily from 19:00, #41, tel. 01 43 54 75 42). There's a near-food-fight clone next door at **Nos Ancêtres Les Gaulois** ("Our Ancestors the Gauls," 190F *menu*, daily from 19:00, tel. 01 46 33 66 07).

Elegant Dining on the Seine

La Plage Parisienne is a nearly dress-up riverfront place popular with locals, serving elegant, healthy meals at good prices (Port de Javel-Haut, Mo: Javel, tel. 01 40 59 41 00).

Transportation Connections—Paris

Paris is Europe's rail hub, with six major train stations, each serving different regions: Gare de l'Est (east-bound trains), Gare du Nord (northern France and Europe), Gare St. Lazare (north-western France), Gare d'Austerlitz (southwest France and Europe), Gare du Lyon (southeastern France and Italy), and Gare Montparnasse (northwestern France and TGV service to France's southwest). Any train station can give you schedule information, make reservations, and sell tickets for any destination. Buying tickets is handier from an SNCF neighborhood office (e.g., Louvre, Invalides, Orsay, Versailles, airports) or at your neighborhood travel agency—worth their small fee (SNCF signs in their window indicate they sell train tickets). For schedule information, call 08 36 35 35 35 (3F/min, English sometimes available).

Gare du Nord: Serves northern France and several interna-tional destinations. To **Brussels** (10/day, 1.5 hrs), **Bruges** (3/day, 2.5 hrs), **Amsterdam** (10/day, 4 hrs), **Copenhagen** (3/day, 16 hrs), **Koblenz** on the Rhine (3/day, 7 hrs), **London** via Eurostar Chunnel (12/day, 3 hrs, France tel. 08 36 35 35 39, U.S. tel. 800/EUROSTAR, www.raileurope.com, www.eurostar.co.uk).

Gare de l'Est: Serves eastern France and points east. To **Colmar** (6/day, 5.5 hrs, transfer in Strasbourg or Mulhouse), **Strasbourg** (10/day, 4.5 hrs), **Reims** (8/day, 2 hrs), **Verdun** (5/day, 3 hrs), **Munich** (4/day, 8.5 hrs), **Vienna** (3/day, 13 hrs), **Zurich** (4/day, 6 hrs), **Prague** (2/day, 15 hrs).

Gare Montparnasse: Serves Lower Normandy and Brittany

and offers TGV service to Loire Valley and southwestern France. To **Chartres** (10/day, 1 hr), **Mont St. Michel** (2/day, 4.5 hrs, via Rennes), **Dinan** (7/day, 3 hrs, via Rennes and Dol), **Bordeaux** (14/day, 3.5 hrs), **Sarlat** (5/day, 6 hrs, transfer in Bordeaux), **Toulouse** (7/day, 5 hrs, possible transfer in Bordeaux), **Albi** (6.5 hrs, via Toulouse), **Carcassonne** (6.5 hrs, via Toulouse), **Tours** (14/day, 1 hr).

Gare du Lyon: Offers TGV and regular service to south-eastern France, Italy, and other international destinations. To **Beaune** (8/day, 2.5 hrs), **Dijon** (13/day, 1.5 hrs), **Chamonix** (3/day, 9 hrs, transfer in Lyon and St. Gervais, 1 direct night train), **Annecy** (8/day, 4–7 hrs), **Lyon** (16/day, 2.5 hrs), **Avignon** (10/day, 4 hrs), **Arles** (10/day, 5 hrs), **Nice** (8/day, 7 hrs), **Venice** (5/day, 11 hrs), **Rome** (3/day, 15 hrs), **Bern** (5/day, 5 hrs).

Gare St. Lazare: Serves Upper Normandy. To **Giverny** (train to Vernon, 5/day, 45 min; then bus or taxi 10 min to Giverny), **Rouen** (15/day, 75 min), **Honfleur** (6/day, 3 hrs, via Lisieux then bus), **Bayeux** (9/day, 2.5 hrs), **Caen** (12/day, 2 hrs).

Gare d'Austerlitz: Provides non-TGV service to the Loire Valley, southwestern France, and Iberia. To **Amboise** (8/day, 2.5 hrs), **Cahors** (5/day, 7 hrs), **Barcelona** (3/day, 13 hrs), **Madrid** (5/day, 16 hrs), **Lisbon** (1/day, 24 hrs).

Buses: Long-distance buses provide cheaper, if less comfort-able and flexible, transportation to major European cities. The main bus station in Paris is Gare Routière du Paris-Gallieni (avenue du General de Gaulle, in suburb of Bagnolet, Mo: Gallieni, tel. 01 49 72 51 51). Eurolines buses depart from here.

Charles de Gaulle Airport

Paris' primary airport has three main terminals: T-1, T-2, and T-9. (Air France uses T-2; charters dominate T-9.) Terminals are connected every few minutes by a free *navette* (bus), and the RER (Paris subway) stops at T-1 and T-2 terminals. There is no bag storage at the airport.

Those flying to or from the United States will probably use T-1. Here you'll find an American Express cash machine, an auto-matic bill changer (at baggage claim 30), and an exchange window (at baggage claim 18). A bank (with lousy rates) and an ATM are near gate 32. At the Meeting Point, you'll find the TI, which has free maps and information (daily 7:00–22:00), and Relais H, which sells *télécartes* (phone cards). Car-rental offices are on the arrival level from gates 10 to 22; the SNCF (train) office is at gate 22. For flight information, call 01 48 62 22 80.

Transportation between Charles de Gaulle Airport and Paris: There are plenty of choices. Three efficient public transporta-tion routes, taxis, and airport shuttle vans link the airport's T-1 and T-2 terminals with central Paris. At T-1 (where most will land), the free *navette* (bus) runs between gate 36, the lower level (take elevator down to floor 2, walk outside, cross street, and catch green bus), and the **RER Roissy Rail** station, where a train zips you into Paris' subway system in 30 minutes (51F, stops at Gare du Nord, Chatelet, St. Michel, and Luxembourg Gardens). The **Roissy Bus** runs every 15 minutes between gate 30 and the old Opéra Garnier (stop is on rue Scribe, in front of American Express), costs 48F (use automatic ticket machine), and takes 40 minutes, but can be jammed. The **Air France Bus** leaves every 15 minutes from gate 34 and serves the Arc de Triomphe and Porte Maillot in about 40 minutes for 60F, and the Montparnasse Tower in 60 minutes for 75F (from any of these stops you can reach your hotel by taxi). For most people, the RER Roissy Rail works best. A **taxi** ride with luggage costs about 230F; a taxi stand is at gate 16. The **Disneyland Express bus** departs from gate 32. (The RER Roissy Rail, Roissy Bus, and Air France bus described above serve the T-2 terminal as efficiently and economically as T-1.)

For a stress-free trip between either of Paris' airports and downtown, consider an airport shuttle minivan, ideal for single travelers or families of four or more. Reserve from home and they'll meet you at the airport. Consider **Airport Shuttle** (allow 150F for 1 person, 89F per person for 2, cheaper for larger groups and kids, plan on 30-min wait if you ask them to pick you up at airport, tel. 01 45 38 55 72, fax 01 43 21 35 67, www.paris-anglo.com/clients/ashuttle.html, e-mail: ashuttle@club-internet.fr) or **Paris Airport Services** (tel. 01 49 62 78 78, fax 01 49 62 78 79, www.magic.fr/pas, e-mail: pas@magic.fr).

Sleeping at or near Charles de Gaulle Airport: Those with early flights can sleep in T-1 at **Cocoon** (60 cabins, Sb-250F, Db-300F, CC:VM, TV, take elevator down to "boutique level" or walk down from departure level, tel. 01 48 62 06 16, fax 01 48 62 56 97). You get 16 hours of silence buried under the check-in level. **Hôtel Ibis****, at the Roissy Rail station, offers more-normal accommodations (Db-420F, CC:VMA, free shuttle bus to either terminal takes 2 min, tel. 01 49 19 19 19, fax 01 49 19 19 21), as does the similarly priced **Novotel***** (CC:VMA, tel. 01 49 19 27 27, fax 01 49 19 27 99).

Orly Airport

This airport feels small. Orly has two terminals: Sud and Ouest. International flights arrive at Sud. After exiting Terminal Sud's baggage claim (near gate H), you'll be greeted by signs directing you to city transportation, car rental, and so on. Turn left to enter the main terminal area and you'll find exchange offices with bad rates, an ATM machine, the ADP (a quasi-tourist office that offers free city maps and basic sightseeing information, open until 23:00), and an SNCF French rail desk (closes at 18:00, sells train tickets and even Eurailpasses, next to ADP). Downstairs is a sandwich bar, WCs, a bank (same bad rates), a newsstand (buy a *télécarte* phone card), and a post office (great rates for cash or American Express traveler's checks). Car-rental offices are located in the parking lot in front of the terminal. For flight information on any airline serving Orly, call 01 49 75 15 15.

Transportation between Paris and Orly Airport: There are three efficient public-transportation routes, taxis, and a couple of airport shuttle services linking Orly and central Paris. The **Air France bus** (outside gate G) runs to Paris' Invalides Métro stop (45F, 5/hrly, 30 min) and is best for those staying in or near the rue Cler neighborhood (at Paris' Invalides terminal, take Métro 2 stops to École Militaire to reach recommended hotels). The **Jetbus #285** (outside gate F, 28F, 4/hrly) is the quickest way to the Paris subway and the best way to the recommended hotels in the Marais and Contrescarpe neighborhoods (take Jetbus to Villejuif Métro stop, buy a carnet of 10 Métro tickets, then take the Métro to the Sully Morland stop for the Marais area, or the Cardinal Lemoine stop for the Contrescarpe area). The **Orlybus** (outside gate H, 35F, 4/hr) takes you to the Denfert-Rochereau RER-B line and the Métro, offering subway access to central Paris. The **Orlyval trains** are overpriced (57F). **Taxis** are to the far right (gate M) as you leave the terminal. Allow 170F for a taxi into central Paris.

Airport shuttle minivans are ideal for single travelers or families of four or more (see "Charles de Gaulle Airport," above; from Orly, figure about 120F for 1 person, 80F per person for 2, less for larger groups and kids).

Sleeping near Orly Airport: The only reasonable airport hotel is the **Hôtel Ibis**** (Db-420F, CC:VMA, tel. 01 46 87 33 50, fax 01 46 87 29 92). The **Hilton***** offers more comfort for more money (Db-680F, tel. 01 45 12 45 12, fax 01 45 12 45 00). Both offer a free shuttle service to the terminal.

PROVENCE

This magnificent region is shaped like a giant wedge of quiche. From its sunburnt crust fanning out along the Mediterranean coast from Nîmes to Nice, it stretches north along the Rhône Valley to Orange. The Romans were here in force and left many ruins—some of the best anywhere. Seven popes, great artists like van Gogh, Cézanne, and Picasso, and author Peter Mayle all enjoyed their years in Provence. The region offers a splendid recipe of arid climate (but brutal winds known as the *mistral*), captivating cities, exciting hill towns, dramatic scenery, and oceans of vineyards.

Explore the ghost town of ancient Les Baux and France's greatest Roman ruin, Pont du Gard. Spend your starry, starry nights where van Gogh did, in Arles. Uncover its Roman past then find the linger-longer squares and café corners that inspired Vincent. Youthful but classy Avignon bustles in the shadow of its brooding popes' palace.

Planning Your Time
Make Arles or Avignon your sightseeing base (hotels are a far better value in Arles). Italophiles prefer Arles, while poodles pick Avignon. Everything is accessible by public transit. You'll want a full day for sightseeing in Arles (ideally on Wed or Sat, when the morning market rages), a half day for Avignon, and a day or two for the villages and sights in the countryside.

Getting around Provence
By Car: The yellow Michelin map to this region is essential for drivers. Avignon is a headache for drivers; Arles is easier. Park only in well-watched spaces and leave nothing in your car.

By Bus or Train: Public transit is good between cities and

Provence

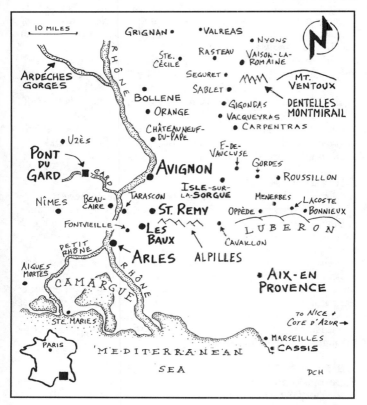

marginal to small towns: Frequent trains link Avignon, Arles, and Nîmes (about 30 min between each), and buses connect smaller towns. Les Baux is accessible by bus from Arles. Pont du Gard and St. Rémy are accessible by bus from Avignon. The TIs in Arles and Avignon have information on bus excursions to regional sights that are hard to reach *sans* car (120F/half day, 200F/full day).

ARLES

By helping Julius Caesar defeat Marseille, Arles earned the imperial nod and was made an important port city. With the first bridge over the Rhône, Arles was a key stop on the Roman road from Italy to Spain, the Via Domitia. After reigning as a political center of the early Christian church (the seat of an archbishopric for centuries) and thriving as a trading city on and off until the 18th century, Arles all but disappeared from the map. Van Gogh settled here a hundred years ago, but left only memories. American bombers destroyed much of Arles in World War II, but today Arles thrives again. This compact city is alive with great Roman ruins, an eclectic assortment of museums, made-for-ice-cream pedestrian zones, and squares that play hide-and-seek with visitors.

Tourist Information: The TI at the train station is open only in summer (June–Sept 9:00–13:00, 14:00–18:00, closed Sun). The main TI is on the ring-road esplanade Charles de Gaulle (daily 9:00–18:40, in winter Mon–Sat 9:00–18:45, Sun 9:00–13:00, tel. 04 90 18 41 20). Pick up the good city map, the "Arles et Vincent Van Gogh" walking tour brochure (5F), the free *Guide Pratique*, and information on the Camargue wildlife area. Ask about bullfights and bus excursions to regional sights.

Arrival in Arles

By Train and Bus: Both stations are next to each other on the river and a 10-minute walk from the center. Lockers are available at the train station. Get the bus schedule to Les Baux at the bus station (tel. 04 90 49 38 01). To reach the old town, walk to the river and turn left.

By Car: Follow signs to *centre-ville*, then follow signs toward the *gare SNCF* (train station). You'll come to a huge roundabout (place Lamartine) with a Monoprix department store to the right. Park along the city wall or in nearby lots (6F/hr, or 17F for 4 hrs; pay attention to no-parking signs on Wed and Sat until 13:00). Theft is a big problem. From place Lamartine, walk into the city through the two stumpy towers.

Helpful Hints

Supermarket: Place Lamartine has a big, handy Monoprix supermarket/department store (Mon–Sat 8:30–19:25, closed Sun).

Banks: Several banks on place de la République across from St. Trophime change money.

Laundromats: One is at 12 rue Portagnel (daily 7:00–21:00). Another, nearby at 6 rue Cavalarie, near place Voltaire (daily 7:00–21:00, later once you're in), has a confusing central-command panel: 20F for wash (push machine number on top row), 10F for 25 minutes of dryer (push dryer number on 3rd row 5 times slowly), 2F for flakes (button #11). Dine at the recommended L'Arlatan restaurant (across the street, see "Eating in Arles," below) while you clean.

Getting around Arles

Arles faces the Mediterranean and turns its back to Paris. Its spaghetti street plan disorients the first-time visitor. Landmarks hide in the medieval tangle of narrow, winding streets. Everything is deceptively close. While Arles sits on the Rhône, it completely ignores the river. The elevated riverside walk provides a direct route to the excellent Ancient History Museum, an easy return to the station, and fertile ground for poorly trained dogs. Hotels have free city maps, but Arles works best if you simply follow street-corner signs pointing you toward the sights and hotels of the town center. Racing cars enjoy Arles' medieval lanes, turning sidewalks into tightropes and pedestrians into leaping targets.

By Minibus: The free "Starlette" shuttle minibus circles the town's major sights twice an hour, but does not serve the Ancient History Museum so isn't very helpful (just wave at the driver and hop in; Mon–Sat 7:30–19:30, never on Sun).

By Bike: Riding to Les Baux (very steep climb) or into the Camargue works from Arles, providing you're in great shape (forget it in the wind). The Peugeot store rents bikes (15 rue du Pont, tel. 04 90 96 03 77), as does the newsstand next to the main TI (tel. 04 90 96 44 20).

By Taxi: Arles' taxis charge a minimum flat 60F fee. Nothing in town is worth a taxi ride (figure 110F to Les Baux, tel. 04 90 96 90 03).

Car Rental: Rent a car at ADA (cheapest, 22 avenue Stalingrad, tel. 04 90 07 87), Avis (at train station, tel. 04 90 96 82 42), and Europcar (downtown at 15 boulevard Victor Hugo, tel. 04 90 93 23 24).

Sights—Arles' Museums

There are two monument passes with reduced entries to Arles' many sights: one that covers all of the sights listed in this section (65F, sold at each sight), or a 55F pass good for all Roman sights but not the Arlaten or Reattu museums. Otherwise, it's 20F per sight and museum (35F apiece for the Ancient History Museum and the Arlaten folk museum). While any sight is worth a few minutes, many aren't worth the individual admission. (All sights except the Ancient History Museum and Arlaten folk museum are open June–mid-Sept 9:00–19:00; April–May and latter half of Sept 9:00–12:30, 14:00–19:00; Oct–March 10:00–12:30, 14:00–17:30.) See listings for the Ancient History Museum and Musée Arlaten, below, for their hours.

▲▲▲**Ancient History Museum (Musée de L'Arles Antique)**— Begin your visit of Arles in this superb, air-conditioned museum. Models and original sculpture (with the help of the free English handout) re-create the Roman city of Arles, making work-a-day life and culture easier to imagine. Notice what a radical improvement the Roman buildings were over the simple mud-brick homes of pre-Roman peoples. Models of Arles' arena even illustrate the moveable stadium cover, good for shade and rain. While virtually nothing is left of Arles' chariot racecourse, the model shows that it must have rivaled Rome's Circus Maximus. Jewelry, fine metal and glass artifacts, and well-crafted mosaic floors make it clear that

Arles

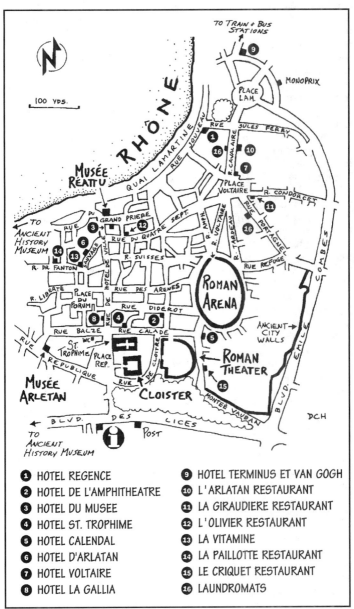

1 HOTEL REGENCE
2 HOTEL DE L'AMPHITHEATRE
3 HOTEL DU MUSEE
4 HOTEL ST. TROPHIME
5 HOTEL CALENDAL
6 HOTEL D'ARLATAN
7 HOTEL VOLTAIRE
8 HOTEL LA GALLIA

9 HOTEL TERMINUS ET VAN GOGH
10 L'ARLATAN RESTAURANT
11 LA GIRAUDIERE RESTAURANT
12 L'OLIVIER RESTAURANT
13 LA VITAMINE
14 LA PAILLOTTE RESTAURANT
15 LE CRIQUET RESTAURANT
16 LAUNDROMATS

Roman Arles was a city of art and culture. The finale is an impressive row of pagan and early Christian sarcophagi (second to fifth centuries). In the early days of the Church, Jesus was often portrayed beardless and as the good shepherd—with a lamb over his shoulder.

Built at the site of the chariot racecourse, this museum is a 20-minute walk from Arles along the river. Turn left at the river and follow it to the big modern building just past the new bridge—or take bus #1 (5.20F) from boulevard des Lices and the TI (35F, daily 9:00–19:00 March–Oct, Nov–Feb 10:00–17:00, tel. 04 90 18 88 88).

▲▲▲**Roman Arena (Amphithéâtre)**—Nearly 2,000 years ago, gladiators fought wild animals here to the delight of 20,000 screaming fans—cruel. Today matadors fight wild bulls to the delight of local fans—still cruel. While the ancient third row of arches is long gone, three towers survive from medieval times, when the arena was used as a fortress. In the 1800s it corralled 200 humble homes and functioned as a town within the town. Climb the tower. Walk through the inner corridors of this 440-by-350-foot oval and notice the similarity to modern-day stadium floor plans. And if you don't mind the gore, a bullfight is an exciting show.

Classical Theater (Théâtre Antique)—Precious little survives from this Roman theater, which served as a handy town quarry throughout the Middle Ages. Two lonely Corinthian columns look from the stage out over the audience. The 10,000 mostly modern seats are still used for concerts and festivals. Take a stroll backstage through broken bits of Rome.

Musée Réattu—Highlights of this mildly interesting museum are a fun collection of 70 Picasso drawings (some two-sided and all done in a flurry of creativity) and a room of Henri Rousseau's Camargue watercolors.

▲**Musée Arlaten**—This cluttered folklore museum, given to Arles by Nobel prize winner Frederic Mistral (see "Place du Forum," below), is filled with interesting odds and ends of Provence life. The employees wear the native costumes. It's like a failed turn-of-the-century garage sale—shoes, hats, wigs, old photos, bread cupboards, and the beetle-dragon monster. If you're into folklore, this museum is for you (35F, April–Sept daily 9:00–12:30, 14:00–18:00, Oct–March closes at 17:00).

▲▲**St. Trophime Cloisters and Church**—This church, named after a third-century bishop of Arles, sports the finest Romanesque west portal (main doorway) I've seen anywhere.

But first enjoy the place de la République. Sit on the steps opposite the church. The **Egyptian obelisk** used to be the centerpiece of Arles' Roman Circus. Watch the peasants—pilgrims, locals, and street musicians. There's nothing new about this scene. Like a Roman triumphal arch, the church trumpets the promise of Judgment Day. The tympanum is filled with Christian symbolism. Christ sits in majesty, surrounded by symbols of the four evangelists

(Matthew—the winged man, Mark—the winged lion, Luke—the ox, and John—the eagle). The Twelve Apostles are lined up below Jesus. Move closer. This is it. Some are saved and others aren't. Notice the condemned—a chain gang on the right bunny-hopping over the fires of hell. For them the tune trumpeted by the three angels on the very top isn't a happy one. Ride the exquisite detail back to a simpler age. In an illiterate medieval world long before the vivid images of our Technicolor time, this message was a neon billboard over this town's square. A chart just inside the church (on the right) helps explain the carvings. On the right side of the nave, a fourth-century early-Christian sarcophagus is used as an altar.

The adjacent **cloisters** are the best in Provence (20F, covered by pass, enter from square, 20 meters to right of church). Enjoy the sculpted capitals of the rounded Romanesque columns (12th century) and the pointed Gothic columns (14th century). The second floor offers only a view of the cloisters from above.

More Sights—Arles

▲▲**Place du Forum**—This café-crammed square is always lively and best at night. Named for the Roman Forum that stood here, only two columns from a second-century temple survive. They are incorporated into the wall of Hôtel Nord Pinus. Van Gogh lounged under these same plane trees—his *Le Café de Nuit* was painted from this square. The bistros on the square, while no place for a fine dinner, put together a good salad, and when you sprinkle in the ambience, that's 50F well spent. The guy on the pedestal is Frederic Mistral; in 1904 he received the Nobel Prize for literature. He used his prize money to preserve and display the folk identity of Provence (by founding the Arlaten folk museum) at a time when France was rapidly centralizing.

▲▲**Wednesday and Saturday Markets**—On these days until noon, Arles' ring road erupts into an outdoor market of fish, flowers, produce, and you-name-it (boulevard Emile Combes on Wed, boulevard Lices on Sat). Join in, buy flowers, try the olives, sample some wine, and swat a pickpocket. On the first Wednesday of the month it's a grand flea market.

Fondation Van Gogh—A two-star sight for his fans, this small gallery features works by several well-known contemporary artists who pay homage to Vincent through their thought-provoking interpretations of his art (30F, not covered by monument passes, April–mid Oct daily 10:00–19:00, mid-Oct–March Tue–Sun 10:00–12:30, 14:00–17:30, facing Roman arena at #24).

Van Gogh in Arles Self-Guided Walking Tour—The 5F "Arles et Vincent Van Gogh" brochure (available at TI) describes several interesting walks through Arles using pavement markers as guides. By far the most worthwhile walk follows the footsteps of Vincent van Gogh.

▲▲**Bullfights (Courses Camarguaise)**—Occupy the same seats fans have been sitting in for nearly 2,000 years and take in one of Arles' most memorable experiences—a bullfight *à la Provençale.* Three classes of bullfights take place here. The *course protection* is for aspiring matadors; it's a daring dodge-bull game of scraping hair off the angry bull's nose for prize money offered by local businesses (no blood). The *trophée de l'avenir* is the next class, with amateur matadors. The *trophée des as excellence* is the real thing *à la Spain:* outfits, swords, spikes, and the whole gory shebang (tickets 30–60F; Easter–Oct Sat, Sun, and holidays; skip the "rodeo" spectacle, tel. 04 90 96 03 70 or ask at TI). There are nearby village bullfights in small wooden bullrings nearly every weekend (TI has schedule).

Sleeping in Arles
(6.50F = about $1, country code: 33, zip code: 13200)
Sleep Code: **S** = Single, **D** = Double/Twin, **T** = Triple, **Q** = Quad, **b** = bathroom, **t** = toilet only, **s** = shower only, **CC** = Credit Card (Visa, MasterCard, Amex), **SE** = Speaks English, **NSE** = No English, * = French hotel rating system (0–4 stars).

Hotels are a great value here though few have elevators. If you're sweating, get a room with air-conditioning. All except the last are central.

Hôtel Régence** sits on the river with immaculate and comfortable rooms, good beds, safe parking, and easy access to the train station. Helpful, gentle Sylvie speaks English (Db-200–300F, Tb-260–360F, Qb-370F, choose river-view or quiet, air-con courtyard rooms, most with cable TV, CC:VM, from place Lamartine turn right immediately after passing through towers, 5 rue Marius Jouveau, tel. 04 90 96 39 85, fax 04 90 96 67 64).

Hôtel Acacias**, next door, was just redone and is owned by Hôtel Régence (above). The rooms are a bit small but provide all the comforts including cable TV, an elevator, and air-conditioning (Db-300–430F, Tb-455–485F, Qb-510F, CC:VM, 1 rue Marius Jouveau, tel. 04 90 96 37 88, fax 04 90 96 32 51).

Hôtel de l'Amphithéâtre**, a boutique hotel, is small, friendly, and *très* cozy, with thoughtfully decorated, air-conditioned rooms and a pleasant atrium breakfast room. It's located one block from the arena toward place du Forum (Db-290–420F, Tb-550F, parking-25F, CC:VMA, 5 rue Diderot, tel. 04 90 96 10 30, fax 04 90 93 98 69, www.hotelamphitheatre.fr, SE).

Hôtel du Musée** is a quiet, delightful manor-home hideaway with comfortable air-conditioned rooms, a terrific two-tiered courtyard, and an art-gallery lounge. The rooms in the new section are worth the few extra francs. The relaxed Dubreuils speak some English (Sb-240–300F, Db-300–400F, Tb-390–420F, Qb-490F, parking-40F, CC:VMA, follow signs to Musée Réattu, 11 rue de la Grande Prieure, tel. 04 90 93 88 88, fax 04 90 49 98 15).

Hôtel St. Trophime is another fine place with a grand entry, charming courtyard, broad halls, large rooms, and helpful owners (Db-300–350F, Tb-400F, huge Qb-450F, CC:VM, 16 rue de la Calade, near place de la République, tel. 04 90 96 88 38, fax 04 90 96 92 19).

Hôtel Calendal should be three stars and is a better value than the Hôtel d'Arlatan (below). It's Provençal chic, with an exquisite outdoor garden, smartly decorated rooms, Internet access, and a seductive ambience (Db-350–480F, Tb-490F, Qb-530F, splurge for a room on the garden, CC:VMA, air-con, strong beds, modern bathrooms, parking-60F, just above the arena on rue Porte de Laure, tel. 04 90 96 11 89, fax 04 90 96 05 84, www .lecalendal.com, SE).

Hôtel d'Arlatan* is classy yet affordable with a pleasant courtyard, air-conditioned, antique-filled rooms, and stiff staff. In the lobby of this 15th-century building, a glass floor looks down into Roman ruins (Db-500–850F, Db/suites-1,000–1,500F, CC:VMA, elevator, parking-70F, very central, a block off place du Forum at 26 rue du Sauvage, tel. 04 90 93 56 66, fax 04 90 49 68 45, www.hotel-arlatan.fr, SE).

Starving artists can afford these two clean but spartan places: friendly **Hôtel Voltaire*** rents 12 small rooms with great balconies overlooking a caffeine-stained square a block below the arena (D-160F, Ds-180F, Db-200F, 3rd or 4th person-50F each, CC:VM, 1 place Voltaire, tel. 04 90 96 49 18, fax 04 90 96 45 49). **Hôtel La Gallia**, with small but clean rooms, is a steal (Ds-140F, Db-150F, above lively café, 22 rue de l'Hôtel de Ville, tel. 04 90 96 00 63).

Hôtel Terminus et Van Gogh* has bright, cheery rooms facing a busy square at the gate of the old town, a block from the train station. This building appears in the painting of van Gogh's house; the artist's house was bombed in World War II (D-150F with no shower available, Ds-185F, Db-225F, CC:VM, 5 place Lamartine, tel. & fax 04 90 96 12 32).

Eating in Arles

Great atmosphere and mediocre food at fair prices await on place du Forum. Elsewhere, near Hôtel Régence, **L'Arlatan** is unpretentious and friendly and serves a fine meal and great desserts (105F *menu*, opposite Laundromat on rue Cavalarie, closed Wed). Just up the street on the place Voltaire, **La Giraudiere** offers excellent regional cooking (115F *menu*, closed Tue, tel. 04 90 93 27 52). Near Hôtel du Musée, **L'Olivier** is my Arles splurge, offering exquisite *Provençale* cuisine (160F *menu*, 1 bis rue Reattu, reserve ahead, tel. 04 90 49 64 88). Vegetarians love **La Vitamine**'s salads and pastas (closed Sat–Sun, just below place du Forum on 16 rue Dr. Fanton, tel. 04 90 93 77 36). Almost next door, **La Paillotte** specializes in traditional *Provençale* cuisine (95F *menu*, 28 rue

Dr. Fanton). **Le Criquet** is cheap, fun, and good (1 block from Hôtel Calendal at 12 Porte de Laure).

Transportation Connections—Arles

By bus to: Les Baux (4/day, 30 min; none on Sun, ideal departure about 8:30 with a return from Les Baux about 11:20 or 12:40, departs Arles bus station and 16 boulevard Clemenceau downtown, service reduced Nov–March, tel. 04 90 49 38 01).

By train to: Paris (2 direct TGVs, 4.5 hrs; otherwise transfer in Avignon, 8/day, 5.5 hrs), **Avignon** (8/day, 20 min, check for afternoon gaps), **Carcassonne** (8/day, 3 hrs, a few direct, most require a painless transfer in Narbonne), **Beaune** (7/day, 5 hrs, transfer in Lyon), **Nice** (8/day, 3.5 hrs, likely transfer in Marseille), **Barcelona** (3/day, 7 hrs, at least 1 transfer), **Italy** (3/day, via Marseille and Nice; from Arles it's 5 hrs to Ventimiglia on the border, 9 hrs to the Cinque Terre, 9 hrs to Milan, 11 hrs to Florence, or 13 hrs to Venice or Rome). Train info: tel. 04 90 96 43 94.

AVIGNON

Famous for its nursery rhyme, medieval bridge, and brooding Palace of the Popes, contemporary Avignon bustles and prospers behind its mighty walls. During the 68 years (1309–1377) that Avignon played Franco Vaticano, it grew from a quiet village to the thriving city it still is. Today this city combines a huge student population with a white-collar, sophisticated-city feel. Street mimes play to international crowds enjoying Avignon's sprawling cafés and chic boutiques. If you're here any time in July, save evening time for Avignon's rollicking theater festival and reserve your hotel early. Clean, polished, and popular Avignon is more impressive for its outdoor ambience than its museums and monuments. Come here to see its pope's palace, then explore its thriving streets and beautiful vistas from the Parc de Rochers des Doms.

Orientation

The cours Jean Jaurés (which turns into the rue de la République) leads from the train station to place de l'Horloge and the Palace of the Popes, splitting Avignon in two. The larger right (southern) half is where the action is. Climb to the parc de Rochers des Doms for a fine view, enjoy the people scene on place de l'Horloge, and meander the backstreets (see "Sights—Walking Tour Of Avignon's Backstreets," below). Avignon's shopping district fills the traffic-free streets where rue de la République meets place de l'Horloge (creamy gelato just off place de l'Horloge, where St. Agricol meets Joseph-Vernet). Walk across Pont Daladier (bridge) for a great view of Avignon and the Rhône River.

Tourist Information: The main TI is between the train

station and the old town at 41 cours Jean Juarés (Mon–Fri 9:00–
18:00, Sat–Sun 9:00–13:00, 14:00–17:00, longer hours during the
July festival, tel. 04 32 74 32 74, www.avignon-tourisme.com.fr).
A branch TI is inside the city wall at the entrance to Pont St.
Bénezet (May–Sept only, daily 9:00–18:00). Pick up the handy
Guide Pratique (info on car and bike rental, hotels, and museums) as
well as their Avignon discovery guide, which includes several good
(but tricky to follow) walking tours. The TI offers English-language
walking tours of Avignon (50F, Tue and Thu at 10:00). They
also have regional bus and train schedules and information on bus
excursions to popular regional sights (including the Camargue).
Note that most of Avignon's sights are closed on Tuesdays.

Arrival in Avignon

By Train: Walk through the city walls onto the cours Jean Juarés
(TI 3 blocks down at #41). The bus station (*gare routière*) and car
rentals are 100 meters to the right of the train station, near the
IBIS hotel.

By Car: Drivers enter Avignon following "centre-ville" signs.
Park along the wall close to Pont St. Bénezet (ruined old bridge)
and use that TI. Hotels have advice for smart overnight parking.
Leave nothing in your car.

Sights—Avignon

▲**Palace of the Popes (Palais des Papes)**—In 1309 a French
pope was elected (Pope Clement V). At the urging of the French
king, His Holiness decided he'd had enough of unholy Italy. So
he loaded his carts and moved north to peaceful Avignon for a
steady rule under a supportive king. The Catholic Church literally bought Avignon, then a two-bit town, and popes resided here
until 1403. From 1378 on, there were twin popes, one in Rome
and one in Avignon, causing a split in the Catholic Church that
wasn't fully resolved until 1417.

The pope's palace is two distinct buildings, one old and one
older. Along with lots of big, barren rooms, you'll see frescoes,
tapestries, and some beautiful floor tiles. The audiophone self-
guided tours do a good job of overcoming the lack of furnishings
and give a thorough history lesson while allowing you to tour this
vast place at your own pace. Enjoy the view and windswept café
at the tower (45–55F, occasional supplements for special exhibits,
April–Oct daily 9:00–19:00, until 20:00 in summer, off-season
9:00–17:45, ticket office closes 1 hr earlier, tours in English twice
daily March–Oct, call 04 90 27 50 74 to confirm).

▲**Musée du Petit Palais**—This palace superbly displays medieval
Italian painting and sculpture. Since the Catholic Church was the
patron of the arts, all 350 paintings deal with Christian themes.
Visiting this museum before going to the Palace of the Popes

gives you a sense of art and life during the Avignon papacy (30F, June–Sept Wed–Mon 10:00–12:00, 14:00–18:00, Oct–May Wed–Mon 9:30–13:00, 14:00–17:30, closed Tue).

▲**Parc de Rochers des Doms and Pont St. Bénezet**—Hike above the Palace of the Popes for a panoramic view over Avignon and the Rhône valley. At the far end, drop down a few steps for a good view of Pont St. Bénezet. This is the famous "sur le Pont d'Avignon," whose construction and location were inspired by a shepherd's religious vision. Imagine a 22-arch, 1,000-meter-long bridge extending across two rivers to that lonely Tower of Philippe the Fair, the bridge's former tollgate, on the distant side, (equally great view from that tower back over Avignon). The island the bridge spanned is now filled with campgrounds. You can pay 15F to walk along a section of the ramparts and do your own jig on the Pont St. Benezet (nice view, otherwise nothing special). The castle on the right, the St. André Fortress, was once another island in the Rhône. Cross Daladier Bridge for the best view of the old bridge and Avignon's skyline.

Fondation Angladon Dubrujeaud—This museum mixes a small but enjoyable collection of art from Post-Impressionists (including Cézanne, van Gogh, Daumier, Degas, and Picasso) with recreated art studios and furnishings from many periods. It's a quiet place with a few superb paintings (30F, Wed–Sun 13:00–18:00, closed Tue, 5 rue Laboureur).

Musée Calvet—This fine-arts museum impressively displays its good collection without any English explanations (30F, Wed–Mon 10:00–12:00, 14:00–18:00, closed Tue, on quieter northern half of Avignon at 65 rue Jospeh Vernet, its antiquities collection is a few blocks away at 27 rue de la République, same hours and ticket).

Walking Tour of Avignon's Backstreets—Use the TI's barely adequate, single-sheet-of-paper city map to navigate and the Avignon Discovery Guide (Strolling the Old Streets tour) to narrate this one-hour walk. Begin at the Agricol Perdiguier Park by the TI and work your way to the triangular place des Corps Saints. Walk up to the rue des Lices, turn right, then turn right again after about five minutes on the rue des Tenturiers, ground-zero in Avignon for all that's hip. Earthy cafés, cheap restaurants, galleries, and a small stream line this atmospheric street. Go as far as the waterwheel then return, crossing back over the rue des Lices. Now angle up rue de la Bonterre to the modern market hall, Les Halles (produce, meats, fish until 12:30). Cross over to the cafés of place Pie, then up rue Gal Leclerc. Make a left on rue Carnot, then veer right on the first street, rue Peyrolle, and continue to place des Chataignes. Work your way around the church of St. Pierre to charming place St. Pierre (recommended restaurant, L'Épicerie, see "Eating," below). Then head back down to place Carnot and enter Avignon's thriving network of pedestrian streets.

Sleeping in Avignon
(6.50F = about $1, country code: 33, zip code: 84000)
Hotel values in Avignon pale in comparison to Arles. These hotels
are listed in the order you would pass them from the train station.
The first three are a right turn off the cours Jean Jaurés on rue
Agricol Perdiguier.

At **Hôtel Splendid***, friendly Madame Prel-Lemoine rents
firm beds in good rooms for a fair price near the station (Db-
210F–290F, on small park near TI, 17 rue Agricol Perdiguier,
tel. 04 90 86 14 46, fax 04 90 85 38 55). Across the street at #18,
Hôtel du Parc's tastefully designed rooms with small beds are
a good value (D-170–210F, Ds-220–270F, Db-230–290F, tel. 04
90 82 71 55, fax 04 90 85 64 86).

Hôtel Colbert**, one block down, is a simple two-star hotel
with air-conditioning and cheap rates (Sb-190–260F, Db-240–
340F, Tb-270–370F, 7 rue Agricol Perdiguier, tel. 04 90 86 20 20,
fax 04 90 85 97 00).

Hôtel Blauvac** offers cozy rooms with stone walls in an old
manor home near the pedestrian zone (Sb-350–400F, Db-380–470F,
Tb/Qb-470–550F, CC:VMA, 1 block off rue de la République, 11
rue de La Bancasse, tel. 04 90 86 34 11, fax 04 90 86 27 41).

Hôtel Danieli** is a hello-dolly fluff-ball of a place with
good modern rooms needing new carpeting (Db-330–475F, Tb-
470–570F, CC:VM, tel. 04 90 86 46 82, fax 04 90 27 09 24).

Hôtel Medieval** is a fine value in an old mansion with
friendly owners. Kitchenettes are in all of its unimaginative
but comfortable and fairly spacious rooms (Db-250–360F, Tb-
390F, extra bed-50F, 5 blocks east of place de l'Horloge, behind
Église St. Pierre, 15 rue Petite Saunerie, tel. 04 90 86 11 06,
fax 04 90 82 08 64).

For predictable, ultramodern comfort with air-conditioning
and a great location, try one of two **Hôtel Mercures***** (Db-
550–650F). One is just inside the walls near Pont St. Bénezet
(Quartier de la Balance, tel. 04 90 80 93 93, fax 04 90 80 93 94);
the other is within spitting distance of the Palace of the Popes
and has many rooms with good views (Cité des Papes, 1 rue Jean
Vilar, tel. 04 90 80 93 00, fax 04 90 80 93 01, e-mail: H1952
@accor-hotels.com).

You'll find dirt cheap beds across Pont Daladier on the Island
(*Île de la*) Barthelasse at the **Auberge Bagatelle's hostel/
campground**, which has a pool, laundry, a cheap café, and
campers for neighbors (dorm bed-64F, Ile de la Barthelasse,
tel. 04 90 86 30 39).

Eating in Avignon
L'Épicerie, charmingly located on a tiny square a few blocks
east of place de l'Horloge, offers a good selection of à la carte

items (open daily, 10 place St. Pierre, tel. 04 90 82 74 22). I also like strolling the cafés that line the rue des Tenturiers (see "Sights—Walking Tour of Avignon's Backstreets," above), where you'll find several inexpensive places.

Transportation Connections—Avignon

By train to: Arles (8/day, 20 min), **Orange** (hrly, 15 min), **Nîmes** (hrly, 20 min), **Isle sur la Sorgue** (6/day, 30 min), **Nice** (10/day, 4 hrs; a few direct, most require transfer in Marseille), **Carcassonne** (8/day, 3 hrs, possible transfer in Narbonne), **Lyon** (14/day, 2.5 hrs), **Paris'** Gare du Lyon (10 TGVs/day, 4 hrs), **Barcelona** (2/day, 5 hrs, possible transfer in Narbonne; direct night train is convenient).

By bus to: St. Rémy (6/day, 45 min handy way to visit its Wed market), **Pont du Gard** (6/day in summer, 4/day off-season, 40 min): The stop is at Auberge Blanche, a 15-minute walk from Pont du Gard (STD Gard buses, tel. 04 66 29 27 29). Off-season service can leave you stranded for hours. Consider visiting Pont du Gard, continuing on to Nîmes or Uzès (both merit exploration), and returning to Avignon from there. Try these plans: Take the 12:00 bus from Avignon, arriving at Pont du Gard at 12:45. Then take either the 14:45 bus from there to Nîmes, where trains run hourly back to Avignon, or a 16:00 bus (Mon–Fri) on to Uzès, arriving at 16:30, with a return bus to Avignon at 18:30. Make sure you're waiting for the bus on the right side of the road at the Pont du Gard Auberge Blanche stop (ask at the small inn: "*Nîmes? Uzès? Avignon? Par ici?*"). The Avignon TI should have schedules. Service is reduced or non-existent on Sunday and holidays. In Avignon, the bus station (tel. 04 90 82 07 35) is adjacent to the train station.

Sights—Provence

A car is a dream come true here. However you tour this magnificent area, notice the wind-buffeting rows of bamboo and cypress and how buildings are oriented south, with few or no windows facing north.
▲▲▲**Les Baux**—This rock-top ghost town is worth visiting for the lunar landscape alone. Arrive by 9:00 or after 17:00 to avoid ugly crowds. A 12th-century regional powerhouse with 6,000 fierce residents, Les Baux was razed in 1632 by a paranoid Louis XIII, who was afraid of these troublemaking upstarts. What remains is a reconstructed "live city" of tourist shops and snack stands and the "dead city" ruins carved into, out of, and on top of a 200-meter-high rock. Spend your time in the dead city—best in the morning or early-evening light. Don't miss the slideshow on van Gogh, Gaugin, and Cézanne in the small chapel near the entry. Spend some time in the small museum as you enter (good exhibits) and pick up the English explanations. In the tourist-trampled live city, you'll find shops, some Renaissance homes, and a fine exhibit of paintings by Yves

Brayer (20F), who spent his final years here (39F for dead city, includes entry to all the town's sights, Easter–Oct 9:00–19:00, until 20:00 in summer, Nov–Easter 9:30–17:00, pick up the interesting brochure, "A Sense of Place," at TI, tel. 04 90 54 34 39). To best experience the bauxite rock quarries and a great view of Les Baux, go one kilometer up D-27 and sample wines with atmosphere at **Caves de Sarragnan** (until 19:00, tel. 04 90 54 33 58). Nearby, **Cathedrale d'Images** uses 48 projectors showing 3,000 images inside a rock quarry to immerse its visitors in themes from the region (43F, daily 10:00–18:00, just above Les Baux on the D-27). If you're tempted to spend the night, try the enchanting **Hôtel Reine Jeanne****, 50 meters to your right after the main entry to the live city (Db-280–380F, great family suite-550F, ask for a *chambre avec terasse*, CC:VM, good *menus* from 110F, 13520 Les Baux, tel. 04 90 54 32 06, fax 04 90 54 32 33).

Four daily buses serve Les Baux from the Arles bus station (see "Transportation Connections—Arles," above).
St. Rémy—This chic Provençal town is a scenic ride over the hill from Les Baux. Here you'll find a thriving Wednesday market (until 13:00), the sprawling, crumbled ruins of Glanum, and the mental ward where Vincent van Gogh was sent after cutting off his ear.
Glanum—This was a once-thriving Roman city located at the crossroads of two ancient trade routes between Italy and Spain. The setting is beautiful. Walk to the gate and peek in to appreciate its size. The ruins are worth the effort if you haven't been to Pompeii or Ephesus. Get the English handout (35F, April–Sept daily 9:00–12:00, 14:00–19:00, Oct–March 9:30–12:00, 14:00–17:00). Across the street, opposite the entrance, is a Roman arch and tower. The arch marked the entry into Glanum. The tower is a memorial to the grandsons of Emperor Augustus.

Across the street from Glanum is the still-functioning mental hospital that took care of van Gogh: **St Paul de Mausole Monastery** (Clinique St. Paul). Wander into the small chapel and intimate cloisters. Vincent's favorite walks outside the hospital are signposted. Glanum and the Clinique St. Paul are 800 meters from St. Rémy on the road to Les Baux (D-5).

In St. Rémy, sleep dead center at the simple **Hôtel du Cheval Blanc**** (Db-290–310F, CC:VM, streetside rooms are noisy, 6 avenue Fauconnet, tel. 04 90 92 09 28, fax 04 90 92 69 05) or just east of town at the tranquil and comfortable **Canto Cigalo** (Db-290–360F, extra bed-100F, chemin Canto Cigalo, tel. 04 90 92 14 28, fax 04 90 92 24 48, e-mail: hotel.cantocigalo@wanadoo.fr).
▲▲▲Pont du Gard—One of Europe's great treats, this perfectly preserved Roman aqueduct was built before the time of Christ. It was the missing link of a 35-mile canal that, by dropping one foot for every 300, supplied 44 million gallons of water to Nîmes daily. Study it up close. There's no mortar—just expertly cut

stones. Signs direct you to "panoramas" above the bridge on either side. The best view of the aqueduct is from the cool of the river below, floating flat on your back—bring a swimsuit and sandals for the rocks (always open and free). Consider renting a canoe from Collas to Remoulins, ending at the Pont du Gard (2-hr trip, 185F per 2-person canoe; shuttle to bus stop, car park, or Remoulins included; Collas Canoes, tel. 04 66 22 85 54).

Buses run to Pont du Gard from Nîmes, Uzès, and Avignon. Combine Uzès (see below) and Pont du Gard for an ideal day excursion from Avignon (see "Transportation Connections—Avignon," above). By car, Pont du Gard is an easy 30-minute drive due west of Avignon (follow signs to Nîmes) and 45 minutes northwest of Arles (via Tarascon). Park on the *rive gauche* side (you'll see signs) and leave nothing in your car.

Uzès—An intriguing, less-trampled town near Pont du Gard, Uzès is best seen slowly on foot, with a long coffee break in its mellow main square, the place aux Herbes (not so mellow during the colorful Sunday-morning market). You can tour the round Tour Fenestrelle (all that remains of a 12th-century cathedral) and the palace of the Duché de Uzès (55F, French-only tour, get English handout). Uzès is a short hop west (by bus) of Pont du Gard and is well served by bus from Nîmes (9/day) and Avignon (3/day). Uzès is officially in Languedoc, not Provence.

The Camargue—This is one of the few truly "wild" areas of France, where pink flamingos, wild bulls, and the famous white horses wander freely amid rice fields, lagoons, and mosquitoes. It's a three-star sight for nature lovers and boring for others. The D-37 that follows the Étang du Vaccares has some of the best viewing. The Camargue's biggest town is Aigue Mortes. That means "dead town," and it should stay that way.

▲▲Orange—This most northern town in Provence is notable for its Roman arch and theater. The 20-meter-tall Roman Arc de Triomphe (from 25 B.C., north of city center) honors Julius Caesar's defeat of the Gauls in 49 B.C., but is lightweight compared to its best-preserved Roman theater (*Théâtre Antique*) in existence. Find a seat up high to appreciate the acoustics and contemplate that 2,000 years ago Orange residents enjoyed grand spectacles with high-tech sound and lights affects like thunder, lightning, and rain. A huge awning could be unfurled from that awesome 40-meter-high stage wall to provide shade that you might appreciate right now. It still seats 10,000 (30F, April–Sept 30 daily 9:00–18:30, Oct–March 9:00–12:00, 13:30–17:00; ticket includes entrance to city museum across street, which has more Roman art; Orange TI tel. 04 90 34 70 88). Trains run hourly between Avignon and Orange (15 min). From Orange's train station to the old town and theater, it's a 20-minute walk or 10-minute ride on bus #2.

BAVARIA
AND TIROL

Two hours south of Munich, between Germany's Bavaria and
Austria's Tirol, is a timeless land of fairy-tale castles, painted
buildings shared by cows and farmers, and locals who still yodel
when they're happy.

In Germany's Bavaria, tour "Mad" King Ludwig's ornate
Neuschwanstein Castle, Europe's most spectacular. Stop by the
Wieskirche, a textbook example of Bavarian rococo bursting with
curly curlicues, and browse through Oberammergau, Germany's
wood-carving capital and home of the famous Passion Play.

In Austria's Tirol, hike to the Ehrenberg ruined castle,
scream down a nearby ski slope on an oversized skateboard, then
catch your breath for an evening of yodeling and slap dancing.

In this chapter I'll cover Bavaria first, then Tirol. Austria's
Tirol is easier and cheaper than touristy Bavaria. My favorite
home base for exploring Bavaria's castles is actually in Austria, in
the town of Reutte. Füssen, in Germany, is a handier home base
for train travelers.

Planning Your Time
While locals come here for a week or two, the typical speedy
American traveler will find two days' worth of sightseeing. With
a car and more time you could enjoy three or four days, but the
basic visit ranges anywhere from a long day trip from Munich to
a three-night, two-day visit. If the weather's good and you're not
going to Switzerland, be sure to ride a lift to an Alpine peak.

A good schedule for a one-day circular drive from Reutte is:
7:30–Breakfast, 8:00–Depart hotel, 8:15–Arrive at Neuschwanstein
to get admission times for two castles, tour both Hohenschwangau
and Neuschwanstein, 13:00–Drive to the Wieskirche (20-minute

Highlights of Bavaria and Tirol

stop) and on to Linderhof, 14:30–Tour Linderhof, 16:30–Drive along scenic Plansee back into Austria, 17:30–Back at hotel, 19:00–Dinner at hotel and perhaps a folk evening (or the Ludwig II Musical). In peak season you might arrive later at Linderhof to avoid the crowds. The next morning you could stroll through Reutte, hike to the Ehrenberg ruins, and ride the luge on your way to Innsbruck, Munich, Venice, Switzerland, or wherever.

Train travelers can base in Füssen and bus or bike the short distance to Neuschwanstein. Reutte, which will likely lose its train station in 2001, is connected by bus with Füssen (5/day, none on Sun). If you base in Reutte, you can bike to Neuschwanstein, Ehrenberg ruins, and the Tegelberg luge (and hike to Neuschwanstein from the recommended Gutshof zum Schluxen).

Getting around Bavaria and Tirol

By Car: This region is ideal by car. All the sights are within an easy 60-mile loop from Reutte or Füssen.

By Train and Bus: It can be frustrating by train. Local bus
service in the region is spotty for sightseeing. If you're rushed
and without wheels, Reutte, the Wieskirche, and the luge rides
are probably not worth the trouble (but the Tegelberg luge near
Neuschwanstein is within walking distance).

Füssen (with a 2-hour train ride to/from Munich every
hour, transfer in Buchloe) is five kilometers from Neuschwanstein
Castle with easy bus and bike connections. Reutte is a 30-minute
bus ride from Füssen (5/day, not Sun). Oberammergau (2-hour
trains from Munich every hour with 1 change) has decent bus connections to nearby Linderhof Castle. Oberammergau to Füssen is
sparse (1 bus/day, 2 hrs).

By Rental Car: You can rent a car in Füssen (or in Reutte,
if you're a guest at the Hotel Maximilian).

By Tour: If you're interested only in Bavarian castles, consider an all-day organized bus tour of the Bavarian biggies as a side
trip from Munich (offered by Panorama Tours, tel. 089/593-889).

By Bike: This is great biking country. Many shops near train
stations (such as in Füssen) and hotels rent bikes for 15 to 20 DM
per day. The rides from Reutte to Neuschwanstein, Ehrenberg
ruins, and the luge are great for those with the time and energy.

By Thumb: Hitchhiking, always risky, is a slow-but-possible
way to connect the public transportation gaps.

FÜSSEN

Füssen has been a strategic stop since ancient times. Its main street
sits on the Via Claudia Augusta, which crossed the Alps (over Bren-
ner Pass) in Roman times. The town was the southern terminus of
the medieval trade route known among modern tourists as the
"Romantic Road." Dramatically situated under a renovated castle
on the lively Lech River, Füssen just celebrated its 700th birthday.

Unfortunately, in the summer Füssen is entirely overrun by
tourists. Traffic can be exasperating, but by bike or on foot it's
not bad. Off-season the town is a jester's delight.

Apart from Füssen's cobbled and arcaded town center, there's
little real sightseeing here. The striking-from-a-distance castle
houses a boring picture gallery. The mediocre city museum in the
monastery below the castle exhibits lifestyles of 200 years ago and the
story of the monastery, and offers displays on the development of the
violin, for which Füssen was famous (5 DM, Tue–Sun 11:00–16:00,
closed Mon, explanations in German only). Halfway between Füssen
and the border (as you drive, or a woodsy walk from the town) is the
Lechfall, a thunderous waterfall with a handy potty stop.

Orientation (area code: 08362)

Füssen's train station is a few blocks from the TI, the town
center (a cobbled shopping mall), and all my hotel listings (see

"Sleeping," below). The TI has a room-finding service (Mon–Fri 9:00–18:00, Sat 9:00–14:00, shorter hours off-season, 3 blocks down Bahnhofstrasse from station, tel. 08362/93850, fax 08362/938-520, www.fuessen.de). After-hours the little self-service info pavilion near the front of the TI dispenses Füssen maps for 3 DM.

Arrival in Füssen: Exit left as you leave the train station (lockers available) and walk a few straight blocks to the center of town and the TI. To go to Neuschwanstein or Reutte, catch a bus from the station.

Bike Rental: Rent at Preisschranke next to the station (15 DM/day, Mon–Sat 9:00–20:00, tel. 08362/921-544) or, for a bigger selection and less convenient location, check out Rad Zacherl (14 DM/day, mountain bikes-20 DM, passport number for deposit, Mon–Fri 9:00–12:00, 14:00–18:00, Sat 9:00–13:00, 2 km out of town at Kempterstrasse 119, tel. 08362/3292).

Car Rental: Antes & Huber is more central (Kemptenenerstrasse 59, tel. 08362/91920) than Hertz (Füssenerstrasse 112, tel. 08362/986-580).

Sights—Neuschwanstein Castle Area, Bavaria

The most popular tourist destination in Bavaria is the "King's Castles" (Konigschlosser). With fairy-tale turrets in a fairy-tale Alpine setting built by a fairy-tale king, it's understandably popular. The well-organized visitor can have a great four-hour visit. Others will just stand in line and perhaps not even see the castle. The key: arrive early. You can see both castles, consider fun options nearby (mountain lift, luge course, Füssen town) and get out by early afternoon.

Ludwig II (a.k.a. "Mad" King Ludwig), a tragic figure, ruled Bavaria for 23 years until his death in 1886 at the age of 41. Politically, his reality was to "rule" either as a pawn of Prussia or a pawn of Austria. Rather than deal with politics in Bavaria's capital, Munich, Ludwig frittered away most of his time at his family's hunting palace, Hohenschwangau. He spent most of his adult life constructing his fanciful Neuschwanstein castle—much like a kid builds a tree house—on a neighboring hill upon the scant ruins of a medieval castle. Although Ludwig spent 17 years building Neuschwanstein, he lived in it only 172 days. Ludwig was a true Romantic living in a Romantic age. His best friends were artists, poets, and composers such as Richard Wagner. His palaces are wallpapered with misty medieval themes—especially those from Wagnerian operas. Eventually he was declared mentally unfit to rule Bavaria and taken away from Neuschwanstein. Two days after this eviction, Ludwig was found dead in a lake. To this day people debate whether the king was murdered or committed suicide.

▲▲▲**Neuschwanstein Castle**—Imagine King Ludwig as a boy, climbing the hills above his dad's castle, Hohenschwangau (below),

Neuschwanstein

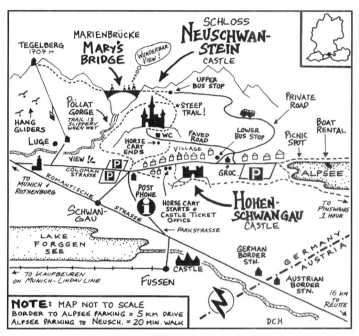

dreaming up the ultimate fairy-tale castle. He had the power
to make his dream concrete and stucco. Neuschwanstein was
designed by a painter first...then an architect. It looks medieval,
but it's only about as old as the Eiffel Tower. It feels like something you'd see at a home show for 19th-century royalty. Built
from 1869 to 1886, it's a textbook example of the Romanticism
that was popular in 19th-century Europe. Construction stopped
with Ludwig's death (only a third of the interior was finished) and
within six weeks, tourists were paying to go through it. Guides
herd groups of 60 through the castle giving an interesting if
rushed 30-minute tour. You'll go up and down more than 300
steps through lavish Wagnerian dream rooms, a royal state-of-the-
19th-century-art kitchen, the king's gilded-lily bedroom, and his
extravagant throne room. You'll see 15 rooms with their original
furnishings and fanciful wall paintings. After the tour you'll see a
room lined with fascinating drawings (described in English) of the
castle plans, construction, and 1883 drawings of Falkenstein—
a fanciful over-the-top but never-built castle which made Neuschwanstein look stubby and occupied Ludwig's fantasies the year he
died. After the tour, a 20-minute slide show (alternating German

and English) plays continuously. If English is on, pop in. If not, it's not worth waiting for.

▲▲**Hohenschwangau Castle**—Standing quietly below Neuschwanstein, the big yellow Hohenschwangau Castle was Ludwig's boyhood home. Originally built in the 12th century, it was ruined by Napoleon. Ludwig's father Maximilian rebuilt it, and you'll see it as it looked in 1836. It's more lived-in and historic, and excellent 30-minute tours actually give a better glimpse of Ludwig's life than the more visited and famous Neuschwanstein castle tour.

Getting Tickets for the Castles: Every tour bus in Bavaria converges on Neuschwanstein and tourists flush in each morning from Munich. A new reservation system sorts out the chaos for smart travelers. If you arrive late without a reservation you'll spend two hours in the ticket line and may find all tours for the day booked. A ticket center for both Neuschwanstein and Hohenschwangau castles is located a few blocks from the TI toward the Alpsee (street level between the 2 castles—not at either castle). The ticket booth opens at 7:30. Tickets come with admission times. (Miss this time and you don't get in.) First tours go at 8:45. Arrive by 8:30 (arriving before 8:00 accomplishes nothing) and you'll be touring by 9:00. To tour both castles you must do Hohenschwangau first (logical since this gives a better introduction to Ludwig's short life). You'll get two castle tour times: Hohenschwangau and then, two hours later, Neuschwanstein. The ticket office claims you can telephone for a reservation (minimum 48 hrs in advance, 08362/930-8322 or 08362/930-8324), but you'll likely get a long recording telling you first in German, then in English, how to fax or e-mail for a reservation (fax 08362/930-8320, www.ticket-center-hohenschwangau.de).

Cost and Hours: Each castle costs 14 DM, both castles are 26 DM, and children are free (April–Sept daily 8:30–17:30, Thu until 19:30, March and Oct 9:30–16:30, Neuschwanstein Nov–Feb 10:00–16:00, Hohenschwangau closed in winter, no photography inside).

Getting to the Castles: From the ticket booth, Hohenschwangau is an easy five-minute climb. Neuschwanstein is a steep 30-minute hike. To minimize hiking, you can take a shuttle bus or horse carriage, but neither gets you to the castle doorstep. The frequent shuttle buses drop you off at Mary's Bridge, leaving you a steep 10-minute downhill walk to the castle—be sure to see the view from Mary's Bridge before hiking down to castle (3.50 DM up; 5 DM round-trip not worth it since you have to hike up to bus stop for return trip). Horse carriages (8 DM up, 4 DM down) are slower than walking and stop below Neuschwanstein, leaving you a five-minute uphill hike. Note: If it's less than an hour until your Neuschwanstein tour time, you'll need to hike—at a brisk pace it's still 20 minutes.

Mary's Bridge: Before or after the tour, climb up to Mary's Bridge to marvel at Ludwig's castle, just as Ludwig did. This bridge was quite an engineering accomplishment 100 years ago. From the bridge, the frisky can hike even higher to the "Beware— Danger of Death" signs and an even more glorious castle view. For the most interesting descent (15 min longer and extremely slippery when wet), follow signs to the Pöllat Gorge.

Castle Village: The "village" at the foot of Europe's "Disney" castle feeds off the droves of hungry, shop-happy tourists. The Bräustüberl serves the cheapest grub (often with live folk music). The Alpsee lake is ideal for a picnic; the souvenir shop (open daily) nearest the Bräustüberl restaurant has a microwave fast-food machine and the makings for a skimpy lunch. Picnic at the lakeside park or in one of the old-fashioned rowboats (rented by the hour in summer). The bus stop, post/telephone office, and helpful TI cluster around the main intersection (TI open daily 9:00–18:00, until 16:00 Oct–March, tel. 08362/819-840).

Getting to the Castles from Füssen or Reutte: There's plenty of parking (all lots-7 DM). Get there early and you'll park conveniently at lot D next to the lake. Those without cars can bus from Füssen (2.50 DM one-way, 5 DM round-trip, 2/hrly, 10 min, 5 kilometers, from train station) or ride a rental bike. From Reutte, it's a bus ride to Füssen (5/day except Sun, 30 min, then city bus to castle).

For a romantic twist, hike or mountain bike from the trail-head at the recommended hotel Gutshof zum Schluxen in Pin-swang (see "Sleeping near Reutte," below). When the dirt road forks at the top of the hill, go right (downhill), cross the Austria-Germany border (marked by a sign and deserted hut), and follow the narrow paved road to the castles. It's a 60- to 90-minute hike or a great circular bike trip (allow 90 min from Reutte or 30 min from Gutshof zum Schluxen; return by bus via Füssen).

▲**Tegelberg Gondola**—Just north of Neuschwanstein is a fun play zone around the mighty Tegelberg gondola. Hang gliders circle like vultures. Their pilots jumped from the top of the Tegelberg Gondola. For 28 DM you can ride high to the 5,500-foot summit and back down (daily from 9:00, last lift at 16:30, tel. 08362/98360). On a clear day you get great views of the Alps and Bavaria and the vicarious thrill of watching hang gliders and parasailors leap into airborne ecstasy. Weather permitting, scores of German thrill seekers line up and leap from the launch ramp at the top of the lift. With one leaving every two or three minutes, it's great spectating. Thrill seekers with exceptional social skills may talk themselves into a tandem ride with a parasailor. From the top of Tegelberg, it's a steep 2.5-hour hike down to Ludwig's castle. At the base of the gondola, you'll find a playground, cheery eatery, and a very good luge ride.

▲**Tegelberg Luge**—Next to the lift is a luge course. A luge is like a bobsled on wheels (for more details, see "Sights—Tirol, Near Reutte," below). The track, made of stainless steel, is often open when drizzly weather shuts down the concrete luges. It's not as scenic as Bichlbach and Biberwier (see below), but it's handy (5 DM per run, daily 10:00–18:00, closed in rain, tel. 08362/98360). A funky cable system pulls lugers to the top without a ski lift.

▲**Ludwig II Musical**—A spectacular opera/musical based on the romantic life and troubled times of Ludwig debuted in a grand new lakeside theater in 2000. While called a musical, "Ludwig II, Longing for Paradise" felt like opera to me—with an orchestra in the pit, creative stage sets, fine singing, wonderful acoustics, and an easy-to-follow story line about Ludwig abandoning the normal, guy-thing rush of political power to pal around with his muses (three vampy women dressed in purple). It's Bismarck the realistic politician on one side versus Wagner the romantic composer on the other as "art triumphs" (and Ludwig disappears into the lake).

The music is wonderful and the show's a hit with Germans. It's clearly top classical quality, but the superscripts in English are tough to read and tickets are pricey. The state-of-the-art theater is romantically set on a lake (Forgensee) with a view of floodlit Neuschwanstein in the distance (85–230 DM per seat, Tue–Fri at 19:30, Sat–Sun at 13:00 and 18:00, Jan–Dec, English subtitles, 3 hrs including intermission, plenty of chances to eat a good light meal, parking-6 DM—have coins, about 1.5 kilometers north of Füssen—follow signs for "musical," book well in advance, for tickets call 01805/583-944, www.ludwigmusical.com).

More Sights—Bavaria

These are listed in driving order from Füssen.

▲▲**Wies Church (Wieskirche)**—Germany's greatest rococo-style church, Wieskirche ("the church in the meadow") is newly restored and looking as brilliant as the day it floated down from heaven. Overripe with decoration but bright and bursting with beauty, this church is a divine droplet, a curly curlicue, the final flowering of the Baroque movement. The ceiling depicts the Last Judgment—but the most positive one around. Jesus, rather than sitting on the throne to judge, rides high on a rainbow, giving any sinners the feeling that there is still time to repent and plenty of mercy on hand.

This is a pilgrimage church. In the early 1700s a carving of Christ too graphic to be accepted by that generation's church was the focus of worship in a peasant's private chapel. Miraculously, it wept. And pilgrims came from all around.

Bavaria's top rococo architects, the Zimmermann brothers, were then commissioned to build the Wieskirche, which features the amazing carving above its altar and still attracts countless pilgrims (donation requested, daily 8:00–20:00, less off-season).

Take a commune-with-nature-and-smell-the-farm detour back
through the meadow to the car park.

Wieskirche is 30 minutes north of Neuschwanstein.
The northbound Romantic Road bus tour stops here for 15
minutes. Füssen–Wieskirche buses run several times a day.
By car, head north from Füssen, turn right at Steingaden, and
follow the signs.

If you can't visit Wieskirche, visit one of the other
churches that came out of the same heavenly spray can:
Oberammergau's church, Munich's Asam Church, the Würzburg Residenz Chapel, or the splendid Ettal Monastery (free
and near Oberammergau).

If you're driving from Wieskirche to Oberammergau, you'll
cross the Echelsbacher Bridge, which arches 70 meters over the
Pöllat Gorge. Thoughtful drivers let their passengers walk across
(for the views) and meet them at the other side. Any kayakers?
Notice the painting of the traditional village wood-carver (who
used to walk from town to town with his art on his back) on the
first big house on the Oberammergau side, a shop called Almdorf
Ammertal. It has a huge selection of overpriced carvings and
commission-hungry tour guides.

▲**Oberammergau**—The Shirley Temple of Bavarian villages
and exploited to the hilt by the tourist trade, Oberammergau
wears way too much makeup. If you're passing through anyway,
it's worth a wander among the half-timbered houses painted with
Bible scenes and famous fairy-tale characters. Browse through
wood-carvers' shops—small art galleries filled with very expensive
whittled works. Pilat's house on Ludwig Thomastrasse is a living
workshop full of wood-carvers and painters in action (daily
13:00–18:00, off-season weekends only). Or see folk art at the
town's Heimatmuseum (TI tel. 08822/92310, closed weekends
off-season, www.oberammergau.de).

Visit the church, a poor cousin of the one at Wies. This
church looks richer than it is. Put your hand on the "marble"
columns. If they warm up, they're painted fakes. Wander through
the graveyard. Ponder the deaths that two wars dealt Germany.
Behind the church are the photos of three Schneller brothers,
all killed within two years in World War II.

Passion Play: Still making good on a deal the townspeople
made with God when they were spared devastation by the Black
Plague, once each decade Oberammergau performs the Passion
Play. It happened in 2000 when 5,000 people a day for 100 summer days attended Oberammergau's sold-out, all-day dramatic
story of Christ's crucifixion. Until the next performance in 2010,
you'll have to settle for reading the Book, seeing Nicodemus
tool around town in his VW, or browsing through the theater's
exhibition hall (4 DM, daily 9:30–12:00, 13:30–16:00, closed

Mon off-season, tel. 08822/32278). Consider a guided tour of the
Passion Play theatre (call TI for details).

Gasthaus zum Stern is friendly, serves good food (closed
Tue off-season), and is a good value for this touristy town (Sb-50
DM, Db-100 DM, Dorfstrasse 33, 82487 Oberammergau, tel.
08822/867, fax 08822/7027). **Hotel Bayerische Lowe** is central
with a good restaurant and comfortable rooms (Db-99 DM,
Dedlerstrasse 2, tel. 08822/1365). Oberammergau's modern
youth hostel is on the river a short walk from the center (20-DM
beds, open all year, tel. 08822/4114).

Driving into town from the north, cross the bridge, take the
second left, follow "Polizei" signs, and park by the huge gray Pas-
sionsspielhaus. Leaving town, head out past the church and turn
toward Ettal on Road 23. You're 30 kilometers from Reutte via
the scenic Plansee. Oberammergau is connected to Füssen by six
direct two-hour buses per day.

▲▲**Linderhof Castle**—This homiest of "Mad" King Ludwig's castles is small and comfortably exquisite—good enough
for a minor god. Set in the woods 15 minutes from Oberammergau by car or bus (3 buses/day, fewer off-season) and surrounded by fountains and sculpted, Italian-style gardens, it's
the only palace I've toured that actually had me feeling envious.
Don't miss the grotto—15-minute tours included with palace
ticket (11 DM, daily 9:00–17:30, Thu until 19:30, Oct–March
10:00–16:00 with lunch break, parking-4 DM, fountains
often erupt on the hour, English tours when 20 gather—easy
in summer but sparse off-season, tel. 08822/92030). Plan for
lots of walking and a two-hour stop to fully enjoy this royal
park. Pay at entry and get admission time. Visit outlying sights
to pass any wait time.

▲▲**Zugspitze**—The tallest point in Germany is a border crossing. Lifts from Austria and Germany go to the 10,000-foot summit of the Zugspitze. Straddle the border between two great
nations while enjoying an incredible view. Restaurants, shops, and
telescopes await you at the summit.

On the German side, the 75-minute trip from Garmisch
costs 79 DM round-trip; family discounts are available (buy a
combo cogwheel train and cable car ride, tel. 08821/7970).
Hikers enjoy the easy 10-kilometer walk around the lovely Elbsee
lake (German side, 5 minutes downhill from cable "Seilbahn").

On the Austrian side, from the less crowded Talstation
Obermoos above the village of Erwald, the tram zips you to
the top in 10 minutes (420 AS or 61 DM round-trip, late
May–Oct daily 8:40–16:40, tel. in Austria 05673/2309).

The German ascent is easier for those without a car, but
buses do connect the Erwald train station and the Austrian
lift almost every hour.

Sleeping in Füssen
(2 DM = about $1, country code: 49,
area code: 08362, zip code: 87629)
Sleep Code: **S** = Single, **D** = Double/Twin, **T** = Triple, **Q** = Quad,
b = bathroom, **t** = toilet only, **s** = shower only, **CC** = Credit Card
(**V**isa, **M**asterCard, **A**mex).

Unless otherwise noted, breakfast is included, hall showers
are free, and English is spoken. Prices listed are for one-night
stays. Some places give a discount for longer stays. Always ask.
Competition is fierce, and off-season prices are soft.

While I prefer sleeping in Reutte (see below), convenient
Füssen is just five kilometers from Ludwig's castles and offers a
cobbled, riverside retreat. But it also happens to be very touristy
(notice *das* sushi bar). It has just about as many rooms as tourists,
though, and the TI has a free room-finding service. All places
I've listed (except the hostel) are within a few blocks of the train
station and the town center. They are used to travelers getting in
after the Romantic Road bus arrives (20:05) and will hold rooms
for a telephone promise. Parking is easy at the station.

Hotel Kurcafé is deluxe, with spacious rooms and all of
the amenities. Its bakery can ruin your budget any time of year
(Sb-99–169 DM, Db-149–209 DM, Tb-179–249 DM, Q-199–279
DM, less off-season, CC:VM, on the tiny traffic circle a block in
front of train station at Bahnhofstrasse 4, tel. 08362/6369, fax
08362/39424, www.kurcafe.com). The attached restaurant has
good and reasonable daily specials.

Altstadt-Hotel zum Hechten offers all the modern comforts
in a friendly, traditional shell right under the Füssen Castle in the
old-town pedestrian zone (S-65 DM, Sb-80–90 DM, D-100 DM,
Db-130–150 DM, Tb-180 DM, Qb-200 DM, these prices and free
parking promised with this book in 2001, cheaper off-season and
for multinight stays, fun mini–bowling alley in basement; from TI,
walk down pedestrian street, take second right to Ritterstrasse 6,
tel. 08362/91600, fax 08362/916-099, www.hotel-hechten.com,
Frau Margaret has taken fine care of travelers for 40 years). The
attached restaurant Zum Hechten serves hearty Bavarian specialties
and specializes in pike (*Hecht*), pulled from the Lech River.

American **Suzanne's B&B**, though run with an iron hand,
offers fresh eggs, local cheese, a children's yard, affordable laundry, bright rooms, and feel-good balconies. Big families should
ask about her "attic special," and the budget-conscious should
ask about her "backpacker's special" (D-100 DM, Db-140 DM,
Tb-180 DM, Qb-210 DM, room for up to six-220–240 DM,
nonsmoking, low ceilings, backtrack 2 blocks from station,
Venetianerwinkel 3, tel. 08362/38485, fax 08362/921-396,
www.suzannes.org, e-mail: svorbrugg@t-online.de).

The funky, old, ornately furnished **Pension Garni Elisabeth**

Füssen

1 HOTEL KURCAFE

2 HOTEL HECHTEN

3 SUZANNE'S B & B

4 HAUS PETERS

5 PENSION ELISABETH

6 GASTHOF KRONE

7 HOTEL BRÄUSTÜBERL

8 YOUTH HOSTEL

9 BIKE RENTAL

10 HOTEL SONNE

exudes an Addams-family friendliness. Floors creak, dust balls wander, and the piano is never played (S-55 DM, D-90–100 DM, Db-120–180 DM, T-135 DM, Tb-180–195 DM, showers-6 DM, Augustenstrasse 10, 2 blocks from the station toward town, take second left, tel. 08362/6275).

Haus Peters, across the street, is comfy, smoke free, and friendly, but will be closed May, June, and September (Db-86 DM, Tb-120 DM, Augustenstrasse 5 1/2, tel. 08362/7171).

Gasthof Krone, a rare bit of pre-glitz Füssen in the pedestrian zone, has dumpy halls and stairs and standard, comfy rooms at good prices (S-58 DM, D-106 DM, extra bed-53 DM, prices drop 6 DM for 2-night stays, CC:VMA, reception in restaurant, from TI, head down pedestrian street, take first left to Schrannengasse 17, tel. 08362/7824, fax 08362/37505).

Hotel Bräustüberl, run with indifference, has decent rooms attached to a gruff and musty old beer hall–type place at fair rates (Sb-55 DM, Db-100 DM, Rupprechtstrasse 5, a block from the station, tel. 08362/7843, fax 08362/941-361).

Hotel Sonne is a splurge in the heart of the town with 32 quaint yet plush rooms with all the extras (Sb-160 DM, Db-195 DM, Tb-240 DM, CC:VMA, free parking, kitty-corner from TI on Reichenstrasse 37, tel. 08362/9080, fax 08362/908-100, www.hotel-sonne.de).

Füssen Youth Hostel, a fine, German-run youth hostel, welcomes travelers under 27 (2- to 6-bed rooms, bed and breakfast-23 DM, dinner-7 DM, sheets-5.50 DM, laundry-7 DM/load, non-smoking, Mariahilferstrasse 5, tel. 08362/7754, fax 08362/2770). From the station, backtrack 10 minutes along the tracks.

Sleeping in Hohenschwangau, near Neuschwanstein Castle
(country code: 49, area code: 08362, zip code: 87645)

Inexpensive farmhouse *Zimmer* (B&Bs) abound in the Bavarian countryside around Neuschwanstein and are a good value. Look for signs that say "Zimmer Frei" ("room free," or vacancy). The going rate is about 80 DM per double including breakfast. **Pension Weiher** has lots of balconies and floodlit Neuschwanstein views (S-38 DM, D-80 DM, Db-100 DM, Hofwiesenweg 11, tel. & fax 08362/81161). **Pension Schwansee** has clean, basic rooms (Db-100–120 DM, CC:VM, bike rental, 2.5 kilometers from the castle, right on the road to Füssen at Parkstrasse 9, 87645 Alterschrofen, tel. 08362/8353, fax 08362/987-320, family Strössner).

For more of a hotel, try **Alpenhotel Meier**. It's located in a rural setting within walking distance of the castle, just beyond the lower parking lot. Its rooms have new furnishings and porches (Sb-80–90 DM, Db-130–150 DM, 2-night discounts, larger rooms available, easy parking, Schwangauerstrasse 37, tel. 08362/81152, fax 08362/987-028, e-mail: alpenhotelmeier@firemail.de).

Eating in Füssen

Infooday is a clever and modern self-service eatery that sells its hot meals and salad bar by weight and offers English newspapers (filling salad-6 DM, meals-10 DM, Mon–Fri 10:30–18:30, Sat 10:30–14:30, closed Sun, under Füssen Castle in Hotel zum Hechten, Ritterstrasse 6). Nearby **Ritterstuben** offers reasonable and delicious fish and salads (Tue–Sun 11:30–14:30, 17:30–23:00, closed Mon, next to Altstadt-Hotel zum Hechten at Ritterstrasse 4, tel. 08362/7759). A couple of blocks away, **Pizza Blitz** is a dive that offers good take-out or eat-at-the-counter pizzas and hearty salads for about 10 DM apiece (Mon–Sat 11:00–23:00, Sun 12:00–23:00, Luitpoldstrasse 14). Picnickers can shop at **Woolworth's** plentiful supermarket (Mon–Fri 9:00–19:00, Sat 9:00–16:00, closed Sun, Reichenstrassse 11, tel. 083621/91840).

Transportation Connections—Füssen
To: Neuschwanstein (2 buses/hrly, 10 min, 2.50 DM one-way, 5 DM round-trip; taxis cost 20 DM), **Reutte** (5 buses/day, 30 min, no service on Sun; taxis cost 40 DM), **Munich** (hrly trains, 2 hrs, transfer in Buchloe).

Romantic Road Buses: The northbound Romantic Road bus departs Füssen at 8:00; the southbound bus arrives at Füssen at 20:05 (bus stops at train station). Railpasses get you a 75 percent discount on the Romantic Road bus (and, best of all, the ride doesn't use up a day of a flexipass)—this is a great value. For more information, see the Rothenburg chapter.

REUTTE, AUSTRIA
(15 AS = about $1)
Reutte (ROY-teh, rolled "r"), a relaxed town of 5,500, is located 20 minutes across the border from Füssen. It's far from the international tourist crowd, but popular with Germans and Austrians for its climate. Doctors recommend its "grade 1" air. Reutte's one claim to fame with Americans: As Nazi Germany was falling in 1945, Hitler's top rocket scientist Werner von Braun joined the Americans (rather than the Russians) here in Reutte. You could say the American space program began in Reutte.

Reutte isn't in any other American guidebook. Its charms are subtle, though its generous sidewalks are filled with smart boutiques and lazy coffeehouses. It never was rich or important. Its castle is ruined, its buildings have painted-on "carvings," its churches are full, its men yodel for each other on birthdays, and lately its energy is spent soaking its Austrian and German guests in *Gemütlichkeit*. Most guests stay for a week, so the town's attractions are more time-consuming than thrilling. If the weather's good, hike to the mysterious Ehrenberg ruins, ride the luge, or rent a bike. For a slap-dancing bang, enjoy a Tirolean folk evening. For accommodations, see "Sleeping," below.

Orientation (area code: 05672)
Tourist Information: Reutte's TI is a block in front of the train station (Mon–Fri 8:00–12:00, 14:00–18:00, Sat 8:30–12:00, tel. 05672/62336 or, from Germany, 0043-5672/62336). Go over your

sightseeing plans, ask about a folk evening, pick up city and biking maps, and ask about discounts with the hotel guest cards.

Bike Rental: In the center, the Heinz Glatzle rents good bikes (city and mountain bikes–200 AS, kids' bikes–100 AS, Obermarkt 61, tel. 05672/62752). Several recommended hotels loan or rent bikes to guests. Most of the sights described in this chapter make good biking destinations. Ask about the bike path (*Radwanderweg*) along the Lech River.

Kids' Play Areas: Reutte's excellent pool (see below) has a playground. The TI can recommend several others.

Laundry: Don't ask the TI about a Laundromat. Unless you can infiltrate the local campground, Hotel Maximilian, or Gutshof zum Schluxen (see "Sleeping," below), the town has none.

Sights—Reutte

▲▲**Ehrenberg Ruins**—The brooding ruins of Ehrenberg Castle are 1.5 kilometers outside of Reutte on the road to Lermoos and Innsbruck. This is a pleasant walk or a short bike ride from Reutte; bikers can use the trail—*Radwanderweg*—along the Lech River (the TI has a good map).

Ehrenberg, a 13th-century rock pile, provides a great contrast to King Ludwig's "modern" castles and a super opportunity to let your imagination off its leash.

At the parking lot at the base of the ruin-topped hill, you'll find the café/guest house Gasthor Klaus (closed Wed), which offers a German-language flyer about the castle and has a wall painting of the intact castle.

The parking lot lies on the ancient Roman road, Via Claudia, and the medieval salt road. The **fortification** at the parking lot was a castle built over the road to control traffic and levy tolls on all that passed this strategic valley. (This ruin will open as a museum of European castle ruins in about 2004.)

Hike up 20 minutes from the parking lot for a great view from your own private ruins. Facing the hill from the parking lot, find the gravelly road at the Klaus sign. Follow the road to the saddle between the two hills. From the saddle notice how the castle stands high on the horizon. This is Ehrenberg (which means "mountain of honor"), built in 1290. Thirteenth-century castles were designed to stand boastfully tall. With the advent of gunpowder, castles dug in. Notice the **ramparts** around you. They are 18th century. Approaching Ehrenberg castle, look for the small door to the left. It's the night entrance (tight and awkward, therefore safer in a surprise invasion).

Hiking up the hill you go through two doors. Castles allowed step-by-step retreat, giving defenders time to regroup and fight back against invading forces.

Before making the final and steepest ascent, follow the path

Reutte

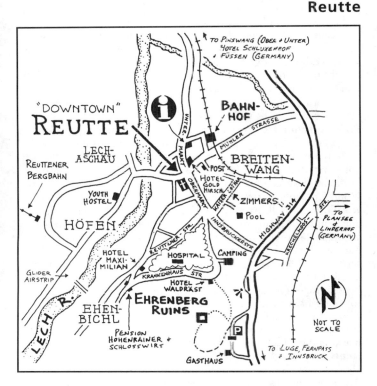

around to the right to a big, grassy courtyard with commanding views and a fat, newly restored **turret**. This stored gunpowder and held a big cannon that enjoyed a clear view of the valley below. In medieval times, all the trees approaching the castle were cleared to keep an unobstructed view.

Look out over the valley. The pointy spire marks **Breitenwang**, which was a stop on the ancient Via Claudia. In A.D. 46, there was a Roman camp here. In 1489, after the Reutte bridge crossed the Lech River, Reutte (marked by the onion-domed church) was made a market town and eclipsed Breitenwang in importance. Any gliders circling? They launch from just over the river in Hofen (see "Flying and Gliding," below).

For centuries, this castle was the seat of government—ruling an area called the "judgement of Ehrenberg" (roughly the same as today's "district of Reutte"). When the emperor came by, he stayed here. In 1604, the ruler moved downtown into more comfortable quarters and the castle was no longer a palace.

Climb the steep hill to the top of the castle. Take the high ground. There was no water supply here, just kegs of wine, beer, and a cistern to collect rain.

Ehrenberg repelled 16,000 Swedish soldiers in the defense of Catholicism in 1632. Ehrenberg saw three or four other battles, but its end was not glorious. In the 1780s, a local businessman bought the castle in order to sell off its parts. Later, when vagabonds moved in, the roof was removed to make squatting miserable. With the roof gone, deterioration quickened, leaving this evocative shell and a whiff of history.

Folk Museum—Reutte's Heimatmuseum, offering a quick look at the local folk culture and the story of the castle, is more cute than impressive and comes without English explanations (20 AS, Tue–Sun 10:00–12:00, 14:00–17:00, closed Mon and off-season, in the bright green building on Untermarkt, around corner from Hotel Goldener Hirsch, 1 block away).

▲▲**Tirolean Folk Evening**—Ask the TI or your hotel if there's a Tirolean folk evening scheduled. About three times a week in the summer, Reutte or a nearby town puts on an evening of yodeling, slap dancing, and Tirolean frolic usually worth the 80 to 120 AS and short drive. Off-season, you'll have to do your own yodeling. There are also weekly folk concerts in the park (summer only, ask at TI).

Swimming—Plunge into Reutte's Olympic-size swimming pool to cool off after your castle hikes (65 AS, daily 10:00–21:00, off-season 14:00–21:00 and closed Mon, new pool planned for 2001 at same site, 15 min on foot from Reutte center, head out Obermarkt and turn left on Kaiser-Lothar Strasse).

Reuttener Bergbahn—This mountain lift swoops you high above the tree line to a starting point for several hikes and an Alpine flower park with special paths leading you past countless local varieties (good bike ride with an uphill at the end).

Flying and Gliding—For a major thrill on a sunny day, drop by the tiny airport in Hofen across the river, and fly. A small single-prop plane can buzz the Zugspitze and Ludwig's castles and give you a bird's-eye peek at Reutte's Ehrenberg ruins (2 people for 30 min-1,350 AS, 1 hr-2,400 AS, tel. 05672/63207). Or, for something more angelic, how about *Segelfliegen*? For 370 AS you get 30 minutes in a glider for two (you and the pilot). Just watching the towrope launch the graceful glider like a giant, slow-motion rubber-band gun is thrilling (late May–Oct 11:00–19:00, in good weather only, tel. 05672/71550).

Sights—Tirol, Near Reutte

▲▲**The Luge (***Sommerrodelbahn***)**—Near Lermoos, on the road from Reutte to Innsbruck, you'll find two exciting luge courses, or *Sommerrodelbahn*. To try one of Europe's great $5 thrills, take the lift up, grab a sledlike go-cart, and luge down. The concrete course banks on the corners, and even a novice can go very, very fast. Most are cautious on their first run, speed demons on their second (and bruised and bloody on their third). A woman once showed me her journal illustrated with her husband's dried five-inch-long luge scab. He disobeyed the only essential rule of luging: Keep both hands on your stick. To avoid getting into a bumper-to-bumper traffic jam, let the person in front of you get way ahead before you start. No one emerges from the course without a windblown hairdo and a smile-creased face. Both places charge the same price (80 AS per run, 5- and 10-trip discount cards) and shut down at the least hint of rain (call ahead to make sure they're open; you're more likely to encounter an English-speaker if you call the TIs, numbers listed below). If you're without a car, these are not worth the trouble (consider the luge near Neuschwanstein instead, see "Tegelberg Luge," above).

The short and steep luge: Bichlbach, the first course (100-meter drop over 800-meter course), is six kilometers beyond Reutte's castle ruins. Look for a chair lift on the right and exit on the tiny road at the Almkopfbahn Rosthof sign (open only Sat–Sun 10:00–17:00 in mid-May, then daily June–Oct, call first, tel. 05674/5350, or contact the local TI at 05674/5354).

The longest luge: The Biberwier Sommerrodelbahn is a better luge and, at 1,300 meters, the longest in Austria (15 min farther from Reutte than Bichlbach, just past Lermoos in Biberwier—the first exit after a long tunnel). The only drawbacks are its short season and hours (open only Sat–Sun 9:00–16:30 from mid-May, then daily 9:00–16:30 through Sept, call first, tel. 05673/2111, TI tel. 05673/2922).

▲**Fallerschein**—Easy for drivers and a special treat for those who may have been Kit Carson in a previous life, this extremely remote log-cabin village is a 4,000-foot-high, flower-speckled world of serene slopes and cowbells. Thunderstorms roll down the valley like it's God's bowling alley, but the pint-size church on the high ground, blissfully simple in a land of Baroque, seems to promise that this huddle of houses will survive and the river and breeze will just keep flowing. The couples sitting on benches are mostly Austrian vacationers who've rented cabins here. Many of them, appreciating the remoteness of Fallerschein, are having affairs.

For a rugged chunk of local Alpine peace, spend a night in the local **Matratzenlager Almwirtschaft Fallerschein**, run by Kerle Erwin (about 120 AS per person with breakfast, 27 cheap beds in a very simple loft dorm, good, inexpensive meals; open, if weather permits, mid-May–Oct, 6671 Weissenbach Pfarrweg 18, Reutte, tel. 05678/5142, rarely answered, and then not in English). It's crowded only on weekends. Fallerschein, at the end of the two-kilometer Berwang Road, is near Namlos and about 45 minutes southwest of Reutte.

Sleeping in and near Reutte
(15 AS = about $1, country code: 43, area code: 05672, zip code: 6600)
Reutte is a mellow Füssen with fewer crowds and easygoing locals with a contagious love of life. Come here for a good dose of Austrian ambience and lower prices. Those with a car should home-base here; those without should consider it. (To call Reutte from Germany, dial 00-43-5672, then the local number.) You'll drive across the border without stopping. Reutte is popular with Austrians and Germans who come here year after year for one- or two-week vacations. The hotels are big, elegant, and full of comfy, carved furnishings and creative ways to spend so much time in one spot. They take great pride in their restaurants, and the owners send their children away to hotel management schools. All include a generally great breakfast but few accept credit cards.

Hotels and Guest Houses
Moserhof Hotel is a plush Tirolean splurge with polished service and facilities. The dining room is elegant (older but fine Db-900 AS, newer and larger Db-980 AS, extra person-460 AS, all rooms with balconies, elevator, from downtown Reutte walk to post office roundabout then to Planseestrasse 44, in village of Breiten-wang, tel. 05672/62020, fax 05672/620-2040).

Hotel Goldener Hirsch, located in the center of Reutte just two blocks from the station, is a grand old hotel renovated with a mod Tirolean Jugendstil flair. It includes minibars, cable TV, and one lonely set of antlers (Sb-620 AS, Db-940 AS, 2-night discounts, CC:VMA, a few family rooms, elevator, quality food in their restaurant, 6600 Reutte-Tirol, tel. 05672/62508, fax 05672/625-087, www.goldener-hirsch.at, e-mail: gold.hirsch@netway.at, Monika, Helmut—who can be unpleasant, and daughter Vanessa).

The next four listings are a few miles upriver from Reutte in the village of Ehenbichl; all are along an enjoyable hike to Ehrenberg ruins.

Hotel Maximilian is a fine splurge. It includes free bicycles, Ping-Pong, a sauna, a children's playroom, and the friendly service of the Koch family. Daughter Gabi speaks flawless English and is clearly in charge. There always seems to be a special event here, and the Kochs host many Tirolean folk evenings (Sb-450–500 AS, Db-940–1,000 AS, cheaper for families, no CC, laundry service available even to nonguests, good restaurant, A-6600 Ehenbichl-Reutte, tel. 05672/62585, fax 05672/625-8554, www.maxihotel.com, e-mail: maxhotel@netway.at). From central Reutte, go south on Obermarkt and turn right on Reuttenerstrasse. They rent cars to guests only (one VW Golf, one VW van, must book in advance).

Pension Hohenrainer is a quiet, good value with some castle-view balconies (Sb-280–350 AS, Db-620–700 AS). The same family runs the simpler **Gasthof Schlosswirt** across the green field (S-180–200 AS, D-400–480 AS, no CC, traditional Tirolean-style restaurant). Both are up the road behind Hotel Maximilian (turn right and continue 100 meters to Unterreid 3, A-6600 Ehenbichl, tel. 05672/62544, fax 05672/62052, e-mail: hohenrainer@aon.at).

Gasthof-Pension Waldrast, separating a forest and a meadow, is run by the farming Huter family. The place feels hauntingly quiet and has no restaurant, but it does include 10 very nice rooms with sitting areas and castle-view balconies (Sb-400 AS, Db-700 AS, Tb-900 AS, Qb-1,200 AS, includes small breakfast, nonsmoking, a mile from Reutte just off the main drag toward Innsbruck, past the campground and under the castle ruins, on Ehrenbergstrasse, 6600 Reutte-Ehenbichl, tel. & fax 05672/62443, www.waldrast.com, e-mail: info@waldrast.com).

Closer to Füssen but still in Austria, **Gutshof zum Schluxen**, run by helpful Hermann, gets the "remote-old-hotel-in-an-idyllic-setting" award. This family-friendly working farm offers modern rustic elegance draped in goose down and pastels, and a chance to pet a rabbit and feed the deer. Its picturesque meadow setting will turn you into a dandelion picker, and its proximity to Neuschwanstein will turn you into a hiker (Sb-560 AS, Db-1,120 AS, extra person-300 AS, 3-night discounts, free pickup from Reutte, CC:VM, good restaurant, fun bar, self-service laundry, mountain bike rental, between Reutte and Füssen in village of Pinswang, A-6600 Pinswang-Reutte, tel. 05677/8903, fax 05677/890-323, www.schluxen.com, e-mail: welcome@schluxen.com).

Private Homes in Breitenwang, near Reutte

The Reutte TI has a list of more than 50 private homes (*Zimmer*) that rent out generally good rooms with facilities down the hall, pleasant communal living rooms, and breakfast. Most charge 200 AS per person per night and speak little if any English. Reservations are nearly impossible for one- or two-night stays. But short stops are welcome if you just drop in and fill in available gaps. Most *Zimmer* charge 15 AS to 20 AS extra for heat in winter (worth it). The TI can always find you a room when you arrive.

Right next door to Reutte is the older and quieter village of Breitenwang. It has all the best *Zimmer*, the recommended Moserhof Hotel (above), and a bakery (a 20-minute walk from the Reutte train station—at the post office roundabout, follow Planseestrasse past the onion dome to the pointy straight dome; unmarked Kaiser Lothar Strasse is the first right past this church). The following three *Zimmer* are comfortable, quiet, have few stairs, and are within two blocks of the Breitenwang church steeple: **Helene Haissl** (S-200 AS, D-400 AS, 2-night discounts, fine rooms, beautiful garden, separate entrance for rooms, across

from the big Alpenhotel at Planseestrasse 63, tel. 05672/67913);
Inge Hosp (S-220 AS, D-400 AS, an old-fashioned place, includes
antlers over the breakfast table, Kaiser Lothar Strasse 36, tel.
05672/62401); and **Walter and Emilie Hosp**, Inge's more formal
cousins, who have a modern house across the street (D-400 AS,
extra person-160 AS, Kaiser Lothar Strasse 29, tel. 05672/65377).

Hostel
The homey hostel **Jugendgästehaus Graben** has two to six beds
per room and includes breakfast and sheets. The Reyman family
keeps the place traditional, clean, and friendly and serves a great
90-AS dinner for guests only. This is a super value. If you've never
hosteled and are curious (and have a car or don't mind a bus ride),
try it. They accept nonmembers of any age (dorm bed-210 AS,
Db-570 AS, laundry service, no curfew, smoke-free rooms, bus
connection to Neuschwanstein; about 3 kilometers from Reutte,
from downtown Reutte, cross the bridge and follow the main road
left along the river, or take the bus—1 bus/hrly until 18:00, ask
for Graben stop; Graben 1, A-6600 Reutte-Höfen, tel. 05672/
626-440, fax 05672/626-444, www.tirol.com/jgh-hoefen, e-mail:
jgh-hoefen@tirol.com).

Eating in Reutte
Hotels in this region take great pleasure in earning the loyalty of
their guests by serving local cuisine at reasonable prices. Rather
than go to a cheap restaurant, eat at your hotel. For cheap food,
the **Metzgerei Storf** (Mon–Fri 8:30–15:00), above the deli across
from the Heimatmuseum on Untermarkt Street, is good. The
modern **Alina** restaurant in Breitenwang is a fine Italian establishment with decent prices (near recommended *Zimmer*, 2 blocks
behind church at Bachweg 17).

Transportation Connections—Reutte
To: Füssen (5 buses/day, 30 min, no service on Sun; taxis cost 40
DM). In 2001 Reutte will probably lose its train service. Buses will
likely connect the town with Garmisch and Innsbruck from which
trains will connect to Munich and Salzburg.

ROTHENBURG AND THE ROMANTIC ROAD

From Munich or Füssen to Frankfurt, the Romantic Road takes you through Bavaria's medieval heartland, a route strewn with picturesque villages, farmhouses, onion-domed churches, Baroque palaces, and walled cities.

Dive into the Middle Ages via Rothenburg (ROE-ten-burg), Germany's best-preserved walled town. Countless travelers have searched for the elusive "untouristy Rothenburg." There are many contenders (such as Michelstadt, Miltenberg, Bamberg, Bad Windsheim, and Dinkelsbühl), but none holds a candle to the king of medieval German cuteness. Even with crowds, over-priced souvenirs, Japanese-speaking night watchmen, and, yes, even with *Schneebälle*, Rothenburg is best. Save time and mileage and be satisfied with the winner.

Planning Your Time

The best one-day look at the heartland of Germany is the Romantic Road bus tour. Eurail travelers, who get a 60 percent discount, pay about 54 DM for the ride (daily, Frankfurt to Munich or Füssen, and vice versa). Drivers can follow the route laid out in the tourist brochures (available at any TI). The only stop worth more than a few minutes is Rothenburg. Twenty-four hours is ideal for this town. Two nights and a day are a bit much, unless you're actually relaxing on this trip.

Rothenburg in a day is easy, with four essential experiences: the Medieval Crime and Punishment Museum, the Riemenschneider wood carving in St. Jakob's Church, the city walking tour, and a walk along the wall. With more time there are several mediocre but entertaining museums, walking and biking in the nearby countryside, and lots of cafés and shops. Make a point to

Rothenburg

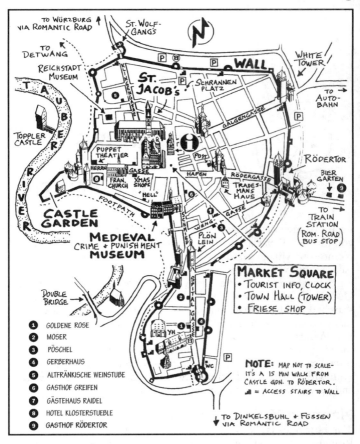

TO WÜRZBURG
VIA ROMANTIC ROAD
ST. WOLF-
GANGS
TO
DETWANG
REICHSTADT
MUSEUM

WHITE
TOWER
T
A
U
B
E
R
ST.
JACOB'S
WALL
SCHRANNEN
PLATZ
TO
AUTO-
BAHN
GALGENGASSE
TOPPLER
CASTLE
PUPPET
THEATER
HERRN
GASSE
FRAN.
CHURCH
XMAS
SHOPS
HELL
POST
HAFEN
RÖDERGASSE
TRADES-
MAN'S
HAUS
RÖDERTOR
BIER
GARTEN
R
I
V
E
R
CASTLE
GARDEN
FOOTPATH
MEDIEVAL
CRIME + PUNISHMENT
MUSEUM
GASSE
PLÖN
LEIN
TO
TRAIN
STATION
(ROM. ROAD
BUS STOP)
DOUBLE
BRIDGE
S
P
I
T
A
L
G
A
S
S
E
YH
WC

MARKET SQUARE
• TOURIST INFO, CLOCK
• TOWN HALL (TOWER)
• FRIESE SHOP

① GOLDENE ROSE
② MOSER
③ PÖSCHEL
④ GERBERHAUS
⑤ ALTFRÄNKISCHE WEINSTUBE
⑥ GASTHOF GREIFEN
⑦ GÄSTEHAUS RAIDEL
⑧ HOTEL KLOSTERSTUEBLE
⑨ GASTHOF RÖDERTOR

NOTE: MAP NOT TO SCALE-
IT'S A 15 MIN WALK FROM
CASTLE GDN. TO RÖDERTOR.
▟ = ACCESS STAIRS TO WALL

TO DINKELSBUHL + FÜSSEN
VIA ROMANTIC ROAD

spend at least one night. The town is yours after dark when the
groups vacate and the town's floodlit cobbles wring some romance
out of any travel partner.

ROTHENBURG

In the Middle Ages, when Frankfurt and Munich were just wide
spots on the road, Rothenburg was Germany's second-largest free
imperial city, with a whopping population of 6,000. Today it's her
best-preserved medieval walled town, enjoying tremendous tourist
popularity without losing its charm. Get medievaled in Rothenburg.

During Rothenburg's heyday, from 1150 to 1400, it was the
crossing point of two major trade routes: Tashkent–Paris and

Hamburg–Venice. Today the great trade is tourism; two-thirds
of the townspeople are employed to serve you. Too often
Rothenburg brings out the shopper in visitors before they've
had a chance to appreciate the historic city. True, this is a great
place to do your German shopping, but first see the town.
While 2.5 million people visit each year, a mere 500,000 spend
the night. Rothenburg is most enjoyable early and late, when
the tour groups are gone.

Orientation (area code: 09861)

To orient yourself in Rothenburg, think of the town map as a
human head. Its nose—the castle garden—sticks out to the left,
and the neck is the skinny lower part, with the hostel and my
favorite hotels in the Adam's apple. The town is a joy on foot.
No sight or hotel is more than a 15-minute walk from the train
station or each other.

Most of the buildings you'll see were built by 1400. The
city was born around its long-gone castle—built in 1142,
destroyed in 1356, and now the site of the castle garden. You
can see the shadow of the first town wall, which defines the
oldest part of Rothenburg, in its contemporary street plan.
A few gates from this wall still survive. The richest and biggest houses were in this central part. The commoners built
higgledy-piggledy (read: picturesquely) farther from the center
near the present walls.

Tourist Information

The TI is on Market Square (Mon–Fri 9:00–12:30, 13:00–18:00,
unreliably Sat–Sun 10:00–15:00, shorter hours off-season, tel.
09861/40492, after-hours board lists rooms still available). Pick up
a map and the *Sights Worth Seeing and Knowing* brochure (a virtual
walking guide to the town). The free "Hotels and Pensions of
Rothenburg" map has the greatest detail and names all of the
streets. Confirm sightseeing plans and ask about the daily 14:00
walking tour (April–Oct) and evening entertainment. The best
town map is available free at the Friese shop, two doors from the
TI in the direction of Rothenburg's "nose."

Arrival in Rothenburg: Exit left from the train station and
turn right on the first busy street (Ansbacher Strasse). It'll take
you to Rothenburg's Market Square within 10 minutes. Leave
luggage in lockers at the station (2 DM). The travel agency in
the station is the place to arrange train and *couchette*/sleeper reservations. Taxis wait at the station and can take you to any hotel
for 10 DM. Drivers will find many parking lots outside the town
walls that range from no charge up to 7 DM per day. Park outside
of town and walk five minutes to the center. Only those with a
hotel reservation can park within the walls after hours.

Helpful Hints

Festivals: Rothenburgers dress up in medieval costumes and beer gardens spill out into the street to celebrate Mayor Nusch's Meistertrunk victory (Whitsun, 7 weeks after Easter, on June 3 in 2001, see story below under "Sights—Meistertrunk Show") and 700 years of history in the Imperial City Festival (second weekend in September, with fireworks).

    Internet Access: Try Planet Internet (9 DM/hr, Paradeisgasse 5, tel. 09861/934-415).

Tours of Rothenburg

The TI on Market Square offers one-hour guided walking tours in English (6 DM, April–Oct daily at 14:00 from Market Square). A bit less informative but wonderfully entertaining, the **Night Watchman's Tour** takes tourists on his one-hour rounds each evening at 20:00 (6 DM, April–Dec, in English). This is the best evening activity in town. Or you can hire a **private guide**. For 98 DM, a local historian who's an intriguing character as well brings the ramparts alive. Eight hundred years of history are packed between Rothenburg's cobbles. Anita Weinzierl (tel. 09868/7993) and Manfred Baumann (tel. 09861/4146) are good guides. If you prefer riding to walking, **horse-and-buggy rides** last 30 minutes and cost 10 DM per person for a minimum of three people.

Sights—Rothenburg's Town Hall Square

▲▲**Town Hall Tower**—The best view of Rothenburg and the surrounding countryside and a close-up look at the interior of an old tiled roof are yours for 2 DM and a rigorous (214 steps, 180 feet) but interesting climb (daily 9:30–12:30, 13:00–17:00, off-season weekends 12:00–15:00 only). The entrance is on Market Square. Women, beware: Some men find the view best from the bottom of the ladder just before the top.

Meistertrunk Show—Be on Market Square at 11:00, 12:00, 13:00, 14:00, 15:00, 20:00, 21:00, or 22:00 for the ritual gathering of the tourists to see the less-than-breathtaking reenactment of the Meistertrunk story. In 1631 the Catholic army took the Protestant town and was about to do its rape, pillage, and plunder thing when, as the story goes, the mayor said, "Hey, if I can drink this entire three-liter tankard of wine in one gulp, will you leave us alone?" The invading commander, sensing he was dealing with an unbalanced person, said, "Sure." Mayor Nusch drank the whole thing, the town was saved, and the mayor slept for three days. Hint: For the best show, don't watch the clock; watch the open-mouthed tourists gasp as the old windows flip open. At the late shows, the square flickers with flash attachments. While you wait for the show, give yourself the spin tour below.

Market Square Spin Tour—Stand at the bottom of Market

Square (10 feet below the wooden post) and spin 360 degrees clockwise starting with the city hall tower. Now, do it slower following these notes: 1) The city's tallest **tower**, at 200 feet, stands atop the old city hall, a white, Gothic, 13th-century building. Notice the tourists enjoying the view from the black top of the tower. 2) When the town had more money and Gothic went out of style, a new **town hall** was built in front of the old one. This is in Renaissance style from 1570. (Access to the old town hall tower is through the middle of the new town hall arcade.) 3) At the top of the square stands the proud **Councilors' Tavern** (clock tower, from 1466). In its day, the city council drank here. Today it's the TI and the focus of all the attention when the little doors on either side of the clock flip open and the wooden figures (from 1910) reenact the Meistertrunk. 4) Across the street, the green building is the oldest **pharmacy** in town—Löwen Apotheke, from 1374—peek inside. 5) On the bottom end of the square, the gray building is a fine **print shop** (see "Shopping," below, free brandy). 6) Adjoining that is the **Baumeister's House** with its famous Renaissance façade featuring statues of the seven virtues and the seven vices—the former supporting the latter. 7) The green house below that is the former house of Mayor Toppler, today the fine old **Greifen Hotel**; next to it is a famous Scottish restaurant with golden arches. 8) Continue circling to the big 17th-century **St. George's fountain**. The long metal gutters slid, routing the water into the villagers' buckets. Rothenburg's many fountains had practical functions beyond providing drinking water. The water was used for fighting fires and the fountains were stocked with fish during times of siege. Two fine buildings behind the fountain show the old-time lofts with warehouse doors and pulleys on top for hoisting. All over town, lofts were filled with grain and corn. A year's supply was required by the city so they could survive any siege. The building on the left is a free art gallery showing off the work of Rothenburg's top artists. The other is another old-time pharmacy. 9) The broad street running under the town hall tower is **Herrngasse**. The town originated with its castle (1142). Herrngasse leads from the castle (now gone) to Market Square where you stand now.

▲**Historical Town Hall Vaults**—Under the town hall tower is a city history museum that gives a waxy but good look at medieval Rothenburg. With the best English descriptions in town, it offers a look at "the fateful year 1631," a replica of the famous Meistertrunk tankard, and a dungeon complete with three dank cells and some torture lore (3 DM, 9:00–18:00, closed in winter, well described in English).

Sights—Rothenburg

▲▲**Walk the Wall**—Just over a mile around, providing great views and a good orientation, this walk can be done by those under six feet tall and without a camera in less than an hour, and requires no special sense of balance. Photographers go through lots of film, especially before breakfast or at sunset, when the lighting is best and the crowds are fewest. The best fortifications are in the Spitaltor (south end). Walk from there counterclockwise to the "forehead." Climb the Rödertor en route. The names you see along the way are people who donated money to rebuild the wall after World War II.

▲**Rödertor**—The wall tower nearest the train station is the only one you can climb. It's worth the hike up for the view and a fascinating rundown on the bombing of Rothenburg in the last weeks of World War II when the northeast corner of the city was destroyed (2 DM, daily 9:00–17:00, closed Nov–March, photos, English translation).

▲▲**St. Jakob's Church**—Built in the 14th century, it's been Lutheran since 1544. Take a close look at the Twelve Apostles altar in front (from 1546, left permanently in its open festival-day position). Six saints are below Christ. St. James (Jakob in German) is the one with the staff. He's the saint of pilgrims, and this was on the medieval pilgrimage route to Santiago de Compostela in Spain. Study the painted panels. Around the back (upper left) is a great painting of Rothenburg's Market Square in the 15th century looking like it does today. Before leaving the front of the church, notice the old medallions above the carved choir stalls featuring the coats of arms of Rothenburg's leading families and portraits of early Reformation preachers.

Next, climb the stairs in the back. Behind the pipe organ stands the artistic highlight of Rothenburg and perhaps the most wonderful woodcarving in all Germany: the glorious 500-year-old, 30-foot-high *Altar of the Holy Blood*. Tilman Riemenschneider, the Michelangelo of German wood-carvers, carved this from 1499 to 1504 to hold a precious rock crystal capsule set in a cross containing a drop of the holy blood (1270). Below, in the scene of the Last Supper, Jesus gives Judas a piece of bread marking him as the traitor while John lays his head on Christ's lap. On the left: Jesus entering Jerusalem. On the right: Jesus praying in the Garden of Gethsemane (2.50 DM, Mon–Sat 9:00–17:30, Sun 10:45–17:30, off-season 10:00–12:00, 14:00–16:00, free helpful English info sheet).

▲▲**Medieval Crime and Punishment Museum**—It's the best of its kind, full of fascinating old legal bits and *Kriminal* pieces, instruments of punishment and torture, even a special cage complete with a metal gag—for nags. Exhibits are well described in English (6 DM, 10 DM combo includes Imperial City Museum, daily 9:30–18:00, shorter hours in winter, fun cards and posters).

Museum of the Imperial City (Reichsstadt Museum)—This less sensational museum, housed in the former Dominican Convent, gives a more scholarly look at old Rothenburg. Highlights include *The Rothenburg Passion*, a 12-panel series of paintings from

1492 showing scenes leading up to Christ's crucifixion, an exhibit of Jewish culture through the ages in Rothenburg, and a 14th-century convent kitchen (5 DM, daily 9:30–17:30, Oct–March 13:00–16:00). The convent garden is a peaceful place to work on your tan.

▲**Toy Museum**—Two floors of historic *Kinder* cuteness is a hit with many (6 DM, 12 DM per family, daily 9:30–18:00, just off Market Square, downhill from the fountain, Hofbronneng 13).

▲▲**Herrngasse and the Castle Garden**—Any town's *Herrngasse*, where the richest patricians and merchants (the *Herren*) lived, is your chance to see its finest old mansions. Wander from Market Square down Herrngasse (past Rothenburg's old official measurement rods on the city hall wall) and drop into the lavish front rooms of a ritzy hotel or two. Pop into the Franciscan Church (free, Mon–Sat 10:00–12:00, 14:00–16:00, Sun 14:00–16:00, built in 1285—the oldest in town, with a Riemenschneider altar piece), continue on down past the old-fashioned puppet theater, through the old gate (notice the tiny after-curfew door in the big door and the frightening mask mouth from which hot Nutella was poured onto attackers), through the garden and to the end of what used to be the castle (great picnic spots and Tauber Riviera views at sunset). This is the popular kissing spot for romantic Rothenburg teenagers.

▲**Walk in the Countryside**—Just below the *Burggarten* (castle garden) in the Tauber Valley is the cute, skinny, 600-year-old castle/summer home of Mayor Toppler (2 DM, Fri–Sun 13:00–16:00, closed Mon–Thu, 1.5 kilometers from town center). On the top floor, notice the photo of bombed-out Rothenburg in 1945. Then walk on past the covered bridge and huge trout to the peaceful village of Detwang. Detwang (from 968, the second-oldest village in Franconia) is actually older than Rothenburg and also has a Riemenschneider altar piece in its church. For a scenic return, loop back to Rothenburg through the valley along the river, past a café with outdoor tables, great desserts, and a town view to match.

Swimming—Rothenburg has a fine modern recreation center with an indoor/outdoor pool and sauna. It's just a few minutes' walk down the Dinkelsbühl Road (Fri–Wed 9:00–20:00, Thu 10:00–20:00, tel. 09861/4565).

Sightseeing Lowlights—St. Wolfgang's Church is a fortified Gothic church built into the medieval wall at Klingentor. Its dungeonlike passages and shepherd's dance exhibit are pretty lame (2 DM, daily 10:00–13:00, 14:00–17:00, closed Nov–March). The cute-looking Bäuerliches Museum (farming museum) next door is even worse. The Rothenburger Handwerkerhaus (tradesman's house, 700 years old) shows the typical living situation of a Rothenburger in the town's heyday (3 DM, daily 10:00–18:00, closed in winter, Alter Stadtgraben 26, near the Markus Tower).

Sights—Near Rothenburg

Franconian Bike Ride—For a fun, breezy look at the countryside around Rothenburg, rent a bike from Rad & Tat (25 DM/day, Mon–Fri 9:00–18:00, Sat 9:00–14:00, closed Sun, Bensenstrasse 17, outside of town behind the "neck," near corner of Bensenstrasse and Erlbacherstrasse, no deposit except passport number, tel. 09861/87984). Return the bike the next morning before 10:00. For a pleasant half-day pedal, bike south down to Detwang via Topplerschlosschen. Go north along the level bike path to Tauberscheckenbach, then huff and puff uphill about 20 minutes to Adelshofen and south back to Rothenburg.

Franconian Open-Air Museum—A 20-minute drive from Rothenburg in the undiscovered "Rothenburgy" town of Bad Windsheim is a small, open-air folk museum that, compared with others in Europe, isn't much. But it's trying very hard and gives you the best look around at traditional rural Franconia (6 DM, Tue–Sun 9:00–18:00, closed Mon and Nov–Feb, tel. 09841/66800).

Shopping

Be careful...Rothenburg is one of Germany's best shopping towns. Do it here and be done with it. Lovely prints, carvings, wineglasses, Christmas-tree ornaments, and beer steins are popular. Warning: Shipping is so expensive that it's probably not worth it for purchases under $200.

The Käthe Wohlfahrt Christmas trinkets phenomenon is spreading across the half-timbered reaches of Europe. In Rothenburg tourists flock to two **Käthe Wohlfahrt Christmas Villages** (on either side of Herrngasse, just off Market Square). This Christmas wonderland is filled with enough twinkling lights to require a special electric hookup, instant Christmas mood music (best appreciated on a hot day in July), and American and Japanese tourists hungrily filling little woven shopping baskets with 10- to 15-DM goodies to hang on their trees. (OK, I admit it, my Christmas tree sports a few KW ornaments.) Note: Prices have hefty tour-guide kickbacks built into them. The Käthe Wohlfahrt discount store sells damaged and discontinued items. It's unnamed at Kirchgasse 5 across from the entrance of St. Jakob's Church (Mon–Fri 9:00–18:00, less on weekends, closed Jan–Feb, tel. 09861/4090).

The **Friese shop** offers a charming contrast (just off Market Square, west of TI, on corner across from public WC). Cuckoo with friendliness, it gives shoppers with this book tremendous service: a 10 percent discount, 16 percent tax deducted if you have it mailed, and a free map. Anneliese, who runs the place with her sons, Frankie and Berni, charges only her cost for shipping, changes money at the best rates in town with no extra charge, and lets tired travelers leave their bags in her back room for free.

For fewer crowds and better service, visit after 14:00. Her pricing is good, but to comparison shop, go here last.

The Ernst Geissendörfer **print shop** sells fine prints, etchings, and paintings. If you show this book they'll offer 10 percent off marked prices for all purchases in cash (or credit-card purchases of at least 100 DM) and a free shot of German brandy whether you buy anything or not (enter through bear shop in gray building on corner where Market Square hits Schmiedgasse; go to first floor).

For characteristic wineglasses and onkology gear, drop by the **Weinladen am Plonlein** (Plonlein 27).

Shoppers who mail their goodies home can get handy boxes at the **post office** two blocks east of Market Square (Mon–Fri 9:00–12:30, 14:00–17:00, Milchmarkt 5) or the post office at the shopping center across from the train station (similar weekday hours and Sat 9:00–13:00).

Those who prefer to eat their souvenirs shop the *Bäckereien* (bakeries). Their succulent pastries, pies, and cakes are pleasantly distracting. Skip the bad-tasting Rothenburger *Schneebälle*.

Sleeping in Rothenburg
(2 DM = about $1, country code: 49, area code: 09861, zip code: 91541)

Sleep Code: **S** = Single, **D** = Double/Twin, **T** = Triple, **Q** = Quad, **b** = bathroom, **t** = toilet only, **s** = shower only, **CC** = Credit Card (Visa, MasterCard, Amex), **SE** = Speaks English, **NSE** = No English. Unless otherwise indicated, room prices include breakfast.

Rothenburg is crowded with visitors. But when the sun sets, most retreat to the predictable plumbing of their big-city high-rise hotels. Except for the rare Saturday night and festivals (see "Orientation," above), room finding is easy throughout the year. Unless otherwise noted, enough English is spoken.

Many hotels and guest houses will pick up desperate heavy packers at the station. You may be greeted at the station by *Zimmer* skimmers who have rooms to rent. If you have reservations, resist and honor your reservation. But if you haven't booked ahead, try talking yourself into one of these more desperate bed-and-breakfast rooms for a youth-hostel price. Be warned: These people are notorious for taking you to distant hotels and then charging you for the ride back if you decline a room.

A handy **Laundromat** is near the station (Johannitergasse 8, tel. 09861/2775).

Hotels
I like **Hotel Goldene Rose**, where scurrying Karin serves breakfast and stately Henni keeps everything in good order. Besides its annex and apartment, the hotel has one shower on each floor of rooms, but the rooms are clean, and you're surrounded by cobbles,

flowers, and red-tiled roofs (S-40 DM, D-68 DM, Ds-85 DM, Db-90 DM; some triples, spacious family apartment: for four-200 DM, for five-240 DM; CC:VMA; streetside rooms can be noisy, closed Jan–Feb, kid friendly, ground-floor rooms in annex, Spital-gasse 28, tel. 09861/4638, fax 09861/86417, Henni SE). The Fav-etta family also serves good, reasonably priced meals. Remember to keep your key to get in after they close (at the side gate in the alley). The hotel is a 15-minute walk from the station or a seven-minute walk downhill from Market Square.

Gasthof Greifen, once the home of Mayor Toppler, is a big, traditional, 600-year-old place with large rooms and all the comforts. It's run by a fine family staff and creaks just the way you want it to (small Sb-64 DM, Sb-80 DM, one big D-74 DM with no shower available, Db-115–135 DM, Tb-180 DM, fourth person-30 DM, 10 percent off for three-night stay, CC:VMA, laundry self- or full-service, free and easy parking, half a block downhill from Market Square at Obere Schmiedgasse 5, tel. 09861/2281, fax 09861/86374, Brigitte and Klingler family).

Gasthof Marktplatz, right on Market Square, has nine tidy rooms and a cozy atmosphere (S-40 DM, D-72 DM, Ds-82 DM, Db-90 DM, T-95 DM, Ts-108 DM, Tb-118 DM, Grüner Markt 10, tel. & fax 09861/6722, www.gasthof-marktplatz.de, Herr Rosner SE).

Gästehaus Raidel, a creaky 500-year-old house packed with antiques, offers 14 large rooms with cramped facilities down the hall. Run by grim people who make me want to sing the *Addams Family* theme song, it works in a pinch (S-35 DM, Sb-69 DM, D-69 DM, Db-89 DM, Wenggasse 3, tel. 09861/3115, fax 09861/935-255, www.romanticroad.com/raidel, e-mail: Gaestehaus -Raidel@t-online.de, Herr Raidel speaks a little English).

Hotel Gerberhaus, a classy new hotel in a 500-year-old build-ing, is warmly run by Inge and Kurt, who mix modern comforts into bright and airy rooms while maintaining a sense of half-timbered elegance. Enjoy the great buffet breakfasts and pleasant garden in back (Sb-80 DM, Db-100–140 DM depending on size, Tb-165 DM, Qb-185 DM, all with TV and telephones, CC:VM or pay cash for 5 percent off and a free *Schneebälle*, Spitalgasse 25, tel. 09861/94900, fax 09861/86555, www.gerberhaus.rothenburg .de). The downstairs café serves good salads and sandwiches.

Hotel Klosterstueble, deep in the old town near the castle garden, is even classier. Jutta greets her guests while husband Rudolf does the cooking (Sb-100 DM, Db-130–170 DM, Tb-210 DM, some luxurious family rooms, 10 DM extra on weekends, discounts for families, CC:VM, Heringsbronnengasse 5, tel. 09861/6774, fax 09861/6474, www.klosterstueble.de).

Bohemians enjoy the **Hotel Altfränkische Weinstube am Klosterhof**. Mario and lovely Hanne run this dark and smoky pub in a 600-year-old building. Upstairs they rent six cozy rooms with upscale Monty Python atmosphere, TVs, modern showers, open-beam ceilings, and *"Himmel"* beds—canopied four-poster "heaven" beds (Sb-79 DM, Db-89 DM, Tb-109–119 DM, CC:VM, most rooms have tubs with hand-held showers, kid friendly, walk under St. Jakob's Church, take second left off Klingengasse at Klosterhof 7, tel. 09861/6404, fax 09861/6410). Their pub is a candlelit classic, serving hot food until 22:30 and closing at 01:00. Drop by on Wednesday evening (19:30–24:00) for the English Conversation Club.

Gasthof Rödertor offers 15 decent rooms in a quiet setting one block from the Rodertor tower (Sb-75–90 DM, Db-120–150 DM, third person-30 DM, most rooms with TV and phone, Ansbacher Strasse 7, tel. 09861/2022, fax 09861/86324, e-mail: hotel@roedertor.com).

Top Private Rooms

For the best real, with-a-local-family, comfortable, and homey experience, stay with **Herr und Frau Moser** (D-70 DM, T-100 DM, no single rooms, Spitalgasse 12, tel. 09861/5971). This charming retired couple speak little English but try very hard. Speak slowly, in clear, simple English. Reserve by phone and please reconfirm by phone one day ahead of arrival.

Pension Pöschel is friendly with seven cozy rooms on the second floor of a concrete but pleasant building (S-35 DM, D-60 DM, T-90 DM, small kids free, Wenggasse 22, tel. 09861/3430, e-mail: pension.poeschel@t-online.de).

Frau Guldemeister, who rents two simple ground-floor rooms, takes reservations by phone only, no more than a day or two in advance (Ss-40 DM, Ds with twin beds-60 DM, bigger Db-70 DM, breakfast in room, minimum two-night stay, off Market Square behind the Christmas shop, Pfaffleinsgasschen 10, tel. 09861/8988, some English).

Last-Resort Accommodations

These are all decent places, just lesser values compared to the places mentioned above. **Pension Kreuzerhof** has seven big, modern, ground-floor, motel-style rooms with views of parked cars on a quiet street (Sb-48–55 DM, Db-78–88 DM, Millergasse 6, tel. 09861/3424, fax 09861/936-730, http://home.debitel.net/user/maltz/Kreuzerhof). **Erich Endress** offers five airy, comfy rooms above his grocery store (S-45 DM, D-80 DM, Db-110 DM, nonsmoking, Rodergasse 6, tel. 09861/2331, fax 09861/935-355). The **Zum Schmolzer** restaurant at Rosengasse 21 rents 14 nice but drab-colored rooms (Sb-55 DM, Db-90 DM, Stollengasse 29, tel. 09861/3371, fax 09861/7204, e-mail: pension-hofmann-oe@t-online.de, SE). **Cafe Uhl** offers 10 fine, slightly frayed rooms over a bakery (Sb-58–75 DM, Db-98–120 DM, third person-35 DM, fourth person-25 DM, CC:VMA, Plonlein 8, tel. 09861/4895,

fax 09861/92820, e-mail: hotel@uhl.de). **Gästehaus Flemming** has
seven plain yet comfortable rooms behind St. Jakob's Church (Db-
93 DM, Klingengasse 21, tel. & fax 09861/92380). **Gästehaus
Viktoria** is a peaceful and cheery little place with a tiny garden and
two rooms (Ds-75 DM, Klingenschütt 4, tel. 09861/87682, Hanne).

In the modern world, a block from the train station, **Pension
Then** has six decent rooms and is worth a look (D-100 DM,
Db-120 DM, Yohaneiter 8A, tel. 09861/5177, fax 09861/86014).

Hostel

Here in Bavaria, hosteling is limited to those under 27, except for
families traveling with children under 18. The fine **Rossmühle
Youth Hostel** has 184 beds in two buildings. The droopy-eyed
building (the old town horse mill, used when the town was under
siege and the river-powered mill was inaccessible) houses groups
and the office. The adjacent hostel is mostly for families and individuals (dorm beds-28 DM, Db-66 DM, includes breakfast, dinner-10
DM, self-serve laundry, Muhlacker 1, tel. 09861/94160, fax 09861/
941-620, www.djh.de, e-mail: jhrothenburg@djh-bayern.de, SE).
This popular place takes reservations (even more than a year
in advance) and will hold rooms until 18:00.

Sleeping in Nearby Detwang and Bettwar

The town of Detwang, a 15-minute walk below Rothenburg, is
loaded with quiet *Zimmer*. The clean, quiet, and comfortable old
Gasthof zum Schwarzes Lamm in Detwang (D-85 DM, Db-110–
130 DM, CC:VM, tel. 09861/6727, fax 09861/86899, e-mail:
hotelschwarzeslamm@t-online.de) has 30 rooms and serves good
food, as does the popular and very local-style **Eulenstube** next
door. **Gästehaus Alte Schreinerei** offers good food and 18 quiet,
comfy, reasonable rooms a little farther down the road in Bettwar
(Db-76 DM, 9168 Bettwar, tel. 09861/1541, fax 09861/86710,
e-mail: alte.schreinerei@t-online.de).

Eating in Rothenburg

Most places serve meals only from 11:30 to 13:30 and 18:00 to
20:00. At **Goldene Rose** (see "Sleeping," above), Reno cooks up
traditional German fare at good prices (Tue 11:30–14:00, Wed–
Mon 11:30–14:00, 17:30–21:00, in sunny weather the leafy garden
terrace is open in the back, Spitalgasse 28).

Galgengasse (Gallows Lane) has two cheap and popular standbys: **Pizzeria Roma** (11:30–24:00, 12-DM pizzas and normal schnitzel fare, Galgengasse 19) and **Gasthof zum Ochsen** (Fri–Wed
11:30–13:30, 18:00–20:00, closed Thu, uneven service but decent
15-DM meals, Galgengasse 26). **Landsknechtstuben**, at Galgengasse 21, is pricey but friendly, with some cheaper schnitzel choices.

Gasthaus Siebersturm serves up tasty, reasonable meals in a bright, airy dining room (Spitalgasse, tel. 09861/3355). For a break from schnitzel, **Lotus China** serves good Chinese food daily (2 blocks behind TI near the church, Eckele 2, tel. 09861/86886). **Gasthaus Greifen** serves typical Rothenburg cuisine at moderate prices (just below Market Square, tel. 09861/2281).

Two **supermarkets** are near the wall at Rödertor (the one outside the wall to the left is cheaper; the one inside is nicer).

Evening Fun and Beer Drinking

For beer-garden fun on a summer evening, you have three fine choices: **Gasthof Rödertor** is just outside the wall at the Rödertor (red gate, near discos, see below). In the valley along the river, a worthy 20-minute hike is **Unter den Linden** beer garden. A more central and touristy beer garden is behind Hotel Eisenhut (nightly until 22:00, access from Burggasse or via the hotel off Herrngasse).

Trinkstube zur Hölle (Hell) is dark and foreboding. But they serve good ribs from 18:00 and offer thick wine-drinking atmosphere until late (a block past Criminal Museum on Burggasse, with devil hanging out front, tel. 09861/4229). For mellow ambience, try the beautifully restored **Alte Keller's Weinstube** under walls festooned with old pots and jugs (closed Tue, Alter Keller 8). Wine lovers enjoy the **Glocke Hotel's Stube** (Plonlein 1). And perhaps the most elegant place in town is the courtyard of **Baumeister Haus** (behind statue-festooned facade a few doors below Market Square).

Two popular **discos** are near the Gasthof Rödertor's beer garden, a few doors farther out near the Sparkasse bank (G-Spot at Ansbacher 15, in alley next to bank, open Wed, Fri–Sat; the other is Club 23, around the corner from the bank, open Wed, Fri–Sun).

For a rare chance to mix it up with locals who aren't selling anything, bring your favorite slang and tongue twisters to the **English Conversation Club** at Mario's Altfränkische Weinstube (Wed 19:30–24:00, Anneliese from the Friese shop is a regular). This dark and smoky pub is an atmospheric hangout any night but Tuesday, when it's closed (Klosterhof 7, off Klingengasse, behind St. Jakob's Church, tel. 09861/6404).

Transportation Connections—Rothenburg

The Romantic Road bus tour takes you in and out of Rothenburg each afternoon (April–Oct) heading to Munich, Frankfurt, or Füssen. See the Romantic Road bus schedule on page 251 (or check www.euraide.de/ricksteves).

A tiny train line runs between Rothenburg and Steinach (almost hrly, 15 min, last train at 21:00, train often leaves from the "B" section of track, away from the middle of the station).

Steinach by train to: Würzburg (hrly, 30 min), **Munich** (hrly, 3 hrs), **Frankfurt** (hrly, 3 hrs, change in Würzburg). Train connections in Steinach are usually within a few minutes.

Romantic Road

ROMANTIC ROAD

The Romantic Road (*Romantische Strasse*) winds you past the most beautiful towns and scenery of Germany's medieval heartland. Once Germany's medieval trade route, now it's the best way to connect the dots between Füssen, Munich, and Frankfurt.

Wander through quaint hills and rolling villages, and stop wherever the cows look friendly or a town fountain beckons. My favorite sections are from Füssen to Landsberg and Rothenburg to Weikersheim. (If you're driving with limited time, you can connect Rothenburg and Munich by autobahn, but don't miss these two best sections.) Caution: The similarly promoted "Castle Road," which runs between Rothenburg and Mannheim, sounds intriguing but is nowhere near as interesting.

Throughout Bavaria you'll see colorfully ornamented maypoles decorating town squares. Many are painted in Bavaria's

Romantic Road Bus Schedule (Daily, April–October)

These times are based on the 2000 schedule. Check www.euraide.de/ricksteves for updates.

Frankfurt	8:00	—
Würzburg	10:00	—
Arrive Rothenburg	12:45	—
Depart Rothenburg	14:30	—
Arrive Dinkelsbühl	15:25	—
Depart Dinkelsbühl	16:15	15:30
Munich	19:50	—
Füssen	—	20:05
Füssen	8:00	—
Arrive Wieskirche	8:35	—
Depart Wieskirche	8:55	—
Munich	—	9:00
Arrive Dinkelsbühl	12:45	12:45
Depart Dinkelsbühl	—	14:00
Arrive Rothenburg	—	14:50
Depart Rothenburg	—	16:15
Depart Würzburg	—	18:45
Frankfurt	—	20:30

colors, blue and white. The decorations that line each side of the pole symbolize the crafts or businesses of that community. Each May Day they are festively replaced. Traditionally, rival communities try to steal each other's maypole. Locals will guard their new pole night and day as May Day approaches. Stolen poles are ransomed only with lots of beer for the clever thieves.

Getting around the Romantic Road

By Bus: The Europa Bus Company runs buses daily between Frankfurt and Munich in each direction (April–Oct). A second route goes daily between Dinkelsbühl and Füssen. Buses leave from train stations in towns served by a train. The 134-DM, 11-hour ride is offered at a 60 percent discount (about 54 DM, plus 3 DM per bag) to travelers who have a German railpass, Eurailpass, Europass, or Eurail Selectpass—if Germany is one of the selected countries. Buses stop in Rothenburg (about 2 hrs) and Dinkelsbühl (only Munich-bound buses stop here, about 1 hr) and briefly at a few other attractions, and have a usually mediocre guide who hands out brochures and narrates the journey in English. There is no quicker or easier way to travel across Germany and get such a hearty dose of its countryside. Bus reservations are free, easy, and smart—without one you can lose your seat to someone who has one (especially on summer weekends; call Munich's EurAide office at 089/593-889 at least one day in advance to reserve). You can start, stop, and switch over where you like, but you'll be guaranteed a seat only if you reserve each segment.

By Car: Follow the brown *Romantische Strasse* signs.

Sights along the Romantic Road

These sights are listed from south to north.

Füssen—This town, the southern terminus of the Romantic Road, is two miles from the startlingly beautiful Neuschwanstein Castle, worthy of a stop on any sightseeing agenda. (See the Bavaria and Tirol chapter for description and accommodations.)

▲▲**Wieskirche**—This is Germany's most glorious Baroque-Rococo church. Heavenly! It's in a sweet meadow and is newly restored. Northbound Romantic Road buses stop here for 15 minutes. (See the Bavaria and Tirol chapter.)

Rottenbuch—This is a nondescript village with an impressive church in a lovely setting.

▲**Dinkelsbühl**—Rothenburg's little sister is cute enough to merit a short stop. A moat, towers, gates, and a beautifully preserved medieval wall surround this town and its interesting local museum. The Kinderzeche children's festival turns Dinkelsbühl wonderfully on end in mid-July (TI tel. 09851/90240). On Neustädtlein you'll find 80-DM doubles with baths and TV s at friendly Haus Küffner (tel. 09851/1247) and Zur Linde (tel. 09851/3465).

▲▲▲**Rothenburg**—See opening of this chapter for information on Germany's best medieval town.

▲**Herrgottskapelle**—This peaceful church, graced with Tilman Riemenschneider's greatest carved altar piece (daily 9:15–17:30), is one mile from Creglingen and across the street from the Fingerhut thimble museum (daily 9:00–18:00). The southbound Romantic Road bus stops here for 15 minutes, long enough to see one or the other.

Weikersheim—This untouristy town has a palace with fine Baroque gardens (luxurious picnic spot), a folk museum, and a picturesque town square.

▲▲**Würzburg**—This historic city, though freshly rebuilt since
World War II, is worth a stop for its impressive Prince Bishop's
Residenz, the bubbly Baroque chapel (Hofkirche) next door, and
the palace's sculpted gardens. The helpful TI is on the Marktplatz
(Mon–Sat 10:00–18:00, tel. 0931/372-355). The Residenz is a Fran-
conian Versailles, with grand rooms, 3-D art, and a tennis-court-
sized fresco by Tiepolo (5 DM, April–Oct Tue–Sun 9:00–18:00,
Nov–March 10:00–16:00, last entry 30 min before closing, tel. 0931/
355-170). English tours are offered on weekends at 11:00 and 15:00
(April–Oct, confirm at TI or call ahead). To get a tour on weekdays,
take the TI's walking tour at 11:00, which includes a tour of the
Residenz along with a walk through the "old" city (15 DM, daily
May–Oct, 2 hrs, all in English, includes admission to Residenz).
The elaborate Hofkirche chapel is next door (as you exit the palace,
go left) and the entrance to the picnic-worthy garden is just beyond.
Easy parking is available. Don't confuse the Residenz (a 15-min walk
from the train station) with the fortress on the hilltop.

FRANKFURT
Frankfurt, the northern terminus of the Romantic Road, is
actually pleasant for a big city and offers a good look at today's
no-nonsense urban Germany.

Orientation (area code: 069)
Tourist Information: For a quick look at the city, pick up a
1-DM map at the TI in the train station (Mon–Fri 8:00–21:00,
Sat–Sun 9:00–18:00, tel. 069/2123-8849).

It's a 20-minute walk from the station down Kaiserstrasse
past Goethe's house (great man, mediocre sight, Grosser Hirsch-
graben 23) to the lively **market square**, Römerberg (or you can
take subway U-4 or U-5 from the station to Römerberg). Just
across the river along Schaumainkai is a string of **museums**
(Tue–Sun 10:00–17:00, Wed until 20:00, closed Mon). The TI
also has info on **bus tours** of the city (44 DM, 10:00 and 14:00 in
summer, 14:00 only off-season, 2.5 hrs).

A browse through Frankfurt's **red-light district** offers a fascinating way to kill time between trains. Wander down Taunusstrasse two blocks in front of the station and you'll find 20 "eros
towers," each a five-story-tall brothel filled with prostitutes. Climbing through a few of these may be one of the more memorable
experiences of your European trip. It feels safe, the atmosphere
is friendly, and browsing is encouraged (40 DM, daily).

Romantic Road Bus: If you're taking the bus out of Frankfurt, you can buy your ticket either at the train station or the
Deutsches Touring office, which is part of the train station
complex but has an entrance outside (Mon–Fri 7:30–18:00, Sat
7:30–14:00, Sun 7:30–14:00, CC:VMA, enter at Mannheimer

Strasse 4, to your left as you face the station, tel. 069/230-735);
or pay cash when you board the bus.

Travelers with railpasses (German, Eurail, Europass, or
Eurail Selectpass), who get a 60 percent discount, pay about 54 DM
(plus 3 DM per bag). The bus waits at stall #9 (right of the train
station as you leave).

Sleeping in Frankfurt
**(2 DM = about $1, country code: 49, area code: 069,
zip code: 60329)**
Avoid driving or sleeping in Frankfurt, especially during the city's
numerous trade fairs (about 5 days a month), which send hotel
prices skyrocketing. Pleasant Rhine or Romantic Road towns are
just a quick train ride or drive away. But if you must spend the
night in Frankfurt, here are some places within a block of the train
station (and its handy train to the airport). This isn't the safest
neighborhood; be careful after dark. For a rough idea of directions
to hotels, stand with your back to the main entrance of the station:
Using a 12-hour clock, Hotel Manhattan is across the street at
10:00, Pension Schneider at 12:00, Hotel Europa and Wiesbaden
at 4:00, and Hotel Paris at 5:00. Breakfast is included in all listings
and English is spoken.

Hotel Manhattan, with sleek, arty rooms, is expensive—
best for a splurge on a first or last night in Europe (Sb-145 DM,
Db-175 DM, show this book to get a break during nonconvention
times, CC:VMA, elevator, riffraff in front of hotel, Düsseldorfer
Strasse 10, tel. 069/269-5970, fax 069/2695-97777, e-mail:
manhattan-hotel@t-online.de).

Pension Schneider is a strange little oasis of decency and
quiet three floors above the epicenter of Frankfurt's red-light
district, two blocks in front of the train station. The street is safe
in spite of the pimps and pushers. Its 10 rooms are big, bright,
and comfortable (S-70 DM, D-100 DM, Db-120 DM, Tb-150
DM, CC:VM, elevator, corner of Moselstrasse at Taunusstrasse
43, tel. 069/251-071, fax 069/259-228).

Hotel Europa, with 50 well-maintained rooms, is a fine value
(Sb-80 DM, Db-120 DM, Tb-150 DM, prices soft on weekends,
some nonsmoking rooms, garage, CC:VMA, Baseler Strasse 17,
tel. 069/236-013, fax 069/236-203).

Hotel Wiesbaden has worn rooms and a kind manager
(S-80 DM, Sb-115 DM, Db-140–165 DM depending on size,
Tb-180–200 DM, CC:VMA, a little smoky, elevator, Baseler
Strasse 52, tel. 069/232-347, fax 069/252-845).

Hotel Paris, with modern, Impressionist rooms, is the
most cushy of my listings (Sb-110 DM, Db-150 DM, CC:VMA,
Karlsruherstrasse 8, tel. 069/273-9963, fax 069/2739-9651).

Farther from the station is **Pension Backer** (S-50 DM,

D-60 DM, showers-3 DM, near botanical gardens, take S-Bahn 2 stops to Hauptwache, then transfer to U-6 or U-7 for 2 stops to Westend; Mendelssohnstrasse 92, tel. 069/747-992).

The **hostel** is open to members of any age (8-bed rooms, 35 DM per bed with sheets and breakfast, bus #46 from station to Frankenstein Place, Deutschherrnufer 12, tel. 069/610-0150, fax 069/610-01599, e-mail: jugendherberge_frankfurt@t-online.de).

Transportation Connections—Frankfurt

By train to: Rothenburg (hrly, 3 hrs, changes in Würzburg and Steinach; the tiny Steinach–Rothenburg train often leaves from the "B" section of track, away from the middle of the station, shortly after the Würzburg train arrives), **Würzburg** (hrly, 90 min), **Munich** (hrly, 3.5 hrs), **Baden-Baden** (2/hr, 90 min), **Freiburg** (hrly, 2 hrs, change in Mannheim), **Bonn** (hrly, 2 hrs), **Koblenz** (hrly, 90 min), **Köln** (hrly, 2 hrs), **Berlin** (hrly, 5 hrs), **Amsterdam** (8/day, 5 hrs), **Bern** (14/day, 4.5 hrs, changes in Mannheim and Basel), **Brussels** (6/day, 5 hrs), **Copenhagen** (3/day, 10 hrs), **London** (5/day, 9.5 hrs), **Milan** (6/day, 9 hrs), **Paris** (4/day, 6.5 hrs), **Vienna** (7/day, 7.5 hrs).

Frankfurt's Airport

The airport (*Flughafen*) is a 12-minute train ride from downtown (4/hrly, 6.10 DM, ride included in Frankfurt's 8.5-DM all-day city transit pass). The airport is user-friendly. It offers showers, a baggage check, fair banks with long hours, a grocery store, a train station, a lounge where you can sleep overnight, a business lounge (Europe City Club—30 DM for anyone with a plane ticket), easy rental-car pickup, plenty of parking, an information booth, and even McBeer. McWelcome to Germany. Airport English-speaking info: tel. 069/6901 (will transfer you to any of the airlines for booking or confirmation). Lufthansa—069/255-255, American Airlines—069/690-21781, Delta—069/690-28751, Northwest—0180-525-4650.

To Rothenburg: Train travelers can validate railpasses or buy tickets at the airport station and catch a train to Würzburg, connecting to Rothenburg via Steinach (hrly, 3 hrs). If driving to Rothenburg, follow autobahn signs to Würzburg.

Flying Home from Frankfurt: The airport has its own train station, and many of the trains from the Rhine stop there on their way into Frankfurt (e.g., hrly 90-min rides direct from Bonn; hrly 2-hr rides from Bacharach with a change in Mainz; earliest train from Bacharach to Frankfurt leaves just before 6:00). By car, head toward Frankfurt on the autobahn and follow the little airplane signs to the airport.

RHINE AND
MOSEL VALLEYS

These valleys are storybook Germany, a fairy-tale world of Rhine legends and robber-baron castles. Cruise the most castle-studded stretch of the romantic Rhine as you listen for the song of the treacherous Loreley. For hands-on castle thrills, climb through the Rhineland's greatest castle, Rheinfels, above the town of St. Goar. Then, for a sleepy and laid-back alternative, mosey through the neighboring Mosel Valley.

Spend your nights in a castle-crowned village. On the Rhine, I choose between St. Goar and Bacharach. On the Mosel, choose Zell.

Planning Your Time

The Rhineland does not take much time to see. The blitziest tour is an hour at the Köln cathedral (see below) and an hour looking at the castles from your train window. For a better look, however, cruise in, tour a castle or two, sleep in a genuine medieval town, and take the train out. If you have limited time, cruise less and be sure to get into a castle.

Ideally, spend two nights here, sleep in Bacharach, cruise the best hour of the river (from Bacharach to St. Goar), and tour the Rheinfels Castle. Those with more time can ride the riverside bike path. With two days and a car, visit the Rhine and the Mosel. With two days by train, see the Rhine. With three days, actually relax on the Rhine, and with four days include Trier and a sleepy night in the Mosel River Valley.

If your train travels take you through Köln, pop out to see Germany's greatest Gothic cathedral (located next to station and TI), then continue on your way (Köln has nearly hourly train connections to nearby Rhine villages).

Rhine and Mosel Valleys

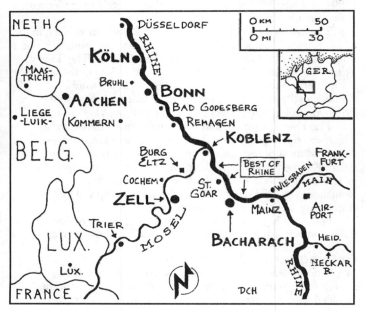

THE RHINE

Ever since Roman times, when this was the Empire's northern boundary, the Rhine has been one of the world's busiest shipping rivers. You'll see a steady flow of barges with 1,000- to 2,000-ton loads. Tourist-packed buses, hot train tracks, and highways line both banks.

Many of the castles were "robber-baron" castles, put there by petty rulers (there were 300 independent little countries in medieval Germany) to levy tolls on passing river traffic. A robber baron would put his castle on, or even in, the river. Then, often with the help of chains and a tower on the opposite bank, he'd stop each ship and get his toll. There were 10 customs stops between Mainz and Koblenz alone (no wonder merchants were early proponents of the creation of larger nation-states).

Some castles were built to control and protect settlements, and others were the residences of kings. As times changed, so did the lifestyles of the rich and feudal. Many castles were abandoned for more comfortable mansions in the towns.

Most Rhine castles date from the 11th, 12th, and 13th centuries. When the pope successfully asserted his power over the German emperor in 1076, local princes ran wild over the rule of their emperor. The castles saw military action in the 1300s and 1400s, as emperors began reasserting their control over Germany's many silly kingdoms.

The castles were also involved in the Reformation wars, in which Europe's Catholic and "protesting" dynasties fought it out using a fragmented Germany as their battleground. The Thirty Years' War (1618–1648) devastated Germany. The outcome: Each ruler got the freedom to decide if his people would be Catholic or Protestant, and one-third of Germany was dead. Production of Gummi Bears ceased entirely.

The French—who feared a strong Germany and felt the Rhine was the logical border between them and Germany— destroyed most of the castles prophylactically (Louis XIV in the 1680s, the revolutionary army in the 1790s, and Napoleon in 1806). They were often rebuilt in neo-Gothic style in the Romantic Age—the late 1800s—and today are enjoyed as restaurants, hotels, hostels, and museums.

For more information on the Rhine, visit www.loreleytal.com (heavy on hotels but has maps, photos, and a little history).

Getting around the Rhine

While the Rhine flows north from Switzerland to Holland, the stretch from Mainz to Koblenz hoards all the touristic charm. Studded with the crenelated cream of Germany's castles, it bustles with boats, trains, and highway traffic. Have fun exploring with a mix of big steamers, tiny ferries, bikes, and trains.

By Boat: While many travelers do the whole trip by boat, the most scenic hour is from St. Goar to Bacharach. Sit on the top deck with your handy Rhine map-guide (or the kilometer-keyed tour in this chapter) and enjoy the parade of castles, towns, boats, and vineyards.

There are several boat companies, but most travelers sail on the bigger, more expensive and romantic Köln-Düsseldorf (K-D) line (free with a consecutive-day Eurailpass or a dated Eurail flexi-pass, Europass, Eurail Selectpass, or German railpass, otherwise about 15.40 DM for the first hr, then progressively cheaper per hr; the recommended Bacharach–St. Goar trip costs 15.40 DM one-way, 18.80 DM round-trip; tel. 06741/1634 in St. Goar, www .k-d.com, schedule at www.euraide.de/ricksteves). Boats run daily in both directions from April through October, with fewer boats off-season. Complete, up-to-date schedules are posted in any station, Rhineland hotel, TI, or current Thomas Cook Timetable. Purchase tickets at the dock up to five minutes before departure. The boat is rarely full. (Confirm times at your hotel the night before.)

The smaller Bingen-Rüdesheimer line is 25 percent cheaper than K-D (railpasses not valid, buy tickets on boat,

tel. 06721/14140), with three two-hour round-trip St. Goar–
Bacharach trips daily in summer (about 12 DM one-way, 17 DM
round-trip; departing St. Goar at 11:00, 13:10, and 16:10, departing Bacharach at 10:10, 12:30, and 15:00).

Drivers have these options: (1) skip the boat; (2) take a round-
trip cruise from St. Goar or Bacharach; (3) draw pretzels and let
the loser drive, prepare the picnic, and meet the boat; (4) rent a
bike, bring it on the boat for free, and bike back; or (5) take the
boat one-way and return by train.

By Train: Hourly milk-run trains down the Rhine hit every
town: St. Goar–Bacharach, 12 min; Bacharach–Mainz, 60 min;
Mainz–Frankfurt, 45 min. Some train schedules list St. Goar but
not Bacharach as a stop, but any schedule listing St. Goar also
stops at Bacharach. Tiny stations are unmanned—buy tickets at
the platform machines or on the train.

By Bike: In Bacharach try Hotel Hillen (10 DM/half day,
15 DM/day, cheaper for guests, 20 bikes) or Hotel Gelberhof
(25 DM/day for 10-speeds, 25 DM for trekking bikes, 5 DM
for child's seat, tel. 06743/910-100, ring bell when closed). In
St. Goar, it's Hermy's Garden (18 DM/day, Reine Strasse, tel.
06741/1360). The best riverside bike path is from Bacharach to
Bingen (leaving Bacharach, after you pass campground, head down
to path bordering river). The path is also good from St. Goar to
Bacharach, but it's closer to the highway. Consider renting a bike
in Bacharach and taking it on the boat to Bingen and biking back,
visiting Rheinstein Castle (you're on your own to wander the
well-furnished castle) and Reichenstein Castle (admittance with
groups), and maybe even taking a ferry across the river to Kaub
(where a tiny boat shuttles sightseers to the better-from-a-distance
castle on the island). While there are no bridges between Koblenz
and Mainz, several small ferries do their job constantly and cheaply.

Sights—The Romantic Rhine

These sights are listed from north to south, Koblenz to Bingen.
▲▲▲**Der Romantische Rhein Blitz Zug Fahrt**—One of
Europe's great train thrills is zipping along the Rhine in this fast
train tour. Here's a quick and easy, from-the-train-window tour
(also works for car, bike, or best by boat, you can cut in anywhere)
that skips the syrupy myths that fill normal Rhine guides. For
more information than necessary, buy the handy *Rhine Guide from
Mainz to Cologne* (7-DM book with foldout map, at most shops).

Sit on the left (river) side of the train or boat going south
from Koblenz. While nearly all the castles listed are viewed from
this side, clear a path to the right window for the times I yell,
"Crossover!"

You'll notice large black-and-white kilometer markers along
the riverbank. I erected these years ago to make this tour easier

Best of the Rhine

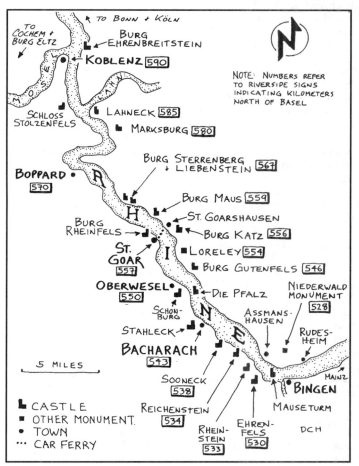

NOTE: Numbers refer to riverside signs indicating kilometers north of Basel

Legend:
🅛 CASTLE
■ OTHER MONUMENT.
• TOWN
⋯ CAR FERRY

5 MILES

TO BONN + KÖLN
TO COCHEM + BURG ELTZ
BURG EHRENBREITSTEIN
KOBLENZ 590
MOSEL
LAHN
SCHLOSS STOLZENFELS
LAHNECK 585
MARKSBURG 580
BURG STERRENBERG + LIEBENSTEIN 567
BOPPARD 570
RHEIN
BURG MAUS 559
ST. GOARSHAUSEN
BURG RHEINFELS
BURG KATZ 556
ST. GOAR 557
LORELEY 554
BURG GUTENFELS 546
OBERWESEL 550
DIE PFALZ
NIEDERWALD MONUMENT 528
SCHON-BURG
ASSMANS-HAUSEN
STAHLECK
RUDES-HEIM
BACHARACH 543
SOONECK 538
REICHENSTEIN 534
MAUSETURM
RHEIN-STEIN 533
EHREN-FELS 530
BINGEN
MAINZ
DCH

to follow. They tell the distance from the Rhinefalls where the Rhine leaves Switzerland and becomes navigable. Now the river-barge pilots have accepted these as navigational aids as well. We're tackling just 36 miles of the 820-mile-long Rhine. Your Blitz Rhine Tour starts at Koblenz and heads upstream to Bingen. If you're going the other direction, it still works. Just hold the book upside down.

Km 590: Koblenz—This Rhine blitz starts with Romantic Rhine thrills—at Koblenz. Koblenz is not a nice city (it was really hit hard in World War II), but its place as the historic

Rhine Cruise Schedule

Koblenz	Boppard	St. Goar	Bacharach
—	9:00	10:15	11:35
9:00	10:50	12:05	13:15
11:00	12:50	14:05	15:15
14:00	15:50	17:05	18:15
11:05*	11:30*	11:50*	12:10*
13:00	11:40	10:45	10:00
14:20	13:10	12:15	11:30
—	14:00	13:15	12:30
18:00	16:40	15:45	15:00
20:00	18:50	18:00	17:20

* *Hydrofoil, Koblenz–Bacharach, 25 DM one-way and 45 DM round-trip with Eurail, 90 DM without.*
Note: Schedule applies May through September and mostly April and October; no boats run November through March.

Deutsche-Ecke (German corner)—the tip of land where the Mosel joins the Rhine—gives it a certain historic charm. Koblenz, Latin for "confluence," has Roman origins. Walk through the park, noticing the reconstructed memorial to the Kaiser. Across the river, the yellow Ehrenbreitstein Castle now houses a hostel. It's a 30-minute hike from the station to the Koblenz boat dock.

Km 585: Burg Lahneck—Above the modern autobahn bridge over the Lahn River, this castle (*Burg*) was built in 1240 to defend local silver mines, ruined by the French in 1688 and rebuilt in the 1850s in neo-Gothic style. Burg Lahneck faces the yellow Schloss Stolzenfels (out of view above the train, a 10-minute climb from tiny car park, open for touring, closed Mon).

Km 580: Marksburg—This castle (black and white with the three modern chimneys behind it, just after town of Spay) is the best looking of all the Rhine castles and the only surviving medieval castle on the Rhine. Because of its commanding position, it was never attacked. It's now open as a museum with a medieval interior second only to the Mosel's Burg Eltz (9 DM, daily 10:00–17:00, call ahead to see if a rare English tour is scheduled, tel. 02627/206).

Km 570: Boppard—Once a Roman town, Boppard has

some impressive remains of fourth-century walls. Notice the Roman towers and the substantial chunk of Roman wall near the Boppard's train station. Boppard is worth a stop. Just above the main square are the remains of the Roman wall. Below the square is a fascinating church. Notice the carved Romanesque crazies at the doorway. Inside, to the right of the entrance, you'll see Christian symbols from Roman times. Also notice the painted arches and vaults. Originally most Romanesque churches were painted this way. Down by the river, look for the high water (*Hochwasser*) marks on the arches from various flood years. (You'll find these flood marks throughout the Rhine and Mosel Valleys.)

Km 567: Burg Sterrenberg and Burg Liebenstein— These are the "Hostile Brothers" castles, across from Bad Salzig. Take the wall between the castles (actually designed to improve the defenses of both castles), add two greedy and jealous brothers and a fair maiden, and create your own legend. The castles are restaurants today.

Km 559: Burg Maus—The Maus ("Mouse") got its name because the next castle was owned by the Katzenelnbogen family. ("Katz" means "cat.") In the 1300s it was considered a state-of-the-art fortification . . . until Napoleon had it blown up in 1806 with state-of-the-art explosives. It was rebuilt true to its original plans around 1900.

Km 557: St. Goar and Rheinfels Castle—Cross to the other side of the train. The pleasant town of St. Goar was named for a sixth-century hometown monk. It originated in Celtic times (really old) as a place where sailors would stop, catch their breath, send home a postcard, and give thanks after surviving the seductive and treacherous Loreley crossing. St. Goar is worth a stop to explore its mighty Rheinfels Castle. (For information on a guided castle tour and accommodations, see below.)

Km 556: Burg Katz—From the town of St. Goar, you'll see Burg Katz (Katzenelnbogen) across the river. Together, Burg Katz (built in 1371) and Rheinfels Castle had a clear view up and down the river and effectively controlled traffic. There was absolutely no duty-free shopping on the medieval Rhine. Katz got Napoleoned in 1806 and rebuilt around 1900. Today it's a convalescent home.

About Km 555: You'll see the statue of the Loreley, the beautiful but deadly nymph (see next listing for legend), at the end of a long spit—built to give barges protection from vicious icebergs that occasionally rage down the river in the winter. The actual Loreley, a cliff, is just ahead.

Km 554: The Loreley—Steep a big slate rock in centuries of legend and it becomes a tourist attraction, the ultimate Rhinestone. The Loreley (two flags on top, name painted near shoreline), rising 450 feet over the narrowest and deepest point of the Rhine, has long been important. It was a holy site in pre-Roman

River Trade and Barge Watching

The river is great for barge watching. Since ancient times this has been a highway for trade. Today the world's biggest port (Rotterdam) waits at the mouth of the river. Barge workers are almost a subculture. Many own their own ships. The captain (and family) live in the stern. Workers live in the bow. The family car often decorates the bow like a shiny hood ornament. In the Rhine town of Kaub there's even a boarding school for the children of the Rhine merchant marine. The flag of the boat's home country flies in the stern (German, Swiss, Dutch—horizontal red, white, and blue; or French—vertical red, white, and blue). Logically, imports go upstream (Japanese cars, coal, and oil) and exports go downstream (German cars, chemicals, and pharmaceuticals). A clever captain manages to ship goods in each direction.

At this point tugs can push a floating train of up to five barges at once. Upstream it gets steeper and they can push only one at a time. Before modern shipping, horses dragged boats upstream (the faint remains of the towpaths survive at points along the river). From 1873 to 1900 they actually laid a chain from Bonn to Bingen, and boats with cogwheels and steam engines hoisted themselves slowly upstream. Today 265 million tons are shipped each year along the 528 navigable miles from Basel on the Swiss border to Rotterdam on the Atlantic.

While riverside navigational aids are ignored by camera-toting tourists, they are of vital interest to captains who don't wish to meet the Loreley. Boats pass on the right unless they clearly signal otherwise with a large blue sign. Since downstream ships can't stop or maneuver as freely, upstream boats are expected to do the tricky do-si-do work. Cameras monitor traffic all along and relay warnings of oncoming ships via large triangular signals posted before narrow and troublesome bends in the river. There may be two or three triangles per signpost, depending upon how many "sectors," or segments, of the river are covered. The lowest triangle indicates the nearest stretch of river. Each triangle tells if there's a ship in that sector. When the bottom side of a triangle is lit, that sector is empty. When the left side is lit, an oncoming ship is in that sector.

days. The fine echoes here—thought to be ghostly voices—
fertilized the legendary soil.

Because of the reefs just upstream (at kilometer 552), many
ships never made it to St. Goar. Sailors (after days on the river)
blamed their misfortune on a *wunderbares Fräulein* whose long
blonde hair almost covered her body. Heinrich Heine's *Song of
Loreley* (the Cliffs Notes version is on local postcards) tells the
story of a count who sent his men to kill or capture this siren
after she distracted his horny son, causing him to drown. When
the soldiers cornered the nymph in her cave, she called her father
(Father Rhine) for help. Huge waves, the likes of which you'll
never see today, rose from the river and carried Loreley to safety.
And she has never been seen since.

But alas, when the moon shines brightly and the tour buses
are parked, a soft, playful Rhine whine can still be heard from the
Loreley. As you pass, listen carefully ("Sailors . . . sailors . . . over
my bounding mane").

Km 552: Killer reefs, marked by red-and-green buoys, are
called the "Seven Maidens."

Km 550: Oberwesel—Cross to the other side of the train.
Oberwesel was a Celtic town in 400 B.C., then a Roman military
station. It now boasts some of the best Roman wall and tower
remains on the Rhine and the commanding Schönburg Castle.
Notice how many of the train tunnels have entrances designed
like medieval turrets—they were actually built in the Romantic
19th century. OK, back to the riverside.

**Km 546: Burg Gutenfels and Pfalz Castle: The Classic
Rhine View**—Burg Gutenfels (see the white painted "Hotel" sign)
and the shipshape Pfalz Castle (built in the river in the 1300s)
worked very effectively to tax medieval river traffic. The town of
Kaub grew rich as Pfalz raised its chains when boats came and
lowered them only when the merchants had paid their duty. Those
who didn't pay spent time touring its prison, on a raft at the bottom
of its well. In 1504 a pope called for the destruction of Pfalz, but a
six-week siege failed. Notice the overhanging "outhouse" (tiny white
room with the faded medieval stains between the two wooden ones).
Pfalz is tourable but bare and dull (3-DM ferry from Kaub, 4 DM,
Tue–Sun 9:00–13:00, 14:00–18:00, closed Mon, tel. 06774/570).

In Kaub a green statue honors the German General Blücher.
He was Napoleon's nemesis. In 1813, as Napoleon fought his way
back to Paris after his disastrous Russian campaign, he stopped at
Mainz—hoping to fend off the Germans and Russians pursuing
him—by controlling that strategic bridge. Blücher tricked Napoleon. By building the first major pontoon bridge of its kind,
here at the Pfalz Castle, he crossed the Rhine and outflanked the
French. Two years later Blücher and Wellington teamed up to
defeat Napoleon once and for all at Waterloo.

Km 544: The "Raft Busters"—Immediately before Bacharach, at the top of the island, buoys mark a gang of rocks notorious for busting up rafts. The Black Forest is upstream. It was poor, and wood was its best export. Black Foresters would ride log booms down the Rhine to the Ruhr (where their timber fortified coal-mine shafts) or to Holland (where logs were sold to shipbuilders). If they could navigate the sweeping bend just before Bacharach and then survive these "raft busters," they'd come home reckless and romantic, the German folkloric equivalent of American cowboys after payday.

Km 543: Bacharach and Burg Stahleck—Cross to the other side of the train. Bacharach is a great stop (see details and accommodations below). Some of the Rhine's best wine is from this town, whose name means "altar to Bacchus." Local vintners brag that the medieval Pope Pius II ordered it by the cartload. Perched above the town, the 13th-century Burg Stahleck is now a hostel.

Km 540: Lorch—This pathetic stub of a castle is barely visible from the road. Notice the small car ferry (3/hrly, 10 min), one of several between Mainz and Koblenz, where there are no bridges.

Km 538: Castle Sooneck—Cross back to the other side of the train. Built in the 11th century, this castle was twice destroyed by people sick and tired of robber barons.

Km 534: Burg Reichenstein, and **Km 533: Burg Rheinstein**—Stay on the other side of the train to see two of the first castles to be rebuilt in the Romantic era. Both are privately owned, tourable, and connected by a pleasant trail.

Km 530: Ehrenfels Castle—Opposite Bingerbrück and the Bingen station, you'll see the ghostly Ehrenfels Castle (clobbered by the Swedes in 1636 and by the French in 1689). Since it had no view of the river traffic to the north, the owner built the cute little *Mäuseturm* (Mouse Tower) on an island (the yellow tower you'll see near the train station today). Rebuilt in the 1800s in neo-Gothic style, today it's used as a Rhine navigation signal station.

Km 528: Niederwald Monument—Across from the Bingen station on a hilltop is the 120-foot-high Niederwald monument, a memorial built with 32 tons of bronze in 1877 to commemorate "the reestablishment of the German Empire." A lift takes tourists to this statue from the famous and extremely touristy wine town of Rüdesheim.

Our tour is over. From Bingen you can continue your journey (or return to Koblenz) by train or boat.

BACHARACH

Once prosperous from the wine and wood trade, Bacharach is now just a pleasant half-timbered village working hard to keep its tourists happy.

The slick new **TI** is on the main street in the Posthof court-yard next to the church (Mon–Fri 9:00–17:00, Sat 10:00–16:00, closed Sun, Internet access-12 DM/hr, Oberstrasse 45, from station turn right and walk down main street with castle high on your left and walk about 5 blocks, tel. 06743/919-303).

The **Jost beer stein "factory outlet"** carries most every-thing a shopper could want. It has one shop across from the church in the main square and a slightly cheaper shop (housing the post office) a block away on Rosenstrasse 16 (Mon–Fri 8:30–18:00, Sat 8:30–17:00, Sun 10:00–17:00, ships overseas, 10 percent discount with this book, CC:VMA, tel. 06743/1224).

Get acquainted with Bacharach by taking a **walking tour**. Charming Herr Rolf Jung, retired headmaster of the Bacharach school, is a superb English-speaking guide (50 DM, 90 min, call him to reserve a tour, tel. 06743/1519). The TI also has a list of other guides, or take the self-guided walk, described below. For accommodations, see "Sleeping on the Rhine," below.

Sights—Bacharach

▲▲**Introductory Bacharach Walk**—Start at the Köln-Düssel-dorf ferry dock (next to a fine picnic park). View the town from the parking lot—a modern landfill. The Rhine used to lap against Bacharach's town wall, just over the present-day highway. Every few years the river floods, covering the highway with several feet of water. The **castle** on the hill is a youth hostel. Two of its original 16 towers are visible from here (up to five if you look real hard). The huge roadside wine keg declares this town was built on the wine trade.

Reefs up the river forced boats to unload upriver and reload here. Consequently, Bacharach became the biggest wine trader on the Rhine. A riverfront crane hoisted huge kegs of prestigious "Bacharach" wine (which in practice was from anywhere in the region). The tour buses next to the dock and the flags of the biggest spenders along the highway remind you today's economy is basically tourism.

At the big town map and public WC, take the underpass, ascend on the right, make a U-turn, then walk under the train tracks through the medieval gate (one out of an original six 14th-century gates) and to the two-tone Protestant **church**, which marks the town center.

From this intersection, Bacharach's main street (Oberstrasse) goes right to the half-timbered, red-and-white Altes Haus (from 1368, the oldest house in town) and left way down to the train station. To the left (or south) of the church, the golden horn hangs over the old **Posthof** (and new TI). The post horn symbol-izes the postal service throughout Europe. In olden days, when the postman blew this, traffic stopped and the mail sped through.

Bacharach

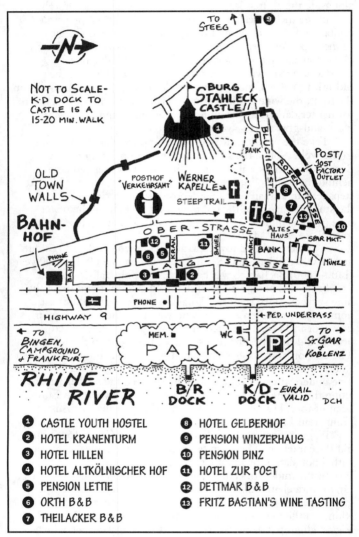

1. CASTLE YOUTH HOSTEL
2. HOTEL KRANENTURM
3. HOTEL HILLEN
4. HOTEL ALTKÖLNISCHER HOF
5. PENSION LETTIE
6. ORTH B & B
7. THEILACKER B & B
8. HOTEL GELBERHOF
9. PENSION WINZERHAUS
10. PENSION BINZ
11. HOTEL ZUR POST
12. DETTMAR B & B
13. FRITZ BASTIAN'S WINE TASTING

Step into the courtyard. Notice the fascist eagle (from 1936, on the left as you enter) and the fine view of a chapel and church. This post station dates from 1724, when stagecoaches ran from Köln to Frankfurt.

Two hundred years ago this was the only road along the

Rhine. Napoleon widened it to fit his cannon wagons. The steps alongside the church lead to the castle. Return to the church.

Inside the church you'll find grotesque and brightly painted capitals and a mix of round Romanesque and pointed Gothic arches. In the upper left corner some medieval frescoes survive where an older Romanesque arch was cut by a pointed Gothic one.

Continue down Oberstrasse past the Altes Haus to the **old mint** (*Münze*), marked by a crude coin in its sign. Across from the mint, the wine garden of Fritz Bastian is the liveliest place in town after dark. Above you in the vineyards stands a ghostly black-and-gray tower—your destination.

Take the next left (Rosenstrasse) and wander 30 meters up to the **well**. Notice the sundial and the wall painting of 1632 Bacharach with its walls intact. Climb the tiny-stepped lane behind the well up into the vineyard and to the tower. The slate steps lead to a small path that deposits you at a viewpoint atop the stubby remains of the old town wall, just above the tower's base (if signs indicate that the path is closed, get as close to the tower base as possible).

A grand medieval town spreads before you. When Frankfurt had 15,000 residents, medieval Bacharach had 6,000. For 300 years (1300–1600) Bacharach was big, rich, and politically powerful.

From this perch you can see the chapel ruins and six of the nine surviving **city towers**. Visually trace the wall to the castle, home of one of seven electors who voted for the Holy Roman Emperor in 1275. To protect their own power, these elector princes did their best to choose the weakest guy on the ballot. The elector from Bacharach helped select a two-bit prince named Rudolf von Hapsburg (from a two-bit castle in Switzerland). The underestimated Rudolf brutally silenced the robber barons along the Rhine and established the mightiest dynasty in European history. His family line, the Hapsburgs, ruled the Austro-Hungarian Empire until 1918.

Plagues, fires, and the Thirty Years' War (1618–1648) finally did Bacharach in. The town has slumbered for several centuries, with a population of about a thousand.

In the mid-19th century, artists and writers such as Victor Hugo were charmed by the Rhineland's romantic mix of past glory, present poverty, and rich legend. They put this part of the Rhine on the old "grand tour" map as the "Romantic Rhine." Victor Hugo pondered the ruined 15th-century chapel, which you can see under the castle. In his 1842 travel book, *Rhein Reise* (*Rhine Travels*), he wrote, "No doors, no roof or windows, a magnificent skeleton puts its silhouette against the sky. Above it, the ivy-covered castle ruins provide a fitting crown. This is Bacharach, land of fairy tales, covered with legends and sagas." If you're enjoying the Romantic Rhine, thank Victor Hugo and company.

To get back into town, take the path that leads along the wall up the valley to the next tower, then down onto the street. Follow the road under the gate and back into the center.

ST. GOAR

St. Goar is a classic Rhine town—its hulk of a castle overlooking a half-timbered shopping street and leafy riverside park busy with sightseeing ships and contented strollers. From the boat dock, the main drag—a pedestrian mall—cuts through town before winding up to the castle. Rheinfels Castle, once the mightiest on the Rhine, is the single best Rhineland ruin to explore.

The St. Goar **TI**, which offers a free left-luggage service, is on the pedestrian street, three blocks from the K-D boat dock (May–Oct Mon–Fri 8:00–12:30, 14:00–17:00, Sat 10:00–12:00, closed Sun and earlier in winter; if you're coming from train station, take a quick right, go around church, walk toward river and turn left on Herr Strasse, TI is 100 meters down on the right; tel. 06741/383).

St. Goar's waterfront park is hungry for a picnic. The small EDEKA **supermarket** on the main street is great for picnic fixings (Mon–Fri 8:00–19:00, Sat 8:00–16:00, limited hours on Sun in summer). **Bike rental** is available from Hermy's Garden (18 DM/day, Reine Strasse, tel. 06741/1360).

The friendly and helpful Montag family in the shop under Hotel Montag has Rhine guidebooks (Koblenz-Mainz), fine steins, and copies of this year's *Rick Steves' Germany, Austria & Switzerland* guidebook. They offer 10 percent off any of their souvenirs for travelers with this book (10 DM minimum purchase) and offer Internet access (12 DM/hr).

For a good two-hour **hike** from St. Goar to the Loreley viewpoint, catch the ferry across to St. Goarshausen (2.5-DM roundtrip, 4/hrly), hike up past the Katz castle (now a convalescent home), and traverse along the hillside, always bearing right toward the river. You'll pass through a residential area, hike down a 50-meter path through trees, then traverse a wheat field until you reach an amphitheater adjacent to the Loreley overview (restaurant available). From here it's a steep 15-minute hike down to the river where a riverfront trail takes you back to the St. Goarshausen–to–St. Goar ferry.

Sights—St. Goar's Rheinfels Castle

▲▲▲**Self-Guided Tour**—Sitting like a dead pit bull above St. Goar, this mightiest of Rhine castles rumbles with ghosts from its hard-fought past. Burg Rheinfels (built in 1245) withstood a siege of 28,000 French troops in 1692. But in 1797 the French Revolutionary army destroyed it.

Rheinfels was huge. In fact, it was the biggest castle on

St. Goar

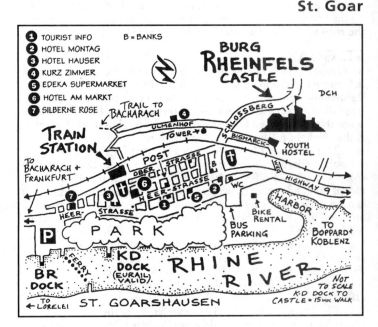

the Rhine and was used as a quarry. Today this hollow but interesting shell offers your single best hands-on ruined castle experience on the river (6 DM, daily 9:00–18:00, last entry at 17:00,
only Sat–Sun in winter, gather 15 English-speaking tourists and
get a nearly free English tour, tel. 06741/7753). The castle map
is mediocre (.30 DM); the English booklet is better, with history
and illustrations (3.50 DM).

If planning to explore the underground passages, bring a
flashlight, buy a tiny one (5 DM at entry), or do it by candlelight
(museum sells candles with matches, 1 DM). To get to the castle
from St. Goar's boat dock or train station, take a steep 15-minute
hike, a 9-DM taxi ride (11 DM for a minibus, tel. 06741/93100),
or the goofy tourist train (5 DM, 3/hrly, 10:00–18:00, runs from
square between station and dock, complete with lusty music).
A handy WC is in the castle courtyard by the restaurant entry.
If it's damp, be careful of slippery stones.

Rather than wander aimlessly, visit the castle by following
this tour: From the ticket gate walk straight and uphill. Pass
Grosser Keller on the left (where we'll end this tour), walk
through an internal gate past the *zu den gedeckten Wehrgängen* sign
on the right (where we'll pass later) to the museum (daily
9:00–12:00, 13:00–17:30) in the only finished room of the castle.

1. Museum and castle model: The seven-foot-tall carved stone (*Keltische Säule von Pfalzfeld*) immediately inside the door—a tombstone from a nearby Celtic grave—is from 600 years before Christ. There were people here long before the Romans...and this castle. The chair next to the door is an old library chair. Fold it up and it becomes stairs for getting to the highest shelves.

The castle history exhibit in the center of the room is well described in English. The massive fortification was the only Rhineland castle to withstand Louis XIV's assault during the 17th century. At the far end of the room is a model reconstruction of the castle showing how much bigger it was before French revolutionary troops destroyed it in the 18th century. Study this. Find where you are (hint: look for the tall tower). This was the living quarters of the original castle, which was only the smallest ring of buildings around the tiny central courtyard (13th century, marked by red well). The ramparts were added in the 14th century. By 1650, the fortress was largely complete. Ever since its destruction by the French in 1797, it's had no military value. While no WWII bombs were wasted on this ruin, it served St. Goar as a quarry for generations. The basement of the museum shows the castle pharmacy and an exhibit on Rhine region odds and ends, including tools and an 1830 loom.

Exit the museum and walk 30 meters directly out, slightly uphill into the castle courtyard.

2. Medieval castle courtyard: Five hundred years ago the entire castle circled this courtyard. The place was self-sufficient and ready for a siege with a bakery, pharmacy, herb garden, animals, brewery, well (top of yard), and livestock. During peacetime, 300 to 600 people lived here; during a siege there would be as many as 4,500. The walls were plastered and painted white. Bits of the original 13th-century plaster survive.

Continue through the courtyard, out *Erste Schildmauer*, turn left into the next courtyard, and walk to the two old, black, upright posts. Find the pyramid of stone catapult balls.

3. Castle garden: Catapult balls like these were too expensive not to recycle. If ever used, they'd be retrieved after the battle. Across from the balls is a well—essential for any castle during the age of sieging. The old posts are for the ceremonial baptizing of new members of the local trading league. While this guild goes back centuries, today it's a social club that fills this court with a huge wine party the first weekend of each August.

If weary, skip to 5; otherwise, climb the cobbled path up to the castle's best viewpoint up where the German flag waves.

4. Highest castle tower lookout: Enjoy a great view of the river, castle, and the forest that was once all part of this castle. Remember, the fortress once covered five times the land it does today. Originally this castle was no bigger than the two you see over the river. Notice how the other castles don't poke above the top of the Rhine canyon. That would make them easy for invading armies to see.

Return to the catapult balls, walk down the road, go through the tunnel, veer left through the arch marked *zu den Gedeckten Wehrgängen*, go down two flights of stairs, and turn left into the dark covered passageway. We now begin a rectangular walk taking us completely around the perimeter of the castle.

5. Covered defense galleries: Soldiers—the castle's "minutemen"—had a short commute: defensive positions on the outside, home in the holes below on the left. Even though these living quarters were padded with straw, life was unpleasant. A peasant was lucky to live beyond age 28.

Continue straight through the gallery and to the corner of the castle, where you'll see a white painted arrow at eye level.

6. Corner of castle: Look up. A three-story, half-timbered building originally rose beyond the highest stone fortification. The two stone tongues near the top just around the corner supported the toilet. (Insert your own joke here.) Turn around. The crossbow slits below the white arrow were once steeper. The bigger hole on the riverside was for hot pitch, etc.

Follow that white arrow along the outside to the next corner. Midway you'll pass stairs leading down *zu den Minengängen* (sign on upper left). Adventurers with flashlights can detour here. You may come out around the next corner. Otherwise, stay with me, walking level to the corner. At the corner, turn left.

7. Thoop...you're dead. Look ahead at the smartly placed crossbow arrow slit. While you're lying there, notice the stone work. The little round holes were for scaffolds used as they built up. They indicate this stonework is original. Notice also the fine stonework on the chutes. More boiling oil...now you're toast too. Continue along. At the railing, look up the valley and uphill where the fort existed. Below, just outside the wall, is land where attackers would gather.

To the left you'll find a metal gate and stairs. Walk down into small, dark tunnels that were once filled with explosives and ran under the land just outside the walls. Keep your bearings by following the faded white marks on the ceiling. To protect their castle, the Rheinfellers cleverly built tunnels topped by thin slate roofs and packed with explosives. By detonating the explosives when under attack, they could kill hundreds of approaching invaders without damaging the castle. In 1626 a handful of underground Protestant Germans blew 300 Catholic Spaniards to—they figured—hell.

Continue along the perimeter, jog left, go down five steps and into an open field, and walk toward the wooden bridge. You may detour here into the passageway marked "13 Hals Graben." The old wooden bridge is actually modern. Angle left through two arches and through the rough entry to *Verliess* on the left.

8. Prison: This is one of six dungeons. You walked through a door prisoners only dreamed of 400 years ago. They came and went through the little square hole in the ceiling. The holes in the walls supported timbers that politely gave as many as 15 residents something to sit on to keep them out of the filthy slop that gathered on the floor. Twice a day they were given bread and water. Some prisoners actually survived five years in here. The town could torture and execute. The castle had permission only to imprison criminals in these dungeons.

Continue through the next arch, under the white arrow, and turn left and walk 40 yards to the *Schlachthaus*.

9. Slaughterhouse: A castle was prepared to survive a six-month siege. With 4,000 people, that's a lot of provisions. The cattle that lived within the walls were slaughtered here. Notice the drainage gutters for water and blood. "Running water" came through from above...one bucket at a time.

Back outside, climb the modern stairs to the left. A skinny passage leads you into...

10. The big cellar: This *Grosser Keller* was a big pantry. When the castle was smaller, this was the original moat—you can see the rough lower parts of the wall. The original floor was five feet deeper. When the castle expanded, the moat became the cellar. Above the entry, holes mark spots where timbers made a storage loft, perhaps filled with grain. Kegs of wine lined the walls. Part of a soldier's pay was three liters of wine a day. In the back, an arch leads to the wine cellar where finer wine was kept. The castle consumed 200,000 liters of wine a year. The count owned the surrounding farmland. Farmers got to keep 20 percent of their production. Later, in more liberal feudal times, the nobility let them keep 40 percent. Today the German government leaves the workers with 60 percent...and provides a few more services.

Climb out, turn right, and leave. For coffee on a great view terrace, visit the Rheinfels Castle Hotel, opposite the entrance (good WC at base of steps).

Sleeping on the Rhine
(2 DM = about $1)
Sleep Code: **S** = Single, **D** = Double/Twin, **T** = Triple, **Q** = Quad, **b** = bathroom, **t** = toilet only, **s** = shower only, **CC** = Credit Card (Visa, MasterCard, Amex), **SE** = Speaks English, **NSE** = No English. All hotels speak some English. Breakfast is included unless otherwise noted.

The Rhine is an easy place for cheap sleeps. *Zimmer* and *Gasthäuser* with 40-DM beds abound (and *Zimmer* normally discount their prices for longer stays). A few exceptional Rhine-area hostels offer 20-DM beds (for travelers of any age). Each town's TI is eager to set you up, and finding a room should be easy any time of year (except for wine-festy weekends in September and October). Bacharach and St. Goar, the best towns for an overnight stop, are about 10 miles apart, connected by milk-run trains, riverboats, and a riverside bike path. Bacharach is more interesting and less touristy, but St. Goar has the famous castle (see "St. Goar," above). Parking in Bacharach is simple along the highway next to the tracks (3-hour daytime limit is generally not enforced) or in the boat parking lot. Parking in St. Goar is tighter; ask at your hotel.

Sleeping in Bacharach
(country code: 49, area code: 06743, zip code: 55422)

Hotels
Hotel Kranenturm gives you castle ambience without the climb. It offers a good combination of comfort and hotel privacy with *Zimmer* coziness, a central location, and a medieval atmosphere. Every room is different. Run by hardworking Kurt Engel, his intense but friendly wife, Fatima, and faithful Schumi, this hotel is actually part of the medieval fortification. Its former *Kran* (crane) towers are now round rooms—great for medievalists. When the riverbank was higher, cranes on this tower loaded barrels of wine onto Rhine boats. Hotel Kranenturm is five meters from the train tracks, but a combination of medieval sturdiness, triple-paned windows, and included earplugs makes the riverside rooms sleepable (Sb-75–80 DM, Db-105–110 DM, Tb-145–150 DM, Qb-175–180 DM with this book, prices include breakfast, the lower price is for off-season or stays of at least 3 nights in high season, CC:VMA but prefer cash, Rhine views come with ripping train noise, back rooms—some with castle views—are quieter, all rooms with cable TV, kid friendly, Langstrasse 30, tel. 06743/1308, fax 06743/1021, e-mail: hotel-kranenturm@t-online.de). Kurt, a good cook, serves 12- to 27-DM dinners; try his ice-cream special for dessert. Trade travel stories on the terrace with new friends over dinner, letting screaming trains punctuate your conversation. Drivers park along the highway at the Kranenturm tower. Eurailers walk down Oberstrasse, then turn right on Kranenstrasse.

Hotel Hillen, a block south of the Hotel Kranenturm, has less charm and more train noise, with friendly owners, great food, and lots of rental bikes. To minimize train noise, ask for *"ruhige Seite,"* the quiet side (S-50 DM, Sb-65 DM, D-80 DM, Ds-85 DM, Db-90–100 DM, Tb-140 DM, includes breakfast, 10 percent less for 2 nights, Langstrasse 18, tel. 06743/1287, fax 06743/1037, Iris speaks some English).

Hotel Altkölnischer Hof, a grand old building near the church, rents 20 rooms with modern furnishings and bathrooms, some with balconies over an Old World restaurant. Public rooms are old-time elegant (Sb-90–95 DM, Db-120–130 DM, Db with terrace-160–170 DM, with balcony-150–170 DM, CC:VA, TV in rooms, elevator, tel. 06743/1339 or 06743/2186, fax 06743/2793, e-mail: tscherba@sparkasse.net, SE).

Hotel Gelberhof, a few doors up from the Jost store, has spiffy public spaces but unimaginative rooms (S-55 DM, Sb-75–85 DM, small Db-110 DM, Db-120–140 DM, 3-night discounts, CC:VM, popular with groups, elevator, bike rental, Blücherstrasse 26, tel. 06743/910-100, fax 06743/910-1050, www.hotelgelberhof.com).

Pensions and Private Rooms

At **Pension Lettie**, effervescent and eager-to-please Lettie offers four modern, bright rooms (Sb-60 DM, Db-80 DM, Tb-110 DM with this book and cash, discount for 3-night stays, strictly nonsmoking, no train noise, a few doors inland from Hotel Kranenturm, Kranenstrasse 6, tel. & fax 06743/2115, e-mail: pension.lettie@ t-online.de). Lettie speaks English (worked for the U.S. Army before we withdrew) and does laundry (18 DM per load).

Delightful **Ursula Orth** rents five, airy rooms—a great value, around the corner from Pension Lettie (Sb-35 DM, Db-60–65 DM, Tb-75 DM for 1 night and less for 2, nonsmoking, Rooms 4 and 5 on ground floor—easy access, from Hotel Hillen walk up Spurgasse, her *Zimmer* is on the right at #3, tel. 06743/1557, minimal English spoken).

On the main street, the cozy home of **Herr und Frau Theilacker** is a German-feeling *Zimmer* offering comfortable rooms and a pleasant stay. It's likely to have a room when others don't (S-30 DM, D-60 DM, in the town center, walk 30 steps straight out of Restaurant Braustube to Oberstrasse 57, no outside sign, tel. 06743/1248, NSE).

Pension Winzerhaus, a 10-room place run by Herr and Frau Petrescu, is 200 meters up the valley from the town gate, so the location is less charming, but it has no train noise and easy parking. Rooms are simple, clean, and modern (Sb-50 DM, Db-85 DM, Tb-90 DM, Qb-95 DM, 10 percent off with this book, free bikes for guests, Blücherstrasse 60, tel. 06743/1294, fax 069/283-927).

Pension Binz offers slightly older rooms and an apartment in a serene location (Sb-65 DM, Db-98 DM, third person-35 DM, apartment-120–150 DM, fine breakfast, CC:VM, Koblenzer Strasse 1, tel. 06743/1604, cheery Carla SE).

Hotel zur Post has 16 quiet rooms, fine furniture, dark hallways, and a hint of character (Sb-85 DM, Db-95–110 DM, Tb-135 DM, Qb-145 DM, CC:V, Oberstrasse Strasse 38, tel. 06743/1277, fax 06743/2807, e-mail: hzp.scherschlicht@t-online.de).

Annelie und Hans Dettmar, entrepreneurial and curiously lacking in warmth, rent several smoke-free rooms and two great family rooms with kitchenette (20 DM to use it) in a modern house on the main drag (big Sb-50 DM, Db-55–70 DM, Tb-75–90 DM, Qb-100–120 DM, includes breakfast, free use of 2 old bikes, laundry-17 DM, Oberstrasse 8, tel. 06743/2661, fax 06743/919-396, a little English spoken). Readers give this couple mixed reviews, but their rooms are good. Their son **Jürgen Dettmar**, who smiles occasionally, rents five fine, very central rooms with a common kitchen and small bathrooms, near the church behind Restaurant Braustube. Ask for a room with balcony for a bird's-eye view over the town center (D-60 DM, Db-80 DM, Tb-105 DM, Oberstrasse 64, tel. & fax 06743/1715, www.pension-dettmar.bacharach-rhein.de, SE).

Bacharach's hostel, **Jugendherberge Stahleck**, is a 12th-century castle on the hilltop—500 steps above Bacharach—with a royal Rhine view. Open to travelers of any age, this is a newly redone gem with eight beds and a private modern shower and WC in each room. A steep 15-minute climb on the trail from the town church, the hostel is warmly run by Evelyn and Bernhard Falke (FALL-kay), who serve hearty, 9.70-DM buffet, all-you-can-eat dinners. The hostel pub serves cheap local wine until midnight (26-DM dorm beds with breakfast and sheets, 6 DM extra without a card or in a double, couples can share rooms, groups pay 35.40 DM per bed with breakfast and dinner, no smoking in rooms, easy parking, beds normally available but call and leave your name, they'll hold a bed until 18:00, tel. 06743/1266, fax 06743/2684, e-mail: jh-bacharach@djh-info.de, SE).

Eating in Bacharach

Several places offer good, inexpensive, and atmospheric indoor or outdoor dining in Bacharach, all for about 20 to 30 DM. The oldest building in town, **Altes Haus** (dead center by the church, closed Wed), and **Kurpfälzische Münze** (open daily, in the old mint, a half block down from Altes Haus; claims to be even older) are both good values with great ambience. **Weingut zum Gruner Baum** offers delicious appetizers (also next to Altes Haus with good ambience indoors and out). **Hotel Kranenturm** is another good value with hearty meals and good main course salads (see hotel listing above).

Wine Tasting: Drop in on entertaining Fritz Bastian's **Weingut zum Grüner Baum** wine bar (just past Altes Haus, eves only, closed Thu, tel. 06743/1208). As the president of the local vintner's club, Fritz's mission is to give travelers an understanding of the subtle differences among the Rhine wines. Groups of two to six people pay 26 DM for a "carousel" of 15 glasses of 14 different white wines, one lonely red, and a basket of bread. Your mission: Team up with others with this book to rendezvous here after dinner. Spin the lazy Susan, share a common cup, and discuss the taste. Fritz insists, "After each wine, you must talk to each other."

Sleeping in St. Goar
(country code: 49, area code: 06741, zip code: 56329)
Hotel am Markt, well run by Herr and Frau Velich, is rustic with all the modern comforts. It features a hint of antler with a pastel flair and bright rooms and a good restaurant. It's a good value and a stone's throw from the boat dock and train station (Ss-65 DM, Sb-80 DM, Db-110 DM, Tb-140 DM, Qb-160 DM, cheaper off-season, closed Dec–Feb, CC:VMA, Am Markt 1, tel. 06741/1689, fax 06741/1721, e-mail: hotel.am.markt@gmx.de).

Hotel Hauser, facing the boat dock, is another good deal, warmly run by another Frau Velich and Sigrid (S-42 DM, D-88 DM, Db-98 DM, great Db with Rhine-view balconies-110 DM, small bathrooms, show this book to get these prices, cheaper in off-season, CC:VMA, Heerstrasse 77, telephone reservations easy, tel. 06741/333, fax 06741/1464, SE).

Hotel Montag is on the castle end of town just across the street from the world's largest free-hanging cuckoo clock. Manfred and Maria Montag and their son Mike speak New Yorkish. Even though the hotel gets a lot of bus tours, it's friendly, laid-back, and comfortable; ask about its luxurious apartments (Sb-70 DM, Db-130 DM, price can drop if things are slow, CC:VMA, Internet access-12 DM/hr, Heerstrasse 128, tel. 06741/1629, fax 06741/2086, e-mail: hotelmontag@1019freenet.de). Check out their adjacent crafts shop (heavy on beer steins).

A few doors away, the strangely vacant **Rhein Hotel** has modern, unimaginative rooms (Sb-70–80 DM, Db-90–130 DM, Heerstrasse 71, tel. 06741/355, fax 06741/2835, e-mail: blecic@t-online.de). Next door, **Hotel Silberne Rose** is musty with older decor and some rooms with Rhine views (Sb-60–70 DM, Db-100–120 DM, Tb-125–140 DM, cheaper price for longer stays, CC:VM, across from K-D dock, Heerstrasse 63, tel. 06741/7040, fax 06741/2865).

St. Goar's best *Zimmer* deal is the home of **Frau Kurz**, "which comes with a breakfast terrace, garden, fine view, easy parking, and most of the comforts of a hotel (S-37 DM, D-60–64 DM, Db-70 DM, showers-5 DM, 1-night stays cost extra, free parking, confirm prices, honor your reservation or call to cancel, Ulmenhof 11, tel. & fax 06741/459, some English spoken). It's a steep five-minute hike from the train station (exit left from station, take immediate left at the yellow phone booth, go under tracks to paved path, take a right partway up stairs, climb a few more stairs to Ulmenhof).

The Germanly run **St. Goar Hostel**, the big beige building under the castle (veer right off the road up to the castle), has two to twelve beds per room, a 22:00 curfew, and hearty 10-DM dinners (22-DM beds with breakfast, open all day, check-in preferred 17:00–18:00 and 19:00–20:00, Bismarckweg 17, tel. 06741/388, e-mail: jl-st-goar@djh-info.de, SE).

Rheinfels Castle Hotel is the town splurge. Actually part
of the castle, but an entirely new building, this luxury place is
good for those with money and a car (Db-240–285 DM depending
on river views and balconies, CC:VMA, elevator, free parking,
dress-up restaurant, Schlossberg 47, tel. 06741/8020, fax 06741/
802-802, www.schlosshotel-rheinfels.de, e-mail: rheinfels
.st.goar@t-online.de).

Eating in St. Goar
Hotel Am Markt and **Hotel Hauser** offer excellent meals at fair
prices. For your Rhine splurge, walk, taxi, or drive up to **Rheinfels Castle Hotel** for its incredible view and elegant setting,
and consider a sunset drink on the view terrace (see hotel listing
above; reserve a table by the window).

Transportation Connections—Rhine
Milk-run trains stop at all Rhine towns each hour starting as
early as around 6:00. Koblenz, Boppard, St. Goar, Bacharach,
Bingen, and Mainz are each about 15 minutes apart. From
Koblenz to Mainz takes 75 minutes. To get a faster big train,
go to Mainz or Koblenz.
   From Mainz by train to: Bacharach/St. Goar (hrly, 1 hr),
Cochem (hrly, 2.5 hrs, changing in Koblenz), **Köln** (3/hrly, 90
min), **Baden-Baden** (hrly, 2.5 hrs), **Munich** (hrly, 4 hrs), **Frank-
furt** (3/hrly, 45 min), **Frankfurt Airport** (3/hrly, 25 min).
   From Frankfurt by train to: Koblenz (hrly, 90 min),
Rothenburg (hrly, 3 hrs, transfers in Würzburg and Steinach),
Würzburg (hrly, 90 min), **Munich** (hrly, 3.5 hrs), **Amsterdam**
(8/day, 5 hrs), **Paris** (4/day, 6.5 hrs).

MOSEL VALLEY
The misty Mosel is what some visitors hoped the Rhine would
be—peaceful, sleepy, romantic villages slipped between the steep
vineyards and the river; fine wine; a sprinkling of castles; and lots
of friendly *Zimmer*. Boat, train, and car traffic here is a trickle
compared to the roaring Rhine. While the swan-speckled Mosel
moseys 300 miles from France's Vosges Mountains to Koblenz,
where it dumps into the Rhine, the most scenic piece of the valley
lies between the towns of Bernkastel-Kues and Cochem. I'd savor
only this section. Zell makes a pleasant home base.
   Throughout the region on summer weekends and during the
fall harvest time, wine festivals with oompah bands, dancing, and
colorful costumes are powered by good food and wine.

Getting around the Mosel Valley
By Train and Bus: The train zips you to Cochem, Bullay, or
Trier in a snap. Frequent buses connect Zell with the Bullay

Mosel Valley

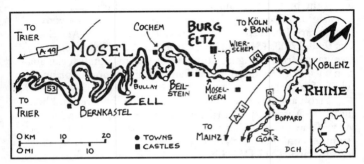

station in 10 minutes, and six buses a day connect tiny Beilstein with Cochem in 20 minutes (last bus about 15:10). Four buses a day link Zell and Beilstein.

By Boat: A few daily departures allow you to cruise the most scenic stretch between Cochem, Beilstein, and Zell: between Cochem and Zell (2/day, May–Oct, but none on Fri and Mon May–June, 3 hrs, 23 DM one-way, 35 DM round-trip, on Kolb-Line); between Cochem and Beilstein (5/day, 60 min, 14 DM one-way, 19 DM round-trip, tel. 02671/7387); and between Zell and Beilstein (1/day May–Oct, 2 hrs, 18 DM one-way, 26 DM round-trip). The K-D (Köln-Düsseldorf) line sails once a day in each direction but only as far as Cochem (May–Sept, Koblenz to Cochem 10:00–14:30, or Cochem to Koblenz 15:40–20:10, free with consecutive-day Eurailpass or a dated Eurail flexipass, Europass, Eurail Selectpass, or German railpass).

By Bike: You can rent bikes in most Mosel towns (see village listings below).

Cochem

With a majestic castle and picturesque medieval streets, Cochem is the very touristic hub of this part of the river.

Tourist Information: The information-packed TI is by the bridge at the main bus stop. They book rooms (same day only) and keep a thorough 24-hour room listing in the window. Their free map includes the town's history and a walking tour. Ask about public transportation to Burg Eltz (see below) and pick up the well-done *Moselle Wine Road* brochure and info on area hikes (May–Oct Mon–Sat 10:00–17:00, Sun 10:00–12:00, off-season closed weekends and at lunch, tel. 02671/60040). For accommodations, see "Sleeping," below.

Arrival in Cochem: Make a hard right out of the station (lockers available) and walk about 10 minutes to the town center and TI (just past the bus lanes). Drivers can park near the bridge

(TI right there). To get to the main square (*Markt*), continue under the bridge, then angle right and follow Bernstrasse.

Sights: The pointy Cochem Castle is the work of overly imaginative 19th-century restorers (7 DM, daily mid-March–Oct 9:00–17:00, 15-minute walk from Cochem, follow one of the frequent German-language tours while reading English explanation sheets or call ahead to see if any English tours are planned, tel. 02671/255).

Stroll along the pleasant paths that line the river and hike up to the Aussichtspunkt (the cross on the hill) for a great view. You can rent bikes from the K-D boat kiosk at the dock (summers only) or year-round from Kreutz near the station on Ravenstrasse 42 (7 DM/4 hrs, 14 DM/day, no deposit required, just your passport number, tel. 02671/91131). Consider taking a bike on the boat and riding back. If stranded, many hitchhike.

Connections: Cochem has frequent train service to Koblenz (hrly, 60 min), Bullay (hrly, 10 min), and Trier (hrly, 60 min).

Sights—Mosel Valley

▲▲▲**Burg Eltz**—My favorite castle in all of Europe lurks in a mysterious forest. It's been left intact for 700 years and is furnished throughout as it was 500 years ago. Thanks to smart diplomacy and clever marriages, Burg Eltz was never destroyed. (It survived one five-year siege.) It's been in the Eltz family for 820 years. The countess arranges for new flowers in each room weekly. The only way to see the castle is with a one-hour tour (included in admission ticket). German tours (with helpful English fact sheets, 1 DM) go constantly. Call ahead to see if an English-language tour is scheduled, or organize your own by corralling 20 English-speakers in the inner courtyard—they'll thank you for it. Then push the red button on the white porch and politely beg for an English guide. This is well worth a short wait (9 DM, April–Oct daily 9:30–17:30, tel. 02672/950-500, www.burg-eltz.de). To get to Burg Eltz from Cochem, you can taxi (70 DM, 02671/980-098), drive, or train-and-hike.

Arrival by Train: Get off at the Moselkern station midway between Cochem and Koblenz (no lockers at station, but, if you ask politely, clerk will store luggage in office). When leaving the station, exit right and follow Burg Eltz signs for about 15 minutes through town, then take the marked trail (slippery when wet, slightly steep near end). It's a pleasant 60-minute hike between the station and castle through a pine forest where sparrows carry crossbows, and maidens, disguised as falling leaves, whisper "watch out."

Arrival by Car: Drivers often get lost on the way to Burg Eltz. Use your map and do this: Leave the river at Hatzenport (shortest drive) following the white "Burg Eltz

Park & Ride" signs through the towns of Münstermaifeld and Wierschem. The castle parking lot is two kilometers past Wierschem. From the lot, hike 10 minutes downhill or wait for the red castle shuttle bus (2 DM). There are three "Burg Eltz" parking lots; only the lot two kilometers south of Wierscheim is close enough for an easy walk. Another option is to park at the Moselkern station and follow the "park and walk" signs (see "Arrival by Train," above).

Burg Eltz Area

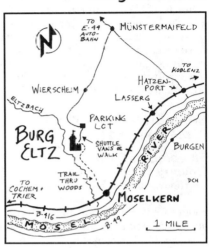

▲**Beilstein**—Farther upstream is the quaintest of all Mosel towns (see "Sleeping," below). Beilstein is Cinderella land. Explore the narrow lanes, ancient wine cellar, resident (and very territorial) swans, and ruined castle. The small 2-DM ferry goes constantly back and forth across the river. A shop rents bikes for the pleasant riverside ride (toward Zell is best). The TI is in Café Klapperburg (summer Tue–Sun 9:00–18:00, closed Mon, tel. 02673/1417). Four buses a day connect Zell and Beilstein.

▲**Zell**—This is the best Mosel town for an overnight stop (see "Sleeping," below). It's peaceful, with a fine riverside promenade, a pedestrian bridge over the water, plenty of *Zimmer*, and a long pedestrian zone filled with colorful shops, restaurants, *Weinstuben* (wine bars), and a fun oompah folk band on weekend evenings on the main square.

The TI is on the pedestrian street, four blocks downriver from the pedestrian bridge (Mon–Fri 8:00–12:30, 13:30–17:00, Sat 10:00–13:00, off-season closed Sat, tel. 06542/4031). The fine little Wein und Heimatmuseum features Mosel history (same building as TI, Wed and Sat 15:00–17:00). Walk up to the medieval wall's gatehouse and through the cemetery to the old munitions tower for a village view. You can rent bikes from Frau Klaus (Hauptstrasse 5, tel. 06542/2589). For Internet access, try the relaxing Berliner Kaffe-Kännchen (30 min/5 DM, 7:00–18:30 Thu–Tue, closed Wed, across pedestrian bridge opposite bus stop at Baldninen Strasse 107, tel. 06542/5450).

Locals know Zell for its Schwarze Katz (Black Cat) wine. Franz Josef Weis (who was once a POW in England) and his son Peter give an entertaining and free tour of their 40,000-bottle-per-year wine cellar. The clever tour starts at 17:00 (call ahead to reserve, tel. 06542/41398); buy a bottle or two to keep this fine tour going. A green flag marks their *Weinkeller* south of town, past the bridge, at Notenau 30. They also rent two fine apartments (see "Sleeping in Zell," below).

Sleeping on the Mosel
(2 DM = about $1)

Sleeping in Cochem
(country code: 49, area code: 02671, zip code: 56812)
All rooms come with breakfast.

Weingut Rademacher offers a good value and beautiful rooms, wedged between vineyards and train tracks, with a pleasant garden and a big common kitchen. Charming hostess Andrea (SE) and her husband sometimes give tours of their wine cellar; houseguests enter for free. If there is no tour, visitors are welcome to taste the wine (Sb-50 DM, Db-90 DM, family deals, ground-floor rooms, from station take a quick right on Ravenestrasse, turn right on Pinnerstrasse, pass under train tracks, curve right for another 50 meters, Pinnerstrasse 10, tel. 02671/4164, fax 02671/91341).

Just above a local *Weinstube*, the light-hearted and ever-so-funky **Gasthaus Ravene** offers six rooms varying in size and comfort (several are spacious and airy). The stairway needs new carpeting, but the rooms are fine (Sb-60 DM, Db-80–100 DM, Tb-135 DM, CC:VM, Ravenestrasse 43, tel. 02671/980-177, fax 02671/91119, www.gasthaus-ravene.de, NSE).

The rustic **Hotel Lohspeiche**r, just off the main square on a tiny-stepped street, is for those who want a real hotel—with much higher prices—in the thick of things (Sb-95 DM, Db-170 DM, CC:VMA, some nonsmoking rooms, includes breakfast, restaurant, elevator, closed Feb, Obergasse 1, tel. 02671/3976, fax 02671/1772, Ingo SE).

Haus Andreas has many small but modern rooms at fair prices (S-25 DM, Sb-40 DM, Db-60 DM, Schlosstrasse 9, tel. 02671/1370 or 02671/5155, fax 02671/1370). From the main square, take Herrenstrasse; after a block, angle right uphill on Schlosstrasse.

For a top-dollar view of Cochem, cross the bridge and find the balconied rooms at **Hotel Am Hafen** (110–190 DM, skip cheaper no-view rooms, Uferstrasse 3, cross bridge to reach hotel, tel. 02671/97720, fax 02671/977-227, e-mail: hotel-am-hafen@t-online.de).

Sleeping in Zell
(country code: 49, area code: 06542, zip code: 56856)

If the Mosel charms you into spending the night, do it in Zell. By car, this is a natural. It's also easy by boat (2/day from Cochem) or train (go to Bullay—hrly from Cochem or Trier; from Bullay the bus takes you to little Zell—2.80 DM, 2/hrly, 15 min; bus stop is across street from Bullay train station, check yellow MB schedule for times, last bus at about 19:00). The central Zell stop is called Lindenplatz.

Zell's hotels are a disappointment, but its private homes are great. The owners speak almost no English and discount their rates if you stay more than one night. They can't take reservations long in advance for one-night stays; just call a day ahead. My favorites are on the south end of town, a five-minute walk from the town hall square (TI) and the bus stop. Breakfast is included unless otherwise noted. These places are listed in the order you would find them from the pedestrian bridge.

Friendly **Natalie Huhn** (no sign), your German grand-mother, has the cheapest beds in town in her simple but comfort-able house (S-35 DM, D-60 DM, cheaper for 2-night stays, 2 blocks to left of church at Jakobstrasse 32, tel. 06542/41048).

Weinhaus zum Fröhlichen Weinberg offers cheap, basic rooms (D-70 DM, 60 DM for 2 or more nights, family *Zimmer*, Mittelstrasse 6, tel. 06542/4308, fax 06542/5781) above a *Wein-stube* disco (noisy on Friday and Saturday nights).

Homey **Gästehaus am Römerbad** is a few blocks from the church and a decent value (Db-80 DM, Am Römerbad 5, tel. 06542/41602, Elizabeth Münster).

Zell's best *Zimmer* values lie at the end of the pedestrian street about five blocks from the pedestrian bridge:

Gasthaus Gertrud Thiesen is classy, with a TV-living-breakfast room and a river view. The Thiesen house has big, bright rooms and is on the town's first corner overlooking the Mosel from a great terrace (S or D-70 DM, Balduinstrasse 1, tel. 06542/4453, SE). Notice the high-water flood marks on the wall across the street.

Gästezimmer Rosa Mesenich is another little place facing the river (S-35 DM, Sb-40 DM, D-76 DM, Db-80 DM, Branden-burg 48, tel. 06542/4297, NSE).

Almost next door, the vine-strewn doorway of **Gastehaus Eberhard** leads to gregarious owners, cushy rooms, and potential wine tastings (Db-70 DM, Brandenburg 42, tel. 06542/41216, NSE).

If you're looking for room service, a sauna, a pool, and an ele-vator, sleep at **Hotel Grüner Kranz** (Sb-85 DM, Db-160 DM, CC:VMA, tel. 06542/98610, fax 06542/986-180).

Weinhaus Mayer, a classy—if stressed-out—old pen-sion next door, is perfectly central with Mosel-view rooms

(Db-120–160 DM, Balduinstrasse 15, tel. 06542/4530, fax 06542/61160). They have newly renovated rooms with top comforts, many with river-view balconies (ask for *Neues Gastehaus*, view Db-180 DM, big Tb-240 DM, tel. & fax 06542/61169).

The freshly remodeled **Hotel Ratskeller** (above a classy pizzeria) has rooms on the pedestrian street that are less cozy but sharp with tile flooring and fair rates (Sb-70–85 DM, Db-120–145 DM, CC:VM, Balduinstrasse 36, tel. 06542/98620, fax 06542/986-244).

Franz Josef Weis and son Peter of the **Schwarze Katz** winery rent two luxurious apartments with kitchens and fireplaces and free use of a funky old grape-pressing room (Db-100 DM, extra person-20 DM, breakfast-10 DM, CC:VMA, look for green flag marking their *Weinkeller* south of town, past bridge, at Notenau 30, tel. 06542/41398, fax 06542/961-178, e-mail: f.j.weis@t-online.de).

Sleeping in Beilstein
(country code: 49, area code: 02673, zip code: 56814)
Cozier and farther north, Beilstein (BILE-shtine) is very small and quiet (no train; 5 buses/day to nearby Cochem, fewer buses on weekends, 15 min; taxi from Cochem-25 DM). Breakfast is included.

Hotel Haus Lipmann is your chance to live in a medieval mansion with hot showers and TVs. A prizewinner for atmosphere, it's been in the Lipmann family for 200 years. The creaky wooden staircase and the elegant dining hall, with long wooden tables surrounded by antlers, chandeliers, and feudal weapons, will get you in the mood for your castle sightseeing, but the riverside terrace may mace your momentum (5 rooms, Db-140–160 DM, tel. 02673/1573, fax 02673/1521, e-mail: hotel.haus.lipmann@t-online.de).

Gasthaus Winzerschenke an der Klostertreppe is comfortable and a great value, right in the tiny heart of town (Db-75 DM, bigger Db-95 DM, discount for 2-night stays, tel. & fax 02673/1354, Frau Sausen).

The half-timbered, riverfront **Altes Zollhaus Gästezimmer** has packed all the comforts into eight tight, bright, and modern rooms (Db-110 DM, deluxe Db-145 DM, closed Nov–Feb, tel. 02673/1574, fax 02673/1287, e-mail: lipmann@t-online.de).

Hotel Gute Quelle offers more half-timbers, 13 comfortable rooms, and a good restaurant (Db-80–120 DM, CC:VMA, Marketplatz 34, tel. 02673/1437, fax 02673/1399, Susan SE).

BERLIN

No tour of Germany is complete without a look at its historic and reunited capital, a construction zone called Berlin. Stand over ripped-up tracks and under a canopy of cranes and watch the rebirth of a European capital. Enjoy the thrill of walking over what was the Wall and through Brandenburg Gate.

Berlin has had a tumultuous history. The city was devastated in World War II then divided by the Allied powers: with the American, British, and French sectors being West Berlin, and the Russian sector, East Berlin. The division was set in stone when the East built the Berlin Wall in 1961. The Berlin Wall lasted 28 years. In 1990, less than a year after the Wall fell, Germany was formally reunited. When the dust settled, Berliners from both sides of the once-divided city faced the monumental challenge of reunification.

The last decade has taken Berlin through a frenzy of rebuilding. And, while there's still plenty of work to be done, a new Berlin is emerging. Berliners joke they don't need to go anywhere because the city's always changing. Spin a postcard rack to see the news. A five-year-old guidebook on Berlin covers a different city.

Unification has had its negative side, and the Wall survives in the minds of some people. Some "Ossies" (impolite slang for Easterners) miss their security. Some "Wessies" miss their easy ride (military deferrals, subsidized rent, and tax breaks). To free spirits, walled-in West Berlin was a citadel of freedom within the East.

The city government has been eager to charge forward with little nostalgia for anything that was "Eastern." Big corporations and the national government have moved in, and the dreary swath of land that was the Wall has been transformed. City planners are boldly taking Berlin's reunification and the return of the national government as a good opportunity to make Berlin a great capital once again.

During the grind of World War II, Hitler enjoyed rolling out the lofty plans for a post-war Berlin as capital of a Europe united under his rule. As Europe unites, dominated by a muscular Germany with its shiny new capital in the works, Hitler's dream of a grand post-war Berlin seems about to come true....

Planning Your Time

Because of the city's location, try to enter and/or leave by either night train or plane. On a three-week trip through Germany, Austria, and Switzerland, I'd give Berlin two days and spend them this way:

Day 1: 10:00-Take a guided walking tour (offered by Original Berlin Walks, see "Tours of Berlin," below). After lunch, take my Do-It-Yourself Orientation Tour, stopping midway to scale the new dome of the Reichstag building, then finishing with a walk through Eastern Berlin. Stop at the Deutscher Dom (German Cathedral) to devour the "Questions on Germany History" exhibit. Finish your day at the Pergamon Museum.

Day 2: Spend the morning lost in the painted art of the Gemäldegalerie, explore Potsdamer Platz center, hike to the Topography of Terror exhibit and along the surviving Zimmerstrasse stretch of Wall to the Museum of the Wall at Checkpoint Charlie.

If you are maximizing your sightseeing you could start Day 2 with a visit to the Egyptian and Picasso museums at Charlottenburg. Remember that the Museum of the Wall is open late and most museums are closed on Monday.

Orientation (area code: 030)

Berlin is huge, with nearly four million people. But the tourist's Berlin can be broken into four digestible chunks:

1. The area around Bahnhof Zoo and the grand Kurfürstendamm (called Ku'damm) Boulevard (transportation, tours, information, hotel, shopping hub).

2. Former downtown East Berlin (Brandenburg Gate, Unter den Linden Boulevard, Pergamon Museum, and the area around Oranienburger Strasse).

3. The new center: Kulturforum museums, Potsdamer Platz, and Wall-related sights.

4. Charlottenburg Palace and museums.

Tourist Information

Berlin's TIs are run by a for-profit agency working for the city's big hotels, which colors the information they provide. The main TI is five minutes from the Bahnhof Zoo train station, in the Europa Center (with Mercedes symbol on top, enter outside to left, on Budapester Strasse, Mon–Sat 8:30–20:30, Sun 10:00–18:00,

Berlin Sightseeing Modules

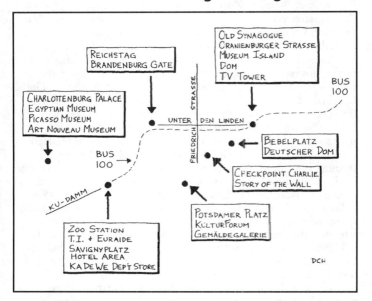

tel. 030/250-025, www.btm.de). A smaller TI is in the Brandenburg Gate (daily 9:30–18:00). The TIs sell city maps (1 DM—
get it), the *Berlin Programm* (a 3-DM German-language monthly
listing upcoming events and museum hours, www.berlin.de), the
Museumspass (16-DM, 3-day pass to state museums, see "Helpful
Hints," below), and the German-English quarterly *Berlin* magazine
(4 DM, with timely features on Berlin and a partial calendar of
events). Ask for the free *What's On in Berlin* monthly entertainment
magazine. The TIs also offer a 5-DM room-finding service (but
only to hotels that give them kickbacks—many don't). Most hotels
have free city maps.

EurAide's information office, in the Bahnhof Zoo, provides a
great service. They have answers to all your questions about Berlin
or train travel around Europe. Staffed by Americans, communica-
tion is simple and they have a knack for predicting your needs and
then publishing free fliers to answer them (daily 10:00–18:00 with
a 12:00–13:00 lunch break in summer, off-season Mon–Sat 10:00–
16:30, closed Sun, at the back of station near lockers, great opportunity to get all future *couchette* reservations nailed ahead of time,
Prague Excursion passes available, www.euraide.de). EurAide also
sells one-day bus/metro passes and city maps (making a trip to the
TI probably unnecessary). To get the most out of EurAide, organize your questions and needs before your visit.

Arrival in Berlin

By Train at Bahnhof Zoo: Berlin's central station is called Bahnhof Zoologischer Garten (because it's near Berlin's famous zoo)... "Zoo" for short. Coming from Western Europe, you'll probably land at Zoo (rhymes with "toe"). It's small, well organized, and handy.

Upon arrival by train, orient yourself like this: Inside the station, follow signs to Hardenbergplatz. Step into this busy square filled with city buses, taxis, the transit office, and derelicts. "The Original Berlin Walks" start from the curb immediately outside the station at the top of the taxi stand (see "Tours of Berlin," below). Between you and the McDonald's across the street is the stop for bus #100 (departing to the right for the Do-It-Yourself Orientation Tour, described below). Turn right and tiptoe through the riffraff to the eight-lane highway, Hardenbergstrasse. Walk to the median strip and stand with your back to the tracks. Ahead you'll see the black, bombed-out hulk of the Kaiser Wilhelm Memorial Church and the Europa Center (Mercedes symbol spinning on roof), which houses the main TI. Just ahead on the left amid the traffic is the BVG transport information kiosk. (Buy a 8.70-DM day pass covering the subway and buses, and pick up a free subway map.) If you're facing the church, my recommended hotels are behind you to your right.

If you arrive at Berlin's other train stations (trains from most of Eastern Europe arrive at Ostbahnhof), no problem: Ride another train (fastest option) or the S-Bahn or U-Bahn (runs every few minutes) to Bahnhof Zoo and pretend you arrived here.

By Plane: See "Transportation Connections," below.

Getting around Berlin

Berlin's sights spread far and wide. Right from the start, commit yourself to the fine public transit system. The *On the Move* booklet (from BVG and EurAide) explains it all.

By Subway and Bus: The U-Bahn, S-Bahn, and all buses are consolidated into one "BVG" system that uses the same tickets. Here are your options:

• Basic ticket (*Einzel Fahrschein*) for two hours of travel on buses or subways (4 DM; *Erwachsener* means adult—anyone 14 or older).

• A day pass (*Tages Karte*) covering zones A and B—the city proper—8.70 DM, good till 03:00 the morning after. To get out to Potsdam you need a ticket covering zone C (9.90 DM). Small groups from three to five people should consider the all-day *Kleingruppenkarte* which costs 21 DM (25 DM to include Zone C for Potsdam).

• A cheap short-ride ticket (*Kurzstrecke Erwachsener*) for a single short ride of six bus stops or three subway stations, with one transfer (2.50 DM).

• Berlin/Potsdam WelcomeCard gives you three days of transportation and three days of minor sightseeing discounts (32 DM, valid for an adult and up to 3 kids—generally only worthwhile for traveling families).

Buy your tickets or cards from machines at U- or S-Bahn stations or at the BVG pavilion in front of Bahnhof Zoo. To use the machine, first select the type of ticket you want, then load in the coins or paper. Punch your ticket in a red or yellow clock machine to validate it (or risk a 60-DM fine). The double-decker buses are a joy (can buy ticket on bus) and the subway is a snap. The S-Bahn is free with a validated Eurailpass.

By Taxi: Taxis are easy to flag down, and taxi stands are common. A typical ride within town costs 15 DM. A local law designed to help people get safely and affordably home from their subway station late at night is handy for tourists any time of day: A short ride of no more than two kilometers is a flat 5 DM. (Ask for "*Kurzstrecke, fünf Mark, bitte.*")

By Bike: In western Berlin you can rent bikes at the Bahnhof Zoo; in the east, go to Fahhradstation at Hackesche Höfe (25 DM/day, Mon–Fri 10:00–19:00, Sat 10:00–16:00, closed Sun, Rosenthaler Strasse 40). Be careful, in Berlin motorists don't brake for bikers.

Helpful Hints

Most **museums** are closed on Monday. Save Monday for Berlin Wall sights, the Reichstag building, the Do-It-Yourself Orientation Tour (see below), walking/bus tours, churches, the zoo, or shopping along Kurfurstendamm (Ku'damm) Boulevard or at the Kaufhaus des Westens (KaDeWe) department store. (When Monday is a holiday—as it is several times a year—museums are open then and closed Tuesday.)

City museums—such as the Käthe Kollwitz Museum, Bröhan Museum, and Jewish Museum—are free on the first Sunday of each month. All **state museums**, including the Pergamon Museum and Gemäldegalerie (plus others noted in "Sights," below), are covered by one Museumspass (8 DM/1 day, 16 DM/3 consecutive days, not valid for special exhibitions, purchase at TI or participating museum).

Many **Berlin streets** are numbered with odd and even numbers on the same side of the street, often with no connection to the other side (i.e., Ku'damm #212 can be across the street from #14). To save steps, check the white street signs on curb corners; many list the street numbers covered on that side of the block.

Reiseburo im Europa Center specializes in **last-minute tickets** (e.g., fly to London tomorrow for 200 DM, next to TI in Europa Center, tel. 030/2655-1050, www.lastminuteflugboerse.de).

Do-It-Yourself Orientation Tour

Here's an easy ▲▲▲ introduction to Berlin. Half the tour is by bus; the other half is on foot. Berlin's bus #100 is a sightseer's dream, stopping at Bahnhof Zoo, Europa Center/Hotel Palace, Siegessäule, Reichstag, Brandenburg Gate, Unter den Linden, Pergamon Museum, and ending at Alexanderplatz. If you have the 33 DM and 90 minutes for a hop-on hop-off bus tour (described below), take that instead. But this short 4-DM tour is a fine city introduction. Buses leave from Hardenbergplatz in front of the Zoo Station (and nearly next door to the Europa Center TI, in front of Hotel Palace). Buses come every 10 minutes, and single tickets are good for two hours—so take advantage of hop on and off privileges. Climb aboard, stamp your ticket (giving it a time), and grab a seat on top. You could ride the bus all the way, but I'd get out at the Reichstag and walk to Alexanderplatz.

Part 1: By Bus #100 from Bahnhof Zoo to the Reichstag

(This is about a 10-minute ride.)

☛ Around the corner, then straight ahead, before descending into the tunnel, you'll see: the bombed-out hulk of the Kaiser Wilhelm Memorial Church, with its post-war sister church (described below) and the Europa Center. This is the west end shopping district with the big department stores nearby.

☛ At the stop in front of Hotel Palace: on the left, the Berlin Zoo entrance and its aquarium (described below).

☛ Driving down Kurfürstenstrasse, turning left into Tiergarten: The Victory Column (Siegessäule, with the gilded angel, described below), towers above a vast city park once a royal hunting grounds, now nicknamed the "green lungs of Berlin."

☛ On the left a block after leaving the Siegessäule: The 18th-century late-rococo Bellevue Palace is the German "White House," once a Nazi VIP guesthouse, now the residence of the federal president (whose "power" is mostly ceremonial). If the flag's out, he's in.

☛ Driving along the Spree River: This park area was a residential district before World War II. Now, on the left-hand side, it's filled with the buildings of the new national government. The huge brick "brown snake" complex was built to house government workers—but it didn't sell—so now its apartments are available to anyone. Beyond that is the new and huge chancellory. A Henry Moore sculpture floats in front of the slope-roofed House of World Cultures (left side, nicknamed "the pregnant oyster"). The modern tower (next on left) is a carillon with 68 bells (1987).

☛ While you could continue on bus #100, it's better on foot from here. Leap out at the House of World Cultures (Haus der Kulturen der Welt). Before you stands the Reichstag. Visit this and continue the walk below.

Berlin

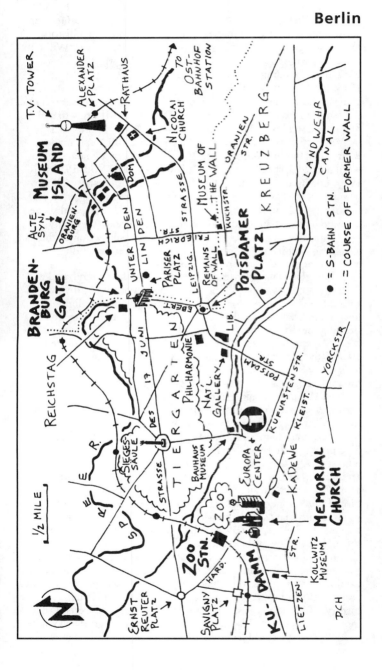

▲▲▲**Reichstag Building**—This building—the heart of German democracy—has a short but complicated and emotional history. When inaugurated in the 1890s, the last emperor, Kaiser Wilhelm, disdainfully called it the "house for chatting." It was from this Parliament building that the German Republic was proclaimed in 1918. In 1933 this symbol of democracy nearly burned down. It's believed Hitler planned the fire, using it as a handy excuse to frame the Communists and grab power. As World War II drew to a close, Stalin ordered his troops to take the Reichstag from the Nazis by May 1 (the worker's holiday). More than 1,500 Nazis made their last stand here—extending World War II by two days. On April 30, 1945, it fell to the Allies. It was not used from 1933 to 1999. For its 101st birthday, in 1995, the Bulgarian artist Christo wrapped it in silvery-gold cloth. It was then wrapped again in scaffolding, rebuilt by British architect Sir Norman Foster, and turned into the new parliamentary home of the Bundestag (Germany's lower house). To many Germans, the proud resurrection of the Reichstag—which no longer has a hint of Hitler—symbolizes the end of a terrible chapter in German history.

The **glass cupola** rises 48 meters above the ground, and a double staircase winds 230 meters to the top for a grand view. Inside the dome a cone of 360 mirrors reflects natural light into the legislative chamber. Lit from inside at night, this gives Berlin a memorable new night-light.

Visit the Reichstag (free, daily 8:00–22:00, most crowded 10:00–16:00, wait in line to go up—good street musicians, some hour-long English tours, tel. 030/2273-2152). As you approach the building, look above the door, surrounded by stone patches from WWII bomb damage, to see the motto and promise: *Dem Deutschen Volke* (to the German people). The open and airy lobby towers 30 meters (about 30 yards) high with 20-meter tall colors of the German flag. Glass doors show the **central chamber**. The message: there will be no secrets in government. Look inside. The seats are "Reichstag blue," a lilac blue color designed by the architect to brighten the otherwise gray interior. The German eagle (a.k.a. the "fat hen") spreads his wings behind the podium. Notice the doors marked "yes," "no," or "abstain" . . . the Bundestag's traditional "sheep jump" way of counting votes (for critical and close votes, all 669 members leave and vote by walking through the door of their choice).

Ride the elevator to the base of the glass dome. Take time to study the photos and read the circle of captions—an excellent exhibition telling the Reichstag story. Then study the surrounding architecture: a broken collage of old on new, like Germany's history. Notice the dome's giant and unobtrusive sunscreen that moves as necessary with the sun. Peer down through the skylight to look over the shoulders of the elected representatives at work.

For Germans, the best view is down—keeping a close eye on their government.

Wind up to the top of the double staircase. Take a 360-degree survey of the city as you hike: First, the big park is the Tiergarten, the "green lung" of Berlin. Beyond that is the Teufelsberg—Devil's Hill (built of rubble from the bombed city in the late 1940s and famous during the Cold War as a powerful ear of the West—notice the telecommunications tower on top). Given the violent and tragic history of Berlin, a city blown apart by bombs and covered over by bulldozers, locals say, "You have to be suspicious when you see the nice green park." Find the Seigessäule, the Victory Column (moved by Hitler in the 1930s from in front of the Reichstag to its present position in the Tiergarten). Next, scenes of the new Berlin spiral into your view—Potsdamer Platz marked with the conical glass tower that houses Sony's European headquarters. The yellow building to the right is the Berlin Philharmonic Concert Hall. Continue circling left, and find the green chariot atop the Brandenburg Gate. A monument to the Gypsy Holocaust will be built between the Reichstag and Brandenburg Gate. (Gypsies, as disdained by the Nazis as the Jews, lost the same percentage of their population to Hitler.) Next, you'll see former East Berlin and what will become the city's next huge construction zone, with a forest of 100-meter-tall skyscrapers in the works. Notice the TV tower (with the Pope's Revenge—explained below), the Berlin Cathedral's massive dome, the red tower of the city hall, the golden dome of the New Synagogue, and the Reichstag's roof garden restaurant (Dachgarten, 25-DM meals with a view, open until 17:00, tel. 030/2262-9933). Follow the train tracks in the distance to the left toward a huge construction zone marking the future central Berlin train station. Complete your spin tour with the blocky Chancellory. It may look like a pharaoh's tomb, but it's the office of Germany's most powerful person, the Chancellor and his team.

Part 2: Walking Tour from Brandenburg Gate up Unter den Linden to Alexanderplatz

Allow a comfortable hour for this walk through Eastern Berlin, including time for dawdling but not museum stops.

▲▲**Brandenburg Gate**—The historic Brandenburg Gate (1791, the last survivor of 14 gates in Berlin's old city wall), crowned by a majestic four-horse chariot with the Goddess of Peace at the reins, was the symbol of Berlin and then the symbol of divided Berlin. Napoleon took the statue to the Louvre in Paris in 1806. When the Prussians got it back, she was renamed the Goddess of Victory. The gate sat, part of a sad circle dance called The Wall, for more than 25 years. (TI within gate, open daily 9:30–18:00.)

Now postcards all over town show the ecstatic day—November 9, 1989—when the world enjoyed the sight of happy

Berliners jamming the gate like flowers on a parade float. Pause a minute and think about struggles for freedom—past and present.

▲**Pariser Platz**—From Brandenburg Gate, face Pariser Platz (into the east). Unter den Linden leads to the TV tower in the distance (the end of this walk). The space used to be filled with important government buildings—all bombed to smithereens. Today, Pariser Platz is unrecognizable from the deserted no-man's land it became under the Communist regime. Sparkling new banks, embassies (the French embassy rebuilt where it was pre–World War II), and a swanky hotel have filled in the void.

Crossing through the Gate, look to your right to a stretch of empty land—formerly the "death strip." The U.S. Embassy once stood here. Plans to rebuild it here are stalled because of new American setbacks for embassy safety requirements. The new Holocaust memorial (probably under construction in 2001) will stand behind that.

Brandenburg Gate, the center of old Berlin, sits on a major boulevard, running east-west through Berlin. The western segment, called Strasse des 17 Juni, stretches for 10 miles from the Siegessäule to the Olympic Stadium. For our walk, we'll follow this city axis in the opposite direction, east, up what is known as Unter den Linden, into the core of old imperial Berlin and past what was once the palace of the Hohenzollern family of Prussia, and then of Germany's imperial rulers. The palace—the reason for just about all you'll see—is a phantom sight...long gone.

▲▲**Unter den Linden**—This is the heart of former East Berlin. In Berlin's good old days, Unter den Linden was one of Europe's grand boulevards. In the 15th century, this horseway led from the palace to the hunting grounds (today's big park). In the 17th century, Hohenzollern princes and princesses moved in and built their palaces here so they could be near the Prussian emperor.

Named centuries ago for its thousand linden trees, this was the most elegant street of Prussian Berlin before Hitler's time and the main drag of East Berlin after his reign. Hitler replaced the venerable trees—many 250 years old—with Nazi flags. Popular discontent actually drove him to replant linden trees. Today Unter den Linden is no longer a depressing Cold War cul-de-sac, and its pre-Hitler strolling café ambience is returning.

As you walk toward the giant TV tower, the first big building you see on your right is the **Hotel Adlon**. It hosted such notables as Charlie Chaplin, Albert Einstein, and Greta Garbo. (This was where Garbo said, "I want to be alone," during the filming of *Grand Hotel*.) Destroyed in World War II, the grand Adlon was rebuilt in 1996. See how far you can get inside.

On your right, several doors down (past the S-Bahn station), is the **Russian embassy** (guarded by German police)—not quite as important now as it was a few years ago, but immense as ever. It

Unter den Linden

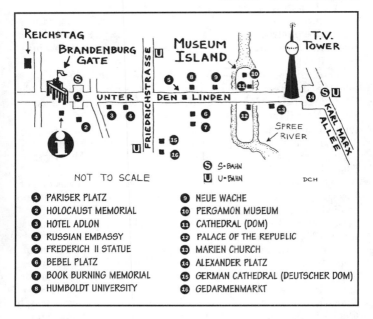

REICHSTAG
BRANDENBURG GATE
FRIEDRICHSTRASSE
MUSEUM ISLAND
T.V. TOWER
UNTER DEN LINDEN
SPREE RIVER
KARL MARX ALLEE
NOT TO SCALE

S S-BAHN
U U-BAHN
DCH

1 PARISER PLATZ
2 HOLOCAUST MEMORIAL
3 HOTEL ADLON
4 RUSSIAN EMBASSY
5 FREDERICH II STATUE
6 BEBEL PLATZ
7 BOOK BURNING MEMORIAL
8 HUMBOLDT UNIVERSITY

9 NEUE WACHE
10 PERGAMON MUSEUM
11 CATHEDRAL (DOM)
12 PALACE OF THE REPUBLIC
13 MARIEN CHURCH
14 ALEXANDER PLATZ
15 GERMAN CATHEDRAL (DEUTSCHER DOM)
16 GEDARMENMARKT

flies the Russian white, red, and blue. Find the hammer-and-sickle motif decorating the window frames. Continuing past the Aeroflot Airline offices, you come to the back of the Komische Oper (comic opera, program, and view of ornate interior posted in window). While the exterior is ugly, the fine old theater interior, amazingly missed by WWII bombs, survives.

The West lost no time in consuming the East; consequently, some are feeling a wave of nostalgia—**Ost-algia**—for the old days of East Berlin. But one symbol of that era has been given a reprieve. At Friedrichstrasse, look at the DDR–style pedestrian lights and you'll realize someone had a sense of humor back then. The perky red and green men—*Ampelmannchen*—were under threat of replacement by the far less jaunty Western signs. Fortunately, the DDR lights will be kept after all.

At **Friedrichstrasse**, look right. Before the war, the Unter den Linden/Friedrichstrasse intersection was the heart of Berlin. In the '20s this was the cabaret drag, a springboard to stardom for young and vampy entertainers like Marlene Dietrich. Today, this boulevard, lined with super department stores (like Galeries Lafayette—with its cool marble and glass waste-of-space interior) and big-time hotels (like Hilton and Four Seasons)—hopes to replace Ku'damm as the grand commerce and café boulevard of Berlin. Unfortunately, no one expects the new Friedrichstrasse to have the café/strolling ambience of the old one. It's a no-man's-land after dark.

Continue down Unter den Linden a few more blocks, past the large equestrian statue of **Frederick II** ("the Great"), and turn right into the square (Bebelplatz). Stand on the glass window in the center.

Frederick the Great—who ruled from 1740 to 1786— established Prussia as a military power. This square was center of Frederick's Berlin. Much of Frederick's palace actually survived World War II but was torn down by the Communists since it symbolized the imperialist past.

Look around: **Bebelplatz** is bounded by the German State Opera, former state library, and the round Catholic St. Hedwig's Church.

Humboldt University (across Unter den Linden) was one of Europe's greatest. Marx and Lenin (not the brothers or the sisters) studied here along with Grimm (both brothers) and 22 Nobel Prize winners. Einstein taught here until taking a spot at Princeton in 1932 (smart guy).

Look down through the glass you're standing on: The room of empty bookshelves is a memorial to the notorious Nazi **book burning**. It was on this square in 1933 that staff and students from the university threw 20,000 newly forbidden books (like Einstein's) into a huge bonfire on the orders of the Nazi propaganda minister Joseph Goebbels. Continue down Unter den Linden. The next square on your right holds the Opernpalais' restaurants (see "Eating," below).

On the university side of Unter den Linden, the Greek templelike building is the **Neue Wache** (New Guardhouse, from 1816). When the Wall fell, this memorial to the victims of fascism was transformed into a new national memorial. Look inside where a replica of the Käthe Kollwitz statue, *Mother with Her Dead Son*, is surrounded by thought-provoking silence. The inscription in front reads, "To the victims of war and tyranny."

Just before the bridge (where the pink German History Museum will reopen in 2002), wander left along the canal through the tiny but colorful flea market (weekends only). Canal tour boats leave from here.

Cross the bridge to **Museum Island**, home of Germany's first museums and today famous for its Pergamon Museum (described below). The museum complex starts with an imposing neoclassical facade on the left (a musty museum of antiquities). For 300 years the square has flip-flopped between military parade ground and people-friendly park. In 1999 it was made into a park again.

The towering church (ahead, before the next bridge) is the 100-year-old **Berlin Cathedral**, or *Dom* (8 DM, 10 DM including access to the dome, organ concerts offered most Wed, Thu, and Fri at 15:00 for free with regular admission). Inside, the great reformers stand around the brilliantly restored dome like stern saints guarding their theology. Frederick I rests in an ornate tomb (right transept, near entry to dome). The crypt downstairs is not worth a look.

Across the street is the **Palace of the Republic** (with the copper-tinted windows). A symbol of the Communist days, it was East Berlin's parliament building and futuristic entertainment complex. Although it officially has a date with the wrecking ball, many easterners want it saved, and its future is still uncertain.

Before crossing the next bridge (and leaving Museum Island), look right. The pointy twin spires of the 13th-century Nikolai Church mark the center of medieval Berlin. This *Nikolai-Viertel* (district) was restored by the DDR and was trendy in the last years of socialism. Today it's dull and, with limited time, not worth a visit.

As you cross the bridge, look left in the distance to see the gilded **New Synagogue**, rebuilt after WWII bombing (described below).

Walk toward **Marien Church** (from 1270, interesting but very faded old *Dance of Death* mural inside door) at the base of the TV tower. The big, red brick building past the trees on the right is the city hall, built after the revolution of 1848 and arguably the first democratic building in the city.

The 400-meter-tall **Fernsehturm (TV Tower)** offers a fine view from 200 meters (9 DM, daily 9:00–01:00). Consider a kitchsy trip to the top for the view and lunch in its revolving restaurant. Built (with Swedish know-how) in 1969, the tower was meant to show the power of the atheistic state at a time when DDR leaders were having the crosses removed from church domes and spires. But when the sun shines on their tower, the greatest spire in East Berlin, a huge cross reflects on the mirrored ball. Cynics called it "The Pope's Revenge."

Farther east, pass under the train tracks into **Alexanderplatz**. This, especially the Kaufhof, was the commercial pride and joy of East Berlin. Today it's still a landmark, with a major U-Bahn and S-Bahn station.

For a ride through workaday eastern Berlin, with its Lego-hell apartments (dreary even with their new face-lifts), hop back on bus #100 from here. It loops five minutes to the end of the line and then, after a couple minutes break, heads on back. (This bus retraces your route, finishing back at Bahnhof Zoo.) Consider extending this foray into eastern Berlin to Karl Marx Allee (described below).

Tours of Berlin
▲▲▲**City Walking Tours**—"The Original Berlin Walks" offers a variety of worthwhile tours led by enthusiastic guides who are native English speakers. The company, run by Englishman Nick Gay, offers a three-hour "Discover Berlin" introductory walk daily

at 10:00 (all year) and 14:30 (April–Oct) for 18 DM (14 DM if you're under 26). Just show up at the taxi rank in front of Zoo Station. Their high-quality, high-energy guides also offer tours of "Infamous Third Reich Sites," most mornings in high season at 10:00, "Jewish Life in Berlin," and Potsdam. Many of the Third Reich and Jewish history sites are difficult to pin down without these excellent walks. Confirm the schedule at EurAide or by phone with Nick or his wife and partner Serena (private tours also available, tel. 030/301-9194, www.berlinwalks.com).

▲**City Bus Tours**—For bus tours you have two choices:
1) Full-blown, three-hour bus tours. Contact Severin & Kühn (39 DM, live guides in 2 languages, daily 10:00 and 14:00, 2/day in summer, from Ku'damm 216, tel. 030/880-4190) or take BVG buses from Ku'damm 225 (tel. 030/885-9880).
2) Hop-on hop-off circle tours. Several companies do the "City-Circle Sightseeing" tour. The tour offers unlimited hop-on hop-off privileges for its 12-stop route (33 DM, 2/hrly, 2-hr loop, April–October, taped guides, frequent buses). The TI has the brochures. Just hop on where you like and pay the driver. On a sunny day when the double-decker buses go topless, these are a photographer's delight.

Sights—Western Berlin

Western travelers still think of Berlin's "West End" as the heart of the city. While it's no longer that, the West End still has the best infrastructure to support your visit and works well as a home base. Here are a few sights within an easy walk of your hotel and the Zoo station.

▲**Kurfürstendamm**—In the 1850s, when Berlin became a wealthy and important capital, her new rich chose Kurfürsten-damm as their street. Bismarck made it Berlin's Champs-Élysées. In the 1920s it became a chic and fashionable drag of cafés and boutiques. During the Third Reich, as home to an international community of diplomats and journalists, it enjoyed more freedom than the rest of Berlin. Throughout the Cold War, economic subsidies from the West made sure that capitalism thrived on Ku'damm, as western Berlin's main drag is popularly called. And today, while much of the old charm has been hamburgerized, Ku'damm is still a fine place to feel the pulse of the city and enjoy the elegant shops (around Fasanenstrasse), department stores, and people watching. Ku'damm, starting at Kaiser Wilhelm Memorial Church, does its commercial cancan for two miles.

▲**Kaiser Wilhelm Memorial Church (Gedächtniskirche)**—The church was originally a memorial to the first emperor of Germany, who died in 1888. Its bombed-out ruins have been left standing as a memorial to the destruction of Berlin in World War II. Under a fine mosaic ceiling, a small exhibit features interesting

Western Berlin

photos about the bombing (free, Mon–Sat 10:00–16:00, closed Sun). Next to it, a new church (1961) offers a world of 11,000 little blue windows. The blue glass was given to the church by the French as a reconciliation gift. The lively square between this and the Europa Center (a shiny high-rise shopping center built as a showcase of Western capitalism during the Cold War) usually attracts street musicians.

▲**Käthe Kollwitz Museum**—This local artist (1867–1945), who experienced much of Berlin's stormiest century, conveys some powerful and mostly sad feelings about motherhood, war, and suffering through the black-and-white faces of her art (8 DM, Wed–Mon 11:00–18:00, closed Tue, free on first Sun of month, a block off Ku'damm at Fasanenstrasse 24).

▲**Kaufhaus des Westens (KaDeWe)**—The "department store of the West," with a staff of 2,400 to help you sort through its vast selection of 380,000 items, is the biggest department store

on the Continent. You can get everything from a haircut and
train ticket to souvenirs (third floor). A cyber bar is on the fourth
floor (5 DM/30 min). The theater and concert box office on the
sixth floor charges an 18 percent booking fee, but they know all
your options. The sixth floor is also a world of gourmet taste
treats. This biggest selection of deli and exotic food in Germany
offers plenty of classy opportunities to sit down and eat. Ride the
glass elevator to the seventh floor's glass-domed Winter Garden
self-service cafeteria—fun but pricey (Mon–Fri 9:30–20:00,
Sat 9:00–16:00, closed Sun, tel. 030/21210, U-Bahn: Wittenbergplatz). The Wittenbergplatz U-Bahn station (in front of
KaDeWe) is a unique opportunity to see an old-time station in
Berlin. Enjoy its interior.

Berlin Zoo—More than 1,400 different kinds of animals call
Berlin's famous zoo home—or so the zookeepers like to think.
Germans enjoy seeing the pandas at play (straight in from the
entry). I enjoy seeing the Germans at play (13 DM for zoo or
world-class aquarium, 21 DM for both, children half price, daily
9:00–18:30, feeding times—*Fütterungszeiten*—posted on map just
inside entry, enter near Europa Center in front of Hotel Palace,
Budapester Strasse 32, tel. 030/254-010).

Erotic Art Museum—This offers three floors of graphic (mostly
18th-century) Oriental art, a tiny theater showing erotic silent
movies from the early 1900s, and a special exhibit on the queen
of German pornography, Beate Uhse. This amazing woman, a
former test pilot for the Third Reich and ground-breaking
purveyor of condoms and sex ed in the 1950s, is now the female
Hugh Hefner of Germany and CEO of a huge chain of porn
shops. If you're traveling far and are sightseeing selectively, the
sex museums in Amsterdam or Copenhagen are much better.
This one, while well described in English, is little more than
prints and posters (10 DM, daily 9:00–24:00, hard-to-beat gift
shop, at corner of Kantstrasse and Joachimstalerstrasse, a block
from Bahnhof Zoo). If you just want to see sex, you'll see much
more for half the price in a private video booth next door.

Sights—Central Berlin

Hitler and The Third Reich—While many come to Berlin to see
Hitler sights, these are essentially invisible. The German Resistance
Museum (described below) is in German only and difficult for the
tourist to appreciate. The Topography of Terror (Gestapo headquarters) is a fascinating exhibit but—again—only in German, and
all that remains of the building is its foundation. "Hitler's Bunker" is
completely gone and built over. Your best bet for "Hitler sights" is
to take the "Infamous Third Reich Sites" walking tour offered by
Berlin Walks (see "City Walking Tours," above). EurAide has a
good flier listing and explaining sights related to the Third Reich.

Tiergarten/Siegessäule—Berlin's "Central Park" stretches two miles from Bahnhof Zoo to Brandenburg Gate. Its centerpiece, the Siegessäule (Victory Column), was built to commemorate the Prussian defeat of France in 1870. The pointy-helmeted Germans rubbed it in, decorating the tower with French cannons and paying for it all with francs received as war reparations. The three lower rings commemorate Bismarck's victories. I imagine the statues of Moltke and other German military greats goose-stepping around the floodlit angel at night. Originally standing at the Reichstag, the Siegessäule was moved to this position by Hitler to complement his anticipated victory parades. Climbing its 285 steps earns you a fine Berlin-wide view (2 DM, Mon–Thu 9:30–18:30, Fri–Sun 9:30–19:00, bus #100). From the tower, the grand Strasse des 17 Juni (named for a workers' uprising against the DDR government in the 1950s) leads to the Brandenburg Gate.

German Resistance Memorial (Gedenkstätte Deutscher Widerstand)—This memorial and museum tells the story of the German resistance to Hitler. The Benderblock was a military headquarters where an ill-fated attempt to assassinate Hitler was plotted. Stauffenberg and his co-conspirators were shot in the courtyard. While explanations are in German only, the spirit that haunts the place is multilingual (free, Mon–Fri 9:00–18:00, Thu until 20:00, Sat–Sun 10:00–18:00, printed English translation for sale, just south of Tiergarten at Stauffenbergstrasse 13, bus #129, tel. 030/2699-5000).

▲**Potsdamer Platz**—The Times Square of Berlin and possibly the busiest square in Europe before World War II, it was cut in two by the Wall and left a deserted no-man's-land for 40 years. This immense commercial/residential/entertainment center (with the European corporate headquarters of Sony and others) sitting on a futuristic transportation hub was a vision begun in 1991 when it was announced that Berlin would resume its position as capital of Germany. Sony, Daimler-Chrysler, and other huge corporations have turned it once again into a center of Berlin. Stroll the arcade (like any huge modern American mall) and find the Sony Center Platz under the towering tent roof. The "Sony Music Box" is a huge interactive center for music fun.

Sights—Kulturforum, in Central Berlin

Just off Potsdamer Platz, with several top museums and Berlin's concert hall, is the city's cultural heart (admission to all sights covered by 8-DM day card, free on first Sun of month, S- and U-Bahn: Potsdamer Platz). Of its sprawling museums, only the Gemäldegalerie is a must.

▲▲▲**Gemäldegalerie**—Germany's top collection of 13th-through 18th-century European paintings (over a thousand canvases) is beautifully displayed in a building which is a work of art in itself. The central hall is part medieval (like three parallel naves) and part Renaissance (pillars converge as they move toward the back wall, giving the place the illusion of greater depth—a trick popular with the Renaissance artists). Follow the excellent and free audioguide. The North Wing starts with German paint- ings of the 13th to 16th centuries—including eight by Dürer. Then come the Dutch and Flemish—Jan van Eyck, Brueghel, Rubens, Van Dyck, Hals, and Vermeer. The wing finishes with German, English, and French 18th-century art—Gainsborough and Watteau. An octagonal hall at the end features one of the best collections of Rembrandts anywhere. The South Wing is saved for the Italians—Giotto, Botticelli, Titian, Raphael, and Caravaggio (8 DM, covered by Museumspass, Tue–Sun 10:00– 18:00, closed Mon, S- and U-Bahn: Potsdamer Platz, or bus #200 to Philharmonie).

New National Gallery (Neue Nationalgalerie)—This features 20th-century art (8 DM, covered by Museumspass, Tue–Fri 10:00–18:00, Sat–Sun 11:00–18:00, closed Mon, Potsdamer Strasse 50, tel. 030/266-2662).

Museum of Arts and Crafts (Kunstgewerbemuseum)— This shows off a thousand years of applied arts—porcelain, fine Jugendstil furniture, art deco, and reliquaries. There are no crowds and no English descriptions (4 DM, covered by Museumspass, Tue–Fri 10:00–18:00, Sat–Sun 11:00–18:00, closed Mon). The huge National Library is across the courtyard (free, English periodicals).

▲**Music Museum**—This impressive hall is filled with 600 exhibits from the 16th century to modern times. Wander among old key- board instruments and funny-looking tubas. There's no English, but it's fascinating if you're into pianos (4 DM, Tue–Fri 9:00– 17:00, Sat–Sun 10:00–17:00, closed Mon, facing the Philharmonic Concert Hall, circle around to left, tel. 030/254-810). Poke into the lobby of Berlin's Philharmonic Concert Hall and see if there are tickets available for your stay (must purchase tickets in person, box office tel. 030/2548-8132).

Sights—Eastern Berlin

▲▲**Pergamon Museum**—Of the museums on Museumsinsel (Museum Island), just off Unter den Linden, only the Pergamon Museum is essential. Its highlight is the fantastic Pergamon Altar. From a second-century B.C. Greek temple, it shows the Greeks under Zeus and Athena beating the giants in a dramatic pig pile of mythological mayhem. Check out the action spilling onto the stairs. The Babylonian Ishtar Gate (glazed blue tiles from sixth century B.C.) and many ancient Greek and Mesopotamian trea- sures are also impressive (8 DM, covered by Museumspass, free

Eastern Berlin

on first Sun of month, Tue–Sun 10:00–18:00, Thu until 22:00, closed Mon, café, tel. 030/2090-5555). The excellent audioguide (free with admission) cover the museum's highlights.

Old National Gallery—Also on the museum island, this gallery shows German paintings of the 19th century (closed for renovation until Dec 2001).

▲▲**The Berlin Wall**—The 100-mile "Anti-Fascist Protective Rampart," as it was called by the East German government, was erected almost overnight in 1961 to stop the outward flow of people (3 million leaked out between 1949 and 1961). It was 13 feet high with a 16-foot tank ditch, 30 to 160 feet of no-man's-land, and 300 sentry towers. In its 28 years there were 1,693 cases when border guards fired, more than 250 deaths, 3,221 arrests, and 5,043 documented successful escapes (565 of these were East German guards). The carnival atmosphere of those first years after the Wall fell has faded away, but hawkers still sell "authentic" pieces of the Wall, DDR (East German) flags, and military paraphernalia to gawking tourists.

▲▲▲**Haus am Checkpoint Charlie Museum**—While the famous border checkpoint between the American and Soviet sectors is long gone, its memory is preserved by one of Europe's most interesting museums: The House at Checkpoint Charlie. During the Cold War it stood defiantly—spitting distance from the border guards—showing off all the clever escapes over, under, and through the Wall.

Today, while the drama is over and hunks of the Wall stand like victory scalps at its door, the museum still tells a gripping history of the Wall, recounts the many ingenious escape attempts, and includes plenty of video and film coverage of those heady days when people-power tore down the Wall (10 DM, daily 9:00–22:00, U-Bahn to Kochstrasse, Friedrichstrasse 44, tel. 030/253-7250). If you're pressed for time, this is a good after-dinner sight.

Americans and Russians, the major forces behind the Cold War, have the biggest appetite for Wall-related sights. Where the gate once stood, notice the thought-provoking post with a young American soldier facing east and a young Russian soldier facing west. What do their young faces tell us? A few meters away (on Zimmerstrasse) a glass panel describes the former Checkpoint. From there a double row of cobbles in Zimmerstrasse marks where the Wall once stood. Follow it down Zimmerstrasse to a surviving stretch of Wall.

When it fell, the Wall was literally carried away by the euphoria. What survived has been nearly devoured by a decade of persistent "wall peckers." The park behind the Zimmerstrasse Wall marks the site of the command center of Hitler's Gestapo and SS (explained by English plaques throughout). It's been left undeveloped as a memorial to the tyranny once headquartered here. In the park is ...

The Topography of Terror—Now temporarily housed in the excavated foundations of the Gestapo and SS buildings, this exhibit tells the story of National Socialism and its victims in Berlin (free, info booth open daily 10:00–18:00, English translation-2 DM, tel. 030/2548-6703).

East Side Gallery—The biggest remaining stretch of the Wall is now "the world's longest art gallery." It stretches for a mile and is covered with murals painted by artists from around the world. The murals are routinely whitewashed so new ones can be painted. This length of the Wall makes a poignant walk. From Schlesisches Tor (end of Kreuzberg), walk across the river on the bridge, turn left, and follow the Wall to the Ostbahnhof. For a quick look, just go to Ostbahnhof station and look around. The gallery only survives until a land ownership dispute can be solved when it will likely be developed like the rest of the city. (Given the recent history, imagine the complexity of finding rightful owners of all this suddenly very valuable land.)

Kreuzberg—This district—once butted against the dreary Wall and inhabited largely by poor Turkish guest laborers and their families—is still run-down, with graffiti-riddled buildings and plenty of student and Turkish street life. It offers a great look at melting-pot Berlin in a city where original Berliners are as rare as old buildings. Berlin is the fourth-largest Turkish city in the world, and Kreuzberg is its "downtown." But to call it a "little Istanbul" insults the big one. You'll see mothers wearing scarves, *döner kebab* stands, and spray paint–decorated shops. For a dose of Kreuzberg without getting your fingers dirty, joyride on bus #129. For a colorful stroll, take U-bahn to Kottbusser Tor and wander— ideally on Tuesday and Friday from 12:00 to 18:00, when the Turkish Market sprawls along the bank of the Maybachufer Canal.

▲▲**German Cathedral**—The Deutscher Dom houses the great and thought-provoking "Questions on German History" exhibit, a wonderful coverage of the story of German nationalism from medieval times to unification. It's impressive how openly and honestly Germany is dealing with its fascist past. There are no English descriptions, but you can follow a fine and free hour-long audio- guide or buy the excellent 10-DM book (free, Tue–Sun 10:00– 18:00, summer until 19:00, closed Mon, on Gendarmenmarkt just off Friedrichstrasse, tel. 030/2273-2141).

▲▲**New Synagogue**—A shiny gilded dome marks the New Synagogue, now a museum and cultural center on Oranienburger Strasse. Only the dome and facade have been restored, and a window overlooks a vacant field marking what used to be the synagogue. The largest and finest synagogue in Berlin before World War II, it was desecrated by Nazis on "Crystal Night" in 1938, bombed in 1943, and partially rebuilt in 1990. Inside, past tight security, there's a small but moving exhibit on the Berlin Jewish community through the centuries with some good English descriptions (ground floor and first floor). The *Vergesst es nie* message on its facade means "Never forget." It was put up by East Berlin Jews in 1966. East Berlin had only a few hundred Jews, but now that the city is united, the Jewish community numbers about 10,000 (8 DM, Sun–Thu 10:00–18:00, Fri 10:00–14:00, closed Sat, at Oranienburger Tor U-Bahn stop). Oren, a popular near- kosher café, is next to the synagogue (see "Eating," below). Note: If you're heading for the Pergamon Museum, take the shortcut (leaving synagogue, turn left, then right on Monbijoustrasse, cross canal, and turn left to museum).

A block from the Synagogue, go 50 meters down Grosse Hamburger Strasse to a little park. This street was known for 200 years as the "street of tolerance" for its many religions. Hitler turned it into the street of death (*Todes Strasse*), bulldozing 12,000 graves of the city's oldest Jewish cemetery and turning a Jewish old-folks home into a deportation center. Note the two memorials—one erected by the former East Berlin government and one built later by the city's unified government. Somewhere nearby, a plainclothes police officer keeps watch on this park.

▲**Oranienburger Strasse**—Berlin is developing so fast it's impossible to predict what will be "in" next year. The area around Oranienburger Strasse is definitely trendy (but is being challenged by hip Friedrichshain farther east).

While the area immediately around the Synagogue is dull, 100 meters away things get colorful. The streets behind Grosse Hamburger Strasse flicker with atmospheric cafés, *Kneipen* (pubs), and art galleries.

At night "techno-prostitutes" line Oranienburger Strasse. Prostitution is legal here, but there's a big debate about taxation. Since they don't get unemployment insurance, why should they pay taxes?

A block in front of the Hackescher Markt S-Bahn station is Hackesche Höfe—with eight courtyards bunny-hopping through a wonderfully restored 1907 Jugendstil building. It's full of trendy restaurants, theaters, and cinema (playing movies in their original languages). This is a fine example of how to make huge city blocks livable—Berlin's apartments are organized around courtyard after courtyard off the main roads.

Jewish Museum Berlin—Berlin's new Jewish museum opens in October 2001. The striking zinc-walled building (built 1993–1998) is already drawing crowds. Designed by the American architect Daniel Libeskind, the building's zigzag shape is pierced by voids symbolic of the irreplaceable cultural loss caused by the Holocaust. While it promises to be a great museum, it's in a nondescript neighborhood a 10-minute walk from the Checkpoint Charlie museum. Unless you're an architect, see the wonderful exhibits at the New Synagogue before trekking out here (Lindenstrasse 9).

Karl Marx Allee—The buildings along Karl Marx Allee in east Berlin (just beyond Alexanderplatz) were completely leveled by the Soviets in 1945. When Stalin decided this main drag should be a showcase street, he had it rebuilt with lavish Soviet aid and named Stalin Allee. Today, this street, done in the bold Stalin Gothic style so common in Moscow back in the 1950s, has been restored (and named after Karl Marx), providing a rare look at Berlin's communist days. Cruise down Karl Marx Allee by taxi or ride the U-bahn to Strausberger Platz and walk to Schillingstrasse. You might cap the experience with a stop at the ice cream shop across the street from the Moskwa restaurant—it was an institution in communist times.

Natural History Museum (Museum für Naturkunde)—This place is worth a visit just to see the largest dinosaur skeleton ever assembled. While you're there, meet "Bobby," the stuffed ape (5 DM, Tue–Sun 9:30–17:00, closed Mon, U-6 to Zinnowitzer Strasse, at Invalidenstrasse 43).

Sights—Around Charlottenburg Palace

The Charlottenburg District—with a cluster of fine museums across the street from a grand palace—makes a good side trip from downtown. Ride U-1 to Sophie-Charlotte Platz and walk 10 minutes up the tree-lined boulevard (following signs to "Schloss"), or—much faster—catch bus #145 direct from Bahnhof Zoo. For a Charlottenburg lunch, the Luisen Brau is a comfortable brew-pub restaurant with a copper and woody atmosphere, good local "microbeers" (*dunkles*—dark, *helles*—light), and traditional German grub (10-DM meals, fun for groups, daily 9:00–24:00, across from palace at Luisenplatz 1, tel. 030/341-9388).

▲**Charlottenburg Palace (Schloss)**—If you've seen the great palaces of Europe, this Baroque Hohenzollern palace comes in at about number 10 (behind Potsdam, too). It's even more disappointing since the main rooms can be toured only with a German guide (8 DM, 45-minute tour, Tue–Fri 10:00–18:00, Sat–Sun 11:00–18:00, closed Mon, tel. 030/3209-1275).

The **Knöbelsdorff Wing** of the palace is used for two painting galleries. Facing the palace, walk to the right wing where one desk sells tickets to two galleries. For a quick look at a few royal apartments, go upstairs (5 DM) and take a substantial hike through restored-since-the-war, gold-crusted, white rooms filled with Frederick the Great's not-so-great collection of Baroque paintings. The ground floor of the Knöbelsdorff wing is the **Galerie der Romantik**, a delightful collection of 19th-century German Romantic art: man against nature, Greek ruins dwarfed in enchanted forests, medieval churches, and powerful mountains (5 DM, covered by Museumspass).

▲▲**Egyptian Museum**—Across the street from the palace, the Egyptian Museum offers one of the great thrills in art appreciation—gazing into the still-young and beautiful face of 3,000-year-old Queen Nefertiti, the wife of King Akhenaton (8 DM, covered by Museumspass, Tue–Sun 10:00–18:00, closed Mon, Schlosstrasse 70).

This bust of Queen Nefertiti, from 1340 B.C., is perhaps the most famous piece of Egyptian art in Europe. Discovered in 1912, she was the Marilyn Monroe of the early 20th century, with all the right beauty marks: long neck, symmetrical face, and just the right makeup. The bust never left its studio but served as a master model for all other portraits of the queen. (That's probably why the left eye was never inlaid.) Buried over 3,000 years, she was found by a German team who, by agreement with the Egyptian

Charlottenburg Palace Area

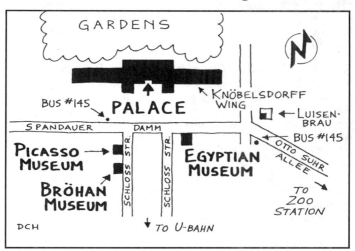

government, got to take home any workshop models they found. Although this bust is not representative of Egyptian art, it's become a symbol for Egyptian art by popular acclaim. Don't overlook the rest of the impressive museum: wonderfully lit and displayed but with little English.

▲▲**Berggruen Collection: Picasso and His Time**—This tidy little museum is a pleasant surprise. Climb three floors through a fun and substantial collection of Picasso. Along the way you'll see plenty of notable work by Matisse, van Gogh, and Cézanne, and enjoy a great chance to meet Paul Klee (8 DM, covered by Museumspass, Tue–Fri 10:00–18:00, Sat–Sun 11:00–18:00, closed Mon, tel. 030/2090-5566).

▲**Bröhan Museum**—Wander through a dozen beautifully furnished Art Nouveau (Jugendstil) and art deco living rooms, a curvy organic world of lamps, glass, silver, and posters. While you're there, go to the second floor to see a fine collection of Impressionist paintings by Karl Hagemeister (6 DM, free first Sun of month, Tue–Sun 10:00–18:00, closed Mon, next to Egyptian Museum, across street from Charlottenburg Palace).

Sights—Near Berlin

▲**Sanssouci Palace and Park, Potsdam**—With a lush park strewn with the extravagant whimsies of Frederick the Great, the sleepy town of Potsdam has long been Berlin's holiday retreat. Frederick's super-rococo Sanssouci Palace is one of Germany's most dazzling. His equally extravagant New Palace (Neues Palais), built to disprove rumors that Prussia was running out of money after the costly Seven Years' War, is on the other side of the park. While Potsdam is easy to reach (30 min direct on S-Bahn from Bahnhof Zoo to Potsdam Stadt), Sanssouci Palace can be visited only by German-language tour—which can be booked for hours (unless you take TI tour; see below). The palaces of Vienna, Munich, and even Würzburg offer equal sightseeing thrills with fewer headaches. Even though *Sanssouci* means "without a care," get your appointment immediately upon arrival so you know how much time to kill or if you need to come back and try again tomorrow (Sanssouci: 10 DM, Tue–Sun 9:00–12:30, 13:00–17:00, closed Mon, shorter hours off-season, tel. 0331/969-4190; New Palace: 8 DM, Sat–Thu 9:00–12:30, 13:00–17:00, closed Fri). Sanssouci Palace and the New Palace are a 30-minute walk apart.

Potsdam's TI offers a handy walking tour that includes Sanssouci Palace (39 DM covers guided German/English tour of palace park and admission and tour of Sanssouci without any wait, 11:00 except Mon, 5-minute walk from S-Bahn stop, depart from Film Museum in downtown Potsdam, 3.5 hrs, book by phone, tel. 0331/291-100). Otherwise, upon arrival, catch bus #695 from S-Bahn to the palace. Use the same bus (3/hrly) to shuttle between the sights in the park. Potsdam's much-promoted Wannsee boat rides are torturously dull.

An interesting "Discover Potsdam" walking tour, offered by "The Original Berlin Walks" and led by a well-qualified English-speaking guide, leaves from Berlin Tuesday, Thursday, and Saturday (28 DM, or 21 DM if under age 26, meet at 9:00 at taxi stand at Zoo Station, public transportation not included but can buy ticket from guide, no booking necessary, tel. 030/301-9194). This tour takes you to Cecilienhof Palace (site of post-war Potsdam conference attended by Churchill, Stalin, and Truman), through pleasant green landscapes to the historic heart of Potsdam for lunch, and to Sanssouci Park (palace not included).

Other Day Trips—EurAide has researched and printed a "Get Me Outta Here" flier describing good day trips to small towns and another on the nearby Sachsenhausen Concentration Camp.

Nightlife in Berlin

"What's On in Berlin" is a small, free English entertainment listing available at EurAide. For the young and determined sophisticate, *Zitty* and *Tip* are the top guides to alternative culture (German, sold at kiosks). The TI's *Berlin Programm* lists the nonstop parade of concerts, plays, exhibits, and cultural events (www.berlin.de).

Tourists stroll the Ku'damm after dark. Oranienburger Strasse's trendy scene (described above) is already being eclipsed by the action at Friedrichshain and Kollwitzplatz farther east.

Greater Berlin

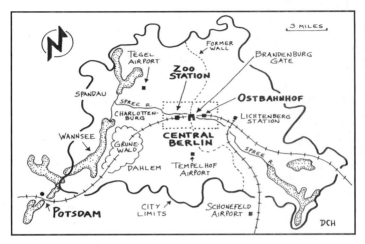

Visit KaDeWe's ticket office for your music and theater options (sixth floor, 18 percent fee but access to all tickets). Ask about "competitive improvisation" and variety shows.

For jazz (blues and boogie, too) near recommended Savignyplatz hotels, consider **A Trane Jazz Club** (Bleibtreustrasse 1, tel. 030/313-4629) and **Quasimodo Live** (Kantstrasse 12a, under Delphi Cinema, tel. 030/312-8086). For quality blues and New Orleans–style jazz, stop by **Ewige Lampe** (from 21:00, Niebuhrstrasse 11a, tel. 030/324-3918).

Sleeping in Berlin
(2 DM = about $1, country code: 49, area code: 030)
Sleep Code: **S** = Single, **D** = Double/Twin, **T** = Triple, **Q** = Quad, **b** = bathroom, **t** = toilet only, **s** = shower only, **CC** = Credit Card (**V**isa, **M**asterCard, **A**mex), **SE** = Speaks English, **NSE** = No English. Unless otherwise noted, a buffet breakfast is included.

I've concentrated my hotel recommendations around Savignyplatz. While the Bahnhof Zoo and Ku'damm are no longer the center of Berlin, trains, TI, and walking tours are all still handy to Zoo. And the streets around the tree-lined Savignyplatz (a five-minute walk behind the station) have a neighborhood charm. While towering new hotels are being built in the new center, simple, small, and friendly good value places abound only here. My listings are generally located a couple of flights up in big, run-down buildings. Inside they are clean, quiet, and spacious enough so that their well-worn character is actually charming. Rooms in back are on quiet courtyards.

The city is packed and hotel prices go up on holidays, including Green Week in mid-January, Easter weekend, first weekend in May, Ascension weekend in May, the Love Parade (a huge techno-Woodstock, second weekend in July), Germany's national holiday (Oct 2–4), Christmas, and New Year's.

During slow times, the best values are actually business-class rooms on the push list booked through the TI. But as the world learns what a great place Berlin is to visit, a rising tide of tourists will cause these deals to fade away.

Sleeping near Zoo Station at Savignyplatz (zip code: 10623, unless otherwise noted)

These hotels and pensions are a 5- to 15-minute walk from Bahnhof Zoo (or take S-Bahn to Savignyplatz). Hotels on Kantstrasse have street noise. Ask for a quieter room in back. The area has an artsy charm going back to the cabaret days in the 1920s, when it was the center of Berlin's gay scene. Wasch Salon is a handy **Laundromat** (daily 6:00–22:00, 8–16 DM wash and dry, Leibnizstrasse 72, near intersection with Kantstrasse).

Business-Class Splurges near Zoo

Hotel Astoria is a friendly, three-star, business-class hotel with 32 comfortably furnished rooms and affordable summer and weekend rates (high season Db-289 DM, prices drop to Sb-186 DM, Db-220 DM during low season of July–Aug, Nov–Feb, or any 2 weekend nights or if slow; rooms with showers are cheaper than rooms with baths, CC:VMA, around corner from Bahnhof Zoo at Fasanenstrasse 2, tel. 030/312-4067, fax 030/312-5027, www.home.t-online.de/home/astoriahotel, e-mail: astoriahotel@t-online.de).

Heckers Hotel is an ultramodern, three-star business hotel with all the sterile Euro-comforts (Sb-260 DM, Db-310 DM, breakfast-25 DM, summer and weekends breakfast included, CC:VMA, smoke-free rooms, between Savignyplatz and Ku'damm at Grolmanstrasse 35, tel. 030/88900, fax 030/889-0260, www.heckers-hotel.com).

Hotel Askanisherhof is the oldest *Zimmer* in Berlin. Posh as can be, you get porters, valet parking, and 16 sprawling antique-furnished rooms. Photos on the walls brag of famous movie-star guests. Frau Glinicke offers Old World service and classic Berlin atmosphere (Sb-195 DM, Db-250 DM, CC:VMA, no-smoking rooms, elevator, Kurfurstendamm 33, tel. 030/881-8033, fax 030/881-7206).

Inexpensive Pensions near Savignyplatz

These hotels are clean but well worn, unless otherwise stated.

Pension Peters, run by a German-Swedish couple, is sunny

Berlin's Savignyplatz Neighborhood

1 PENSION PETERS	**8** HOTEL ASTORIA	**14** HOTEL BOGOTA
2 HOTEL CRYSTAL GARNI	**9** PENSION SAVOY	**15** HOTEL PENSION FUNK
3 PENSION ALEXIS	**10** HOTEL ATLANTA	**16** DICKE WIRTIN
4 HOTEL CARMER 16	**11** HECKERS HOTEL	**17** ZILLEMARKT RESTAURANT
5 JUGENDGASTEHAUS AM ZOO	**12** HOTEL ASKANISHERHOF	**18** SCHELL RESTAURANT
6 PENSION KNESEBECK	**13** HOTELS AUSTRIANA, RÜGEN,	**19** KÄTHE KOLLEWITZ MUSEUM
7 PENSION SILVA	CURTIS, HOTEL-PENSION BELLA,	**20** TAXI STAND
	WEYERS CAFE RESTAURANT	

and central with a cheery breakfast room. Decorated sleek Scandinavian, with every room renovated, it's a winner (S-60–80 DM, Ss-90–100 DM, D-100–110 DM, Ds-120–130 DM, Db-130–150 DM, extra bed-15 DM, kids under 12 free, family room, CC:VMA, 10 meters off Savignyplatz at Kantstrasse 146, tel. 030/3150-3944, fax 030/312-3519, e-mail: penspeters@aol.com, Annika and Christoph SE). They also rent apartments (ideal for small groups and longer stays) and bikes (10 DM/day).

Hotel Crystal Garni is professional, with small, well-worn but comfortable rooms and a *vollkorn* breakfast room (S-70 DM, Sb-80 DM, D-90 DM, Ds-110 DM, Db-130–150 DM, CC:VMA, elevator, a block past Savignyplatz at Kantstrasse 144, tel. 030/312-9047, fax 030/312-6465, run by John and Dorothy Schwarzrock and Herr Glasgow Flasher).

Pension Alexis is a classic, old-European, four-room pension in a stately 19th-century apartment run by Frau and Herr

Schwarzer. This, more than any other Berlin listing, has you feeling at home with a faraway aunt (S-75 DM, D-110 DM, T-155 DM, Q-220 DM, big rooms, Carmerstrasse 15, tel. 030/312-5144, enough English spoken).

Hotel Carmer 16, with 40 bright, airy rooms, feels like a big professional hotel (S-90–110 DM, Sb-130–140 DM, D-130 DM, Db-180–200 DM, CC:VMA, smoke-free rooms, Carmerstrasse 16, tel. 030/3110-0500, fax 030/3110-0510, e-mail: carmer16@t-online.de).

Pension Knesebeck rents nine comfy—if cheaply furnished—rooms just off Savignyplatz (S-65–75 DM, Ss-85 DM, D-120 DM, Ds-130–140 DM, Ts-180 DM, Qs-200 DM, laundry-8 DM/load, Knesebeckstrasse 86, tel. 030/312-7255, fax 030/313-9507, Brigitta SE).

Pension Silva is another basic place just off Savignyplatz with 15 spacious well-furnished rooms (S-55 DM, Sb-90 DM, Db-100 DM, Tb-150 DM, 10 DM less without breakfast, CC:VM, Knesebeckstrasse 29, tel. 030/881-2129, fax 030/885-0435).

Pension Savoy rents 16 rooms with all the amenities. You'll love the cheery old pastel breakfast room (S-120 DM, Ss-140 DM, Db-195 DM, CC:VM, Meinekestrasse 4, 10719 Berlin, elevator, tel. 030/881-3700, fax 030/882-3746).

Hotel Atlanta is in an older building half a block south of Ku'damm. It's next to Gucci, on an elegant shopping street, with big leather couches (Sb-130–165 DM, Db-160–195 DM, extra person-10 DM, family friendly, smoke-free rooms, CC:VMA, Fasanenstrasse 74, 10719 Berlin, tel. 030/881-8049, fax 030/881-9872, e-mail: hatlanta68266759@aol.com).

Hotel Bogota has 125 big and comfortable rooms in a sprawling, well-worn old building. The service is brisk and hotel-esque (S-78 DM, Ss-100 DM, Sb-130 DM, D-125 DM, Ds-145 DM, Db-170–190 DM, extra person-45 DM, children under 15 free, elevator, CC:VMA, smoke-free rooms, bus #109 from Bahnhof Zoo to Schlüterstrasse 45, tel. 030/881-5001, fax 030/883-5887, e-mail: hotel.bogota@t-online.de).

Hotel-Pension Funk is the former home of a 1920s silent-movie star. It offers 14 elegant, richly furnished old rooms (S-70 DM, Ss-100 DM, Sb-120 DM, D-120 DM, Ds-140 DM, Db-160 DM, extra person-45 DM, CC:VMA but prefer cash, Fasanenstrasse 69, a long block south of Ku'damm, tel. 030/882-7193, fax 030/883-3329).

Hotel Pension Eden am Zoo is another nondescript place with well-worn rooms in a big, old, well-located building (25 rooms, D-100 DM, Ds-120 DM, Db-150 DM, Uhlandstrasse 184, tel. 030/881-5900, www.rheingold-hotel.de).

Jugendgastehaus am Zoo is a bare-bones, cash-only youth hostel that takes no reservations and hardly has a reception desk.

It's far less comfortable and only marginally cheaper than simple hotels (85 beds, 40 DM dorms, S-52 DM, D-90 DM, with sheets, without breakfast, Hardenbergstrasse 9a, tel. 030/312-9410).

Sleeping South of Ku'damm
(zip code: 10707)
Several small hotels are nearby in a charming, café-studded neighborhood 300 meters south of Ku'damm near the intersection of Sächsische Strasse and Pariser Strasse (bus #109 from Bahnhof Zoo). They are less convenient from the station than the Savignyplatz listings above.

Hotel Austriana, with 25 modern and bright rooms, is warmly and energetically run by Thomas (S-65 DM, Ss-85 DM, Sb-100 DM, Ds-120 DM, Db-150 DM, cheaper off-season, CC:VMA, Pariser Strasse 39, tel. 030/885-7000, fax 030/8857-0088, e-mail: Austriana@t-online.de). Two other pensions are in the same building: the ornate and eastern-feeling **Hotel Rügen** (Ds-130 DM, CC:VM, Pariser Strasse 39, tel. 030/884-3940, fax 030/884-39-437); and hip, piney, and basic **Pension Curtis** (S-70 DM, Ds-110–130 DM, cheaper for slow-time drop-ins, Pariser Strasse 39, tel. 030/883-4931, fax 030/885-0438).

Hotel-Pension Bella, a clean, simple, masculine-feeling place with high ceilings and an cheery, attentive management, rents nine big, comfortable rooms (S-80 DM, D-110 DM, Ds-140–150 DM, Ts-170 DM, Qs-200 DM, CC:VM, bus #249 from Zoo, Ludwigkirchstrasse 10a, tel. 030/881-6704, fax 030/8867-9074, e-mail: pension.bella@t-online.de).

More Berlin Hotels
Near Augsburgerstrasse U-Bahn stop: Consider **Hotel-Pension Nürnberger Eck** (D-130 DM, Db-150 DM, Nürnberger Strasse 24a, tel. 030/235-1780, fax 030/2351-7899) or, just upstairs, **Pension Fischer** (D-70 DM, Ds-90–130 DM, breakfast-10 DM, Nürnberger Strasse 24a, tel. 030/218-6808, fax 030/213-4225), or **Hotel Arco** (S-110–140 DM, Db-140–175 DM, Geisbergerstrasse 30, tel. 030/235-1480, fax 030/2147-5178, www.arco-hotel.de).

Near Güntzelstrasse U-Bahn stop: The **Hotel Pension München** (D-80 DM, Db-115–130 DM, breakfast-9 DM, Güntzelstrasse 62, tel. 030/857-9120, fax 030/8579-1222), **Pension Güntzel** (Ds-100–140 DM, also Guntzelstrasse 62, tel. 030/857-9020, fax 030/853-1108), or **Pension Finck** (Ds-110 DM, Güntzelstrasse 54, tel. 030/861-2940).

In eastern Berlin: The **Hotel Unter den Linden** is ideal for those nostalgic for the days of Soviet rule, although nowadays at least, the management tries to be efficient and helpful. Formerly one of the best hotels in the DDR, this huge blocky hotel, right

on Unter den Linden in the heart of what was East Berlin, is
reasonably comfortable and reasonably priced. Built in 1966
with prisonlike corridors, its 331 rooms are modern, plain, and
comfy (Sb-110–220 DM, standard Db-160–230 DM, superior
Db-180–290 DM, only a tiny difference between standard and
superior, some nonsmoking rooms, CC:VMA, at intersection
of Friedrichstrasse, Unter den Linden 14, 10117 Berlin, tel. 030/
238-110, fax 030/2381-1100).

Studenten Hotel Berlin is open to all and has no curfew
(D-84 DM, 40-DM-per-bed quads with sheets and breakfast, near
city hall on JFK Platz, Meiningerstrasse 10, U-Bahn: Rathaus
Schoneberg, tel. 030/784-6720, fax 030/788-1523).

Eating in Berlin

Don't be too determined to eat "Berlin style." The city is
known only for its mildly spicy sausage, curry wurst. Still there
is a world of restaurants in this ever-changing city to choose
from. Your best approach may be to choose a neighborhood
rather than a particular restaurant.

For quick and easy meals, colorful pubs—called *Kneipen*—
offer light meals and the fizzy local beer, Berliner Weiss. Ask for
it *mit Schuss* for a shot of fruity syrup in your suds. If the kraut
is getting wurst, try one of the many Turkish, Italian, or Balkan
restaurants. Eat cheap at *Imbiss* snack stands, bakeries (sandwiches), and falafel/kebab places. Bahnhof Zoo has several
bright and modern fruit-and-sandwich bars and a grocery (daily
6:00–24:00).

Self-Service Cafeterias near Bahnhof Zoo

The top floor of the famous department store, **KaDeWe**,
holds the Winter Garden Buffet view cafeteria, and its sixth-floor
deli/food department is a picnicker's nirvana. Its arterials are
clogged with more than 1,000 kinds of sausage and 1,500 types
of cheese (hours similar to Wertheim's, below). The **Wertheim**
department store, a half block from the Memorial Church, has
cheap food counters in the basement and a city view from its fine
self-service cafeteria, Le Buffet, located up six banks of escalators
(Mon–Fri 9:30–20:00, Sat 9:00–16:00, closed Sun, U-Bahn:
Ku'damm). The **Marche**, popping up in big cities all over Germany, is another decent self-service cafeteria within a half block
of the church (daily 8:00–24:00, CC:VMA, Ku'damm 14, enter
on ground floor of mall).

Eating near Savignyplatz

Several good places are within 100 meters of Savignyplatz:

Dicke Wirtin is a smoky old pub with good *Kneipe* atmosphere and famous *Gulaschsuppe* for 6 DM (daily from noon until

late, just off Savignyplatz at Carmerstrasse 9). **Die Zwölf Apostel**
restaurant is trendy for leafy candlelit ambience and Italian food.
A dressy local crowd packs the place for 20-DM pizzas and
30-DM meals. Late-night party goers appreciate Apostel's great
breakfast (daily 24 hrs, immediately across from Savigny S-Bahn
entrance, Bleibtreustrasse 49, tel. 030/312-1433). **Ristorante San
Marino** is another good Italian place, this one on the square and
serving cheaper pasta and pizza (Savignyplatz 12, tel. 030/313-
6086). **Zillemarkt Restaurant** feels like an old-time Berlin beer
garden. It offers seating in the garden or in the rustic candlelit
interior and serves traditional Berlin specialties (20-DM meals,
daily until late, no English menu—that's good—a block from
Savigny S-Bahn station, under the tracks at Bleibtreustrasse 48a,
tel. 030/881-7040).

   Schell Restaurant is a dressy place (named for a gas station
that once stood there) serving high Italian cuisine to a completely
German crowd that seems in-the-know (40-DM dinner plates,
daily, a block off Savignyplatz at Knesebackstrasse 22, tel. 030/
312-8310). **Bistrot Hegel** is a mellow little Russian piano bar
with light meals right on Savignyplatz. Late at night there may
be some balalaika music (open from 18:00 on, Savignyplatz 2,
tel. 030/312-1948).

   Weyers Cafe Restaurant, serving quality international/
German cuisine, is a great value and worth a short walk. It's trendy
with white tablecloths but not stuffy (20-DM dinner plates, daily,
seating indoors or outside on the leafy square, Pariser Strasse 16,
reservations smart after 20:00, tel. 030/881-9378).

   Ullrich Supermarkt is the neighborhood grocery store
(Mon–Sat 9:00–20:00, Sun 9:00–16:00, Kantstrasse 7, under
the tracks near Bahnhof Zoo). There's plenty of fast food near
Bahnhof Zoo and on Ku'damm.

Eating along Unter den Linden
near Pergamon Museum

The Opernpalais, preening with fancy pre-war elegance, hosts a
number of pricey restaurants. Its **Operncafé** has the best desserts
(longest dessert bar in Europe, across from university and war
memorial at Unter den Linden 5). The shady beer/tea garden in
front has a cheap self-service *Imbiss* (wurst, meatball sandwiches,
and so on) and a *creperie*. More students and fewer tourists eat in
the café at Humboldt University across the street (off courtyard,
enter building, café on right).

   Oren Restaurant/Café is a trendy, stylish, near-kosher/
vegetarian place next to the New Synagogue. The food is pricey
but good, and the ambience is happening (daily 12:00–24:00,
north of Museum Island about 5 blocks away at Oranienburger
Strasse 28, tel. 030/282-8228).

Transportation Connections—Berlin

Berlin has three train stations. Bahnhof Zoo was the West Berlin train station and still serves Western Europe: Frankfurt, Munich, Hamburg, Paris, and Amsterdam. The Ostbahnhof (former East Berlin's main station) still faces east, serving Prague, Warsaw, Vienna, and Dresden. The Lichtenberg Bahnhof (eastern Berlin's top U- and S-Bahn hub) also handles a few eastbound trains. Expect exceptions. All stations are conveniently connected by subway and even faster, by train. Train info: tel. 0180/599-6633.

By train to: **Frankfurt** (14/day, 5 hrs), **Munich** (8/day, 7 hrs, 10 hrs overnight), **Köln** (hrly, 6.5 hrs), **Amsterdam** (4/day, 7 hrs), **Budapest** (3/day, 13 hrs), **Copenhagen** (4/day, 8 hrs), **London** (4/day, 15 hrs), **Paris** (6/day, 13 hrs), **Zurich** (12/day, 10 hrs), **Prague** (8/day, 4.5 hrs), **Warsaw** (4/day, 8 hrs), **Vienna** (2/day, 12 hrs via Czech Republic; for second-class ticket, Eurailers pay an extra 45 DM if under age 26 or 60 DM if age 26 or above; otherwise, take the Berlin-Vienna via Passau train—nightly at 20:00), **Prague** (5/day, 6 hrs, no overnight); Eurailpasses don't cover the Czech Republic. The Prague Excursion pass picks up where Eurail leaves off, getting you from any border into Prague and then back out to Eurail country again within seven days (60 DM-second class, 90 DM-first class, buy at EurAide in Berlin and get reservations—5 DM—at the same time).

Berlin is connected by overnight trains from Bonn, Köln, Frankfurt, Munich, and Vienna. A *Liegeplatz*, or berth (30–40 DM), is a great deal; inquire at EurAide at Bahnhof Zoo for details. Beds cost the same whether you have a first- or second-class ticket or railpass. Trains are rarely full, but get your bed reserved a few days in advance from any travel agency or major train station in Europe. Note: Since the Paris–Berlin night train goes through Belgium, Europass or Eurail Selectpass holders can't travel on it unless they've added or selected Belgium.

Berlin's Three Airports

Allow 25 DM for a taxi ride to or from any of Berlin's airports. **Tegel Airport** handles most flights from the United States and Western Europe (6 kilometers from center, catch the faster bus #X9 to Bahnhof Zoo or bus #109 to Ku'damm and Bahnhof Zoo for 3.90 DM). Flights from the east usually arrive at **Schönefeld Airport** (20 km from center, short walk to S-Bahn, catch S-9 to Zoo Station). **Templehof Airport**'s future is uncertain (in Berlin, bus #119 to Ku'damm or U-Bahn 6 or 7). The central telephone number for all three airports is 0180-500-0186. British Air (tel. 030/254-0000), Delta (tel. 0180-333-7880), SAS and Lufthansa (tel. 0180-6951-2841).

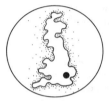

LONDON

London is more than 600 square miles of urban jungle. With 9 million struggling people—many of whom speak English—it's a world in itself and a barrage on all the senses. On my first visit I felt very, very small. London is much more than its museums and famous landmarks. It's a living, breathing, thriving organism.

London has changed dramatically in recent years, and many visitors are surprised to find how "un-English" it is. Whites are now a minority in major parts of the city that once symbolized white imperialism. Arabs have nearly bought out the area north of Hyde Park. Chinese take-outs outnumber fish-and-chips shops. Many hotels are run by people with foreign accents (who hire English chambermaids), while outlying suburbs are home to huge communities of Indians and Pakistanis. London is learning—sometimes fitfully—to live as a microcosm of its formerly vast empire. Many see the English Channel Tunnel as another foreign threat to the Britishness of Britain.

With just a few days here, you'll get no more than a quick splash in this teeming human tidal pool. But, with a quick orientation, you'll get a good taste of its top sights, history, and cultural entertainment, as well as its ever-changing human face.

Have fun in London. Blow through the city on the open deck of a double-decker orientation tour bus, and take a pinch-me-I'm-in-Britain walk through downtown. Ogle the crown jewels at the Tower of London, hear the chimes of Big Ben, and see the Houses of Parliament in action. Hobnob with the tombstones in Westminster Abbey, duck WWII bombs in Churchill's underground Cabinet War Rooms, and brave the earthshaking Imperial War Museum. Overfeed the pigeons at Trafalgar Square. Visit with Leonardo, Botticelli, and Rembrandt in the National Gallery.

The Party's Not Over

Last year, London was hell-bent on hosting the world's grandest millennium celebrations. The year 2000 brought London revamped museums, a huge Ferris wheel, and a giant dome at Greenwich.

After the stardust of the millennium settled, what's left?

Only Greenwich's Millennium Dome has been a disappointment. It needed to draw 35,000 people a day to recoup its huge costs. But its crowds kept away bigger crowds.

To celebrate the millennium, the British Museum opened its glass-domed Great Court, giving the museum a formal entry and offering visitors a classy place to hang out after the museum closes—to shop, dine, people watch, or attend a lecture. Marx (Karl not Groucho) enjoyed the museum's Round Reading Room, freshly restored and once again open to the public.

The London Eye Ferris Wheel, for the silly thrill of it, is a delightful way to see London from a 450-foot-high perch. The towering Wheel adds a carnival whirl to London's stodgy skyline.

The striking Tate Modern, which opened in 2000, is as modern as its art. The new pedestrian Millennium Bridge links the old, sedate St. Paul's Cathedral with the new great Tate. Gracefully spanning the Thames, the Millennium Bridge connects old and new, religious and secular, the heart of London with the art of the world.

London gambled big on the millennium, and you're the winner.

Whisper across the dome of St. Paul's Cathedral and rummage through our civilization's attic at the British Museum. Cruise down the Thames River. You'll enjoy some of Europe's best people watching at Covent Garden and snap to at Buckingham Palace's Changing of the Guard. Just sit in Victoria Station, at a major tube station, at Piccadilly Circus, or in Trafalgar Square, and observe. Spend one evening at a theater and the others catching your breath.

Planning Your Time

The sights of London alone could easily fill a trip to Britain. It's a great one-week getaway. On a three-week tour of Britain I'd give it three busy days. If you're flying in, consider starting your trip in Bath and make London your British finale. Especially if you hope to enjoy a play or concert, a night or two of jet lag is bad news.

Here's a suggested schedule:

Day 1: 9:00–Tower of London (Beefeater tour, crown jewels), 12:00–Munch a sandwich on the Thames while cruising from the Tower to Westminster Bridge, 13:00–Follow the self-guided Westminster Walk (see below) with a quick visit to the Cabinet War Rooms, 15:30–Trafalgar Square and National Gallery, 17:30–Visit the Britain Visitors Centre near Piccadilly, planning ahead for your trip, 18:30–Dinner in Soho. Take in a play or 19:30 concert at St. Martin-in-the-Fields.

Day 2: 8:30–If traveling around Britain, spend 30 minutes in a phone booth getting all essential elements of your trip nailed down. If you know where you'll be and when, call those B&Bs now. 9:00–Take the Round London bus tour (consider hopping off near the end for the 11:30 Changing of the Guard at Buckingham Palace), 12:30–Covent Gardens for lunch and people watching, 14:00–Tour the British Museum. Have a pub dinner before a play, concert, or evening walking tour.

Days 3 and 4: Choose among these remaining London highlights: Tour Westminster Abbey, British Library, Imperial War Museum, the two Tates (Tate Modern on the south bank for modern art, Tate Britain on the north bank for British art), St. Paul's Cathedral, Museum of London, or London Eye Ferris Wheel; cruise to Kew or Greenwich; do some serious shopping at one of London's elegant department stores or open-air markets; or consider another historic walking tour.

After considering nearly all of London's tourist sights, I have pruned them down to just the most important (or fun) for a first visit of up to seven days. You won't be able to see all of these, so don't try. You'll keep coming back to London. After 25 visits myself, I still enjoy a healthy list of excuses to return.

Orientation
(area code: 020)
To grasp London comfortably, see it as the old town without the modern, congested sprawl. Most of the visitor's London lies between the Tower of London and Hyde Park—about a three-mile walk. Mentally—maybe even physically—scissor down your map to include only the area between the Tower, King's Cross Station, Paddington Station, the Victoria and Albert Museum, and Victoria Station. With this focus and a good orientation, you'll find London manageable and even fun.

Tourist Information
The **Britain Visitors Centre** is the best information service in town (Mon-9:30–18:30, Tue–Fri 9:00–18:30, Sat–Sun 10:00–16:00, July–Sept until 17:00 on Sat, booking service, just off Piccadilly Circus at 1 Lower Regent Street, tel. 020/8846-9000,

www.visitbritain.com). It's great for London information; buy your city map here (£1). If you're traveling beyond London, take advantage of its well-equipped London/England desk, Wales desk (tel. 020/7803-3838), Ireland desk (tel. 020/7493-3201), and Scotland desk. At the center's extensive bookshop, gather whatever guidebooks, hostel directories, maps, and information you'll need. If venturing beyond London, consider the *Michelin Green Guide* to London or Britain (£9.25), the Britain road atlas (£10), and Ordnance Survey maps for areas you'll be exploring by car. There's also a travel agency upstairs plus computers displaying only www.visitbritain.com (no Internet access).

Nearby you'll find the **Scottish Tourist Centre** (mid-June–mid-Sept Mon–Fri 9:00–18:00, Sat 10:00–17:00, otherwise Mon–Fri 9:30–17:30, Sat 12:00–16:00, Cockspur Street, tel. 020/7930-8661, www.holiday.scotland.net) and the slick **French National Tourist Office** (Mon–Sat 9:00–17:30, closed Sun, 178 Piccadilly Street, tel. 0891-244-123).

Unfortunately **London's Tourist Information Centres** (TIs) are now owned by the big hotels and are simply businesses selling advertising space to companies with fliers to distribute. They are reasonably helpful but biased; the London map they sell for £1.40 is littered with hotels. Avoid their 50p-per-minute telephone information service (instead try the **Britain Visitors Centre** at 020/8846-9000). Locations include Heathrow Airport's Terminal 3 (daily 6:00–23:00, most convenient and least crowded); Heathrow Airport's Terminal 1 and 2 tube station (daily 8:00–18:00); Victoria Station (daily 8:00–18:00, crowded and commercial); and Waterloo International Terminal Arrivals Hall (daily 8:30–22:30, serving trains from Paris; if you arrive by train when TI is mobbed, skip the TI, buy city map at a newsstand upstairs in station lobby, then return downstairs to catch tube to your hotel).

At any of the TIs, bring your itinerary and a checklist of questions. Pick up these publications: *London Planner* (a great free monthly that lists all the sights, events, and hours), walking-tour schedule fliers, a theater guide, and the Thames River Services brochure. Of all the TIs, only the Britain Visitors Centre on Regent Street sells a good city map (£1, free from British Tourist Authority in U.S.A.: tel. 800/462-2748, 551 Fifth Avenue, 7th floor, New York, NY 10176, www.travelbritain.org). Bensons Mapguide of London is the best map of London I've seen (£2, sold at newsstands).

TIs sell BT phone cards, long-distance bus tickets and passes, British Heritage Passes, and tickets to plays (steep booking fee). And they book rooms (avoid their £5 booking fee by calling hotels direct). Skip the pricey London Pass, which covers 50 mostly minor sights (1 day/£17.50).

TIs also sell "Fast Track" tickets to some of London's

attractions (at no extra cost), allowing you to skip the queue at the sights; these are worthwhile for places notorious for long ticket lines: Tower of London, London Eye Ferris Wheel, and Madame Tussaud's Wax Museum.

Helpful Hints

U.S. Embassy: 24 Grosvenor Square (for passport concerns, open Mon–Fri 8:30–11:30 plus Mon, Wed, Fri 14:00–16:00, tube: Bond Street, tel. 020/7499-9000).

Theft Alert: The Artful Dodger is alive and well in London. Be on guard, particularly on public transportation and in places crowded with tourists. Tourists, considered naive and rich, are targeted. Over 7,500 handbags are stolen annually at Covent Garden alone. Thieves paw you so you don't feel the pickpocketing.

Changing Money: ATMs are the way to go. For changing traveler's checks, standard transaction fees at banks are £2–4. American Express Offices offer a fair rate and change any brand of traveler's checks for no fee. Handy Amex offices are at Heathrow's Terminal 4 tube station (daily 7:00–19:00) and near Piccadilly (30 Haymarket, June–Sept Mon–Fri 8:30–20:00, Sat 9:00–18:30, Sun 10:00–17:00; Oct–May Mon–Sat 9:00–17:30, Sun 10:00–17:00; tel. 020/7484-9600). Avoid changing money at exchange bureaus. Their latest scam: they advertise very good rates with a same-as-the-banks fee of 2 percent. But the fine print explains that the fee of 2 percent is for buying pounds. The fee for *selling* pounds is 9.5 percent. Ouch!

What's Up: For the best listing of what's happening (plays, movies, restaurants, concerts, exhibitions, protests, walking tours, shopping, and children's activities) and a look at the trendy London scene, pick up a current copy of *Time Out* (£1.85, www.timeout .co.uk) or *What's On* at any newsstand. The TI's free monthly *London Planner* lists sights, plays, and events at least as well. For a chatty, *People* magazine–type Web site on London's entertainment, theater, restaurants, and news, go to www.thisislondon.com.

Free Sights: The British Museum, British Library, National Gallery, National Portrait Gallery, Tate Britain (British art), and Tate Modern (modern art) are always free—though special exhibitions cost extra. The following museums are free from 16:30 to closing (17:30 or 18:00), saving you £5 or so: The Imperial War Museum, Museum of London, Natural History Museum, and Victoria and Albert Museum. More museums will be free in the next few years.

Internet Access: The astonishing easyEverything offers up to 500 computers per store, 24 hours daily. Depending on demand, a mere £1 ticket buys anywhere from 40 minutes to six hours of computer time; the ticket is valid for four weeks and multiple visits at any of their five branches: Victoria Station (across from front of station, near taxis and buses), Trafalgar

Square, Tottenham Court Road, Oxford Street, and Kensington High Street.

Travel Bookstores: Stanfords Travel Bookstores is good and stocks current editions of my books at Covent Garden (12 Long Acre, tel. 020/7836-1321) and 156 Regent Street (tel. 020/7434-4744). Waterstones Bookstore, on the corner of Trafalgar Square, is also handy, with a fine travel selection next to the Coffee Republic café (WC upstairs, tel. 020/7839-4411).

Travel Agency: The student travel agency, USIT, across from Victoria Station, has great deals on flights for people of all ages (Mon–Fri 9:00–18:00, Sat–Sun 10:00–17:00, Internet access, Buckingham Palace Road, tel. 020/7823-5363, www.usitcampus .co.uk). Also, look in the Sunday *Times* travel section for great deals on flights.

Beatles: Fans of the still Fabulous Four can take one of the Beatles walks (5/weekly, offered by Original London Walks, under "Tours of London," below); visit the Beatles Shop (231 Baker Street, next to Sherlock Holmes Museum, tube: Baker Street); or go to Abbey Road and walk the famous crosswalk (at intersection with Carlton Hill, tube: St. John's Wood).

Arrival in London

By Train: London has eight train stations, all connected by the tube (subway), all with exchange offices and luggage storage. From any station, ride the tube or taxi to your hotel.

By Bus: The bus station is one block southwest of Victoria Station, which has a TI and tube entrance.

By Plane: For detailed information on getting from London's airports to downtown London, see "Transportation Connections" at the end of this chapter.

Getting around London

London's taxis, buses, and subway system make a private car unnecessary. To travel smart in a city this size, you must get comfortable with public transportation. For tube and bus information 24 hours a day, call 020/7222-1234 (www.londontransport.co.uk).

By Taxi: London is the best taxi town in Europe. Big, black, carefully regulated cabs are everywhere. I never met a crabby cabbie in London. They love to talk and know every nook and cranny in town. I ride in one a day just to get my London questions answered. Rides start at £1.50 and cost about £1.50 per tube stop. Connecting downtown sights is quick and easy and will cost you about £4 (e.g., St. Paul's to the Tower of London). For a short ride, three people in a cab travel at tube prices. Groups of four or five should taxi everywhere. If a cab's top light is on, just wave it down. (Drivers flash lights when they see you.) They have a tiny turning radius, so you can wave at cabs going both directions. If waving doesn't work, ask someone where you can find a taxi stand. Stick with metered cabs. While telephoning a cab gets one in minutes, it's generally not necessary and adds to the cost. London is such a great wave-'em-down taxi town that most cabs don't even have a radio phone.

By Bus: London's extensive bus system is easy to follow. Just pick up a free "Central London bus guide" map from a TI or tube station. Signs at stops list routes clearly. Conductors are terse but helpful. Ask to be reminded when it's your stop. Just hop on, tell the driver where you're going, pay what he says (usually £1) grab a ticket, take a seat, and relax. (The best views are upstairs.) If the driver is not taking money, hop in and grab a seat. The conductor will eventually sell you a ticket. If you have a Travel Card (see below), get in the habit of hopping buses for quick little straight shots, even just to get to a metro stop. During bump-and-grind rush hours (8:00–10:00 and 16:00–19:00), you'll go faster by tube.

By Tube: London's subway is one of this planet's great people movers and the fastest—and cheapest—long-distance transport in town (runs daily about 5:00–24:00). Any ride in the Central Zone (on or within the Circle Line, including virtually all my recommended sights and hotels) costs £1.50. You can avoid ticket window lines in tube stations by buying tickets from coin-op machines; practice on the punchboard to see how the system works (hit "adult single" and your destination). Again, nearly every ride will be £1.50. (These tickets are valid only on the day of purchase.) Beware: Overshooting your zone will get you a £10 fine.

Most city maps include a tube map with color-coded lines and names (free at any station window). Each line has a name (such as Circle, Northern, or Bakerloo) and two directions (indicated by end stop). In stations you'll have a choice of two platforms per line. Navigate by signs leading to the platforms (usually labeled north, south, east, or west) which clearly list the stops served by each line, or ask a local or an orange-vested staff person for help. All city maps have north on top. If you know which general direction you're heading, tube navigation suddenly becomes easier. Some tracks are shared by several lines, and electronic signboards announce which train is next and the minutes remaining until various arrivals. Each train has its final destination or line name above its windshield. Depending on the particular line, trains run roughly every 3 to 10 minutes. Bring something to do to make your wait productive. And always . . . mind the gap.

You can't leave the system without feeding your ticket to the turnstile. Save time by choosing the best street exit (look at the maps on the walls). "Subway" means pedestrian underpass in "English."

London Tube and Bus Passes: Consider using these passes, valid on both the tube and buses (all passes are available for more zones and are purchased as easily as a normal ticket at any station):

London

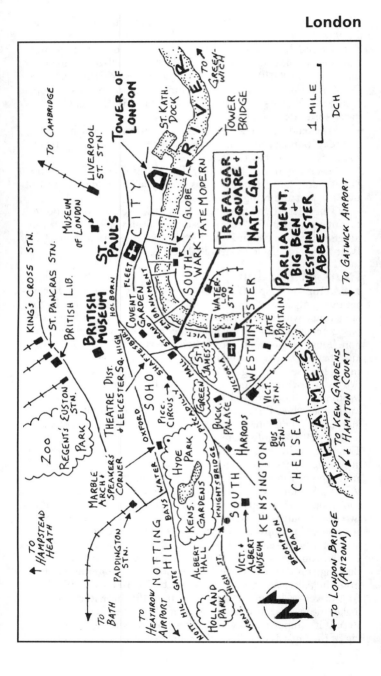

One Day passes: If you figure you'll take three rides in a day, a day pass is a good deal. The "One Day Travel Card," covering Zones 1 and 2, gives you unlimited travel for a day, starting after 9:30 and anytime on weekends, for £3.90. The all-zone version of this card costs £4.70 (and includes Heathrow airport). The "One Day LT Card," covering Zones 1 and 2 with no time restriction, costs £5. Families save with the one-day "Family Travel Card" (price varies depending on number in family).

Weekend pass: The "Weekend Travel Card," which covers Saturday, Sunday, and Zones 1 and 2 for £5.80, costs 25 percent less than two one-day cards.

Seven-day pass: The "7-Day Travel Card" costs £18, covers Zones 1 and 2, and requires a passport-type photo (cut one out of any snapshot and bring it from home).

Ten rides: If you want to travel a little each day or if you're part of a group, a £11 "carnet" is a great deal: you get 10 separate tickets for tube travel in Zone 1 (£1.10 per ride rather than £1.50). Wait for the machine to lay all 10 tickets.

Tours of London

▲▲▲Hop-on Hop-off Double-Decker Bus Tours—Two competitive companies ("Original" and "Big Bus") offer essentially the same tours, with buses that have live (English-only) guides as well as some marked buses with a tape-recorded, dial-a-language narration. This two-hour, once-over-lightly bus tour drives by all the most famous sights, providing a stressless way to get your bearings and at least see the biggies. You can sit back and enjoy the entire two-hour orientation tour (a good idea if you like the guide and the weather) or "hop on and hop off" at any of the nearly 30 stops and catch a later bus. Buses run about every 10 to 15 minutes in summer, every 20 minutes in winter. It's an inexpensive form of transport as well as an informative tour. Grab one of the maps from a TI and study it. Buses run daily except Christmas (from about 9:00 in summer—9:30 in winter—until early evening in summer, late afternoon in winter), stopping at Victoria Street (1 block north of Victoria Station), Marble Arch, Piccadilly Circus, Trafalgar Square, and so on. Each company offers a core two-hour overview tour and two other routes (buy ticket from driver, CC sometimes accepted at some major stops such as Victoria Station, ticket good for 24 hours, bring a sweater and extra film). Note: If you start at Victoria at 9:00, you can hop off near the end of the two-hour loop at the Buckingham Palace stop (Bressenden Place), a five-minute walk from the palace and the Changing of the Guard (at 11:30); ask your driver—who knows about current traffic diversions—if it makes more sense to walk to the palace from the Victoria Station stop. If it's important to you to get a close-up view of the Changing of the Guards or to take in the guards' inspection at 11:00 at

Wellington Barracks, save the bus tour for another day. Sunday morning, with light traffic and many museums closed, is a fine time for a tour.

Original London Sightseeing Bus Tour: Live guided buses have a Union Jack flag and a yellow triangle on the front of the bus. If the front has many flags or a green triangle, it's a tape-recorded multilingual tour—avoid it, unless you have kids who'd enjoy the more entertaining recorded kids' tour (£12.50, £2.50 off with this book—limit 2 discounts per book, they'll rip off the corner of this page, ticket good for 24 hours, tel. 020/8877-1722).

Big Bus Hop-on Hop-off London Tours: These are also good. For £15 you get the same basic tour plus coupons for three different one-hour London walks and the scenic and entertainingly guided Thames boat ride (normally £4.80) between Westminster Pier and the Tower of London. The pass and extras (which you could just barely do in a day) are valid for 24 hours. Buses with live guides are marked in front with a picture of a blue bus; buses with tape-recorded spiels display a picture of a yellow bus and head-phones. While the price is steeper, Big Bus guides seem more dynamic than the Original guides, and the Big Bus system is probably better organized (office a block from Victoria Station at 48 Buckingham Palace Road, daily 8:30–17:30, CC accepted, or pay driver cash, tel. 020/7233-9533, www.bigbus.co.uk).

At Night: To do it at night, consider the London by Night Sightseeing Tour, which runs basically the same circuit as the other companies (£9, pay driver or buy tickets at Victoria Station TI, April–Oct, 2-hr tour with live guide, can hop on and off, leaves at 20:00, 21:00, and 22:00 from Victoria Station, Taxi Road, Stop E, at front of station, tel. 020/8646-1747).

▲▲**Walking Tours**—Many times a day top-notch local guides lead small groups through specific slices of London's past. Schedule fliers litter the desks of TIs, hotels, and pubs. *Time Out* lists many but not all scheduled walks. Simply show up at the announced location, pay £5, and enjoy two chatty hours of Dickens, the Plague, Shakespeare, Legal London, the Beatles, Jack the Ripper, or whatever is on the agenda. Original London Walks, the dominant company, lists their extensive daily schedule in a beefy, plain, black-and-white *Original London Walks* brochure; they also run Explorer day trips, a good option for those with limited time and transportation (different trip daily: Stonehenge/Salisbury, Oxford/Cotswolds, York, Bath, and so on; walks offered year-round—even Christmas, get schedule at hotel or TI, or call 020/7624-3978, private tours for £80, www.walks.com).

Here are a few private guides; for any of these, book well in advance: Robina Brown, who winters in Seattle (a bizarre concept), leads tours on foot or with small groups in her Toyota Previa. For car and guiding she charges £155 for three hours and about £275 to £360 per day trip per group (tel. & fax 020/7228-2238, e-mail: robina.brown@which.net). Brit Lonsdale, an energetic mother of twins, is another registered London guide (tel. 020/7386-9907, fax 020/7386-9807). Chris Salaman and his colleague, Rich Parks, both tailor specialty walks (Chris's favorite: industrial tours); their daylong private walks, including lunch, a tube travel card, and museum admissions, cost £120 for up to six people (Chris, tel. 020/8672-1270; Rich, tel. 020/8464-4369). For other guides call 020/7403-2962 (www.touristguides.org.uk); standard rates for registered guides: £83/4 hrs, £132/8 hrs.

▲▲**Cruise the Thames**—Boat tours with an entertaining commentary sail regularly from Westminster Pier (at the base of Westminster Bridge under Big Ben). You can cruise to the Tower of London (£4.80, only the one-way is included with Big Bus London tour, round-trip £6, 2/hrly, 10:20–21:00 April–Oct, until 15:45 Nov–March, 30 min, tel. 020/7930-9033), Greenwich (£6.30, round-trip £7.60, 2/hrly, 9:00–16:00, 50 min, tel. 020/7930-4097), and Kew Gardens (£7, round-trip £11, 5/day, 10:15–14:00, 90 min, 30 min narrated, some boats continue on to Hampton Court for extra £3, tel. 020/7930-2062). For pleasure and efficiency, consider combining a one-way cruise with a tube ride back.

Frog Tours—A bright yellow, amphibious vehicle takes you streetside past some famous sights (Big Ben, Buckingham Palace, Piccadilly Circus), then splashes into the Thames for a 30-minute cruise (£13, daily 10:00–18:00, live commentary, 80 min, departs from County Hall near London Eye Ferris Wheel, tube: Waterloo or Westminster, tel. 020/7928-3132, www.frogtours.com).

Sights—From Westminster Abbey to Trafalgar Square

▲▲**Westminster Walk**—Just about every visitor to London strolls the historic Whitehall boulevard from Big Ben to Trafalgar Square. Beneath London's modern traffic and big-city bustle lies 2,000 fascinating years of history. This three-quarter-mile, self-guided orientation walk (see map on next page) gives you a whirlwind tour and connects the sights listed in this section.

Start halfway across **Westminster Bridge** (#1 on map) for that "Wow, I'm really in London!" feeling. Get a close-up view of the **Houses of Parliament** and **Big Ben** (floodlit at night). Downstream (#2) you'll see the **London Eye Ferris Wheel**. Downstairs are boats to the Tower of London and Greenwich.

En route to Parliament Square, you'll pass a statue of Boadicea (#3), the Celtic queen defeated by Roman invaders in A.D. 60.

To thrill your loved ones (or bug the envious), call home from a pay phone near Big Ben at about three minutes before the hour. You'll find a phone on Great George Street, across from Parliament Square. As Big Ben chimes, stick the receiver outside

Westminster Walk

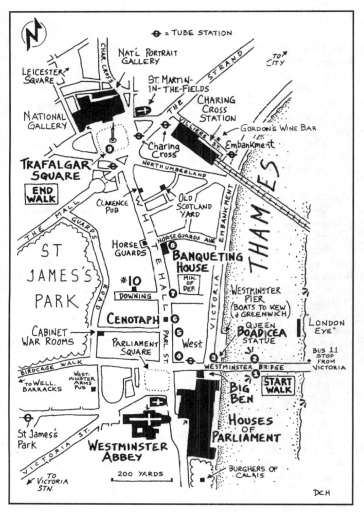

the booth and prove you're in London: Ding dong ding dong... dong ding ding dong.

Wave hello to Churchill in Parliament Square (#4). To his right is **Westminster Abbey** with its two stubby, elegant towers.

Walk north up Parliament Street (which turns into White-hall) toward Trafalgar Square. You'll see the thought-provoking **Cenotaph** (#6) in the middle of the street, reminding passersby of Britain's many war dead. To visit the Cabinet War Rooms (see "Sights," below) take a left before the Cenotaph, on King Charles Street (#5).

Continuing on Whitehall, stop at the barricaded and guarded little **10 Downing Street** to see the British "White House" (#7), home of the prime minister. Break the bobby's boredom and ask him a question.

Nearing Trafalgar Square, look for the **Horse Guards** behind the gated fence (11:00 inspection Mon–Sat, 10:00 on Sun; dismounting ceremony daily at 16:00) and the 17th-century **Banqueting House** across the street (#8; see "Sights," below).

The column topped by Lord Nelson marks **Trafalgar Square** (#9). The stately domed building on the far side of the square is the **National Gallery** (free) which has a classy café (upstairs in the Sainsbury wing). To the right of the National Gallery is **St. Martin-in-the-Fields Church** and its Café in the Crypt.

To get to Piccadilly from Trafalgar Square, walk up Cockspur Street to Haymarket, then take a short left on Coventry Street to colorful **Piccadilly Circus.**

Near Piccadilly you'll find the **Britain Visitors Centre** and piles of theaters. **Leicester Square** (with its half-price ticket booth for plays) thrives just a few blocks away. Walk through seedy **Soho** (north of Shaftesbury Avenue) for its fun pubs (see "Eating," below, for "Food is Fun" Dinner Crawl). From Piccadilly or Oxford Circus, you can taxi, bus, or tube home.

▲▲▲**Westminster Abbey**—England's historic coronation church is a crowded collection of famous tombs. Like a stony refugee camp huddled outside St. Peter's gates, this is an English hall of fame. Consider a tour (audioguide-£2 or live-£3), an evensong service (weekdays except Wed at 17:00, Sat and Sun at 15:00), and the Sunday 17:45 organ recital (£5 for abbey entry, tours extra, Mon–Fri 9:15–16:45 plus Wed 18:00–19:45, Sat 9:00–14:45, technically no visitors on Sun, last admission 1 hr before closing, photography prohibited, lattés in cloister, tube: Westminster or St. James' Park, call for tour schedule, tel. 020/7222-7110). Since the church is often closed to the public for special services, it's wise to call first. Praying is free, thank God (in two chapels set aside for private prayer), but you must inform the marshal at the door of your intention.

▲▲**Houses of Parliament (Palace of Westminster)**—This neo-Gothic icon of London, the royal residence from 1042 to 1547, is now the meeting place of the legislative branch of government. While Parliament is too tempting to terrorists to be opened wide to tourists, you can view debates in either the bickering House of Commons or the genteel House of Lords if they're in session—indicated by a flag flying atop the Victoria Tower. It's not worth a long wait and the actual action is generally extremely dull, but it is a thrill to be inside and see the British government in action (House of Commons:

Mon–Wed 14:30–22:30, Thu 11:30–19:30, Fri 9:30–15:00, generally less action and no lines after 18:00, use St. Stephen's entrance, tube: Westminster, tel. 020/7219-4272 for schedule, www.parliament.uk). The House of Lords has more pageantry, shorter lines, and less-interesting debates (Mon–Wed 14:30 until they finish, Thu from 15:00 on, sometimes Fri from 11:00 on, tel. 020/7219-3107 for schedule). If confronted with a too-long House of Commons line, see the House of Lords first. Once you've seen the Lords (hide your HOL flier), you can often slip directly to the Commons—joining the gang waiting in the lobby. If there's only one line outside, it's for the House of Commons. Go to the gate and tell the guard you want the Lords. You may pop right in.

After passing security, slip to the left and study the big dark **Westminster Hall,** which survived the 1834 fire. The hall is 11th century, and its famous self-supporting hammer-beam roof was added in 1397. The Houses of Parliament are located in what was once the Palace of Westminster, long the palace of England's medieval kings, until it was largely destroyed by fire in 1834. The palace was rebuilt in Victorian Gothic style (a move away from neoclassicism back to England's Christian and medieval heritage, true to the Romantic age). It was completed in 1860; only a few of its 1,000 rooms are open to the public.

The **Jewel Tower** is (along with Westminster Hall) about the only surviving part of the old Palace of Westminster. It contains a fine little exhibit on Parliament: first floor—history, second floor—Parliament today, with a 45-minute video and lonely picnic-friendly benches (£1.50, April–Sept daily 10:00–18:00, until 17:00 Oct, until 16:00 Nov–March, across street from St. Stephens Gate, tel. 020/7222-2219).

The clock tower (315 feet high) is named for its 13-ton bell, Ben. The light above the clock is lit when the House of Commons is sitting. For a hip HOP view, walk halfway over Westminster Bridge.

▲▲**Cabinet War Rooms**—This is a fascinating walk through the underground headquarters of the British government's fight against the Nazis in the darkest days of the Battle for Britain. The 21-room nerve center of the British war effort was used from 1939 to 1945. Churchill's room, the map room, and so on, are just as they were in 1945. For all the blood, sweat, toil, and tears details, pick up an audioguide at the entry and follow the included and excellent 30-minute tour; be patient—it's worth it (£5, April–Oct daily 9:30–18:00, Nov–March 10:00–17:15, last entry 45 min before closing, on King Charles Street 200 yards off Whitehall, follow the signs, tube: Westminster, tel. 020/7930-6961). For a nearby pub lunch, try the Westminster Arms (on Storey's Gate, a couple blocks south of War Rooms).

Horse Guards—The Horse Guards change daily at 11:00 (10:00 on Sun), and there's a colorful dismounting ceremony daily at

National Gallery Highlights

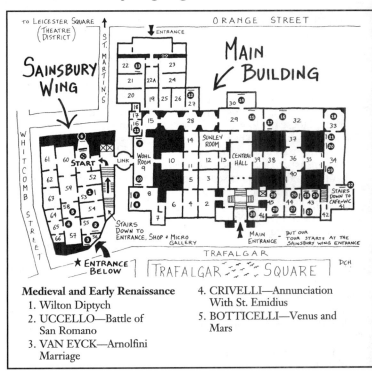

Medieval and Early Renaissance

1. Wilton Diptych
2. UCCELLO—Battle of San Romano
3. VAN EYCK—Arnolfini Marriage
4. CRIVELLI—Annunciation With St. Emidius
5. BOTTICELLI—Venus and Mars

16:00. The rest of the day they just stand there—terrible for camcorders (on Whitehall, between Trafalgar Square and #10 Downing Street, tube: Westminster). While Buckingham Palace pageantry is canceled when it rains, the horse guards change regardless of the weather.

▲**Banqueting House**—England's first Renaissance building was designed by Inigo Jones around 1620. It's one of the few London landmarks spared by the 1666 fire and the only surviving part of the original Palace of Whitehall. Don't miss its Rubens ceiling, which, at Charles I's request, drove home the doctrine of the legitimacy of the divine right of kings. In 1649, divine right ignored, Charles I was beheaded on the balcony of this building by a Cromwellian parliament. Admission includes a restful 18-minute audiovisual history, which shows the place in banqueting action, a 30-minute tape-recorded tour that is interesting only to history buffs, and a look at a fancy banqueting hall (£3.80, Mon–Sat 10:00–17:00, last entry at 16:30, subject to closure for

High Renaissance

6. LEONARDO DA VINCI—Virgin and Child (painting and cartoon)

7. MICHELANGELO—Entombment

8. RAPHAEL—Pope Julius II

Venetian Renaissance

9. TINTORETTO—Origin of the Milky Way

10. TITIAN—Bacchus and Ariadne

Northern Protestant Art

11. VERMEER—Young Woman Standing at a Virginal

12. REMBRANDT—Self Portrait

13. REMBRANDT—Belshazzar's Feast

Baroque and Rococo

14. RUBENS—The Judgment of Paris

15. VAN DYCK—Charles I on Horseback

16. VELÁZQUEZ—The Rokeby Venus

17. CARAVAGGIO—Supper at Emmaus

18. BOUCHER—Pan and Syrinx

British

19. CONSTABLE—The Hay Wain

20. TURNER—The Fighting Téméraire

21. TURNER—Rain, Steam, Speed

Impressionism and Beyond

22. DELAROCHE—The Execution of Lady Jane Grey

23. MONET—Gare St. Lazare

24. MANET—The Waitress (La Servante de Bocks)

25. DEGAS— Miss La La at the Cirque Fernando

26. RENOIR—The Umbrellas

27. SEURAT—Bathers at Asnieres

28. VAN GOGH—Sunflowers

29. CÉZANNE—Bathers

30. MONET—Water Lilies

government functions, aristocratic WC, immediately across White-hall from the Horse Guards, tube: Westminster, tel. 020/7930-4179). Just up the street is Trafalgar Square.

Sights—Trafalgar Square

▲▲**Trafalgar Square**—London's central square is a thrilling place to just hang out. Lord Nelson stands atop his 185-foot-tall fluted granite column, gazing out to Trafalgar, where he lost his life but defeated the French fleet. Shot by a sniper during the battle, Nelson died gasping, "Thank God, I have done my duty." Part of this 1842 memorial is made from the melted-down cannons of his victims at Trafalgar. He's surrounded by giant lions, hordes of people, and even more pigeons. Buy a 25p cup of bird-pleasing seed. To make the birds explode into flight, you don't need to yell; simply toss a sweater into the air. This high-profile square is the climax of most marches and demonstrations (tube: Charing Cross).

▲▲▲**National Gallery**—Wonderfully renovated, displaying

Britain's top collection of European paintings from 1250 to 1900 (works by Leonardo, Botticelli, Velázquez, Rembrandt, Turner, van Gogh, and the Impressionists), this is one of Europe's great galleries. While the collection is huge, following the 30-stop route suggested on the map on previous page will give you my best quick tour. The audioguide tours are the best I've used in Europe (£4 donation requested). Don't miss the "Micro Gallery," a computer room even your dad could have fun in (closes 30 minutes earlier than museum); you can study any artist, style, or topic in the museum and even print out a tailor-made tour map (free, daily 10:00–18:00, Wed until 21:00, free one-hour overview tours daily at 11:30 and 14:30 plus Wed at 18:30, photography prohibited, on Trafalgar Square, tube: Charing Cross or Leicester Square, tel. 020/7747-2885).

▲**National Portrait Gallery**—Put off by halls of 19th-century characters who meant nothing to me, I used to call this "as interesting as someone else's yearbook." But a select walk through this five-centuries-long Who's Who of British history is quick and free and puts faces on the story of England. A bonus is the chance to admire some great art by painters such as Holbein, Van Dyck, Hogarth, Reynolds, and Gainsborough. The collection is well described, not huge, and in historical sequence, from the 16th century on the top floor to today's royal family on the bottom.

Some highlights: Henry VIII and wives; several fascinating portraits of the "Virgin Queen" Elizabeth I, Sir Francis Drake, and Sir Walter Raleigh; the only real-life portrait of Shakespeare; Oliver Cromwell and Charles I with his head on; self-portraits and other portraits by Gainsborough and Reynolds; the Romantics (Blake, Byron, Wordsworth, and company); Queen Victoria and her era; and the present royal family, including the late Princess Diana. For more information, follow the fine audioguide (£3 donation requested, tells more about history than art, hear actual interviews with 20th-century subjects) or get the 60p quick overview guidebooklet (free, Mon–Sat 10:00–18:00, Sun 12:00–18:00, entry 100 yards off Trafalgar Square, around the corner from the National Gallery, opposite Church of St. Martin-in-the-Fields, tel. 020/7306-0055).

▲**St. Martin-in-the-Fields**—This church, built in the 1720s, with a Gothic spire placed upon a Greek-type temple, is an oasis of peace on wild and noisy Trafalgar Square. St. Martin cared for the poor. "In the fields" was where the first church stood on this spot (in the 13th century), between Westminster and the City. Stepping inside, you still feel a compassion for the needs of the people in this community. The church is famous for its concerts. Consider a free lunchtime concert (Mon, Tue, and Fri at 13:05) or an evening concert (Thu, Fri, and Sat at 19:30, £6–16, CC:VM, box office tel. 020/7839-8362, church tel. 020/7930-0089). Downstairs you'll find

a ticket office for concerts, a good shop, a brass-rubbing centre, and
a fine budget support-the-church cafeteria (see "Eating," below).

More Top Squares:
Piccadilly, Soho, and Covent Garden

▲▲**Piccadilly Circus**—London's touristy square got its name from
the fancy ruffled shirts—picadils—made in the neighborhood long
ago. Today the square is surrounded by fascinating streets and
swimming with youth on the rampage. The Rock Circus offers a
commercial but serious history of rock music with Madame Tussaud
wax stars. While overpriced, it's an entertaining hour under radio
earphones for rock 'n' roll romantics—many enter with a beer
buzz and sing happily off-key under their headphones—nearly as
entertaining as the exhibit itself (£8.25, daily 10:00–21:00, plenty of
photo ops, tube: Piccadilly Circus, tel. 020/7734-8025). For over-
stimulation, drop by the extremely trashy Pepsi Trocadero Center's
"theme park of the future" for its Segaworld virtual reality games,
nine-screen cinema, and thundering IMAX theater (admission to
Trocadero is free; individual attractions cost £2–8; find a discount
ticket at brochure racks at TI or hotels before paying full price for
IMAX; between Coventry and Shaftesbury, just off Piccadilly).
Chinatown, to the east, has swollen since Hong Kong lost its independence. Nearby Shaftesbury Avenue and Leicester Square teem
with fun seekers, theaters, Chinese restaurants, and street singers.

Soho—North of Piccadilly, seedy Soho is becoming trendy and
is well worth a gawk. Soho is London's red-light district, where
"friendly models" wait in tiny rooms up dreary stairways and scant-
ily clad con artists sell strip shows. While venturing up a stairway to
check out a model is interesting, anyone who goes into any one of
the shows will be ripped off. Every time. Even a £3 show comes
with a £100 cover or minimum (as it's printed on the drink menu)
and a "security man." You may accidentally buy a £200 bottle of
bubbly. And suddenly, the door has no handle. By the way, telephone sex is hard to avoid these days in London. Phone booths
are littered with racy fliers of busty ladies "new in town." Some
travelers gather six or eight phone booths' worth of fliers and take
them home for kinky wallpaper.

▲▲**Covent Garden**—This boutique-ish shopping district is a
people watcher's delight with cigarette eaters, Punch-and-Judy
acts, food that's good for you (but not your wallet), trendy crafts,
sweet whiffs of pot, two-tone hair (neither natural), and faces that
could set off a metal detector (tube: Covent Garden). For better
Covent Garden lunch deals, walk a block or two away from the
eye of this touristic hurricane (check out the places a block or two
north of the tube station along Endell Street and Neal Street—
try Food for Thought at #31), and for a "Food is Fun" dinner-
crawl from Covent Garden to Soho, see "Eating," below.

Central London

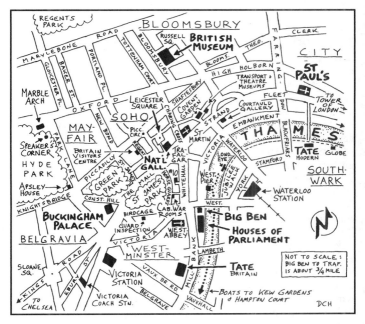

Museums near Covent Garden

▲**Courtauld Gallery**—While far less impressive than the National Gallery, this generally overlooked yet wonderful collection of paintings is a joy. Part of the Courtauld Institute of Art, the thoughtful descriptions of each piece of art remind visitors that the gallery is still used for teaching. You'll see medieval European paintings, and works by Rubens, Impressionists (Manet, Monet, Degas, Seurat), and Post-Impressionists (Cézanne). An additional fee or combo ticket gets you into the Gilbert Collection, a glittering display of gold, silver, and tiny mosaics from the 15th to 19th centuries (£4 apiece, £7 combo includes Courtauld and Gilbert, both free Mon 10:00–14:00, Mon–Sat 10:00–18:00, Sun 12:00–18:00, located in Somerset House, near Waterloo Bridge, enter on Strand, tube: Temple or Covent Garden, tel. 020/7848-2526).

▲**London Transport Museum**—This wonderful museum is a delight for kids. Whether you're cursing or marveling at the buses and tube, the growth of Europe's biggest city has been made possible by its public transit system. Watch the growth of the tube, then sit in the simulator to "drive" a train (£5.50, Sat–Thu 10:00–18:00, Fri 11:00–18:00, 30 yards southeast of Covent Garden's marketplace, tel. 020/7836-8557).

Theatre Museum—This earnest museum, probably worthwhile only for theater buffs, traces the development of British theater from Shakespeare to today (£4.50, Tue–Sun 10:00–18:00, closed Mon, a block east of Covent Garden's marketplace down Russell Street, call about guided tours, makeup demos, and costume workshops, tel. 020/7943-4700).

Sights—North London

▲▲▲**British Museum**—This is the greatest chronicle of our civilization anywhere. Visiting this immense museum is like hiking through Encyclopedia Britannica National Park.

The museum has undergone a major transformation for the millennium and for its 250th birthday in 2003. With more than 6 million visitors a year, Britain's most popular museum was due for an upgrade.

Entering on Great Russell Street, you'll step into the **Great Court**, the new glass-domed hub of a two-acre cultural complex. This bustling people zone of shops, restaurants, and lecture halls stays open after the museum closes for the day. The Round Reading Room (Marx's hangout), located within the Great Court, has been restored and is once again public. The new Ethnographic Galleries contain collections on life in Africa, Asia, and the Americas.

After an overview ramble, cover just two or three sections of your choice more thoroughly. The Egyptian, Mesopotamian (Assyrian), and Greek (Parthenon) sections are highlights.

The huge winged lions (which guarded Assyrian palaces 800 years before Christ) guard the museum's three great ancient galleries. For a brief tour, connect these ancient dots:

Start with the **Egyptian.** Wander from the Rosetta Stone past the many statues. At the end of the hall, climb the stairs to mummy land.

Back at the winged lions, wander through the dark, violent, and mysterious **Assyrian** rooms. The Nimrud Gallery is lined with royal propaganda reliefs and wounded lions.

The most modern of the ancient art fills the **Greek** section. Find room 1 behind the winged lions and start your walk through Greek art history with the simple and primitive Cycladic fertility figures. Later, painted vases show a culture really into partying. The finale is the Elgin Marbles. The much-wrangled-over bits of the Athenian Parthenon (from 450 B.C.) are even more impressive than they look. To best appreciate these ancient carvings, take the free audioguide tour and read through the orientation material in the tiny area between rooms 7 and 8. (Free, £2 donation requested, Mon–Sat 10:00–17:00, Sun 12:00–18:00, least crowded weekday late afternoons, Great Russell Street, tube: Tottenham Court Road, tel. 020/7323-8000 or 020/7388-2227, www.thebritishmuseum.ac.uk.)

There are three types of **tours**: Highlights tours (£7, 4/day, 90 min), Focus tours (£5, 2/day, 60 min), and Eye Openers (free, nearly hrly, 50 min). For tour times, call ahead or check schedule and brochures at entry.

▲▲▲**British Library**—In the new and impressive British Library, wander through the manuscripts that have enlightened and brightened our lives for centuries. While the library contains 180 miles of bookshelves in London's deepest basement, one beautiful room filled with state-of-the-art glass display cases shows you the treasures: ancient maps, early Gospels on papyrus, illuminated manuscripts from the early Middle Ages, the Gutenberg Bible, the Magna Carta, pages from Leonardo's notebooks, and original writing by the titans of English literature, from Chaucer and Shakespeare to Dickens and Wordsworth. There's also a wall dedicated to music, with manuscripts from Beethoven to the Beatles. To virtually flip through the pages of a few precious books, drop by the "Turning the Pages" room (free, Mon–Fri 9:30–18:00, Tue 9:30–20:00, Sat 9:30–17:00, Sun 11:00–17:00; 60-minute tours for £4 usually offered Mon, Wed, and Fri–Sun at 15:00, also Tue 18:30, Sat 10:30, and Sun 11:30, call 020/7412-7332 to confirm schedule and reserve, great cafeteria/restaurant upstairs from café, tube: King's Cross, leaving station, turn right and walk a block to 96 Euston Road, library tel. 020/7412-7000, www.bl.uk).

▲**Madame Tussaud's Waxworks**—This is expensive but dang good. The original Madame Tussaud did wax casts of heads lopped off during the French Revolution (e.g., Marie Antoinette). She took her show on the road and ended up in London. And now it's much easier to be featured. The gallery is one big Who's Who photo op—a huge hit with the kind of travelers who skip the British Museum. Don't miss the "make a model" exhibit (showing Jerry Hall getting waxed) or the gallery of has-been heads that no longer merit a body (such as Sammy Davis Jr. and Nikita Khrushchev). After looking a hundred famous people in the glassy eyes and surviving a silly hall of horror, you'll board a Disney-type ride and cruise through a kid-pleasing "Spirit of London" time trip (£11.50, kids-£8, under age 5 free; combo ticket for Tussaud's and Planetarium-£14, kids-£9.50; Jan–Sept daily 9:00–17:30, Oct–Dec Mon–Fri 10:00–17:30, Sat–Sun 9:30–17:30, Marylebone Road, tube: Baker Street). Avoid a wait by either booking ahead to get a ticket with an entry time (tel. 0870/400 3000, online at www.madame-tussaud.com, or at TI) or arriving late in the day— 90 minutes is plenty of time for the exhibit.

Sir John Soane's Museum—Architects and fans love this quirky place crammed with art and architectural bric-a-brac (free, Tue– Sat 10:00–17:00, also first Tue of month 18:00–21:00, closed Sun– Mon, 13 Lincoln's Inn Fields, 5 blocks east of British Museum, tube: Holborn, tel. 020/7405-2107).

Sights—Buckingham Palace

▲**Buckingham Palace**—This lavish home has been the royal residence since 1837. When the queen's at home, the royal standard flies; otherwise the Union Jack flaps in the wind (£10.50 for state apartments and throne room, open Aug and Sept only, daily 9:30–16:30, only 8,000 visitors a day—come early to get an appointed visit time or call 020/7321-2233 and reserve a ticket with CC, tube: Victoria).

▲▲**Changing of the Guard at Buckingham Palace**—The guards change with much fanfare at 11:30 daily May through August and generally every even-numbered day September through April (no band when wet; worth a 50p phone call any day to confirm that they'll change, tel. 0891-505-452). Join the mob at the back of the palace (the front faces a huge and extremely private park). You'll need to be early or tall to see much of the actual changing of the guard, but for the pageantry in the street you can pop by at 11:30. Stake out the high ground on the circular Victoria Monument for the best general views. The marching troops and bands are colorful and even stirring, but the actual changing of the guard is a non-event. It is interesting, however, to see nearly every tourist in London gathered in one place at the same time. Hop into a big black taxi and say, "Buck House, please." The show lasts about 30 minutes: three troops parade by, the guard changes with much shouting, the band plays a happy little concert, and then they march out. On a balmy day, it's a fun happening.

For all the color with none of the crowds, see the **Inspection of the Guard Ceremony** at 11:00 in front of the **Wellington Barracks**, 500 yards east of the palace on Birdcage Walk. Afterwards, stroll through nearby St. James' Park (tube: Victoria, St. James' Park, or Green Park).

Sights—West London

▲**Hyde Park and Speakers' Corner**—London's "Central Park"—originally Henry VIII's hunting ground—has more than 600 acres of lush greenery, a huge man-made lake, the royal Kensington Palace (not worth touring), and the ornate neo-Gothic Albert Memorial across from the Royal Albert Hall. Early afternoons on Sunday, Speakers' Corner offers soapbox oratory at its best (tube: Marble Arch). "The grass roots of democracy" is actually a holdover from when the gallows stood here and the criminal was allowed to say just about anything he wanted to before he swung. I dare you to raise your voice and gather a crowd—it's easy to do.

▲**Apsley House (Wellington Museum)**—Having beat Napoleon at Waterloo, the Duke of Wellington was the most famous man in Europe. He was given London's ultimate address, #1 London. His newly refurbished mansion offers one of London's best palace experiences. An 11-foot-tall marble statue (by Canova) of Napoleon clad only in a fig leaf greets you. Downstairs is a small gallery of Wellington memorabilia (including a 30-minute video and a pair of Wellington boots). The lavish upstairs shows off the duke's fine collection of paintings, including works by Velázquez and Steen (well described by included audioguide, £4.50, Tue–Sun 11:00–17:00, closed Mon, 20 yards from Hyde Park Corner tube station, tel. 020/7499-5676). Hyde Park's pleasant and picnic-wonderful rose garden is nearby.

▲▲Victoria and Albert Museum—The world's top collection of decorative arts is a gangly (150 rooms over 12 miles of corridors) but surprisingly interesting assortment of artistic stuff from the West as well as Asian and Islamic cultures. The V&A, which grew out of the Great Exhibition of 1851—that ultimate festival celebrating the Industrial Revolution and the greatness of Britain—was originally for manufactured art. But after much support from Queen Victoria and Prince Albert, it was renamed after the royal couple, and its present building was opened in 1909. The idealistic Victorian notion that anyone can be continually improved by education and example remains the driving force behind this museum.

While just wandering works well here, consider catching one of the regular 60-minute orientation **tours**, buying the fine £5 "Hundred Highlights" guidebook, or walking through these ground-floor highlights: **Medieval Treasury** (room 43, well-described treasury of Middle Age European art), the finest collection of **Indian decorative art** outside India (room 41), the **Dress Gallery** (room 40, 400 years of English fashion corseted into 40 display cases), the **Raphael Gallery** (room 48a, seven huge water-color "cartoons" painted as designs for tapestries to hang in the Sistine Chapel, among the greatest art treasures in Britain and the best works of the High Renaissance), reliefs by the Renaissance sculptor **Donatello** (room 16), a close-up look at **medieval stained glass** (room 28, much more upstairs), the fascinating **Cast Courts** (rooms 46a and 46b, filled with plaster copies of the greatest art of our civilization—such as Trajan's Column and Michelangelo's *David*—made for the benefit of 19th-century art students who couldn't afford a railpass), and the hall of "great" **fakes and forgeries** (room 46). Upstairs you can walk through the **British Galleries** for centuries of aristocratic living rooms (£5, daily 10:00–18:00, free after 16:30, £3 admission on Wed 18:30–21:30, open Wed eve year-round except mid-Dec–mid-Jan; the museum café is in the delightfully ornate Gamble Room from 1868, just off room 14, tube: South Kensington, a long tunnel leads directly from the tube station to the museum, tel. 020/7938-8500).

▲Natural History Museum—Across the street from the Victoria and Albert Museum, this mammoth museum is housed in a giant

and wonderful Victorian neo-Romanesque building. Built in the
1870s specifically to house the huge collection (50 million speci-
mens), it presents itself in two halves: the Life Galleries (creepy-
crawlies, human biology, the origin of the species, "our place in
evolution," and awesome dinosaurs) and the Earth Galleries
(meteors, volcanoes, earthquakes, and so on). Exhibits are wonderfully explained with lots of creative interactive displays (£7.50,
children under 16 free, free to anyone after 16:30 on weekdays
and after 17:00 on weekends—pop in if only for the wild collection of dinosaurs, Mon–Sat 10:00–17:50, Sun 11:00–17:50, a
long tunnel leads directly from South Kensington tube station
to museum, tel. 020/7938-9123, www.nhm.ac.uk).

Sights—East London: "The City"

▲▲**The City of London**—When Londoners say "The City," they
mean the one-square-mile business, banking, and journalism center
that 2,000 years ago was Roman Londinium. The outline of the
Roman city walls can still be seen in the arc of roads from Blackfriars Bridge to Tower Bridge. Within the City are 24 churches
designed by Christopher Wren, mostly just ornamentation around
St. Paul's Cathedral. Today, while home to only 5,000 residents, the
City thrives with over 500,000 office workers coming and going
daily. It's a fascinating district to wander, but since almost nobody
actually lives there, it's dull on Saturday and Sunday.

▲**Old Bailey**—To see the British legal system in action—lawyers
in little blond wigs speaking legalese with a British accent—spend
a few minutes in the visitors' gallery at "Old Bailey" (free, Mon–
Fri 10:00–13:00, 14:00–14:30 most weeks, no kids under 14, no
bags or cameras, purses OK, you can check your bag at the SPAR
grocery across the street for £1, 2 blocks northwest of St. Paul's on
Old Bailey Street, follow signs to public entrance, tube: St. Paul's,
tel. 020/7248-3277).

▲▲▲**St. Paul's Cathedral**—Wren's most famous church is the
great St. Paul's, its elaborate interior capped by a 365-foot dome.
The crypt (included with admission) is a world of historic bones
and memorials, including Admiral Nelson's tomb and interesting
cathedral models. The great West Door is opened only for great
occasions, such as the wedding of Prince Charles and the late
Princess Diana in 1981. Stand at the back of the church and imagine how Diana felt before making the hike to the altar with the
world watching. Sit under the second-largest dome in the world
and eavesdrop on guided tours.

Since World War II, St. Paul's has been Britain's symbol of
resistance. Despite 57 nights of bombing, the Nazis failed to
destroy the cathedral, thanks to the St. Paul's volunteer fire watch
who stayed on the dome. Climb the dome for a great city view and
some fun in the whispering gallery—where the precisely designed

East London: "The City"

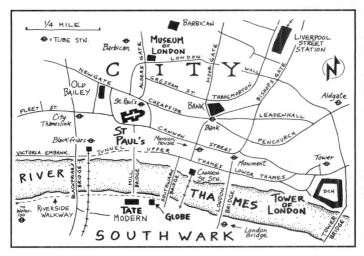

barrel of the dome lets sweet nothings circle audibly around to
the opposite side (£5 entry, Mon–Sat 8:30–16:30, last entry 16:00,
closed Sun except for worship, allow an hour to climb up and
down dome—closed Sun, no photography allowed within church,
£2.50 for guided 90-minute "super tours" of cathedral and crypt
offered at 11:00, 11:30, 13:30, and 14:00 or £3 for an audioguide
tour anytime, Sun services at 8:00, 10:15, 11:30, and 15:15—
evensong, good restaurant, and cheap and cheery café in the
crypt, tube: St. Paul's, tel. 020/7236-8348).

The **evensong** services are free, though visitors are not allowed
to linger afterward (Mon–Sat at 17:00, Sun at 15:15, 40 min).
▲**Museum of London**— London, a 2000-year-old city, is so littered with Roman ruins that when a London builder finds Roman
antiquities he doesn't stop work. He simply documents the finds,
moves the artifacts to a museum, and builds on. If you're asking,
"Why did the Romans build their cities underground?," a trip to
the creative and entertaining London Museum is a must. Stroll
through London history from pre-Roman times through the Blitz
up to today. This regular stop for the local schoolkids gives the
best overview of London history in town (£5, free after 16:30,
Mon–Sat 10:00–18:00, Sun 12:00–18:00, tube: Barbican or St.
Paul's, tel. 020/7600-3699).
Geffrye Decorative Arts Museum—Walk through British
front rooms from 1600 to 1990 (free, Tue–Sat 10:00–17:00,
Sun 12:00–17:00, closed Mon, tube: Liverpool Street, then bus
149 or 242 north, tel. 020/7739-9893).

▲▲▲**Tower of London**—The Tower has served as a castle in wartime, a king's residence in peace, and, most notoriously, as the prison and execution site of rebels. This historic fortress is host to more than 3 million visitors a year. Enjoy the free, and riotously entertaining, 50-minute Beefeater tour (leaves regularly from inside the gate, last one is usually at 15:30 in summer, 14:30 off-season). The crown jewels, dating from the Restoration, are the best on earth—and come with hour-long lines for most of the day. To avoid the crowds, arrive at 9:00 and go straight for the jewels, doing the tour and tower later—or do the jewels after 16:30 (£11, one-day combo ticket with Hampton Court Palace-£18.50, March–Oct Mon–Sat 9:00–18:00, Sun 10:00–18:00, Nov–Feb Tue–Sat 9:00–17:00, Sun–Mon 10:00–17:00, last entry 1 hr before closing, the long but fast-moving ticket line is worst on Sun, no photography allowed of jewels or in chapels, tube: Tower Hill, tel. 020/7709-0765, recorded info: 020/7680-9004).

Ceremony of the Keys: Every night at 21:30, with pageantry-filled ceremony, the Tower of London is locked up (as it has been for the last 700 years). To attend this free 30-minute event, you need to request an invitation at least two to three months before your visit. Write to: Ceremony of the Keys, H.M. Tower of London, London EC3N 4AB. Include your name; the addresses, names, and ages of all people attending (up to 7 people, nontransferable, no kids under 8 allowed); requested date; alternative dates; and an international reply coupon (buy at U.S. post office).

Sights next to the Tower—The best remaining bit of London's **Roman Wall** is just north of the tower (at the Tower Hill tube station). Freshly painted and restored, **Tower Bridge**—the neo-Gothic maritime gateway to London—has an 1894 to 1994 history exhibit (£6.25, daily 10:00–18:30, last entry at 17:15, good view, poor value, tel. 020/7403-3761). The chic **St. Katherine Yacht Harbor**, just east of the Tower Bridge, has mod shops and the classic old Dickens Inn, fun for a drink or pub lunch. Across the bridge is the South Bank, with the upscale Butlers Wharf area, museums, and promenade.

Sights—South London, on the South Bank

The South Bank is a thriving arts and cultural center tied together by a riverside path. This trendy, pub-crawling walk—called the Jubilee Promenade—stretches from the Tower of London bridge past Westminster Bridge, where it offers grand views of the Houses of Parliament. (The promenade hugs the river except just east of London Bridge, where it cuts inland for a couple of blocks.)

▲▲**Globe Theater**—The original Globe Theater has been rebuilt—half-timbered and thatched—exactly as it was in Shakespeare's time. Open as a museum and working theater, it hosts authentic old-time performances of Shakespeare's plays. The

The South Bank

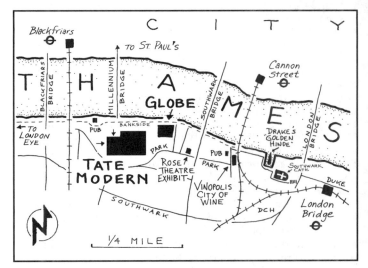

theater can be toured when there are no plays. The Globe's exhibition on Shakespeare is the world's largest, with interactive displays and film presentations, a sound lab, a script factory, and costumes (£7.50, mid-May–Sept daily 9:00–12:00, Oct–mid-May 10:00–17:00, includes guided 30-minute tour offered on the half hour, on the South Bank directly across the Thames over Southwark Bridge from St. Paul's, tube: Mansion House or London Bridge, tel. 020/7902-1500, www.shakespeares-globe.org, for details on seeing a play, see "Entertainment," on page 349).

▲▲**Tate Modern**—Dedicated in spring of 2000, this striking new museum across the river from St. Paul's opened the new century with art from the old one (remember the 20th century?). Its powerhouse collection of Monet, Matisse, Dalí, Picasso, Warhol, and much more is displayed in a converted power house (museum free, fee for special exhibitions, daily 10:00–18:00, Fri–Sat until 22:00—a good time to visit, audioguide-£1, free guided tours, call for schedule, view café on top floor, walk the new Millennium Bridge from St. Paul's or tube: Southwark plus a 7-minute walk, tel. 020/7887-8008, www.tate.org.uk). From May through September, a river-bus service will connect Tate Modern with Tate Britain—ask for schedule at either Tate.

▲▲**Millennium Bridge**—This new pedestrian bridge links St. Paul's Cathedral and Tate Modern across the Thames. Its sleek minimalist design—370 meters long, 4 meters wide, stainless steel with teak planks—has clever aerodynamic handrails to deflect wind over the heads of pedestrians. This is London's only pedestrian bridge and its first new bridge in a century (free, always open).

▲▲▲**London Eye Ferris Wheel**—Towering above London opposite Big Ben, this is the world's highest observational wheel—and a chance to fly British Air without leaving London. Built like a giant bicycle wheel, it's a pan-European undertaking: British steel and Dutch engineering, with Czech, German, French, and Italian mechanical parts. It's also very "green," running extremely efficiently and virtually silently. Twenty-five people ride in each of its 32 air-conditioned capsules for the 30-minute rotation (each capsule has a bench, but most people stand).

The "flight" is as tame as an elevator ride, but fun for the grand views. From the top of this 450-foot-high wheel—the highest public viewpoint in the city, Big Ben looks small. You only go around once; save a shot on top for the glass capsule of people next to yours.

A big hit with Londoners and tourists alike, the ride gets booked up fast, especially on weekends. To save time and guarantee a spot, book a time slot a day ahead—at a London TI, in person at the office near the base of the wheel, at the Big Bus Information Centre (daily 8:30–17:30, 48 Buckingham Palace Road, a block from Victoria Station), or possibly through your hotel (ask). You can also book by phone, but allow at least five days before your ticket is available (pick up ticket at office at Wheel, 50p charge, automated booking tel. 0870-500-0600). Whether you book ahead or just stand in line, you'll be assigned—or you can request—a half-hour time slot (such as 9:00–9:30); you must arrive at the Wheel during this time (earlier is better) to ensure getting on. Advance booking, which costs nothing extra, allows you to skip the queue to buy tickets. No one escapes the second queue, the ticket-holders' line to get on the Wheel (line starts forming 10 minutes before your half-hour time slot begins; listen for announcement). The long line moves quickly; the many purple-shirted staff are there to help and herd you.

Freewheeling types who don't care for lines or prebooking will have the best luck spinning the Wheel at night; it's open until 22:00 in peak season (last boarding 21:30); if you're lucky, you can waltz right on (£8.50, April–mid-Sept 9:00–22:00, mid-Sept–March 10:00–18:00, at County Hall, WCs, coffee, shop that has binoculars for rent, on river Thames, with its own ferry dock, tube: Waterloo or Westminster, www.ba-londoneye.com). The Wheel is slated to be dismantled in 2005 and moved to a lower-profile location.

▲▲**Imperial War Museum**—This impressive museum covers the wars of this century, from heavy weaponry to love notes and Varga Girls, from Monty's Africa campaign tank to Schwartzkopf's Desert Storm uniform. You can trace the development of the machine gun, watch footage of the first tank battles, hold your breath through the gruesome WWI trench experience, and buy WWII–era toys in the fun museum shop. Rather than glorify war, the museum does its best to shine a light on the powerful human side of one of mankind's most persistent traits (£5.50, free for kids under 16, daily 10:00–18:00, free for anyone after 16:30, 90 minutes is enough time for most visitors, tube: Lambeth North, tel. 020/7416-5000).

Bramah Tea and Coffee Museum—Aficionados of tea or coffee will find this small museum fascinating. It tells the story of each drink almost passionately. The owner, Mr. Bramah, comes from a big tea family and wants the world to know how the advent of commercial television, with breaks not long enough to brew a proper pot of tea, required a faster hot drink. In came the horrible English instant coffee. Tea countered with finely chopped leaves in tea bags, and it's gone downhill ever since. (£4, daily 10:00–18:00, in the Butlers Wharf complex just across the bridge from the Tower, behind the Design Museum, tel. 020/7378-0222). Its café, which serves more kinds of coffees and teas than cakes, is open to the public.

Sights—South London, on the North Bank

▲▲**Tate Britain**—One of Europe's great art houses, Tate Britain specializes in British painting: 16th century through the 20th, including Pre-Raphaelites. Commune with the mystical Blake and romantic Turner (free, daily 10:00–17:50, fine £3 audioguide, free tours: 11:30—Turner, 14:30 and 15:30—British Highlights, call to confirm schedule, no photography allowed, tube: Pimlico plus 7-minute walk, or arrive directly at museum by taking bus #88 from Oxford Circus or #77A from National Gallery or the river-bus from Tate Modern, tel. 020/7887-8000, recorded info tel. 020/7887-8888, www.tate.org.uk).

Sights—Greater London

▲**Kew Gardens**—For a fine riverside park and a palatial greenhouse jungle to swing through, take the tube or the boat to every botanist's favorite escape, Kew Gardens. While to most visitors the Royal Botanic Gardens of Kew is simply a delightful opportunity to wander among 33,000 different types of plants, it's run by a hardworking organization committed to understanding and preserving the botanical diversity of our planet. The Kew tube station drops you in an herbal little business community a two-block walk from Victoria Gate (the main garden entry). Pick up a map brochure with a monthly listing of best blooms.

Garden lovers could spend days exploring Kew's 300 acres. For a quick visit, spend a fragrant hour wandering through three buildings: the Palm House—a humid Victorian world of iron, glass, and tropical plants—built in 1844; a Waterlily House—hottest in the gardens—that Monet would swim for; and the Princess of Wales Conservatory—a modern greenhouse with many different climate zones growing countless cacti,

Greater London

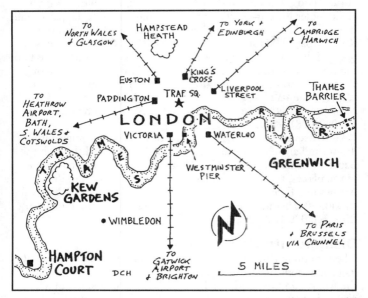

bug-munching carnivorous plants, and more (£5, Mon–Sat 9:30–18:00, Sun 9:30–19:30, until 16:30 or sunset off-season, galleries and conservatories close 45 minutes earlier, entry discounted to £3.50 at 45 minutes before closing, consider £2.50 narrated floral joyride on little train departing from Victoria Gate, tube: Kew Gardens, tel. 020/8332-5000). For a sun-dappled lunch, hike 10 minutes from the Palm House to the Orangery (£6 hot meals, daily 10:00–17:30). For tea, consider the Maids of Honor (280 Kew Road, near garden entrance, tel. 020/8940-2752).

▲**Hampton Court Palace**—Fifteen miles up the Thames from downtown (£15 taxi ride from Kew Gardens) is the 500-year-old palace of Henry VIII. Actually, it was the palace of his minister, Cardinal Wolsey. When Wolsey, a clever man, realized Henry VIII was experiencing a little palace envy, he gave it to his king. The Tudor palace was also home to Elizabeth I and Charles I. And parts were updated by Christopher Wren for William and Mary. The palace stands stately overlooking the Thames and includes some impressive Tudor rooms, including a Great Hall, with its magnificent hammer-beam ceiling. The industrial-strength Tudor kitchen was capable of keeping 600 schmoozing courtesans thoroughly—if not well—fed. The sculpted garden features a rare Tudor tennis court and a popular maze. The palace, fully restored since its 1986 fire, tries hard to please, but it doesn't quite sparkle. From the information center in the main courtyard, visitors book times for tours with tired costumed guides or grab audioguides for self-guided tours of various wings of the palace (all free). The Tudor Kitchens, Henry VIII's Apartments, and the King's Apartments are most interesting. The Georgian Rooms are pretty dull. The maze in the nearby garden is a curiosity some find fun (maze only-£2.50). The train (2/hrly, 30 min) from London's Waterloo station drops you just across the river from the palace (£10.50, one-day combo ticket with Tower of London-£18.50, Mon 10:00–18:00, Tue–Sun 9:30–18:00, Nov–March until 16:30, tel. 020/8781-9500).

RAF Museum—A hit with aviation enthusiasts, this huge aerodrome and airfield contain planes from World War I through the Battle of Britain up to the Gulf War. You can climb inside some of the planes, try your luck in a cockpit, and fly with the Red Arrows in a flight simulator (£7, daily 10:00–18:00, café, shop, car parking, Grahame Park Way, tube: Colindale—on the Northern Line, tel. 020/8205-2266, www.rafmuseum.org.uk).

Disappointments of London

The venerable BBC broadcasts from Broadcasting House. Of all its productions, its "BBC Experience" tour for visitors is among the worst. On the South Bank, the London Dungeon, a much-visited but amateurish attraction, is just a highly advertised, over-priced haunted house—certainly not worth the £10 admission, much less your valuable London time. It comes with long and rude lines. Wait for Halloween and see one in your hometown to support a better cause. The Design Museum (next to Bramah Tea and Coffee Museum) and "Winston Churchill's Britain at War Experience" (next to London Dungeon) waste your time. The Kensington Palace State Apartments are lifeless and not worth a visit.

Shopping in London

Harrods—Filled with wonderful displays, Harrods is London's most famous and touristy department store. Big yet classy, Harrods has everything from elephants to toothbrushes. The food halls are sights to savor, with cafeterias (Mon, Tue, and Sat 10:00–18:00, Wed–Fri 10:00–19:00, closed Sun, on Brompton Road, tube: Knightsbridge, tel. 020/7730-1234). Many readers report that Harrods is overpriced (its £1 toilets are the most expensive in Europe), snooty, and teeming with American and Japanese tourists. Still, it's the palace of department stores—an experience for even nonshoppers. The nearby Beauchamp Place is lined with classy and fascinating shops.

Harvey Nichols—The late Princess Diana's favorite, this is still the department store *du jour*. Its fifth floor is a food fest with a fancy restaurant and a Yo! Sushi bar. Consider a take-away tray of sushi to eat on a bench in the Hyde Park rose garden two blocks away (Mon–Tue and Sat 10:00–19:00, Wed–Fri 10:00–20:00, Sun 12:00–18:00, near Harrods, 109 Knightsbridge, tube: Knightsbridge).

Toys—The biggest toy store in Britain is **Hamley's** (Mon–Sat 10:00–20:00, Sun 12:00–18:00, 188 Regent Street, tube: Oxford Circus, tel. 020/7494-2000).

Street Markets—Antique buffs, people watchers, and folks who brake for garage sales love London's street markets. There's good early morning market activity somewhere any day of the week. The best are Portobello Road (Fri–Wed 9:00–18:00, Thu 9:00–13:00, go on Sat for antiques until 16:00—plus the regular junk, clothes, and produce; tube: Notting Hill Gate) and Camden Market (Sat–Sun 10:00–18:00, trendy arts and crafts, tube: Camden Town). The tourist office has a complete, up-to-date list. If you like to haggle, there are no holds barred in London's street markets. Warning: Markets attract two kinds of people—tourists and pickpockets.

Famous Auctions—London's famous auctioneers welcome the curious public for viewing and bidding. For schedules, call Sotheby's (Mon–Fri 9:00–16:30, 34 New Bond Street, tube: Oxford Circus or Bond Street, tel. 020/7293-5000, www.sothebys .com) or Christie's (Mon–Fri 9:00–17:00, 8 King Street, tube: Green Park, tel. 020/7839-9060, www.christies.com).

Entertainment and Theater in London

London bubbles with top-notch entertainment seven days a week. Everything's listed in the weekly entertainment magazines, available at newsstands. Choose from classical, jazz, rock, and far-out music, Gilbert and Sullivan, dance, comedy, Baha'i meetings, poetry readings, spectator sports, film, and theater.

London's theater rivals Broadway's in quality and beats it in price. Choose from the Royal Shakespeare Company, top musicals, comedy, thrillers, sex farces, and more. Performances are nightly except Sunday, usually with one matinee a week. Matinees (Wed, Thu, or Sat) are cheaper and rarely sold out. Tickets range from about £8 to £35.

Most theaters, marked on tourist maps, are in the Piccadilly-Trafalgar area. Box offices, hotels, and TIs have a handy "Theater Guide" brochure listing what's playing.

To book a seat, simply call the theater box office directly, ask about seats and dates available, and buy one with your credit card. You can call from the U.S.A. as easily as from England (photocopy your hometown library's London newspaper theater section or check out www.officiallondontheatre.co.uk). Pick up your ticket 15 minutes before the show.

Ticket agencies are scalpers with an address. Booking through an agency (at most TIs or scattered throughout London) is quick and easy, but prices are inflated by a standard 25 percent fee. If buying from an agency, look at the ticket carefully (your price should be no more than 30 percent over the printed face value; the 17 percent VAT tax is already included in the face value) and understand where you're sitting according to the floor plan (if your view is restricted it will state this on ticket). Agencies are worthwhile only if a show you've got to see is sold out at the box office. They scarf up hot tickets, planning to make a killing after the show is sold out. U.S. booking agencies get their tickets from another agency, adding even more to your expense by involving yet another middleman. Many tickets sold on the streets are forgeries. With cheap international phone calls and credit cards, there's no reason not to book direct.

Theater lingo: stalls (ground floor), dress circle (first balcony), upper circle (second balcony), balcony (sky-high third balcony).

Cheap theater tricks: Most theaters offer cheap returned tickets, standing room, matinee, and senior or student standby deals. These "concessions" are indicated with a *conc* or *s* in the listings. While theaters won't technically discount tickets, during slow times they'll offer to sell you a cheap seat and "upgrade" it to an expensive one for free—it doesn't hurt to ask. Picking up a late return can get you a great seat at a cheap-seat price. Standing room can be very cheap. If a show is "sold out," there's usually a way to get a seat. Call the theater box office and ask how. I buy the second-cheapest tickets directly from the theater box office.

The famous "half-price booth" in Leicester (pronounced "Lester") Square sells discounted tickets for good seats to shows on the push list the day of the show only (Mon–Sat 12:00–18:30). The real half-price booth is a free-standing kiosk at the edge of the garden actually in Leicester Square. Several dishonest outfits advertise "official half-price tickets" at agencies closer to the tube station. Avoid these.

Many theaters are so small that there's hardly a bad seat. After the lights go down, "scooting up" is less than a capital offense. Shakespeare did it.

Royal Shakespeare Company—If you'll ever enjoy Shakespeare, it'll be in Britain. The RSC performs at the Barbican Centre in London from December through May (box office open daily 9:00–20:00, call 020/7638-8891 to book with credit card, or for recorded information, call 020/7628-9760) and year-round at the Royal Shakespeare Theatre in Stratford (box office tel. 01789/295-623). To get a schedule, you can either request it by phone (tel. 020/7638-8891) or write to the Royal Shakespeare Theatre (Stratford-upon-Avon, CV37 6BB Warwickshire). You can also visit www.rsc.org.uk. Tickets for London performances range in price from £10 to £30. The best way to book is direct, by telephone and credit card. You can pick up your ticket at the door (Barbican

Centre, Silk Street, tube: Barbican). Students, seniors, and those under 16 can get tickets for half price.

Shakespeare at the Globe Theater—To see Shakespeare in an exact replica of the theater for which he wrote his plays, attend a play at the Globe. This thatch-roofed, open-air round theater does the plays as Shakespeare intended (with no amplification). There are performances from mid-May through September (usually Tue–Sat 14:00 and 19:30, Sun at either 13:00 and 18:30 or at 16:00 only, and no plays on Mon). You'll pay £5 to stand and £10 to £26 to sit (usually on a backless bench; only a few rows and the pricier Gentlemen's Rooms have seats with backs). The £5 "yard" (or "groundling") tickets—while the only ones open to rain—are most fun. You're a crude peasant. You can walk around, munch a picnic dinner, lean your elbows on the stage, and even interact with the actors. I've never enjoyed Shakespeare as much as here, performed as it was meant to be in the "wooden O." The theater is on the South Bank directly across the Thames over Southwark Bridge from St. Paul's (tube: Mansion House, tel. 020/7902-1500, box office tel. 020/7401-9919). Plays are long. Many groundlings leave before the end. If you like, hang out an hour before the finish and beg or buy a ticket off someone leaving early (groundlings are allowed to come and go). The Globe is far from public transport, but the courtesy phone in the lobby gets a minicab in minutes. Confirm the cost, but they seem to be much cheaper than the official black cabs (£5–6 to Victoria Station).

Music—For easy, cheap, or free concerts in historic churches, check the TI's listings for lunch concerts (especially Wren's St. Bride's Church, tel. 020/7353-1301; St. James at Piccadilly; and St. Martin-in-the-Fields, Mon, Tue, and Fri at 13:05, church tel. 020/7930-0089). St. Martin-in-the-Fields also hosts fine evening concerts by candlelight (Thu, Fri, and Sat at 19:30, £6–16, CC:VM, box office tel. 020/7839-8362). For a fun classical event (mid-June–early Sept only), attend a "Prom Concert." This is an annual music festival with nightly concerts in the Royal Albert Hall at give-a-peasant-some-culture prices (£3 standing-room spots sold at the door; £5–65 seats, most £21.50, CC:VM, tube: South Kensington, tel. 020/7589-8212, www.royalalberthall.com).

Cruises—Of the Thames River evening cruises that offer four-course meals and dancing, London Showboat offers the best value (£45, 3.5 hrs, 4-course meal, April–Oct Wed–Sun departs 19:00 from Westminster Pier, tel. 020/7237-5134, www.citycruises.com). For more on cruising, get the Thames River Services brochure from a London TI.

Day Trips from London

You could fill a book with the many easy and exciting day trips from London (Earl Steinbicker did: *Daytrips London: Fifty One-Day*

London Day Trips

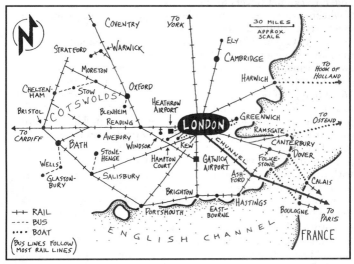

Adventures by Rail or Car, in and around London and Southern England). Several tour companies take London-based travelers out and back every day. Original London Walks offers a variety of Explorer day trips using the train for about £10 plus transportation costs (see their walking-tour brochure, tel. 020/7624-3978, www.walks.com).

A big bus tour can be used by those without a car as a "free" way to get to Bath (saving you, for instance, the £31 London–Bath train ticket). Evan Evans' tours leave from the Victoria Coach Station daily every morning (with your bag stowed under the bus), include a day of sightseeing, and leave you in Bath before returning to London (£48 for fully guided version offered year-round; £33 for Low Cost version offered April–Oct—bus transportation only—there's a small chance this cheaper version won't be offered in 2001). You can book the tour at the Victoria Station TI, the Evan Evans' office (258 Vauxhall Bridge Road, near Victoria Station, tel. 020/7950-1777, www.evanevans.co.uk), or at Green Line Travel Office (4a Fountain Square, across from Victoria Coach Station, tel. 020/7950-1777)—please note that you have to specifically ask about the Low Cost version of the tour. Golden Tours also offers a similar, daily, fully guided tour of Stonehenge and Bath for similar prices (about £48, departs from Fountain Square, across from Victoria Coach Station, tel. 020/7233-6668, www.goldentours.co.uk).

The British rail system uses London as a hub and normally offers round-trip fares (after 9:30) that cost virtually the same as one-way fares. "Day return" tickets are best (and cheapest) for day trips. You can save a little money if you purchase Super Advance tickets before 18:00 on the day before your trip. But given the high cost of big-city living and the charm of small-town England, rather than side-tripping, I'd see London and get out.

Sleeping in London
(£1 = about $1.60, country code: 44, area code: 020)
Sleep Code: **S** = Single, **D** = Double/Twin, **T** = Triple, **Q** = Quad, **b** = bathroom, **t** = toilet only, **s** = shower only, **CC** = Credit Card (Visa, MasterCard, Amex). Unless otherwise noted, prices include a generous breakfast and all taxes.

London is expensive. For £50 ($80), you'll get a sleepable double with breakfast in a safe, cramped, and dreary place with minimal service. For £60 ($95) you'll get a basic, clean, reasonably cheery double in a usually cramped, cracked-plaster building or a soulless but comfortable room without breakfast in a huge Motel 6–type place. My London splurges, at £100 to £140 ($170–240), are spacious, thoughtfully appointed places you'd be happy to entertain or make love in. Hearty English or generous buffet breakfasts are included unless otherwise noted, and TVs are nearly standard in rooms.

Reserve your London room with a phone call or e-mail as soon as you can commit to a date. A few places will hold a room with no deposit if you promise to arrive by midday. Most take your credit-card number as security. Most have expensive cancellation policies. Some fancy £120 rooms rent for half price if you arrive late on a slow day and ask for a deal.

Sleeping in Victoria Station Neighborhood, Belgravia
The streets behind Victoria Station teem with budget B&Bs. It's a safe, surprisingly tidy, and decent area without a hint of the trashy touristy glitz of the streets in front of the station. Here in Belgravia, your neighbors include Andrew Lloyd Webber and Margaret Thatcher (her policeman stands outside 73 Chester Square). Decent eateries abound (see "Eating," below). The cheaper listings are dumpy. Don't expect £90 cheeriness in a £50 room. Off-season save money by arriving late without a reservation and checking around. Fierce competition softens prices, especially for multinight stays. Particularly for Warwick Way hotels (and on hot summer nights), request a quiet back room. All are within a five-minute walk of the Victoria tube, bus, and train stations. There's an £8-per-day garage, a nearby **launderette** (daily 8:00–20:30, self-serve or full-serve, past Warwick Square at 3 Westmoreland Terrace, tel. 020/7821-8692), and an easygoing little dance club (Club D'Jan, £5 includes drink, Wed–Sat, 63 Wilton Road).

London, Victoria Station Neighborhood

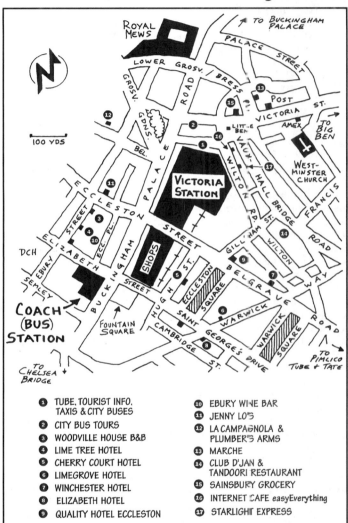

● 1 TUBE, TOURIST INFO, TAXIS & CITY BUSES
● 2 CITY BUS TOURS
● 3 WOODVILLE HOUSE B&B
● 4 LIME TREE HOTEL
● 5 CHERRY COURT HOTEL
● 6 LIMEGROVE HOTEL
● 7 WINCHESTER HOTEL
● 8 ELIZABETH HOTEL
● 9 QUALITY HOTEL ECCLESTON

● 10 EBURY WINE BAR
● 11 JENNY LO'S
● 12 LA CAMPAGNOLA & PLUMBER'S ARMS
● 13 MARCHE
● 14 CLUB D'JAN & TANDOORI RESTAURANT
● 15 SAINSBURY GROCERY
● 16 INTERNET CAFE easyEverything
● 17 STARLIGHT EXPRESS

Winchester Hotel is family run and perhaps the best value, with 18 fine rooms, no claustrophobia, and a wise and caring management (Db-£80, Tb-£105, Qb-£125, no CC, no groups, no small children, 17 Belgrave Road, London SW1V 1RB, tel. 020/7828-2972, fax 020/7828-5191, run by Jimmy).

In **Woodville House,** the quarters are dollhouse tight, showers are down the hall, and several rooms are on the noisy street (doubles on quiet backside, twins and singles on street), but this well-run, well-worn place is a good value, with lots of travel tips and friendly chat—especially about the local rich and famous—from Rachel Joplin (S-£42, D-£62, bunky family deals-£80–110 for up to 5, CC:VM, 107 Ebury Street, SW1W 9QU, tel. 020/7730-1048, fax 020/7730-2574, www.woodvillehouse.co.uk, e-mail: woodville.house@cwcom.net).

Lime Tree Hotel, enthusiastically run by David and Marilyn Davies, comes with spacious and thoughtfully decorated rooms and a fun-loving breakfast room. While priced a bit steep, the place has character plus (Sb-£75, Db-£100–110, Tb-£140, family room-£145, David deals in slow times and is creative at helping travelers in a bind, CC:VM, 135 Ebury Street, SW1W 9RA, tel. 020/7730-8191, fax 020/7730-7865).

Elizabeth House feels institutional and a bit bland—as you might expect from a former YMCA—but the rooms are clean and bright, and the price is right (S-£30, D-£50, Db-£60, T-£75, Q-£85, CC:VM, 118 Warwick Way, SW1 4JB, tel. 020/7630-0741, fax 020/7630-0740, e-mail: elizabethhouse@compuserve.com).

Quality Hotel Eccleston is big, modern, well located, and a fine value for no-nonsense comfort (Db-£108, on slow days drop-ins can ask for "saver prices"—33 percent off on first night, breakfast extra, CC:VMA, nonsmoking floor, elevator, 82 Eccleston Square, SW1V 1PS, tel. 020/7834-8042, fax 020/7630-8942, e-mail: admin@gb614.u-net.com).

Astors Hotel has a helpful staff and 22 decent rooms, some with high ceilings (Db-£72, CC:VM, discount for payment in cash, 110 Ebury Street, SW1W 9QD, tel. 020/7730-3811, fax 020/7823-6728, www.astors.uk.com).

Georgian House Hotel has 50 pleasant rooms, with a cheaper annex that attracts backpackers (D-£40, Db-£66, annex Db-£55, CC:VM, small breakfast, Internet access, 35 St. George's Drive, SW1V 4DG, tel. 020/7834-1438, fax 020/7976-6085, www.georgianhousehotel.co.uk).

Enrico Hotel, with 26 simple rooms, is basic, older, clean, and affordable (S-£45, D-£55, Ds-£60, 77 Warwick Way, SW1V 1QP, tel. 020/7834-9583, fax 020/7233-9995, www.enricohotel .fsnet.co.uk).

These three places come with cramped rooms and claustrophobic halls. While they generate a lot of reader complaints, I list them because they offer cheap beds at youth hostel prices and are beautifully located a few minutes' walk from Victoria Station: **Cherry Court Hotel** is run by the friendly and industrious Patel family (S-£30, Sb-£42, Db-£48, T-£55, Tb-£70, price promised with this book, CC:VMA, using CC adds

5 percent extra, non-smoking, Internet access, TV, phones, fruit basket breakfast in room, no twins—only double beds, 23 Hugh Street, SW1V 1QJ, tel. 020/7828-2840, fax 020/7828-0393, www.cherrycourthotel.co.uk). **Cedar Guest House,** run by a Polish organization to help Poles afford London, welcomes all (D-£40, Db-£50, T-£60, 30 Hugh Street, SW1V 1RP, tel. 020/ 7828-2625). **Limegrove Hotel,** run by harried Joyce, more musty and run-down, serves a humble breakfast in the room (S-£28, D-£38, Db-£50, T-£48, Tb-£60, cheaper off-season, lots of stairs, 101 Warwick Way, SW1V 1QL, tel. 020/7828-0458). Back rooms are quieter.

Big, Cheap, Modern Hotels

These places—popular with budget tour groups—are well run and offer elevators and all the modern comforts in a no-frills practical package. The doubles for £60 to £70 are a great value for London.

    London County Hall Travel Inn, literally down the hall from a $400-a-night Marriott Hotel, fills one end of London's massive former City Hall. This place is wonderfully located, near the base of the London Eye Ferris Wheel, and across the Thames from Big Ben. Its 300 slick and no-frills rooms come with all the necessary comforts (Db-£70 for 2 adults and up to 2 kids under age 15, couples can request a bigger family room—same price, breakfast extra, book in advance, no-show rooms are released at 16:00, elevator, some smoke-free and easy-access rooms, CC:VMA, 500 yards from Westminster tube stop and Waterloo Station where the Chunnel train leaves for Paris, Belvedere Road, SE1 7PB, tel. 020/7902-1600, fax 020/7902-1619, www.travelinn.co.uk).

    Other London Travel Inns charging about £60 per room include **London Euston** (141 Euston Road, NW1 2AU, tube: Euston), **Tower Bridge** (tube: London Bridge), and **London Putney Bridge** (farther out, tube: Putney Bridge). For any of these, contact tel. 0870-242-8000 (fax 0870-241-9000).

    Hotel Ibis London Euston, which feels classier than a Travel Inn, is located on a quiet street a block behind Euston Station (Sb-£64, Db-£70, breakfast extra, CC:VMA, nonsmoking floor, 3 Cardington Street, NW1 2LW, tel. 020/7388-7777, fax 020/7388-0001, e-mail: h0921@accor-hotels.com).

    Jurys Inn rents 200 mod, compact, and comfy rooms near King's Cross station (Db/Tb-£84, 2 adults and 2 kids—under age 12—can share one room, breakfast extra, CC:VMA, nonsmoking floors, 60 Pentonville Road, Islington, N1 9LA, tube: Angel, tel. 020/7282-5500, fax 020/7282-5511, www.jurys.com).

    Premier Lodge opens in spring of 2001 near the Globe Theatre on the South Bank (55 rooms, Db for up to 2 adults and 2 kids-£64.50, Bankside, 34 Park Street, London SE1, tube: Canon, tel. 0870-201-0203, fax 0870-700-1457).

South Kensington Neighborhood

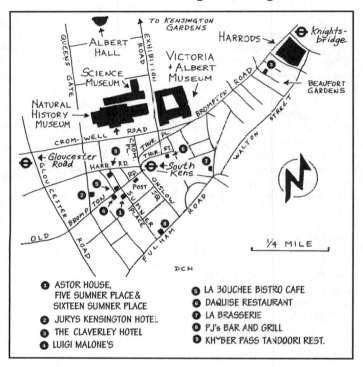

- **1** ASTOR HOUSE, FIVE SUMNER PLACE & SIXTEEN SUMNER PLACE
- **2** JURYS KENSINGTON HOTEL
- **3** THE CLAVERLEY HOTEL
- **4** LUIGI MALONE'S
- **5** LA BOUCHEE BISTRO CAFE
- **6** DAQUISE RESTAURANT
- **7** LA BRASSERIE
- **8** PJ's BAR AND GRILL
- **9** KHYBER PASS TANDOORI REST.

"South Kensington," She Said, Loosening His Cummerbund

To live on a quiet street so classy it doesn't allow hotel signs, surrounded by trendy shops and colorful restaurants, call "South Ken" your London home. Shoppers like being a short walk from Harrods and the designer shops of King's Road and Chelsea. When I splurge, I splurge here. Sumner Place is just off Old Brompton Road, 200 yards from the handy South Kensington tube station (on Circle Line, two stops from Victoria Station, direct Heathrow connection). There's a taxi rank in the meridian at the end of Harrington Road. The handy "Wash & Dry" **Laundromat** is on the corner of Queensberry Place and Harrington Road (daily 8:00–21:00, bring 20p and £1 coins).

Aster House Hotel—run by friendly and accommodating Simon and Leona Tan—has a sumptuous lobby, lounge, and breakfast room. Its newly renovated rooms are comfy and quiet, with TV, phone, air-conditioning, and fridge. Enjoy breakfast or just lounging in the whisper-elegant Orangery, a Victorian greenhouse (Sb-£65–85, Db-£125, deluxe four-poster Db-£145, CC:VM, entirely nonsmoking, 3 Sumner Place, SW7 3EE, tel. 020/7581-5888, fax 020/7584-4925, www.asterhouse.com).

Five Sumner Place Hotel was recently voted "the best small hotel in London." In this 150-year-old building, rooms are tastefully decorated and the breakfast room is a Victorian-style conservatory/greenhouse (13 rooms, Sb-£100, Db-£153, third bed-£22; CC:VMA, TV, phones, and fridge in rooms by request, nonsmoking rooms, elevator, 5 Sumner Place, South Kensington, SW7 3EE, tel. 020/7584–7586, fax 020/7823-9962, www.sumnerplace.com, e-mail: reservations@sumnerplace.com, run by Tom).

Sixteen Sumner Place—a lesser value for classier travelers—has over-the-top formality and class packed into its 37 unnumbered but pretentiously named rooms, plush lounges, and quiet garden (closed Jan–June for renovations, reopens in July, Db-£160 with showers, £185 with baths, CC:VMA, breakfast in your room, elevator, 16 Sumner Place, SW7 3EG, tel. 020/7589-5232, fax 020/7584-8615, U.S. tel. 800/592-5387, e-mail: reservations@numbersixteenhotel.co.uk).

Jurys Kensington Hotel is big and stately (Sb/Db/Tb-£100–170 depending upon "availability," ask for a deal, breakfast extra, CC:VMA, piano lounge, nonsmoking floor, elevator, Queen's Gate, South Kensington, SW7 5LR, tel. 020/7589-6300, fax 020/7581-1492).

The Claverley, two blocks from Harrods, is on a quiet street similar to Sumner Place. The warmly furnished rooms come with all the comforts (S-£70, Sb-£85–115, Db-£130–155, sofa bed Tb-£160–215, flexible during slow times, CC:VMA, plush lounge, nonsmoking rooms, elevator, 13–14 Beaufort Gardens, SW3 1PS, tube: Knightsbridge, tel. 020/7589-8541, fax 020/7584-3410, U.S. tel. 800/747-0398, www.claverleyhotel.co.uk).

Sleeping in Notting Hill Gate Neighborhood

Residential Notting Hill Gate has quick bus and tube access to downtown, is on the A2 Airbus line from Heathrow, and, for London, is very "homely." It has a self-serve launderette, an artsy theater, a late-hours supermarket, and lots of fun budget eateries (see "Eating," below).

Westland Hotel is comfortable, convenient, and hotelesque, with a fine lounge and spacious 1970s-style rooms (Sb-£80, Db-£95, cavernous deluxe Db-£110, sprawling Tb-£120, gargantuan Qb-£135, 10 percent discount with this book through 2001 for first stay only, CC:VMA, elevator, free garage—7 spaces, between Notting Hill Gate and Queensway tube stations, 154 Bayswater Road, W2 4HP, tel. 020/7229-9191, fax 020/7727-1054, www.westlandhotel.co.uk).

Vicarage Private Hotel, understandably popular, is family

London, Notting Hill Gate Neighborhood

Key to map:

1. WESTLAND HOTEL
2. VICARAGE & ABBEY HOUSE HOTELS
3. NORWEGIAN YWCA
4. GARDEN COURT HOTEL
5. KENSINGTON GARDENS HOTEL
6. VANCOUVER STUDIOS
7. PHOENIX HOTEL
8. LONDON HOUSE BUDGET
9. LADBROKE ARMS PUB
10. CHURCHILL ARMS PUB
11. GEALE'S FISH & CHIPS
12. MODHUBON INDIAN REST.
13. MAGGIE JONES REST.
14. MR. WU'S CHINESE REST.

run and elegantly British in a quiet, classy neighborhood. It has 19 rooms furnished with taste and quality, a TV lounge, and facilities on each floor. Mandy, Richard, and Tere maintain a homey and caring atmosphere. Reserve long in advance. There's no better room for the price (S-£45, D-£74, Db-£98, T-£90, Q-£98, a 6-minute walk from the Notting Hill Gate and High Street Kensington tube stations, near Kensington Palace at 10 Vicarage Gate, Kensington, W8 4AG, tel. 020/7229-4030, fax 020/7792-5989, www.londonvicaragehotel.com).

Abbey House Hotel, next door, is similar, but—while also a fine value—it has no lounge and is less cozy (16 rooms, S-£45, D-£74, T-£90, Q-£100, Quint-£110, 11 Vicarage Gate, Kensington, W8 4AG, tel. 020/7727-2594, Rodrigo).

Norwegian YWCA (Norsk K.F.U.K.) is for women under

30 only (and men with Norwegian passports). Located on a quiet, stately street, it offers nonsmoking rooms, a study, TV room, piano lounge, and an open-face Norwegian ambience. They have mostly quads, so those willing to share with strangers are most likely to get a place (July–Aug: Ss-£27, bed in shared double-£25, shared triple-£21 apiece, shared quad-£18 apiece, with breakfast; Sept–June: same prices include dinner; CC:VMA, 52 Holland Park, W11 3RS, tel. & fax 020/7727-9897, www.kfuk.dial.pipex .com). With each visit I wonder which is easier to get—a sex change or a Norwegian passport?

Sleeping on Kensington Gardens

Several big old hotels line the quiet Victorian Kensington Gardens, a block off the bustling Queensway shopping street near the Bayswater tube station. Popular with young travelers from around the world, Queensway is a multicultural festival of commerce and lively eateries (such as Mr Wu's Chinese buffet, stuffing locals for £4.50, on Queensway, see "Eating," below). These hotels come with the least traffic noise of all my downtown recommendations. **Brookford Wash & Dry** is at Queensway and Bishop's Bridge Road (daily 7:00–19:30, service from 9:00–17:30, computerized pay point takes all coins).

Garden Court rents 34 large, comfortable rooms, offering one of London's best accommodations values. The breakfast room is sticky, and the public bathrooms are a bit unkempt, but it's friendly, with a great lounge and super prices (S-£34, Sb-£50, D-£54, Db-£82, T-£72, Tb-£90, Q-£80, Qb-£96, CC:VM, 30 Kensington Gardens Square, W2 4BG, tel. 020/7229-2553, fax 020/7727-2749, www.gardenhotel.co.uk, e-mail: info@garden-courthotel.co.uk).

Kensington Gardens Hotel laces 16 fine, fresh rooms together in a tall, skinny place with lots of stairs (S-£53, Sb-£58, Db-£79, 9 Kensington Gardens Square, W2 4BH, tel. 020/7221-7790, fax 020/7792-8612, www.kensingtongardenshotel.co.uk).

Vancouver Studios is a different concept, giving you a fully equipped kitchenette (utensils, stove, microwave, and fridge) rather than breakfast (Sb-£55–72, Db-£90–105, Tb-£123, Q-£160, CC:VMA, homey lounge and private garden, rooms with all the modern comforts, 30 Prince's Square, W2 4NJ, tel. 020/7243-1270, fax 020/7221-8678, www.vienna-group.co.uk, e-mail: hotels @vienna-group.co.uk).

Phoenix Hotel, a Best Western modernization of a 130-room hotel, offers American business-class comforts; spacious, plush public spaces; and big, fresh, modern-feeling rooms (Sb-£89, Db-£120, Tb-£145, CC:VMA, nonsmoking rooms, elevator, 1–8 Kensington Gardens Square, W2 4BH, tel. 020/7229-2494, fax 020/7727-1419, U.S. tel. 800/528-1234, www.phoenixhotel.co.uk).

London House Budget Hotel is a threadbare, nose-ringed slumbermill renting 220 beds in 76 stark but sleepable rooms (S-£40, twin-£54, dorm bed-£20, includes continental breakfast, CC:VMA, lots of school groups, 81 Kensington Gardens Square, W2 4DJ, tel. 020/7727-0696, fax 020/7243-8626).

Sleeping in Other Neighborhoods

Euston Station: The **Methodist International Centre** (new in 1998) is a youthful Christian residence, its lower floors filled with international students and its top floor open to travelers. Rooms are modern and simple yet comfortable, with fine bathrooms, phones, and desks. The atmosphere is friendly, safe, clean, and controlled, with a spacious lounge and game room (Sb-£38, Db-£58, Tb-£70, includes breakfast, three-course buffet dinner-£11, CC:VM, nonsmoking rooms, elevator, on a quiet street a block southwest of Euston Square, 81–103 Euston Street, not Euston Road, W1 2EZ, tube: Euston Station, tel. 020/7380-0001, fax 020/7387-5300, e-mail: sales@micentre.com).

Cottage Hotel is tucked away a block off the west exit of Euston Station. Established in 1950—a bit tired, cramped, and smoky—it feels like 1950. But it's cheap, quiet, and has a fine breakfast room (40 rooms, S-£35, Sb-£45, D-£45, Db-£55, T-£65, Tb-£75, Qb-£85, 67 Euston Street, tel. 020/7387-6785, fax 020/7383-0859).

Downtown near Baker Street: For a less hotelesque alternative in the center, consider renting one of 18 stark, hardwood, comfortable rooms in **22 York Street B&B** (Db-£94, Tb-£141, CC:VMA, strictly smoke free, inviting lounge, social breakfast, from Baker Street tube station walk 2 blocks down Baker Street and take a right, 22 York Street, tel. 020/7224-3990, fax 020/7224-1990, www.myrtle-cottage.co.uk/callis.htm, energetically run by Liz and Michael).

Near St. Paul's: The **City of London Youth Hostel** is clean, modern, friendly, and well run. You'll pay about £25 for a bed in three- to five-bed rooms, £26 in a single (hostel membership required, 200 beds, CC:VM, cheap meals, 36 Carter Lane, EC4V 5AD, tube: St. Paul's, tel. 020/7236-4965, fax 020/7236-7681).

South London: Caroline Cunningham's humble guest house is on a quiet street in a well-worn neighborhood south of Victoria Station near Clapham Common (3 rooms, S-£15, D-£30 with English breakfast, 98 Hambalt Road, Clapham Common, London SW4 9EJ, tel. 020/8673-1077). It's 15 minutes by tube to Clapham Common, then a bus ride or a 12-minute walk—exit left down Clapham South Road, left on Elms, right on Abbeville Road, left on Hambalt. Rooms in Caroline's brother's house are a lesser value. A good, cheap Thai restaurant (the Pepper Tree) is near the tube station.

Near Gatwick Airport: The **Gatwick Travelodge** is a budget hotel two miles from the airport (Db-£50, free shuttle to/from south terminal, Church Road, Lowfield Heath, Crawley, tel. 0870-905-6343). These two B&Bs are both in the peaceful countryside and have tennis courts, small swimming pools, and a good pub within walking distance: **Barn Cottage,** a converted 17th-century barn, has two wood-beamed rooms, antique furniture, and a large garden that makes you forget Gatwick is 10 minutes away (S-£35, D-£50, can drive you to airport or train station for £5–6—a taxi costs £10— Leigh, Reigate, Surrey, RH2 8RF, tel. 01306/611-347, warmly run by Pat and Mike Comer). The idyllic **Crutchfield Farm B&B** offers three comfortable rooms, a great sitting room, and an elegant dining room in a 600-year-old renovated farmhouse surrounded by lots of greenery and a pond. Gillian Blok includes a ride to the airport and its train station, whether you're leaving Britain or day-tripping to London (Sb-£55, Db-£75, Tb-£85, Qb-£95, two miles from Gatwick Airport—£5 by taxi, 30 minutes by train from London, at Hookwood, Surrey, RH6 0HT, tel. 01293/863-110, fax 01293/863-233, e-mail: TonyBlok@compuserve.com).

Near Heathrow Airport: It's so easy to get to Heathrow from central London, I see no reason to sleep there. But for budget beds near the airport, consider the **Heathrow Ibis** (Db-£60, breakfast extra, CC:VMA, shuttle bus to terminals except to T-4, 112 Bath Road, tel. 020/8759-4888, fax 020/8564-7894, www.ibishotel.com). **Heathrow Airport Travelodge** is another option (300 rooms, Db-£70, free shuttle to/from all terminals, Bath Road, off A4, behind Le Meridien Excelsior Hotel, half mile from airport, tel. 0870-905-6343).

Eating in London

If you want to dine (as opposed to eat), check out the extensive listings in the weekly entertainment guides sold at London newsstands (or catch a train for Paris). The thought of a £30 meal in Britain generally ruins my appetite, so my London dining is limited mostly to easygoing, fun, but inexpensive alternatives. I've listed places by neighborhood—handy to your sightseeing or hotel.

Your £6 budget choices are pub grub, a café, fish and chips, pizza, ethnic, or picnic. Pub grub is the most atmospheric budget option. Many of London's 7,000 pubs serve fresh, tasty buffets under ancient timbers, with hearty lunches and dinners priced from £6 to £8. (While pubs are going strong, the new phenomenon is coffee shops: Starbucks and its competitors have sprouted up all over town providing cushy and social watering holes with comfy chairs, easy WCs, £1.50 lattes, and a nice break between sights.)

Ethnic restaurants from all over the world add spice to England's lackluster cuisine scene. Eating Indian or Chinese is "going local" in London. It's also going cheap (cheaper if you take out). Most large museums (and many churches) have inexpensive, cheery cafeterias. Sandwich shops are a hit with local workers eating on the run. Of course, picnicking is the fastest and cheapest way to go. Good grocery stores and sandwich shops, fine park benches, and polite pigeons abound in Britain's most expensive city.

Eating near Trafalgar Square

For a tasty meal on a monk's budget sitting on somebody's tomb in an ancient crypt, descend into the **St. Martin-in-the-Fields Café in the Crypt** (Mon–Sat 10:00–20:00, Sun 12:00–20:30, £5–7 cafeteria plates, cheaper sandwich bar, profits go to the church; underneath St. Martin-in-the-Fields on Trafalgar Square, tel. 020/7839-4342).

Chandos Bar's Opera Room floats amazingly apart from the tacky crush of tourism around Trafalgar Square. Look for the pub opposite the National Portrait Gallery (corner of William Street and St. Martin's Lane) and climb the stairs to the Opera Room. They serve £6 pub lunches and dinners (last orders at 19:00, 18:00 on weekends, tel. 020/7836-1401). This is a fine Tragalfar rendezvous point—smoky, but wonderfully local.

Gordon's Wine Bar is ripe with atmosphere. A simple steep staircase leads into a 14th-century cellar filled with candlelight, dusty old wine bottles, faded British memorabilia, and local nine-to-fivers (hot meals only for lunch, fine plate of cheeses or various cold cuts with salad buffet all day until 21:00—one plate of each feeds two for £7). While it's crowded, you can normally corral two chairs and grab the corner of a table (Mon–Sat 11:00–23:00, closed Sun, arrive before 18:00 to get a seat, 2 blocks from Trafalgar Square, bottom of Villiars Street at #47, near Embankment tube station, tel. 020/7930-1408).

Down Whitehall, a block south of Trafalgar Square, you'll find the touristy but atmospheric **Clarence Pub** (decent grub, lunch only) and cheaper cafeterias and pizza joints.

For a classy lunch in the National Gallery, eat at the moderately priced **Crizelli's Garden** (open daily, first floor of Sainsbury Wing).

Simpson's in the Strand serves a stuffy, aristocratic, old-time carvery dinner—where the chef slices your favorite red meat from a fancy trolley at your table—in their elegant smoky old dining room (£20, coat and tie required, Mon–Sat 12:15–14:30, 17:30–23:00, tel. 020/7836-9112).

Eating near Piccadilly

Hungry and broke in the theater district? Head for Panton Street (off Haymarket, 2 blocks southeast of Piccadilly Circus) for a line of decent eateries. **Stockpot** is a mushy-peas kind of place, famous and rightly popular for its edible, cheap meals (Mon–Sat 8:00–23:00, Sun 8:00–22:00, 38 Panton Street). The **West End Kitchen** (across the street at #5, same hours and menu) is a competitor that's just as good. The original **Stockpot**, a few blocks away, has better atmosphere (daily 12:00–23:00, a block north of Shaftesbury near Cambridge Circus at 18 Old Compton Street tel. 020/7287-1066).

The palatial **Criterion Brasserie** serves a special £15 two-course "Anglo-French" menu (or £18 for 3 courses) under gilded tiles and chandeliers in a dreamy Byzantine church setting from 1880. It's right on Piccadilly Circus but a world away from the punk junk. The house wine is great and so is the food (specials available Mon–Sat 12:00–14:30 and 17:30–18:30, pricier later, CC:VM, closed Sun, tel. 020/7930-0488).

Just off Leicester Square, **Luigi Malone's**, a chain restaurant, serves inexpensive salads and pasta (12 Irving Street, tel. 020/7925-0457).

Eating in the City, near St. Paul's

The **Counting House**, formerly an elegant old bank, offers great £7 lunches, nice homemade meat pies, fish, and fresh vegetables (gets really busy with the button-down 9–5 crowd after 12:15 Mon–Fri, 50 Cornhill, near Mansion House in the City, tel. 020/7283-7123).

The "Food Is Fun" Dinner Crawl: From Covent Garden to Soho

London has a trendy, generation X scene that most Beefeater seekers miss entirely. For a multicultural movable feast and a chance to sample some of London's most popular eateries, consider sampling these. Start around 18:00 to avoid lines, get in on early specials, and find waiters willing to let you split a meal. Prices, while reasonable by London standards, add up. Servings are large enough to share. All are open nightly.

Suggested nibbler's dinner crawl for two: Arrive before 18:00 at **Belgo** and split the early-bird dinner special: a kilo of mussels, fries, and dark Belgian beer; at **Yo! Sushi,** have beer or sake and a few dishes; slurp your last course at **Wagamama**; for dessert, people watch at Leicester Square, where the serf's always up.

Belgo Centraal is a space-station world overrun with Trappist monks serving hearty Belgian specialties. The classy restaurant section requires reservations, but just grabbing a bench in the boisterous beer hall is more fun. Belgians claim they eat as well as the French and as hearty as the Germans. Specialties include mussels, great fries, and a stunning array of dark, blond, and fruity Belgian beers. Belgo actually makes things Belgian trendy—a formidable feat (£14 meals; open daily until very late; Mon–Fri 17:00–18:30 "beat the clock" meal specials cost only the time… £5 to £6.30, and you get mussels, fries, and beer; no meal splitting after 18:30; £5 lunch special daily, 12:00–17:00; one block north of Covent Garden tube station at intersection of Neal and Shelton Streets, 50 Earlham Street, tel. 020/7813-2233).

From Covent Garden to Soho, "Food is Fun"

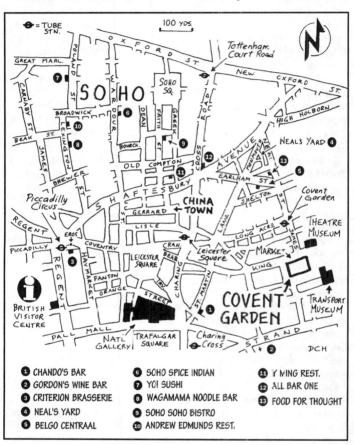

❶ CHANDO'S BAR	❻ SOHO SPICE INDIAN	⓫ Y WING REST.
❷ GORDON'S WINE BAR	❼ YO! SUSHI	⓬ ALL BAR ONE
❸ CRITERION BRASSERIE	❽ WAGAMAMA NOODLE BAR	⓭ FOOD FOR THOUGHT
❹ NEAL'S YARD	❾ SOHO SOHO BISTRO	
❺ BELGO CENTRAAL	❿ ANDREW EDMUNDS REST.	

Soho Spice Indian is where modern Britain meets Indian tradition—fine Indian cuisine in a trendy jewel-tone ambience. The £15 "Tandoori selections" meal is the best "variety" dish and big enough for two (daily 11:30–24:00, nonsmoking section available Sun–Tue, CC:VM, 5 blocks due north of Piccadilly Circus at 124 Wardour Street, tel. 020/7434-0808).

Yo! Sushi is a futuristic Japanese food extravaganza experience. With thumping rock music, Japanese cable TV, a 60-meter-long conveyor-belt sushi bar (the world's longest), automated sushi machines, and a robotic drink trolley, just sipping a sake on a bar stool here is a trip. For £1 you get unlimited tea (on request), water (from spigot at bar, with or without gas), or miso soup. Grab dishes as they rattle by (priced by color of dish; see their chart) and a drink off the trash-talking robot (daily 12:00–24:00, two blocks south of Oxford Street, where Lexington Street becomes Poland Street, 52 Poland Street, tel. 020/7287-0443). For more serious drinking on tatami mats, go downstairs into "Yo Below."

Wagamama Noodle Bar is a noisy, pan-Asian slurp-athon. As you enter, check out the kitchen and listen to the roar of the basement, where benches rock with happy eaters. Everything's organic—stand against the wall to feel the energy of all this "positive eating" (daily 12:00–23:00, crowded after 20:00, smoke free, 10A Lexington Street, tel. 020/7292-0990).

More possibilities: Soho Soho French Bistro-Rotisserie is a chance to go French in a Matisse-esque setting. The ground floor is a trendy wine bar and brasserie. Upstairs is an oasis of peace serving £16 three-course French "pre-theater specials"—order from 17:30 to 19:00 (CC:VMA, near Cambridge Circus, 2 blocks east of Charing Cross Road at 11 Frith Street, tel. 020/7494-3491).

Near Covent Garden, the area around Neal's Yard is busy with fun cafés. One of the best is **Food for Thought** (serving until 20:15, Sun 12:00–16:15, good £5 vegetarian meals, nonsmoking, 2 blocks north of tube: Covent Garden, 31 Neal Street, tel. 020/7836-0239). Neal's Yard itself is a food circus of trendy, healthy eateries.

All Bar One, a modern English restaurant chain popular with the young black-clad crowd, offers good fast food in a rustic mod setting with plain wooden tables (£5 light meals, £8–10 meals). In Covent Garden, try the location at the intersection of Cross Road and Shaftesbury Avenue. Other locations include 19 Henrietta Street/Covent Garden, 84 Cambridge Circus, 36 Dean Street in Soho, 48 Leicester Square, 289 Regent Street, and 126 Notting Hill.

Y Ming Chinese Restaurant, across Shaftesbury Avenue from the ornate gates, clatter, and dim sum of Chinatown, has clean European decor, serious but helpful service, and authentic Northern Chinese cooking (good £10 meal deal offered 12:00–18:00, Mon–Sat 12:00–23:30, closed Sun, 35 Greek Street, tel. 020/7734-2721).

Andrew Edmunds Restaurant is a tiny candlelit place where you'll want to hide your camera and guidebook and act as local as possible. The modern-European cooking is worth the splurge (3 courses for £25, 12:30–15:00, 18:00–22:45, 46 Lexington Street in Soho, reservations are smart on weekends, tel. 020/7437-5708).

Eating near Recommended Victoria Station Accommodations

Here are places a couple of blocks southwest of Victoria Station where I've enjoyed eating (see map on page 354):

Jenny Lo's Tea House is a simple, for-the-joy-of-good-food kind of place serving up £5 Chinese-style meals to locals in the know (Mon–Sat 12:00–15:00, 18:00–22:00, 14 Eccleston Street, tel. 020/7259-0399).

For pub grub with good local atmosphere, consider the **Plumbers Arms** (filling £6 hot meals Mon–Fri, cheaper sandwiches anytime, indoor/outdoor seating, ask about the murdered nanny, 14 Lower Belgrave Street, tel. 020/7730-4067).

Next door, the small but classy **La Campagnola** is Belgravia's favorite budget Italian restaurant (£12–15, Mon–Sat 12:00–15:00, 18:00–23:30, closed Sun, 10 Lower Belgrave Street, tel. 020/7730-2057).

Across the street, the **Maestro Bar** is the closest thing to an English tapas bar I've seen, with salads, sandwiches, and 10 bar stools (very cheap, closed Sat).

The **Ebury Wine Bar** offers a French candlelit ambience and pricey but delicious meals (£15, daily 12:00–15:00, 18:00–22:30, CC:VM, 139 Ebury Street, at intersection with Elizabeth Street, near bus station, tel. 020/7730-5447). Several cheap places are around the corner on Elizabeth Street (#23 for take-out or eat-in fish and chips). **Goya**, a Spanish restaurant nearby, is popular for its fine tapas (Elizabeth Street).

The **Duke of Wellington** pub is good, if smoky, for dinner (£6 meals, Mon–Sat 12:00–15:00, 18:00–21:30, Sun 12:00–15:00, 63 Eaton Terrace, at intersection with Chester Row). **Peter's Restaurant** is the cabbie's hangout for cheap food, smoke, and chatter—men would feel more comfortable here than women (closed Sun, end of Ebury, at intersection with Pimlico).

The **Country Pub in London** lives up to its name and serves good £6 to £12 meals (12:00–15:00, 18:30–21:30, corner of Warwick and Cambridge Streets, tel. 020/7834-5281).

Jomuna Tandoori serves quality Indian cuisine (daily 12:00–15:00, 18:00–23:30, 74 Wilton Road, near Eccleston Hotel, tel. 020/7828-7509).

The **Marche** is an easy cafeteria a couple of blocks north of Victoria Station at Bressenden Place (Mon–Sat 7:30–23:00, Sun 11:00–21:00, CC:VM, tel. 020/7630-1733). If you miss America, there's a mall-type food circus at Victoria Place, upstairs in Victoria Station. **Cafe Rouge** is probably the best food there.

Groceries: The late-hours **Whistle Stop** at the station has decent sandwiches and a fine salad bar (daily, 24 hrs). A larger grocery, **Sainsbury Local**, is on Victoria Street in front of the station, just past the buses (daily 6:00–24:00).

Eating at Notting Hill Gate
To locate restaurants, see map on page 359.

The exuberantly rustic and very English **Maggie Jones** serves my favorite £20 London dinner. You'll get solid English cuisine, with huge plates of crunchy vegetables, by candlelight (daily

18:30–23:00, CC:VMA, 6 Old Court Place, just east of Kensington Church Street, near High Street Kensington tube stop, reservations recommended, tel. 020/7937-6462). If you eat well once in London, eat here (and do it quick, before it burns down).

The **Churchill Arms** pub is a local hangout, with good beer and old English ambience in front and hearty £5 Thai plates in an enclosed patio in the back (you can bring the Thai food into the more atmospheric pub section, Mon–Sat 12:00–15:00, 18:00–21:30, closed Sun, 119 Kensington Church Street, tel. 020/7792-1246).

The friendly **Ladbroke Arms Pub** serves country-style meals that are one step above pub grub in quality and price (£10–12 meals, June–Sept daily 11:00–23:00, Oct–May daily 12:00–14:30, 19:00–22:00, great indoor/outdoor ambience, 54 Ladbroke Road, near Holland Park tube station, tel. 020/7727-6648).

For fish and chips, the almost-too-popular **Geale's** has long been considered one of London's best (£8, Mon–Sat 12:00–15:00, 18:00–23:00, Sun 18:00–23:00, 2 Farmer Street, just off Notting Hill Gate behind Gate Cinema, tel. 020/7727-7528). Get there early for a place to sit (they take no reservations) and the best selection of fish.

The **Modhubon** Indian restaurant is not too spicy, "vedy, vedy nice," and has cheap lunch specials (Sun–Fri 12:00–15:00, 18:00–24:00, Sat 12:00–24:00, 29 Pembridge Road, tel. 020/7727-3399). Next door is the cheap **Slowboat** Chinese take-out (daily 17:30–24:00, 19 Pembridge Road) and the tiny **Organic Restaurant** at #35, which busily keeps yuppie vegetarians as well as carnivores happy (£10, 100 percent organic, Mon–Fri 17:30–23:00, Sat–Sun 11:00–22:00, CC:VM, 35 Pembridge Road, tel. 020/7727-9620).

Cafe Diana is a healthy little sandwich shop decorated with photos of Princess Diana (daily 8:00–22:30, 5 Wellington Terrace, on Bayswater Road, opposite Kensington Palace Garden Gates, tel. 020/7792-9606).

Mr. Wu's Chinese Restaurant serves a 10-course buffet in a bright and cheery little place. Just grab a plate and help yourself (£4.50, daily 12:00–23:00, check quality of buffet—right inside entrance—before committing, pickings can get slim, across from Bayswater tube station, 54 Queensway, tel. 020/7243-1017). Queensway is lined with lively and inexpensive eateries.

Supermarket: Europa is a half-block from the Notting Hill Gate tube stop (Mon–Fri 8:00–23:00, Sun 12:00–18:00, 112 Notting Hill Gate, near intersection with Pembridge Road).

Eating near Recommended Accommodations in South Kensington

Popular eateries line Old Brompton Road and Thurloe Street (tube: South Kensington). See map on page 357.

Luigi Malone's is an Italian-food chain restaurant serving good £8 salads and pasta (73 Old Brompton Road, tel. 020/7584-4323). Its twin brother is just off Leicester Square at 12 Irving Street.

La Bouchee Bistro Café is a classy hole-in-the-wall touch of France serving early-bird, three-course, £11 meals before 19:30 and *plats du jour* for £8 all *jour* (daily 12:00–23:00, CC:VM, 56 Old Brompton Road, almost directly across street from Luigi Malone's, tel. 020/7589-1929).

Daquise, an authentic-feeling Polish place, is ideal if you're in the mood for kielbasa and kraut. It's fast, cheap, family run, and a part of the neighborhood (£8 meals, daily until 23:00, nonsmoking, 20 Thurloe Street, tel. 020/7589-6117).

La Brasserie fills a big, plain, tiled room with ceiling fans, a Parisian ambience, and good French-style food at reasonable prices (2-course £14 "regional menu," £12 bottle of house wine, CC:VMA, nightly until 24:00, 272 Brompton Road, tel. 020/7581-3089).

PJ's Bar and Grill is popular with the yuppie Chelsea crowd for a good reason. Traditional "New York Brasserie"–style yet trendy, it serves modern Mediterranean cuisine (£15 meals, nightly until 24:00, 52 Fulham Road, at intersection with Sydney Street, tel. 020/7581-0025).

For Indian food, the **Khyber Pass Tandoori Restaurant** is a nondescript but handy place serving good £12 dinners nightly (12:00–14:30, 18:00–23:30, CC:VM, 21 Bute Street, tel. 020/7589-7311).

Transportation Connections—London

Flying into London's Heathrow Airport

Heathrow Airport is the world's busiest. Think about it: 60 million passengers a year on 425,000 flights from 200 destinations riding 90 airlines . . . some kind of global maypole dance. While many complain about it, I like it. It's user-friendly. Read signs, ask questions. For Heathrow's airport, flight, and transfers information, call the switchboard at 0870-000-0123 (or 020/8759-4321). It has four terminals: T-1 (mostly domestic flights), T-2 (mostly European flights), T-3 (mostly flights from the U.S.), T-4 (British Air trans-Atlantic flights).

Each terminal has an airport information desk, car-rental agencies, exchange bureaus and ATMs, a pharmacy, a VAT refund desk (VAT info tel. 020/8910-3682; you must present the VAT claim form from the retailer here to get your 17.5 percent tax rebate on items purchased in Britain), and a £3.50/day baggage check desk (open 5:30–23:00). There's a post office in T-2 and T-4. Each terminal has cheap eateries (such as the cheery **Food Village** self-service cafeteria in T-3). The American Express desk, in the tube station at Terminal 4 (daily 7:00–19:00), has rates similar to the exchange bureaus upstairs, but they don't charge a commission (typically 1.5 percent) for cashing any type of traveler's check.

Heathrow's small TI gives you all the help that London's Victoria Station does, with none of the crowds (daily 8:30–18:00, a 5-minute walk from Terminal 3 in the tube station, follow signs to "underground"; bypass the queue for transit info to reach the window for London questions); if you're riding the Airbus into London, have your partner stay with the bags at the terminal. At the TI get a free simple map and brochures, and if you're taking the tube (subway) into London, buy a Travel Card day pass to cover the ride (see below).

Transportation to London from Heathrow Airport

By Tube (Subway): For £3.50, the tube takes you 14 miles to downtown London in 50 minutes (6/hrly, depending on your destination, may require one change). Even better, buy a £4.70 Travel Card that covers your trip into London and all your tube travel for the day (starting at 9:30). Buy it at the ticket window at the tube.

By Airport Bus: The Airbus, running between the airport and London's King's Cross station, serves the Notting Hill Gate and Bayswater neighborhoods—see recommended hotels, above (departs from each terminal, £7, 2/hrly 6:30–21:15, 60 min, buy ticket from driver, tel. 020/8571-2233). The tube works fine, but with baggage I prefer the Airbus—there are no connections underground and a lovely view from the top of the double-decker bus. Ask the driver to remind you when to get off. If you're going to the airport, exact pick-up times are clearly posted at each bus stop.

If you're staying in London's Victoria Station neighborhood, consider the National Express bus that runs between Heathrow's central bus station and Victoria Coach Station (£6, 2/hrly, 7:45–24:00 from Victoria, 5:40–21:45 from Heathrow, 40 min, tel. 08705-808-080).

By Taxi: Taxis from the airport cost about £35–50. Especially for four people traveling together this can be a deal. Hotels can often line up a cab back to the airport for £30. For the cheapest taxi to the airport don't order one from your hotel. Simply flag down a few and ask them for their best "off-meter" rate (I managed a ride for £25).

By Heathrow Express Train: This slick train service zips air travelers between Heathrow Airport and London's Paddington Station; at Paddington, you're in the thick of the tube system, with easy access to any of my recommended neighborhoods—Notting Hill Gate is just two stops away (£12 but ask about discount promos at Heathrow ticket desk, children under 16 ride free if you buy tickets before boarding, CC:VMA, covered by Britrail, 4/hrly, 5:10–23:30, 15 min to downtown from Terminals 1, 2, 3; 20 min from T-4; works as a free transfer between terminals, tel. 0845-600-1515, www.heathrowexpress.co.uk); a "Go Further" ticket for £13 includes one tube ride to get you to your hotel (valid only on same day and in Zone 1, saves 50p). For one person, combining the Heathrow Express with either a tube or taxi ride (between your hotel and Paddington) is as fast and half the cost of using solely a cab to (or from) the airport.

If you're flying out of Heathrow, check in at London's Paddington station. Take advantage of the calm, easy airline check-in at Paddington. If you're using any of the 26 represented airlines (including British Airways, British Midland, American, Lufthansa, SAS, Swiss Air, United Airlines, Air Canada, and Canadian Airlines), you can get a boarding pass and check your luggage (daily 5:00–21:00, last check-in 2 hrs before departure). You avoid the crowded chaos of check-in at Heathrow, and, even better, you'll have a little more time to sightsee instead of wasting three or four hours at the airport (on the morning of my departure, I checked my luggage at Paddington—6 hrs before my flight— then went on the London Eye Ferris Wheel, which I'd booked the day before). Catch your breath, then catch the Heathrow Express to arrive one hour before your plane leaves.

Buses from Heathrow to Destinations beyond London

The **National Express Central Bus Station** offers direct bus connections to **Cheltenham** (11/day, 2 hrs, £10.25), **Gatwick Airport** (2/hrly, 1 hr, £8), and **Bath** (11/day, at 8:40, 10:10, 11:40, 13:10, 14:40, 16:40, 18:10, 19:10, 20:10, 20:40, 21:40, 2.5 hrs, £11.25, direct, tel. 08705-808-080). Britrail passholders may prefer the 2.5-hour Heathrow–Bath bus/train connection via Reading (free with pass, otherwise £29.20, payable at desk in terminal, CC:VM); catch the twice-hourly RailAir Link shuttle bus to Reading (pron. REDing), then hop on the hourly express train to Bath. Most Heathrow buses depart from the common area serving terminals 1, 2, and 3, although some depart from T-4 (tel. 08705-747-777).

Flying into London's Gatwick Airport

More and more flights, especially charters, land at Gatwick Airport, halfway between London and the southern coast (airport tel. 01293/535-353). Trains—clearly the best way into London from here—shuttle conveniently between Gatwick and London's Victoria Station (£10.20, £19.50 round-trip, can purchase tickets on train at no extra charge, runs 24 hrs daily, 4/hrly during day, 1–2/hrly at night, 30 min, tel. 08705-301-530, www.gatwickexpress.co.uk).

London's Other Airports

If you're flying into or out of **Stansted** (airport tel. 01279/680-500), take the Airbus between the airport and downtown London's

Victoria Coach Station (£8, 2/hrly, from 4:00–24:00, 1.75 hrs, picks up and stops throughout London, tel. 08705-747-777). For **Luton** (airport tel. 01582/405-100, www.london-luton.com), try Green Line's bus #757 to get to or from London's Victoria Station at Buckingham Palace Road—stop 6 (£7.50, 2/hrly, 1–1.25 hrs depending on time of day, from 4:30–24:00, tel. 0870-608-7261, www.greenline.co.uk).

Discounted Flights from London

With any of these discount airlines, the farther you book in advance (up to about 9–12 months or as few as 3 weeks), the cheaper the fares. Cheap seats sell out first, leaving more expensive seats for latecomers. British Midland has been around the longest, but Virgin Express and Ryanair generally offer cheaper flights.

British Midland, the local discount airline, is sometimes cheaper than the train. You can fly inexpensively to Edinburgh (as little as £70 round-trip if you stay over Sat); to Dublin, Ireland (as little as £99 round-trip over Sat); to Paris (as little as £78 round-trip over Sat); and more. For the latest, call British tel. 0870-607-0555 or U.S. tel. 800/788-0555 (www.britishmidland.com).

Virgin Express is a British-owned company with good rates (book by phone and pick up ticket at airport an hour before your flight, tel. 020/7744-0004, www.virgin-express.com). Virgin Express flies from London to Shannon, Ireland (£40 from Stansted) and to Brussels (£50 from Heathrow, £40 from Gatwick). From its hub in Brussels you can connect cheaply to Barcelona, Madrid, Nice, Berlin, Copenhagen, Rome, or Milan (e.g., London–Milan, £50).

Ryanair is a creative Irish airline that prides itself on offering the lowest fares. They fly from London (mostly Stansted airport) to Dublin, Glasgow, Frankfurt, Lyon, Stockholm, Oslo, Venice, Turin, and many others. Sample fares: London–Dublin—£40 round-trip, London–Frankfurt—£40 round-trip (Irish tel. 01/609-7800, British tel. 0870-333-1231, www.ryanair.com). If you're the spontaneous sort, this airline is probably the best choice to try first. Because they offer promotional deals any time of year, it's not as essential that you book long in advance to get the best deals.

Trains and Buses

London, Britain's major transportation hub, has a different train station for each region. Waterloo handles the Eurostar to Paris (tel. 800/EUROSTAR). King's Cross covers northeast England and Scotland (tel. 08457-225-225). Paddington covers west and southwest England (Bath) and South Wales (tel. 08457-000-125). For the others, call 08457-484-950. Also see the BritRail map in the introduction.

National Express's excellent bus service is considerably cheaper

than trains. (For a busy signal, call 08705-808-080, or visit www
.nationalexpress.co.uk or the bus station a block southwest of
Victoria Station.)

To Bath: Trains leave London's Paddington Station every
hour (at a quarter after) for the 75-minute ride to Bath (costs
roughly £31 if you leave after 9:30). As an alternative, consider taking a guided bus tour from London to Stonehenge and Bath and
abandoning the tour in Bath (for details, see page 352).

To points north: Trains run hourly from London's King's
Cross Station, stopping in York (2 hrs), Durham (3 hrs), and
Edinburgh (5 hrs).

Crossing the English Channel

By Eurostar Train: The fastest and most convenient way to get
from Big Ben to the Eiffel Tower is by rail. In London, advertisements claim "more businessmen travel from London to Paris on
the Eurostar than on all airlines combined." Eurostar is the speedy
passenger train that zips you (and up to 800 others in 18 sleek cars)
from downtown London to downtown Paris (12/day, 3 hrs) or
Brussels (6/day, 3 hrs) faster and easier than flying. The train goes
80 mph in England and 190 mph on the Continent. (When the
English segment gets up to speed the journey time will shrink to
2 hours.) The actual Tunnel crossing is a 20-minute black, silent,
100 mph nonevent. Your ears won't even pop. You can go direct
to Disneyland Paris (1/day, more frequent with transfer at Lille) or
change at Lille to catch a TGV to Paris' Charles de Gaulle airport.

Channel fares (essentially the same to Paris or Brussels) are
reasonable but complicated. For the latest, call 800/EUROSTAR
in the U.S. These are U.S. prices: The "Leisure Ticket" is reasonable ($139 second class, $219 first class, 50 percent refundable
up to 3 days before departure). "Full Fare" first class costs $279
and includes a meal (a dinner departure nets you more grub than
breakfast); second class (or "standard") costs $199 (fully refundable
even after departure date). Discounts are given to railpass holders
($155-first, $75-second), youth under 26 ($165-first, $79-second),
and children under 12 (about half the fare of your ticket). Leisure
round-trip fares offer a decent value ($248-first, $158-second, not
refundable, 2 night minimum stay).

Cheaper seats can sell out. Book from home if you're ready to
commit to a date and time. Compare fares sold by U.S. rail agents
(www.raileurope.com) and British agents (www.eurostar.co.uk).
If you're ready to commit to a date, time, and U.S. prices, you can
book by calling 800/EUROSTAR, visiting www.raileurope.com,
or having your travel agent do it all for you (prices do not include
FedEx ticket delivery). For the British fares, book by calling
08705-186-186 or 1233-617-575 or visiting www.eurostar.co.uk
(pick up ticket at station).

Buying your Eurostar ticket in London is easy. Here are some sample London-Paris standard—that's second-class—fares (London-Brussels fares are up to £20 less). Avoid the "standard flexi" fare: one way for £165, round-trip for £290. Those with a railpass pay £50 one way, any day. Without a railpass, a same-day round-trip on a Saturday or Sunday costs £70. The various second-class round-trip Leisure Tickets (for stays over a Sat) are affordable: Leisure Flexi—£140 (partially refundable if not used), Leisure—£110 (not refundable), Leisure Apex 7—£90 (not refundable, purchase at least 7 days in advance), Leisure Apex 14—£70 (not refundable, purchase at least 14 days in advance, stay 2 nights or over a Sat). One-way tickets for departures after 14:00 Friday or anytime Saturday or Sunday cost £100. Youth tickets (for those under 26) are £45 one-way to either Paris or Brussels (£75 round-trip, exchangeable but not refundable). First-class and business-class fares are substantially higher. Remember, round-trip tickets over a Saturday are much cheaper than the basic one-way fare... you know the trick.

In Europe, you can get your Eurostar ticket at any major train station (in any country) or at any travel agency that handles train tickets (expect a booking fee). In Britain, you can book and pay for tickets over the phone with a credit card by calling 08705-186-186; pick up your tickets at London's Waterloo station an hour before the Eurostar departure. Note: Britain's time zone is one hour earlier than the Continent's. Times listed on tickets are local times.

By Bus and Boat or Train and Boat: The old-fashioned way of crossing the Channel is competitive and cheaper than Eurostar; it's also twice as romantic, complicated, and time-consuming. You'll get better prices arranging your trip in London than you would in the U.S. Taking the bus is cheapest, and round-trips are a bargain. By bus to Paris, Brussels, or Amsterdam from Victoria Coach Station: £35 one-way, £51 round-trip; 8.5 hrs to Paris—6/day; 8.25 hrs to Brussels—5/day; 11.25 hrs to Amsterdam—6/day; day or overnight, on Eurolines (tel. 08705-143-219, www.eurolines.co.uk; for Hoverspeed ferry only, call 0870-240-8070, www.hoverspeed.co.uk). By train and ferry from London to Paris: £39 one-way, £49 round-trip with five-day return, £59 round-trip over more than five days (tel. 0870-600-0613).

By Plane: Typical fares are £110 regular, less for student stand-by. Call in London for the latest fares. Consider British Midland (see "Discounted Flights," above) for its cheap round-trip fares to Paris.

BATH

Any tour of Britain that skips Bath stinks. Two hundred years ago this city of 80,000 was the trendsetting Hollywood of Britain. If ever a city enjoyed looking in the mirror, Bath's the one. It has more "government-listed" or protected historic buildings per capita than any other town in England. The entire city, built of the creamy warm-tone limestone called "Bath stone," beams in its cover-girl complexion. An architectural chorus line, it's a triumph of the Georgian style. Proud locals remind visitors that the town is routinely banned from the "Britain in Bloom" contest to give other towns a chance to win. Bath's narcissism is justified. Even with its mobs of tourists, it's a joy to visit.

Long before the Romans arrived in the first century, Bath was known for its hot springs. What became the Roman spa town of Aquae Sulis has always been fueled by the healing allure of its 116-degree mineral hot springs. The town's importance carried through Saxon times, when it had a huge church on the site of the present-day Abbey and was considered the religious capital of Britain. Its influence peaked in 973, when England's first king, Edgar, was crowned in the Abbey. Bath prospered as a wool town.

Bath then declined until the mid-1600s, when it was just a huddle of huts around the Abbey and some hot springs, with 3,000 residents oblivious to the Roman ruins 18 feet below their dirt floors. Then, in 1687, Queen Mary, fighting infertility, bathed here. Within 10 months she gave birth to a son...and a new age of popularity for Bath.

The town boomed as a spa resort. Ninety percent of the buildings you'll see today are from the 18th century. Local archi-tect John Wood was inspired by the Italian architect Palladio to build a "new Rome." The town bloomed in the neoclassical style, and streets were lined not with scrawny sidewalks but with wide "parades," upon which the women in their stylishly wide dresses could spread their fashionable tails.

Beau Nash (1673–1762) was Bath's "master of ceremonies." He organized both the daily regimen of the aristocratic visitors and the city, lighting and improving street security, banning swords, and opening the Pump Room. Under his fashionable baton, Bath became a city of balls, gaming, and concerts and the place to see and be seen in England. This most civilized place became even more so with the great neoclassical building spree that followed.

Planning Your Time

Bath needs two nights even on a quick trip. There's plenty to do, and it's a joy to do it.

Here's how I'd spend a day in Bath: 9:00–Tour the Roman Baths, 10:30–Catch the free city walking tour, 12:30–Picnic on the open deck of a Guide Friday bus tour, 14:30–Free time in the shopping center of old Bath, 16:00–Tour the Costume Museum.

Evening: Consider a Bizarre Bath Walk.

Orientation (area code: 01225)

Bath's town square, three blocks in front of the bus and train station, is a bouquet of tourist landmarks, including the Abbey, Roman and medieval baths, and the royal Pump Room.

Tourist Information: The TI is in the Abbey church-yard (Mon–Sat 9:30–18:00, Sun 10:00–16:00; Oct–April Mon–Sat closes at 17:00, tel. 01225/477-101, www.visitbath.co.uk). Pick up the 50p Bath map/guide (called *Leisure Attractions in and around Bath*) and the free, info-packed *This Month in Bath*. Browse through scads of fliers, books, and maps. Skip their room-finding service (£3 fee for walk-ins, £5 for callers) and book direct. An American Express office is tucked into the TI (decent rates, no commission on any checks, open same hours as TI).

Arrival in Bath: The Bath train station is a pleasure (small-town charm, an international tickets desk, and a Guide Friday office masquerading as a TI). The bus station is immediately in front of the train station. To get to the TI, walk two blocks up Manvers Street from either station and turn left at the triangular "square," following the small TI arrow on signpost. My recommended B&Bs are all within a 10- or 15-minute walk or a £3.50 taxi ride from the station.

Driving within Bath is a nightmare of one-way streets. Nearly everyone gets lost. Ask for advice from your hotelier and minimize driving in town.

Helpful Hints

Festivals: The International Music Festival bursts into song from May 18 to June 3 in 2001(classical, folk, jazz, contemporary, tel. 01225/462-231) overlapped by the eclectic Fringe Festival from late May to mid-June (theatre, walks, talks, bus trips, tel. 01225/480-079, www.bathfringe.co.uk). The Mozart festival strikes a universal chord every November. Bath's box office sells tickets for most every event (2 Church Street, tel. 01225/463-362, www.bathfestivals.org.uk).

Internet Access: The best in town is Click Café, with two branches, one across from the railway station and the other on 19 Broad Street, near the YMCA (£2.50/30 min, daily 10:00–22:00, tel. 01225/337-711). Other places offering Internet access are the Itchy Feet Café & Travel Store (4 Bartlett Street, near Costume Museum) and the Bath Backpackers Hostel (13 Pierrepont Street; coming from train station, you pass hostel on your way to the TI).

Farmers' Market: First and third Saturday of the month at Green Park Station (9:00–15:00).

Car Rental: Avis (behind the station and over the river at Unit 4B Riverside Business Park, Lower Bristol Road, tel. 01225/446-680), Enterprise (Lower Bristol Road, tel. 01225/443-311), and Hertz (just outside the train station, tel. 01225/442-911) are all trying harder. Most offices are a 10-minute walk from most recommended accommodations. Consider hotel delivery (usually £5, free with Enterprise). Most offices close Saturday afternoon and all day Sunday, complicating weekend pickups. Ideally, pick up your car only on the way out and into the countryside. Take the train or bus from London to Bath and rent a car as you leave Bath rather than in London.

Regional Tours: "Mad Max" minibus tours are thoughtfully organized, informative, and inexpensive (£16, 6-14 people). They last from 8:45 to 16:40 and cover 110 miles with stops in Avebury, Stonehenge, and two cute villages—Lacock and Castle Combe. Castle Combe, the southernmost Cotswold village, is as cute as they come. The Mad Max bus picks up passengers at 8:45 at the statue on Cheap Street (behind Bath Abbey). To reserve a seat, call the Bath YMCA (tel. 01225/325-900, please honor or cancel your seat reservation, e-mail: maddy@madmax.abel.co.uk).

If Mad Max is booked up, don't fret. Plenty of companies in Bath offer tours of varying lengths, prices, and destinations. Danwood Tours offers a daily day-long City Safari tour of the southern Cotswolds, Avebury, Stonehenge, Salisbury, and Longleat for £16.50 (departs outside Abbey Hotel at 10:00, book at Bath TI or call 07977-929-486 or 01373/461-135, private car hire also available). Or try Andrews Country Tours (£15 for tour that includes Wells, Glastonbury, and more, 15-seat minivan, narrated trip, tel. 01761/416-362, Chris Andrews). The cost of admission to sites is usually not included with any tour.

Tours of Bath

▲▲**City Bus Tours**—The Guide Friday green-and-cream open-top tour bus makes a 70-minute figure-eight circuit of Bath's main sights with an exhaustingly informative running commentary. For one £8.50 ticket (buy from driver), tourists can stop and go at will for a whole day. The buses cover the city center and the surrounding hills (17 signposted pick-up points, 3/hrly spring and fall—runs 9:30–17:00, 4/hrly in summer—9:30–18:00, hrly in winter—9:30–15:30, tel. 01225/464-446). This is great in sunny weather and a feast for photographers. You can munch a sandwich, work on a tan, and sightsee at the same time. Several competing hop-on hop-off tour bus companies offer basically the same tour, but in 45 minutes and without the swing through the countryside, for a couple pounds less. (Ask a local what he or she thinks about all of these city-tour buses.) Generally, the Guide Friday guides are better. Save your ticket to get a £1 discount on a Guide Friday tour in another town.

▲▲▲**Walking Tours**—These two-hour tours, offered free by trained local volunteers who want to share their love of Bath with its many visitors, are a chatty, historical, gossip-filled joy, essential for your understanding of this town's amazing Georgian social scene. How else will you learn that the old "chair ho" call for your sedan chair evolved into today's "cheerio" greeting? Tours leave from in front of the Pump Room (year-round daily at 10:30, plus May–Oct at 14:00 Mon–Fri, 14:30 Sun, and 19:00 on Tue, Fri, and Sat). For Ghost Walks and Bizarre Bath Comedy Walks, see "Nightlife," below. For a private walking tour from a local gentleman who's an excellent guide, contact Patrick Driscoll (£42/2 hrs, tel. 01225/462-010).

Sights—Bath

▲▲▲**Roman and Medieval Baths**—In ancient Roman times, high society enjoyed the mineral springs at Bath. From Londinium, Romans traveled so often to Aquae Sulis, as the city was called, to "take a bath" that finally it became known simply as Bath. Today a fine museum surrounds the ancient bath and is, with its well-documented displays, a one-way system leading you past Roman artifacts, mosaics, a temple pediment, and the actual mouth of the spring, piled high with Roman pennies. Enjoy some quality time looking into the eyes of Minerva, goddess of the hot springs. The included self-guided tour audio-wand makes the visit easy and plenty informative. For those with a big appetite for Roman history, in-depth 40-minute tours leave from the end of the museum at the edge of the actual bath (included, on the hour, a poolside clock is set for the next departure time). You can revisit the museum after the tour (£6.90, £8.90 combo ticket includes Costume Museum at a good savings, family combo-£23.50, combo

Bath

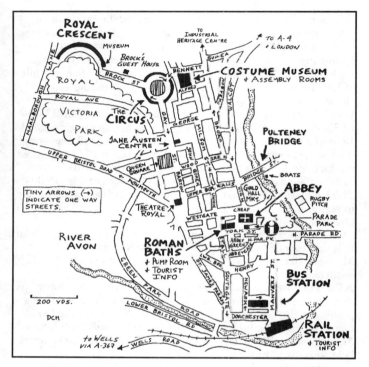

tickets good for 1 week; April–Sept daily 9:00–18:00, in Aug until 21:30, Oct–March until 17:00, tel. 01225/477-000). In 2002, when a new spa facility opens (near the museum), people will once again be able to bathe in the hot springs of Bath.

▲**Pump Room**—After a centuries-long cold spell, Bath was re-heated when the previously barren Queen Mary bathed here and in due course bore a male heir to the throne (1687). Once Bath was back on the aristocratic map, high society soon turned the place into one big pleasure palace. The Pump Room, an elegant Georgian hall just above the Roman baths, offers the visitor's best chance to raise a pinky in this Chippendale elegance. Drop by to sip coffee or tea to the rhythm of a string trio or pianist (live music all year 10:00–12:00, summers until 17:00, tea/coffee and pastry available for £6 anytime except during lunch, a £9 traditional high tea served after 14:30). Above the newspaper table and sedan chairs a statue of Beau Nash himself sniffles down at you. Now's your chance to have a famous (but forgettable) "Bath bun" and split (and spit) a 50p drink of the awfully curative water.

Public WCs are in the entry hallway that connects the Pump Room with the Baths.

▲**Abbey**—Bath town wasn't much in the Middle Ages. But an important church has stood on this spot since Anglo-Saxon times. In 973, Edgar, the first king of England, was crowned here. Dominating the town center, the present church—the last great medieval church of England—is 500 years old and a fine example of Late Perpendicular Gothic, with breezy fan vaulting and enough stained glass to earn it the nickname "Lantern of the West" (worth the £2 donation, Mon–Sat 9:00–18:00, Sun 13:00–17:30, closes at 16:30 in winter, handy flier narrates a self-guided 18-stop tour). The schedule for concerts, services, and **evensong** (Sun at 15:15 year-round, plus most Sat in Aug at 17:00) is posted on the door. **Church bells** ring before services from 10:15 to 11:00 on Sunday; practice is usually on Monday evening (19:00–21:00; a glorious time to take an evening walk). Take a moment to really appreciate the Abbey's architecture from the Abbey Green square.

The Abbey's **Heritage Vaults**, a small but interesting exhibit, tells the story of Christianity in Bath since Roman times (£2, Mon–Sat 10:00–16:00, closed Sun, entrance just outside church, south side).

▲**Pulteney Bridge and Cruises**—Bath is inclined to compare its shop-lined Pulteney Bridge to Florence's Ponte Vecchio. That's pushing it. To best enjoy a sunny day, pay £1 to enter the Parade Gardens below the bridge (daily 10:00–19:00, until 20:00 June–Aug, free after 20:00, includes deck chairs, ask about the concerts held some Sun at 15:00 in summer).

Across the bridge at Pulteney Weir, tour boats run cruises from under the bridge (£4.50, up to 7/day if the weather's good, 50 minutes to Bathampton and back, WCs on board). Just take whatever boat is running. Avon Cruisers stop in Bathampton if you'd like to walk back; Pulteney Cruisers come with a sundeck ideal for picnics.

▲▲**Royal Crescent and the Circus**—If Bath is an architectural cancan, these are the kickers. These first elegant Georgian "condos" by John Wood (the Elder and the Younger) are well explained in the city walking tours. "Georgian" is British for "neoclassical," or dating from the 1770s. As you cruise the Crescent, pretend you're rich. Pretend you're poor. Notice the "ha ha fence," a drop in the front yard offering a barrier, invisible from the windows, to sheep and peasants. The round Circus is a colosseum turned inside out. Its Doric, Ionic, and Corinthian capital decorations pay homage to its Greco-Roman origin.

▲▲**Georgian House at #1 Royal Crescent**—This museum (on the corner of Brock Street and the Royal Crescent) offers your best look into a period house. It's worth the £4 admission to get

behind one of those classy exteriors. The volunteers in each
room are determined to fill you in on all the fascinating details
of Georgian life...like how high-class women shaved their eye-
brows and pasted on carefully trimmed strips of furry mouse
skin in their place (Tue–Sun 10:30–17:00, closed Mon, closes
at 16:00 in Nov, closed Dec–mid-Feb, "no stiletto heels, please,"
tel. 01225/428-126).

▲▲▲**Costume Museum**—One of Europe's great museums,
displaying 400 years of fashion—one frilly decade at a time—is
housed within Bath's Assembly Rooms. Follow the included, excellent audioguide tour (£4, an £8.90 combo ticket covers Roman
Baths, family combo-£23.50, daily 10:00–17:00, tel. 01225/477-789).
The Assembly Rooms, which you'll see en route to the museum,
are big, elegant, empty rooms where card games, concerts, tea, and
dances were held in the 18th century before the advent of fancy
hotels with grand public spaces made them obsolete.

▲▲**Museum of Bath at Work**—This is the official title for Mr.
Bowler's Business, a 1900s engineer's shop, brass foundry, and
fizzy-drink factory with a Dickensian office. It's just a pile of
meaningless old gadgets until a volunteer guide lovingly resurrects
Mr. Bowler's creative genius. Fascinating hour-long tours go regularly; just join the one in session upon arrival. (£3.50, plus a few
pence for a glass of genuine Victorian lemonade, April–Oct daily
10:00–17:00, weekends only in winter, 2 blocks up Russell Street
from Assembly Rooms, call to be sure a volunteer is available to
give a tour, café upstairs, tel. 01225/318-348.)

Jane Austen Centre—This new exhibition focuses on Jane
Austen's five years in Bath (around 1800) and the influence Bath
had on her writing. While the exhibit is thoughtfully done and is a
hit with "Jane-ites," there is little of historic substance here. You'll
walk through a Georgian townhouse which she didn't live in and
see mostly enlarged reproductions of things associated with her
writing. After a live intro explaining how this romantic but down-
to-earth girl dealt with the silly, shallow, and arrogant aristocrat's
world where "the doing of nothings all day prevents one from
doing anything," you see a 13-minute video and wander through
the rest of the exhibit (£4, Mon–Sat 10:00–17:30, Sunday 10:30–
17:30, 40 Gay Street between Queen's Square and the Circus,
tel. 01225/443-000, www.janeausten.co.uk).

The Building of Bath Museum—This offers a fascinating look
behind the scenes at how the Georgian city was actually built. It's
just one large room of exhibits, but those interested in construction find it worth the £4 (Tue–Sun 10:30–17:00, closed Mon, near
the Circus on a street called "the Paragon," tel. 01225/333-895).

Microworld—This dark two-room museum glows with a couple
dozen glass bubbles of light, containing the smallest sculptures
you've ever seen—the creations of two artists. Ussa's work borders

on hokey (flea riding a bicycle), but Wigan's work is remarkable. Wigan actually carves his minute work—out of a sugar grain, a match head, a bit of boxwood (look for the Statue of Liberty in the eye of a needle). As a dyslexic kid, labeled "nothing" by a racist teacher, he was determined to make something out of nothing (£3.50, daily 10:00–18:00, Kingsmead Square, near Theatre Royal, tel. 01225/333-003).

Royal Photographic Society—A hit with shutterbugs, this focuses on the earliest cameras, photos, and their development, (£4, daily 9:30–17:30, on Milsom Street, tel. 01225/462-841).

Views—For the best views of Bath, try Alexander Park (south of city, 10-minute walk from train station), Camden Crescent (10–15 minute walk north), or Becksford Tower (steep 20-minute walk north up Lansdown Road, www.bath-preservation-trust.org.uk).

▲**American Museum**—I know, you need this in Bath like you need a Big Mac. But this museum offers a fascinating look at colonial and early-American lifestyles. Each of 18 completely furnished rooms (from the 1600s to the 1800s) is hosted by an eager guide waiting to fill you in on the candles, maps, bedpans, and various religious sects that make domestic Yankee history surprisingly interesting. One room is a quilter's nirvana (£5.50, Tue–Sun 14:00–17:00, closed Mon and early Nov–late March, at Claverton Manor, tel. 01225/460-503). The museum is outside of town and a headache to reach if you don't have a car (15-minute walk from the nearest Guide Friday stop or a 10-minute walk from bus #18).

Activities in Bath

Walking, Biking, and Swimming—The Bath Skyline Walk is a six-mile wander around the hills surrounding Bath (70p leaflet at TI). For more options, get *Country Walks around Bath*, by Tim Mowls (£4.50 at TI).

Consider the idyllic walk up the canal path to Bathampton: from downtown, walk over Pulteney Bridge, through Sydney Gardens, turn left on canal, and in 30 minutes you'll hit Bathampton, with its much-loved Old George Pub. Sailors enjoy the river cruise up to Bathampton; hikers like walking back (see "Pulteney Bridge and Cruises," above). From Bathampton it's two hours along the canal to the fine old town of Bradford-on-Avon, from which you can train back to Bath. You can bike this route (rent bikes at Avon Valley Cyclery behind train station, £9/half day, £14/all day, tel. 01225/442-442). The scenic 12-mile path along the old Bath–Bristol train tracks is also popular.

The Bath Sports and Leisure Centre has a swimming pool and more (£2.50, daily 8:00–22:00, just across North Parade Bridge, call for free swim times, tel. 01225/462-563).

The Bath Boating Station, in an old Victorian boathouse, rents boats and punts (£4.50/first hr per person, then £1.50/hr,

April–Sept 10:00–18:00, tearoom, Forester Road, a mile northeast of center, tel. 01225/466-407).

Shopping—There's great browsing between the Abbey and the Assembly Rooms (Costume Museum). Shops close at 17:30, later on Thursday. Explore the antique center on Bartlett Street just below the Assembly Rooms. You'll find the most stalls open on Wednesday. Pick up the local paper (usually out on Friday) and shop with the dealers at estate sales and auctions listed in "What's On."

Nightlife in Bath

This Month in Bath (available at TI) lists events.

Plays—The Theatre Royal, newly restored and one of England's loveliest, offers a busy schedule of London West End–type plays, including many "pre-London" dress rehearsal runs (£11–25, cheaper matinees as low as £5, tel. 01225/448-844). Forty standby tickets per evening show go on sale starting at 12:00 on the day of the performance (either pay cash at box office or call and book with CC, 2 tickets maximum). Or you can buy a last-minute seat at a reduced price 30 minutes before "curtain up."

Evening Walks—For a walking comedy act "with absolutely no history or culture," follow J. J. or Noel Britten on their creative and entertaining **Bizarre Bath** walk. This 90-minute "tour," which plays off local passersby as well as tour members, is a kick (£4.50, 20:00 nightly April 9–Sept 30, heavy on magic, careful to insult all minorities and sensitivities, just racy enough but still good family fun; leave from Huntsman pub near the Abbey, confirm at TI or call 01225/335-124, www.bizarrebath.co.uk). **Ghost Walks** are another way to pass the after-dark hours (£4, 20:00, 2 hrs, unreliably Mon–Sat April–Oct; in winter Fridays only; leave from Garrick's Head pub near Theatre Royal, tel. 01225/463-618). Scholarly types can try the **free walking tours** offered several times a week (19:00 on Tue, Fri, and Sat, 2 hrs, May–Oct, leave from Pump Room, confirm at TI).

Sleeping in Bath

(£1 = about $1.60, country code: 44, area code: 01225)
Sleep Code: **S** = Single, **D** = Double/Twin, **T** = Triple, **Q** = Quad, **b** = bathroom, **t** = toilet only, **s** = shower only, **CC** = Credit Card (Visa, MasterCard, Amex).

Bath is a busy tourist town. To get a good B&B, make a telephone reservation in advance. Competition is stiff, and it's worth asking any of these places for a weekday, three-nights-in-a-row, or off-season deal. Friday and Saturday nights are tightest, especially if you're staying only one night, since B&Bs favor those staying longer. If staying only Saturday night, you're very bad news. At B&Bs (and cheaper hotels), expect lots of stairs and no lifts.

Launderettes: The Spruce Goose Launderette is around the corner from Brock's Guest House on the pedestrian lane called Margaret's Buildings (£4 self-serve, £7 full-service on same day if dropped off by 10:30, Sun–Fri 8:00–20:00, Sat 8:00–19:00, tel. 01225/483-309). The scruffier Monmouth Place Launderette, closer to the Marlborough Lane listings, is on Upper Bristol Road (£4 self-serve, £6 full-service—drop off by noon for same-day return, daily 9:00–20:00, tel. 01225/429-378). East of Pulteney Bridge, the humble Lovely Wash is on Daniel Street (daily 9:00–21:00, self-serve only).

Sleeping in B&Bs near the Royal Crescent

From the train station, these listings are all a 10- to 15-minute uphill walk or an easy £3.50 taxi ride. Or take the Guide Friday bus tour from the station and get off at the stop nearest your B&B (for Brock's, Assembly Rooms; for Marlborough listings, Royal Avenue; for Armstrong's, Upper Bristol Road—confirm with driver), check in, then finish the tour later in the day. All of these B&Bs are nonsmoking.

Brock's Guest House will put bubbles in your Bath experience. Marion and Geoffrey Dodd have redone their Georgian townhouse (built by John Wood in 1765) in a way that would make the famous architect proud. It's located between the prestigious Royal Crescent and the elegant Circus (Db-£62–70, 1 deluxe Db-£72–75, Tb-£85–87, Qb-£99–105, reserve with a credit-card number far in advance, CC:VM, strictly nonsmoking, little library on top floor, 32 Brock Street, BA1 2LN, tel. 01225/338-374, fax 01225/334-245, www.brocksguesthouse.co.uk, e-mail: marion@brocks.force9.net). Marion can occasionally arrange a reasonable private car hire.

On Marlborough Lane: The **Woodville House** is run by Anne and Tom Toalster. This grandmotherly little house has three tidy, charming rooms, one shared shower/WC, an extra WC, and a TV lounge. Breakfast is served at a big, family-style table (D-£40, minimum 2 nights, strictly nonsmoking, below the Royal Crescent at 4 Marlborough Lane, BA1 2NQ, tel. & fax 01225/319-335, e-mail: toalster@compuserve.com).

Elgin Villa, also a fine value, has five comfy, well-maintained rooms (Ds-£45, Db-£50, discounts for 3-night stays, kids £15 extra, continental breakfast served in room, parking, nonsmoking, 6 Marlborough Lane, BA1 2NQ Bath, tel. & fax 01225/424-557, www.elginvilla.co.uk, Alwyn and Carol Landman).

Athelney Guest House, which also serves a continental breakfast in your room, has three spacious rooms with two shared bathrooms (D-£40–42, T-£60–63, nonsmoking, parking, 5 Marlborough Lane, BA1 2NQ, tel. & fax 01225/312-031, Sue and Colin Davies, e-mail: colin-davies@supanet.com).

Parkside Guest House is more upscale, renting four classy Edwardian rooms (Db-£65, nonsmoking, access to pleasant

backyard, 11 Marlborough Lane, BA1 2NQ, tel. & fax 01225/
429-444, e-mail: parkside@lynall.freeserve.co.uk, Erica and
Inge Lynall).

Marlborough House is both Victorian and vegetarian, with
seven comfortable rooms—well furnished with antiques—and
optional £15 organic veggie dinners (Sb-£45–75, Db-£65–85
depending on season, CC:VM, varied breakfast menu, room service,
nonsmoking,1 Marlborough Lane, BA1 2NQ, tel. 01225/318-175,
fax 01225/466-127, www.s-h-systems.co.uk/hotels/marlbor1.html,
Americans Laura and Charles).

Prior House B&B, with four well-kept rooms, is run by
helpful Lynn and Keith Shearns (D-£40, Db-£45, CC:VM, nonsmoking, 3 Marlborough Lane, tel. 01225/313-587, fax 01225/
443-543, e-mail: priorhouse@greatplaces.co.uk).

On Upper Bristol Road: The **Armstrong House B&B**
is well run and closer to town on a busier road, with five pleasant
rooms behind double-paned windows (Db-£55, continental breakfast in room, nonsmoking, 41 Crescent Gardens, Upper Bristol
Road, BA1 2NB, tel. 01225/442-211, fax 01225/460-665, Tony
Conradi).

Sleeping in B&Bs East of the River
These listings are about a 10-minute walk from the city center.

Near North Parade Road: The **Holly Villa Guest House,**
with a cheery garden, six bright rooms, and a cozy TV lounge, is
enthusiastically and thoughtfully run by Jill and Keith McGarrigle
(Ds-£45, Db-£50, Tb-£70, strictly nonsmoking, easy parking,
8-minute walk from station and city center, 14 Pulteney Gardens,
BA2 4HG, tel. 01225/310-331, fax 01225/339-334, e-mail:
hollyvilla.bb@ukgateway.net). From the city center, walk over
North Parade Bridge, take the first right, then the second left.

Near Pulteney Road: Muriel Guy's B&B is another good
value, mixing Georgian elegance with homey warmth, artistic
taste, and fine city views (5 rooms, 1 S with private bath upstairs-
£25, Db-£50, nonsmoking, 10-minute walk from city center, go
over bridge on North Parade Road, left on Pulteney Road, cross
to church, Raby Place is first row of houses on hill, 14 Raby Place,
BA2 4EH, tel. 01225/465-120, fax 01225/465-283).

The Ayrlington, next door to a lawn-bowling green, has
attractive rooms that hint of a more genteel time. Though this
well-maintained hotel fronts a busy street, it feels tranquil inside,
with double-paned windows. Rooms in the back have pleasant
views of sports greens and Bath beyond. For the best value,
request a standard double with a view of Bath (standard Db-
£80–95, superior Db-£90–110, deluxe Db with Jacuzzi-£99–125,
prices decrease midweek and increase weekends, no Sat night only,
CC:VMA, access to garden in back, easy parking, 10-minute walk

from center, 24/25 Pulteney Road, BA2 4EZ, tel. 01225/425-495, fax 01225/469-029, www.ayrlington.com, Simon and Mee-Ling).

In Sydney Gardens: The **Sydney Gardens Hotel** is a classy Casablanca-type place with six tastefully decorated rooms, an elegant breakfast room, garden views, and an entrance to Sydney Gardens park (Db-£69/weekdays, £75/weekends, Tb-£95, CC:VM, 2 nights preferred, request garden view, located on busy road between park and canal, easy parking, 10-minute walk from center, Sydney Road, BA2 6NT, tel. 01225/464-818, fax 01225/484-347, Geraldine and Peter Beaven).

Sleeping East of Pulteney Bridge

These are just a few minutes' walk from the city center.

The **Kennard Hotel** is comfortable, with 14 charming Georgian rooms. Richard Ambler runs this place warmly, giving careful attention to guests (S-£48, Db-£88–98 depending upon size, CC:VMA, no kids under 12, nonsmoking, just over Pulteney Bridge, turn left at Henrietta, 11 Henrietta Street, BA2 6LL, tel. 01225/310-472, fax 01225/460-054, www.kennard.co.uk, e-mail: kennard@dircon.co.uk).

Laura Place Hotel is another elegant Georgian place (8 rooms, 2 on the ground floor, Db-£70–90 from small and high up to huge and palatial, 2-night minimum stay, must show this book to get 10 percent discount with cash, CC:VMA, family suite, nonsmoking, easy parking, 3 Laura Place, Great Pulteney Street, BA2 4BH, just over Pulteney Bridge, tel. 01225/463-815, fax 01225/310-222, Patricia Bull).

Villa Magdala, with 18 spacious rooms in a freestanding Victorian townhouse opposite a park, is centuries away from a Motel 6 (Db-£85–£105, depending on size, type of bed, and plumbing; nonsmoking, in quiet residential area, parking, Henrietta Road, Bath BA2 6LX, tel. 01225/466-329, fax 01225-483-207, www .villamagdala.co.uk).

Henrietta Hotel has simple, tidy, and decent rooms, giving you a budget hotel option in an elegant neighborhood (10 rooms, Db-£45–75, discounts for cash and 2-night stay Sun–Thu, CC:VM, 32 Henrietta Street, tel. 01225/447-779, fax 01225/444-150).

Sleeping in the City Center

Harington's of Bath Hotel, with 13 newly renovated rooms on a quiet street in the town center, is run by Susan and Desmond Pow (Db-£78–98, Tb-£110–120, prices decrease midweek and increase weekends, CC:VMA, nonsmoking, lots of stairs, attached restaurant/bar serves simple meals and pastries throughout day, extremely central at 10 Queen Street, BA1 1HE, tel. 01225/461-728, fax 01225/444-804, www.haringtonshotel.co.uk).

Parade Park Hotel, in a Georgian building, has a central

Hotels in Bath

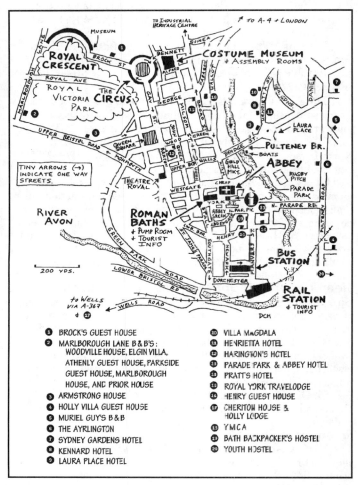

- ❶ BROCK'S GUEST HOUSE
- ❷ MARLBOROUGH LANE B&B'S:
  WOODVILLE HOUSE, ELGIN VILLA,
  ATHENLY GUEST HOUSE, PARKSIDE
  GUEST HOUSE, MARLBOROUGH
  HOUSE, AND PRIOR HOUSE
- ❸ ARMSTRONG HOUSE
- ❹ HOLLY VILLA GUEST HOUSE
- ❺ MURIEL GUY'S B&B
- ❻ THE AYRLINGTON
- ❼ SYDNEY GARDENS HOTEL
- ❽ KENNARD HOTEL
- ❾ LAURA PLACE HOTEL
- ❿ VILLA MAGDALA
- ⓫ HENRIETTA HOTEL
- ⓬ HARINGTON'S HOTEL
- ⓭ PARADE PARK & ABBEY HOTEL
- ⓮ PRATT'S HOTEL
- ⓯ ROYAL YORK TRAVELODGE
- ⓰ HENRY GUEST HOUSE
- ⓱ CHERITON HOUSE &
  HOLLY LODGE
- ⓲ YMCA
- ⓳ BATH BACKPACKER'S HOSTEL
- ⓴ YOUTH HOSTEL

location, helpful owners, and comfortable rooms decorated in a
modern style (35 rooms, Db-£60–65, 4-poster Db-£75, Tb-£80,
Qb-£105, CC:VM, nonsmoking, beaucoup stairs, 10 North
Parade, BA2 4AL, tel. 01225/463-384, fax 01225/442-322,
www.paradepark.co.uk, Nita and David Derrick).

Pratt's Hotel is as proper and old English as you'll find in
Bath. Its creaks and frays are aristocratic. Its public places make
you want to sip a brandy, and its 46 rooms are bright, spacious,
and come with all the comforts (Sb-£75, Db-£110, prices promised

with this book in 2001, dogs £2.95 but children free, CC:VMA, attached restaurant/bar, elevator, 2 blocks immediately in front of the station on South Parade, BA2 4AB, tel. 01225/460-441, fax 01225/448-807, e-mail: admin@prattshotel.demon.co.uk).

The **Royal York Travelodge** offers American-style characterless, comfortable rooms, worrying B&Bs and hotels alike with its reasonable prices (Db-£69, 1 York Bldg, George Street, BA1 3EB, tel. 01225/448-999).

The Abbey Hotel, a Best Western hotel, has 60 good-quality rooms with a super location, and offers a rare elevator as well as some ground floor rooms (standard Db-£120, deluxe Db-£130, CC:VMA, attached restaurant, nonsmoking rooms available, North Parade, BA1 1LF, tel. 01225/461-603, fax 01225/447-758, e-mail: ahres@compasshotels.co.uk).

Henry Guest House is a plain, simple, old, vertical, eight-room, family-run place two blocks in front of the train station on a quiet side street. Nothing matches—not the curtains, wallpaper, carpeting, throw rugs, or bedspreads—but it is the cheapest hotel in the center (S-£22.50, D-£45, T-£67.50, TVs in rooms, lots of narrow stairs, 2 showers and WCs for all, 6 Henry Street, BA1 1JT, tel. 01225/424-052, e-mail: cox@thehenrybath.freeserve.co.uk).

Sleeping in B&Bs South of the Train Station

Up a hill an eight-minute walk south of the train station are a string of classy, upscale B&Bs with views of Bath. Here are two good ones (request a view room): **Cheriton House**, with nine well-furnished rooms (Db-£58–66, larger Db-£68–76, CC:VM, garden, 9 Upper Oldfield Park, BA2 3JX, tel. 01225/429-862, e-mail: cheriton @which.net, Mrs. Iris Wroe-Parker), and **Holly Lodge**, with six frilly, Victorian-style rooms and a view gazebo in the garden (Sb-£48–55, Db-£75–94, add £5 for 4-poster, CC:VM, no smoking, phones, tel. 01225/339-187, fax 01225/481-138, Mr. George Hall).

Sleeping in Dorms

The **YMCA,** wonderfully central on a leafy square down a tiny alley off Broad Street, has industrial-strength rooms and scuff-proof halls (S-£15, D-£28, T-£42, Q-£56, beds in big dorms-£11, cheaper for 2-night stays, includes continental breakfast, families offered a day nursery for kids under 5, cheap dinners, CC:VM, Broad Street Place, BA1 5LH, tel. 01225/460-471, fax 01225/ 462-065, e-mail: info@ymcabath.u-net.com).

Bath Backpackers Hostel bills itself as a totally fun-packed, mad place to stay. This Aussie-run dive/hostel rents bunk beds in 6- to 10-bed coed rooms (£12 per bed, 2 D-£30, no lockers, Internet access for nonguests as well, a couple of blocks toward the city center from the station, 13 Pierrepont Street, tel. 01225/446-787, fax 01225/446-305, e-mail: stayinbath@backpackers-uk.demon.co.uk).

The **Youth Hostel** is in a grand old building on Bathwick Hill outside of town (£11 per bed without breakfast in 2- to 12-bed rooms, bus #18 from station, tel. 01225/465-674).

Eating in Bath

While not a great pub grub town, Bath is bursting with quaint eateries. There's something for every appetite and budget—just stroll around the center of town. A picnic dinner of deli food or take-out fish 'n' chips in the Royal Crescent Park is ideal for aristocratic hobos.

Eating between the Abbey and the Station

Three fine and popular places share North Parade Passage, a block south of the Abbey: **Tilley's Bistro** serves healthy French, English, and vegetarian meals with ambience (£10 3-course lunches, £15–20 dinners, Mon–Sat 12:00–14:30, nightly 18:30–23:00, closed Sun lunch, CC:VM, nonsmoking, North Parade Passage, tel. 01225/484-200). **Sally Lunn's House** is a cutesy, quasi-historic place for expensive doily meals, tea, pink pillows, and lots of lace (£5–8, nightly, CC:VM, 4 North Parade Passage, tel. 01225/461-634). It's fine for tea and buns, and customers get a free peek at the basement Kitchen Museum (otherwise 30p). Next door, **Demuth's Vegetarian Restaurant** serves good three-course £15 meals (daily 10:00–22:00, CC:VM, vegan options available, tel. 01225/446-059).

Crystal Palace Pub, with hearty meals under rustic timbers or in the sunny courtyard, is a handy standby (£6 meals, Mon–Fri 11:00–20:30, Sat 11:00–15:30, Sun 12:00–14:30; children welcome on patio, not indoors; 11 Abbey Green, tel. 01225/423-944).

Evans is considered the best fish 'n' chips joint in town, but it's mainly open only for lunch and is perpetually on the verge of being bought out (Mon–Fri 11:30–15:30, Sat 11:30–19:00, on Abbeygate, near Marks & Spencer). A good fallback is **Seafoods** (daily 12:00–23:00, 27 Kingsmeads Street, just off Kingsmead Square). For more cheap meals, try **Spike's Fish and Chips** (open very late) and the neighboring café just behind the bus station.

Eating between the Abbey and the Circus

George Street is lined with cheery eateries: Thai, Italian, wine bars, and so on. **Caffé Martini** is purely Italian with class (£10 entrees, £7 pizzas, daily 12:00–14:30, 18:00–22:00, CC:VM, 9 George Street, tel. 01225/460-818), while the **Mediterraneo,** also Italian, is homier (12 George Street, CC:VMA, tel. 01225/429-008).

Eastern Eye serves Indian food under the domes of a Georgian auction hall (£15 meals, £9 minimum, daily 12:00–14:30, 18:00–23:00, CC:VMA, 8a Quiet Street, tel. 01225/422-323). **Jamuna** makes a mean curry (Mon–Sun 12:00–14:30, 18:00–24:00, Abbey views, 9–10 High Street, tel. 01225/464-631).

The **Old Green Tree Pub** on Green Street is a rare pub with good grub, locally brewed real ales, and a nonsmoking room (lunch only, served 12:00–14:30, no children, live jazz Sun–Mon 20:30 until closing, tel. 01225/448-259).

Browns, a popular, modern chain, offers affordable English food throughout the day (£6 lunch special, Mon-Sat 11:00–23:30, Sun 12:00–23:30, CC:VMA, half block east of Abbey, Orange Grove, tel. 01225/461-199).

The Moon and Sixpence, prized by locals, gives British cooking a needed international flair and flavor (£7 lunch, 3-course dinner menu for £18–22, daily 12:00–14:30, 17:30–22:30, CC:VM, indoor/outdoor seating, 6a Broad Street, tel. 01225/460-962).

All Bar One, offering inexpensive meals, is a trendy, modern-day pub popular with the younger crowd (12 High Street, tel. 01225/324-021).

Devon Savouries serves greasy, delicious take-out pasties, sausage rolls, and vegetable pies (Mon–Sat 9:00–17:30, hours vary on Sun; on Burton Street, the main walkway between New Bond Street and Upper Borough Walls).

Pasta Galore serves decent (sometimes so-so) Italian food and homemade pasta outside on a patio or inside—the ground floor beats the basement (daily 12:00–14:30, 18:00–22:30, CC:VM, 31 Barton Street, tel. 01225/463-861).

If you're missing California, try the popular **Firehouse Rotisserie** (daily 12:00–14:30, 18:00–23:00, reserve on weekends, John Street, tel. 01225/482-070).

Guildhall Market, across from Pulteney Bridge, is fun for browsing and picnic shopping, with an inexpensive Market Café if you'd like to sip tea surrounded by stacks of used books, bananas on the push list, and honest-to-goodness old-time locals (Mon–Sat 9:00–17:00, closed Sun, main entrance on High Street, a block north of Abbey).

The **Cornish Bakehouse**, near the Guildhall Market, has good take-away pasties (11a The Corridor, off High Street, tel. 01225/426-635).

Supermarkets: Waitrose, at the Podium shopping center, is great for groceries (Mon–Fri 8:30–20:00, Sat 8:30–19:00, Sun 11:00–17:00, salad bar, just west of Pulteney Bridge and across from post office on High Street). **Marks & Spencer,** near the train station, has a good grocery at the back of its department store (Mon–Sat 9:00–17:30, Sun 11:00–17:00, Stall Street).

Eating East of Pulteney Bridge

For a classy, intimate setting and "new English" cuisine worth the splurge, dine at **No. 5 Bistro** (main courses with vegetables £12–15, Mon and Tue are "bring your own bottle of wine" nights—no corkage charge, Mon–Sat 18:30–22:00, closed Sun, just over Pulteney Bridge at 5 Argyle Street, smart to reserve, tel. 01225/444-499). **Rajpoot Tandoori,** next door to No. 5, serves good Indian food. **Cappeti's,** across the street from No. 5, is a pasta pleaser (Tue–Sat 12:00–14:00, 18:30–22:30, closed Mon, 12 Argyle Street, tel. 01225/442-299).

Eating near the Circus and Brock's Guest House

Circus Restaurant is intimate and a good value, with Mozartian ambience and candlelight prices: £17 for a three-course dinner special including great vegetables and a selection of fine desserts (daily 12:00–14:00, 18:30–22:00, CC:VM, 34 Brock Street, tel. 01225/318-918, Felix Rosenow).

Woods Restaurant serves modern English cuisine to well-dressed locals in a sprawling candlelit brasserie (lunches-£7, 3-course dinners-£13–25, daily 12:00–15:00, 18:00–22 30 except closed Sun eve, CC:VM, 9–13 Alfred Street, near Assembly Rooms, tel. 01225/314-812).

Transportation Connections—Bath

To London's Paddington Station: By train (2/hrly, 75 min, £31 one-way after 9:30), or cheaper by National Express bus (nearly hrly, up to 3.25 hrs, £11.25 one-way, £19.50 round-trip but £23 on Fri, ask about £12 day returns). To get from London to Bath, consider an all-day Stonehenge-and-Bath organized bus tour from London. For about the same cost as the train ticket, you can see Stonehenge, tour Bath, and leave the tour before it returns to London (stow your bag underneath). Evan Evans offers daily Stonehenge/Bath day trips from London (£48 for fully guided version includes admissions, offered year-round; also has a £33 Low Cost version providing bus transportation only, offered April–Oct only, but may not run in 2001—ask, departs Victoria Coach Station, tel. 020/7950-1777, www.evanevans.co.uk). Golden Tours offers a similar fully guided tour at similar prices (about £48, departs from Fountain Square, across from Victoria Coach Station, tel. 020/7233-6668, www.goldentours.co.uk). Train info: tel. 08457-484-950.

To London's airports: By National Express bus to **Heathrow** Airport—and continuing on to London (10/day, leaving Bath at 5:00, 6:30, 7:30, 8:45, 10:00, 12:00, 13:30, 15:00, 16:30, and 18:30, 2.5 hrs, £11.50, tel. 08705-808-080), and to **Gatwick** (2/hrly, 4.5 hrs, £19.50, change at Heathrow). Trains are faster but more expensive (hrly, 2.5 hrs, £29.20). Coming from Heathrow, you can take the Heathrow Express train from the airport to London's Paddington station, then catch the Exeter train to Bath (about £45 total).

By train to: York (hrly, 5 hrs, 2–3 transfers), **Edinburgh** (hrly, 9 hrs, 2–3 transfers).

YORK

Historical York is loaded with world-class sights. Marvel at the York Minster, England's finest Gothic church. Ramble through the Shambles, York's wonderfully preserved medieval quarter. Enjoy a walking tour led by an old Yorker. Hop a train at Europe's greatest Railway Museum, travel to the 1800s in York Castle Museum, and head back a thousand years to Viking York at the Jorvik exhibit.

York has a rich history. In A.D. 71 it was Eboracum, a Roman provincial capital. Constantine was proclaimed emperor here in A.D. 306. In the 5th century, as Rome was toppling, a Roman emperor sent a letter telling England it was on its own, and York became Eoforwic, the capital of the Anglo-Saxon kingdom of Northumbria. A church was built here in 627, and the town was an early Christian center of learning. The Vikings later took the town, and from about 860 to 950 it was a Danish trading center called Jorvik. The invading and conquering Normans destroyed then rebuilt the city, giving it a castle and the walls you see today. Medieval York, with 9,000 inhabitants, grew rich on the wool trade and became England's second city. Henry VIII spared the city's fine Minster and used York as his Anglican church's northern capital. The Archbishop of York is second only to the Archbishop of Canterbury in the Anglican Church. In the Industrial Age, York was the railway hub of North England. When it was built, York's train station was the world's largest. Today, York's leading industry is tourism. Its leading drug? Starbucks and Costa are doing their best to turn high tea into high coffee.

Planning Your Time

York rivals Edinburgh as the best sightseeing city in Britain after London. On even a 10-day trip through Britain, it deserves two nights and a day. For the best 36 hours, follow this plan: Catch the 19:00 city walking tour on the evening of your arrival. The next morning be at Jorvik at 9:00 when it opens (to avoid the midday crowds—or prebook at least a day ahead; see Jorvik under "Sights," below). The nearby Castle Museum is worth the rest of the morning (10:00–noon, I could spend even more time here). Three options for your early afternoon: shoppers browse the Shambles, train buffs tour the National Railway Museum, and scholars do the Yorkshire Museum. Tour the Minster at 16:00 before catching the 17:00 evensong service. Finish your day with an early evening stroll along the wall and perhaps through the abbey gardens. This schedule assumes you're there in the summer (evening orientation walk) and that there's an evensong on. Confirm your plans with the TI.

Orientation (area code: 01904)

The sightseer's York is small. Virtually everything is within a few minutes' walk: the sights, train station, TI, and B&Bs. The longest walk a visitor might take (from a B&B across the old town to the Castle Museum) is 15 minutes.

Bootham Bar, a gate in the medieval town wall, is the hub of your York visit. At Bootham Bar (and on Exhibition Square facing it) you'll find the TI, the starting points for most walking tours and bus tours, handy access to the medieval town wall, Gillygate (pronounced "jilly-gate," lined with good eateries), and Bootham Street, which leads to the recommended B&Bs. (In York, a "bar" is a gate and a "gate" is a street. Go ahead, blame the Vikings.)

Tourist Information: The TI at Bootham Bar sells a 75p "York Map and Guide." Ask for the free monthly *What's On* guide and the monthly *Gig Guide* for live music (April–Oct Mon–Sat 9:00–18:00, Sun 9:00–16:00; July–Aug until 19:00; Nov–March Mon–Sat 9:00–17:30, Sun 10:00–16:00, tel. 01904/621-756, pay WCs next door). The TI books rooms for a £3 fee and sells theatre tickets and Guide Friday city bus tours (£8.50, CC:VM). The train station TI is smaller but provides all the same information and services (April–Sept Mon–Sat 9:00–20:00, Sun 9:30–17:00, shorter hours off-season).

Arrival in York: The station is a five-minute walk from town; turn left down Station Road and follow the crowd toward the Gothic towers of the Minster. After the bridge, a block before the Minster, signs to the TI send you left on St. Leonard's Place. Recommended B&Bs are a five-minute walk from there. (For a shortcut to B&B area from station, walk 1 block toward Minster, cut through parks to riverside, cross railway bridge/pedestrian walkway, cross parking lot for B&Bs on St. Mary's Street, or duck through pedestrian walkway under tracks to B&Bs on Sycamore and Queen Anne's Road.) With lots of luggage, consider a quick

York

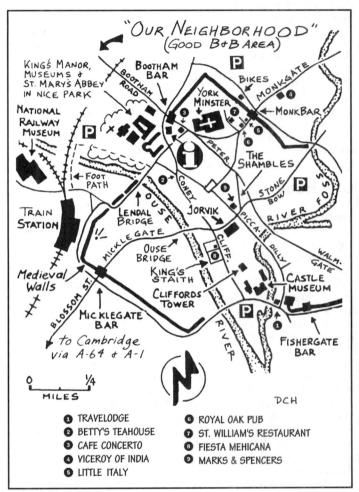

"OUR NEIGHBORHOOD"
(GOOD B&B AREA)

KING'S MANOR,
MUSEUMS &
ST. MARY'S ABBEY
IN NICE PARK

BOOTHAM
BAR

BOOTHAM ROAD

MONKGATE

BIKES

NATIONAL
RAILWAY
MUSEUM

YORK
MINSTER

MONKBAR

PETER

THE
SHAMBLES

FOOT
PATH

CONEY

OUSE

STONE
BOW

RIVER FO

TRAIN
STATION

LENDAL
BRIDGE

MICKLEGATE

JORVIK

PICCA-

CLIFF.

DILLY

WALM.
GATE

OUSE
BRIDGE

Medieval
Walls

BLOSSOM ST.

MICKLEGATE
BAR

KING'S
STAITH

CLIFFORDS
TOWER

CASTLE
MUSEUM

RIVER

FISHERGATE
BAR

to Cambridge
via A-64 & A-1

0   ¼
MILES

N

DCH

❶ TRAVELODGE
❷ BETTY'S TEAHOUSE
❸ CAFE CONCERTO
❹ VICEROY OF INDIA
❺ LITTLE ITALY

❻ ROYAL OAK PUB
❼ ST. WILLIAM'S RESTAURANT
❽ FIESTA MEHICANA
❾ MARKS & SPENCERS

taxi ride (£3.50–4). Luggage storage at York's train station: £1.50 (Mon–Sat 8:30–20:30, Sun 9:00–20:30, platform 1).

Helpful Hints

Study Ahead: York has a great Web site: www.york.gov.uk.
    Internet Access: Try Internet Exchange (Mon–Sat 8:00–20:00, Sun 10:00–18:00, 13 Stonegate), Gateway (Mon–Sat 10:00–20:00, Sun 12:00–16:00, 26 Swinegate), or comms.port

(Mon–Thu 8:00–18:00, Fri–Sat 8:00–20:00, Sun 10:00–17:00, on St. Helen's Square, above Costas coffee shop, near Betty's, Coney Street 2a, first floor, tel. 01904/658-270).

Festivals: The Viking Festival in late February (tentatively Feb 22–25 in 2001) is a lot of fun, with lur-blowing, warrior drills, and recreated battles. The Early Music Festival zings its strings in mid-July (July 6–15 in 2001). The York Festival of Food and Drink takes a 10-day bite out of the last half of September. Book a room well in advance during festival times and weekends any time of year.

Bike Rental: Trotters, just outside Monk Bar, has free cycle maps. The riverside path is fun (£8/day, helmets-£2, Mon–Sat 9:00–17:30, Sun 10:00–16:00, tel. 01904/622-868). Europcar at the train station also rents bikes (£7.50/day, platform 1).

Car Rental: If you're nearing the end of your trip, consider dropping your car upon arrival in York. The money saved by turning it in early nearly pays for the train ticket that whisks you effortlessly to Edinburgh or London. Avis (1 Layerthorpe, closed Sun, tel. 01904/610-460), Hertz (at train station, daily including Sun 9:00–13:00 April–Sept, tel. 01904/612-586), Kenning Car & Van Rental (Micklegate, closed Sun, tel. 01904/659-328), Budget (Leeman Road, next to National Railway Museum, daily including Sun 9:00–11:00, tel. 01904/644-919), and Europcar (train station, platform 1, also Sun 9:00–13:00, tel. 1904/656-161) all have offices in York. Beware, car rental agencies close Saturday afternoon and some close all day Sunday—when dropping off is OK but picking up is impossible.

Tours of York

▲▲▲**Walking Tours**—Charming local volunteer guides give energetic, entertaining, and free two-hour walks through York (daily 10:15 all year, plus 14:15 April–Oct, plus 19:00 June–Aug, from Exhibition Square across from TI). There are many other commercial York walking tours. YorkWalk Tours, for example, has reliable guides and many themes to choose from, such as Roman York, City Walls, or Snickleways—small alleys (£4.50, tel. 01904/622-303, TI has schedule). Most of the ghost tours, all offered after nightfall, are more fun than informative. Haunted Walk, though, relies on storytelling and history rather than masks and surprises (£3, April–Nov daily at 20:00, 90 min, just show up, depart from Exhibition Square, across street from TI, end in the Shambles, tel. 01904/621-003 or 01904/411-578).

▲**Guide Friday Hop-on Hop-off Bus Tours**—York's Guide Friday offers tour guides on speed who can talk enthusiastically to sleeping tourists in a gale on a topless double-decker bus for an hour without stopping. Buses make the 60-minute circuit, covering secondary York sights that the city walking tours skip—the work-a-day perimeter of town (£8.50, pay driver cash, can also buy from TI with CC, departures every 15 min from 9:15 until around 17:00, includes vouchers for discounts on York's sights, read brochure, tel. 01904/640-896). While you can hop on and off all day, the York route is of no value from a transportation-to-the-sights point of view. I'd catch it at the Bootham Bar TI and ride it for an orientation all the way around or get off at the Railway Museum, skipping the last five minutes. Guide Friday's competitors give you a little less for a little less.

Boat Cruise—The York Boat does a lazy 60-minute lap along the River Ouse (£4.50, daily Feb–Nov from 10:30 on, narrated cruise, leaves from Lendal Bridge and King's Staith landing), and also offers themed evening cruises: ghost, dinner, floodlit, and so on (boat rentals possible, tel. 01904/628-324, www.yorkboat.co.uk).

Sights—York Minster

▲▲▲**Minster**—The pride of York, this largest Gothic church north of the Alps (540 feet long, 200 feet tall) brilliantly shows that the High Middle Ages were far from dark. The word "minster" means a place from which people go out to minister or spread the word of God.

Your first impression might be the spaciousness and brightness of the **nave** (built 1280–1350). The nave—from the middle period of Gothic, called "Decorated Gothic"—is one of the widest Gothic naves in Europe. Notice the Great West Window (1338) above the entry. The heart in the tracery is called "the heart of Yorkshire."

Look down the nave. The mysterious gold-and-red dragon's head (in the middle of the nave, sticking out of the side) was probably used as a crane to lift a font cover.

The north and south **transepts** are the oldest part of today's church (1220–1270). The oldest complete window in the minster is the entire wall of glass in the north transcept (1260). Known as the Five Sister's Window, these 50-foot-high panels were made of modern-looking grisaille (gray-silver) glass.

The fanciful choir and the east end (high altar) is from the last stage of Gothic, Perpendicular (1360–1470). The **Great East Window** (1405), the largest medieval glass window in existence, shows the beginning and the end of the world, with scenes from Genesis and the book of Revelation. A chart (on the right, with a tiny, more helpful chart within) highlights the core Old Testament scenes in this hard-to-read masterpiece. Enjoy the art close up on the chart and then step back and find the real thing.

There are three more extra visits to consider. The **Chapter House,** an elaborately decorated 13th-century Gothic dome, features playful details carved in the stonework (pointed out in the flier that comes with the £1 admission, enter from north transept).

You can scale the 275-step **tower** for £3 and a great view (south transcept). The **Undercroft,** also in the south transcept, consists of the crypt, treasury, and foundations (£3). The crypt is an actual bit of the Romanesque church, featuring 12th-century Romanesque art, excavated in modern times. The foundations give you a chance to climb down—archaeologically and physically—through the centuries to see the roots of the much smaller, but still huge, Norman church (Romanesque, 1100) that stood on this spot and, below that, the Roman excavations. Constantine was proclaimed Roman emperor here in A.D. 306. Peek also at the modern concrete save-the-church foundations.

Hours and Tours: The cathedral opens daily at 7:00. The closing time flexes with the season (roughly 20:30 July–Aug, 19:30 May–June and Sept, 18:00 Oct–April, tel. 01904/624-426). The Chapter House, tower, and Undercroft have shorter hours, usually 9:30 to 18:00 (Oct–April 10:00–16:30). Activities are limited Sunday morning during services.

While a donation of £2.50 to visit the church is reasonably requested, by visiting all the small extra spots inside I give that (and more) in the form of those admissions. Just pay for and enjoy all the little extras. The recent £1 photography fee, which applies to everyone, may or may not last due to obvious problems of enforcement.

Follow the "Welcome to the York Minster" flyer and ask about a free guided tour at the reception desk at the entry (tours go frequently, even with just one or two people; you can join one in progress). The helpful blue-armbanded Minster guides are happy to answer your questions.

Evensong and Church Bells: To experience the cathedral in musical and spiritual action, attend an evensong (Tue–Sat 17:00, Sat–Sun 16:00); when the choir is off on school break (mid-July–Aug), visiting choirs usually fill in. If you're a fan of church bells, Sunday morning (around 10:00) and Tuesday evening practice (19:30–21:30) are heavenly.

Sights—York

▲**City Walls**—The historic walls of York provide a fine two-mile walk. Walk from Bootham Bar (gate) to Monk Bar for outstanding cathedral views. The walls are open from dawn until dusk (barring attacks) and free.

▲**The Shambles**—This is the most colorful old York street in the half-timbered, traffic-free core of town. Ye olde downtown York, while very touristy, is a window-shopping, busker-filled, people-watcher's delight. Don't miss the more frumpy Newgate Market or the old-time candy store just opposite the bottom end of the Shambles. For a cheap lunch, consider the cute, tiny **St. Crux Parish Hall,** a medieval church now used by a medley of charities selling tea and simple snacks (Mon–Sat 10:00–16:00, at bottom end of the Shambles, at intersection with Pavement).

▲▲▲**York Castle Museum**—Truly one of Europe's top museums, this is a Victorian home show, the closest thing to a time-tunnel experience England has to offer. It includes the 19th-century Kirkgate, a fine collection of old shops well stocked exactly as they were 150 years ago, along with the new "From Cradle to Grave" exhibit, plus costumes, armor, and an eye-opening Anglo-Saxon helmet (from A.D. 750). The one-way plan allows you to see everything: a working water mill (April–Oct), prison cells, man traps, WWII fashions, and old toys (£5.25, daily 9:30–17:00, Nov–March daily 9:30–16:30, cafeteria midway through museum, shop, car park; the £2.50 guidebook, while not necessary, makes a nice souvenir; CC:VM, tel. 01904/653-611). Clifford's Tower (across from Castle Museum, not worth the £1.80, daily 10:00–18:00, until 16:00 Oct–March) is all that's left of York's castle (13th century, site of a 1190 massacre of local Jews—read about this at base of hill).

▲**Jorvik**—Sail the "Pirates of the Caribbean" north and back 800 years and you get Jorvik—more a ride than a museum. Innovative 10 years ago, the commercial success of Jorvik (yor-vik) inspired copycat ride/museums all over England. You'll ride a little Disney-type train car for 13 minutes through the recreated Viking street of Coppergate. It's the year 948, and you're in the village of Jorvik. Next your little train takes you through the actual excavation sight that inspired this. Finally you'll browse through a small gallery of Viking shoes, combs, locks, and other intimate glimpses of that red-headed culture (£6, daily 9:00–17:30, Nov–March closing varies from 15:30–16:30, last entry 30 minutes before closing, tel. 01904/643-211, www.jorvik-viking-centre.co.uk).

Midday lines can be an hour long, and even past the turnstile there's a 25-minute wait. Avoid the line by going very early or very late in the day or by prebooking (call 01904/543-403 at least a day ahead, Mon–Fri 9:00–17:00, office closed on weekends, CC:VM, you're given a time slot, add £1 per ticket for entry 10:00–16:00). Some love this "ride"; others call it a gimmicky rip-off. If you're looking for a serious museum, see the Viking exhibit at the York-shire Museum. It's better. If you're thinking Disneyland with a splash of history, Jorvik's great. I like Jorvik, but it's not worth a long line.

▲▲**National Railway Museum**—This thunderous museum shows 150 fascinating years of British railroad history. Fanning out from a grand roundhouse is an array of historic cars and engines, including Queen Victoria's lavish royal car and the very first "stagecoaches on rails." There's much more, including exhibits on dining cars, post cars, sleeping cars, train posters, and videos. This biggest and best railroad museum anywhere is interesting even to people who think "Pullman" is Japanese for "tug-o-war" (£6.50, kids under 17 free, CC:VM, daily 10:00–18:00, tel. 01904/621-261). Cute little "road trains" shuttle you between the Minster and the Railway Museum (£1.50, leaves Railway Museum every 30 minutes from 12:00–17:30 on the top and bottom of the hour, leaves Minster—from Duncombe Place—every 30 minutes at :15 and :45 after the hour).

▲**Yorkshire Museum**—Located in a lush and lazy park next to the stately ruins of St. Mary's Abbey, Yorkshire Museum is the city's forgotten serious "archaeology of York" museum. While the hordes line up at Jorvik, the best Viking artifacts are here—with no crowds and in a better historical context. You have to walk through this museum, but the stroll takes you through Roman, Saxon, Viking, Norman, and Gothic York. Its prize piece is the delicately etched 15th-century pendant called the Middleham Jewel. The video about the creation of the abbey is worth a look (£4, various exhibitions can increase price, daily 10:00–17:00, tel. 01904/629-745).

Theatre Royal—Fine plays, usually British comedies, entertain the locals (20:00 almost nightly, 19:30 Sept–May, tickets easy to get, £10–15, CC:VMA, closes for 6-week period starting in June, on St. Leonard's Place next to TI and a 5-minute walk from recommended B&Bs, recorded info tel. 01904/610-041, booking tel. 01904/623-568, www.theatre-royal-york.co.uk).

Honorable Mention

York has a number of other sights and activities (described in TI material) that, while interesting, pale in comparison to the biggies. **Fairfax House** is perfectly Georgian inside, with docents happy to talk with you (£4, Sat–Thu 11:00–17:00 except Sun 13:30–17:00, closed Fri except in Aug; guided tours offered at 11:00 and 14:00 on Friday during summer—confirm in advance at TI; a tour helps bring this well-furnished building to life; on Castlegate, near Jorvik, tel. 01904/655-543). The **Hall of the Merchant Adventurers** claims to be the finest medieval guildhall in Europe (from 1361). It's basically a vast half-timbered building with marvelous exposed beams and 15 minutes worth of interesting displays about life and commerce back in the days when York was England's second city (£2, daily 8:30–17:00, early Nov–mid-March until 15:30, below the Shambles off Piccadilly). The **Richard III "Museum"** is interesting only for Richard III enthusiasts (£1.50, daily 9:00–17:00, Nov–Feb until 16:00, Monk Bar). The **ARC, or Archaeological Resource Center,** is a big former church full of genuine archaeological artifacts that visitors—mostly school groups—can study as pretend archaeologists (£3.60, Mon–Fri 10:00–16:00, closed Sat–Sun, great for kids, welcomes adults, plenty of microscopes, hands-on fun, and helpful volunteers; just off Shambles on St. Saviourgate, tel. 01904/543-402). The **York Dungeon** is gimmicky but, if you insist on papier-mâché gore, is better than the London Dungeon (£6, daily 10:00–18:30, Oct–March until 17:30, 12 Clifford Street). The **antique shops** are a fun browse (41 Stonegate near the Minster, and 2 Lendal near Museum Garden). At the **bowling green** on Sycamore Place near the recommended B&Bs, visitors are welcome (tell them which B&B you're staying at) to buy a pint of beer and watch the action.

Sights—Near York
Eden Camp—Once an internment camp for German and Italian POWs during World War II, this is now a theme museum on Britain's war experience. Various barracks detail the rise of Hitler and the fury of the Blitz (with the sound of bombs, the acrid smell of burning, and quotes such as "Hitler will send no warning— so always carry your gas mask.") This award-winning museum energetically conveys the spirit of a country Hitler couldn't conquer (£3.50, daily 10:00–17:00, closed late-Dec–mid-Jan, mess-kitchen cafeteria, Malton, 18 miles northeast of York, tel. 01653/697-777, www.edencamp.co.uk). To get to the camp from York, catch the Coastliner bus at the York Railway Station (leaves from front of station, on station side of road). Buses are marked with the destination "Whitby" or "Pickering" and are numbered #840, #842, or #X40, depending on the time of day (Mon–Sat 11/day, 50 min, fewer on Sun, £4 round-trip).

Sleeping in York
(£1 = about $1.60, country code: 44, area code: 01904)
Sleep Code: **S** = Single, **D** = Double/Twin, **T** = Triple, **Q** = Quad, **b** = bathroom, **t** = toilet only, **s** = shower only, **CC** = Credit Card (**V**isa, **M**asterCard, **A**mex).

I've listed peak-season, book-direct prices. Don't use the TI. Outside of July and August some prices go soft. B&Bs will sometimes turn away one-night bookings, particularly for peak-season Saturdays. (York is worth two nights.)

Sleeping in B&Bs near Bootham
These recommendations are in the handiest B&B neighborhood, a quiet residential neighborhood just outside the old-town wall's Bootham gate, along the road called Bootham. All are within a five-minute walk of the Minster and TI and a 10-minute walk or taxi ride (£3.50–4) from the station. If driving, head for the cathedral and follow the medieval wall to the gate called Bootham Bar. Bootham "street" leads away from Bootham Bar.

These B&Bs are all small, nonsmoking, and family run and come with plenty of steep stairs but no traffic noise. For a good selection, call well in advance. B&Bs will generally hold a room

York, Our Neighborhood

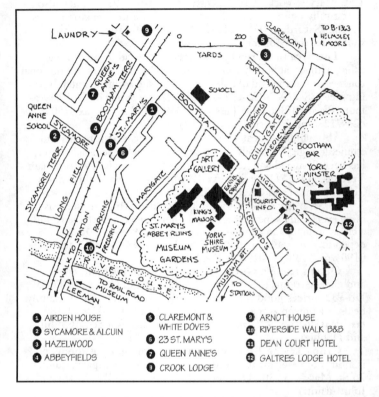

- ❶ AIRDEN HOUSE
- ❷ SYCAMORE & ALCUIN
- ❸ HAZELWOOD
- ❹ ABBEYFIELDS
- ❺ CLAREMONT & WHITE DOVES
- ❻ 23 ST. MARY'S
- ❼ QUEEN ANNE'S
- ❽ CROOK LODGE
- ❾ ARNOT HOUSE
- ❿ RIVERSIDE WALK B&B
- ⓫ DEAN COURT HOTEL
- ⓬ GALTRES LODGE HOTEL

with a phone call and work hard to help their guests sightsee and eat smartly. Most have permits for street parking. And most don't take credit cards.

Laundry: Regency Dry Cleaning does small loads for £8 (drop off by 9:30 for same-day service, Mon–Fri 8:30–18:00, Sat 9:00–17:00, closed Sun, 75 Bootham, at intersection with Queen Anne's, tel. 01904/613-311). The cheaper Washeteria launderette is a 10 to 15 minute walk from the B&B neighborhood (£5 self-serve, £6 full-serve—drop off by 12:00 for same-day service, Mon–Fri 8:00–18:00, Sat 8:00–17:30, Sun 8:00–16:30, last wash 2 hrs before closing, 124 Haxby Road, at north end of Gillygate, continue on Clarence, then Haxby, tel. 01904/623-379).

Airden House, the most central of my Bootham-area listings, has eight spacious rooms, a grandfather clock–cozy TV lounge, and brightness and warmth throughout. Susan and Keith Burrows, a great source of local travel tips, keep their place simple, clean, comfortable, and friendly (D-£40–42, Db-£50–52, 1 St. Mary's, York YO30 7DD, tel. 01904/638-915). They also rent a fully equipped apartment and a house for weeklong stays starting Saturdays (Db-£210–250, Qb-£320–350, a 5-minute walk from the Minster).

The Sycamore, run by Margaret and David Tyce, is a fine value, with seven homey rooms strewn with silk flowers and personal touches. It's at the end of a dead end opposite a fun-to-watch bowling green (S-£20–24, D-£32–34, Db-£42–44, family deals, 19 Sycamore Place off Bootham Terrace, YO30 7DW, tel. & fax 01904/624-712, e-mail: thesycamore@talk21.com).

Abbeyfields Guest House has nine cozy, bright rooms and a quiet lounge. This doily-free place, which lacks the usual clutter, has been designed with care (S-£23, Sb-£33, Db-£52, 19 Boothham Terrace, YO30 7DH, tel. & fax 01904/636-471, www.abbeyfields .co.uk, Richard and Gwen Martin).

23 St. Mary's is extravagantly decorated. Mrs. Hudson has done everything supercorrectly and offers nine comfortable rooms, a classy lounge, and all the doily touches (Sb-£34–36, Db-£64–75 depending on season and size, 23 St. Mary's, YO30 7DD, tel. 01904/622-738, fax 01904/621-168).

Queen Anne's Guest House has seven pleasant, clean, and cheery rooms (May–Sept D-£34, Db-£36, Oct–April D-£30, Db-£32, prices good through 2001 with this book, CC:V, family deals, 24 Queen Anne's Road, Y030 7AA, tel. 01904/629-389, fax 01904/619-529, e-mail: info@queenannes.fsnet.co.uk, Phil and Debbie).

Crook Lodge B&B, with seven charming, tight rooms, is a bit more elegant than the rest (Db-£46–56, car park, quiet, 26 St. Mary's, Y030 7DD, tel. & fax 01904/655-614, Susan and John Arnott).

Alcuin Lodge is a good value, with seven flowery rooms and solid-wood furnishings (Db-£42–50, 1 small top-floor D-£35, no kids, CC:VM, 15 Sycamore Place, Y030 7DW, tel. 01904/632-222, fax 01904/626-630, e-mail: Alcuinlodg@aol.com, Susan Taylor).

Arnot House, run by a friendly daughter-and-mother team, is homey, cluttered, and lushly decorated with early 1900s memorabilia. The four well-furnished rooms have little libraries (Db-£52–56, CC:VM, minimum 2-night stay, nonsmoking, 17 Grosvenor Terrace, Y030 7AG, tel. & fax 01904/641-966, www.arnothouseyork.co.uk, Kim and Ann Robbins).

Riverside Walk B&B, on a pedestrian street along the river, has 14 small shipshape rooms, steep stairs, narrow hallways, and a breakfast room decorated in nautical green that feels like a fisherman's cottage. Request a river view or you'll overlook a car park (2 D-£45, Db-£52–57, nonsmoking, sun terrace on river, quiet, CC:VM for 3.5 percent extra, 8 Earlsborough Terrace, Y030 7BQ,

tel. 01904/620-769, fax 01904/646-249, www.riversidewalkbb
.demon.co.uk, Julie Mett).

York's Youth Hotel is well run, with lots of extras, like a
kitchen, launderette, bar, and game room (S-£16, D-£30, £14 in
4- to 6-bed dorms, less for multinight stays, cheaper in larger
dorms, same-sex or coed possible, continental breakfast-£2,
CC:VM, 10-minute walk from station at 11 Bishophill Senior
Road, YO1 1EF, tel. 01904/625-904, fax 01904/612-494, e-mail:
info@yorkyouthhotel.demon.co.uk).

B&Bs nearer the Center
These are off Gillygate, a two minutes' walk to Bootham Bar.

Claremont Guest House is a friendly house offering two
delightful rooms and many thoughtful touches, including £3
laundry service (D-£32–40, Db-£36–50, telephone shower, 18
Claremont Terrace off Gillygate, YO31 7EJ, tel. 01904/625-158,
e-mail: claremont.york@dial.pipex.com, run by Gill—pronounced
Jill—and Martyn Cornell).

White Doves is a cheery little Victorian place with a comfy
lounge and three tastefully decorated rooms in soothing pastels
(Db-£50–52, family deals, 20 Claremont Terrace off Gillygate,
YO31 7EJ, tel. 01904/625-957, Pauline and David Pearce).

The Hazelwood, my most hotelesque listing in this neighborhood, is plush, though it lacks the friendly warmth of a B&B. This
spacious house has 14 beautifully decorated rooms with modern
furnishings (Db-£65–85 depending on room size, 2 ground-floor
rooms, classy breakfast, CC:VM, quiet for being so central, laundry
service-£5; a fridge, ice, and great travel library in the pleasant
basement lounge; 24 Portland Street, Gillygate, YO31 7EH, tel.
01904/626-548, fax 01904/628-032, e-mail: hazwdyork@aol.com).

Sleeping in Hotels in the Center
Travelodge, newly opened, offers 90 identical, affordable rooms
near the Castle Museum (Db-£60, CC:VM, attached restaurant,
1 Piccadilly, central reservations tel. 0870-905-6343).

Dean Court Hotel, facing the Minster, is a big, stately place
marketed by Best Western that has classy lounges and 40 comfortable rooms (small Db-£105, standard Db-£130, superior Db-£145
includes fruit, spacious deluxe Db-£160, includes breakfast,
CC:VMA, some nonsmoking rooms, tearoom, restaurant, elevator
to most rooms, Duncombe Place, YO1 7EF, tel. 01904/625-082,
fax 01904/620-305, www.deancourt-york.co.uk).

Galtres Lodge Hotel, a block from the Minster, offers
comfy rooms above a restaurant in the old town center (S-£25,
Sb-£35, Dt-£50, Db-£65, one refurbished Db-£75 and worth it,
CC:VM, nonsmoking, 54 Low Petergate, YO1 7HZ, tel. 01904/
622-478, fax 01904/627-804).

Eating in York

Traditional Tea

York is famous for its elegant teahouses. Drop into one around 16:00 for tea and cakes. Ladies love **Betty's Teahouse** (£5 cream tea, CC:VM, daily 9:00–21:00, piano music nightly 18:00–21:00, mostly nonsmoking, St. Helen's Square, fine people watching from a window seat on the main floor; downstairs near WC is a mirror signed by WWII bomber pilots). If there's a line for Betty's, it moves quickly. Or it's easy to come back at dinnertime, when the line disappears—because for the English, "tea time" is over, but tea time is any time at Betty's. If Betty's is just too crowded, many other tearooms can satisfy your king- or queen-for-a-day desires.

Eating near the Minster

Café Concerto, a French-style bistro, has a loyal following for good reason. Their food was the best I've had in York (daily 10:00–22:00, serves meals all day, CC:VM, Petergate 21, under Bootham Bar, smart to reserve at 01904/610-478).

The Viceroy of India—just outside Monk Bar and therefore outside the tourist zone—serves great Indian food at good prices to mostly locals; if you've yet to eat Indian on your trip, do it here (nightly 18:00–24:00, £8 plates, friendly staff, CC:VM, continue straight through Monk Bar to 26 Monkgate, notice the big old "Bile Beans keep you healthy, bright-eyed, and slim" sign on your left, tel. 01904/622-370). **Bengal Brasserie,** which serves Indian food, is also good (minimum charge-£8, Sun–Fri 12:00–14:30, 18:00–24:00, Sat 12:00–24:00, 21 Goodramgate, just inside Monk Bar, tel. 01904/640-066).

For Italian food, consider the popular **Little Italy** (£6–12, Tue–Sun 17:00–23:00, plus Sat 12:00–14:00, closed Mon, Goodramgate 12, just inside Monk Bar, tel. 01904/623-539).

There's a pub serving grub on every block. Eat where you see lots of food. The **Royal Oak** offers £5 pub grub throughout the day, a small nonsmoking room, and hand-pulled ale (daily 11:00–20:00, CC:VM, Goodramgate, a block from Monk Bar, a block east of the Minster, tel. 01904/653-856). The **Golden Slipper,** next door, is also good.

St. Williams Restaurant, just behind the great east window of the Minster in a wonderful half-timbered, 15th-century building, serves quick and tasty lunches and elegant candlelit dinners (daily 10:00–22:00, £10 early bird special 17:30–18:45, otherwise 2 courses-£13, 3 courses-£16, traditional and Mediterranean, CC:VM, College Street, tel. 01904/634-830).

For the closest you'll get to Mexico in Britain, try **Fiesta Mehicana** (nightly 18:00–22:00, take-out available and early bird discount for sit-down dinner before 19:00 except Sat, CC:VM, 14 Clifford Street, tel. 01904/610-243).

Eating near Bootham Bar and Your B&B

Walk along Gillygate and choose from an enjoyable array of eateries: For authentic Italian, consider **Mama Mia's** (£6–9, daily 11:30–14:00, 17:30–23:00, fun, leisurely Italian service, indoor/outdoor patio, CC:VM, 20 Gillygate, tel. 01904/622-020). **Gillygate Fisheries** is a wonderfully traditional little fish-and-chips joint where tattooed people eat in and housebound mothers take out (Mel serves £3–4 meals, "eat your mushy peas," Mon 17:00–23:30, Tue–Fri 11:30–13:30, 17:00–23:30, Sat 11:30–23:30, closed Sun, smoke-free seating, 59 Gillygate).

Pubs: The **Waggon and Horses** pub has local color and £5 meals (Mon–Sat 11:30–21:00, Sun 12:00–15:00, across from Fisheries joint, Gillygate 48, tel. 01904/654-103). The **Coach House** has consistently good quality (£8–11, CC:VM, nightly 18:30–21:30, 20 Marygate, tel. 01904/652-780). The **Grange Hotel's Brasserie** is easy, a couple of blocks from the B&Bs, and classier than a pub. Go downstairs—avoid the pricey ground-floor restaurant (£9 meals, Mon–Sat 12:00–14:00, 18:00–22:00, Sun 18:00–22:00, CC:VM, 1 Clifton, tel. 01904/644-744). The people who run your B&B know the latest on what's good.

Grocery stores: In the B&B neighborhood you'll find **Spar** (daily 9:00–21:00, on 61 Bootham, at intersection with Queen Anne's Road) and **Jacksons** (a little run-down but open late, daily 7:00–23:00, near Bootham Bar, on Bootham). In the old town is **Marks & Spencers** (Mon–Sat 9:30–18:00, Sun 11:00–17:00, on Parliament Street); go to the top floor for a striking view of the south wall of the Minster from the menswear department.

Most atmospheric picnic spot: In the Museum Gardens (near Bootham Bar), at the evocative 12th-century ruins of **St. Mary's Abbey.**

Transportation Connections—York

By train to: Durham (hrly, 60 min), **Edinburgh** (2/hrly, 2 hrs), **London** (2/hrly, 2 hrs), **Bath** (via Bristol, hrly, 5 hrs), **Birmingham** (8/day, 3 hrs). Train info: tel. 08457/484-950.

The **York Bus Information Centre** is at 20 Hudson Street, near the train station (Mon–Fri 8:30–17:00, Sat 9:00–12:30, Sun 8:00–14:00, tel. 01904/551400, phone answered Mon–Sat 8:00–20:00, Sun 8:00–14:00).

EDINBURGH

Edinburgh, the colorful city of Robert Louis Stevenson, Sir Walter Scott, and Robert Burns, is Scotland's showpiece and one of Europe's most entertaining cities. Historical, monumental, fun, and well organized, it's a tourist's delight.

Promenade down the Royal Mile through the Old Town. Historic buildings pack the Royal Mile between the castle (on the top) and Holyrood Palace (on the bottom). Medieval skyscrapers stand shoulder to shoulder, hiding peaceful courtyards connected to High Street by narrow lanes or even tunnels. This colorful jumble—in its day the most crowded city in the world—is the tourist's Edinburgh.

Edinburgh (ED'n-burah) was once two towns divided by a lake. To alleviate crowding, the lake was drained, and a magnificent Georgian city, today's New Town, was laid out to the north. Georgian Edinburgh, like the city of Bath, shines with broad boulevards, straight streets, square squares, circular circuses, and elegant mansions decked out in colonnades, pediments, and sphinxes in the proud, neoclassical style of 200 years ago.

While the Georgian city celebrated the union of Scotland and England (with streets and squares named after English kings and emblems), "devolution" is the latest craze. In a 1998 election the Scots voted for more autonomy and to bring their parliament home. Though Edinburgh has been the historic capital of Scotland for centuries, parliament has not met in Scotland since 1707. In 2000—while London still calls the strategic shots—Edinburgh resumed its position as home to the Scottish Parliament. And a strikingly modern new parliament building, opening in 2003, will be one more jewel in Edinburgh's crown.

Planning Your Time

While the major sights can be seen in a day, I'd give Edinburgh two days and three nights.

Day 1: Tour the castle. Then consider catching one of the city bus tours (from castle parking lot) for a 60-minute loop, returning to the castle. Explore the Royal Mile, going downhill—lunching, museum-going, shopping, taking a walking tour (leaves at 14:00 from Mercat Cross). If you tour Holyrood Palace, do it near the end of the day and the bottom of the Mile. Evening–Scottish show, folk music at pub, literary pub crawl, or haunted walk.

Day 2: Tour the National Gallery and stroll the adjacent Princes Street Gardens. After lunch, choose among browsing the New Town/Georgian House, touring the Museum of Scotland (tours at 14:15), visiting the ship *Britannia* (booking advisable), or hiking up King Arthur's Seat. Evening–Show, pubs, walks, whatever you didn't do last night.

Orientation (area code: 0131)

The center of Edinburgh holds the Princes Street Gardens park and Waverley Bridge, where you'll find the TI, Waverley Shopping and Eating Center, train station, bus info office (starting point for most city bus tours), National Gallery, and a covered dance-and-music pavilion. Weather blows in and out—bring your sweater.

Tourist Information: The crowded TI is as central as can be atop the Waverley Market on Princes Street (May–June & Sept: Mon–Sat 9:00–19:00, Sun 10:00–19:00; July–Aug: daily until 20:00; Nov–March: daily until 17:00, ATM outside entrance, tel. 0131/473-3800). Buy a map (£1) and ask for the free monthly entertainment *Gig Guide* if you're interested in late-night music. For a longer visit, consider the *Essential Guide to Edinburgh* (£1), which lists additional sights and services. Book your room direct without the TI's help (and £3 charge). Browse the racks (tucked away in hallway at back of TI) for brochures on the various Scottish folk shows, walking tours, and regional bus tours. Connect@edinburgh, a small **Internet café**, is beyond the brochure racks (see "Hints," below). The best monthly entertainment listing, *The List*, is sold for £1.95 at newsstands.

Haggis Backpackers Ltd has **budget travel information** (Mon–Sat 8:00–18:00, Sun 14:00–18:00, 60 High Street, at Blackfriars Street, tel. 0131/557-9393).

Arrival in Edinburgh: Arriving by train at Waverley Station puts you in the city center and below the TI (go up the many stairs until you surface at street level, TI to your left) and the city bus to my recommended B&Bs (see "Sleeping," below, for directions to B&B neighborhood by bus). Both Scottish Citylink and National Express buses use the bus station two blocks north of the train station on St. Andrew Square in the New Town.

Edinburgh

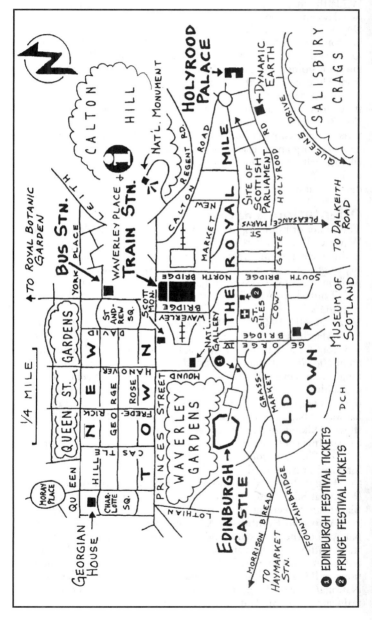

Edinburgh's slingshot-of-an-airport is 10 miles northwest of the center and well connected by shuttle buses with Waverley Bridge (LRT "Airline" bus #100, £3.30 or £4.20 with all-day "Airsaver" city bus pass, 4/hrly, 30 min, roughly 6:00–22:00). Flight info: tel. 0131/333-1000, British Midland tel. 0870-607-0555, British Air tel. 0345-222-111). Taxi to airport: £15.

Helpful Hints

Sunday Activities: Many sights close on Sunday, but there's still a lot to do: Royal Mile walking tour, Edinburgh Castle, St. Giles Cathedral, Holyrood Palace, Royal Botanic Gardens, Arthur's Seat hike, and city bus tour. An open-air market including antiques is held every Sunday from 10:00 to 16:00 at New Street Car Park near Waverley Center. The Georgian House and National Gallery open Sunday afternoon.

Internet Access: It's a cinch to get plugged in. Try connect @edinburgh at the TI (£1/20 min, Mon–Sat 9:00–18:00, Sun 10:00–18:00, as you enter TI head back to the left down a corridor, tel. 0131/473-3600); International Telecom Centre on the Royal Mile (£1/15 min, daily 8:00–23:00, also has cheap phones with rare sit-down booths, 52 High Street, half block east of Tron Kirk and South Bridge); or Café Cyberia in the New Town (£1.50/30 min, daily 10:00–22:00, 88 Hanover Street, near recommended restaurants, a few blocks northeast of TI).

Car Rental: Avis is at 100 Dairy Road in Haymarket suburb (tel. 0131/337-6363).

Getting around Edinburgh

Nearly all Edinburgh sights are within walking distance. City buses are handy and inexpensive (average fare-80p, LRT office, Old Town end of Waverley Bridge, tel. 0131/555-6363). Tell the driver where you're going, have change handy (most buses require exact change; you lose any excess), take your ticket as you board, push the stop button as you near your stop (so your stop isn't skipped), and exit from the middle door. Two companies handle the city routes: Lothian (or LRT) does most of it and First does the rest (e.g., route #C3 and #86). Day passes sold by each company are valid only on their buses (£2.20, or £1.50 after 9:30 weekdays and all day weekends, buy from driver). Buses run from about 6:00 to 23:00. Taxis are reasonable (easy to flag down, average ride between downtown and B&B district-£5).

Bus Tours of Edinburgh

▲**Hop-on Hop-off City Bus Tours**—Three companies offer 60-minute bus tours that circle the town center stopping at the biggies—Waverley Bridge, the castle, Royal Mile, Georgian New Town, and Princes Street—with pickups about every 10 to 15 minutes and an informative narration. You can hop on and off with one ticket all day, not 24 hours. Hop on at any stop or go to Waverley Bridge to comparison shop.

Guide Friday has a live guide (£8.50; can use CC if you buy ticket at TI, at office at 133 Canongate—near bottom of Royal Mile, or possibly at Waverley Bridge, tel. 0131/556-2244). LRT's "Edinburgh Classic Tour," which runs a little more frequently, uses headphones with a recorded narration (£7.50, usually includes price break on trip to Britannia, tel. 0131/555-6363). Mac Tours' "Edinburgh by Vintage Bus" has a live guide, fewer buses, and a shorter route (£7.50, 3/hrly, 50 min, ticket bought after 17:00 also valid the next day).

On sunny days they go topless (the buses) but can suffer from traffic noise and congestion. Buses run year-round. First and last buses leave Waverley Bridge around 9:00 through 19:00 mid-June through early September (off-season, last buses leave at 17:15).

Sights—Edinburgh

▲▲▲**Edinburgh Castle**—The fortified birthplace of the city 1,300 years ago, this imposing symbol of Edinburgh sits proudly on a rock high above the city. While the castle has been both a fort and a royal residence since the 11th century, most of the buildings today are from its more recent use as a military garrison (£7.50, CC:VM, daily 9:30–18:00, Oct–March until 17:00, cafeteria, tel. 0131/225-9846; consider avoiding the long uphill walk from the nearest city bus stop by taking a cab to the castle gate).

Entry Gate: Start with the wonderfully droll 30-minute guided introduction tour (free with admission, departs every 15 minutes from entry, see clock for the next departure; few tours run off-season). The CD-ROM audio guide is excellent, with four hours of quick digital dial descriptions (free with admission, pick up at entry gate before meeting the live guide). The clean WC at the entry annually wins "British Loo of the Year" awards (see plaques near men's room), but they use a one-way mirror showing the sink area in the women's room (women: pop your head into office near men's room to complain or make sure mirror is curtained).

In the castle there are four essential stops: Crown Jewels, Great Hall, National War Memorial, and St. Margaret's Chapel with city view. The newly refurbished National War Museum of Scotland is also worth considering. All are at the highest and most secure point—on or near the castle square, where your guided tour ends.

The **Royal Palace** (facing castle square under the flag pole) has two unimpressive rooms (through door reading 1566). Remember, Scottish royalty only lived here when safety or protocol required. They preferred the **Holyrood Palace** at the bottom of the Royal Mile. The line of tourists leads from the square directly to the jewels. Skip this line and enter the building around to the left where you'll get to the jewels via a wonderful *Honors of Scotland* exhibition about the crown jewels.

Scotland's **Crown Jewels** are older than England's. While Cromwell destroyed England's, the Scots hid theirs successfully. Longtime symbols of Scottish nationalism, they were made in Edinburgh—of Scottish gold, diamonds, and gems—in 1540 for a 1543 coronation. They were last used to crown Charles II in 1651. Apparently there was some anxiety about the Act of Union, which dissolved Scotland's parliament into England's to create the United Kingdom in 1707—the Scots locked up and hid their jewels. In 1818 Walter Scott and a royal commission rediscovered the jewels intact.

The **Stone of Scone** sits plain and strong next to the jewels. This big gray chunk of rock is the coronation stone of Scotland's ancient kings (ninth century). Swiped by the English, it sat under the coronation chair at Westminster Abbey from 1296 until 1996. With major fanfare, Scotland's treasured Stone of Scone returned to Edinburgh on November 15, 1996. Talk to the guard for more details.

Enter the **Mary Queen of Scots room**, where in 1666 the queen gave birth to James VI of Scotland, who later became King James I of England. The **Presence Chamber** leads into **Laich Hall** (Lower Hall), the dining room of the royal family.

The **Great Hall** was the castle's ceremonial meeting place in the 16th and 17th centuries. In modern times it was a barracks and a hospital. While most of what you see is Victorian, two medieval elements survive: the fine hammer-beam roof and the iron-barred peephole (above fireplace on right). This allowed the king to spy on his partying subjects.

The imposing **Scottish National War Memorial** commemorates the 148,000 Scottish soldiers lost in World War I, the 57,000 lost in World War II, and the 750 lost in British battles since. Each bay is dedicated to a particular Scottish regiment. The main shrine, featuring a green Italian-marble memorial containing the original WWI rolls of honor, actually sits upon an exposed chunk of the castle rock. Above you, the archangel Michael is busy slaying the dragon. The bronze frieze accurately shows the attire of various wings of Scotland's military. The stained glass starts with Cain and Abel on the left and finishes with a celebration of peace on the right.

St. Margaret's Chapel, the oldest building in Edinburgh, is dedicated to Queen Margaret, who died here in 1093 and was sainted in 1250. Built in 1130 in the Romanesque style of the Norman invaders, it is wonderfully simple, with classic Norman zigzags decorating the round arch that separates the tiny nave from the sacristy. Used as a powder magazine for 400 years, very little survives. You'll see an 11th-century Gospel book of St. Margaret's and small windows featuring St. Margaret, St. Columba (who brought Christianity to Scotland via Iona), and William Wallace (the brave defender of Scotland). The place is popular for weddings and, since it seats only 20, particularly popular with brides' fathers.

Belly up to the bannister (across the terrace outside the chapel) to enjoy the great view. Below you are the guns—which fire the one o'clock salute—and a sweet little line of doggie tombstones, the **soldier's pet cemetery**. Beyond stretches the **Georgian New Town** (read the informative plaque).

The **National War Museum of Scotland**, reopened after renovation, thoughtfully covers the last 400 years of Scottish military history. Instead of the usual musty, dusty displays of endless armor, this museum has an interesting mix of short films, uniforms, weapons, medals, mementos, and eloquent excerpts from soldiers' letters.

The castle has more to offer (for instance, below, in the vaults, you can see Mons Meg—a huge 15th-century siege cannon that fired 500-pound stones nearly 2 miles), but you've seen the essentials.

When leaving the castle, turn around and look back at the gate. There stand King Robert the Bruce (on the left, 1274–1329) and Sir William Wallace (Braveheart—on the right, 1270–1305). Wallace (newly famous, thanks to Mel Gibson) fought long and hard against English domination before being executed in London—his body cut to pieces and paraded through the far corners of jolly olde England. Bruce beat the English at Bannockburn in 1314. Bruce and Wallace still defend the spirit of Scotland.

Sights—Along the Royal Mile

These are listed in walking order, from top to bottom. (Bus #35 runs along the Mile, handy for going up after you've hit bottom.)
▲▲▲**Royal Mile**—This is one of Europe's most interesting historic walks. Start at the top and amble down to the palace. The Royal Mile, which consists of a series of four different streets—Castlehill, Lawnmarket, High Street, and Canongate—is actually 100 yards longer than a mile. And every inch is packed with shops, cafés, and lanes leading to tiny squares. By poking down the many side alleys, you'll find a few rough edges of a town well on its way to becoming a touristic mall. See it now. In a few years tourists will be slaloming through the postcard racks on bagpipe skateboards.

Royal Mile Terminology: A "close" is a tiny alley between two buildings (originally with a door that closed it at night). A close usually leads to a "court" or courtyard. A "land" is a tenement block of apartments. A "pend" is an arched gateway. A "wynd" is a narrow winding lane. And "gate" is from an old Scandinavian word for street.

Royal Mile Walking Tours: Mercat Tours offers two-hour guided walks of the Mile—more entertaining than historic (£6, April–Sept daily at 11:00 and 14:00, Oct–March daily 11:15 only,

Royal Mile

from Mercat Cross on the Royal Mile, tel. 0131/557-6464). The guides, who enjoy making a short story long, ignore the big sights, taking you behind the scenes with piles of barely historic gossip, bully-pulpit Scottish pride, and fun but forgettable trivia. They also offer a variety of other tours. In August only, the Voluntary Guides Association leads free tours of Edinburgh; call for schedule (tel. 0131/664-7180).

Castle Esplanade—At the top of the Royal Mile, the big parking lot leading up to the castle was once a military parade ground. It's often cluttered with bleachers under construction for the military tattoo—a spectacular massing of the bands that fills the square nightly for most of August (see "Edinburgh Festival," below). At the bottom, on the left, the tiny witch's fountain memorializes 300 women who were accused of witchcraft and burned here. Scotland burned more witches per capita than any other country—17,000 between 1479 and 1722. But in a humanitarian gesture, rather than burning them alive as was the custom in the rest of Europe, Scottish "witches" were strangled to death before they were burned. The plaque shows two witches: one good and one bad. (For 90 minutes of this kind of Royal Mile trivia, take the guided tour described above.)

Scotch Whiskey Heritage Centre—This touristy ambush is designed only to distill £5.50 out of your pocket. You get a free sample, video history, short talk, and a little whiskey-keg train-car ride before finding yourself in the shop 45 minutes later. If you say you're in a hurry, you'll likely be offered the unadvertised quickie—a sample and a whiskey-keg ride for £3.60. People do seem to enjoy it, but that might have something to do with the sample (tel. 0131/220-0441). The Camera Obscura, across the street, is just as rewarding.

▲▲**Gladstone's Land**—Take a good look at this typical

16th- to 17th-century merchant's house, complete with a lived-in furnished interior and guides in each room who love to talk (£3.50, Mon–Sat 10:00–17:00, Sun 14:00–17:00, last entry at 16:30). For a good Royal Mile photo, lean out the upper-floor window (or simply climb the curved stairway outside the museum to the left of the entrance).

▲**Writers' Museum at Lady Stair's House**—This interesting house, built in 1622, is filled with manuscripts and knickknacks of Scotland's three greatest literary figures: Robert Burns, Sir Walter Scott, and Robert Louis Stevenson. It's worth a few minutes for anyone and is fascinating for fans (free, Mon–Sat 10:00–17:00, closed Sun). Wander around the courtyard here. Edinburgh was a wonder in the 17th and 18th centuries. Tourists came here to see its skyscrapers, which towered 10 stories and higher. No city in Europe was so densely populated as "Auld Reekie."

Deacon Brodie's Tavern—This is a decent place for a light meal (see "Eating," below). Read the story of its notorious name-sake on the wall facing Bank Street.

Visitors Centre of the Scottish Parliament—This new center, at the southwest corner of High Street and George IV Bridge, proudly introduces the new Scottish Parliament, with exhibits explaining how it works and models showing the building where it will work (currently an expensive hole in the ground near Holyrood Palace). At the Visitors Centre, you can sign up (free) to witness the new Parliament debating and creating Scottish history in their temporary quarters, a few steps off the Royal Mile, tucked away in Mylnes Court, across from The Hub (debates Wed 14:30–17:30, Thu 9:30–12:30, 14:30–17:30, day bags allowed after scanning, tel. 0131/348-5411).

▲**St. Giles Cathedral**—Wander through Scotland's most important church. Stepping inside, find John Knox's statue. Look into his eyes from 10 inches away. Knox, the great reformer and founder of austere Scottish Presbyterianism, first preached here in 1559. His insistence that every person should be able to read the word of God gave Scotland an educational system 300 years ahead of the rest of Europe. For this reason it was Scottish minds that led the way in math, science, medicine, engineering, and so on. Voltaire called Scotland "the intellectual capital of Europe."

The neo-Gothic **Chapel of the Knights of the Thistle** (from 1911, in far right corner), with its intricate wood carving, was built in two years entirely with Scottish material and labor. Find the angel tooting the bagpipes (from inside chapel, look above the door to the right). The Scottish crown steeple from 1495 is a proud part of Edinburgh's skyline (April–Sept daily 9:00–19:00, Oct–March until 17:00; ask about concerts—some are free, usually Thu at 13:00; fine café downstairs; see "Eating," below).

Scottish Words

aye	yes	**inch, innis**	island
ben	mountain	**inver**	river, mouth
bonnie	beautiful	**kyle**	strait
carn	heap of stones	**loch**	lake
creag	rock, cliff	**neeps**	turnips
tattie	potato		
haggis	rich assortment of oats and sheep organs stuffed into a chunk of sheep intestine, liberally seasoned, boiled, and eaten mostly by tourists. Usually served with "neeps and tatties." Tastier than it sounds.		

John Knox is buried out back—austerely, under the parking lot, at spot 44. The statue among the cars shows King Charles II riding to a toga party back in 1685.

Parliament House—Stop in to see the grand hall with its fine 1639 hammer-beam ceiling and stained glass. This hall housed the Scottish Parliament until the Act of Union in 1707 (explained in history exhibition adjacent) and now holds the law courts. Today it's busy with wigged and robed lawyers hard at work in the old library (peek through the door) or pacing the hall deep in discussion. Greater eminence...longer wig. The friendly doorman is helpful (free, public welcome Mon–Fri 9:00–16:30, best action midmornings Tue–Fri, open-to-the-public trials 10:00–16:00—doorman has day's docket, entry behind St. Giles Cathedral near parking spot 21).

Mercat Cross—This chunky pedestal, on the downhill side of St. Giles, holds a slender column topped with a white unicorn. Royal proclamations were read from here in the 14th century. Today it's the meeting point of various walking tours. Pop into the police information center, a few doors downhill, for a little local law-and-order history (free, daily 10:00–22:00).

▲**Tron Kirk**—This fine old building (staffed by volunteers and open at irregular times) houses a free, interesting Old Town history display and sometimes a TI.

▲**Museum of Childhood**—This five-story playground of historical toys and games—called the noisiest museum in the world because of its delighted tiny visitors—is rich in nostalgia and history (free, Mon–Sat 10:00–16:30, closed Sun). Just downhill is a fragrant fudge shop offering free samples.

▲**John Knox House**—Fascinating for Reformation buffs, this fine 16th-century house offers a well-explained look at the life of the great reformer (£2, Mon–Sat 10:00–16:30, closed Sun, 43 High

Street). While Knox never actually lived here, it was called "his house" to save it from the wrecking ball in 1850.

▲**People's Story**—This interesting exhibition traces the lot of the working class through the 18th, 19th, and 20th centuries (free, Mon–Sat 10:00–17:00, closed Sun). Curiously, while this museum is dedicated to the proletariat, immediately around the back is the tomb of Adam Smith—the author of *Wealth of Nations* and the father of modern capitalism (1723–1790).

▲**Huntly House**—Another old house full of old stuff, Huntly is worth a look for its early Edinburgh history and handy ground-floor WC. Don't miss the original copy of the National Covenant (written in 1638 on an animal skin) or the sketches of pre-Georgian Edinburgh with its lake still wet (free, Mon–Sat 10:00–17:00, closed Sun). Just a toot farther downhill is Bagpipes Galore.

White Horse Close—Step into this 17th-century courtyard (bottom of Canongate, on the left, a block before Holyrood Palace). It was from here that the Edinburgh stagecoach left for London. Eight days later, the horse-drawn carriage pulled into its destination: Scotland Yard.

▲**Holyrood Palace**—The palace marks the end of the Royal Mile. The queen spends a week in Scotland each summer, during which this is her official residence and office. The abbey—part of a 12th-century Augustinian monastery—stood here first. It was named for a piece of the cross brought here as a relic by queen-then-saint Margaret. Scotland's royalty preferred living here to the blustery castle on the rock, and, gradually, the palace grew. The building is rich in history and decor. But without information or a guided tour ("there's none of either," snickered the guy who sells the boring £3.70 museum guidebooks), you're just another peasant in the dark. Docents in each room are happy to give you the answer if you know the question. After wandering through the elegantly furnished rooms and a few dark older rooms filled with glass cases of historic bits and Scottish pieces that must be fascinating, you're free to wander through the ruined abbey and the queen's gardens (£6, CC:VM, daily 9:30–18:00, Nov–April until 16:30—guided tour mandatory off-season, last admission 45 minutes before closing; closed last 2 weeks in May, 10 days in early July, when the queen's home, and whenever a prince drops in; tel. 0131/556-7371).

The building lot near the palace entrance is the site of the new Scottish Parliament, slated for completion in 2003. As a conversation starter, ask a local what he/she thinks about the building's architect, expense, design, and so on.

More Bonnie Wee Sights

▲**Georgian New Town**—Cross Waverley Bridge and walk through Georgian Edinburgh. The grand George Street, connecting St. Andrew and Charlotte Squares, was the centerpiece of the elegantly planned New Town. The entire city plan—laid out in the late 18th century when George was king—celebrates the notion of the United Kingdom. Look at the map. You'll see George Street, Queen Street, and Hanover (the royal family surname) Street. Even Thistle and Rose Streets are emblems of the two happily paired nations. Rose Street, mostly pedestrian-only, is fun to wander. Where it hits St. Andrew's Square, Rose Street is flanked by the venerable Jenners department store and a Sainsbury supermarket. Sprinkled with popular restaurants and bars, the stately New Town is turning trendy.

▲▲**Georgian House**—This refurbished Georgian house, set on Edinburgh's finest Georgian square, is a trip back to 1796. A volunteer guide in each room is trained in the force-feeding of stories and trivia. Start your visit with two interesting videos (architecture/Georgian lifestyles) totaling 30 minutes (£5, Mon–Sat 10:00–17:00, Sun 14:00–17:00, new touch screens provide extra info, 7 Charlotte Square, tel. 0131/225-2160).

Princes Street Gardens—This grassy park, a former lake bed, separates Edinburgh's New and Old Towns and offers a wonderful escape from the city. There are plenty of free concerts and country dances in the summer and the oldest floral clock in the world. Join the local office workers for a picnic lunch break.

▲**National Gallery**—This elegant neoclassical building has a small but impressive collection of European masterpieces, from Raphael to van Gogh, and offers the best look you'll get at Scottish paintings (free, Mon–Sat 10:00–17:00, Sun 12:00–17:00, tel. 0131/624-6200).

▲**Walter Scott Monument**—Built in 1840, this elaborate, neo-Gothic monument honors the great author, one of Edinburgh's many illustrious sons. The 200-foot monument shelters a marble statue of Scott, surrounded by busts of 16 great Scottish poets and 64 characters from his books. Climb 287 steps for a fine view of the city (£2.50, Mon–Sat 9:00–18:00, Nov–Feb until 16:00, closed Sun).

Museum of Scotland—Learn the story of Scotland, from 2,400 million years ago through today. Take advantage of their free 60-minute tours, usually offered daily at 14:15 (orientation) and 15:15 (on a theme), plus Tuesday at 18:00 (orientation). Or take the included audioguide tour (£3, free Tue 16:30–20:00; Mon–Sat 10:00–17:00, Tue until 20:00, Sun 12:00–17:00, Chambers Street, off George IV bridge, 2 long blocks south of Royal Mile, tel. 0131/247-4422, www.nms.ac.uk). Admission includes entry to the Royal Museum, next door.

Dynamic Earth—Best for younger kids, this is a little tame for Americans raised on a steady diet of computers and science museums. The museum's grand goal is to showcase the power of the planet. Standing in a time tunnel, you watch time rewind from Churchill to dinosaurs to that first big bang. After several short films on stars, tectonic plates (interesting), and ice caps, you're freed to wander past salty pools, a recreated rain forest, and various TV screens, ending your visit with a 12-minute continuous film shown on the domed ceiling of a room with few seats (£7, family deals, April–Oct daily 10:00–18:00, Nov–March Wed–Sun 10:00–17:00, last ticket sold 1.25 hrs before closing, on Holyrood Road, near palace and park, tel. 0131/550-7800).

Royal Botanic Garden—Britain's second-oldest botanical garden, established in 1670 for medicinal herbs, is now one of Europe's best (free, Feb/Oct 9:30–17:00, March/Sept 9:30–18:00, April–Aug 9:30–19:00, Nov–Jan 9:30–16:00, 90-minute "rain forest to desert" tours daily at 11:00 and 14:00 for £2 April–Sept, 1 mile north of center at Inverleith Row, tel. 0131/552-7171).

Sights—Near Edinburgh

Britannia—This elegant vessel, which has carted around Britain's royal family for over 40 years and 900 voyages, is moored at Edinburgh's Port of Leith and open to the public. After watching a video about the ship, wander through the museum. Then, armed with the included audioguide, take the stairs or elevator up to the ship (BYO crown). Enjoy views of the Firth of Forth from the deck. Tour the bridge, dining room, and living quarters, following in the historic footsteps of such notables as Churchill, Gandhi, and Reagan. Book in advance—or risk a wait on site—by calling 0131/555-5566 (CC:VM); weekends are busiest (£8, April–Oct daily 9:30–18:00, in Aug Fri–Sun until 21:00, Nov–March 10:30–17:00, last ticket sold 1.5 hrs before closing; to get to ship from Edinburgh, catch city bus X50 bus at Waverley Bridge—£3 round-trip—or take the Guide Friday bus—£3.50 round-trip; cheap café on site, www .royalyachtbritannia.co.uk).

Edinburgh Crystal—Blowing, molding, cutting, polishing, and engraving, the Edinburgh Crystal Company glassworks tour smashes anything you'll see in Venice (£3, 35-minute tours offered year-round Mon–Fri 9:15–15:30, April–Sept weekends 11:00–14:30, kids under 8 not admitted). There is a shop full of "bargain" second-quality pieces, a video show, and a cafeteria. A free minibus shuttle service from Waverley Bridge departs at the top of the hour (April–Sept Mon–Fri 10:00–15:00, Sat–Sun 11:00–14:00), or you can drive 10 miles south of town on A701 to Penicuik. You can schedule a more expensive supertour where you actually blow and cut glass (tel. 01968/675-128).

Activities in Edinburgh

▲▲**Arthur's Seat Hike**—A 45-minute hike up the 822-foot volcanic mountain (surrounded by a fine park overlooking Edinburgh), starting from the Holyrood Palace, gives you a rewarding view. You can drive up most of the way from behind (follow the one-way street from the palace, park by the little lake) or run up like they did in *Chariots of Fire*. From the parking lot (immediately south of Holyrood Palace), you'll see two trails going up. For an easier grade, take the wide path to the left and skip the steeper path that begins with steps and skirts the base of the cliffs. You can also hike up to the Seat from the Dalkeith B&B neighborhood. Take the road (Holyrood Park Road) that borders the Commonwealth pool, turn right (on Queen's Drive), and continue to a small car park. From here, it's a 20-minute hike.

Brush Skiing—If you'd rather be skiing, the Midlothian Ski Centre in Hillend has a hill on the edge of town with a chairlift, two slopes plus jump slope, and rentable skis, boots, and poles (£6.50/first hr, then £2.60/hr, includes gear, Mon–Sat 9:30–21:00, Sun 9:30–19:00, closed last 2 weeks of June, probably closed if it snows, LRT bus #4 from Princes Street—garden side, tel. 0131/445-4433).

▲**Royal Commonwealth Games Swimming Pool**—The biggest pool I've ever seen is open to the public, with a well-equipped fitness center (£5.10, includes swim), sauna (£6.50 extra), and a cafeteria overlooking the pool (£2.70 for pool admission only, Mon–Fri 6:00–21:00, Sat–Sun 10:00–16:00, closed 9:00–10:00 every Wed, no towels or suit rentals, tel. 0131/667-7211).

More Hikes—You can hike along the river (called Water of Leith) through Edinburgh. Locals favor the stretch between Roseburn and Dean Village, but the 1.5-mile walk from Dean Village to the Royal Botanic Garden is also good. This and other hikes are described in the TI's "Walks in and around Edinburgh" (ask for the free one-page flyer, not their £2 guide to walks).

Shopping—The best shopping is along Princes Street (look for elegant old Jenners department store), Victoria Street (antiques galore), and the Royal Mile (touristy but competitively priced, shops usually open 9:00–17:30, later on Thu, some closed Sun).

Bus Tours to Countryside—Many companies offer day trips to regional sights (such as Loch Ness). Comparison-shop at the brochure rack at the TI.

Edinburgh Festival

One of Europe's great cultural events, Edinburgh's annual festival turns the city into a carnival of culture. There are enough music, dance, art, drama, and multicultural events to make even the most jaded traveler drool with excitement. Every day is jammed with formal and spontaneous fun. A number of festivals—official, fringe, book, film, and jazz and blues—rage simultaneously for about three weeks each August, with the Military Tattoo starting a week earlier (the best overall Web site is www.edinburghfestivals.co.uk). Many city sights run on extended hours, and those that normally close on Sunday (Writers' Museum, Huntly House, People's Story, and

Museum of Childhood) open in the afternoon. It's a glorious time to be in Edinburgh.

The official festival (August 12–September 1 in 2001) is the original, more formal and likely to get booked up first. Major events sell out well in advance. The ticket office is at The Hub, a churchlike building (with café, ATM, and WC), located near the top of the Royal Mile as you approach the castle (tickets-£4–55, CC:VMA, booking from mid-April on, office open Mon–Sat 9:30–17:30, in Aug until 20:00 plus Sun 10:00–17:00, tel. 0131/473-2000, fax 0131/473-2003, can book online, www.eif.co.uk).

The less-formal **Fringe Festival** features "on the edge" comedy and theater (CC:VM, Aug 5–27 in 2001, ticket/info office just below St. Giles Cathedral on the Royal Mile, 180 High Street, tel. 0131/226-5257, bookings tel. 0131/226-5138, can book online from mid-June on, www.edfringe.com). Tickets are usually available at the door, but popular shows can sell out.

Other festivals in August: jazz and blues (tel. 0131/467-5200, e-mail: info@assemblydirect.ednet.co.uk), film (tel. 0131/229-2550, e-mail: info@edfilmfest.org.uk), and book (tel. 0131/228-5444, e-mail: admin@edbookfest.co.uk).

The **Military Tattoo** is a massing of the bands, drums, and bagpipes with groups from all over what was the British Empire. Displaying military finesse with a stirring lone-piper finale, this grand spectacle fills the castle esplanade nightly except Sunday, normally from a week before the festival starts until a week before it finishes: August 3 to 25 in 2001 (£10–27, CC:VMA, booking starts in Jan, Fri–Sat shows sell out first, office open Mon–Fri 10:00–16:30, 33 Market Street, behind—and south of—Waverley train station, tel. 0131/225-1188, www.edintattoo.co.uk). If nothing else, it is a really big show.

If you do manage to hit Edinburgh during the festival, book a room far in advance and extend your stay by a day or two. While Fringe tickets and most Tattoo tickets are available the day of the show, you may want to book a couple of official events in advance. Do it directly by telephone, leaving your credit-card number. Pick up your ticket at the office the day of the show. Several publications—including the festival's official schedule, the *Edinburgh Festivals Guide Daily*, *The List*, the *Fringe Program*, and the *Daily Diary*—list and evaluate festival events.

Nightlife in Edinburgh

▲▲**Evening Walking Tours**—These walks, more than a pile of ghost stories, are an entertaining and cheap night out (offered nightly, usually 19:00 and 21:00, easy socializing for solo travelers). The theatrical and creatively staged **Witchery Tours,** the most established of the ghost tours, offer two different walks: "Ghosts and Gore" and "Murder and Mystery" (£7, 90 min, leave from the Royal

Mile, reservations required, book your spot by calling 0131/225-6745). The fascinating-for-those-who-care **Literary Pub Tour** leaves from the Beehive Pub on Grassmarket, lasts two hours, and includes two actors and four pub stops (£7, April–May and Oct at 19:30 from Thu–Sun; July–Aug daily at 14:00,18:00, and 20:30; Nov–March Fri only at 19:30; tel. 0131/226-6665).

▲**Scottish Folk Evenings**—These £35 to £40 dinner shows, generally for tour groups, are held in huge halls of expensive hotels. (Prices are bloated to include 20 percent commissions.) Your "traditional" meal is followed by a full slate of swirling kilts, blaring bagpipes, and Scottish folk dancing with an "old-time music hall"–type emcee. You can often see the show without dinner for about half price. The TI has fliers on all the latest venues. **Carlton Highland Hotel** offers its Scottish folk evening with or without dinner, nearly nightly—ask when the next show is scheduled (£19.50 for show at 20:45–22:30, £39.50 includes dinner at 19:30, CC:VM, at High Street and North Bridge, tel. 0131/556-7277).

▲▲**Folk Music in Pubs**—Edinburgh is a good place for folk music. There's always a pub or two with a folk evening on. The monthly *Gig Guide* (free at TI and various pubs, www.gigguide .co.uk) lists most of the live music action. **Whistle Binkies** offers nightly ad-lib traditional music, which can start as early as 19:30 or as late as 22:30 and goes until the wee hours (just off the Royal Mile on South Bridge, another entrance on Niddry Street, tel. 0131/557-5114).

　　Grassmarket Street (below the castle) is sloppy with live music—mostly folk. This noisy nightlife center is fun to just wander through late at night. **Finnigan's Wake** has live music—often Irish folk songs—nightly (starts at 22:00, a block off Grassmarket at 9 Victoria Street, tel. 0131/226-3816). The **Fiddlers Arms, Biddy Mulligan,** and **White Hart Inn**, among others, all feature live folk music. By the noise and crowds you'll know where to go and where not to. Have a beer and follow your ear.

Theater—Even outside of festival time, Edinburgh is a fine place for lively and affordable theater. Pick up *The List* for a complete rundown of what's on.

Sleeping in Edinburgh
(£1 = about $1.60, country code: 44, area code: 0131)
Sleep Code: **S** = Single, **D** = Double/Twin, **T** = Triple, **Q** = Quad, **b** = bathroom, **t** = toilet only, **s** = shower only, **CC** = Credit Card (Visa, MasterCard, Amex).

　　Book ahead! The annual festival fills Edinburgh each August—when prices for accommodations are at their peak. Conventions, school holidays, and weekends can make finding a room tough at almost any time of year. Call in advance or pay 30 percent extra for a relative dump. For the best prices, book directly rather than through the TI, which charges a £3 booking fee. "Standard" rooms, with toilets and showers a tissue-toss away, save you £10 a night.

Room prices in this section are usually listed as a range, from low season (winter) to high season (July–Sept), though prices can go even higher during the August festival. Prices get soft off-season, for longer visits, and sometimes for midweek stays outside of summer.

Sleeping off Dalkeith Road

These recommendations are south of town near the Royal Commonwealth Pool, just off Dalkeith Road. This comfortably safe neighborhood is a 20-minute walk or 10-minute bus ride from the Royal Mile. All listings are nonsmoking, on quiet streets, a two-minute walk from a bus stop, and well served by city buses. B&Bs are unlikely to accept bookings for one-night stays in August.

Near the B&Bs you'll find plenty of eateries (see "Eating," below), easy free parking, and the handy **Capital Launderette** (Mon–Sat 8:30–17:00, £4 for self-serve, £5.50 if they do it, drop off by 11:00 for same-day service, June–Sept they'll deliver your clean clothes to your B&B for free, 208 Dalkeith Road, tel. 0131/667-0825).

To reach the hotel neighborhood from the train station, TI, or Scott Monument, cross Princes Street and wait at the bus stop under the small C&A sign on the department store (80p, buses #C3, #14, #21, #33, #82, or #86; tell driver your destination is "Dalkeith Road," red bus: exact change or pay more; green bus: makes change; ride 10 minutes to first stop 100 yards after the pool, push the button, exit middle door). These buses also stop at the corner of North Bridge and High Street on the Royal Mile. Buses generally run from about 6:00 to 23:00, except on Sunday morning—buses don't start running from Dalkeith Road into town until 9:00. Taxi fare between the station or Royal Mile and the B&Bs is about £5.

Plusher B&Bs off Dalkeith Road

Turret Guest House is teddy-on-the-beddy cozy, with a great bay-windowed family room and a vast breakfast menu that includes haggis and vegetarian options (7 rooms, S-£20–23, S-£23–28, D-£46–56, Db-£44–58, £2-per-person discount with this book and cash, 8 Kilmaurs Terrace, EH16 5DR, tel. 0131/667-6704, www.turret.clara.net, Mrs. Jackie Cameron).

Amaragua Guest House, next door to Turret, is an inviting Victorian home away from home, decorated with a Malaysian twist—art and some furniture accumulated when the English owners lived in Kuala Lumpur (7 rooms, S-£18–25, Db-£36–55, £2-per-person discount with this book, 10 Kilmaurs Terrace, EH16 5DR, tel. & fax 0131/667-6775, cellular 0789-987-8722, e-mail: amaragua @cableinet.co.uk, run by gracious Helen and Dave Butterworth).

Edinburgh, Our Neighborhood

TO
EDINBURGH
CITY CENTER
(10 MIN BY BUS)

SALISBURY
CRAGS →

HOLYROOD
PARK

ARTHUR'S
SEAT
823'

QUEEN'S DRIVE

← CLIFFS

LION'S
HAUNCH

ROYAL
COMMONWEALTH
POOL

TO
ARTHUR'S
SEAT

PRESTONFIELD

MARCHALL
PLACE

MARCHALL ROAD

GOLF COURSE

EAST MAYFIELD

QUEEN'S
CRESCENT

PRIESTFELD AVE.

CEMETERY

DCH

DALKEITH ROAD
BECOMES A-68
SOUTH TO BORDERS
& ENGLAND

¼ MILE

1 MILLFIELD GUEST HOUSE	**9** BELFORD G.H.
2 TURRET G.H. HIGHLAND PARK, AMARAGUA B&Bs	**10** WINEGLASS PUB, CHINATOWN & CHATTERBOX
3 DUNEDIN & KENVIE G.H.	**11** LAUNDRETTE, GROCERIES & JADE PALACE
4 ARD-NA-SAID B&B	**12** FENWICK'S REST.
5 DORSTAN HOTEL	**13** MINTO REST.
6 HOTEL CEILIDH-DONIA	**14** WILD ELEPHANT & BRATTISANI'S
7 SALISBURY HOTEL	**15** AIRDENDAIR GUEST HOUSE
8 PRIESTVILLE HOTEL	

Dunedin Guest House (pron. dun-EE-cin) is bright, plush, Scottish, and a good value (7 rooms, 1 S-£20–30, Db-£40–70, family rooms and deals, strong showers, good lighting, TVs with satellite channels, no 1-nights stays in Aug, 8 Priestfield Road, EH16 5HH, tel. 0131/668-1949, fax 0131/668-3636, e-mail: dunedin-guesthouse@edinburgh-EH16.freeserve.co.uk, Marcella Bowen).

Dorstan Private Hotel is personable but professional and hotelesque, with all the comforts. Several of its 14 thoughtfully decorated rooms are on the ground floor (2 Ds-£60, Db-£66, family rooms, no clothes washing except for "smalls," CC:VMA, 7 Priestfield Road, EH16 5HJ, tel. 0131/667-6721, fax 0131/668-4644, e-mail: reservations@dorstan-hotel.demon.co.uk, Mairae Campbell).

Hotel Ceilidh-Donia (pron. caledonia) has 13 rooms: half are state-of-the-art new and comfortable, and the other half—slated for renovation—are decent. Owners Max and Annette Preston offer dinner (£6–7), run a bar, and have a high-tech security system (2 D-£40–50, standard Db-£43–55, deluxe Db-£55–70, CC:VM, Internet access, nonsmoking except in part of bar, minibus tours possible, 14 Marchhall Crescent, EH16 5HL, tel. 0131/667-2743, fax 0131/668-2181, www.hotelceilidh-donia.freeserve.co.uk).

Ard-Na-Said B&B is an elegant 1875 Victorian house with a comfy lounge and classy rooms (reconfirm your reservation, 1 S-£22–28, Db-£44–60, family deals, 5 Priestfield Road, EH16 5HH, tel. 0131/667-8754, fax 0131/271-0960, www.ardnasaid.freeserve .co.uk, enthusiastically run by Jim and Olive Lyons).

Simpler B&Bs off Dalkeith Road

Millfield Guest House, run graciously by Liz and Ed Broomfield, is thoughtfully furnished with antique class, a rare sit-and-chat ambience, and a comfy TV lounge. Since the showers are down the hall, you'll get spacious rooms and great prices (S-£21–23, D-£38–40, T-£48–52, CC reservation allows for late arrival but pay in cash, 12 Marchhall Road, EH16 5HR, tel. & fax 0131/667-4428). Decipher the breakfast prayer by Robert Burns. Then try the "Taste of Scotland" breakfast option. See how many stone (14 pounds) you weigh in the elegant throne room. This place is worth calling well in advance.

Kenvie Guest House, well and warmly run by Dorothy Vidler, comes with six pleasant rooms and lots of personal touches (1 small twin-£40, D-£42, Db-£50, family deals, 3 percent more with CC, 16 Kilmaurs Road, EH16 5DA, tel. 0131/668-1964, fax 0131/668-1926, www.kenvie.co.uk, e-mail: dorothy@kenvie.co.uk).

Airdenair Guest House, offering views and homemade scones, has five attractive rooms with a lofty above-it-all feeling (Sb-£25–35, Db-£40–50, CC:VM, 29 Kilmaurs Road, EH16 5DB, tel. 0131/668-2336, http://airdenair.edinburghnet.co.uk/, Jill McLennan).

Highland Park House, bright and friendly, has homey rooms with double-glazed windows to shut out noise and keep in warmth (S-£20–25, D-£40–44, Db-£44–52 with this book, family deals, 16 Kilmaurs Terrace, EH16 5DR, tel. & fax 0131/667-9204, e-mail: highlandparkhouse@hotmail.com, Margaret and Brian Love).

Colquhoun Guest House, in an elegant building, has seven fine rooms, several on the ground floor (S-£22–25, D-£40,

Db-£50, across street from Millfield House, 5 Marchhall Road, EH16 5HR, tel. 0131-667-8481, cellular 0411-561066, run by amazing Grace McAinsh).

Priestville B&B, a spacious place, has six cozy rooms, each with a VCR and access to a video library (D-£40–50, Db-£45–60, CC:VM with 3 percent charge, family deals, Internet access, small fridge per floor, 10 Priestfield Road, EH16 5HJ, tel. & fax 0131/667-2435, e-mail: priestville@hotmail.com, Angela and Alan Aberdein).

Belford House is a tidy, homey place offering seven good rooms and a warm welcome (D-£40–44, Db-£50–54, family deals, CC:VM, 13 Blacket Avenue, tel. 0131/667-2422, fax 0131/667-7508, Isa and Tom Borthwick).

The Salisbury, more like a hotel than its neighbors, fills a classy old Georgian building with 12 rooms, a large lounge, tired carpeting, and even a dumbwaiter in the breakfast room (D-£44–56, Db-£50–62, 5 percent off with cash and this book, CC:VM, 45 Salisbury Road, EH16 5AA, tel. & fax 0131/667-1264, http://members.edinburgh.org/salisbury/, Brenda Wright).

Big, Modern Hotels

Four of these listings are cheap as hotels go, and offer more comfort than character; book in advance. One's a splurge. In each case, I'd skip the pricey breakfast and eat out.

Sleeping cheap near the Royal Mile: Travelodge, the cheapest hotel in the center, has 193 no-nonsense, central rooms all decorated in dark blue decor (Db-£50–70, breakfast-£8, CC:VMA, most rooms nonsmoking, 33 St. Mary's Street, a block off the Royal Mile, tel. 0870-905-6343, www.travelodge.co.uk).

Ibis Hotel, mid–Royal Mile behind Tron Church, is perfectly located and has 98 soulless but clean and comfy rooms and American charm (Sb-£54–70, Db-£62–70, continental breakfast-£4.50, CC:VMA, nonsmoking rooms available, elevator, 6 Hunter Square, EH1 1QW, tel. 0131/240-7000, fax 0131/240-7007, e-mail: H2039@accor-hotels.com).

Jurys Inn is another cookie-cutter place, with 186 dependably comfortable rooms. Prices fluctuate wildly, dropping in winter and soaring in August (Db-£39–82, CC:VM, breakfast-£7.50, nonsmoking rooms available, some views, pub/restaurant, on quiet street just off Royal Mile, 43 Jeffrey Street, EH1 1DG, tel. 0131/200-3300, fax 0131/200-0400, www.jurys.com).

Splurge near the Royal Mile: MacDonald, my only fancy listing, offers its best value outside of August. With its classy marble-and-wood decor, fitness center, and pool, it's hard to leave. On a gray winter day in Edinburgh, this could be worth it. Prices vary wildly (standard Db: £75 in winter, £90–110 May–July, up to £200 in Aug, breakfast-£11, CC:VM, near bottom of Mile, across from

Dynamic Earth, Holyrood Road, EH8 6AE, tel. 0131/550-4500, fax 0131/528-8191, www.macdonaldhotels.co.uk). If you call, mention you're on holiday—not business—and ask if there's a Leisure Break (prices usually don't drop, but breakfast is thrown in).

Away from the center: Travel Inn, the biggest hotel in Edinburgh, has even less character but a great price and a mediocre location about a mile west of the Mile. Each of its 280 rooms is modern and comfortable, with a sofa that folds out for two kids if necessary (Db-£50 for 2 adults and up to 2 kids under 15, breakfast is extra, CC:VMA, elevators, nonsmoking rooms, weekends booked long in advance, near Haymarket station west of the castle at 1 Morrison Link, EH3 8DN, tel. 0131/228-9819, fax 0131/228-9836, www.travelinn.co.uk).

Hostels

Although Edinburgh's hostels are open to all and well run, providing Internet access, laundry facilities, and £12 bunk beds (about a £9–12 savings over B&Bs), they are scruffy and don't include breakfast.

Castle Rock Hostel is hip and easygoing, offering cheap beds, plenty of friends, and a great central location just below the castle and above the pubs with all the folk music (15 Johnston Terrace, tel. 0131/225-9666). Their sister hostels are nearly across the street from each other: **High Street Hostel** (laundry-£2.50, kitchen, 8 Blackfriars Street, just off High Street/Royal Mile, tel. 0131/557-3984) and **Royal Mile Backpackers** (105 High Street, tel. 0131/557-6120).

For more regulations and less color, try the IYH hostels: **Bruntsfield Hostel** (near golf course, 6–12 beds per room, 7 Bruntsfield Crescent, buses #11, #15, and #16 from Princes Street, tel. 0131/447-2994) and **Edinburgh Hostel** (4–10 beds per room, 18 Eglinton Crescent, 5-minute walk from Haymarket station, tel. 0131/337-1120).

Eating in Edinburgh

Eating along the Royal Mile

Historic pubs and doily cafés with reasonable, unremarkable meals abound. Here are some handy, affordable places for a good bite to eat (listed in downhill order). **Deacon Brodie's Pub** serves soup, sandwiches, and snacks on the ground floor and good £7 meals upstairs in the restaurant. As in all Edinburgh pubs, kids are allowed only in the restaurant section (open daily 12:00–22:00, CC:VM, tel. 0131/225-6531). Or munch prayerfully in the **Lower Aisle** restaurant under St. Giles Cathedral (Mon–Fri 8:30–16:30; July–Sept also Sun 11:00–14:00). The **Filling Station** makes good burgers (daily 12:00–22:30, 235 High Street, near North Bridge, tel. 0131/226-2488). **Bann UK,** an upscale vegetarian café, serves carnivore-pleasing cuisine that goes way beyond tofu and granola (daily 11:00–23:00, CC:VM, just off South Bridge behind the Tron Church at 5 Hunter Square, tel. 0131/226-1112). **Food Plantation** has good, inexpensive, fresh sandwiches to eat in or take out (Mon–Fri 8:30–15:30, 274 Canongate). **Brambles Tea Room** serves light lunches and Starbucks coffee (Mon–Sat 10:30–16:45, Sun 11:00–16:45, next to Huntly House at 158 Canongate). **Clarinda's Tea Room,** near the bottom of the Royal Mile, is a charming and tasty place for a break after touring the Mile or palace (daily 9:30–16:45).

For a break from the touristic grind, consider the **Elephant House,** where locals browse newspapers, listen to classic rock, and sip coffee or munch a light meal (Mon–Fri 8:00–23:00, Sat–Sun 9:00–23:00, 3 blocks south of Royal Mile at 21 George IV Bridge, tel. 0131/220-5355).

Grassmarket Street, below the castle, is lined with sloppy eateries and noisy pubs. This is the place for live folk music. If you want dinner to melt into your beer, eat here.

Eating in the New Town

Waverley Center Food Court, below the TI and above the station, is a food circus of sticky fast-food joints littered with paper plates and shoppers (Mon–Sat 8:30–18:00, Thu until 19:00, Sun 11:00–17:00). If you'd prefer pubs, browse Rose Street.

The **Undercroft,** in the basement of St. Andrew's church, is the cheapest place in town for lunch (£1 sandwich or soup and roll, Mon–Fri 12:00–14:00, on George Street, just off St. Andrew's Square).

For a generation, New Town vegetarians have munched hearty cuisine and salads at **Henderson's Salad Table and Wine Bar** (£5–6, CC:VM, Mon–Sat 8:00–22:45, closed Sun, nonsmoking section, strictly vegetarian, pleasant live music nightly, between Queen and George Streets at 94 Hanover Street, tel. 0131/225-2131).

Local office workers pile into the friendly and family-run **La Lanterna** for good Italian food (Mon–Sat 12:00–14:00, 17:15–22:00, closed Sun, CC:VMA, 83 Hanover Street, 2 blocks off Princes Street, dinner reservations wise, tel. 0131/226-3090).

Browns, a chain restaurant that's like an upscale Denny's, offers predictably good food throughout the day (£8–11, daily 12:00–22:30, family scene at dinner, nonsmoking section, CC:VMA, at west end of George Street, near Georgian House, intersection with Charlotte Street, 131 George Street, tel. 0131/225-4442).

All Bar One, the hip, mod chain of light-wood pubs offering pasta and quesadillas, bumps and grinds on the corner of George and Hanover Streets (£4 meals, Mon–Sat 12:00–24:00, Sun 12:30–23:00, order at bar, 29 George Street).

Supermarket: The glorious **Sainsbury** supermarket, with a

Edinburgh's New Town

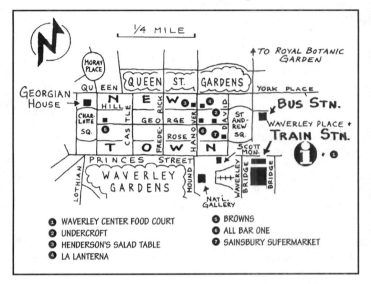

Map legend:
- ❶ WAVERLEY CENTER FOOD COURT
- ❷ UNDERCROFT
- ❸ HENDERSON'S SALAD TABLE
- ❹ LA LANTERNA
- ❺ BROWNS
- ❻ ALL BAR ONE
- ❼ SAINSBURY SUPERMARKET

tasty assortment of take-away food and specialty coffee, is just one block from the Walter Scott Monument and the lovely picnic-perfect Princes Street Gardens (Mon–Sat 7:00–21:00, Sun 10:00–19:00, CC:VM, on corner of Rose Street, on St. Andrew's Square). Across the street is Jenners, the classy department store.

Eating in Dalkeith Road Area, near Your B&B

All of these places except Howie's are within a five-minute walk of the recommended B&Bs. The following eateries are on or near the intersection of Newington and East Preston Streets. For a fun local atmosphere, the smoky **Wine Glass Pub** serves filling meals (£4, daily 12:00–14:30, 17:00–20:00 but no dinner on Fri, closes 19:30 on Sat). **Chinatown,** next to the Wine Glass, is a delightful—though not cheap—Chinese restaurant (£7–10, Tue–Fri 12:00–14:00, 17:30–23:00, Sat–Sun 17:30–23:00, closed Mon, CC:VM, reservations smart on weekend nights, tel. 0131/662-0555). The **Wild Elephant,** a few doors down on the same block, serves decent Thai food (£4–6, Tue–Sun 16:30–22:30, closed Mon, CC:VM, also does take-away, 21 Newington Road, tel. 0131/662-8822). **Chatterbox,** on the other side of the Wine Glass Pub, is fine for a light meal with tea (£4 meals, Mon–Fri 8:30–18:00, Sat 9:00–18:00, Sun 11:00–18:00). **Brattisanis** is your basic fish-and-chips joint serving lousy milkshakes and great haggis (daily 11:30–24:00, 87 Newington Road).

Two affordable splurges feature Scottish cooking with a

French flair, are open daily, and charge about £5 to £7 for lunch and £17 for a three-course dinner. **Fenwicks** is cozy and reliable, with tasty food (daily 12:00–14:00, dinner 18:00–late, all day Sunday, CC:VM, 15 Salisbury Place, tel. 0131/667-4265). **Howies,** with a more adventurous menu, is a bit pricier and a longer walk, about 10 minutes north of the B&B neighborhood; you could get off the bus at the Clerk Street stop on the way home (Tue–Sun 12:00–14:00, daily 18:00–22:00, can bring own wine for £2 corkage fee, 75 St. Leonard's Street, tel. 0131/668-2917).

Hotel Ceilidh-Donia, one of the recommended hotels, serves dinner (£6–7, Mon–Fri eves plus Sun lunch 12:00–14:30), runs a bar with a nonsmoking section, and is open to the public (CC:VM, Internet access, 14 Marchhall Crescent, tel. 0131/667-2743).

On Dalkeith Road, the huge Commonwealth Pool's noisy **cafeteria** is for hungry swimmers and budget travelers alike (pass the entry without paying, Mon–Fri 10:00–20:00, Sat–Sun 10:00–17:00).

Jade Palace, several blocks south of the pool, has tasty Chinese food—takeout only (Wed–Mon 16:30–23:00, closed Tue, 212 Dalkeith Road, tel. 0131/667-9030).

Minto Hotel's bar/restaurant serves a filling high tea—hot meaty dinner with tea and scones—for £7 to £10 (Mon–Sat 17:00–21:15, Sun 16:00–21:15, CC:VM, on Minto Street just north of intersection with Mayfield Terrace, tel. 0131/668-1234).

Supermarket: The nearest supermarket, **Tesco,** is located between the Royal Mile and B&B neighborhood (Mon–Sat 8:00–21:00, Sun 9:00–19:00, on Nicolson, just south of intersection with W. Richmond Street, 5 long blocks south of the Royal Mile).

Transportation Connections—Edinburgh
By train to: Inverness (7/day, 4 hrs), **Oban** (3/day, change in Glasgow, 4.5 hrs), **York** (hrly, 2.5 hrs), **London** (hrly, 5 hrs), **Durham** (hrly, 2 hrs, less frequent in winter), **Newcastle** (hrly, 1.5 hrs), **Lake District** (south past Carlisle to Penrith, catch bus to Keswick; hrly except Sun 3/day, 40 min), **Birmingham** (6/day, 4.5 hrs), **Crewe** (6/day, 3.5 hrs), **Bristol,** near Bath (hrly, 6–7 hrs). Train info: tel. 08457-484-950.

By bus to: Oban (1/day, 4 hrs), **Fort William** (1/day, 4 hrs), **Inverness** (hrly, 4 hrs), **Blackpool** (1/day, 5 hrs), **York** (1/day, 5 hrs). For bus info, call Scottish Citylink (tel. 08705-505-050, www.citylink.co.uk) or National Express (tel. 08705-808-080).

ROME
(ROMA)

Rome is magnificent and brutal at the same time. Your ears will ring, if you're careless you'll be run down or pickpocketed, you'll be frustrated by the kind of chaos that only an Italian can understand. You may even come to believe Mussolini was a necessary evil. But Rome is required, and in the wake of improvements made for Jubilee Year 2000, it's more exciting and easier than ever.

If your hotel provides a comfortable refuge, if you pace yourself and accept and even partake in the siesta plan, if you're well organized for sightseeing, and if you protect yourself and your valuables with extra caution and discretion, you'll do fine. You'll see the sights and leave satisfied.

Rome at its peak meant civilization itself. Everything was either civilized (part of the Roman Empire, Latin- or Greek-speaking) or barbarian. Today Rome is Italy's political capital, the capital of Catholicism, and a splendid... "junk pile" is not quite the right term... of Western civilization. As you peel through its fascinating and jumbled layers, you'll find its buildings, cats, laundry, traffic, and 2.6 million people endlessly entertaining. And then, of course, there are its magnificent sights.

Tour St. Peter's, the greatest church on earth, and scale Michelangelo's 100-meter-tall dome, the world's largest. Learn something about eternity by touring the huge Vatican Museum. You'll find the story of creation—bright as the day it was painted—in the newly restored Sistine Chapel. Do the "Caesar Shuffle" through ancient Rome's Forum and Colosseum. Savor Europe's most sumptuous building—the Borghese Gallery—and take an early evening *"Dolce Vita* Stroll" down the Via del Corso with Rome's beautiful people. Enjoy an after-dark walk from Trastevere to the Spanish Steps, lacing together Rome's Baroque and bubbly night spots.

Rome Area

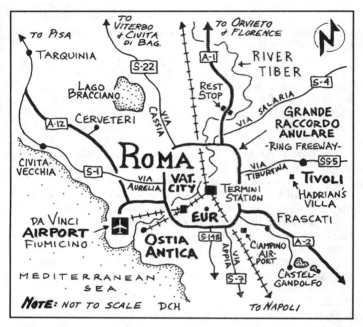

TO PISA
TARQUINIA
TO VITERBO + CIVITA DI BAG.
S·22
LAGO BRACCIANO
A·12
CERVETERI
VIA CASSIA
TO ORVIETO + FLORENCE
A·1
RIVER TIBER
REST STOP
S·4
VIA SALARIA
GRANDE RACCORDO ANULARE
-RING FREEWAY-
CIVITA-VECCHIA
S·1
VIA AURELIA
RoMA
VAT. CITY
VIA TIBURTINA
SS·5
TIVOLI
HADRIAN'S VILLA
TERMINI STATION
DA VINCI AIRPORT FIUMICINO
EUR
S·148
FRASCATI
A·2
OSTIA ANTICA
VIA APPIA
CIAMPINO AIR-PORT
MEDITERRANEAN SEA
S·7
CASTEL GANDOLFO
NOTE: NOT TO SCALE   DCH
TO NAPOLI

Planning Your Time

For most travelers, Rome is best done quickly. It's a great city, but it's exhausting. Time is normally short, and Italy is more charming elsewhere. To "do" Rome in a day, consider it as a side trip from Orvieto or Florence and maybe before the night train to Venice. Crazy as that sounds, if all you have is a day, it's a great one.

Rome in a day: Vatican (2 hours in the museum and Sistine Chapel and 1 hour in St. Peter's), taxi over the river to the Pantheon (munch a bar-snack picnic on its steps), then hike over Capitol Hill, through the Forum, and to the Colosseum. Have dinner on Campo de' Fiori and dessert on Piazza Navona.

Rome in two days: Do the "Caesar Shuffle" from the Colosseum and Forum over Capitol Hill to the Pantheon. After a siesta, join the locals strolling from Piazza del Popolo to the Spanish Steps. Have dinner near your hotel. On the second day, see Vatican City (St. Peter's, climb the dome, tour the Vatican Museum). Spend the evening walking from Trastevere to Campo de' Fiori (atmospheric place for dinner) to the Trevi Fountain. With a third day, add the Borghese Gallery (reservations required) and the National Museum of Rome.

Orientation

The modern sprawl of Rome is of no interest to us. Our Rome actually feels small when you know it. It's the old core—within the triangle formed by the train station, Colosseum, and Vatican. Get a handle on Rome by considering it in these layers:

The ancient city had a million people. Tear it down to size by walking through just the core. The best of the classical sights stand in a line from the Colosseum to the Pantheon.

Medieval Rome was little more than a hobo camp of 50,000—thieves, mean dogs, and the pope, whose legitimacy required a Roman address. The medieval city, a colorful tangle of lanes, lies between the Pantheon and the river.

Window-shoppers' Rome twinkles with nightlife and ritzy shopping near medieval Rome, on or near Rome's main drag— Via del Corso—and around the ritzy Spanish Steps.

Vatican City is a compact world of its own with two great, huge sights: St. Peter's Basilica and the Vatican Museum.

Trastevere, the seedy, colorful, wrong-side-of-the-river neighborhood/village, is Rome at its crustiest—and perhaps most "Roman."

Baroque Rome is an overleaf that embellishes great squares throughout the town with fountains and church facades.

Since no one is allowed to build taller than St. Peter's dome, the city has no modern skyline. And the Tiber River is ignored. It's not navigable, and after the last floods (1870), the banks were built up very high and Rome turned its back on its naughty river.

Tourist Information

While Rome has three main tourist information offices (abbreviated in this book as TI), the dozen or so handy TI kiosks scattered around the town at major tourist centers are handy and just as helpful. If all you need is a map, forget the TI and pick one up at your hotel.

You'll find TIs at the airport (daily 8:15–19:00, tel. 06-6595-6074) and the train station (daily 8:00–21:00, off-season 9:00–20:00, near track 3, accessible from platforms or lobby, marked "Informazioni Turistiche/Tourist Info," crowded, combined with travel agency, tel. 06-4890-6300).

The **central TI** office, near Piazza della Repubblica's huge fountain, covers the city and the region. It's a five-minute walk out the front of the train station (Mon–Fri 8:15–19:15, Sat 8:15–13:30, next to Saab dealership, Via Parigi 5, tel. 06-4889-9253). It's air-conditioned, less crowded, and more helpful than the station TI, and it has a table to plan on—or sit under to overcome your frustration.

At any TI, ask for a city map, a listing of sights and hours (in the free *Tesori di Roma* booklet), and *L'Evento*, the free bimonthly

Rome

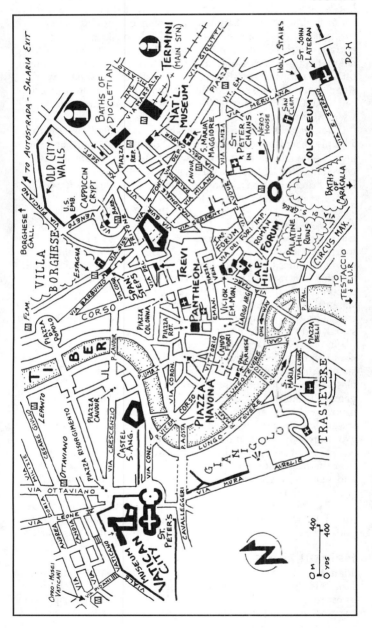

Map labels (as shown):

TO AUTOSTRADA - SALARIA EXIT · TERMINI (MAIN STN.) · ST. JOHN LATERAN · DCH · HOLY STAIRS · VIA GIOLITTI · PIAZZA · VIT. EM. · BATHS OF DIOCLETIAN · VIA MARSALA · NAT'L. MUSEUM · VIA MERULANA · SAN CLEM. · COLOSSEUM · OLD CITY WALLS · FLAM. · VIA FLAG. · PIAZZA REP. · S. MARIA MAGGIORE · VIA LANZA · ST. PETER IN CHAINS · NERO'S HOUSE · VIA S. STEFANO · VIA DI SETT. · CAPPUCCIN CRYPT · VIA NAZIONALE · VIA CAVOUR · BATHS OF CARACALLA · VIA PINCIANA · U.S. EMB. · VIA VENETO · VIA BARB. · VIA DEL TRITONE · VIA QUIR. · VIA SERPENTI · FORI IMP. · VIA DEI FORI IMP. · S. GREGA · VIA DI S. GREGORIO · BORGHESE GALL. · VILLA BORGHESE · VIA SIST. · PZA. · TREVI · ROMAN FORUM · PALATINE HILL RUINS · CIRCUS MAX. · VIA FLAM. · ESPAGNA · SPAN. STEPS · VIA DEL BAB. · PANTHEON · CAP. HILL · TO TESTACCIO · EUR · PIAZZA DEL POPOLO · CORSO · VIA COND. · PIAZZA COLONNA · PIAZZA ROT. · EMAN. · VIA EM. MON. · PIAZZA VEN. · VIA DEL CORSO · P. PAL. · PIAZZA BELLI · T I B E R · VIA P. CAVOUR · VIA DI RIPETTA · CORSO V. EMAN. · LARGO ARG. · VITTORIO · CORONARI · PIAZZA NAVONA · VIA LUNG. · S. MARIA · TRASTEVERE · VIA CRESCENZIO · PIAZZA CAVOUR · PUMP. · CAMPO FIORI · PZA. FARNESE · LUNGO - TEVERE · VIA SISTO · VIA CESARE GIULIO · LEPANTO · OTTAVIANO · PIAZZA RISORGIMENTO · VIA CONC. · CASTEL S. ANG. · GIANICOLO · VIA AURELIA · VIA OTTAVIANO · VIA DORIA · ANDREA LEONE · CANDIA · VIA IV · VIA CONC. · CAVALLEGGERI · VIA MURA · AURELIA · CIPRO - MUSEI VATICANI · VIA PISANI · VIALE VATICANO · MUSEUM VATICAN CITY · ST. PETER'S · VIA MILITE · 400 · 0 M · 0 YDS · N periodical entertainment guide for evening events and fun. All hotels list an inflated rate to cover the hefty commission any TI room-finding service charges. Save money by booking direct.

Smaller TIs (daily 9:00–18:00) include kiosks near the entrance to the Forum (on Piazza del Tempio della Pace), at Via del Corso (on Largo Goldoni), in Trastevere (on Piazza Sonnino), on Via Nazionale (at Palazzo delle Esposizioni), at Castel Sant' Angelo, and at San Giovanni in Laterano. For more information, call 06-3600-4399 (daily 9:00–19:00, www.comune.roma.it, www.informaroma.it).

Roma c'è is a cheap little weekly entertainment guide with a helpful English section (at the back) on musical events and the pope's schedule for the week (new edition every Thu, sold at newsstands for L2,000, www.romace.it, Web site in Italian). Fancy hotels carry a free English monthly, *Un Ospite a Roma* (A Guest in Rome).

Arrival in Rome

By Train: Rome's main train station, Termini, is a minefield of tourist services: a TI (daily 8:00–21:00, off-season 9:00–20:00), train info office (daily 7:00–21:45), ATMs, late-hours banks, public showers (downstairs), luggage lockers (near track 24), 24-hour thievery, a pharmacy (daily 7:30–22:00, downstairs, at west end of station), the main city-bus hub (in front of train station), a subway stop, a grocery (oddly named "Drug Store," daily 7:00–24:00, downstairs), and the handy, cheery Chef Express Self-Service Ristorante (daily 11:00–22:30, easy WC at entrance, near east end of station; although there are several Chef Express bars scattered throughout station, the most comfortable is this sit-down Ristorante). The closest Internet point is downstairs near Dunkin Donuts (Thenetgate, daily 6:00–23:30, cheapest to buy a L10,000 60-minute card, can return or use at branches at Trevi Fountain or Vatican). The station has some sleazy sharks with official-looking cards. In general, avoid anybody selling anything at the station if you can.

Most of my hotel listings are easily accessible by foot (those near the train station) or by Metro (those in the Colosseum and Vatican neighborhoods). The train station has its own Metro stop (Termini).

By Plane: If you arrive at the airport, catch a train (hrly, 30 min, L16,000) to Rome's train station or take (or share) a taxi to your hotel. For details, see "Transportation Connections," below.

Helpful Hints

Plan Ahead: The marvelous Borghese Gallery and Nero's Golden House both require reservations. For the Borghese Gallery, it's safest to make reservations well in advance before your trip. You can wait until you're in Rome to call for a reservation time at

Nero's Golden House, though it's wise to book farther ahead. For specifics on these museums, look in "Sights," below.

Museums: Outdoor sights like the Colosseum, the Forum, and Ostia Antica are open roughly 9:00 to 18:00. The Vatican Museum is closed on Sunday (except for last Sun of month when it's free and crowded), some sights close early on Sunday (such as the Pantheon and E.U.R.'s Museum of Roman Civilization), and some close all day Monday (National Museum of Rome, Borghese Gallery, Capitol Hill Museum, Castel Sant' Angelo, Ostia Antica, and more). Some museums stay open later in summer (usually on Sat). The helpful TI booklet, *Tesori di Roma*, has a current listing of museum hours, or check the last pages of the daily *Messaggero* newspaper. On holidays, expect shorter hours or closures. Hours listed anywhere can vary. Confirm sightseeing plans each morning with a quick L200 telephone call asking, "Are you open today?" ("*Aperto oggi?*"; ah-PER-toh OH-jee) and "What time do you close?" ("*A che ora chiuso?*"; ah kay OH-rah kee-OO-zoh). I've included telephone numbers for this purpose.

A combo ticket—covering the National Museum of Rome, Colosseum, Palatine Hill, and Baths of Caracalla—which was offered in 2000 may be offered again in 2001 (around L30,000, basically allows you to see 4 sights for price of 3, purchase at participating sites, valid for 5 days).

Churches: Churches generally open early (around 7:00), close for lunch (roughly 12:00–15:00), and close late (around 19:00). Kamikaze tourists maximize their sightseeing hours by visiting churches before 9:00 and seeing the major sights that stay open during the siesta (St. Peter's, Colosseum, Forum, Capitol Hill Museum, National Museum of Rome) while Romans are taking it cool and easy. Many churches have "modest dress" requirements, which means no bare shoulders, miniskirts, or shorts—for men or women. This dress code is strictly enforced at St. Peter's (elsewhere you'll see many tourists in shorts touring many churches).

Shops: Shops are usually open 9:00 to 13:00 and 16:00 to 19:00. Grocery stores are often closed on Sunday. While the summer break is not what it used to be, during the holiday month of August many shops and restaurants still close up for vacation, and "*Chiuso per ferie*" signs decorate locked doors all over town.

Travel Agencies: Your hotel can direct you to the nearest travel agency. Buy train tickets and get railpass-related reservations and supplements at travel agencies rather than dealing with the congested train station. The cost is usually the same as at the station (otherwise a minimal charge worth paying).

Books: The American Bookstore sells all the major guidebooks (Via Torino 136, Metro: Repubblica, tel. 06-474-6877).

Dealing with (and Avoiding) Problems

Theft Alert: With sweet-talking con artists meeting you at the station, well-dressed pickpockets on buses, and thieving gangs of children at the ancient sites, Rome is a gauntlet of rip-offs. There's no great physical risk, but green tourists will be ripped off. Thieves strike when you're distracted. Don't trust kind strangers. Keep nothing important in your pockets. Assume you're being stalked. (Then relax and have fun.) Be most on guard while boarding and leaving buses and subways. Thieves crowd the door, then stop and turn while others crowd and push from behind. The sneakiest thieves are well-dressed business men (generally with something in their hands); lately many are posing as tourists with Tevas, fanny packs, and cameras. Scams abound: Don't give your wallet to self-proclaimed "police" who stop you on the street, warn you about counterfeit (or drug) money, and ask to see your wallet.

If you know what to look out for, the gangs of children picking the pockets and handbags of naive tourists are no threat but an interesting, albeit sad, spectacle. Gangs of city-stained children (sometimes as young as 8–10 years old), too young to prosecute but old enough to rip you off, troll through the tourist crowds around the Colosseum, Forum, Piazza Repubblica, and train and Metro stations. Watch them target tourists who are overloaded with bags or distracted with a video camera. The kids look like beggars and hold up newspapers or cardboard signs to confuse their victims. They scram like stray cats if you're onto them. A fast-fingered mother with a baby is often nearby. The terrace above the bus stop near the Colosseum Metro stop is a fine place to watch the action and maybe even pick up a few moves of your own.

Reporting Losses: To report lost or stolen passports and documents or to file an insurance claim, you must file a police report (with Polizia at track 1 or with Carabinieri at track 20, also at Piazza Venezia). To replace a passport, file the police report, then go to your embassy (see below). To report lost traveler's checks, call your bank (Visa tel. 800-874-155, Thomas Cook/Mastercard tel. 800-872-050, American Express tel. 800-872-000; these toll-free 800 numbers are Italian, not American), then file a police report. To report stolen or lost credit cards, call the company (Visa tel. 800-877-232, Mastercard tel. 800-870-866, American Express tel. 800-874-333), then file a police report.

Embassies: United States (Mon–Fri 8:30–13:00, 14:00–17:30, Via Veneto 119, tel. 06-46741) and Canada (Via Zara 30, tel. 06-445-981).

Emergency Numbers: Police tel. 113. Ambulance tel. 118.

Hit and Run: Walk with extreme caution. Scooters don't need to stop at red lights, and even cars exercise what drivers call the "logical option" of not stopping if they see no oncoming traffic. As Vespa scooters become electric, they'll get quieter (hooray) but more dangerous for pedestrians. Follow locals like a shadow when you cross a street (or spend a good part of your visit stranded on curbs).

Staying/Getting Healthy: The siesta is a key to survival in summertime Rome. Lie down and contemplate the extraordinary power of gravity in the eternal city. I drink lots of cold, refreshing water from Rome's many drinking fountains (the Forum has three). There's a pharmacy (marked by a green cross) in every neighborhood, including a handy one in the train station (daily 7:30–22:00, located downstairs, at west end). A 24-hour pharmacy is on Piazza dei Cinquecento 51 (next to train station on Via Cavour, tel. 06-488-0019). Embassies can recommend English-speaking doctors. Consider MEDline, a 24-hour home medical service (tel. 06-808-0995, doctors speak English). Anyone is entitled to free emergency treatment at public hospitals. The hospital closest to the train station is Policlinico Umberto 1 (entrance for emergency treatment on Via Lancisi, translators available, Metro: Policlinico).

Getting around Rome

Sightsee on foot, by city bus, or by taxi. I've grouped your sightseeing into walkable neighborhoods.

Public transportation is efficient, cheap, and part of your Roman experience. It starts running around 5:30 and stops around 23:30, sometimes earlier. After midnight there are a few very crowded night buses, and taxis become more expensive and hard to get. Don't try to hail one—go to a taxi stand.

Buses and subways use the same ticket. You can buy tickets at newsstands, tobacco shops, or at major Metro stations or bus stops, but not on board (L1,500, good for 75 minutes—one Metro ride and unlimited buses); all-day bus/Metro passes cost L6,000 (for more info, visit www.atac.roma.it).

Buses (especially the touristic #64) and the subway are havens for thieves and pickpockets. Assume any commotion is a thief-created distraction.

By Subway: The Roman subway system (Metropolitana) is simple, with two clean, cheap, fast lines. While much of Rome is not served by its skimpy subway, these stops are helpful: Termini (train station, National Museum of Rome at Palazzo Massimo, recommended hotels), Repubblica (Baths of Diocletian/Octagonal Hall, main TI, recommended hotels), Barberini (Cappuccin Crypt, Trevi Fountain), Spagna (Spanish Steps, Villa Borghese, classy shopping area), Flaminio (Piazza del Popolo, start of recommended Via del Corso Dolce Vita stroll), Ottaviano (St. Peter's and Vatican City), Cipro-Musei Vaticani (Vatican Museum, recommended hotels), Colosseo (Colosseum, Roman Forum, recommended hotels), and E.U.R. (Mussolini's futuristic suburb).

Metropolitana: Rome's Subway

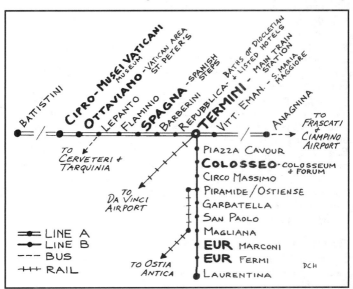

By Bus: Bus routes are clearly listed at the stops. Punch your ticket in the orange stamping machine as you board—or you are cheating. Riding without a stamped ticket on the bus, while relatively safe, is stressful. Inspectors fine even innocent-looking tourists L100,000. If you hop a bus without a ticket, locals who use tickets rather than a monthly pass can sell you a ticket from their wallet bundle. Ideally buy a bunch of tickets so you can hop a bus without first having to search for an open tobacco shop.

Learn which buses serve your neighborhood. Here are a few worth knowing about:

#64: Termini (train station), Piazza della Repubblica, Via Nazionale (recommended hotels), Piazza Venezia (near Forum), Largo Argentina (near Pantheon), St. Peter's Basilica. Ride it for a city overview and to watch pickpockets in action (can get horribly crowded).

#8: This tram connects Largo Argentina with Trastevere (get off at Piazza Mastai).

Electrico #116: Through the medieval core of Rome from Campo de' Fiori to Piazza Barberini via the Pantheon (runs daily except Sun).

By Taxi: Taxis start at about L5,000 (surcharges of L2,000 on Sun, L5,000 for night hours of 22:00–7:00, L2,000 surcharge for luggage, L14,000 extra for airport, tip about 10 percent by rounding up to the nearest thousand lire). Sample fares: Train station to Vatican-L16,000; train station to Colosseum-L10,000; Colosseum to Trastevere-L12,000. Three or four companions with more money than time should taxi almost everywhere. It's tough to wave down a taxi in Rome. Find the nearest taxi stand. (Ask a local or in a shop "*Dov'è* [DOH-vay] *una fermata dei tassi*?" Some are listed on my maps.) Unmarked, unmetered taxis at train stations and the airport are usually a rip-off. Taxis listing their telephone number on the door have fair meters—use them. To save time and energy, have your hotel call a taxi; the meter starts when the call is received. (Some Rome cab telephone numbers: 06-6645, 06-8822, and 06-3570.)

Tours of Rome

Scala Reale—Tom Rankin (an American architect in love with Rome and his Roman wife) runs Scala Reale, a company committed to sorting out the rich layers of Rome for small groups with a longer-than-average attention span. Their excellent walking tours vary in length from two to four hours and start at L30,000 per person. Try to book in advance since their groups are limited to six and fill up fast. Their fascinating "Rome Orientation" walks lace together lesser-known sights from antiquity to the present, helping you get a sense of how Rome works (U.S. tel. 888/467-1986, Italy tel. 06-445-1477, www.scalareale.org, e-mail: info@scalareale.org.

Through Eternity—This company offers four tours, all led by native English speakers with relevant university degrees and an emphasis on storytelling: St. Peter's and Vatican Museum (L50,000, museum entry not included, 5.5 hrs, daily except Sun, meet at 10:00 at Piazza Pio XII); Colosseum and Roman Forum (L30,000, 2.5 hrs, starts daily at 13:00 at Arch of Constantine); Rome at Twilight (L30,000, starts nightly at 19:00 at fountain at base of Spanish Steps); and a Wine Sampling Tour (L30,000, nightly at 19:00 at central fountain in Piazza Navona). Confirm details and book in advance (max of 25 people, tel. 06-700-9336, cellular 0347-336-5298, private tours possible, www.througheternity.com).

Walks of Rome—Students working for "Walks of Rome" give free 45-minute tours of the Colosseum in order to promote their other guided walks. The tours bring the Colosseum to life and they hope you'll join—and pay for—their other walks: Ancient City (L30,000, 2 hrs), Vatican City (L50,000/full day of St. Peter's/Vatican Museum; L30,000 for just Vatican Museum Tour), Roman Sunset (L30,000, great Renaissance and Baroque squares, nightly at 19:00), and Catacombs (L50,000, 3 hrs, by bus with some of the city included). Admissions cost extra. Their pub crawl tours meet at 20:00 at the Spanish Steps (March–Sept) and at the Colosseum Metro stop (year-round) and finish at a disco six pubs later around midnight. I've never seen 50 young, drunk people having so much fun (tel. 06-484-853 or cellular 0347-795-5175, private tours possible, www.walksofeurope.com, e-mail: walkingtours@yahoo.com).

Hop-on Hop-off Bus Tour—The ATAC city bus tour offers your best budget orientation tour of Rome. In 1.75 hours you'll have 80 sights pointed out to you (by a live guide in English and maybe one other language) and have a chance to get out at nine different stops and catch a later bus. The stops are: Piazza Barberini, Via Veneto, Villa Borghese, Piazza Cavour, St. Peter's Square, Corso Vittorio Emanuele (for Piazza Navona), Piazza Venezia, Colosseum, and Via Nazionale (L15,000, bus #110 departs every 30 minutes—at top and bottom of hour, runs 9:00–20:00 March–Sept, 10:00–18:00 Oct–Feb, departs from front of station, near platform C, buy tickets at info kiosk there—marked "i metro," tel. 06-4695-2252). Avoid their unprofessional competitor, Stop 'n' Go, which runs only at whim.

Sights—From the Colosseum Area to Capitol Hill

▲**St. Peter-in-Chains Church (San Pietro in Vincoli)**—Built in the fifth century to house the chains of St. Peter, this church is most famous for its Michelangelo statue. Check out the much-venerated chains under the high altar and then focus on *Moses* (free, but pop in L500 to light the statue, Mon–Sat 7:00–12:30, 15:30–19:00, Sun 7:30–12:30, a short 5- to 10-minute walk uphill from Colosseum; modest dress required).

Pope Julius II commissioned Michelangelo to build a massive tomb with 48 huge statues crowned by a grand statue of this egomaniac pope. When Julius died, the work had barely started, and no one had the money or concern for Julius to finish the project. Michelangelo finished one statue, *Moses*, and left a few unfinished statues: *Leah* and *Rachel* flanking *Moses* in this church, the *Prisoners* now in Florence's Accademia, and the *Slaves* now in Paris' Louvre. Study the powerful statue; it's mature Michelangelo. He worked on it in fits and starts for thirty years. Moses has received the Ten Commandments. As he holds the stone tablets, his eyes show a man determined to stop his tribe from worshiping the golden calf and idols...determined to win salvation for the people of Israel. Why the horns? Centuries ago, the Hebrew word for "rays" was mistranslated as "horns."

▲▲**Nero's Golden House (Domus Aurea)**—The remains of Emperor Nero's "Golden House" were recently opened to the public. Nero's huge house used to sprawl across the valley where the Colosseum now stands. Nero was your quintessential bad emperor: killed his mother and crucified St. Peter. The story goes that he fiddled while Rome burned in A.D. 64; Romans suspected he started the fires to clear land for an even bigger house. While only hints of the splendid colored frescoes survive, the towering vaults and basic immensity of the place is impressive. As you wander, look up at the holes in the ceiling and imagine how much of Rome hides underground . . . and why the subway is limited to two lines.

Visits are allowed only with an escort (25 people every 15 minutes) and a reservation (L12,000, Wed–Mon 9:00–19:45, last entry at 18:45, closed Tue, tour lasts 45 min, escort speaks Italian, audioguides-L3,000, 200 meters northeast of Colosseum, through a park gate, up a hill and on the left). To reserve a place, call 06-3996-7700. If you just show up (particularly on a late afternoon on a weekday), you could luck out and get on a tour; if tours aren't booked up, the remaining seats are sold to drop-ins.

▲▲**Colosseum**—This 2,000-year-old building is the great example of Roman engineering. Using concrete, brick, and their trademark round arches, Romans constructed much larger buildings than the Greeks. But in deference to the higher Greek culture, notice how they finished their no-nonsense megastructure by pasting all three orders of Greek columns (Doric, Ionic, and Corinthian) as exterior decorations. The Flavian Amphitheater's popular name, "Colosseum," comes from the colossal statue of Nero that once stood in front of it.

Romans were into "big." By putting two theaters together, they created a circular amphitheater. They could fill and empty its 50,000 numbered seats as quickly and efficiently as we do our superstadiums. Teams of sailors hoisted canvas awnings over the stadium to give fans shade. This was where ancient Romans, whose taste for violence was the equal of modern America's, enjoyed their Dirty Harry and *Terminator*. Gladiators, criminals, and wild animals fought to the death in every conceivable scenario. The floor of the Colosseum is missing, exposing underground passages. Animals in cages were kept here and then lifted up in elevators; they'd pop out from behind blinds into the arena. The gladiator didn't know where, when, or by what he'd be attacked.

Cost, Hours, Tours: L10,000, daily 9:00–19 00, off-season 9:00–15:00 (public WC is behind Colosseum, face ticket entrance and go right—WC under stairway; Metro: Colosseo, tel. 06-3974-9907). As you stand in the ticket line, students may offer you a free tour. The tours are good (and free because they'll try to get you to pay for their other tours—see "Tours of Rome," above). The stairs to the upper level are near the exit (west end). Beware of young pickpockets—ragged children carrying cardboard or newspapers—between the Colosseum and its Metro stop (see "Theft Alert," above).

▲**Arch of Constantine**—The well-preserved arch that stands between the Colosseum and the Forum commemorates a military coup and, more important, the acceptance of Christianity in the

The Forum Area

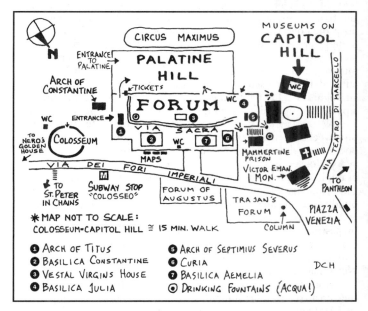

1 ARCH OF TITUS
2 BASILICA CONSTANTINE
3 VESTAL VIRGINS HOUSE
4 BASILICA JULIA

5 ARCH OF SEPTIMIUS SEVERUS
6 CURIA
7 BASILICA AEMELIA
⊙ DRINKING FOUNTAINS (ACQUA!)

DCH

Roman Empire. In A.D. 312, Emperor Constantine (who had a vision he could win under the sign of the cross) defeated his rival Maxentius. Constantine promptly legalized Christianity.

▲▲▲**Roman Forum (Foro Romano)**—Ancient Rome's birthplace and civic center, the Forum was the common ground between Rome's famous seven hills (free admission to Forum, L12,000 for Palatine Hill, both keep the same hours: daily 9:00–19:30 or an hour before dark, off-season 9:00–15:00, Metro: Colosseo, tel. 06-3974-9907).

To help resurrect this confusing pile of rubble, study the before-and-after pictures in the cheap city guidebooks sold on the streets. (Check out the small red *Rome, Past and Present* books with plastic overlays to un-ruin the ruins. They're priced at L20,000—pay no more than L15,000.) With the help of the map in this section, follow this basic walk (assuming you enter from the Colosseum side near the Arch of Constantine):

1. Start by the small **Arch of Titus** (drinking fountain opposite) overlooking the remains of what was the political, social, and commercial center of the Roman Empire. The Via Sacra—the main street of ancient Rome—cuts through the Forum from here to Capitol Hill and the Arch of Septimius Severus on the opposite side. On the left a ticket booth welcomes you to the Palatine Hill (described below)—once filled with the palaces of Roman emperors. Study the Arch of Titus—carved with propaganda celebrating the A.D. 70 defeat of the Jews, which began the Diaspora that ended with the creation of Israel in 1947. Notice the gaggle of soldiers carrying the menorah.

2. Ahead of you on the right are the massive ruins of the **Basilica of Constantine.** Follow the path leading there from the Via Sacra. Only the giant barrel vaults remain, looming crumbly and weed eaten. As you stand in the shadow of the Basilica of Constantine, reconstruct it in your mind. The huge barrel vaults were just side niches. Extend the broken nub of an arch out over the vacant lot and finish your imaginary Roman basilica with rich marble and fountains. People it with plenty of toga-clad Romans. Yeow.

3. Next hike past the semicircular Temple of Vesta to the **House of the Vestal Virgins.** Here, the VVs kept the eternal flame lit. A set of ponds and a marble chorus line of Vestal Virgins mark the courtyard of the house.

4. The grand **Basilica Julia,** a first-century law court, fills the corner opposite the Curia. Notice how the Romans passed their time; ancient backgammon-type game boards are cut into the pavement.

5. The **Arch of Septimius Severus,** from about A.D. 200, celebrates that emperor's military victories. In front of it a stone called Lapis Niger covers the legendary tomb of Romulus. To the left of the arch, the stone bulkhead is the Rostra, or speaker's platform. It's named for the ship's prows that used to decorate it as big shots hollered, "Friends, Romans, countrymen...."

6. The plain, intact brick building near the Arch of Septimius Severus was the **Curia,** where the Roman senate sat. (Peek inside.) Roman buildings were basically brick and concrete, usually with a marble veneer, which in this case is long lost.

7. The **Basilica Aemilia** (second century B.C.) shows the floor plan of an ancient palace. This pre-Christian "basilica" design was later adopted by medieval churches. From here a ramp leads up and out (past a WC and a fun headless statue to pose with). The entire area between here and Trajan's Column may eventually become an archeological park.

Palatine Hill—The hill above the Forum contains scanty remains of the Imperial palaces and the Roman Quadrata (Iron Age huts and the legendary house of Romulus—under corrugated tin roof in far corner). We get our word *palace* from this hill, where the emperors chose to live. The Palatine was once so filled with palaces that later emperors had to build out. (Looking up at it from the Forum you see the substructure that supported these long-gone palaces.) The newly opened Palatine museum has sculptures and fresco fragments but is nothing special. From the pleasant garden, you'll get an overview of the Forum. On the far side, look down into an emperor's private stadium and then beyond at the dusty Circus Maximus, once a chariot course. Imagine the cheers, jeers, and furious betting. But considering how ruined the ruins are, the heat, the hill to climb, the L12,000 entry fee, and the relative difficulty in understanding what you're looking at, the Palatine Hill is a disappointment (same hours as Forum, above).

▲**Mammertine Prison**—The 2,500-year-old cisternlike prison that once imprisoned saints Peter and Paul is worth a look. Stepping into the room you hit a modern floor. Erase that in your mind and look up at the hole in the ceiling through which prisoners were lowered. Then take the stairs down to the actual prison floor level. Imagine humans, amid rotting corpses, awaiting slow deaths. Then consider the legend of the saints baptizing the prisoners from a miraculous spring. On the walls near the entry are lists of notable prisoners (Christian and non-Christian) and how they were executed: *strangolati*, *decapitato*, *morto di fame*...(donation requested, daily 9:00–12:00, 14:30–18:00).

Leaving the prison, turn right and climb the stairs leading to Capitol Hill. Halfway up, you'll find a refreshing water fountain. Block the spout with your fingers; it spurts up for drinking. Romans, who call this *il nasone* (the nose), joke that cheap Roman boys take their dates out for a drink at *il nasone*.

▲▲**Capitol Hill (Campidoglio)**—This hill was the religious and political center of ancient Rome. It's still the home of the city's government. Michelangelo's Renaissance square is bounded by two buildings of the Capitol Hill Museum and the mayoral palace. Its centerpiece is a copy of the famous equestrian statue of Marcus Aurelius (the original is behind glass in the adjacent museum). To approach the great square the way Michelangelo wanted you to, walk halfway down the grand stairway toward Piazza Venezia, spin around, and walk back up. This was the new Renaissance face of Rome, with its back to the Forum and facing the new city. Notice how Michelangelo gave the buildings the "giant order," with huge pilasters making the existing two-story buildings feel one story and a more harmonious part of the new square. Notice also how the statues atop these buildings first welcome you and then draw you in. There's a fine view of the Forum from the terrace just past the mayor's palace (downhill on the right).

▲▲**Capitol Hill Museum**—This museum encompasses two buildings (Palazzo dei Conservatori and Palazzo Nuovo), connected by an underground passage that leads to the Tabularium and a panoramic overlook of the Forum (L12,000, free on last Sun of month, Tue–Sun 9:00–19:00, shorter hours off-season, last entry 60 min before closing, closed Mon, tel. 06-3996-7800 or 06-6710-2071).For an orientation to the museum's two buildings, face the equestrian statue on Capitol Hill Square (with your back to the grand stairway). The Palazzo Nuovo is on your left and the Palazzo dei

Conservatori is on your right (closer to the river). Ahead is the
mayor's palace (Palazzo Senatorio); below it and out of sight is
the Tabularium and underground passage.

You can buy your ticket at either building (but if you want
to rent an L7,000 audioguide, go to Palazzo dei Conservatori).

The **Palazzo dei Conservatori** is one of the world's oldest
museums, at 500 years old. Outside the entrance, notice the marriage announcements and, very likely, wedding-party photo ops.
Inside the courtyard, have a look at giant chunks of a statue of
Emperor Constantine; when intact, this imposing statue held
court in the Basilica of Constantine in the Forum. The museum
is worthwhile, with lavish rooms and several great statues. Tops
is the original (500 B.C.) Etruscan *Capitoline Wolf* (the little statues
of Romulus and Remus were added in the Renaissance). Don't
miss the *Boy Extracting a Thorn* or the enchanting *Commodus
as Hercules*. The second-floor painting gallery—except for two
Caravaggios—is forgettable. The café upstairs has a splendid
patio with city views (lovely at sunset).

Connect the two museums with the underground passage that
leads to the **Tabularium**. Built in the first century A.D., this once
held the archives of ancient Rome. The word *Tabularium* comes
from tablet, on which the Romans wrote their laws. You won't see
any tablets, but you will see a superb head-on view of the Forum
from the windows.

The **Palazzo Nuovo** houses mostly portrait busts of forgotten emperors. But it has three must-see statues: the *Dying Gaul*,
the *Capitoline Venus* (both on the first floor up), and the original
gilded bronze equestrian statue of Marcus Aurelius (behind glass
in museum courtyard). This greatest surviving equestrian statue
of antiquity was the original centerpiece of the square. While
most such pagan statues were destroyed by Dark Age Christians,
Marcus was mistaken as Constantine (the first Christian emperor)
and therefore spared.

From Capitol Hill to Piazza Venezia—Leaving Capitol Hill,
descend the stairs leading to Piazza Venezia. At the bottom of the
stairs, look left several blocks down the street to see a condominium
actually built around surviving ancient pillars and arches of Teatro
Marcello—perhaps the oldest inhabited building in Europe.

Still at the bottom of the stairs, look up the long stairway
to your right (which pilgrims climb on their knees) for a good
example of the earliest style of Christian church. While pilgrims
find it worth the climb, sightseers can skip it. As you walk toward
Piazza Venezia, look down into the ditch on your right and see
how everywhere modern Rome is built on the forgotten frescoes
and mangled mosaics of ancient Rome.

Piazza Venezia—This vast square is the focal point of modern Rome. The Via del Corso, starting here, is the city's axis,

surrounded by Rome's classiest shopping district. From the Palazzo Venezia's balcony above the square (to your left with back to Victor Emmanuel Monument), Mussolini whipped up the nationalistic fervor of Italy. Fascist masses filled the square screaming, "Four more years!" or something like that. (Fifteen years later, they hung him from a meat hook in Milan.)

Victor Emmanuel Monument—This oversized monument to an Italian king was part of Italy's rush to overcome the new country's strong regionalism and to create a national identity after unification in 1870. Romans think of it not as an altar of the fatherland but as "the wedding cake," "the typewriter," or "the dentures." It wouldn't be so bad if it weren't sitting on a priceless acre of ancient Rome. The good news is that it was recently opened to the public, offering a new city viewpoint. Soldiers guard Italy's Tomb of the Unknown Soldier as the eternal flame flickers. Stand directly in front of it and see how Via del Corso bisects Rome.

▲**Trajan's Column, Market, and Forum**—This offers the grandest column and best example of "continuous narration" from antiquity. Over 2,500 figures scroll around the 40-meter-high column telling of Trajan's victorious Dacian campaign (circa A.D. 103, in present-day Romania), from the assembling of the army at the bottom to the victory sacrifice at the top. The ashes of Trajan and his wife were held in the mausoleum at the base while the sun once glinted off a polished bronze statue of Trajan at the top. Today St. Peter is on top. Study the propaganda that winds up the column like a scroll, trumpeting Trajan's wonderful military exploits. You can view this close-up for free (it's just off Piazza Venezia, across the street from the Victor Emmanuel Monument). Viewing balconies once stood on either side, but it seems likely Trajan fans only came away with a feeling that the greatness of their emperor and empire was beyond comprehension (for a rolled-out version of the Column's story, visit the Museum of Roman Civilization at E.U.R., below). This column marked **Trajan's Forum**, built to handle the shopping needs of a wealthy city of over a million. Commercial, political, religious, and social activities all mixed in the Forum.

For a fee, you can go inside **Trajan's Market** and part of Trajan's Forum; the entrance is uphill from the column on Via IV Novembre. The market was once filled with shops selling goods from all over the Roman Empire (L12,000, summer Tue–Sun 9:00–18:30, winter 9:00–16:30, closed Mon).

Rome is in the slow process of excavating Trajan's Forum, closing down the busy street Via dei Fori Imperiali (controversial for the traffic problems this would create), and turning the entire area into a vast archaeological park.

Sights—Heart of Rome

▲▲▲**Pantheon**—For the greatest look at the splendor of Rome, antiquity's best-preserved interior is a must (free, Mon–Sat 9:00–18:30, Sun and holidays 9:00–13:00, tel. 06-6830-0230). Because it became a church dedicated to the martyrs just after the fall of Rome, the barbarians left it alone, and the locals didn't use it as a quarry. The portico is called Rome's umbrella—a fun local gathering in a rainstorm. Walk past its one-piece granite columns (biggest in Italy, shipped from Egypt) and through the original bronze doors. Sit inside under the glorious skylight and enjoy classical architecture at its best.

The dome, 47 meters (142 feet) high and wide, was Europe's biggest until the Renaissance. Michelangelo's dome at St. Peter's, while much higher, is one meter smaller. The brilliance of its construction astounded architects through the ages. During the Renaissance, Brunelleschi was given permission to cut into the dome (see the little square hole above and to the right of the entrance) to analyze the material. The concrete dome gets thinner and lighter with height—the highest part is volcanic pumice.

This wonderfully harmonious architecture greatly inspired Raphael and other artists of the Renaissance. Raphael, along with Italy's first two kings, chose to be buried here.

As you walk around the outside of the Pantheon, notice the "rise of Rome"—about 5 meters (15 feet) since it was built.

▲▲**Curiosities near the Pantheon**—The only Gothic church you'll see in Rome is **Santa Maria sopra Minerva**. On a little square behind the Pantheon to the east, past the Bernini statue of an elephant carrying an Egyptian obelisk, this Dominican church was built *sopra* (over) a pre-Christian temple of Minerva. Before stepping in, notice the high-water marks on the wall (right of door). Inside you'll see that the lower parts of the frescoes were lost to floods. (After the last great flood, in 1870, Rome built the present embankments, finally breaking the spirit of the Tiber River.)

Rome was at its low ebb, almost a ghost town, through much of the Gothic period. Little was built during this time (and much of what was built was redone Baroque). This church is a refreshing exception.

St. Catherine's body lies under the altar (her head is in Siena). In the 1300s, she convinced the pope to return from France to Rome, thus saving Italy from untold chaos.

Left of the altar stands a little-known Michelangelo statue, *Christ Bearing the Cross*. Michelangelo gave Jesus an athlete's or warrior's body (a striking contrast to the more docile Christ of medieval art) but left the face to one of his pupils. Fra Angelico's simple tomb is farther to the left, on the way to the back door. Before leaving, head over to the right (south transept), pop in a

Heart of Rome

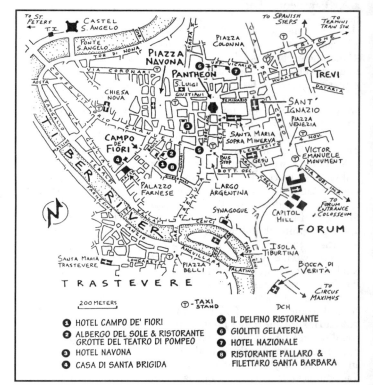

1. HOTEL CAMPO DE' FIORI
2. ALBERGO DEL SOLE & RISTORANTE
   GROTTE DEL TEATRO DI POMPEO
3. HOTEL NAVONA
4. CASA DI SANTA BRIGIDA
5. IL DELFINO RISTORANTE
6. GIOLITTI GELATERIA
7. HOTEL NAZIONALE
8. RISTORANTE PALLARO &
   FILETTARO SANTA BARBARA

L500 coin for light, and enjoy a fine Filippo Lippi fresco showing scenes from the life of St. Thomas Aquinas.

Exit the church via its rear door (behind the Michelangelo statue), walk down Fra Angelico lane (spy any artisans at work), turn left, and walk to the next square. On your right you'll find the **Chiesa di St. Ignazio** church, a riot of Baroque illusions. Study the fresco over the door and the ceiling in the back of the nave. Then stand on the yellow disk on the floor between the two stars. Look at the central (black) dome. Keeping your eyes on the dome, walk under and past it. Church building project runs out of money? Hire a painter to paint a fake, flat dome. (Both churches open early, take a siesta—Santa Maria sopra Minerva closes at 12:00, St. Ignazio at 12:30—reopen around 15:30, and close at 19:00. Modest dress is recommended.)

A few blocks away, back across Corso Vittorio Emanuele, is the rich and Baroque **Gesu Church**, headquarters of the

Jesuits in Rome. The Jesuits powered the Church's Counter-Reformation. While Protestants were teaching that all roads to heaven didn't pass through Rome, the Baroque churches of the late 1500s were painted with spiritual road maps that said they did.

Walk out the Gesu Church and two blocks down Corso V. Emanuele to the **Sacred Area** (Largo Argentina), an excavated square facing the boulevard, about four blocks south of the Pantheon. Walk around this square looking into the excavated pit at some of the oldest ruins in Rome. It was here that Caesar was assassinated. Today this is a refuge for cats. Some 250 cats are cared for by volunteers. You'll see them—and their refuge—at the far (west) side of the square.

Sights—Near the Train Station

These sights are within a three- to 10-minute walk northwest of the train station. By Metro, use the Piazza Repubblica stop for all of these sights except the National Museum of Rome and the Museum of the Bath (Metro: Termini).

▲▲▲**National Museum of Rome in Palazzo Massimo**—Rome's National Museum houses the greatest collection of ancient Roman art I've seen anywhere. The ground floor is a historic yearbook of marble statues from the second century B.C. to the second century A.D., with rare Greek originals.

The first floor is peopled by statues from the first through fourth centuries A.D. The second floor (which requires an appointment) contains frescoes and mosaics that once decorated the walls and floors of Roman villas. Finally, descend into the basement to see a mummified eight-year-old girl, fine gold jewelry, dice, an abacus, and vault doors leading into the best coin collection in Europe, with fancy magnifying glasses maneuvering you through cases of coins from ancient Rome to modern times.

Cost and Hours: L12,000, Tue–Sun 9:00–18:45, closed Mon, last entry 60 min before closing (L7,000 audioguide available at bookshop after you buy ticket). The second floor can be visited only with a guide (get time for 45-minute tour—in Italian—upon arrival, not possible to reserve in advance). The museum is about 100 meters from the Termini train station. As you leave the station, it's the sandstone-brick building on your left. Enter at the far end, at Largo di Villa Peretti (Metro: Termini, tel. 06-481-5576).

Baths of Diocletian—Around A.D. 300, Emperor Diocletian built the largest baths in Rome. This sprawling meeting place, with baths and schmoozing spaces to accommodate 3,000 bathers at a time, was a big deal in ancient Rome. While much of it is still closed, three sections are open: the Octagonal Hall, the Church of St. Mary of the Angels and Martyrs (both face Piazza della Repubblica), and the Museum of the Bath (across from the train station).

▲▲**Octagonal Hall**—The Aula Ottagona or Rotunda of Diocletian was a private gymnasium in the Baths of Diocletian. Built
around A.D. 300, these functioned until 537, when the barbarians
cut Rome's aqueducts. The floor would have been seven meters
lower (look down the window in the center of the room). The
graceful iron grid supported the canopy of a 1928 planetarium.
Today, the hall's a gallery, showing off fine bronze and marble
statues—the kind that would have decorated the baths of imperial
Rome. Most are Roman copies of Greek originals...gods,
athletes, portrait busts. Two merit a close look: the *Defeated
Boxer* (first century B.C., Greek and textbook Hellenistic) and
the *Roman Aristocrat*. The aristocrat's face is older than the body.
This cat-bronze statue is typical of the day: take a body modeled
on Alexander the Great and pop on a portrait bust. (Free, Tue–
Sat 9:00–14:00, Sun 9:00–13:00, closed Mon.)

▲**Church of St. Mary of the Angels and Martyrs (Santa Maria
degli Angeli e dei Martiri)**—From Piazza della Repubblica, step
through the Roman wall into what was the great central hall of the
baths and is now a church (since the 16th century) designed by
Michelangelo. When the church entrance was moved to Piazza
Repubblica, the church was reoriented 90 degrees, turning the
nave into long transepts and the transepts into a short nave.
The 12 red granite columns still stand in their ancient positions.
The classical floor was 15 feet lower. Project the walls down and
imagine the soaring shape of the Roman vaults.

**Museum of the Bath (Museo Nazionale Romano—Terme di
Diocleziano)**—This newly opened museum, located on the grounds
of the ancient Baths of Diocletian, has a misleading name. Rather
than featuring the Baths, it displays ancient Roman inscriptions on
tons of tombs, steles, and tablets. Although well displayed and
described in English, the museum is difficult to appreciate quickly,
and most travelers will find more history presented on a grander
scale in the National Museum of Rome a block away (L8,000,
Tue–Sun 9:00–19:45, closed Mon, audioguide-L7,000—confirm it's
in English, Viale E. De Nicola 79, entrance faces Termini station,
tel. 06-488-0530).

▲**Santa Maria Della Vittoria**—This church houses Bernini's
statue of a swooning *St. Theresa in Ecstasy* (free, daily 6:30–11:30,
16:30–19:00, Largo Susanna, about 5 blocks northwest of the
train station, Metro: Repubblica).

Sights—North Rome

▲**Villa Borghese**—Rome's unkempt "Central Park" is great
for people watching (plenty of modern-day Romeos and Juliets).
Take a row on the lake or visit its fine museums.

▲▲▲**Borghese Gallery** (Galleria Borghese)—This private
museum, filling a cardinal's mansion in the park, offers one of

Europe's most sumptuous art experiences. Because of the gallery's slick mandatory reservation system, you'll enjoy its collection of world-class Baroque sculpture, including Bernini's *David* and his exciting statue of Apollo chasing Daphne, as well as paintings by Caravaggio, Raphael, Titian, and Rubens, with manageable crowds.

The essence of the collection is the connection of the Renaissance with the classical world. Notice the second-century Roman reliefs with Michelangelo-designed panels above either end of the portico as you enter. The villa was built in the early 17th century by the great art collector Cardinal Borghese, who wanted to prove that the glories of ancient Rome were matched by the Renaissance.

In the main entry hall, opposite the door, notice the thrilling relief of the horse falling (first century A.D., Greek). Pietro Bernini, father of the famous Bernini, completed the scene by adding the rider.

Each room seems to feature a Baroque masterpiece. The best of all is in Room 3: Bernini's Apollo chasing Daphne. It's the perfect Baroque subject—capturing a thrilling, action-filled moment. In the mythological story, Apollo races after Daphne. Just as he's about to reach her, she turns into a tree. As her toes turn to roots and branches spring from her fingers, Apollo is in for one rude surprise. Walk slowly around. It's more air than stone.

Cost, Hours, Reservations: L14,000, Tue–Sun 9:00–21:00, maybe until 23:00 on Sat June–Sept, closed Mon. No photos are allowed.

Reservations are mandatory and easy to get in English over the Internet (www.ticketeria.it) or by phone: call 06-32810 (if you get an Italian recording, press 2 for English; office hours: Mon–Fri 9:00–19:00, Sat 9:00–13:00, office closed Sat in Aug). Every two hours, 360 people are allowed to enter the museum. Entry times are 9:00, 11:00, 13:00, 15:00, 17:00, and 19:00 (plus 21:00 on Sat). Reserve a minimum of several days in advance for a weekday visit, at least a week ahead for weekends. When you reserve, request a day and time (which you'll be given if available), and you'll get a claim number. While you'll be advised to come 30 minutes before your appointed time, you can arrive a few minutes beforehand, but don't be late as no-show tickets are given to standbys.

Visits are strictly limited to two hours. Concentrate on the first floor but leave yourself 30 minutes for the paintings of the Pinacoteca upstairs; highlights are marked by the audioguide icons. The fine bookshop and cafeteria are best visited outside your two-hour entry window.

If you don't have a reservation, just show up (or call first and ask if there are openings; a late afternoon on a weekday is usually your best bet). Reservations are tightest at 11:00 and on weekends. No-shows are released a few minutes after the top of the hour.

Generally out of 360 reservations a few will fail to show (but more than a few may be waiting to grab those spots).

Tours: Guided English tours are offered at 9:10 and 11:10 for L8,000; reserve with entry reservation (or consider the excellent audioguide tour-L8,000).

Location: The museum is in the Villa Borghese park. A taxi (tell the cabbie your destination: gah-leh-REE-ah bor-GAY-zay) can get you within 100 meters of the museum. Otherwise, Metro to Spagna and take a 15-minute walk through the park.

▲**Cappuccin Crypt**—If you want bones, this is it. It's below the church Santa Maria della Immaculata Concezione on Via Veneto, just off Piazza Barberini. The bones of over 4,000 monks who died between 1528 and 1870 are in the basement, all artistically arranged for the delight—or disgust—of the always-wide-eyed visitor. The soil in the crypt was brought from Jerusalem 400 years ago, and the monastic message on the wall explains that this is more than just a macabre exercise. Pick up a few of Rome's most interesting postcards (donation, Fri–Wed 9:00–12:00, 15:00–18:00, closed Thu, Metro: Barberini). A painting of St. Francis by Caravaggio is upstairs. Just up the street you'll find the American embassy, Federal Express, and fancy Via Veneto cafés filled with the poor and envious looking for the rich and famous.

Castel Sant' Angelo—Built as a tomb for Emperor Hadrian; used through the Middle Ages as a castle, prison, and place of last refuge for popes under attack; and hosting a museum today, this giant pile of ancient bricks is packed with history (L10,000, Tue–Sun 9:00–20:00, closed Mon, Metro: Lepanto or bus #64, near Vatican City, tel. 06-681-9111).

Sights—Vatican City

This tiny independent country of just over 100 acres, contained entirely within Rome, has its own postal system, armed guards, helipad, mini–train station, and radio station (KPOP). Politically powerful, the Vatican is the religious capital of 800 million Roman Catholics. If you're not one, become a Catholic for your visit.

Small as it is, Vatican City has two huge sights: St. Peter's Basilica and the Vatican Museum (with the Sistine Chapel). A helpful TI is just to the left of St. Peter's Basilica (Mon–Sat 8:30–18:30, closed Sun, tel. 06-6988-1662, Vatican switchboard tel. 06-6982, www.vatican.va; facing the church, WCs are to the right and left—near TI, and also on roof). Nearest Metro stops are still a 10-minute walk away from either sight: for St. Peter's, the closest stop is Ottaviano; for the Vatican Museum, it's Cipro-Musei Vaticani.

Post Office: The Vatican post, with an office in the Vatican Museum and one on St. Peter's Square, is more reliable than the Italian mail service (comfortable writing rooms,

Vatican City Overview

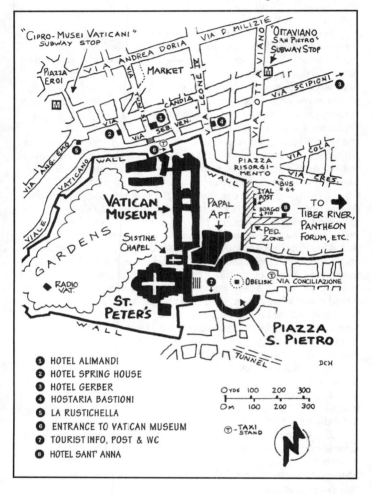

- ❶ HOTEL ALIMANDI
- ❷ HOTEL SPRING HOUSE
- ❸ HOTEL GERBER
- ❹ HOSTARIA BASTIONI
- ❺ LA RUSTICHELLA
- ❻ ENTRANCE TO VATICAN MUSEUM
- ❼ TOURIST INFO, POST & WC
- ❽ HOTEL SANT' ANNA

Mon–Fri 8:30–19:00, Sat 8:30–18:00). The stamps are a collectible bonus (Vatican stamps are good throughout Rome; Italian stamps are not good at the Vatican).

Tours: The Vatican TI conducts free 90-minute tours of St. Peter's (depart from TI at 15:00 on Mon, Wed, and Fri, no need to book ahead but do confirm schedule with TI, tel. 06-6988-1662). Tours of the Vatican Gardens offer the only way to see the gardens; book tours at least one day in advance by calling 06-6988-4466 (L17,000, Mon–Sat 10:00–12:00). For a tour of the necropolis of St. Peter's and the saint's tomb, fax the Excavations Office at 06-6988-5518 (L15,000, 2 hrs, office open Mon–Fri 9:00–17:00, tel. 06-6988-5318).

Seeing the Pope: Your best chances for a sighting are on Sundays and Wednesdays. Because he's a travelin' man, the following schedule can vary. The pope gives a blessing at noon on Sunday from his apartment on St. Peter's Square (except Aug–Sept when he speaks at his summer residence at Castel Gandolfo, 40 km from Rome; train leaves Rome's Termini station at 8:35, returns after his talk). On Wednesday at 10:00, the pope blesses the crowds at St. Peter's from a balcony or canopied platform on the square (except in winter, when he speaks at 11:00 in 7,000-seat Aula Paola VI Auditorium, next to St. Peter's Basilica). To find out the pope's schedule or to book a free spot for the Wednesday blessing (either for a seat on the square or in the auditorium), call 06-6988-3017. Smaller ceremonies celebrated by the pope require reservations. The weekly entertainment guide *Roma c'è* always has a "Seeing the Pope" section. If you don't want to see the pope, minimize crowd problems by avoiding these times.

▲▲▲**St. Peter's Basilica**—There is no doubt: This is the richest and most impressive church on earth. To call it vast is like calling God smart. Marks on the floor show where the next-largest churches would fit if they were put inside. The ornamental cherubs would dwarf a large man. Birds roost inside, and thousands of people wander about, heads craned heavenward, hardly noticing each other. Don't miss Michelangelo's *Pietà* (behind bullet-proof glass) to the right of the entrance. Bernini's altar work and seven-story-tall bronze canopy (*baldacchino*) are brilliant.

For a quick self-guided walk through the basilica, follow these points (see map on page 455):

1. The atrium is larger than most churches. Notice the historic doors (the Holy Door, on the right, won't be opened until the next Jubilee Year, in 2025—see point 13 below).

2. The purple circular porphyry stone marks the site of Charlemagne's coronation in A.D. 800 (in the first St. Peter's church that stood on this site). From here get a sense of the immensity of the church, which can accommodate 95,000 worshippers standing on its six acres.

3. Michelangelo planned a Greek-cross floor plan rather than the Latin-cross standard in medieval churches. A Greek cross, symbolizing the perfection of God, and by association the goodness of man, was important to the humanist Michelangelo. But accommodating large crowds was important to the Church in the fancy Baroque age, which followed Michelangelo, so the original nave length was doubled. Stand halfway up the nave and imagine the stubbier design Michelangelo had in mind.

4. View the magnificent dome from the statue of St. Andrew.

St. Peter's Basilica

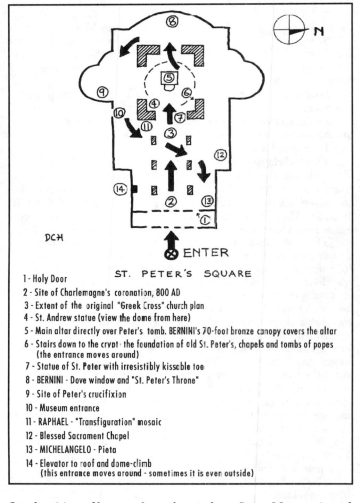

N

ST. PETER'S SQUARE

DCH

ENTER

1 - Holy Door
2 - Site of Charlemagne's coronation, 800 AD
3 - Extent of the original "Greek Cross" church plan
4 - St. Andrew statue (view the dome from here)
5 - Main altar directly over Peter's tomb. BERNINI's 70-foot bronze canopy covers the altar
6 - Stairs down to the crypt - the foundation of old St. Peter's, chapels and tombs of popes
    (the entrance moves around)
7 - Statue of St. Peter with irresistibly kissable toe
8 - BERNINI - Dove window and "St. Peter's Throne"
9 - Site of Peter's crucifixion
10 - Museum entrance
11 - RAPHAEL - "Transfiguration" mosaic
12 - Blessed Sacrament Chapel
13 - MICHELANGELO - Pieta
14 - Elevator to roof and dome-climb
    (this entrance moves around - sometimes it is even outside)

See the vision of heaven above the windows: Jesus, Mary, a ring of saints, rings of angels, and, on the very top, God the Father.

5. The main altar sits directly over St. Peter's tomb and under Bernini's 70-foot-tall bronze canopy.

6. The stairs lead down to the crypt to the foundation, chapels, and tombs of popes. (Do this last since it leads you out of the church.)

7. The statue of St. Peter, with an irresistibly kissable toe, is one of the few pieces of art that predate this church. It adorned the first St. Peter's church.

8. St. Peter's throne and Bernini's star-burst dove window is the site of a daily mass (Mon–Sat at 17:00, Sun at 17:45).

9. St. Peter was crucified here when this location was simply "the Vatican Hill." The obelisk now standing in the center of St. Peter's square marked the center of a Roman racecourse long before a church stood here.

10. For most, the treasury (in the sacristy) is not worth the admission.

11. The church is filled with mosaics, not paintings. Notice the mosaic version of Raphael's *Transfiguration*.

12. Blessed Sacrament Chapel.

13. Michelangelo sculpted his *Pietà* when he was 24 years old. A pietà is a work showing Mary with the dead body of Christ taken down from the cross. Michelangelo's mastery of the body is obvious in this powerfully beautiful masterpiece. Jesus is believably dead, and Mary, the eternally youthful "handmaiden" of the Lord, still accepts God's will…even if it means giving up her son.

The Holy Door (just to the right of the *Pietà*) was bricked shut at the end of the Jubilee Year 2000 and won't be opened until 2025. Every 25 years the Church celebrates an especially festive year derived from the Old Testament idea of the Jubilee Year (originally every 50 years), which encourages new beginnings and the forgiveness of sins and debts. In the Jubilee Year 2000, the pope tirelessly promoted debt relief for the Third World.

14. An elevator leads to the roof and the stairway up the dome. The dome, Michelangelo's last work, is (you guessed it) the biggest anywhere. Taller than a football field is long, it's well worth the sweaty climb for a great view of Rome, the Vatican grounds, and the inside of the basilica—particularly heavenly while there is singing. Look around—Rome has no modern skyline. No building is allowed to exceed the height of St. Peter's. The elevator takes you to the rooftop of the nave. From there a few steps take you to a balcony at the base of the dome looking down into the church interior. After that the one-way, 300-step climb (for some people claustrophobic) to the cupola begins.

The rooftop level (below the dome) has a gift shop, WC, drinking fountain, and a commanding view (L8,000 elevator, allow an hour to go up and down, May–Sept daily 8:30–18:00, Oct–April daily 8:30–17:00).

The church strictly enforces its dress code: no shorts or bare shoulders (men and women); no miniskirts. You might be required to check any bags at a free cloakroom near the entry.

Hours: St. Peter's is open daily May through September from 7:00 to 19:00, until 18:00 October through April (ticket booth to treasury closes 1 hour earlier). All are welcome to join in the hour-long mass at the front altar (Mon–Sat at 17:00, Sun at 17:45).

The church is particularly moving at 7:00, while tourism is still sleeping. Volunteers who want you to understand and appreciate St. Peter's give free 90-minute tours (3/week, see "Tours," above); these are generally excellent but non-Christians can find them preachy. Seeing the *Pietà* is neat; understanding it is divine.

▲▲▲**Vatican Museum**—Too often the immense Vatican Museum is treated as an obstacle course, with four nagging miles of displays separating the tourist from the Sistine Chapel. Even without the Sistine, this is one of Europe's top three or four houses of art. It can be exhausting, so plan your visit carefully, focusing on a few themes. Allow two hours for a quick visit, three or four for time to enjoy it. The museum has a nearly impossible-not-to-follow, one-way system (although, for the rushed visitor, the museum does clearly mark out 4 color-coded visits of different lengths—A is shortest, D longest).

Start, as civilization did, in Egypt and Mesopotamia. Next, the Pio Clementino collection features **Greek and Roman statues**. Decorating its courtyard are some of the best Greek and Roman statues in captivity, including the *Laocoön* group (1st century B.C., Hellenistic) and the *Apollo Belvedere* (a 2nd-century Roman copy of a Greek original). The centerpiece of the next hall is the *Belvedere Torso* (just a 2,000-year-old torso, but one that had a great impact on the art of Michelangelo). Finishing off the classical statuary are two fine fourth-century porphyry sarcophagi; these royal purple tombs hold the remains of Constantine's mother and daughter. Crafted in Egypt at a time when a declining Rome was unable to do such fine work, the details are fun to study.

After long halls of tapestries, old maps, broken penises, and fig leaves, you'll come to what most people are looking for: the Raphael Rooms (or *stanza*), and Michelangelo's Sistine Chapel.

These outstanding works are frescoes. A fresco (meaning "fresh" in Italian) is technically not a painting. The color is mixed into wet plaster, and, when the plaster dries, the painting is actually part of the wall. This is a durable but difficult medium, requiring speed and accuracy as the work is built slowly, one patch at a time.

After fancy rooms illustrating the "Immaculate Conception of Mary" (a hard-to-sell, 19th-century Vatican doctrine) and the triumph of Constantine (with divine guidance, which led to his conversion to Christianity), you enter the first room completely done by **Raphael** and find the newly restored *School of Athens*. This is remarkable for its blatant pre-Christian classical orientation wallpapering the apartments of Pope Julius II. Raphael honors the great pre-Christian thinkers—Aristotle, Plato, and company—who are portrayed as the leading artists of Raphael's day. The bearded figure of Plato is Leonardo da Vinci. Diogenes, history's first hippie, sprawls alone in bright blue on the stairs, while Michelangelo broods in the foreground—supposedly added late. Apparently Raphael snuck a peek at the Sistine Chapel and decided that his arch competitor was so good he had to put their personal differences aside and include him in this tribute to the artists of his generation. Today's St. Peter's was under construction as Raphael was working. In the *School of Athens*, he gives us a sneak preview of the unfinished church.

Next (unless you detour through the refreshingly modern Catholic art section) is the brilliantly restored **Sistine Chapel**. The Sistine Chapel, the pope's personal chapel, is where, upon the death of the ruling pope, a new pope is elected. The College of Cardinals meets here and votes four times a day until a two-thirds-plus-one majority is reached and a new pope is elected.

The Sistine is famous for Michelangelo's pictorial culmination of the Renaissance, showing the story of Creation, with a powerful God weaving in and out of each scene through that busy first week. This is an optimistic and positive expression of the High Renaissance and a stirring example of the artistic and theological maturity of the 33-year-old Michelangelo, who spent four years on this work.

Later, after the Reformation wars had begun and after the Catholic army of Spain had sacked the Vatican, the reeling Church began to fight back. As part of its Counter-Reformation, a much older Michelangelo was commissioned to paint the *Last Judgment* (behind the altar). Brilliantly restored, the message is as clear as the day Michelangelo finished it: Christ is returning, some will go to hell and some to heaven, and some will be saved by the power of the rosary.

In the recent and controversial restoration project, no paint was added. Centuries of dust, soot (from candles used for lighting and mass), and glue (added to make the art shine) were removed, revealing the bright original colors of Michelangelo. Photos are allowed (without a flash) elsewhere in the museum, but as part of the deal with the company who did the restoration, no photos are allowed in the Sistine Chapel.

For a shortcut, a small door at the rear of the Sistine Chapel allows tour groups and speedy individuals (without an audioguide) to escape directly to St. Peter's Basilica (ignore sign saying "Tour Groups Only"). If you squirt out here, you're done with the museum. The Pinacoteca is the only important part left. Consider doing it at the start. Otherwise it's a 10-minute, heel-to-toe slalom through tourists from the Sistine Chapel to the entry/exit.

After this long march to the entry/exit, you'll find the **Pinacoteca** (the Vatican's small but fine collection of paintings, with Raphael's *Transfiguration*, Leonardo's unfinished *St. Jerome*, and Caravaggio's *Deposition*), a cafeteria (long lines, mediocre food), and the underrated early-Christian-art section, before you exit via the souvenir shop.

Cost: L18,000, free on last Sunday of each month.

Hours: March–Oct Mon–Fri 8:45–16:45, Sat 8:45–13:45, Nov–Feb Mon–Sat 8:45–13:45, closed Sun except last Sun of the month (when it's free and open 8:45–13:45). The last entry is 75 minutes before closing time. The Sistine Chapel closes 30 minutes early. The museum is closed on many holidays, including: Jan 1 and 6, Feb 11, March 19, Easter and Easter Monday, May 1, Ascension Day, Corpus Christi, June 29, Aug 15 plus 14 or 16, Nov 1, Dec 8, 25, and 26.

It's generally hot and crowded. Saturday, the last Sunday of the month, and Monday are the worst; late afternoons are best. Modest dress (no short shorts or bare shoulders) is appropriate and often required.

Information: An information window is in the entry hall (look for "i" symbol; it's probably in the bank of windows to your left, under "Special Permits"; some English spoken). Also in the entry you'll find a book kiosk plus a bookshop just up the stairs (with other shops scattered throughout the museum). You can rent an audioguide (L10,000) after you buy your ticket. Tel. 06-6988-4947 or 06-6988-3333.

Sights—South Rome

Baths of Caracalla (Terme di Caracalla)—Today it's just a shell—a huge shell—with all of its sculptures and most of its mosaics moved to museums. Inaugurated by Emperor Caracalla in A.D. 216, this massive complex could accommodate 1,600 visitors at a time. Today you'll see a huge two-story, roofless brick building surrounded by a garden, bordered by ruined walls. The two huge rooms at either end of the building were used for exercise. In between the exercise rooms was a pool flanked by two small mosaic-floored dressing rooms. Niches in the walls once held statues. In its day, this was a remarkable place to hang out. For ancient Romans, the baths were a social experience.

The Baths of Caracalla functioned until Goths severed the aqueducts in the sixth century. In modern times, operas were held here from 1938 to 1993. For the same reason concerts no longer occur in the Forum—to keep the ruins from getting more ruined— operas were discontinued here (L8,000, Mon 9:00–14:00, Tue– Sun 9:00–19:15, ask if audioguides are available, fine L15,000 guidebook—can read in shaded garden while sitting on a chunk of column, Metro: Circus Maximus, and a 5-minute walk south along Via delle Terme di Caracalla). Look for Caracalla's statues in Rome's Octagonal Hall and Naples' Archaeological Museum.

E.U.R.—In the late 1930s, Italy's dictator, Mussolini, planned an international exhibition to show off the wonders of his fascist society. But the "wonders of fascism" brought us World War II first, and Il Duce's celebration never happened. Italy made the best of the unfinished mega-project, finishing it in the 1950s to house government offices and big obscure museums. If Hitler and Mussolini had won the war, our world might look like E.U.R. (pronounced "ai-oor"). From the Magliana subway stop, stairs lead uphill to E.U.R.'s skyscraper, the blocky **Palace of the Civilization of Labor** (Palazzo del Civilta del Lavoro). With its giant, no-questions-asked, patriotic statues and its black-and-white simplicity, this is the essence of fascist architecture. It's understandably nicknamed the "Square Colosseum."

The **Museum of Roman Civilization** (Museo della Civilta Romana) fills 59 rooms with plaster casts and models illustrating the greatness of classical Rome. It also has a scrolled-out version of Trajan's Column, but the highlight is the 1:250 scale model of Constantine's Rome—c. A.D. 300 (L8,000, Tue–Sat 9:00–18:45, Sun 9:00–13:30, closed Mon, Piazza G. Agnelli, Metro: E.U.R. Fermi, tel. 06-592-6041).

Sights—Near Rome
▲▲**Ostia Antica**—Rome's ancient seaport, less than an hour from downtown, is the next best thing to Pompeii. Ostia had 80,000 people at the time of Christ, later became a ghost town, and is now excavated. Start at the 2,000-year-old theater, buy a map, explore the town, and finish with its fine little museum (note that museum closes at 14:00). To get there take the subway's B Line to the Piramide stop and then catch the Lido train to Ostia Antica (2/hrly), walk over the overpass, go straight to the end of that road, and follow the signs to (or ask for) "*scavi* Ostia Antica" (L8,000, Tue–Sun 9:00–18:00 in summer, 9:00–16:00 in winter, closed Mon, museum closes at 14:00, tel. 06-5635-8099). Just beyond is Rome's filthy beach (*lido*).

Self-Guided Walks of Rome
▲▲▲**Floodlit Rome Hike: Trastevere to the Spanish Steps**—Rome can be grueling. But a fine way to enjoy this historian's rite of passage is an evening walk lacing together Rome's floodlit night spots. Enjoying fine urban spaces, observing real-life theater vignettes, sitting so close to a Bernini fountain that traffic noises evaporate, watching water flicker its mirror on the marble, jostling with local teenagers to see all the gelato flavors, enjoying lovers straddling more than the bench, jaywalking past flak-proof vested *polizia*, marveling at the ramshackle elegance that softens this brutal city for those who were born here and can imagine living nowhere else—these are the flavors of Rome best tasted after dark. This walk is about three kilometers (2 miles) long; for a shortcut, start at Campo de' Fiori.

Taxi or ride the bus (from Vatican area, take #23; from Via

Nazionale hotels, take #64, #70, #115, or #640 to Largo Argentina
and then transfer to #8) to Trastevere, the colorful neighborhood
across (*tras*) the Tiber (*tevere*) River.

Trastevere offers the best look at medieval-village Rome.
The action all marches to the chime of the church bells. Go to
Trastevere and wander. Wonder. Be a poet on Rome's Left Bank.
This proud neighborhood was long an independent working-
class area. Now becoming trendy, high rents are driving out the
source of so much color. Still, it's a great people scene, especially
at night. Start your exploratory stroll at Piazza di Santa Maria in
Trastevere. While today's fountain is 17th century, there's been a
fountain here since Roman times.

Santa Maria in Trastevere, one of Rome's oldest churches,
was made a basilica in the fourth century, when Christianity was
legalized (free, daily 7:30–13:00, 15:00–19:00). It was the first
church dedicated to the Virgin Mary. The portico (covered area
just outside the door) is decorated with fascinating ancient fragments filled with early Christian symbolism. Most of what you see
today dates from around the 12th century, but the granite columns
come from an ancient Roman temple, and the ancient basilica
floor plan (and ambience) survives. The 12th-century mosaics
behind the altar are striking and notable for their portrayal of
Mary—the first showing her at the throne with Jesus in heaven.
Look below the scenes from the life of Mary to see ahead-of-
their-time paintings (by Cavallini, from 1300) that predate the
Renaissance by 100 years.

Before leaving Trastevere, wander the back streets (if you're
hungry, see "Eating," below). Then, from the church square
(Piazza di Santa Maria), take Via del Moro to the river and cross
on Ponte Sisto, a pedestrian bridge with a good view of St. Peter's
dome. Continue straight ahead for one block. Take the first left,
which leads down Via di Capo di Ferro through the scary and narrow darkness to Piazza Farnese, with its imposing Palazzo Farnese.
Michelangelo contributed to the facade of this palace, now the
French embassy. The fountains of the square feature huge one-
piece granite hot tubs from the ancient Roman Baths of Caracalla.

One block from there (opposite the palace) is **Campo de' Fiori**
(Field of Flowers), which is my favorite outdoor dining room after
dark (see "Eating," below). The statue of Giordano Bruno, a heretic
who was burned in 1600 for believing the world was round and not
the center of the universe, marks the center of this great and colorful
square. Bruno overlooks a busy produce market in the morning and
strollers after dark. This neighborhood is still known for its free
spirit. When the statue of Bruno was erected in 1889, local riots
overcame Vatican protests against honoring a heretic. Bruno faces
his executioner, the Vatican Chancellory (the big white building in
the corner a bit to his right), while his pedestal reads: "And the

flames rose up." The square is lined and surrounded by fun eateries. Bruno also faces La Carbonara, which gave birth to pasta carbonara. The Forno, next door, is a popular place for hot and tasty take-out *pizza bianco* (plain but spicy pizza bread).

If Bruno did a hop, step, and jump forward and turned right and marched 200 meters, he'd cross the busy Corso Vittorio Emanuele and find **Piazza Navona**. Rome's most interesting night scene features street music, artists, fire eaters, local Casanovas, ice cream, outdoor cafés (splurge worthy if you've got time to sit and enjoy the human river of Italy), and fountains by Bernini, the father of Baroque art. The Tartufo "death by chocolate" ice cream (L5,500 to go, L12,000 at a table) made the Tre Scalini café (left of obelisk) world famous among connoisseurs of ice cream and chocolate alike. This oblong piazza is molded around the long-gone stadium of Domitian, an ancient chariot racetrack.

Leave Piazza Navona directly across from Tre Scalini café, go (east) past rose peddlers and palm readers, jog left around the guarded building, and follow the brown sign to the **Pantheon** straight down Via del Salvatore (cheap pizza place on left just before the Pantheon, easy WC at McDonald's). Sit for a while under the Pantheon's floodlit, moonlit portico.

With your back to the Pantheon, head right, passing Bar Pantheon on your right. The Tazza d'Oro Casa del Caffè, one of Rome's top coffee shops, dates back to the days when this area was licensed to roast coffee beans. Look back at the fine view of the Pantheon from here.

With the coffee shop on your right, walk down Via degli Orfani to Piazza Capranica, with the big plain Florentine Renaissance–style Palazzo Capranica. Big shots, like the Capranica family, built stubby towers on their palaces—not for any military use . . . just to show off. Leave the piazza to the right of the palace, between the palace and the church. Via in Aquiro leads to a sixth-century B.C. Egyptian **obelisk** (taken as a trophy by Augustus after his victory in Egypt over Mark Antony and Cleopatra). Walk into the guarded square past the obelisk and face the huge parliament building. A short detour to the left (past Albergo National) brings you to some of Rome's best gelato. Gelateria Caffè Pasticceria Giolitti is cheap to go or elegant, pricey, and worthwhile for a sit among classy locals (open daily until very late, your choice: cone or *bicchierini*—cup, Via Uffici del Vicario 40). Or head directly from the parliament into the next, even grander, square.

Piazza Colonna features a huge second-century column honoring Marcus Aurelius, the philosopher-emperor. The big, important-looking palace is the prime minister's residence. Cross Via del Corso, Rome's noisy main drag, and jog right (around the Y-shaped shopping gallery from 1928) and head down Via dei Sabini to the roar of the water, light, and people of the Trevi Fountain.

The **Trevi Fountain** is an example of how Rome took full advantage of the abundance of water brought into the city by its great aqueducts. This watery Baroque avalanche was built in 1762 by a pope celebrating his reopening of the ancient aqueduct that powers it. Romantics toss two coins over their shoulder thinking it will give them a wish and assure their return to Rome. That may sound silly, but every year I go through this touristic ritual...and it actually seems to work.

Take some time to people watch (whisper a few breathy *bello*s or *bella*s) before leaving. Facing the fountain, go past it on the right down Via delle Stamperia to Via del Triton. Cross the busy street and continue to the Spanish Steps (ask, *"Dov'è Piazza di Spagna?"*; doh-vay pee-aht-zah dee spahn-yah) a few blocks and thousands of dollars of shopping opportunities away.

The **Piazza di Spagna** (rhymes with "lasagna"), with the very popular Spanish Steps, got its name 300 years ago, when this was the site of the Spanish Embassy. It's been the hangout of many Romantics over the years (Keats, Wagner, Openshaw, Goethe, and others). The Boat Fountain at the foot of the steps, which was done by Bernini's father, Pietro Bernini, is powered by an aqueduct. (All of Rome's fountains are aqueduct powered; their spurt is determined by the water pressure provided by the various aqueducts. This one, for instance, is much weaker than Trevi's gush.) The piazza is a thriving night scene. Facing the steps, walk to your right about a block to tour one of the world's biggest and most lavish McDonald's. About a block on the other side of the steps is the Spagna Metro stop, which (usually until 23:30) will zip you home.

▲**The Dolce Vita Stroll down Via del Corso**—This is the city's chic and hip "cruise" from Piazza del Popolo (Metro: Flaminio) down a wonderfully traffic-free section of Via del Corso and up Via Condotti to the Spanish Steps each evening around 18:00 (Sat and Sun are best). Strollers, shoppers, and flirts on the prowl fill this neighborhood of Rome's most fashionable stores (open after siesta 16:30–19:30). Throughout Italy, early evening is time to stroll.

Start on **Piazza Popolo**. Historians: This area was once just inside medieval Rome's main entry. The delightfully car-free square is marked by an obelisk that was brought to Rome by Augustus after he conquered Egypt. (It once stood in the Circus Maximus.) The Baroque Church of **Santa Maria del Popolo**—with Raphael's Chigi Chapel (pron. kee-gee, third chapel on left) and two Caravaggio paintings (side paintings in chapel left of altar)—is next to the gate in the old wall, on the far side of Piazza del Popolo, to the right as you face the gate (church open Mon–Sat 7:00–12:00, 16:00–19:00, Sun 8:00–13:30, 16:30–19:30).

From Piazza del Popolo, shop your way down **Via del Corso**. To rest your feet, join the locals sitting on the steps of various churches along the street.

At Via Pontefici, historians turn right and walk a block to see the massive, rotting, round brick **Mausoleum of Augustus**, topped with overgrown cypress trees. Beyond it, next to the river, is Augustus' Ara Pacis, or Altar of Peace (due to reopen in 2001 . . . maybe).

From the mausoleum, return to Via del Corso and the 21st century, continuing straight until **Via Condotti**. Shoppers, take a left to join the parade to the **Spanish Steps**. The streets that parallel Via Condotti to the south (Borgogno and Frattini) are just as popular. You can catch a taxi home at the taxi stand a block south of the Spanish Steps (at Piazza Mignonelli, near American Express and McDonald's).

Historians: Ignore Via Condotti. Continue a kilometer down Via del Corso—straight since Roman times—to the Victor Emmanuel Monument. Climb Michelangelo's stairway to his glorious (especially when floodlit) square atop Capitol Hill and catch the lovely views of the Forum (from either side of the mayor's palace) as the horizon reddens and cats prowl the unclaimed rubble of ancient Rome.

Sleeping in Rome
(L2,000 = about $1, country code: 39)
Sleep Code: **S** = Single, **D** = Double/Twin, **T** = Triple, **Q** = Quad, **b** = bathroom, **t** = toilet only, **s** = shower only, **CC** = Credit Card (**V**isa, **M**asterCard, **A**mex), **SE** = Speaks English, **NSE** = No English. Breakfast is normally included in the expensive places.

The absolute cheapest doubles in Rome are L70,000, without shower or breakfast. You'll pay L30,000 in a backpacker-filled dorm or hostel. A nicer hotel (L240,000 with a bathroom and air-conditioning) provides an oasis and refuge, making it easier to enjoy this intense and grinding city. If you're going door to door, prices are soft—so bargain. Built into a hotel's official price list is a kickback for a room-finding service or agency; if you're coming direct, they pay no kickback and may lower the price for you. Many hotels have high-season (mid-March–June, Sept–Oct) and low-season prices. Room rates are lowest in sweltering August. Easter and September are most crowded and expensive. On Easter, April 25, and May 1, the entire city gets booked up.

Some of my recommended hotels are small, with huge, murky entrances that make you feel like a Q-Tip in a gas station. English works in all but the cheapest places. Traffic in Rome roars, so my challenge has been to find friendly places on quiet streets. With the recent arrival of double-paned windows and air-conditioning, night noise is not the problem it was. Even so, light sleepers should always ask for a *tranquillo* room. Many prices here are promised only to people who show this book and come direct without using a room-finding service.

Scala Reale, the company that runs tours (see "Tours of Rome," above), can help you find short-term accommodations if you contact them in advance (U.S. tel. 888/467-1986, Italy tel. 06-445-1477, www.scalareale.org, e-mail: info@scalareale.org).

Your hotel can point you to the nearest **Laundromat** (usually open daily 8:00–22:00, about L12,000 to wash and dry a 15-pound load). The Bolle Blu chain comes with Internet access (L8,000/hr, near train station at Via Milazzo 20, Via Palestro 59, and Via Principe 116, tel. 06-446-5804).

Sleeping on Via Firenze *(zip code: 00184)*

I generally stay on Via Firenze because it's tranquil, safe, handy, and central. It's a 10-minute walk from the central train station and airport shuttle, and two blocks beyond the Piazza della Repubblica and TI. The defense ministry is nearby, and you've got heavily armed guards all night. Virtually all the orange buses that rumble down Via Nazionale (#64, #70, #115, #640) take you to Piazza Venezia (Forum) and Largo Argentina (Pantheon). From Largo Argentina, #8 goes to Trastevere (first stop after crossing the river) and #64 (jammed with people and thieves) continues to St. Peter's.

Hotel Oceania is a peaceful slice of air-conditioned heaven. This nine-room manor house–type hotel is spacious and quiet, with newly renovated and spotless rooms, run by a pleasant father-and-son team (Sb-L190,000, Db-L240,000, Tb-L300,000, Qb-L355,000, these prices through 2001 with this book only, additional 20 percent off in Aug and winter, includes breakfast, phones, English newspaper, CC:VMA, Via Firenze 38, tel. 06-482-4696, fax 06-488-5586, www.hoteloceania.it, e-mail: hoceania@tin.it, son Stefano SE, dad Armando serves world-famous coffee).

Hotel Aberdeen is classier and more professional for about the same price. It has mini-bars, phones, and showers in its 36 modern, air-conditioned, and smoke-free rooms; includes a fine breakfast buffet; and is warmly run by Annamaria, with support from her cousins Sabrina and Cinzia, and trusty Reda riding shotgun after dark (Sb-L180,000, Db-L250,000, Tb-L300,000, Qb-L350,000, prices through 2001 with this book only, L60,000 less per room in Aug and winter, CC:VMA, garage-L40,000, Via Firenze 48, tel. 06-482-3920, fax 06-482-1092, check for deals on Web, www.travel.it/roma/aberdeen, e-mail: hotel .aberdeen@travel.it, SE).

Residence Adler, with its wide halls, garden patio, and eight quiet, elegant, and air-conditioned rooms in a great locale, is another good deal. It's run the old-fashioned way by a charming family (Db-L200,000, Tb-L280,000, Qb-L340,000, includes breakfast, prices through 2001 with this book only, CC:VMA, additional 5 percent off if you pay cash, elevator, Via Modena 5, tel. 06-484-466, fax 06-488-0940, NSE).

Rome's Train Station Neighborhood

1. HOTEL OCEANIA & NARDIZZI
2. HOTEL ABERDEEN
3. RESIDENCE ADLER
4. HOTEL REX
5. HOTEL BRITTANIA
6. HOTEL SONYA
7. HOTEL PENSIONE ITALIA
8. HOTEL CORTINA & CAFFETTERIA NAZIONALE
9. YWCA CASA STUDENTESSE
10. SUORE SANTA ELISABETTA
11. HOTEL MONTREAL
12. HOTEL FENICIA & MAGIC
13. ALBERGO SILEO
14. HOTEL DUCA D'ALBA
15. HOTEL GRIFO
16. SUORE DI SANT ANNA
17. SNACK BAR GASTRONOMIA
18. PASTICCERIA DAGNINO
19. HOSTARIA ROMANA
20. RISTORANTE GIOVANNI
21. PHARMACY
22. RIST. CINESE INT'L.
23. BEEHIVE HOSTEL
24. CASA OLMATA HOSTEL

Hotel Nardizzi Americana, with its 18 simple, pleasant, air-conditioned rooms and a rooftop terrace, is loosely run (Sb-L150,000, Db-L200,000, Tb-L240,000, Qb-L260,000, prices through 2001 with this book only, includes breakfast, discounts for off-season and long stays, CC:VMA, additional 10 percent off with cash, elevator, drinks available evenings, Via Firenze 38, tel. 06-488-0368, fax 06-488-0035, SE).

Hotel Seiler is a quiet, serviceable place with 30 decent rooms (Sb-L160,000, Db-L230,000, Tb-L280,000, these discounted prices good only with this book, includes continental breakfast, CC:VMA, fans, elevator, Via Firenze 48, tel. 06-485-550, fax 06-488-0688, e-mail: acropoli@rdn.it, Silvio and Alessia SE).

Hotel Texas Seven Hills, a stark institutional throwback to the 1960s, rents 18 quiet but depressing rooms (D-L160,000, Db-L200,000, often soft prices, CC:VMA, air-con planned for 2001, Via Firenze 47, elevator, tel. 06-481-4082, fax 06-481-4079, e-mail: what's that?, NSE).

Sleeping between Via Nazionale and Basilica Santa Maria Maggiore

Hotel Pensione Italia, in a busy, interesting, handy locale, is placed safely on a quiet street next to the Ministry of the Interior. Thoughtfully run by English-speaking Andrea, Lena, and Alberico, it's comfortable, airy, clean, and bright (31 rooms, Sb-L130,000, Db-L180,000, Tb-L240,000, Qb-L280,000, includes breakfast, prices through 2001 with this book and cash only, all rooms 20 percent off in mid-July–Aug and winter, elevator, air-con for L15,000 extra, Via Venezia 18, just off Via Nazionale, 00184 Roma, tel. 06-482-8355, fax 06-474-5550, www.hotelitaliaroma .com, e-mail: hitalia@pronet.it). Their singles are all on the quiet courtyard and the nine annex rooms across the street are a cut above the rest.

Hotel Sonya is a small, family-run but impersonal place with 20 comfortable, well-equipped rooms, a great location, and low prices; reserve well in advance (Db-L220,000, Tb-L250,000, Qb-L290,000, CC:VMA, air-con, elevator, facing the Opera at Via Viminale 58, tel. 06-481-9911, fax 06-488-5678, Francesca SE).

Hotel Cortina rents 14 modern, air-conditioned rooms for a decent price on a busy street. Ask for a quieter room on the courtyard or side street (Db-L250,000, includes breakfast, CC:VMA, 10 percent discount with this book and cash only, Via Nazionale 18, 00184 Roma, tel. 06-481-9794, fax 06-481-9220, www.travel.it/roma/hotelcortina, John Carlo and Angelo SE).

YWCA Casa Per Studentesse accepts men and women. It's an institutional place, filled with white-uniformed maids, more-colorful Third World travelers, and 75 single beds. It's closed from midnight to 7:00; in case of an emergency, a live-in

manager can let people out, but not in (L50,000 per person in 3-
and 4-bed rooms, S-L70,000, Sb-L90,000, D-L120,000, Db-
L140,000, includes breakfast except on Sun, elevator, Via C. Balbo
4, 00184 Roma, tel. 06-488-0460, fax 06-487-1028). The YWCA
faces a great little street market.

Suore di Santa Elisabetta is a heavenly Polish-run convent
booked long in advance, but it's an incredible value (Sb-L63,000,
Db-L115,000, Tb-L148,000, Qb-L180,000, includes breakfast,
CC:VM, elevator, fine view roof terrace, a block southwest of
Basilica Santa Maria Maggiore at Via dell' Omata 9, tel. 06-488-
8271, fax 06-488-4066).

Hotel Montreal, run with care, is a bright, solid, business-
class place on a big street a block southeast of Santa Maria
Maggiore (Db-L220,000 most of year, L170,000 in July–Aug,
L150,000 in winter, CC:VMA, 21 of its 27 rooms have air-con,
elevator, good security, 1 block from Metro: Vittorio, 3 blocks
west of train station, Via Carlo Alberto 4, 00185 Roma, tel.
06-445-7797, fax 06-446-5522, www.hotelmontrealroma.com).

Splurges: Hotel Britannia stands like a marble fruitcake,
offering all the comforts in tight quarters on a quiet and safe-
feeling street. Lushly renovated with over-the-top classical motifs,
its 32 air-conditioned rooms are small but comfortable with bright,
modern bathrooms (Db-L430,000 in May–June and Sept–Oct,
Db-L275,00 in Aug, Db-L380,000 the rest of the year, extra
bed-L90,000, children up to 10 stow away for free, babysitting
service, CC:VMA, phones, TV, safes, mini-bar, free parking,
Via Napoli 64, 00184 Roma, tel. 06-488-3153, fax 06-488-2343,
e-mail: britannia@venere.it).

Hotel Rex is a business-class Art Deco fortress—a quiet,
plain, and stately four-star place with all the comforts (50 rooms,
Sb-L370,000, Db-L470,000, Tb-L550,000, CC:VMA, elevator,
air-con, some smoke-free rooms, 2 phones per room—next to bed
and toilet, 2 blocks south of Via Nazionale at Via Torino 149, tel.
06-482-4828, fax 06-488-2743, e-mail: hotel.rex@alfanet.it, SE).

Sleeping Cheap, Northeast of the Train Station

The cheapest hotels in town are northeast of the station.
Some travelers feel this area is weird and spooky after dark.
With your back to the train tracks, turn right and walk two
blocks out of the station.

Hotel Fenicia rents 11 comfortable, well-equipped rooms
at a fine price. Their bigger rooms are on fourth floor—quiet
but there's no elevator (Sb-L85,000, Db-L135,000, Tb-L185,000,
prices through 2001 with this book only, air-con-L20,000/day,
breakfast-L10,000, CC:VMA, TVs, safes, 2 blocks from station at
Via Milazzo 20, tel. & fax 06-490-342, www.fenicia.web-page.net,
e-mail: hotel.fenicia@tiscalinet.it, Georgio and Anna SE).

Hotel Magic, a clean, marbled place run by a mother-daughter team, is high enough off the road to escape the traffic noise (10 rooms, Sb-L90,000, one D-L100,000, Db-L130,000, Tb-L180,000, Qb-L200,000, air-con-L20,000/day, breakfast-L7,000, prices through 2001 with this book only, cheaper in Aug and winter, CC:VM, thin walls, phones, safes, TV, midnight curfew, Via Milazzo 20, 3rd floor, 00185 Roma, tel. & fax 06-495-9880, little English spoken).

Albergo Sileo is a shiny-chandeliered, 10-room place with an elegant touch that has a contract to house train conductors who work the night shift. With maids doing double time, they offer simple, pleasant rooms from 19:00 to 9:00 only. If you can handle this, it's a great value. During the day they store your luggage, and though you won't have access to a room, you're welcome to hang out in their lobby or bar (D-L75,000, Db-L90,000, Tb-L115,000, elevator, Via Magenta 39, tel. & fax 06-445-0246, Alessandro and Maria Savioli NSE).

Sleeping near the Colosseum *(zip code: 00184)*

These places are buried in a very Roman world of exhaust-stained medieval ambience. For the first three, take the subway one stop from the train station to Metro: Cavour). The handy electrico bus line #117 connects you with the sights.

Hotel Duca d'Alba is a tight and modern pastel-marble-hardwood place just half a block from the Metro station (Sb-L260,000, Db-L390,000, much cheaper July–Aug and winter, extra bed-L40,000, breakfast buffet, CC:VMA, air-con, safes, phones, TV, elevator, Via Leonina 14, tel. 06-484-471, fax 06-488-4840, check Web site for deals, www.hotelducadalba.com, SE).

Hotel Grifo has a homey, tangled floor plan with 20 modern rooms and a roof terrace. The double-paned windows almost keep out the Vespa noise (Db-L230,000, L210,000 in July, CC:VMA, elevator, air-con, some rooms have terraces, 2 blocks off Via Cavour at Via del Boschetto 144, tel. 06-487-1395, fax 06-474 2323, e-mail: alez@dds.nl, son Alessandro SE).

Suore di Sant Anna was built for Ukrainian pilgrims. The sisters are sweet. It's difficult (little English plus 23:00 curfew), but once you're in, you've got a comfortable home in a classic Roman-village locale. Reserve well in advance (Sb-L65,000, Db-L120,000, Tb-L180,000, includes breakfast, consider dinner for L29,000, off the corner of Via dei Serpenti and Via Baccina at Piazza Madonna dei Monti 3, Metro: Cavour, tel. 06-485-778, fax 06-487-1064, e-mail: santasofia@tiscalinet.it).

Pensione Per Pelligrini is another nun-run place with simple, clean rooms and lots of twin beds. The language barrier is a challenge, but the price is right (39 rooms, S-L60,000, Sb-L80,000, D-L128,000, Db-L148,000, Tb-L172,000, breakfast-L8,000, closed

Aug, just off Piazza Vittorio Emmanuele II with morning market scene, Istituto Buon Salvatore, Via Leopardi 17, from station take bus # 714, #649, or #360, tel. 06-446-7147 or 06-446-7225, fax 06-4461382, Sister Anna Maria SE).

Near the Palatine: The **Hotel Casa Kolbe**, located in a former monastery, rents out monkish, spartan rooms with no fans or air-conditioning. But the location is magical, across from the Palatine ruins on a quiet side street about a block from a little-used entrance to the Forum. This place isn't for everybody but perfect for some—you know who you are. Ask for a room with a view of Palatine Hill (63 rooms, Sb-L120,000, Db-L150,000, Qb-L210,000, breakfast-L8,000, CC:VM, elevator, garden, courtyard, Via S. Teodoro 44, tel. 06-679-4974 or 06-679-8866, fax 06-6994-1550, Maurizio SE).

Sleeping near Campo de' Fiori and Piazza Navona (zip code: 00186)

Hotel Campo de' Fiori is ideal for wealthy bohemians who value centrality over peace and comfort. Just off Campo de' Fiori, it has an unreal rooftop terrace, 27 smallish rooms, and rickety windows and furniture (D-L180,000–190,000, Db-L280,000, includes breakfast, CC:VM, narrow hallways, fans, lots of stairs and no elevator, Via del Biscione 6, tel. 06-6874886, fax 06-687-6003, Andreas and others SE). They also have apartments very close by that can house five or six people (Db-L280,000, extra person-L50,000); these are a better (roomier) deal than staying at the hotel.

Albergo del Sole, with 60 simply decorated rooms, is impersonal and filled with German groups but well located (D-L150,000, small Db-L180,000, Db-L220,000, no breakfast, fans, elevator, multitiered terrace, Via del Biscione 76, tel. 06-6880-6873, fax 06-689-3787, www.venere.it/roma/sole, e-mail: sole@italyhotel.com).

Casa di Santa Brigida, also near the characteristic Campo de' Fiori, overlooks the elegant Piazza Farnese. With soft-spoken sisters gliding down polished hallways, and pearly gates instead of doors, this lavish convent makes the exhaust-stained Roman tourist feel like he's died and gone to heaven. If you're unsure of your destiny (and don't need a double bed), this is worth the splurge (23 rooms, Sb-L150,000, Db-L260,000, 4 percent extra with CC, great-value dinners, roof garden, plush library, air-con, walk-in address: Monserrato 54, mailing address: Piazza Farnese 96, reserve months in advance, tel. 06-6889-2596, fax 06-6889-1573, e-mail: hesselblad@tiscalinet.it, many of the sisters are from India and speak English).

Piazza Navona: **Hotel Navona** is a fine value, offering 35 basic rooms in an ancient building in a perfect locale a block off Piazza Navona. The rooms on the top floor come with more character (wood beams) and more stairs (D-L160,000, Db-L190,000, Db with air-con-L230,000, family rooms, Via dei Sediari 8, tel. 06-686-4203, fax 06-6880-3802, www.hotelnavona.com, run by a friendly Australian named Corry). **Residenza Zanardelli**, also owned by Corry, has six airy, pleasant rooms two blocks north of Piazza Navona (Db-L260,000, CC:VM but prefer cash, TV, phone, air-con, on busy street but double-paned windows minimize noise, Via G. Zanardelli 7, look for tiny name next to buzzer at door, tel. 06-6821-1392 or 06-6880-9760, fax 06-6880-3802).

Hotel Nazionale, a four-star landmark, is a 16th-century palace sharing a well-policed square with the national parliament. Its 90 rooms are served by lush public spaces, fancy bars, and a uniformed staff. It's a big hotel and even has a revolving front door, but if you want security, comfort, and the heart of old Rome at your doorstep (the Pantheon is 3 blocks away and Rome's top gelateria is just around the corner), this is a worthy splurge (Sb-L360,000, Db-L560,000, extra person-L120,000, suites-L850,000—gasp, less in Aug and winter, CC:VMA, air-con, elevator, Piazza Montecitorio 131, tel. 06-695-001, fax 06-678-6677, www.nazionaleamontecitorio.it, e-mail: nazionale@montecitorio.it, SE).

Sleeping "Three Stars" near the Vatican Museum (zip code: 00192)

To locate hotels, see map on page 453.

Hotel Alimandi is a good value, run by the friendly and entrepreneurial Alimandi brothers: Paolo, Enrico, Luigi, and Germano. Their 35 rooms are air-conditioned, modern, and marbled in white (Sb-L160,000 or L170,000 with breakfast; Db-L240,000 or L260,000 with breakfast; Tb-L280,000 or L315,000 with breakfast; 5 percent discount with this book and cash, CC:VMA, grand breakfast-L15,000 unless included in room price—see above, elevator, great roof garden, self-service washing machines, Internet access-L5,000, pool table, free parking, down the stairs directly in front of Vatican Museum, Via Tunisi 8, near Metro: Cipro-Musei Vaticani, reserve by phone, no reply to fax means they are full, tel. 06-3972-6300, toll free in Italy tel. 800-122-121, fax 06-3972-3943, www.alimandi.org, e-mail: alimandi@tin.it, SE). They offer their guests free airport pickup and drop off (saving you L80,000 if you were planning on taking a taxi), though you must reserve when you book your room and conform to their set schedule (which can mean waiting). Maria Alimandi rents out three rooms in her apartment, a 20-minute bus ride from the Vatican (Db-L140,000, see Web site above).

Hotel Spring House, with a hotelesque feel, offers 51 attractive rooms—some with balconies which don't cost extra

(ask for a balcony). Mention this book to get a special price
(Db-L250,000 instead of normal L280,000 rate, includes breakfast,
5 percent discount for cash payment, 15 percent discount July–
Aug and winter, Internet access-L10,000/30 min, CC:VMA,
phones, TV, air-con, fridges in room, elevator, parking-L25,000/
day, Metro: Cipro-Musei Vaticani, Via Mocenigo 7, 2 blocks
from Vatican Museum, tel. 06-3972-0948, fax 06-3972-1047,
www.hotelspringhouse.com, Stefano Gabbani).

Hotel Gerber is sleek, modern, air-conditioned, business-
like, and set in a quiet residential area (27 rooms, S-L120,000,
Sb-L180,000, Db-L250,000, Tb-L290,000, Qb-L330,000, 10
percent discount with this book, includes breakfast buffet, air-con,
CC:VMA, 1 block from Lepanto subway stop, Via degli Scipioni
241, at intersection with Ezio, tel. 06-321-6485, fax 06-321-7048,
www.hotelgerber.it, Peter SE).

Hotel Sant' Anna is much pricier than the rest but closer
to the city center and located on a charming-for-Rome pedestrian
street that fills with restaurant tables at dinnertime. Its 20 rooms
are overly decorated with classical themes, but the furnishings
are comfy (Db-L350,000, Db-L280,000 in July–Aug and winter,
CC:VM, air-con, elevator, courtyard, Borgo Pio 133, near intersection with Mascherino, a couple blocks from entrance of
St. Peter's, tel. 06-6880-1602, fax 06-6830-8717, www.travel.it/
roma/santanna, SE).

Sleeping in Hostels and Dorms

Rome's one real youth hostel is big, institutional, and not central
or worth the trouble. For cheap dorm beds, consider the following
places:

Near Basilica Santa Maria Maggiore: Casa Olmata is a
laid-back backpackers' place midway between the Termini train
station and Colosseum (beds in shared quads-L30,000, S-L60,000,
bunkbed D-L70,000, one queen-size D-L100,000, lots of stairs,
laundry service, free Internet access, video rentals, games, roof-top
terrace, communal kitchen, dinners twice weekly, English dominant language, a block southwest of Basilica Santa Maria Maggiore,
Via dell' Omata 36, 3rd floor, tel. 06-483-019, fax 06-474-2854,
www.casaolmata.com, e-mail: casaolmata30@hotmail.com, Mirella
and Marco). **The Beehive** is especially good for older travelers.
This tidy little place, with three six-bed dorms, some doubles, and
a guests' kitchen on one floor, is thoughtfully run by a friendly
young American couple, Steve and Linda (L30,000 dorm beds,
D-L50,000, Db-L75,000, CC:VM, closed 13:00–16:00, 2 blocks
south of Basilica Santa Maria Maggiore at Via Giovanni Lanza 99,
tel. 06-474-0719, fax 06-4788-1190, www.the-beehive.com). The
Beehive has doubles in a building a 15-minute walk away
(S-L50,000, D-L100,000, T-L150,000, reserve and check in at

Beehive) and can also refer you to B&Bs, private rooms, and apartments elsewhere in Rome (www.cross-pollinate.com).

Near the Vatican: Pensione Ottaviano offers a fun, easy-going clubhouse feel and a good location near the Vatican (25 beds in 2- to 7-bed rooms, L30,000 per bed with sheets, D-L90,000, 6 blocks south of Ottaviano Metro stop, Via Ottaviano 6, near Piazza Risorgimento, reservations only after 21:00 the night before, tel. 06-3973-7253, www.pensioneottaviano.com).

Eating in Rome

Romans spend their evenings eating rather than drinking and the preferred activity is to simply enjoy a fine, slow meal buried deep in the old city. Rome's a fun and cheap place to eat, with countless little eateries serving fine $20 meals. Tourists wander the streets just before midnight wondering, "Why did I eat so much?"

Although I've listed a number of restaurants, I recommend that you just head for a scenic area and explore. Piazza Navona, the Pantheon area, Campo de' Fiori, and Trastevere are neighborhoods full of places ranging from expensive sit-down to cheap take-out.

Eating in Trastevere

Guidebooks list Trastevere's famous places, but I'd wander the fascinating maze of streets near Piazza Santa Maria in Trastevere and find a mom-and-pop place with barely a menu. Check out the tiny streets north of the church. You might consider these places before making a choice:

For outdoor seating on romantic Piazza della Scala, check out **Taverna della Scala**, the local choice for pizza (Wed–Mon 12:30–15:00, 19:00–24:00, closed Tue, tel. 06-581-4100) and **La Scala**, chic and popular with Generation X Romans (daily 12:00–15:00, 19:00–24:00, tel. 06-580-3763). Don't miss the fine little *gelatería* with oh-wow pistachio (across from church on Piazza della Scala).

At **Taverna del Moro da Tony**, Tony scrambles—with a great antipasti table—to keep his happy eaters well fed and returning (but too much mayo on bruschetta, Tue–Sun 14:00–02:00, closed Mon, off Via del Moro at Vicolo del Cinque 36, tel. 06-580-9165). For a basic meal with lots of tourists, you can eat cheap at **Mario's** (Mon–Sat 12:00–14:00 19:00–24:00, closed Sun, 3 courses with wine and service for L20,000, Via del Moro 53, tel. 06-580-3809).

Ristorante Alle Fratte di Trastevere is lively and inexpensive (closed Tue, Via dell Fratte di Trastevere, tel. 06-583-5775).

Da Otello, on Piazza San Edigio, has good antipasti and pizzas, and cooks up meat dishes on a wood-burning stove in the dining room (Thu–Tue 12:30–14:30, 19:30–24:00, closed Wed, Via della Pelliccia 47, tel. 06-589-6848).

Eating on and near Campo de' Fiori

For the ultimate romantic square setting, eat at whichever place looks best on Campo de' Fiori. Circle the square, considering each place. **La Carbonara** claims to be the birthplace of pasta carbonara (closed Tue). Meals on small nearby streets are a better value but lack that Campo de' Fiori magic. Bars and pizzerias seem to be overwhelming the popular square. The **Taverna** and **Vineria** at numbers 16 and 15 offer good perches from which to people watch and nurse a glass of wine.

Nearby, on the more elegant and peaceful Piazza Farnese, **Ostaria Da Giovanni Ar Galletto** has a dressier local crowd, great outdoor seating, moderate prices, and fine food (closed Sun, tucked in corner of Piazza Farnese at #102, tel. 06-686-1714).

Filetti de Baccala is a tradition for many Romans. Basically a fish bar with paper tablecloths and cheap prices, its grease-stained, hurried waiters serve old-time favorites—fried cod fillets, a strange bitter *puntarelle* salad, and delightful anchovies with butter—to nostalgic locals (Mon–Sat 17:30–23:10, closed Sun, a block east of Campo de' Fiori tumbling onto a tiny and atmospheric square, Largo dei Librari 88, tel. 06-686-4018).

Trattoria der Pallaro has no menu but plenty of return eaters. Paola Fazi, with a towel wrapped around her head turban-style, and her family serve up a five-course festival of typically Roman food for L33,000, including wine, coffee, and a wonderful mandarin liqueur. Their slogan: "Here, you'll eat what we want to feed you." Look like Oliver asking for more soup and get seconds on the mandarin liqueur (Tue–Sun 12:00–15:30, 19:30–24:00, closed Mon, indoor/outdoor seating on quiet square, a block south of Corso Vittorio Emanuele down Largo del Chiavari to Largo del Pallaro 15, tel. 06-6880-1488).

Ristorante Grotte del Teatro di Pompeo, sitting atop an ancient theater, serves good food at fair prices with a smile (closed Mon, Via del Biscione 73, tel. 06-6880-3686).

For interesting bar munchies, try **Cul de Sac** on Piazza Pasquino (daily 12:00–18:00, 19:00–24:00, a block southwest of Piazza Navona). **L'Insalata Ricca**, a popular chain that specializes in hearty and healthy salads, is next door (daily 12:00–15:45, 18:45–22:00, Piazza Pasquino 72, tel. 06-6830-7881). Another branch is nearby with more spacious outdoor seating (just off Corso Vittorio Emanuele on Largo del Chiavari).

Brek, on Largo Argentina just south of the Pantheon, is an appealing, new self-service restaurant—which it calls "free flow" (daily 12:00–15:30, 18:30–23:00, sandwiches and pizza slices downstairs, "free flow" upstairs, northwest corner of square, Largo Argentina 1, tel. 06-6821-0353).

Il Delfino, also on Largo Argentina and near Brek, is a tired but handy self-service cafeteria that serves throughout the day (daily 7:00–21:00, not cheap but fast). Across the side street, **Frullati di Frutta** sells refreshing fruity frappés. The *alimentari* (grocery store) on the Pantheon square will make you a sandwich for a temple-porch picnic.

Eating near Via Firenze and Via Nazionale Hotels
Snack Bar Gastronomia is a great local hole-in-the-wall for lunch or dinner (daily 7:00–21:00, really cheap hot meals dished up from under glass counter, tap water with a smile, Via Firenze 34). There's an *alimentari* across the street.

Pasticceria Dagnino, popular for its top-quality Sicilian specialties—especially pastries and ice cream—is where those who work at my recommended hotels eat (daily 7:00–22:00, in Galleria Esedra off Via Torino, a block from hotels, tel. 06-481-8660). Their *arancino*—a rice, cheese, and ham ball—is a greasy Sicilian favorite. Direct the construction of your meal at the bar, pay for your trayful at the cashier, and climb upstairs, where you'll find the dancing Sicilian girls (free).

Hostaria Romana is a great place for traditional Roman cuisine. For an air-conditioned, classy local favorite run by a jolly group of men who enjoy their work, eat here (closed Sun, midway between Trevi fountain and Piazza Barberini, Via del Boccaccio 1, at intersection with Via Rasella, no reservations needed before 20:00, tel. 06-474-5284). Go ahead and visit the antipasto bar in person to assemble your plate. They're happy to serve an *antipasti misto della casa* and pasta dinner. Take a hard look at their *Specialita Romane* list.

Ristorante da Giovanni is a serviceable, hardworking place that has been feeding locals and travelers for 50 years (L23,000 menu, Mon–Sat 12:00–15:00, 19:00–22:30, closed Sun, CC:VM, just off Via XX Septembre at Via Antonio Salandra 1, tel. 06-485-950).

Cafetteria Nazionale, with woody elegance, offers light lunches—including salads—at reasonable prices (set menu or buffet, Mon–Sat 7:00–20:00, closed Sun, CC:VM, Via Nazionale 26–27, at intersection with Via Agostino de Pretis, tel. 06-4899-1716).

Ristorante Cinese Internazionale is your best neighborhood bet for Chinese (daily 12:00–15:00, 18:00–23:00, inexpensive, no pasta, just off Via Nazionale behind Hotel Luxor at Via Agostino de Pretis 98, tel. 06-474-4064).

The **McDonald** restaurants on Piazza della Repubblica (free piazza seating outside), Piazza Barberini, and Via Firenze offer air-conditioned interiors and salad bars.

Flann O'Brien Irish Pub is a great place for a quick light meal (pasta or something *other* than pasta), fine Irish beer, and the most Italian crowd of all (daily 7:30–01:00, Via Nazionale 17, at intersection with Via Napoli, tel. 06-488-0418).

Eating near the Vatican Museum

Antonio's Hostaria dei Bastioni is tasty and friendly. It's conveniently located midway between your walk from St. Peters' to the Vatican Museum, with noisy streetside seating and a quiet interior (hot when hot—no air-con, Mon–Sat 12:00–15:00, 19:00–23:30, closed Sun, L10,000–12,000 pastas, L15,000 *secondi*, no cover charge, at corner of Vatican wall, Via Leone IV 29, tel. 06-3972-3034).

La Rustichella has a great and fresh antipasti buffet (L15,000, enough for a meal) and fine pasta dishes. Arrive when they open at 19:30 to avoid a line and have the pristine buffet to yourself (Tue–Sun 12:30–15:00, 19:30–23:00, closed Mon, near Metro: Cipro-Musei Vaticani stop, opposite church at end of Via Candia, Via Angelo Emo 1, tel. 06-3972-0649). Consider the fun and fruity **Gelatería Millennium** next door.

Avoid the restaurant pushers handing out fliers near the Vatican: bad food, expensive menu tricks. Viale Giulio Cesare is lined with cheap **Pizza Rustica** shops and fun eateries, such as **Cipriani Self-Service Rosticcería** (closed Mon, pleasant outdoor seating, near Ottaviano subway stop, Viale Guilio Cesare 195).

Turn your nose loose in the wonderful **Via Andrea Doria** open-air market three blocks north of the Vatican Museum (Mon–Sat roughly 7:00–13:30, until 16:30 on Tue and Fri except summer, between Via Tunisi and Via Andrea Doria). If the market is closed, try the nearby **IN's supermarket** (Mon–Sat 8:30–13:30, 16:00–20:00 but closed Thu eve, a half block straight out from Via Tunisi entrance of open-air market, Via Francesco 18).

Transportation Connections—Rome

Termini is the central station. Long-distance buses (e.g., from Siena) arrive at Rome's small Tiburtina station, which is on Metro line B, with easy connections to the main train station (a straight shot 4 stops away) and the entire Metro system.

By train from Rome to: Venice (6/day, 5–8 hrs), **Florence** (12/day, 2 hrs, stop at Orvieto en route), **Pisa** (8/day, 3–4 hrs), **Genova** (7/day, 6 hrs, overnight possible), **Milan** (12/day, 5 hrs, overnight possible), **Naples** (6/day, 2 hrs), **Brindisi** (2/day, 9 hrs), **Amsterdam** (2/day, 20 hrs), **Bern** (5/day, 10 hrs), **Frankfurt** (4/day, 14 hrs), **Munich** (5/day, 12 hrs), **Nice** (2/day, 10 hrs), **Paris** (5/day, 16 hrs), **Vienna** (3/day, 13–15 hrs).

Rome's Airports

Rome's two airports—Fiumicino (a.k.a. Leonardo da Vinci) and the small Ciampino—share the same Web site (www.adr.it).

Fiumicino Airport: Rome's major airport has a TI (daily 8:15–19:00, tel. 06-6595-4471), ATMs, banks, luggage storage, shops, and bars.

A slick, direct train connects the airport and Rome's central

Termini train station in 30 minutes. Trains run twice hourly in both directions from roughly 7:30 to 21:30. From the airport, trains depart at :07 and :37 past the hour (from airport's arrival gate, follow signs to "Stazione/Railway Station"; buy ticket from a machine or the Biglietteria office; L16,000, CC:VM, or free with first-class railpass). From Termini, trains depart at :21 and :51 past the hour from Track 25 (L16,000, buy ticket from any *Tabacchi* shop in station or at Alitalia desk near entrance to Track 25; to reach Track 25, walk along Track 24 midway through the station, then follow signs that take you inside—to Alitalia desk—and down the escalator). Read the ticket. If validation is required, stamp it in a yellow machine on the platform.

Your hotel can arrange a taxi to the airport at any hour for about L80,000. To get from the airport into town cheaply by taxi, try teaming up with any tourist also just arriving (most are heading for hotels near yours in the center). Splitting a taxi and hopping out once downtown at a taxi stand to take another to your hotel will save you L30,000. Avoid unmarked, unmetered taxis.

Airport information (tel. 06-65951 or 06-6595-3640) can connect you directly to your airline. (British Air tel. 147-812-266, Alitalia tel. 06-65643, Delta tel. 800-864-114, KLM tel. 06-652-9286, SAS tel. 06-6501-0771, TWA tel. 800-841-843, United tel. 0266-7481, Lufthansa tel. 06-6568-4004, Swiss Air tel. 06-847-0555.)

Ciampino Airport: Rome's smaller airport (tel. 06-794-941) handles budget and charter flights. To get to downtown Rome from the airport, take the LILA/Cotral bus (2/hrly) to the Anagnina Metro stop, where you can connect by Metro to the stop nearest your hotel.

Driving in Rome

Greater Rome is circled by the Grande Raccordo Anulare. This ring road has spokes that lead you into the center. Entering from the north, leave the autostrada at the Settebagni exit. Following the ancient Via Salaria (and the black-and-white "Centro" signs), work your way doggedly into the Roman thick of things. This will take you along the Villa Borghese park and dump you right on Via Veneto (where there's an Avis office). Avoid rush hour and drive defensively: Roman cars stay in their lanes like rocks in an avalanche. Parking in Rome is dangerous. Park near a police station or get advice at your hotel. The Villa Borghese underground garage is handy (L35,000/day, Metro: Spagna).

Consider this: Your car is a worthless headache in Rome. Avoid a pile of stress and save money by parking at the huge, easy, and relatively safe lot behind the Orvieto station (follow "P" signs from autostrada) and catch the train to Rome (every 2 hrs, 75 min).

FLORENCE (FIRENZE)

Florence, the home of the Renaissance and birthplace of our modern world, is a "supermarket sweep," and the groceries are the best Renaissance art in Europe.

Get your bearings with a Renaissance walk. Florentine art goes beyond paintings and statues—there's food, fashion, and handicrafts. You can lick Italy's best *gelato* while enjoying some of Europe's best people watching.

Planning Your Time

If you're in Europe for three weeks, Florence deserves a well-organized day. (Siena, an easy 75-minute bus ride away, has no awesome sights but is a more enjoyable home base.) For a day in Florence, see Michelangelo's *David*, tour the Uffizi Gallery (best Italian paintings anywhere), tour the underrated Bargello (best statues), and do the Renaissance ramble (explained below). Art lovers will want to chisel another day out of their itinerary for the many other Florentine cultural treasures. Shoppers and ice-cream lovers may need to do the same. Plan your sightseeing carefully. Mondays and afternoons can be sparse. While many spend several hours a day in lines, thoughtful travelers do not. Consider eating long and slow at lunch (it's hot out and prices are better). See any sights in the evening that you can.

Orientation

The Florence we're interested in lies mostly on the north bank of the Arno River. Everything is within a 20-minute walk of the train station, cathedral, or Ponte Vecchio (Old Bridge). The less impressive but more characteristic Oltrarno (south

Florence Schematic

bank) area is just over the bridge. The huge red-tiled dome of the cathedral (the Duomo) and its tall bell tower (Giotto's Tower) mark the center of historic Florence.

Tourist Information

There are three TIs in Florence. The TI across the square from the train station can be plagued by long lines (Mon–Sat 8:30–19:00, Sun 8:30–13:00; off-season Mon–Sat 8:30–17:30, Sun 8:30–13:00, handy train schedule posted in lobby; with your back to tracks, TI is straight ahead, across square in wall near corner of church, look for "i" sign; Piazza Stazione, tel. 055-212-245). Note: In the station, avoid the Hotel Reservations "Tourist Information" window (marked Informazioni Turistiche Alberghiere) near the McDonald's; it's not a real TI but a hotel reservation business. The TI near Santa Croce Church is pleasant, helpful, and uncrowded (Mon–Sat 9:00–19:00, Sun 9:00–14:00, shorter hours off-season, Borgo Santa Croce 29 red, tel. 055-234-0444). Another winner is the TI three blocks north of the Duomo (Mon–Sat 8:15–19:15, Sun 8:30–18:30, shorter hours off-season, Via Cavour 1 red, tel. 055-290-832 or 055-290-833; international bookstore across street, see "Helpful Hints," below). TI Web site: www.firenze.turismo.toscana.it.

At the TI pick up a map, a current museum-hours listing (extremely important since hours are constantly in flux), and any information on entertainment. They even have a brochure on where to find public WCs in Florence. The free monthly *Florence Concierge Information* magazine lists museums plus lots that I

Greater Florence

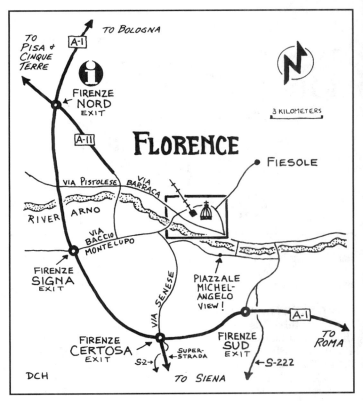

To Bologna

To Pisa & Cinque Terre

A-1

FIRENZE NORD EXIT

A-11

3 KILOMETERS

FLORENCE

FIESOLE

VIA PISTOLESE   VIA BARRACA

RIVER   ARNO

VIA BACCIO MONTELUPO

FIRENZE SIGNA EXIT

PIAZZALE MICHELANGELO VIEW!

VIA SENESE

FIRENZE CERTOSA EXIT

SUPER-STRADA

S-2

A-1

TO ROMA

FIRENZE SUD EXIT

S-222

TO SIENA

DCH

don't: concerts and events, markets, sporting events, church services, shopping ideas, bus and train connections, and an entire similar section on Siena. Get yours at the TI or from any expensive hotel (pick one up, as if you're staying there).

Arrival in Florence

By Train: The station soaks up time and generates dazed and sweaty crowds. Try to get your tourist information and train tickets elsewhere. (You can get onward tickets and information at American Express—see "Helpful Hints," below.) With your back to the tracks, to your left are most of my recommended hotels, a 24-hour pharmacy (Farmacia Comunale, near McDonald's), city buses, and the entrance to the underground mall/passage to Santa Maria Novella (but because the surface point near the church is frequented by pickpockets, stay above ground).

By Car: From the autostrada (north or south), take the Certosa exit (follow signs to Centro, at Porta Romana go to the left of the arch and down Via Francesco Petrarca). After driving and trying to park in Florence, you'll understand why Leonardo never invented the car. Cars flatten the charm of Florence. Don't drive in Florence and don't risk parking illegally (fines up to L300,000). The city has plenty of lots. For a short stay, consider the underground lot at the train station (L3,000/hr). The Fortezza da Basso is clearly marked in the center (L36,000/24 hrs). The least expensive lot is Parcheggio Parterre (Firenze Parcheggi, L15,000/24 hrs with hotel reservation). For parking information, call 055-234-0444.

Helpful Hints

Museums and Churches: Hours of sights are certain to change without warning. Pick up the latest listing of museum hours at a TI, or you'll miss out on something you came to see. Visit everyone's essential sight, *David*, right off. In Italy a masterpiece seen and enjoyed is worth two tomorrow; you never know when a place will unexpectedly close for a holiday, strike, or restoration. The Uffizi has one- to two-hour lines on busy days (make reservations at least a day in advance before 18:30 when the ticket office closes, see Uffizi, under "Sights," below). Some museums close at 14:00 and stop selling tickets 30 minutes before that. The biggies (Uffizi and Accademia) close on Monday. The *Concierge Information* magazine thoughtfully lists which sights are open afternoons, Sundays, and Mondays (best attractions open Mon: Museo dell' Opera del Duomo, Giotto's Tower, Brancacci Chapel, Michelangelo's Casa Buonarroti, Dante's House, Science Museum, Palazzo Vecchio, and churches). In 2001, a combo ticket may cover the Accademia (*David*), Bargello, and the Medici Chapel (L25,000, available at participating sites). Churches usually close from 12:30 to 15:00 or 16:00. Local guidebooks are cheap and give you a map and a decent commentary on the sights.

Theft Alert: Florence has particularly hardworking thief gangs. They specialize in tourists and hang out where you do: near the train station, the station's underpass (especially where the tunnel surfaces), and major sights. American tourists—especially older ones—are considered the easiest targets.

Medical Help: For a doctor who speaks English, call 055-475-411 (reasonable hotel calls, cheaper if you go to clinic at Via L. Magnifico 59, 24-hour pharmacy at the train station). The TI has a list of English-speaking doctors.

Addresses: Street addresses list businesses in red and residences in black or blue (color coded on the actual street number and indicated by a letter following the number in printed addresses: n = black, r = red). *Pensioni* are usually black but can be either. The red and black numbers each appear in roughly consecutive order on streets but bear no apparent connection with each other.

American Express: Amex offers all the normal services but is most helpful as an easy place to get your train tickets, reservations, supplements (all the same price as at station), or even just information on train schedules. It's north of the Palazzo Vecchio on Via Dante Alighieri 22 red (Mon–Fri 9:00–17:30, Sat 9:00–12:30, CC:VMA!, tel. 055-50981).

Long-Distance Telephoning: Small newsstand kiosks and dreary hole-in-the-wall phone shops all over town sell PIN phone cards giving you cheap (3 minutes/$1) phone calls to the United States.

Books: Feltrinelli International, a fine bookstore that sells fiction and guidebooks in English, is a few blocks north of the Duomo and across the street from the TI on Via Cavour (Mon–Sat 9:00–19:30, Via Cavour 20 red). Paperback Exchange also sells fiction and guidebooks (daily 9:00–19:30, shorter hours in Aug, at corner of Via Fiesolana and Via dei Pilastri, 6 blocks east of Duomo, tel. 055-247-8154).

Tours: Walking Tours of Florence offers a variety of tours (up to 4 a day) Monday through Saturday featuring downtown Florence, Uffizi highlights, or the countryside, presented by informative, entertaining guides who are fluent in English (L35,000 for 3-hr Original Florence walk, office open Mon–Sat 8:30–12:15, 14:15–18:00, Piazza Santo Stefano 2 black, a short block north of Ponte Vecchio; go east on tiny Vicolo San Stefano, in Piazza Santo Stefano go left to #2 and up the stairs; booking necessary for Uffizi tour, private tours also available even on Sun, tel. 055-264-5033 or cellular 0329-613-2730, www.florencewalkingtours.com). Their office serves as the meeting point for the tours (offered year-round, regardless of weather, maximum of 18, extra guide available if more than 18 show up).

Getting around Florence

I organize my sightseeing geographically and do it all on foot. A L1,500 ticket gives you one hour on the buses, L2,500 gives you three hours, and L6,000 gets you 24 hours (tickets not sold on bus, buy in *tabacchi* shops or newsstands, validate on bus). Minimum taxi ride: L7,000, or, after 22:00, L9,500 (rides in the center of town should be charged as tarif #1). A taxi ride from the train station to Ponte Vecchio costs about L15,000.

A Florentine Renaissance Walk

Even during the Dark Ages people knew they were in a "middle time." It was especially obvious to the people of Italy—sitting on the rubble of Rome—that there was a brighter age before them. The long-awaited rebirth, or Renaissance, began in Florence for good

Florence

TO PIAZZA LIBERTÀ
SAN MARCO
ACCADEMIA
TRAIN STN.
GUELFA
S. ZANOBI
SAN MARCO
BUS STN.
MERCATO CENTRALE
SAN LORENZO
MEDICI CHAPEL
STREET MKT.
FIUME
FAENZA
NAZ.
RICAS.
SOLI
PIAZZA ANNUNZIATA
S. MARIA NOVELLA
VIA PANZANI
LAUR. LIB.
CERRETANI
MEDICI PALACE
SERVI
D. SCALA
DUOMO
CATHEDRAL MUSEUM
BAPT.
BARGELLO
PALLAZ.
FOSSI
SOLE
VIGNA NOVA
TORNABUON
AGLI
P. REP.
CORSO
CASA DI DANTE
ORI.
Vivoli's
CASA BUONARROTI
GHIB.
CARAIA
RIVER
ORSANMICHELE
PORTA ROSSA
COV. MKT.
G
S. CROCE
D. GRECI
P.
SANTA CROCE
OLTRARNO
B. S. JACAR.
GUIZEI
MAGGIO
S. SPIRITO
G
MAZETA
PALAZZO VECCHIO
G SCI. MUS.
TINTORI
PAZZI CHAPEL
PONTE VECCHIO
UFFIZI
ARNO
GRAZIE
PITTI PALACE
FORTE BELVEDERE
DCH
BOBOLI GARDENS
PIAZZALE MICHELANGELO
★ PIAZZA SIGNORIA
VIEW
G = GELATERIA
400 METERS

reason. Wealthy because of its cloth industry, trade, and banking; powered by a fierce city-state pride (locals would pee into the Arno with gusto, knowing rival city-state Pisa was downstream); and fertile with more than its share of artistic genius (imagine guys like Michelangelo and Leonardo attending the same high school)— Florence was a natural home for this cultural explosion.

Take a walk through the core of Renaissance Florence by starting at the Accademia (home of Michelangelo's *David*) and cutting through the heart of the city to Ponte Vecchio on the Arno River. (A 10-page, self-guided tour of this walk is outlined in my museum guidebook, *Rick Steves' Mona Winks;* otherwise, you'll find brief descriptions below.)

At the Accademia you'll look into the eyes of Renaissance man—humanism at its confident peak. Then walk to the cathedral (Duomo) to see the dome that kicked off the architectural Renaissance. Step inside the baptistery to view a ceiling covered with preachy, flat, 2-D, medieval mosaic art. Then, to learn what happened when art met math, check out the realistic 3-D reliefs on the doors. The painter, Giotto, designed the bell tower—an early example of how a Renaissance genius excelled in many areas. Continue toward the river on Florence's great pedestrian mall, Via de' Calzaiuoli (or "Via Calz"), which was part of the original grid plan given the city by the ancient Romans. Down a few blocks, compare medieval and Renaissance statues on the exterior of the Orsanmichele Church. Via Calz connects the cathedral with the central square (Piazza della Signoria), the city palace (Palazzo Vecchio), and the Uffizi Gallery, which contains the greatest collection of Italian Renaissance paintings in captivity. Finally, walk through the Uffizi courtyard—a statuary think tank of Renaissance greats—to the Arno River and Ponte Vecchio.

Sights—On Florence's Renaissance Walk

▲▲▲**Accademia (Galleria dell' Accademia)**—This museum houses Michelangelo's *David* and powerful (unfinished) *Prisoners*. Eavesdrop as tour guides explain these masterpieces. More than any other work of art, when you look into the eyes of *David*, you're looking into the eyes of Renaissance man. This was a radical break with the past. Man was now a confident individual, no longer a plaything of the supernatural. And life was now more than just a preparation for what happened after you died.

The Renaissance was the merging of art and science. In a humanist vein, *David* is looking at the crude giant of medieval darkness and thinking, "I can take this guy." Back on a religious track (and speaking of veins), notice *David*'s large and overdeveloped right hand. This is symbolic of the hand of God that powered David to slay the giant . . . and enabled Florence to rise above its crude neighboring city-states.

Beyond the magic marble are two floors of interesting pre-Renaissance and Renaissance paintings, including a couple of dreamy Botticellis.

Cost, Hours, Location: L15,000 (ask about combo ticket that covers Bargello and Medici Chapel). Open Tue–Sun 8:30–18:50, Sat until 22:00, closed Mon, shorter hours off-season (Via Ricasoli 60, tel. 055-238-8609).

Nearby: Piazza Santissima Annunziata, behind the Accademia, features lovely Renaissance harmony. Brunelleschi's Hospital of the Innocents (Spedale degli Innocenti, not worth going inside), with terra-cotta medallions by Luca della Robbia, was built in the 1420s and is considered the first Renaissance building.

▲▲**Duomo**—Florence's mediocre Gothic cathedral has the third-longest nave in Christendom (free, Mon–Wed and Fri–Sat 10:00–17:00, Thu 10:00–15:30, Sun 13:30–17:00, first Sat of month 10:00–15:30). The church's noisy neo-Gothic facade from the 1870s is covered with pink, green, and white Tuscan marble. Since nearly all of its great art is stored in the Museo dell' Opera del Duomo, behind the church, the best thing about the interior is the shade. The inside of the dome is decorated by one of the largest paintings of the Renaissance, a huge (and newly restored) *Last Judgment* by Vasari and Zuccari. The cathedral's claim to artistic fame is Brunelleschi's magnificent dome—the first Renaissance dome and the model for domes to follow. Ascend 463 steps and enjoy an inside look at the construction (L10,000, Mon–Fri 8:30–19:00, Sat 8:30–17:00, closed Sun, first Sat of month 8:30–15:20). When planning St. Peter's in Rome, Michelangelo said, "I can build a dome bigger, but not more beautiful, than the dome of Florence."

Giotto's Tower—Climbing Giotto's 82-meter-tall tower (or Campanile) beats climbing the neighboring Duomo's dome because it's 50 fewer steps, faster, not so crowded, and offers the same view plus the dome (L10,000, daily 8:30–19:30).

▲▲**Museo dell' Opera del Duomo**—The underrated cathedral museum, behind the church at #9, is great if you like sculpture. It has masterpieces by Donatello (a gruesome wood carving of Mary Magdalene clothed in her matted hair, and the *cantoria*, a delightful choir loft bursting with happy children) and della Robbia (another choir loft, lined with the dreamy faces of musicians praising the Lord). Look for a late Michelangelo *Pietà* (Nicodemus, on top, is a self-portrait), Brunelleschi's models for his dome, and the original restored panels of Ghiberti's doors to the baptistery. This is one of the few museums in Florence open on Monday (L10,000, Mon–Sat 9:30–18:30, Sun 8:00–14:00, tel. 055-230-2885).

▲**Baptistery**—Michelangelo said its bronze doors were fit to be the gates of Paradise. Check out the gleaming copies of Ghiberti's bronze doors facing the Duomo and the famous competition doors around to the right (north). Making a breakthrough in perspective, Ghiberti used mathematical laws to create the illusion of receding distance on a basically flat surface. Go inside Florence's oldest building and sit and savor the medieval mosaic ceiling. Compare that to the "new, improved" art of the Renaissance (L5,000 interior open Mon–Sat 12:00–18:30, Sun 8:30–13:30, bronze doors are on the outside so always "open" and free; original panels are in the Museo dell' Opera del Duomo).

▲**Orsanmichele**—Mirroring Florentine values, this was a combination church-granary. The glorious tabernacle by Orcagna takes you back (1359). Notice the grain spouts on the pillars inside. Also study the sculpture on its outside walls. You can see man stepping out of the literal and figurative shadow of the church in the great

Renaissance sculptor Donatello's *St. George* (free, daily 9:00–12:00,
16:00–18:00, closed first and last Mon of month, on Via Calzaiuoli; can be closed due to staffing problems, try going through
the back door). Across the street is Museo Orsanmichele...

▲**Museo Orsanmichele**—For some peaceful time alone with
the original statues that filled the niches of Orsanmichele, climb
to the top of the church (entry behind church, across street). Be
there during the few minutes at 9:00, 10:00, and 11:00 on weekdays when the door is open and art lovers in the know climb four
flights of stairs to this little known museum, containing statues by
Ghiberti, Donatello, and others (info in Italian, but picture guides
on wall help you match art with artists). Upstairs is a tower room
with city views. On Saturday and Sunday, the museum is wide
open from 9:00 to 13:00 and 16:00 to 18:00 (free, closed first and
last Mon of month; benches on both floors).

▲**Palazzo Vecchio**—This fortified palace, once the home of the
Medici family, is a Florentine landmark. But if you're visiting only
one palace interior in town, the Pitti Palace is better. The Palazzo
Vecchio interior is wallpapered with mediocre magnificence,
worthwhile only if you're a real Florentine art and history fan.
The museum's most famous statues are Michelangelo's *Genius of
Victory*, Donatello's static *Judith and Holerfernes*, and Verrocchio's
Winged Cherub (a copy tops the fountain in the free courtyard at
entrance, original inside).

Scattered throughout the museum are a dozen computer
terminals with information in English on the Medici family,
Palazzo Vecchio, and the building's architecture and art, including
Michelangelo's *David* (with jerky animation showing how the
original *David* was moved to the square in front of the Palazzo
Vecchio). The computer info, combined with English descriptions
labeling the art, make this otherwise-numbing museum more
meaningful. Overeager to clock out, guards start turning off
computer terminals 30 minutes before closing (L11,000, Sun
9:00–14:00, Mon–Wed and Fri–Sat 9:00–19:00, Thu 9:00–14:00,
in summer open until 23:00 on Mon and Fri, buy ticket in office
in second courtyard, then ascend stairs between first and second
courtyard to reach museum; WC in second courtyard; tel. 055-
276-8465). The gift shop sells Art Cubes (next to cash register)
that can be manipulated into different paintings (L25,000, so cool
they're probably sold out, but worth asking about; entrance to
shop next to ticket office, no need to pay admission). A new
"Secret Routes" tour takes you up hidden stairs to the Duke of
Athens' private chambers and studio (L13,000, includes Palazzo
Vecchio, book in advance; stop by Palazzo Vecchio or call 055-
276-8224 between 9:30 and 12:00).

Even if you don't go to the museum, do step into the free
courtyard (behind the fake *David*) just to feel the essence of the

Medici. Until 1873 Michelangelo's *David* stood at the entrance, where the copy is today. While the huge statues in the square are important only as the whipping boys of art critics and rest stops for pigeons, the nearby Loggia dei Lanzi has several important statues. Look for Cellini's bronze statue of Perseus (with the head of Medusa). The plaque on the pavement in front of the fountain marks the spot where Savonarola was burned in MCCCCXCVIII.

▲▲▲**Bargello (Museo Nazionale)**—This underrated sculpture museum is behind Palazzo Vecchio in a former prison that looks like a mini–Palazzo Vecchio. It has Donatello's painfully beautiful *David* (the very influential first male nude to be sculpted in a thousand years), works by Michelangelo, and rooms of Medici treasures cruelly explained in Italian only—mention that English descriptions would be wonderful (L8,000, daily 8:30–13:50 but closed first, third, and fifth Sun and second and fourth Mon of each month, Via del Proconsolo 4, tel. 055-238-8606).

▲▲▲**Uffizi Gallery**—The greatest collection of Italian paintings anywhere is a must, with plenty of works by Giotto, Leonardo, Raphael, Caravaggio, Rubens, Titian, and Michelangelo and a roomful of Botticellis, including his *Birth of Venus*. There are no official tours, so buy a book on the street before entering (or follow *Mona Winks*). Because only 600 visitors are allowed inside the building at any one time, during the day there's generally a very long wait. The good news: no Louvre-style mob scenes. The museum is nowhere near as big as it is great: Few tourists spend more than two hours inside. The paintings are displayed on one comfortable floor in chronological order from the 13th through 17th centuries.

Essential stops are (in this order) the Gothic altarpieces (narrative, prerealism, no real concern for believable depth); Giotto's altarpiece in the same room, which progressed beyond "totem-pole angels"; Uccello's *Battle of San Romano*, an early study in perspective (with a few obvious flubs); Fra Filippo Lippi's cuddly Madonnas; the Botticelli room, filled with masterpieces, including a pantheon of classical fleshiness and the small *La Calumnia*, showing the glasnost of Renaissance free-thinking being clubbed back into the darker age of Savonarola; two minor works by Leonardo; the octagonal classical sculpture room with an early painting of Bob Hope and a copy of Praxiteles' *Venus de Medici*—considered the epitome of beauty in Elizabethan Europe; Michelangelo's only surviving easel painting, the round *Holy Family*; Raphael's noble *Madonna of the Goldfinch*; Titian's voluptuous *Venus of Urbino*; and views from the café terrace at the end.

Cost, Hours, Reservations: L12,000, open Tue–Sun 8:30–18:50, Sat until 22:00, closed Mon (last entry 45 min before closing, take elevator or climb 4 long flights of stairs; Sat eve is least crowded).

Avoid the two-hour peak season midday wait by making a reservation. It's easy, slick, and costs only L3,000. Simply telephone during their office hours, choose a time, leave your name, and they'll give you a 15-minute entry time window and a five-digit confirmation number (call 055-294-883, Mon–Fri 8:30–18:30, Sat 9:00–12:00). You can reserve from months ahead to the day before (sometimes even on same day, but no guarantee). At the Uffizi, walk briskly past the 200-meter-long line to the special entrance for those with reservations (labeled in English "Entrance for Reservations Only"), give your name and number, pay (cash only), and scoot right in. You can reserve in advance for other museums—including the Bargello, Accademia (*David*), and Medici Chapel, though the only other one I'd consider reserving would be the Accademia.

If you haven't called ahead, you may be able to book directly at the Uffizi. Ask the clerk (who stands at the entrance for people with reservations) if you can make a reservation in person. He may direct you to the ticket office where you can secure a reservation for later in the day or the next day (depends on luck and availability).

Enjoy the Uffizi square, full of artists and souvenir stalls. The surrounding statues honor the earthshaking: artists, philosophers (Machiavelli), scientists (Galileo), writers (Dante), explorers (Amerigo Vespucci), and the great patron of so much Renaissance thinking, Lorenzo (the Magnificent) de Medici.

▲**Ponte Vecchio**—Florence's most famous bridge is lined with shops that have traditionally sold gold and silver. A statue of Cellini, the master goldsmith of the Renaissance, stands in the center, ignored by the flood of tacky tourism. Notice the "prince's passageway" above. In less secure times, the city leaders had a fortified passageway connecting the Palace Vecchio and Uffizi with the mighty Pitti Palace, to which they could flee in times of attack. This passageway, called the Vasari Corridor, is open to the persistent by request only (L12,000, Tue–Sat at 9:30, closed Mon, tel. 055-265-4321).

More Sights—Central Florence

▲▲**Santa Croce Church**—This 14th-century Franciscan church, decorated by centuries of precious art, holds the tombs of great Florentines (free, Mon–Sat 8:00–18:30, Sun 15:00–17:30, in winter Mon–Sat 8:00–12:30, 15:00–17:30, Sun 15:00–17:30, modest dress code enforced, tel. 055-244-619). The loud 19th-century Victorian Gothic facade faces a huge square ringed with tempting touristy shops and littered with tired tourists. Escape into the church.

Working counterclockwise from the entrance you'll find the tomb of Michelangelo (with the allegorical figures of painting, architecture, and sculpture), a memorial to Dante (no body...he was banished by his hometown), the tomb of Machiavelli (the originator of hardball politics), a relief by Donatello of the Annunciation, and the tomb of the composer Rossini. To the right of the altar, step into the sacristy where you'll find the bit of St. Francis' cowl (he is supposed to have founded the church around 1290) and old sheets of music with the medieval and mobile C clef (two little blocks on either side of the line determined to be middle C). In the bookshop notice the photos high on the wall of the devastating flood of 1966. Beyond that is a touristy—but mildly interesting—"leather school." The chapels lining the front of the church are richly frescoed. The Bardi Chapel (far left of altar) is a masterpiece by Giotto featuring scenes from the life of St. Francis. On your way out you'll pass the tomb of Galileo (allowed in by the church long after his death). The neighboring Pazzi Chapel (by Brunelleschi) is considered one of the finest pieces of Florentine Renaissance architecture.

▲▲**Museum of San Marco**—One block north of the Accademia on Piazza San Marco, this museum houses the greatest collection anywhere of medieval frescoes and paintings by the early Renaissance master Fra Angelico. You'll see why he thought of painting as a form of prayer and couldn't paint a crucifix without shedding tears. Each of the monks' cells has a Fra Angelico fresco. Don't miss the cell of Savonarola, the charismatic monk who rode in from the Christian right, threw out the Medici, turned Florence into a theocracy, sponsored "bonfires of the vanities" (burning books, paintings, and so on), and was finally burned himself when Florence decided to change channels (L8,000, daily 8:30–13:50, Sat until 19:00, but closed the first, third, and fifth Sun and the second and fourth Mon of each month, tel. 055-238-8608).

▲**Medici Chapel (Cappella dei Medici)**—This chapel, containing two Medici tombs, is drenched in incredibly lavish High Renaissance architecture and sculpture by Michelangelo (L11,000, daily 8:30–17:00 but closed the second and fourth Sun and the first, third, and fifth Mon of each month, tel. 055-233-8602). Behind San Lorenzo on Piazza Madonna is a lively market scene that I find just as interesting. Take a stroll through the huge double-decker central market one block north.

Science Museum (Museo di Storia della Scienza)—This is a fascinating collection of Renaissance and later clocks, telescopes, maps, and ingenious gadgets. One of the most talked-about bottles in Florence is the one here containing Galileo's finger. English guidebooklets are available. It's friendly, comfortably cool, never crowded, and just downstream from the Uffizi (L12,000, Mon and Wed–Fri 9:30–17:00, Tue and Sat 9:30–13:00, closed Sun, Piazza dei Giudici 1, tel. 055-239-8876).

▲**Michelangelo's Home, Casa Buonarroti**—Fans enjoy Michelangelo's house, which has some of his early, much-less-monumental statues and sketches (L12,000, Wed–Mon 9:30–14:00, closed Tue, English descriptions, Via Ghibellina 70).

Casa di Dante—Dante's house is five rooms in an old building with little of substance to show but lots of photos relating to the life and work of Dante. Although it's well described in English, it's interesting only to his fans (L5,000, Mon and Wed–Sat 10:00–18:00, Sun 10:00–14:00, closed Tue, across the street and around the corner from Bargello, at Via S. Margherita 1).

Church of Santa Maria Novella—This 13th-century Dominican church is rich in art. Along with crucifixes by Giotto and Brunelleschi, there's every textbook's example of the early Renaissance mastery of perspective: *The Holy Trinity* by Masaccio (free, Mon–Sat 7:00–12:00, 15:00–18:00, Sat until 17:00, Sun 15:00–17:00).

A palatial perfumery is around the corner at 16 Via della Scala. Thick with the lingering aroma of centuries of spritzes, it started as the herb garden of the Santa Maria Novella monks. Well-known even today for its top-quality products, it is extremely Florentine. Pick up the history sheet at the desk and wander deep into the shop. From the back room you can peek at the S. M. Novella cloister, with its dreamy frescoes, and imagine a time before Vespas and tourists.

Museum of Precious Stones (Museo dell' Opificio delle Pietre Dure)—This unusual gem of a museum features mosaics of inlaid marble and semiprecious stones, along with oil-painting copies (L4,000, Mon–Sat 8:15–14:00, Tue until 19:00, closed Sun, Via degli Alfani 78, around corner from Accademia).

Sights—Florence, South of the Arno River

▲▲**Pitti Palace**—From the Uffizi follow the elevated passageway (closed to non-Medicis) across the Ponte Vecchio bridge to the gargantuan Pitti Palace, which has five separate museums.

The **Palatine Gallery/Royal Apartments** features palatial room after chandeliered room, its walls sagging with paintings by the great masters. Its Raphael collection is the biggest anywhere (first floor, L14,000, Tue–Sun 8:30–18:50, Sat until 22:00, closed Mon, shorter hours off-season).

The **Modern Art Gallery** features Romanticism, neoclassicism, and Impressionism by 19th- and 20th-century Tuscan painters (second floor, L8,000, daily 8:30–13:50 but closed second and fourth Sun and first, third, and fifth Mon).

The **Grand Ducal Treasures**, or Museo degli Argenti, is the Medici treasure chest entertaining fans of applied arts with jeweled crucifixes, exotic porcelain, gilded ostrich eggs, and so on (ground floor, L4,000, same hours as Modern Art Gallery).

Behind the palace, the huge landscaped **Boboli Gardens** offer a shady refuge from the city heat (L4,000, Tue–Sun 9:00–18:30, until 19:30 June–Aug, until 16:30 in winter, closed first and last Mon of month).

▲**Brancacci Chapel**—For the best look at the early Renaissance master Massaccio, see his restored frescoes here (L6,000, Mon and Wed–Sat 10:00–17:00, Sun 13:00–17:00, closed Tue, cross Ponte Vecchio and turn right a few blocks to Piazza del Carmine). Since only a few tourists are let in at a time, seeing the chapel often involves a wait. The neighborhoods around here are considered the last surviving bits of old Florence.

▲**Piazzale Michelangelo**—Across the river overlooking the city (look for the huge statue of *David*), this square is worth the 30-minute hike, drive, or bus ride (either #12 or #13 from the train station) for the view of Florence and the stunning dome of the Duomo. After dark it's packed with local schoolkids feeding their dates slices of watermelon. Just beyond it is the stark and beautiful, crowd-free Romanesque San Miniato Church.

Experiences—Florence

▲▲*Gelato*—*Gelato* is an edible art form. Italy's best ice cream is in Florence—one souvenir that can't break and won't clutter your luggage. But beware of scams at touristy joints on busy streets that turn a simple request of a cone into a L15,000 "tourist special." The **Gelateria Carrozze** is very good (daily in summer 11:00–01:00, closed Wed in winter, on riverfront 30 meters from Ponte Vecchio toward the Uffizi, Via del Pesce 3). **Gelateria dei Neri**—considered by many to be the best in central Florence— is worth finding. It's two blocks east of Palazzo Vecchio at Via Dei Neri 20 red (daily in summer 12:00–23:00, closed Wed in winter). **Vivoli's** is a longtime favorite (Tue–Sun 8:00–01:00, closed Mon, the last 3 weeks in Aug, and winter; opposite the Church of Santa Croce, go down Via Torta a block, turn right on Via Stinche; before ordering, try a free sample of their *riso*— rice). The **Cinema Astro**, across the street from Vivoli's, plays English/American movies in their original language (closed Mon).

Shopping

Florence is a great shopping town. Busy street scenes and markets abound, especially near San Lorenzo, near Santa Croce, and on Ponte Vecchio (plus 3 blocks north of bridge at Mercato Nuovo—a covered market square). Leather (often better quality for less than the U.S. price), gold, silver, art prints, and tacky plaster "mini-*Davids*" are most popular. Prices are soft in the markets. Many spend entire days shopping. Shops usually have promotional stalls in the market squares. For ritzy Italian fashions, browse along Via de Tornabuoni, Via della Vigna Nuova, and Via Strozzi. Typical chain department stores are Coin (Mon–Sat 9:30–20:00, Sun 11:00–20:00, on Via Calzaiuoli, near Orsanmichele church) and Standa (Mon–Sat 9:00–19:55, closed Sun, at intersection of Via Panzani and Via del Giglio, near train station). For shopping ideas, ads, and a list of markets, see the *Florence Concierge Information* magazine described under "Tourist Information," above (free from TI and many hotels).

Side Trips to Fiesole and Siena

For a candid peek at **Fiesole**—a Florentine suburb—ride bus #7 (3/hrly, from Piazza Adua, northeast side of the station and from Piazza San Marco) for about 25 minutes through neighborhood gardens, vineyards, orchards, and large villas to the last stop—Fiesole. Fiesole is a popular excursion from Florence because of its small eateries and its good views of Florence. Catch the sunset from the terrace just below the La Reggia restaurant; from the Fiesole bus stop, face the bell tower and take the very steep Via San Francisco on your left. You'll find the view terrace near the top of the hill.

Connoisseurs of peace and small towns who aren't into art or shopping (and who won't be seeing Siena otherwise) should consider riding the bus to **Siena** (75 minutes if you take the *corse rapide* via the autostrada). This can be a day trip or an evening trip. Siena is magic after dark. Confirm when the last bus returns. For more on Siena, see the chapter on Hill Towns of Central Italy.

Sleeping in Florence
(L2,000 = about $1, country code: 39)

Sleep Code: **S** = Single, **D** = Double/Twin, **T** = Triple, **Q** = Quad, **b** = bathroom, **s** = shower only, **CC** = Credit Card (**V**isa, **M**aster-Card, **A**mex), **SE** = Speaks English, **NSE** = No English. Unless otherwise noted, breakfast is included (but usually optional). English is generally spoken.

The accommodations scene varies wildly with the season. Spring and fall are very tight and expensive, while mid-July through August are wide open and discounted. November through February is also generally empty. With good information and a phone call ahead, you can find a stark, clean, and comfortable double with breakfast for L120,000, with a private shower for L170,000 (less at the smaller places, such as the *soggiornos*). You get elegance for L200,000. Many places listed are old and rickety. I can't imagine Florence any other way. Rooms with air-conditioning cost around L200,000—worth the extra lire in the summer. Virtually all of the places are central, within minutes of the great sights.

Call direct to the hotel. Do not use the TI, which costs your host and jacks up the price. In slow times, budget travelers call around and find soft prices. Ask if you'll get a discount for paying in cash or for staying for three or more nights (or both). And ask if you can skip breakfast (these overpriced breakfasts are legally optional, though some hotels pretend otherwise).

Call ahead. I repeat, call ahead. Places will hold a room

Florence Hotels and Restaurants

1 - HOTEL ACCADEMIA
2 - HOTEL MORANDI
3 - CASA RABATTI
4 - SOGGIORNO PEZZATI
5 - HOTEL ENZA
6 - SOGGIORNO MAGLIANI
7 - HOTEL LOGGIATO DEI SERVITI
8 - DUE FONTANE HOTEL
9 - HOTEL MONNA LISA & OBLATE
10 - SOGGIORNO LA PERGOLA
11 - PALAZZO CASTIGLIONI & HOTEL ALDOBRANDINI

12 - HOTEL BELLETTINI
13 - HOTEL BASILEA
14 - PENSIONE CENTRALE
15 - PICNIC SPOT IF NOT TOO HOT
16 - OSTERIA BELLEDONNE
17 - HOTEL PENDINI
18 - PENSIONE MAXIM
19 - HOTEL RITZ
20 - HOTEL ELITE
21 - ALBERGO MONTREALE
22 - PENSIONE SOLE

23 - PENSIONE BRETAGNA
24 - FLORENCE WALKING TOURS
25 - TORRE GUELFA, APOSTOLI & ALESSANDRA HOTELS
26 - TRATTORIA IL CONTADINO
27 - TRATTORIA DA GIORGIO
28 - GROTTA DI LEO
29 - TRATTORIA BURRASCA
30 - HYDRA PIZZERIA
31 - ROSTICCERIA GIULIANO
32 - OSTERIA SAPORI
33 - CANTINETTA VERRAZZANO

until early afternoon. If they say they're full, mention you're using this book.

Laundromats: The Wash & Dry Lavarapido chain offers long hours and efficient self-service Laundromats at several locations (daily 8:00–22:00, tel. 055-580-480). Close to recommended hotels: Via dei Servi 105 red (near *David*), Via del Sole 29 red and Via della Scala 52 red (between station and river), and Via dei Serragli 87 red (across the river). East of the station another handy modern launderette is just off Via Cavour at Via Guelfa 22 red (daily 8:00–22:00, 12 pounds wash and dry for L12,000).

Sleeping between the Station and Duomo (zip code: 50123)

Hotel Accademia is an elegant two-star hotel with marble stairs, parquet floors, attractive public areas, 16 pleasant rooms, and a floor plan that defies logic (S with private bath down hall-L150,000, Sb-L160,000, Db-L230,000, Tb-L290,000, these discounted prices only with this book, CC:VMA, air-con, TV, tiny courtyard, Via Faenza 7, tel. 055-293-451, fax 055-219-771, www.accademiahotel.net, e-mail: info@accademiahotel.net).

Hotel Bellettini has 33 bright, cool, well-cared-for rooms with tile floors, inviting lounges, and a touch of class. Its five rooms in an annex two blocks away are three-star quality with all the comforts, but you need to come to the main hotel for breakfast (Sb-L150,000, Db-L200,000, Tb-L270,000, Qb-L340,000, CC:VMA, 5 percent discount with this book, buffet breakfast, air-con, free Internet access, Via de' Conti 7, tel. 055-213-561, fax 055-283-551, www.firenze.net/hotelbellettini, e-mail: hotel.bellettini@dada.it).

Residenza Dei Pucci, a block north of the Duomo, has 12 tastefully decorated rooms—in soothing earth tones—with good furniture and tweed carpeting. Just opened last year, it's fresh and bright. The suite has a huge view of the dome (Db-L230,000, Db suite-L315,000, these discounted prices good only with this book, includes breakfast—served in room, CC:VM, treats and beverages available in afternoon, Via dei Pucci 9, tel. 055-281-886, fax 055-264-314, SE).

Palazzo Castiglioni, newly opened, offers six grand rooms with all the conveniences in a 19th-century palazzo package. Most rooms are spacious, several have frescoes, and all make a fine splurge (Db-L320,000, Db suite-L400,000, includes breakfast, CC:VM, air-con, elevator, Via del Giglio 8, tel. 055-214-886, fax 055-274-0521, e-mail: torre.guelfa@flashnet.it, Giancarlo and Sabina).

Pensione Centrale, a happy and traditional-feeling place, is indeed central. Run by aristocratic Marie Therese Blot, spunky Margherita, and Franco, you'll feel right at home

(18 rooms, D-L170,000, Db-L200,000 with an "American" breakfast, CC:VMA, quiet, some air-con rooms, often filled with American students, elevator, Via de' Conti 3, tel. 055-215-761, fax 055-215-216). They sometimes send people to a nearby, noisier pension; confirm that your reservation is for this place.

Hotel Aldobrandini, a good budget choice, has 15 decent, clean, affordable rooms, with the San Lorenzo market at its doorstep and the entrance to the Medici Chapel a few steps away (Ss-L80,000, Sb-L100,000, D-L120,000, Db-L150,000, includes breakfast, CC:VM, noisy in front, quieter rooms in back, lots of stairs, Piazza Madonna Degli Aldobrandini 8, tel. 055-211-866, fax 055-267-6281, e-mail: welcome@srl.com).

Sleeping near the Central Market
(zip code: 50129)

Hotel Basilea features a rare ground-floor lobby and offers predictable three-star, air-conditioned comfort in its 38 modern rooms (Db-L200,000–280,000 depending on season, CC:VM, elevator, terrace, free e-mail service, Via Guelfa 41, at intersection with Nazionale—a busy street, ask for rooms in the back, tel. 055-214-587, fax 055-268-350, e-mail: basilea@dada.it).

Casa Rabatti is the ultimate if you always wanted to be a part of a Florentine family. It's simple, clean, friendly, and run with motherly warmth by Marcella and her husband Celestino, who speak minimal English (4 rooms, D-L85,000, Db-L100,000, L40,000 per bed in shared quad or quint, prices good with this book, no breakfast, no sign other than on doorbell, 5 blocks from station, Via San Zanobi 48 black, tel. 055-212-393).

Soggiorno Pezzati Daniela is another quiet little place with six homey rooms (Sb-L78,000, Db-L105,000, Tb-L150,000, Qb-L180,000, no breakfast, marked only by small sign near door, Via San Zanobi 22, tel. 055-291-660, fax 055-287-145, e-mail: 055291660@iol.it, Daniela SE). If you get an Italian recording when you call, hang on—your call is being transferred to a cell phone.

Hotel Enza rents 16 quirky rooms. While Eugenia's chihuahua, Tricky, is tiny, her rooms are spacious (S-L80,000, Sb-L85,000, D-L100,000, Ds-L120,000, Db-L135,000, T-L135,000, Tb-L175,000, family loft, no breakfast provided, CC to reserve but pay cash, Via San Zanobi 45 black, tel. 055-490-990, fax 055-473-672).

Central and humble **Soggiorno Magliani** feels and smells like a great-grandmother's place (7 rooms, S-L60,000, D-L80,000, double-paned windows don't quite keep out street noise, near corner of Via Guelfa and Via Reparata, Via Reparata 1, tel. 055-287-378, run by a friendly family duo, Vincenza and English-speaking daughter Cristina).

Sleeping East of the Duomo

The first two listings are near the Accademia, on Piazza Annunziata (zip code: 50122).

Hotel Loggiato dei Serviti, at the most prestigious address in Florence on the most Renaissance square in town, gives you Renaissance romance with a place to plug in your hair dryer (29 rooms, Sb-L250,000, Db-L380,000, family suites from L500,000, book a month ahead during peak season, discounts in Aug, CC:VMA, elevator, square noisy at night, Piazza S.S. Annunziata 3, tel. 055-289-592, fax 055-289-595, e-mail: loggiato_serviti@italyhotel.com, SE). Stone stairways lead you under open-beam ceilings through this 16th-century monastery's elegant public rooms. The cells, with air-conditioning, TVs, mini-bars, and telephones, wouldn't be recognized by their original inhabitants.

Le Due Fontane Hotel faces the same great square but fills its old building with a smoky, 1970s, business-class ambience. Its 57 air-conditioned rooms are big and comfortable (Sb-L190,000, Db-L260,000, Tb-L370,000, buffet breakfast, CC:VMA, phones, TVs, elevator, they're trying to make third floor nonsmoking, Piazza S.S. Annunziata 14, tel. 055-210-185, fax 055-294-461, SE).

At **Hotel Morandi alla Crocetta**, a former convent, you're enveloped in a 16th-century cocoon. Located on a quiet street, with period furnishings throughout the hotel, parquet floors, and wood-beamed ceilings, it draws you in (Sb-L160,000, Db-L270,000, CC:VM, Via Laura 50, a block off Piazza S.S. Annunziata, tel. 055-234-4747, fax 055-248-0954, www.hotelmorandi.it, e-mail: welcome@hotelmorandi.it).

Hotel Monna Lisa, my only four-star listing in this neighborhood, is an art-filled convent-turned-palace with an elegant garden, palatial public spaces, and professional service. It's steeped in history. Judging from the guest book, its visitors are happy to have paid the ransom (30 rooms, Db-L370,000 most of the year but L550,000 mid-March–mid-July and Sept–Oct, CC:VMA, air-con, parking, 3 blocks east of Duomo at Borgo Pinti 27, tel. 055-247-9751, fax 055-247-9755, www.monnalisa.it, e-mail: monnalis@ats.it).

The **Oblate Sisters of the Assumption** run a small hotel in a Renaissance building with a dreamy garden and a quiet, institutional feel (S-L65,000, D-L120,000, Db-L130,000, big L25,000 dinners, elevator, Borgo Pinti 15, 50121 Firenze, tel. 055-248-0582, fax 055-234-6291, NSE).

Soggiorno La Pergola is a homey, air-conditioned place with 14 rooms, some with kitchenettes (Db-L150,000–190,000, Qb-L200,000–250,000 depending on season, Via della Pergola 23, tel. & fax 055-700-896).

Sleeping on or near Piazza Repubblica
(zip code: 50123)

These are the most central of my accommodations recommendations, though given Florence's walkable core, nearly every hotel can be considered central.

Hotel Pendini, a three-star hotel with 42 elegant rooms (8 with views of the square), is popular and central, overlooking Piazza Repubblica (Sb–from L200,000, Db–from L280,000 depending on season, CC:VMA, elevator, fine lounge and breakfast room, air-con, Via Strozzi 2, reserve ASAP, tel. 055-211-170, fax 055-281-807, e-mail: pendini@dada.it).

Pensione Maxim, right on Via Calz, is a big, institutional-feeling place as close to the sights as possible. Its halls are narrow, but the 26 rooms are comfortable and well maintained (Sb–L150,000, Db–L170,000, Tb–L225,000, Qb–L280,000, with breakfast, add L10,000 per person per day for air-con June–Sept, CC:VMA but pay first night in cash, Internet access, phones, elevator, no curfew, Via dei Calzaiuoli 11, tel. 055-217-474, fax 055-283-729, www.firenzealbergo.it/home/hotelmaxim, e-mail: hotmaxim@tin.it, Paolo and Nicola Maioli).

Soggiorno Battistero, next door to the Baptistery, has seven simple, airy rooms, most with urban noise but great views overlooking the Baptistery and square. You're in the heart of Florence (S-L80,000, D-L120,000, Db-L150,000, Tb-L180,000, breakfast extra—served in room, Internet access, CC:VM, Piazza San Giovanni 1, third floor, tel. 055-295-143, fax 055-268-189, www.venere.it/firenze/battistero, e-mail: battistero@dada.it, run by Italian Luca and American wife Kelly).

Sleeping South of the Train Station near Piazza Santa Maria Novella
(zip code: 50123)

From the station, follow the Galleria S.M. Novella tunnel (with back to tracks, outside on the left) to Piazza Santa Maria Novella, a pleasant square by day that becomes a little sleazy after dark. Note: Theft alert in the tunnel, where the tunnel surfaces, and at night. The square is handy—only three blocks from the cathedral and near a good **launderette** (Lavarapido, daily 8:00–22:00, Via della Scala 52 red) and cheap restaurants (on Via Palazzuolo, see below).

Hotel Pensione Elite, with eight comfortable rooms and a charm rare in this price range, is a fine basic value run warmly by Maurizio and Nadia (Ss-L90,000, Sb-L120,000, Ds-L130,000, Db-L150,000, breakfast-L10,000, at south end of square with back to church, go right to Via della Scala 12, second floor, tel. & fax 055-215-395, SE).

The nearby **Albergo Montreal** is OK for backpackers, with 18 clean, airy, characterless, although renovated, rooms

(S-L75,000, Db-L120,000, Tb-L160,000, mention this book when reserving to get these prices, no breakfast, Via della Scala 43, tel. 055-238-2331, fax 055-287-491, e-mail: info@hotelmontreal.com, SE).

Pensione Sole, a clean, cozy, family-run place with seven bright, modern rooms, is just off Santa Maria Novella toward the river (Db-L120,000–130,000, no breakfast; air-con, phone, elevator, Via del Sole 8, third floor, tel. & fax 055-239-6094, friendly Anna NSE).

Sleeping near Arno River and Ponte Vecchio (zip code: 50123)

Pensione Bretagna is an Old World–elegant place. It's run by the helpful, English-speaking Antonio, Maura, and Sara. Imagine eating breakfast under a painted, chandeliered ceiling overlooking the Arno River (S-L80,000, Ss-L90,000, Sb-L100,000, D-L130,000, Ds-L145,000, Db-L175,000, Tb-L220,000, Qb-L245,000, including optional L5,000 breakfast, family deals, prices special with this book through 2001, CC:VMA, air-con, elevator, just past Ponte San Trinita, Lungarno Corsini 6, tel. 055-289-618, fax 055-289-619, www.bretagna.it, e-mail: hotel@bretagna.it). They also run Althea, a cheaper place with nicer rooms, near Piazza San Spirito in the Oltrarno neighborhood (Db-L120,000, no breakfast, no reception desk, call Bretagna to book).

Hotel Torre Guelfa is topped with a fun medieval tower with a panoramic rooftop terrace and a huge living room. Its 16 rooms vary wildly in size (Sb-L180,000, small Db-L250,000, Db-L290,000–300,000). Number 15, with a private terrace—L350,000—is worth reserving several months in advance (elevator, air-con, a couple blocks northwest of Ponte Vecchio, Borgo S.S. Apostoli 8, tel. 055-239-6338, fax 055-239-8577, http://home .venere.it/firenze/torreguelfa, e-mail: torre.guelfa@flashnet.it, Giancarlo, Carlo, and Luigi all SE).

Residenza Apostoli, in the same building, is bright, spacious, and modern, with parquet floors and 12 air-conditioned rooms all buried in a very old building on a quiet street one block off the river (Sb-L190,000–200,000, Db-L200,000–250,000 depending on season, breakfast in room, CC:VM, 10 percent discount with this book, stay-awhile TV lounge, elevator, Borgo Santi Apostoli 8, tel. 055-284-837, fax 055-268-790, run by Mirella).

Hotel Pensione Alessandra is an old 16th-century, peaceful place with 25 big rooms (S-L120,000, Sb-L190,000, D-L190,000, Db-L250,000, T-L250,000, Tb-L330,000, Q-L280,000, Qb-L370,000, includes breakfast, CC:VMA, most rooms have air-con, 2 have views, Borgo S.S. Apostoli 17, tel. 055-283-438, fax 055-210-619, www.hotelalessandra.com).

Hotel Ritz is a grand, riverside, four-star place with all the comforts, (Db-L200,000–320,000, Lungarno della Zecca Vecchia 24, 50122 Firenze, tel. 055-234-0650, fax 055-24-0863, e-mail: ritz@dada.it).

Sleeping in Oltrarno, South of the River (zip code: 50125)

Across the river in the Oltrarno area, between the Pitti Palace and Ponte Vecchio, you'll still find small traditional crafts shops, neighborly piazzas, and family eateries. The following places are a few minutes' walk from Ponte Vecchio.

Hotel La Scaletta is elegant, friendly, and clean, with a dark, cool, labyrinthine floor plan, lots of Old World lounges, and a romantic and panoramic roof terrace. Owner Barbara, her son Manfredo, and daughters Bianca and Diana run this well-worn but loved place. If Manfredo is cooking dinner, eat here (S-L100,000, Sb-L180,000, D-L190,000, Db-L210,000–240,000, Tb-L250,000–270,000, Qb-L280,000–300,000, higher price is for quieter rooms in back, L10,000–20,000 discount if you pay cash, CC:VM, air-con in 3 rooms and fans in others, elevator, bar, Via Guicciardini 13 black, 150 meters south of Ponte Vecchio, tel. 055-283-028, fax 055-289-562, www.lascaletta.com, e-mail: lascaletta.htl@dada.it). Reserve by phone, confirm by fax, then send a personal or traveler's check.

Hotel Silla, a classic three-star hotel with 36 cheery, spacious, pastel, and modern rooms, is a fine value. It faces the river and overlooks a park opposite the Santa Croce Church (Db-L290,000, includes breakfast, CC:VMA, elevator, air-con, Via dei Renai 5, 50125 Florence, tel. 055-234-2888, fax 055-234-1437, www.hotelsilla.it, e-mail: hotelsilla@tin.it, SE).

Pensione Sorelle Bandini is a ramshackle, 500-year-old palace on a perfectly Florentine square, with cavernous rooms, museum-warehouse interiors, a musty youthfulness, cats, a balcony lounge-loggia with a view, and an ambience that, for romantic bohemians, can be a highlight of Florence. Mimmo or Sr. Romeo will hold a room until 16:00 with a phone call (D-L172,000, Db-L200,000, T-L240,000, Tb-L290,000, includes breakfast, elevator, Piazza Santo Spirito 9, tel. 055-215-308, fax 055-282-761).

Soggiorno Pezzati Alessandra is a warm and friendly place renting five great rooms in the Oltrarno neighborhood (Sb-L78,000, Db-L105,000, Tb-L150,000, Qb-L180,000, no breakfast, Via Borgo San Frediano 6, tel. 055-290-424, fax 055-264-6742, e-mail: alex170169@libero.it, Alessandra). If you get an Italian recording when you call, hang on—your call is being transferred to a cell phone.

Istituto Gould is a Protestant Church–run place with 33 clean but drab rooms with twin beds and modern facilities (S-L55,000, Sb-L65,000, D-L78,000, Db-L86,000, Tb-L114,000,

Florence's Oltrarno Neighborhood

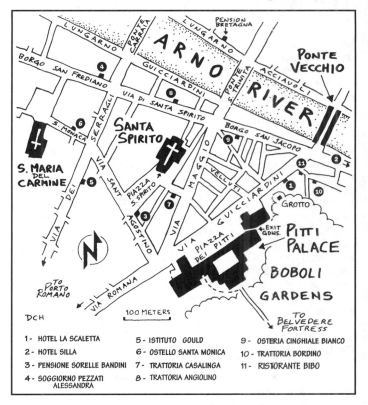

1 - HOTEL LA SCALETTA
2 - HOTEL SILLA
3 - PENSIONE SORELLE BANDINI
4 - SOGGIORNO PEZZATI ALESSANDRA
5 - ISTITUTO GOULD
6 - OSTELLO SANTA MONICA
7 - TRATTORIA CASALINGA
8 - TRATTORIA ANGIOLINO
9 - OSTERIA CINGHIALE BIANCO
10 - TRATTORIA BORDINO
11 - RISTORANTE BIBO

L37,000 in quads, L33,000 in quints, no breakfast, quieter rooms in back, Via dei Serragli 49, tel. 055-212-576, fax 055-280-274, e-mail: gould.reception@dada.it). You must arrive when the office is open (Mon–Fri 9:00–13:00, 15:00–19:00, Sat 9:00–13:00, no check-in Sun).

Ostello Santa Monaca, a cheap hostel, is a few blocks south of Ponte Alla Carraia, one of the bridges over the Arno (L26,000 beds, 10-bed rooms, breakfast extra, 01:00 curfew, Via Santa Monaca 6, tel. 055-268-338, fax 055-280-185).

Sleeping Away from the Center

Hotel Ungherese, warmly run by Sergio and Rosemary, is good for drivers. It's northeast of the city center (near Stadio, en route to Fiesole), with easy, free street parking and quick bus access (#11 and #17) into central Florence (Sb-L120,000, Db-L210,000, these discounted prices available with this book, pay cash for additional 7 percent discount, rooms are 20 percent less off-season, includes breakfast, CC:VM, most rooms air-con, Via G. B. Amici 8, tel. & fax 055-573-474, www.prato.dada.it/ungherese, e-mail: hotel .ungherese@dada.it, NSE). It has great singles and a backyard garden terrace (ask for a room on the garden). On the downside, no restaurants are nearby (eat in Florence).

Villa Camerata, classy for an IYHF hostel, is on the outskirts of Florence (L25,000 per bed with breakfast, 4- to 12-bed rooms, no reservations, show up 9:00–13:00, ride bus #17 to Salviatino stop, Via Righi 2, tel. 055-601-451).

Eating in Florence

To save money and time for sights, you can keep meals fast and simple, eating in one of the countless self-service places and pizzerias or just picnicking (try juice, yogurt, cheese, and a roll for L10,000). Or consider the following.

Eating in Oltrarno, South of the River

For a change of scene, I'd eat across the river in Oltrarno. Here are a few good places just over Ponte Vecchio and on or near Piazza Santo Spirito.

A block south of Ponte Vecchio is the unpretentious and happy Piazza San Felicita, with two great restaurants to consider. **Ristorante Bibo** serves *"cucina tipica Fiorentina"* with smart and friendly service, an air-conditioned interior, and leafy candlelit outdoor seating (good L28,000 3-course meal, CC:VMA, reserve for outdoor seating, Fri–Wed 11:00–15:00, 19:00–24:00, closed Thu, Piazza San Felicita 6 red, tel. 055-239-8554). The cozier **Trattoria Bordino**, just up the street, is similar, serving fine Florentine cuisine (L40,000 dinners, cheaper options, Mon–Sat 12:00–14:30, 19:30–22:30, closed Sun, Via Stracciatella 9 red).

Piazza Santo Spirito is a classic Florentine square (and therefore touristy) with two classy and popular little restaurants offering good local cuisine every night of the week, indoor and on-the-square seating (reserve for on-the-square), moderate prices, and impersonal service: **Borgo Antico** (Piazza Santo Spirito 6 red, tel. 055-210-437) and **Osteria Santo Spirito** (Piazza Santo Spirito 16 red, tel. 055-238-2383).

The **Ricchi Caffè**, next to Borgo Antico, has fine gelati and shaded outdoor tables across the street. Notice how plain the facade of the Brunelleschi church facing the square is. Then step inside, grab a coffee, and ponder the many proposals on how it might be finished.

Trattoria Casalinga is an inexpensive standby. Famous for its home cooking, it's now filled with tourists rather than locals. But it sends them away full, happy, and with lire left for *gelato* (closed Sun, plus all of Aug, just off Piazza Santo Spirito, near the church at Via dei Michelozzi 9 red, tel. 055-218-624).

Consider **Osteria del Cinghiale Bianco** (Borgo S. Jacopo 43 red, air-con, closed Tue–Wed, tel. 055-215-706), **Trattoria Angiolino** (closed Mon, Via Santo Spirito 36 red, tel. 055-239-8976), or other inviting places along Via Santo Spirito.

Eating North of the River

Eating near Santa Maria Novella and the Train Station
Osteria Belledonne is a crowded and cheery hole-in-the-wall serving great food at good prices. I loved the meal but had to correct the bill—read it carefully (Mon–Fri 12:00–14:30, 19:00–22:30, closed Sat–Sun, Via delle Belledonne 16 red, tel. 055-238-2609). **Ristorante La Spada**, nearby, is another local favorite serving typical Tuscan cuisine with less atmosphere and more menu (L23,000 lunch special, air-con, near Via della Spada at Via del Moro 66 red, tel. 055-218-757).

Twin chow houses for local workers offer a L17,000, hearty, family-style, fixed-price menu with a bustling working-class/budget-Yankee-traveler atmosphere (Mon–Sat 12:00–14:30, 18:15–21:30 or 22:00, closed Sun, 2 blocks south of train station): **Trattoria il Contadino** (Via Palazzuolo 69 red, tel. 055-238-2673) and **Trattoria da Giorgio** (across the street at Via Palazzuolo 100 red). Arrive early or wait.

The touristy **La Grotta di Leo** (a block away) has a cheap, straightforward menu and edible food and pizza (daily 11:00–01:00, Via della Scala 41 red, tel. 055-219-265).

Eating near the Central and San Lorenzo Markets
For mountains of picnic produce or just a cheap sandwich and piles of people watching, visit the huge, multistoried Central Market—**Mercato Centrale** (Mon–Sat 7:00–14:00, closed Sun), a block north of the San Lorenzo street market.

Trattoria la Burrasca is a small, inexpensive place serving local-style dishes in a characteristic setting (Fri–Wed 12:00–15:00, 19:00–22:00, closed Thu, Via Panicale 6 black, at north corner of Central Market, tel. 055-215-827).

Hydra Pizzeria Spaghetteria, two blocks south, is brighter and more modern (closed Tue off-season, CC:VM, across from entrance of Medici Chapel, amid San Lorenzo street market, Canto de' Nelli 38 red, tel. 055-218-922).

Eating near Palazzo Vecchio
The cozy **Rosticceria Giulano Centro**, a few blocks east of the Palazzo Vecchio, serves fine food to go or enjoy there (Tue–Sat 8:00–15:30, 17:00–21:30, closed Sun–Mon, Via Dei Neri 74 red).

Osteria Vini e Vecchi Sapori is a colorful hole-in-the-wall serving traditional food, including plates of mixed sandwiches (L1,500 each), half a block north of the Palazzo Vecchio (Tue–Sun 9:30–22:30, closed Mon, Via dei Magazzini 3 red, facing the bronze equestrian statue in Piazza della Signoria, go behind its tail to your left).

Cantinetta dei Verrazzano is a long-established bakery/café/wine bar serving elegant sandwich plates and hot focaccia sandwiches in an elegant old-time setting (until 21:00, closed Sun, just off Via Calzaiuoli on a side street across from Orsanmichele at Via dei Tavolini 18, tel. 055-268-590).

For a reasonably priced pizza with a Medici-style view, consider one of the pizzerias on Piazza della Signoria.

Transportation Connections—Florence

By train to: Assisi (3/day, 2 hrs, more frequent with transfers, direction: Foligno), **Orvieto** (6/day, 2 hrs), **Pisa** (2/hrly, 1 hr), **La Spezia** (for the Cinque Terre, 2/day direct, 2 hrs, or change in Pisa), **Venice** (7/day, 3 hrs), **Milan** (12/day, 3–5 hrs), **Rome** (hrly, 2.5 hrs), **Naples** (2/day, 4 hrs), **Brindisi** (3/day, 11 hrs with change in Bologna), **Frankfurt** (3/day, 12 hrs), **Paris** (1/day, 12 hrs overnight), **Vienna** (4/day, 9–10 hrs). Train info: tel. 147-888-088.

Buses: The SITA bus station, a block west of the Florence train station, is user-friendly (but remember, bus service drops dramatically on Sunday). Schedules are posted everywhere with TV monitors indicating imminent departures. You'll find buses to: **San Gimignano** (hrly at :40 past the hour, 1.75 hrs), **Siena** (hrly at :10 past the hour, 75-min *corse rapide* fast buses, faster than the train, avoid the 2-hr *diretta* slow buses), and the **airport** (hrly, 15 min). Bus info: tel. 055-214-721 from 9:30 to 12:30; some schedules are in the *Florence Concierge Information* magazine.

VENICE (VENEZIA)

Soak all day in this puddle of elegant decay. Venice is Europe's best-preserved big city. This car-free urban wonderland of 100 islands—laced together by 400 bridges and 2,000 alleys—survives on the artificial respirator of tourism.

Born in a lagoon 1,500 years ago as a refuge from barbarians, Venice is overloaded with tourists and is slowly sinking (unrelated facts). In the Middle Ages, the Venetians, becoming Europe's clever middlemen for east-west trade, created a great trading empire. By smuggling in the bones of St. Mark (San Marco, in about A.D. 830), Venice gained religious importance as well. With the discovery of America and new trading routes to the Orient, Venetian power ebbed. But as Venice fell, her appetite for decadence grew. Through the 17th and 18th centuries, Venice partied on the wealth accumulated through earlier centuries as a trading power.

Today Venice is home to about 70,000 people in its old city, down from a peak population of around 200,000. While there are about 500,000 in greater Venice (counting the mainland, not counting tourists), the old town has a small-town feel. Locals seem to know everyone. To see small-town Venice through the touristic flak, get away from the Rialto-San Marco tourist zone and savor the town early and late without the hordes of vacationers day-tripping in from nearby beach resorts. A 10-minute walk from the madness puts you in an idyllic Venice few tourists see.

Planning Your Time

Venice is worth at least a day on even the speediest tour. Hyper-efficient train travelers take the night train in and/or out. Sleep in the old center to experience Venice at its best: early and late. For a one-day visit, cruise the Grand Canal, do the major sights on

Venice

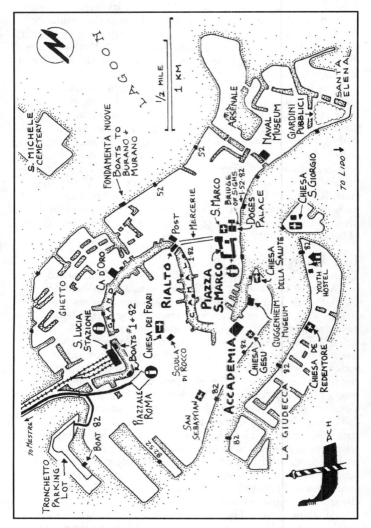

St. Mark's Square (the square itself, Doge's Palace, St. Mark's Basilica), see the Church of the Frari (Chiesa dei Frari) for art, and wander the back streets on a pub crawl (see "Eating," below). Venice's greatest sight is the city itself. Make time to simply wander. While doable in a day, Venice is worth two. It's a medieval cookie jar, and nobody's looking.

Orientation

The island city of Venice is shaped like a fish. Its major thoroughfares are canals. The Grand Canal winds through the middle of
the fish, starting at the mouth where all the people and food enter,
passing under the Rialto Bridge, and ending at St. Mark's Square
(San Marco). Park your 21st-century perspective at the mouth and
let Venice swallow you whole.

Venice is a carless kaleidoscope of people, bridges, and odor-
less canals. The city has no real streets, and addresses are hope-
lessly confusing. There are six districts: San Marco (most touristy),
Castello (behind San Marco), Cannaregio (from the station to the
Rialto), San Polo (other side of the Rialto), Santa Croce, and Dorsoduro. Each district has about 6,000 address numbers. Luckily it's
easy to find your way, since many street corners have a sign pointing you to the nearest major landmark, such as San Marco, Accademia, Rialto, and Ferrovia (the train station). To find your way,
navigate by landmarks, not streets. Obedient visitors stick to the
main thoroughfares as directed by these signs and miss the charm
of backstreet Venice.

Tourist Information

There are TIs at the train station (daily 8:10–18:50, crowded
and surly), at the far end of St. Mark's Square (Mon–Sat 9:00–
17:00, friendly), and near St. Mark's Square on the lagoon (daily
10:00–18:00, sells *vaporetto* tickets, rents audioguides for self-
guided walking tours). For a quick question, save time by phoning
(tel. 041-529-8711, www.turismovenezia.it). At any TI, pick up a
free city map and the free *Leo* bimonthly magazine, which comes
with an insert, *Leo Bussola*, that lists museum hours, exhibitions,
and musical events (in Italian and English). Confirm your sightseeing plans. Ask for the fine brochures outlining three offbeat
Venice walks. The free periodical entertainment guide *Un Ospite
de Venezia* (a monthly listing of events, nightlife, museum hours,
train and *vaporetto*—motorized bus-boat—schedules, emergency
telephone numbers, and so on) is available at the TI or fancy hotel
reception desks. The cheap Venice map on sale at postcard racks
has much more detail than the TI map. Also consider the little
guidebook (sold alongside the postcards), which comes with a
city map and explanations of the major sights.

Walking Tours: The TI offers audioguides for self-guided
walking tours of Venice's neighborhoods (5 to choose from: San
Marco, Rialto, Santa Croce, Cannaregio, and Castello; prices range
from L4,000 for 1 tour to L30,000 for all; available at TI at lagoon
near St. Mark's Square—maybe also at other TIs in 2001).

Local guide Alessandro Schezzini gets beyond the clichés and
into offbeat Venice (L175,000, 2.5 hrs, tel. & fax 041-534-5367,
cellular 033-5530-9024, e-mail: venische@tiscalinet.it).

Arrival in Venice

A three-kilometer-long causeway (with highway and train lines) connects Venice to the mainland. Mestre, Venice's sprawling mainland industrial base, has fewer crowds, cheaper hotels, plenty of parking lots, but no charm. Don't stop here (unless you're parking your car in a lot). Trains regularly connect Mestre with Venice's Santa Lucia station (6/hrly, 5 min).

By Train: Venice's Santa Lucia train station plops you right into the old town on the Grand Canal, an easy *vaporetto* ride or fascinating 40-minute walk from St. Mark's Square. Upon arrival, skip the station's crowded TI (the two TIs at St. Mark's Square are better); it's not worth a long wait for a miminal map (if you want a map now, buy one at a newsstand). Confirm your departure plan (stop by train info desk or just study the *partenze*—departure—posters on walls). Consider storing unnecessary heavy bags, although it's not worth it if the lines for baggage check are long, sweaty, and dreary (baggage check at platform 14, L5,000/12 hrs, L10,000/24 hrs, daily 03:45–00:30; or lockers at platform 1—L3,000–5,000, often either in use or broken). Then walk straight out of the station to the canal. The dock for *vaporetti* #1 and #82 is on your left (for downtown Venice, most recommended hotels, and Grand Canal Tour); the dock for #51 and #52 is on your right (for two recommended hotels). Buy a L6,000 ticket at the ticket window and hop on a boat for downtown (direction: Rialto or San Marco).

By Car: The freeway ends at Venice. Follow the green lights directing you to a parking lot with space, probably Tronchetto (across the causeway and on the right), which has a huge, multi-storied garage (L30,000/day, half price with discount coupon from your hotel). From there you'll find travel agencies masquerading as TIs and *vaporetto* docks for the boat connection (#82) to the town center. Don't let taxi boatmen con you out of the cheap (L6,000) *vaporetto* ride. Parking in Mestre is easy and cheap (open-air lots L8,000/day, L10,000/day, garage across from Mestre train station).

By Plane: Romantics can jet to St. Mark's Square by Alilaguna speedboat (L17,000, hrly, 70 min, 6:15–24:00 from airport, 4:50–22:50 from St. Mark's Square). Or, catch a bus from the airport to the Tronchetto *vaporetto* stop: either the handy blue ATVO shuttle bus (L5,000, 2/hrly, 20 min, 5:30–20:40 to airport, 8:30–24:00 from airport, www.atvo.it) or the cheaper orange ACTV bus #5 (L1,500, 1–3/hrly, 20–40 min, 4:40–01:00). Airport info: tel. 041-260-611, flight info: tel. 041-260-9260.

Helpful Hints

The Venice fly trap lures us in and takes our money any way it can. Count your change carefully—I catch someone shortchanging me about once a day. Accept the fact that Venice was a tourist town 400 years ago. It was, is, and always will be crowded. While 80 percent of Venice is actually an untouristy place, 80 percent of the tourists never notice. Hit the back streets.

Get Lost: Venice is the ideal town to explore on foot. Walk and walk to the far reaches of the town. Don't worry about getting lost. Get as lost as possible. Keep reminding yourself, "I'm on an island, and I can't get off." When it comes time to find your way, just follow the directional arrows on building corners or simply ask a local, *"Dov'è San Marco?"* ("Where is St. Mark's?"). People in the tourist business (that's most Venetians) speak some English. If they don't, listen politely, watching where their hands point, say *"Grazie,"* and head off in that direction. If you're lost, pop into a hotel and ask for their business card—it comes with a map and a prominent "you are here."

Rip-Offs, Theft, and Help: While pickpockets work the crowded main streets, docks, and *vaporetti,* the dark, late-night streets of Venice are safe. A service called Venezia No Problem tries to help tourists who've been mistreated by any Venetian business (toll-free tel. 800-355-920, for complaints only, not for information).

Water: Venetians pride themselves on having pure, safe, and tasty tap water piped in from the foothills of the Alps (which you can actually see from Venice bell towers on crisp, clear winter days).

Money: ATMs are plentiful and the easiest way to go. Bank rates vary. I like the Banca di Sicilia, a block toward St. Mark's Square from Campo San Bartolomeo. The American Express change desk is just off St. Mark's Square (Mon–Sat 8:30–20:00). Thomas Cook's two offices waive their commission on Thomas Cook checks but charge 4.5 percent for others (Mon–Sat 9:00–19:45, Sun 9:30–17:00, at St. Mark's Square, nearly under the tower with digital clock; or Mon–Sat 9:00–19:45, Sun 9:30–17:00, at Rialto *vaporetto* dock). Nonbank exchange bureaus like Exacto will cost you $10 more than a bank for a $200 exchange. A 24-hour cash machine near the Rialto *vaporetto* stop exchanges U.S. dollars and other currencies for lire at fair rates.

Travel Agencies: If you need to get train tickets, pay supple-ments, or make reservations, try Kele & Teo Viaggi e Turismo (cash only, Mon–Fri 8:30–12:30, 15:00–18:00, Sat 9:00–12:00, at Ponte dei Bareteri on the Mercerie midway between Rialto and St. Mark's Square, tel. 041-520-8722) or American Express (Mon–Fri 9:00–17:30, Sat 9:00–12:30, CC:A for rail tickets, CC:VMA for supplements and reservations; also offer tours of Venice April–Oct; just off St. Mark's Square at 1471, en route to the Accademia, tel. 041-520-0844). Either agency saves travelers time-consuming trips to the train station (sold at the same price as at the station).

Post Office: A large post office is off the far end of St. Mark's Square (on the side of square opposite the St. Mark's church, Mon–Sat 8:10–18:00, shorter hours off-season), and a branch is near the Rialto (on St. Mark's side, Mon–Fri 8:10–13:30, Sat 8:10–12:30).

Church Services: The San Zulian Church offers a mass in English at 9:30 on Sunday (May–Sept, 2 blocks toward Rialto off St. Mark's Square). Gregorians would enjoy the sung Gregorian mass at 11:00 on Sunday at San Giorgio Maggiore church (on island of San Giorgio Maggiore, visible from Doge's Palace, catch *vaporetto* #10 or #20 from San Zaccaria dock). Confirm times of mass at TI.

The "Rolling Venice" Youth Discount Pass: This worthwhile L5,000 pass gives those under 30 discounts on sights and transportation plus information on cheap eating and sleeping. In summer, they have a kiosk in front of the train station (July–Sept daily 8:00–20:00). Their main office, near St. Mark's Square, is open year-round (Mon–Fri 9:30–13:00, from American Express head toward St. Mark's Square, first left, first left again through "Contarina" tunnel, follow white sign to Commune di Venezia and see the sign, Corte Contarina 1529, third floor, tel. 041-274-7651).

Pigeon Poop: If bombed by a pigeon, resist the initial response to wipe it off immediately—it'll just smear into your hair. Wait until it dries and flake it off cleanly.

Laundry: Near St. Mark's Square and many of my hotel listings is the full-service Lavanderia Gabriella (Mon–Fri 8:00–19:00, 985 Rio Terra Colonne, near St. Mark's Square, from San Zulian Church go over Ponta dei Ferali, take first right down Calle dei Armeni, tel. 041-522-1758). Near the Rialto is Lavanderia S.S. Apostoli (Mon–Sat 8:30–12:00, 15:00–19:00, closed Sun, just off Campo S.S. Apostoli on Salizada del Pistor, tel. 041-522-6650). At either place you can get nine pounds of laundry washed and dried for L30,000—confirm price carefully. Drop it by in the morning; pick it up that afternoon. (Call to be sure they're open.) Don't expect to get your clothes back ironed, folded, or even entirely dry. The modern and much cheaper Bea Vita self-serve *lavanderia* is across the canal from the station (daily 8:00–22:00, go over bridge, take first right, first left, first right).

Etiquette: Walk on the right and don't loiter on bridges. Picnicking is technically forbidden (keep a low profile). Dress modestly. Men should keep their shirts on. When visiting St. Mark's or other major churches, men, women, and even children should cover their knees and shoulders (or risk being turned away).

Haircuts: I've been getting my hair cut at Coiffeur Benito for 15 years. Benito has been keeping local men and women trim for 25 years. He's an artist—actually a "hair sculptor"—and a cut is a fun diversion from the tourist grind (L35,000, Tue–Sat 8:30–13:30, 15:30–19:30, behind San Zulian Church near St. Mark's Square, Calle S. Zulian Gia del Strazzanol 592A, tel. 041-528-6221).

Downtown Venice

LODGING:

❶ GUERATTO	⓫ BEL SITO	㉑ GIORGIONE
❷ STURION	⓬ MARIN	㉒ AMERICAN
❸ CANADA	⓭ LEVI	㉓ BELLE ARTI
❹ ASTORIA	⓮ GAMBERO	㉔ LA CALCINA
❺ CANEVA	⓯ CAMPIELLO	㉕ CHIESA VALDESE
❻ RIVA	⓰ PAGANELLI	
❼ PIAVE	⓱ ACCADEMIA	
❽ FONTANA	⓲ GALLERIA	
❾ DONI	⓳ ALBORETTI	
❿ CORONA	⓴ ALLA SCALA	

```
● 1·82 VAPORETTI STOPS
      w/ LINE #'S
●···· TRACHETTO ROUTES
```

Getting around Venice

The public transit system is a fleet of motorized bus-boats called *vaporetti*. They work like city buses except that they never get a flat, the stops are docks, and if you get off between stops, you may drown. For most, only two lines matter: #1 is the slow boat, taking 45 minutes to make every stop along the entire length of the Grand Canal, and #82 is the fast boat that zips down the Grand

Canal in 25 minutes, stopping mainly at Tronchetto (car park), Piazzale Roma (bus station), Ferrovia (train station), Rialto Bridge, and San Marco. Buy a L6,000 ticket ideally before boarding or from a conductor on board. (Families of 3 or more pay L5,000 per person.) A round-trip (*andata e ritorno*) costs L10,000 (good for 2 trips within a day on any line).

You can buy a pass for a 24-hour period (L18,000, families of 3 or more pay L15,000 apiece), 72 hours (L35,000), and one week (L60,000)—it's fun to be able to hop on and off spontaneously. Technically, luggage costs the same as dogs—L6,000—but I've never been charged. Riding free? There's a one-in-six chance a conductor will fine you L32,000.

Only three bridges cross the Grand Canal, but *traghetti* (little L700 ferry gondolas, marked on better maps) shuttle locals and in-the-know tourists across the Grand Canal at several handy locations (see Downtown Venice map). Take advantage of these time savers. They can also save money. For instance, while most tourists take the L6,000 *vaporetto* to connect St. Mark's with Salute Church, a L700 *traghetto* also does the job.

Grand Canal Tour of Venice

For a ▲▲▲ joyride, introduce yourself to Venice by boat. You can ride boat #82 (too fast, 25 minutes, be certain you're on a "San Marco via Rialto" boat) or #1 (slow, 45 minutes). Either way, cruise the entire Canale Grande from Tronchetto (car park) or Ferrovia (train station) to San Marco. If you can't snag a front seat, lurk nearby and take one when it becomes available or find an outside seat in the stern. This ride has the best light and least crowds early in the morning. Twilight is also good. While Venice is a barrage on the senses that hardly needs a narration, these notes give the cruise a little meaning and help orient you to this great city. Some city maps (on sale at postcard racks) have a handy Grand Canal map on the back.

Venice, built in a lagoon, sits on pilings—pine trees driven 15 feet into the clay. About 25 miles of **canals** drain the city, dumping like streams into the Grand Canal. Technically, there are three canals (Grand, Giudecca, and Cannaregio), and the other 45 "canals" are rivers.

Venice is a city of **palaces**. The most lavish were built fronting this canal. This cruise is the only way to really appreciate the front doors of this unique and historic chorus line of mansions from the days when Venice was the world's richest city. Strict laws prohibit any changes in these buildings, so while landowners gnash their teeth, we can enjoy Europe's best-preserved medieval city—slowly rotting. Many of the grand buildings are now vacant. Others harbor chandeliered elegance above mossy, empty ground floors.

Start at **Tronchetto** (the bus and car park) or the **train**

station. The station, one of the few modern buildings in town, was built in 1954. It's been the gateway into Venice since 1860, when the first station was built. "F.S." stands for "Ferrovie dello Stato," the Italian state railway system. The bridge at the station is the first of only three that cross the Canale Grande.

The **ghetto** is shortly after the train tation, on the left. Look down Cannaregio Canal (opposite the Riva di Biasio stop). The twin pink six-story buildings (known as the "skyscrapers") are a reminder of how densely populated the world's original ghetto was. Set aside as the local Jewish quarter in 1516, the area became extremely crowded. This urban island (behind the San Marcuola stop) developed into one of the most closely knit business and cultural quarters of all Jewish communities in Italy.

As you cruise, notice the traffic signs. Venice's main thoroughfare is busy with traffic. You'll see all kinds of **boats**: taxis, police boats, garbage boats, and even brown-and-white UPS boats. Venice's sleek, black, graceful **gondolas** are a symbol of the city. While used gondolas cost around $10,000, new ones run up to $30,000 apiece. They're built with a slight curve so that one oar propels them in a straight line. Today, with over 500 gondoliers joyriding around the churning *vaporetti*, there's a lot of congestion on the Grand Canal. Listen to your *vaporetto* driver curse the gondoliers.

Opposite the San Stae stop look for the faded frescoes. Imagine the facades of the Grand Canal in its day: frescoed by masters like Tintoretto and glittering with mosaics.

At the Ca d'Oro stop notice the lacy Gothic palace. Named the **"House of Gold"**—the frilly edge of the roof was once gilded—it's considered the most elegant Venetian Gothic palace on the canal. Unfortunately there's little to see inside (L6,000, daily 8:15–16:00, free peek through hole in door of courtyard).

On the right, the outdoor **fish and produce market** bustles with people in the morning but is quiet the rest of the day. (This is a great scene to wander through—even though new European hygiene standards required a less-colorful remodeling job last year.) Can you see the *traghetto* gondola ferrying shoppers—standing like Washingtons crossing the Delaware—back and forth? Ahead, above the post office, the golden angel of the Campanile faces the wind and marks St. Mark's Square (where this tour ends). The huge **post office**, with *servizio postale* boats moored at its blue posts, is on the left just before the Rialto Bridge.

A major landmark of Venice, the **Rialto Bridge** is lined with shops and tourists. The third bridge on this spot, it was built in 1592. Earlier Rialto Bridges could open to let in big ships. After 1592, the Grand Canal was closed to shipping and became a canal of palaces. With a span of 42 meters and foundations stretching 200 meters on either side, the Rialto was an impressive engineering feat in its day. Locals call the summit of this bridge the "icebox of Venice" for its cool breeze. Tourists call it a great place to kiss. *Rialto* means "high river." The restaurants beyond the bridge feature high prices and low quality.

The Rialto, a separate town in the early days of Venice, has always been the commercial district, while San Marco was the religious and governmental center. Today a street called the Mercerie connects the two, providing travelers with human traffic jams and a gauntlet of shopping temptations.

Beyond the Rialto on the left, notice the long stretch of **merchants' palaces**, each with proud and different facades. Many feature the Roman palace design of twin towers flanking a huge set of central windows. These were showrooms designed to let in maximum sunlight.

Take a deep whiff of Venice. What's all this nonsense about stinky canals? All I smell is my shirt. By the way, how's your captain? Smooth dockings? To get to know him, stand up in the bow and block his view.

The rising water level takes its toll. Many canal-level floors are abandoned. Notice how many buildings have a foundation of waterproof white stone (*pietra d'Istria*) upon which the bricks sit high and dry. The posts—historically painted gaily with the equivalent of family coats of arms—don't rot under water. But the wood at the water line does rot. Notice how the rich marble facades are just a veneer covering no-nonsense brick buildings. Look up at the characteristic chimneys.

After the San Silvestro stop you'll see (on the right) a **13th-century admiral's palace**. Venetian admirals marked their palaces with twin obelisks.

After the San Tomá stop look down the side canal (on the right) before the bridge to see the traffic light, the **fire station**, and the fireboats ready to go.

These days, when buildings are being renovated, huge murals with images of the building mask the ugly scaffolding. Corporations hide the scaffolding out of goodwill (and get their name— e.g., Frette—on the mural).

The wooden Accademia Bridge crosses the Grand Canal and leads to the **Accademia Gallery** (neoclassical facade just after the British consulate on the right), filled with the best Venetian paintings. The bridge was put up in 1932 as a temporary fix for the original iron one. Locals liked it, so it stayed.

Cruising under the bridge, you'll get a classic view of the **Salute Church** (ahead), built as a thanks to God when the devastating plague of 1630 passed. It's claimed that more than a million trees were piled together to build a foundation upon the solid clay 35 meters below sea level. Much of the surrounding countryside was deforested by Venice. Trees were needed both to fuel the furnaces of its booming glass industry and to prop up this city in the mud.

The low white building on the right (between the bridge and the church) is the **Peggy Guggenheim Gallery**. She willed the city a fine collection of modern art. The Salviati building (with the fine mosaic) is a glass factory.

Just before the Salute stop (on the right), the house with the big view windows and the red and wild Andy Warhol painting on the living-room wall (often behind white drapes) was lived in by Mick Jagger. In the 1970s this was famous as Venice's rock-and-roll-star party house.

The building on the right with the golden ball is the **Dogana da Mar**, a 16th-century customs house. Its two bronze Atlases hold a statue of Fortune riding the ball. While there are no hotels on this side, all the buildings on the left are fancy Grand Canal hotels.

As you prepare to deboat at San Marco, look from left to right out over the lagoon. A wide harborfront walk leads past the town's most elegant hotels to the green area in the distance. This is the public garden, the only sizable park in town. Farther out is the **lido**, Venice's beach. It's tempting, with its sand and casinos, but its car traffic breaks into the medieval charm of Venice.

The dreamy church that seems to float is the architect Palladio's **San Giorgio Maggiore**. It's just a *vaporetto* ride away (#10 or #20 from San Zaccaria dock). Find the Tintoretto paintings in the church (such as the *Last Supper*) and take the elevator up the tower for a terrific view (L3,000, daily 9:30–13:00, 14:30–18:30, Gregorian mass at 11:00 on Sun, tel. 041-522-7827). Across the lagoon (to your right) is a residential island called Giudecca.

Get out at the San Marco stop. Directly ahead is Harry's Bar. Hemingway drank here when it was a characteristic no-name *osteria* and the gondoliers' hangout. Today, of course, it's the overpriced hangout of well-dressed Americans who don't mind paying triple for their Bellinis (peach juice with Prosecco wine) to make the scene. St. Mark's Square is just around the corner.

For more *vaporetto* fun, ride a boat around the city and out into the lagoon and back (ask for the *circulare;* pron. cheer-koo-LAH-ray). Plenty of boats leave from San Marco for the beach (*lido*), and speedboats offer tours of nearby islands: Burano is a quiet, picturesque fishing and lace town, Murano specializes in glassblowing, and Torcello has the oldest churches and mosaics but is otherwise dull and desolate. Boat #12 takes you to these remote points slower and cheaper.

Sights—Venice, on St. Mark's Square

▲▲▲**St. Mark's Square (Piazza San Marco)**—Surrounded by splashy and historic buildings, Piazza San Marco is filled with music, lovers, pigeons, and tourists by day and is your private rendezvous with the Middle Ages late at night. Europe's greatest dance floor is the romantic place to be. In a hard rain, St. Mark's Square is the first place in Venice to flood (you might see stacked wooden benches; when the square floods, these are put end to end to make elevated sidewalks).

Venice's best **TIs** (and WCs) are here; one TI is on the square, the other on the lagoon. To find the TI on the square, stand with your back to the church, and go to the far corner on your left; the office is tucked away in the arcade (daily 9:00–17:00, near this TI is a L1,000 WC open daily 8:00–21:00—it's a few steps beyond St. Mark's Square en route to American Express office and Accademia; see Albergo Diorno—marked on pavement). The other TI is on the lagoon (daily 10:00–18:00, walk out to water by Doge's Palace, go right; nearby WCs open daily 9:00–19:00).

With your back to the church, survey one of Europe's great urban spaces and the only square in Venice to merit the title "Piazza." Nearly two football fields long, it's surrounded by the offices of the republic. On the right are the "old offices" (16th-century Renaissance). On the left are the "new offices" (17th-century Baroque). Napoleon, after enclosing the square with the more simple and austere neoclassical wing across the far end, called this "the most beautiful drawing room in Europe."

The **clock tower**, a Renaissance tower built in 1496, marks the entry to the Mercerie, the main shopping drag, which connects St. Mark's Square with the Rialto. From the piazza you can see the bronze men (Moors) swing their huge clappers at the top of each hour. In the 17th century one of them knocked an unsuspecting worker off the top and to his death—probably the first-ever killing by a robot. Notice the world's first "digital" clock on the tower facing the square (with dramatic flips every 5 minutes).

For a slow and pricey evening thrill, invest L12,000 (plus L7,000 if the orchestra plays) in a beer or coffee in one of the elegant cafés with the **dueling orchestras**. If you're going to sit awhile and savor the scene, it's worth the splurge. For the most thrills L2,000 can get you in Venice, buy a bag of pigeon seed and become popular in a flurry. To get everything airborne, toss your sweater in the air.

▲▲**St. Mark's Basilica**—Since about A.D. 830 this basilica has housed the saint's bones. The mosaic above the door at the far left of the church shows two guys carrying Mark's coffin into the church. Mark looks pretty grumpy after the long voyage from Egypt.

To enter the church, modest dress is required even of kids (no shorts or bare shoulders); T-shirt sales at kiosks outside the entrance are brisk. In peak season, there can be long lines of people waiting to get into the church. People who ignore the dress code hold up the line while they plead fruitlessly with—or put on extra clothes under the watchful eyes of—the dress code police.

Floods and a Dying City

Venice floods about 60 times a year—normally in winter. Venetian floods start in St. Mark's Square. The entry of the church is the lowest spot in town. The meters at the base of the outside of the bell tower, or campanile (near the exit, facing the grand square), show the current sea level (*livello marea*). Find the mark showing the high-water level from the terrible floods of 1966 (waist level on right). When wind and tide combine to raise the water level to one meter, a warning siren sounds. It repeats if a serious flood is imminent.

In 1965 Venice's population was over 150,000. Since the flood of 1966 the population has been shrinking. Today the population is about 70,000 . . . and geriatric. Sad, yes, but imagine raising a family here: the fragile nature of things means piles of regulations (no biking, and so on), and costs are high—even though the government is now subsidizing rents to keep people from moving out. You can easily get glass and tourist trinkets, but it's hard to find groceries. And floods and the humidity make house maintenance an expensive pain.

The church has 4,000 square meters of **Byzantine mosaics**, the best and oldest of which are in the atrium (turn right as you enter and stop under the last dome—this may be roped off, but dome is still partially visible). Facing the church, gape up (it's OK, no pigeons), and read clockwise the story of Adam and Eve that rings the bottom of the dome. Now, facing the piazza, look domeward for the story of Noah, the ark, and the flood (two by two, the wicked being drowned, Noah sending out the dove, a happy rainbow, and a sacrifice of thanks).

Step inside the church (stairs on right lead to bronze horses) and notice the rolling mosaic marble floor. As you shuffle under the central dome, look up for the Ascension (free, no photos, Mon–Sat 9:45–17:30, Sun 14:00–17:00, tel. 041-522-5205). See the schedule board in the atrium listing two free English guided tours (July–Aug Mon–Fri up to 4 tours/day, Sat 1/day, off-season 2/weekly, 30–90 minutes depending on guide and group). The church is particularly beautiful when lit (unpredictable schedule, maybe middays 11:00–12:00, Sat–Sun 14:00–17:00 plus 18:45 mass on Sat).

In the **museum** upstairs (L3,000, daily 9:45–16:00, sometimes until 17:00, enter from atrium either before or after you tour church), you can see an up-close mosaic exhibition, a fine view of the church interior, a view of the square from the horse balcony, and (inside, in their own room) the newly restored original bronze horses. These well-traveled horses, made during the days of Alexander the Great (4th century B.C.), were taken to Rome by Nero, to Constantinople/Istanbul by Constantine, to Venice by crusaders, to Paris by Napoleon, back "home" to Venice when Napoleon fell, and finally indoors and out of the acidic air.

The **treasury** and **altarpiece** of the church (L3,000 each, daily 9:45–17:10, 16:10 in winter) give you the best chance outside of Istanbul or Ravenna to see the glories of Byzantium. Venetian crusaders looted the Christian city of Constantinople and brought home piles of lavish loot (until the advent of TV evangelism, perhaps the lowest point in Christian history). Much of this plunder is stored in the treasury (*tesoro*) of San Marco. As you view these treasures, remember most were made in A.D. 500, while Western Europe was still rutting in the mud. Beneath the high altar lies the body of St. Mark ("Marxus") and the Pala d'Oro, a golden altarpiece made with 80 Byzantine enamels (A.D. 1000–1300). Each shows a religious scene set in gold and precious stones. Both of these sights are interesting and historic, but neither is as much fun as two bags of pigeon seed.

▲▲▲**Doge's Palace (Palazzo Ducale)**—The seat of the Venetian government and home of its ruling duke, or doge, this was the most powerful half acre in Europe for 400 years (April–Oct daily 9:00–19:00, Nov–March daily 9:00–17:00, last entry 90 minutes before closing, tel. 041-522-4951). The L18,000 combo ticket includes admission to a number of lesser museums: Museo Correr (see below), Palazzo Mocenigo (textiles and costumes, closed Mon), Museo del Vetro di Murano (glass museum on Murano, closed Wed), and Museo del Merletto di Burano (lace museum on Burano, closed Tue). The ticket is valid for three months.

While each room in the Doge's Palace has a short English description, the fast-moving, 90-minute, tape-recorded guided tour wand is wonderfully done and worth the L7,000 if you don't have *Rick Steves' Mona Winks* and you're planning to really understand the Palace. Vagabond lovers, sightseeing cheek to cheek, can crank up the volume and split one wand. Audioguides are rentable up to two hours before closing (until 17:00 April–Oct, until 15:00 Nov–March).

The new "Secret Itineraries Tour," which follows the Doge's tracks into rooms not included in the general admission price, must be booked in advance (L24,000, at 10:00 and 11:30 in English, 1.25 hrs, call 041-522-4951 to confirm times and to reserve).

The palace was built to show off the power and wealth of the republic and remind all visitors that Venice was number one. In typical Venetian Gothic style, the bottom has pointy arches, and the top has an Eastern or Islamic flavor. Its columns sat on pedestals, but in the thousand years since they were erected, the palace has settled into the mud, and the bases have vanished.

Enjoy the newly restored **facades** from the courtyard. Notice a grand staircase (with nearly naked Moses and Paul Newman at the top). Even the most powerful visitors climbed this to meet the doge. This was the beginning of an architectural power trip. The doge, the elected-for-life king of this "dictatorial republic," lived with his family on the first floor near the halls of power. From his lavish quarters you'll follow the one-way tour through the public rooms of the top floor, finishing with the Bridge of Sighs and the prison. The place is wallpapered with masterpieces by Veronese and Tintoretto. Don't worry much about the great art. Enjoy the building.

In room 12, the **Senate Room**, the 200 senators met, debated, and passed laws. From the center of the ceiling, Tintoretto's *Triumph of Venice* shows the city in all her glory. Lady Venice, in heaven with the Greek gods, stands high above the lesser nations who swirl respectfully at her feet with gifts.

The **Armory** shows remnants of the military might the empire employed to keep the east-west trade lines open (and the local economy booming). Squint out the window at the far end for a fine view of Palladio's San Giorgio Maggiore Church and the lido (cars, casinos, crowded beaches) in the distance.

After the huge brown globes, you'll enter the giant **Hall of the Grand Council** (180 feet long, capacity 2,000), where the entire nobility met to elect the senate and doge. Ringing the room are portraits of 76 doges (in chronological order). One, a doge who opposed the will of the Grand Council, is blacked out. Behind the doge's throne, you can't miss Tintoretto's monsterpiece, *Paradise*. At 1,700 square feet, this is the world's largest oil painting. Christ and Mary are surrounded by a heavenly host of 500 saints.

Walking over the **Bridge of Sighs**, you'll enter the prisons. The doges could sentence, torture, and jail their opponents secretly and in the privacy of their own homes. As you walk back over the bridge, squeeze your arm through the marble lattice window and wave to the gang of tourists gawking at you.

▲▲**Museo Civico Correr**—The city history museum is now included (whether you like it or not) with the Doge's Palace admission. In the Napoleon Wing you'll see fine neoclassical works by Canova. Then peruse armor, banners, and paintings recreating festive days of the Venetian Republic. The top floor lays out a fine overview of Venetian art. And just before the cafeteria a room is filled with traditional games. There are fine English descriptions and great Piazza San Marco views throughout (L18,000 combo ticket with Doge's Palace and other museums, enter in arcade directly opposite church, April–Oct daily 9:00–19:00, Nov–March daily 9:00–17:00, tel. 041-522-4951).

▲**Campanile di San Marco**—Ride the elevator 300 feet to the top of the bell tower for the best view in Venice. This tower crumbled into a pile of bricks in 1902, a thousand years after it

was built. For an ear-shattering experience, be on top when the
bells ring (L10,000, daily 9:00–21:00 in summer, until 19:00
otherwise). The golden angel at its top always faces into the wind.
Beat the crowds and enjoy crisp air at 9:00.

More Sights—Venice

▲▲Galleria dell' Accademia—Venice's top art museum, packed
with highlights of the Venetian Renaissance, features paintings
by Bellini, Veronese, Tiepolo, Giorgione, Testosterone, and Cana-
letto. It's just over the wooden Accademia Bridge. Expect long lines
in the late morning because they allow only 300 visitors in at a
time; visit early or late to miss crowds (L12,000, Mon 8:15–14:00,
Tue–Sun 8:15–19:15, shorter hours off-season, audioguide-L7,000
or L10,000 with 2 earphones, English info sheets in some rooms,
guidebook-L15,000, no photos, tel. 041-522-2247). Hour-long
guided tours run Monday through Friday at 10:00, 11:00, and 12:00
for L10,000 (you can skip to the front of the line if buying a tour).

There's a decent pizzeria at the bridge (Pizzeria Accademia
Foscarini; see "Eating," below), a public WC under it, and usually
a classic shell game going on on top of it (study the system as
partners in the crowd win big money).

▲Peggy Guggenheim Collection—This popular collection of
far-out art offers one of Europe's best reviews of the art styles
of the 20th century. Stroll through Cubism (Picasso, Braque),
surrealism (Dalí, Ernst), futurism (Boccione, Carra), American
abstract expressionism (Pollock), and a sprinkling of Klee, Calder,
and Chagall (L12,000, Wed–Mon 10:00–18:00, Sat until 22:00
April–Oct, closed Tue, audioguide-L8,000, guidebook-L8,000,
free baggage check, photos allowed only in garden and terrace—
overlooking Grand Canal, near Accademia, tel. 041-240-5411).

▲▲Chiesa dei Frari—This great Gothic Franciscan church, an
artistic highlight of Venice featuring three great masters, offers
more art per lira than any other Venetian sight. Freeload on English-language tours to get the most out of the Titian *Assumption*
above the high altar. Then move one chapel to the right to see
Donatello's wood carving of St. John the Baptist almost live. And,
for the climax, continue right through an arch into the sacristy to
sit before Bellini's *Madonna and the Saints*. The genius of Bellini,
perhaps the greatest Venetian painter, is obvious in the pristine
clarity, believable depth, and reassuring calm of this three-paneled
altar piece. Notice the rich colors of Mary's clothing and how
good it is to see a painting in its intended setting. For many, these
three pieces of art make a visit to the Accademia Gallery unnecessary (or they may whet your appetite for more). Before leaving,
check out the neoclassical, pyramid-shaped tomb of Canova and
(opposite that) the grandiose tomb of Titian the Venetian.
Compare the carved marble Assumption behind his tombstone

portrait with the painted original above the high altar (L4,000, Mon–Sat 9:00–18:00, Sun 13:00–18:00).

▲**Scuola di San Rocco**—Next to the Frari Church, another lavish building bursts with art, including some 50 Tintorettos. The best paintings are upstairs, especially the *Crucifixion* in the smaller room. View the neck-breaking splendor with one of the mirrors (*specchio*) available at the entrance (L9,000, daily 9:00–17:30). For *molto* Tiepolo (14 stations of the cross), drop by the nearby Church of San Polo.

Ca' Rezzonico—This 18th-century Grand Canal *palazzo* is the Museo del '700 Veneziano, offering a good look at the life of Venice's rich and famous in the 1700s (at a *vaporetto* stop of the same name, tel. 041-522-4543). It will probably be closed for restoration through spring of 2001.

Santa Elena—For a pleasant peek into a completely untouristy residential side of Venice, catch the boat from St. Mark's Square to the neighborhood of Santa Elena (at the fish's tail). This 100-year-old suburb lives as if there were no tourism. You'll find a kid-friendly park, a few lazy restaurants, and beautiful sunsets over San Marco.

Gondola Rides

A rip-off for some, this is a traditional must for romantics. Gondoliers charge about L120,000 for a 40-minute ride during the day; from 20:00 on, figure on L150,000 to L200,000 (for *musica*—singer and accordionist, it's an additional L170,000 during day, L190,000 after 20:00). You can divide the cost—and the romance—among up to six people (only 2 people get to sit side by side). Glide through nighttime Venice with your head on someone else's shoulder. Follow the moon as it sails past otherwise unseen buildings. Silhouettes gaze down from bridges while window glitter spills onto the black water. You're anonymous in the city of masks as the rhythmic thrust of your striped-shirted gondolier turns old crows into songbirds. This is extremely relaxing (and I think worth the extra to experience at night). Since you might get a narration plus conversation with your gondolier, talk with several and choose one you like who speaks English well.

For a glimpse at the only **gondola workshop** in Venice, visit the Accademia neighborhood. Walk down the Accademia side of the canal Fondamenta Nani. As you approach Giudecca Canal you'll see the beached gondolas on your right across the Nani Canal.

For cheap gondola thrills, stick to the L700 one-minute ferry ride on a Grand Canal *traghetto* or hang out on a bridge along the gondola route and wave at (or drop leftover pigeon seed on) romantics.

Festivals

Venice's most famous is **Carnevale** (Feb. 17–27 in 2001). Carnevale, which means "farewell to meat," originated centuries ago as a wild two-month-long party leading up to the austerity of Lent. In Carnevale's heyday—the 1600s and 1700s—you could do pretty much anything with anybody from any social class if you were wearing a mask. These days it's a tamer 10-day celebration, culminating in a huge dance lit with fireworks on St. Mark's Square. Sporting masks and costumes, Venetians from kids to businessmen join in the fun. Drawing the biggest crowds of the year, Carnevale has nearly been a victim of its success, driving away many Venetians (who skip out on the craziness to go ski in the Dolomites).

The **Feast of the Redeemer** features a parade and fireworks (July 21 in 2001). The colorful **Historical Regatta** fills the Grand Canal with old-time boats and pageantry (Sept 2 in 2001).

Shopping

Shoppers like Carnevale masks, lace (a specialty of Burano, see below, but sold in Venice as well), empty books with handmade covers, and paintings—especially of Venice. If you're buying a substantial amount from nearly any shop, bargain. It's accepted and almost expected. Offer less and offer to pay cash; merchants are very conscious of the bite taken by credit-card companies.

Popular Venetian glass is available in many forms: vases, tea sets, decanters, glasses, jewelry, lamps, sculptures (such as solid-glass aquariums), and on and on. Shops will ship it home for you (snap a photo of it before it's packed up). If you're serious about glass, visit the small shops on Murano Island. Murano's glass-blowing demonstrations are fun; you'll usually see a vase and a "leetle 'orse" made from molten glass. In Venice, demos are given by various companies around St. Mark's Square, but they're only for groups; to see a demo, you'd have to sneak in with a group waiting outside. In Venice, glass-bead necklaces—simple, packable souvenirs—are cheap at vendors' stalls, expensive at shops.

Salizada San Samuele is a nontouristy street with several artsy shops. Livio de Marchi's wood sculpture shop is delightful even when it's closed. Check out the window displays for his latest creations: socks, folded shirts, teddy bears, "paper" sacks, all carved from wood (Mon–Fri 9:30–12:30, 13:30–18:30, nearest major landmark is Accademia Bridge—on St. Mark's side, Salizada San Samuele 3157, *vaporetto* stop: San Samuele, or if approaching by foot, follow signs to Palazzo Grassi, tel. 041-528-5694, www.liviodemarchi.com).

Sights—Venice Lagoon

Several interesting islands hide out in the Venice Lagoon. **Burano**, famous for its lace, is a sleepy island with a sleepy

Venice Lagoon

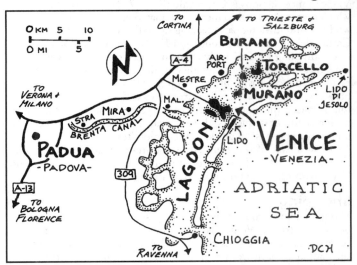

community—village Venice without the glitz. Lace fans enjoy Scuola di Merletti (L8,000, Wed–Mon 10:00–17:00, closed Tue, tel. 041-730-034).

Torcello, another lagoon island, is dead except for its church, which claims to be the oldest in Venice (L5,000, daily 10:30–17:30, tel. 041-730-084). It's impressive for its mosaics but not worth a look on a short visit unless you really have your heart set on Ravenna but can't make it there.

The island of **Murano**, famous for its glass factories, has the Museo Vetrario, which displays the very best of 700 years of Venetian glassmaking (L8,000, Thu–Tue 10:00–17:00, closed Wed, tel. 041-739-586).

The islands are reached easily, cheaply, and slowly by *vaporetto* (depart from San Zaccaria dock nearest the Bridge of Sighs/Doge's Palace, line #12 connects all 3 islands, can also take #41 to Murano, then #12 to the other islands). Four-hour speed-boat tours of these three lagoon destinations leave twice a day (usually 9:30 and 14:30; 1/day winter at 14:30, L30,000, tel. 041-523-8835) from the dock near the Doge's Palace; the tours are indeed speedy, stopping for roughly 35 minutes at each island.

Nightlife in Venice

Venice is quiet at night, as tour groups are back in the cheaper hotels of Mestre, and the masses of day-trippers return to their beach resorts. **Gondolas** cost nearly double but are doubly romantic and relaxing under the moon. *Vaporettos* are nearly empty, and it's a great time to cruise the Grand Canal on the slow boat #1.

Take your pick of traditional Vivaldi **concerts** in churches throughout town. Vivaldi is as trendy here as Strauss in Vienna and Mozart in Salzburg. In fact, you'll find frilly young Vivaldis all over town hawking concert tickets. The TI has a list of this week's concerts (tickets from L35,000). If you see a concert at Scuola di San Rocco, you can enjoy the art (which you're likely to pay L9,000 for during the day) for free during the intermission.

On St. Mark's Square, the **dueling café orchestras** entertain. Every night, enthusiastic musicians play the same songs, creating the same irresistible magic. Hang out for free behind the tables (which allows you to easily move on to the next orchestra when the musicians take a break) or spring for a seat and enjoy a fun and gorgeously set concert. If you sit awhile it can be L20,000 well spent (drink L12,000 plus a one-time L7,000 fee for entertainment).

You're not a tourist, you're a living part of a soft Venetian night... an alley cat with money. Streetlamp halos, live music, floodlit history, and a ceiling of stars make St. Mark's magic at midnight. In the misty light, the moon has a golden hue. Shine with the old lanterns on the gondola piers where the sloppy Grand Canal splashes at the Doge's Palace... reminiscing. Comfort the small statues of the four frightened tetrarchs (ancient Byzantine emperors) where the Doge's Palace hits the basilica. Cuddle history.

Sleeping in Venice
(L2,000 = about $1, country code: 39)
Sleep Code: **S** = Single, **D** = Double/Twin, **T** = Triple, **Q** = Quad, **b** = bathroom, **t** = toilet only, **s** = shower only, **CC** = Credit Card (Visa, MasterCard, Amex), **SE** = Speaks English, **NSE** = No English. Breakfast is included unless otherwise noted. Air-conditioning, when available, is usually only turned on in summer. See map on page 510 for hotel locations. Virtually all of these hotels are central.

Reserve a room as soon as you know when you'll be in town. Book direct—not through any tourist agency. Call first to see what's available. Follow up with a fax or phone call to reconfirm. Most places will take a credit card for a deposit. If everything's full, don't despair. Call a day or two in advance and fill in a cancellation. If you arrive on an overnight train, your room may not be ready. Drop your bag at the hotel and dive right into Venice.

I've listed prices for peak season: April, May, June, September, and October. Prices can get soft in July, August, and winter. Hotels sometimes give discounts if you stay at least three nights and/or pay cash. If on a budget, ask for a cheaper room or a discount. Always ask. I've listed rooms in two neighborhoods: in the Rialto-San Marco action and in a quiet Dorsoduro area behind the Accademia Gallery. If a hotel has a Web site, check it.

Hotel Web sites are particularly valuable for Venice, because they often come with a map that at least gives you the illusion you can easily find the place.

Sleeping between St. Mark's Square and Campo Santa Maria di Formosa (zip code: 30122)

Hotel Riva, with gleaming marble hallways and bright modern rooms, is romantically situated on a canal along the gondola serenade route. You could actually dunk your breakfast rolls in the canal (but don't). Sandro may hold a corner (*angolo*) room if you ask. Confirm prices and reconfirm reservations, as readers have had trouble with both (2 D with adjacent showers-L170,000, Db-L200,000, Tb-L280,000, Ponte dell' Angelo, #5310 Castello, 30122 Venezia, tel. 041-522-7034, fax 041-528-5551, unenthusiastic receptionists don't speak English). Face St. Mark's cathedral, walk behind it on the left along Calle de la Canonica, take the first left (at blue "Pauly & C" mosaic in street), continue straight, go over the bridge, and angle right to the hotel.

Locanda Piave, with 15 fine rooms above a bright and classy lobby, is fresh, modern, and comfortable (Db-L260,000, Tb-L340,000, family suites-L370,000 for 3, L410,000 for 4, L420,000 for 5 people, prices with this book, CC:VMA but 10 percent discount with cash, air-con; *vaporetto* #1 to San Zaccaria, to the left of Hotel Danieli is Calle de le Rasse, take it, turn left at end, turn right nearly immediately at square—S.S. Filippo e Giacomo—on Calle Rimpeto La Sacrestie, go over bridge, take second left, hotel is two short blocks ahead on Ruga Giuffa #4838/40, Castello, 30122 Venezia, tel. 041-528-5174, fax 041-523-8512, www.elmoro.com/alpiave, e-mail: hotel.alpiave@iol.it, Mirella, Paolo, and Ilaria SE, faithful Molly NSE). They have a couple of apartments for L350,000 to L440,000 (for 3–5 people, cash only, includes kitchenette, 2-night minimum during high season: mid-March–mid-July, Sept–mid-Nov, cheaper in Aug for 2-night stays).

Sleeping on or near the Waterfront, East of St. Mark's Square

These places, about one canal down from the Bridge of Sighs on or just off the Riva degli Schiavoni waterfront promenade, rub drainpipes with Venice's most palatial five-star hotels. The first three—while pricey for the location and not particularly friendly—are professional and comfortable. Ride *vaporetto* #1 to San Zaccaria.

Hotel Campiello, a lacy and bright little 16-room, air-conditioned place, was once part of a 19th-century convent. It's ideally located 50 meters off the waterfront (Sb-L200,000, Db-L230,000–300,000, includes buffet breakfast, CC:VMA,

5 percent discount with cash, 30 percent discount mid-Nov–Feb excluding Christmas and Carnevale; behind Hotel Savoia, up Calle del Vin off the waterfront street—Riva Schiavoni, San Zaccaria #4647, tel. 041-520-5764, fax 041-520-5798, www.hcampiello.it, e-mail: campiello@hcampiello.it, family run for 4 generations, sisters Monica and Nicoletta).

Albergo Paganelli is right on the waterfront—on Riva degli Schiavoni—and has a few incredible view rooms (S-L160,000, Sb-L220,000, D-L220,000, Db-L260,000–350,000, Db with view-L350,000, request *"con vista"* for view, CC:VMA, air-con, prices often soft, at San Zaccaria *vaporetto* stop, Riva degli Schiavoni #4182, Castello, 30122 Venezia, tel. 041-522-4324, fax 041-523-9267, www.gpnet.it/paganelli, e-mail: hotelpag@tin.it). With spacious rooms, carved and gilded headboards, chandeliers, and hair dryers, this hotelesque place is a good value. Seven of their 22 rooms are in a less interesting but equally comfortable *dependencia* a block off the canal.

Albergo Doni is a dark, hardwood, clean, and quiet place with 12 dim-but-classy rooms run by a likable smart aleck named Gina (D-L130,000, Db-L170,000, T-L180,000, Tb-L230,000, ceiling fans, air-con for L20,000 extra per night, use credit card to secure telephone reservations but must pay in cash, Riva Schiavoni, San Zaccaria N. #4656 Calle del Vin, tel. & fax 041-522-4267, Niccolo and Gina SE). Leave Riva Degli Schiavoni on Calle del Vin and go 100 meters with a left jog.

Hotel Fontana is a cozy, two-star, family-run place with 14 rooms and lots of stairs on a touristy square two bridges behind St. Mark's Square (Sb-L100,000–180,000, Db-L150,000–270,000, family rooms, fans, 10 percent discount with cash, CC:VMA; *vaporetto* #1 to San Zaccaria, find Calle de le Rasse—to left of Hotel Danieli—take it, turn right at end, continue to first square, Campo San Provolo, Castello 4701, tel. 041-522-0579, fax 041-523-1040, www.hotelfontana.it).

Albergo Corona is a clean, confusing, Old World place with eight basic rooms (D-L105,000, lots of stairs; *vaporetto* #1 to San Zaccaria dock, take Calle de le Rasse—to left of Hotel Daneli, turn left at end, take right at square—Campo S.S. Filippo e Giacomo—on Calle Rimpeto La Sacrestie, take first right, then next left on Calle Corona to #4464, tel. 041-522-9174, SE).

Sleeping North of St. Mark's Square

Hotel Astoria is a clean, simple place with 28 comfortable rooms tucked away a few blocks off St. Mark's Square (D-L180,000, Db-L240,000, July–Aug Db-L180,000, closed mid-Nov–mid-March, CC:VMA, 2 blocks from San Zulian Church at Calle Fiubera #951; from Rialto *vaporetto* #1 dock go straight inland on Calle le Bembo, which becomes Calle dei Fabbri, turn left on Calle Fiubera, tel. 041-522-5381, fax 041-520-0771, e-mail: hotelastoria@inwind.it).

Locanda Gambero, with 27 rooms, is the biggest one-star hotel in the San Marco area (S-L110,000, old D-L170,000, new Db-L250,000, T-L220,000, Tb-L320,000, CC:VM, rooms with bath also have TV and air-con; from Rialto *vaporetto* #1 dock go straight inland on Calle le Bembo, which becomes Calle dei Fabbri; or from St. Mark's Square go through Sotoportego dei Dai then down Calle dei Fabbri to #4687, at intersection with Calle del Gambero, tel. 041-522-4384, fax 041-520-0431, e-mail: hotgamb@tin.it). Gambero runs the pleasant Art Deco–style La Bistrot on the corner, which serves old-time Venetian cuisine.

Sleeping West/Northwest of St. Mark's Square
Hotel Bel Sito, friendly for a three-star hotel, has Old World character and a picturesque location—facing a church on a small square between St. Mark's Square and the Accademia. With solid wood furniture, its rooms feel elegant, even the few with peely paint (Sb-L204,000–238,000, Db-L227,000–362,000, includes breakfast, CC:VM, air-con, some rooms with canal or church views, *vaporetto* #1 to Santa Maria del Giglio stop, take narrow alley to square, hotel at far end to your right, San Marco 2517, Santa Maria del Giglio, tel. 041-522-3365, fax 041-520-4083, e-mail: belsito@iol.it).

Alloggi Alla Scala, a comfy and tidy five-room place run by Senora Andreina della Fiorentina, is homey, central, and tucked away on a quiet square that features a famous spiral stairway called Scala Contarini del Bovolo (small Db-L130,000, big Db-L150,000, extra bed-L40,000, breakfast-L12,000, CC:VM, Campo Manin #4306, San Marco, tel. 041-521-0629, fax 041-522-6451, daughter SE). From Campo Manin follow signs to (on statue's left) "Scala Contarini del Bovolo" (L4,000, daily 10:00–17:30, views from top).

Sleeping near the Rialto Bridge
(zip code: 30125)
The first three hotels are located on the west side of the Rialto Bridge (away from St. Mark's Square).

Locanda Sturion, with air-conditioning and all the modern comforts, is pricey because it overlooks the Grand Canal (Db-L230,000–340,000, Tb-L350,000–450,000, family deals, canal-view rooms cost about L50,000 extra, includes breakfast, CC:VMA, miles of stairs, 100 meters from Rialto Bridge opposite *vaporetto* dock, San Polo, Rialto, Calle Sturion #679, 30125 Venezia, tel. 041-523-6243, fax 041-522-8378, www.locandasturion.com, e-mail: sturion@tin.it, SE). They require a personal check or traveler's check for a deposit.

Hotel Locanda Ovidius, with an elegant view terrace, wood-beamed-ceilinged breakfast room, and nine bright, comfortable rooms, is also on the Grand Canal. It has far fewer stairs than the Locanda Sturion next door (Sb-L150,000–300,000, Db-L200,000–390,000, Db with view-L300,000–450,000, off-season deal: get 1 night free for 4-night stay during Sun–Thu, CC:VMA, air-con, Calle del Sturion #677a, tel. 041-523-7970, fax 041-520-4101, www.hotelovidius.com, e-mail: info@hotelovidius.com).

Albergo Guerrato, overlooking a handy and colorful produce market, one minute from the Rialto action, is run by friendly, creative, and hardworking Roberto and Piero. Giorgio takes the night shift. Their 800-year-old building is Old World simple, airy, and wonderfully characteristic (D-L140,000, Db-L185,000, T-L180,000, Tb-L240,000, Q-L190,000, Qb-L280,000, including a L4,000 city map, prices promised through 2001 with this book, cash only; walk over the Rialto away from St. Mark's Square, go straight about 3 blocks, turn right on Calle drio la Scimia—not Scimia, the block before—and you'll see the hotel sign, Calle drio la Scimia #240a, 30125 San Polo, tel. & fax 041-522-7131 or 528-5927, e-mail: hguerrat@tin.it, SE). My tour groups book this place for 50 nights each year. Sorry. If you fax without calling first, no reply within three days means they are booked up. (It's best to call first.)

The next three hotels are located on the east side of the Rialto Bridge (St. Mark's side).

Hotel Canada has 25 small, pleasant rooms (S-L150,000, Sb-L210,000, 2 D with adjacent bath-L220,000, Db-L270,000, Tb-L330,000, Qb-L420,000, CC:VM, air-con L15,000 extra per night, rooms on canal come with view, noise, and aroma, rooms facing church are quiet and fresh, Castello San Lio #5659, 30122 Venezia, tel. 041-522-9912, fax 041-523-5852, SE). Canada is ideally located on a small, lively square, just off Campo San Lio between the Rialto and St. Mark's Square.

Hotel Caneva is an institutional, vinyl feeling, canalside place with plain, big, bright rooms and a tired management (S-L70,000, Sb-L110,000, Db-L155,000, Tb-L205,000, prices good with this book and cash, CC:VMA but prices increase with a credit card; midway between Rialto and St. Mark's Square near Chiesa la Fava; coming from San Bartolomeo square—at east end of Rialto Bridge—take a left at Stagneri/Disney store, go straight over bridge, then right—around church, Ramo Dietro La Fava #5515, 30122 Venezia, tel. 041-522-8118, fax 041-520-8676).

Hotel Giorgione, a four-star hotel in a 15th-century palace on a quiet lane, is superprofessional, with plush public spaces, pool tables, Internet access, a garden terrace, and 70 spacious over-the-top rooms with all the comforts (Sb-L170,000–280,000, Db-L250,00–430,000, pricier superior rooms and suites available, extra bed-L100,000, 20 percent off in July and August, check Web for discounts, CC:VMA, elevator, air-con, Piazza S.S. Apostoli #4587, tel. 041-522-5810, fax 041-523-9092, www.hotelgiorgione.com).

Sleeping near S.S. Giovanni e Paoli

Locanda la Corte, with three stars, has 16 attractive, high-ceilinged, wood-beamed rooms—done in pastels—bordering a small, quiet courtyard (Sb-L180,000, standard Db-L320,000, superior Db-350,000, suites available, CC:VM, air-con; *vaporetto* #52 from train station to Fondamente Nove, exit boat to your left, follow waterfront, turn right after second bridge to get to S.S. Giovanni e Paolo square; facing Rosa Salva bar, take street to left—Calle Bressana, hotel is a short block away at bridge; Castello 6317, tel. 041-241-1300, fax 041-241-5982, www.locanda.lacorte.it).

Sleeping near the Accademia

When you step over the Accademia Bridge, the commotion of touristy Venice is replaced by a sleepy village laced with canals. This quiet area, next to the best painting gallery in town, is a 10-minute walk from St. Mark's Square and the Rialto. All are within 12 minutes from the station or car park and three minutes from St. Mark's Square on the fast boat #82. The hotels are located near the south end of the Accademia Bridge except for the last listing (Fondazione Levi), which is at the north end of the bridge (St. Mark's side).

Pensione Accademia fills the 17th-century Villa Maravege. While its 27 comfortable and air-conditioned rooms are nothing extraordinary, you'll feel aristocratic gliding through its grand public spaces and lounging in its breezy garden (Sb-L150,000–220,000, standard Db-L240,000–350,000, superior Db-L290,000–420,000, family deals, CC:VMA; facing Accademia Gallery, take first right, cross first bridge, go right, Dorsoduro #1058, 30123 Venezia, tel. 041-523-7846, fax 041-523-9152, www .pensioneaccademia.it, e-mail: pensione.accademia@flashnet.it).

Hotel Galleria is a compact and velvety little 10-room place (S-L100,000, D-L150,000–160,000, Db-L180,000, big Db-L220,000, CC:VMA, fans, includes breakfast in room, views overlooking Grand Canal, near Accademia Gallery and next to recommended Foscarini restaurant, Dorsoduro #878a, 30123 Venezia, tel. 041-523-2489, tel. & fax 041-520-4172, www .galleria.it, e-mail: galleria@tin.it, SE).

Hotel Agli Alboretti is a cozy, family-run, 25-room place in a quiet neighborhood a block behind the Accademia Gallery. With red carpeting and wood-beamed ceilings, it feels elegant (Sb-L175,000, 2 small Db-L215,000, Db-L270,000, Tb-L320,000, Qb-L370,000, includes breakfast, CC:VMA, air-con; 100 meters from the Accademia *vaporetto* stop on Rio Terra a Foscarini at #884 Accademia; facing Accademia Gallery, go left, then forced right, tel. 041-523-0058, fax 041-521-0158, www.cash.it/alboretti, e-mail: alborett@gpnet.it, SE).

Hotel American is a small, cushy, three-star place on a lazy canal next to the delightful Campo San Vio (a tiny over-looked square facing the Grand Canal). At this Old World hotel with 18 rooms, you'll get better rates Sundays through Thursdays (Sb-L150,000–280,000, Db-L230,000–400,000, Db with view-L260,000–450,000, rates vary by day and season, extra bed-L50,000–100,000, includes big buffet breakfast, CC:VMA, air-con, 30 meters off Campo San Vio and 200 meters from Accademia Gallery; facing Accademia Gallery, go left, forced right, take second left—following yellow sign to Guggenheim Museum, cross bridge, take immediate right, 628 Accademia, 30123 Venezia, tel. 041-520-4733, fax 041-520-4048, check www.hotelamerican.com for deals).

Hotel Belle Arti is the place if you want to be in the old center without the commotion and intensity of Venice. With a grand entry and all the American hotel comforts, it's a big 67-room, modern, three-star place sitting on a former schoolyard (Sb-L200,000–240,000, Db-L280,000–360,000, Tb-L360,000–440,000, the cheaper rates apply to July–Aug and winter, CC:VMA, includes buffet breakfast, plush public areas, air-con, quiet, elevator, 100 meters behind Accademia Gallery; facing Gallery, take left, then forced right, Via Dorsoduro 912, tel. 041-522-6230, fax 041-528-0043, www.hotelbellearti.com, info@hotelbellearti.com).

Domus Cavanis, nearly across the street from—and owned by—Belle Arti, is a two-star hotel that recently opened and still feels new. Its 27 simple rooms are quiet and affordable (Db-L200,000, includes breakfast at Hotel Belle Arti, elevator, TV, phones, Dorsoduro 896, tel. 041-528-7374, fax 041-522-8505).

Pensione La Calcina, the home of English writer John Ruskin in 1876, comes with all the three-star comforts in a professional yet intimate package. Its 29 rooms are squeaky clean, with good wood furniture, hardwood floors, and a peaceful canalside setting facing Giudecca (S-L110,000–130,000, Sb-L150,000, Sb with view-L170,000, Db-L200,000–230,000, Db with view-L260,000–300,000, depending on size and season, CC:VMA, air-con, can reserve rooftop terrace for 60-minute visit, canalside buffet breakfast terrace, Dorsoduro #780, at the south end of Rio di San Vio, tel. 041-520-6466, fax 041-522-7045, e-mail: la.calcina@libero.it). From the car park or station catch *vaporetto* #51 to Zattere (at *vaporetto* stop, exit right, and walk along canal to hotel).

Locanda San Trovaso is sparkling new, with seven classy, spacious rooms—three with canal views—and a peaceful location on a small canal (Sb-L150,000, Db-L200,000, CC:VM, small

roof terrace, Dorsoduro 1351, take *vaporetto* #82 from Tronchetto
or #51 from Piazzale Roma or train station, get off at Zattere,
exit left, cross bridge, continue along canal, turn right at tiny
Calle Trevisan, cross bridge, cross adjacent bridge, take immediate right, first left, tel. 041-277-1146, fax 041-277-7190,
www.locandasantrovaso.com, e-mail: s.trovaso@tin.it).

Fondazione Levi, a guest house run by a foundation that
promotes research on Venetian music, offers 18 quiet, comfortable
rooms (Sb-L110,000, Db-L180,000, Tb-L210,000, Qb-L240,000,
only twin beds, elevator; 80 meters from base of Accademia
Bridge on St. Mark's side; from Accademia *vaporetto* stop, cross
Accademia Bridge, take immediate left—crossing the bridge
Ponte Giustinian and going down Calle Giustinian directly to the
Fondazione, buzz the "Foresteria" door to the right, San Vidal
#2893, 30124 Venezia, tel. 041-786-711, fax 041-786-766, SE).

Sleeping near the Train Station

Hotel Marin is three minutes from the train station but completely out of the touristic bustle of the Lista di Spagna. Just
renovated, cozy, and cheery, it seems like a 19-bedroom home
the moment you cross the threshold and is one of the best values
in town (S-L100,000, D-L125,000, Db-L155,000, T-L170,000,
Tb-L200,000, Q-L205,000, Qb-L225,000, prices good with this
book and if you pay cash, pricier with CC:VMA, San Croce
#670b, tel. 041-718-022, fax 041-721-485, www.hotelmarin.it).
It's family run by helpful, friendly, English-speaking Bruno,
Nadia, and son Samuel (they have city maps). It's immediately
across the canal from the train station, behind the green dome
(over bridge, right, first left, first right, first right). There's an
Internet café and handy **Laundromat** nearby.

Dormitory Accommodations

Foresteria della Chiesa Valdese, warmly run by a Protestant
church, offers cheap dorm beds and doubles in a handy location
(halfway between St. Mark's Square and Rialto). This run-down
but charming old palace has elegant paintings on the ceilings
(dorm bed-L35,000, D-L90,000, Db-L120,000, includes breakfast,
more expensive for 1-night stays, some larger apartments for
families with up to 5 people-L190,000, office open Mon–Sun
9:00–13:00, 18:00–20:00, from Campo Santa Maria di Formosa,
walk past Bar all' Orologio to the end of Calle Lunga and cross
the bridge, Castello #5170, reserve 3 months in advance, tel. &
fax 041-528-6797, fax 041-241-6328).

The **Venice youth hostel**, on Giudecca Island, is crowded,
cheap, and newly remodeled (L30,000 beds with sheets and breakfast in 10- to 16-bed rooms, membership required, office open
daily 7:00–9:30, 13:30–23:00, catch *vaporetto* #82 from station to

Zittele, tel. 041-523-8211). Their budget cafeteria welcomes nonhostelers (nightly 17:00–23:30).

Eating in Venice

While touristy restaurants are the scourge of Venice, there are plenty of good alternatives. The first trick: Walk away from triple-language menus.

Eating between Campo Santi Apostoli and Campo S.S. Giovanni e Paolo

Trattoria da Bepi caters to a local crowd and specializes in fresh seafood and Venetian cuisine. Bepi's son, Loris, who speaks English, makes a smooth *panna cotta* (pudding) and a mean licorice grappa (Fri–Wed 12:00–14:30, 19:00–22:00, closed Thu, CC:VM, allow L65,000 per person, on Salizada del Pistor next to Santi Apostoli Church, tel. 041-528-5031).

Antiche Cantine Ardenghi de Lucia e Michael is a leap of local faith and an excellent splurge. Michael—an effervescent former Murano glass salesman—and his wife, Lucia, cook for a handful of people each night by reservation only. You must call first. You pay L80,000 per person and trust them to wine, dine, and serenade you with Venetian class. The evening can be quiet or raucous depending on who and how many are eating. When you call, ask for a festival of fruit and vegetables or you'll get nothing but crustaceans. There's no sign, and the door's locked. Find #6369 and knock. The password: La Repubblica Serenissima. From Campo S.S. Giovanni e Paolo, pass the churchlike hospital (notice the illusions painted on its facade), go over the bridge to the left, and take the first right—the street is Calle della Testa—to #6369 (Tue–Sat 20:00–24:00, closed Sun–Mon, tel. 041-523-7691).

Two colorful *osterias* are good for *cicchetti*, (munchies) wine tasting, or a simple, rustic, sit-down meal surrounded by a boisterous local ambience: **Osteria da Alberto** (Mon–Sat 12:00–15:00, 18:00–21:30, closed Sun, CC:VM, midway between Campo Santi Apostoli and Campo S.S. Giovanni e Paolo, next to Ponte de la Panada on Calle Larga Giacinto Gallina, tel. 041-523-8153) and **Osteria Candela** on Calle de l'Oca. You'll find local pubs in the side streets opposite Campo St. Sofia across Strada Nueva.

For great local cuisine far beyond the crowds in a rustic Venetian setting, hike to **Osteria Al Bacco** in Cannaregio (closed Mon, Fondamenta Capuzine, Cannaregio #3054, reservations wise, tel. 041-717-493).

Eating near the Accademia

Restaurant/Pizzeria Accademia Foscarini, next to the Accademia Bridge and Galleria, offers decent L9,000 to L13,000 pizzas in a great canalside setting (Wed–Mon 7:00–23:00, closed Tue).

Trattoria Al Cugnai is an unpretentious place run by three sisters serving good food at a good price with friendly service (Tue–Sun 12:00–15:00, 19:00–22:00, closed Mon, midway between the Accademia Gallery and the forgotten and peaceful Campo San Vio, tel. 041-528-9238). They are happy to let you sip your sweet *fragolino bianco* (L2,000) on Campo San Vio (benches with Grand Canal view) and return the glass.

Taverna San Trovaso is a restaurant/pizzeria with nice gnocchi and a good L30,000 menu (Tue–Sun 12:00–14:50, 19:00–21:50, closed Mon, CC:VM, air-con, 100 meters from Accademia Gallery on San Trovaso canal; facing Accademia take a right, then a forced left at canal).

Just west of St. Mark's Square, consider **Osteria Da Carla** (a.k.a. Pietro Panizzolo), a fun and very local hole-in-the-wall where the food is good, the price is right, and Carla mothers you (Mon–Sat 7:00–23:00, closed Sun; from American Express head toward St. Mark's Square, first left, first left again through "Contarina" tunnel, at Sotoportego e Corte Contarina, tel. 041-523-7855).

The Stand-Up Progressive Venetian Pub-Crawl Dinner

A tradition unique to Venice in Italy is a *giro di ombre* (pub crawl)—ideal in a city with no cars. My favorite Venetian dinner is a pub crawl. I've listed plenty of pubs in walking order for a quick or extended crawl below. If you've crawled enough, most of these bars make a fine one-stop, sit-down dinner. *Ombre* means shade, from the old days when a wine bar scooted with the shadow of the Campanile across St. Mark's Square.

Venice's residential back streets hide plenty of characteristic bars with countless trays of interesting toothpick-munchie food (*cicchetti*). This is a great way to mingle and have fun with the Venetians. Real *cicchetti* pubs are getting rare in these fast-food days, but locals appreciate the ones that survive.

Try fried mozzarella cheese, gorgonzola, calamari, artichoke hearts, and anything ugly on a toothpick. Ask for a *piatto misto* (mixed plate). Or try a plate of assorted appetizers for L10,000 (or more, depending on how hungry you are); ask for *"Un classico piatto di cicchetti misti da dieci mila lire"* (pron. oon KLAH-see-koh pee-AH-toh dee chee-KET-tee MEE-stee dah dee-AY-chee MEE-lah LEE-ray). Drink the house wines. A small glass of house red or white wine (*ombre rosso* or *ombre bianco*) or a small beer (*birrino*) costs about L2,000. *Vin bon*, Venetian for fine wine, may run you from L3,000 to L5,000 per little glass. Meat and fish (*pesce:* PAY-shay) munchies are expensive; veggies (*verdure*) are cheap, around L6,000 for a meal-sized plate. Bread sticks (*grissini*) are free for the asking. A good last drink is *fragolino*, the local sweet wine—*bianco* or *rosso*. A liter of house wine costs around L7,000. Bars don't stay open very late, and the *cicchetti* selection

Venice Pub Crawl

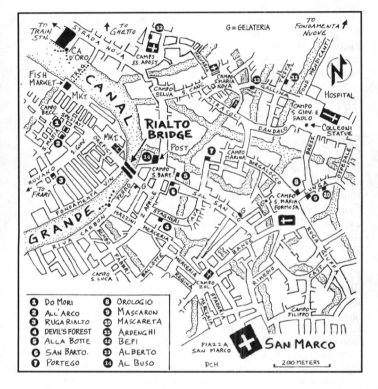

Map legend:

G = GELATERIA

1. Do Mori
2. All'Arco
3. Ruga Rialto
4. Devil's Forest
5. Alla Botte
6. San Barto.
7. Portego
8. Orologio
9. Mascaron
10. Mascareta
11. Ardenghi
12. Bepi
13. Alberto
14. Al Buso

200 METERS

is best early, so start your evening by 18:00. Most bars are closed on Sunday. You can stand around the bar or grab a table in the back—usually for the same price.

Cicchetteria *West of the Rialto Bridge*

Cantina Do Mori is famous with locals (since 1462) and savvy travelers (since 1962) as a classy place for fine wine and *francobollo* (a spicy selection of 20 tiny sandwiches called "stamps"). Choose from the featured wines in the barrel on the bar. Order carefully, or they'll rip you off. From Rialto Bridge walk 200 meters down Ruga degli Orefici away from St. Mark's Square—then ask (Mon–Sat 17:00–20:30, closed Sun, stand up only, arrive early before *cicchetti* are gone, San Polo 429, tel. 041-522-5401). The rough-and-tumble **Cantina All' Arco** across the lane is worth a quick *ombre*.

Antica Ostaria Ruga Rialto is less expensive than Do Mori and offers tables, a busier/younger crowd, and a better selection of munchies (closed Mon, past the blue Chinese restaurant sign, on corner of Ruga Vecchia S. Giovanni and Ramo del Sturion, San Polo 692, tel. 041-521-1243).

These small restaurants, which serve meals and *cicchetti* snacks, are a few steps from the Rialto fish market: **Vini da Pinto** faces the west entrance of the fish market on the small square, Sestier de S. Polo (Tue–Sun 7:30–15:00, 17:30–21:00). As you face Vini da Pinto, **Ostaria Sora al Ponte** is to your right, on the bridge (closed Mon), and **Cantina do Spade** is directly behind Vini da Pinto (head around building to your left, take a right through archway; closed Sun).

Eating near Campo San Bartolomeo, East of the Rialto Bridge

Osteria "Alla Botte" Cicchetteria is an atmospheric place packed with a young, local, bohemian jazz clientele. It's good for a light meal or a *cicchetti* snack with wine (2 short blocks off Campo San Bartolomeo in the corner behind the statue—down Calle de la Bissa, notice the "day after" photo showing a debris-covered Venice after the notorious 1989 Pink Floyd open-air concert, tel. 041-520-9775).

If the statue on the Campo San Bartolomeo walked backward 20 meters, turned left, and went under a passageway, he'd hit **Rosticceria San Bartolomeo.** This cheap—if confusing—self-service restaurant on the ground floor has a likably surly staff (good L9,000 pasta, great fried mozzarella *al* prosciutto for L2,300, delightful fruit salad, and L2,000 glasses of wine, prices listed on wall behind counter, no cover or service charge, daily 9:30–21:30, tel. 041-522-3569). Good but pricier meals are served at the full-service restaurant upstairs. Take out or grab a table.

From Rosticceria San Bartolomeo, continue over a bridge to Campo San Lio (a good landmark), go left at Hotel Canada, and walk straight over another bridge into **Osteria Al Portego** (at #6015). This fine, friendly, and local-style bar has plenty of *cicchetti* (Mon–Fri 9:00–22:00, closed Sat–Sun, tel. 041-522-9038). The *cicchetti* here can make a great meal. If pub crawling from here, ask *"Dov'è Santa Maria di Formosa?"*

The **Devil's Forest Pub,** an air-conditioned bit of England tucked away a block from the crowds, is—strangely—more Venetian these days than the *tipico* places. Locals come here for good English and Irish beer on tap, big salads (L12,000, lunch only), hot bar snacks, and an easygoing ambience (no cover or service charge, fine prices, backgammon and chess boards available-L3000, meals daily 12:00–15:30, bar snacks all the time, closed Sun in Aug, a block off Campo San Bartolomeo on Calle dei Stagneri, tel. 041-520-0623). Across the street, **Bora Bora Pizzeria** serves pizza and salads from an entertaining menu (daily 12:00–15:00, 19:00–22:30, closed Wed in winter, CC:VM, tel. 041-523-6583).

For a Grand Canal view, consider **Al Buso**, at the northeast end of the Rialto Bridge. Of the several restaurants that hug the canal near the Rialto, this is recommended by locals as offering the best value (daily 9:00–24:00, Ponte di Rialto 5338, tel. 041-528-9078).

Eating near Campo Santa Maria di Formosa

Campo Santa Maria di Formosa is just plain atmospheric (as most squares with a Socialist Party office seem to be). For a balmy outdoor sit, you could split a pizza with wine on the square. **Bar all' Orologio** has a good setting and friendly service but mediocre "freezer" pizza (happy to split a pizza for pub crawlers, Mon–Sat 6:00–23:00, closed Sun). For a pizza snack on the square, cross the bridge behind the canalside *gelateria* and grab a slice to go from **Cip Ciap Pizza** (Wed–Mon 9:00–21:00, closed Tue; facing *gelateria*, take bridge to the right; Calle del Mondo Novo). Pub crawlers get a salad course at the fruit-and-vegetable stand next to the water fountain (open until about 19:30, closed Sun).

From Campo Santa Maria di Formosa, follow the yellow sign to "S.S. Giov e Paolo" down Calle Longa Santa Maria di Formosa and head down the street to **Osteria al Mascaron** (#5225, Gigi's bar, Mon–Sat 12:00–15:00, 19:00–23:00, best selection by 19:30, closed Sun). Gigi also runs **Enoteca Mascareta**, a wine bar, 30 meters farther down the street (#5183, Mon–Sat 18:00–01:00, closed Sun, tel. 041-523-0744). The piano sounds like they dropped it in the canal, but the wine was saved.

A *gelateria* is on the canal at Campo Santa Maria di Formosa (for more, see "*Gelato*," below).

Cheap Meals

A key to cheap eating in Venice is bar snacks, especially stand-up mini-meals in out-of-the-way bars. Order by pointing. *Panini* (sandwiches) are sold fast and cheap at bars everywhere. Pizzerias are cheap and easy—try for a sidewalk table at a scenic location. For budget eating, I like small *cicchetti* bars (see "Pub-Crawl Dinner," above); for speed, value, and ambience, you can get a filling plate of local-style tapas at nearly any of the bars.

The **produce market** that sprawls for a few blocks just past the Rialto Bridge (best 8:00–13:00, closed Sun) is a great place to assemble a picnic. The nearby street, Ruga Vecchia, has good bakeries and cheese shops. Side lanes in this area are speckled with fine little hole-in-the-wall munchie bars.

The **Mensa DLF**, the public transportation workers' cafeteria, is cheap and open to the public (daily 11:00–14:30, 18:00–22:00). Leaving the train station, turn right on the Grand Canal, walk about 150 meters along the canal, up eight steps, and through the unmarked door.

Gelato

La Boutique del Gelato is one of the best *gelaterias* in Venice (daily 10:00–21:00, closed Dec–Jan, 2 blocks off Campo Santa Maria di Formosa on corner of Salizada San Lio and Calle Paradiso, next to Hotel Bruno, #5727). A decent *gelateria* is canalside on Campo Santa Maria di Formosa.

For late-night *gelato* at Rialto, try **Michielangelo**, next to the McDonald's on Campo San Bartolomeo, on the St. Mark's side of the Rialto Bridge (daily 10:00–23:30, closed Wed in winter). At St. Mark's Square, the **Al Todaro** *gelateria* opposite the Doge's Palace is open late (daily 8:00–24:00, closed Mon in winter).

Transportation Connections—Venice

By train to: Verona (hrly, 90 min), **Florence** (6/day, 3 hrs), **Dolomites** (8/day to Bolzano, 4 hrs with 1 transfer; catch bus from Bolzano into mountains), **Milan** (hrly, 3–4 hrs), **Rome** (6/day, 5 hrs, slower overnight), **Naples** (change in Rome, plus 2–3 hrs), **Brindisi** (3/day, 11 hrs), **Cinque Terre** (2 La Spezia trains go directly to Monterosso al Mare daily, 6 hrs, at 9:58 and 14:58), **Bern** (4/day, change in Milan, 8 hrs), **Munich** (5/day, 8 hrs), **Paris** (3/day, 11 hrs), **Vienna** (4/day, 9 hrs). Train and *couchette* reservations (about L35,000) are easily made at the American Express office near St. Mark's Square. Venice train info: tel. 147-888-088 or 041-785-570.

HILL TOWNS OF CENTRAL ITALY

Break out of the Venice-Florence-Rome syndrome. There's more to Italy! Experience the slumber of Umbria, the texture of Tuscany, and the lazy towns of Lazio. For starters, here are a few of my favorites.

Siena seems to be every Italy connoisseur's pet town. In my office, whenever Siena is mentioned, someone moans, "Siena? I luuuv Siena!" San Gimignano is the quintessential hill town, with Italy's best surviving medieval skyline and most unusual sausage—*einghiale* (boar). Orvieto, one of the most famous hill towns, is close to Rome (75 min by train) and an ideal springboard for a bus trip to tiny, sparsely populated Civita. Stranded alone on its pinnacle in a vast canyon, Civita's the most lovable.

Planning Your Time
Siena, the must-see town, has the easiest train and bus connections. On a quick trip, consider spending three nights in Siena (with a whole-day side trip into Florence and a day to relax and enjoy Siena). Whatever you do, enjoy a sleepy medieval evening in Siena. After an evening in Siena, its major sights can be seen in half a day.

San Gimignano is an overrun, pint-sized Siena. Don't rush Siena for San Gimignano (with less than 24 hours for Siena, skip San Gimignano).

Orvieto, an easy train stop, is worth a short visit for its cathedral and provides the carless traveler with the best launchpad for a trip to Civita.

Civita di Bagnoregio is the great pinnacle town. A night in Bagnoregio (via Orvieto bus) with time to hike to the town and spend three hours makes the visit worthwhile.

Hill Towns of Central Italy

SIENA

Seven hundred years ago, Siena was a major military power in a class with Florence, Venice, and Genoa. With a population of 60,000, it was even bigger than Paris. In 1348 a disastrous plague weakened Siena. Then, in the 1550s, her bitter rival, Florence, really salted her, making Siena forever a nonthreatening backwater. Siena's loss became our sightseeing gain, as its political and economic irrelevance pickled it purely Gothic. Today Siena's population is still 60,000, compared to Florence's 420,000.

Siena's thriving historic center, with red-brick lanes cascading every which way, offers Italy's best Gothic city experience. Most people do Siena, just 50 kilometers south of Florence, as a day trip, but it's best experienced after dark. While Florence has the blockbuster museums, Siena has an easy-to-enjoy soul: Courtyards sport flower-decked wells, alleys dead-end at rooftop views, and the sky is a rich blue dome. Right off the bat, Siena becomes an old friend.

For those who dream of a Fiat-free Italy, pedestrians rule in the old center of Siena. Sit at a café on the red-bricked main square. Take time to savor the first European city to eliminate automobile traffic from its main square (1966) and then, just to be silly, wonder what would happen if they did it in your city.

Hill Towns: Public Transportation

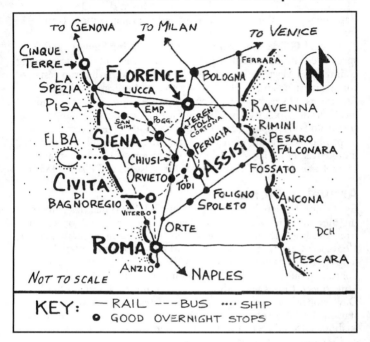

KEY: — RAIL --- BUS ···· SHIP
● GOOD OVERNIGHT STOPS

Orientation

Siena lounges atop a hill, stretching its three legs out from Il
Campo. This main square, the historic meeting point of Siena's
neighborhoods, is pedestrians only. And most of those pedestrians
are students from the local university. Everything I mention is
within a 15-minute walk of the square. Navigate by landmarks,
following the excellent system of street-corner signs. The typical
visitor sticks to the San Domenico–Il Campo axis.

Siena is one big sight. Its essential individual sights come in
two little clusters: the square (city hall, museum, tower) and the
cathedral (baptistery, cathedral museum with its surprise viewpoint). Check these sights off and you're free to wander.

Tourist Information: Pick up a free town map from the
main TI on Il Campo (#56, look for the yellow "Change" sign—
bad rates, good information, Mon–Sat 8:30–19:30, mid–Nov–
mid–March Mon–Sat 8:30–14:00, 15:00–19:00, tel. 0577-280-551,
www.siena.turismo.toscana.it). The little TI at San Domenico is
for hotel promotion only and and sells a Siena map for L1,000.
For a longer stay, consider buying the combo ticket (*biglietto*

cumulativo) for L29,000 that covers nine sights, including the Museo Civico, Santa Maria della Scala, Museo dell' Opera, Baptistery, Piccolomini Library (in cathedral), and more (valid for 7 days, sold at participating sites).

Local Guide: Roberto Bechi, a hardworking Sienese guide, specializes in off-the-beaten-path tours of Siena and the surrounding countryside. Married to an American (Patti) and having run restaurants in Siena and the U.S., Roberto communicates well with Americans. His passions are Sienese culture, Tuscan history, and local cuisine. Book well in advance for full-day tours (ranging in cost from $60–90 per person). Half days ($30–50 per person) cannot be pre-booked during high season, but may be available at the last minute (tel. & fax 0577-704-789, www.zaslon.si/roberto, e-mail: tourrob@tin.it; for U.S. contact, fax Greg Evans at 540/434-4532).

Arrival in Siena

By Train: At Siena's train station, buy a L1,400 bus ticket from the blue machine near the door (exact change needed), or, easier, from the Bus Ticket Office across from the machine (daily 5:50–19:30, ask for city map—it's free and just a bus route map, but helps get you started). Then cross the square (and street) and board any bus heading for Piazza Gramsci, Piazza del Sale, or Stufa Secco (buses leave about every 7 minutes, fewer on Sun). Day-trippers can store luggage at the *deposito bagagli* at the train station (L3,000). The cost of a taxi from the station to your hotel is about L15,000. Siena taxi numbers: at the station (tel. 0577-44504) and elsewhere (tel. 0577-49222).

To get to Siena's train station from the center of Siena, catch a bus at Piazza del Sale or Stufa Secco; note that bus stops are not usually marked by a sign but by a yellow rectangle and the word "bus" marked on the pavement. Confirm with the driver that the bus is going to the *stazione* (stat-zee-OH-nay). Remember to purchase your ticket in advance from a *tabacchi* shop.

By Bus: Some buses arrive at the train station (see "Arrival By Train," above), others at Piazza Gramsci (a few blocks from city center), and some stop at both. You can store baggage underneath Piazza Gramsci in Sotopassaggio la Lizza (L5,000, daily 7:00–19:30, no overnight).

By Car: Drivers coming from the autostrada take the Porta San Marco exit and follow the "Centro" then "Stadio" signs (stadium, soccer ball). The soccer-ball signs take you to the stadium lot (Parcheggio Stadio, L2,500/hr, L24,000/day) at the huge, bare-brick San Domenico Church. The Fortezza lot nearby charges the same. Or park in the lot underneath the railway station. You can drive into the pedestrian zone (a pretty ballsy thing to do) only to drop bags at your hotel. You can park free in the lot below the Albergo Lea, in white-striped spots behind Hotel Villa Liberty, and behind the Fortezza. (The signs showing a street cleaner and a day of the week indicate which day the street is cleaned; there's a L200,000 tow-fee incentive to learn the days of the week in Italian.)

Sights—Siena's Main Square

▲▲▲**Il Campo**—Siena's great central piazza is urban harmony at its best. Like a people-friendly stage set, its gently tilted floor fans out from the tower and city hall backdrop. It's the perfect invitation to loiter. Think of it as a trip to the beach without sand or water. Il Campo was located at the historic junction of Siena's various competing districts, or *contrada*, on the old marketplace. The brick surface is divided into nine sections, representing the council of nine merchants and city bigwigs who ruled medieval Siena. At the square's high point, look for the Fountain of Joy, the two naked guys about to be tossed in, and the pigeons politely waiting their turn to gingerly tightrope down slippery snouts to slurp a drink. At the base of the tower, the Piazza's chapel was built in 1348 as a thanks to God for ending the Black Plague (after it killed more than a third of the population). The market area behind the city hall, a wide-open expanse since the Middle Ages, originated as a farming area within the city walls to feed the city in times of siege (now the Wednesday morning market is held here).

To say Siena and Florence have always been competitive is an understatement. In medieval times a statue of Venus stood on Il Campo (where the Fountain of Joy is today). After the plague hit Siena, the monks blamed this pagan statue. The people cut it to pieces and buried it along the walls of Florence.

▲**Museo Civico**—The Palazzo Pubblico (City Hall), at the base of the tower, has a fine and manageable museum housing a good sample of Sienese art. In the following order you'll see the Sala Risorgimento, with dramatic scenes of Victor Emmanuel's unification of Italy (surrounded by statues that don't seem to care); the chapel, with impressive inlaid wood chairs in the choir; and the Sala del Mappamondo, with Simone Martini's *Maesta* (Enthroned Virgin) facing the faded *Guidoriccio da Fogliano* (a mercenary providing a more concrete form of protection). Next is the Sala della Pace—where the city's fat cats met. Looking down on the oligarchy during their meetings were two interesting frescoes showing the effects of good and bad government. Notice the whistle-while-you-work happiness of the utopian community ruled by the utopian government (in the better-preserved fresco) and the fate of a community ruled by politicians with more typical values (in a terrible state of repair). The message: Without justice there can be no prosperity. The rural view out the window is essentially the view from the top of the big stairs—enjoy it from here (L12,000, combo ticket with tower-L18,000, daily March–Oct 10:00–17:00,

Siena

1 - PICCOLO HOTEL ETRURIA	8 - ALMA DOMUS	15 - OSTERIA DA DIVO
2 - ALBERGO TRE DONZELLE	9 - HOTEL CHIUSARELLI	16 - IL VERROCHIO
3 - ALBERGO LA PERLA	10 - ALBERGO LEA & HOTEL LIBERTY	17 - LAUNDROMAT
4 - HOTEL DUOMO	11 - PIZZERIA SPADAFORTE	18 - PALIO MOVIE
5 - HOTEL CANNON D'ORO	12 - CIAO CAFETERIA	19 - PENSIONE PAL. RAVIZZA
6 - LOCANDA GARIBALDI	13 - RISTORANTE GALLO NERO	20 - HOTEL SANTA CATARINA & PALAZZO VALLI
7 - ALBERGO BERNINI	14 - OSTERIA IL TAMBURINO	21 - SOTTOPASSAGGIO LA LIZZA

July–Sept 10:00–23:00, Nov–Jan 10:00–16:00, last entry 45
minutes before closing, tel. 0577-292-111). Leave Mauro Civai
(the director of this museum) a polite note requesting that a little
English information be shared with his paying guests.

▲**City Tower (Torre del Mangia)**—Siena gathers around its
city hall, not its church. It was a proud republic, and its "declaration of independence" is the tallest secular medieval tower in Italy,
the 100-meter-tall Torre del Mangia (named after a hedonistic
watchman who consumed his earnings like a glutton consumes
food; his chewed-up statue is in the courtyard, to the left as you
enter). Its 300 steps get pretty skinny at the top, but the reward
is one of Italy's best views (L10,000, combo ticket with Museo
Civico-L18,000, daily 10:00–19:00, until 20:30 mid-July–mid-
Aug, closed in rain, sometimes long lines, limit of 30 towerists
at a time, avoid midday crowd).

▲**Pinacoteca (National Picture Gallery)**—Siena was a power
in Gothic art. But the average tourist, wrapped up in a love affair
with the Renaissance, hardly notices. This museum takes you on
a walk through Siena's art, chronologically from the 12th through
the 15th centuries. For the casual sightseer, the Sienese art in the
city hall and cathedral museums is adequate. But art fans enjoy this
opportunity to trace the evolution of Siena's delicate and elegant
art (L8,000, Sun–Mon 8:30–13:15, Tue–Sat 8:15–19:15, plus
possibly 20:30–23:30 on Sat in summer, tel. 0577-281-161). From
the Campo, walk out Via di Città to Piazza di Postierla and go
left on San Pietro.

Sights—Siena's Cathedral Area

▲▲▲**Duomo**—Siena's cathedral is as Baroque as Gothic gets.
The striped facade is piled with statues and ornamentation; the
interior is decorated from top to bottom. The heads of 172 popes
peer down from the ceiling over the fine inlaid art on the floor.
This is one busy interior.

To orient yourself in this *panforte* of Italian churches, stand
under the dome and think of the church floor as a big clock.
You're the middle, and the altar is high noon: you'll find the
Slaughter of the Innocents roped off on the floor at 10:00, Pisano's
pulpit between two pillars at 11:00, Bernini's chapel at 3:00, two
Michelangelo statues (next to snacks, shop, and WC) at 7:00, the
library at 8:00, and a Donatello statue at 9:00. Take some time
with the floor mosaics in the front. Nicola Pisano's wonderful
pulpit is crowded with delicate Gothic storytelling from 1268.
To understand why Bernini is considered the greatest Baroque
sculptor, step into his sumptuous *Cappella della Madonna del Voto*.
This last work in the cathedral, from 1659, is enough to make a
Lutheran light a candle. Move up to the altar and look back at the
two Bernini statues: St. Jerome playing the crucifix like a violinist

lost in beautiful music, and Mary Magdalene in a similar state of spiritual ecstasy. The Piccolomini altar is most interesting for its two Michelangelo statues (the lower big ones). Paul, on the left, may be a self-portrait. Peter, on the right, resembles Michelangelo's more famous statue of Moses. Originally contracted to do 15 statues, Michelangelo left the project early (1504) to do his great *David* in Florence. The Piccolomini Library—worth the L2,000 entry—is brilliantly frescoed with scenes glorifying the works of a pope from 500 years ago. It contains intricately decorated, illuminated music scores and a Roman copy of three Greek graces (library open Sun 14:30–19:30, Tue–Sat same as church hours, below). Donatello's bronze statue of St. John the Baptist, in his famous rags, is in a chapel to the right of the library (church open daily 9:00–19:30 but Sun 10:15–13:30 is reserved for worship only, Nov–mid-March 10:00–13:00, 14:30–17:00, modest dress required).

▲▲**Santa Maria della Scala**—This renovated old hospital (opposite the Duomo entrance) displays a rich treasury and a lavishly frescoed hall. The frescoes in the Pellegrinaio Hall show medieval Siena's innovative health care and social welfare system in action (c. 1442, wonderfully described in English). Downstairs are statues from the *Fountain of Gaia* by Jacopo della Quercia (L10,000, daily 10:00–18:00, until 23:00 Fri–Sat in summer, off-season 11:00–16:30). The chapel just inside the door to your left is free (English description inside chapel entrance).

▲**Baptistery**—Siena is so hilly that there wasn't enough flat ground on which to build a big church. What to do? Build a big church and prop up the overhanging edge with the baptistery. This dark and quietly tucked-away cave of art is worth a look (and L3,000) for its cool tranquility and the bronze panels and angels—by Ghiberti, Donatello, and others—adorning the pedestal of the baptismal font (daily mid-March–Sept 9:00–19:30, Oct 9:00–18:00, Nov–mid-March 10:00–13:00, 14:30–17:00).

▲▲**Cathedral Museum (Museo dell'Opera e Panorama)**—Siena's most enjoyable museum, on the Campo side of the church (look for the yellow signs), was built to house the cathedral's art. The ground floor is filled with the cathedral's original Gothic sculpture by Giovanni Pisano (who spent 10 years here carving and orchestrating the decoration of the cathedral in the late 1200s) and a fine Donatello *Madonna and Child*. Upstairs to the left awaits a private audience with Duccio's *Maesta* (Enthroned Virgin). Pull up a chair and study one of the great pieces of medieval art. The flip side of the *Maesta* (displayed on the opposite wall), with 26 panels—the medieval equivalent of pages—shows scenes from the Passion of Christ. Climb onto the "Panorama dal Facciatone." From the first landing, take the skinnier second spiral for Siena's surprise view. Look back over the Duomo and consider this:

When rival republic Florence began its grand cathedral, proud
Siena decided to build the biggest church in all Christendom. The
existing cathedral would be used as a transept. You're atop what
would have been the entry. The wall below you, connecting the
Duomo with the museum of the cathedral, was as far as Siena got
before a plague killed the city's ability to finish the project. Were
it completed, you'd be looking straight down the nave—white
stones mark where columns would have stood (L6,000, worthwhile
L5,000 40-minute audioguide, daily mid-March–Sept 9:00–19:30,
Oct 9:00–18:00, Nov–mid-March 9:00–13:30, tel. 0577-283-048).

Sights—Siena's San Domenico Area
Church of San Domenico—This huge brick church is worth a
quick look. The bland interior fits the austere philosophy of the
Dominicans. Walk up the steps in the rear for a look at various
paintings from the life of Saint Catherine, patron saint of Siena.
Halfway up on the right you'll see a wooden bust of Saint Catherine and her finger in a case. And in the adjacent chapel, you'll see
her actual head (free, daily April–Oct 7:00–12:55, 15:00–18:30,
Nov–March 9:00–12:55, 15:00–18:00).

Sanctuary of Saint Catherine—A few downhill blocks toward the
center from San Domenico (follow signs to the Santuario di Santa
Caterina), step into Catherine's cool and peaceful home. Siena
remembers its favorite hometown girl, a simple, unschooled, but
almost mystically devout girl who, in the mid-1300s, helped get
the pope to return from France to Rome. Pilgrims have come here
since 1464. Since then, architects and artists have greatly embellished what was probably a humble home (her family worked as
wool dyers). Enter through the courtyard and walk to the far end.
The chapel on your right was built over the spot where Saint
Catherine received the stigmata while praying. The chapel on
your left used to be the kitchen. Go down the stairs next to the
chapel/kitchen to reach the saint's room. Once a bare cell, it's
been frescoed, coffered, and honored beyond recognition. Much
of the art throughout the sanctuary depicts scenes from the saint's
life (free, daily 9:00–12:30, 14:30–18:00, winter 9:00–12:30, 15:30–
18:00, Via Tiratoio).

Siena's Palio
In the Palio, the feisty spirit of Siena's 17 *contrada* (neighborhoods)
lives on. These neighborhoods celebrate, worship, and compete
together. Each even has its own historical museum. *Contrada* pride
is evident any time of year in the colorful neighborhood banners
and parades. (If you hear distant drumming, run to it for the
medieval action.) But *contrada* pride is most visible twice a year—
on July 2 and August 16—when they have their world-famous
Palio di Siena. Ten of the 17 neighborhoods compete (chosen by

lot), hurling themselves with medieval abandon into several days of trial races and traditional revelry. On the big day, Il Campo is stuffed to the brim with locals and tourists, as the horses charge wildly around the square in this literally no-holds-barred race. Of course, the winning neighborhood is the scene of grand celebrations afterward. The grand prize: simply proving your *contrada* is numero uno. All over town, sketches and posters depict the Palio. This is not some folkloristic event. It's a real medieval moment. If you're packed onto the square with 15,000 people who each really want to win, you won't see much, but you'll feel it. While the actual Palio packs the city, you could side trip in from Florence to see horse-race trials each of the three days before the big day (usually at 9:00 and 19:45).

▲**Palio al Cinema**—This 20-minute film helps recreate the craziness of the Palio. See it at the Cinema Moderno in Piazza Tolomei, two blocks from the Campo (L10,000, L8,000 or 2 for L15,000 with this book, Mon–Fri 9:30–17:30, Sat 9:30–15:30, maybe until 17:30 on Sat July–Aug, English showings generally hourly at :30 past the hour, closed Sun, tel. 0577-289-201). Call or drop by to confirm when the next English showing is scheduled— there are usually nine each day.

Shopping
Shops line Via Banchi di Sopra, the *passeggiata* route (see "Nightlife," below). For a department store, try Upim on Piazza Mateotti (Mon–Sat 9:30–19:50, closed Sun). The large, colorful scarves/flags, each depicting the symbol of one of Siena's 17 different neighborhoods, are easy-to-pack souvenirs, fun for decorating your home (L10,000 apiece, sold at souvenir stands).

Nightlife
Join the evening *passeggiata* (peak strolling time is 19:00) along Via Banchi di Sopra with *gelato* in hand. **Nannini's** at Piazza Salimbeni has fine *gelato* (daily 11:00–24:00).

The **Enoteca Italiana** is a good wine bar in a cellar in the Fortezza (Mon 12:00–20:00, Tue–Sat 12:00–01:00, closed Sun, sample glasses in 3 different price ranges: L3,000, L5,000, L10,000, bottles and snacks available, CC:VM, tel. 0577-288-497).

Sleeping in Siena
(L2,000 = about $1, country code: 39, zip code: 53100)
Sleep Code: **S** = Single, **D** = Double/Twin, **T** = Triple, **Q** = Quad, **b** = bathroom, **t** = toilet only, **s** = shower only, **CC** = Credit Card (**V**isa, **M**asterCard, **A**mex), **SE** = Speaks English, **NSE** = No English. Breakfast is generally not included. Have breakfast on Il Campo or in a nearby bar.

Finding a room is tough during Easter or the Palio in early

July and mid-August. Call ahead any time of year, as Siena's few budget places are listed in all the budget guidebooks. While day-tripping tour groups turn the town into a Gothic amusement park in midsummer, Siena is basically yours in the evenings and off-season. Nearly all listed hotels lie between Il Campo and the Church of San Domenico (see map on page 542). About a third of the listings don't take credit cards. If "CC:VM" isn't mentioned in a listing, they don't take plastic, no matter how earnestly you ask. Cash machines are plentiful on the main streets.

The TI lists private homes that rent rooms for around L60,000 per person. Some are central, and some require a stay of several days (tel. 0577-280-551).

Siena has two modern, self-service **Laundromats:** Lavarapido Wash and Dry (daily 8:00–21:00, Via di Pantaneto 38) and Onda Blu (daily 8:00–22:00, Via del Casato di Soto 17).

Sleeping near Il Campo

Each of these first listings is forgettable but inexpensive and just a horse wreck away from one of Italy's most wonderful civic spaces.

Piccolo Hotel Etruria, a good bet for a hotel with 19 decent rooms but not much soul, is just off the square (S-L70,000, Sb-L80,000, Db-L130,000, Tb-L165,000, Qb-L210,000, breakfast-L8,000, CC:VMA, with your back to the tower, leave Il Campo to the right at 2:00, Via Donzelle 1–3, tel. 0577-288-088, fax 0577-288-461, e-mail: hetruria@tin.it).

Albergo Tre Donzelle is a plain, institutional place next door to Piccolo Hotel Etruria that makes sense only if you think of Il Campo as your terrace (S-L60,000, D-L85,000, Db-L110,000, CC:VMA, Via Donzelle 5, tel. 0577-280-358, fax 0577-223-933, Senora Iannini SE).

Hotel Cannon d'Oro, a few blocks up Via Banchi di Sopra, is spacious and group friendly (30 rooms, Sb-L112,000, Db-L137,000, Tb-L181,000, these discounted prices promised through 2001 with this book, family deals, breakfast-L10,000, CC:VMA, Via Montanini 28, tel. 0577-44321, fax 0577-280-868, e-mail: cannonsi@tin.it, Maurizio and Debora SE).

Locanda Garibaldi is a modest, very Sienese restaurant/*albergo*. Gentle Marcello wears two hats, as he runs a fine, busy restaurant downstairs and seven pleasant rooms up a funky metal staircase (Db-L120,000, Tb-L150,000, family deals, takes reservations only a few days in advance, half a block downhill off the square at Via Giovanni Dupre 18, tel. 0577-284-204, NSE).

Albergo La Perla is a funky, jumbled, 13-room place. Its narrow maze of hallways, stark rooms, old bedspreads, miniscule bathrooms, and laissez-faire environment works for backpackers (Sb-L80,000, Db-L110,000, Tb-L150,000, a block off the square on Piazza Independenza at Via della Terme 25, tel. 0577-47144).

Attilio and his American wife, Deborah, take reservations only a day or two ahead. Ideally, call the morning you'll arrive.

Splurges: Hotel Duomo is the best in-the-old-town splurge, a classy place with 23 spacious, elegant rooms (Sb-L200,000, Db-L250,000, Tb-L330,000, Qb-L360,000, includes breakfast, CC:VMA, air-con, picnic-friendly roof terrace, free parking, follow Via di Città, which becomes Via Stalloreggi, to Via Stalloreggi 38, 10-minute walk to Il Campo, tel. 0577-289-088, fax 0577-43043, www.hotelduomo.it, e-mail: hduomo@comune.siena.it, Stefania SE). If you arrive by train, take a taxi (L15,000); if you drive, go to Porta San Marco and follow the signs to the hotel, drop off your bags, and then park in nearby "Il Campo" lot.

Pensione Palazzo Ravizza has an aristocratic feel and a peaceful garden. Classy and friendly, it's a 10-minute walk from Il Campo (Db-L380,000–550,000, includes breakfast and dinner, cheaper mid-Nov–Feb, CC:VMA, elevator, back rooms face open country, good restaurant, parking, Via Pian dei Mantellini 34, tel. 0577-280-462, fax 0577-221-597).

Sleeping near San Domenico Church

These hotels are listed in order of closeness to Il Campo—maximum 10-minute walk. The first two enjoy views of the old town and cathedral (which sits floodlit before me as I type) and are the best values in town.

Albergo Bernini makes you part of a Sienese family in a modest, clean home with nine fine rooms. Friendly Nadia and Mauro welcome you to their spectacular view terrace for breakfast and picnic lunches and dinners. Mauro, an accomplished accordionist, might play "Happy Birthday" if you say it's your birthday (Sb-L95,000, D-L110,000, Db-L130,000, breakfast-L12,000, less in winter, midnight curfew, on the main San Domenico–Il Campo drag at Via Sapienza 15, tel. & fax 0577-289-047, www.albergobernini.com, e-mail: hbernin@tin.it, their son, Alessandro, SE).

Alma Domus is ideal—unless nuns make you nervous, you need a double bed, or you plan on staying out past the 23:30 curfew (no mercy given). This quasi hotel (not a convent) is run with firm but angelic smiles by sisters who offer clean and quiet rooms for a steal and save the best views for foreigners. Bright lamps, quaint balconies, fine views, grand public rooms, top security, and a friendly atmosphere make this a great value. The check-out time is strictly 10:00, but they will store your luggage in their secure courtyard (Db-L105,000, Tb-L130,000, Qb-L160,000, breakfast-L11,000, ask for view room—*con vista*, elevator, from San Domenico walk downhill with the church on your right toward the view, turn left down Via Camporegio, make a U-turn at the little chapel down the brick steps to

Via Camporegio 37, tel. 0577-44177 and 0577-44487, fax 0577-47601, NSE).

Hotel Chiusarelli, a proper hotel in a beautiful building with a handy location, comes with lots of traffic noise at night—ask for a quieter room in the back (50 rooms, S-L102,000 without breakfast; the following include a big buffet breakfast: S-L130,000, Db-L190,000, Tb-L255,000, suites available, CC:VMA, air-con, pleasant garden terrace, across from San Domenico at Viale Curtatone 15, tel. 0577-280-562, fax 0577-271-177, e-mail: chiusare@tin.it, SE).

Albergo Lea is a sleepable place in a residential neighborhood a few blocks away from the center (past San Domenico) with easy parking (11 rooms, S-L100,000, Db-L160,000, Tb-L185,000 Qb-L200,000, cheaper in winter, includes breakfast, rooftop terrace, CC:VMA, Viale XXIV Maggio 10, tel. & fax 0577-283-207, e-mail: hotellea@libero.it, SE). **Hotel Villa Liberty** has 18 big, bright, comfortable rooms (S-L140,000, Db-L220,000, includes breakfast, CC:VMA, only one room with twin beds, elevator, bar, air-con, TVs, courtyard, etc., facing the fortress at Viale V. Veneto 11, tel. 0577-44966, fax 0577-44770, SE).

Sleeping Farther from the Center, near Porta Romana

Splurges: Hotel Santa Caterina is a three-star, 18th-century place best for drivers who need air-conditioning. It's peaceful with a delightful garden, and professionally run with real attention to quality (Sb-L185,000, small Db-L185,000, Db-L230,000, Tb-L290,000, mention this book to get these prices, includes breakfast, CC:VMA, request quiet garden side, fridge in room, parking-L10,000/day—request when you reserve, 100 meters outside Porta Romana at Via E.S. Piccolomini 7, tel. 0577-221-105, fax 0577-271-087, e-mail: hsc@sienanet.it, Stefania SE). Easy parking and shuttle bus (Mon–Sat 4/hrly, Sun 2/hrly) to town center. A taxi to/from the station runs L15,000.

Palazzo di Valli, with 11 big, peaceful rooms, a fine TV lounge, and a garden, is 800 meters beyond Porta Romana (the Roman gate). It's a straight shot into town on the shuttle bus (Mon–Sat 4/hrly, Sun 2/hrly) and it feels like it's in the country (Db-L250,000 with breakfast for travelers with this book in 2001, CC:VMA, parking, Via E.S. Piccolomini, tel. 0577-226-102, fax 0577-222-255, Camarda family). From the autostrada exit at Siena Sud in the direction of Porta Romana.

Cheaper Options: The homespun **Casa Laura** has five clean, well-maintained rooms, some with brick-and-beam ceilings (Db-L160,000, breakfast-L15,000 for 2, CC:VM, Via Roma 3, tel. 0577-226-061, fax 0577-225-240, e-mail: labenci@tin.it).

Siena's **Guidoriccio Youth Hostel** has 120 cheap beds, but, given the hassle of the bus ride and the charm of downtown Siena at night, I'd skip it (office open 15:00–01:00, L24,000 beds in doubles, triples, and dorms with sheets and breakfast, bus #10 from train station or bus #15 from Piazza Gramsci, Via Fiorentina 89 in Stellino neighborhood, tel. 0577-52212, SE).

Eating in Siena

Budget eaters look for *pizza al taglio* shops, scattered throughout Siena, selling pizza by the slice. Picnickers enjoy the open-air market on Wednesday morning (Piazza Mercato, just behind Il Campo).

Sienese restaurants are reasonable by Florentine and Venetian standards. Even with higher prices, lousy service, and lower-quality food, consider eating on Il Campo—a classic European experience. **Pizzeria Spadaforte**, at the edge of the Campo, has a decent setting, mediocre pizza, and tables steeper than its prices (daily 12:00–16:00, 19:30–22:30, CC:VM, to the far right of city tower as you face it, tel. 0577-281-123). At the bottom of the Campo, a **Ciao** cafeteria offers easy self-service meals, no ambience, and no views. The crowded **Spizzico**, a pizza counter in the front half of Ciao, serves huge, inexpensive quarter pizzas; people take the pizza, trays and all, out on the Campo for a picnic (daily 12:00–15:00, 19:00–21:00, nonsmoking section—*non fumatori*—in back, CC:VM only in cafeteria, to left of city tower as you face it).

For authentic Sienese dining at a fair price, eat at **Locanda Garibaldi**, down Via Giovanni Dupre at #18, within a block of Il Campo (L27,000 menu, Sun–Fri opens at 12:00 for lunch and 19:00 for dinner, arrive early to get a table, closed Sat). Marcello does a nice little L5,000 *piatto misto dolce*, featuring several local desserts with sweet wine.

Ristorante Gallo Nero, a friendly "grotto" for authentic Tuscan cuisine, is a good student-type place. This "black rooster" serves a mean *ribollita* (hearty Tuscan bean soup) and offers a L40,000 "medieval menu" (L28,000 Tuscan menu, daily 12:00–15:30, 19:00–24:00, CC:VMA, 3 blocks down Via del Porrione from the Campo at #65, tel. 0577-284-356). A block away, **Il Verrochio** serves a decent L22,000 menu (CC:VM, Logge del Papa 1).

Osteria il Tamburino is friendly, small, and intimate and serves up tasty meals (Mon–Sat 12:00–14:30, 19:00–20:30, closed Sun, CC:VM, follow Via di Città off Campo, becomes Stalloreggi, Via Stalloreggi 11, tel. 0577-280-306).

Antica Osteria Da Divo is the place for a fine L80,000 meal. The kitchen is creative, the food is fresh and top notch, and the ambience is candlelit. You'll get a basket of exotic fresh breads. The "black pearls"—with a truffle sauce—are sumptuous. The lamb goes baaa in your mouth. And the chef is understandably proud of his desserts (daily 12:00–14:30, 19:00–22:00, CC:VMA, facing baptistery door, take the far right, reserve for summer eves, Via Franciosa 29, tel. 0577-284-381).

Osteria la Chiacchera, while touristy, is an atmospheric, tasty, and affordable hole-in-the-brick-wall (daily 12:00–14:30, 19:00–24:00, CC:VM, below Pension Bernini at Costa di San Antonio 4, reservations wise, tel. 0577-280-631).

Le Campane, two blocks off the Campo, is also good (indoor/outdoor seating, CC:VM, a few steps off Via di Città at Via delle Campane 6, tel. 0577-284-035).

Snack with a view from a balcony overlooking the Campo. Survey these three places from the Campo to see which has a free table: **Gelateria Artigiana** (perhaps Siena's best ice cream), **Bar Paninoteca** (sandwiches, closed Mon), or **Bar Barbero d'Oro** (*panforte*—L3,500/100 grams—and cappuccino, best balcony, closed Sun), all of which are on Via di Città.

Sienese Sweets: All over town, Prodotti Tipici shops sell Sienese specialties. Siena's claim to caloric fame is its *panforte*, a rich, chewy concoction of nuts, honey, and candied fruits that impresses even fruitcake haters (although locals prefer a white macaroon-and-almond cookie called *ricciarelli*).

Transportation Connections—Siena

By bus to: Rome (6/day, 3 hrs, by Sena bus, arrives at Rome's Tiburtina station), **Assisi** (3/day, 2 hrs, by Sena bus; 1 goes direct to Assisi, the other 2 go to S. Maria Angeli, from here catch a local bus to Assisi, 2/hrly, 20 min), **San Gimingano** (hrly, 1 hr, by Train bus), **Florence** (2/hrly, 1.25–2 hrs, by Train bus). Schedules get sparse on Sunday.

Buses depart Siena from Piazza Gramsci, the train station, or both. Confirm when you buy your ticket. You can buy tickets for the confusingly named Train (pron. TRAH-een) buses or Sena buses at the train station (Train bus office: Mon–Sat 5:50–19:30; for Sena, buy tickets at *tabacchi* shop unless they've opened a new office in the station), or even easier and more central, at Sottopassaggio La Lizza under Piazza Gramsci (Train bus office: daily 5:50–19:30, tel. 0577-204-246, toll-free 800-373-760; Sena bus office: Mon–Sat 7:45–19:45, Sun 15:15–19:45, tel. 0577-283-203).

Sottopassaggio La Lizza has a cash machine (neither office accepts credit cards), luggage storage (L5,000, daily 7:00–19:30), posted bus schedules, TV monitors (listing imminent departures), and expensive WCs. The fastest buses are marked "*corse rapide*," the *diretto* makes a few stops, and the misnamed *accellerata* stops everywhere. These milk-run buses are much slower but more scenic, offering an interesting glimpse of small-town and rural Tuscany.

If you plan to depart Siena after the bus offices close, either buy a ticket in advance from a nearby *tabacchi* shop, or on the bus from the driver (this is discouraged, but possible).

Buses run from Siena to **Viterbo** for Civita connections (usually 1/day, departs Siena in afternoon); get tickets in Siena at the
train station or at Balzana Viaggi travel agency (Via Montanini 73,
near Piazza Gramsci, tel. 0577-285-013).

By train to: Florence (9/day, 1.75 hrs, last one at 21:00).

SAN GIMIGNANO

The epitome of a Tuscan hill town, with 14 medieval towers
still standing (out of an original 72!), San Gimignano is a perfectly preserved tourist trap so easy to visit and visually pleasing
that it's a good stop. In the 13th century, back in the days of
Romeo and Juliet, towns were run by feuding noble families.
They'd periodically battle things out from the protective bases
of their respective family towers. Pointy skylines were the norm
in medieval Tuscany. But in San Gimignano, fabric was big
business, and many of its towers were built simply to hang
dyed fabric out to dry.

While the basic three-star sight here is the town of San
Gimignano itself, there are a few worthwhile stops. From the
town gate, shop straight up the traffic-free town's cobbled main
drag to Piazza del Cisterna (with its 13th-century well). The
town sights cluster around the adjoining Piazza del Duomo.
Thursday is market day (8:00–13:00), but, for local merchants,
every day is a sales frenzy.

Tourist Information: The TI is in the old center on Piazza
Duomo (daily March–Oct 9:00–13:00, 15:00–19:00, Nov–Feb
9:00–13:00, 14:00–18:00, changes money, tel. 0577-940-008,
www.sangimignano.com, e-mail: prolocsg@tin.it). To see virtually
all of the city's sights, consider a L20,000 combo ticket (covers
Collegiata, Torre Grossa, Museo Civico, archaeological museum,
and more).

Sights—San Gimignano

The **Collegiata**, with the round windows and wide steps, is a
Romanesque church filled with fine Renaissance frescoes (L6,000,
Mon–Fri 9:30–19:30, Sat 9:30–17:00, Sun 13:00–17:00).

You can climb the city's tallest tower, **Torre Grossa**
(L8,000, 60 meters tall, March–Oct daily 9:30–19:20; Nov–Feb
Sat–Thu 10:30–16:20, closed Fri), but the free *rocca* (castle), a
short hike behind the church, offers a better view and a great
picnic perch, especially at sunset.

The **Museo Civico**, in Piazza Popolo, has a classy little
painting collection with a 1422 altarpiece by Taddeo di Bartolo
honoring Saint Gimignano. You can see him with the town in
his hands, surrounded by events from his life (L7,000, L12,000
combo ticket with Torre Grossa, has the same hours as Torre
Grossa).

Sleeping and Eating in San Gimignano
(L2,000 = about $1, country code: 39, zip code: 53037)
Carla Rossi offers rooms—most with views—throughout the town (Db-from L100,000, Via di Cellole 81, tel. & fax 0577-955-041, cellular 036-8352-3206, www.appartamentirossicarla.com). For a listing of private rooms, stop by or call **Associazione Strutture Extralberghiere** (Db-L100,000, no breakfast, Piazza della Cisterna, tel. 0577-943-190). **Osteria del Carcere** has good food and prices (Via del Castello 13, just off Piazza della Cisterna, tel. 0577-941-905). Shops guarded by wild boar statues sell boar by the gram; carnivores buy some boar (*cinghiale*—cheen-GAH-lay), cheese, bread, and wine and enjoy a picnic in the garden by the castle.

Transportation Connections—San Gimignano
To: Florence (hrly buses, 75 min, change in Poggibonsi; or catch the frequent 20-min shuttle bus to Poggibonsi and train to Florence), **Siena** (hrly buses, 90 min, change in Poggibonsi to bus or train), **Volterra** (6 buses/day, 2 hrs, change in Poggibonsi and Colle di Val d'Elsa). Bus tickets are sold at the bar just inside the town gate. San Gimignano has no baggage-check service.
   Drivers: You can't drive within the walled town of San Gimignano, but a car park awaits just a few steps outside.

ORVIETO
Umbria's grand hill town, while no secret, is still worth a quick look. Just off the freeway, with three popular claims to fame (its cathedral, Classico wine, and ceramics), it's loaded with tourists by day and quiet by night. Drinking a shot of wine in a ceramic cup as you gaze up at the cathedral lets you experience Orvieto all at once.
   Ride the back streets of Orvieto into the Middle Ages. The town sits majestically on a big chunk of tufa. Streets lined with buildings made from the exhaust-stained volcanic stuff seem to grumble Dark Ages.
   Piazza Cahen is a key transportation hub at the entry to the hilltop town. It has a ruined fortress with a garden, a commanding view, and the Pozzo San Patrizio, an impressive, although over-priced, double helix well carved into tufa rock.
   Tourist Information: The TI is at Piazza Duomo 24 on the cathedral square (Mon–Fri 8:15–14:00, 16:00–19:00, Sat 10:00–13:00, 16:00–19:00, Sun 10:00–12:00, 16:00–18:00, tel. 0763-341-772). The TI sells a "Carta Unica" (L20,000) that covers entry to the Archaeological Museum, Underground Orvieto Tours, and other sights, plus your public transportation (bus and funicular) for one day.
   Arrival in Orvieto: A handy funicular/bus shuttle takes visitors quickly from the train station and car park to the top of the town (4/hrly, L1,600 ticket includes Piazza Cahen–Piazza Duomo

Orvieto

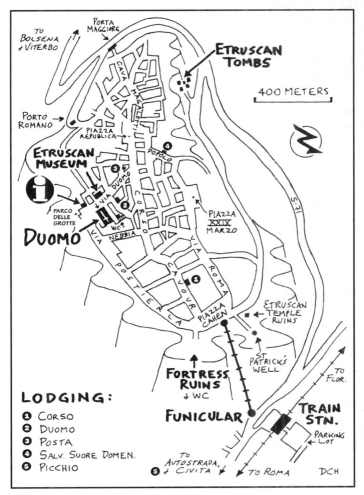

To the map labels:

- TO BOLSENA & VITERBO
- PORTA MAGGIORE
- ETRUSCAN TOMBS
- 400 METERS
- PORTO ROMANO
- PIAZZA REPUBLICA
- ETRUSCAN MUSEUM
- POPOLO
- VIA DUOMO
- PARCO DELLE GROTTE
- WC
- DUOMO
- VIA NEBBIA
- VIA POSTIERLA
- CORSO
- CAVOUR
- PIAZZA XXIX MARZO
- VIA ROMA
- S-1
- PIAZZA CAHEN
- ETRUSCAN TEMPLE RUINS
- ST PATRICK'S WELL
- TO FLOR.
- FORTRESS RUINS & WC
- FUNICULAR
- TRAIN STN.
- PARKING LOT

LODGING:

1. CORSO
2. DUOMO
3. POSTA
4. SALV. SUORE DOMEN.
5. PICCHIO

- TO AUTOSTRADA, & CIVITA
- TO ROMA
- DCH

minibus transfer, where you'll find everything that matters; or L1,200 for funicular only—best choice if you're staying at Hotel Corso; funicular runs Mon–Sat 7:15–20:30, Sun 8:00–20:30).

Buy your ticket at the entrance to the funicular (look for "*biglieterria*" sign) or at the train station *tabacchi* shop across the street. At the top of the funicular, get on the waiting orange bus. The shuttle bus drops you at the TI (last stop, in front of Duomo). Drivers park at the base of the hill at the huge, free lot behind the

Orvieto train station (follow the "P" and "funicolare" signs) or at the pay lot to the right of Orvieto's cathedral (L1,500 for first hour, L1,000/hrly thereafter).

Sights—Orvieto

▲▲**Duomo**—Orvieto's cathedral has Italy's most striking facade (from 1330). Grab a *gelato* (to the left of the church) and study this fascinating mass of mosaics and sculpture (daily 7:30–12:45, 14:30–19:15, closes at 18:15 March and Oct, closes at 17:15 Nov–Feb). Inside the cathedral notice how the downward-sloping floor diminishes the perspective, giving it the illusion of being shorter than it is. Notice also the alabaster windows.

To the right of the altar, the Chapel of St. Brizio features Luca Signorelli's brilliantly lit and recently restored frescoes of the Apocalypse. Step into the chapel and you're surrounded by vivid scenes showing the Preaching of the Antichrist, the End of the World, the Resurrection of the Bodies, the Last Judgment, and a gripping pietà. For a bonus, check out Fra Angelico's painting of Jesus, the angels, and the prophets on the ceiling. This room is Orvieto's artistic must-see (get L3,000 ticket at the TI or the shop across the square; chapel sometimes free 7:30–10:00—drop by to check, only 24 people allowed in chapel at a time, closed on Sun). A good book about the chapel is Dugald McLellan's *Signorelli's Orvieto Frescoes.*

Public toilets are just off the square, down the stairs from the left transept. To find the viewpoint park, face the cathedral and go right (past parking lot) for a one-minute walk.

Archaeological Museum (Museo Civico)—Across from the entrance of the cathedral is a fine Etruscan art museum combined with a city history museum (L8,000, daily 9:30–18:00; Oct–March Tue–Sun 10:00–13:00, 14:30–17:00).

Underground Orvieto Tours (Parco delle Grotte)—Guides weave a good archaeological history into an hour-long look at about 100 meters of caves (L10,000, tours daily at 11:00, 12:15, 16:00, and 17:15 from TI, tel. 0763-344-891 or the TI). Orvieto is honeycombed with Etruscan and medieval caves. You'll see only the remains of an old olive press, two impressive 40-meter-deep Etruscan well shafts, and the remains of a primitive cement quarry, but if you want underground Orvieto, this is the place to get it.

Sleeping in Orvieto
(L2,000 = about $1, country code: 39, zip code: 05018)
Here are five places in the old town and one in a more modern neighborhood near the station (see map on page 554).

Hotel Corso is small, clean, and friendly, with comfy, modern rooms, some with balconies and views (Sb-L110,000, Db-L150,000, 10 percent discount if you show this book, buffet breakfast-L12,500, CC:VM, elevator, air-con at no extra charge, garage on the main street up from funicular toward Duomo at Via Cavour 339, tel. & fax 0763-342-020).

Hotel Virgilio is a decent hotel with bright and modern—if overpriced—rooms shoehorned into an old building ideally located on the main square facing the cathedral (Sb-L120,000, Db-L175,000, includes breakfast, send personal or traveler's check for first night's deposit, CC:VM, elevator, noisy church bells, Piazza Duomo 5, tel. 0763-341-882, fax 0763-343-797, SE). They also have a cheaper *dependencia*—a double and quad in a one-star hotel a few doors away (Db-L110,000, Qb-L200,000).

Hotel Duomo is a funky, brightly colored, Old World place with 17 not-quite-clean rooms and a great location (renovated for 2001, Db–maybe L100,000, a block from Duomo, behind *gelateria* at Via di Maurizio 7, tel. 0763-341-887, fax 0763-341-105).

Hotel Posta is a five-minute walk from the cathedral into the medieval core. It's a big, old, formerly elegant but well-cared-for-in-its-decline building with a breezy garden, a grand old lobby, and spacious, clean, plain rooms with vintage rickety furniture and springy beds (20 rooms, S-L60,000, Sb-L70,000, D-L80,000, Db-L100,000, breakfast-L10,000, Via Luca Signorelli 18, tel. & fax 0763-341-909).

The sisters of the **Istituto Salvatore Suore Domenicane** rent 15 spotless twin rooms in their heavenly convent (Sb-L55,000, Db-L90,000, 2-night minimum, breakfast-L5,000, just off Piazza del Populo at Via del Populo 1, tel. & fax 0763-342-910).

Hotel Picchio is a concrete-and-marble place, more comfortable but with less character than others in the area. It's in the lower, plain part of town, 300 meters from the train station (S-L35,000, Sb-L60,000, D-L65,000, Db-L85,000, Tb-L105,000, ask for the Rick Steves discount; some rooms with air-con, fridge, and phone; Via G. Salvatori 17, 05019 Orvieto Scalo, tel. 0763-301-144 or 0763-90246, family run by Marco and Picchio). A trail leads from here up to the old town.

Transportation Connections—Orvieto

By train to: Rome (14/day, 75 min, consider leaving your car at the large car park behind the Orvieto station), **Florence** (14/day, 90 min), **Siena** (10/day, 2–3 hrs, change in Chiusi).

By bus to Bagnoregio: It's a 50-minute, L3,000 bus ride (departures in 2000 from Orvieto's Piazza Cahen on blue Cotral bus: 9:10, 12:40, 13:55, 15:45, 17:40, and 18:35, each bus stops at Orvieto's train station five minutes later, runs daily except Sun, buy tickets on bus or from "café snack bar" at station, confirm return times with the conductor, tel. 0763-792-237). If the bus is empty, develop a relationship with your driver. He may let you jump out in Lubriano for a great photo of distant Civita.

Orvieto Area

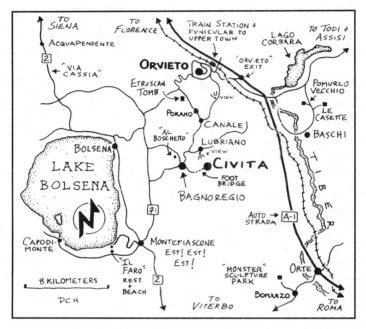

CIVITA DI BAGNOREGIO

Perched on a pinnacle in a grand canyon, the traffic-free village of Civita is Italy's ultimate hill town. Curl your toes around its Etruscan roots.

Civita is terminally ill. Only 15 residents remain, as, bit by bit, it's being purchased by rich big-city Italians who escape here. Apart from its permanent (and aging) residents and those who have weekend homes here, there is a group of Americans— introduced to the town through a small University of Washington architecture program—who have bought into the rare magic of Civita. When the program is in session, 15 students live with residents and study Italian culture and architecture.

Civita is connected to the world and the town of Bagnoregio by a long pedestrian bridge. While Bagnoregio lacks the pinnacle-town romance of Civita, it is a pure and lively bit of small-town Italy. It's actually a healthy, vibrant community (unlike Civita, the suburb it calls "the dead city"). Get a haircut, sip a coffee on the square, walk down to the old laundry (ask, *"Dov'è la lavanderia vecchia?"*). A lively market fills the parking lot each Monday.

From Bagnoregio, yellow signs direct you along its long, skinny spine to its older neighbor, Civita. Enjoy the view as you walk up the bridge to Civita. Be prepared for the little old ladies of Civita, who have become aggressive at getting lire out of visitors—tourists are their only source of support. Off-season Civita, Bagnoregio, and Al Boschetto (see "Sleeping," below) are all deadly quiet—and cold. I'd side trip in quickly from Orvieto or skip the area altogether.

Civita Orientation Walk

Civita was once connected to Bagnoregio. The saddle between the separate towns eroded away. Photographs around town show the old donkey path, the original bridge. It was bombed in World War II and replaced in 1965 with the new bridge you'll climb today. The town's hearty old folks hang on the bridge's hand railing when fierce winter weather rolls through.

Entering the town you'll pass through a cut in the rock (made by Etruscans 2,500 years ago) and under a 12th-century Romanesque arch. This was the main Etruscan road leading to the Tiber Valley and Rome.

Inside the town gate on the left notice the old laundry (in front of the WC). On the right a fancy door and windows lead to thin air. This was the **facade** of a Renaissance palace—one of five that once graced Civita. It fell into the valley riding a chunk of the ever-eroding rock pinnacle. Today the door leads to a remaining chunk of the palace—complete with Civita's first hot tub—owned by the "Marchesa," a countess who married into Italy's biggest industrialist family.

Poke through the **museum** next door and check out the viewpoint around the corner near the long-gone home of Civita's one famous son, Saint Bonaventure, known as the "second founder of the Franciscans."

Now wander to the town square in front of the church, where you'll find Civita's only public phone, bar, and restaurant—and a wild donkey race on the first Sunday of June and the second Sunday of September. The **church** marks the spot where an Etruscan temple, and then a Roman temple, once stood. The pillars that stand like giants' bar stools are ancient—Roman or Etruscan.

Go into the church and find Anna. She'll give you a tour, proudly pointing out frescoes and statues from "the school of Giotto" and "the school of Donatello," a portrait of the patron saint of your teeth (notice the scary-looking pincers), and an altar dedicated to Marlon Brando (or St. Ildebrando). Tip her and buy your postcards from her.

The basic grid street plan of the ancient town survives. Just around the corner from the church, on the main street, is Rossana and Antonio's cool and friendly **wine cellar**. Pull up a stump and let them or their children, Arianna and Antonella, serve you *panini* (sandwiches), *bruschetta* (garlic toast with optional tomato topping),

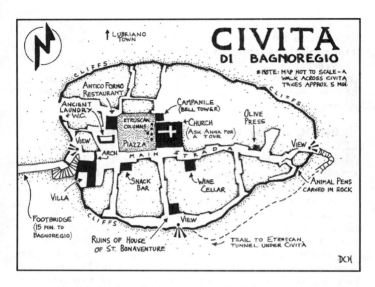

wine, and a local cake called *ciambella*. Climb down into the cellar and note the traditional wine-making gear and the provisions for rolling huge kegs up the stairs. Tap on the kegs in the cool bottom level to see which are full.

The rock below Civita is honeycombed with ancient cellars (for keeping wine at the same temperature all year) and cisterns (for collecting rainwater, since there was no well in town). Many of these date from Etruscan times.

Explore farther down the street but remember, nothing is abandoned. Everything is still privately owned. After passing an ancient Roman tombstone on your left, you'll come to **Vittoria's Antico Mulino**, an atmospheric collection of old olive presses (donation requested, give about L1,500). Her sons Sandro and Felice, running the local equivalent of a lemonade stand, toast delicious *bruschetta* on weekends and holidays. Choose your topping (chopped tomato is super) and get a glass of wine for a fun, affordable snack.

Farther down the way, Maria (for a donation of about L1,500) will show you through her garden with a grand view (Maria's Giardino) and share historical misinformation (she says Civita and Lubriano were once connected).

At the end of town the main drag peters out, and a trail leads you down and around to the right to a **tunnel** that has cut through the hill under the town since Etruscan times. It was widened in the 1930s so farmers could get between their scattered fields easier.

Evenings on the town square are a bite of Italy. The same people sit on the same church steps under the same moon, night after night, year after year. I love my cool late evenings in Civita. If you visit in the cool of the morning, have cappuccino and rolls at the small café on the town square.

Whenever you visit, stop halfway up the donkey path and listen to the sounds of rural Italy. Reach out and touch one of the monopoly houses. If you know how to turn the volume up on the crickets, do so.

Sleeping in Civita and Bagnoregio
(L2,000 = about $1, country code: 39, zip code: 01022)
When you leave the tourist crush, life as a traveler in Italy becomes easy, and prices tumble. Finding a room is easy in small-town Italy.

Franco, who runs Civita's only restaurant, **Antico Forno**, rents three remodeled rooms on Civita's main square. Call a minimum of one day in advance. Franco will meet you at the base of the bridge to beam up your luggage (Db-L120,000, D-L100,000, the more expensive rooms overlook the square, L20,000 more for optional half pension, CC:VM, Piazza Del Duomo Vecchio, 01022 Civita di Bagnoregio, tel. 0761-760-016, cellular 034-7611-5426, e-mail: fsala@pelagus.it, Franco Sala SE).

For information about a fully furnished and equipped two-bedroom **Civita apartment** with a terrace and cliffside garden that's rentable May through October ($700/week, $2,200/month, one-week minimum Sat to Sat), call Carol Watts in Kansas (tel. 785/539-0815, evenings).

Hotel Fidanza, in Bagnoregio near the bus stop, is tired but decent and the only hotel in town. Of its 25 rooms, #206 and #207 have views of Civita (Sb-L90,000, Db-L120,000, breakfast-L10,000, attached restaurant, Via Fidanza 25, Bagnoregio/Viterbo, tel. & fax 0761-793-444).

Just outside Bagnoregio is **Al Boschetto.** The Catarcia family speaks no English. Have an English-speaking Italian call for you (Sb-L65,000, D-L85,000, Db-L95,000, breakfast-L6,000, CC:V, Strada Monterado, Bagnoregio/Viterbo, tel. 0761-792-369, walking and driving instructions below). Most rooms, while very basic, have private showers (no curtains, slippery floors—be careful not to flood the place; sing in search of your shower's resonant frequency). The Catarcia family (Angelino, his wife Perina, sons Gianfranco and Domenico, daughter-in-law Giuseppina, and the grandchildren) offer a candid look at rural Italian life. Meals are sometimes hearty, and the men are often tipsy (can pose a problem for women). If the men invite you down deep into the gooey, fragrant bowels of the cantina, be warned: The theme song is *"Trinka Trinka Trinka,"* and there are no rules unless the female participants set them. The Orvieto bus drops you at the town gate. (Remember, no bus service at all on Sunday.) Al Boschetto is a 15-minute walk out of town past the old arch (follow "Viterbo" signs); turn left at the pyramid monument and right at the first fork (follow "Montefiascone" sign). Civita is a pleasant 45-minute walk (back through Bagnoregio) from Al Boschetto.

Casa San Martino, in the village of Lisciano Niccone (near Cortona and Perugia), is a 250-year-old farmhouse run as a B&B by American Italophile Lois Martin. Using this comfortable hill-top countryside as a home base, those with a car can tour Assisi, Orvieto, and Civita. While Lois reserves the summer for one-week stays, she'll take guests staying a minimum of three nights for the rest of the year (Db-$140, 10 percent discount with this book, includes breakfast, views, pool, washer/dryer, house rental available, Casa San Martino 19, Lisciano Niccone, tel. 075-844-288, fax 075-844-422). When she's booked, she refers people to her neighbors Ernestina and Gisbert Schwanke, who rent a charming two-bedroom apartment for less than Lois' (minimum 4-night stay, San Martino 36, tel. & fax 075-844-309, SE).

For drivers only: Outside the village of Baschi is the out-standing **Agriturismo Le Cassette**, with rooms in several restored stone farmhouses clustered around a grassy lawn and a swimming pool with a fabulous view of the green Umbrian land-scape (Db-L180,000, includes breakfast and home-cooked dinner, minimum 1-week stays preferred July–Aug, tel. 0744-957-645, fax 0744-950-500, www.argoweb.it/agriturismo_pomurlovecchio, e-mail: pomurlovecchio@tiscalinet.it, run by charming Minghelli family, Daniela speaks "a leetle" English). The same family also owns **Pomurlo Vecchio**, a 12th-century tower house with three rooms a few kilometers away (same prices and phone numbers).

Eating in and near Civita

In Civita, try **Trattoria Antico Forno**, which serves up pasta at affordable prices (daily for lunch at 12:30 and dinner at 19:30, on the main square, also rents rooms, tel. 0761-760-016).

Hostaria del Ponte offers light, creative cuisine at the car park at the base of the bridge to Civita (Tue–Sat 12:30–16:00, 19:30–24:00, Sun 12:30–16:00, closed Mon, great view terrace, tel. 0761-793-565).

In Bagnoregio, check out **Ristorante Nello il Fumatore** (closed Fri, on Piazza Fidanza). You'll get country cooking—such as bunny—served at **Al Boschetto,** just outside Bagnoregio (see "Sleeping," above).

Transportation Connections—Bagnoregio

To Civita: It's a 30-minute walk. Taking the shuttle bus from Bagnoregio (10-min ride, first bus at 7:45, last at 17:50, 2/hrly except during 13:00–15:00 siesta) still involves a 15-minute walk up the pedestrian bridge from the bus stop.

To Orvieto: Public buses (8/day, 50 min) connect Bagnoregio to the rest of the world via Orvieto (2000 departures from Bagnoregio: 5:30, 6:35, 6:55, 9:30, 10:15, 13:00, 13:35, 14:25, 16:40, 17:20, runs daily except Sun, see "Connections—Orvieto," above). While there's no official baggage-check service in Bagnoregio, I've arranged with Laurenti Mauro, who runs the Bar Enoteca just outside the Bagnoregio old-town gate, to let you leave your bags there (open 6:00–24:00 with a short lunch break, closed Thu, from the Orvieto bus stop walk downhill and turn right on first street). Pay him L2,000 per bag or buy breakfast there.

Driving from Orvieto to Bagnoregio: Orvieto overlooks the autostrada (and has its own exit). The shortest way to Civita from the freeway exit is to turn left (below Orvieto) and follow the signs to Lubriano and Bagnoregio. The more winding and scenic route takes 20 minutes longer: From the freeway, pass under hill-capping Orvieto (on your right, signs to Lago di Bolsena, on Viale I Maggio); take the first left (direction: Bagnoregio), winding up past great Orvieto views through Canale, and through farms and fields of giant shredded wheat to Bagnoregio, where the locals (or rusty old signs) will direct you to Al Boschetto, just outside town. Either way, just before Bagnoregio, follow the signs left to Lubriano and pull into the first little square by the church on your right for a breathtaking view of Civita. Then return to the Bagnoregio road. Drive through Bagnoregio (following yellow "Civita" signs) and park at the base of the steep pedestrian bridge leading up to the traffic-free, 2,500-year-old, canyon-swamped pinnacle town of Civita di Bagnoregio.

More Hill Towns

Italy is spiked with hill towns. **Perugia**, big and reeking with history, is famous for its fragrant Perugina candy factory and its well-known university for sweet-toothed foreigners bent on learning Italian. **Cortona** is smaller and has a fine youth hostel (tel. 0575-601-765). **Todi** is nearly untouristed. **Pienza**, a Renaissance-planned town, and **Montepulciano**, with its dramatic setting, are also worth the hill town–lover's energy and time. **Sorano** and **Pitigliano** have almost no tourism. **Bevagna**, near Assisi, is as dazed as its town fool, who stands between the twin dark Romanesque churches on its main square. Paranoid **Orte** filled its tufa perch so completely that there's no room for charm, and traffic circulates on a single, skinny, one-way lane. You'll see Orte, Orvieto's poor cousin, from the freeway 30 minutes north of Rome (consider La Ciocciola B&B, Db-L170,000, Seripola, 01028 Orte, tel. & fax 0761-402-734). Wine lovers flock to **Montalcino** for its wonderful Brunello, best enjoyed in the atmospheric *enoteca* built inside the fortress. Train travelers often use the town of **Chiusi** as a home base for the hill towns. The region's trains (to Siena, Orvieto, Assisi) go through or change at this hub, and there are several reasonable hotels near the station.

THE CINQUE TERRE

The Cinque Terre (CHINK-wuh TAY-ruh), a remote chunk of the Italian Riviera, is the traffic-free, lowbrow, underappreciated alternative to the French Riviera. There's not a museum in sight. Just sun, sea, sand (well, pebbles), wine, and pure unadulterated Italy. Enjoy the villages, swimming, hiking, and evening romance of one of God's great gifts to tourism. For a home base, choose among five villages, each of which fills a ravine with a lazy hive of human activity—calloused locals, sunburned travelers, and no Vespas. While the place is now well discovered (and has its own Web site: www.cinqueterre.it), I've never seen happier, more relaxed tourists. Vernazza is my favorite home base.

The area was first described in medieval times as "the five castles." Tiny communities grew up in the protective shadows of the castles ready to run inside at the first hint of a Turkish "Saracen" pirate raid. Many locals were kidnapped and ransomed or sold into slavery somewhere far to the east. As the threat of pirates faded, the villages grew, with economies based on fish and grapes. Until the advent of tourism in this generation, the towns were very remote. Even today, traditions survive, and each of the five villages comes with a distinct dialect and proud heritage. The region has just become a UNESCO World Heritage Site and a national park, and its natural and cultural wonders will be carefully preserved.

Now that the Cinque Terre is a national park, there are plans to charge entry fees. Starting March 1, hikers and overnight visitors will pay L5,000 for a pass (at train stations, hotels, and possibly booths at trailheads; includes hiking map). When you arrive, see if your hotel offers free passes for guests (if not, buy pass at hotel or back at station). The fees will be used for trail repair. The pass

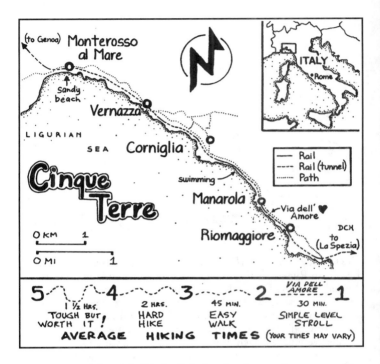

covers your entire visit. To include local train travel, get a combination pass (L10,000/1 day, L20,000/3 days, L30,000/week). Look for the latest on www.ricksteves.com/update.

Over the next decade, Italy has quiet plans for the Cinque Terre. For the sake of tranquility, a new train line will be built inland for the noisy fast trains, leaving the Cinque Terre tracks for just the pokey milk-run trains.

Sadly, a few ugly, noisy Americans are giving tourism a bad name here. Even hip young locals are put off by loud, drunk tourists. They say (and I agree) the Cinque Terre is a special place. It deserves a special dignity. Party in Viareggio but be mellow in the Cinque Terre. Talk softly. Help keep it clean. In spite of the tourist crowds, it's still a real community, and we are guests.

Planning Your Time

The ideal minimum stay is two nights and a completely uninterrupted day. The Cinque Terre is served by the milk-run train from Genoa and La Spezia. Speed demons arrive in the morning, check their bags in La Spezia, take the five-hour hike through all five towns, laze away the afternoon on the beach or rock of their choice, and zoom away on the overnight train to somewhere back in the real world. But be warned: The Cinque Terre has a strange way of messing up your momentum.

The towns are each just a few minutes apart by hourly train or boat. There's no checklist of sights or experiences; just a hike, the towns themselves, and your fondest vacation desires. Study this chapter in advance and piece together your best day, mixing hiking, swimming, trains, and a boat ride. For the best light and coolest temperatures, start your hike early.

Market days perk up the towns (8:00–13:00, Tue in Vernazza, Wed in Levanto, Thu in Monterosso, and Fri in La Spezia— near train station).

Getting around the Cinque Terre

By Train: The city of La Spezia is the gateway to the Cinque Terre. In La Spezia's train station, the milk-run Cinque Terre train schedule is posted at the information window, and the La Spezia TI hands out the schedule for free. Also ask about the nifty "Footpaths Along The Cinque Terre" brochure/map (daily in summer 9:00–13:00, 15:00–18:00; winter Mon–Sat 9:00–13:00, 14:00–17:00, Sun 9:00–13:00; look for "i" on platform, tel. 0187-718-997).

Buy your L2,300 ticket and take the half-hour train ride into the Cinque Terre town of your choice. Once in the villages, you'll get around cheapest by train but more conveniently and scenically by boat.

Cinque Terre Train Schedule: Since the train is the Cinque Terre lifeline, many shops and restaurants post the current schedule (train info tel. 0187-817-458). Pick up a photocopied schedule—it'll come in handy.

Trains leave La Spezia for the Cinque Terre villages (last year's schedule) at 7:17, 8:10, 10:00, 11:23, 12:40, 13:20, 14:16, 15:00, 16:32, 17:19, 18:16, 19:16, 21:09, and 23:05.

Trains leave Monterosso al Mare for La Spezia (departing Vernazza about 10 minutes later, last year's schedule) at 6:30, 7:06, 8:07, 9:04, 10:16, 11:00, 12:13, 13:05, 13:43, 14:08, 15:12, 16:15, 17:23, 18:24, 19:14, 20:07, and 23:31.

Do not rely on these train times. Check the current posted schedule and then count on half the trains being 15 minutes or so late (unless you're late, in which case they are right on time).

To orient yourself, remember that directions are "*per* [to] Genoa" or "*per* La Spezia," and any train that stops at any of the villages other than Monterosso will stop at all five. (Note that many trains leaving La Spezia skip them all or stop only in Monterosso.) The five towns are just minutes apart by train. Know your stop. After leaving the town before your destination, go to the door to slip out before mobs pack in. Since the stations are small and the trains are long, you might need to get off the train deep in a tunnel, and you might need to open the door yourself.

New for 2001, the train stations should be staffed at all five Cinque Terre towns. They sell train tickets, the national park entry pass (L5,000), and the combination pass, which covers the park fee and train travel on the Cinque Terre (L10,000/1 day, L20,000/3 days, and L30,000/week).

It's cheaper to buy individual tickets to travel between the towns. Since a one-town hop costs the same as a five-town hop (L1,900) and every ticket is good for six hours with stopovers, save money and explore the region in one direction on one ticket. Stamp the ticket at the station machine before you board.

The combination pass, which includes the national park entry fee, isn't a great value. Since the trains are so inexpensive, you'll save money if you pay for the national park entry (L5,000) and your train travel separately. Don't spend one of your valuable rail-pass flexi-days on the cheap Cinque Terre.

By Boat: From Easter to late October (through Nov if weather is good), a daily boat service connects Monterosso, Vernazza, Manarola, Riomaggiore, and Portovenere. This provides a scenic way to get from town to town and survey what you just hiked. It's also the only efficient way to visit the nearby resort of Portovenere (the alternative is a tedious train/bus connection via La Spezia). In good weather, the boats are more reliable than the trains. Boats go about hourly, from 10:00 until 18:00 (about L5,000 per single hop or L20,000 for an all-day pass to the Cinque Terre towns, L30,000 to add Portovenere, buy tickets at little stands at each town's harbor, tel. 0187-777-727). A more frequent boat service connects Monterosso and Vernazza (tel. 0187-817-452). Schedules are posted at docks, harbor bars, and hotels. If you're in a jam, Gianni in Monterosso runs a taxi boat service (cellular 033-9761-0022).

By Foot: A scenic trail runs along the coast, connecting each of the five Cinque Terre towns (see "Hiking," below).

VERNAZZA

With the closest thing to a natural harbor—overseen by a ruined castle and an old church—and only the occasional noisy slurping up of the train by the mountain to remind you of the modern world, Vernazza is my Cinque Terre home.

The action is at the harbor, where you'll find a kids' beach, plenty of sunning rocks, outdoor restaurants, a bar hanging on the edge of the castle (great for evening drinks), and a tailgate-party street market every Tuesday morning. In the summer, the beach becomes a soccer field where teams fielded by local bars and restaurants provide late night entertainment. In the dark, locals fish off the promonotory, using glowing bobs that shine in the waves.

The town's 500 residents, proud of their Vernazzan heritage, brag that "Vernazza is locally owned. Portofino has sold out."

Vernazza

Fearing the change it would bring, keep-Vernazza-small proponents stopped the construction of a major road into the town and
region. Families are tight and go back centuries; several generations stay together. Leisure time is devoted to the *passeggiata*—
strolling lazily together up and down the main street. Sit on a
bench and study the passersby. Then explore the characteristic
alleys called *carugi*. In October the cantinas are draped with
drying grapes. In the winter the population shrinks, as many
people move to more comfortable big-city apartments.

A steep five-minute hike in either direction from Vernazza
gives you a classic village photo op (for the best light, head
toward Corniglia in the morning, toward Monterosso in the
evening). Franco's Bar, with a panoramic terrace, is at the tower
on the trail toward Corniglia.

Vernazza has ATMs and two banks (center and top of town).
The Blue Marlin bar (run by Franco and Massimo) offers **Internet**

access and a self-service **laundry** (L9,000 wash, L9,000 dry, super-easy machines with automatic detergent and English instructions, buy tokens at adjacent bar daily except Thu, laundry open daily 8:00–22:00, Via Roma 49, 30 meters below train station).

At least at this moment, the Vernazza train station is staffed (daily 7:00–20:00), stores luggage, and can help you find a room when you arrive (tel. 0187-812-533, NSE). Accommodations are listed at the end of this chapter.

Vernazza honors its patron saint, St. Margaret, on July 20 with a religious festival.

Sights—Vernazza

▲▲**Vernazza Top-Down Orientation Walk**—Walk uphill until you hit the parking lot—with a bank, a post office, and a barrier that keeps all but service vehicles out. The tidy new square is called Fontana Vecchia, after a long-gone fountain. Older locals remember the river filled with townswomen doing their washing. Begin your saunter downhill to the harbor.

Just before the "Pension Sorriso" sign you'll see the ambulance barn (big brown wood doors) on your right. A group of volunteers is always on call for a dash to the hospital, 30 minutes away in La Spezia. Opposite that is a big empty lot next to Pension Sorriso. Like many landowners, Sr. Sorriso had plans to expand, but the government said no. The old character of these towns is carefully protected.

Across from Pension Sorriso is the honorary clubhouse for the ANPI (members of the local WWII resistance). Only five ANPI old-timers survive. Cynics consider them less than heroes. After 1943 Hitler called up Italian boys over 15. Rather than die on the front for Hitler, they escaped to the hills. Only to remain free did they become "resistance fighters."

A few steps farther you'll see a monument (marble plaque in wall to your left) to those killed in World War II. Not a family was spared. Study this: Soldiers *morti in combattimento* fought for Mussolini, some were deported to Germania, and "partisans" were killed later fighting against Mussolini.

The tiny monorail *trenino* (as you're facing plaque, look up on the wall on your right) is parked quietly here except in September and October, when it's busy helping locals bring down the grapes. The path to Corniglia leaves from here (it runs above plaque, starting at your left). Behind you is a tiny square playground, decorated with three millstones, which no longer grind local olives into oil. From here, Vernazza's tiny river goes underground.

In the tunnel under the railway tracks, you'll see a door marked "Croce Verde" (Green Cross). Posted on the other side of the tunnel is the "P.A. Croce Verde Vernazza," the list of volunteers ready for ambulance duty each day of the month.

The train tracks are above you. The second set of tracks (nearer harbor) was recently renovated to lessen the disruptive noise; locals say it made no difference.

Follow the road downhill. Until the 1950s, Vernazza's river ran open through the center of town from here to the *gelateria*.

Wandering through this main business center you'll pass many locals doing their *vasca* (laps) past the entrepreneurial Blue Marlin bar (about the only nightspot in town) and the tiny Chapel of Santa Marta (the small stone building with iron grillwork over the window, across from Bar Il Baretto), where mass is celebrated only on special Sundays. Next you'll see a grocery, *gelateria*, bakery, pharmacy, another grocery, and another *gelateria*.

On the left, in front of the second *gelateria*, an arch leads to what was a beach and where the river used to flow out of town. Continue on down to the harbor square and breakwater. Vernazza, with the only natural harbor of the Cinque Terre, was established as the only place boats could pick up the fine local wine. (It's named for a kind of wine.) Peek into the tiny street behind the Vulnetia restaurant with the commotion of arches. Vernazza's most characteristic side streets, called *carugi*, lead up from here. The trail (above the church toward Monterosso) leads to the classic view of Vernazza (best photos just before sunset).

▲▲▲**The Burned-Out Sightseer's Visual Tour of Vernazza**—Sit at the end of the harbor breakwater (perhaps with a glass of local white wine or something more interesting from Bar Capitano—borrow the glass, they don't mind), face the town, and see…

The harbor: In a moderate storm you'd be soaked, as waves routinely crash over the *molo* (breakwater, built in 1972). The train line (to your left), constructed 130 years ago to tie a newly united Italy together, linked Turin and Genoa with Rome. A second line (hidden in a tunnel at this point) was built in the 1960s. The yellow building was Vernazza's first train station. You can see the four bricked-up alcoves where people once waited for trains. Vernazza's fishing fleet is down to three small fishing boats (with the net spools); the town's restaurants buy up everything they catch. Vernazzans are more likely to own a boat than a car. In the '70s tiny Vernazza had one of the top water polo teams in Italy, and the harbor was their "pool." Later, when a real pool was required, Vernazza dropped out of the league.

The castle: On the far right, the castle, which is now a grassy park with great views, still guards the town (L2,000, daily 10:00–19:30, from harbor, take stairs by Trattoria Gianni and follow signs to Castello restaurant, tower is a few steps beyond, see the photo and painting gallery rooms). It's called *Belforte*, or "loud screams," for the warnings it made back in pirating days. The lowest deck is great for a glass of wine (follow the rope to the

Belforte Bar, open until 24:00, closed Tue; inside the submarine-strength door, a photo of a major storm shows the entire tower under a wave). The highest umbrellas mark the recommended Castello restaurant (see "Eating," below).

The town: Vernazza has two halves. *"Sciuiu,"* on the left (literally "flowery"), is the sunny side, and *"luvegu,"* on the right (literally "dank"), is the shady side. The houses below the castle were connected by an interior arcade—ideal for fleeing attacks. The pastel colors are regulated by a commissioner of good taste in the community government. The square before you is locally famous for some of the region's finest restaurants. The big red central house, the 12th-century site where Genoan warships were built, used to be a kind of guardhouse.

Above the town: The small tower above the "guardhouse," another part of the city fortifications, reminds us of Vernazza's importance in the Middle Ages, when it was an important ally of Genoa (whose arch enemies were the other maritime republics of Pisa, Amalfi, and Venice). Franco's Bar, just behind the tower, welcomes hikers finishing, starting, or simply contemplating the Corniglia–Vernazza hike with great town views. Vineyards fill the mountainside beyond the town. Notice the many terraces. Someone calculated that the vineyard terraces of the Cinque Terre have the same amount of stonework as the Great Wall of China. Wine production is down nowadays, as the younger residents choose less physical work. But locals still work their plots and proudly serve their family wine. A single steel train line winds up the gully behind the tower. This is for the vintner's *trenino*, the tiny service train.

The church, school, and city hall: Vernazza's Ligurian Gothic church, built with black stones quarried from Punta Mesco (the distant point behind you), dates from 1318. The gray-and-red house above and to the left of the spire is the local elementary school (which about 25 children attend). High school is in the "big city," La Spezia. The red building to the right of (and below) the schoolhouse is the former monastery and present city hall. Vernazza and Corniglia function as one community. Through most of the 1990s, the local government was Communist. In 1999 they elected a coalition of many parties working to rise above ideologies and simply make Vernazza a better place. Finally, on the top of the hill, with the best view of all, is the town cemetery, where most locals plan to end up.

Cinque Terre Hiking and Swimming
▲▲▲**Hiking**—All five towns are connected by good trails. Experience the area's best by hiking from one end to the other. The entire 11-kilometer hike can be done in about four hours, but allow five for dawdling. While you can detour to dramatic hilltop sanctuaries (one trail leads from Vernazza's cemetery uphill),

I'd keep it simple by following the easy red-and-white-marked low trails between the villages. A good L7,000 hiking map (sold everywhere, not necessary for this described walk) covers the expanded version of this hike, from Porto Venere through all five Cinque Terre towns to Levanto, and more serious hikes in the high country.

Since I still get the names of the Cinque Terre towns mixed up, I think of the towns by number: Riomaggiore (town #1), Manarola (#2), Corniglia (#3), Vernazza (#4), and resorty Monterosso (#5).

Riomaggiore–Manarola (20 min): Facing the front of the train station in Riomaggiore (town #1), go up the stairs to the right, following signs for the Via dell' Amore. The film-gobbling promenade—wide enough for baby strollers—leads down the coast to Manarola. While there's no beach here, stairs lead down to sunbathing rocks.

Manarola–Corniglia (45 min): The walk from the Manarola (#2) to Corniglia (#3) is a little longer and a little more rugged than that from #1 to #2.

Ask locally about the more difficult six-mile inland hike to Volastra. This tiny village, perched between Manarola and Corniglia, offers great views and the Five-Terre wine co-op; stop by the Cantina Sociale. If you take this high road between Manarola and Corniglia, allow two hours, in return, you'll get sweeping views and a closer look at the vineyards.

Corniglia–Vernazza (90 min): The hike from Corniglia (#3) to Vernazza (#4)—the wildest and greenest of the coast—is most rewarding. From the Corniglia station and beach, zigzag up to the town. Ten minutes past Corniglia toward Vernazza you'll see the well-hung Guvano beach far below (see below). The trail leads past a bar and picnic tables, through lots of fragrant and flowery vegetation, and scenically into Vernazza.

Vernazza–Monterosso (90 min): The trail from Vernazza (#4) to Monterosso (#5) is a scenic up-and-down-a-lot trek. Trails are rough (and some readers report "very dangerous") but easy to follow. Camping at the picnic tables midway is frowned upon. The views just out of Vernazza are spectacular.

▲**Swimming**—Wear your walking shoes and pack your swim gear. Each beach has showers (no shampoo, please) that may work better than your hotel's. Underwater sightseeing is full of fish; goggles are sold in local shops. Here's a beach review:

Riomaggiore: The beach is rocky but clean and peaceful and has a diving center (follow the roped path from the harbor 100 meters to the left; shower at beach).

Manarola: Manarola has no sand but the best deepwater swimming of all. The first "beach" with a shower, ladder, and wonderful rocks (with daredevil high divers) is my favorite.

The second (follow paved path around the point) has tougher access and no shower but feels more remote and pristine.

Corniglia: This hilltop town has a rocky man-made beach below its station. It's clean and uncrowded, and the beach bar has showers, drinks, and snacks.

The nude Guvano (GOO-vah-noh) beach (between Corniglia and Vernazza) made headlines in Italy in the 1970s as clothed locals in a makeshift armada of dinghies and fishing boats retook their town beach. But big-city nudists still work on all-around tans in this remote setting. From the Corniglia train station (follow the road north, go over the tracks, then zigzag below the tracks, follow signs to the tunnel in the cliff), travelers buzz the intercom, and the hydraulic *Get Smart*–type door is opened from the other end. After a 15-minute hike through a cool, moist, and dimly lit unused old train tunnel, you'll emerge at the Guvano beach—and be charged L5,000 (L4,000 with this guidebook). The beach has drinking water, but no WC. A steep (free) trail leads from the beach up to the Corniglia–Vernazza trail. The crowd is Italian counterculture: pierced nipples, tattooed punks, hippie drummers in dreads, and nude exhibitionist men. The ratio of men to women is about three to two. About half the people on the pebbly beach keep their swimsuits on.

Vernazza: The village has a sandy children's cove, sunning rocks, and showers by the breakwater. There's a ladder on the breakwater for deepwater access. The tiny *acque pendente* (waterfall) cove which locals call their *laguna blu*, between Vernazza and Monterosso, is accessible only by small hired boat.

Monterosso: The town's beaches, immediately in front of the train station, are easily the Cinque Terre's best and most crowded. It's a sandy resort with everything rentable...lounge chairs, umbrellas, paddleboats, and usually even beach access. Beaches are free only where you see no umbrellas.

Cinque Terre Towns

(Note: Readers of this book fill Vernazza. For this reason you might prefer to stay in one of these towns with fewer Americans. See "Sleeping," below, for accommodations for each town.)

▲▲**Riomaggiore (town #1)**—The most substantial nonresort town of the group, Riomaggiore is a disappointment from the train station. But walk through the tunnel next to the train tracks (or ride the elevator through the hillside to the top of town) and you land in a fascinating tangle of pastel homes leaning on each other as if someone stole their crutches. There's homemade *gelato* at the Bar Central on main street, and, if Ivo is there, you'll feel right at home. When Ivo closes, the gang goes down to the harborside with a guitar.

Riomaggiore's TI is inside the train station (Mon–Sat

Riomaggiore and Manarola

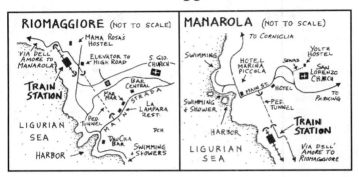

RIOMAGGIORE (NOT TO SCALE)

MAMA ROSA'S HOSTEL
VIA DELL' AMORE TO MANAROLA
ELEVATOR TO HIGH ROAD
S. GIO. CHURCH
TRAIN STATION
BAR CENTRAL
MAR MAR
STRADA
LA LAMPARA REST.
PED. TUNNEL
LIGURIAN SEA
DAUCILA BAR
PCH
SWIMMING + SHOWERS
HARBOR

MANAROLA (NOT TO SCALE)

TO CORNIGLIA
SWIMMING
YOUTH HOSTEL
HOTEL MARINA PICCOLA
SENAS
SAN LORENZO CHURCH
MAIN ST.
HOTEL
TO PARKING
SWIMMING + SHOWER
PED. TUNNEL
TRAIN STATION
HARBOR
LIGURIAN SEA
VIA DELL' AMORE TO RIOMAGGIORE

14:30–17:30, sometimes also mornings, tel. 0187-920-633). A little orange electric bus shuttles locals and tourists up and down Riomaggiore's steep main street (free with park pass, 2/hrly, just flag it down); a larger blue bus helps out in the morning.

If you arrive in Riomaggiore by train (rather than boat), here's an easy loop trip through town that maximizes views and minimizes walking uphill. From the station, take the elevator up to the top of town (free, entrance just before railway tunnel). At the top, follow the walkway—with spectacular sea views—around the cliff. Ignore the steps marked "Marina Sea Coast" (harbor). Instead, continue on the path; it's a five-minute, fairly level walk to the church. Continue past the church and then take either the stairs or the road down to Via Columbo, Riomaggiore's main street. Stroll down Via Columbo past the colorful, small shops. (The flower boxes blocking the road can be electrically pulled back on a track to let the little electric bus get past.) When Via Columbo dead-ends, on your left you'll find the stairs down to the harbor, boat dock, and a short 100-meter trail to the beach (*spiaggia*). To your right is the tunnel, running alongside the tracks, that takes you directly to the station. Either take a train or hop a boat (from the harbor) to your next destination.

For hikes from Riomaggiore, consider the cliff-hanging trail that leads from the beach to a hilltop botanical garden and old WWII bunkers. Another climbs scenically to the Madonna di Montenero sanctuary high above the town. Riomaggiore also has a diving center (scuba, snorkeling, boats, Via San Giacomo, tel. 0187-920-011).

Riomaggiore honors its patron saint, John the Baptist, on June 24 with a procession.

▲**Manarola (town #2)**—Like town #1, #2 is attached to its station by a 200-meter-long tunnel. Manarola is tiny and picturesque, a tumble of buildings bunny-hopping down its ravine

Corniglia and Monterosso

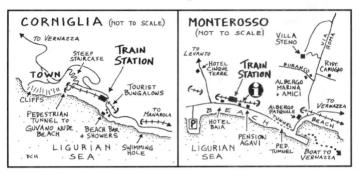

to the fun-loving harbor. Notice how the I-beam crane launches the boats. As you face the harbor, a hillside is to your right, dotted with a bar in the middle. It's Punta Bonfiglio, an entertaining park/game area/bar with the best view playground on the coast. The gate at the top of the hillside is the entrance to the cemetery. From here you can get poster-perfect views of Manarola (2-minute walk from the harbor on path to Corniglia).

Within Manarola, a little electric bus shuttles people between main street and the parking lot (free with park pass, 2/hrly, just flag it down). In the middle of town, across from the railway tunnel, you'll see Bar Aristide, which shows outdoor movies in August by hanging a screen over part of the tunnel entrance. At the top of the town you'll find great views, the church, and a cluster of accommodations, including a super hostel (see "Sleeping," below).

On August 10, Manarola holds a religious festival for its patron saint, St. Lawrence.

▲▲**Corniglia (town #3)**—From the station a footpath zigzags up 370 stairs to the only town of the five not on the water (electric bus planned for 2001, free with park pass). Originally settled by a Roman farmer who named it for his mother, Cornelia (which is how Corniglia is pronounced), its ancient residents produced a wine so famous that vases found at Pompeii touted its virtues. Today its wine is still its lifeblood. Follow the pungent smell of ripe grapes into an alley cellar and get a local to let you dip a straw into her keg. Remote and less visited, Corniglia has fewer tourists, cooler temperatures, a windy belvedere (on its promontory), a few restaurants, and plenty of private rooms for rent. Continue past the train station (toward Manarola) to find Corniglia's beach.

The festival of St. Peter and St. Paul, patron saints of Corniglia, is on June 29.

▲▲▲**Vernazza (town #4)**—See beginning of chapter.

▲▲**Monterosso al Mare (town #5)**—This is a resort with cars, hotels, rentable beach umbrellas, and crowds. The town is split into the old and new, connected by a tunnel. The train station is in the new town, along with the TI (daily Mon–Sat 9:30–12:30, 15:30–17:30, closed Mon and Nov–Easter, exit station and go left a few doors, tel. 0187-817-506), several recommended accommodations, and a statue—*Il Gigante*. This 14-meter-tall statue, which once held a shell and trident, looks as if it were hewn from the rocky cliff, but it's made of reinforced concrete, and dates from the beginning of the 20th century.

The old town contains Old World charm, small crooked streets, and nearly hourly boats to Vernazza and points beyond. From the breakwater (and the new town), you can see all the towns of the Cinque Terre (though just a "corner" of Riomaggiore).

You can easily take the short tunnel between the new and old towns, but hikers will prefer the trail. It's like a mini–Cinque Terre trail, combining scenery and greenery, a world away from the resort town below. Heading from the station to the old town, take the path to the right of the tunnel entrance. The path leads to views of a German WWII bunker below on the rocks (worth seeing, but not worth climbing down to). Continuing on the path gets you into the old town. Or, at the point where you see the bunker, take the path up to the top of the hill (where you'll see a statue of St. Francis), and up farther still through the woods to reach a gate leading to a church with a Van Dyck painting of the Crucifixion (accommodations next to church, see "Sleeping," below). Then take the trail down into the old town. (Reversing this, if you're going from the old town to the new town, take the trail to the right of the tunnel entrance). Allow a total of a half hour if you include the church and gawking at the views.

Monterosso celebrates a number of festivals: Lemon Festival (May 26), Corpus Domini (June 17, a procession passes on carpet of flowers), Festival of St. John the Baptist (June 24), Ascension of Mary (Aug 15, a holiday throughout Italy), Maria Nascente ("Rising Mary," Sept 8, fair with handicrafts), and the intriguing Walnut Festival (near end of Sept, ancient games played with walnuts).

Cinque Terre Cuisine 101

A few menu tips: *Accuighe* (pron. ah-CHOO-gay) are anchovies, a local specialty—always served the day they're caught. If you've always hated anchovies (the harsh, cured-in-salt American kind), try them fresh here. *Tegame alla Vernazza* is the most typical main course: anchovies, potatoes, tomatoes, white wine, oil, and herbs. *Pansotti* is ravioli with ricotta and spinach, often served with a hazelnut sauce…delightful. While antipasto is cheese and salami in Tuscany, here you'll get *antipasti di mare*, a big plate of mixed fruits of the sea and a fine way to start a meal. For many, splitting this and a pasta dish is plenty. Try the fun local dessert: "grandmother's cake" with a glass of *sciacchetrà* for dunking (see "Wine," below).

▲▲**Pesto**—This is the birthplace of pesto. Basil, which loves the temperate Ligurian climate, is mixed with cheese (half *Parmigiano* cow cheese and half pecorino sheep cheese), garlic, olive oil, and pine nuts and then poured over pasta. Try it on spaghetti, *trenette*, or *trofie* (made of flour with a bit of potato, designed specifically for pesto). Many also like pesto lasagna. If you become addicted, small jars of pesto are sold in the local grocery stores.

▲▲**Wine**—The *vino delle Cinque Terre*, famous throughout Italy, flows cheap and easy throughout the region. It is white—great with the local seafood. D.O.C. is the mark of top quality. For a sweet, sherrylike wine, the local *sciacchetrà* wine is worth the splurge (L5,000 per glass, often served with a cookie). While 10 kilos of grapes yield seven liters of local wine, *sciacchetrà* is made from near-raisins, and 10 kilos of grapes make only 1.5 liters of *sciacchetrà*. The word means "push and pull"...push in lots of grapes, pull out the best wine. If your room is up a lot of steps, be warned: *sciacchetrà* is 18 percent alcohol, while regular wine is only 11 percent. In the cool, calm evening, sit on the Vernazza breakwater with a glass of wine and watch the phosphorescence in the waves. While red wine is sold as Cinque Terre wine, it's a fantasy designed to please the tourists.

Sleeping and Eating on the Cinque Terre
(L2,000 = about $1, country code: 39)
Sleep Code: **S** = Single, **D** = Double/Twin, **T** = Triple, **Q** = Quad, **b** = bathroom, **t** = toilet only, **s** = shower only, **CC** = Credit Card (**V**isa, **M**asterCard, **A**mex), **SE** = Speaks English, **NSE** = No English. Breakfast is included only in real hotels.

If you're trying to avoid my readers, stay away from Vernazza. Rich, sun-worshiping softies (who prefer firm reservations for hotels with private bathrooms) like Monterosso. Wine lovers and mountain goats prefer Corniglia. Budget travelers sleep cheap in Riomaggiore. Sophisticated Italians and Germans choose Manarola.

While the Cinque Terre is too rugged for the mobs that ravage the Spanish and French coasts, it's popular with Italians, Germans, and Americans in the know. Hotels charge the most and are packed on Easter, in August, and on summer Fridays and Saturdays. August weekends are worst. But L50,000 beds in private rooms abound throughout the year. Outside of August weekends, you can land a comfortable L100,000 double in a private home on any day by just arriving in town (ideally by noon) and asking around at bars and restaurants or simply approaching locals on the street. This seems scary, but it's true.

For the best value, visit three private rooms and snare the best. Going direct cuts out a middleman and softens prices.

Plan on paying cash. Private rooms are generally bigger and more comfortable than those offered by the pensions.

If you want the security of a reservation, make it long in advance for a hotel (small places generally don't take reservations made weeks ahead). If you don't get a reply to your faxed request for a room, assume the place is fully booked.

Sleeping in Vernazza
(zip code: 19018)

Vernazza, the essence of the Cinque Terre, is my favorite. There are three pensions and piles of private rooms for rent. Anywhere you stay here will require some climbing. Night noises can be a problem if you're near the station or the church bell tower. Address letters to 19018 Vernazza, Cinque Terre, La Spezia.

Albergo Barbara, on the harbor square, is run by kindly Giuseppe and his Swiss wife, Patricia. Their nine, clean, modern rooms share three public showers and WCs (S-L70,000–90,000 depending on season, D without view-L80,000, D with small view-L85,000, D with big view-L100,000, bunky family Q-L130,000, 2-night stay preferred, loads of stairs, fans, closed Dec–Jan, Piazza Marconi 30, call to reserve instead of fax, tel. & fax 0187-812-398, cellular 032-8221-9688, SE). The big doubles on the main floor come with grand harbor views and are the best value (top-floor doubles have small windows and small views). The office is on the top floor of the big, red, vacant-looking building facing the harbor.

Trattoria Gianni rents 23 small rooms just under the castle. The funky ones are artfully decorated à la shipwreck and are up lots of tight, winding, spiral stairs, and most have tiny balconies and grand views. The new, comfy rooms lack views but have modern bathrooms and a superscenic, cliff-hanger private garden. Marisa (who doles out smiles like a rich gambler on a losing streak) requires a two-night minimum and check-in before 16:00 (S-L65,000, D-L90,000, sinks and bathrooms down the hall; Db-L120,000, Tb-L150,000, CC:VMA but 10 percent discount for cash, Piazza Marconi 5, closed Jan–Feb, tel. & fax 0187-812-228, tel. 0187-821-003). Pick up your keys at Trattoria Gianni's restaurant/reception on the harbor square and hike up the stairs to #41 (funky, *con vista mare*) or #47 (new, *nuovo*) at the top. As a matter of principle, no English is spoken here. (Note: My tour company books this place 50 nights of the season.) Telephone three days in advance and leave your first name and time of arrival.

Pension Sorriso knows it's the only real pension in town. Don't expect an exuberant welcome. Prices include breakfast and an obligatory dinner (D-L180,000, Db-L200,000, cash only, 50 meters up from station, minimal views, closed Nov–Feb, tel. 0187-812-224, fax 0187-821-198, some English spoken). While train sounds rumble through the front rooms of the main building, the annex up the street is quieter.

Affitta Camere are the best values in Vernazza. The town is honeycombed year-round with pleasant, rentable private rooms and apartments with kitchens (cheap for families). They are reluctant to reserve rooms far in advance. It's easiest to call a day or two in advance or simply show up by morning and look around. All are comfortable and inexpensive (L30,000–50,000 per person, depending on the view and plumbing). Some are lavish with killer views, and cost the same as a small dark place on a back lane over the train tracks. Little or no English is spoken at these places. Any main-street business has a line on rooms for rent.

Filippo Camere has eight sharp, new rooms run by dreadlocked Filippo and his mother, Rita (Db-L100,000, 2 rooms have views, Via A. Del Santo 62—take stairs across street from phone booths by railroad tracks, tel. 0187-812-244).

Tonino Basso rents four pleasant rooms near the post office at the top of town—with bath, without views (Db-L120,000, tel. 0187-821-264, tel. & fax 0187-821-260, cellular 0335-269-436, when you arrive, call cellular number from train station—phones at bottom of stairs—and Tonino will meet you; or the Gambero Rosso restaurant at harbor can find him—but then you'll have to backtrack to get to rooms).

Mike and Franca Castiglione, who speak New Yorkish, rent a room with a small private garden with a grand sea view (Via Carratino 16, turn left at pharmacy, climb Via Carattino to #16, tel. 0187-812-374). Farther up the same street, consider **Affitta Camere da Anna-Maria** (D-L80,000, Db-L100,000 with view or terrace, Via Carattino 64, tel. 0187-821-082).

The woman at the grocery store near the harbor can check if **Giuseppina's Villa** is available—a modern, deluxe apartment without a view (Db-L80,000, Qb-L140,000, Via S. Giovanni Battista 7, tel. 0187-812-026).

Martina Callo rents three fine rooms overlooking the square up miles of steps near the church tower (Db-L110,000, room #1-Db with harbor view, room #2-Qb is huge family room with no view, room #3-Db with great view terrace, prices drop to L90,000 Nov–March, heating in winter, ring bell at Piazza Marconi 26, tel. & fax 0187-812-365, e-mail: roomartina@supereva.it).

Franca Maria Dimartino rents two comfortable rooms overlooking the harbor square (Db-L90,000–130,000, Qb-L160,000–200,000 depending on season, only a few steps up from harbor, Piazza Marconi 30, tel. 0187-812-002).

Pizzeria Vulnetia on the harbor rents two rooms, one with a view (Db-L120,000, Qb with terrace and view-L240,000, no reservations taken, just show up at restaurant—opens for lunch at

12:30 but doors open much earlier, closed Mon, Piazza Marconi 29, tel. 0187-821-193).

Working Holiday: Consider the work camp offered by Protect the Landscape of Vernazza (run by the city of Vernazza and the Italian Environmental Impact Assessment Center in Milan). You pay about L750,000 and do three days of work (such as repairing walls and trails and picking grapes depending on the season). In return, you get room and board in Vernazza plus guided tours in English (tel. 02-7601-5672, fax 02-782-485, www.protectvernazza.org).

Eating in Vernazza

If you're into Italian cuisine, Vernazza's restaurants are worth the splurge. All take pride in their cooking and have similar prices. At about 20:00 wander around and compare the ambience.

The **Castello**, run by gracious and English-speaking Monica, her husband Massimo, kind Mario, and the rest of her family, serves great food with great views just under the castle (Thu–Tue 12:00–15:00 for lunch, 15:00–19:00 for drinks and snacks, 19:00–22:00 for dinner, closed Wed and Nov–April, tel. 0187-812-296).

Four fine places fill the harborfront with happy eaters: **Gambero Rosso**, considered Vernazza's best restaurant, feels classy and costs only a few thousand lire more than the others (Tue–Sun 12:00–15:00, 19:00–22:00, closed Mon and Nov–March, Piazza Marconi 7, tel. 0187-812-265). **Trattoria del Capitano** might serve the best food for the lire (Thu–Tue 12:00–15:00, 19:00–22:30, closed Wed except in Aug, closed Dec–Jan, Paolo speaks English). **Trattoria Gianni** is also good, especially for seafood (daily 12:30–15:00, 18:30–22:00 in July–Aug, otherwise closed Wed). **Pizzeria Vulnetia** serves the best harborside pizza (Tue–Sun 12:30–15:00, 19:00–23:00, closed Mon, Piazza Marconi 29).

Trattoria da Sandro mixes Genovese and Ligurian cuisine with friendly service but no view (Wed–Mon 12:00–15:00, 19:00–22:00, closed Tue, CC:VM, just below train station, Via Roma 60, tel. 0187-812-223). The more offbeat and intimate **Trattoria da Piva** may come with late-night guitar strumming (Tue–Sun 12:00–15:30, 19:00–01:00, closed Mon, Via Carattino 6, around corner from pharmacy).

For great food, a grand view, and perfect peace, hike to Franco's **Ristorante "La Torre"** for a dinner at sunset (Wed–Mon 20:00–21:30, closed Tue, on trail toward Corniglia, tel. 0187-821-082).

The main street is creatively finding tourist needs and filling them. The **Blue Marlin** bar offers a good selection of sandwiches, salads, and *bruschetta*. Try the bakery and bars for good focaccia and pizza by the slice. Grocery stores make inexpensive sandwiches to order (Mon–Sat 7:30–13:00, 17:00–19:30, Sun 7:30–13:00).

The town's two *gelaterias* are good. Most harborside bars will let you take your glass on a breakwater stroll.

Breakfast: Locals take breakfast about as seriously as flossing. A cappuccino and a pastry or a piece of focaccia does it. The two harborfront bars offer the most ambience; the **Ananas Bar** often decorates the foam on a cup of cappuccino with an artistic design (can either sit down at their indoor or outdoor tables, or, even cheaper, get your cappuccino to go, sit on a harborfront picnic bench, then return the cup). The **bakery** is open early and makes ham and cheese on toast. Many tourists start their day at the **Blue Marlin**. Consider their L12,000 special breakfast: ham and cheese focaccia, tiny slices of three local pastries, juice, and cappuccino (Fri–Wed 7:00–24:00, closed Thu, just below station, tel. 0187-821-149).

Sleeping and Eating in Riomaggiore
(zip code: 19017)

Riomaggiore has organized its private room scene better than its neighbors. Several agencies within a few meters of each other on the main drag (with regular office hours, English-speaking staff, and e-mail addresses) manage a corral of local rooms for rent. Expect lots of stairs.

Edi's Rooms is open daily from 8:00 to 20:00 and has a line on 10 fine rooms and 20 apartments (Db-L80,000, Qb-L160,000, CC:V, some with views—especially the apartments, Via Colombo 111, tel. & fax 0187-920-325, tel. 0187-760-842, e-mail: edi-vesigna@iol.it).

Mar Mar Rooms, run by Mario Franceschetti, has pleasant rooms and a mini-hostel (L40,000 dorm beds, Db-L90,000–100,000, bunky family deals, can request kitchen and balcony, CC:VMA, Internet access and small self-service laundry in office, 30 meters above train tracks on the main drag next to Lampara restaurant, Via Malborghetto 8, tel. & fax 0187-920-932, e-mail: marmar5t@tin.it). Mar Mar also rents kayaks (double kayaks L15,000/hr, cheaper by the half day).

Michielini Anna rents four clean, decent apartments with kitchens and no views (L50,000 per person June–Sept, otherwise L40,000 per person, CC to reserve but please pay cash, cheaper for longer stays, 2 nights preferred June–Sept, across from Bar Central at Colombo 143, tel. 0187-920-950 for friendly Daniela who speaks good English, tel. & fax 0187-920-411 for solo-Italiano-speaking mother, e-mail: anna.michielini@tin.it, another e-mail: michielinis@yahoo.it).

Luciano and Roberto Fazioli have five apartments, nine rooms, and a basic 11-bed mini-hostel (L30,000–40,000 for dorm bed, D-L70,000, Db-L120,000, apartments-L50,000–100,000 per person, prices increase with view and demand, Via Colombo 94, tel. 0187-920-904 or 0187-920-822).

At **Bar Central**, friendly Ivo and Alberto can help you find a room (Via Colombo 144, tel. 0187-920-208, e-mail: barcentr@tin.it). Ivo lived in San Francisco, fills his bar with only the best San Francisco rock, and speaks great English. His Bar Central, a good stop for breakfast, cheeseburgers, and Internet access, is a shady place to relax with other travelers. It's the only lively late-night place in town. And there's prizewinning *gelato* next door.

Hotel: If you want a real hotel, consider **Villa Argentina**. It's near the top of town, with 15 crisply clean modern rooms, fine balconies (for 9 rooms), and sea views. The little electric bus which shuttles people (and their luggage) twice hourly between the top and bottom of town makes this hotel an option even for train travelers (Db-L200,000, breakfast extra, no CC, Via de Gasperi 37, go through tunnel from station, wait for bus, tel. 0187-920-213, fax 0187-920-213, www.emmeti.it/hvillaargentina).

Hostel: **Youth Hostel Mama Rosa** is a hard-to-forget slum that gives vagabonds a reason to bond. It's run by Rosa Ricci (an aggressively friendly character who snares backpackers at the train station), her husband Carmine (a.k.a. "Papa Rosa"), and their English-speaking son, Silvio. It's a jumble of bunk beds with the ambience of a YMCA locker room (L30,000–40,000 beds in 9 coed, poorly ventilated dorms, meager washroom, no curfew, 20 meters in front of station—angle left as you exit station and then enter courtyard, no sign, Via T. Signovini 673G, just show up without a reservation—the earlier the better, no telephone). This is one of those rare places where perfect strangers become good friends with the slurp of spaghetti, and wine supersedes the concept of ownership—organize and cook a co-op dinner.

Eating: Eat well at **Ristorante La Lampara**. Check out the *frutti di mare* pizza, the *trenete al pesto*, and my favorite 5-Terre pasta experience: the aromatic *spaghetti al cartoccio*—spaghetti with mixed seafood cooked in foil (L25,000 tourist menu, Wed–Mon 12:00–15:30, 18:00–24:00, CC:VMA, closed Tue, on Via Colombo just above tracks, tel. 0187-920-120). Groceries and delis (such as Il Bomber) on Via Columbo sell food to go including pizza slices (picnic at the harbor). While the late-night action is at Ivo's Bar Central, take a walk down to the harborside **Dau Cila** bar for jazz, nets, and mellow *limoncino* (a drink of lemon juice, sugar, and pure alcohol—a.k.a. *limoncello* elsewhere in Italy).

Sleeping in Manarola
(zip code: 19010)

Manarola has plenty of private rooms. Ask in bars and restaurants. Otherwise you'll find a modern three-star place halfway up the main drag, a cluster of great values around the church at the peaceful top of town a five-minute hike above the train tracks, and a salty old place on the harbor.

Up the hill, the utterly normal **Albergo ca' d'Andrean** is quiet, comfortable, modern, and very hotelesque, with 10 big, sunny rooms and a cool garden oasis complete with lemon trees (Sb-L95,000, Db-L120,000, breakfast-L9,000, closed Nov, Via A. Discovolo 101, tel. 0187-920-040, fax 0187-920-452, Simone SE).

Affitta Camere de Baranin rents eight airy, refreshing rooms (Db-L100,000–120,000, Internet access, includes breakfast, CC to reserve but please pay cash, climb stairway against wall beyond church square—with your back to the church, stairway is at 7:00, follow sign to Trattoria dal Billy, Via Rollandi 29, tel. & fax 0187-920-595, www.baranin.com, Sara and Silvia SE).

La Torretta has two compact apartments with kitchens, four doubles, and a single, all attractively designed by the young English-speaking architect/manager Gabriele Baldini (Sb-L40,000–60,000, Db-L70,000–90,000, apartment for 2 people-L90,000–120,000, extra bed-L30,000, prices vary with season, breakfast-L10,000, views, big garden, with your back to church, it's at 10:00—look left across the square toward the sea, Piazza della Chiesa, Vico Volto 14, tel. & fax 0187-920-327, check Web for deals involving their Tuscan mountain villa, www .cinqueterre.net/torretta/, e-mail: torretta@cdh.it).

Casa Capellini rents four rooms (D-L80,000, L70,000 for 2 or more nights, Db-L90,000, L80,000 for 2 or more nights; the *alta camera* on the top, with a kitchen, private terrace, and knock-out view-L110,000, L100,000 for 2 or more nights, 2 doors down the hill from the church, with your back to the church, it's at 2:00, Via Ettore Cozzani 12, tel. 0187-920-823 or 0187-736-765, NSE).

Ostello 5-Terre, Manarola's modern and well-run hostel, stands like a Monopoly hotel behind the church square. It's smart to reserve at least two weeks in advance in high season (one week in off-season). You book with your credit card number; if you cancel with less than three days' notice, you'll be charged (June–mid-Sept: beds-L30,000, Qb-L120,000, off-season: beds-L25,000, Qb-L100,000, closed mid-Jan–mid-Feb, CC:VMA, 48 beds in 4- to 6-bed rooms, office closed 13:00–17:00, rooms closed 10:00–17:00, curfew-01:00, open to anyone of any age, laundry, Internet access, elevator, breakfast and dinner, great roof terrace with showers and sunsets, Via B. Riccobaldi 21, tel. 0187-920-215, fax 0187-920-218, www.cinqueterre.net/ostello/, e-mail: ostello@cdh.it). They rent bikes, kayaks, and snorkeling gear.

Marina Piccola has 10 bright, modern rooms on the water, so they figure a warm welcome is unnecessary (Db-L130,000 for 1-day stays, otherwise half-pension required at L120,000 per person, CC:VMA, Via Discovolo 192, tel. 0187-920-103, fax 0187-920-966, e-mail: marijes@tin.it).

Sleeping in Corniglia
(zip code: 19010)

Perched high above the sea on a hilltop, this town has plenty of private rooms (generally Db-L100,000). There is a slim chance someone will be waiting for stray travelers at the station with a car to run you up to their place in the town—otherwise, prepare for a 15-minute uphill hike. From the station, you reach the town by either a long road or many stairs. At the top of the stairs, turn left to reach the town (if you've taken the road, just stay on the road). The main drag is Via Fieschi, stretching to the tip of the promontory and its viewpoint park.

For this first listing, take the road (rather than the stairs) up from the station. **Domenico Spora** has 10 rooms scattered throughout town, all with views and private bath (Db-L100,000, Qb-L200,000, Via Villa 19, tel. 0187-812-293, NSE). Her place is about three-fourths of the way up the hill from the station.

For the following listings, take the stairs leading up from the station (turn left to reach the center). These are listed in the order you'll encounter them as you walk up Via Fieschi. At the main square, you'll see **La Lanterna** bar, which rents a dozen rooms (Db-L100,000, tel. 0187-812-291). Continue up Via Fieschi. Detour right—up the stairs—on Via Solferino to find #34 for **Pelligrini** (3 rooms, tel. 0187-812-184). Return to Via Fieschi. Next comes **Villa Sandra** (Db-L90,000, Via Fieschi 212, tel. 0187-812-384), followed by...

Louisa Christiana rents a great apartment with three doubles and a big comfy living room/kitchen with view terrace on the tiny soccer court at the top of the town (Db-L100,000, grand apartment for 2 people-L200,000, for 4 people-L220,000, for 6 people-L250,000, Via Fieschi 215, tel. 0187-812-345 or English-speaking daughter Cristiana at Bar Matteo on Via Fieschi, below main square, tel. 0187-812-236; daughter rents small apartment for L110,000). Finally, near the town promontory, you'll see the door for **Signora Silvana** (Via Fieschi 220, tel. 0187-513-830) and next door, **Maria Guelfi** (Via Fieschi 222, tel. 0187-812-178); both offer rooms at this scenic cliff-hanging edge of town.

Villa Cecio is more of a hotel (on the main road 200 meters toward Vernazza, views, tel. 0187-812-043).

Sleeping in Monterosso
(zip code: 19016)

Monterosso al Mare, the most beach-resorty of the five Cinque Terre towns, offers maximum comfort and ease. There are plenty of hotels and rentable beach umbrellas, shops, and cars. The TI (Pro Loco) can find you a L50,000-per-person double (pricier for a single) in a private home (below the station, Mon–Sat 10:00–12:00, 15:30–17:30, Sun 10:00–12:00, tel. 0187-817-506).

Monterosso is 30 minutes off the freeway (exit: Carrodano). Parking is easy in the huge beachfront guarded lot (L12,000/day). Via Roma at the top of the old town has banks, a post office, and a self-serve laundry. Another self-serve **laundry** in the old town is more central (daily 9:00–12:00, 15:00–21:00, Via Mazzini 4, off Via Roma).

The following hotel listings are in the order you'll see them as you leave the station heading right (5 hotels) or left (the rest of the hotels). My favorite is Hotel Villa Steno, listed near the end.

Turn right leaving the station to the central, waterfront **Hotel Baia** (Db-L250,000, includes breakfast, CC:VMA, elevators, balconies, request view—same price, Via Fegina 88, tel. 0187-817-363, fax 0187-817-512).

Consider the newly remodeled **Hotel Punta Mesco** (Db-L150,000, Tb-L180,000, no views, exit right from station, take first right, Via Molinelli 35, tel. 0187-817-495, www.cinqueterre .it/belvedere) or the cheaper **Affitta Camere Villa Mario** (5 rooms, Db-L120,000, exit right from station, take second right, Via Padre Semeria 28, tel. & fax 0187-818-030).

Hotel Cinque Terre, a slick new building with 54 similar rooms, is often the last to fill (Db-L240,000–260,000, includes breakfast, skip dinner deal, closed Nov–March, CC:VM, reconfirm reservations, easy parking, exit right from station, walk along waterfront, turn right at Via IV Novembre, 300 meters off beach, Via IV Novembre 21, tel. 0187-817-543, fax 0187-818-380, Giovanna and Vittorio). Next door is . . .

Villa Adriana, run by brusque Austrian nuns, has 55 decent, clean rooms divided between a 19th-century villa and an adjacent, modern annex. With a strict 23:00 curfew, a lofty setting (up off the street with a tropical garden as its front yard), and a religious, institutional atmosphere, it's peaceful (Db-L180,000–200,000, includes breakfast, extra for optional half-pension, CC:VM, double and twins available, some views, attached chapel, parking, Via IV Novembre 23, reception at back of building, tel. 0187-818-109, fax 0187-818-128, SE).

Turn left out of the station to the bright, airy **Pension Agavi** (8 rooms, Db-L140,000–160,000, refrigerators, Fegina 30, tel. 0187-817-171, fax 0187-818-264, cellular 0336-258-467, spunky Hillary SE). The tunnel then leads to the old town.

Albergo Pasquale is the first hotel you'll see as you exit the tunnel. Run by the same family who own Hotel Villa Steno (see listing below), this is a decent place with more comfort than character. It's just a few steps from the beach. The air-conditioning (used with closed windows) minimizes train noise (Db-L210,000, Tb-L250,000, Qb-L280,000, includes breakfast, CC:VMA, L20,000 discount per room per night if you pay cash and show this book, readers get a free glass of the local sweet wine—*sciacchetrà*—at check-in, Via

Fegina 4, tel. 0187-817-550 or 0187-817-477, fax 0187-817-056, e-mail: pasquale@pasini.com, Felicita and Marco SE).

The next two places push half-pension during peak season: the fancy, nicer **Albergo degli Amici** (36 rooms, Db-L160,000–170,000 with breakfast, cheaper without breakfast, Db with half-pension-L240,000—technically not required but encouraged July–Aug, CC:VMA, air-con, no views from rooms, peaceful above-it-all view garden with "sun beds"—lawn chairs with movable sun shades, Via Buranco 36, tel. 0187-817-544, fax 0187-817-424) and **Albergo Marina** (23 rooms, Db with required half-pension-L200,000–240,000, CC:VM, elevator, some air-con, garden with lemon trees, next door at Via Buranco 40, tel. & fax 0187-817-242 or 0187-817-613). To get to the Amici and Marina from the old town harbor, go to the left of the arcaded building with the bell tower; for the next listing go to the right of the arcaded building up Via Roma.

Ristorante al Carugio rents 10, no-view rooms in an apartment flat at the no-character top end of town (Db-L120,000, CC:VM, office at Via S. Pietro 15—just off Via Roma, rooms at Via Roma 100, tel. & fax 0187-817-453). **Hotel La Colonnina**, a comfy, modern place on a sleepy side street, usually takes only long-term reservations but rents fine rooms to those who call a day in advance (Db-L160,000, no breakfast, elevator, garden, Via Zuecca 6, tel. 0187-817-439). Near the harbor playground is a square with a statue of Garibaldi; Via Zuecca is directly behind him.

Farther on is the best place in town: the lovingly managed **Hotel Villa Steno**, featuring great view balconies, private gardens off some rooms, TVs, telephones, air-conditioning, and the friendly help of English-speaking Matteo. Of his 16 rooms, 12 have view balconies (Sb-L140,000, Db-L210,000, Tb-L250,000, Qb-L280,000, includes hearty buffet breakfast, CC:VMA, L20,000 discount per room per night if you pay with cash and show this book. Internet access, 10-minute hike from the station to the top of the old town at Via Roma 109, tel. 0187-817-028 or 0187-818-336, fax 0187-817-354, www.pasini.com, e-mail: steno@pasini.com). Readers get a free glass of the local sweet wine, *sciacchetrà*, when they check in—ask. The Steno has a tiny parking lot (free, but call to reserve a spot).

For the hardy: The religious **Convento dei Cappuccini** rents 14 spartan rooms, named after monks, on the hill above the tunnel that connects the old and new parts of town. Their terrace, overlooking the garden and a long stretch of coastline, has a tremendous panoramic view. But it's a steep hike (D-L140,000, all twins, attached church and cloister, either call when you arrive or reserve 2–3 days in advance, honor your reservation or fear the afterlife, tel. 0187-817-531, truly NSE). From the station, go through the tunnel, then take a hairpin left. Zigzag up the side of the hill until you reach the gate, church (Chiesa Cappuccin), and *convento* (15-minute walk from station).

Eating in Monterosso

Ristorante Belvedere is a good bet for good value in the old town (Wed–Mon 12:00–14:30, 19:00–22:00, closed Tue, CC:VM, right on the harbor, across from Albergo Pasquale). Lots of shops and bakeries sell pizza and focaccia, which make an easy picnic at the beach. **Il Frantoia** makes tasty pizza to go (Via Gioberti 1, off Via Roma in old town). For a splurge in the new town, try **Il Pirata** (closed Wed, reserve in advance—even if only a half hour in advance—because they have just a few tables, CC:VM, Via Molinelli 8, exit right from train station, take first right, tel. 0187-817-536).

Transportation Connections—Cinque Terre

The five towns of the Cinque Terre are on a milk-run train line described earlier in this chapter. Hourly trains connect each town with the others, La Spezia, and Genoa. While a few of the milk-run trains go to more distant points (Milan or Pisa), it's faster to change in La Spezia or Monterosso to a bigger train. Train info: tel. 0187-817-458 or 147-888-088.

From La Spezia by train to: Rome (10/day, 4 hrs), **Pisa** (hrly, 1 hr), **Florence** (hrly, 2.5 hrs, change at Pisa), **Milan** (hrly, 3 hrs, possible change in Genoa), **Venice** (2 direct 6-hr trains/day).

From Monterosso by train to: Venice (2/day, 6 hrs), **Milan** (3/day, 3 hrs), **Genova** (9/day, 1.25 hrs), **Turin** (5/day, 3.25 hrs), **Pisa** (3/day, 1.5 hrs), **Sestri Levante** (hrly, 15 min, most trains to Genova stop here), **La Spezia** (nearly hrly, 20 min), **Levanto** (nearly hrly, 6 min).

Parking: It's possible to snake your car down the treacherous little road into the Cinque Terre and park above the town, but you're likely to park a mile above Vernazza. Don't even try this on weekends or in August, when Italian day-trippers clog the region. Monterosso has a big, guarded beachfront parking lot that fills only on August weekends (L12,000/day). There is no adequate parking near Vernazza (park in Levanto or Monterosso and take the train to Vernazza). Riomaggiore has a huge but expensive garage and an orange shuttle bus to get you into town. Manarola also has parking and a shuttle bus to the center.

You can park your car near the train station in La Spezia. Spots on Via Paleocapa below the station are free for long stays. Confirm that parking is OK and leave nothing inside to steal. The "Autorimessa Stationi" garage immediately below the station can store your car for about L20,000 per day.

LA SPEZIA

When all else fails, you can stay in a noisy, bigger town like La Spezia. While a quick train ride into the fanciful Five-Terre, La Spezia feels like work-a-day Italy.

The TI is at the station (daily 9:00–13:00, 15:00–18:00 in

summer; Mon–Sat 9:00–13:00, 14:00–17:00, Sun 9:00–13:00 in winter, look for "i" on platform, tel. 0187-718-997).

Sights are slim. On Friday morning a huge open-air market sprawls along Via Garibaldi (about 6 blocks from station). The Museo Amedeo Lia displays Italian paintings and statues from the 13th to 18th centuries (L12,000, Tue–Sun 10:00–18:00, closed Mon, 10-minute walk from station at Via Prione 234, tel. 0187-731-100).

Sleeping in La Spezia
(L2,000 = about $1, country code: 39, zip code: 19122)
The first three hotels are within a block of the train station; the fourth is a five-minute walk from the station. The last is for drivers only. Only the first has air-conditioning.

The grand, old, but newly restored **Hotel Firenze e Continentale** has 68 rooms with all the classy comforts (Db-L200,000, maybe L180,000 in slow time, includes buffet breakfast, CC:VMA, air-con, some nonsmoking rooms, elevator, no parking, Via Paleocapa 7, tel. 0187-713-200, fax 0187-714-930, SE). **Hotel Venezia**, across the street, has a plain lobby but its 22 rooms are pleasant and modern (Db-L170,000, CC:VM, elevator, Via Paleocapa 10, tel. & fax 0187-733-465, NSE). **Albergo Parma**, tight, bright, and bleachy clean, with TVs in the rooms, is located just below the station, down the stairs (D-L80,000, Db-L95,000, CC:VM, Via Fiume 143, 19100 La Spezia, tel. 0187-743-010, fax 0187-743-240, some English spoken). **Hotel Astoria**, with 56 decent rooms, has a lobby and breakfast room as large as a school cafeteria. It's a fine backup if the hotels nearer to the station are full (Db-L170,000–190,000, includes breakfast, elevator, Via Roma 139, take street left of Albergo Parma—Via Milano, go 3 blocks and turn left on Via Roma, tel. 0187-714-655, fax 0187-714-425).

Il Gelsomino, for drivers only, is a small B&B in the hills above La Spezia (3 rooms, D-L120,000, Db-L140,000, Tb-L160,000, views, Via dei Viseggi 9, tel. & fax 0187-704-201, run by Carla massi).

AMSTERDAM

Amsterdam is a progressive way of life housed in Europe's most 17th-century city. Physically, it's a city built upon millions of pilings. But, more than that, it's a city built on good living, cozy cafés, great art, street-corner jazz, stately history, and a spirit of live and let live. It has 800,000 people and as many bikes. It also has more canals than Venice and as many tourists. While Amsterdam may box your Puritan ears, this great, historic city is an experiment in freedom.

Planning Your Time

While I'd sleep in nearby Haarlem, Amsterdam is worth a full day of sightseeing on even the busiest itinerary. While the city has a couple of must-see museums, its best sight is its own breezy ambience. The city's a joy on foot. It's a breezier and faster joy by bike. And the sights are conveniently laced together by the circular tram #20. Here are the essential stops for a day in Amsterdam:

Start the day with a circular orientation tour on tram #20 (described below). Break this morning overview with a stop at the city's two great art museums: Van Gogh and the Rijksmuseum (cafeteria for lunch). Walk to Spui from the museums via Leidsestraat (or pick up tram #20 where you got off and complete the circle back to the station).

Spend midafternoon taking a relaxing hour-long canal cruise from the dock at Spui. Near Spui consider seeing the peaceful Begijnhof, Amsterdam Historical Museum, and flower market.

Visiting the Anne Frank House after 18:00 (it's open until 21:00) will save you an hour in line.

On a balmy evening, Amsterdam has a Greek-island ambience. Wander the Jordaan for the idyllic side of town and wander down Leidsestraat to Leidseplein for the roaring café and people scene. Wander the Red-Light District while you're at it.

With extra time: With two days in Holland, I'd side trip by bike, bus, or train to an open-air folk museum and visit Edam or Haarlem. With a third day I'd do the other great Amsterdam museums. With four days I'd do the "historic triangle" or visit The Hague.

Amsterdam Overview

Orientation (area code: 020)

Amsterdam's central train station is your starting point (TI, bike rental, and trams—including #20—fanning out to all points). Damrak is the main street axis, connecting the station with Dam Square (people watching and hangout center) and its Royal Palace. From this spine the city spreads out like a fan, with 90 islands, hundreds of bridges, and a series of concentric canals (named "Prince's," "Gentleman's," and "Emperor's") laid out in the 17th century, Holland's golden age. Amsterdam's major sights are within walking distance of Dam Square.

Tourist Information

Avoid Amsterdam's inefficient VVV offices if you can ("VVV" is Dutch for tourist information office; TI in train station open Mon–Sat 8:00–19:30, Sun 9:00–17:00). Most people wait 30 minutes just to pick up information brochures and get a room. At the VVV in front of the station, avoid this line by studying the display of publications for sale and going straight to the sales desk (where everyone ends up anyway, since any information of substance will cost you). Consider buying a city map (f4), *What's On* (f4, monthly entertainment calendar), and any of the f4 walking-tour brochures ("Discovery Tour through the Center," "The Former Jewish Quarter," "Walks through Jordaan"). The Amsterdam Culture & Leisure Pass, offering free or discounted admissions to some sights and boat rides, isn't worth the clutter or cost (f40, doesn't include Anne Frank House). Nor does it make sense to stand in line at the VVV to buy prepaid same-cost admissions to various Amsterdam sights.

The TI on Leidsestraat is less crowded (daily 9:00–17:00).

But for f1 a minute, you can save yourself a trip by calling the tourist information toll line at 0900-400-4040 (Mon–Fri 9:00–17:00). If you're staying in nearby Haarlem, use the helpful Haarlem TI (see next chapter) to answer most of your Amsterdam questions and provide you with the brochures.

At Amsterdam's Central Station, GWK Change has two hotel reservations windows that sell phone cards and cheaper city maps (f3) and answer basic tourist questions. The lines are shorter. They also change money, including coins, for a hefty f5 fee (near lockers, at right end of station as you leave platform).

Don't use the TI (or GWK) to book a room; you'll pay f5 and your host loses the 13 percent deposit. The phone system is easy, everyone speaks English, and the listings in this book are a better value than the potluck booking you'd be charged for at the TI.

Helpful Hints

Theft Alert: Tourists are considered green and rich, and the city has more than its share of hungry thieves—especially on trams. Wear your moneybelt.

Street Smarts: A *plein* is a square, *gracht* means canal, and most canals are lined by streets with the same name.

Shop Hours: Many shops close all day Sunday and Monday morning.

Telephones: Calling the United States from a phone booth is now very cheap—you'll get about five minutes for a dollar. Handy telephone cards (f10, f25, or f50) are sold at TIs, the GVB public-transit office (in front of station), tobacco shops, post offices, and train stations.

Internet Access: It's easy at cafés all over town. The Internet Café is a couple blocks from the station (f2.50 per 30 min, Sun–Thu 9:00–01:00, Fri–Sat 9:00–3:00, must buy at least 1 beverage, Martelaarsgracht 11, tel. 020/627-1052). A monstrous Internet café, easyEverything, has several hundred computers and cheap access (daily 24 hrs, Reguliersbreestraat 22, next to Rembrandtplein). Coffeeshops (which sell marijuana) also offer Internet access.

Arrival in Amsterdam

By Train: Amsterdam swings, and the hinge that connects it to the world is its perfectly central Central Station. Walk out the door and you're in the heart of the city. You'll nearly trip over trams ready to take you anywhere your feet won't. Straight ahead is Damrak Street, leading to Dam Square. With your back to the entrance of the station, the TI and GVB public-transit offices and circular tram #20A are just ahead and to your left.

By Plane: From Schiphol Airport, take the train to Amsterdam (6/hrly, 20 min, f6.25). If you're staying in Haarlem, take a direct express bus to Haarlem (#236 or #362, 2/hrly, 30 min, f7).

Getting around Amsterdam

The helpful GVB transit-information office is next to the TI (the glass building with revolving sign in front of train station). Its free multilingual "Tourist Guide to Public Transport" includes a transit map, explains ticket options and tram connections to all the sights, and describes the Circle Tram #20 route, listing all the stops and nearby sights (#20A goes clockwise, #20B goes counterclockwise).

By Bus, Tram, and Metro: Individual tickets cost f3 and give you an hour on the buses, trams, and metro system (on trams and buses pay as you board; buy metro tickets from machines). **Strip cards** are cheaper than individual tickets. Any downtown ride costs two strips (good for 1 hr of transfers). A card with 15 strips costs f12.25 at the GVB public-transit office, train stations, post offices, airport, or tobacco shops throughout the country; shorter strip tickets (2, 3, and 8 strips) are also sold on some buses and trams. Strip cards are good on buses all over the Netherlands (e.g., 6 strips for Haarlem to the airport), and you can share them with your partner. An f10 **Day Card** gives you unlimited transportation on the buses and metro for a day in Amsterdam; you'll almost break even if you take three trips (valid until 6:00 the following morning; buy as you board or at the GVB public-transit office, which also sells a better-value 2-day version for f15). If you get lost in Amsterdam, 10 of the city's 17 trams take you back to the central train station.

By Foot: The longest walk a tourist would take is 45 minutes from the station to the Rijksmuseum. Watch out for silent but potentially painful bikes, trams, and crotch-high curb posts.

By Bike: One-speed bikes, with "brrringing" bells and two locks (use them both; bike thieves are bold and brazen here), rent for f10 per day at the central train station (daily 8:00–22:00, deposit of f200 or your credit-card imprint and passport required, entrance to the left down the ramp as you leave the station, tel. 020/624-8391). In the summer, arrive early or make a telephone reservation (they hold bikes until 10:30). If the station has rented all its bikes, walk 10 minutes to Rent-a-Bike Damstraat on Dam Square (f15/day, daily 9:00–18:00, deposit of f50 or credit-card imprint and I.D., Damstraat 20, tel. 020/625-5029).

By Boat: While the city is great on foot or bike, there is a "Museum Boat" and a similar "Canal Bus" with an all-day ticket that shuttles tourists from sight to sight. Tickets cost f29 (with discounts to sights worth about f5). The sales booths in front of the central train station (and the boats) offer handy free brochures with museum times and admission prices. The narrated ride takes 90 minutes if you don't get off (every 30 min in summer, every 45 min off-season, 7 stops, live quadrilingual guide, departures 10:00–17:00, discounted after 13:00 to f24, tel. 020/622-2181). If you're looking for a floating (nonstop) tour, the real canal tour boats (without the stops) give more information, cover more ground, and cost less (see "Tours of Amsterdam," below).

By Taxi: Amsterdam's taxis are expensive (f6 drop and f3 for each kilometer). Given the fine tram system, taxis are only a good value for airport connections (Schiphol Airport to Amsterdam costs f60).

By Car: Forget it—frustrating one-ways, terrible parking.

Circle Tram #20 Orientation Tour

For a ▲▲ self-guided tour, orient yourself for f3 in less than an hour by riding this designed-for-tourists circle route from the station. Catch #20A (not #20B) from tram lane (or *spoor*) #2 on the left as you leave the station. The free tourist guidebooklet—there's a stack on the desk in the transit office 50 meters away—comes with a route map and lists each stop. You could buy the f6 one-day tram #20 pass. Tram #20 runs every 10 minutes from 9:00 to 18:00 only.

0. Train Station: Leaving the station you pass both the canal bus and museum boat docks (left). The "Rondvaart" sign (right) means round-trip. Boats like these all over town offer similar one-hour city tours. Gliding up the tacky commercial cancan called the Damrak (which was once the Amstel River), you're following the same route taken by boats loaded with spices and goodies from the East Indies in the city's early trading days. The buildings across the water are Amsterdam's oldest. Behind them is the Red-Light District and the old sailor's quarter. The huge redbrick Beurs building (left) is the Dutch stock exchange.

1. The Dam Square: This is the city center, where the original dam was built across the Amstel River, giving the town its name. To your right is the Royal Palace (1655); next to it is the New Church, the coronation church of Dutch royalty. To your left is the World War I Memorial (1956), now becoming a generic peace memorial; behind that is a strip of head shops. Straight ahead is one of many "diamond polishing centers." Beyond the Dam Square you continue down Rokin. Parallel and a block to the right is the bustling Kalverstraat pedestrian shopping mall.

2. Spui Square: This marked the end of the city in the 14th century. It's near the Begijnhof and the University of Amsterdam's archaeology museum, which has a fine Egyptian collection.

3. Muntplein: This lively area is marked by the Mint Tower from 1620 (on the right). Behind that a charming flower market lines the Singel Canal (see the row of greenhouses, thriving Mon–Sat 9:00–17:00). Turning left you enter a noisy neon nightlife center.

4. Rembrandtplein: Look for Rembrandt's statue in the leafy park (right). This is the center of gay Amsterdam. You'll pass lots of discos and a Planet Hollywood, and a bridge will take you over the Amstel River. The modern brown-and-white building (left) is

Amsterdam

the city hall. Adjacent is the round Opera House. Notice the charming counterbalance bridges (right).

5. Waterlooplein: This is famous for its flea market (daily except Sun, on left). The Jewish Quarter (right) features the impressive new Jewish History Museum (renovated brick synagogues with blue-and-white banner). Crossing the bridge (funny paintings revealed when opened) you enter green Amsterdam (gardens and hothouses of University of Amsterdam all around, zoo nearby).

6. Plantage Kerklaan: Immediately to the right of this tram stop, the white facade of the old Dutch Theater (*Hollandsche Schouwburg*) survives. Used by Nazis as a holding zone for Jews being deported, today it's a memorial. The Dutch Resistance

Museum and the zoo are half a block to the left. Passing through many University of Amsterdam buildings, notice the "XXX" symbol of the city (the three Xs stand for the adversities the Amsterdammers have overcome throughout their history: fire, plague, and floods). Crossing the Amstel River again, see the city hall and the opera house again in the distance (right), the palatial Amstel Hotel (behind on the left), and, in the distance, Holland's tallest skyscraper—the Phillips corporate headquarters.

7. Frederiksplein: Notice the houseboats; they're a common sight in Amsterdam. Also in Frederiksplein, you'll see the huge Albert Cuyp Market, perhaps the town's most interesting market, showing off the ethnic mix daily except Sunday. Now, passing through a nondescript area, notice how the city works: Shops at street level—with homes above—keep neighborhoods vital, people-friendly, and safe. Bike lanes even have their own little traffic lights. New buildings still lean out and come with planks and pulleys for hoisting furniture past too-narrow stairways. Many of these are brick and built in the Art Deco "Amsterdam School" from the 1920s—a time when architects considered entire blocks as integrated works of art. Notice street signs with the district listed. You're in the *oud-zuid* (old south) quarter. Mail slots have green and orange decals saying yes or no to junk mail. And now public phone booths stand next to curbside computers for Internet access (locals use prepaid "chip cards"—the first step toward the cash-free society of the future—to access things such as these).

8. Museumplein: A huge park (right) leads to the grand red-brick Rijksmuseum (built in 1885 by the same guy who designed Central Station). The new addition to the Van Gogh Museum (opened 1999) juts into the park in the foreground. The Concertgebouw (on the left) is Amsterdam's main concert hall. A huge underground parking lot keeps things uncluttered.

9. Van Baerlestraat: Rounding the corner, you stop at the Stedelijk Modern Art Museum (right) and the Van Gogh Museum (see crowd on right). An ice rink (right) faces the Coster Diamond House (left).

10. Hobbenmastraat: This is the stop for the Rijksmuseum (right). A fancy gate marks the entrance to the sprawling, in-love-with-life Vondelpark (left). Pass a casino (right) as you cross a canal and enter the noisy, people-filled Leidseplein area.

11. Leidseplein: Your tram just skirts Amsterdam's liveliest café, people-watching, and entertainment district. Be sure to loiter in Leidseplein later on. The huge modern parking lot (Texaco station, left) marks the line between the protected old town (right) and the anything-goes new one (left). Turning right you cut through the proud, fashionable, and trendy Jordaan district. Ahead stands the much-loved tallest church spire in town, marking the Westerkerk (West Church). Anne Frank hid out just down the street. As you continue ahead, the canal system is evident as you cross the Prince's, Keizers (kings), Herren (medieval business fat cats), and Singel Canals and head toward the back side of the Royal Palace we saw at the Dam Square. Hop out here or glide back to your starting point at the Central Station.

Sights—Amsterdam's Museum Neighborhood

▲▲▲**Rijksmuseum**—Built to house the nation's greatest art, the Rijksmuseum packs several thousand paintings into 200 rooms. To survive, focus on the Dutch masters: Rembrandt, Hals, Vermeer, and Steen. For a list of the top 20 paintings, pick up the cheap f1 leaflet "A Tour of the Golden Age" and plan your attack (or follow the self-guided tour, one of 20, in my *Mona Winks* guidebook, written with Gene Openshaw). Audioguide tours are available, allowing you to dial up descriptions of over 200 paintings (f7.50).

Follow the museum's chronological layout to see painting evolve from narrative religious art, to religious art starring the Dutch love of good living and eating, to the golden age when secular art dominated. With no local church or royalty to commission big canvases in the post-1648 Protestant Dutch republic, artists had to find different patrons. They specialized in portraits of the wealthy city class (Hals), pretty still lifes (Claesz), and nonpreachy slice-of-life art (Steen). The museum has four quietly wonderful Vermeers. And, of course, a thoughtful brown soup of Rembrandt, including *Night Watch*. Works by Rembrandt show his excellence as a portraitist for hire (*De Staalmeesters*) and offer some powerful psychological studies, such as *St. Peter's Denial*—with a betrayed Jesus in the murky background (f15, daily 10:00–17:00, great bookshop, decent cafeteria, tram #2, #5, or #20 from station, Stadhouderskade 42, tel. 020/674-7000).

▲▲▲**Van Gogh Museum**—Near the Rijksmuseum, this outstanding and user-friendly museum was opened in 1973 to house the 200 paintings owned by Vincent's younger brother Theo. Newly renovated in 1999, it's a stroll through a beautifully displayed garden of van Gogh's work and life (f15, daily 10:00–18:00, Paulus Potterstraat 7, tel. 020/570-5200). The museum also focuses on the late-19th-century art that influenced van Gogh (it happened to be in his brother Theo's collection). The new exhibition hall (included with admission) features art from 1840 to 1920. The f8.50 audioguide includes insightful commentaries about van Gogh's paintings along with related quotations from Vincent himself.

Stedelijk Modern Art Museum—Next to the Van Gogh Museum, this place is fun, far-out, and refreshing. It has mostly post-1945 art but also a sometimes-outstanding collection of Monet, van Gogh, Cézanne, Picasso, and Chagall, and a lot of special exhibitions (f10, daily 11:00–17:00, tel. 020/573-2737).

Sights—Near Dam Square

▲▲**Anne Frank House**—A virtual pilgrimage for many, this house offers a fascinating look at the hideaway of young Anne when the Nazis occupied the Netherlands. Pick up the English pamphlet at the door. Recently expanded, the exhibit now offers more thorough coverage of the Frank family, the diary, the stories of others who hid out, and the Holocaust. Why do thousands endure hour-long daytime lines when they can walk right in by arriving after 18:00? Last entrance is 20:30. Visit after dinner (f12.50, April–Aug daily 9:00–21:00, closes daily at 19:00 Sept–March, 263 Prinsengracht, tel. 020/556-7100). For an interesting glimpse of Holland under the Nazis, rent the powerful movie *Soldier of Orange* before you leave home.

Westerkerk—Near the Anne Frank House, this landmark church has a barren interior, Rembrandt somewhere under the pews, and Amsterdam's tallest steeple. It's worth climbing for the view (f3, ascend only with a guide, departures on the hour, April–Sept Mon–Sat 10:00–17:00, closed Sun, tel. 020/612-6856).

Royal Palace (Koninklijk Paleis)—The palace, right on Dam Square, was built as a lavish city hall for Amsterdam, part of the proud new Dutch Republic. Amsterdam was awash in profit from trade. When this building was constructed (around 1660), it was one of Europe's finest. Today it's the official (but not actual) residence of the queen. Its sumptuous interior is worth a look (f5, June–Aug daily 12:30–17:00, less off-season).

▲**Begijnhof**—Step into this tiny, idyllic courtyard in the city center to escape into the charm of old Amsterdam. Notice house #34, a 500-year-old wooden structure (rare since repeated fires taught city fathers a trick called brick). Peek into the hidden Catholic church, opposite the English Reformed church, where the pilgrims worshiped while waiting for their voyage to the New World (marked by a plaque near the door). Be considerate of the people who live here (free, on Begijnensteeg Lane, just off Kalverstraat between #130 and #132, pick up flyer at office near entrance).

Amsterdam Historical Museum—Offering the town's best look into the age of the Dutch masters, this creative and hardworking museum features Rembrandt's paintings, fine English descriptions, and a carillon loft. The loft comes with push-button recordings of the town bell tower's greatest hits and a self-serve carillon "keyboard" to ring a few bells yourself (f12, Mon–Fri 10:00–17:00, Sat–Sun 11:00–17:00, good-value restaurant, next to Begijnhof, Kalverstraat 92, tel. 020/523-1822). Its free pedestrian corridor is a powerful teaser.

Sights—East Amsterdam

To reach these sights from the train station, take tram #9, #14, or #20. The first six sights listed make an interesting walk.

Rembrandt's House—Rembrandt's reconstructed house is filled with exactly what his bankruptcy inventory of 1656 said he owned. You'll find no paintings but 65 of his etchings (f12.50, Mon–Sat 10:00–17:00, Sun 13:00–17:00, 10-min English video upon request, Jodenbreestraat 4, tel. 020/520-0400).

Holland Experience—Bragging "Experience Holland in 30 minutes," this show takes you traveling with three clowns through an idealized montage of Dutch clichés. There are no words but lots of images and special effects as you rock with the boat and get spritzed with perfume while viewing the tulips (f17.50, 2 enter for price of 1 with this book, or show this book and get f2.50 off the f25 combo Rembrandt's House/Experience ticket, daily 10:00–18:00, Jodenbreestraat 8, near Rembrandt's House and Waterlooplein street market, metro: Waterlooplein, tel. 020/422-2233. www.holland-experience.nl). The men's urinal is a trip to the beach. Plan for it.

Waterlooplein Flea Market—For over a hundred years, the flea market of the Jewish Quarter has raged daily except Sunday behind the Rembrandt House.

Jewish History Museum—Four historic synagogues have been joined by steel and glass to make one modern complex telling the story of the Jews in Amsterdam through the centuries (f10, daily 11:00–17:00, good kosher café, Jonas Daniel Meijerplein 2, tel. 020/626-9945).

Dutch Theatre (Hollandsche Schouwburg)—This is a moving memorial. Once a great theater in the Jewish neighborhood, this was used as an assembly hall for local Jews destined for Nazi concentration camps. On the wall, 6,700 family names pay tribute to the 104,000 Jews deported and killed by the Nazis. There's little to actually see but plenty to think about (free, daily 11:00–16:00, Plantage Middenlaan 24, tel. 020/626-9945).

▲▲Dutch Resistance Museum (Verzetsmeuseum)—This is a new and impressive look at how the Dutch resisted their Nazi occupiers from 1940 to 1945. You'll see propaganda movie clips, study forged ID cards under a magnifying glass, and read of ingenious, clever, and courageous efforts to hide local Jews from the Germans (f8, Tue–Sun 12:00–17:00, closed Mon, well described in English, tram #9 or #20A from station, Plantage Kerklaan 61, tel. 020/620-2535). Amsterdam's famous zoo is just across the street.

▲Tropenmuseum (Tropical Museum)—As close to the Third World as you'll get without lots of vaccinations, this imaginative museum offers wonderful re-creations of tropical-life scenes and explanations of Third World problems (f12.50, Mon–Fri 10:00–17:00, Sat–Sun 12:00–17:00, tram #9 to Linnaeusstraat 2, tel. 020/568-8215).

Netherlands Maritime (Scheepvaart) Museum—This huge collection of model ships, maps, and sea-battle paintings fills the

Central Amsterdam

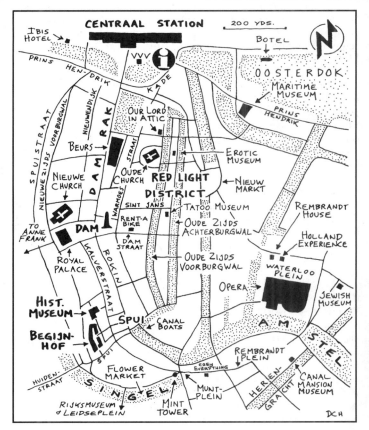

300-year-old Dutch Navy Arsenal. Given the Dutch seafaring heritage, I expected a killer museum but found it lifeless and boring. Sailors may disagree, but—even with its re-creation of an 18th-century Dutch East India Company ship manned with characters in old costumes—the museum disappoints (f14.50, daily 10:00–17:00, closed Mon off-season, English explanations, don't waste your time with 30-min movie, bus #22 or #32 to Kattenburgerplein 1, tel. 020/523-2222).

Sights—Red-Light District

Our Lord in the Attic (Amstelkring)—Near the station, in the Red-Light District, you'll find a fascinating hidden church filling the attic of a hollowed-out row of 17th-century merchants' houses.

This dates from 1661, when post-Reformation Dutch Catholics couldn't worship in public (f10, Mon–Sat 10:00–17:00, Sun 13:00–17:00, Oudezijds Voorburgwal 40, tel. 020/624-6604).
▲**Red-Light District**—Europe's most touristed ladies of the night shiver and shimmy in display-case windows between the Oudezijds Achterburgwal and Oudezijds Voorburgwal, surrounding the Oude Kerk (Old Church). Druggies make the streets uncomfortable late at night, but it's a fascinating walk at any other time after noon (S&F, f75–100).

Amsterdam has two sex museums, one in the Red-Light District and one a block in front of the train station on Damrak. While visiting one can be called sightseeing, visiting both is hard to explain. Here's a comparison:

The Red-Light District sex museum is less offensive, with five sparsely decorated rooms relying heavily on badly dressed dummies acting out the roles that women of the neighborhood play. It also has videos, phone-sex phones, and a lot of uninspired paintings, old photos, and sculpture (f5, daily 11:00–24:00, along the canal at Oudezijds Achterburgwal 54).

The Damrak sex museum goes deeper and has more rooms. It tells the story of pornography from Roman times through 1960. Every sexual deviation is uncovered in its various displays, and the nude and pornographic art is a cut above the other sex museum's. Also interesting are the early French pornographic photos and memorabilia from Europe, India, and Asia. You'll find a Marilyn Monroe tribute and some S&M displays, too (f5, daily 10:00–23:30, Damrak 18, a block in front of station).

More Sights—Amsterdam
▲**Herengracht Canal Mansion (Willet Holthuysen Museum)**—This 1687 patrician house offers a fine look at the old rich of Amsterdam, with a good 20-minute English introductory film and a 17th-century garden in back (f8, Mon–Fri 10:00–17:00, Sat–Sun 11:00–17:00, tram #1, #2, #4, #5, or #9 to Herengracht 605, tel. 020/523-1870).
Vondelpark—This huge and lively city park is popular with the Dutch—families with little kids, romantic couples, hippies sharing blankets and beers, and oldsters strolling. It's the scene of free concerts in the summer (tel. 020/523-7790).
Amsterdam Film Museum—This museum, next to Vondelpark, has a massive archive and a theater that shows a variety of films, from small foreign productions to 70-mm classics (f12.50, at least 3 showings/night, often English subtitles, Vondelstraat 69, tel. 020/523-7790, www.filmmuseum.nl).
Leidseplein—Brimming with cafés, this people- and pigeon-watching square is an impromptu stage for street artists, accordionists, jugglers, and unicyclists. Sunny afternoons are liveliest.

Stroll nearby Lange Leidsedwarsstraat (1 block north) for a taste-bud tour of ethnic eateries from Greece to Indonesia.

Shopping—Amsterdam brings out the browser even in those who were not born to shop. Ten general markets, open six days a week, keep folks who brake for garage sales pulling U-ies. Shopping highlights include Waterlooplein (the flea market); the huge Albert Cuyp street market; various flower markets (such as the Singel Canal market near mint tower/*Munttoren*, daily except Sun); diamond dealers (free cutting and polishing demos at shops behind the Rijksmuseum and on Dam Square); and Kalverstraat, Amsterdam's teeming pedestrian/shopping street (parallel to Damrak).

Tours of Amsterdam

▲▲**Canal-Boat Tour**—These long, low, tourist-laden boats leave continually from several docks around the town for a relaxing, if uninspiring, one-hour quadrilingual introduction to the city (f14, 2/hrly, more frequent in summer). One very central company is at the corner of Spui and Rokin, about five minutes from Dam Square (daily 10:00–22:00, tel. 020/623-3810). No fishing allowed—but bring your camera. Some prefer to cruise at night, when the bridges are illuminated.

Biking Tours—The Yellow Bike Tour company offers a city tour (f34, 3 hrs) and a tour of the countryside (f42.50, 6 hrs, 35 km; daily April–Nov, Nieuwezijds Kolk 29, 3 blocks from train station, tel. 020/620-6940).

Do-It-Yourself Bike Tour of Amsterdam—A day enjoying the bridges, bike lanes, and sleepy off-the-beaten-path canals on your own one-speed is the essential Amsterdam experience. The real joys of Europe's best-preserved 17th-century city are the countless intimate glimpses it offers: the laid-back locals sunning on their porches under elegant gables, rusted bikes that look as if they've been lashed to the same lamppost since the '60s, wasted hedonists planted on canalside benches, happy sailors permanently moored but still manning the deck.

For a good day, rent a bike at the station. Head west down Haarlemmerstraat, working your wide-eyed way down the Prinsengracht (along the canal) and detouring through the gentrified small streets of the Jordaan area before popping out at Westerkerk under the tallest spire in the city.

Pedal past the palace, through Dam Square, and down Kalverstraat (the city's bustling pedestrian mall), and poke into the sleepy Begijnhof. Catch the hour-long cruise at Spui. Continue down Rokin to the Mint Tower, biking along the Singel Canal flower market to Leidsestraat. Dodge trams and people down Leidsestraat. Enjoy the lush and peaceful Vondelpark. Then pedal back to the Dam Square. To detour through seedy, sexy, pot-smoking Amsterdam, roll down Damstraat and then turn left down Oudezijds Voorburgwal through the land of Rastafarian "coffee shops," Red-Lights over black tights, and sailors lost without the sea. You'll pop out near the station.

To finish your day, escape into the countryside by hopping on the free ferry behind the Amsterdam station. In five minutes Amsterdam will be gone, and you'll be rolling through your very own Dutch painting. (See "Getting around Amsterdam," above, for info on bike rental).

Brewery Tour—The infamous Heineken brewery tours are in full slosh Monday through Friday at 9:30, 11:00, 13:00, and 14:30 (f2, 2 hrs, tours also Sat in summer; must be over age 18, tram #16, #24, or #25, Stadhouderskade 78, near Rijksmuseum, tel. 020/523-9666). Try to arrive a little early.

Wetlands Safari, Nature Canoe Tours Near Amsterdam— If you'd like to "turn your back on Amsterdam" and get a dose of the *polder* country and village life along with some exercise, consider this tour. Majel Tromp, a village girl who speaks great English, takes groups of no more than 15. The program: Meet at the VVV tourist office outside the station, catch a bus, stop for coffee, take a canoe trip with several stops, munch a village picnic lunch (included), canoe, and bus back into the big city by 14:30 (f58, May–mid-Sept Mon–Fri, call to reserve, tel. 020/686-3445 or 06/53-552-669, www.wetlandssafari.nl).

Sleeping in Amsterdam
(f1 = about 40 cents, country code: 31, area code: 020)
Sleep Code: **S** = Single, **D** = Double/Twin, **T** = Triple, **Q** = Quad, **b** = bathroom, **t** = toilet only, **s** = shower only, **CC** = Credit Card (Visa, MasterCard, Amex). Nearly everyone speaks English in the Netherlands, and prices include breakfast unless noted.

While I prefer sleeping in cozy Haarlem (see next chapter), those into more urban charms will find that Amsterdam has plenty of beds. Summer weekends are booked well in advance.

Sleeping near the Station
Amstel Botel, the city's only remaining "boat hotel," is a shipshape, bright, and clean floating hotel with 175 rooms (Sb-f141, Db-f159, Tb-f180, worth the extra f10 for canalside view, breakfast-f14, f40/ day parking pass, CC:VMA, elevator, 400 meters from train station, on your left as you leave station, you'll see the sign, Oosterdokskade 2-4, 1011 AE Amsterdam, tel. 020/626-4247, fax 020/639-1952).

Ibis Amsterdam Hotel is a modern and efficient 180-room place towering over the station. It offers a central location, comfort, and good value without a hint of charm (Db-f298, family-f368, skip breakfast and save f24 per person, CC:VMA, book long in advance, air-con, smoke-free floors, Stationsplein 49, tel. 020/638-3080, fax 020/620-0156, www.ibishotel.com).

Amsterdam Hotels

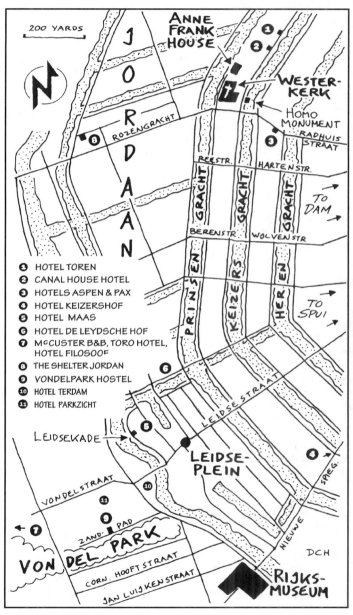

200 YARDS

N

JORDAAN

ANNE FRANK HOUSE

WESTER-KERK

HOMO MONUMENT

RADHUIS STRAAT

ROZENGRACHT

REESTR.

HARTEN STR.

BERENSTR.

WOLVEN STR

TO DAM

TO SPUI

PRINSEN GRACHT

KEIZERS GRACHT

HEREN GRACHT

❶ HOTEL TOREN
❷ CANAL HOUSE HOTEL
❸ HOTELS ASPEN & PAX
❹ HOTEL KEIZERSHOF
❺ HOTEL MAAS
❻ HOTEL DE LEYDSCHE HOF
❼ McCUSTER B&B, TORO HOTEL, HOTEL FILOSOOF
❽ THE SHELTER JORDAN
❾ VONDELPARK HOSTEL
❿ HOTEL TERDAM
⓫ HOTEL PARKZICHT

LEIDSEKADE

LEIDSE-PLEIN

LEIDSE STRAAT

VONDELSTRAAT

ZAND-PAD

VON DEL PARK

CORN. HOOFT STRAAT

JAN LUIJKEN STRAAT

NIEUWE

SPIEG.

DCH

RIJKS-MUSEUM

Sleeping between Dam Square and the Anne Frank House

Hotel Toren is a chandeliered historic mansion in a pleasant, quiet canalside setting in downtown Amsterdam. This splurge is classy yet friendly, two blocks northeast of the Anne Frank House, and still run by the Toren family: Elsje, Lisa, and Eric (Sb-f240–260, Db-f260–290, Tb-f300–375, bridal suites for f425–450 make you want to get married, prices vary with view and Jacuzzi, 10 percent discount for 3 nights and cash with this book, CC:VMA, air-con, Keizersgracht 164, 1015 CZ Amsterdam, tel. 020/622-6352, fax 020/626-9705, www.toren.nl).

Well-heeled readers enjoy the similar 17th-century **Canal House Hotel**, a few doors down, for its beautiful antique interiors, candlelit evenings, and soft music (Db-f285–365, CC:VMA, elevator, Keizersgracht 148, 1015 CX Amsterdam, tel. 020/622-5182, fax 020/624-1317, www.canalhouse.nl).

Cheap hotels line the convenient but noisy main drag between the town hall and the Anne Frank House. Expect a long, steep, and depressing stairway, noisy front rooms, and quieter rooms in the back. **Hotel Aspen**, a good value for a budget hotel, is tidy, stark, and well maintained (S-f60, D-f85, Db-f130, Tb-f150, Qb-f180, no breakfast, CC:VMA, Raadhuisstraat 31, 1016 DC Amsterdam, tel. 020/626-6714, fax 020/620-0866, run by Esam, e-mail: hotelaspen@planet.nl). A few doors away, **Hotel Pax** has large, plain, but airy backpacker-type rooms (S-f55-75, D-f80–125, T-f110–150, Q-f120–170, no breakfast, prices vary with size and season, CC:VMA, 2 showers for 8 rooms, Raadhuisstraat 37, tel. 020/624-9735, run by brothers Philip and Peter).

Calendula Goldbloom's B&B, run by an American couple, offers two comfortable rooms in a classy old home in a quiet Jordaan neighborhood a five-minute walk northwest of the Anne Frank House (D-f200, extra bed f60, 3-night minimum, good breakfasts, Goudsbloemstraat 132, tel. 020/428-3055, fax 020/776-0075, www.calendulas.com, Lynn and Dennis).

Sleeping in the Leidseplein Area

The area around Amsterdam's museum square (Museumplein) and the rip-roaring nightlife center (Leidseplein) is colorful, comfortable, convenient, and affordable. These three canalside places are a five- to ten-minute walk from Leidseplein.

Hotel Keizershof is wonderfully Dutch, with six bright, airy rooms in a 17th-century canal house. A steep spiral staircase leads to rooms named after old-time Hollywood stars. The enthusiastic hospitality of the De Vries family has made this place a treat for 38 years (S-f100, D-f130–140, Ds-f150, Db-f180, T-f175, Tb-f200, 3-night minimum, CC:VM, nonsmoking, classy breakfast, tram #16, #24, or #25 from station, where Keizers canal crosses

Spiegelstraat at Keizersgracht 618, 1017 ER Amsterdam, tel. 020/622-2855, fax 020/624-8412, e-mail: keizershof@vdwp.nl).

Hotel Maas is a big, well-run, elegant, quiet, and stiffly hotelesque place (S-f125, 1 D-f145, Db-f295–345, suite-f425, prices vary with view and room size, extra person-f50, CC:VMA, hearty breakfast, air-con, elevator, tram #1, #2, #5, or #20 from station, Leidsekade 91, 1017 PN Amsterdam, tel. 020/623-3868, fax 020/622-2613, www.hotelmaas.nl).

Hotel De Leydsche Hof is canalside with simple, quiet rooms. Its peaceful demeanor almost helps you overlook the flimsy cots and old carpets (Ds-f110, Tb-f150, Qb-f200, no breakfast, near where Keizersgracht hits Leidsegracht, Leidsegracht 14, 10-min walk from Leidseplein, 1016 CK Amsterdam, tel. 020/623-2148, run by friendly Mr. Piller).

Best Western Hotel Terdam is a 90-room American-style hotel well situated on a quiet street just across the bridge from bustling Leidseplein (Db-f260–340 depending on season and air-con, CC:VMA, elevator, Tesselschadestraat 23, tel. 020/612-6876, fax 020/683-8313, www.hospitality.nl/ams).

Sleeping near Vondelpark

These options connect you with the sights via an easy tram ride, a pleasant 15-minute walk, or a short bike ride through Vondelpark.

Karen McCuster, a friendly Englishwoman, rents cozy rooms in her shoes-off home. Rooms are clean, white, and bright, with red carpeting and green plants. One room has a private rooftop patio (D-f120–160 depending on room size, includes buffet breakfast, tram #2 from station to Amstelveenseweg, Zeilstraat 22, 3rd floor, 1075 SH Amsterdam, tel. 020/679-2753, fax 020/670-4578, e-mail: p.galdermans@chello.nl).

Toro Hotel, in a peaceful residential area at the edge of Vondelpark, is your personal 19th-century hotel/mansion, with a plush lounge, elegant dining hall, and 22 rooms with TVs, safes, and phones. Rooms in the back overlook the park, canal, and garden, which is yours for relaxing. Mr. Plooy fusses over his guests (Ss-f200, Sb-f255, Db-f308, Tb-f363, CC:VMA, elevator, metered parking at door, tram #2 from station to Koningslaan, then walk to intersection of Emmalaan and Koningslaan, Koningslaan 64, 1075 AG Amsterdam, tel. 020/673-7223, fax 020/675-0031).

Hotel Filosoof greets you with Aristotle and Plato in the foyer and classical music in its lobby. Its 28 rooms are decorated with themes; the Egyptian room has a frieze of hieroglyphics. Philosophers' sayings hang on walls as thoughtful travelers wander down the halls or sit in the garden, rooted deep in discussion. The rooms are small (and split between two buildings), but the hotel is endearing (Sb-f185–215, Db-f205–235, Tb-f255–285, Qb-f275, CC:VMA, all rooms have TV and phone, elevator,

Anna Vondelstraat 6, 5-min walk from tram #1 line, get off at Constantyn Huygenstraat, tel. 020/683-3013, fax 020/685-3750, www.xs4all.nl/~filosoof, e-mail: filosoof@xs4all.nl).

Hotel Parkzicht is an old-time place with lots of extremely steep stairs and 14 big plain rooms on a quiet street bordering Vondelpark (S-f65, Sb-f95, Db-f150–175, as low as f100 in winter, Tb-f220, Qb-f250, CC:VMA, tram #1, #2 or #5 from station, exit Leidseplein, Roemer Visscherstraat 33, tel. 020/618-1954, fax 020/618-0897, e-mail: hotel@parkzicht.nl).

Hostels

The Shelter Jordan is scruffy, friendly, well run, and in a great neighborhood. These are Amsterdam's best budget beds, in 20-bed dorms (f28, includes sheets and breakfast, maximum age 35, nonsmoking, 02:00 curfew, near Anne Frank House, Bloemstraat 179, tel. 020/624-4717, www.shelter.nl, e-mail: jordan@shelter.nl). It serves hot meals, runs a snack bar, offers lockers, leads nightly Bible studies, and closes the dorms from 10:00 to 12:30. Its sister Christian hostel, **The Shelter City**, in the Red-Light District, is similar but definitely not preaching to the choir (f28, includes breakfast, maximum age 35, curfew, Barndesteeg 21, tel. 020/625-3230, e-mail: city@shelter.nl).

The city's two IYHF hostels are **Vondelpark**, Amsterdam's top hostel (f33–49 with breakfast, S-f90, D-f135, nonmembers pay f5 extra, lots of school groups, 4–20 beds per dorm, right on the park at Zandpad 5, tel. 020/589-8996, fax 020/589-8955, www.njhc.org/vondelpark) and **Stadsdoelen YH** (f33–37 with breakfast, f5 extra without YH card, just past Dam Square, Kloveniersburgwal 97, tel. 020/624-6832, fax 020/639-1035, e-mail: stadsdoelen@njhc.org). While generally booked long in advance, a few beds open up each day at 11:00.

Eating in Amsterdam

Dutch food is basic and hearty. *Eetcafés* are local cafés serving budget sandwiches, soup, eggs, and so on. Cafeterias, *broodje* (sandwich shops), and automatic food shops are also good bets for budget eaters. Picnics are cheap and easy. A central supermarket is **Albert Heijn**, at the corner of Koningsplein and Singel Canal near the flower market (Mon–Sat 10:00–20:00, Sun 12:00–18:00).

Of Amsterdam's thousand-plus restaurants, no one knows which are best—especially us. I pick an area and wander. The major action is around Leidseplein. Wander along restaurant row: Leidsedwarsstraat. For fewer crowds and more charm, find something in the Jordaan. The best advice: your hotel's. Most keep a reliable eating list for their neighborhood. Here are a few handy places to consider:

Eating near Spui in the Center

The city university's **Atrium** is a great budget cafeteria (f9 meals, Mon–Fri 11:30–14:30, 17:00–19:30; from Spui, walk west down Landebrug Steeg to the canalside Café 't Gasthuys 3 blocks to Oudezijds Achterburgwal 237, go through arched doorway on the right, tel. 020/525-3999). **Café 't Gasthuys**, one of Amsterdam's many "brown" cafés (named for their smoke-stained walls), makes good sandwiches and offers indoor or canalside seating (daily 12:00–01:00, walk west down Landebrug Steeg to Grimburgwal 7, tel. 020/624-8230).

La Place, a cafeteria on the ground floor of the Vroom Dreesmann department store, has islands of entrées, veggies, fruits, desserts, and beverages (Mon–Sat 10:00–20:00, Thu until 21:00, Sun 12:00–20:00, near Mint Tower, corner of Rokin and Muntplein, tel. 020/620-2364).

De Jaren Café ("The Years") features eclectic energy, an upstairs restaurant, and drinks at its canalside patio (daily 10:00–01:00, Nieuwe Doelenstraat 20–22, just up from Muntplein, tel. 020/625-5771).

Eating in the Train Station

The train station has a surprisingly classy budget self-service **Stationsrestauratie** on platform 1 (Mon–Sat 7:00–22:00, Sun from 8:00).

Eating near the Anne Frank House

For pancakes in a family atmosphere, try the **Pancake Bakery** (f18 pancakes, splitting is OK, offers an Indonesian pancake for those who want 2 experiences in 1, daily 12:00–21:30, Prinsengracht 191, 1 block north of Anne Frank House, tel. 020/625-1333). Across the canal, **De Bolhoed** serves serious vegetarian food (daily 12:00–22:00, Prinsengracht 60, tel. 020/626-1803). **Dimitri's** is the place for a hearty salad (f20 main course salads, daily 8:00–22:00, Prinsenstraat 3, tel. 020/627-9393).

Eating near the Rijksmuseum, on Leidseplein

The Art Deco **American Hotel** dining room serves an all-you-can-eat f16 salad bar (available 11:00–15:00, 17:00–23:00, where Leidseplein hits Singel Canal). On the café-packed street called Lange Leidsedwarsstraat, **Bojo** is a reasonably-priced Indonesian restaurant at #51 (daily from 16:00–02:00, 020/622-7434). If hunger hits in the **Rijksmuseum**, head for the cafeteria in the west wing's ground floor.

Eating near Vondelpark

Café Vertigo offers an international melange of sushi, soups, and pastas. Grab an outdoor table and watch the world spin by (daily 11:00–01:00, next to Film Museum, Vondelpark 3, tel. 020/612-3021).

Bars

Try a *jenever* (Dutch gin), the closest thing to an atomic bomb in a shot glass. While cheese gets harder and sharper with age, *jenever* grows smooth and soft. Old *jenever* is best.

Drugs

Amsterdam, Europe's counterculture mecca, thinks the concept of a "victimless crime" is a contradiction. While hard drugs are definitely out, marijuana causes about as much excitement as a bottle of beer. Throughout the Netherlands "coffee shops" are pubs selling marijuana. Menus dangling from strings look like the inventory of a drug bust. Display cases show various joints or baggies for sale. The Dutch roll a little tobacco into their joints. To avoid the tobacco, you need to get a baggie and papers. Baggies usually cost f25—smaller contents...better quality. Walk east from Dam Square on Damstraat for a few blocks and then down to Nieuwmarkt. While several touristy Bulldog Cafés are hits with tourists, less-glitzy neighborhood places (farther from the tourists) offer a better value and a more comfortable atmosphere.

Pot should never be bought on the street in Amsterdam. Well-established coffee shops are considered much safer. Up to five grams of marijuana per person per day can be sold in coffee shops. Minimum age for purchase: 18 years.

The tiny **Grey Area** coffee shop is a cool, welcoming, and smoky hole-in-the-wall appreciated among local aficionados as a seven-time winner of Amsterdam's Cannabis Cup award. Judging by the proud autographed photos on the wall, many of America's most famous heads have dropped in. You're welcome to just nurse a bottomless cup of coffee (open high noon to 21:00, closed Mon, between Dam Square and Anne Frank House at Oude Leliestraat 2, tel. 020/420-4301, www.greyarea.nl, Steven and John).

Near the corner of Leidsestraat and Prinsengracht, **Tops** coffee shop has Internet access. **Homegrown Fantasy's** coffee shop and gallery, about two blocks northwest of Dam Square, has a gentle Dutch atmosphere, cosmic restroom, and a grow shop next door (daily 12:00–24:00, Nieuwe Zijds Voorburgwal 87a, tel. 020/627-5683).

▲**Marijuana and Hemp Museum**—This is a collection of dope facts, history, science, and memorabilia (f12.50, daily 11:00–22:00, Oudezijds Achterburgwal 148, tel. 020/623-5961). While small, it has a shocker finale: the high-tech grow room in which dozens of varieties of marijuana are cultivated in optimal hydroponic (among other) environments. Some plants stand five feet tall and shine under the intense grow lamps. The view is actually through glass walls into the neighboring "Sensi Seed Bank" Grow Shop, which sells carefully cultivated seeds and all the gear needed to grow them. It's an interesting neighborhood. The Cannabis College Foundation, "dedicated to ending the global war against the cannabis plant through public education," is next door at #124 (tel. 020/423-4420, www. cannabiscollege.com or www.marijuananews.com). As you wander through the Foundation, ponder the 400,000 Americans serving time in jail because of U.S. marijuana laws.

Transportation Connections—Amsterdam

Amsterdam's train-information center requires a long wait. Save lots of time by getting train tickets and information in a small-town station or travel agency. For phone information, dial 0900-9292 for local trains or 0900-9296 for international trains (75 cents/min, daily 7:00–24:00, wait through recording and hold... hold...hold...).

By train to: **Schiphol Airport** (6/hrly, 20 min, f7), **Haarlem** (6/hrly, 15 min, f12 round-trip), **The Hague** (4/hrly, 45 min), **Rotterdam** (4/hrly, 1 hr), **Brussels** (hrly, 3 hrs), **Ostende** (hrly, 4 hrs, change in Roosendaal), **Paris** (5/day, 5 hrs, required fast train from Brussels with f24 supplement; there's one slow, 4-hr, no-supplement train a day), **London** (4/day, 10–12 hrs), **Copenhagen** (5/day, 11 hrs), **Frankfurt** (10/day, 5 hrs), **Munich** (8/day, 8 hrs, change in Mannheim), **Bonn** (10/day, 3 hrs), **Bern** (8/day, 9 hrs, change in Basel).

Amsterdam's Schiphol Airport: The airport, like most of Holland, is English speaking, user-friendly, and below sea level. Its banks offer fair rates (24 hrs daily, in arrival area). Schiphol Airport has easy bus and train connections (11 kilometers) into Amsterdam or Haarlem. The airport also has a train station of its own. (You can validate your Eurailpass and hit the rails immediately or, to stretch your train pass, buy the inexpensive ticket today and start the pass later.) Schiphol flight information (tel. 0900-0141) can give you flight times and your airline's Amsterdam number for reconfirmation before going home (f1/min to climb through its phone tree). To reach airlines, dial KLM at 020/649-9123 and Martainair at 020/601-1222.

HAARLEM

Cute, cozy, yet real and handy to the airport, Haarlem is a fine home base, giving you small-town, overnight warmth with easy access (15 minutes by train) to wild and crazy Amsterdam.

Haarlem is a busy Dutch market town buzzing with shoppers biking home with fresh bouquets. Enjoy the market on Saturday (general) and Monday (clothing), when the square bustles like a Brueghel painting with cheese, fish, flowers, and families. Make yourself at home here. Buy some flowers to brighten your hotel room.

Orientation (area code: 023)

Tourist Information: Haarlem's VVV, at the train station, is friendlier, more helpful, and less crowded than Amsterdam's. Ask your Amsterdam questions here (Mon–Fri 9:30–17:30, Sat 10:00–14:00, closed Sun, tel. 0900-616-1600, f1/min, helpful parking brochure, their f4 *Haarlem* magazine is not necessary).

Arrival in Haarlem: As you walk out of the train station (has lockers), the TI is on your right and the bus station is across the street. Two parallel streets flank the train station (Kruisweg and Jansweg). Head up either one and you'll reach the town square and church within 10 minutes. If you're uncertain of the way, ask a local person, "*Grote Markt?*" ("Main Square?"), and they'll point you in the right direction.

Helpful Hints

The handy GWK change office at the station offers fair exchange rates (Mon–Fri 8:00–20:00, Sat 9:00–18:00, Sun 10:00–17:00). The train station rents bikes (f10/day, f100 deposit and passport number, Mon–Sat 6:00–24:00, Sun 7:30–24:00). For Internet access (f7.50/30 min), nonguests are welcome to use Hotel Amadeus' computer (facing Market Square) and nonsmokers are welcome at High Times (Lange Veerstraat 47).

Sights—Haarlem

▲▲**Market Square (Grote Markt)**—Haarlem's market square is the town's delightful centerpiece. To enjoy a coffee or beer here simmering in Dutch good living is a quintessential European experience. In a recent study, the Dutch were found to be the most content people in Europe. And later, the people of Haarlem were found to be the most content in the Netherlands. Observe. Just a few years ago trolleys ran through the square and cars were parked everywhere. But today it's a people zone, with market stalls filling the square on Mondays and Saturdays and café tables on others. The local drunk used to hang out on the bench in front of the town hall, where he'd expose himself to newlyweds. The Dutch, rather than arrest the man, moved the bench. The big statue in the square is of Coster, the man only Haarlemers think invented printing. The little shops around the cathedral have long been church owned and rented to bring in a little cash. The fine building nearest the cathedral is the old meat hall—decorated with carved bits of early advertising.

▲**Church (Grote Kerk)**—This 15th-century Gothic church (now Protestant) is worth a look, if only for its Oz-like organ (from 1738, 30 meters high, its 5,000 pipes impressed both Handel and Mozart). Note how the organ, which fills the west end, seems to steal the show from the altar. Pick up the English flyer, which lists spots of interest, including Frans Hals' tomb (under black lantern in choir). To enter, find the small "Entrée" sign behind the church (f2.75, Mon–Sat 10:00–16:00). Consider attending (even part of) a concert to hear Holland's greatest pipe organ (regular free concerts Tue at 20:15 mid-May–mid-Oct, additional concerts Thu at 15:00 July–Aug, confirm schedule at TI).

▲▲**Frans Hals Museum**—Haarlem is the hometown of Frans Hals, and this refreshingly easy museum—an almshouse for old men back in 1610—displays many of his greatest paintings (f10, Mon–Sat 11:00–17:00, Sun 12:00–17:00, tel. 023/511-5775). Enjoy lots of Frans Hals group portraits (rooms 21, 26, 28) and take-me-back paintings of old-time Haarlem (room 22). Peter Brueghel the Younger's painting *Proverbs* (outside room 24) illustrates 72 old Dutch proverbs. To peek into old Dutch ways, identify some with the help of the English-language key.

History Museum—Across the street from the Frans Hals Museum, this small, free museum gives a peek into old Haarlem. Request the English version of the 10-minute video. Study the large-scale model of Haarlem in 1822 before the town's fortifications were demolished (Tue–Sat 12:00–17:00, Sun 13:00–17:00,

Haarlem

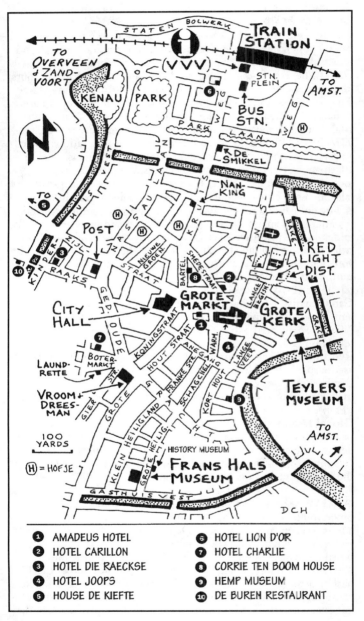

STATEN BOLWERK

TRAIN STATION

TO OVERVEEN & ZANDVOORT

VVV

KENAU PARK

STN. PLEIN

TO AMST.

BUS STN.

PARK LAAN

DE SMIKKEL

HUIS VEST

NAN-KING

TO

POST

RED LIGHT DIST.

NIEUWE GROEN STRAAT

BARTEL

SMEDESTRAAT

BAKE

RAAKS

KINDER

GROTE MARKT

GROTE KERK

CITY HALL

GED. OUDE

KONINGSTRAAT

HOUT STRAAT

BOTER-MARKT

LAUND-RETTE

VROOM+ DREES-MAN

GIER STR.

GROTE

FRANKE STR

SCHAGCHEL

WARM.

LANGE VEEK

KORT HOUT

TEYLERS MUSEUM

TO AMST.

100 YARDS

KLEIN HEILLIGLAND

GROTE HEILIG.

HISTORY MUSEUM

FRANS HALS MUSEUM

Ⓗ = HOFJE

GASTHUIS VEST

DCH

❶	AMADEUS HOTEL	❻	HOTEL LION D'OR
❷	HOTEL CARILLON	❼	HOTEL CHARLIE
❸	HOTEL DIE RAECKSE	❽	CORRIE TEN BOOM HOUSE
❹	HOTEL JOOPS	❾	HEMP MUSEUM
❺	HOUSE DE KIEFTE	❿	DE BUREN RESTAURANT

closed Mon, Groot Heiligland 47, tel. 020/542-2427). The
adjacent architecture museum (also free) is of conceivable
interest to architects.

Corrie Ten Boom House—Haarlem is home to Corrie Ten
Boom, popularized by *The Hiding Place*, an inspirational book and
movie about the Ten Boom family's experience hiding Jews from
Nazis. The Ten Boom House is open for 60-minute English tours
(donation accepted, April–Oct Tue–Sat 10:00–16:00, Nov–March
Tue–Sat 11:00–15:00, closed Mon, 50 meters off Market Square
at Barteljorisstraat 19, the clock-shop people get all wound up if
you go inside—wait at the door, where tour times are posted, tel.
023/531-0823). The Ten Boom family had for generations hosted
a prayer meeting for peace here for Jews and Christians. On the
100th anniversary of the prayer meetings, the Gestapo came,
looking for the hiding place. It's a great and inspirational story
(although some may be put off by the preaching mixed in).

▲**Teylers Museum**—Famous as the oldest museum in Holland,
it's interesting mainly as a look at a 200-year-old museum—fossils,
minerals, and primitive electronic gadgetry. New exhibition halls
(with rotating exhibits) have freshened up the place. Stop by if
you enjoy mixing, say, Renaissance sketches with pickled coela-
canths (f10, Tue–Sat 10:00–17:00, Sun 12:00–17:00, Spaarne 16,
tel. 023/531-9010).

Canal Cruise—Making a scenic loop through and around Haarlem, these little trips are more relaxing than informative (f12.50,
70 min, 5/day, across from Teylers Museum at Spaarne 11a,
tel. 023/535-7723).

Red Lights—Wander through a little red-light district as precious
as a Barbie doll (2 blocks northeast of Market Square, off Lange
Begijnestraat, no senior or student discounts). Don't miss the
mall marked by the red neon sign reading "t'Steegje." The nearby
t'Poortje (office park) costs f7.50.

Global Hemp Museum—More a hemp-products store and hub
of Haarlem's coffee-shop action, this friendly place runs a humble
hemp museum out back (shop free, museum f5, Internet access-
f3/30 min, Mon–Sat 11:00–18:00, summer Sun 12:00–18:00, down
the canal from Teylers Museum at Spaarne 94, tel. 023/534-9939).

Amsterdam to Haarlem Train Tour

Since you'll be commuting from Amsterdam to Haarlem, here's
a tour to keep you entertained. Departing from Amsterdam, grab
a seat on the right (with your back to Amsterdam, top deck if
possible). Everything is on the right unless I say on the left.

You're riding the oldest train line in Holland. Across the
harbor behind the Amsterdam station, the tall brown skyscraper
is the corporate office of **Shell Oil**. The Dutch had the first multi-
national corporation (the United East India Company back in the

17th century). And today this international big-business spirit survives with companies like Shell and Phillips.

Leaving Amsterdam you'll see the cranes and ships of its harbor—sizable but nothing like the world's biggest in nearby Rotterdam.

On your left find the old **windmill**. In front of it the little garden plots and cottages are escapes for big-city people who probably don't even have a balcony.

Coming into the Sloterdijk Station (where trains connect for Amsterdam airport), you'll see huge office buildings, such as Dutch Telecom KPN. These grew up after the station made commuting easy.

A kilometer past Sloterdijk Station, about 50 meters to the right of the tracks, a yellow sign says, "Tippel Zone—open 21:00." (*Tippel* is the sound a mouse makes when it runs through the house at night.) This is a **drive-in brothel**. See the oval driveway with pink "bus stops" for browsing, the lounge building, and the blue privacy stalls behind (including 2 for bikers). The lounge has a clinic with a nurse and counselors to keep the women healthy. If a prostitute is diagnosed with AIDS, she gets a subsidized apartment to encourage her to quit the business. Shocking as this may seem to some, it's a good example of a pragmatic solution to a problem—getting the most dangerous prostitutes off the streets and combating AIDS.

Passing through a forest and by some houseboats, you enter a *polder*—reclaimed land. This is an ecologically sound farm zone, run without chemicals. Cows, pigs, and chickens run free—they're not raised in cages. The train tracks are on a dike, which provides a solid foundation not susceptible to floods. This way the transportation system functions right through any calamity. Looking out at the distant dike, remember you're in the most densely populated country in Europe. On the horizon, sleek modern windmills whirl.

Passing the tall smokestack and the Sony Music Building, find a big, unnamed, beige-and-white building. This is the **mint**, where the Dutch currency is printed (top security, no advertising). This has long been a family business. Study a bill. Even today you can read who printed it: Johan Enschede en Zonen, imp. (Johan Enschede and Sons, Inc.).

As the train slows down, you're passing through the Netherlands' biggest train-car maintenance facility and entering Haarlem. Look left. The domed building is a **prison**, built in 1901 and still in use. As you cross the Spaarne River you'll see the great **church spire** towering over Haarlem as it has since medieval times—back when a fortified wall circled the town. Hop out into one of Holland's oldest stations. Art Nouveau—decor from 1908—survives all around.

Nightlife in Haarlem

Haarlem's evening scene is great. The bars around the Grote Kerk and Lange Veerstraat are colorful and lively. You'll find plenty of music.

The best show in town: the café scene on Market Square. In good weather, café tables tumble happily out of the bars.

For trendy local crowds, consider a drink at the **Studio** (daily 12:00–02:00, on the square, next to Hotel Carillon) or **Café 1900** across from the Corrie Ten Boom House (daily 9:00–00:30, live music Sun night).

Coffee Shops: Haarlem has 16 "coffee shops" where marijuana is casually sold and smoked by easygoing noncriminal types. The **Frans Hals Coffee Shop** is one of the best established (in front of station at 46 Kruisweg). The display case–type "menu" explains what's on sale (f5 joints, f25 baggies, space cakes—but no alcohol, only soft drinks). At **High Times**, smokers can choose from 16 varieties of joints in racks behind the bar (neatly prepacked in trademarked "Joint Packs," f4-7.50, daily 12:00–23:00, Internet access, 47 Lange Veerstraat). If you don't like the smell of pot, avoid places sporting Rastafarian yellow, red, and green colors; wildly painted walls; or plants in the windows.

Crack is the wild and leathery place to go for loud music, pool, darts, and smoking (Lange Veerstraat 32). **Imperial Café and Bar** has live music Sunday through Thursday (daily 20:00–02:00, best to arrive around 00:30 on weekends, a few doors down from Crack at Korte Veerstraat 3).

Sleeping in Haarlem
(f1 = about 40 cents, country code: 31, area code: 023)

Sleep Code: **S** = Single, **D** = Double/Twin, **T** = Triple, **Q** = Quad, **b** = bathroom, **t** = toilet only, **s** = shower only, **CC** = Credit Card (**V**isa, **M**asterCard, **A**mex).

The helpful Haarlem tourist office ("VVV" at the train station, Mon–Fri 9:30–17:30, Sat 10:00–14:00, closed Sun, tel. 0900-616-1600, f1/min) can nearly always find you a f35 bed in a private home (for a f10-per-person fee plus a cut of your host's money). Avoid this if you can; it's cheaper to call direct.

Haarlem is most crowded in April, on Easter weekend, in May, and in August. Nearly every Dutch person you'll encounter speaks English. The listed prices include breakfast (unless otherwise noted) and usually include the f3.50-per-person-per-day tourist tax. To avoid this town's louder-than-normal street noises, forgo views for a room in the back. Hotels and the TI have a useful parking brochure.

For a **Laundromat**, try My Beautiful Launderette—handy, self-service, and cheap (f11 wash and dry, daily 8:30–20:30, bring coins, including 6 Dutch quarters to dry, near Vroom Dreesman department store at Boter Markt 20).

Sleeping in the Center

Hotel Amadeus, on Market Square, has 15 small, bright, and basic rooms. Some have views of the square. This characteristic hotel, ideally located above an early 20th-century dinner café, is relatively quiet. Its lush old lounge/breakfast room, on the second floor, overlooks the square (Sb-f97.50, Db-f140, Tb-f180, Qb-f200, includes tax, 2-night stay and cash get you a 5 percent discount, 12-min walk from train station, CC:VMA, steep climb to lounge, then an elevator, Grote Markt 10, 2011 RD Haarlem, tel. 023/532-4530, fax 023/532-2328, www.amadeus-hotel.com, Mike takes good care of his guests).

Hotel Carillon also overlooks the town square but comes with a little more traffic and bell-tower noise. Many of the well-worn rooms are small, and the stairs are ste-e-e-p. The front rooms come with great town-square views and street noise (22 rooms, tiny loft singles-f60, Db-f142, Tb-f187.50, Qb-f210, includes tax, no elevator, 12-min walk from train station, CC:VMA, Grote Markt 27, 2011 RC Haarlem, tel. 023/531-0591, fax 023/531-4909, e-mail: fra.baars@wxs.nl). The Carillon also runs the nearby **Die Raeckse Hotel**, which has fewer stairs, less character, more traffic noise, and decent rooms (Sb-f98–115, Db-f143–171, baths cost more than showers, CC:VMA, Raaks 1, 2011 VA Haarlem, tel. 023/532-6629, fax 023/531-7937).

Hotel Joops is an innovative concept. From a reception desk in his furniture store, just behind the cathedral, Mr. Joops administers a corral of 80 rooms, all within a block of the church. He has cheap, well-worn, spacious rooms (S-f80, D-f115, T-f150) and new suites with kitchenettes (Db-f120–160, depending upon size, Tb-f165–195, breakfast—with the furniture—is f17.50 extra, save about 5 percent with cash, CC:VMA, Oude Groenmarkt 20, 2011 HL Haarlem, tel. 023/532-2008, fax 023/532-9549, www .joops.hotelinformation.com, e-mail: joops@hotelinformation.com).

Bed and Breakfast House de Kiefte, your get-into-a-local-home budget option, epitomizes the goodness of B&Bs. Marjet (mar-yet) and Hans, a fun-to-know Dutch couple who speak English fluently, rent four bright, cheery, nonsmoking rooms (with a good breakfast and travel advice) in their quiet, 100-year-old home (Ds-f100, T-f145, Qs-f175, Quint/s-f200, cash only, minimum 2 nights, family loft sleeps up to 5, very steep stairs, kid-friendly, Coornhertstraat 3, 2013 EV Haarlem, tel. 023/532-2980, cellular 06-5474-5272). It's a 15-minute walk or f14 taxi ride from the train station and a five-minute walk from the center. From Grote Markt (Market Square), walk straight out Zijlstraat and over the bridge and take a left on the fourth street.

Hotel Charlie is new and its staff eager to please. With basic rooms and a bizarre floor plan, it's only a three-minute

walk from the Markt (Sb-f100, Db-f140, Qb-f200, near launderette, Botermarkt 7, tel. 023/534-6615, fax 023/551-4488,
friendly Johnny).

Hotel Lion D'Or is a classy business hotel with all the
professional comforts and a handy location. Don't expect a warm
welcome (34 rooms, Sb-f210, Db-f275, extra beds-f50, CC:VMA,
elevator, some nonsmoking rooms, across the street from the
station at Kruisweg 34, 2011 LC Haarlem, tel. 023/532-1750,
fax 023/532-9543, www.goldentulip.nl/hotels/gtliondor).

Sleeping near Haarlem

The 300-room, very American **Hotel Haarlem Zuid** is sterile
but a good value for those interested only in sleeping and eating.
Renovated in 2000, it sits in an industrial zone, a 20-minute walk
from the center on the road to the airport (Db-f173–193 depending upon size of room, add f20 each for a 3rd or 4th person,
breakfast included or skip and save f17.50 each, CC:VMA,
elevator, easy parking, laundry service, fitness center, inexpensive
hotel restaurant, Toekanweg 2, 2035 LC Haarlem, tel. 023/
536-7500, fax 023/536-7980, www.hotelhaarlemzuid.nl, e-mail:
haarlemzuid@valk.com). Buses #5, #70, #72, and #75 connect
the hotel to the station and Market Square every 10 minutes.
Bus #80 makes runs to the beach or Amsterdam. Fast buses (#236
and #362) zip to the airport.

Pension Koning, a 15-minute walk north of the station or a
quick hop on bus #71, has five simple rooms in a row house in a
residential area (S-f45, D-f90, T-f120, 2-night minimum, includes
breakfast, Kleverlaan 179, 2023 JC Haarlem, tel. 023/526-1456).

Hostel Jan Gijzen, completely renovated and with all the
youth-hostel comforts, charges f39–43 for beds (breakfast) in
eight-bed dorms (f5 extra for nonmembers, a few D-f82, daily
7:30–24:00, Jan Gijzenpad 3, 3 kilometers from Haarlem station—
take bus #2, or a 5-min walk from Santpoort Zuid train station,
tel. 023/537-3793, fax 023/537-1176, e-mail: haarlem@njhc.org).

Eating in Haarlem

Eating between Market Square (Grote Markt) and Train Station

Enjoy an Indonesian rijsttafel feast at the **Nanking Chinese-
Indonesian Restaurant** (daily 16:00–22:00, Kruisstraat 16, a few
blocks off Grote Markt, tel. 023/532-0706). Couples eat plenty,
heartily, and cheaply by splitting a f26 Indonesian "rice table" for
one; each eater should order a drink. Say hi to gracious Ai Ping
and her daughter, Fan. Don't let them railroad you into a Chinese
(their heritage) dinner. They also do cheap and tasty takeout.

Pancakes for dinner? **Pannekoekhuis "De Smikkel"** serves

a selection of over 50 dinner (meat, cheese, etc.) and dessert pancakes. The pancakes (f18 each) are filling. With the f2.50-per-person cover charge, splitting is OK (daily 16:00–22:00, closed Mon in winter, 2 blocks in front of station, Kruisweg 57, tel. 023/532-0631).

Eat well and surrounded by trains and 1908 architecture in the classy **Brasserie Haarlem Station Restaurant** (f30 for 3 courses, daily 9:00–21:00, between tracks #3 and #6).

Eating on or near Zijlstraat

Eko Eet Café is great for a cheery, tasty vegetarian meal (f20 *menu*, daily 17:30–21:30, Zijlstraat 39, tel. 023/532-6568). Because they serve only fresh food, the *menu* gets sparse by 21:00.

Vincent's Eethuis serves the best cheap, basic Dutch food in town. This former St. Vincent's soup kitchen now feeds more gainfully employed locals than poor (f10, free seconds on veggies, friendly staff, Mon–Fri 12:00–14:00, 17:00–19:30, Nieuwe Groenmarkt 22).

The friendly **De Buren** offers handlebar-mustache fun and traditional Dutch food (such as *draadjesvlees*, beef stew with applesauce; and *oma's kippetje*, grandmother's chicken) to happy locals (f25 dinners, Wed–Sun 17:00–22:00, closed Mon–Tue, outside the tourist area at Brouwersvaart 146, follow Raaks Straat west across the canal from Die Raeckse Hotel, tel. 023/534-3364). Gerard and Marjo love their work. Enjoy their creative menu, made especially for you.

Eating between the Market Square and Frans Hals Museum

Jacobus Pieck Eetlokaal is popular with locals for its fine-value "global cuisine" (f18 plate of the day, Mon–Sat 10:00–22:00, Sun 12:00–22:00, Warmoesstraat 18, tel. 023/532-6144).

For a (f3) cone of old-fashioned French fries, drop by **Friethuis de Vlaminck** on Warmoesstraat 3 (Tue–Sat until 18:00). Notice the old-time shop sign cobbled into Warmoesstraat's brick sidewalk.

La Plume steak house is noisy with a happy, local, and carnivorous crowd (f30 meals, daily from 17:30, CC:VMA, Lange Veerstraat 1).

Bastiaan serves good "Mediterranean" cuisine in a classy atmosphere (f30 dinners, Tue–Sun from 18:00, closed Mon, CC:VMA, Lange Veerstraat 8).

De Lachende Javaan ("The Laughing Javanese") serves the best real Indonesian food in town. Their f37 rijsttafel is great (light eaters can split this extravaganza—f5 for extra plate, Tue–Sun from 17:00, closed Mon, CC:VMA, Frankestraat 25, tel. 023/532-8792).

For a candlelit dinner of cheese and wine, consider **In't Goede Uur** (Tue–Sun from 17:30, closed Mon, Korte Houtstraat 1).

For a healthy budget lunch with Haarlem's best view, eat at **La Place**, on the top floor or roof garden of the Vroom Dreesman department store (Mon–Sat 9:30–17:30, Thu until 20:30, closed Sun, on the corner of Grote Houtstraat and Gedempte Oude Gracht).

Picnic shoppers head to the **DekaMarkt** supermarket (Mon–Sat 8:30–20:00, closed Sun, Gedemple Oude Gracht 54, between Vroom Dreesman department store and post office).

Transportation Connections—Haarlem

By train to: Amsterdam (6/hrly, 15 min, f7 one-way, f12 same-day return, ticket not valid on "Lovers Train," a misnamed private train that runs hrly), **Delft** (2/hrly, 38 min), **Hoorn** (4/hrly, 1 hr), **The Hague** (4/hrly, 35 min), **Alkmaar** (2/hrly, 30 min), **Schiphol Airport** (2/hrly, 40 min, f10, transfer at Amsterdam-Sloterdijk); the direct buses #236 (use a strip card) and #362 (local cash) to the airport are faster (2/hrly, 30 min, f7); by taxi it's f70.

Sights—Near Haarlem and Amsterdam

The Netherlands are tiny. The sights listed below are an easy day trip by bus or train from Haarlem or Amsterdam. Match your interest with the village's specialty: flower auctions, folk museums, cheese, delft porcelain, beaches, or modern art.

▲▲**Enkhuisen's Zuiderzee Museum**—This lively, open-air folk museum in the salty old town of Enkhuizen has a "Living on Urk" village populated by people who do a convincing job of role-playing no-nonsense 1905 Dutch villagers. No one said "Have a nice day" back then. You can eat herring hot out of the old smoker and see barrels and rope made. Children enjoy the dress-up chest, the old-time game zone, and making sailing ships out of old wooden shoes (f18.50, early April–late Oct daily 10:00–17:00, free tours at 14:00, private guide for f80, tel. 0228/351-111). Take the train from Amsterdam direct to Enkhuisen, where a boat shuttles you to the museum, avoiding a pleasant 15-minute walk.

▲**Zaanse Schans**—This 17th-century Dutch village turned open-air folk museum puts Dutch culture—from cheese making to wooden-shoe carving—on a lazy Susan. Climb to the top of a whirring windmill (gather a group and ask for a tour). Located in the town of Zaandijk, this is your easiest one-stop look at traditional Dutch culture and the Netherlands' best collection of windmills (free, daily 8:30–18:00, until 17:00 in winter, parking f7.50/1 hr, f15/day, tel. 075/616-8218). It's 15 minutes by train north of Amsterdam; take the Alkmaar-bound train to Station Koog-Zaandijk and then walk, following the signs—past a fragrant chocolate factory—for 10 minutes.

▲▲**Aalsmeer Flower Auction**—Get a bird's-eye view of the huge Dutch flower industry. Wander on elevated walkways

Day Trips from Haarlem and Amsterdam

(through what's claimed to be the biggest building on earth) over literally trainloads of freshly cut flowers. About half of all the flowers exported from Holland are auctioned off here in six huge auditoriums (f7.50, Mon–Fri 7:30–11:00, the auction wilts after 9:30 but the warehouse swarms, gift shop, cafeteria; bus #172 from Amsterdam's station, 2/hrly, 1 hr; from Haarlem take bus #140, 2/hrly, 1 hr; tel. 0297/393-939). Aalsmeer is close to the airport and a handy last fling before catching a morning weekday flight.

▲▲▲**Keukenhof**—This is the greatest bulb-flower garden on earth. Each spring 6 million flowers, enjoying sandy soil behind the Dutch dunes, conspire to make even a total garden hater enjoy them. This 100-acre park is packed with tour groups daily from about March 22 to May 24 for the 2001 spring show (f20, 8:00–19:30, last tickets sold at 18:00) and from August 2 to September 16 for the 2001 summer exhibition (f15.50, 9:00–18:00, last ticket sold at 17:00, catch bus #50 or #51 from Haarlem, tel. 0252/465-555, www.keukenhof.nl). Go late in the day for the best light and the fewest groups.

The 2001 flower parade will be held April 21. This all-day parade, featuring floats decorated with blossoms instead of crepe paper, runs through eight towns, including Lisse and Haarlem.

▲**Hoorn**—This is an elegant, quiet, and typical 17th-century Dutch town north of Amsterdam. Its TI can rent you a bike or give you a walking-tour brochure. Any TI offers the flier describing the "Historic Triangle," an all-day excursion from Amsterdam that connects Hoorn, Medemblik, and Enkhuizen by steam train and boat (f30 plus f6.25 for train back to Haarlem, 2/day, tel. 0229/214-862).

▲**Delft**—Peaceful as a Vermeer painting (he was born here) and lovely as its porcelain, Delft is a typically Dutch town with a special soul. Enjoy it best by simply wandering around, watching people, munching local syrup-waffles, or daydreaming from the canal bridges. The town bustles during its Saturday antiques market (9:00–17:00). Its colorful Thursday food-and-flower market attracts many traditional villagers (9:00–17:00). The TI on the main square has a f3.50 brochure outlining Delft's sights, including a "Historical Walk through Delft" (Mon–Fri 9:00–17:30, Sat 9:00–17:30, Sun 11:00–15:00, tel. 015/212-6100). The town is a museum in itself, but if you need a turnstile, it has an impressive Army Museum (f6, Mon–Fri 10:00–17:00, Sat–Sun 13:00–17:00). Or tour the Royal Porcelain Works to watch the famous 17th-century blue delftware turn from clay into art (f5, Mon–Sat 9:00–17:00, summer Sun 9:30–17:00, tel. 015/256-9214).

▲**Alkmaar**—Holland's cheese capital is especially fun (and touristy) during its weekly cheese market (Friday 10:00–12:00).

▲▲**Edam**—This tiny town is sweet but palatable, and 30 minutes by bus from Amsterdam (2/hrly). The Edam Museum is a small, quirky house offering a fun peek into a 400-year-old home and a floating cellar (f4.50, Tue–Sat 10:00–16:30, Sun 13:30–16:30, closed in winter, on the main square). Wednesday is the town's market day (9:00–13:00). In July and August, market day includes a traditional cheese market (10:30–12:30). TI tel. 0299/315-125.

▲**Rotterdam**—This city, the world's largest port, bounced back after being bombed flat in World War II. See its towering Euromast, take a harbor tour, and stroll its great pedestrian zone (TI tel. 0900/403-4065, toll call-f1/min).

▲▲**The Hague (Den Haag)**—Locals say the money is made in Rotterdam, divided in The Hague, and spent in Amsterdam. The Hague is the Netherlands' seat of government and the home of several engaging museums. The Hague's TI is at the train station (Mon–Sat 9:00–17:30, later in summer, Sun 10:00–17:00, tel. 06/3403-5051, f1/min).

The **Mauritshuis'** delightful, easy-to-tour art collection stars Vermeer and Rembrandt (f12.50, Tue–Sat 10:00–17:00, Sun 11:00–17:00, Korte Vijverberg 8, tel. 070/302-3456). Across the pond, the **Torture Museum** (Gevangenpoort) shows the medieval mind at its worst (f8, Tue–Fri 11:00–16:00, Sat–Sun 12:00–16:00, closed Mon, required tours on the hour, last one at 16:00, ask ticket-taker if film and talk will be in English before you commit, tel. 070/346-0861). For a look at the 19th century's attempt at virtual reality, tour **Panorama Mesdag**, a 360-degree painting of nearby Scheveningen in the 1880s with a 3-D sandy-beach foreground (f9.50, Mon–Sat 10:00–17:00, Sun 12:00–17:00, Zeestraat 65, tel. 070/310-6665). The nearby **Peace Palace**, a gift from Andrew Carnegie, houses the International Court of Justice (f5, Mon–Fri, required guided tours only at 10:00, 11:00, 14:00, or 15:00, closes without warning—call ahead or check at TI, tram #7 or #8 from station, tel. 070/302-4137).

Scheveningen, the Dutch Coney Island, is liveliest on sunny summer afternoons (take tram #7). Madurodam, a mini-Holland amusement park, is a kid pleaser (f21, kids 4–11 f14, daily 9:00–17:00, until 20:00 March–June, until 23:00 July–Aug, tram #1 or #9, tel. 070/355-3900).

Utrecht—The Museum von Speelklok tot Pierement has free and necessary guided 50-minute tours on the hour demonstrating its musical clocks, calliopes, and street organs (f12, Tue–Sat 10:00–17:00, Sun 12:00–17:00, closed Mon, last tour at 16:00, 10-min walk from station, Buurkerkhof 10, tel. 030/231-2789).

▲▲**Arnhem's Open-Air Dutch Folk Museum**—An hour east of Amsterdam, Arnhem has the Netherlands' first and biggest folk museum. You'll enjoy a huge park of windmills, old farms, traditional crafts in action, and a pleasant education-by-immersion in Dutch culture. The English guidebook (f7.50) explains each historic building (f22.50, April–Oct daily 10:00–17:00, tel. 026/357-6111). The park has several good budget restaurants and covered picnic areas. Its rustic Pancake House serves hearty (splittable) Dutch flapjacks.

Trains make the 70-minute trip from Amsterdam to Arnhem twice an hour (likely transfer in Utrecht). At Arnhem station, take bus #3 or, even better, #13 (faster, 4/hrly, 15 min) to the Openlucht Museum.

▲▲**Kröller-Müller Museum and Hoge Veluwe National Park**—Near Arnhem, Hoge Veluwe National Park is the Netherlands' largest (13,000 acres) and is famous for its Kröller-Müller Museum. This huge, striking modern-art collection, including 55 paintings by van Gogh, is set deep in the forest. The park has hundreds of white bikes you're free to use to make your explorations more fun. After you pay f9.50 at the park entrance, the museum is "free" (Tue–Sun 10:00–17:00, easy parking, tel. 055/378-1441). Pick up information at the Amsterdam or Arnhem TI (tel. 026/442-6767). Bus #12 connects the Arnhem train station with the Kröller-Müller Museum (March–Oct, check ahead for times as #12 runs infrequently). A visit to the park and the open-air museum makes a great day trip from Amsterdam.

COPENHAGEN

Copenhagen (København), Denmark's capital, is the gateway to Scandinavia. And now, with the new bridge connecting Sweden and Denmark, Copenhagen is energized and ready to de-throne Stockholm as Scandinavia's powerhouse city. Spend a busy day cruising the canals, wandering through the palace, and taking an old-town walk. This will give you your historical bearings. Then, after another day strolling the Strøget (Europe's greatest pedestrian shopping mall), biking the canals, and sampling the Danish good life, you'll feel right at home.

Copenhagen is Scandinavia's cheapest and most fun-loving capital. So live it up.

Planning Your Time

A first visit deserves two days.

Day 1: Catch the 10:30 city walking tour. After a Riz-Raz lunch, visit the Use It information center and catch the relaxing canal boat tour out to *The Little Mermaid* and back. Enjoy the rest of the afternoon tracing Denmark's cultural roots in the National Museum and touring the Ny Carlsberg Glyptotek art gallery. Spend the evening strolling Strøget (follow "Heart and Soul" walk described below) or dipping into Christiania.

Day 2: At 10:00 explore the subterranean Christiansborg Castle ruins under today's palace or go neoclassical at Thorvaldsen's Museum. At 11:00 take the 50-minute guided tour of Denmark's royal Christiansborg Palace. After a *smørrebrød* lunch in a park, spend the afternoon seeing the Rosenborg Castle/crown jewels, Nazi Resistance museum, or riding the hop-on hop-off bus (or train) across the new bridge to Sweden and back. Spend the evening at Tivoli Gardens.

Orientation

Nearly all of your sightseeing is in Copenhagen's compact old town. By doing things by bike or on foot you'll stumble into some charming bits of Copenhagen that many miss.

Study the map to understand the city: The medieval walls are now roads that define the center: Vestervoldgade (literally, "western wall street"), Nørrevoldgade, and Østervoldgade. The fourth side is the harbor and the island of Slotsholmen where København ("merchants' harbor") was born in 1167. The next of the city's islands is Amager, where you'll find the local "Little Amsterdam" district of Christianshavn. What was Copenhagen's moat is now a string of pleasant lakes and parks, including Tivoli Gardens. You can still make out some of the zigzag pattern of the moats in the city's greenbelt. In 1850 Copenhagen's 120,000 residents all lived within this defensive system. Building in the "no man's land" outside the walls was only allowed with the understanding that in the event of an attack you'd burn your dwellings to clear the way for a good defense. Today, the buildings of historic importance lie within the *voldgade* ring. In the 17th century, King Christian IV extended the fortifications to the north, doubling the size of the city, adding a grid plan of streets and his Rosenborg Castle. This old "new town" has the Amalienborg Palace and *The Little Mermaid*.

For most visitors, the core of the town is the axis formed by the train station, Tivoli Gardens, Rådhus (City Hall) Square, and the Strøget pedestrian street. Bubbling with street life and colorful pedestrian zones, Copenhagen's great on foot. But be sure to get off the Strøget.

You need to remember one character in Copenhagen's history: Christian IV. Ruling from 1588 to 1648, he was Denmark's Renaissance king. The royal Danish party animal, his personal energy kindled a golden age when Copenhagen prospered and many of the city's grandest buildings were built. Locals love to tell wild stories of everyone's favorite king.

Tourist Information

The tourist office is a for-profit company called "Wonderful Copenhagen." This colors the advice and information it provides. Drop by to get a city map, *Copenhagen This Week* (a free, handy, and misnamed monthly guide to the city, worth reading for its good maps, museum hours with telephone numbers, sightseeing tour ideas, shopping suggestions, and calendar of events, including free English tours and concerts), to browse its racks of brochures, and get your questions answered (May–Aug Mon–Sat 9:00–20:00, Sun 10:00–20:00, Sept–April Mon–Fri 9:00–16:30, Sat 9:00–13:30, closed Sun, across from train station on Bernstorffsgade, tel. 33 25 38 44, www.ctw.dk, www.dt.dk).

Tivoli's weekly entertainment is posted near the front door.

Use It (a 10-minute walk from the station) is a better information service. Government-sponsored and student-run, it caters to Copenhagen's young but welcomes travelers of any age. It's a friendly, driven-to-help, energetic, no-nonsense source of budget travel information, offering a free budget room-finding service, free Internet access, a jazz bar, a ride-finding board, free condoms, and free luggage lockers. Their free *Playtime* publication has Back Door–style articles on Copenhagen and the Danish culture, special budget tips, and self-guided tours for bikers, walkers, and those riding scenic bus #6. They have a list of private rooms (300-kr doubles). From the station, head down Strøget, then turn right on Rådhustræde for three blocks to #13 (mid-June–mid-Sept daily 9:00–19:00; otherwise Mon–Wed 11:00–16:00, Thu 11:00–18:00, Fri 11:00–14:00, closed Sat–Sun; tel. 33 73 06 20).

The two essential publications you need—a map and *Copenhagen This Week*—are free at the airport TI, the TI across from the station, the Interrail Center, Use It, and the lobby of City Hall.

The **Copenhagen Card** covers the public transportation system and admissions to nearly all the sights in greater Copenhagen, which stretches from Helsingør to Roskilde. It includes virtually all the city sights, Tivoli, and the train from the airport. It's available at any TI (including the airport's): 24 hours–155 kr; 48 hours–255 kr; 72 hours–320 kr (www.woco.dk). It's hard to break even, unless you take the train (included) to outlying sights. It comes with a handy book explaining the 60 included sights, such as: Christiansborg Palace (normally 40 kr), Christiansborg Castle ruins (20 kr), National Museum (40 kr), Ny Carlsberg Glyptotek (30 kr), and Tivoli (50 kr).

Arrival in Copenhagen

By Train: The main train station is called Hovedbanegården (HOETH-ban-gorn; learn that word—you'll need to recognize it). It's a temple of travel and a hive of travel-related activity, offering lockers (25–35 kr/day), a garderobe (40 kr/day per rucksack), a post office, a grocery store (daily 8:00–24:00), 24-hour thievery, and bike rentals. The Interail Center, a service the station provides for mostly young travelers (but anyone with a railpass is welcome), is a pleasant lounge with 10-kr showers, free (if risky) luggage storage, city maps, *Playtime* magazines, snacks, information, and other young travelers (June–mid-Sept daily 06:30–10:30 and 16:00–22:00).

The station has ATMs and two long-hours exchange desks (both open daily 08:00–20:00). You'll get a few more kroner at FOREX (daily 08:00–21:00, 10-kr fee per travelers check) than at Den Danske Bank (which charges the standard 40-kr minimum or 20-kr-per-check fee for traveler's checks).

While you're in the station, you can reserve an overnight

train seat or *couchette* out (at Rejse-bureau, Mon–Fri 10:00–17:00). International rides and all IC trains require reservations (usually 20 kr). To get to Christianshavn B&Bs, catch bus #8 (4/hrly, in front of station on near side of Bernstorffsgade). Note the time the bus departs, then stop by the TI (across the street) and pick up a free Copenhagen city map that shows bus routes.

By Plane: Copenhagen's International Airport is a traveler's dream, with a TI, bank (standard rates), post office, telephone center, shopping mall, grocery store, and bakery. You can use U.S. dollars at the airport and get change back in kroner (airport info tel. 32 31 24 47 or 32 32 22 12, SAS ticket office 70 10 20 00). Need to kill a night at the airport? Try the fetal rest cabins, called *hvilekabiner* (Sb-360 kr, Db-530 kr for 8 hrs, prices vary for 4- to 16-hr periods, reception open 6:00–22:00, easy telephone reservations, CC:VMA, sauna and showers also available, tel. 32 31 24 55, fax 32 31 31 09).

Getting Downtown from the Airport: Taxis are fast, civil, accept credit cards, and, at about 150 kr to the town center, are a good deal for foursomes. The Air Rail train (18 kr, 3/hrly, 12 min) links the airport with the train station, Norreport, and Osterport. City bus #250s gets you downtown (City Hall Square, TI) in 40 minutes for 18 kr (6/hrly, across the street and to the right as you exit airport). If you're going from the airport to Christianshavn, ride #9 just past Christianshavn Torv and get off before Knippels Bridge.

Helpful Hints

Jazz Festival: The Copenhagen Jazz Festival—10 days starting the first Friday in July (July 6–15 in 2001)—puts the town in a rollicking slide-trombone mood. The Danes are Europe's jazz enthusiasts and this music festival fills the town with happiness. The TI prints up an extensive listing of each year's festival events.

Telephones: Use the telephone liberally. Everyone speaks English, and *This Week* and this book list phone numbers for everything you'll be doing. All telephone numbers in Denmark are eight digits, and there are no area codes. Calls anywhere in Denmark are cheap; calls to Norway and Sweden cost 6 kr per minute from a booth (half that from a private home). Get a phone card (from newsstands, starting at 30 kr).

Pharmacy: Steno Apotek is across from the train station (open 24 hrs daily, Vesterbrogade 6g, tel. 33 14 82 66).

U.S. Embassy: Dag Hammerskjolds Alle 24, tel. 35 55 31 44.

Getting around Copenhagen

By Bus and Subway: A fine bus and subway system called S-tog (Eurail valid on S-tog) makes getting around Copenhagen easy. A 12-kr two-zone ticket (pay as you board) gets you an hour's travel within the center. Consider the blue two-zone *klippekort* (80 kr for 10 one-hour "rides") and the 24-hour pass (70 kr, both sold at stations and the TI). Assume you'll be within the middle two zones. Drivers are patient, have change, and speak English. City maps list bus and subway routes. Locals are friendly and helpful. Copenhagen is a bit torn up as it puts together a slick new subway expansion that will open in a year or two.

By Bus Tour: Open Top Tour buses do a hop-on hop-off 90-minute circle connecting the city's top sights—Tivoli, Royal Palace, National Museum, Little Mermaid, Rosenborg Castle, Nyhavn, and more—with a taped narration (100 kr, 2/hrly, daily 9:00–18:00; you can get off, see a sight, and catch a later bus; bus departs City Hall below Lur Blowers statue or at many other stops throughout city, pay driver, ticket good for 48 hrs; for more information on bus tours, see "Tours of Copenhagen," below).

Budget do-it-yourselfers simply ride city bus #6: from the Carlsberg Brewery, it stops at Tivoli, City Hall, National Museum, Royal Palace, Nyhavn, Amalienborg Castle, Kastellet, and *The Little Mermaid* (12 kr for a stop-and-go hour). The entire tour is described in Use It's *Playtime* magazine.

By Taxi: Taxis are plentiful and easy to call or flag down (22-kr drop charge, then 10 kr per km, CC:VMA). For a short ride, four people spend about the same by taxi as by bus (e.g., 50 kr from train station to Christianshavn B&Bs). Calling 35 35 35 35 will get you a taxi within minutes.

By Bike—Free! Copenhagen's radical "city bike" program is great for sightseers (though bikes can be hard to find at times). From May through November, 1,500 clunky but practical little bikes are scattered around the old-town center (basically the terrain covered in the Copenhagen map in this chapter). Simply locate one of the 150 racks, unlock a bike by popping a 20-kr coin into the handlebar, and pedal away. When you're done, plug your bike back into any other rack and your deposit coin will pop back out (if you can't find a rack, just abandon it and a bum will take it back and pocket your coin). These simple bikes come with "theft-proof" parts (unusable on regular bikes) and—they claim—computer tracer chips embedded in them so bike patrols can retrieve strays. These are constructed with prison labor and funded by advertisements painted on the wheels and by a progressive electorate. Try this once and you'll find Copenhagen suddenly a lot smaller and easier.

For a serious bike tour, rent a more comfortable bike at Central Station's Cykelcenter (50 kr/day, Mon–Fri 8:00–18:00, Sat 9:00–13:00, summer Sun 10:00–13:00, closed Sun off-season, tel. 33 33 86 13). Bikers see more, save time and money, and really feel like temporary locals by doing everything by bike. Consider it.

Tours of Copenhagen
▲**Walking Tours**—Once upon a time, American Richard Karpen visited Copenhagen and fell in love with the city (and one of its

women). He gives daily two-hour walking tours of his adopted hometown covering its people, history, and contemporary scene. Richard offers four entertaining tours: three city walks—each about 1.5 miles with breaks, covering different parts of the historic center—and a Rosenborg Castle tour (city tours depart from TI May–Sept Mon–Sat at 10:30, 50 kr, kids under 12 free; the Rosenborg Castle tour leaves from the castle turnstile at 13:30 Mon and Thu, 100 kr, which includes 50-kr castle admission; pick up schedule at TI or call Richard at 32 84 74 35). Richard has an infectious love of Copenhagen. His tours, while different, complement each other and are of equal "introduction" value.

Bus Tours—A variety of guided bus tours depart from City Hall Square in front of the Palace Hotel. Copenhagen Excursions runs both city tours and jaunts into the countryside (with themes like Vikings, castles, and Legos, tel. 32 54 06 06, www.copenhagen-excursions.dk). Their hop-on hop-off **Open Top Tours** do the basic 90-minute circle of the city sights with a tape-recorded spiel (100 kr, 2/hrly, ticket valid for 48 hrs, departs below Lur Blowers statue to the left of City Hall). One of their HOHO tours includes the Oresund Bridge and Malmo in Sweden—with stops at the Oresund Link exhibition centers on both shores, a chance to enjoy a trip over Europe's new mega-bridge from the windy open top of a double-decker bus, and a narrated swing through Malmo (130 kr, tel. 32 54 06 06). For information on the Oresund Bridge, see page 638.

▲▲Harbor Cruise and Canal Tours—Two companies offer essentially the same live, three-language, 50-minute tours through the city canals (April–late Oct daily 10:00–17:00, later in July, at least 2/hrly, dress warmly—boats are open-top). Both boats leave from near Christiansborg Palace, cruise around the palace and Christianshavn area, and then proceed into the wide-open harbor. It's a relaxing way to see the Mermaid and munch a lazy picnic during the slow-moving narration. The low-overhead 20-kr Netto-Bådene tour boats leave from Holmen's Bridge in front of the palace (wait at the dock where a sign indicates the next departure, tel. 32 54 41 02). The competition, Canal Tours Copenhagen, does the same tour for 50 kr (from Gammel Strand, 200 meters away; and from Nyhavn). They also do a "water bus" hop-on hop-off version (tel. 33 93 42 60). Go with Netto. There's no reason to pay double. Netto boats have no roof (until Sept).

Bike Tours—City Safari offers two-hour guided bike tours of Copenhagen (June–Aug daily 10:00 and 13:00, 150 kr includes bike, in English and Danish as needed, depart near train station's Cykelcenter—ignore the bums, tel. 33 23 94 90, www.citysafari.dk, or ask at Use It; energetic Steen is a one-man show and speaks fine English).

Copenhagen

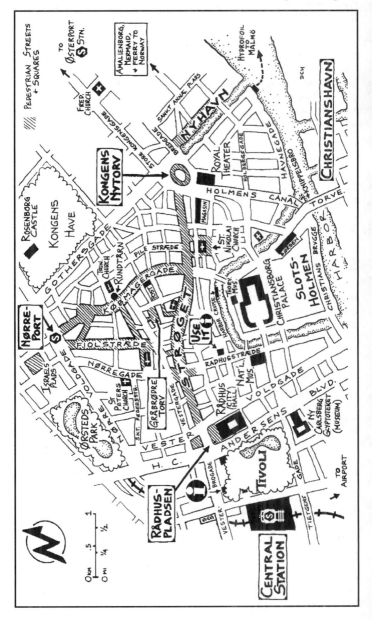

Do-It-Yourself Orientation Walk: "Strøget and Copenhagen's Heart and Soul"

Start from **Rådhuspladsen** (City Hall Square), the bustling heart of Copenhagen, dominated by the spire of City Hall. This was Copenhagen's fortified west end. The king cleverly quelled a French Revolution–type thirst for democracy by giving his people Europe's first great public amusement park. **Tivoli** was built just outside the city walls in 1843. When the train lines came, the station was placed just beyond Tivoli.

Step inside the **City Hall** (Mon–Fri 7:45–17:00—described under "Sights," below). Old **Hans Christian Andersen** sits to the right of City Hall, almost begging to be in another photo (as he did in real life). On a pedestal left of City Hall, note the *Lur Blowers* sculpture. The *lur* is a horn that was used 3,500 years ago. The ancient originals (which still play) are displayed in the National Museum. (City tour buses leave from below these horns.)

The **golden girls** high up on the building on the square opposite the Strøget's entrance tell the weather: on a bike (fair) or with an umbrella. These two have been called the only women in Copenhagen you can trust. Here in the traffic hub of this huge city you'll notice...not many cars. Denmark's 200 percent tax on car purchases makes the bus or bike a sweeter option.

The American trio of Burger King, 7-Eleven, and KFC marks the start of the otherwise charming **Strøget**. Copenhagen's 25-year-old experimental, tremendously successful, and most-copied pedestrian shopping mall is a string of lively (and individually named) streets and lovely squares that bunny-hop through the old town from City Hall to Nyhavn, which is a 15-minute stroll (or "*strøget*") away.

As you wander down this street, remember that the commercial focus of a historic street like Strøget drives up the land value, which generally trashes the charm and tears down the old buildings. While Strøget has become hamburgerized, historic bits and charming pieces of old Copenhagen are just off this commercial cancan.

After one block (at Kattesundet) side trip two blocks left into Copenhagen's colorful **university district**. Formerly the old brothel area, today this "Latin Quarter" is Soho chic. At Studiesstraede turn right and walk two blocks to the big neoclassical church (with John the Baptist up where the Greek mythological gods would normally be). Enter and find statues of Christ and the 12 apostles—masterpieces by the great Danish sculptor Torvaldsen—all looking quite Greek. On the corner across the street from the church you can see how Golden Age Copenhagen (early 1800s) fancied itself a Nordic Athens. To the left is the university. And 300 meters to your right is the Greek Temple–like law courts.

Step into the university (up the middle steps of the big building) into a colorful lobby starring Athena and Apollo. The frescoes celebrate high thinking and themes such as the triumph of wisdom over barbarism. Notice how harmoniously the architecture, sculpture, and painting work together.

Rejoin Strøget (down where you see the law courts) at **Gammel Torv** and **Nytorv** (Old Square and New Square). This was the old town center. The Oriental-looking kiosk was one of the city's first community telephone centers before phones were privately owned—look at the reliefs ringing its top: an airplane with bird wings (c. 1900) and two women talking on the new-fangled phone. (It was thought business would popularize the telephone but actually it was women...Now, 100 years later, look at the cell phones.) The squirting woman and boy on the very old fountain were so offensive to people from the Victorian age that the pedestal was added, raising it—they hoped—out of view.

Walk down Amager Torv to the stately brick Holy Ghost church (note the fine spire, typical of old Danish churches). Under the step gable was a hospital run by monks. A block behind the church (walk down Valkendorfsgade and through a passage under a rust-colored building) is the leafy and caffeine-stained **Gråbrødretorv** (Grey Brothers' Square)—a popular place for an outdoor meal or drink in the summer—surrounded by fine old buildings. At the end of the square, the street Niels Hemmingsens Gade returns (past the Copenhagen Jazz House—good place for live music tonight?) to Strøget. Continue down the pedestrian zone to the next square with the stork fountain.

Amager Torv delights shoppers. Spin around and see Royal Copenhagen Porcelain (with demos), Copenhagen Crystal, George Jensen Jewelry and Silverware, and Illums Bolighus (modern design, Mon–Sat 10:00–18:00, Sun 12:00–17:00). Café Norden is a smoky but good place for a coffee with a view. From here you can see the imposing Parliament building (from where canal boat tours leave). A block toward the canal, running parallel to Strøget, starts Straedet, a second Strøget with cafés, antique shops, and no fast food. In the other direction a broad pedestrian mall leads past the Museum of Erotica to Christian IV's Round Tower.

The final stretch of Strøget leads past **Pistolstræde** (a cute lane of shops in restored 18th-century buildings leading off Strøget to the right from Østergade; wander way back into half-timbered section), McDonald's (good view from top floor), and major department stores (Illum and Magasin—see "Shopping," below) to Kongens Nytorv. **Kongens Nytorv** is the biggest square in town and is home to the Royal Theater, the French Embassy, and the venerable Hotel D'Angleterre. On the right, Hviids Vinstue, the oldest wine cellar in town (from 1723), is a colorful if smoky spot for an open-face sandwich and a beer (Kongens Nytorv 19). The statue in the middle celebrates Christian V who, in the 1670s, extended Copenhagen, adding this "King's

New Square" (Kongens Nytorv). Across the square is a trendy dead-end canal.

Nyhavn, a recently gentrified sailors' quarter, is just opposite Kongens Nytorv. This formerly sleazy harbor is an interesting mix of tattoo parlors, taverns, and trendy cafés lining a canal filled with glamorous old sailboats of all sizes. Any historic sloop is welcome to moor here in Copenhagen's ever-changing boat museum. Hans Christian Andersen lived and wrote his first stories here (in the red double-gabled building on the right).

Continuing north along the harborside (from end of Nyhavn canal, turn left), you'll pass a huge ship that sails to Oslo every evening (at 17:00—see "Transportation Connections"). Follow the waterfront to the modern fountain of Amaliehave Park.

The **Amalienborg Palace and Square** (a block inland, behind the fountain) is a good example of orderly Baroque planning. Queen Margrethe II and her family live in the palace to your immediate left as you enter the square from the harbor side. Her son and heir to the throne, Frederik, recently moved into the palace directly opposite his mother's. While the guards change with royal fanfare at noon only when the queen is in residence, they shower every morning.

Leave the square on Amaliegade, heading north to Kastellet (Citadel) Park and past Denmark's World War II Resistance Museum. A short stroll past the Gefion fountain (showing the mythological story of the goddess who was given one night to carve a chunk out of Sweden to make into Denmark's main island, Zealand—which you're on) and a church built of flint brings you to the overrated, overfondled, and overphotographed symbol of Copenhagen, *Den Lille Havfrue—The Little Mermaid.*

You can get back downtown on foot, by taxi, or on bus #1, #6, or #9 from Store Kongensgade on the other side of Kastellet Park (a special bus may run from the Mermaid in summer).

Sights—Copenhagen

▲**Copenhagen's City Hall (Rådhus)**—This city landmark, between the station/Tivoli/TI and Strøget pedestrian mall, offers private tours and trips up its 350-foot-high tower. It's draped, inside and out, in Danish symbolism. Bishop Absalon (the city's founder) stands over the door. The polar bears climbing on the rooftop symbolize the giant Danish protectorate of Greenland. Step inside. The courtyard is inspired by the city hall in Siena (with the necessary addition of a glass roof). Huge functions fill this grand hall (the square in center is a lift for the necessary furniture, etc.) while the busts of three illustrious local boys— the storyteller Hans Christian Andersen, the sculptor Bertel Thorvaldsen, and the physicist Niels Bohr—look on. Underneath the floor are national archives dating back to 1275—popular with

Danes researching their family roots. The city hall is free and open to the public (Mon–Fri 07:45–17:00). You're welcome to wander throughout the building and into the peaceful garden out back. Guided tours (in English), which get you into more private, official rooms, are dry but interesting (30 kr, 45 min, year-round Mon–Fri at 15:00, Sat at 10:00). Tourists romp up the tower's 300 steps for the best aerial view of Copenhagen (20 kr, Mon–Fri 10:00, 12:00, and 14:00, Sat 12:00; off-season Mon–Sat 12:00; tel. 33 66 25 82). The lobby has racks of tourist information (city maps and *This Week*).

▲▲**Christiansborg Palace**—A complex of government buildings stands on the ruins of Copenhagen's original 12th-century castle: the Parliament, Supreme Court, Prime Minister's headquarters, a slick new library, several museums, and the royal palace.

While the current palace dates only from 1928 and the royal family moved out 200 years ago, it's the third to stand here in 800 years and is rich with tradition. The information-packed 50-minute English language tours of the royal reception rooms are excellent. As you slip-slide on protect-the-floor slippers through 22 rooms, you'll gain a good feel for Danish history, royalty, and politics. (For instance, the family portrait of King Christian IX shows why he's nicknamed the father-in-law of Europe—with children eventually marrying royalty in Russia, Greece, Britain, and Norway.) The highlight is the dazzling new set of tapestries—Danish-designed but Gobelin—made in Paris. This gift, given to the queen on her 60th birthday in 2000, celebrates 1,000 years of Danish history with wild wall-hangings from the Viking age to our chaotic age (admission by tour only, 40 kr, May–Sept daily 11:00, 13:00, and 15:00; Oct–April Tue, Thu, Sat, and Sun 11:00 and 15:00; from the equestrian statue in front, go through the wooden door, past the entrance to the Christiansborg Castle ruins, into the courtyard, and up the stairs on the right; tel. 33 92 64 92).

▲**Christiansborg Castle Ruins**—An exhibit in the scant remains of the first castle built by Bishop Absalon—the 12th-century founder of Copenhagen—lies under the palace. There's precious little to see, but it's old and very well described (20 kr, daily May–Sept 9:30–15:30, closed off-season Mon, Wed, and Sat, good 1-kr guide). Early birds note that this sight opens 30 minutes before other nearby sights.

▲**Thorvaldsen's Museum**—This museum tells the story and shows the dreamy work of the great Danish neoclassical sculptor Bertel Thorvaldsen (1770–1844). Considered Canova's equal among neo-classical sculptors, Thorvaldsen spent 40 years in Rome. He was lured home to Copenhagen with the promise to showcase his work in a fine museum—which opened in the revolutionary year of 1848 as Denmark's first public art gallery (20 kr, Tue–Sun 10:00–17:00, closed Mon, well-described, located in neoclassical building with colorful walls next to Christiansborg Palace, tel. 33 32 15 32).

National Library—Copenhagen's new "Black Diamond" library is a striking black glass building leaning over the harbor at the edge of the palace complex. Wander through the old and new sections, surf the Web (piles of free computers with super Internet connections), read a magazine, or enjoy a classy or cheap lunch (Mon–Sat 8:00–23:00, closed Sun; library hours: Mon–Fri 10:00–19:00, Sat 10:00–14:00).

▲▲▲**National Museum**—Focus on the excellent and curiously enjoyable Danish collection, which traces this civilization from its ancient beginnings. Exhibits are laid out chronologically and described in English. Pick up the museum map. The free (with deposit) headsets describe the highlights but add nothing to the printed descriptions you'll find inside. Start with room #1 (opposite the entrance) and follow the numbers through the "prehistory" section on the ground floor—oak coffins with still-clothed and armed skeletons from 1300 B.C., ancient and still-playable *lur* horns, the 200-year old Gunderstrup Cauldron of art-textbook fame, lots of Viking stuff, and a bitchin' collection of well-translated rune stones. Then go upstairs, find room #101, and carry on—fascinating dirt on the Reformation, everyday town life in the 16th and 17th centuries, and, in room 126, a unique "cylinder perspective" of the royal family (from 1656) and two peep shows. The next floor takes you into modern times (40 kr, Tue–Sun 10:00–17:00, free Wed, closed Mon, mandatory bag check, cafeteria, enter at Ny Vestergade 10, tel. 33 13 38 50).

▲**Ny Carlsberg Glyptotek**—Scandinavia's top art gallery—with especially intoxicating Egyptian, Greek, and Etruscan collections; the best of Danish Golden Age (early 19th century) painting; and a heady, if small, exhibit of 19th-century French paintings (in the new "French Wing," including Géricault, Delacroix, Manet, Impressionists, Gauguin before and after Tahiti)—is an impressive example of what beer money can do. Linger with marble gods under the palm leaves and glass dome of the very soothing winter garden. Designers, figuring Danes would be more interested in a lush garden than classical art, used this wonderful space as leafy bait to cleverly introduce locals to a few Greek and Roman statues. (It works for tourists, too.) One of the original Rodin *Thinkers* (wondering how to scale the Tivoli fence?) is in the museum's backyard. This collection is artfully displayed and thoughtfully described (30 kr, Tue–Sun 10:00–16:00, closed Mon, free Wed and Sun, 2-kr English brochure/guide, classy cafeteria under palms, behind Tivoli, Dantes Plads 7, tel. 33 41 81 41).

▲▲**Rosenborg Castle**—This finely furnished Dutch Renaissance–style castle was built by Christian IV in the early 1600s as a summer castle. Today it houses the Danish crown jewels and 500 years of royal knickknacks, including some great Christian IV memorabilia . . . like the shrapnel he pulled from his eye after a naval battle and made into earrings for his girlfriend. It would be fascinating if anything were explained in English. If you don't want to buy and read the palace guidebook or follow Richard Karpen's guided tour (2/wk, see "Tours of Copenhagen," above), here are a few highlights:

In the Long Hall, the **throne** is made of unicorn horns (actually narwhal tusks from Greenland). Unicorn horn was believed to bring protection from evil and poison. The military themes decorating the room celebrate Danish victories over archenemy Sweden. The delightful **royal porcelain** display in a side room shows off the herbs and vegetables found in the realm.

The **treasury** (downstairs) will dazzle you. The two sparkling saddles were Christian IV's—the first for his coronation, the second for his son's wedding (constructed lavishly when the kingdom was nearly bankrupt to impress visiting dignitaries and bolster Denmark's credit rating). The tall, two-handed, 16th-century coronation sword was drawn by the new king who cut crosses into the air in four directions, symbolically promising to defend the realm from all attacks. See if you can find the golden ring—a gift from a jealous king—with the hand of a promiscuous queen shaking hands with a penis. (Hint: it sits above a brooch of cupid complete with bow and arrow.) Some consider Christian IV's coronation crown (from 1596, 7 pounds of gold and precious stones) the finest Renaissance crown in Europe. It radiates symbolism. Find: the symbols of justice (sword and scales); charity (a woman nursing—meaning the king will love God and his people as a mother loves her child); and fortitude (a woman on a lion with a sword). Climb the footstool to look inside. The shields of various Danish provinces remind the king that he's surrounded by all Denmark. The painting shows the coronation of Christian V at Fredericksburg in 1671 (50 kr, daily May–Sept 10:00–16:00, Oct 11:00–15:00, Nov–April 11:00–14:00,S-train: Nørreport, tel. 33 15 32 86).

▲**Rosenborg Gardens**—The Rosenborg Castle is surrounded by the royal pleasure gardens, a rare plant collection, and, on sunny days, a minefield of sunbathing Danish beauties and picnickers. When the royal family is in residence, there's a daily changing-of-the-guard mini-parade from Rosenborg Castle (at 11:30) to Amalienborg Castle (at 12:00). The King's Rosegarden (across the canal from the palace) is a royal place for a picnic (cheap open-face sandwiches to go at Lorraine's, nearby at the corner of Borgergade and Dronningenstværgade). The fine statue of Hans Christian Andersen in the park, actually erected in his lifetime (and approved by H. C. A.), is meant to symbolize how his stories had a message even for adults.

▲**Denmark's Resistance Museum (Frihedsmuseet)**—The

fascinating story of Denmark's heroic Nazi resistance struggle (1940–1945) is well explained in English (free, May–mid-Sept Tue–Sun 10:00–16:00, closed Mon; off-season Tue–Sun 11:00–15:00; between the Queen's Palace and *The Little Mermaid*, bus #1, #6, or #9, tel. 33 13 77 14). If you're prioritizing, the Resistance Museum in Oslo is more interesting.

▲**Our Savior's (Vor Frelsers) Church**—The church's bright Baroque interior, with the pipe organ supported by the royal elephants, is worth a look (free, helpful English flier, daily 11:00–16:30, Dec–Feb 10:00–15:30, bus #8, tel. 31 57 27 98). The unique spiral spire that you'll admire from afar can be climbed for a great city view and a good aerial view of the Christiania commune below (311 feet high, 400 steps, 20 kr).

Lille Mølle—This tiny intimate museum shows off a 1916 Christianshavn house (40 kr, visits by guided tour only at 13:00, 14:00, 15:00, 16:00, closed Mon; just off south end of Torvgade, tel. 33 47 38 38). A fine café serves light lunches, dinners, and huge weekend brunches in its terrace garden.

Carlsberg Brewery Tour—Denmark's beloved source of legal intoxicants, Carlsberg shows off its plant (with tasting, Mon–Fri 10:00–16:00) and has an old brewery museum (Mon–Fri 10:00–15:00, bus #6 or #18 to Ny Carlsberg Vej 140, tel. 33 27 13 14).

Museum of Erotica—This museum's focus: the love life of *Homo sapiens*. Better than the Amsterdam equivalents, it offers a chance to visit a porno shop and call it a museum. It took some digging, but they've documented a history of sex from Pompeii to present day. Visitors get a peep into the world of 19th-century Copenhagen prostitutes and a chance to read up on the sex lives of Mussolini, Queen Elizabeth, Charlie Chaplin, and Casanova. After reviewing a lifetime of *Playboy* centerfolds, realizing how dull Marilyn Monroe's dress is without her in it, visitors sit down for the arguably artistic experience of watching the "electric *tabernakel*," a dozen silently slamming screens of porn (worth the 65-kr entry fee only if fascinated by sex, daily May–Sept 10:00–23:00, Oct–April 11:00–20:00, a block north of Strøget at Købmagergade 24, tel. 33 12 03 11). For a look at the real thing—unsanitized but free—wander Copenhagen's dreary little red-light district along Istedgade behind the train station.

Hovedbanegården—The great Copenhagen train station is a fascinating mesh of Scandinavian culture and transportation efficiency. Even if you're not a train traveler, check it out (fuller description under "Orientation," above).

Nightlife—For the latest on Copenhagen's hopping jazz scene, inquire at the TI or pick up the "alternative" *Playtime* magazine at Use It. The Copenhagen Jazz House is a good bet for live jazz (around 90 kr, Tue–Thu and Sun at 20:30, Fri–Sat at 21:30, closed Mon, 10 Niels Hemmingsensgade, tel. 33 15 47 00).

Tivoli

The world's grand old amusement park—over 150 years old—
is 20 acres, 110,000 lanterns, and countless ice-cream cones of
fun. You pay one admission price and find yourself lost in a Hans
Christian Andersen wonderland of rides, restaurants, games,
marching bands, roulette wheels, and funny mirrors. Tivoli is
wonderfully Danish. It doesn't try to be Disney (50 kr, April–
late-Sept Sun–Thu 11:00–24:00, Fri–Sat 11:00–01:00, also open
for "Christmas Market" mid-Nov–Dec daily 11:00–22:00—with
ice skating on Tivoli Lake, tel. 33 15 10 01, www.tivoli.dk).
Rides range in price from 10 to 50 kr (180 kr for all-day pass).
All children's amusements are in full swing by 11:30; the rest of
the amusements open by 14:00.

    Entertainment in Tivoli: Upon arrival (through main entry,
on right in shop), pick up a map and events schedule. Take a
moment to sit down and plan your entertainment for the evening.
Events are spread between 15:00 and 23:00; the 19:30 concert in
the concert hall can be free or cost up to 500 kr, depending on the
performer. If the Tivoli Symphony is playing, it's worth paying
for. (Concert hall tickets include your Tivoli entry so purchase
before entering park—box office tel. 33 15 10 12). Free concerts,
mime, ballet, acrobats, puppets, and other shows pop up all over
the park, and a well-organized visitor can enjoy an excitingeven-
ing of entertainment without spending a single kroner. The
children's theater, Valmuen, plays excellent traditional fairy tales
daily at 12:00, 13:00, and 14:00 (13:00 show is in English in
summer). Friday evenings feature a (usually free) rock or pop
show at 22:00. On Wednesday and Saturday at 23:45, fireworks
light up the sky. If catching an overnight train, Tivoli (across from
the station) is the place to spend your last Copenhagen hours.

    Eating at Tivoli: Generally, you'll pay amusement-park prices
for amusement park–quality food inside. **Søcafeen**, by the lake,
allows picnics if you buy a drink. The *pølse* (sausage) stands are
cheap. **Færgekroen** is a good lakeside place for typical Danish food,
beer, and an impromptu sing-along with a bunch of drunk Danes.
The Croatian restaurant, **Hercegovina**, serves a 129-kr lunch buffet
and a 159-kr dinner buffet. For a cake and coffee, consider the
Viften café. **Georg**, to the left of the Concert Hall, has tasty 40-kr
sandwiches and 100-kr dinners (dinner includes glass of wine).

Christiania

In 1971 the original 700 Christianians established squatters'
rights in an abandoned military barracks just a 10-minute walk
from the Danish parliament building. A generation later this "free
city"—an ultra-human mishmash of 1,000 idealists, anarchists,
hippies, dope fiends, nonmaterialists, and people who dream
only of being a Danish bicycle seat—not only survives, it thrives.

This is a communal cornucopia of dogs, dirt, soft drugs, and dazed people, or a haven of peace, freedom, and no taboos, depending on your perspective. Locals will remind judgmental Americans that a society must make the choice: allow for alternative lifestyles...or build more prisons.

For 25 years Christiania was a political hot potato; no one in the Danish establishment wanted it—or had the nerve to mash it. These days Christiania is connecting better with the rest of society—paying its utilities, taxes, and even offering daily walking tours (see below).

Passing under the city gate you'll find yourself on "Pusher Street"...the main drag. This is a line of stalls selling hash, pot, pipes, and souvenirs leading to the market square and a food circus beyond. Make a point of getting past this touristy side of Christiania. You'll find a fascinating ramshackle world of moats and earthen ramparts, alternative housing, unappetizing falafel stands, carpenter shops, hippie villas, children's playgrounds, and peaceful lanes. Be careful to distinguish between real Christianians and Christiania's uninvited guests—motley lowlife vagabonds from other countries who hang out here in the summer, skid row–type Greenlanders, and gawking tourists.

Soft Drugs: While hard drugs are out, hash and pot are sold openly (individual joints—30 kr, senior discounts) and smoked happily. While locals will assure you you're safe within Christiania, they'll remind you that it's risky to take pot out—Denmark is required by Uncle Sam to make a token effort to snare tourists leaving the "free city" with pot. Beefy marijuana plants stand on proud pedestals at the market square. Beyond that an open-air food circus (or the canal-view perch above it, on the earthen ramparts) creates just the right ambience to lose track of time.

Graffiti on the wall declares "a mind is a wonderful thing to waste." If you agree, buy a joint on Pusher Street, buy a drink and light up in a bar that allows smoking, then wander. Find the Manefiskeren (Moonfish) bar...Brueghel 2001. Cap your evening cruising through Tivoli with an ice-cream cone and singing, "Wonderful Wonderful Copenhagen."

Nitty-Gritty: Christiania is open all the time and visitors are welcome (down Prinsessegade behind Vor Frelsers' spiral church spire in Christianshavn). Photography is absolutely forbidden on Pusher Street (if you value your camera, don't even sneak a photo). Otherwise, you're welcome to snap photos, but ask residents before you photograph them. Guided tours are supposed to leave from the front entrance of Christiania at 15:00 (daily June–Aug, 25 kr, in English and Danish, tel. 32 95 65 07 to confirm). Morgenstedet is a good, cheap vegetarian place (left after Pusher Street). Spiseloppen is the classy, good-enough-for-Republicans restaurant (see "Eating," below).

More Sights—Copenhagen

The National Art Museum (Statens Museum for Kunst) fills an impressive building with Danish and European paintings from the 14th century until today. Of most interest is probably the Danish Golden Age of paintings—1800–1850 (40 kr, Tue–Sun 10:00–17:00, closed Mon, Solvgade 48, tel. 33 74 84 94).

The noontime **changing of the guard** at the Amalienborg Palace is boring—all they change is places.

Nyhavn, with its fine old ships, tattoo shops (pop into Tattoo Ole at #17—fun photos, very traditional), and jazz clubs, is a wonderful place to hang out.

The **Round Tower**, built in 1642 by Christian IV, connects a church, library, and observatory (the oldest functioning observatory in Europe) with a ramp that spirals up to a fine view of Copenhagen (15 kr, June–Aug Mon–Sat 10:00–20:00, Sun 12:00–20:00; Sept–May Mon–Sat 10:00–17:00, Sun 12:00–17:00; nothing to see but the ramp and the view, just off Strøget on Købmagergade).

Copenhagen's **Open Air Folk Museum (Frilandsmuseet)** is a park filled with traditional Danish architecture and folk culture (40 kr, March–Sept Tue–Sun 10:00–17:00, closed Mon, shorter hours off-season, outside of town in the suburb of Lyngby, S-train to Lyngby then bus #184 or #194 to museum, tel. 33 13 44 11).

Danes gather at Copenhagen's other great amusement park, **Bakken** (free, April–Aug daily 12:00–24:00, S-train: Klampenborg, then walk 10 minutes through the woods, tel. 39 63 35 44).

For a look at small-town Denmark, consider a trip a few minutes out of Copenhagen to the fishing village of **Dragør** (bus #250s from station 5 stops at Sundbyvesterplads, change to #350s).

Sights near Copenhagen: Oresund Bridge (pron: ora-sohn) is new, and opened in July 2000, connecting Denmark and Sweden. This 10-mile-long link, which has a motorway for cars (230 kr toll) and a two-track train line, is the final section of a grand scheme to tie together the main islands of Denmark with Europe and Sweden. The $4-billion project consists of a 2.5-mile tunnel, a 2.5-mile artificial island called Peberholm, and a 5-mile-long bridge. With speedy connecting trains, Malmo is now an easy half-day side trip by train from Copenhagen and a fun way to slip a taste of Sweden into your visit (60 kr each way, 3/hrly, 35 min). The easiest way to see the bridge and Malmo is on one of Copenhagen's hop-off-hop-on bus tours (described above, on page 627).

The **Oresund Exhibition Center** on the Danish end of the link has a 50-foot-long model of the project with interactive videos and piles of info on the project's environmental impact, cost, and role in this new business zone (20 kr, daily 10:00–17:00, bus #9 from Kongens Nytorv or #250s from City Hall Square, at Kastrup Strandpark 9, tel. 32 50 55 22).

Shopping

Copenhagen's colorful flea market is small but feisty and surprisingly cheap (summer Sat 8:00–14:00 at Israels Plads). An antique market enlivens Nybrogade (near the palace) every Friday and Saturday. For other street markets, ask at the TI.

Shops are open Monday through Friday from 10:00 to 19:00 and Saturday from 9:00 to 16:00. For a street's worth of shops selling "Scantiques," wander down Ravnsborggade from Nørrebrogade.

The city's top department stores (Illum at Østergade 52, tel. 33 14 40 02; and Magasin at Kongens Nytorv 13, tel. 33 11 44 33) are open until 20:00 and offer a good, if expensive, look at today's Denmark. Both are on Strøget and have fine cafeterias on their top floors. The department stores and the Politiken Bookstore on the Rådhus Square have a good selection of maps and English travel guides.

If you buy anything substantial from a shop displaying the Danish Tax-Free Shopping emblem, you can get back 70 percent of the 25 percent VAT (MOMS in Danish). If you have your purchase mailed, the tax can be deducted from your bill. For example: a 1,000-kr sweater includes 250 kr in MOMS tax, of which you can get 143 kr back. The shop gives you the receipt, you turn it in after customs at the airport, and pocket the cash—fast and simple. For details, call 32 52 55 66 (Mon–Fri 7:00–22:00), see *Copenhagen This Week*, or ask a merchant.

Sleeping in Copenhagen
(8 kr = about $1, country code: 45)

Sleep Code: **S** = Single, **D** = Double/Twin, **T** = Triple, **Q** = Quad, **b** = bathroom, **CC** = Credit Card (Visa, MasterCard, Amex). Breakfast is generally included at hotels but not at private rooms or hostels.

I've listed cheap rooms in private homes in great neighborhoods an easy bus ride from the station, the best budget hotels in the center, and a few backpacker dorm options.

Sleeping in Rooms in Private Homes

Lots of travelers seem shy about rooms in private homes. Don't be. They are as private or social as you want them to be, offering great "at home in Denmark" experiences in good neighborhoods for a third the price of hotels. You'll get a key and come and go as you like. Always call ahead—they book in advance. Most are in apartments, run by single professional women supplementing their income. All speak English and afford a fine peek into Danish domestic life. Rooms generally have no sink. While they usually don't include breakfast, you'll have access to the kitchen. If their rooms are booked up, the women can often find you a place with a neighbor. You can trust the quality of their referrals. I almost always sleep in a private home.

Private Homes in Christianshavn

This area is a never-a-dull-moment hodgepodge of the chic, artistic, hippie, and hobo, with beer-drinking Greenlanders littering streets in the shadow of fancy government ministries. Colorful with lots of shops, cafés, and canals, it's an easy 10-minute walk to the center and has good bus connections to the airport and downtown. There's a **Laundromat** just off Christianshavn's main square at Dronningensgade 42. Take buses #8 or #28 to the central station (from just outside the 7-Eleven store); bus #2 to City Hall; and bus #9 to the airport.

Annette and Rudy Hollender enjoy sharing their 300-year-old home with my readers. Even with a long and skinny staircase, sinkless rooms, and two rooms sharing one toilet/shower, it's a comfortable and cheery place to call home (S-300 kr, D-350 kr, T-400 kr, half a block off Torvegade at Wildersgade 19, 1408 Copenhagen K, closed Nov–April, tel. 32 95 96 22, e-mail: hollender@adr.dk).

Chicken's Private Pension Deluxe, run by Morten Frederiksen—a laid-back, ponytailed sort of guy, rents five spacious rooms and two four-bed suites in a mod-funky-pleasant old house. The stairs are steep and the furniture is old-time rustic but elegant. It's a clean, comfy, good look at today's hip Danish lifestyle in a great location right on Christianshavn's main drag (S-225 kr, D-350 kr, T-475 kr, Q-600 kr, extra bed-100 kr, Torvegade 36, tel. 32 95 32 73, cellular 20 41 92 73, e-mail: morten@chickens.dk).

Britta Krogh-Lund rents two spacious doubles in an old, Christianshavn house. This easygoing place faces a peaceful courtyard off a quiet cobbled lane (S-250 kr, D-350 kr, T-450 kr, Amagergade 1c, 1423 Copenhagen K, tel. 32 95 55 85).

South of Christianshavn, **Gitte Kongstad** rents two apartments, each taking up an entire spacious floor in her flat. You'll have a kitchenette, little garden, and your own bike (D-375 kr, extra bed-125 kr, family-friendly, bus #9 or #19 from airport, bus #12 or #13 from station, a 10-minute pedal past Christianshavn to Badensgade 2, 2300 Copenhagen, tel. & fax 32 97 71 97, e-mail: g.kongstad@post.tele.dk). While it's not central, you'll feel at home here and the bike ride into town (or to the beach) is a snap.

Private Rooms a Block from Amalienborg Palace

Amaliegade is a stately cobbled street in a quiet neighborhood (a 10-min walk north of Nyhavn and Strøget). You can look out your window and see the palace guards changing. Many people rent rooms to travelers here.

Puk and Line are artistic and professional women who rent out two rooms in their wonderfully mod and Danish flats: **Puk** (pook) **De La Cour** (D-400 kr with breakfast, kitchen/family room available, Amaliegade 34, fourth floor, tel. 33 12 04 68,

Christianshavn

TO "DOWNTOWN" COPENHAGEN
TO NYHAVN
200 YARDS
BRYGGE
BOR
HAR
TO TRAIN STN.
CHRISTIANS-
GADE
VOR FRELSERS CHURCH
BURMEISTER
PRINSESSE
CHRISTIANIA
"PUSHER" STREET
CHRISTIANS CHURCH
MAIN SQ.
GADE
STRÆDE
STADS-GRAVEN
PATH
VOLD
MEDIEVAL RAMPARTS
DRON-NING-PRIN-
AMAGER
TO AIRPORT

1 HOLLENDER HOUSE
2 BRITTA KROGH-LUND HOUSE
3 CHICKEN'S PRIVATE PENSION DELUXE
4 CAFE WILDER
5 CAFE LUNA
6 RAVELIN RESTAURANT
7 LOVEN & BASTIONEN RESTAURANT

8 SPISELOPPEN RESTAURANT
9 BASE CAMP RESTAURANT
10 BAKERY
11 FAERGE CAFEEN
12 SPICY KITCHEN
13 LAUNDROMAT

e-mail: creme@get2net.dk) and **Line** (lee-nuh) **Voutsinos** (May–Sept only, D-425 kr with breakfast, extra bed-150 kr, Amaliegade 34, third floor, tel. & fax 33 14 71 42). Down the street, **Mrs. Thordahl** also rents rooms (D-350 kr, no breakfast, Amaliegade 26, tel. 33 12 05 78).

Solveig Diderichsen rents three rooms in her comfortable, high-ceilinged, ground-floor apartment home in a quiet embassy/residential neighborhood just past Østre Anlæg park (S-300 kr, D-350 kr, extra bed-125 kr, no breakfast but kitchen access, easy S-tog connection to Østerport station, then a 3-min walk to Upsalagade 26, 2100 Copenhagen Ø, tel. 35 43 39 58, fax 35 43 22 70, cellular 40 11 39 58). Solveig's an avid dogsledder.

If unable to get a place in any of these homes, the TI or Use It would love to send you to one from their stable of locals renting out rooms.

Good Hotels in Central Copenhagen

These are listed in geographical order from the train station. Prices include breakfast unless noted otherwise. All are big and modern places with elevators and smoke-free rooms, and all accept credit cards.

Hotel Nebo, a calm refuge with a friendly welcome and comfy, spacious rooms, is half a block from the station at the start of Copenhagen's sleazy street (S-450/400 kr, Sb-750/660 kr, D-650/510 kr, older Db-860/720 kr, newly renovated Db-990/820 kr, lower prices are for Oct–April, extra bed-250 kr, Istedgade 6, tel. 33 21 12 17, fax 33 23 47 74, e-mail: nebo@email.dk).

Excelsior Hotel is similar but with a little less warmth and slightly higher prices (Sb-995 kr, Db-1,195 kr, a block from station and a block off busy Vesterbrogade at Colbjørnsensgade 4, DK-1652 Copenhagen, tel. 33 24 50 85, fax 33 24 50 87, www .excelsior.dk).

Webers Scandic Hotel, my classiest hotel by the train station, faces busy Vesterbrogade but has a peaceful garden courtyard (nice for breakfast). It has a classy, modern, and inviting interior and generous weekend/summer rates (late June–July and Fri–Sun all year: Sb-795 kr, Db-795/1,100/1,250/1,350 kr depending on size/grade of room; high season: Sb-1,045/1,250 kr, Db-1, 245/1,445 kr; sauna/ exercise room, Vesterbrogade 11B, DK-1620 Copenhagen, tel. 33 31 14 32, fax 33 31 14 41, e-mail: webers.webers@scandic-hotels.com).

Ibsen's Hotel is a newly-renovated 118-room hotel in a charming neighborhood away from the station commotion and a short walk from the old center (Sb-845/945 kr, Db-1,050–1,250 kr, high prices for bigger rooms, they deal on slow days, third person-200 kr, Vendersgade 23, DK-1363 Copenhagen, bus #14, #16, or #40 from the station, or S-train: Nørreport, tel. 33 13 19 13, fax 33 13 19 16, e-mail: hotel@ibsenshotel.dk).

Sophie Amalie Hotel is a classy and modern Danish-style hotel a block from the big cruise-ship harbor and a block from trendy Nyhavn (134 rooms, Sb-700/910/970 kr, Db-1,000/1,110/ 1,170 kr, prices vary with size of room from pretty tight to very spacious, breakfast costs extra here, CC:VMA but pay with cash and get 10 percent off, Sankt Annae Plads 21, tel. 33 13 34 00, fax 33 11 77 07, www.remmen.dk).

Special Cheaper Hotels in Central Copenhagen

Hotel Sankt Jørgen has 19 big, friendly-feeling rooms with plain old wooden furnishings. Brigitte and Susan offer a warm welcome and a great value, though the rooms are musty from smokers (S-475 kr, D-575 kr, special prices promised with this book through 2001, third person-150 kr, 5-bed family rooms, 10 percent less in winter, breakfast served in your room, elevator, a 12-min walk from station or catch bus #13 to first stop after lake,

Copenhagen Hotels

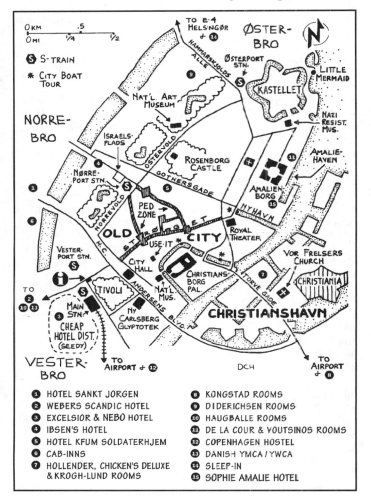

S S-TRAIN

✳ CITY BOAT TOUR

NORRE-BRO

ØSTER-BRO

NAT'L. ART MUSEUM

ISRAELS-PLADS

NORRE-PORT STN.

VESTER-PORT STN.

OLD CITY

USE-IT

CITY HALL

TIVOLI

NAT'L. MUS.

MAIN STN.

CHEAP HOTEL DIST. (SEEDY)

NY CARLSBERG GLYPTOTEK

VESTER-BRO

ROSENBORG CASTLE

GOTHERSGADE

PED ZONE

CHRISTIANS BORG PAL.

AMALIEN BORG

NYHAVN

ROYAL THEATER

VOR FRELSERS CHURCH

CHRISTIANIA

CHRISTIANSHAVN

ØSTERPORT STN.

KASTELLET

LITTLE MERMAID

NAZI RESIST. MUS.

AMALIE-HAVEN

TO E-4 HELSINGØR

TO AIRPORT

TO AIRPORT

DCH

❶ HOTEL SANKT JORGEN	❽ KONGSTAD ROOMS
❷ WEBERS SCANDIC HOTEL	❾ DIDERICHSEN ROOMS
❸ EXCELSIOR & NEBO HOTEL	❿ HAUGBALLE ROOMS
❹ IBSEN'S HOTEL	⓫ DE LA COUR & VOUTSINOS ROOMS
❺ HOTEL KFUM SOLDATERHJEM	⓬ COPENHAGEN HOSTEL
❻ CAB-INNS	⓭ DANISH YMCA / YWCA
❼ HOLLENDER, CHICKEN'S DELUXE & KROGH-LUND ROOMS	⓮ SLEEP-IN
	⓯ SOPHIE AMALIE HOTEL

Julius Thomsensgade 22, DK-1632 Copenhagen V, tel. 35 37 15 11, fax 35 37 11 97, e-mail: st.jorgen@teliamail.dk).

Hotel KFUM Soldaterhjem, originally for soldiers, rents eight singles and two doubles on the fifth floor, with no elevators and a soldier-friendly game room (S-315 kr. S used as D with hide-abed-425 kr, D-480 kr, extra bed-110 kr, no breakfast, Gothersgade 115, Copenhagen K, tel. 33 15 40 44). The reception is on the first floor up (Mon–Fri 8:30–23:00, Sat–Sun 15:00–23:00).

Cab-Inn is a radical innovation: 86 identical, mostly collapsible, tiny but comfy, cruise ship–type staterooms, all bright and shiny with TV, coffeepot, shower, and toilet. Each room has a single bed that expands into a twin with one or two fold-down bunks on the walls. The staff will hardly give you the time of day, but it's tough to argue with this efficiency (Sb-475 kr, Db-585 kr, Tb-695 kr, Qb-805 kr, breakfast 45-kr extra, easy parking-45 kr, CC:VMA, e-mail either mentioned below at cab-inn@cab-inn.dk). There are two virtually identical Cab-Inns in the same neighborhood (a 15-min walk north-west of the station): **Cab-Inn Copenhagen** (Danasvej 32-34, 1910 Frederiksberg C, tel. 33 21 04 00, fax 33 21 74 09) and **Cab-Inn Scandinavia** (its "Commodore" rooms have a real double bed for 100-kr extra, Vodroffsvej 55, tel. 35 36 11 11, fax 35 36 11 14).

Sleeping in Hostels

Copenhagen energetically accommodates the young vagabond on a shoestring. The Use It office is your best source of information. Each of these places charges about 100 kr per person for a bed and breakfast. Some don't allow sleeping bags, and if you don't have your own hostel bedsheet you'll normally have to rent one for around 30 kr. IYHF hostels normally sell noncardholders a "guest pass" for 25 kr.

The modern **Copenhagen Hostel** (IYHF) is huge, with 60 240-kr doubles and five-bed dorms at 90 kr per bed (sheets extra, no curfew, excellent facilities, breakfast not included, cheap meals, self-serve laundry). Unfortunately, it's on the edge of town (30 min from center by bus #250s with change to #100s, Vejlands Alle 200, 2300 Copenhagen S, tel. 32 52 29 08, fax 32 52 27 08, www.danhostel.dk).

The following two big, grungy, central crash pads are open in July and August only: **Danish YMCA/YWCA** (dorm bed-80 kr, 4- to 10-bed rooms, breakfast-25 kr, Valdemarsgade 15, 10-min walk from train station or bus #3, #6, or #16, tel. 33 31 15 74) and **Sleep-In** (80 kr plus 30 kr for sheets, 4- or 6-bed cubicles in a huge 452-bed coed room, no curfew or breakfast, lockers, always has room and free condoms, Blegdamsvej 132, bus #1 or #6 to "Triangle" stop and look for sign, tel. 35 26 50 59).

Sleep-in Green, the "ecological hostel," is very young and cool. It's open all year (85-kr bunks, in a quiet spot a 15-min walk from the center, off Norrebrogade at Ravnsborggade 18, tel. 35 37 77 77).

Eating in Copenhagen

Picnics

Viktualiehandler (small delis) and bakeries, found on nearly every corner, sell fresh bread, tasty pastries (a *wienerbrød* is what we call a "Danish"), juice, milk, cheese, and yogurt (drinkable, in tall liter boxes). **Irma** (in arcade on Vesterbrogade next to Tivoli) and **Brugsen** are the two largest supermarket chains. **Netto** is a cut-rate outfit with the cheapest prices. The little grocery store in the central station is expensive but handy (daily 8:00–24:00).

Smørrebrød

Denmark's 300-year-old tradition of open-face sandwiches survives. Find a *smørrebrød* take-out shop and choose two or three that look good (around 15 kr each). You'll get them wrapped and ready for a park bench. With a cold drink, it makes for a fine, quick, and very Danish lunch. Tradition calls for three sandwich courses: herring first, then meat, then cheese. Downtown you'll find these handy local alternatives to Yankee fast-food chains: **Tria Cafe** (Mon–Fri 8:00–14:00, closed Sat–Sun, Gothersgade 12, near Kongens Nytorv); **Café Halvejen** for sit-down *smørrebrød* (lunch only, on Kristalgade); a place in Nyhavn (corner of Holbergsgade and Peder Skrams Gade); and, my favorite, **Domhusets Smørrebrød** (Mon–Fri 07:00–14:30, Kattesundet 18, tel. 33 15 98 98).

The Pølse

The famous Danish hot dog, sold in *pølsevogn* (sausage wagons) throughout the city, is another typically Danish institution that has resisted the onslaught of our global, Styrofoam-packaged, fast-food culture. Study the photo menu for variations of the Danish hot dog. These are fast, cheap, tasty, and—like their American cousins—almost worthless nutritionally. Even so, what the locals call the "dead man's finger" is the dog kids love to bite.

There's more to getting a *pølse* than simply ordering a hotdog. Employ these handy phrases: *rød* (red, the basic weenie); *medister* (spicy, better quality); *knæk* (short, stubby, tastier than *rød*); *ristet* (fried); *brød* (a bun, usually smaller than the sausage); *svøb* ("swaddled" in bacon); *Fransk* (French style, buried in a long skinny hole in the bun with sauce); and *flottenheimer* (a fat one with onions and sauce). *Sennep* is mustard and *ristet løg* are crispy, fried onions. Wash everything down with a *sodavand* (soda pop).

By hanging around a *pølsevogn* you can study this institution. Denmark's "cold feet cafés" are a form of social care: people who have difficulty finding jobs, such as the handicapped, are licensed to run these wiener-mobiles. As they gain seniority they are promoted to work at more central locations. Danes like to gather here for munchies and *pølsesnak* ("sausage talk"), the local slang for empty chatter.

Inexpensive Restaurants near Strøget

Riz-Raz, around the corner from the canal boat rides at Kompagnistræde 20, serves a healthy all-you-can-eat 49-kr Mediterranean/vegetarian buffet lunch (daily 11:30–17:00) and an even bigger 59-kr dinner buffet (until 24:00, tel. 33 15 05 75). The dinner has to be the best deal in town. And they're happy to serve free water with your meal.

Det Lille Apotek, the "little pharmacy," is a reasonable, candlelit place that's been popular with locals for 200 years (sandwich lunches, traditional dinners for 100–150 kr nightly from 17:30, just off Strøget, between Frue Church and Round Tower at St. Kannikestræde 15, tel. 33 12 56 06). Their specialty is "Stone Beef," a big slab of tender, raw steak plopped down in front of you on a scalding-hot lava stone. Flip it over a few times and it's cooked within minutes.

Den Grimme Aelling is a practical place offering an inviting red meat and salad buffet for 115 kr (daily 12:00–15:00, 17:30–22:30, across from Det Lille Apotek at Store Kannikestraede 19, tel. 33 11 20 30).

Cafe Norden, smoky and very Danish with fine pastries, overlooks Amagertorv by the swan fountain. They have good light meals and salads and great people-watching from window seats on the second floor (order at the bar upstairs).

Grabrodretorv is perhaps the most popular square in the old center for a meal. It's a food circus—especially in good weather. Choose from Greek, Mexican, Danish, or a meal in the old streetcar #14.

At **El Porron**, you'll find good Spanish tapas (Vendersgade 10, a block from Ibsen's Hotel near Norreport).

Department stores serving cheery, reasonable meals in their cafeterias include **Illum** (head to the elegant glass-domed top floor, Østergade 52), **Magasin** (Kongens Nytorv 13), and **Dælls Varehus** (Nørregade 12).

Gammel Strand serves "Danish-inspired French" cuisine and is ideal for a dressy splurge in the old center (3-course menu-300 kr, Mon–Sat 17:30–22:00, closed Sun, reservations wise, across from the canal tour boats at Gammel Strand 42, tel. 33 91 21 21).

To explore your way through a world of traditional Danish food, try a Danish *koldt bord* (an all-you-can-eat buffet). The central station's **Bistro Restaurant** is handy but touristy (150 kr dinner, served daily 11:30–22:00, tel. 33 69 21 12).

Eating in Christianshavn

This neighborhood is so cool, it's worth combining an evening wander with dinner even if you don't live here.

Faerge Cafeen is a fun-loving pub with a local following serving inexpensive traditional Danish specialties indoors or along the canal (daily specials about 70 kr, 17:00–21:00, Strandgade 50, tel. 32 54 46 24).

Twin cafés serve creative and hearty dinner salads by candlelight to a trendy local clientele: **Café Wilder** serves a three-salad plate (61 kr with bread) and a budget dinner plate for around 85 kr (tel. 32 54 71 83). Across the street, **Luna Café** is also good and serves a slower-paced meal. Each are open daily until 24:00 (reservations smart) and located at the corner of Wildersgade and Skt. Annæ Gade, a block off Torvegade.

Ravelin Restaurant, on a tiny island on the big road just south of Christianshavn, serves good and traditional Danish-style food at reasonable prices to happy local crowds. Either dine indoors or on the lovely lakeside terrace (*smørrebrød* lunches 40–100 kr, dinners 100–170 kr, Torvegade 79, tel. 32 96 20 45).

Bastionen & Løven, at the little windmill (Lille Mølle), serves Scandinavian nouveau cuisine on a Renoir terrace or in its Rembrandt interior (55-kr lunch specials, 130–200-kr dinners, 285 kr for 3-course *menu, menu* is small but fresh, Voldgade 50, walk to the end of Torvegade and follow the ramparts up to the restaurant, at south end of Christianshavn, daily 10:00–24:00, tel. 32 95 09 40).

Lagkagehuset, with a big selection of pastries and excellent fresh-baked bread and focaccia, is a great place for breakfast (coffee and pastries for 15 kr, Torvegade 45).

In Christiania, the wonderfully classy **Spiseloppen** (meaning "the flea eats") serves great 120-kr vegetarian meals and 150-kr meaty ones by candlelight. Christiania is the free city/squatter town, located three blocks behind the spiral spire of Vor Frelser's church (restaurant open Tue–Sun 17:00–22:00, closed Mon, on top floor of old brick warehouse, turn right just inside Christiania's gate, reservations often necessary on weekends, tel. 32 57 95 58).

Spicy Kitchen serves cheap and good Bangladeshi food "(56 Torvegade).

Transportation Connections—Copenhagen
By train to: Hillerød/Frederiksborg (6/hrly, 30 min), **Louisiana Museum** (Helsingør train to Humlebæk, 3/hrly, 30 min), **Roskilde** (1–3/hrly, 30 min), **Odense** (2/hrly, 2 hrs), **Helsingør** (ferry to Sweden, 40/day, 50 min), **Stockholm** (5/day, 8 hrs), **Oslo** (4/day, 9 hrs), **Växjö** (via Alvesta, 10/day, 5 hrs), **Kalmar** (10/day, via Alvesta and Växjö, 7 hrs), **Berlin** (via Hamburg, 4/day, 9 hrs), **Amsterdam** (2/day, 11 hrs), **Frankfurt/Rhine** (4/day, 8 hrs). Convenient overnight trains from Copenhagen run directly to Stockholm, Oslo, Amsterdam, and Frankfurt. National train info: tel. 70 13 14 15. International train info: tel. 70 13 14 16. Cheaper bus trips are listed at Use It.

BARCELONA

Barcelona is Spain's second city and the capital of the proud and distinct region of Catalunya. With Franco's fascism now history, Catalunyan flags wave once again. Language and culture are on a roll in Spain's most cosmopolitan and European corner.

Barcelona bubbles with life in its narrow Gothic Quarter alleys, along the grand boulevards, and throughout the chic, grid-planned new town. While Barcelona had an illustrious past as a Roman colony, Visigothic capital, 14th-century maritime power, and, in more modern times, a top Mediterranean trading and manufacturing center, it's most enjoyable to throw out the history books and just drift through the city. If you're in the mood to surrender to a city's charms, let it be in Barcelona.

Planning Your Time

Sandwich Barcelona between flights or overnight train rides. There's little of earth-shaking importance within eight hours by train. It's as easy to fly into Barcelona as into Madrid or Paris for most travelers from the United States. After you visit Barcelona, leave by overnight train (to Madris, Paris, etc.).

On the shortest visit, Barcelona is worth one night, one day, and an overnight train out. Consider starting your visit with an orientation tour on the new Tourist Bus. The Ramblas is two different streets by day and by night. Stroll it from top to bottom at night and again the next morning, grabbing breakfast on a stool in a market café. Wander the Gothic Quarter, see the cathedral, and have lunch in Eixample (eye-SHAM-plah). The top two sights in town, Gaudí's Sacred Family Church and the Picasso Museum, are usually open until 20:00. The illuminated fountains (located on Montjuïc, near Plaça Espanya) are a good finale for your day.

Barcelona

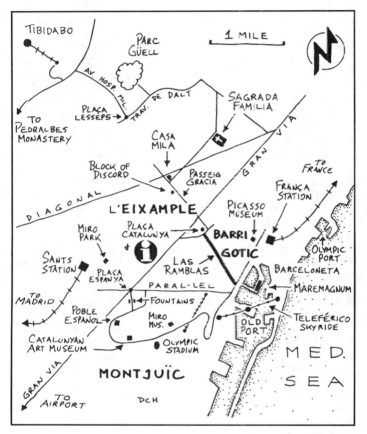

Of course, Barcelona in a day is insane. To better appreciate the city's ample charm, spread your visit over two or three days.

Orientation

Orient yourself mentally by locating these essentials on the map: Barri Gòtic/Ramblas (Old Town), Eixample (fashionable modern town), Montjuïc (hill covered with sights and parks), and Sants Station (train to Madrid). The soul of Barcelona is in its compact core—the Barri Gòtic (Gothic Quarter) and the Ramblas (main boulevard). This is your strolling, shopping, and people-watching nucleus. The city's sights are widely scattered, but with a map and a willingness to figure out the sleek subway system (or a few dollars for taxis), all is manageable.

Tourist Information

There are four useful TIs in Barcelona: at the airport (tel. 93-478-4704), at the Sants train station (near track 6), on Plaça de Catalunya (daily 9:00–21:00, on main square near my hotel recommendations, look for red sign, Gothic Quarter walking tours in English Sat–Sun at 10:00 from TI, 950 ptas, 2 hrs, call to reserve, tel. 93-304-3232; fair rates at TI exchange desk—open daily, room-finding service, half-price ticket booth from 3 hrs before show time), and at Paseo de Gàrcia 107—which covers all Catalunya (Mon–Sat 10:00–19:00, Sun 10:00–13:00, tel. 93-238-4000). Pick up the large city map, brochure on public transport, and the free quarterly "See Barcelona" guide with practical information (museum hours, restaurants, transportation, history, festivals, and so on).

Arrival in Barcelona

By Train: Although many international trains use the França Station, all domestic (and some international) trains use Sants Station. Both França and Sants have baggage lockers and subway stations: França's is "Barceloneta" (2 blocks away), and Sants' is "Sants Estacio" (under the station). Sants Station has a good TI, a world of handy shops and eateries, and a classy "Sala Euromed" lounge for travelers with first-class reservations (quiet, plush, TV, free drinks, study tables, coffee bar). Subway or taxi to your hotel. Most trains to/from France stop at the subway station Passeig de Gràcia, just a short walk from the center (Plaça de Catalunya, TI, hotels).

By Plane: Barcelona's El Prat de Llobregat Airport is 12 kilometers southwest of town and connected cheaply and quickly by Aerobus (immediately in front of arrivals lobby, 4/hrly until 24:00, 20 min to Plaça de Catalunya, buy 500-ptas ticket from driver, tel. 93-412-0000) or by RENFE train (walk the tunnel overpass from airport to station, 2/hrly at :13 and :43, 20 min to Sants Station and Plaça de Catalunya, 335 ptas). A taxi to or from the airport costs under 3,000 ptas. The airport has a post office, pharmacy, left luggage, and ATMs (far-left end of arrival hall as you face the street). Airport info: tel. 93-298-3838.

Getting around Barcelona

Subway: Barcelona's Metro, among Europe's best, connects just about every place you'll visit. It has five color-coded lines (L1 is red, L2 is lilac, L3 is green, L4 is yellow, L5 is blue). Rides cost 150 ptas. A T-1 Card gives you 10 tickets good for the bus or Metro for 825 ptas. Pick up the TI's guide to public transport. One, two, and five-day passes are available.

Hop-on hop-off bus: The handy Tourist Bus (*Bus Turistic*) offers two multi-stop circuits in colorful double decker buses (red route covers north Barcelona—most Gaudí sights, blue route covers south—Barri Gòtic, Montjuïc) with multilingual guides (April–Dec

Pronunciation Guide for Place Names:

Barcelona	barth-ah-LOH-nah
Placa de Catalunya	PLAS-sah duh cat-ah-LOON-yah
Eixample	eye-SHAM-plah
Passeig de Gràcia	PAH-sage duh grass-EE-ah
Catedral	CAH-tah-dral
Barri Gòtic	BAH-ree GAH-zeek
Montjuïc	MOHN-jew-eek

9:00–21:30, buses run every 10–20 min, buy tickets on bus). Ask for a brochure at the TI. The one-day (2,000 ptas) and two-day (2,500 ptas) tickets include discounts on the city's major sights.

Taxis: Barcelona is one of Europe's best taxi towns. Taxis are plentiful and honest (300-ptas drop charge, 110 ptas/km, extras posted in window). Save time by hopping a cab (Ramblas to Sants Station—600 ptas, luggage—100 ptas/piece).

Helpful Hints

Theft Alert: Barcelona feels safer than it did. Still, you're more likely to be pickpocketed here—especially on the Ramblas—than about anywhere in Europe. Be on guard. Leave valuables in your hotel. Keep no money in your pockets. If you stop for any show or commotion on the Ramblas, put your hands in your pockets before someone else does.

American Express: Amex offices are at Paseo de Gràcia 101 (Mon–Fri 9:30–18:00, Sat 10:00–12:00, tel. 93-415-2371, Metro: Diagonal) and at La Ramblas 74 opposite the Liceu Metro station (daily 9:00–24:00, tel. 93-301-1166).

U.S. Consulate: Passeig Reina Elisenda 23 (tel. 93-280-2227).

Emergency Phone Numbers: Police–092, Emergency–061.

Pharmacy: At the corner of Ramblas and Carrer de la Porta-ferrissa (daily 9:00–22:00, 24-hour info line: tel. 010).

Local Guides: The Barcelona Guide Bureau is a co-op with plenty of excellent local guides who give personalized four-hour tours for 25,000 ptas (Via Laietana 54, tel. 93-310-7778).

Internet Access: A handy choice among the many Internet cafés is Cybermundo Internet Center, a block off Plaça de Catalunya (daily 9:00–24:00, no line likely in morning, Carrer Bargara 3, tel. 93-317-7142).

Language: Although Spanish is understood here (and the basic survival words are the same), Barcelona speaks a different language—Catalan. (Most place-names in this chapter are listed in Catalan.) Here are the essential Catalunyan phrases:

Hello	*Hola*	(OH-lah)
Please	*Si us plau*	(see oos plow)

Thank you	*Gracies*	(GRAH-see-es)
Goodbye	*Adeu*	(ah-DAY-oo)
Exit	*Sordida*	(sor-DEE-dah)
Long live Catalunya!	*Visca Catalunya!*	(BEE-skah . . .)

Introductory Walk: From Plaça de Catalunya down the Ramblas

A ▲▲▲ sight, Barcelona's central square and main drag exert a powerful pull as many visitors spend a major part of their time here doing laps on the Ramblas. Here's an orientation walk:

Plaça de Catalunya—This vast central square—littered with statues of Catalunyan heroes—divides old and new Barcelona and is the hub for the Metro, bus, airport shuttle, and both hop-on and hop-off buses (red/northern route leaves from El Corte Inglés, blue/southern route from west side of Plaça). The grass around its fountain is the best public place in town for serious necking. Overlooking the square, the huge El Corte Inglés department store offers everything from bonsai trees to a travel agency, plus one-hour photo developing, haircuts, and cheap souvenirs (Mon–Sat 10:00–21:30, closed Sun, supermarket in basement, ninth-floor terrace cafeteria with great city view—take elevator from near entrance, tel. 93-306-3800). Four great boulevards start here: the Ramblas, the fashionable Passeig de Gràcia, the cozier but still fashionable Rambla Catalunya, and the stubby, shop-filled, pedestrian-only Portal de L'Angel. Homesick Americans even have a Hard Rock Café. Locals traditionally start or end a downtown rendezvous at the venerable Café Zurich. Cross the street from the café to reach . . .

Ramblas Walk Stop #1: The Top of the Ramblas—Begin your ramble 20 meters down at the ornate fountain (near #129). Grab a chair—a man will collect 50 ptas—and observe.

More than a Champs-Élysées, this grand boulevard takes you from rich at the top to rough at the port in a one-mile, 20-minute walk. You'll raft the river of Barcelonan life past a grand opera house, elegant cafés, plain prostitutes, pickpockets, con men, artists, street mimes, an outdoor bird market, great shopping, and people looking to charge more for a shoeshine than you paid for the shoes. When Hans Christian Andersen saw this street he wrote there's no doubt Barcelona is a great city.

Rambla means "stream" in Arabic. The Ramblas used to be a drainage ditch along the medieval wall that once defined what's now called the Gothic Quarter. The boulevard consists of five separately named segments, but address numbers treat it as a single mile-long street.

Open up your map and read some history into it: You're about to walk right across medieval Barcelona from Plaça de Catalunya to the harbor. Notice how the higgledy-piggledy street plan of the medieval town was contained within the old town walls—now gone but traced by a series of roads named Ronda (meaning "to go around"). Find the Roman town, occupying about 10 percent of what became the medieval town—with tighter roads yet around the cathedral. The sprawling modern grid plan beyond the Ronda roads is from the 19th century. Breaks in this urban waffle show where a little town was consumed by the growing city. The popular Passeig de Gràcia boulevard was literally the road to Gràcia (once a town, now a characteristic Barcelona neighborhood).

"Las Ramblas" is plural, a succession of streets. You're at Rambla Canaletes, named for the fountain. The black and gold **Fountain of Canaletes** is the beginning point for celebrations and demonstrations. All along the Ramblas you'll see newspaper stands (open 24 hours, selling phone cards) and ONCE booths (selling lottery tickets which support Spain's organization of the blind, a powerful advocate for the needs of disabled people).

Got some change? As you wander downhill, drop coins into the cans of the human statues (the money often kicks them into entertaining gear). Warning: Wherever people stop to gawk, pickpockets are at work.

Walk 100 yards downhill to #115 and...

Ramblas Walk Stop #2: Rambla of the Little Birds—Traditionally kids bring their parents here to buy pets (especially on Sundays). Apartment dwellers find birds, turtles, and fish easier to handle than dogs and cats. Balconies with flowers are generally living spaces, those with air-conditioning are generally offices. The Academy of Science's clock (#115) marks official Barcelona time—synchronize. The supermarket (#113) has cheap groceries and a handy deli with cooked food to go. Across the street, 50 meters behind the big modern Citadines Hotel, is a park with a newly discovered **Roman necropolis** (worth a look). Local apartment dwellers blew the whistle on local contractors who hoped they could finish their building before anyone noticed the antiquities they had unearthed. Imagine the tomb-lined road leading into the Roman city of Barcino 2,000 years ago.

Another hundred yards takes you to #109, Carrer del Carme, and...

Ramblas Walk Stop #3: Baroque Church—The big plain church lining the boulevard is Baroque, rare in Barcelona. While Barcelona's Gothic age was rich (with buildings to prove it), the Baroque age hardly left a mark (the city's importance dropped when New World discoveries shifted lucrative trade to ports on the Atlantic). The Bagues jewelry shop across Carrer del Carme from the church is known for its Art Nouveau jewelry (from the molds of Masriera, displayed in the window). At the shop's side entrance, step on the old-fashioned scales (free, in kilos) and head down the lane opposite (behind the church, 30 meters) to a place

From Plaça de Catalunya down the Ramblas

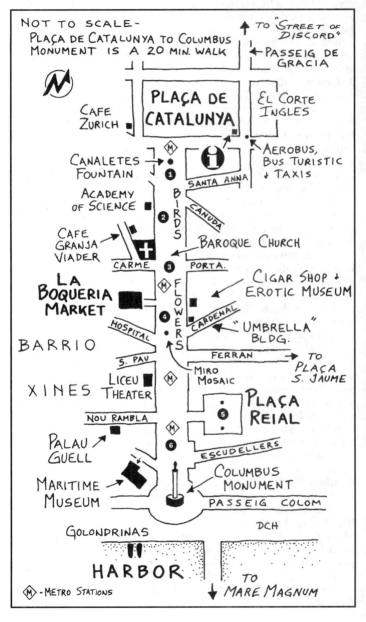

NOT TO SCALE -
PLAÇA DE CATALUNYA TO COLUMBUS
MONUMENT IS A 20 MIN. WALK

TO "STREET OF DISCORD"

← PASSEIG DE GRACIA

CAFE ZURICH

PLAÇA DE CATALUNYA

EL CORTE INGLES

CANALETES FOUNTAIN

SANTA ANNA

Aerobus, Bus Turistic & Taxis

ACADEMY OF SCIENCE

BIRDS

CANUDA

CAFE GRANJA VIADER

BAROQUE CHURCH

CARME

PORTA.

CIGAR SHOP & EROTIC MUSEUM

LA BOQUERIA MARKET

FLOWERS

CARDENAL

"UMBRELLA" BLDG.

HOSPITAL

BARRIO

S. PAU

FERRAN

TO PLAÇA S. JAUME

XINES

LICEU THEATER

MIRO MOSAIC

PLAÇA REIAL

NOU RAMBLA

PALAU GUELL

ESCUDELLERS

COLUMBUS MONUMENT

MARITIME MUSEUM

PASSEIG COLOM

GOLONDRINAS

DCH

Ⓜ - METRO STATIONS

HARBOR

TO MARE MAGNUM

expert in making you heavier. Café Granja Viader (see "Eating," below) has specialized in baked and dairy delights since 1870.

Stroll through the Ramblas of Flowers to the subway stop marked by the red M (near #100), and . . .

Ramblas Walk Stop #4: La Boqueria—This lively produce market is an explosion of chicken legs, bags of live snails, stiff fish, delicious oranges, and sleeping dogs (#91, Mon–Sat 8:00–20:00, best mornings after 9:00, closed Sun). The Conserves shop sells 25 kinds of olives (straight in, near back on right, 100-gram minimum, 40–70 ptas). Full legs of ham (*jamón serrano*) abound; *Paleta Iberica de Bellota* are best and cost about 20,000 ptas ($110) each. Beware: *Huevos de toro* are bull testicles—surprisingly inexpensive . . . but oh so good. Drop by Mario and Alex's Café Central for an *espresso con leche* (far end of main aisle on left) or breakfast. Ask for Mario's "breakfast special" (potato omelet with whatever's fresh).

Further down the Ramblas at #83, the Art Nouveau Escriba Café—an ornate world of pastries, little sandwiches, and fine coffee—still looks like it did on opening day in 1906 (daily 8:30–21:00, indoor/outdoor seating, tel. 93-301-6027).

The **Museum of Erotica** (1,000 ptas, daily 10:00–24:00, across from market at #96) is your standard European sex museum—neat if you like nudes and a chance to hear phone ssssex in four languages.

At #100, Gimeno sells cigars (appreciate the dying art of cigar boxes). Go ahead . . . buy a Cuban cigar (singles from 100 ptas). Tobacco shops sell stamps.

Walk past **Liceu Theater** (reopened after a 1994 fire, tickets on sale 14:00–20:30, tel. 90-233-2211) to #46; turn left down an arcaded lane to a square filled with palm trees . . .

Rambla Walk Stop #5: Plaça Reial—This elegant neoclassical square comes complete with old-fashioned taverns, modern bars with patio seating, a Sunday coin and stamp market (10:00–14:00), Gaudí's first public works (the 2 helmeted lampposts), and characters who don't need the palm trees to be shady. **Herbolari Ferran** is a fine and aromatic shop of herbs, with fun souvenirs such as top-quality saffron or "safra" (Mon–Sat 9:30–14:00, 16:30–20:00, closed Sun, downstairs at #18 Placa Reial). The small streets stretching toward the water from the square are intriguing, seedy, and dangerous.

Back across the Ramblas, the **Palau Güell** offers an enjoyable look at a Gaudí interior (400 ptas, usually open Mon–Sat 10:00–13:00, 16:00–19:00, Carrer Nou de la Rambla 3–5, tel. 93-317-3974). If you'll see Casa Milà, skip the climb to this rooftop.

Farther downhill, on the right-hand side, is . . .

Ramblas Walk Stop #6: Chinatown—This is the world's only Chinatown with nothing even remotely Chinese in or near it. Named for the prejudiced notion that Chinese immigrants go hand in hand with poverty, prostitution, and drug dealing, the actual inhabitants are poor Spanish, Arab, and Gypsy people. At night the Barri Xines features prostitutes, many of them transvestites, who cater to sailors wandering up from the port. A nighttime visit gets you a street-corner massage—look out.

Ramblas Sights at the Harbor

Columbus Monument (Monument a Colóm)—Marking the point where the Ramblas hits the harbor, this 50-meter-tall monument built for an 1888 exposition offers an elevator-assisted view from its top (250 ptas, daily 9:00–20:30, off-season 10:00–13:30, 15:30–19:30, the harbor cable car offers a better—if less handy—view). It's interesting that Barcelona would so honor the man whose discoveries ultimately led to its downfall as a great trading power. It was here in Barcelona that Ferdinand and Isabel welcomed Columbus home after his first trip to America.

Maritime Museum (Museo Maritim)—This museum—housed in the old royal shipyards—covers the salty history of ships and navigation from the 13th to 20th centuries. Its 45-minute infrared multimedia tour (delivered in English via headphone) shows off the Catalunyan role in the development of maritime technology (e.g., the first submarine was Catalunyan). With fleets of seemingly unimportant replicas of old boats explained in Catalan and Spanish, landlubbers may find it dull (800 ptas, daily 10:00–19:00, closed Mon off-season).

Golondrinas—Little tourist boats at the foot of the Columbus Monument make half-hour harbor tours (290 ptas across harbor or 485 ptas round-trip, 11:00–20:00). Consider this ride or the harbor steps here for a picnic.

La Rambla de Mar—This "Rambla of the Sea" is a modern extension of the boulevard into the harbor. A popular wooden pedestrian bridge—with waves like the sea—leads to Maremagnum, a soulless Spanish mall with a cinema, huge aquarium, restaurants, and piles of people out for the night.

Sights—Gothic Quarter (Barri Gòtic)

The Barri Gòtic is a bustling world of shops, bars, and nightlife packed between hard-to-be-thrilled-about 14th- and 15th-century buildings. The area around the port is seedy. But the area around the cathedral is a tangled yet inviting grab bag of undiscovered courtyards, grand squares, schoolyards, Art Nouveau storefronts, baby flea markets, musty junk shops, classy antique shops, street musicians strumming Catalunyan folk songs, and balconies with domestic jungles behind wrought-iron bars. Go on a cultural scavenger hunt. Write a poem.

▲**Cathedral**—As you stand in the square facing the cathedral, you're facing what was Roman Barcelona. To your right, letters spell out BARCINO—the city's Roman name. The three towers

Barcelona's Gothic Quarter

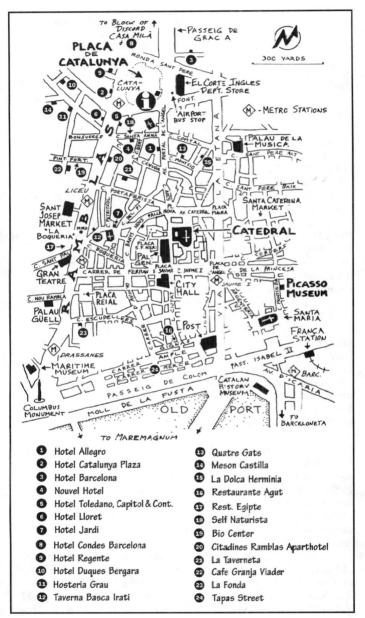

❶	Hotel Allegro	⓭	Quatre Gats
❷	Hotel Catalunya Plaza	⓮	Meson Castilla
❸	Hotel Barcelona	⓯	La Dolca Herminia
❹	Nouvel Hotel	⓰	Restaurante Agut
❺	Hotel Toledano, Capitol & Cont.	⓱	Rest. Egipte
❻	Hotel Lloret	⓲	Self Naturista
❼	Hotel Jardi	⓳	Bio Center
❽	Hotel Condes Barcelona	⓴	Citadines Ramblas Aparthotel
❾	Hotel Regente	㉑	La Taverneta
❿	Hotel Duques Bergara	㉒	Cafe Granja Viader
⓫	Hosteria Grau	㉓	La Fonda
⓬	Taverna Basca Irati	㉔	Tapas Street

on the building to the right are mostly Roman (wander inside for good Roman Wall views).

The colossal **cathedral**—started in about 1300—took 600 years to complete. Rather than stretching toward heaven, it makes a point to be simply massive (similar to the Gothic churches of Italy). The west front, while built according to the original plan, is only 100 years old (cathedral 8:00–13:30, 16:00–19:30; cloisters 9:00–13:00, 16:00–19:00; tel. 93-315-1554).

The spacious interior—characteristic of Catalunyan Gothic—was supported by buttresses. These provided walls for 28 richly ornamented chapels. While the main part of the church is fairly plain, the chapels—sponsored by local guilds—show great wealth. Located in the community's most high-profile space, they provided a kind of advertising to illiterate worshippers. Find logos and symbols of the various trades represented. The Indians Columbus brought to town were supposedly baptized in the first chapel on the left.

The **chapels** ring a finely carved 15th-century choir (*coro*). Pay 125 ptas for a close-up look (with the lights on) at the ornately carved stalls and the emblems representing the various Knights of the Golden Fleece who once sat here. The chairs were folded up, giving VIPs stools to lean on during the standing parts of the mass. Each was creatively carved and—since you couldn't sit on sacred things—the artists were free to enjoy some secular fun here. Study the upper tier of carvings.

The **high altar** sits upon the tomb of Barcelona's patron saint, Eulalia. She was a 13-year-old local girl tortured 13 times by Romans for her faith and finally crucified on an X-shaped cross. Her X symbol is carved on the pews.

Ride the **elevator** to the roof and climb a tight spiral staircase up the spire for a commanding view (200 ptas, Mon–Fri 10:30–12:30, 16:30–18:30, start from chapel left of high altar).

Enter the **cloister** (through arch, right of high altar). In the cloister, look back at the arch, an impressive mix of Romanesque and Gothic. A tiny statue of St. George slaying the dragon stands in the garden. Jordi (George) is the patron saint of Catalunya and by far the most popular boy's name here. While cloisters are generally found in monasteries, this church added it to accommodate more chapels—good for business. Again, notice the symbols of the trades or guilds. Even the pavement is filled with symbols—similar to Americans getting their name on a brick for helping to pay for something.

Long ago the resident geese—there's always 13 in memory of Eulalia—functioned as a sophisticated alarm system. Any commotion would get them honking, alerting the monk in charge.

From St. Jordi, circle to the right (past a WC). The skippable little 100-ptas **museum** (far corner) is one plush room with a dozen

Barcelona's Cathedral

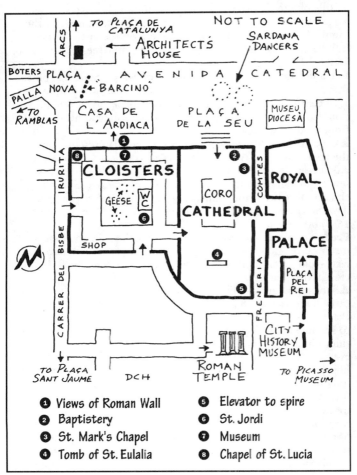

TO PLAÇA DE CATALUNYA

NOT TO SCALE

ARCS

ARCHITECT'S HOUSE

SARDANA DANCERS

BOTERS PLAÇA A V E N I D A C A T E D R A L

PALLA

NOVA "BARCINO"

TO RAMBLAS

CASA DE L'ARDIACA

PLAÇA DE LA SEU

MUSEU DIOCESÀ

CLOISTERS

IRURITA

CORO

ROYAL

GEESE W C

CATHEDRAL

COMTES

SHOP

PALACE

CARRER DEL BISBE

PLAÇA DEL REI

FRENERIA

TO PLAÇA SANT JAUME

DCH

ROMAN TEMPLE

CITY HISTORY MUSEUM

TO PICASSO MUSEUM

1 Views of Roman Wall
2 Baptistery
3 St. Mark's Chapel
4 Tomb of St. Eulalia
5 Elevator to spire
6 St. Jordi
7 Museum
8 Chapel of St. Lucia

old religious paintings. In the corner the dark, barrel-vaulted Romanesque Chapel of Santa Lucia was a small church predating the cathedral and built into the cloister. The candles outside were left by people hoping for good eyesight (Santa Lucia's specialty). Farther along, the Chapel of Santa Rita (in charge of impossible causes) usually has the most candles. Complete the circle and exit at the door just before the place you entered.

Walk uphill, following the church. From the end of the apse turn right 50 meters up Carrer del Paradis to the **Roman**

Temple (Temple Roma d' August). In the corner a sign above a millstone in the pavement marks "Mont Tabor, 16.9 meters." Step into the courtyard for a peek at a surviving corner of the imposing temple which once stood here on the city's highest hill, keeping a protective watch over Barcino (free, 10:00–14:00, 16:00–20:00).

Plaza del Rei—The Royal Palace sat on King's Square (a block from the cathedral) until Catalunya became part of Spain in the 15th century. Then it was the headquarters of the local inquisition. Columbus came here to show King Ferdinand his souvenirs from what he thought was India.

▲**City History Museum**—After a multimedia presentation on the history of the city, an elevator takes you down 20 meters (and 2,000 years) to walk the streets of Roman Barcelona. You'll see sewers, models of domestic life, and bits of an early Christian church. Nearly nothing remains of the Royal Palace (700 ptas, Tue–Sat 10:00–20:00, Sun 10:00–14:00, closed Mon and 14:00–16:00 off-season).

Frederic Mares Museum—This classy collection combines medieval religious art with a quirky bundle of more modern artifacts—old pipes, pinups, toys, and so on (Tue–Sun 10:00–15:00, closed Mon, between Plaza del Rei and cathedral).

▲**Sardana Dances**—The patriotic Sardana dances are held at the cathedral (often at 18:00 on Sat and most Sun at 12:00) and at Plaça de Sant Jaume (often at 18:00 Sun). Locals of all ages seem to spontaneously appear. They gather in circles after putting their things in the center—symbolic of community and sharing (and the ever-present risk of theft). Then they raise and hold hands as they hop and sway gracefully to the band. The band (*cobla*) consists of a long flute, tenor and soprano oboes, strange-looking brass instruments, and a tiny bongolike drum (*tambori*). The rest of Spain mocks this lazy circle dance, but it is a stirring display of local pride and patriotism.

Shoe Museum (Museu del Calcat)—Shoe lovers enjoy this two-room shoe museum (with a we-try-harder attendant) on the delightful Plaça Sant Felip Neri (200 ptas, Tue–Sun 11:00–14:00, closed Mon, 1 block beyond outside door of cathedral cloister, behind Plaça de G. Bachs). The huge shoe at the entry is designed to fit the foot of the Columbus memorial at the bottom of the Ramblas.

Plaça de Sant Jaume—On this stately central square of the Gothic Quarter, two of the top governmental buildings in Catalunya face each other: the Barcelona city hall (Ajuntament, free, Sat–Sun 10:00–14:00) and the seat of the autonomous government of Catalunya (Palau de la Generalitat). Sardana dances take place here many Sundays at 18:00 (see "Sardana Dances," above).

▲▲▲**Picasso Museum**—This is the best collection of Picasso's

(1881–1973) work in Spain, and the best collection of his early works anywhere. It's scattered through two Gothic palaces, six blocks from the cathedral.

Picasso's personal secretary, Sabartes, amassed a huge collection of his work and bequeathed it to the city. Picasso, happy to have a fine museum showing off his work in the city of his youth, added to the collection throughout his life. (Sadly, since Picasso vowed never to set foot in a fascist Spain, and he died 2 years before Franco, the artist never saw the museum.)

This is a great chance to see Picasso's earliest art and better understand his genius (725 ptas, Tue–Sat 10:00–20:00, Sun 10:00–15:00, closed Mon, free and required bag check, Montcada 15–19, Metro: Jaume, tel. 93-319-6310).

There's no English information inside but the art is presented chronologically. If you follow the rooms in numerical order and take this quick room-by-room tour, you can see Picasso's art evolve:

Room 4 (1895): With this earliest art, a budding genius emerges at age 12.

Room 6 (1896): Pablo moves to Barcelona and gets serious about art. The portraits (left as you enter, Padre del Artista) are of Pablo's first teacher, his father. The glass case is filled with what you do at art school. Every time Pablo starts breaking rules, he's sent back to the standard classic style.

Room 9 (1896)—reached through room 4: More school assignments. The goal: Sketch models to capture human anatomy accurately.

Room 10 (1896): On the left you see three self-portraits with a self-awareness of his genius showing in his eyes. The woman (Retrato de la Madre del Artista) is Pablo's mother. Fifteen-year-old Pablo is working on the fine details and gradients of white in her blouse. Pablo was closer to his mom than his dad. Spaniards keep both parents' surnames: Pablo Ruiz Picasso. Eventually he kept just his mom's name.

Room 11: During a short trip to Málaga, Picasso dabbles in Impressionism (unknown in Spain at the time).

Room 12: As a 15-year-old, Pablo does his first big painting for a fine-arts exhibition in Barcelona. While forced to show a religious subject (First Communion), Pablo uses it as an excuse to paint his family.

Room 13: *Science and Charity*, a prize-winning fine-arts exhibition piece, got Picasso the chance to study in Madrid. His little sister (perhaps portrayed in the arms of the nun) had just died. Here for the first time we see Picasso conveying real feeling. The doctor (Pablo's father) represents science. The nun represents charity and religion. But nothing can help and the woman is clearly dead (notice her face and lifeless hand). Pablo painted a little trick: Notice how the bed stretches and shrinks as you walk across the room. Four small studies for this painting hang in the back of the room.

Room 14: Fine-arts school in stuffy Madrid was boring. But Pablo enjoyed hanging out in the Prado Gallery and copying the masters (such as Velázquez' portrait of Phillip IV).

Room 15 (1900): Back in Barcelona, Art Nouveau is the rage. Upsetting his dad, Pablo quits art school and falls in with the avant-garde crowd. These bohemians congregate daily at the Four Cats (slang for "a few crazy people"—see "Eating," below). Declaring his artistic freedom, we see portraits of his new friends and nothing more of his family.

Room 17 (1900): Picasso goes to Paris, a city bursting with life, light, and love.

Room 18: Dropping the surname Ruiz, Pablo establishes his commercial brand name: "Picasso." Here we see the explorer Picasso befriending prostitutes and painting like Toulouse-Lautrec. La Espera (Margot)—with her bold outline and strong gaze—pops out from the Impressionistic background. Painting a dwarf (La Nana), Picasso, like Velázquez and Toulouse-Lautrec, sees "the beauty in ugliness."

Room 19 (1902): The bleak weather and poverty Picasso experienced in Paris leads to his "Blue Period." For three years he cranks out piles of blue art just to stay housed and fed. With blue—the coldest color—backgrounds and depressing subjects, this period was revolutionary in art history. Now the artist is painting not what he sees but what he feels.

Room 20 (1902)—across the hall, through two glass doors: Back home in Barcelona, Picasso paints his hometown at night from rooftops (Terrats de Barcelona). Still blue, here we see proto-cubism . . . five years before the first real cubist painting. The woman in pink (Retrato de la Sra. Canals), painted with classic "Spanish melancholy," finally lifts Picasso out of his funk, replacing the blue period with the happier pink period (of which this museum has only one painting).

Room 21 (1917): Jumping 15 years, we see Picasso is a painter of many styles. In the age of the camera, the cubist gives just the basics (a man with a bowl of fruit) and lets you finish it. We see a little post-Impressionistic Pointillism and a portrait look-ing like a classical statue (inspired by a trip to Rome). The chrome-framed painting of a spool of cable (between the information sheets on the wall) is remarkably realistic. The expressionist horse sym-bolizes to Spaniards the innocent victim. In bullfights, the horse—with blinders and pummeled by the bull—has nothing to do with the fight. Picasso used the horse—guts spilling out near the bull's horn—to show the suffering of war. (This shows up again in his future masterpiece, *Guernica*, which you can see in Madrid.)

Room 22 (1957): Notice the print of Velázquez' *Las Meninas* to the left of the doorway. Picasso, who had great respect for Velázquez, painted 60 interpretations of the painting many consider the greatest painting by anyone ever (it's in Madrid's Prado). In the big black-and-white canvas, Picasso plays with perspectives within the painting. The king and queen (reflected in the mirror in the back of the room) are hardly seen while the self-portrait of the painter towers above everyone. The two women of the court on the right look like they're in a tomb—but they're wearing party shoes. In this room and room 23, see the fun Picasso had playing paddleball with Velázquez' masterpiece.

Rooms 24 and 26 (1957): All his life Picasso said, "Paintings are like windows open to the world." Here we see the French Riviera. As a child, Picasso was forced to paint as an adult. Now, at age 60 (with little kids of his own and an also-childish artist Matisse for a friend), he paints like a child.

To exit, hike up the stairs through rooms 28 to 32 and lots of Picasso etchings and engravings, and out.

Textile and Garment Museum (Museu Textil i de la Indumentaria)—If fabrics from the 4th to 16th centuries leave you cold, have a *café con leche* on the museum's beautiful patio (museum, 400 ptas, Tue–Sat 10:00–20:00, Sun 10:00–15:00, closed Mon, patio is outside the museum but within the walls, 30 meters from Picasso Museum at Montcada 12–14).

▲▲Catalana Concert Hall (Palau de la Música Catalana)— This concert hall, finished in 1908, features the best moderniste interior in town. Inviting arches lead you into the 2,000-seat hall. A kaleidoscopic skylight features a choir singing around the sun while playful carvings and mosaics celebrate music and Catalunyan culture. Admission is by tour only, and starts with a relaxing 20-minute video (700 ptas, 1 hr, in English, daily on the hour 10:00–15:00, maybe later, tel. 93-268-1000). Ask about concerts (300 per year, inexpensive tickets).

Sights—Eixample

Uptown Barcelona is a unique variation on the common grid-plan city. Barcelona snipped off the building corners to create light and spacious eight-sided squares at every intersection. Wide sidewalks, hardy shade trees, chic shops, and plenty of Art Nouveau fun make the Eixample a refreshing break from the Old Town. For the best Eixample example, ramble Rambla Catalunya (unrelated to the more famous Ramblas) and pass through Passeig de Gràcia (described below, Metro: Passeig de Gràcia for Block of Discord or Diagonal for Casa Mila).

The 19th century was a boom time for Barcelona. By 1850 it was busting out of its medieval walls. A new town was planned to follow a gridlike layout. The intersection of three major thoroughfares—Gran Vía, Diagonal, and Meridiana—would shift the city's focus uptown.

The Eixample, or "Enlargement," was a progressive plan in which everything was accessible to everyone. Each 20-block-square district would have its own hospital and large park, each 10-block-square area would have its own market and general services, and each five-block-square grid would house its own schools and day-care centers. The hollow space found inside each "block" of apartments would form a neighborhood park.

While much of that vision never quite panned out, the Eixample was an urban success. Rich and artsy big shots bought plots along the grid. The richest landowners built as close to the center as possible. For this reason, the best buildings are near the Passeig de Gràcia. Adhering to the height, width, and depth limitations, they built as they pleased—often in the trendy new moderniste style.

Sights—Gaudí's Art and Architecture

Barcelona is an architectural scrapbook of the galloping gables and organic curves of hometown boy Antonio Gaudí. A devoted Catalan and Catholic, he immersed himself in each project, often living on-site. He called Parc Güell, La Pedrera, and the Sagrada Familia all home.

▲▲**Sagrada Familia (Sacred Family) Church**—Gaudí's most famous and persistent work is this unfinished landmark. He worked on the church from 1883 to 1926; your 800-ptas admission helps pay for the ongoing construction (daily 9:00–20:00, off-season 9:00–18:00, Metro: Sagrada Familia, tel. 93-207-3031).

When finished, 12 100-meter spires (representing the apostles) will stand in groups of four and mark the three ends of the building. The center tower (honoring Jesus), reaching 170 meters up, will be flanked by 125-meter-tall towers of Mary and the four evangelists. A unique exterior ambulatory will circle the building like a cloister turned inside out.

The nativity facade really shows the vision of Gaudí. It was finished in 1904, before Gaudí's death, and shows scenes from the birth and childhood of Jesus along with angels playing musical instruments. (Because of ongoing construction, you may need to access this area—opposite the entrance, viewed from outside— by walking through the museum. Don't miss it.)

The little on-site **museum** displays physical models used for the church's construction. Gaudí lived on the site for more than a decade and is buried in the crypt. When he died in 1926, only the stubs of four spires stood above the building site. Judge for yourself how the controversial current work fits in with Gaudí's original formulation.

With the cranking cranes, rusty forests of rebar, and

Gaudí Sights

scaffolding requiring a powerful faith, the Sagrada Familia Church offers a fun look at a living, growing, bigger-than-life building. Take the lift (200 ptas) or the stairs (free but often miserably congested) up to the dizzy lookout bridging two spires. You'll get a great view of the city and a gargoyle's-eye perspective of the loopy church. If there's any building on earth I'd like to see, it's the Sagrada Familia...finished.

▲**Palau Güell**—This is a good chance to enjoy a Gaudí interior (see "Introductory Tour," above). Curvy.

▲▲**Casa Milà (La Pedrera)**—This Gaudí exterior laughs down on the crowds filling Passeig de Gràcia. Casa Milà, also called La Pedrera (the Quarry), has a much-photographed roller coaster of melting-ice-cream eaves. This is Barcelona's quintessential moderniste building.

Visits come in three parts: apartment, attic, and rooftop. Buy the 1,000-ptas ticket to see all three. Starting with the apartment, an elevator whisks you to the *Life in Barcelona 1905–1929* exhibit (well-described in English). Then you walk through a sumptuously furnished Art Nouveau apartment. Upstairs in the attic, wander under brick arches—enjoying a multimedia exhibit of models, photos, and videos of Gaudí's works. From there a stairway leads to the fanciful rooftop where chimneys play volleyball with the clouds (daily 10:00–20:00—even on Mon, Passeig de Gràcia 92, Metro: Diagonal, tel. 93-484-5995, most days there are apartment tours in English at 16:30 and attic/rooftop tours at 18:00). At the ground level of Casa Milà is the original entrance courtyard for the Fundacio Caixa de Cataluyna, dreamily painted in pastels (free). The first floor hosts free art exhibits.

▲**The Block of Discord**—Four blocks from Casa Milà you can survey a noisy block of competing turn-of-the-century facades. Several of Barcelona's top moderniste mansions line Passeig de Gràcia (Metro: Passeig de Gràcia). Because the structures look as though they are trying to outdo each other in creative twists, locals nicknamed the block between Consell de Cent and Arago, "The Block of Discord." First (at #43) and most famous is Gaudí's Casa Batllo, with skull-like balconies and a tile roof of cresting waves...or is it a dragon's back? (If you're tempted to frame your photos from the middle of the street, be careful—Gaudí died under a streetcar.) Next door, at Casa Amatller (#41, desk sells Moderniste Route combo tickets), check out architect Puig i Cadafalch's creative mix of Moorish and Gothic and iron grillwork. On the corner (at #35) is Casa Lleo Morera (by Lluís Domènechi Muntaner who did the Catalana Concert Hall—you'll see similarities). The perfume shop halfway down the street has a free and interesting little perfume museum in the back. The Hostal de Rita restaurant, just around the corner on Calle Arago, serves a fine three-course lunch for a great price at 13:00 (see "Eating," below).

Park Güell—Gaudí fans find the artist's magic in this colorful park (free, daily 9:00–20:00) and small Gaudí Museum (200 ptas, daily 10:00–20:00, closes off-season at 18:00, Metro: Vallcarca but easier by bus #24 from Plaça de Catalunya; 1,000 ptas by taxi). Gaudí intended this to be a planned garden city rather than a park. As a high-income housing project, it flopped. As a park...even after I reminded myself that Gaudí's work is a careful rhythm of color, shapes, and space, it was disappointing.

Modern Art Museum (Museu d'Art Modern)—East of the França train station in Parc de la Ciutadella, this manageable museum exhibits Catalunyan sculpture, painting, glass, and furniture by Gaudí, Casas, Llimona, and others (500 ptas, Tue–Sat 10:00–19:00, Sun 10:00–14:30, closed Mon).

Sights—Barcelona's Montjuïc

The Montjuïc (Mount of the Jews), overlooking Barcelona's hazy port, has always been a show-off. Ages ago it had the impressive fortress. In 1929 it hosted an international fair, from which most of today's sights originated. And in 1992 the Summer Olympics directed the world's attention to this pincushion of attractions.

There are many ways to reach Montjuïc: on the blue Bus Turistic route (see "Getting around Barcelona," above); bus #50 from the corner of Gran Vía and Passeig de Gràcia (150 ptas, every 10 min); subway to Metro: Parallel and catch the funicular (250 ptas one way, 375 ptas round-trip, daily 11:00–22:00, Sat–Sun only in winter); or taxi. The first three options leave you at the *teleférico* (cable car), which you can take to the Castle of Montjuïc (475 ptas one way, 675 ptas round-trip, daily 11:00–22:00, less off season, tel. 93-443-0859). Alternatively, from the same spot, you can walk uphill 20 minutes through the pleasant park. Only a taxi gets you doorstep delivery. From the port, the fastest and most scenic way to Montjuïc is via the 1929 Trasbordador Aereo (at tower in port, ride elevator up to catch dangling gondola, 1,200 ptas round-trip, 4/hrly, daily 10:30–19:00, tel. 93-443-0859).

Castle of Montjuïc—This offers great city views and a military museum (250 ptas, Tue–Sun 10:00–20:00, closed Mon). The seemingly endless museum houses a dull collection of guns, swords, and toy soldiers. An interesting section on the Spanish-American War covers Spain's valiant fight against American aggression (from its perspective). Unfortunately, there are no English descriptions. Those interested in Jewish history will find a fascinating collection of 9th-century Jewish tombstones.

▲**Fountains (Font Magica)**—Music, colored lights, and huge amounts of water make an artistic and coordinated splash on summer nights (Fri–Sun, 20-min shows start on the half-hour, 21:30–24:00, summer Thu eves also, from Metro: Plaça Espanya, walk toward towering National Palace).

Spanish Village (Poble Espanyol)—This tacky five-acre model village uses fake traditional architecture from all over Spain as a shell to contain gift shops. Craftspeople do their clichéd thing only in the morning (not worth your time or 950 ptas). After hours it becomes a popular local nightspot.

▲▲**Catalunyan Art Museum (Museo Nacional d'Art de Catalunya)**—Often called "the Prado of Romanesque art," this is a rare, world-class collection of Romanesque art taken mostly from remote Catalunyan village churches in the Pyrenees (saved from unscrupulous art dealers—many American).

The Romanesque wing features frescoes, painted wooden altar fronts, and ornate statuary. This classic Romanesque art—with flat 2-D scenes, each saint holding his symbol, and Jesus (easy to identify by the cross in his halo)—is impressively displayed on replicas of the original church ceilings.

In the Gothic wing, fresco murals give way to vivid 14th-century paintings of Bible stories on wood. A roomful of paintings by the Catalunyan master Jaume Huguet (1412–1492) deserves a close look.

Before you leave, ice skate under the huge dome over to the air-conditioned cafeteria. This was the prime ceremony room and dance hall for the 1929 International Exposition (museum-800 ptas, Tue–Sat 10:00–19:00, Sun 10:00–14:30, closed Mon, tel. 93-622-0375). The museum is in the massive National Palace building above the fountains, near Plaça Espanya (Metro: Plaça Espanya, then hike up or ride the bus; the Bus Turistic and bus #50 stop close by).

▲Fundació Joan Miró—For something more up-to-date, this museum showcases the modern-art talents of yet another Catalunyan artist and is considered the best collection of Joan Miró art anywhere. You'll also see works by other modern Spanish artists; don't miss the *Mercury Fountain* by Alexander Calder. This museum leaves those who don't like abstract art scratching their heads (800 ptas, Oct–June Tue–Sat 10:00–20:00, Thu until 21:30, Sun 10:00–14:30, closed Mon, July–Sept closes at 20:00).

Sleeping in Barcelona
(180 ptas = about $1, country code: 34)
Sleep Code: **S** = Single, **D** = Double/Twin, **T** = Triple, **Q** = Quad, **b** = bathroom, **t** = toilet only, **s** = shower only, **CC** = Credit Card (**V**isa, **M**asterCard, **A**mex), **NSE** = No English.

Book ahead. If necessary, the TI at Plaça de Catalunya has a room-finding service.

Barcelona is Spain's most expensive city. Still, it has reasonable rooms. Cheap places are more crowded in summer; fancier business-class places fill up in winter and offer discounts on weekends and in summer. Prices listed do not include the 7 percent tax or breakfast (ranging from simple 500-ptas spreads to 2,200-ptas buffets) unless otherwise noted. While many recommended places are on pedestrian streets, night noise is a problem almost everywhere (especially in cheap places with single-pane windows). For a quiet night, ask for "*tranquilo*" rather than "*con vista.*"

Sleeping in Eixample
For an elegant and boulevardian neighborhood, sleep in Eixample, a 10-minute walk from the Ramblas action.

Hotel Condes de Barcelona, a four-star business hotel in a grand moderniste building, rents 183 stylish and spacious rooms with all the comforts (Db-31,000 ptas, special Db price—26,000 ptas or less—offered with this book on weekends all year and daily June–mid-Sept, extra bed-5,000 ptas, CC:VMA, air-con, smoke-free floor, elevator, Gaudí-pleasing rooftop sun garden with Jacuzzi, intersection of Mallorca and Passeig de Gracia at Passeig de Gracia 73, 08008 Barcelona, tel. 93-467-4780, fax 93-467-4781, www. condesdebarcelona.com, e-mail: cbhotel@condesdebarcelona.com).

Hotel Regente, another big four-star place, is a notch below Condes de Barcelona but still a fine splurge (80 rooms, Db-23,000 ptas, less June–Aug, CC:VMA, air-con, elevator, roof terrace, Rambla Catalunya 76, 08008 Barcelona, tel. 93-487-5989, fax 93-487-3227, e-mail: regente@hoteles-centro-ciudad.es).

Hotel Gran Vía, filling a palatial mansion built in the 1870s, offers Botticelli and chandeliers in the public rooms; a sprawling, peaceful sun garden; and 54 spacious, comfy, air-conditioned rooms. It's an excellent value (Sb-10,500 ptas, Db-14,500 ptas with this book through 2001, CC:VMA, Internet access, elevator, quiet, Gran Vía de les Corts Catalanes 642, 08007 Barcelona, tel. 93-318-1900, fax 93-318-9997).

Hotel Residencia Neutral, with a classic Eixample address and 35 basic rooms, is popular with backpackers (tiny Sb-3,700 ptas, big Sb-6,000 ptas, Ds-5,500 ptas, Db-6,500 ptas, extra bed-1,500 ptas, includes tax, CC:VM, elevator, thin walls and some street noise, elegantly located 2 blocks north of Gran Vía at Rambla Catalunya 42, 08007 Barcelona, tel. 93-487-6390).

Sleeping near Plaça de Catalunya and at the top of the Ramblas
(zip code: 08002 unless otherwise noted)

The first five of these places are on big but quiet streets within a block or two of Barcelona's exuberant central square. The next are on or near the top of the Ramblas, also just off Plaça de Catalunya. The last is buried in the Gothic Quarter. See map on page 657.

Hotel Duques de Bergara boasts four stars with splashy public spaces, slick marble and hardwood floors, 150 comfortable rooms, and a garden courtyard with a pool a world away from the big-city noise (Sb-22,000 ptas, Db-27,000 ptas, extra bed-3,000 ptas, CC:VMA, air-con, elevator, a half block off Plaça de Catalunya at Bergara 11, tel. 93-301-5151, fax 93-317-3442, www.hoteles-catalonia.es, e-mail: cataloni@hoteles-catalonia.es).

Hotel Occidental Reding, a five-minute walk west of the Ramblas and Plaça de Catalunya action on a quiet street, keeps business travelers fat and happy with 44 comfortable rooms (Db-19,000 ptas, extra bed-5,400 ptas, CC:VMA, air-con, elevator, near University metro stop at Gravina 5, 08001 Barcelona, tel. 93-412-1097, fax 93-268-3482, e-mail: reding@occidental-hoteles.com).

Hotel Allegro elegantly fills a renovated old palace with wide halls, hardwood floors, and modern rooms with all the comforts. It overlooks a thriving pedestrian boulevard. Front rooms have views. Balcony rooms on the back are quiet and come with sun terraces (Db-27,000 ptas, extra bed-3,000 ptas, CC:VMA, family rooms, air-con, elevator, a block down from Plaça de Catalunya at Portal de l'Angel 17, tel. 93-318-4141, fax 93-301-2631).

Catalunya Plaza, an impersonal business hotel right on the square, has all the air-conditioning and minibar comforts (Sb-21,000 ptas, Db-26,000 ptas, includes breakfast, CC:VMA, elevator, air-con, free nuts at the desk, Plaça de Catalunya 7, tel. 93-317-7171, fax 93-317-7855, e-mail: catalunya@city-hotels.es).

Hotel Barcelona is another big, American-style hotel with bright, prefab, and comfy rooms (Sb-19,000 ptas, Db-27,000 ptas, Db with terrace-34,000 ptas, CC:VMA, air-con, elevator, a block from Plaça de Catalunya at Caspe 1–13, tel. 93-302-5858, fax 93-301-8674, e-mail: hotelbarcelona@husa.es).

Nouvel Hotel, an elegant Victorian-style building on a fine pedestrian street, has royal lounges and 70 comfy rooms (Sb-13,000 ptas, Db-19,000 ptas, includes breakfast, manager Gabriel promises 10 percent discount with this book, CC:VMA, air-con, Carrer de Santa Ana 18, tel. 93-301-8274, fax 93-301-8370).

Hotel Toledano's, overlooking the Ramblas, is suitable for backpackers and popular with dust-bunnies. Small, folksy, and borderline dumpy, it's warmly run by Juan Sanz, his son Albert, and trusty Daniel on the nightshift (Sb-4,400 ptas, Db-7,600 ptas, Tb-9,500 ptas, Qb-10,600 ptas, cheaper off-season, CC:VMA, Rambla de Canaletas 138, tel. 93-301-0872, fax 93-412-3142, e-mail: Toledano@ibernet.com). They run **Hostal Residencia Capitol** one floor above—quiet, plain, cheaper, and also appropriate for backpackers (S-3,200 ptas, D-5,200 ptas, Ds-5,800 ptas, cheap 5-bed room).

Hotel Continental has comfortable rooms, double-thick mattresses, and wildly clashing carpets and wallpaper. To celebrate 100 years in the family, José includes a free breakfast and an all-day complimentary coffee bar. Choose a Ramblas-view balcony or quiet back room (Db-10,000–13,000 ptas, extra bed-2,000 ptas, special family room, CC:VMA, fans in rooms, elevator, Internet access, Las Ramblas 138, tel. 93-301-2570, fax 93-302-7360, www.hotelcontinental.com, e-mail: ramblas@hotelcontinental.com).

Hotel Lloret is a big, dark, old-world place on the Ramblas with plain neon-lit rooms (Sb-6,500 ptas, Db-9,500 ptas, Tb-11,000 ptas, extra beds-1,000 ptas each up to quints, choose a noisy Ramblas balcony or *tranquilo* in the back, CC:VMA, air-con in summer, elevator dominates stairwell, Rambla de Canaletas 125, tel. 93-317-3366, fax 93-301-9283).

Hosteria Grau is a homey, almost alpine place, family-run with 27 clean and woody rooms just far enough off the Ramblas (S-4,000 ptas, D-6,500 ptas, Ds-7,500 ptas, Db-8,500 ptas, family suites with 2 bedrooms-16,000 ptas, 1,000 ptas extra charged July–Sept, CC:VMA, fans, 200 meters up Calle Tallers from the

Ramblas at Ramelleres 27, 08001 Barcelona, tel. 93-301-8135, fax 93-317-6825, www.intercom.es/grau, e-mail: hgrau@lix .intercom.es, Monica SE).

Meson Castilla is clean, comfy and handy, but it's also pricey, a bit sterile, and in all the American guidebooks. It's three blocks off the Ramblas in an appealing university neighborhood (56 rooms, Sb-12,000 ptas, Db-15,000 ptas, Tb-20,000 ptas, Qb apartment-24,000 ptas, includes buffet breakfast, CC:VMA, air-con, elevator, Valldoncella 5, 08001 Barcelona, tel. 93-318-2182, fax 93-412-4020, e-mail: hmesoncastilla@teleline.es).

Citadines Ramblas Aparthotel is a clever concept offering apartments by the day in a bright modern building right on the Ramblas. Prices range with the seasonal demand and rooms come in three categories (studio apartment for 2 with sofa bed and kitchenette-18,000–21,000 ptas, hotel room for 2 with real bed-22,000–24,000 ptas, apartment with real bed and sofa bed for up to 4 people-27,000–31,000 ptas, includes tax, CC:VMA, laundry, Ramblas 122, tel. 93-270-1111, fax 93-412-7421, e-mail: barca @citadines.com).

Hotel Jardi is a hardworking, clean, plain place on the happiest little square in the Gothic Quarter. Balcony rooms overlooking the peaceful leafy square are most expensive (Sb-4,000–7,500 ptas, Db-5,800–7,500 ptas, Tb-6,800–8,500 ptas, extra bed-1,500 ptas, includes tax, 10 percent off with cash, CC:VMA if bill totals at least 15,000 ptas, air-con, elevator, halfway between Ramblas and cathedral on Plaça Sant Josep Oriol #1, tel. 93-301-5900, fax 93-318-3664, e-mail: sgs110sa@retemail.es, Albert SE). Rooms with balconies enjoy an almost Parisian ambiance and minimal noise.

Humble Places Buried in Gothic Quarter with Youth-Hostel Prices

Pensio Vitoria has loose tile floors and 12 basic rooms, each with a tiny balcony. It's more dumpy than homey, but consider the price (D-3,500 ptas, Db-4,500 ptas, CC:VM, a block off day-dreamy Plaça dei Pi at Carrer la Palla 8, tel. & fax 93-302-0834).

Hostal Campi—big, quiet, and ramshackle—is a few doors off the Ramblas (D-5,500 ptas, Db-6,500 ptas, T-7,500 ptas, Canuda 4, tel. & fax 93-301-3545). **Huéspedes Santa Ana** is plain and claustrophobic, with head-to-toe twins (S-3,000 ptas, D-5,000 ptas, Db-7,000 ptas, T-7,500 ptas, Carrer de Santa Ana 23, tel. 93-301-2246). **Hostal Residencia Lausanne**, filled with backpackers, has only its location and price going for it (S-3, 500 ptas, D-5,500 ptas, Ds-6,500 ptas, Db-7,500 ptas, TV room, Avenida Portal de l'Angel 24, tel. & fax 93-302-1139, friendly Javier SE). **Hostal Rembrandt** keeps backpackers happy with 26 simple rooms and a good location (S-3,200 ptas,

Sb-4,300 ptas, D-5,000 ptas, Db-7,000 ptas, Tb-8,500 ptas, break-fast costs 400 ptas, Portaferrisa 23, tel. & fax 93-318-1011). **Pension Fina**, next to Hostal Rembrandt, offers more cheap sleeps (S-3,500 ptas, D-5,000 ptas, Db-6,000 ptas, Portaferrissa 11, tel. & fax 93-317-9787).

Eating in Barcelona
Barcelona, the capital of Catalunyan cuisine, offers a tremendous variety of colorful places to eat. Many restaurants are closed in August (or sometimes July), when the owners are on vacation.

Eating near the Ramblas and in the Gothic Quarter
Taverna Basca Irati serves 25 kinds of hot and cold Basque *pintxos* for 150 ptas each. These are open-faced sandwiches—like Basque sushi but on bread. Muscle in through the hungry local crowd. Get an empty plate from the waiter, then help yourself. It's a Basque honors system: You'll be charged by the number of toothpicks left on your plate when you're done. Wash it down with *sidra* (apple wine, 150 ptas) poured from on high to bring out the flavor (Tue–Sat 12:00–15:00, 19:00–23:00, Sun 12:00–15:00, closed Mon, a block off the Ramblas, behind the arcade at Calle Cardenal Casanyes 17, near Metro: Liceu, tel. 93-302-3084). **Juicy Jones**, next door, is a tutti-frutti vegetarian place with a hip menu and a stunning array of fresh-squeezed juices (#7, daily 10:00–23:30).

Ria de Vigo III, a nondescript local eatery, is filled with blue-collar workers and cheap, no-nonsense food (open until 21:30, closed Sun, 3 blocks off Ramblas at Carrer Tallers 69, tel. 93-318-4724).

La Taverneta, an artists' bistro, brags it doesn't cater to tourists. It serves good Catalan food seasoned in the evenings with live music (1,200-ptas lunch menus, Mon–Sat 13:00–16:30, 19:00–24:00, closed Sun, 2 blocks off Ramblas near Plaza Villa de Madrid at Pje. Duque de la Victoria 3, tel. 93-302-6152).

Café Granja Viader is a quaint time-trip, family-run since 1870. This feminine place—specializing in baked and dairy delights, toasted sandwiches, and light meals—is ideal for a traditional breakfast (note the "Esmorzars" specials posted). Try a glass of Orxata (Horchata, almond milk, summer only), Llet Mallorquina (Majorca-style milk with cinnamon, lemon, and sugar), or "Suis" (literally Switzerland, hot chocolate with a snowcap of whipped cream). It's a block off the Ramblas behind El Carme church (9:00–13:45, 17:00–20:45, closed Sun and Mon morning, Xucla 4, tel. 93-318-3486).

Egipte offers decent food, indifferent service, and late-19th-century ambience on the Ramblas (daily 13:00–16:00, 20:00–24:00, Rambla 79, downhill from Boqueria, tel. 93-317-7480).

For **groceries**, consider El Corte Ingles on Plaça de Catalunya or the Champion Supermarket at 113 Ramblas (Mon–Sat 9:15–21:15, closed Sun). For a good pizza at the top of the Ramblas, consider **La Poma** (La Ramblas 117).

Restaurants in the Gothic Quarter

A chain of three bright, modern restaurants with high-quality traditional cuisine in classy bistro settings with great prices has stormed Barcelona. Each can be crowded so arrive early if you can: **La Fonda** (daily 13:00–15:30, 20:30–23:30, a block from Plaça Reial at Escudellers 10, tel. 93-301-7515), **La Dolca Herminia** (2 blocks toward Ramblas from Catalan Concert Hall at Magdalenes 27, tel. 93-317-0676), and **Les Quinze Nits** (on trendy La Plaça Reial at #6—you'll see the line, tel. 93-317-3075).

Els Quatre Gats, Picasso's hangout, still has a bohemian feel in spite of its tourist crowds. Before it was founded in 1897, the idea of a café for artists was mocked as a place where only *quatre gats* ("four cats," meaning only crazies) would go (3,000-ptas meals, Mon–Sat 8:30–02:00, Sun 17:00–01:30, live piano nightly from 21:00, CC:VMA, Montsio 3, tel. 93-302-4140).

Restaurante Agut, buried deep in the Gothic Quarter four blocks off the harbor, is a fine place for local-style food in a local-style setting (Tue–Sat 21:00–24:00, closed Sun, Mon, and July or Aug, Calle Gignas 16, tel. 93-315-1709).

Vegetarian near Plaça de Catalunya

Self Naturista is a quick, no-stress buffet that will make vegetarians and health-food lovers feel right at home. Others may find a few unidentifiable plates and drinks. The food seems tired—pick what you like and microwave it (Mon–Sat 11:30–22:00, closed Sun, near several recommended hotels, just off the top of Ramblas at Carrer de Santa Ana 11–17).

Bio Center, a Catalan soup and salad place popular with local vegetarians, is better but not as handy (Mon–Sat 13:00–17:00, closed Sun, Pintor Fortuny 25, Metro: Catalunya, tel. 93-318-0343). The street has several other good vegetarian places.

Eating in the Eixample

The people-packed boulevards of the Eixample (Passeig de Gràcia and Rambla Catalunya) are lined with appetizing places with breezy outdoor seating. Many trendy and touristic tapas bars offer a cheery welcome and aggressively slam out the appetizers.

La Bodegueta is an unbelievably atmospheric below-street-level bodega serving hearty wines and *flauta* (sandwich on flute-thin baguette, Mon–Sat 8:00–02:00, Sun 19:00–01:00, Rambla Catalunya 100, at intersection with Provenza, Metro: Diagonal, tel. 93-215-4894).

El Hostal de Rita is a fresh and dressy little place serving Catalunyan cuisine just around the corner from Casa Milà. Their three-course-with-wine lunch (1,100 ptas, Mon–Fri at 13:00) and dinner (2,000 ptas, daily from 20:30) specials are a great value (Arago 279, tel. 93-487-2376).

The classy **Quasi Queviures** serves upscale tapas, sandwiches, or the whole nine yards—classic food with modern decor (Passeig de Gràcia 24).

El Café de Internet provides an easy way to munch a sandwich while sending e-mail messages to Mom (600 ptas/30 min, Mon–Sat 9:00–24:00, closed Sun, Gran Vía 656, Metro: Passeig de Gràcia, tel. 93-412-1915, www.cafeinternet.es).

Sandwich Shops
Bright, clean and inexpensive sandwich shops are proudly holding the cultural line against the fast-food invasion hamburgerizing the rest of Europe. You'll find great sandwiches at **Pans & Company** and **Bocatta**, two chains with outlets all over town. Catalunyan sandwiches are made to order with crunchy French bread. Rather than butter, locals prefer *pa amb tomaquet* (pah ahm too-MAH-kaht), a mix of crushed tomato and olive oil. Study the instructive multilingual menu fliers to understand your options.

Eating near the Harbor in Barceloneta
Barceloneta is a charming beach suburb of the big city. A grid plan of long, narrow, laundry-strewn streets surrounds the central Plaça Poeta Boscan. For an entertaining evening, wander around this corner. Drop by the two places listed here or find your own restaurant (15-min walk or Metro: Barceloneta). During the day a lively produce market fills one end of the square. At night kids play soccer and Ping-Pong.

Cova Fumada is the neighborhood eatery. Josep Maria and his family serve famously fresh fish (Mon–Fri 17:30–20:30, closed July, Carrer del Baluarte 56, on the corner at Carrer Sant Carles, tel. 93-221-4061). Their *sardinas a la plancha* (grilled sardines, 350 ptas) are fresh and tasty. *Bombas* (potato croquets with pork, 150 ptas) are the house specialty. It's macho to have it *picante* (spicy with chili sauce); gentler taste buds prefer it with garlic cream (alioli). Catalunyan *bruschetta* is *pan tostado* (toast with oil and garlic, 140 ptas). Wash it down with *vino tinto* (house red wine, 80 ptas).

At **Bar Electricidad**, Arturo Jordana Barba is the neighborhood source for cheap wine. Drop in. It's 180 ptas per liter; the empty plastic water bottles are for takeaway. Try a 75-ptas glass of Torroja Tinto, the best local red, or Priorato Dulce, a wonderfully sweet red (Mon–Sat 8:00–13:00, 15:00–19:00, across the square from Cova Fumada, Plaça del Poeta Bosca, #61, NSE).

The Olympic Port, a swanky marina district, is lined with

harborside restaurants and eaters enjoying what locals claim is the freshest fish in town (a short taxi ride from the center past Barceloneta).

Tapas on Carrer Merce in the Gothic Quarter
Tapas aren't as popular in Catalunya as they are in the rest of Spain, but Barcelona boasts great *tascas*—colorful local tapas bars. Get small plates (for maximum sampling) by asking for "*tapas*," not "*raciones*."

While trendy uptown places are safer, better lit, and come with English menus and less grease, these places will stain your journal.

From the bottom of the Ramblas (near the Columbus monument), hike east along Carrer Clave. Then follow the small street that runs along the right side of the church (Carrer Merce), stopping at the *tascas* that look fun.

La Jarra is known for its tender *jamón canario con patatas* (baked ham with salty potatoes). Across the street, **La Pulperia** serves up fried fish. A block down the street, **Tasca El Corral** makes one of the neighborhood's best chorizo *al diablo* (hell sausage), which you sauté yourself. It's great with the regional specialty, *pan con tomate*. Across the street, **La Plata** keeps things wonderfully simple, serving extremely cheap plates of sardines and small glasses of keg wine. **Tascael Corral** serves northern Spain mountain favorites such as *queso de cabrales* (very moldy cheese) with *sidra* (apple wine). Have a chat with the parrot at **Bar la Choza del Sopas**. At the end of Carrer Merce, **Bar Vendimia** serves up tasty clams and mussels. Carrer Ample and Carrer Gignas, the streets paralleling Carrer Merce inland, have more refined barhopping possibilities.

Transportation Connections—Barcelona
By train to: Lisbon (1/day, 17 hrs with change in Madrid, $70 with *couchette*), **Madrid** (6/day, 7–9 hrs, $40 with *couchette*), **Paris** (3/day, 11–15 hrs, $100 with *couchette*, night train, reservation required), **Sevilla** (4/day, 11 hrs, $45 with couchette), **Málaga** (3/day, 14 hrs), **Nice** (1/day, 12 hrs, change in Cerbere). Train info: tel. 93-490-0202; international train info: tel. 93-490-1122. RENFE tel. 93-490-0202.

By bus to: Madrid (12/day, 8 hrs, half the price of a train ticket, departs from station Barcelona Nord at Metro: Marina).

By plane: To avoid 10-hour train trips, check the reasonable flights from Barcelona to Sevilla or Madrid. Iberia Air (tel. 93-412-5667) and Air Europe (tel. 90-224-0042) offer $80 flights to Madrid. Airport info: tel. 93-298-3838.

MADRID

Today's Madrid is upbeat and vibrant, still enjoying a post-Franco renaissance. You'll feel it. Even the statue-maker beggars have a twinkle in their eyes.

Madrid is the hub of Spain. This modern capital—Europe's highest, at more than 2,000 feet—has a population of more than 4 million and is young by European standards. Only 400 years ago, King Philip II decided to move the capital of his empire from Toledo to Madrid. One hundred years ago Madrid had only 400,000 people, so 90 percent of the city is modern sprawl surrounding an intact, easy-to-navigate historic core.

Dive headlong into the grandeur and intimate charm of Madrid. The lavish Royal Palace, with its gilded rooms and frescoed ceilings, rivals Versailles. The Prado has Europe's top collection of paintings. The city's huge Retiro Park invites you for a shady siesta and a hopscotch through a mosaic of lovers, families, skateboarders, pets walking their masters, and expert bench-sitters. Make time for Madrid's elegant shops and people-friendly pedestrian zones. Enjoy the shade in an arcade. On Sundays, cheer for the bull at a bullfight or bargain like mad at a mega–flea market. Lively Madrid has enough street singing, barhopping, and people-watching vitality to give any visitor a boost of youth.

Planning Your Time

Madrid's top two sights, the Prado and the palace, are worth a day. On a Sunday (Easter–Oct), consider allotting extra time for a bullfight. Ideally, give Madrid two days and spend them this way:

Day 1: Breakfast of *churros* (see "Eating," below) before a brisk, good-morning-Madrid walk for 20 minutes from Puerta del Sol to the Prado; 9:00–12:00 at the Prado; afternoon siesta in Retiro

Park or modern art at Centro Reina Sofia (Guernica) and/or Thyssen-Bornemisza Museum; dinner at 8:00, with tapas around Plaza Santa Ana.

Day 2: Follow this book's "Puerta del Sol to Royal Palace Walk" (see below); tour the Royal Palace, lunch near Plaza Mayor; afternoon free for other sights or shopping. Be out at the magic hour—before sunset—when beautifully lit people fill Madrid.

Note that the Prado, Thyssen-Bornemisza Museum, and El Escorial are closed on Monday. Sunday is market day: the huge El Rastro flea market rages off Plaza Mayor while a sedate stamp-and-coin market is held *on* Plaza Mayor.

Orientation

The historic center is enjoyably covered on foot. No major sight is more than a 20-minute walk or a 600-ptas taxi ride from Puerta del Sol, Madrid's central square. Divide your time between the city's two major sights—the Royal Palace and the Prado—and its barhopping, contemporary scene.

The Puerta del Sol marks the center of Madrid and of Spain itself; notice the "kilometer zero" marker, from which all of Spain is surveyed (southwest corner). The Royal Palace to the west and the Prado Museum and Retiro Park to the east frame Madrid's historic center.

Southwest of Puerta del Sol is a 17th-century district with the slow-down-and-smell-the-cobbles Plaza Mayor and memories of pre-industrial Spain.

North of Puerta del Sol runs Gran Vía, and between the two are lively pedestrian shopping streets. Gran Vía, bubbling with expensive shops and cinemas, leads to the modern Plaza de España. North of Gran Vía is the gritty Malasana quarter, with its colorful small houses, shoemakers' shops, sleazy-looking hombres, milk vendors, bars, and hip night scene.

Tourist Information

Madrid has four Turismos: on Plaza Mayor (#3, Mon–Sat 10:00–20:00, Sun 10:00–15:00, tel. 91-588-1636); near the Prado Museum (behind Palace Hotel, Mon–Fri 9:00–19:00, Sat 9:00–13:00, Duque de Medinaceli 2, tel. 91-429-4951); at the Chamartin train station (Mon–Fri 8:00–20:00, Sat 9:00–13:00, tel. 91-315-9976) and at the airport (same hours, tel. 91-305-8656).

During the summer small temporary TI stands with yellow umbrellas and yellow-shirted student guides pop up (at places such as Puerta del Sol), happy to help out lost tourists. Confirm your sightseeing plans and pick up a city map and *Enjoy Madrid*. If interested, ask at the TI about bullfights and Zarzuela (the local light opera).

For entertainment listings, the TI's free *En Madrid* is not as

Madrid

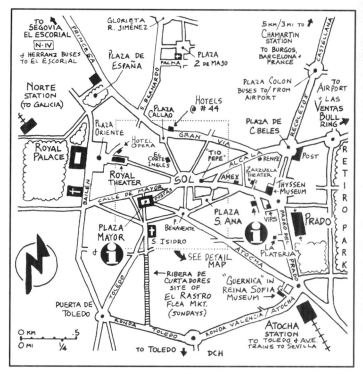

good as the easy-to-decipher Spanish weekly entertainment guide *Guía del Ocio* (150 ptas, sold at newsstands), which lists events, restaurants, and movies ("v.o." means a movie is in its original language rather than dubbed).

If you're heading to other destinations in Spain, ask any Madrid TI for free maps and brochures. Since many small-town TIs keep erratic hours and run out of these pamphlets, get what you can here. Get bus schedules, too, to avoid unnecessary trips to the various bus stations. The TI's free and amazingly informative *Mapa de Comunicaciones España* lists all the Turismos and highway SOS numbers with a road map of Spain. (If they're out, ask for the Paradores Hotel chain-sponsored route map.)

Arrival in Madrid

By Train: Madrid's two train stations, Atocha and Chamartin, are both on subway lines with easy access to downtown Madrid. Each station has all the services (but there's no TI at Atocha). In Spain, train rides longer than about three hours require reservations, even if you have a Eurailpass. To avoid needless running around, arrange your departure upon arrival.

Chamartin handles most international trains. Atocha runs AVE trains to Sevilla. Both stations offer long-distance trains (*largo recorrido*) as well as local trains to nearby destinations (*cercanías*). Atocha is split into two halves (local and long-distance trains) with separate schedules; this can be confusing if you're in the wrong side of the building. Atocha also has two helpful (necessary) customer-service offices called Atención al Cliente (daily 7:00–23:00)—one office for each half of the building. The Chamartin station is less confusing (customer-service office beside the ticket windows in the middle of the building, TI opposite track #20).

Club AVE in Atocha (upstairs) is a lounge reserved solely for AVE business or first-class ticket-holders or Eurailers with a reservation (free drinks, newspapers, showers, info service, and so on). The Club Intercity lounge in the Chamartin station is less exclusive—you can get in if you have a first-class railpass and first-class seat or sleeper reservations.

Both train stations have Metro stops: Chamartin and Atocha RENFE. (Note that there are 2 Atocha Metro stops in Madrid; the train station's Metro station is "Atocha RENFE"). If you're traveling between Chamartin and Atocha, the Cercanias trains (6/hrly, 12 min, free with railpass—show it at ticket window in the middle of the turnstiles) are far quicker than the subway. These trains depart from Atocha's track 2. At Chamartin, check the Salidas Immediatas board for the next departure.

The downtown RENFE office offers train information, reservations, and tickets (Mon–Fri 9:30–19:00, credit cards accepted, go in person, 2 blocks north of the Prado at Calle Alcala 44, tel. 902-240-202).

By Bus: Madrid's three key bus stations, all connected by Metro, are: Larrea (for Segovia, Metro: Príncipe Pío), Estación Sur Autobuses (for Toledo, Àvila, and Granada, Metro: Méndez Alvaro, tel. 91-468-4200), and Estación Herranz (for El Escorial, in the Metro: Moncloa).

By Plane: Madrid's Barajas Airport, 10 miles east of downtown, has a 24-hour bank with fair rates, an ATM, a TI, a telephone office (which sells phone cards), a RENFE desk for rail information, a pharmacy, on-the-spot car-rental agencies, and easy public transportation into town. Airport info: tel. 91-393-6000, flight info tel. 90-235-3570. By public transport, take the yellow bus from the airport to Madrid (to Plaza Colón, 385 ptas, 4/hrly, 20 min); then, from Plaza Colón, take a taxi (insist on meter, ride to hotel should be far less than 1,000 ptas) or subway to your hotel (to get to the subway, walk up the stairs and face the blue "URBIS" sign high on a building—the subway stop, M. Serrano, is 50 yards to your right).

The airport's Metro stop, Aeropuerto, provides a cheap (150 ptas) but time-consuming (45 min with changes) way into town (access Metro at check-in level, transfer at Mar de Cristal to brown line #4—direction Arguelles, transfer at Goya to red line #3 to Sol).

For a taxi to or from the airport, allow 3,000 ptas (400-ptas airport supplement is legal). Cabbies routinely try to get 5,000 ptas—a rip off. At the airport, get a rough idea of the price before you hop in. Ask "*¿Cuanto cuesta a Madrid, más o menos?*" ("How much is it to Madrid, more or less?")

Getting around Madrid

By Subway: Madrid's subway is simple, speedy, and cheap (160 ptas/ride). The 735-ptas, 10-ride Metrobus ticket can be shared by several travelers and works on both the Metro and buses (available at kiosks or tobacco shops or in Metro). The city's broad streets can be hot and exhausting. A subway trip of even a stop or two can save time and energy. Pick up a free map (*Plano del Metro*) at most stations. Navigate by subway stops (shown on city maps). To transfer, follow signs to the next subway line (numbered and color-coded). End stops are used to indicate directions. Insert your ticket in the turnstile, then retrieve it as you pass through. Green *Salida* signs point to the exit. Using neighborhood maps and street signs to exit smartly can save lots of walking.

By Bus: City buses, while not as easy as the Metro, can be useful (bus maps at TI or info booth on Puerta del Sol, 160-ptas tickets sold on bus, or 735 ptas for a 10-ride Metrobus—see "By Subway," above).

By Taxi: Taxis are easy to hail and reasonable (180-ptas drop, 100 ptas per km; supplements for airport, train station, and bags). Threesomes travel as cheap by taxi as by subway. A ride from the Royal Palace to the Prado costs only 500 ptas.

Helpful Hints

Theft Alert: Be wary of pickpockets, anywhere, anytime, but particularly on Puerta del Sol (main square), the subway, and crowded streets. Wear your money belt. The small streets north of Gran Vía are particularly dangerous even before nightfall. Fortunately, violent crime against tourists is rare.

Museum Pass: If you plan to visit the Prado, Reina Sofia (*Guernica*), and Thyssen-Bornemisza museums, save 33 percent by buying the Paseo del Arte pass (1,300 ptas, sold at each museum).

Travel Agency and Free Maps: The grand department store, El Corte Inglés, has a travel agency (Mon–Sat 10:00–21:30, just off Puerta del Sol) and gives free Madrid maps (at the information desk, immediately inside the door, just off Puerta del Sol at intersection of Preciados and Tetuan).

Telephones: The telephone office, centrally located at Gran

Vía 30, has metered phones and accepts credit cards for charges over 500 ptas (daily 10:00–23:00).

American Express: The Amex office is at Plaza Cortes 2 (opposite Palace Hotel, 2 blocks from Metro: Banco de España, Mon–Fri 9:00–17:30, Sat 9:00–12:00, tel. 91-322-5455).

Embassies: The U.S. Embassy is at Serrano 75 (tel. 91-587-2200); the Canadian Embassy is at Nuñez de Balboa 35 (tel. 91-431-2350).

Laundromat: The self-service Lavamatique is funky but central (Mon–Fri 9:00–20:00, Sat 9:00–17:00, Cervantes 1).

Internet Access: Zahara is at the corner of Gran Vía and Mesoneros (Mon–Fri 9:00–0:30, Sat–Sun 9:00–01:30).

Tours of Madrid

Hop-on hop-off Bus Tours—Several companies offer virtually identical 15-stop circuits of the city with two or three buses per hour allowing you to hop on and off at the various sights all day. They come with tape-recorded or live commentaries (1,600 ptas, under 15 and over 65 half price, 10:00–18:30).

Private Guided Tour—EuropGuide, a local guide's association, offers excellent private tours (4-hr guided walks for 14,000 ptas, tel. 91-447-0114, www.nauta.es/europguide).

Walking Tours—British expatriate Stephen Drake-Jones gives entertaining, informative walks of historic old Madrid almost nightly (along with more specialized walks, such as "Hemingway," "Civil War," and "Bloody Madrid"). A historian with a passion for the memory of Wellington (the man who stopped Napoleon), Stephen is the founder of the Wellington Society. For 2,500 ptas you become a member of the society and get a free two-hour tour that includes stops at two bars for local drinks and tapas. Eccentric Stephen takes you back in time to sort out Madrid's Habsburg and Bourbon history. Stephen likes his drink. If that's a problem, skip the tour. Tours start at the statue on Puerta del Sol (maximum 10 people, tel. 60-914-3203—a cell phone number that will cost you 100 ptas—to confirm tour and reserve a spot; Stephen also does inexpensive private tours for small groups, e-mail: sdrake _jones@hotmail.com).

Introductory Walk: From Madrid's Puerta del Sol to the Royal Palace

Connect the sights with the following walking tour. Allow an hour for this half-mile walk, not including your palace visit.

▲▲**Puerta del Sol**—Named for a long-gone medieval gate with the sun carved onto it, Puerta del Sol is ground zero for Madrid. It's a hub for the Metro, buses, and pickpockets. The statue of the bear pawing the strawberry bush and the Madrono trees in the big planter boxes are symbols of Madrid.

Heart of Madrid

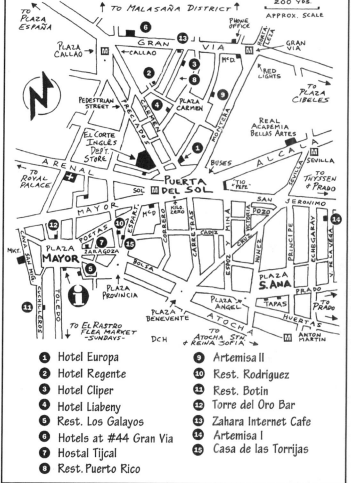

➊	Hotel Europa	➒	Artemisa II
➋	Hotel Regente	➓	Rest. Rodriguez
➌	Hotel Cliper	⓫	Rest. Botin
➍	Hotel Liabeny	⓬	Torre del Oro Bar
➎	Rest. Los Galayos	⓭	Zahara Internet Cafe
➏	Hotels at #44 Gran Via	⓮	Artemisa I
➐	Hostal Tijcal	⓯	Casa de las Torrijas
➑	Rest. Puerto Rico		

Stand by the statue of **King Charles III** and survey the square. Because of his enlightened urban policies, Charles III (who ruled until 1788) is affectionately called the "best mayor of Madrid." He decorated the city squares with fine fountains, got those meddle-some Jesuits out of city government, established the public school system, made the Retiro a public park rather than a royal retreat, and generally cleaned up Madrid. The huge palace he faces was the first post office (which Charles established in the 1760s). Today it's remembered for being Franco's police headquarters. An amazing number of those detained and interrogated by the Franco police "tried to escape" by flying out the windows to their deaths. Notice the hats of the civil guardsmen at the entry. It's said the hats have square backsides so they can lean against the wall while enjoying a cigarette.

Crowds fill the square on New Year's Eve. As Spain's "Big Ben" atop the post office chimes 12 times, Madrillinos eat one grape for each ring to bring good luck through the coming year.

A plaque on the post office wall marks the spot where the war against Napoleon started. Napoleon wanted his brother to be king of Spain. Trying to finagle this, Napoleon brought nearly the entire Spanish royal family to France for negotiations. An anxious crowd gathered outside the post office awaiting word of the fate of their royal family. This was just after the French Revolution, and there was a general nervousness between France and Spain. The French guard appeared and the 2nd of May, 1808, massacre took place. Goya, who worked just up the street, observed the event and captured the tragedy in his paintings *2nd of May, 1808,* and *3rd of May, 1808,* which you'll see in the Prado.

Walking from Puerta del Sol to Plaza Mayor: On the corner of Calle Mayor and Puerta del Sol (across from McDonalds), step into the busy *confiteria,* Salon la Mallorquina. It's famous for its sweet Napolitana (creme-filled pastry) or savory, meat-filled *agujas* pastries (200 ptas)—if you can't finish yours, the beggar at the front door would love to; notice the racks with goodies hot out of the oven. Look back toward the entrance and notice the tile above the door with the 18th-century view of the Puerta del Sol. Compare this with the view out the door. This was before the square was widened, when a church stood where the Tío Pepe sign stands today. The French used this church to hold local patriots awaiting execution. (That venerable sign, advertising a famous sherry for over 100 years, is Madrid's first billboard.)

Cross busy Calle Mayor, round McDonald's, and veer left up the pedestrian alley called Calle de Postas. The street sign shows the post coach heading for that famous first post office. Medieval street signs came with pictures so the illiterate could "read" them. After 50 yards, take a left up Calle San Cristobal (passing the local feminist bookshop). At the square notice the big brick 17th-century Ministry of Foreign Affairs building (with the pointed spire)—originally a prison for rich prisoners who could afford the best cells. Turn right and walk down Calle de Zaragoza under the arch into...

Plaza Mayor—This square, built in 1619, is a vast, cobbled, traffic-free chunk of 17th-century Spain. Each side of the square is uniform, as if a grand palace were turned inside out. The statue is of Philip III, who ordered the square's construction. Upon this stage, much Spanish history was played out: bullfights, fires, royal pageantry, and events of the gruesome Inquisition. Reliefs serving as seatbacks under the lampposts tell the story. During the Inquisition, many were tried here. The guilty would parade around the square (bleachers were built for bigger audiences, the wealthy rented balconies) with billboards listing their many sins. They were then burned. Some were slowly strangled with a *garrotte*; they'd hold a crucifix and hear the reassuring words of a priest as this life was squeezed out of them. The square is painted a democratic shade of burgundy—the result of a citywide vote. Since Franco's 1975 death, there's been a passion for voting here. Three different colors were painted as samples on the walls of this square, and the city voted for its favorite.

Throughout Spain, lesser *plazas mayores* provide peaceful pools for the river of Spanish life. A stamp-and-coin market bustles here on Sundays from 10:00 to 14:00, and on any day it's a colorful and affordable place to enjoy a cup of coffee. The TI is at #3.

Finish your Plaza Mayor visit with a drink at the **Torre del Oro Bar Andalu**—a temple to bullfighting. Warning: They push expensive tapas on tourists. A *caña* (small beer) shouldn't cost more than 200 ptas. The bar's ambience is "*Andalu*"…Andalusian. Look under the stuffed head of "Barbero" the bull. At eye level you'll see a *puntilla*, the knife used to put a bull out of its misery at the arena. This was the knife used to kill Barbero.

Notice the incredible action caught in the bar's many photographs. Near Barbero, follow the black and white photo series of a wannabe bullfighter who jumped into the ring and was killed by the bull. Above that is a series of photos showing the scandalous fight in which a banderillero (the guy who puts the arrows into the bull's back) was in trouble and his partners just stood by watching in horror as the man was killed. At the end of the bar in a glass case is the "suit of lights" El Cordobes wore in his ill-fated 1967 fight. With Franco in attendance, El Cordobes went on and on, long after he could have ended the fight, until finally the bull gored him. El Cordobes survived; the bull didn't. Find Franco with El Cordobes at the far end. Under Segador the Bull is a photo of El Cordobes' illegitimate son, El Cordobes, kissing a bull. Disowned by El Cordobes and using his dad's famous name after a court battle, El Cordobes is one of this generation's top fighters.

Walking from Plaza Mayor to the Royal Palace: Leave Plaza Mayor on Calle Cuidad Rodrigo (far right corner from where you entered), passing a series of fine turn-of-the-century storefronts and shops famous for their fried squid-ring sandwiches (*bocadillos calamares*). From the archway you'll see the covered Mercado de San Miguel (green iron posts, on left). Wander

Plaza Mayor to Royal Palace

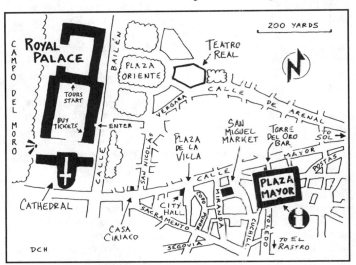

through this produce market, leaving on the opposite (downhill) side and following the pedestrian lane left. At the first corner, turn right, and cross the small plaza to the modern brick **convent**. The door on the right says "venta de dulces"; to buy sweets from cloistered nuns, buzz and follow the sign to *torno*, the lazy Susan which lets the sisters sell their baked goods without being seen (smallest quantities: half or *medio* kilo). Follow Calle del Codo (see the street sign—where those in need of bits of armor shopped) around the convent to Plaza de la Villa, the city-hall square. Ahead the flags of city, state, and nation grace the city hall. The statue in the garden is of Don Bazan—mastermind of the Christian victory over the Moslems at the naval battle of Lepanto in 1571. This pivotal battle ended the Moslem threat to Christian Europe. The mayor's office is behind Don.

From here, busy Calle Mayor leads downhill a couple more blocks to the Royal Palace. Halfway down (on the left) there's a tiny square opposite the recommended Casa Ciriaco restaurant (#84). The statue memorializes the 1906 anarchist bombing that killed 23 people as the royal couple paraded by on their wedding day. While the crowd was throwing flowers, an anarchist threw a bouquet lashed to a bomb from a balcony of #84 (which was a hotel at the time). Amazing photos of the event hang just inside the door in the back room of the restaurant.

▲▲**Royal Palace (Palacio Real)**—Europe's third-greatest palace (after Versailles and Vienna's Schonbrunn) is packed with tourists and royal antiques. After a fortress burned down on this site, King Phillip V commissioned this huge 18th-century palace as a replacement. How huge is it? Over 2,000 rooms with miles of lavish tapestries, a king's ransom of chandeliers, priceless porcelain, paintings, and lots of clocks (Charles IV was a huge collector). While the royal family lives in a mansion a few miles away, the place still functions as a royal palace and is used for formal state receptions and tourist daydreams.

A simple one-floor, 24-room, one-way circuit is open to the public. You can wander on your own or join an English tour (get time of next tour and decide as you buy your ticket; tours depart about every 20 minutes). The tour guides, like the museum guidebook, show a passion for meaningless data (900 ptas without a tour, 1,000 ptas with a tour, Mon–Sat 9:00–19:00, Sun 9:30–14:30; Oct–March Mon–Sat 9:30–18:00, Sun 9:00–14:00, last tickets sold an hour before closing; Metro: Opera, tel. 91-559-7404). Your ticket includes the armory and the pharmacy, both on the courtyard.

If you tour on your own, here are a few details you won't find on the little English descriptions posted in each room:

The Grand Stairs: Fancy carpets are rolled down (notice the little metal bar-holding hooks) for formal occasions. At the top of the first landing, the blue and red coat of arms is of the current—and popular—constitutional monarch, Juan Carlos. While Franco chose him to be the next dictator, J.C. knew Spain was ripe for democracy. Rather than become "Juan the Brief" (as some were nicknaming him), he turned real power over to the parliament. At the top of the stairs (before entering first room, right of door) is a bust of J.C.'s great-great-g-g-g-great-grandfather Phillip V. Grandson of France's King Louis XIV, he began the Bourbon dynasty in 1700. The dynasty survives today with Juan Carlos.

Throne Room: Red velvet walls and lions symbolize the monarchy in this rococo riot. The chandeliers are the best in the house. The thrones are only from 1977. This is where ambassadors give their credentials to the king, who receives them relatively informally... standing rather than seated in the throne.

Gasparini Anteroom (2 rooms after the throne room): The paintings are of King Charles IV and his wife—all by Goya. Velázquez's masterpiece *Las Meninas* originally hung here.

Gasparini Room: This was the royal dressing room. Dressing, for a divine monarch, was a public affair. The court bigwigs would assemble here as the king, standing on a platform—notice the height of the mirrors—would pull on his leotards. In the next room, the silk wallpaper is new—notice the J.C.S. initials of the king and Sofia (the queen).

Gala Dining Room: Five or six times a year the king entertains up to 150 guests at this bowling lane-sized table. The table in the next room would be lined with an exorbitantly caloric dessert buffet. In the next room you can ogle at glass cases filled with the silver tableware used for these functions.

Stradivarius Room: The queen likes classical music and when you perform for her, you do it with these precious 300-year-old violins. About 300 Antonius Stradivarius-made instruments survive. This is the only matching quartet: two violins, a viola, and a cello.

Royal Chapel: The Royal Chapel is used only for baptisms and funerals. The royal tomb sits here before making the sad trip to El Escorial to join the rest of Spain's past royalty.

Billiards and Smoking Rooms: The billiards room and the smoking room were for men only. The porcelain and silk of the smoking room imitates a Chinese opium den.

Queen's Boudoir: The next room was for the ladies, decorated just after Pompeii was excavated and therefore in fanciful ancient-Roman style. You'll exit down the same grand stairway you climbed 24 rooms ago.

The **Cathedral of Almudena**, Madrid's new cathedral, is ahead of you as you leave the palace. It's worth a look while you're here. Built between 1883 and 1993, its exterior is a contemporary mix and its interior is neo-Gothic with a colorful ceiling.

Sights—Madrid's Museum Neighborhood

These three worthwhile museums are in east Madrid. From Prado to the Thyssen-Bornemisza Museum is a five-minute walk; Prado to Reina Sofía is a 10-minute walk.

▲▲▲**Prado Museum**—The Prado holds my favorite collection of paintings anywhere. With more than 3,000 canvases, including entire rooms of masterpieces by Velázquez, Goya, El Greco, and Bosch, it's overwhelming. Take a tour or buy a guidebook (or bring me along by ripping out and packing the Prado chapter from *Rick Steves' Mona Winks*). Focus on the Flemish and northern (Bosch, Dürer, Rubens), the Italian (Fra Angelico, Raphael, Botticelli, Titian), and the Spanish art (El Greco, Velázquez, Goya).

Follow Goya through his stages, from cheery (*The Parasol*) to political (*2nd of May, 1808* and *3rd of May, 1808*) to dark ("Negras de Goya": e.g., *Saturn Devouring His Children*). In each stage, Goya asserted his independence from artistic conventions. Even the standard court portraits from his "first" stage reflect his politically liberal viewpoint, subtly showing the vanity and stupidity of his royal patrons by the looks in their goony eyes. His political stage, with paintings like the *3rd of May, 1808*, depicting a massacre of Spaniards by Napoleon's troops, makes him one of the first artists with a social conscience. Finally, in his gloomy "dark stage," Goya probed the inner world of fears and nightmares, anticipating our modern-day preoccupation with dreams. Also, seek out Bosch's *The Garden of Earthly Delights*—a three-paneled

altarpiece showing creation, the "transparency of earthly plea-
sures," and the resulting hell. Bosch's self-portrait looks out from
hell (with the birds leading naked people around the brim of his
hat) surrounded by people suffering eternal punishments appropriate for their primary earthly excesses.

The art is constantly rearranged by the Prado's fidgety management, so even the Prado's own maps and guidebooks are out of
date. Regardless of the latest location, most art is grouped by
painter, and better guards can point you in the right direction if
you say "*¿Dónde está ... ?*" and the painter's name as Españoled as
you can (e.g., Titian is "Ticiano" and Bosch is "El Bosco"). The
Murillo entrance—at the end closest to the Atocha Station—
usually has shorter lines. Lunchtime, from 14:00 to 16:00, is least
crowded (500 ptas, free on Sat afternoon, all day Sun, and to
anyone under 18 and over 65; Tue–Sat 9:00–19:00, Sun 9:00–
14:00, closed Mon; Paseo de Prado, Metro: Banco de España
or Atocha—each a 15-minute walk from the museum, tel.
91-330-2800 or 91-420-2836).

▲▲**Thyssen-Bornemisza Museum**—This stunning museum
displays the impressive collection that Baron Thyssen (a wealthy
German married to a former Miss Spain) sold to Spain for $350
million. It's basically minor works by major artists and major
works by minor artists (the real big guns are over at the Prado).
But art lovers appreciate how the good baron's art complements
the Prado's collection by filling in where the Prado is weak (Impressionism). For a delightful walk through art history, ride the
elevator to the top floor and do the rooms in numerical order.
It's across from the Prado at Paseo del Prado 8 in the Palacio de
Villahermosa (700 ptas, Tue–Sun 10:00–19:00, closed Mon,
Metro: Banco de España or Atocha, tel. 91-369-0151). Tired ones
can hail a cab at the gate and zip straight to Centro Reina Sofia.

▲▲**Centro Reina Sofia**—In this exceptional modern-art
museum, ride the elevator to the second floor and follow the room
numbers for art from 1900 to 1950. The fourth floor continues
the collection from 1950 to 1980. The museum is most famous
for Picasso's *Guernica*, a massive painting showing the horror of
modern war. Guernica, a village in northern Spain, was the target
of the world's first saturation-bombing raid, approved by Franco
and carried out by Hitler. Notice the two rooms of studies for
Guernica filled with iron-nail tears and screaming mouths.
Guernica was exiled in America until Franco's death, and now it
reigns as Spain's national piece of art.

The museum also houses an easy-to-enjoy collection of other
modern artists, including more of Picasso (3 rooms divided among
his pre-civil-war work, *Guernica*, and his post-civil-war art) and a
mind-bending room of Dalís. Enjoy a break in the shady courtyard
before leaving (500 ptas, free Sat afternoon and all day Sun; Mon

and Wed–Sat 10:00–21:00, Sun 10:00–14:30, closed Tue; Santa Isabel 52, Metro: Atocha, across from Atocha train station, look for exterior glass elevators, tel. 91-467-5062).

More Sights—Madrid

Chapel San Antonio de la Florida—Goya's tomb stares up at a splendid cupola filled with his own frescoes (300 ptas, Tue–Fri 10:00–14:00, 16:00–20:00, Sat–Sun 10:00–14:00, closed Mon, July and Aug only 10:00–14:00, Glorieta de San Antonio de la Florida, Metro: Príncipe Pío, tel. 91-542-0722).

Royal Tapestry Factory (Real Fabrica de Tapices)—Have a look at the traditional making of tapestries (250 ptas, some English tours, Mon–Fri 10:00–14:00, closed Aug, Calle Fuenterrabia 2, Metro: Menendez Pelayo, take Gutenberg exit, tel. 91-434-0551).

▲Retiro Park—Siesta in this 350-acre green and breezy escape from the city. At midday on Saturday and Sunday, the area around the lake becomes a street carnival, with jugglers, puppeteers, and lots of local color. These peaceful gardens offer great picnicking and people watching. From the Retiro Metro stop, walk to the big lake (El Estanque), where you can rent a rowboat (450 ptas for 45 min). Past the lake, a grand boulevard of statues leads to the Prado.

Charles III's Botanical Garden (Real Jardín Botánico)—After your Prado visit, consider a lush and fragrant break in this sculpted park wandering among trees from around the world (entry just opposite Prado's Murillo entry, 250 ptas, daily 9:00–21:00, Plaza de Murillo 2).

Moncloa Tower—This tower offers the best skyscraper view in town (200 ptas, elevator takes you 100 meters up).

Teleferico—For a break from the big city, ride this cable car from downtown over Madrid's sprawling city park to Casa de Campo (535 ptas round-trip, daily from 12:00, departs from Paseo del Pintor Rosales, Metro: Arguelles, tel. 91-541-7450).

Shopping

Shoppers can focus on the colorful pedestrian area between Gran Vía and Puerta del Sol. The giant Spanish department store, El Corte Inglés, is a block off Puerta del Sol and a handy place to pick up just about anything you need (Mon–Sat 10:00–21:30, closed Sun, free maps at info desk, supermarket in basement).

▲El Rastro—Europe's biggest flea market, held on Sundays and holidays, is a field day for shoppers, people watchers, and thieves (9:00–15:00, best before 12:00). Thousands of stalls titillate more than a million browsers with mostly new junk. If you brake for garage sales, you'll pull a U-turn for El Rastro. Start at the Plaza Mayor and head south or take the subway to Tirso de Molina. Hang on to your wallet. Munch on a *relleno* or *pepito* (meat-filled pastry). Europe's biggest stamp market thrives simultaneously on Plaza Mayor.

Nightlife

▲▲▲**Bullfight**—Madrid's Plaza de Toros hosts Spain's top bullfights on most Sundays and holidays from Easter through October and nearly every day mid-May through early June. Top fights sell out in advance. Fights start punctually at 19:00. Tickets range from 500 to 10,000 ptas. There are no bad seats at Plaza de Toros; paying more gets you in the shade and/or closer to the gore (*filas* 8, 9, and 10 tend to be closest to the action). Booking offices and hotels are convenient but they add 20 percent and don't sell the cheap seats (Calle de Victoria 3, tel. 91-531-2732). If you want to save money, stand in the bullring ticket line. Tickets go on sale the day of the fight at 10:00; 10 percent of the seats are kept available to be sold two hours before the fight (Calle Alcala 237, Metro: Ventas, tel. 91-356-2200, www.las-ventas.com). The bullfighting museum (Museo Taurino) is next to the bullring (free, 9:30–14:30, closed Sat and Mon and early on fight days, Calle Alcala 237, tel. 91-725-1857).

▲▲**Zarzuela**—For a delightful look at Spanish light opera that even English speakers can enjoy, try Zarzuela. Guitar-strumming Napoleons in red capes; buxom women with masks, fans, and castanets; Spanish-speaking pharaohs; melodramatic spotlights; and aficionados clapping and singing along from the cheap seats where the acoustics are best—this is Zarzuela . . . the people's opera. Madrid's Theater Zarzuela is at Jovellanos 4 (Metro: Banco de España, tel. 91-524-5400). The TI's monthly guide has a special Zarzuela listing.

Flamenco—This uniquely Spanish dance is fun, sexy, and riveting. Taberna Casa Patas offers flamenco in a small intimate setting, with one drink included and no hassling after that (tickets around 3,000 ptas, shows at 22:00, smoky Canizares 10, near Plaza Santa Ana, reservations tel. 91-369-0496). The Flamenco House is more touristy (Calle Torija 7, just off Plaza Mayor).

Sleeping in Madrid
(180 ptas = about $1, country code: 34)

Sleep Code: **S** = Single, **D** = Double/Twin, **T** = Triple, **Q** = Quad, **b** = bathroom, **t** = toilet only, **s** = shower only, **CC** = Credit Card (**V**isa, **M**asterCard, **A**mex), **SE** = Speaks English, **NSE** = No English. Breakfast is not included unless noted. In Madrid, the 7 percent IVA tax is generally, but not always, included in the price.

Madrid has plenty of centrally located budget hotels and *pensiónes*. You'll have no trouble finding a sleepable double for $30, a good double for $60, and a modern air-conditioned double with all the comforts for $100. Prices are the same throughout the year, and it's almost always easy to find a place. Anticipate full hotels May 15 to 25 (the festival of Madrid's patron Saint Isidro) and the last week in September (conventions). The accommodations I've listed are within a few minutes' walk of Puerta del Sol.

Sleeping in the Pedestrian Zone between Puerta del Sol and Gran Vía (zip code: 28013)

Predictable and away from the seediness, these are good values for those wanting to spend a little more. Their formal prices may be inflated, and some offer weekend and summer discounts whenever it's slow. Metro: Sol. See map on page 682 for location.

Hotel Europa has red-carpet charm: a royal salon, plush halls with happy Muzak, polished wood floors, attentive staff, and 80 squeaky-clean rooms with balconies overlooking the pedestrian zone or an inner courtyard—which amplifies voices, grunts d'amour, and TV noise. For a better night's sleep, remind the management to enforce the no-TV-after-midnight rule (Sb-6,900 ptas, Db-8,900 ptas, Tb-12,600 ptas, Qb-14,800 ptas, fine lounge on second floor, elevator, fans, easy phone reservations with credit card, CC:VMA, Calle del Carmen 4, tel. 91-521-2900, fax 91-521-4696, www.hoteleuropa.net, e-mail: info@hoteleuropa.net, Antonio Garaban and his very helpful staff SE). The convenient Europa cafeteria/restaurant next door is a great scene and a fine value any time of day.

Hotel Regente is a big, traditional, and impersonal place with 145 plain but comfortable air-conditioned rooms and a great location (Sb-6,500 ptas, Db-11,000 ptas, Tb-12,500 ptas, CC:VMA, midway between Puerta del Sol and Plaza del Callao at Mesonero Romanos 9, tel. 91-521-2941, fax 91-532-3014).

Euromadrid Hotel is like a Motel 6 with 43 nondescript rooms in a modern but well-worn shell (Sb-8,600 ptas, Db-11,500 ptas, Tb-14,000 ptas, includes tax and breakfast, CC:VMA, aircon, Mesonero Romanos 7, tel. 91-521-7200, fax 91-521-4582).

Hotel Cliper is spick-and-span with once-elegant character and basic rooms on a fairly quiet street (Sb-6,300 ptas, Db-8,500 ptas, Tb-9,500 ptas, includes tax and breakfast, fine lounge, aircon, elevator, CC:VMA, Chincilla 6, near Plaza Carmen, tel. 91-531-1700, fax 91-531-1707, e-mail: reservas@hotelclipper.com).

The huge **Hotel Liabeny** feels classy and new, with 222 plush, spacious rooms and all the comforts. It's a business-class hotel that decided to lower its prices to get the tourist trade (Sb-11,900 ptas, Db-16,200 ptas, Tb-19,000 ptas; mid-July and Aug Db-12,000 ptas; CC:VMA, air-con, if one room is smoky ask for another, off Plaza Carmen at Salud 3, tel. 91-531-9000, fax 91-532-7421, e-mail: liabeny@apunte.es).

Hotel Opera, a serious 79-room hotel with all the comforts, is located just off Plaza Isabel II, a ten-minute walk from Puerta del Sol toward the Royal Palace (Sb-12,000 ptas, Db-16,800 ptas, Tb-21,800 ptas, 10 percent off on weekends and in the summer, CC:VMA, air-con, elevator, ask for a higher floor—there are eight—to avoid street noise, consider their "singing dinners," Cuesta de Santo Domingo 2, tel. 91-541-2800, fax 91-541-6923, www.hotelopera.com, e-mail: reservas@hotelopera.com).

Sleeping at Gran Vía #44
(zip code: 28013)

The pulse (and noise) of today's Madrid is best felt along the Gran Vía. This main drag in the heart of the city stays awake all night. Despite the dreary pile of prostitutes just a block north, there's a certain urban decency about it. My choices (all at Gran Vía #44) are across from Plaza del Callao, which is four colorful blocks (of pedestrian malls) from Puerta del Sol. Although many rooms are high above the traffic noise, cooler and quieter rooms are on the back side. The Café & Te next door provides a classy way to breakfast. The Callao Metro stop is at your doorstep, and the handy Gran Vía stop (direct to Atocha) is two blocks away.

Hostal Residencia Miami is clean and quiet, with 11 well-lit rooms, padded doors, and plastic-flower decor throughout. It's like staying at your eccentric aunt's in Miami Beach (S-3,000–4,000 ptas, D-5,000 ptas, Db-7,000 ptas, T-7,000 ptas, Tb-8,000 ptas, includes tax, CC:VM, eighth floor, tel. & fax 91-521-1464).

Across the hall, **Hostal Alibel**, like Miami with less sugar, rents seven big, airy, quiet rooms (D-5,000 ptas, Ds-5,500 ptas, Db-6,000 ptas, tel. 91-521-0051, grandmotherly Terese NSE).

These next two are threadbare and suffer from street noise. **Hostal Residencia Valencia** is a tired old place with 32 big, stark rooms. The friendly manager, Antonio Ramirez, speaks English (Sb-4,400 ptas, Ds-6,000 ptas, Db-6,200 ptas, Tb-8,200 ptas, Qb-9,200 ptas, CC:VMA, fifth floor, tel. 91-522-1115, fax 91-522-1113). A bit smoky and with less character, **Hostal Residencia Continental** is downstairs and closer to the traffic (Sb-4,400 ptas, Db-5,800 ptas, CC:VMA, third floor, tel. 91-521-4640, fax 91-521-4649, e-mail: continental@mundivia.es, SE).

Sleeping on or near Plaza Santa Ana
(zip code: 28012 unless otherwise noted)

The Plaza Santa Ana area has plenty of small, cheap places. While well worn and noisy at night, it has a rough but charming ambience, with colorful bars and a central location (3 min from Puerta del Sol's "Tío Pepe" sign; walk down Calle San Jeronimo and turn right on Príncipe; Metro: Sol). At most of these hotels, fluent Spanish is spoken, bathrooms are down the hall, and there's no heat during winter. To locate hotels, see map on page 697.

Hopeless romantics might enjoy playing corkscrew around the rickety cut-glass elevator to the very simple yet homey **Pensión La Valenciana**'s old and funky rooms with springy beds. All rooms have balconies; three of them overlook the square (S-1,600 ptas, D-3,500 ptas, Príncipe 27, fourth floor, right on Plaza Santa Ana next to the theater with flags, tel. 91-429-6317, Esperanza NSE).

Because of the following two places, I list no Madrid youth hostels. For super-cheap beds in a dingy time warp, consider **Hostal Lucense** (S-1,500 ptas, D-2,800 ptas, Ds-3,000 ptas, Ts-3,500 ptas, 200 ptas per shower, cheaper for 2 nights, Nuñez de Arce 15, tel. 91-522-4888, run by Sr. and Sra. Muñoz, both interesting characters, Sr. SE) and **Casa Huéspedes Poza** (same prices, street noise, and owners—but Sr. does the cleaning, at Nuñez de Arce 9, tel. 91-522-4871).

Hostal R. Veracruz II, between Plaza Santa Ana and Puerta del Sol, rents decent, quiet rooms (Sb-4,800 ptas, Db-6,500 ptas, Tb-8,200 ptas, CC:VM, elevator, air-con, Victoria 1, third floor, tel. 91-522-7635, fax 91-522-6749, NSE).

Splurges: To be on the same square and spend in a day what others spend in a week, luxuriate in **Hotel Reina Victoria** (Sb-24,000 ptas, Db-30,000 ptas, prices generally discounted to "weekend rate" of Db-16,500 on Fri, Sat, Sun in summer and all of July, when this becomes a fine value, CC:VMA, Plaza Santa Ana 14, tel. 91-531-4500, fax 91-522-0307, e-mail: reinavictoria@trypnet .com). For a royal, air-conditioned breather, spit out your gum, step into its lobby, grab a sofa, and watch the bellboys push the beggars back out the revolving doors.

Suite Prado, two blocks toward the Prado from Plaza Santa Ana, is a better value, offering 18 sprawling, air-conditioned suites with a homier feel (Db suite-23,500 ptas, suites are modern and comfortable with refrigerators and sitting rooms, extra adult-4,000 ptas, extra kid free, elevator, CC:VMA, Manuel Fernandez y Gonzalez 10, at intersection with Venture de la Vega, 28014 Madrid, tel. 91-420-2318, fax 91-420-0559, www.suiteprado.com, Monica and Anna SE). Across the street, **Residencia Hostal Lisboa** is also a good value (Sb-6,000 ptas, Db-7,100 ptas, Tb-9,100 ptas, CC:VMA, elevator, Ventura de la Vega 17, tel. 91-429-4676, fax 91-429-9894).

Sleeping Elsewhere in Central Madrid

Halfway between the Prado Museum and Plaza Santa Ana are two good places at #34 Cervantes (28014 Madrid, Metro: Anton Martin). The spotless and comfortable **Hotel Gonzalo**—well-run by friendly and helpful Javier—is in all the guidebooks (Sb-4,900 ptas, Db-5,900 ptas, Tb-7,500 ptas, CC:VMA, elevator, 15 rooms, third floor, tel. 91-429-2714, fax 91-420-2007). The equally polished **Hotel Cervantes** is also good (Sb-5,000 ptas, Db-6,500 ptas, Tb-8,500 ptas, CC:VMA, second floor, tel. & fax 91-429-2745).

Hostal Tijcal is comfortable, with tons of extras; and just half a block east of the elegant Plaza Mayor on a quiet, traffic-free street (that can attract unsavory characters late at night). Run with pride by Gabriel Caraballo and his parents, the hotel name is an acronym for: work, equality, justice, culture, amigos, and liberty (S-4,500 ptas, Sb-6,000 ptas, D-6,700 ptas, Db-7,500 ptas, includes tax, air-con–1,000 ptas extra per day, elevator, CC:VM, Zaragoza 6, third floor, 28012 Madrid, Metro: Sol, tel. 91-365-5910, fax 91-364-5260, www.hostaltijcal.com).

Eating in Madrid

In Spain, only Barcelona rivals Madrid for taste-bud thrills. You have three dining choices: an atmospheric sit-down meal in a well-chosen restaurant, an unmemorable basic sit-down meal, or a stand-up meal of tapas in a bar or (more likely) in several bars. Many restaurants are closed in August (especially through the last half).

Eating near Puerta del Sol and Plaza Mayor

Many Americans are drawn to Hemingway's favorite, **Sobrino del Botín** (daily 13:00–16:00, 20:00–24:00, Cuchilleros 17, a block downhill from Plaza Mayor, tel. 91-366-4217). It's touristy, pricey, and the last place he'd go now, but still, people love it, and the food is excellent. If phoning to make a reservation, choose between the downstairs (for dark, medieval-cellar ambience) or upstairs (for a still-traditional but airier and lighter elegance).

Restaurante Los Galayos is less touristy and plenty *tipico* with good local cuisine (daily lunch specials, lunch from 13:00, dinner from 20:30, arrive early or make a reservation, 30 meters off Plaza Mayor at Botoneras 5, tel. 91-366-3028). For many, dinner right on the square is worth the premium (consider Restaurante Pulpito, behind the horse).

Plaza Mayor is famous for its *bocadillos calamares*. For a cheap and tasty squid-ring sandwich, line up at **Casa Rua** on Plaza Mayor's southwest corner (behind and to the right of the horse statue).

Restaurante Rodriguez serves basic food which locals return for (closed July, San Cristobal 15, 1 block toward Puerta del Sol from Plaza Mayor, tel. 91-231-1136).

La Casa de las Torrijas, looking much like it did on opening day in 1907, serves cheap home-cooked lunch specials, tapas, and good wine. The sign under the mirror reads: "For hygienic reasons, no spitting on the floor" (Mon–Sat 13:00–16:00, 18:00–24:00, closed Sun, a block off Puerta del Sol at Calle Paz 4, tel. 91-532-1473).

For a fine meal with no tourists and locals who appreciate good local-style cooking, try **Casa Ciriaco** (3,000-ptas meals, Thu–Tue 13:30–16:00, 20:30–24:00, closed Wed and Aug, halfway between Puerta del Sol and Royal Palace at Calle Mayor 84,

tel. 91-548-0620). It was from this building in 1906 that an anarchist threw a bomb at the royal couple on their wedding day (for
details, see "Introductory Walk," above). Photos of the carnage
are on the wall in the dining room.

Restaurante Puerto Rico has good food, great prices, and
few tourists (Mon–Sat 13:00–16:30, 20:30–24:00, closed Sun,
Chinchilla 2, between Puerta del Sol and Gran Vía, on same
street as Hotel Cliper, tel. 91-532-2040).

Hotel Europa Cafeteria is a fun high-energy scene with a
mile-long bar, traditionally clad waiters, great people watching,
local cuisine, and super prices (next to Hotel Europa, 50 meters
off Puerta del Sol at Calle del Carmen 4, tel. 91-521-2900).

Eating near the Prado
Each of the big-three art museums has a decent cafeteria. These
two cafés are near the Prado: **La Platería** is a hardworking little
café/wine bar with a good menu for tapas, light meals, and hearty
salads. Its tables spill onto the leafy little Plaza de Platarias de
Matinez (daily 8:00–24:00, directly across busy highway from
Atocha end of Prado, tel. 91-429-1722). Good-looking young tour
guides eat cheap and filling salads at **VIPS**, a bright modern place
engulfed in a big bookstore (daily 9:00–24:00, in Galeria del Prado
at Prado end of San Jeronimo under Palace Hotel).

Vegetarian
Artemisia II is a hit with vegetarians who like good, healthy food
in a smoke-free room (great 1,400-ptas 3-course lunch menu, daily
13:30–16:00, 21:00–24:00, closed last half of Aug, CC:VMA, 2 blocks
north of Puerta Sol at Tres Cruces 4, just off Plaza Carmen, tel. 91-
521-8721). **Artemisia I** is like its sister (4 blocks east of Puerta Sol
at Ventura de la Vega 4 off San Jeronimo, tel. 91-429-5092).

Fast Food, Picnics, and Breakfast
Fast Food: For an easy, light, cheap meal, try **Rodilla**—a popular
sandwich bar on the northeast corner of Puerta del Sol at #13 (daily
8:30–20:30). **Pans & Company**, with shops throughout Spain, offers
healthy, tasty sandwiches and great chef's salads (daily 9:00–24:00, on
Puerta del Sol, Plaza Callão, Gran Vía 30, and many more).

Picnics: The department store **El Corte Inglés** has a well-
stocked **deli**, but its produce is sold only in large quantities (Mon–
Sat 10:00–21:00, closed Sun). A perfect place to assemble a cheap
picnic is downtown Madrid's neighborhood market, **Mercado de
San Miguel.** How about breakfast surrounded by early-morning
shoppers in the market's café? (Mon–Fri 9:00–14:30, 17:15–20:15,
Sat 9:00–14:30, closed Sun; from Plaza Mayor, face the colorful
building and exit from the upper left-hand corner.)

***Churros con chocolate* for breakfast:** If you like hash browns

and eggs in American greasy-spoon joints, you must try the Spanish equivalent: greasy *churros* dipped in thick, hot chocolate. **Bar
Valladolid** is a good bet for *churros* (open daily from 7:00, 2 blocks
off Tío Pepe end of Puerta del Sol, south on Espoz y Mina, turn
right on Calle de Cadiz). With luck, the *churros* machine in the
back will be cooking. Notice the expressive WC signs.

Tapas: The Madrid Pub-Crawl Dinner

For maximum fun, people, and atmosphere, go mobile and do the
"tapa tango," a local tradition of going from one bar to the next,
munching, drinking, and socializing. Tapas are the toothpick
appetizers, salads, and deep-fried foods served in most bars.
Madrid is Spain's tapa capital—tapas just don't get any better.
Grab a toothpick and stab something strange—but establish the
prices first. Some items are very pricey, and most bars push larger
raciónes rather than smaller tapas. *Un pincho* is a bite-sized serving
(not always available), *una tapa* is a snack, and *una ración* is half a
meal. *Un bocadillo* is a tapa on bread. A *caña* (can-yah) is a small
glass of draft beer. A *chato* is a small glass of house wine.

   Prowl the area between Puerta del Sol and Plaza Santa Ana.
There's no ideal route, but the little streets (in this book's map)
between Puerta del Sol, San Jeronimo, and Plaza Santa Ana hold
tasty surprises. Nearby, Jesus de Medinaceli is also lined with
popular tapas bars. Below is a seven-stop tapa crawl. These places
are good, but don't be blind to making discoveries on your own.
The action is better after 20:00.

   1. From Puerta del Sol, walk east a block down Carrera de
San Jeronimo to the corner of Victoria Street. Across from Museo
del Jamón, you'll find **La Tourina Cerverecería**, a bullfighters'
Planet Hollywood. Wander among trophies and historic photographs. Each stuffed bull's head is named, along with its farm,
awards, and who killed him. Among the photos study the first
post: It's Che Guevara, Orson Welles, and Salvador Dalí all
enjoying a good fight. Around the corner, the Babe Ruth of
bullfighters, El Cordobes, is wounded in bed. The photo below
shows him in action. Kick off your pub crawl with a drink here.
If inspired, you could go for the *rabo de toro* (bull-tail stew, 1,500
ptas). Across the street at San Jeronimo 5 is…

   2. Museo del Jamón (Museum of Ham), tastefully
decorated—unless you're a pig. This frenetic, cheap, stand-up
bar is an assembly line of fast and deliciously simple *bocadillos*
and *raciónes*. Options are shown in photographs with prices.
For a small sandwich, ask for a *chiquito* (100 ptas, unadvertised).
The pricey *Jamón Iberico*—from pigs who led stress-free lives
in acorn valley—is best. Just point and eat (daily 9:00–24:00,
sit-down restaurant upstairs). Next, forage halfway up Calle
Victoria to the tiny…

Plaza Santa Ana Area

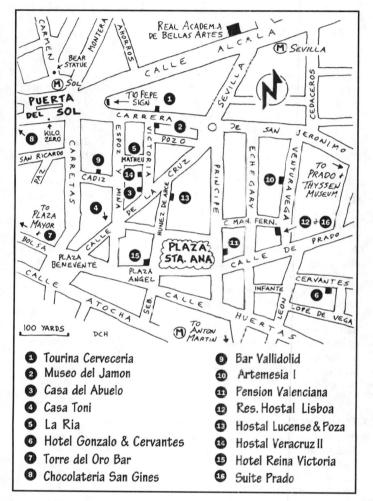

1. Tourina Cerveceria
2. Museo del Jamon
3. Casa del Abuelo
4. Casa Toni
5. La Ria
6. Hotel Gonzalo & Cervantes
7. Torre del Oro Bar
8. Chocolateria San Gines
9. Bar Vallidolid
10. Artemesia I
11. Pension Valenciana
12. Res. Hostal Lisboa
13. Hostal Lucense & Poza
14. Hostal Veracruz II
15. Hotel Reina Victoria
16. Suite Prado

3. La Casa del Abuelo, for shrimp lovers who savor sizzling plates of tasty little *gambas*. Try *gambas a ia plancha* (grilled shrimp, 600 ptas), *gambas al ajillo* (ahh-hheee-yoh, shrimp version of escargot, cooked in oil and garlic and ideal for bread dipping—750 ptas), and a 150-ptas glass of red wine (daily 11:30–15:30, 18:30–23:30, Calle Victoria 12). Continue uphill and around the corner to...

4. Casa Toni, for refreshing bowls of gazpacho—the popular cold tomato-and-garlic soup (250 ptas, open from 19:30, closed

mid-June–mid-July, Calle Cruz 14). Backtrack halfway down
Calle Victoria and turn left, walking through an alley littered
with tourist-filled dining tables to...

5. La Ria, a tapas bar that sells plates of 10 mussels—slurp
out the meat, scoop the juice with the shells, and toss the shells on
the floor as you smack your lips (19:30–23:00, Pasaje Matheu 5).
Mejillones picantes is spicy (460 ptas). Wash each down with the
crude, dry, white Ribeiro wine from Galicia—served in a ceramic
bowl to disguise its lack of clarity. The place is draped in mussels.
Notice the photo showing the floor filled with litter—a reminder
that mussel bars, while lonely these days, have seen better times.
In the 1970s they sold 14 tons a month. Now—with other, more
trendy evening activities entertaining the cruising youth—it takes
a year to sell 14 tons.

6. Head to Plaza Mayor for **La Torre del Oro Bar Andalu**
(26 Plaza Mayor, from 11:00, tel. 91-366-5016). Bullfight aficionados hate the gimmicky Bull Bar across from Museo del Jamón
(stop #1). This one has soul. The walls are lined with grisly bullfight photos from annual photo competitions. Read the gory
description above in the Introductory Walk. Have a drink but be
careful not to let the aggressive staff bully you into high-priced
tapas you don't want.

7. The classy **Chocolatería San Ginés** is much loved locally
for its *churros* (greasy cigar-shaped fritters) and chocolate (Tue–
Sun 22:00–7:00, closed Mon). While empty before midnight, it's
packed with the disco crowd in the wee hours (the popular Joy
disco is next door). Finish off your crawl sweetly, dunking your
churros into the pudding-like hot chocolate, as locals have done
here for over 100 years (from Plaza Mayor, cross Calle Mayor
and go down Calle P. de San Ginés to #5, off Calle Arenal, tel.
93-365-6546).

Transportation Connections—Madrid

By train to: Toledo (9/day, 1 hr, from Madrid's Atocha station,
if day-tripping there's a direct Madrid–Toledo express at 8:34 or
9:44 and a Toledo–Madrid express at 18:56), **Segovia** (9/day, 2
hrs, both Chamartin and Atocha stations), **Avila** (6/day, 90 min,
from Chamartin and Atocha), **Salamanca** (4/day, 2.5 hrs, from
Chamartin), **Barcelona** (6/day, 8 hrs, mostly from Chamartin),
Granada (6–9 hrs, including an overnight train, from Chamartin),
Sevilla (15/day, 2.5 hrs by AVE, 3.5 hrs by Talgo, from Atocha),
Córdoba (16 AVE trains/day, 2 hrs, from Atocha), **Lisbon** (1/day,
10 hrs, overnight from Chamartin), **Paris** (4/day, 12–16 hrs, 1
direct overnight, from Chamartin). Train info: tel. 902-240-202.

GIMMELWALD AND THE BERNER OBERLAND

Frolic and hike high above the stress and clouds of the real world.
Take a vacation from your busy vacation. Recharge your touristic
batteries up here in the Alps, where distant avalanches, cowbells,
the fluff of a down comforter, and the crunchy footsteps of happy
hikers are the dominant sounds. If the weather's good (and your
budget's healthy), ride a gondola from the traffic-free village of
Gimmelwald to a hearty breakfast at Schilthorn's 10,000-foot
revolving Piz Gloria restaurant. Linger among Alpine whitecaps
before riding, hiking, or parasailing down (5,000 feet) to Mürren
and home to Gimmelwald.

Your gateway to the rugged Berner Oberland is the grand
old resort town of Interlaken. Near Interlaken is Switzerland's
open-air folk museum, Ballenberg, where you can climb through
traditional houses from every corner of this diverse country.

Ah, but the weather's fine and the Alps beckon. Head deep
into the heart of the Alps and ride the gondola to the stop just
this side of heaven—Gimmelwald.

Planning Your Time

Rather than tackling a checklist of famous Swiss mountains and
resorts, choose one region to savor—the Berner Oberland. Interlaken is the administrative headquarters and a fine transportation
hub. Use it for business (banking, post office, laundry, shopping)
and as a springboard for Alpine thrills. With decent weather,
explore the two areas (south of Interlaken) that tower above either
side of the Lauterbrunnen Valley: Kleine Scheidegg/Jungfrau and
Schilthorn/Mürren. Ideally, home-base three nights in the village
of Gimmelwald and spend a day on each side of the valley. On a
speedy train trip you can overnight into and out of Interlaken.

For the fastest look, consider a night in Gimmelwald, breakfast at the Schilthorn, an afternoon doing the Männlichen-to-Wengen hike, and an evening or night train out. What? A nature lover not spending the night high in the Alps? Alpus-interruptus.

Getting around the Berner Oberland

For more than 100 years, this has been the target of nature-worshiping pilgrims. And Swiss engineers and visionaries have made the most exciting Alpine perches accessible by lift or train. Part of the fun (and most of the expense) here is riding the many lifts. Generally, scenic trains and lifts are not covered on train passes, but a Eurail, Europass, or Eurail Selectpass gets you a 25 percent discount on even the highest lifts (without the loss of a flexi-day). Ask about discounts for early (and late) trips, youths, seniors, families, groups, and those staying awhile. The Junior Card pays for itself on the first hour of trains and lifts: children under 16 travel free with parents (20 SF for 1 child, 40 SF for 2 or more; available at Swiss train stations but not at gondola stations). Get a list of discounts and the free fare and time schedule at any train station. Study the "Alpine Lifts in the Berner Oberland" chart in this chapter. Lifts generally go at least twice hourly, from about 7:00 until about 20:00 (sneak preview: www.jungfrau.ch). Drivers can park at the gondola station in Stechelberg for the lift to Gimmelwald, Mürren, and the Schilthorn (5 SF/day), or at the train station in Lauterbrunnen for trains to Wengen and Kleine Scheidegg.

INTERLAKEN

When the 19th-century Romantics redefined mountains as something more than cold and troublesome obstacles, Interlaken became the original Alpine resort. Ever since then, tourists have flocked to the Alps because they're there. Interlaken's glory days are long gone, its elegant old hotels eclipsed by the new, more jet-setty Alpine resorts. Today its shops are filled with chocolate bars, Swiss Army knives, and sunburned backpackers.

Orientation (area code: 033)

Efficient Interlaken is a good administrative and shopping center. Take care of business, give the town a quick look, and view the live TV coverage of the Jungfrau and Schilthorn weather in the window of the Schilthornbahn office on the main street (at Höheweg 2, also on TV in most hotel lobbies). Then head for the hills. Stay in Interlaken only if you suffer from alptitude sickness (see "Sleeping in Interlaken," at the end of this chapter).

Tourist Information: The TI has good information for the region, advice on Alpine lift discounts, and a room-finding service (July–Sept Mon–Fri 8:00–18:30, Sat 8:00–17:00, Sun 10:00–12:00, 16:00-18:00; Oct–June Mon–Fri 8:00–12:00, 14:00–18:00,

Interlaken

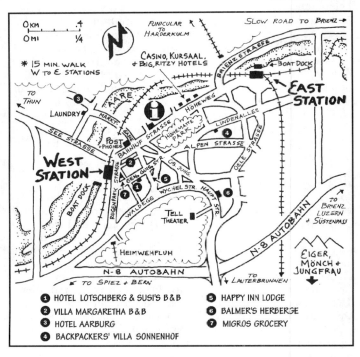

0 KM ____.4
0 MI ____¼

FUNICULAR ↖
TO
HARDERKULM

SLOW ROAD TO BRIENZ →

CASINO, KURSAAL,
& BIG, RITZY HOTELS

BRIENZ STRASSE

★ 15 MIN. WALK
W TO E STATIONS

BOAT DOCK

TO
THUN

AARE

LAUNDRY

HOHEWEG

SEE STRASSE

MARKT

HOHEMATTE
PARK

LINDENALLEE

EAST
STATION

POST
+ PHONES

BAHNHOF STRASSE

ALPEN STRASSE

OELE STRASSE

WEST
STATION →

BOAT DOCK

RUGENPARK STRASSE

GEN. GUIS STR.

CV. JUNG

4

TO
BRIENZ
LUZERN
& SÜSTENPASS

WALDEGG

WYCHEL STR.

HAUPT STR.

6

N-8 AUTOBAHN

TELL
THEATER

HEIMWEHFLUH

N-8 AUTOBAHN

← TO SPIEZ & BERN

TO
LAUTERBRUNNEN ↓

EIGER,
MÖNCH &
JUNGFRAU
↓

❶ HOTEL LOTSCHBERG & SUSI'S B&B
❷ VILLA MARGARETHA B&B
❸ HOTEL AARBURG
❹ BACKPACKERS' VILLA SONNENHOF

❺ HAPPY INN LODGE
❻ BALMER'S HERBERGE
❼ MIGROS GROCERY

Sat 9:00–12:00, closed Sun, tel. 033/826-5300, on main street, 5-minute walk from West station). While the Jungfrau region map costs 2 SF, a good mini-version is included in the free Jungfrau region train timetable. Pick up a Bern map if that's your next destination. The TI organizes town walks in English in summer (10 SF, June–Sept daily at 18:00, 60 min, depart from TI).

Arrival in Interlaken: Interlaken has two train stations: East and West. Most major trains stop at the Interlaken-West station. This station's train information desk answers tourists' questions (Mon–Fri 7:00–20:00, Sat–Sun 8:00–12:00, 14:00–18:00, tel. 033/826-4750), and there's a fair exchange booth next to the ticket windows. Ask at the station about discount passes, special fares, railpass discounts, and schedules for the scenic mountain trains (tel. 033/826-4750).

It's a pleasant 15-minute walk between the West and East stations, or an easy, frequent train connection. From the Interlaken-East station, private trains take you deep into the mountainous Jungfrau region (see "Transportation Connections," at the end of this chapter).

Helpful Hints

Telephone: Phone booths cluster outside the post office near the West station. For efficiency, buy a phone card from a newsstand. (There's a card phone in Gimmelwald that doesn't take coins.)

Laundry: Helen Schmocker's *Wäscherei* (laundry) has a change machine, soap, English instructions, and a pleasant riverside locale (daily, 24 hrs for self-service, or Mon–Sat 8:00–12:00, 13:30–18:00 for full service: drop off 10 pounds in the morning and pick up clean clothes that afternoon, from post office, follow Marktgasse over 2 bridges to Beatenbergstrasse; tel. 033/822-1566).

Grocery: A Migros supermarket is across the street from the train station (Mon–Thu 8:00–18:30, Fri 8:00–21:00, Sat 7:30–16:00, closed Sun).

Sights—Interlaken

Boat Trips—*Interlaken* means "between the lakes." Lazy boat trips explore these lakes (8/day, fewer off-season, free with Eurail/ Euro/Eurail Selectpass, schedules at TI). The boats on **Lake Thun** stop at Beatushöhlen (interesting caves, 30 min from Interlaken, cave entry-14 SF, mid-April–mid-Oct, daily 10:30–17:00) and two visit-worthy towns: Spiez (1 hr from Interlaken) and Thun (1.75 hrs away). The boats on **Lake Brienz** stop at the super-cute and quiet village of Iseltwald (45 min away), and Brienz (1.25 hrs away, near Ballenberg Open-Air Folk Museum).

Adventure Trips—For the adventurer with money and little concern for personal safety, several companies offer high-adrenaline trips such as rafting, canyoning (rappelling down watery gorges), bungee jumping, and paragliding. Most adventure trips cost from 90 to 180 SF. Interlaken companies include: Alpin Raft (Postfach 78, tel. 033/823-4100, www.alpinraft.ch), Alpin Center (near East station, tel. 033/823-5523, www.alpincenter.ch), and Swiss Adventures (tel. 033/773-7373, www.swissadventures.ch).

Recent fatal accidents have understandably hurt the adventure-sport business in the Berner Oberland. In the summer of 1999, 22 tourists died canyoning on the Saxetenbach River, 10 miles from Interlaken (a flash flood pummeled the entire tour group with debris). In the spring of 2000, an American died bungee jumping from the Stechelberg-Mürren gondola (the operator used a 180-meter rope for a 100-meter jump). Also in 2000, a landslide killed several hikers. Enjoying nature up close comes with risks. Adventure sports increase those risks dramatically. Use good judgment.

GIMMELWALD

Saved from developers by its "avalanche zone" classification, Gimmelwald was (before tourism) one of the poorest places in Switzerland. Its traditional economy was stuck in the hay, and its farmers, unable to make it in their disadvantaged trade, survived only by

Gimmelwald

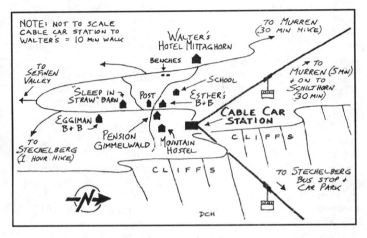

NOTE: NOT TO SCALE
CABLE CAR STATION TO
WALTER'S = 10 MIN WALK

TO MURREN
(30 MIN HIKE)

WALTER'S
HOTEL MITTAGHORN

BENCHES

TO
SEFINEN
VALLEY

SCHOOL

↗ TO
MURREN (5 MIN)
+ ON TO
SCHILTHORN
(30 MIN)

"SLEEP IN
STRAW" BARN

POST

ESTHER'S
B+B

CABLE CAR
STATION

EGGIMAN
B+B

C L I F F S

TO
STECHELBERG
(1 HOUR HIKE)

PENSION
GIMMELWALD

MOUNTAIN
HOSTEL

C L I F F S

TO STECHELBERG
BUS STOP +
CAR PARK

N

DCH

Swiss government subsidies (and working the ski lifts in the winter). For some travelers there's little to see in the village. Others enjoy a fascinating day sitting on a bench and learning why they say, "If heaven isn't what it's cracked up to be, send me back to Gimmelwald." Gimmelwald is my home base in the Berner Oberland (see "Sleeping in Gimmelwald," below).

Take a walk through the town. This place is for real. Most of the 130 residents have the same last name—von Allmen. They are tough and proud. Raising hay in this rugged terrain is labor intensive. One family harvests enough to feed only 15 or 20 cows. But they'd have it no other way and, unlike the absentee landlord town of Mürren, Gimmelwald is locally owned. (When word got out that urban planners wished to develop Gimmelwald into a town of 1,000, locals pulled some strings to secure the town's bogus avalanche-zone building code.)

Do not confuse obscure Gimmelwald with touristy and commercialized Grindelwald just over the Kleine Scheidegg ridge.

A Walk through Gimmelwald

Gimmelwald, while tiny with one zigzag street, gives a fine look at a traditional mountain Swiss community. Here's a quick walking tour.

Gondola Station: When the lift came in the 1960s, this village's back end became Gimmelwald's front door. This was and still is a farm village. Stepping off the gondola you see a sweet little hut. Set on stilts to keep out mice, the hut was used for storing cheese (the rocks on the rooftop keep the shingles on through wild winter winds). Notice the yellow Alpine "street sign" showing where you are, the altitude (1,363 meters), and how many hours and minutes it takes to walk to nearby points. Behind the cheese hut stands the village schoolhouse. In Catholic-Swiss towns, the biggest building is the church. In Protestant towns, it's the school. Gimmelwald's biggest building is the school (2 teachers, 19 students, and a room that doubles as a chapel when the Protestant pastor makes his monthly visit).

In the opposite direction, just beyond the little playground, is Gimmelwald's "Mountain Hostel."

Walk up the lane 50 meters, past the shower in the phone booth, to Gimmelwald's....

"Times Square": From this tiny intersection, we'll follow the only paved road in town. Most of the buildings housed two families and are divided vertically right down the middle. The writing on the post office building is a folksy blessing: "Summer brings green, winter brings snow. The sun greets the day, the stars greet the night. This house will keep you warm. May God give us his blessings." The date indicates when it was built or rebuilt (1911).

Main Street: Walk up Main Street. Notice the town announcement board: one side tourist news, the other for local news. Cross the street and peek into the big new barn dated 1995. This is part of the "Sleep in Straw" association which rents out barn spots to travelers when the cows are in the high country (see "Sleeping," below). To the left of the door is a cow scratcher. Swiss cows have legal rights (e.g., in the winter they must be taken out for exercise at least three times a week). This big barn is built in a modern style. Traditionally, barns were small (like those on the hillside high above) and closer to the hay. But with trucks and paved roads, hay can be moved easier and farther and farms need more cows to be viable. Still, even a well-run big farm hopes just to break even. The industry survives only with government subsidies.

Water Fountain/Trough: This is the site of the town's historic water supply. Local kids love to bathe in this when the cows aren't drinking from it. From here, detour left down a lane about 50 meters (along a wooden fence and past pea-patch gardens) to the next trough and the oldest building in town, "Husmattli," from 1658. Study the log-cabin construction. Many are built without nails.

Back on the paved road, continue uphill. Gimmelwald has a strict building code. For instance, shutters can only be natural, green, or white. Notice the cute cheese hut on the right (with stones on the shingles and Alp cheese for sale). It's full of strong cheese— up to three years old. On the left (at B&B sign) is the home of Olle and Maria (the village school teachers). Gimmelwald heats with wood and, since the wood needs to age a couple of years to burn well, it's stacked everywhere. Fifty meters farther is...

Alpenrose: At the old schoolhouse, big ceremonial cowbells under its uphill eave. These swing from the necks of cows during the Alpine procession from the town to the high Alps (mid-June) and back down (around Sept 20). At the end of town notice the dramatic Sefinen valley. The road switches back at the...

Gimmelwald Fire Station: Check out the notices on the fire station building. Every Swiss male does a year in the military and then a few days a year in the reserves until about age 40. The 2001 Swiss Army calendar tells the reserves when and where to go. The Schiessubungen poster details the shooting exercises required this year. Keeping with the William Tell heritage, each Swiss man does shooting practice annually for the military (or spends 3 days in jail).

High Road: Follow the high road to Hotel Mittaghorn. The resort of Mürren hangs high above in the distance. And high on the left, notice the hay field with terraces. These are from WWII days when Switzerland, wanting self-sufficiency, required all farmers to grow potatoes. From Hotel Mittaghorn, you can return to Gimmelwald's "Times Square" via the stepped path. (For a map and photos of this walk, visit www.gimmelwald-news.ch.)

Gimmelwald After Dark—Evening fun in Gimmelwald is found at the youth hostel (offering a pool table, Internet access, lots of young Alp-aholics, and a good chance to share information on the surrounding mountains) or at Pension Gimmelwald's terrace restaurant next door. Walter's bar is a local farmers' hangout. When they've made their hay, they come here to play. They look like what we'd call hicks, but they speak some English and can be fun to get to know. Sit outside (benches just below the rails, 100 meters down the lane from Walter's) and watch the sun tuck the mountaintops into bed as the moon rises over the Jungfrau.

Alpine Excursions

There are days of possible hikes from Gimmelwald. Many are a fun combination of trails, mountain trains, and gondola rides. Don't mind the fences (but wires can be electrified—solar powered); a hiker has the right-of-way in Switzerland. However, as late as early June, snow can curtail your hiking plans (the Männlichen lift doesn't even open until June 6). Before setting out on any hike, get advice from a knowledgeable local to confirm that it is safe and accessible. Clouds can roll in anytime, but skies are usually clearest in the morning. Refer to maps (within this chapter) as you read about the following hikes.

▲▲▲**The Schilthorn: Hikes, Lifts, and a 10,000-Foot Breakfast**—The Schilthornbahn carries skiers, hikers, and sightseers effortlessly to the 10,000-foot summit of the Schilthorn where the Piz Gloria station (of James Bond movie fame) awaits with a revolving restaurant, shop, and panorama terrace. Linger on top. Piz Gloria has a "touristorama" film room showing a multiscreen slide show and explosive highlights from the James Bond thriller that featured the Schilthorn (free).

Lauterbrunnen Valley: West Side Story

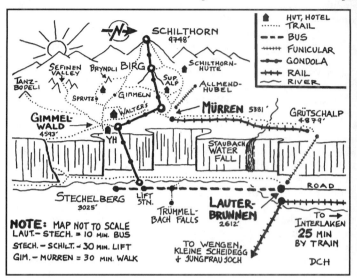

Watch hang gliders set up, psych up, and take off, flying 30 minutes with the birds to distant Interlaken. Walk along the ridge out back. This is a great place for a photo of the "mountain-climber you." For another cheap thrill, ask the gondola attendant to crank down the window (easiest on the Mürren-Birg section). Then stick your head out the window...and you're hang gliding.

The early-bird and afternoon-special **gondola tickets** (about 69 SF, before 9:00 or after 15:30) take you from Gimmelwald to the Schilthorn and back at a discount (normal rate-75 SF, or 90 SF from Stechelberg car park, parking-5 SF/day). Ask the Schilthorn station for a gondola souvenir decal (Schilthornbahn, in Stechelberg, tel. 033/823-1444 or 033/555-2141). For breakfast at 10,000 feet, there's no à la carte, only a 15-SF and a 22.50-SF meal. Ask for more hot drinks if necessary. If you're not revolving, ask them to turn it on.

Lifts go twice hourly, and the ride (including 2 transfers) to the Schilthorn takes 30 minutes. Watch the altitude meter in the gondola. (The Gimmelwald–Schilthorn hike is free if you don't mind a 5,000-foot altitude gain.) You can ride up to the Schilthorn and hike down, but it's tough (weather can change; wear good shoes). Youth hostelers scream down the ice fields on plastic-bag sleds from the Schilthorn mountaintop. (English-speaking doctor in Mürren.) For an easier hike, go halfway down by cable car and walk down from the Birg station (steep and gravelly). Buy the round-trip excursion early-bird fare (cheaper than the Gimmel-wald-Schilthorn-Birg ticket) and decide at Birg if you want to hike or ride down.

Just below Birg is **Schilthorn-Hutte**. Drop in for soup, cocoa, or a coffee schnapps. You can spend the night in the hut's crude loft (bed-20 SF, plus 45 SF if you want breakfast and dinner, open July–Sept, tel. 033/855-5053).

The most interesting **trail** from Birg to Gimmelwald is the high one via Grauseewli Lake and Wasenegg Ridge to Brünli, then down to Spielbodenalp and the Sprutz waterfall. From the Birg lift, hike toward the Schilthorn, taking your first left down to the little, newly made Grauseewli Lake. From the lake a gravelly trail leads down rough switchbacks until it levels out. When you see a rock painted with arrows pointing to "Mürren" and "Rot-stockhütte," follow the path to Rotstockhütte, traversing the cow-grazed mountainside. Follow Wasenegg Ridge left and down along the barbed-wire fence to Brünli. (For maximum thrills, stay on the ridge and climb all the way to the knobby little summit where you'll enjoy an incredible 360-degree view and a chance to sign your name on the register stored in the little wooden box.) A steep trail winds directly down from Brünli toward Gimmelwald and soon hits a bigger, easy trail. The trail bends right (just before the popular restaurant/mountain hut at Spielbodenalp), leading to Sprutz. Walk under the Sprutz waterfall, then follow a steep, wooded trail that will deposit you in a meadow of flowers at the top side of Gimmelwald.

▲▲North Face Trail from Mürren—For a pleasant two-hour hike (6 km, 1,946 meters–1,638 meters), ride the Allmendhubel funicular up from Mürren (cheaper than Schilthorn, good restaurant at top). From there, follow the well-promoted and described route circling around to Mürren (or cut off near the end down to Gimmelwald). You'll enjoy great views, flowery meadows, mountain huts, and a dozen information boards along the way describing the climbing history of the great peaks around you.

▲▲▲The Männlichen–Kleine Scheidegg Hike—This is my favorite easy Alpine hike. It's entertaining all the way with glorious Jungfrau, Eiger, and Mönch views. (That's the Young Maiden being protected from the Ogre by the Monk.)

If the weather's good, descend from Gimmelwald bright and early to Stechelberg. From here, get to the Lauterbrunnen train station by post bus (3.60 SF, bus is synchronized to depart with the arrival of each lift) or by car (parking at the large multistoried pay lot behind the Lauterbrunnen station). At Lauterbrunnen, buy a train ticket to Männlichen. Ride past great valley views to Wen-gen, where you'll walk across town (buy a picnic but don't waste time here if it's sunny) and catch the Männlichen lift (departing every 15 min, from June 6) to the top of the ridge high above you.

Berner Oberland

NOTE: THIS BIRD'S EYE VIEW LOOKS **SOUTH...**

EIGER 13026'   MONCH 13449'   JUNGFRAU 13642'   SCHILT-HORN 9748'

JUNG-FRAU-JOCH

GIMMEL-WALD 4593'

BIRG 8784'

TUNNEL

KLEINE SCHEIDEGG 6762'

W. ALP

MÜRREN 5381'

GRINDEL-WALD 3393'

MÄNN-LICHEN 7317'

STECHEL-BERG 3025'

← NICE WALK

GRÜTSCHALP 4879'

GRUND

← TO FIRST

WENGEN 4180'

LAUTERBRUNNEN 2612'

• ISENFLUH

WILDERSWIL 1916'

SCHYNIGE PLATTE 6454'

ISELT-WALD

SPIEZ

TO LUZERN

E.   W.

TO BERN

LAKE BRIENZ   BRIENZ

INTER-LAKEN 1860'

LAKE THUN

TO BERN

BRIENZ •

• BALLENBERG

PRIVATE RAIL - EURAIL NOT VALID
OTHER RAIL - EURAIL VALID
MTN. LIFTS

--- BUS
•••• BOAT
••••• TRAIL

NOT TO SCALE!

DCH

(Trails may be snowbound into early June. Ask about conditions at the lift stations or local TI. If the Männlichen lift is closed, take the train straight from Lauterbrunnen to Kleine Scheidegg.)

From the tip of the Männlichen lift, hike 20 minutes north to the little peak for that king- or queen-of-the-mountain feeling. From Männlichen, its an easy hour's walk—facing the Alpine panorama views of the north faces of the Eiger, Jungfrau, and Mönch—to Kleine Scheidegg for a picnic or restaurant lunch.

From Kleine Scheidegg you can catch the train to "the top of Europe" (see "Jungfraujoch," below). Or head downhill, riding the train or hiking (30 gorgeous min to Wengeralp station; 90 more steep minutes from there into the town of Wengen). The Alpine views might be accompanied by the valley-filling mellow sound of Alp horns and distant avalanches.

If the weather turns bad or you run out of steam, catch the train early at the little Wengeralp station along the way. After Wengeralp, the trail to Wengen is steep and, while not dangerous, requires a good set of knees. Wengen is a good shopping town.

Alpine Lifts in the Berner Oberland

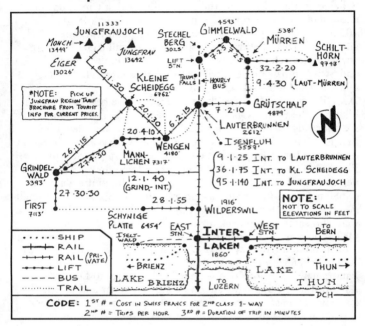

The boring final descent from Wengen to Lauterbrunnen is knee-killer steep—catch the train.

▲▲▲**Jungfraujoch**—The literal high point of any trip to the Swiss Alps is a train ride through the Eiger to the Jungfraujoch. At 11,333 feet, it's Europe's highest train station. The ride from Kleine Scheidegg takes about an hour, including two five-minute stops at stations actually halfway up the notorious North Face of the Eiger. You have time to look out windows and marvel at how people could climb the Eiger and how the Swiss built this train over a hundred years ago.

Once you reach the top, study the Jungfraujoch chart to see your options. There's a restaurant, history exhibit, ice palace (a cavern with a gallery of ice statues), and a 20-minute video (continuous). A tunnel leads outside where you can ski (30 SF for gear and lift ticket), sled (free loaner discs), ride in a dog sled (morning only), or hike 45 minutes across the ice to Mönchsjochhutte (a mountain hut with a small restaurant). An elevator leads to the Sphinx observatory for the highest viewing point from which you can see Aletsch Glacier—Europe's longest at 11 miles—stretch to the south.

Cost: The first trip of the day to Jungfraujoch is discounted; ask for a Good Morning Ticket and return from the top by noon (runs all year, round-trip fares to Jungfraujoch: from Kleine Scheidegg-normally about 100 SF, 60 SF for first trip of day—about 8:00 in summer; from Lauterbrunnen-about 145 SF, 105 SF for first trip—about 7:00 in summer, confirm times and prices, get leaflet on lifts at a local TI or call 033/826-4750, www.jungfrau.ch, discounts for Eurail/Euro/Eurail Selectpass and Swiss railpass holders, trilingual weather info: tel. 033/855-1022, if it's cloudy—skip the trip).

▲▲**Hike from Schynige Platte to First**—The best day I've had hiking in the Berner Oberland was when I made the demanding six-hour ridge walk high above Lake Brienz on one side with all that Jungfrau beauty on the other. Start at Wilderswil train station (just above Interlaken) and catch the little train up to Schynige Platte (2,000 meters). Walk through the Alpine flower display garden and into the wild Alpine yonder. The high point is Faulhorn (2,680 meters, with its famous mountaintop hotel). Hike to a small gondola called "First" (2,168 meters), then descend to Grindelwald and catch a train back to your starting point, Wilderswil. Or, if you have a regional train pass or no car but endless money, return to Gimmelwald via Lauterbrunnen from Grindelwald over Kleine Scheidegg. For an abbreviated ridge walk, consider the Panoramaweg, a short loop from Schynige Platte to Daub Peak.

▲**Mountain Biking**—Mountain biking is popular and accepted (as long as you stay on the clearly marked mountain-bike paths). A popular ride is the round-trip "Mürren Loop" that runs from Mürren-Gimmelwald-Stechelberg-Lauterbrunnen-Grütschalp (by funicular, bike costs same as person-7 SF)-Mürren. You can rent bikes in Mürren (Salomon Sports, 25 SF/half day, 35 SF/24 hrs, 10 SF extra for full suspension, daily 8:30–17:00, at gondola station, tel. 033/855-2330, www.staegersport.ch) or in Lauterbrunnen (Imboden Bike, 25 SF/4 hrs, 35 SF/day, Mon–Sat 8:00–12:00, 13:30–18:00, Sun 9:00–17:30, tel. 033/855-2114).

You can also bike the Lauterbrunnen Valley from Lauterbrunnen to Interlaken. It's a gentle downhill ride via a peaceful bike path over the river from the road. Rent a bike at Lauterbrunnen (see above), bike to Interlaken, and then return to Lauterbrunnen by train (pay 5 SF extra to take bike on train). Or rent a bike at either Interlaken station and take the train to Lauterbrunnen.

▲**More Hikes near Gimmelwald**—For a not-too-tough, three-hour walk (but there's a scary 20-minute stretch) with great Jungfrau views and some mountain farm action, ride the funicular from Mürren to Allmendhubel (1,934 meters) and walk to Marchegg, Saustal, and Grütschalp (a drop of about 500 meters), where you can catch the panorama train back to Mürren. An easier version is the lower Bergweg from Allmenhubel to Grütschalp via Winteregg. For an easy family stroll with grand views, walk from Mürren just above the train tracks to either Winteregg (40 min, restaurant, playground, train station) or Grütschalp (60 min, train station) and catch the panorama train back to Mürren. An easy, go-as-far-as-you-like trail from Gimmelwald is up the Sefinen Valley. Or you can wind from Gimmelwald down to Stechelberg (60 min).

You can get specifics at the Mürren TI. For a description of six diverse hikes on the west side of Lauterbrunnen, pick up the fine and free *Mürren-Schilthorn Hikes* brochure (at stations, hotels, and TIs). The 3-D map of the Mürren mountainside, which includes hiking trails, makes a useful and attractive souvenir (2 SF at TI and lift station). For an extensive rundown on the region, get Don Chmura's fine 8-SF Lauterbrunnen Valley guidebook (includes info on hikes, flora, fauna, culture, and travel tips; available at Mountain Hostel in Gimmelwald).

Rainy-Day Options

If clouds roll in, don't despair. They can roll out just as quickly, and there are some good bad-weather options.

▲▲**Cloudy Day Lauterbrunnen Valley Walk**—There are easy trails and pleasant walks along the floor of the Lauterbrunnen Valley. For a smell-the-cows-and-flowers lowland walk—ideal for a cloudy day, weary body, or tight budget—follow the riverside trail from Stechelberg's Schilthornbahn station for five kilometers to Lauterbrunnen's Staubach Falls, near the town church (you can reverse the route, but it's a gradual uphill to Stechelberg). Detour to Trümmelbach Falls en route (below). There's a fine paved car-free and riverside path all the way.

If you're staying in Gimmelwald: Take the lift down to Stechelberg (5 min), then walk to Lauterbrunnen, detouring to Trümmelbach Falls shortly after Stechelberg. From Lauterbrunnen, take the funicular up to Grütschalp (10 min), then either walk (60 minutes) or take the panorama train (15 min) to Mürren. From Mürren it's a downhill walk (30 min) to Gimmelwald. (This loop trip can be reversed.)

▲**Trümmelbach Falls**—If all the waterfalls have you intrigued, sneak a behind-the-scenes look at the valley's most powerful one, Trümmelbach Falls (10 SF, April–June and Sept–Nov daily 9:00–17:00, July–Aug daily 8:00–18:00, on Lauterbrunnen-Stechelberg road, tel. 033/855-3232). You'll ride an elevator up through the mountain and climb through several caves to see the melt from the Eiger, Mönch, and Jungfrau grinding like God's band saw through the mountain at the rate of up to 20,000 liters a second (nearly double the beer consumption at Oktoberfest). The upper area is the best, so if your legs ache you can skip the lower ones and ride the lift down.

Lauterbrunnen Folk Museum—The Heimatmuseum in Lauterbrunnen shows off the local folk culture (3 SF, mid-June–Sept Tue, Thu, and Sat–Sun 14:00–17:30, just over bridge).

Mürren Activities—This low-key Alpine resort town offers a variety of rainy-day activities, from its shops to its slick Sportzentrum (sports center) with pools, steam baths, squash, and a fitness center (for details, see "Sleeping in Mürren," below).

Interlaken Boat Trips—Consider taking a boat trip from Interlaken (see "Sights—Interlaken," above).

▲▲**Swiss Open-Air Folk Museum at Ballenberg**—Near Interlaken, the Swiss Open-Air Museum of Vernacular Architecture, Country Life, and Crafts in the Bernese Oberland is a rich collection of traditional and historic farmhouses from every region of the country. Each house is carefully furnished, and many feature traditional craftspeople at work. The sprawling 50-acre park, laid out roughly as a huge Swiss map, is a natural preserve providing a wonderful setting for this culture-on-a-lazy-Susan look at Switzerland.

The Thurgau house (#621) has an interesting wattle-and-daub (half-timbered construction) display, and house #331 has a fun bread museum. Use the 2-SF map/guide. The more expensive picture book is a better souvenir than guide. (14-SF entry, half price after 16:00, mid-April–Oct daily 10:00–17:00, houses close at 17:00, park stays open later, craft demonstration schedules are listed just inside the entry, tel. 033/951-1123.) A reasonable outdoor cafeteria is inside the west entrance, and fresh bread, sausage, mountain cheese, and other goodies are on sale in several houses. Picnic tables and grills with free firewood are scattered throughout the park. The little wooden village of Brienzwiler (near the east entrance) is a museum in itself with a lovely little church. Trains run frequently from Interlaken to Brienzwiler, an easy walk from the museum.

Sleeping and Eating in the Berner Oberland
(1.70 SF = about $1, country code: 41, area code: 033)
Sleep Code: **S** = Single, **D** = Double/Twin, **T** = Triple, **Q** = Quad, **b** = bathroom, **t** = toilet only, **s** = shower only, **CC** = Credit Card (**V**isa, **M**asterCard, Amex), **SE** = Speaks English, **NSE** = No English. Unless otherwise noted, breakfast is included and credit cards are not accepted.

Sleeping and Eating in Gimmelwald
(4,500 feet, country code: 41, area code: 033, zip code: 3826)
To inhale the Alps and really hold it in, sleep high in Gimmelwald. Poor but pleasantly stuck in the past, the village has a creaky hotel, happy hostel, decent pension, and a couple of B&Bs. The only bad news is that the lift costs 8 SF each way to get there.

Hotel Mittaghorn, the treasure of Gimmelwald, is run by Walter Mittler, a perfect Swiss gentleman. Walter's hotel is a classic, creaky, Alpine-style place with memorable beds, ancient down comforters (short and fat; wear socks and drape the blanket over your feet), and a million-dollar view of the Jungfrau Alps. The Yodelin' Seniors' loft has a dozen real beds, several sinks, down comforters, and a fire ladder out the back window. The hotel has one shower for 10 rooms (1 SF/5 min). Walter is careful not to let his place get too hectic or big and enjoys sensitive Back Door travelers. He runs the hotel with a little help from Rosemary from the village, and keeps things simple. This is a good place to receive mail from home (check the mail barrel in entry hall).

To some, Hotel Mittaghorn is a fire waiting to happen with a kitchen that would never pass code, lumpy beds, teeny towels, and nowhere near enough plumbing, run by an eccentric old grouch. These people enjoy Interlaken, Wengen, or Mürren, and that's where they should sleep. Be warned, you'll see more of my readers than locals here, but it's a fun crowd—an extended family (D-70–80 SF, T-100 SF, Q-125 SF, Yodelin' Seniors' loft beds-25 SF, all with breakfast, 3-SF surcharge for 1-night stays, cash only, closed Nov–April, CH-3826 Gimmelwald/Bern, tel. 033/855-1658, www.ricksteves.com/mittaghorn). Reserve by telephone only, then reconfirm by telephone the day before your arrival. Walter usually offers his guests a simple 15-SF dinner. Hotel Mittaghorn is at the top of Gimmelwald, a five-minute uphill walk from the town intersection.

Mountain Hostel is a beehive of activity, simple and as clean as its guests, cheap, and very friendly. Phone ahead (2 days maximum) or, to secure one of its 70 dorm beds the same day, call after 9:30 and leave your name. The hostel has low ceilings, a self-service kitchen, a mini-grocery, and healthy plumbing. While it's mostly a college-age crowd with late night sing-a-longs, families and older travelers are welcome. Internet access is 12 SF per hour. Petra Brunner has filled the place with flowers. This relaxed hostel survives with the help of its guests. Read the signs (please clean the kitchen), respect Petra's rules, and leave it cleaner than you found it. The place is one of those rare spots where a family atmosphere spontaneously combusts, and spaghetti becomes communal as it softens (20 SF per bed in 6- to 15-bed rooms, showers-1 SF, no breakfast and no sheets—bring your own, hostel membership not required, 20 meters from lift station, tel. & fax 033/855-1704, e-mail: mountainhostel@tcnet.ch).

Pension Restaurant Gimmelwald, next door, offers 12 basic rooms under low, creaky ceilings (D-110 SF, Db-130 SF, T-150 SF, Q-180 SF, 5-SF surcharge for 1-night stays). It also has sheetless backpacker beds (25–35 SF in small dorm rooms). Prices include a buffet breakfast. The pension has Gimmelwald's scenic terrace overlooking the Jungfrau and the hostel, and is the village's only restaurant (fine meals—their specialty is *Rösti* and bratwurst). It's great for camaraderie but not for peace (closed Nov and first half of May, CC:VM, nonsmoking, 50 meters from gondola station; reserve by phone, plus obligatory reconfirmation by phone 2 or 3 days in advance of arrival, tel. 033/855-1730, fax 033/855-1925, e-mail: pensiongimmelwald@tcnet.ch, run by Liesi and Männi).

Maria and Olle Eggimann rent two rooms—Gimmelwald's most comfortable—in their Alpine-sleek chalet. Fifteen-year town residents, Maria and Olle, who job-share the village's only teaching position and raise three kids of their own, offer visitors a rare inside peek at this community (D-100 SF, Db with kitchenette-180 SF for 2 or 3 people, optional breakfast-18 SF, no CC, last check-in 18:30, 3-night minimum for advance reservations; from gondola continue straight for 200 meters along the town's only road, B&B on left, CH-3826 Gimmelwald, tel. 033/855-3575, e-mail: oeggimann@bluewin.ch, SE fluently).

Esther's Guesthouse, overlooking the main intersection of the village, is like an upscale, mini-hostel with five clean, basic, but comfortable rooms sharing two bathrooms and a great kitchen (S-30 SF, D-70–85 SF, T-90-110 SF, Q-140 SF, 2-night minimum, make your own breakfast, no smoking, tel. 033/855-5488, fax 033/855-5492, e-mail: evallmen@bluewin.ch, some English spoken).

Schlaf im Stroh ("Sleep in Straw") offers exactly that in an actual barn. After the cows head for higher ground in the summer, the friendly von Allmen family hoses out their barn and fills it with straw and budget travelers. Blankets are free, but bring your own sheet, sleep sack, or sleeping bag. No beds, no bunks, no mattresses, no kidding (20 SF, 12 SF for kids under 12, includes breakfast and a modern bathroom, showers-2 SF, open mid-June–mid-Oct, depending on grass and snow levels, almost never full; from lift, continue straight through intersection, barn marked "1995" on right, tel. 033/855-5488, fax 033/855-5492, e-mail: evallmen@bluewin.ch).

Eating in Gimmelwald: Pension Gimmelwald, the only restaurant in town, serves a hearty breakfast buffet for 13.50 SF, fine lunches, and good 15-SF dinners featuring a fine *Rösti* and a sampling of organic produce from the local farmers. The hostel has a decent members' kitchen and a small grocery but serves no food. Hotel Mittaghorn serves dinner only to its guests (15 SF); follow dinner with a Heidi Cocoa (cocoa *mit* peppermint schnapps) or a Virgin Heidi. Consider packing in a picnic meal from the larger towns.

The local farmers sell their produce. Esther (at the main intersection of the village) sells cheese, sausage, and Gimmelwald's best yogurt—but only until the cows go up in June.

Sleeping and Eating in Mürren
(5,500 feet, country code: 41, area code: 033, zip code: 3825)

Mürren—pleasant as an Alpine resort can be—is traffic free, filled with bakeries, cafés, souvenirs, old-timers with walking sticks, GE employees enjoying incentive trips, and Japanese making movies of each other with a Fujichrome backdrop. Its chalets are prefab-rustic. Sitting on a ledge 2,000 feet above the Lauterbrunnen Valley, surrounded by a fortissimo chorus of mountains, it has all the comforts of home (for a price) without the pretentiousness of more famous resorts. With a gondola, train, and funicular, hiking options are endless from Mürren. Mürren has an ATM (by the Co-op grocery), and there are lockers at both the train and gondola stations (located a 10-minute walk apart, on opposite ends of town).

Mürren's helpful **TI** can find you a room, give hiking advice, and change money (mid-July–mid-Sept Mon–Wed 9:00–12:00, 13:00–18:30, Thu until 20:00, Sat 13:00–18:00, Sun 13:00–17:30, less off-season, above the village, follow signs to Sportzentrum, tel. 033/856-8686, www.muerren.ch). The slick **Sportzentrum** (sports center) that houses the TI offers a world of indoor activities (13 SF to use pool and whirlpool, 8 SF for Mürren and Gimmelwald hotel guests, mid-June–Oct Mon–Sat afternoon).

Salomon Sports, right at the gondola station, rents mountain bikes (35 SF/half day, 45 SF/full day), hiking boots (12 SF/day), and is the village Internet station (12 SF/hr, daily 8:30–17:00, tel. 033/855-2330, www.staegersport.ch). **Top Apartments** will do your **laundry** by request (14:00–17:30, across from Hotel Bellevue's backside, look for blue triangle, please call first, tel. 033/855-3706). They also have a few cheap rooms (30–40 SF per person).

Prices for accommodations are often higher during the ski season and from July 15 to August 15.

Guesthouse Eiger offers good budget rooms. This is a friendly, creaky, very wooden home away from home (S-60 SF, D-100 SF, Db-130 SF, 39-SF beds in 2-, 4-, and 6-bunk rooms, with sheets and breakfast, CC:VMA, closed Nov, across from train station, tel. 033/856-5460, fax 033/856-5461, e-mail: eigerguesthouse@muerren.ch, well run by Alan and Veronique). The restaurant serves good, reasonably priced dinners, and its poolroom is a popular local hangout.

Hotel Alpina is a simple, modern place with 24 comfortable rooms and a concrete feeling—a good thing, given its cliff-edge position (Sb-75–85 SF, Db-130–170 SF, Tb-180 SF, Qb-200 SF with awesome Jungfrau views and balconies, CC:VMA, exit left from station, walk 2 min gradually downhill, tel. 033/855-1361, fax 033/855-1049, www.muerren.ch/alpina, Frau and Herr Taugwalder).

Mürren

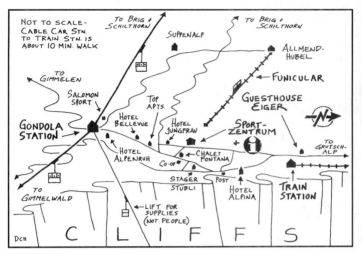

Chalet Fontana, run by a charming Englishwoman, Denise Fussell, is a rare budget option in Mürren with simple, crispy-clean, and comfortable rooms (35–45 SF per person in small doubles or triples with breakfast, 5 SF cheaper without breakfast, 1 apartment with kitchenette-50 SF per person, third and fourth person-10 SF each, closed Nov–April, across street from Stäger-stübli restaurant in town center, tel. 033/855-2686, fax 033/856-8696, cellular 078/642-3485, e-mail: chaletfontana@compuserve .com). If no one's home, check at the Ed Abegglen shop next door (tel. 033/855-1245, off-season only).

Hotel Jungfrau offers two options: a hotel with pricey, modern, and comfortable rooms and an elevator (Db-170–200 SF with view, 150–180 SF without); and a lodge in a basic, blocky, 20-room annex with well-worn but fine rooms and better Jungfrau views (Db-120–190 SF, Tb-156–210 SF, family apartments-280 SF, CC:VMA, near TI and Sportzentrum, tel. 033/855-4545, fax 033/855-4549, www.muerren.ch/jungfrau). All rooms include the same fancy buffet breakfast and free entrance to the Sportzentrum's pools. Without breakfast, deduct 10 SF per person.

Hotel Alpenruh, expensive and yuppie-rustic, is about the only hotel in Mürren open year-round. The comfortable rooms come with views and some balconies (Sb-95–125 SF, Db-180–260 SF depending on season, CC:VMA, elevator, attached restaurant, sauna, free vouchers for breakfast atop Schilthorn, 10 meters from gondola station, tel. 033/856-8800, fax 033/856-8888, e-mail: alpruh@schilthorn.ch).

Hotel Bellevue-Crystal has a homey lounge, great view terrace, and 27 good rooms at fair rates, most with balconies and views. The more expensive rooms are newly renovated and larger (Db-130–200 SF, a few family apartments-225–345 SF, tel. 033/855-1401, fax 033/855-1490, www.muerren.ch/bellevue).

Eating in Mürren: For a rare bit of ruggedness, eat at the **Stägerstübli** (10–30-SF lunches and dinners, closed Tue off-season). The **Kandhar Snack Bar** at the Sportzentrum has fun, creative, and inexpensive light meals, a good selection of teas and pastries, and impressive views. The **Edelweiss** self-serve restaurant is reasonable and wins the best view award (next to Hotel Alpina). Mürren's bakery is excellent. For picnic fixings, shop at the **Co-op** (normally Mon and Wed–Fri 8:00–12:00, 14:00–18:30, Tue and Sat 8:00–12:00 only, closed Sun).

Sleeping in Lauterbrunnen
(2,600 feet, country code: 41, area code: 033, zip code: 3822)

Lauterbrunnen—with a train station, funicular, TI (1 block up from station, tel. 033/855-1955), bank, shops, and lots of hotels—is the valley's commercial center. This is the jumping-off point for Jungfrau and Schilthorn adventures. It's idyllic in spite of the busy road and big buildings. You can rent a bike at Imboden Bike on the main street (25 SF/4 hrs, 35 SF/day, Mon–Sat 8:00–12:00, 13:30–18:00, Sun 9:00–17:30, tel. 033/855-2114).

Hotel Staubbach, a cavernous Old World place—one of the first hotels in the valley—is being lovingly restored by hardworking American Craig and his Swiss wife, Corinne. Its 30 plain, comfortable rooms are family friendly, there's a kids' play area, and the parking is free. Many rooms have great views. They keep their prices down by providing room-cleaning every third day (Db-100–110 SF, figure 40 SF per person in family rooms sleeping up to 6, CC:VM, includes buffet breakfast, elevator, 4 blocks up from station on the left, tel. 033/855-5454, fax 033/855-5484, www.staubbach.ch).

Valley Hostel is practical and comfortable, offering inexpensive beds for quieter travelers of all ages, with a pleasant garden and welcoming owners Martha and Alfred Abegglen (D-50–60 SF, beds in larger family-friendly rooms-22 SF each, ask about their new rooms with balcony, breakfast extra, nonsmoking, Internet access, laundry service, 2 blocks up from train station, tel. & fax 033/855-2008, www.valleyhostel.ch).

Chalet im Rohr, a creaky, old, fire-waiting-to-happen place, has oodles of character and 26-SF beds in big one- to four-bed rooms (no breakfast, common kitchen, below church on main drag, tel. 033/855-2182).

Masenlager Stocki is rustic and humble with the cheapest beds in town (13 SF with sheets in easygoing little 30-bed coed dorm with kitchen, closed Nov–Dec; below the church, take the second road under the train viaduct and walk 200 meters; tel. 033/855-1754).

Sleeping in Interlaken
(country code: 41, area code: 033, zip code: 3800)
I'd head for Gimmelwald or at least Lauterbrunnen (20 min by train or car). Interlaken is not the Alps. But if you must stay...

Hotel Lotschberg, with a sun terrace and wonderful rooms, is run by English-speaking Susi and Fritz and is the best real hotel value in town. Information abounds, and Fritz organizes guided adventures (Sb-100 SF, Db-145 SF, big Db-180 SF, extra bed-20–25 SF, family deals, cheaper Nov–May, CC:VMA, elevator, bar, nonsmoking, laundry service-8 SF, bike rental, cheap e-mail access, discounted parasailing if you "Fly with Fritz," 3-minute walk from station, exit right from West Station, then take a left at traffic circle to General Guisanstrasse 31, tel. 033/822-2545, fax 033/822-2579, www.lotschberg.ch, e-mail: hotel@lotschberg.ch).

Guest House Susi's B&B is Hotel Lotschberg's no-frills, cash-only annex, run by the same people (same address and phone number). It has simple, cozy, cheaper rooms (Db-119 SF, apartments with kitchenettes for 2 people-100 SF; for 4–5 people-175 SF, cheaper Nov–May).

Villa Margaretha B&B, run by English-speaking Frau Kunz-Joerin, offers the best cheap beds in town. It's a big Victorian house with a garden on a quiet residential street three blocks directly in front of the West Station (D-80 SF, T-120 SF, 3 rooms share a big bathroom, kitchenette, 2-night minimum, lots of rules to abide by, Aarmühlestrasse 13, tel. 033/822-1813).

Hotel Aarburg offers 13 plain, peaceful rooms in a beautifully located but run-down old building five minutes' walk from the West Station (D-100 SF, Db-120 SF, next to Laundromat at Beatenbergstrasse 1, tel. 033/822-2615, fax 033/822-6397).

Backpackers' Villa Sonnenhof is a creative guesthouse run by a Methodist Church group. It's fun and youthful but without the frat-party ambience of Balmer's (below). Rooms are comfortable, and half come with Jungfrau-view balconies (D-74–86 SF, dorm beds in 4- to 6-bed rooms with lockers and sheets-29–32 SF each, cheaper if you BYO sheets, includes breakfast, kitchen, garden, Internet access, game room, no curfew, open all day, check-in from 16:00–21:00, 10-minute walk from either station across grassy field from TI, Alpenstrasse 16, tel. 033/826-7171, fax 033/826-7172, www.villa.ch).

Happy Inn Lodge has cheap rooms a five-minute walk from the West Station (D-60–70 SF, dorm beds-19–28 SF, breakfast-7 SF, Rosenstrasse 17, tel. 033/822-3225, fax 033/822-3268, e-mail: happyinn@tcnet.ch).

For many, **Balmer's Herberge** is backpacker heaven. This Interlaken institution comes with movies, Ping-Pong, a Laundromat, bar, restaurant, swapping library, Internet stations, tiny grocery, bike rental, currency exchange, rafting excursions, a shuttle-bus service (which meets every arriving train), and a friendly, hardworking staff. This little Nebraska is home for those who miss their fraternity. Particularly on summer weekends, it's a mob scene (dorm beds-24–26 SF, S-40 SF; D, T, or Q-28–34 SF per person, includes sheets and breakfast, CC:VMA, nonsmoking, open year-round, recommend reservations 5 days in advance, Hauptstrasse 23, in Matten, 15-minute walk from either Interlaken station, tel. 033/822-1961, fax 033/823-3261, www.balmers.com, e-mail: balmers@tcnet.ch).

Transportation Connections—Interlaken

By train to: Spiez (2/hrly, 15 min), **Brienz** (hrly, 20 min), **Bern** (hrly, 1 hr). While there are a few long trains from Interlaken, you'll generally connect from Bern.

By train from Bern to: Lausanne (hrly, 70 min), **Zurich** (hrly, 70 min), **Salzburg** (4/day, 8 hrs, transfers include Zurich), **Munich** (4/day, 5.5 hrs), **Frankfurt** (hrly, 4.5 hrs, transfers in Basel and Mannheim), **Paris** (4/day, 4.5 hrs).

Interlaken to Gimmelwald: Take the train from the Interlaken East (Ost) Station to Lauterbrunnen, then cross the street to catch the funicular to Mürren. Ride up to Grütschalp, where a special scenic train (Panorama Fahrt) will roll you along the cliff into Mürren. From there, either walk an easy, paved 30 minutes downhill to Gimmelwald, or walk 10 minutes across Mürren to catch the gondola (costs 8 SF and once in Gimmelwald, you'll have a 5-minute uphill hike to reach accommodations). A good bad-weather option (or vice versa) is to ride the post bus from Lauterbrunnen station (hrly bus departure coordinated with arrival of train) to Stechelberg and the base of the Schilthornbahn gondola station (tel. 033/823-1444 or 033/555-2141), which will whisk you in five thrilling minutes up to Gimmelwald.

By car it's a 30-minute drive from Interlaken to Stechelberg. The pay parking lot (5 SF/day) at the gondola station is safe. Gimmelwald is the first stop above Stechelberg on the Schilthorn gondola (8 SF, 2 trips/hrly at :25 and :55, get off at first stop). Note that for a week in early May and from mid-November through early December, the Schilthornbahn is closed for servicing.

APPENDIX

European National Tourist Offices in the United States

Austrian National Tourist Office: Box 1142, New York, NY 10108-1142, tel. 212/944-6880, fax 212/730-4568, www.experienceaustria.com, e-mail: info@oewnyc.com. Ask for their "Vacation Kit" with map. Fine hikes and Vienna material.

    Belgian National Tourist Office: 780 3rd Ave. #1501, New York, NY 10017, tel. 212/758-8130, fax 212/355-7675, www.visitbelgium.com, e-mail: info@visitbelgium.com. Hotel and city guides, brochures for ABC lovers—Antiques, Beer, and Chocolates.

    British Tourist Authority: 551 5th Ave., 7th floor, New York, NY 10176, tel. 800/462-2748, fax 212/986-1188, www.travelbritain.org, e-mail: travelinfo@bta.org.uk. Free maps of London and Britain. Updated garden tour map and urban cultural activities brochure.

    Czech Tourist Authority: 1109 Madison Ave., New York, NY 10028, tel. 212/288-0830, fax 212/288-0971, www.czechcenter.com, e-mail: travelczech@pop.net. To get a weighty information package (1-2 lbs, no advertising), send a check for $3.20 to cover postage and specify places of interest. Basic information and map are free.

    Denmark (see Scandinavia)

    French Government Tourist Office: For general information, call 410/286-8310, check the Web site (www.francetourism.com), or contact the nearest office …

    In New York: 444 Madison Ave., 16th floor, New York, NY 10022, tel. 212/838-7800, fax 212/838-7855, e-mail: info@francetourism.com.

    In Illinois: 676 N. Michigan Ave. #3360, Chicago, IL 60611, brochure hotline tel. 312/751-7800, fax 312/337-6339, e-mail: fgto@mcs.net.

    In California: 9454 Wilshire Blvd. #715, Beverly Hills, CA 90212, brochure hotline tel. 310/859-3486, fax 310/276-2835, e-mail: fgto@gte.net.

    German National Tourist Office: 122 E. 42nd St., 52nd floor, New York, NY 10168, tel. 212/661-7200, fax 212/661-7174, www.germany-tourism.de, e-mail: gntony@aol.com. Maps, Rhine schedules, events, city and regional information.

    Italian Government Tourist Board: Check their Web site (www.italiantourism.com) or contact the nearest office …

    In New York: 630 5th Ave. #1565, New York, NY 10111, brochure hotline tel. 212/245-4822, tel. 212/245-5618, fax 212/586-9249.

    In Illinois: 500 N. Michigan Ave. #2240, Chicago, IL 60611,

brochure hotline tel. 312/644-0990, tel. 312/644-0996, fax 312/644-3019, e-mail: enitch@italiantourism.com.

In California: 12400 Wilshire Blvd. #550, Los Angeles, CA 90025, brochure hotline tel 310/820-0098, tel. 310/820-1898, fax 310/820-6357, e-mail: enitla@earthlink.net.

Netherlands Board of Tourism: 355 Lexington Ave., 19th floor, New York, NY 10017, tel. 888/GO-HOLLAND or 212/370-7360, fax 212/370-9507, www.holland.com, e-mail: info@goholland.com. Donation requested for information delivered within two weeks; materials delivered in three to four weeks are free. Great country map.

Scandinavian Tourism: P.O. Box 4649, Grand Central Station, New York, NY 10163, tel. 212/885-9700, fax 212/885-9710, www.goscandinavia.com, e-mail: info@goscandinavia.com. Good general booklets on all the Scandinavian countries. Be sure to also ask for specific country info and city maps.

Tourist Office of Spain: For info, call 888/OKSPAIN, visit their Web site (www.okspain.org), or contact the nearest office…

In New York: 666 5th Ave., 35th floor, New York, NY 10103, tel. 212/265-8822, fax 212/265-8864, e-mail: nyork@tourspain.es.

In Illinois: 845 N. Michigan Ave., Suite 915E, Chicago, IL 60611, tel. 312/642-1992, fax 312/642-9817, e-mail: chicago@tourspain.es. In Florida: 1221 Brickell Ave. #1850, Miami, FL 33131, tel. 305/358-1992, fax 305/358-8223, e-mail: miami@tourspain.es.

In California: 8383 Wilshire Blvd. #960, Beverly Hills, CA 90211, tel. 323/658-7188, fax 323/658-1061, e-mail: losangeles@tourspain.es.

Switzerland Tourism: Check out their Web site (www.myswitzerland.com, e-mail: info.usa@switzerlandtourism.ch) or contact the nearest office in: New York (tel. 212/757-5944, fax 914/682-9093), Chicago (tel. 312/332-9900), San Francisco (tel. 415/362-2260), or Los Angeles (tel. 310/640-8900). Or write to 608 5th Ave., New York, NY 10020. Comprehensive "Welcome to the Best of Switzerland" brochure, great maps and hiking material.

Let's Talk Telephones
In Europe, you can make your calls from public phone booths using a phone card or coins. At post offices in major cities, you'll sometimes find easy-to-use "talk now, pay later" metered phones.

Avoid using hotel room phones, which are rip-offs for anything other than local calls, PIN card calls (see "Telephones" in Introduction for more information), or calling-card calls.

International Access Codes
When dialing direct, first dial the international access code of the country you're calling from. For the U.S.A. and Canada, it's 011. Virtually all European countries use "00" as their international

access code; the only exceptions are Finland (990), Estonia (800), and Lithuania (810).

Country Codes
After you've dialed the international access code, dial the code of the country you're calling.

Austria—43	Finland—358	Norway—47
Belgium—32	France—33	Portugal—351
Britain—44	Germany—49	Spain—34
Canada—1	Greece—30	Sweden—46
Czech Repub.—420	Ireland—353	Switzerland—41
Denmark—45	Italy—39	U.S.A.—1
Estonia—372	Netherlands—31	

Calling Card Operators
Remember, it's much cheaper to dial direct than to use a calling card operator.

	AT&T	MCI	SPRINT
Austria	022-903-011	0800-200-235	0800-200-236
Belgium	0800-10010	0800-10012	0800-10014
Britain	0800-890-011	0800-890-222	0800-890-877
Czech Rep.	00420-00101	00420-00112	00420-87187
Denmark	8001-0010	8001-0022	8001-0877
France	0800-990-011	0800-990-019	0800-990-087
Germany	0130-0010	0800-888-8000	0800-888-0013
Italy	172-1011	172-1022	172-1877
Netherlands	0800-022-9111	0800-022-9122	0800-022-9119
Spain	900-990-011	900-99-0014	900-99-0013
Switzerland	0800-89-0011	0800-89-0222	0800-89-9777

Metric Conversion (approximate)

1 inch = 25 millimeters	32 degrees F = 0 degrees C
1 foot = 0.3 meter	82 degrees F = about 28 degrees C
1 yard = 0.9 meter	1 ounce = 28 grams
1 mile = 1.6 kilometers	1 kilogram = 2.2 pounds
1 centimeter = 0.4 inch	1 quart = 0.95 liter
1 meter = 39.4 inches	1 square yard = 0.8 square meter
1 kilometer = .62 mile	1 acre = 0.4 hectare

Numbers and Stumblers
- Europeans write a few of their numbers differently than we do: 1 = $\mathcal{1}$, 4 = $\mathcal{4}$, 7= $\mathcal{7}$. Learn the difference or miss your train.
- In Europe, dates appear as day/month/year, so Christmas is 25/12/01.
- Commas are decimal points and decimals commas. A dollar and a half is 1,50. There are 5.280 feet in a mile.
- When pointing, use your whole hand, palm downward.

- When counting with fingers, start with your thumb. If you hold up your first finger to request one item, you'll probably get two.
- What we Americans call the second floor of a building is the first floor in Europe.
- Europeans keep the left "lane" open for passing on escalators and moving sidewalks. Keep to the right.

Climate

Here is a list of average temperatures (first line—average daily low; second line—average daily high; third line—days of no rain). This can be helpful in planning your itinerary, but I have never found European weather to be particularly predictable, and these charts ignore humidity

J	F	M	A	M	J	J	A	S	O	N	D

AUSTRIA • Vienna

25°	28°	30°	42°	50°	56°	60°	59°	53°	44°	37°	30°
34°	38°	47°	58°	67°	73°	76°	75°	68°	56°	45°	37°
16	17	18	17	18	16	18	18	20	18	16	16

BELGIUM • Brussels

30°	32°	36°	41°	46°	52°	54°	54°	51°	45°	38°	32°
40°	44°	51°	58°	65°	72°	73°	72°	69°	60°	48°	42°
10	11	14	12	15	15	14	13	17	14	10	12

CZECH REPUBLIC • Prague

23°	24°	30°	38°	46°	52°	55°	55°	49°	41°	33°	27°
31°	34°	44°	54°	64°	70°	73°	72°	65°	53°	42°	34°
18	17	21	19	18	18	18	19	20	18	18	18

DENMARK • Copenhagen

29°	28°	31°	37°	45°	51°	56°	56°	51°	44°	38°	33°
37°	37°	42°	51°	60°	66°	70°	69°	64°	55°	46°	41°
14	15	19	18	20	18	17	16	14	14	11	12

FRANCE • Paris

34°	34°	39°	43°	49°	55°	58°	53°	53°	46°	40°	36°
43°	45°	54°	60°	68°	73°	76°	75°	70°	60°	50°	44°
14	14	19	17	19	18	19	18	17	18	15	15

GERMANY • Berlin

23°	23°	30°	38°	45°	51°	55°	54°	48°	40°	33°	26°
35°	38°	48°	56°	64°	70°	74°	73°	67°	56°	44°	36°
15	12	18	15	16	13	15	15	17	18	15	16

J	F	M	A	M	J	J	A	S	O	N	D

GREAT BRITAIN • London

36°	36°	38°	42°	47°	53°	56°	56°	52°	46°	42°	38°
43°	44°	50°	56°	62°	69°	71°	71°	65°	58°	50°	45°
16	15	20	18	19	19	19	20	17	18	15	16

GREAT BRITAIN • York

33°	34°	36°	40°	44°	50°	54°	53°	50°	44°	39°	36°
43°	44°	49°	55°	61°	67°	70°	69°	64°	57°	49°	45°
14	13	18	17	18	16	16	17	16	16	13	14

GREAT BRITAIN • Edinburgh

34°	34°	36°	39°	43°	49°	52°	52°	49°	44°	39°	36°
42°	43°	46°	51°	56°	62°	65°	64°	60°	54°	48°	44°
14	13	16	16	17	15	14	15	14	14	13	13

ITALY • Rome

40°	42°	45°	50°	56°	63°	67°	67°	62°	55°	49°	44°
52°	55°	59°	66°	74°	82°	87°	86°	79°	71°	61°	55°
13	19	23	24	26	26	30	29	25	23	19	21

NETHERLANDS • Amsterdam

31°	31°	34°	40°	46°	51°	55°	55°	50°	44°	38°	33°
40°	42°	49°	56°	64°	70°	72°	71°	67°	57°	48°	42°
9	9	15	14	17	16	14	13	11	11	9	10

SPAIN • Madrid

35°	36°	41°	45°	50°	58°	63°	63°	57°	49°	42°	36°
47°	52°	59°	65°	70°	80°	87°	85°	77°	65°	55°	48°
23	21	21	21	21	25	29	28	24	23	21	21

SPAIN • Barcelona

43°	45°	48°	52°	57°	65°	69°	69°	66°	58°	51°	46°
55°	57°	60°	65°	71°	78°	82°	82°	77°	69°	62°	56°
26	23	23	21	23	24	27	25	23	22	24	25

SWITZERLAND • Geneva

29°	30°	36°	42°	49°	55°	58°	58°	53°	44°	37°	31°
38°	42°	51°	59°	66°	73°	77°	76°	69°	58°	47°	40°
20	19	22	21	20	19	22	20	20	21	19	21

Road Scholar Feedback for
BEST OF EUROPE 2001

*We're all in the same travelers' school of hard knocks. Your feedback helps us improve this guidebook for future travelers. Please fill this out (or use the on-line version at www.ricksteves.com/feedback), attach more info or any tips/favorite discoveries if you like, and send it to us. As thanks for your help, we'll send you our quarterly travel newsletter free for one year. Thanks! **Rick***

Of the recommended accommodations/restaurants used, which was:

Best _____

      Why? _____

Worst _____

      Why? _____

Of the sights/experiences/destinations recommended by this book, which was:

Most overrated _____

      Why? _____

Most underrated _____

      Why? _____

Best ways to improve this book:

_____

_____

I'd like a free newsletter subscription:

_____ Yes   _____ No   _____ Already on list

_____
Name

_____
Address

_____
City, State, Zip

_____
E-mail Address

Please send to: ETBD, Box 2009, Edmonds, WA 98020

Faxing Your Hotel Reservation

Faxing is more accurate and cheaper than telephoning. Use this handy form for your fax (or find it online at www.ricksteves.com/reservation). Photocopy and fax away.

One-Page Fax

To: _____ @ _____
                hotel   *fax*

From: _____ @ _____
                name   *fax*

Today's date: ____ /_____ /____
                day   *month* *year*

Dear Hotel _____,

Please make this reservation for me:

Name: _____

Total # of people: _____   # of rooms: _____   # of nights: _____

Arriving: ____ /_____ /____ My time of arrival (24-hr clock): _____
             day   *month* *year*   (I will telephone if I will be late)

Departing: ____ /_____ /____
              day   *month* *year*

Room(s):   Single___   Double___   Twin___   Triple___   Quad___

With: Toilet___   Shower___   Bath___   Sink only___

Special needs: View___   Quiet___   Cheap___   Ground Floor___

Credit card: Visa___   MasterCard___   American Express___

Card #: _____

Expiration date: _____

Name on card: _____

You may charge me for the first night as a deposit. Please fax, e-mail, or mail me confirmation of my reservation, along with the type of room reserved, the price, and whether the price includes breakfast. Thank you.

_____
Signature

_____
Name

_____
Address

_____
City   *State*   *Zip Code*   *Country*

_____
E-mail Address

INDEX

FREE TRAVEL GOODIES FROM

Rick Steves

EUROPEAN TRAVEL NEWSLETTER

My *Europe Through the Back Door* travel company will help you travel better *because* you're on a budget—not in spite of it. To see how, ask for my 64-page *travel newsletter* packed full of savvy travel tips, readers' discoveries, and your best bets for railpasses, guidebooks, videos, travel accessories and free-spirited tours.

2001 GUIDE TO EUROPEAN RAILPASSES

With hundreds of railpasses to choose from in 2001, finding the right pass for your trip has never been more confusing. To cut through the complexity, ask for my 64-page *2001 Guide to European Railpasses.* Once you've narrowed down your choices, we give you unbeatable prices, including important extras with every Eurailpass, *free:* my hour-long "How to get the most out of your railpass" video; your choice of one of my 16 country guidebooks and phrasebooks; and written advice on your one-page trip itinerary.

RICK STEVES' 2001 TOURS

We offer 16 different one, two, and three-week tours (160 departures in 2001) for those who want to experience Europe in Rick Steves' Back Door style, but without the transportation and hotel hassles. If a tour with a small group, modest family-run hotels, lots of exercise, great guides, and no tips or hidden charges sounds like your idea of fun, ask for my 48-page 2001 Tours booklet.

YEAR-ROUND GUIDEBOOK UPDATES

Even though the information in my guidebooks is the freshest around, things do change in Europe between book printings. I've set aside a special section at my website (www.ricksteves.com/update) listing *up-to-the-minute changes* for every Rick Steves guidebook.

Call, fax, or visit www.ricksteves.com to get your...

- ☑ **FREE EUROPEAN TRAVEL NEWSLETTER**
- ☑ **FREE 2001 GUIDE TO EUROPEAN RAILPASSES**
- ☑ **FREE RICK STEVES' 2001 TOURS BOOKLET**

Rick Steves' Europe Through the Back Door

130 Fourth Avenue North, PO Box 2009, Edmonds, WA 98020 USA

Rick Steves' Phrase Books

Unlike other phrase books and dictionaries on the market, my well-tested phrases and key words cover every situation a traveler is likely to encounter. With these books you'll laugh with your cabby, disarm street thieves with insults, and charm new European friends.

Each book in the series is 4" x 6", with maps.

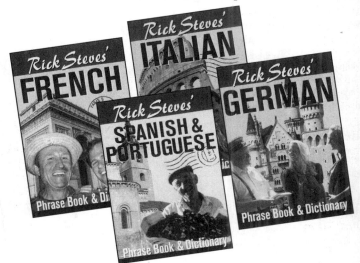

RICK STEVES' FRENCH PHRASE BOOK & DICTIONARY
U.S. $6.95/Canada $10.95

RICK STEVES' GERMAN PHRASE BOOK & DICTIONARY
U.S. $6.95/Canada $10.95

RICK STEVES' ITALIAN PHRASE BOOK & DICTIONARY
U.S. $6.95/Canada $10.95

RICK STEVES' SPANISH & PORTUGUESE PHRASE BOOK & DICTIONARY
U.S. $8.95/Canada $13.95

RICK STEVES' FRENCH, ITALIAN & GERMAN PHRASE BOOK & DICTIONARY
U.S. $8.95/Canada $13.95